# Contents

Introduction	2
N1 Place-value	4
N2 Place-value	4
N3 Addition	6
N4 Addition	6
N5 Addition	6
N6 Subtraction	8
N7 Numbers to 1000	10
N8 Numbers to 1000	10
N9 Multiplication/division	12
N10 Multiplication/division	14
N11 Multiplication/division	16
N12 Fractions	18
N13 Addition/subtraction	20
N14 Addition	20
N15 Place-value	22
N16 Addition	24
N17 Addition/subtraction	24
N18 Money	26
N19 Addition/subtraction	26
N20 Addition/subtraction	26
N21 Counting	28
N22 Odd and even	28
N23 Addition/subtraction	30
N24 Addition	32
N25 Multiplication/division	14
N26 Multiplication/division	12
N27 Multiplication/division	34
N28 Fractions	18
N29 Place-value	36
N30 Addition/subtraction	38
N31 Subtraction	40
N32 Addition/subtraction	40
N33 Addition	38
N34 Addition	42
N35 Addition/subtraction	42
N36 Number patterns	28
N37 Multiplication/division	44
N38 Multiplication/division	44
N39 Multiplication/division	34
N40 Multiplication/division	46
N41 Fractions	48
N42 Addition	50
N43 Addition	50

M1 Length	
M2 Length	52
M3 Time	54
M4 Time	54
M5 Capacity	56
M6 Time	58
M7 Weight	60
M8 Time	58
S1 2-d shape	62
S2 Symmetry	64
S3 Direction	66
S4 3-d shape	68
S5 3-d shape	68
S6 Angle	70
S7 Angle	70
S8 Position	72
D1 Tally charts	74
D2 Frequency tables	74
D3 Bar graphs	74
D4 Pictographs	74
Challenge Master Answers	76

Introduction

Purpose

This book is a resource for providing additional challenging mathematics to that already included in the Abacus 3 materials, to further extend more-able pupils.

It is the responsibility of all teachers to ensure that children are given every opportunity to realise their full mathematical potential. It is important, therefore, that the development of the more-able child is not restricted. There are numerous opportunities, within Abacus 3, for teachers to select tasks appropriate for the more-able child. The Challenge Book provides additional suggestions for such opportunities with a range of structured, challenging and purposeful activities.

Structure

The book is divided into sections relating to Units or groups of Units within Abacus 3.

It is assumed that most children for whom this material is appropriate will have satisfactorily completed the related Abacus Unit(s), and would benefit from further related activity in order to extend their mathematical development.

The suggested Challenges provide the teacher with a wide selection of activities within each Unit for the more-able children. It is not intended that they are all used, but that the teacher will select from this bank of ideas those activities which are appropriate.

Using the Challenges

The activities for each Unit or group of Units are contained in one double-page spread. The left-hand page provides Teacher's Notes relevant to the particular Unit, and the right-hand page is always a photocopiable 'Challenge Master'. The activities are easy to administer, require minimum use of materials, and minimum teacher input.

The Teacher's Notes are arranged under the following headings:

Skills summary
A summary of the key mathematical skills developed within and beyond the particular Abacus 3 Unit.

Core links
Notes with details of how to further extend activities within the existing Abacus 3 Textbooks and Photocopy Masters.

Introduction

Challenge master

Notes relating to the relevant Challenge Master, with details of how to further extend this. The photocopiable Challenge Masters themselves are presented directly to the child and always appear opposite the relevant page of Teacher's Notes.

Challenge activities

Practical activities to further extend the child's understanding of a particular mathematical topic, often using simple materials, e.g. number cards (many of which can be found in the Resource Bank).

Roughly half of all the activities are designed to develop the children's mathematical 'breadth', in which the children seek to broaden their understanding of a piece of mathematics but at the **same** level.

The remainder of the activities are designed to develop the children's mathematical 'depth', and are clearly labelled ⬇. In these activities children extend their study of a particular piece of mathematics, but at a **higher** level.

The suggested activities are often open-ended and of a problem-solving nature, geared towards the development of the children's process skills. It is anticipated that this Challenge Book will develop the child's ability to 'use and apply mathematics' at a higher level.

For many of the Challenge Masters, children can record their work on the sheet. Some Challenge Master activities require the children to record their work on separate sheets or in an exercise book. These sections are highlighted by a recording 'icon':

Children should be encouraged to record their work clearly and systematically.

Numbers to 1000

Skills summary
- To recognise place-value in 3-digit numbers
- To read a 3-digit number written in words, and write the numerals
- To write a 3-digit number in words, given the numerals
- To recognise place-value in 4-digit numbers
- To read a 4-digit number written in words, and write the numerals
- To write a 4-digit number in words, given the numerals

Core links

Number Textbook 1 page 3, top
Write each number in words.

Number Textbook 1 page 4, top
Write how much needs to be added to each number to make 1000.

Number Textbook 1 page 4, Explore
Write all the numbers you can make using any two cards each time.

Number Textbook 1 page 6, top and bottom
Write how much needs to be added to each amount to make £10.

Number Textbook 1 page 8, Explore
Write all the different 4-digit numbers that can be made. Extend to 2-digit numbers.

Photocopy Master 1
Write each number in words.
Write how much needs to be added to each amount to make £10, £5, £20, ...

Photocopy Master 2
Write what must be added to each to make 1000.

Photocopy Master 4
Make some thousand strips, e.g. 2000, 6000. Explore how many 4-digit numbers can be made using these and the other strips. Write ten of the numbers in words.

Challenge Master 1

Extension activities
Round each number to its nearest hundred, and to its nearest thousand.

Challenge Activity
Use a set of numbered cards, 0 to 9. Shuffle them and lay out four to make a 4-digit number. Say the number, then write it in words. Repeat for different numbers.

Name_____

Digit values

Write the value of each underlined digit.

 Add 10 to each number.
Add 100 to each number.

Adding and subtracting

Skills summary

- To recognise that addition can be done in any order
- To know addition pairs to 10
- To know addition pairs to 20
- To add more than two numbers
- To know addition pairs (multiples of 10) to 100 (e.g. 30 + 70 = 100)
- To know addition pairs to other multiples of 10 (e.g. 50, 60)
- To know addition pairs to 100
- To subtract a 1-digit number from a 1-digit number by counting back
- To subtract a 1-digit number from a 2-digit number by counting back
- To use known facts to add and subtract
- To combine addition and subtraction

Core links

Number Textbook 1 page 9, top
Write how many are in each bag if there are 15 (or 30) in each group.

Number Textbook 1 page 11, Explore
Find pairs of cards which make other totals. Investigate how many pairs are possible for each total from 10 to 30.

Number Textbook 1 page 12, top
Write how much more each person needs to make £1.

Number Textbook 1 page 14, Explore
Change the total from 15 to other numbers. Find different ways to use 4 cards to make 15, and other totals.

Number Textbook 1 page 15, top
Write how much needs to be added to each amount to make 50p, £1.

Number Textbook 1 page 17, top
Write the difference between each pair of numbers.

Number Textbook 1 page 18, top
Write how many points are needed by each child to achieve 100 points.

Photocopy Master 8
Use multiples of 10 only on the bottom row of bricks. Investigate different ways of making the same total at the top, e.g. 120, 500 or 1000.

Challenge Master 2

Extension activities
Change the 'Making Up' numbers to other numbers, e.g. 150.

Challenge Activity
Use a set of number cards, 0 to 99. Shuffle them deal out the cards, one at a time, saying the number which makes 100 with the card number.

Name_____

Making 100

Write the missing numbers in the boxes.

20	50	60	80	10	40	90	30	0	70

Make 100

15	5	45	55	25	75	95	35	85	65

Make 100

17	41	28	36	13	35	18	9	25	47

Make 50

Subtracting

Skills summary

- To subtract a 1-digit number from a 1-digit number by counting back
- To subtract a 1-digit number from a 2-digit number by counting back (not crossing a ten)
- To subtract a 1-digit number from a 2-digit number by counting back (crossing a ten)
- To use known subtraction facts, e.g. 9 – 5 = 4 to subtract a 1-digit number from a 2-digit number (not crossing a ten), e.g. 29 – 5 = 24
- To subtract a multiple of 10 from a 2-digit number, e.g. 67 – 30
- To subtract a 2-digit number from a 2-digit number whose units digit is smaller, e.g. 48 – 23
- To subtract a multiple of 10 from a 3-digit number

Core links

Number Textbook 1 page 19, top
Write how much change from 50p.

Number Textbook 1 page 20, top
Write the total reduction on all the tickets when each ticket has been reduced to 20p.

Number Workbook 1 page 21, bottom
Invent your own sequence of winning and losing points. Find ways of finishing with 100 points. Choose any score to start with.

Number Textbook 1 page 22, bottom
Write some of your own adding and subtracting problems like these.

Photocopy Master 13
Invent your own page of 'missing number' subtractions, with answers which are multiples of 10. Write an answer sheet to go with it. Try it out on a partner.

Challenge Master 3

Extension activities
Invent your own set of missing number statements involving subtraction. Write an answer sheet, and give them to a friend to solve. Mark the resulting work.

Challenge Activity
Make a dice by writing 5, 6, 7, 8, 9, 10 on a cube. Start with 100 points. Throw the dice and subtract the dice number from your points total. Continue doing this, writing the score each time, until you reach zero or beyond. How many dice throws did you need? Repeat to see if you can do this in fewer throws.

Name_____

Missing numbers

Write the missing numbers.

1. 48 – ⟨20⟩ = 28

2. 73 – ⬡ = 43

3. 56 – 20 = ⬡

4. 85 – 40 = ⬡

5. ⬡ – 30 = 27

6. ⬡ – 20 = 58

7. 65 – ⬡ = 15

8. 81 – ⬡ = 31

9. ⬡ – 50 = 43

10. ⬡ – 60 = 16

11. 152 – 10 = ⬡

12. 173 – 20 = ⬡

13. 138 – ⬡ = 118

14. 196 – ⬡ = 156

15. 245 – 30 = ⬡

16. 258 – 20 = ⬡

17. 572 – 100 = ⬡

18. 436 – 200 = ⬡

19. 643 – 110 = ⬡

20. 535 – 230 = ⬡

Counting

Skills summary

- To count in ones forwards and backwards from a 1-digit number
- To count in ones forwards and backwards from a 2-digit number
- To count in ones forwards and backwards from a 3-digit number
- To count in tens forwards and backwards from a 2-digit number
- To count in tens forwards and backwards from a 3-digit number
- To count in hundreds forwards and backwards from a 3-digit number
- To recognise the number 1 more/1 less than a 2- or 3-digit number
- To recognise the number 10 more/10 less than a 2- or 3-digit number
- To recognise the number 100 more/100 less than a 2- or 3-digit number
- To count in ones, tens, hundreds, thousands from a 4-digit number
- To recognise the number 1/10/100/1000 more/less than 4-digit number

Core links

Number Textbook 1 page 24, top
Invent some bubble trails with missing numbers which count in tens or hundreds.

Number Textbook 1 page 25, top
Find how much they have between them after 10 weeks, after 20 weeks.

Number Textbook 1 page 28, Explore
Extend to exploring the digit totals for pairs of numbers, one 111 more than the other, or 150 more than the other, ...

Number Textbook 1 page 29, top
Choose your own 4-digit numbers. For each number, write the number 1 more, 10 more, 100 more and 1000 more. Write also the number 1 less, 10 less, 100 less and 1000 less.

Photocopy Master 16
Repeat the game, but as you land on a number you collect Base Ten materials to match the number needed to make 800 with the number you land on. Who collects the most material after five rounds?

Photocopy Master 19
Write the numbers 7 more and 7 less, or 25 more and 25 less.

Challenge Master 4

Extension activities
Investigate making pairs of numbers which have a given total, e.g. 100.
Introduce place-value cards (hundreds). Explore making a pair of numbers so that one is 1 more than the other. Extend to 10 more, 100 more, 50 more and so on.

Doubles and trebles

Use one set of place-value cards (units and tens).

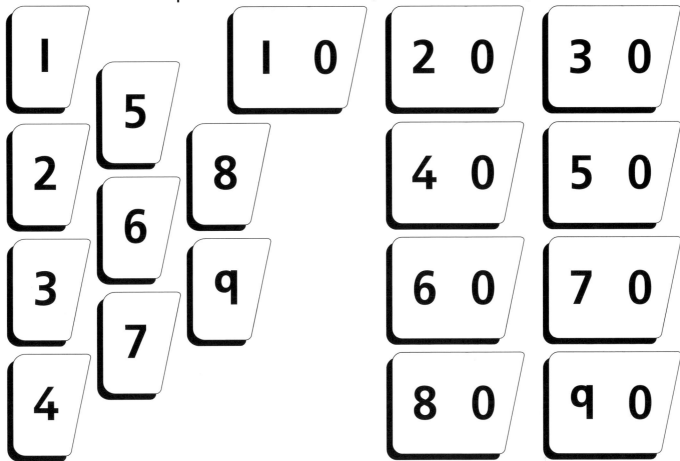

Make a pair of 2-digit numbers so that one number is I more than the other.

How many different pairs can you make?

 Explore how many different pairs you can make so that one number is:

a 10 more than the other
b 50 more than the other
c 5 more than the other
d 75 more than the other

Multiplication and division

Skills summary

- To understand multiplication as repeated addition
- To understand division as repeated subtraction
- To understand multiplication as describing an array
- To recognise that multiplication can be done in any order
- To relate division to multiplication
- To derive the multiplication facts up to 5×5
- To recall the multiplication facts up to 5×5
- To recall the division facts linked to the multiplication facts up to 5×5
- To derive the multiplication facts up to 10×10
- To recall the multiplication facts up to 10×10
- To recall the division facts linked to the multiplication facts up to 10×10

Core links

Number Textbook 1 page 30, top
Write a division for each set.

Number Textbook 2 page 18, top
If each individual stamp costs 5p, write the cost of each set of stamps. Extend this by changing the cost of each stamp to some other amount.

Number Textbook 2 page 19, top
For each board, write multiplications to show how many holes do not contain pegs. For example, in question 2 it could be 3×6 and 2×3. Check that the totals of the multiplications for pegs and holes equals 36.

Number Textbook 2 page 19, Explore
Change the number of counters to 36 or 40.
Explore how many different rectangles can be made for each number of counters from 1 to 30.

Number Textbook 2 page 20, bottom
Use the multiplication table to write six matching divisions which have an answer of 6.

Photocopy Master 21
Draw your own snakes with missing numbers, but for counting in steps of numbers other than 2, e.g. 5, 3, 9, ... Write an answer sheet, then ask a partner to write the missing numbers. Check with your answers.

Photocopy Master 63
Write some of your own sets of multiplication facts, both ways round, with answers, e.g. $7 \times 5 = 5 \times 7 = 35$. How many can you write which have answers between 30 and 50, between 50 and 70, ...?

Challenge Master 5

Extension activities
Find a number which appears four times, and colour, using the same colour, each square containing the number. Repeat for a different number which appears four times using a different colour. Continue like this. Do you notice any patterns in the sets of colours? (They lie on a curve – a 'rainbow' effect).

Multiplication table

x	1	2	3	4	5	6	7	8	9	10
1	1	2	3	4						
2	2	4	6	8						
3	3	6	9	12						
4	4	8	12	16						
5										
6										
7										
8										
9										
10										

Complete the multiplication table.

Which rows of numbers can you say without looking?

Multiplication and division

Skills summary
- To count in 2s (up to and beyond the tenth multiple)
- To know the ×2 multiplication table
- To recall the ×2 multiplication facts
- To count in 10s (up to and beyond the tenth multiple)
- To know the ×10 multiplication table
- To recall the ×10 multiplication facts
- To count in 5s (up to and beyond the tenth multiple)
- To know the ×5 multiplication table
- To recall the ×5 multiplication facts
- To count in 3s
- To know the ×3 multiplication table
- To generate the ×4 facts by doubling the ×2 facts
- To know the ×4 multiplication table

Core links

Number Textbook 1 page 34, top
Write the total number of pairs and the total number of eyes altogether.

Number Textbook 1 page 35, top
Write how much they get for each group if they get 5p or 20p for each can.

Number Textbook 1 page 35, bottom
Choose a new price for the cost of a sticker. Write how much is spent.

Number Textbook 2 page 16, bottom
Suppose you win 10p for each skittle knocked down, and lose 5p for each skittle standing up. Explore all possible scores with 10 skittles.

Number Textbook 2 page 17, top
What are the fewest coins needed to buy each stamp?
Write the cost of a booklet of 10 of each stamp.

Photocopy Master 23
Write twenty different division facts whose answers are more than 5.
Write a multiplication fact which goes with each division fact.

Photocopy Master 61
Write your own page of missing number multiplications, choosing your own multiplication table, e.g. ×6, ×9. Write a set of answers to go with it.

Challenge Master 6

Extension activities
Write a set of numbers to be divided by 5. Make them either 2-digit or 3-digit multiples of 10. To divide by 5, start by dividing by 10, then doubling. Alternatively, start by doubling, then dividing by 10.

Name_____

Multiplying by 5 trick

Multiply by 5, by first multiplying by 10, then halving.

For example:

22 x 5 = 22 x 10 = 220
half of 220 = 110
so, 22 x 5 = 110

 Try these.

1. 31 x 5	**2.** 42 x 5
3. 46 x 5	**4.** 24 x 5
5. 62 x 5	**6.** 48 x 5
7. 84 x 5	**8.** 16 x 5
9. 23 x 5	**10.** 55 x 5
11. 44 x 5	**12.** 26 x 5
13. 66 x 5	**14.** 82 x 5
15. 86 x 5	**16.** 17 x 5

 Choose 10 of your own numbers to multiply by 5.

Doubling and halving

Skills summary

- To understand doubling as two lots of an amount
- To derive doubles of numbers up to 10
- To recall doubles of numbers up to 10
- To understand halving as the reverse of doubling
- To derive doubles of numbers from 10 to 20, and their corresponding halves
- To derive doubles of multiples of 5 from 5 to 50
- To derive halves of multiples of 10 to 100
- To derive doubles of multiples of 50 to 500, and their corresponding halves

Core links

Number Textbook 1 page 37, top
Write a matching half for each set.

Number Textbook 1 page 37, bottom
Explore all the different possible one-dart scores on this board. Extend to two-dart scores.

Number Textbook 1 page 38, top
What are the fewest coins needed to match the double of each amount?

Number Textbook 1 page 38, bottom
Create your own doubling and halving tables using your own numbers.

Photocopy Master 25
Double each planet number. Try doubling it again, and again.
How many times can you keep doubling?

Challenge Master 7

Extension activities
- Investigate all the different possible one counter, two counter, three counter scores.
- Investigate different possible scores on a dartboard in which these numbers are changed. Write some numbers more than 10.

Name_____

Doubles and trebles

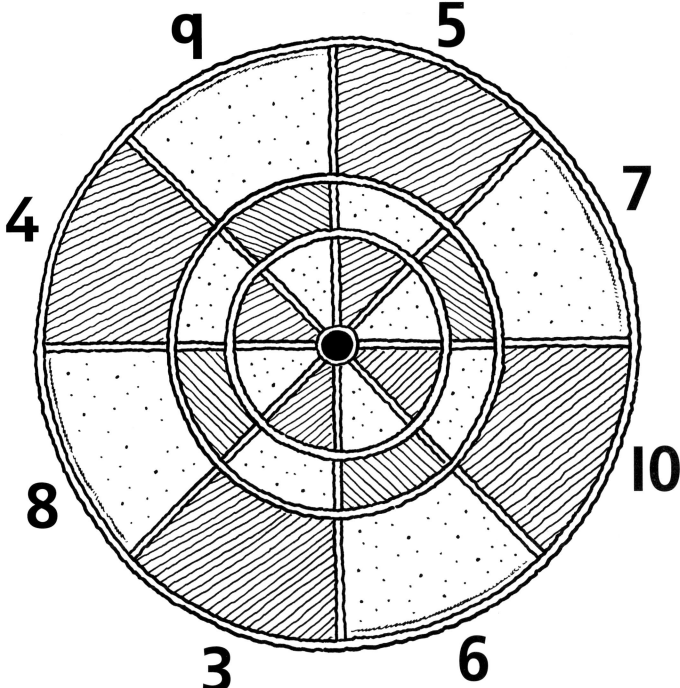

Place counters on the board.
A counter in the outer ring counts single.
A counter in the middle ring counts double.
A counter in the inner ring counts treble.

 Using three counters, find different ways of scoring 30.

 Find different ways of scoring 40 (using three counters).

Fractions

Skills summary

- To recognise one half, one quarter, one third, one eighth of a shape.
- To use fraction notation, e.g. $\frac{1}{2}$, $\frac{1}{4}$
- To recognise other simple fractions (unit numerator, e.g. $\frac{1}{3}$, $\frac{1}{5}$)
- To recognise one half, one quarter and one eighth of a set of objects
- To recognise a fraction of a shape (non-unit numerator, e.g. $\frac{3}{4}$)
- To find fractions of quantities (unit numerator)
- To find fractions of quantities (non-unit numerator)
- To recognise equivalence in fractions, e.g. $\frac{4}{8}$ and $\frac{2}{4}$
- To compare and order fractions on a number line
- To recognise and interpret mixed numbers, e.g. $5\frac{2}{3}$

Core links

Number Textbook 1 page 40, middle
Write what fraction is not coloured.

Number Textbook 1 page 41, top
Write a fraction statement to represent the pieces of mushroom not eaten, e.g. $\frac{3}{4}$ of 8 = 6.

Number Textbook 1 page 42, Explore
Repeat the activity for different pairs of fractions, e.g. quarters and thirds. Make predictions about which numbers will be red and blue.

Number Textbook 2 page 25, top
Imagine that a 2p coin is placed in each square on the grids. Write the fraction of the total which is on the shaded parts and unshaded parts, e.g. in question 1, write $\frac{3}{8}$ of 16p = 6p and $\frac{5}{8}$ of 16p = 10p. Extend by changing the 2p coin to a 20p coin, or 50p coin.

Number Textbook 2 page 26, bottom
Invent three of your own fraction problems like these, and write the answers. Try them out on a partner.

Photocopy Master 28
Write a fraction statement to show how much of each set is not shaded, e.g. in question 1, write '$\frac{2}{3}$ of 9 = 6'.

Photocopy Master 66
Choose a picture and write an equivalent fraction, e.g. in question 1, write $\frac{6}{8} = \frac{3}{4}$. Draw a picture to show the equivalence (e.g. draw a similar square, divide it into eight parts, and colour six of them). Repeat for different pictures on the sheet.

Challenge Master 8

Extension activities

- Explore for each amount, three other fractions which can be found. For example, in amount A, we can state $\frac{1}{3}$ of 60p = 20p, $\frac{2}{3}$ of 60p = 40p, $\frac{1}{4}$ of 60p = 15p.
- Create five different piles of money, then explore which fractions you can find exactly for each.

Name_____

Piles of money

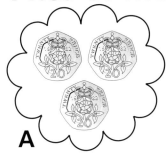

A

B

C

D

E

Write the values of these.

1. $\frac{1}{2}$ of A = ☐ p

2. $\frac{1}{4}$ of B = ☐ p

3. $\frac{1}{3}$ of C = ☐ p

4. $\frac{1}{5}$ of D = ☐ p

5. $\frac{1}{6}$ of E = ☐ p

6. $\frac{1}{8}$ of B = ☐ p

7. $\frac{1}{9}$ of C = ☐ p

8. $\frac{1}{10}$ of D = ☐ p

9. $\frac{1}{3}$ of A = ☐ p

10. $\frac{1}{4}$ of E = ☐ p

11. $\frac{1}{2}$ of B = ☐ p

12. $\frac{1}{6}$ of A = ☐ p

 Explore what fractions you can find exactly for each pile.

N13 Addition/subtraction

N14 Addition

Addition and subtraction

Skills summary
- To recall addition pairs to 10
- To recall addition pairs to 20
- To recall addition pairs of multiples of 10 to 100, e.g. 30 + 70
- To recall addition pairs of multiples of 5 to 100, e.g. 35 + 65
- To use knowledge of addition pairs to 100 to recall change from £1
- To recall addition pairs of 2-digit numbers to 100, e.g. 37 + 63
- To add and subtract 2-digit multiples of 10
- To add and subtract 2-digit multiples of 5
- To add and subtract 3-digit multiples of 10

Core links

Number Textbook 1 page 44, top
Find all the different possible scores with three rings, four rings.

Number Textbook 1 page 46, top
Write the difference between each pair.
Write ten different pairs of cards, which are 2-digit numbers, not multiples of 5 or 10. Write the total and difference for each pair.

Number Textbook 1 page 47, bottom
Write how many drinks each person can afford, and how much they will then have left.

Number Textbook 1 page 49, bottom
Write the total length of all the snakes, end to end. Record these lengths in metres and centimetres.

Number Textbook 1 page 50, top
Write the fewest coins which can be in each bank, and the fewest coins needed to make £1.

Photocopy Master 31
Create your own addition grids using 3-digit numbers which are multiples of 10, e.g. 250, 300, 420, 180, ...

Photocopy Master 34
Write your own sets of pairs of number cards which have numbers that total 1000, or 500.

Challenge Master 9

Extension activities
Create difference tables using 3-digit multiples of 10 or 5.

Challenge Activity
Make a collection of coins and notes. Write the differences between the 1p coin and each of the others. Repeat for each coin and note in turn.

Name_____

Difference table

d				
30				
45				
20				
25				
40				
15				

Write 60, 75, 5, 90 at the top of each column.
Complete the difference table.
Repeat the activity using your own four numbers at the top.

d				
30				
45				
20				
25				
40				
15				

Place-value

Skills summary

- To recognise place-value in 3-digit numbers
- To read a 3-digit number written in words, and write the numerals
- To write a 3-digit number in words, given the numerals
- To compare two 3-digit numbers, recognising which is more and which is less
- To say numbers which lie between two 3-digit numbers
- To order a set of 3-digit numbers
- To say a number which is 1, 10, 100 more/less than a 3-digit number
- To round a 3-digit number to its nearest 100, and nearest 10
- To recognise place-value in 4-digit numbers
- To order a set of 4-digit numbers

Core links

Number Textbook 1 page 51, top
Round each number to its nearest 10.

Number Textbook 1 page 52, top
Round each 'between' number to its nearest 10, and nearest 100.

Number Textbook 1 page 53, top
Write all the balloon numbers, in order, from smallest to largest.

Number Textbook 1 page 53, bottom
Write the difference between the largest and smallest number each time.

Number Textbook 1 page 54, Explore
Extend the activity to finding all the different amounts for other numbers of coins.

Photocopy Master 35
Round each number to its nearest 10 and nearest 100.

Photocopy Master 37
Change the rules so that the player who is nearest to 500 scores 5 points, the next nearest 4 points, etc.
Create a similar game but with four boxes each to create a 4-digit number.

Challenge Master 10

Extension activities
Write the difference between each number and its nearest hundred.
Extend to writing the nearest number to 150, to 250, ...
Explore how many different 4-digit numbers can be created from the four cards. Write which of them are the nearest to 1000, to 2000, ...

Challenge Activity
Use a set of numbered cards, 0 to 9. Shuffle them and lay out four to make a 4-digit number. Repeat for 10 different numbers. List the numbers in order from smallest to largest.
Round each of the above numbers to their nearest thousand, and to their nearest hundred.

Name_____

Four cards
Use these four cards.

 Explore how many different 3-digit numbers you can create, when using any of these four cards. For example:

Write them in order, from smallest to largest.

Write which number is the nearest to 100, 200, 300, …

Nearest to	
100	
200	
300	
400	
500	
600	
700	
800	
900	
1000	

 Repeat the activity, choosing your own four cards.

Adding and subtracting

Skills summary

- To recognise that addition can be done in any order
- To know addition pairs to 10
- To know what must be added to a 2-digit number to make the 'next ten'
- To add a 1-digit number to a 2-digit number by counting on (not crossing a ten)
- To add a 1-digit number to a 2-digit number by counting on (crossing a ten)
- To use known addition facts, e.g. 4 + 3 = 7 to add a 1-digit number to a 2-digit number (not crossing a ten), e.g. 64 + 3 = 67
- To add a 1-digit number to a 2-digit number by partitioning to make a 'ten', e.g. 27 + 5 = 27 + 3 + 2 = 30 + 2
- To add a multiple of 10 to a 2-digit number, e.g. 47 + 30
- To add two or more 2-digit numbers
- To find a small difference between two 2-digit numbers by counting up to and from the 'ten in between'

Core links

Number Textbook 1 page 55, bottom
Write the difference between each successive pair of numbers.

Number Textbook 1 page 56, bottom
Write the heights after one year if the plants grow 6 cm each month.

Number Textbook 1 page 57, Explore
Change the addition sign to a subtraction sign and repeat the activity.

Number Textbook 1 page 59, top
Write how many from the first number to 100.

Number Textbook 1 page 60, top
Write some pairs of your own numbers which have a difference of 17.

Photocopy Master 39
Change the adding machines so that they add different numbers, e.g. 2-digit numbers. Complete the tables for each.

Photocopy Master 42
Create a new game board, with different numbers. Choose numbers between 10 and 100. Play the game again, and take Base Ten material to match the difference each time. The winner is the first to collect 500.

Challenge Master 11

Extension activities
Write pairs of numbers which have differences between 20 and 40. Write the difference each time.

Investigate which pairs have an even difference and which have an odd difference.

Name_____

Difference pairs

Choose pairs from these numbers.

48   98   32   9   65   41

75   37   86   26   56   29

Which pairs of numbers have these differences?

1. ⟶ 6

2. ⟶ 5

3. ⟶ 4

4. ⟶ 3

5. ⟶ 8

6. ⟶ 7

7. ⟶ 10

8. ⟶ 9

9. ⟶ 11

10. ⟶ 12

11. ⟶ 17

12. ⟶ 24

Adding and subtracting

Skills summary

- To add and subtract 2-digit multiples of 10
- To add a multiple of 10 to a 2- or 3-digit number
- To subtract a multiple of 10 from a 2- or 3-digit number
- To add/subtract multiples of 10 pence from amounts of money expressed in pounds and pence, e.g. £2.45
- To add two 2-digit numbers without carrying, e.g. 45 + 23
- To subtract one 2-digit number from another which has a greater units digit, e.g. 48 – 25
- To add two 2-digit numbers with carrying, e.g. 45 + 27
- To subtract one 2-digit number from another which has a smaller units digit, e.g. 45 – 28
- To add and subtract near multiples of 10, e.g. 32 + 29, 34 – 19

Core links

Number Textbook 1 page 63, top
Find the total amount in each row of three banks. Find the total amount in all nine banks.

Number Textbook 1 page 64, top
Suppose the price of each item is reduced by another 25p. Write the new prices.

Number Textbook 1 page 67, top
Write the difference between each pair of scores.

Number Textbook 1 page 68, bottom
Invent some similar squirrel stories, using larger numbers.

Number Textbook 1 page 69, Explore
Repeat the activity, except find the difference between the two numbers, instead of the total.

Number Textbook 1 page 72, bottom
Invent some of your own similar problems.

Photocopy Master 49
Investigate all the different possible two-ball totals. Which of the possible totals have not been included on the sheet?

Challenge Master 12

Extension activities
Write some adding and subtracting rules to make calculations easier, e.g. 'To add 99, you add 100 then take away 1', Make some rules for adding and subtracting 90, 190, 999, 101, ...

Name_____

Ninety-nine

Add 99 by adding 100 first, then taking away 1.

1. 168 + 99 = _____   **2.** 235 + 99 = _____

3. 416 + 99 = _____   **4.** 572 + 99 = _____

5. 385 + 99 = _____   **6.** 754 + 99 = _____

7. 535 + 99 = _____   **8.** 704 + 99 = _____

Subtract 99 by taking away 100, then adding 1.

9. 423 – 99 = _____   **10.** 645 – 99 = _____

11. 175 – 99 = _____   **12.** 408 – 99 = _____

13. 328 – 99 = _____   **14.** 394 – 99 = _____

15. 574 – 99 = _____   **16.** 111 – 99 = _____

Complete these.

17. 144 + 90 = _____   **18.** 256 + 90 = _____

19. 326 – 90 = _____   **20.** 435 – 90 = _____

21. 267 + 199 = _____   **22.** 463 – 299 = _____

21. 714 + 190 = _____   **24.** 387 – 190 = _____

N21 Counting

N22 Odd and even

N36 Number patterns

Counting

Skills summary
- To count in ones forwards and backwards from a 1-, 2- or 3-digit number
- To count in tens forwards and backwards from a 2- or 3-digit number
- To count in hundreds forwards and backwards from a 3-digit number
- To count in fifties forwards and backwards to 1000
- To recognise multiples of 10, multiples of 50, multiples of 100
- To recognise odd and even numbers up to 1000
- To recognise the number 1/10/100/1000 more/less than 3-digit number
- To count in ones, tens, fifties, hundreds, thousands from a 4-digit number
- To recognise the number 1/10/100/1000 more/less than 4-digit number

Core links

Number Textbook 2 page 3, top
- List the numbers which are multiples of 2, multiples of 5.
- List the numbers which are multiples of 3, by checking if the digit total is a multiple of 3.

Number Textbook 2 page 4, bottom
- Write the next four numbers by counting in steps of some other number, e.g. 50, or 40, or 90.

Number Textbook 2 page 7, Explore
- Repeat the activity, but making 3-digit numbers instead. Compare the results of the two different situations.

Number Textbook 2 page 49, Explore
- How many even numbers are there?

Number Textbook 2 page 50, top
- Write how much change for each item from £5.

Photocopy Master 53
- Design your own table, using different numbers, mostly multiples of 10, and choose different column headings, e.g. 'multiples of 4', 'multiples of 15', ... Complete the table with ticks and crosses.

Challenge Master 13

Extension activities
- Investigate similar patterns in multiplication, by multiplying pairs of numbers together which are both even, both odd, and one of each.

Name_____

Odds and evens

Here are five pairs of even numbers.
Write the difference between the numbers in each pair.

1. 8 and 6 ⟶ d = ☐

2. 4 and 10 ⟶ d = ☐

3. 2 and 12 ⟶ d = ☐

4. 6 and 2 ⟶ d = ☐

5. 20 and 14 ⟶ d = ☐

 Choose your own five pairs
of even numbers and write
the difference between them.

What do you notice about
all the differences?

 Repeat the activity by
choosing pairs of numbers
which are:

both odd

one odd and one even

Write about any patterns.

Adding and subtracting

Skills summary
- To recall addition pairs to 10
- To recall addition pairs to 20
- To recall addition pairs of multiples of 10 to 100, e.g. 30 + 70
- To recall addition pairs of multiples of 5 to 100, e.g. 35 + 65
- To use knowledge of addition pairs to 100 to recall change from £1
- To recall addition pairs of 2-digit numbers to 100, e.g. 37 + 63
- To use known facts to add 2-digit numbers, e.g. use 60 + 40 = 100 to add 59 + 40

Core links

Number Textbook 2 page 9, top
- Write pairs of balloons that total other numbers, e.g. 120, 90.

Number Textbook 2 page 10, top
- Write the total cost of all the key rings, and the change from £10.

Number Textbook 2 page 10, Explore
- Use 50p, £1 and £2 coins and find different ways to make £10.

Number Textbook 2 page 11, top
- Write some more additions like these with a given answer, e.g. 110.

Photocopy Master 56
- Investigate pairs, next to each other, which add to 50, to 60, ... to 150.
  If you can't find a pair, which pair has the nearest total to these?

Photocopy Master 57
- Subtract a constant number from each answer, e.g. 25.

Challenge Master 14

Extension activities
- For each addition on the left, of questions 1 to 5, write five other additions which have the same total.

Adding

Complete the addition pairs.

I.   70 + 30 = _____ $\Rightarrow$ 75 + 35 = _____

2.   60 + 40 = _____ $\Rightarrow$ 65 + 45 = _____

3.   15 + 85 = _____ $\Rightarrow$ 16 + 85 = _____

4.   60 + 80 = _____ $\Rightarrow$ 21 + 83 = _____

5.   30 + 70 = _____ $\Rightarrow$ 29 + 69 = _____

Find shortcuts to help you write the total of each row.

46	64
85	21
96	85
71	89
72	35
90	87

151	199
198	234
302	87
160	240
370	530
180	423

Doubling

Skills summary
- To understand doubling as two lots of an amount
- To derive doubles of numbers up to 10
- To recall doubles of numbers up to 10
- To understand halving as the reverse of doubling
- To derive doubles of numbers from 10 to 20, and their corresponding halves
- To derive and recall doubles of multiples of 5 from 5 to 50
- To derive and recall halves of multiples of 10 to 100
- To derive doubles of multiples of 50 to 500, and their corresponding halves
- To derive doubles of 2-digit numbers, with units digit less than 5
- To derive doubles of 2-digit numbers, with units digit 5 or more
- To use known doubles to aid addition, e.g. 15 + 16

Core links

Number Textbook 2 page 12, top
- Double the answers.

Number Textbook 2 page 13, top
- Write the cost of four of each pen by doubling each price, then doubling again. Write the change from £5.
- Write the cost of eight of each pen by doubling, doubling again, then again.

Number Textbook 2 page 14, top
- Write some of your own doubles, then use these to write some additions involving 'near' doubles.

Photocopy Master 58
- Assume that each number, when it comes out, goes back into the machine again, i.e. the answers are doubled again. Write the matching table. Extend this to doubling again. Draw a table which shows what happens to the numbers as they continue to be doubled. How far can you go?

Challenge Master 15

Extension activities
- Double each answer box.
- Repeat the activity, but instead of doubling, try halving each number. Record halves of the odd numbers, 15 for example, as $7\frac{1}{2}$.

Challenge Activity
- Use a set of numbered cards, 0 to 9. Shuffle the cards, and deal out five 2-digit numbers. Try doubling them first mentally, then using written methods. How many can you double in your head? Repeat for different sets of 2-digit numbers.

Name_____

Doubling

Complete each box by doubling.

1.

5	2	7
9	6	4
3	8	1

→

10		

2.

20	70	40
80	50	30
60	10	90

→

3.

55	35	65
75	15	5
45	25	85

→

4.

21	34	43
41	32	24
11	42	52

→

Multiplying and dividing

Skills summary
- To count in 3s
- To know the ×3 multiplication table
- To recall the ×3 multiplication facts
- To recall the ÷3 division facts linked to the ×3 multiplication facts
- To generate the ×4 facts by doubling the ×2 facts
- To count in 4s
- To know the ×4 multiplication table
- To recall the ×4 multiplication facts
- To recall the ÷4 division facts linked to the ×4 multiplication facts
- To count in 3s and 4s beyond the tenth multiple
- To recall the ×2, ×3, ×4, ×5, ×10 multiplication facts, and associated division facts
- To generate the ×6 facts by doubling the ×3 facts
- To generate the ×8 facts by doubling the ×4 facts
- To count in 6s and 8s

Core links

Number Textbook 2 page 22, top
Write the total if each blast is worth a different number of points, e.g. 30 points, 6 points, 50 points.

Number Textbook 2 page 23, Explore
Extend the same activity, but instead of multiplying by 3, try multiplying by other numbers.

Number Textbook 2 page 58, top
If each button costs 6p, write the cost of each set of buttons. What if each button costs 20p?

Number Textbook 2 page 59, top
Find how many squares of edge 1 metre can fit inside each field.
Write the total cost of fencing each field if fencing costs £3 per metre.

Number Textbook 2 page 59, Explore
Extend the activity to colouring numbers in other multiplication tables, and looking for and describing the patterns.

Photocopy Master 93
Complete the same Photocopy Master, but use a different multiplier, e.g. ×6, ×9.

Challenge Master 16

Extension activities
Write a linked multiplication to each division.
Draw your own grids, explore different ways of splitting them into equal parts, then write divisions and multiplication to match each split.

Name_____

Dividing

Complete these sentences.

1.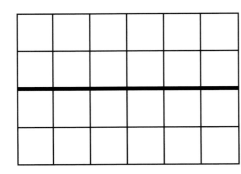
$24 \div 12 =$ _____

2.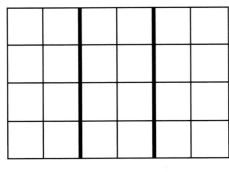
$24 \div 8 =$ _____

3.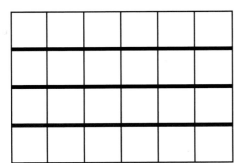
$24 \div 6 =$ _____

 Find some other ways of dividing 24 equally.

Find different ways of dividing these grids.

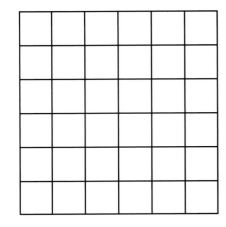

Rounding

Skills summary

- To round a 2-digit number to is nearest 10
- To round a 3-digit number to its nearest 10
- To round a 3-digit number to its nearest 100
- To round a 4-digit number to its nearest 10
- To round a 4-digit number to its nearest 100
- To round a 4-digit number to its nearest 100
- To read and interpret scales

Core links

Number Textbook 2 page 27, top
Write how far away each number is from its nearest 10.

Number Textbook 2 page 27, bottom
Write what must be added to each to make £1.

Number Textbook 2 page 28, top
Write the distances between the birds.

Number Textbook 2 page 28, bottom
Write how many of each creature will have a total weight of 2 kilograms, 10 kilograms.

Number Textbook 2 page 29, top
Write each distance to the nearest 10 miles.

Number Textbook 2 page 29, Explore
Round each number to its nearest 10, and nearest 100.
Try with a different set of four numbers. Is the total of different numbers the same?

Photocopy Master 70
Extend the activity by making different 4-digit numbers, then rounding each to the nearest 1000. Try also rounding each number to its nearest 100 and nearest 10.

Challenge Master 17

Extension activities
Write each number to its nearest thousand.
Write the difference between each padlock number and its nearest hundred. Repeat for nearest thousand.

Challenge Activity
Use a set of numbered cards, 0 to 99. Shuffle them and deal out three cards to make a 3-digit number. Say the nearest ten and hundred. Repeat for different 3-digit numbers. Extend to dealing four cards to create 4-digit numbers, and saying the nearest ten, hundred and thousand.

Name _____

Padlock numbers

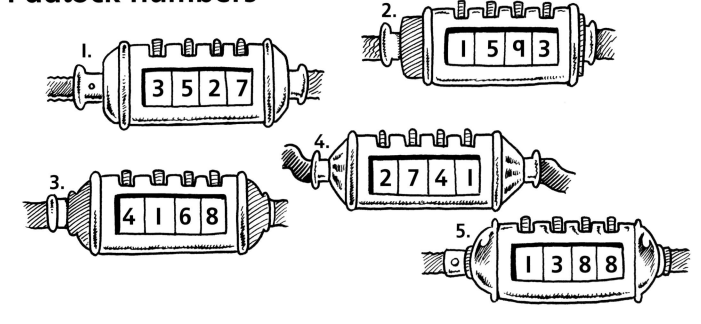

1. 3 5 2 7

2. 1 5 9 3

3. 4 1 6 8

4. 2 7 4 1

5. 1 3 8 8

6. 6 6 3 6

7. 5 3 8 0

8. 4 7 9 1

9. 6 2 7 2

10. 2 0 5 9

11. 4 3 0 8

12. 6 7 4 7

13. 2 3 0 9

Write each number to its nearest 10.
Write each number to its nearest 100.

Adding

Skills summary

- To recall addition pairs to 10, and to 20
- To recall addition pairs of multiples of 10 to 100, e.g. 30 + 70
- To recall addition pairs of multiples of 5 to 100, e.g. 35 + 65
- To add a multiple of 10 to a 2-digit number, e.g. 45 + 30
- To add more than two numbers, and recognise that they can be added in any order
- To use known facts to add 2-digit numbers, e.g. use 60 + 40 = 100 to add 59 + 40
- To use known facts to add three 2-digit numbers, e.g. 25 + 25 + 18
- To recall addition pairs of 2-digit numbers to 100, e.g. 37 + 63
- To add any pair of 2-digit numbers

Core links

Number Textbook 2 page 30, bottom
- Write the cost of ten of each cake.
- Write the cost of all the cakes together, and the amount of change when buying them with a £5 note.

Number Textbook 2 page 31, top
- How much further will each plant need to grow to reach 2 metres?

Number Textbook 2 page 31, Explore
- Investigate how many different ways the three spinners can land to give a particular score, e.g. 50, 75.

Number Textbook 2 page 32
- Investigate all the different possible scores with three glue-balls.

Number Textbook 2 page 39, top
- Write some different sets of three cards which will have a total score of 62.

Number Textbook 2 page 41, top
- Investigate all the different possible total scores for three of these six numbers.

Photocopy Master 78
- Vary the game so that each round involves adding two 3-digit numbers instead of three 2-digit numbers. The player whose answer is closest to 1000 scores 5 points, the next closest 4 points and so on.

Photocopy Master 79
- Investigate the totals if four balls are thrown in a 2 × 2 square arrangement.
- Draw your own 'Glue ball' board, writing numbers which are between 50 and 200. Find the 8 different three-ball totals.

Challenge Master 18

Extension activities
- For each grid, find the total of the three row totals, and the total of the three column totals. Check that they are the same.
- Find the total of all nine numbers in each grid. Which has the largest and which the smallest total?

Rows and columns

Write the row and column totals for each.

1.

15	41	32
18	21	43
31	40	28

2.

26	41	32
43	39	27
28	42	35

Write the missing numbers.

3.

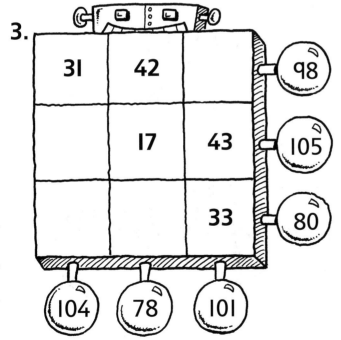

4.

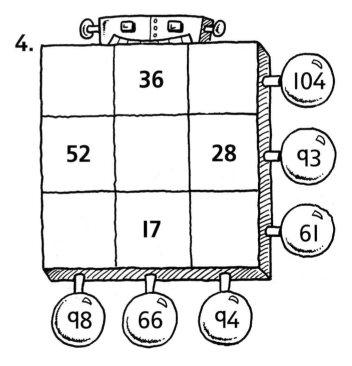

N31 Subtraction

N32 Addition/subtraction

Subtracting

Skills summary
- To recall subtraction facts involving numbers up to 10
- To subtract 2-digit multiples of 10
- To subtract a multiple of 10 from a 2- or 3-digit number
- To subtract multiples of 10 pence from amounts of money expressed in pounds and pence, e.g. £2.45
- To subtract one 2-digit number from another which has a greater units digit, e.g. 48 – 25
- To subtract one 2-digit number from another which has a smaller units digit, e.g. 45 – 28
- To subtract one multiple of 5 from another, numbers up to 100
- To add and subtract near multiples of 10, e.g. 32 + 29, 34 – 19
- To find a small difference between two 2-digit numbers by counting up to and from the 'ten in between'
- To find the difference between any pair of numbers to 100

Core links

Number Textbook 2 page 33, top
Write how many hours and minutes to go on each clock before they show the next hour, then 12 o' clock.

Number Textbook 2 page 34, top
Write the total cost of all the cars at the old prices, then the new prices. What is the difference in the total, and how does it relate to the ten cars? How much change from a £10 note when buying all the cars?

Number Textbook 2 page 36, top
Write all the pairs you can find with a given difference, e.g. 11, 31.

Number Textbook 2 page 37, bottom
Invent your own 'difference' problems like these.

Number Textbook 2 page 38, top
Choose your own difference, e.g. 7. Write several different pairs of card numbers which have this difference. Repeat for a different choice of difference.

Photocopy Master 73
Complete the grids by subtracting different numbers which are not multiples of 10, e.g. 24, 36, 45.

Photocopy Master 76
Create your own difference tables, choosing your own numbers between 20 and 100. Complete the tables.

Challenge Master 19

Extension activities
Extend the activity to reversing pairs of numbers whose digits have a difference of 1, of 2, of 3, ...

Name_____

Next-door numbers

Use number cards 1 to 9.

Choose a pair of 'next-door' numbers, and make a 2-digit number, e.g.

3 4

Reverse the digits to make a new 2-digit number.

4 3

Find the difference between the two numbers.

$$43 - 34 = \underline{\hspace{2cm}}$$

 Repeat this activity for different pairs of 'next-door' numbers. Look for a pattern.

_____

 Try the same activity for cards which are 'next-door-but-one' numbers, e.g.

1 3

Adding and subtracting

Skills summary

- To add and subtract 2-digit multiples of 10
- To add a multiple of 10 to a 2- or 3-digit number
- To subtract a multiple of 10 from a 2- or 3-digit number
- To add two 2-digit numbers without carrying, e.g. 45 + 23
- To subtract one 2-digit number from another which has a greater units digit, e.g. 48 – 25
- To add two 2-digit numbers with units digit total more than 10, e.g. 45 + 27
- To subtract one 2-digit number from another which has a smaller units digit, e.g. 45 – 28
- To add and subtract near multiples of 10, e.g. 32 + 29, 34 – 19
- To add/subtract a 1-digit number to/from a 3-digit number, e.g. 323 + 4
- To add/subtract a multiple of 10 to/from a 3-digit number, e.g. 428 + 60, 428 + 230
- To add/subtract a multiple of 100 to/from a 3-digit number, e.g. 371 + 200
- To add any pair of 3-digit numbers, with units and tens digit totals less than 10
- To add any pair of 3-digit numbers

Core links

Number Textbook 2 page 42, bottom
Add other numbers to each score, e.g. 230, 123.

Number Textbook 2 page 43, top
Find the total amount in all eight sacks. Suppose this total was changed into coins of the same value, e.g. 20p coins. How many coins will there be altogether? Extend to 50p, 5p, ... coins.

Number Textbook 2 page 44, Explore
Repeat the activity, but for subtractions instead of additions.

Number Textbook 2 page 45, top
Write the difference between each pair of numbers of people.

Number Textbook 2 page 46, bottom
Find the total cost of all the items. Write the cost of each item if it was doubled in price. Find the total cost of all items at the doubled price. Compare the two totals. What do you notice?

Photocopy Master 84
Throw two dice and add a matching 3-digit multiple of 10, e.g. throw 2 and 5 add either 250 or 520.

Challenge Master 20

Extension activities
Investigate how many different totals you can make between 400 and 600 using pairs of these numbers.

Invent your own missing pairs of numbers sheet using subtraction instead of addition. Write an answer sheet to go with it.

Name_____

Spot the pair

 315
 234
 452
 220
 340
 207
 147
 610   243
 532
 254
 106
125   302   331
425

Write pairs of these numbers which have these totals:

1. ⬡ + ⬡ = 574   2. ⬡ + ⬡ = 659

3. ⬡ + ⬡ = 817   4. ⬡ + ⬡ = 657

5. ⬡ + ⬡ = 950   6. ⬡ + ⬡ = 617

7. ⬡ + ⬡ = 478   8. ⬡ + ⬡ = 558

9. ⬡ + ⬡ = 864   10. ⬡ + ⬡ = 449

 Write pairs of the numbers which have a total near to 300, to 400, to 500, to 600, to 700 and to 800.

Multiplication

Skills summary
- To derive the multiplication facts up to 5 × 5
- To recall the multiplication facts up to 5 × 5
- To recall the division facts linked to the multiplication facts up to 5 × 5
- To derive the multiplication facts up to 10 × 10
- To recall the multiplication facts up to 10 × 10
- To recall the division facts linked to the multiplication facts up to 10 × 10
- To multiply a 1-digit number by 10
- To multiply a 1-digit number by 100
- To multiply a 2-digit number by 10
- To use known facts to multiply a 1-digit number by 10
- To use multiplication facts, e.g. 7 × 100 to derive associated division facts, e.g. 700 ÷ 100

Core links

Number Textbook 2 page 51, top and bottom
Write a matching division for each multiplication.

Number Textbook 2 page 53, top
Write how many crayons in each set if each box contains 100, or 30, or 50, ...

Number Textbook 2 page 54, top
Find how much each person can save in one year.

Number Textbook 2 page 55, Explore
Repeat the activity, but for division instead of multiplication.

Number Textbook 2 page 56, top
Find different ways of achieving a total score of 200 points, 250 points. How many different ways are possible?

Photocopy Master 89
Write how many 2p coins match each amount. Then write how many 5p coins match each amount. Extend to other coins, e.g. 20p coins.

Photocopy Master 91
Create a similar sheet, but instead of multiplying by 2-digit multiples of 10, include some which multiply by multiples of 100, e.g. 400. This can be extended to some which multiply by 2-digit numbers, e.g. 23.

Challenge Master 21

Extension activities
Explore different multiplications from these tables which have the same answers, e.g. 4 × 20 and 2 × 40. Create some more sets of your own multiplications which have the same answers.

Name_____

Multiplication tables

Complete these multiplication tables.

×	20	50	40	30
4				
3				
2				
5				
6				

×	4	2	5	10
100				
400				
300				
500				
800				

 Invent your own multiplication table, choosing your own numbers.

Division

Skills summary

- To sort small quantities into equal sets
- To share objects equally amongst a small group of people
- To divide by grouping objects into equal sets
- To interpret and use ÷ notation to record division
- To link multiplication to division
- To recall division facts by linking them to known multiplication facts up to 5 × 5
- To recall division facts by linking them to known multiplication facts up to 10 × 10
- To use lists of multiples to recognise multiplication facts.
- To recognise and record remainders when dividing
- To divide a multiple of 10 by 10, e.g. 140 ÷ 10
- To divide a multiple of 100 by 10, e.g. 700 ÷ 10

Core links

Number Textbook 2 page 60, top
If each brick costs 20p, write the total cost of each set of bricks.

Number Textbook 2 page 61, top
Choose your own number of children and write the division and any remainders when they are put into teams of different sizes.

Number Textbook 2 page 61, Explore
Extend the activity by dividing by numbers other than 3.

Number Textbook 2 page 62, bottom
Invent your own division problems. Invent some which divide exactly, and some which involve a remainder.

Photocopy Master 94
Write a multiplication to match each division.

Photocopy Master 95
Write each division and remainder as a fraction, e.g. in question 1, write $2\frac{1}{2}$.

Challenge Master 22

Extension activities
Try making some divisions which involve dividing by numbers more than 9, with and without remainders.
Use an 'x' card and make some multiplications using the number cards.

Divisions with remainders

Use one set of number cards 0 to 9.

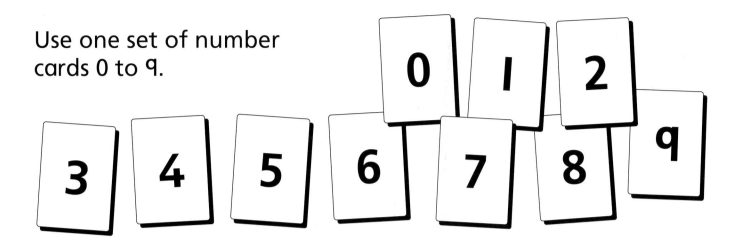

Make and use these cards also.

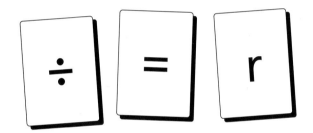

Create some divisions with remainders, e.g.

| 2 | 5 | ÷ | 4 | = | 6 | r | 1 |

Can you make a division for dividing by each of the numbers from 2 to 9?

Fractions

Skills summary

- To recognise one half, one quarter, one third, one eighth of a shape
- To use fraction notation, e.g. $\frac{1}{2}$, $\frac{1}{4}$
- To recognise other simple fractions (unit numerator, e.g. $\frac{1}{3}$, $\frac{1}{5}$)
- To recognise one half, one quarter and one eighth of a set of objects.
- To recognise a fraction of a shape (non-unit numerator, e.g. $\frac{3}{4}$)
- To find fractions of quantities (unit numerator)
- To find fractions of quantities (non-unit numerator)
- To recognise equivalence in fractions, e.g. $\frac{4}{8}$ and $\frac{2}{4}$
- To compare and order simple fractions on a number line
- To recognise and interpret mixed numbers, e.g. $5\frac{2}{3}$
- To construct one fraction equivalent to another
- To construct sets of equivalent fractions

Core links

Number Textbook 2 page 63, bottom
Draw some 3 × 4 grids. Colour pairs of the grids in different ways to show pairs of equivalent fractions, e.g. $\frac{1}{2}$ and $\frac{6}{12}$.

Number Textbook 2 page 64, bottom
Write all the fractions in questions 10, 11 and 12 in order from smallest to largest. Use the number lines to help.

Number Textbook 2 page 65, top
Draw three number lines the same length. Divide one into 3 equal parts, one into 6 equal parts and the other into 12 equal parts. Use these numbers lines to write and mark some sets of equivalent fractions.

Photocopy Master 96
Draw your own set of 10 faces, and give each of them four 2-way attributes, e.g. happy v sad, looking left v looking right, square nose v round nose, ... Can you write a description of the faces which leads to a fraction which is $\frac{1}{10}$, $\frac{2}{10}$, $\frac{3}{10}$, ... $\frac{9}{10}$?

Photocopy Master 98
Draw your own fraction wall which has twenty divisions on the bottom leading to twentieths. Include a layer for tenths, fifths, quarters and halves. Use the fraction wall to write pairs of equivalent fractions.

Challenge Master 23

Extension activities
- Draw some of your own different number lines on squared paper, marking the ends of the lines clearly. Mark different fractions along each line.
- Draw some more grids on squared paper, and colour parts of them to show fractions which appear on the number lines on the photocopy master.

Name_____

Matching fractions

Mark, with a pointer, each fraction on its matching number line.

(a) (b) (c) (d)

(e)

(f) (g) (i)

(h)

(j) (k)

0 ———————————————————— I

0 ———————————————————— I

0 ———————————————————— I

0 ———————————————————— I

0 ———————————————————— I

0 ———————————————————— I

 Write the fractions in order, from smallest to largest.

Abacus Ginn and Company 1999. Copying permitted for purchasing school only. This material is not copyright free.

Adding

Skills summary

- To add a 1-digit number to a 3-digit number, e.g. 323 + 4
- To add a multiple of 10 to a 3-digit number, e.g. 428 + 60, 428 + 230
- To add a multiple of 100 to a 3-digit number, e.g. 371 + 200
- To add any pair of 3-digit numbers, with units and tens digit totals less than 10, using informal recording methods
- To add any pair of 3-digit numbers with carrying, using a standard algorithm
- To add a set of 2- and 3-digit numbers, using a standard algorithm
- To add numbers together which have more than 3 digits, using a standard algorithm

Core links

Number Textbook 2 page 66, top and bottom
- Choose a number to add to each answer. Use a calculator as a check.

Number Textbook 2 page 67, top
- Write how many points each juggler needs to have 1000 points.

Number Textbook 2 page 68, top
- Find the total amount in all the safes. Find the total amount when £300 is added to each. Find the difference between the two totals. How do we know this will be £2100?

Number Textbook 2 page 69, top
- Add 165 to each answer.

Number Textbook 2 page 71, Explore
- Investigate all the different possible answers greater than 500.

Photocopy Master 99
- Investigate all the different possible totals when adding any two of these numbers together. How many totals can you find which do not appear on this sheet?

Photocopy Master 102
- Design a similar score sheet, but for adding two or three 3-digit numbers. Play the game, using the same scoring system.

Challenge Master 24

Extension activities
- Repeat the activity for a different set of five number cards.
- Use the five cards to create a subtraction of a 2-digit number from a 3-digit number. Investigate (a), (b), (c) and (d) for the subtraction.

Five card additions

Use these five number cards.

Arrange them like this to make an addition:

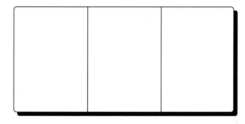

+

_____

 Find:

   a the largest odd answer

   b the largest even answer

   c the smallest odd answer

   d the smallest even answer

   e the additions which have these answers:

      403   709   637   619   727

   f all the possible additions which have answers between 500 and 600

Length

Skills summary
- To measure lengths in whole centimetres
- To estimate lengths in centimetres
- To measure lengths in whole metres
- To estimate lengths in metres
- To recognise relationships between metres and centimetres
- To convert centimetres to metres, and vice versa
- To measure lengths to the nearest centimetre, using a ruler
- To measure lengths in millimetres
- To recognise relationship between metres and kilometres

Core links

Shape, Data and Measures Textbook page 3, top
Measure each length in millimetres.

Shape, Data and Measures Textbook page 4, bottom
Write each distance in both centimetres and in millimetres.

Shape, Data and Measures Textbook page 6, top
Put the lengths of the snakes in order, from smallest to largest. Write the difference in length between each successive pair.

Shape, Data and Measures Textbook page 7, top
Write each new height in metres using decimal notation, then increase each height by another 25 cm, using decimal notation.

Shape, Data and Measures Textbook page 8, bottom
Invent some of your own length problems.

Photocopy Master 103
Measure each length in millimetres. Record the lengths in centimetres and millimetres.

Challenge Master 25

Extension activities
Calculate the difference between each estimate and each accurate measured length.
Convert each length to millimetres.
Collect a range of pens and pencils of different lengths, and repeat the activity.

Pencils

Estimate the length of each pencil in centimetres.

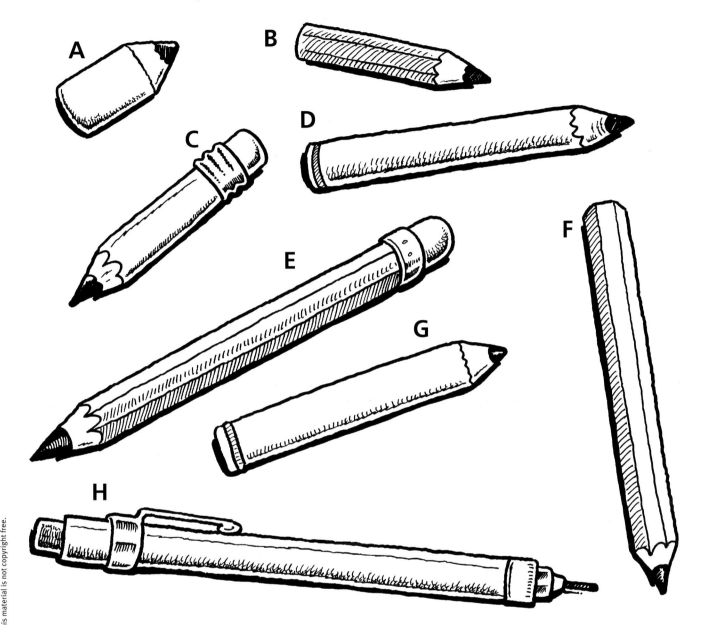

Measure the lengths to check your estimates.

Pencil	A	B	C	D	E	F	G	H
Estimated length								
Measured length								

Time

Skills summary

● To recognise 'o'clock' times on a digital and analogue clock

● To recognise 'quarter past', 'half past' and 'quarter to' the hour times on a digital and analogue clock.

● To tell the time using 5-minute intervals on a digital and analogue clock

● To understand 'past' and 'to' the hour

⊙ To tell the time using 1-minute intervals on a digital and analogue clock

⊙ To calculate time intervals in units of five minutes between two times

⊙ To calculate time intervals in minutes between two times

⊙ To calculate digital and analogue time given a number of minutes (or a number of hours) earlier or later

Core links

Shape, Data and Measures Textbook page 9, top and bottom
● Write each time a given period later, e.g. half an hour, quarter of an hour, ...

Shape, Data and Measures Textbook page 10, top
⊙ Write the fraction of each hour which is coloured.

Shape, Data and Measures Textbook page 12, top
● Write each time as a digital time.

Shape, Data and Measures Textbook page 13, top
● Write each time 45 minutes later. Extend to 35 minutes earlier.

Shape, Data and Measures Textbook page 14, top
⊙ Put all the times in order, then find the difference in minutes between each successive pair of times.

Photocopy Master 106
● Write each time a given number of minutes later, e.g. 20 minutes. Write each time the same number of minutes earlier.

Photocopy Master 109
● Write how many hours and minutes to go to reach 12 o'clock on each clockface. Convert each of these time periods into minutes.

Challenge Master 26

Extension activities
⊙ For each clock, write how long to go before it is 12:00.
⊙ Draw hands on analogue clock faces to show each time, in order, assuming that these times are from midnight to noon.

Minutes

Write for each clock, how many minutes:

past the last hour

until the next hour

1. 5:15

2. 2:25

3. 9:40

4. 9:31

5. 6:23

6. 10:16

7. 7:14

8. 3:37

9. 4:45

10. 12:09

11. 1:52

12. 8:03

13. 11:28

Capacity

Skills summary

- To understand the concept of capacity as a measure of the amount a container will hold
- To measure capacity using non-standard units
- To measure the capacity of a container using a litre measure
- To measure capacity in litres and half-litres
- To measure capacity in units of 100 millilitres
- To recognise the relationship between litres and millilitres
- To measure capacity in units of 10 centilitres
- To recognise the relationships between litres, millilitres and centilitres
- To convert litres to centilitres, and vice versa
- To convert litres to millilitres, and vice versa
- To convert centilitres to millilitres, and vice versa

Core links

Shape, Data and Measures Textbook page 15, top
- Convert each capacity into centilitres.

Shape, Data and Measures Textbook page 16, top
- Write each amount of water in centilitres.
- Write how much water, in litres and millilitres, is required to fill all nine containers.

Shape, Data and Measures Textbook page 17, top
- Write the capacities in order, from smallest to largest. Write the difference in capacity between each successive pair, in both millilitres and centilitres.

Challenge Master 27

Extension activities
- Write each measure in litres and hundredths of a litre, e.g. 350 ml = 35 cl = $\frac{35}{100}$ litre.

Challenge Activity
- Make a large collection of different labels for containers, and sort and order them. Display them according to type or size. Label each using litres, centilitres and millilitres.

Name_____

Centilitres

I litre is the same as 100 centilitres.

$1 \, l = 100 \, cl$

Write how much water each container is holding, in centilitres.

1.

$2 \, l = \underline{\hspace{1cm}} cl$

2.

$\frac{1}{2} \, l = \underline{\hspace{1cm}} cl$

3.

$600 \, ml = \underline{\hspace{1cm}} cl$

4.

$3000 \, ml = \underline{\hspace{1cm}} cl$

5.

$1\frac{1}{2} \, l = \underline{\hspace{1cm}} cl$

6.

$15 \, ml = \underline{\hspace{1cm}} cl$

7.

$100 \, ml = \underline{\hspace{1cm}} cl$

8.

$350 \, ml = \underline{\hspace{1cm}} cl$

9.

$2\frac{1}{4} \, l = \underline{\hspace{1cm}} cl$

10.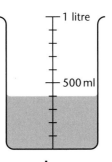

$\underline{\hspace{1cm}} ml = \underline{\hspace{1cm}} cl$

11.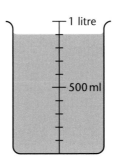

$\underline{\hspace{1cm}} ml = \underline{\hspace{1cm}} cl$

12.

1 litre

500 ml

$\underline{\hspace{1cm}} ml = \underline{\hspace{1cm}} cl$

Time

Skills summary

- To tell the time using 5-minute intervals on a digital and analogue clock
- To understand 'past' and 'to' the hour
- To tell the time using 1-minute intervals on a digital and analogue clock
- To calculate time intervals in units of five minutes between two times
- To calculate time intervals in minutes between two times.
- To calculate digital and analogue time given a number of minutes (or a number of hours) earlier or later
- To measure time in seconds
- To estimate time in seconds
- To recognise the relationship between short units of time, e.g. seconds, minutes, hours, days
- To recognise the relationship between long units of time, e.g. days, weeks, months, years
- To read and interpret a calendar

Core links

Shape, Data and Measures Textbook page 18, top
Write the times in order from shortest to longest, then write the differences between each successive pair in seconds.

Shape, Data and Measures Textbook page 20, top
Use a stopwatch and attempt to estimate each of the race times, in turn. Start the watch, and without looking at it, stop it when you estimate the period of time has passed. Check the period of time on the watch to see how good the estimate is. Record the differences between each time and the estimate.

Shape, Data and Measures Textbook page 24, bottom
Write how many years and months old you are. Convert this into months. How many months have you been alive? Find out how many days you have been alive.

Shape, Data and Measures Textbook page 25, top and bottom
Convert each time into hours.

Challenge Master 28

Extension activities
Create your own lists, choosing your own labels in the left column.

Challenge Activity
Write different fractions of a minute, e.g. $\frac{1}{2}$ a minute is 30 seconds. Start with fractions with unit numerators, e.g. $\frac{1}{3}$, $\frac{1}{4}$, $\frac{1}{5}$, ... and progress to fractions with non-unit numerators, e.g. $\frac{2}{3}$, $\frac{3}{4}$, $\frac{4}{5}$, ...

Name_____

How many?

Complete these lists.

Try them first without a calculator, then use a calculator to check any answers you are unsure about.

How many minutes?	
I hour	
300 seconds	
$\frac{1}{2}$ hour	
10 hours	
I day	
$\frac{3}{5}$ hours	

How many hours?	
I day	
September	
600 minutes	
I week	
10 days	
$\frac{2}{3}$ days	

How many seconds?	
I minute	
I hour	
$\frac{1}{4}$ hour	
3 minutes	
5·5 minutes	
I day	

How many days?	
I week	
August	
I year	
5 years	
360 hours	
March, April, May	

Weight

Skills summary

- To measure weight using non-standard units
- To recognise the kilogram as a unit of weight
- To estimate weights using kilograms
- To compare the weight of an object as more or less than one kilogram
- To weigh objects in units of 100 grams
- To weight objects in kilograms and grams
- To convert gram weights to kilograms/grams
- To convert kilogram/gram weights to grams
- To estimate weights using grams and kilograms
- To weigh objects in units smaller than 100 g, e.g. 10 g

Core links

Shape, Data and Measures Textbook page 21, top
Write how many of each object you need to weigh 1 kilogram.

Shape, Data and Measures Textbook page 22, middle
Find an object or set of objects whose weight matches each of these weights.

Shape, Data and Measures Textbook page 23, bottom
Invent some of your own weight problems.

Photocopy Master 112
Calculate the total weight in grams of all nine objects. Convert this total into kilograms and grams.

Challenge Master 29

Extension activities
Measure a collection of objects which weigh less than 1 kilogram. Write each measure as a fraction of a kilogram.

Challenge Activities
Find an object/set of objects which weigh 100 grams, then 200 grams, then 300 grams, ..., up to 1 kilogram.
Find an object/set of objects which weigh 10 grams, then 20 grams, then 30 grams, ..., up to 100 grams.
Make a large collection of different labels with marked weights, and sort and order them. Display them according to type or size.

Name_____

Grams

Write how many grams each object weighs.

1. _____ g

2. _____ g

3. _____ g

4. _____ g

5. _____ g

6. _____ g

7. _____ g

8. _____ g

9. _____ g

 Write different fractions of a kilogram, and write how many grams each weighs.

For example: $\frac{1}{2}$ kg, $\frac{1}{4}$ kg, $\frac{1}{5}$ kg, …

2-d shape

Skills summary
- To recognise and name 2-d shapes: square, rectangle, triangle, circle, pentagon, hexagon, octagon
- To draw common 2-d shapes
- To sort common 2-d shapes according to their number of sides, type of sides, number of vertices etc
- To construct 2-d shapes by folding and cutting paper/card
- To construct 2-d shapes on a geoboard
- To recognise a polygon as a 2-d shape with straight sides
- To recognise and name a quadrilateral
- To recognise the difference between regular and irregular polygons
- To name polygons with 7 (heptagon), 9 (nonagon) and 10 (decagon) sides

Core links

Shape, Data and Measures Textbook page 27, top
- Copy each shape and mark any right-angles.

Shape, Data and Measures Textbook page 27, bottom
- Find the area of each drawn shape, by counting squares. Which shape has the largest and which the smallest area?

Shape, Data and Measures Textbook page 28
- Find the area of as many shapes as you can by counting squares. Which has the largest and which the smallest area?
- Copy any of the shapes which you think have symmetry. Draw the lines of symmetry.

Shape, Data and Measures Textbook page 29, top
- Estimate the order of the areas of each shape, i.e. write the question numbers, in order, from smallest to largest estimated area. Find the area of each shape, by counting squares, then compare the true order with the estimated order.

Shape, Data and Measures Textbook page 30, Explore
- Investigate the creation of shapes with one-line cuts and three-line cuts.

Photocopy Master 116
- Explore the distance around the boundary ('perimeter') of each shape. Estimate which shape has the largest perimeter, and which the smallest. Put the others in estimated order, from smallest to largest. Measure the lengths of sides of each shape in millimetres, then calculate the perimeters. Compare the estimates with the calculated measures.

Challenge Master 30

Extension activities
- Investigate other shapes which can be drawn on the spotty grid. For example, is it possible to draw a shape with 3-sides, 4-sides, 5-sides, ..., and so on? What is the maximum number of sides possible? Name the 7-, 9-, and 10-sided shapes.
- Investigate the creation of different octagons, or different pentagons.

Shapes on spotty grids

Draw each shape by joining the points on the spotty grids.
Make each pentagon and each hexagon different.

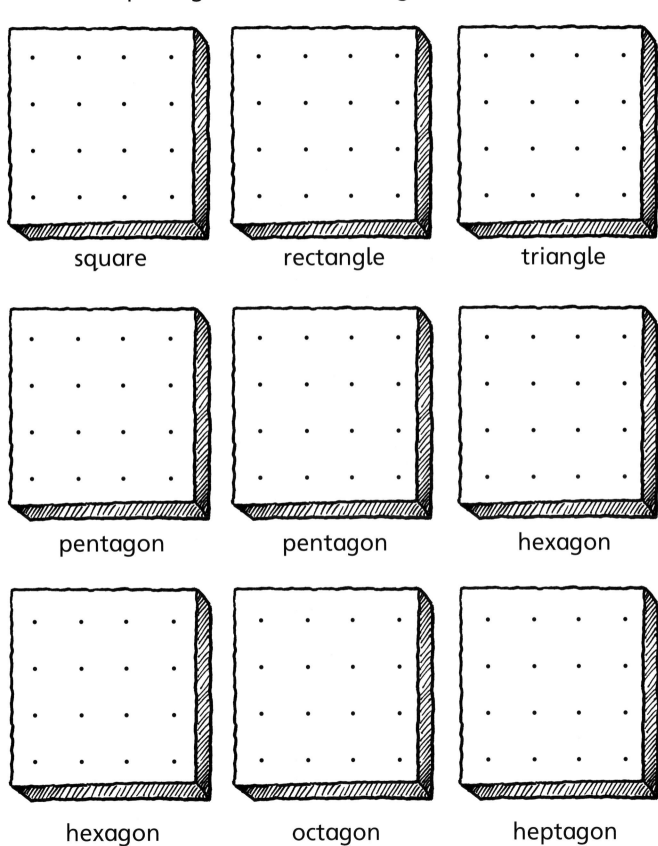

| square | rectangle | triangle |

| pentagon | pentagon | hexagon |

| hexagon | octagon | heptagon |

Abacus Ginn and Company 1999. Copying permitted for purchasing school only. This material is not copyright free.

Symmetry

Skills summary

- To recognise patterns which have line symmetry
- To recognise shapes which have line symmetry
- To locate a line of symmetry on a pattern or shape
- To create symmetrical shapes by folding and cutting paper/card
- To complete a symmetrical pattern, given a line of symmetry and half the pattern
- To complete a symmetrical drawing, given a line of symmetry and half the picture
- To recognise common shapes which are symmetrical, e.g. rectangle.
- To recognise how many lines of symmetry a given shape has
- To understand the meaning of rotational symmetry

Core links

Shape, Data and Measures Textbook page 31, top
Copy any of these shapes which have other lines of symmetry. On each of these, draw all the lines of symmetry.

Shape, Data and Measures Textbook page 32
Find the total area of each shape by counting squares. For a given line of symmetry, find the area of each part divided by the line. Check that each is one half of the whole area.

Shape, Data and Measures Textbook page 33, Explore
Draw round each shape individually. Draw any lines of symmetry.

Photocopy Master 118
Count the number of squares inside each shape (i.e. their areas). Divide the insides of the shapes into squares, half-squares and half-rectangles, in order to find their areas.

Challenge Master 31

Extension activities
Draw large spotty grids, like these, making the spots large enough to contain a counter. Draw a line of symmetry on each. Arrange some red counters in position on one side of the line of symmetry, and complete the symmetrical pattern, using a different colour of counter for the other side.

Make some patterns which look the same as each pattern is given successive half-turns, i.e. patterns with rotational symmetry of order two. Extend to patterns which look the same after each quarter-turn, i.e. patterns with rotational symmetry of order four.

Challenge Activities
Try drawing a shape which has 1 line of symmetry, one which has 2 lines of symmetry, 3 lines of symmetry, and so on.

Use a set of different plastic shapes. Can you find a shape with 1 line, another with 2 lines, another with 3 lines, ... of symmetry?

Symmetry patterns

Colour one more spot on each to make a pattern with symmetry.

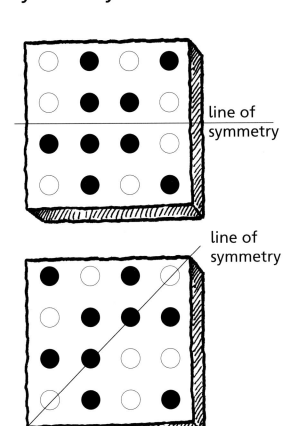

line of symmetry

line of symmetry

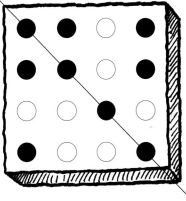

line of symmetry

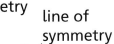

line of symmetry

Colour two more spots on these.

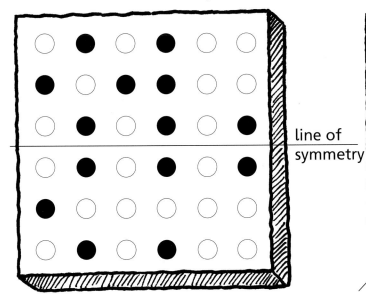

line of symmetry

line of symmetry

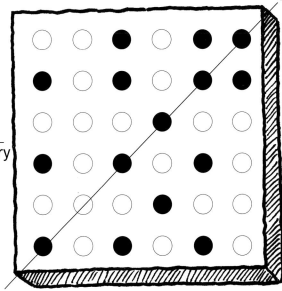

 Make some of your own symmetry patterns.

Direction

Skills summary

- To recognise the four-point compass directions
- To use a direction compass
- To construct a paper-compass, using a direction compass to locate North
- To define the direction of one object from another using the four compass points
- To interpret directions on a map based on the four compass points
- To relate right-angle turns to the four-point compass directions
- To recognise the eight-point compass directions

Core links

Shape, Data and Measures Textbook page 34

- Label each column on the map as 'A', 'B', 'C', etc, and each row on the map as '1', '2', '3', etc. Locate the position of each object on the map using the row and column labels, e.g. lighthouse A6.
- Design a journey from one starting place to each of the other places, travelling in each of the directions N, S, E and W. How far do you have to travel on your journey (i.e. through how many squares must you pass)?

Shape, Data and Measures Textbook page 35

- Describe a journey from the bus stop to visit the church, the phone box and the newspaper shop. How far have you travelled (how many squares have you passed through)? Describe different journeys.
- Design your own map, and draw objects which are north, south, east and west from each other.

Shape, Data and Measures Textbook page 36, top

- Write a description of the journey in reverse, i.e. from p back to a.
- Copy the picture and draw a different journey from a to p, using the four compass directions. Write a description of the journey.

Photocopy Master 119

- Draw some of your own paths on squared paper. Include some diagonal lines. Describe each path using the 8-point compass directions.

Challenge Master 32

Extension activities

- Invent your own map, using an 8 × 8 square grid, and write the directions of objects from each other using the four-point and eight-point compass directions.

Name_____

Shape map

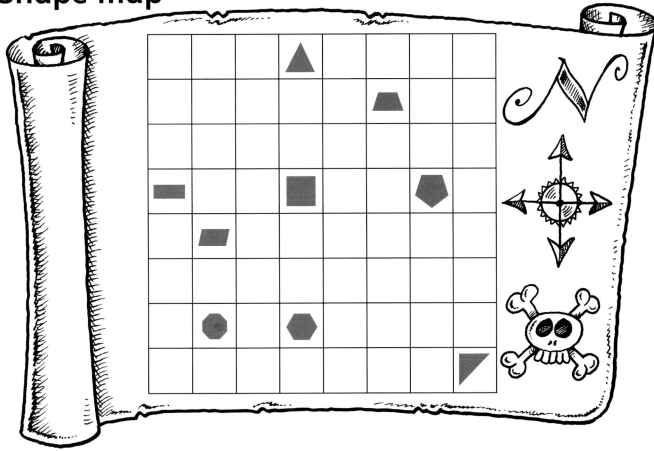

✏️ Which shape is:

1. North from

2. East from

3. West from

4. South from

5. South-east from

6. North-west from

7. South-west from

8. North-east from

✏️ What is the direction from:

9. to

10. to

11. to

12. to

13. to

14. to

3-d shape

Skills summary
- To recognise and name 3-d shapes: cube, cuboid, cylinder, sphere, cone, pyramid, prism, hemi-sphere
- To construct 3-d shapes using construction materials, e.g. Polydron
- To correctly identify the number of faces, edges, and vertices of a 3-d shape
- To recognise the shape of the faces of a 3-d shape
- To sort pyramids according to type, i.e. triangular-based, square-based, etc
- To sort prisms according to type, i.e. triangular, square, pentagonal etc
- To construct 3-d shapes from a net, by cutting, folding and gluing
- To recognise the shape that a given net will produce
- To recognise that there are many different nets of a cube
- To construct different nets of a cube
- To draw a net for a given 3-d shape

Core links

Shape, Data and Measures Textbook page 37, top
- Write the number of faces, edges and vertices of each shape.

Shape, Data and Measures Textbook page 38, top
- Create a table which shows how many faces each type of prism has, e.g. triangular prism – 5 faces, pentagonal prism – 7 faces.

Shape, Data and Measures Textbook page 40, top
- Collect a set of shapes so that one has 10 faces, another has 9 faces, another has 8 faces, and so on. Are some impossible?

Shape, Data and Measures Textbook page 41
- Name each shape.
- How many of the faces in the drawings are squares, rectangles, triangles, ...?

Shape, Data and Measures Textbook page 42, Explore
- Open out flat the packets you have collected to show the 'net' of the prism.

Challenge Master 33

Extension activities
- Design a net for making a different prism. Use plastic shapes, drawing round their edges to help you draw the net. Construct the model from your net.

Challenge Activity
- Investigate the creation of different nets of a cube. How many can you find?

Prism

Guess how many faces, edges and corners this prism will have.

Make the prism by cutting out this net, scoring along the folds, then gluing the tabs. Were you correct?

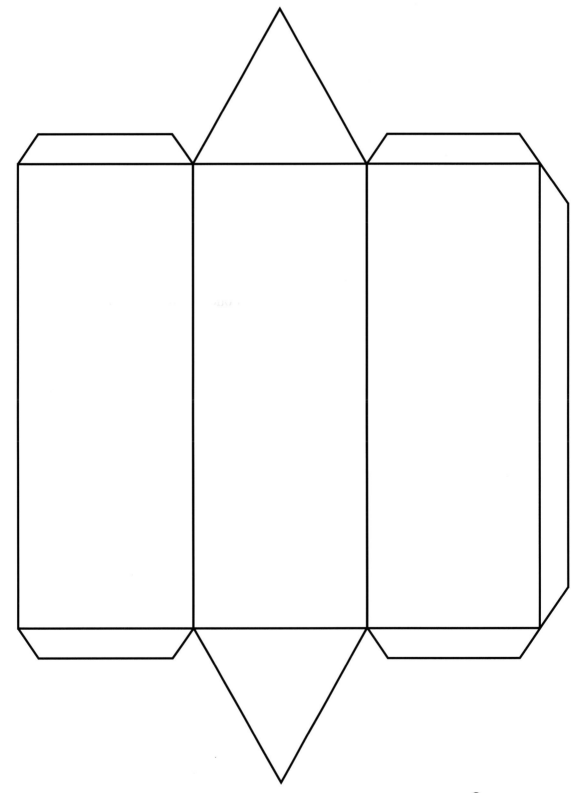

Angle

Skills summary
- To recognise clockwise and anticlockwise turns
- To recognise angle as a measure of an amount of turn
- To measure amounts of turn in right angles
- To relate right angle turns to the four-point compass directions
- To relate right angle and half right angle turns to the eight-point compass directions
- To recognise right angles in shapes
- To recognise angles as 'acute', 'obtuse' or 'reflex'
- To measure angle in degrees
- To measure/draw an angle using a protractor

Core links

Shape, Data and Measures Textbook page 43, top
Write which of the angles are less than one rightangle (i.e. acute), and which are between one and two right angles (i.e. obtuse).

Shape, Data and Measures Textbook page 44, top
Write which of the angles are less than one rightangle (i.e. acute), and which are between one and two right angles (i.e. obtuse).

Shape, Data and Measures Textbook page 45
Write each angle in degrees.

Shape, Data and Measures Textbook page 46, top
If the climbing frame is in the direction North, write the direction faced after each of the turns in the questions.

Shape, Data and Measures Textbook page 48, top
Write each angle in degrees.

Shape, Data and Measures Textbook page 49, Explore
Write different turns that finish facing other directions, using eight-point compass directions, e.g. facing south-east.

Photocopy Master 121
Cut out each of the nine angles. Put them in order from smallest to largest. In cases of uncertainty place one angle over the other to compare.

Challenge Master 34

Extension activities
Write different minute-hand turns in right angles and fractions of a right angle, e.g. from 5 to 6 is one third of a right angle. Write these turns in degrees.

Name_____

Right-angles

Write the new time after each turn by the minute hand.

1. 1 right angle

2. 2 right angles

3. 3 right angles

4. 4 right angles

5. 2 right angles

6. 1 right angle

7. 3 right angles

8. $\frac{1}{3}$ right angle

9. 5 right angles

10. $1\frac{1}{3}$ right angle

11. $2\frac{1}{3}$ right angles

12. 6 right angles

Position

Skills summary

- To state the position of an object on a square grid in which the spaces are labelled
- To mark on object on a square grid, given row and column labels
- To state the position of an object on a square grid (i.e. its coordinates) in which the lines are labelled
- To mark on object on a square grid, given its coordinates
- To draw a shape given the coordinates of its vertices

Core links

Shape, Data and Measures Textbook page 50, top
Draw your own grid, label the rows and columns, and place objects in the spaces in the grid, e.g. counters, cubes, coins. State the position of the objects.

Shape, Data and Measures Textbook page 51, top
Draw a new grid, label the coordinates of the lines 0, 1, 2, ... Draw objects at the intersections of the lines, then state the coordinates of each.

Photocopy Master 123
Describe the positions of different children related to another. For example, 'Starting with Helen, Lisa is two rows back, and five places to the right'.

Challenge Master 35

Extension activities
Name each shape.
Draw your own coordinate grid, and shapes at the intersections of the lines. Write the coordinates of each shape.

Challenge Activities
Use maps in which the spaces are labelled, e.g. a street map. Write the positions of different places on the map.
Play a game for two players. Each player draws a 6 × 6 grid and labels the columns A, B, ..., F, and the rows 1, 2, ..., 6. Players then mark eight targets in different spaces on their grid, unseen by their opponent. Take turns to try to hit an opponent's target by saying the position of a square, e.g. C5. The winner is the first to hit five of their opponent's targets.

Shape positions

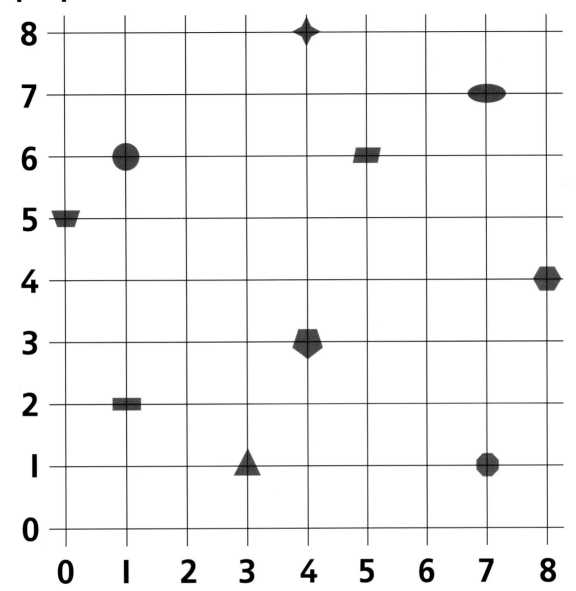

⬣ is at (7, I) – along 7, up I

Write the coordinates of these.

I. ⬤ (,   )   2. ✦ (,   )

3. ▬ (,   )   4. ◼ (,   )

5. ▲ (,   )   6. ⬭ (,   )

7. ⬡ (,   )   8. ▰ (,   )

9. ⬟ (,   )   I0. ▽ (,   )

D1 Tally charts   **D2** Frequency tables

D3 Bar graphs   **D4** Pictographs

Data

Skills summary
- To collect data
- To construct and interpret a tally chart
- To construct and interpret a frequency table
- To construct and interpret a bar graph (vertical frequencies labelled in units)
- To construct and interpret a bar graph (vertical frequencies labelled in twos, fives, tens)
- To construct and interpret a pictograph (one picture per item)
- To construct and interpret a pictograph (one picture per several items)
- To sort data using Venn and Carroll diagrams, and interpret them
- To represent and interpret data generated by a computer

Core links

Shape, Data and Measures Textbook page 53, top and bottom
Draw a bar graph to illustrate the results of the tally charts.

Shape, Data and Measures Textbook page 54, bottom
Draw a bar graph to illustrate the tally chart, labelling the frequencies on the vertical axis in twos or fives.

Shape, Data and Measures Textbook page 55, Explore
Throw two dice 60 times and construct a tally chart to show the totals. Draw a bar graph of the results.

Shape, Data and Measures Textbook page 58, Explore
Investigate the number of letters in the first names of children in the class/year group/whole school. Draw a frequency table and bar graph to show the results.

Shape, Data and Measures Textbook page 61, top
Find how much money there is altogether.
Collect your own set of coins, draw a tally chart, then a bar graph to show their values. Find the total value of all the coins.

Shape, Data and Measures Textbook page 64, Explore
Draw different pictographs for the same set of data, but using a different key each time, e.g. 1 circle represents 2 votes, 1 circle represents 4 votes, ...

Photocopy Master 125
Make a similar list of fruits, draw a frequency table for the vowels, and compare them.
Repeat for consonants in both lists.

Challenge Master 36

Extension activities
Assume that 20 children were asked, instead of 16.

Challenge Activity
Create your own database for numbers. Choose your own descriptions, e.g. 'is a multiple of 3', 'is an odd number', ..., and then choose ten numbers written down the side of the table. Place appropriate ticks and crosses in the table.

Name_____

Ice-cream

Some children were asked about their favourite ice-cream flavour.

Strawberry was the most popular.

Four more preferred chocolate to mint.

Vanilla was the least popular.

16 children were asked altogether.

Draw a possible bar chart to show the votes.

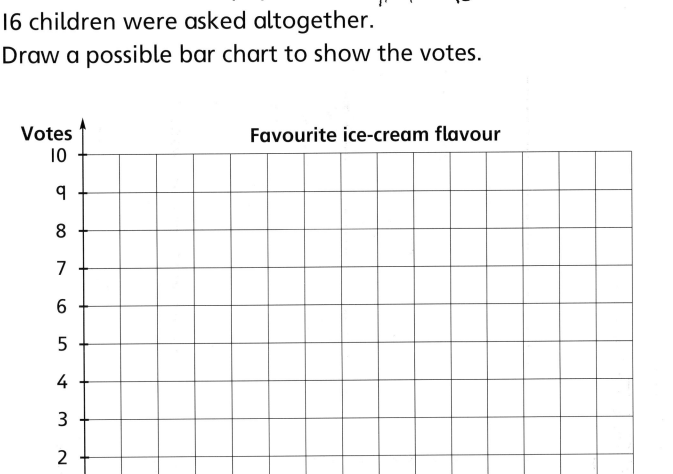

 Draw some different possible bar charts for the same votes.

Challenge Master Answers

Challenge Master 1
1. 400   2. 60   3. 1   4. 60
5. 300   6. 6   7. 4000   8. 600
9. 2000   10. 900   11. 3000 12. 30

Challenge Master 2
80, 50, 40, 20, 90, 60, 10, 70, 100, 30

85, 95, 55, 45, 75, 25, 5, 65, 15, 35

33, 9, 22, 14, 37, 15, 32, 41, 25, 3

Challenge Master 3
1. 20   2. 30   3. 36   4. 45   5. 57
6. 78   7. 50   8. 50   9. 93   10. 76
11. 142 12. 153 13. 20   14. 40   15. 215
16. 238 17. 472 18. 236 19. 533 20. 305

Challenge Master 4
Pairs of numbers with a difference of 1 are:
19, 20   29, 30   39, 40
49, 50, ... 89, 90   8 pairs in total

Pairs of numbers with a difference of 10 are:
10, 20   20, 30   30, 40
40, 50, ... 80, 90   8 pairs in total

Pairs of numbers with a difference of 50 are:
10, 60   20, 70   30, 80
40, 90   4 pairs in total

Pairs of numbers with a difference of 5 are:
15, 20   25, 30   35, 40, ... 85, 90

16, 21   26, 31   36, 41, ... 86, 91

17, 22   27, 32   37, 42, ... 87, 92

18, 23   28, 33   38, 43, ... 88, 93

19, 24   29, 34   39, 44, ... 89, 94   40 pairs in total

Pairs of numbers with a difference of 75 are:
1, 76   2, 77   3, 78   4, 79   5, 80

6, 81   7, 82   8, 83   9, 84   10, 85

11, 86   12, 87   13, 88   14, 89   15, 90

16, 91   17, 92   18, 93   19, 94   20, 95

21, 96   22, 97   23, 98   24, 99   24 pairs in total

Challenge Master 5

x	1	2	3	4	5	6	7	8	9	10
1	1	2	3	4	5	6	7	8	9	10
2	2	4	6	8	10	12	14	16	18	20
3	3	6	9	12	15	18	21	24	27	30
4	4	8	12	16	20	24	28	32	36	40
5	5	10	15	20	25	30	35	40	45	50
6	6	12	18	24	30	36	42	48	54	60
7	7	14	21	28	35	42	49	56	63	70
8	8	16	24	32	40	48	56	64	72	80
9	9	18	27	36	45	54	63	72	81	90
10	10	20	30	40	50	60	70	80	90	100

Challenge Master 6
1. 155   2. 210   3. 230   4. 120
5. 310   6. 240   7. 420   8. 80
9. 115   10. 275 11. 220 12. 130
13. 330 14. 410 15. 430 16. 85

Challenge Master 7
There are many ways of making 30. A systematic
approach is to list all the 'one counter' totals that can
be made:

Single	10	9	8	7	6	5	4	3
Double	20	18	16	14	12	10	8	6
Treble	30	27	24	21	18	15	12	9

Next, take each one in turn, looking for two others
that will make the total up to 30, e.g. (10, 10, 10)
(10, 8, double 6) (10, 8, treble 4) (10, double 4, double 6)
(10, 6, double 7) (10, 5, treble 5) (10, 4, double 8)
(10, double 3, double 7), etc.

Challenge Master 8
1. 30p   2. 10p   4. 12p   4. 10p
5. 8p   6. 5p   7. 9p   8. 5p
9. 20p   10. 12p   11. 20p   12. 10p

Challenge Master 9

d	60	75	5	90
30	30	45	25	60
45	15	30	40	45
20	15	30	40	45
25	35	50	20	65
40	20	35	35	50
15	45	60	10	75

Challenge Master 10

146, 148, 164, 168, 184, 186
416, 418, 461, 468, 481, 486
614, 618, 641, 648, 681, 684
814, 816, 841, 846, 861, 864

Nearest to:
100	146
200	186
300	186
400	416
500	486
600	614
700	684
800	814
900	864
1000	864

Challenge Master 11

1. 32, 26   2. 32, 37   3. 37, 41   4. 32, 29
5. 48, 56   6. 41, 48   7. 65, 75   8. 65, 56
9. 26, 37   10. 86, 98   11. 48, 65   12. 32, 56

Challenge Master 12

1. 267   2. 334   3. 515   4. 671
5. 484   6. 853   7. 634   8. 803
9. 324   10. 546   11. 76   12. 309
13. 429   14. 295   15. 475   16. 12
17. 234   18. 346   19. 236   20. 345
21. 466   22. 164   23. 904   24. 197

Challenge Master 13

1. 2   2. 6   3. 10   4. 4   5. 6

Challenge Master 14

1. 100, 110   2. 100, 110   3. 100, 101
4. 140, 144   5. 100, 98

46	64	110
85	21	106
96	21	117
71	89	160
72	35	107
90	87	177

151	199	350
198	234	432
302	87	389
160	240	400
370	530	900
180	423	603

Challenge Master 15

10	4	14
18	12	8
6	16	2

40	140	80
160	100	60
120	20	180

110	70	130
150	30	10
90	50	170

42	68	86
82	64	48
22	84	104

Challenge Master 16

1. 2   2. 3   3. 4

Other ways of dividing 24 equally:
24 ÷ 24,   24 ÷ 2,   24 ÷ 3,   24 ÷ 4

Ways of dividing 36 equally:
36 ÷ 1, 36 ÷ 2, 36 ÷ 3, 36 ÷ 4,
36 ÷ 6, 36 ÷ 9, 36 ÷ 12, 36 ÷ 18

Ways of dividing 48 equally:
48 ÷ 1, 48 ÷ 2, 48 ÷ 3, 48 ÷ 4,
48 ÷ 6, 48 ÷ 8, 48 ÷ 12, 48 ÷ 16, 48 ÷ 24

Challenge Master 17

1. 3527: 3530, 3500
2. 1593: 1590, 1600
3. 4168: 4170, 4200
4. 2741: 2740, 2700
5. 1388: 1390, 1400
6. 6636: 6640, 6600
7. 5380: 5380, 5400
8. 4791: 4790, 4800
9. 6272: 6270, 6300
10. 2059: 2060, 2100
11. 4308: 4310, 4300
12. 6747: 6750, 6800
13. 2309: 2310, 2300

Challenge Master 18

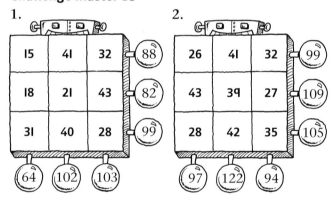

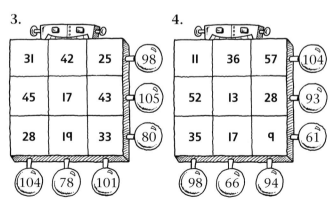

Challenge Master 19

Reversing the digits of 'next door' numbers is effectively the same as adding 9 (i.e. the tens increase by 1 and the units decrease by 1). For example: 34 → 43, 23 → 32. Hence, differences between such pairs will always be 9.

Reversing the digits of 'next door but one' numbers is effectively the same as adding 18 (i.e. the tens increase by 2 and the units decrease by 2). For example: 13 → 31, 46 → 64. Hence, differences between such pairs will always be 18.

Challenge Master 20

To assist them, pupils may find it helpful to make a list of the numbers in order.

1. 234, 340
2. 207, 452
3. 610, 207
4. 532, 125
5. 610, 340
6. 331, 315
7. 147, 331
8. 234, 315
9. 254, 610
10. 147, 302

Challenge Master 21

×	20	50	40	30
4	80	200	160	120
3	60	150	120	90
2	40	100	80	60
5	100	250	200	150
6	120	300	240	180

×	4	2	5	10
100	400	200	500	1000
400	1600	800	2000	4000
300	1200	600	1500	3000
500	2000	1000	2500	5000
800	3200	1600	4000	8000

Challenge Master 22

One example for each divisor:
17 ÷ 2 = 8 r 1
19 ÷ 3 = 6 r 1
13 ÷ 4 = 3 r 1
13 ÷ 5 = 2 r 3
13 ÷ 6 = 2 r 1
15 ÷ 7 = 2 r 1
17 ÷ 8 = 2 r 1
18 ÷ 9 = 2 r 0

Challenge Master 23

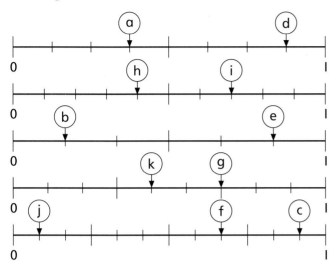

Challenge Master 24

a. 763 + 54 = 817
b. 763 + 45 = 808
c. 346 + 57 = 403
d. 345 + 67 = 412
e. 346 + 57 = 403
   635 + 75 = 709
   573 + 64 = 637
   576 + 43 = 619
   654 + 73 = 727
f. 435 + 67 = 502   437 + 65 = 502
  465 + 37 = 502   467 + 35 = 502

  435 + 76 = 511   436 + 75 = 511
  475 + 36 = 511   476 + 35 = 511

  453 + 67 = 520   463 + 57 = 520
  457 + 63 = 520   467 + 53 = 520

  453 + 76 = 529   473 + 56 = 529
  456 + 73 = 529   476 + 53 = 529

  463 + 75 = 538   465 + 73 = 538
  473 + 65 = 538   475 + 63 = 538

  536 + 47 = 583   537 + 46 = 583
  546 + 37 = 583   547 + 36 = 583

Challenge Master 25

A $3\frac{1}{2}$ cm   B $5\frac{1}{2}$ cm   C 7 cm   D 9 cm
E 13 cm   F $10\frac{1}{2}$ cm   G $8\frac{1}{2}$ cm   H $15\frac{1}{2}$ cm

Challenge Master 26

Past the hour:
1. 15 minutes   2. 25 minutes   3. 40 minutes
4. 31 minutes   5. 23 minutes   6. 16 minutes
7. 14 minutes   8. 37 minutes   9. 45 minutes
10. 9 minutes   11. 52 minutes   12. 3 minutes
13. 28 minutes

Until the next hour:
1. 45 minutes   2. 35 minutes   3. 20 minutes
4. 29 minutes   5. 37 minutes   6. 44 minutes
7. 46 minutes   8. 23 minutes   9. 15 minutes
10. 51 minutes   11. 8 minutes   12. 57 minutes
13. 32 minutes

Challenge Master 27

1. 200 cl   2. 50 cl   3. 60 cl   4. 300 cl
5. 150 cl   6. 1.5 cl   7. 10 cl   8. 35 cl
9. 225 cl   10. 40 cl   11. 90 cl   12. 20 cl

Challenge Master 28

How many minutes?	
I hour	60
300 seconds	5
$\frac{1}{2}$ hour	30
10 hours	600
I day	1440
$\frac{3}{5}$ hours	36

How many hours?	
I day	24
September	720
600 minutes	10
I week	168
10 days	240
$\frac{2}{3}$ days	16

How many seconds?	
I minute	60
I hour	3600
$\frac{1}{4}$ hour	900
3 minutes	180
5·5 minutes	330
I day	86 400

How many days?	
I week	7
August	31
I year	365/366
5 years	1825/1826/1827
360 hours	15
March, April, May	92

Challenge Master 29
1. 1000 g
2. 3000 g
3. 10 000 g
4. 2500 g
5. 500 g
6. 250 g
7. 100 g
8. 3250 g
9. 125 g

Challenge Master 30
Answers will vary.

Challenge Master 31
Colour one more spot:

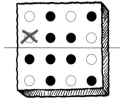 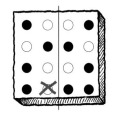

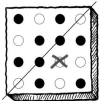 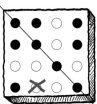

Colour two more spots:

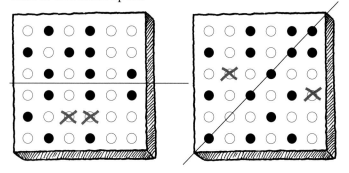

Challenge Master 32
1. Triangle
2. Hexagon
3. Square
4. Hexagon
5. Hexagon
6. Parallelogram
7. Square
8. Pentagon
9. East
10. North-west
11. North-west
12. South-west
13. South-east
14. North-east

Challenge Master 33
Faces: 5   Edges: 7   Corners: 6

Challenge Master 34
1. 25 past 10
2. 5 past 3
3. 5 to 7
4. 20 past 3
5. $\frac{1}{4}$ past 4
6. $\frac{1}{4}$ to 10
7. 25 past 5
8. 5 past 2
9. 10 past 9
10. 5 to 1
11. 20 to 12
12. $\frac{1}{4}$ to 9

Challenge Master 35
1. (1, 6)
2. (4, 8)
3. (1, 2)
4. (3, 5)
5. (3, 1)
6. (7, 7)
7. (8, 4)
8. (5, 6)
9. (4, 3)
10. (0, 5)

Challenge Master 36
One possible bar chart:

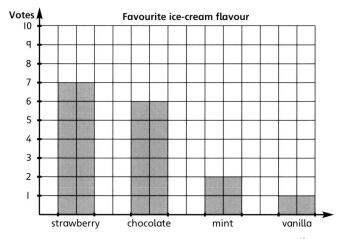

AA

Roa
BRITAIN

C000180429

Scale 1:200,000
or 3.16 miles to 1 inch

35th edition June 2021 © AA Media Limited 2021
Original edition printed 1986.

All cartography in this atlas edited, designed and produced by the Mapping Services Department of AA Media Limited (A05789).

This atlas contains Ordnance Survey data © Crown copyright and database right 2021 and Royal Mail data © Royal Mail copyright and database right 2021. Contains public sector information licensed under the Open Government Licence v3.0.
Ireland mapping and distance chart contains data available from openstreetmap.org © under the Open Database License found at opendatacommons.org

Published by AA Media Limited, whose registered office is Grove House, Lutyens Close, Basingstoke, Hampshire RG24 8AG, UK. Registered number 06112600

ISBN: 978 0 7495 8270 8

A CIP catalogue record for this book is available from The British Library.

The publishers would welcome information to correct any errors or omissions and to keep this atlas up to date. Please write to the Atlas Editor, AA Media Limited, Grove House, Lutyens Close, Basingstoke, Hampshire RG24 8AG, UK.
E-mail: roadatlasfeedback@aamediagroup.co.uk

Acknowledgements: AA Media Limited would like to thank the following for information used in the creation of this atlas:
Cadw, English Heritage, Forestry Commission, Historic Scotland, National Trust and National Trust for Scotland, RSPB, The Wildlife Trust, Scottish Natural Heritage, Natural England, The Countryside Council for Wales. Award winning beaches from 'Blue Flag' and 'Keep Scotland Beautiful' (summer 2019 data): for latest information visit www.blueflag.org and www.keepscotlandbeautiful.org. Road signs are © Crown Copyright 2021. Reproduced under the terms of the Open Government Licence. Transport for London (Central London Map), Nexus (Newcastle district map).
Ireland mapping: Republic of Ireland census 2016 © Central Statistics Office and Northern Ireland census 2016 © NISRA (population data); Irish Public Sector Data (CC BY 4.0) (Gaeltacht); Logainm.ie (placenames); Roads Service and Transport Infrastructure Ireland
Printed by Rotolito SpA, Italy

Contents

Map pages and distance chart	inside front cover
Route planning	**II–XVII**
Route planner	II–VII
Ferries and port plans	VIII–XI
Caravan and camping sites in Britain	XII–XV
Traffic signs	XVI–XVII
Motorways	**XVIII–XXV**
Restricted junctions	XVIII–XXI
M25 London Orbital motorway	XXII
M6 Toll motorway	XXIII
Smart motorways	XXIV–XXV
Map pages	**XXVI**
Road map symbols	**1**
Road maps	**2–173**
Britain 1:200,000 scale	2–169
Some islands are shown at slightly smaller scales	
Ireland 1:1,000,000 scale	170–173
District maps	**174–185**
Birmingham	174–175
Glasgow	176–177
London	178–181
Manchester	182–183
Tyne & Wear	184–185
Street map symbols	**186**
Towns, ports and airports	**187–237**
Town plans	188–234
Major airports	235–237
Port plans	VIII–XI
Channel Tunnel terminals	27
Central London street map and index	**238–253**
Index to place names	**254–302**
County, administrative area map	254
Place name index	255–302
Map pages and distance chart	**inside back cover**

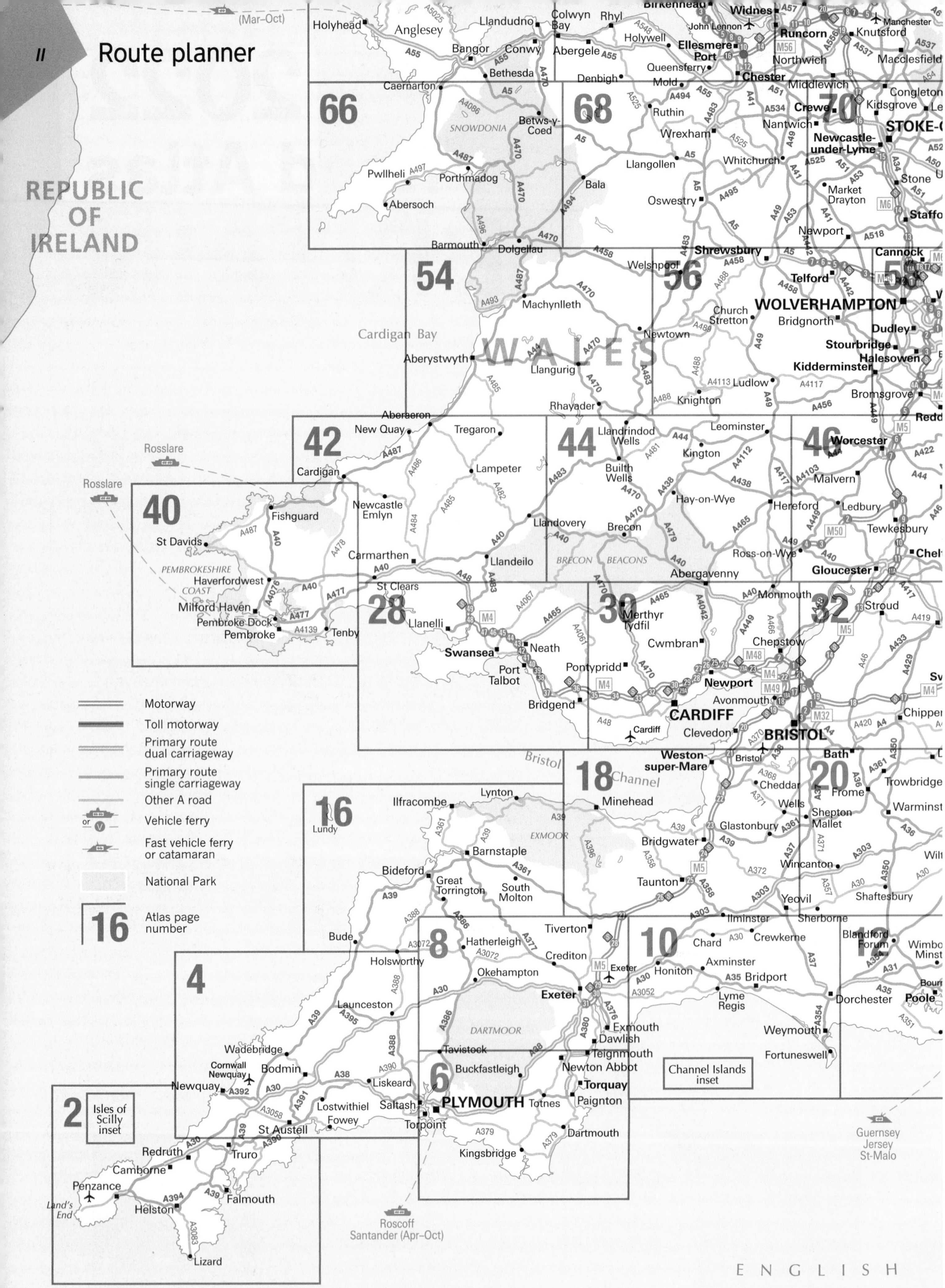

REPUBLIC
OF
IRELAND

WALES

Legend:

	Motorway
	Toll motorway
	Primary route dual carriageway
	Primary route single carriageway
	Other A road
or (V)	Vehicle ferry
	Fast vehicle ferry or catamaran
	National Park
16	Atlas page number

Page numbers on map:
66, 68, 70, 54, 56, 42, 44, 46, 40, 28, 30, 32, 16, 18, 20, 8, 10, 4, 6, 2

Isles of Scilly inset

Channel Islands inset

Place names (by region):

(Mar–Oct)

Holyhead, Anglesey, Llandudno, Colwyn Bay, Rhyl, Birkenhead, Widnes, Manchester
Bangor, Conwy, Abergele, Holywell, John Lennon, Runcorn, Knutsford
Bethesda, Caernarfon, A55, Denbigh, Queensferry, Ellesmere Port, Northwich, Macclesfield
Mold, Chester, Middlewich, Congleton
Snowdonia, Betws-y-Coed, Ruthin, Crewe, Kidsgrove
Pwllheli, Porthmadog, Wrexham, Nantwich, Newcastle-under-Lyme, STOKE-O
Abersoch, Llangollen, Whitchurch, Market Drayton, Stone
Oswestry, Newport, Staffo
Barmouth, Dolgellau, Shrewsbury, Cannock
Welshpool, Telford, Wolverhampton, Dudley, Stourbridge, Halesowen
Machynlleth, Church Stretton, Bridgnorth, Kidderminster
Cardigan Bay, Newtown, Bromsgrove, Redd
Aberystwyth, Llangurig, Ludlow, Knighton
Rhayader, Leominster, Worcester
Aberaeron, New Quay, Tregaron, Llandrindod Wells, Kington, Malvern
Cardigan, Lampeter, Builth Wells, Hay-on-Wye, Hereford, Ledbury, Tewkesbury
Newcastle Emlyn, Llandovery, Brecon, Ross-on-Wye, Gloucester
Fishguard, Carmarthen, Llandeilo, BRECON BEACONS, Abergavenny, Chel
St Davids, PEMBROKESHIRE COAST, St Clears, Monmouth, Stroud
Haverfordwest, Llanelli, Merthyr Tydfil, Chepstow
Milford Haven, Pembroke Dock, Pembroke, Tenby, Neath, Cwmbran, Newport
Swansea, Pontypridd, Avonmouth
Port Talbot, Bridgend, CARDIFF, BRISTOL, Bath
Rosslare, Clevedon, Bristol, Chipper
Weston-super-Mare, Cheddar, Frome, Trowbridge
Lynton, Minehead, Wells, Shepton Mallet, Warminst
Ilfracombe, EXMOOR, Glastonbury
Lundy, Barnstaple, Bridgwater, Wincanton, Wilt
Bideford, Great Torrington, South Molton, Taunton, Yeovil, Shaftesbury
Bude, Hatherleigh, Tiverton, Ilminster, Sherborne, Blandford Forum, Wimbo Minst
Holsworthy, Crediton, Chard, Crewkerne
Okehampton, Exeter, Honiton, Axminster, Bridport, Poole
Launceston, DARTMOOR, Exmouth, Lyme Regis, Dorchester, Bour
Wadebridge, Cornwall Newquay, Bodmin, Tavistock, Dawlish, Teignmouth, Weymouth, Fortuneswell
Newquay, Liskeard, Buckfastleigh, Newton Abbot
St Austell, Lostwithiel, Fowey, Saltash, PLYMOUTH, Totnes, Torquay, Paignton
Redruth, Truro, Torpoint, Dartmouth
Camborne, Falmouth, Kingsbridge
Penzance, Helston, Lizard
Land's End

Isles of Scilly

Roscoff, Santander (Apr–Oct)

Guernsey, Jersey, St-Malo

ENGLISH

Bristol Channel

ENGLISH

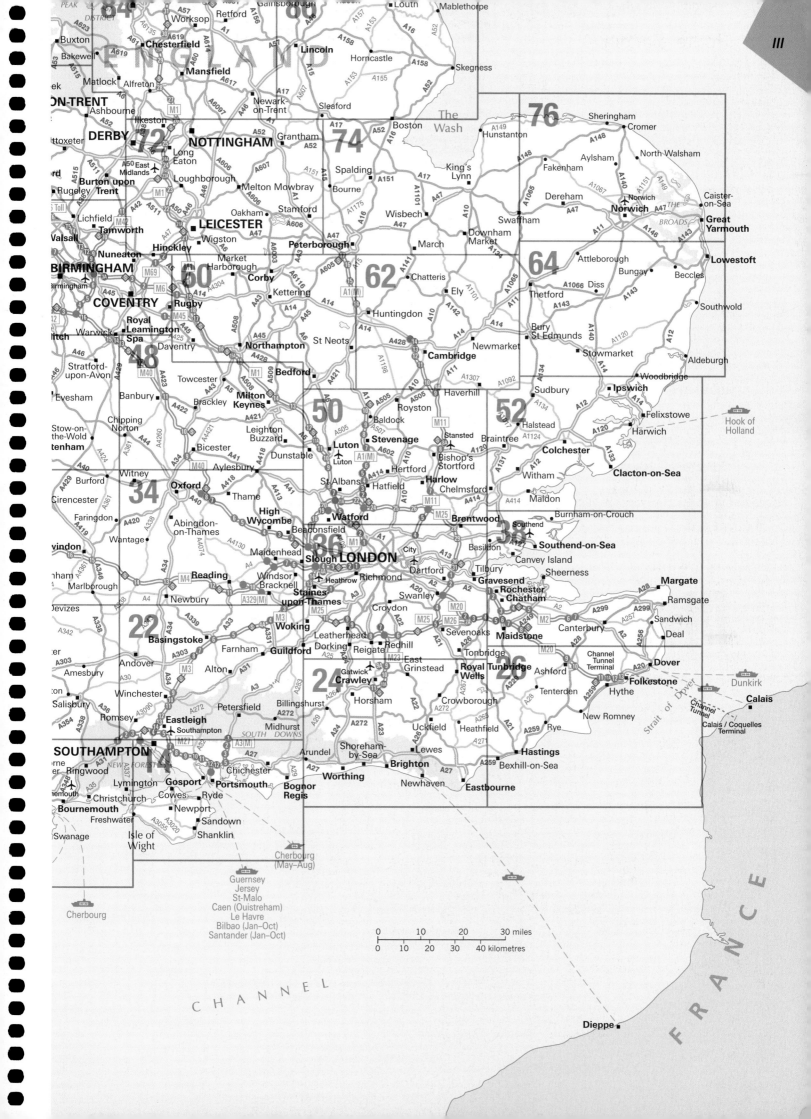

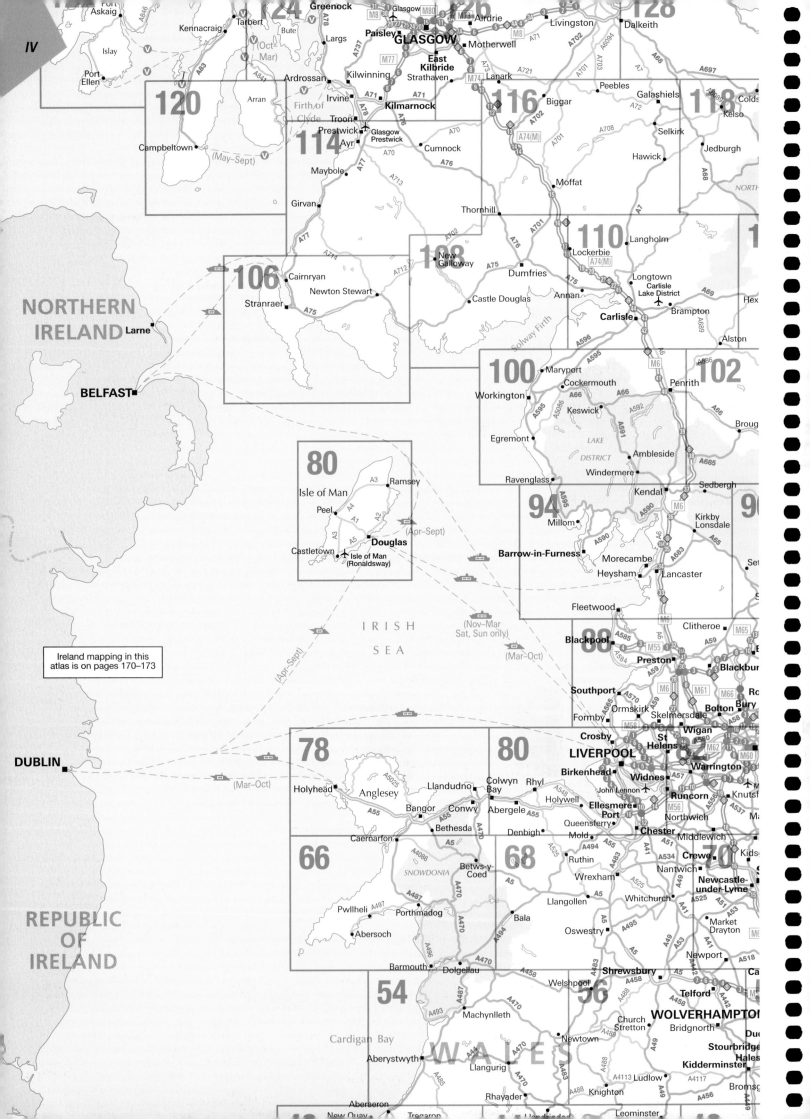

IV

NORTHERN
IRELAND   Larne

BELFAST

REPUBLIC
OF
IRELAND

DUBLIN

Ireland mapping in this
atlas is on pages 170–173

IRISH
SEA

(Apr–Sept)

(Nov–Mar
Sat, Sun only)

(Mar–Oct)

(Mar–Oct)

124   Greenock   Glasgow   126b   Airdrie   Livingston   Dalkeith   128
Kennacraig   Tarbert   M80   Livingston
Askaig   Bute   Paisley   GLASGOW   Motherwell   A702
Islay   Largs   Kilwinning   East   Lanark   Peebles   Galashiels   118   Colds
Port   Arran   120   Irvine   Kilbride   Strathaven   Biggar   Kelso
Ellen   Kilmarnock   116   Selkirk   Jedburgh
Ardrossan   Troon   Glasgow   Cumnock   A702   Hawick
Campbeltown   (May–Sept)   Prestwick   Prestwick   A74(M)   Moffat   NORTH
114   Ayr   A70   Thornhill   110   Langholm
Maybole   A76   Lockerbie   Longtown
Girvan   Dumfries   Carlisle   Brampton
106   Cairnryan   108   New   Castle Douglas   Annan   Lake District   A69   Hex
Newton Stewart   Galloway   Carlisle   Alston
Stranraer   Solway Firth   M6   102
100   Maryport   Cockermouth   Penrith   Broug
Workington   A66   A66
Keswick   LAKE   A66
80   Egremont   DISTRICT   Ambleside
Isle of Man   Ramsey   Ravenglass   Windermere
Peel   Kendal   Sedbergh
Castletown   Douglas   94   Kirkby   90
Isle of Man   Millom   Lonsdale
(Ronaldsway)   Barrow-in-Furness   Morecambe
Heysham   Lancaster   Set
Fleetwood   88   Clitheroe
Blackpool   Preston   Blackbur
78   Southport   Bolton   Bury   Ro
Holyhead   Ormskirk   Skelmersdale
Anglesey   Formby   Wigan
Bangor   Crosby   St   82
Conwy   Llandudno   Colwyn   Rhyl   LIVERPOOL   Helens   Warrington
Bethesda   Bay   Holywell   Birkenhead   Widnes   John Lennon   Runcorn   Knutsf
Caernarfon   Abergele   Queensferry   Ellesmere   Northwich   M
66   Denbigh   Port   Chester   Middlewich
SNOWDONIA   Betws-y-   Mold   68   Ruthin   Crewe   70
Coed   Wrexham   Nantwich   Newcastle-
Pwllheli   Porthmadog   Llangollen   Whitchurch   under-Lyme
Abersoch   Bala   Oswestry   Market
Drayton   Newport
Barmouth   Dolgellau   Shrewsbury   Telford
54   Welshpool   56   WOLVERHAMPTON
Machynlleth   Church   Bridgnorth   Du
Stretton   Stourbridge
Cardigan Bay   Newtown   WALES   Kidderminster   Hales
Aberystwyth   Llangurig   Ludlow   Bromsg
Aberaeron   Rhayader   Knighton   Leominster

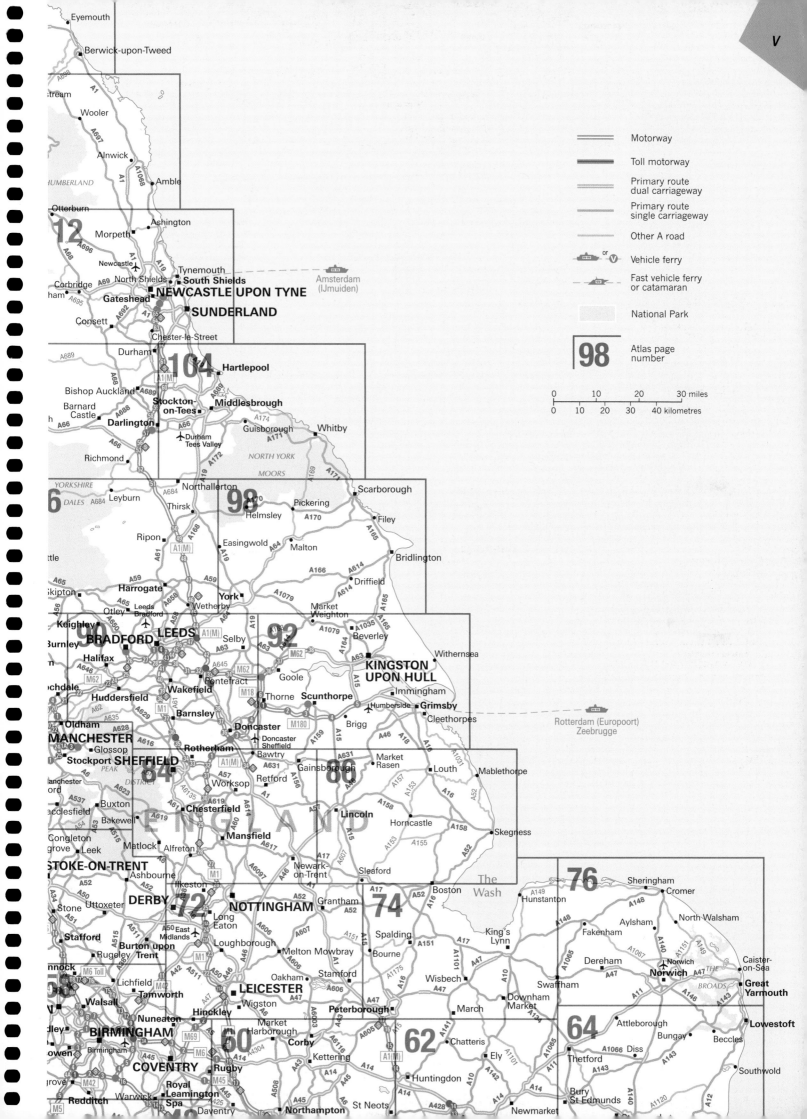

Map Legend

Motorway	
Toll motorway	
Primary route dual carriageway	
Primary route single carriageway	
Other A road	
Vehicle ferry	
Fast vehicle ferry or catamaran	
National Park	
98 Atlas page number	

0   10   20   30 miles
0   10   20   30   40 kilometres

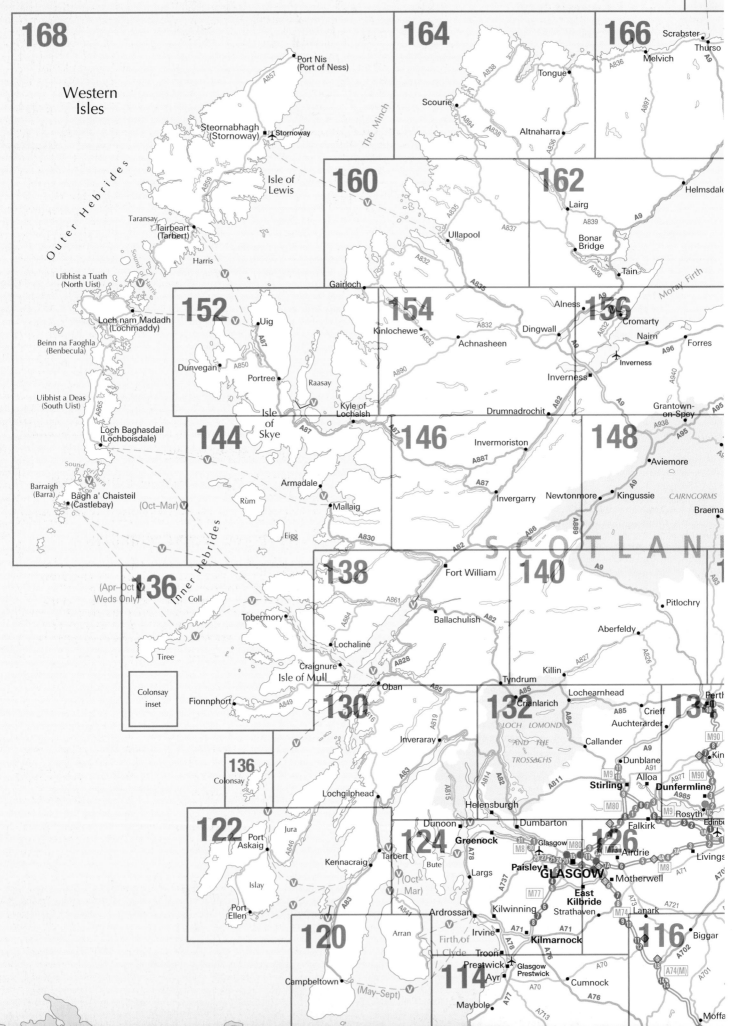

168

Western Isles

Port Nis
(Port of Ness)

Steornabhagh
(Stornoway) ■ Stornoway

Isle of
Lewis

Taransay

Tairbeart
(Tarbert)

Harris

Uibhist a Tuath
(North Uist)

Loch nam Madadh
(Lochmaddy)

Beinn na Faoghla
(Benbecula)

Uibhist a Deas
(South Uist)

Loch Baghasdail
(Lochboisdale)

Barraigh
(Barra)

Bàgh a' Chaisteil
(Castlebay)

(Oct–Mar) V

164

Scourie

Tongue

Altnaharra

166

Scrabster

Thurso

Melvich

160

V

Ullapool

Gairloch

Kinlochewe

Achnasheen

162

Lairg

Bonar
Bridge

Tain

Helmsdale

152

V

Uig

Dunvegan

Portree

Raasay

Isle
of
Skye

Kyle of
Lochalsh

154

Dingwall

Alness

156

V

Cromarty

Nairn

Forres

Inverness

Inverness ■

Drumnadrochit

Grantown-
on-Spey

144

V

Armadale

Mallaig

Rùm

Eigg

146

Invermoriston

Invergarry

148

Newtonmore

Kingussie

Aviemore

CAIRNGORMS

Braemar

136

(Apr–Oct
Weds Only)

Coll

Tobermory

Lochaline

Craignure

Isle of Mull

Tiree

Fionnphort

Colonsay
inset

Inner Hebrides

138

Fort William

Ballachulish

Oban

130

Inveraray

140

Pitlochry

Aberfeldy

Killin

Tyndrum

132

Crianlarich

LOCH LOMOND

AND THE
TROSSACHS

Lochearnhead

Callander

134

Crieff

Auchterarder

Perth

M90

Kin

136

Colonsay

122

Port
Askaig

Jura

Kennacraig

Islay

Port
Ellen

Lochgilphead

Tarbert

Bute

(Oct–
Mar)

Dunoon

124

Greenock

Largs

Dumbarton

Helensburgh

Dunblane

Alloa

Stirling ■

M9

M80

Glasgow
M8

Paisley ■

GLASGOW

East
Kilbride

Motherwell

M77

Dunblane

A91

A977 M90

Dunfermline

Rosyth

Falkirk

M9

Edinb

Airdrie

Livings

126

M8

Lanark

M74

116

Biggar

120

Campbeltown

Arran

(May–Sept)

V

Irvine

114

Ayr

Troon

Prestwick

Glasgow
Prestwick

Kilwinning

Ardrossan

Kilmarnock

Strathaven

Cumnock

Maybole

Moffa

SCOTLAND

The Minch

Outer Hebrides

Moray Firth

Firth of
Clyde

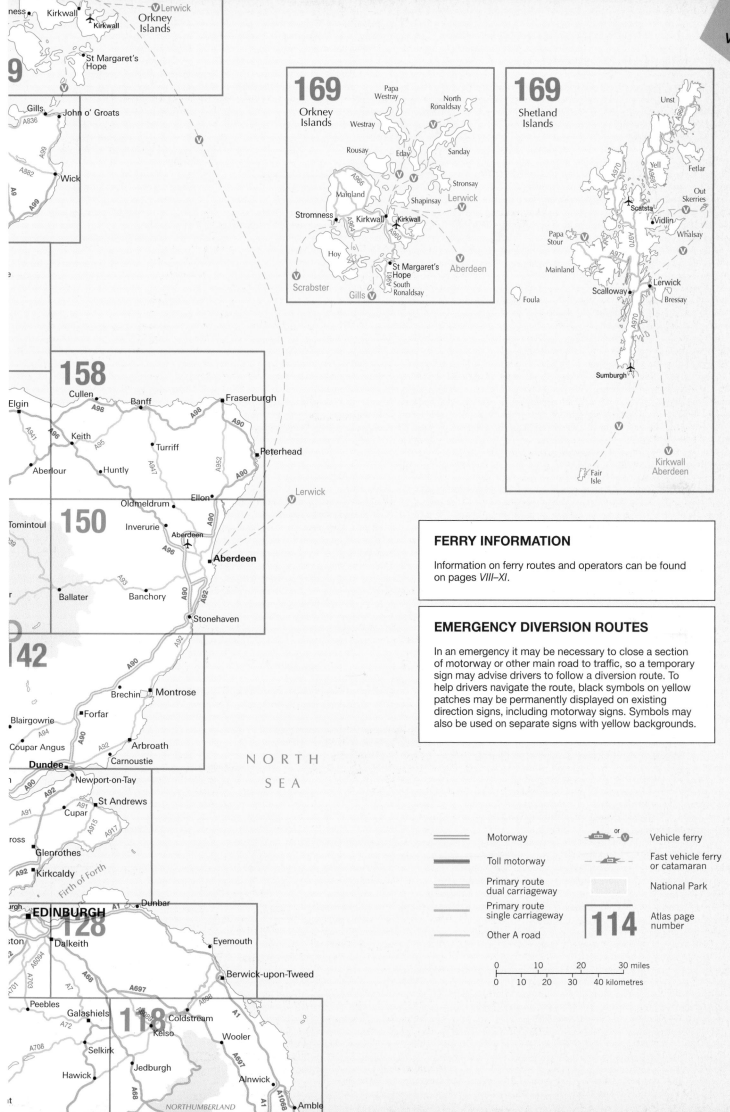

169
Orkney Islands

Papa Westray
North Ronaldsay
Westray
Rousay
Eday
Sanday
Stronsay
Mainland
Shapinsay
Lerwick
Stromness
Kirkwall
Kirkwall
A966
A964
A960
A965
Hoy
St Margaret's Hope
South Ronaldsay
A961
Aberdeen
Scrabster
Gills

169
Shetland Islands

Unst
A968
Yell
A970
Fetlar
Out Skerries
Papa Stour
Scatsta
Vidlin
Whalsay
A971
Mainland
A970
Scalloway
Lerwick
Bressay
Foula
Sumburgh
A970
Fair Isle
Kirkwall Aberdeen

158

Cullen
Banff
Fraserburgh
A98
A98
A90
Elgin
A941
A98
Keith
A95
Turriff
A952
Peterhead
A90
Aberlour
Huntly
A947
Ellon

150

Oldmeldrum
A90
Tomintoul
Inverurie
Aberdeen
A96
Aberdeen
A93
Ballater
Banchory
A90
A92
Stonehaven

42

A90
A92
Brechin
Montrose
Blairgowrie
Forfar
A94
A92
Coupar Angus
Arbroath
Dundee
Carnoustie
A90
A92
Newport-on-Tay
A91
A91
St Andrews
Cupar
A915
A917
Glenrothes
Firth of Forth
A92
Kirkcaldy

Lerwick

9

Kirkwall
Kirkwall
Orkney Islands
St Margaret's Hope
Gills
John o' Groats
A836
A99
A882
Wick
A9
A99

EDINBURGH
A1
Dunbar
128
Dalkeith
Eyemouth
A6094
A68
A7
Berwick-upon-Tweed
A697
A898
A1
Peebles
Galashiels
118
Coldstream
A72
Kelso
Wooler
A708
Selkirk
Jedburgh
A697
Hawick
Alnwick
A68
A1068
NORTHUMBERLAND
Amble

NORTH SEA

FERRY INFORMATION

Information on ferry routes and operators can be found on pages *VIII–XI*.

EMERGENCY DIVERSION ROUTES

In an emergency it may be necessary to close a section of motorway or other main road to traffic, so a temporary sign may advise drivers to follow a diversion route. To help drivers navigate the route, black symbols on yellow patches may be permanently displayed on existing direction signs, including motorway signs. Symbols may also be used on separate signs with yellow backgrounds.

——— Motorway	or Ⓥ Vehicle ferry
——— Toll motorway	Fast vehicle ferry or catamaran
——— Primary route dual carriageway	National Park
——— Primary route single carriageway	**114** Atlas page number
——— Other A road	

0   10   20   30 miles
0 10 20 30 40 kilometres

Channel hopping and the Isle of Wight

For business or pleasure, hopping on a ferry across to France, the Channel Islands or Isle of Wight has never been easier.

The vehicle ferry services listed in the table give you all the options, together with detailed port plans to help you navigate to and from the ferry terminals. Simply choose your preferred route, not forgetting the fast sailings (see ⛴). Bon voyage!

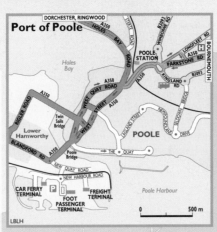

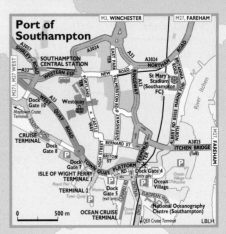

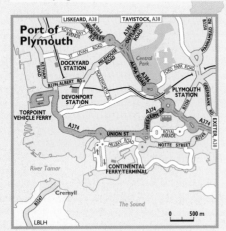

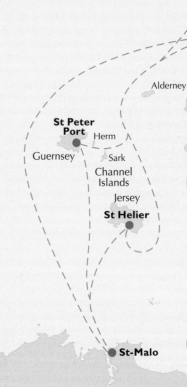

ENGLISH CHANNEL AND ISLE OF WIGHT FERRY CROSSINGS

From	To	Journey time	Operator website
Dover	Calais	1 hr 30 mins	dfdsseaways.co.uk
Dover	Calais	1 hr 30 mins	poferries.com
Dover	Dunkirk	2 hrs	dfdsseaways.co.uk
Folkestone	Calais (Coquelles)	35 mins	eurotunnel.com
Lymington	Yarmouth (IOW)	40 mins	wightlink.co.uk
Newhaven	Dieppe	4 hrs	dfdsseaways.co.uk
Plymouth	Roscoff	6–8 hrs	brittany-ferries.co.uk
Poole	Cherbourg	4 hrs 30 mins	brittany-ferries.co.uk
Poole	Guernsey	3 hrs ⛴	condorferries.co.uk
Poole	Jersey	4 hrs 30 mins ⛴	condorferries.co.uk
Poole	St-Malo	7–12 hrs (via Channel Is.) ⛴	condorferries.co.uk
Portsmouth	Caen (Ouistreham)	6–7 hrs	brittany-ferries.co.uk
Portsmouth	Cherbourg	3 hrs (May–Aug) ⛴	brittany-ferries.co.uk
Portsmouth	Fishbourne (IOW)	45 mins	wightlink.co.uk
Portsmouth	Guernsey	7 hrs	condorferries.co.uk
Portsmouth	Jersey	8–11 hrs	condorferries.co.uk
Portsmouth	Le Havre	5 hrs 30 mins	brittany-ferries.co.uk
Portsmouth	St-Malo	9–11 hrs	brittany-ferries.co.uk
Southampton	East Cowes (IOW)	1 hr	redfunnel.co.uk

The information listed is provided as a guide only, as services are liable to change at short notice and are weather dependent. Services shown are for vehicle ferries only, operated by conventional ferry unless indicated as a fast ferry service (⛴). Please check sailings before planning your journey.

Travelling further afield? For ferry services to Northern Spain see brittany-ferries.co.uk.

ENGLISH

Plymouth

Roscoff

St-Malo

Alderney

St Peter Port

Herm

Guernsey

Sark

Channel Islands

Jersey

St Helier

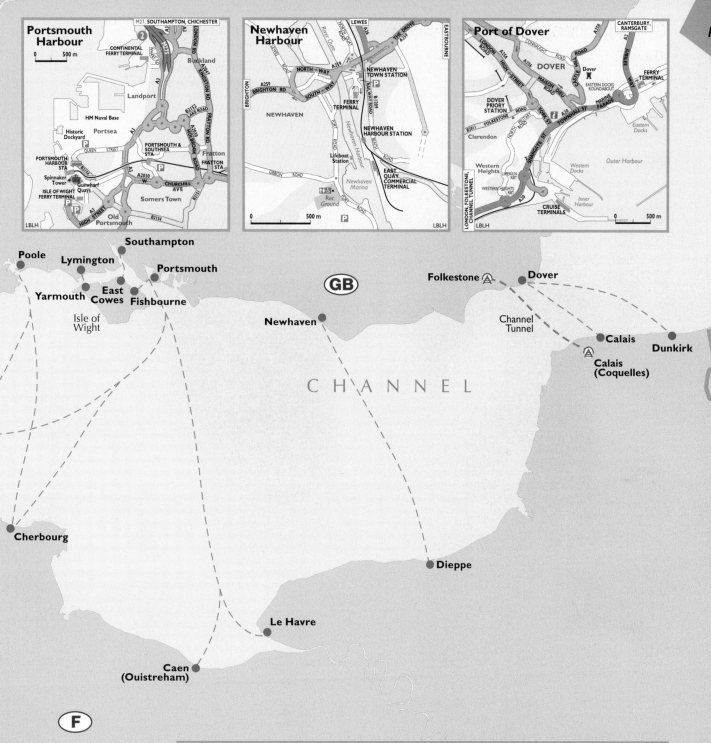

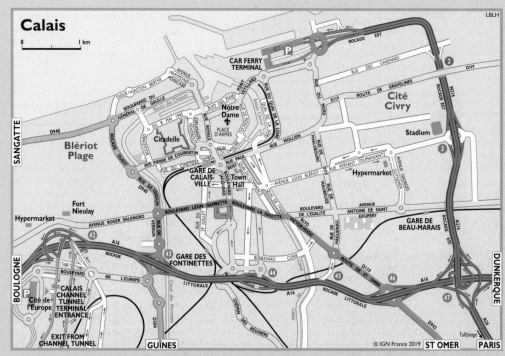

Ferries to Ireland and the Isle of Man

With so many sea crossings to Ireland and the Isle of Man the information provided in the table to the right will help you make the right choice.

IRISH SEA FERRY CROSSINGS

From	To	Journey time	Operator website
Cairnryan	Belfast	2 hrs 15 mins 🚤	stenaline.co.uk
Cairnryan	Larne	2 hrs	poferries.com
Douglas	Belfast	2 hrs 45 mins (April–Sept) 🚤	steam-packet.com
Douglas	Dublin	2 hrs 55 mins (April–Sept) 🚤	steam-packet.com
Fishguard	Rosslare	3 hrs 15 mins	stenaline.co.uk
Heysham	Douglas	3 hrs 45 mins	steam-packet.com
Holyhead	Dublin	2 hrs (Mar–Oct) 🚤	irishferries.com
Holyhead	Dublin	3 hrs 15 mins	irishferries.com
Holyhead	Dublin	3 hrs 15 mins	stenaline.co.uk
Liverpool	Douglas	2 hrs 45 mins (Mar–Oct) 🚤	steam-packet.com
Liverpool	Dublin	8 hrs–8 hrs 30 mins	poferries.com
Liverpool (Birkenhead)	Belfast	8 hrs	stenaline.co.uk
Liverpool (Birkenhead)	Douglas	4 hrs 15 mins (Nov–Mar Sat, Sun only)	steam-packet.com
Pembroke Dock	Rosslare	4 hrs	irishferries.com

The information listed is provided as a guide only, as services are liable to change at short notice and are weather dependent. Services shown are for vehicle ferries only, operated by conventional ferry unless indicated as a fast ferry service (🚤). Please check sailings before planning your journey.

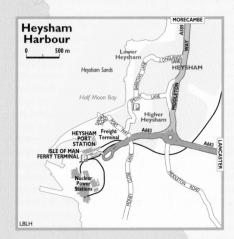

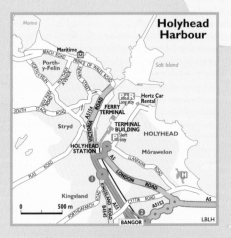

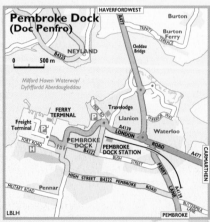

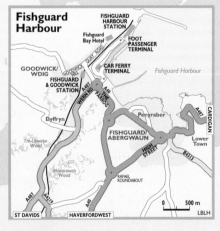

SCOTLAND FERRIES

From	To	Journey time	Operator website
Scottish Islands/west coast of Scotland			
Gourock	Dunoon	20 mins	western-ferries.co.uk
Glenelg	Skye	20 mins (Easter–Oct)	skyeferry.co.uk
Numerous and varied sailings from the west coast of Scotland to Scottish islands are provided by Caledonian MacBrayne. Please visit calmac.co.uk for all ferry information, including those of other operators.			
Orkney Islands			
Aberdeen	Kirkwall	6 hrs	northlinkferries.co.uk
Gills	St Margaret's Hope	1 hr	pentlandferries.co.uk
Scrabster	Stromness	1 hr 30 mins	northlinkferries.co.uk
Lerwick	Kirkwall	5 hrs 30 mins	northlinkferries.co.uk
Inter-island services are operated by Orkney Ferries. Please see orkneyferries.co.uk for details.			
Shetland Islands			
Aberdeen	Lerwick	12 hrs 30 mins	northlinkferries.co.uk
Kirkwall	Lerwick	7 hrs 45 mins	northlinkferries.co.uk
Inter-island services are operated by Shetland Island Council Ferries. Please see shetland.gov.uk/ferries for details.			

Please note that some smaller island services are day and weather dependent and reservations are required for some routes. Book and confirm sailing schedules by contacting the operator.

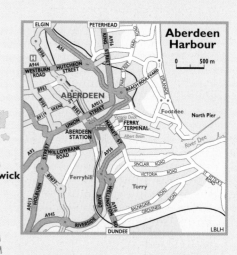

Aberdeen Harbour

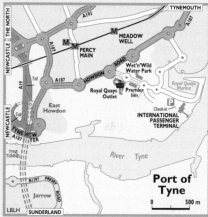

Port of Tyne

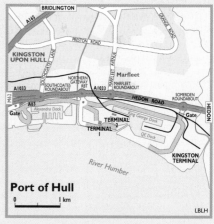

Port of Hull

For a port plan of Harwich see atlas page 53

NORTH SEA FERRY CROSSINGS

From	To	Journey time	Operator website
Harwich	Hook of Holland	7–8 hrs	stenaline.co.uk
Kingston upon Hull	Rotterdam (Europoort)	12 hrs	poferries.com
Kingston upon Hull	Zeebrugge	12 hrs	poferries.com
Newcastle upon Tyne	Amsterdam (IJmuiden)	15 hrs 30 mins	dfdsseaways.co.uk

The information listed on this page is provided as a guide only, as services are liable to change at short notice. Services shown are for vehicle ferries only, operated by conventional ferry. Please check sailings before planning your journey as many are weather dependent.

NORTH SEA

Caravan and camping sites in Britain

These pages list the top 300 AA-inspected Caravan and Camping (C & C) sites in the Pennant rating scheme. Five Pennant Premier sites are shown in green, Four Pennant sites are shown in blue.

Listings include addresses, telephone numbers and websites together with page and grid references to locate the sites in the atlas. The total number of touring pitches is also included for each site, together with the type of pitch available. The following abbreviations are used: **C = Caravan CV = Campervan T = Tent**

To discover AA-rated caravan and camping sites not included on these pages please visit RatedTrips.com

ENGLAND

Alders Caravan Park
Home Farm, Alne, York
YO61 1RY
Tel: 01347 838722 **97 R7**
alderscaravanpark.co.uk
Total Pitches: 91 (C, CV & T)

Andrewshayes Holiday Park
Dalwood, Axminster
EX13 7DY
Tel: 01404 831225 **10 E5**
andrewshayes.co.uk
Total Pitches: 230 (C, CV & T)

Ayr Holiday Park
St Ives, Cornwall
TR26 1EJ
Tel: 01736 795855 **2 E5**
ayrholidaypark.co.uk
Total Pitches: 40 (C, CV & T)

Back of Beyond Touring Park
234 Ringwood Road,
St Leonards, Dorset
BH24 2SB
Tel: 01202 876968 **13 K4**
backofbeyondtouringpark.co.uk
Total Pitches: 83 (C, CV & T)

Bagwell Farm Touring Park
Knights in the Bottom,
Chickerell, Weymouth
DT3 4EA
Tel: 01305 782575 **11 N8**
bagwellfarm.co.uk
Total Pitches: 320 (C, CV & T)

Bardsea Leisure Park
Priory Road, Ulverston
LA12 9QE
Tel: 01229 584712 **94 F5**
bardsealeisure.co.uk
Total Pitches: 171 (C & CV)

Bath Chew Valley Caravan Park
Ham Lane, Bishop Sutton
BS39 5TZ
Tel: 01275 332127 **19 Q3**
bathchewvalley.co.uk
Total Pitches: 45 (C, CV & T)

Bay View Farm C & C Park
Croyde, Devon
EX33 1PN
Tel: 01271 890501 **16 G4**
bayviewfarm.co.uk
Total Pitches: 75 (C, CV & T)

Bay View Holiday Park
Bolton le Sands,
Carnforth
LA5 9TN
Tel: 01524 732854 **95 K7**
holgates.co.uk
Total Pitches: 202 (C, CV & T)

Beacon Cottage Farm Touring Park
Beacon Drive, St Agnes
TR5 0NU
Tel: 01872 552347 **3 J3**
beaconcottagefarmholidays.co.uk
Total Pitches: 70 (C, CV & T)

Beaconsfield Farm Caravan Park
Battlefield, Shrewsbury
SY4 4AA
Tel: 01939 210370 **69 P11**
beaconsfieldholidaypark.co.uk
Total Pitches: 95 (C & CV)

Beech Croft Farm
Beech Croft,
Blackwell in the Peak, Buxton
SK17 9TQ
Tel: 01298 85330 **83 P10**
beechcroftfarm.co.uk
Total Pitches: 30 (C, CV & T)

Beehive Woodland Lakes
Rosliston, Swadlincote,
Derbyshire
DE12 8HZ
Tel: 01283 763981 **71 P11**
beehivefarm-woodlandlakes.co.uk
Total Pitches: 50 (C, CV & T)

Bellingham C & C Club Site
Brown Rigg,
Bellingham
NE48 2JY
Tel: 01434 220175 **112 B4**
campingandcaravanning
club.co.uk/bellingham
Total Pitches: 68 (C, CV & T)

Beverley Park C & C Park
Goodrington Road, Paignton
TQ4 7JE
Tel: 01803 843887 **7 M7**
beverley-holidays.co.uk
Total Pitches: 149 (C, CV & T)

Blue Rose Caravan Country Park
Star Carr Lane, Brandesburton
YO25 8RU
Tel: 01964 543366 **99 N11**
bluerosepark.com
Total Pitches: 114 (C & CV)

Briarfields Motel & Touring Park
Gloucester Road, Cheltenham
GL51 0SX
Tel: 01242 235324 **46 H10**
briarfields.net
Total Pitches: 72 (C, CV & T)

Broadhembury C & C Park
Steeds Lane, Kingsnorth,
Ashford
TN26 1NQ
Tel: 01233 620859 **26 H4**
broadhembury.co.uk
Total Pitches: 120 (C, CV & T)

Burnham-on-Sea Holiday Village
Marine Drive, Burnham-on-Sea
TA8 1LA
Tel: 01278 783391 **19 K5**
haven.com/burnhamonsea
Total Pitches: 781 (C, CV & T)

Burrowhayes Farm C & C Site & Riding Stables
West Luccombe, Porlock,
Minehead
TA24 8HT
Tel: 01643 862463 **18 A5**
burrowhayes.co.uk
Total Pitches: 139 (C, CV & T)

Burton Constable Holiday Park & Arboretum
Old Lodges, Sproatley, Hull
HU11 4LJ
Tel: 01964 562508 **93 L3**
burtonconstableholidaypark.co.uk
Total Pitches: 500 (C, CV & T)

Caister-on-Sea Holiday Park
Ormesby Road, Caister-on-Sea,
Great Yarmouth
NR30 5DH
Tel: 01493 728931 **77 Q9**
haven.com/caister
Total Pitches: 949 (C, CV & T)

Caistor Lakes Leisure Park
99a Brigg Road, Caistor
LN7 6RX
Tel: 01472 859626 **93 K10**
caistorlakes.co.uk
Total Pitches: 36 (C & CV)

Cakes & Ale
Abbey Lane, Theberton,
Leiston
IP16 4TE
Tel: 01728 831655 **65 N9**
cakesandale.co.uk
Total Pitches: 255 (C, CV & T)

Calloose C & C Park
Leedstown, Hayle
TR27 5ET
Tel: 01736 850431 **2 F7**
calloose.co.uk
Total Pitches: 134 (C, CV & T)

Camping Caradon Touring Park
Trelawne, Looe
PL13 2NA
Tel: 01503 272388 **5 L11**
campingcaradon.co.uk
Total Pitches: 75 (C, CV & T)

Capesthorne Hall
Congleton Road, Siddington,
Macclesfield
SK11 9JY
Tel: 01625 861221 **82 H10**
capesthorne.com/caravan-park
Total Pitches: 50 (C & CV)

Carlyon Bay C & C Park
Bethesda, Cypress Avenue,
Carlyon Bay
PL25 3RE
Tel: 01726 812735 **3 R3**
carlyonbay.net
Total Pitches: 180 (C, CV & T)

Carnon Downs C & C Park
Carnon Downs,
Truro
TR3 6JJ
Tel: 01872 862283 **3 L5**
carnon-downs-caravanpark.co.uk
Total Pitches: 152 (C, CV & T)

Cartref C & C
Cartref, Ford Heath,
Shrewsbury, Shropshire
SY5 9GD
Tel: 01743 821688 **56 G2**
cartrefcaravansite.co.uk
Total Pitches: 44 (C, CV & T)

Carvynick Holiday Park
Summercourt,
Newquay
TR8 5AF
Tel: 01872 510716 **4 D10**
carvynick.co.uk
Total Pitches: 47 (C, CV & T)

Castlerigg Hall C & C Park
Castlerigg Hall, Keswick
CA12 4TE
Tel: 017687 74499 **101 J6**
castlerigg.co.uk
Total Pitches: 105 (C, CV & T)

Cheddar Mendip Heights C & C Club Site
Townsend, Priddy, Wells
BA5 3BP
Tel: 01749 870241 **19 P4**
campingandcaravanning
club.co.uk/cheddar
Total Pitches: 92 (C, CV & T)

Clippesby Hall
Hall Lane, Clippesby,
Great Yarmouth
NR29 3BL
Tel: 01493 367800 **77 N9**
clippesbyhall.com
Total Pitches: 120 (C, CV & T)

Cofton Holidays
Starcross, Dawlish
EX6 8RP
Tel: 01626 890111 **9 N8**
coftonholidays.co.uk
Total Pitches: 532 (C, CV & T)

Concierge Camping
Ratham Estate, Ratham Lane,
West Ashling, Chichester
PO18 8DL
Tel: 01243 573118 **15 M5**
conciergecamping.co.uk
Total Pitches: 15 (C & CV)

Coombe Touring Park
Race Plain, Netherhampton,
Salisbury
SP2 8PN
Tel: 01722 328451 **21 L9**
coombecaravanpark.co.uk
Total Pitches: 56 (C, CV & T)

Corfe Castle C & C Club Site
Bucknowle, Wareham
BH20 5PQ
Tel: 01929 480280 **12 F8**
campingandcaravanning
club.co.uk/corfecastle
Total Pitches: 80 (C, CV & T)

Cornish Farm Touring Park
Shoreditch, Taunton
TA3 7BS
Tel: 01823 327746 **18 H10**
cornishfarm.com
Total Pitches: 50 (C, CV & T)

Cosawes Park
Perranarworthal,
Truro
TR3 7QS
Tel: 01872 863724 **3 K6**
cosawes.co.uk
Total Pitches: 59 (C, CV & T)

Cote Ghyll C & C Park
Osmotherley,
Northallerton
DL6 3AH
Tel: 01609 883425 **104 E11**
coteghyll.com
Total Pitches: 95 (C, CV & T)

Country View Holiday Park
Sand Road, Sand Bay,
Weston-super-Mare
BS22 9UJ
Tel: 01934 627595 **19 K2**
cvhp.co.uk
Total Pitches: 255 (C, CV & T)

Crealy Theme Park & Resort
Sidmouth Road,
Clyst St Mary, Exeter
EX5 1DR
Tel: 01395 234888 **9 P6**
crealy.co.uk
Total Pitches: 127 (C, CV & T)

Crows Nest Caravan Park
Gristhorpe, Filey
YO14 9PS
Tel: 01723 582206 **99 M4**
crowsnestcaravan.com
Total Pitches: 263 (C, CV & T)

Deepdale Backpackers & Camping
Deepdale Farm,
Burnham Deepdale
PE31 8DD
Tel: 01485 210256 **75 R2**
deepdalebackpackers.co.uk
Total Pitches: 80 (CV & T)

Diamond C & C Park
Islip Road, Bletchingdon,
Oxfordshire
OX5 3DR
Tel: 01869 350909 **48 F11**
diamondpark.co.uk
Total Pitches: 37 (C, CV & T)

Dibles Park
Dibles Road, Warsash,
Southampton, Hampshire
SO31 9SA
Tel: 01489 575232 **14 F5**
diblespark.co.uk
Total Pitches: 60 (C, CV & T)

Dornafield
Dornafield Farm, Two Mile Oak,
Newton Abbot
TQ12 6DD
Tel: 01803 812732 **7 L5**
dornafield.com
Total Pitches: 135 (C, CV & T)

East Fleet Farm Touring Park
Chickerell, Weymouth
DT3 4DW
Tel: 01305 785768 **11 N9**
eastfleet.co.uk
Total Pitches: 400 (C, CV & T)

Eastham Hall Holiday Park
Saltcotes Road,
Lytham St Annes, Lancashire
FY8 4LS
Tel: 01253 737907 **88 D5**
easthamhall.co.uk
Total Pitches: 274 (C & CV)

Eden Valley Holiday Park
Lanlivery, Nr Lostwithiel
PL30 5BU
Tel: 01208 872277 **4 H10**
edenvalleyholidaypark.co.uk
Total Pitches: 94 (C, CV & T)

Exe Valley Caravan Site
Mill House, Bridgetown,
Dulverton
TA22 9JR
Tel: 01643 851432 **18 B8**
exevalleycamping.co.uk
Total Pitches: 48 (C, CV & T)

Eye Kettleby Lakes
Eye Kettleby, Melton Mowbray
LE14 2TN
Tel: 01664 565900 **73 J7**
eyekettlebylakes.com
Total Pitches: 130 (C, CV & T)

Fen Farm Caravan Site
Moore Lane, East Mersea,
Mersea Island,
Colchester, Essex
CO5 8FE
Tel: 01206 383275 **53 J9**
fenfarm.co.uk
Total Pitches: 180 (C, CV & T)

Fernwood Caravan Park
Lyneal, Ellesmere, Shropshire
SY12 0QF
Tel: 01948 710221 **69 N8**
fernwoodpark.co.uk
Total Pitches: 225 (C, CV & T)

Fields End Water Caravan Park & Fishery
Benwick Road, Doddington,
March
PE15 0TY
Tel: 01354 740199 **62 E2**
fieldsendwater.co.uk
Total Pitches: 52 (C, CV & T)

Fishpool Farm Caravan Park
Fishpool Road, Delamere,
Northwich, Cheshire
CW8 2HP
Tel: 01606 883970 **82 C11**
fishpoolfarmcaravanpark.co.uk
Total Pitches: 51 (C, CV & T)

Flower of May Holiday Park
Lebberston Cliff, Filey,
Scarborough
YO11 3NU
Tel: 01723 584311 **99 M4**
flowerofmay.com
Total Pitches: 503 (C, CV & T)

Freshwater Beach Holiday Park
Burton Bradstock, Bridport
DT6 4PT
Tel: 01308 897317 **11 K6**
freshwaterbeach.co.uk
Total Pitches: 750 (C, CV & T)

Glenfield Caravan Park
Blackmoor Lane, Bardsey, Leeds
LS17 9DZ
Tel: 01937 574657 **91 J2**
glenfieldcaravanpark.co.uk
Total Pitches: 31 (C, CV & T)

Globe Vale Holiday Park
Radnor, Redruth
TR16 4BH
Tel: 01209 891183 **3 J5**
globevale.co.uk
Total Pitches: 195 (C, CV & T)

Glororum Caravan Park
Glororum Farm, Bamburgh
NE69 7AW
Tel: 01670 860256 **119 N4**
northumbrianleisure.co.uk
Total Pitches: 213 (C & CV)

Golden Cap Holiday Park
Seatown, Chideock, Bridport
DT6 6JX
Tel: 01308 422139 **11 J6**
wdlh.co.uk
Total Pitches: 345 (C, CV & T)

Golden Coast Holiday Park
Station Road, Woolacombe
EX34 7HW
Tel: 01271 872302 **16 H3**
woolacombe.com
Total Pitches: 431 (C, CV & T)

Golden Sands Holiday Park
Quebec Road, Mablethorpe
LN12 1QJ
Tel: 01507 477871 **87 N3**
haven.com/goldensands
Total Pitches: 1672 (C, CV & T)

Golden Square C & C Park
Oswaldkirk, Helmsley
YO62 5YQ
Tel: 01439 788269 **98 C5**
goldensquarecaravanpark.com
Total Pitches: 150 (C, CV & T)

Golden Valley C & C Park
Coach Road, Ripley, Derbyshire
DE55 4ES
Tel: 01773 513881 **84 F10**
goldenvalleycaravanpark.co.uk
Total Pitches: 47 (C, CV & T)

Goosewood Holiday Park
Sutton-on-the-Forest, York
YO61 1ET
Tel: 01347 810829 **98 B8**
flowerofmay.com
Total Pitches: 145 (C & CV)

Green Acres Caravan Park
High Knells, Houghton, Carlisle
CA6 4JW
Tel: 01228 675418 **110 H8**
caravanpark-cumbria.com
Total Pitches: 35 (C, CV & T)

Greenhill Farm C & C Park
Greenhill Farm, New Road,
Landford, Salisbury
SP5 2AZ
Tel: 01794 324117 **21 Q11**
greenhillfarm.co.uk
Total Pitches: 160 (C, CV & T)

Greenhills Holiday Park
Crowhill Lane, Bakewell,
Derbyshire
DE45 1PX
Tel: 01629 813052 **84 B7**
greenhillsholidaypark.co.uk
Total Pitches: 245 (C, CV & T)

Grouse Hill Caravan Park
Flask Bungalow Farm,
Fylingdales,
Robin Hood's Bay
YO22 4QH
Tel: 01947 880543 **105 P10**
grousehill.co.uk
Total Pitches: 192 (C, CV & T)

Gunvenna Holiday Park
St Minver, Wadebridge
PL27 6QN
Tel: 01208 862405 **4 F6**
gunvenna.com
Total Pitches: 121 (C, CV & T)

Haggerston Castle Holiday Park
Beal, Berwick-upon-Tweed
TD15 2PA
Tel: 01289 381333 **119 K2**
haven.com/haggerstoncastle
Total Pitches: 1340 (C & CV)

Harbury Fields
Harbury Fields Farm, Harbury,
Nr Leamington Spa
CV33 9JN
Tel: 01926 612457 **48 C2**
harburyfields.co.uk
Total Pitches: 59 (C & CV)

Harford Bridge Holiday Park
Peter Tavy, Tavistock
PL19 9LS
Tel: 01822 810349 **8 D9**
harfordbridge.co.uk
Total Pitches: 198 (C, CV & T)

Haw Wood Farm Caravan Park
Hinton, Saxmundham
IP17 3QT
Tel: 01502 359550 **65 N7**
hawwoodfarm.co.uk
Total Pitches: 115 (C, CV & T)

Heathfield Farm Camping
Heathfield Road,
Freshwater,
Isle of Wight
PO40 9SH
Tel: 01983 407822 **13 P7**
heathfieldcamping.co.uk
Total Pitches: 75 (C, CV & T)

Heathland Beach Holiday Park
London Road,
Kessingland
NR33 7PJ
Tel: 01502 740337 **65 Q4**
heathlandbeach.co.uk
Total Pitches: 263 (C, CV & T)

Hele Valley Holiday Park
Hele Bay,
Ilfracombe
EX34 9RD
Tel: 01271 862460 **17 J2**
helevalley.co.uk
Total Pitches: 133 (C, CV & T)

Hendra Holiday Park
Newquay
TR8 4NY
Tel: 01637 875778 **4 C9**
hendra-holidays.com
Total Pitches: 865 (C, CV & T)

Herding Hill Farm Touring & Camping Site
Shield Hill, Haltwhistle,
Northumberland
NE49 9NW
Tel: 01434 320175 **111 P7**
herdinghillfarm.co.uk
Total Pitches: 22 (C, CV & T)

Highfield Farm Touring Park
Long Road,
Comberton, Cambridge
CB23 7DG
Tel: 01223 262308 **62 E9**
highfieldfarmtouringpark.co.uk
Total Pitches: 120 (C, CV & T)

Highlands End Holiday Park
Eype, Bridport,
Dorset
DT6 6AR
Tel: 01308 422139 **11 K6**
wdlh.co.uk
Total Pitches: 357 (C, CV & T)

Hill of Oaks & Blakeholme
Windermere
LA12 8NR
Tel: 015395 31578 **94 H3**
hillofoaks.co.uk
Total Pitches: 263 (C & CV)

Hillside Caravan Park
Canvas Farm, Moor Road,
Knayton,
Thirsk
YO7 4BR
Tel: 01845 537349 **97 P3**
hillsidecaravanpark.co.uk
Total Pitches: 52 (C & CV)

Holiday Resort Unity
Coast Road, Brean Sands,
Brean
TA8 2RB
Tel: 01278 751235 **19 J4**
hru.co.uk
Total Pitches: 1114 (C, CV & T)

Hollins Farm C & C
Far Arnside, Carnforth
LA5 0SL
Tel: 01524 701767 **95 J5**
holgates.co.uk
Total Pitches: 14 (C, CV & T)

Hylton Caravan Park
Eden Street, Silloth
CA7 4AY
Tel: 016973 32666 **109 P10**
stanwix.com
Total Pitches: 303 (C, CV & T)

Island Lodge C & C Site
Stumpy Post Cross,
Kingsbridge
TQ7 4BL
Tel: 01548 852956 **7 J9**
islandlodgesite.co.uk
Total Pitches: 30 (C, CV & T)

Isle of Avalon Touring Caravan Park
Godney Road,
Glastonbury
BA6 9AF
Tel: 01458 833618 **19 N7**
avaloncaravanpark.co.uk
Total Pitches: 120 (C, CV & T)

Jasmine Caravan Park
Cross Lane, Snainton,
Scarborough
YO13 9BE
Tel: 01723 859240 **99 J4**
jasminepark.co.uk
Total Pitches: 84 (C, CV & T)

Kennford International Holiday Park
Kennford,
Exeter
EX6 7YN
Tel: 01392 833046 **9 M7**
kennfordinternational.co.uk
Total Pitches: 87 (C, CV & T)

King's Lynn C & C Park
New Road, North Runcton,
King's Lynn
PE33 0RA
Tel: 01553 840004 **75 M7**
kl-cc.co.uk
Total Pitches: 170 (C, CV & T)

Kloofs Caravan Park
Sandhurst Lane, Bexhill
TN39 4RG
Tel: 01424 842839 **26 B10**
kloofs.com
Total Pitches: 125 (C, CV & T)

Kneps Farm Holiday Park
River Road, Stanah,
Thornton-Cleveleys,
Blackpool
FY5 5LR
Tel: 01253 823632 **88 D2**
knepsfarm.co.uk
Total Pitches: 86 (C & CV)

Knight Stainforth Hall Caravan & Campsite
Stainforth, Settle
BD24 0DP
Tel: 01729 822200 **96 B7**
knightstainforth.co.uk
Total Pitches: 160 (C, CV & T)

Ladycross Plantation Caravan Park
Egton, Whitby
YO21 1UA
Tel: 01947 895502 **105 M9**
ladycrossplantation.co.uk
Total Pitches: 130 (C & CV)

Lady's Mile Holiday Park
Dawlish, Devon
EX7 0LX
Tel: 01626 863411 **9 N9**
ladysmile.co.uk
Total Pitches: 692 (C, CV & T)

Lakeland Leisure Park
Moor Lane,
Flookburgh
LA11 7LT
Tel: 01539 558556 **94 H6**
haven.com/lakeland
Total Pitches: 977 (C, CV & T)

Lamb Cottage Caravan Park
Dalefords Lane, Whitegate,
Northwich
CW8 2BN
Tel: 01606 882302 **82 D11**
lambcottage.co.uk
Total Pitches: 71 (C, CV & T)

Langstone Manor C & C Park
Moortown, Tavistock
PL19 9JZ
Tel: 01822 613371 **6 E4**
langstonemanor.co.uk
Total Pitches: 76 (C, CV & T)

Lanyon Holiday Park
Loscombe Lane, Four Lanes,
Redruth
TR16 6LP
Tel: 01209 313474 **2 H6**
lanyonholidaypark.co.uk
Total Pitches: 74 (C, CV & T)

Lickpenny Caravan Site
Lickpenny Lane, Tansley, Matlock
DE4 5GF
Tel: 01629 583040 **84 D9**
lickpennycaravanpark.co.uk
Total Pitches: 80 (C & CV)

Lime Tree Park
Dukes Drive, Buxton
SK17 9RP
Tel: 01298 22988 **83 N10**
limetreeparkbuxton.com
Total Pitches: 149 (C, CV & T)

Lincoln Farm Park Oxfordshire
High Street, Standlake
OX29 7RH
Tel: 01865 300239 **34 C4**
lincolnfarmpark.co.uk
Total Pitches: 90 (C, CV & T)

Littlesea Holiday Park
Lynch Lane, Weymouth
DT4 9DT
Tel: 01305 774414 **11 P9**
haven.com/littlesea
Total Pitches: 861 (C, CV & T)

Long Acres Touring Park
Station Road, Old Leake, Boston
PE22 9RF
Tel: 01205 871555 **87 L10**
long-acres.co.uk
Total Pitches: 40 (C, CV & T)

Long Hazel Park
High Street, Sparkford, Yeovil,
Somerset
BA22 7JH
Tel: 01963 440002 **20 B9**
longhazelpark.co.uk
Total Pitches: 52 (C, CV & T)

Longnor Wood Holiday Park
Newtown, Longnor, Nr Buxton
SK17 0NG
Tel: 01298 83648 **71 K2**
longnorwood.co.uk
Total Pitches: 50 (C, CV & T)

Lowther Holiday Park
Eamont Bridge, Penrith
CA10 2JB
Tel: 01768 863631 **101 P5**
lowther-holidaypark.co.uk
Total Pitches: 180 (C, CV & T)

Manor Wood Country Caravan Park
Manor Wood, Coddington,
Chester
CH3 9EN
Tel: 01829 782990 **69 M4**
cheshire-caravan-sites.co.uk
Total Pitches: 66 (C, CV & T)

Marton Mere Holiday Village
Mythop Road, Blackpool
FY4 4XN
Tel: 01253 767544 **88 C4**
haven.com/martonmere
Total Pitches: 782 (C & CV)

Mayfield Park
Cheltenham Road, Cirencester
GL7 7BH
Tel: 01285 831301 **33 K3**
mayfieldpark.co.uk
Total Pitches: 105 (C, CV & T)

Meadow Lakes Holiday Park
Hewas Water, St Austell,
Cornwall
PL26 7JG
Tel: 01726 882540 **3 P4**
meadow-lakes.co.uk
Total Pitches: 232 (C, CV & T)

Meadowbank Holidays
Stour Way, Christchurch
BH23 2PQ
Tel: 01202 483597 **13 K6**
meadowbank-holidays.co.uk
Total Pitches: 221 (C & CV)

Middlewood Farm Holiday Park
Middlewood Lane, Fylingthorpe,
Robin Hood's Bay, Whitby
YO22 4UF
Tel: 01947 880414 **105 P10**
middlewoodfarm.com
Total Pitches: 144 (C, CV & T)

Mill Park Touring C & C Park
Mill Lane, Berrynarbor,
Ilfracombe, Devon
EX34 9SH
Tel: 01271 882647 **17 K2**
millpark.com
Total Pitches: 160 (C, CV & T)

Minnows Touring Park
Holbrook Lane, Sampford Peverell
EX16 7EN
Tel: 01884 821770 **18 D11**
minnowstouringpark.co.uk
Total Pitches: 60 (C, CV & T)

Monkey Tree Holiday Park
Hendra Croft, Scotland Road,
Newquay
TR8 5QR
Tel: 01872 572032 **3 L3**
monkeytreeholidaypark.co.uk
Total Pitches: 700 (C, CV & T)

Moon & Sixpence
Newburn Road,
Waldringfield, Woodbridge
IP12 4PP
Tel: 01473 736650 **53 N2**
moonandsixpence.co.uk
Total Pitches: 275 (C & CV)

Moss Wood Caravan Park
Crimbles Lane,
Cockerham
LA2 0ES
Tel: 01524 791041 **95 K11**
mosswood.co.uk
Total Pitches: 168 (C & CV)

Naburn Lock Caravan Park
Naburn
YO19 4RU
Tel: 01904 728697 **98 C11**
naburnlock.co.uk
Total Pitches: 115 (C, CV & T)

New Lodge Farm C & C Site
New Lodge Farm, Bulwick,
Corby
NN17 3DU
Tel: 01780 450493 **73 P11**
newlodgefarm.com
Total Pitches: 72 (C, CV & T)

Newberry Valley Park
Woodlands, Combe Martin
EX34 0AT
Tel: 01271 882334 **17 K2**
newberryvalleypark.co.uk
Total Pitches: 112 (C, CV & T)

Newlands Holidays
Charmouth, Bridport
DT6 6RB
Tel: 01297 560259 **10 H6**
newlandsholidays.co.uk
Total Pitches: 330 (C, CV & T)

Ninham Country Holidays
Ninham, Shanklin,
Isle of Wight
PO37 7PL
Tel: 01983 864243 **14 G10**
ninham-holidays.co.uk
Total Pitches: 141 (C, CV & T)

North Morte Farm C & C Park
North Morte Road, Mortehoe,
Woolacombe
EX34 7EG
Tel: 01271 870381 **16 H2**
northmortefarm.co.uk
Total Pitches: 253 (C, CV & T)

Northam Farm Caravan & Touring Park
Brean,
Burnham-on-Sea
TA8 2SE
Tel: 01278 751244 **19 K3**
northamfarm.co.uk
Total Pitches: 350 (C, CV & T)

Oakdown Country Holiday Park
Gatedown Lane, Weston,
Sidmouth
EX10 0PT
Tel: 01297 680387 **10 D6**
oakdown.co.uk
Total Pitches: 170 (C, CV & T)

Old Hall Caravan Park
Capernwray,
Carnforth
LA6 1AD
Tel: 01524 733276 **95 L6**
oldhallcaravanpark.co.uk
Total Pitches: 298 (C, CV & T)

Old Oaks Touring & Glamping
Wick Farm, Wick,
Glastonbury
BA6 8JS
Tel: 01458 831437 **19 P7**
theoldoaks.co.uk
Total Pitches: 100 (C, CV & T)

Orchard Farm Holiday Village
Stonegate, Hunmanby,
Filey, North Yorkshire
YO14 0PU
Tel: 01723 891582 **99 N5**
orchardfarmholidayvillage.co.uk
Total Pitches: 137 (C, CV & T)

Ord House Country Park
East Ord,
Berwick-upon-Tweed
TD15 2NS
Tel: 01289 305288 **129 P9**
maguirescountryparks.co.uk
Total Pitches: 344 (C, CV & T)

Otterington Park
Station Farm,
South Otterington,
Northallerton, North Yorkshire
DL7 9JB
Tel: 01609 780656 **97 N3**
otteringtonpark.com
Total Pitches: 67 (C, CV & T)

Oxon Hall Touring Park
Welshpool Road, Shrewsbury
SY3 5FB
Tel: 01743 340868 **56 H2**
morris-leisure.co.uk
Total Pitches: 165 (C, CV & T)

Park Cliffe C & C Estate
Birks Road, Tower Wood,
Windermere
LA23 3PG
Tel: 015395 31344 **94 H2**
parkcliffe.co.uk
Total Pitches: 126 (C, CV & T)

Parkers Farm Holiday Park
Higher Mead Farm,
Ashburton, Devon
TQ13 7LJ
Tel: 01364 654869 **7 K4**
parkersfarmholidays.co.uk
Total Pitches: 118 (C, CV & T)

Park Foot C & C Park
Howtown Road,
Pooley Bridge
CA10 2NA
Tel: 017684 86309 **101 N6**
parkfootullswater.co.uk
Total Pitches: 454 (C, CV & T)

Parkland C & C Site
Sorley Green Cross,
Kingsbridge
TQ7 4AF
Tel: 01548 852723 **7 J9**
parklandsite.co.uk
Total Pitches: 50 (C, CV & T)

Pebble Bank Caravan Park
Camp Road, Wyke Regis,
Weymouth
DT4 9HF
Tel: 01305 774844 **11 P9**
pebblebank.co.uk
Total Pitches: 120 (C, CV & T)

Perran Sands Holiday Park
Perranporth, Truro
TR6 0AQ
Tel: 01872 573551 **4 B10**
haven.com/perransands
Total Pitches: 1012 (C, CV & T)

Petwood Caravan Park
Off Stixwould Road,
Woodhall Spa
LN10 6QH
Tel: 01526 354799 **86 G8**
petwoodcaravanpark.com
Total Pitches: 98 (C, CV & T)

Plough Lane Touring Caravan Site
Plough Lane, Chippenham,
Wiltshire
SN15 5PS
Tel: 01249 750146 **32 H9**
ploughlane.co.uk
Total Pitches: 52 (C & CV)

Polladras Holiday Park
Carleen, Breage,
Helston
TR13 9NX
Tel: 01736 762220 **2 G7**
polladrasholidaypark.co.uk
Total Pitches: 42 (C, CV & T)

Polmanter Touring Park
Halsetown, St Ives
TR26 3LX
Tel: 01736 795640 **2 E6**
polmanter.com
Total Pitches: 270 (C, CV & T)

Porthtowan Tourist Park
Mile Hill, Porthtowan,
Truro
TR4 8TY
Tel: 01209 890256 **2 H4**
porthtowantouristpark.co.uk
Total Pitches: 80 (C, CV & T)

Primrose Valley Holiday Park
Filey
YO14 9RF
Tel: 01723 513771 **99 N5**
haven.com/primrosevalley
Total Pitches: 1549 (C & CV)

Quantock Orchard Caravan Park
Flaxpool, Crowcombe, Taunton
TA4 4AW
Tel: 01984 618618 **18 F7**
quantock-orchard.co.uk
Total Pitches: 75 (C, CV & T)

Ranch Caravan Park
Station Road, Honeybourne,
Evesham
WR11 7PR
Tel: 01386 830744 **47 M6**
ranch.co.uk
Total Pitches: 338 (C & CV)

Ripley Caravan Park
Knaresborough Road, Ripley,
Harrogate
HG3 3AU
Tel: 01423 770050 **97 L8**
ripleycaravanpark.com
Total Pitches: 135 (C, CV & T)

River Dart Country Park
Holne Park, Ashburton
TQ13 7NP
Tel: 01364 652511 **7 J5**
riverdart.co.uk
Total Pitches: 170 (C, CV & T)

River Valley Holiday Park
London Apprentice,
St Austell
PL26 7AP
Tel: 01726 73533 **3 Q3**
rivervalleyholidaypark.co.uk
Total Pitches: 85 (C, CV & T)

Riverside C & C Park
Marsh Lane,
North Molton Road,
South Molton
EX36 3HQ
Tel: 01769 579269 **17 N6**
exmoorriverside.co.uk
Total Pitches: 61 (C, CV & T)

Riverside Caravan Park
High Bentham,
Lancaster
LA2 7FJ
Tel: 015242 61272 **95 P7**
riversidecaravanpark.co.uk
Total Pitches: 267 (C & CV)

**Riverside Meadows Country
Caravan Park**
Ure Bank Top, Ripon
HG4 1JD
Tel: 01765 602964 **97 M6**
flowerofmay.com
Total Pitches: 349 (C)

Robin Hood C & C Park
Green Dyke Lane,
Slingsby
YO62 4AP
Tel: 01653 628391 **98 E6**
robinhoodcaravanpark.co.uk
Total Pitches: 66 (C, CV & T)

**Rose Farm Touring
& Camping Park**
Stepshort, Belton,
Nr Great Yarmouth
NR31 9JS
Tel: 01493 738292 **77 P11**
rosefarmtouringpark.co.uk
Total Pitches: 147 (C, CV & T)

Rosedale Abbey Caravan Park
Rosedale Abbey,
Pickering
YO18 8SA
Tel: 01751 417272 **105 K11**
rosedaleabbeycaravanpark.co.uk
Total Pitches: 141 (C, CV & T)

Ross Park
Park Hill Farm, Ipplepen,
Newton Abbot
TQ12 5TT
Tel: 01803 812983 **7 L5**
rossparkcaravanpark.co.uk
Total Pitches: 110 (C, CV & T)

Rudding Holiday Park
Follifoot, Harrogate
HG3 1JH
Tel: 01423 870439 **97 M10**
ruddingholidaypark.co.uk
Total Pitches: 143 (C, CV & T)

Run Cottage Touring Park
Alderton Road, Hollesley,
Woodbridge
IP12 3RQ
Tel: 01394 411309 **53 Q3**
runcottage.co.uk
Total Pitches: 47 (C, CV & T)

Rutland C & C
Park Lane, Greetham,
Oakham
LE15 7FN
Tel: 01572 813520 **73 N8**
rutlandcaravanandcamping.co.uk
Total Pitches: 130 (C, CV & T)

St Helens in the Park
Wykeham, Scarborough
YO13 9QD
Tel: 01723 862771 **99 K4**
sthelenscaravanpark.co.uk
Total Pitches: 260 (C, CV & T)

St Ives Bay Holiday Park
73 Loggans Road,
Upton Towans, Hayle
TR27 5BH
Tel: 01736 752274 **2 F6**
stivesbay.co.uk
Total Pitches: 507 (C, CV & T)

Salcombe Regis C & C Park
Salcombe Regis,
Sidmouth
EX10 0JH
Tel: 01395 514303 **10 D7**
salcombe-regis.co.uk
Total Pitches: 110 (C, CV & T)

Sand le Mere Holiday Village
Southfield Lane,
Tunstall
HU12 0JF
Tel: 01964 670403 **93 P4**
sand-le-mere.co.uk
Total Pitches: 89 (C & CV)

Searles Leisure Resort
South Beach Road,
Hunstanton
PE36 5BB
Tel: 01485 534211 **75 N3**
searles.co.uk
Total Pitches: 413 (C, CV & T)

**Seaview Gorran Haven
Holiday Park**
Boswinger,
Mevagissey
PL26 6LL
Tel: 01726 843425 **3 P5**
seaviewinternational.com
Total Pitches: 240 (C, CV & T)

Seaview Holiday Park
Preston, Weymouth
DT3 6DZ
Tel: 01305 832271 **11 Q8**
haven.com/seaview
Total Pitches: 347 (C, CV & T)

Severn Gorge Park
Bridgnorth Road,
Tweedale, Telford
TF7 4JB
Tel: 01952 684789 **57 N3**
severngorgepark.co.uk
Total Pitches: 132 (C & CV)

Shamba Holidays
East Moors Lane,
St Leonards, Ringwood
BH24 2SB
Tel: 01202 873302 **13 K4**
shambaholidays.co.uk
Total Pitches: 150 (C, CV & T)

Shrubbery Touring Park
Rousdon,
Lyme Regis
DT7 3XW
Tel: 01297 442227 **10 F6**
shrubberypark.co.uk
Total Pitches: 122 (C, CV & T)

Silverdale Caravan Park
Middlebarrow Plain,
Cove Road, Silverdale,
Nr Carnforth
LA5 0SH
Tel: 01524 701508 **95 K5**
holgates.co.uk
Total Pitches: 427 (C, CV & T)

Skelwith Fold Caravan Park
Ambleside, Cumbria
LA22 0HX
Tel: 015394 32277 **101 L10**
skelwith.com
Total Pitches: 470 (C & CV)

Skirlington Leisure Park
Driffield, Skipsea
YO25 8SY
Tel: 01262 468213 **99 P10**
skirlington.com
Total Pitches: 930 (C, CV & T)

**Sleningford Watermill
Caravan Camping Park**
North Stainley,
Ripon
HG4 3HQ
Tel: 01765 635201 **97 L5**
sleningfordwatermill.co.uk
Total Pitches: 135 (C, CV & T)

Somers Wood Caravan Park
Somers Road, Meriden
CV7 7PL
Tel: 01676 522978 **59 K8**
somerswood.co.uk
Total Pitches: 48 (C & CV)

**South Lytchett Manor
C & C Park**
Dorchester Road,
Lytchett Minster, Poole
BH16 6JB
Tel: 01202 622577 **12 G6**
southlytchettmanor.co.uk
Total Pitches: 154 (C, CV & T)

South Meadows Caravan Park
South Road, Belford
NE70 7DP
Tel: 01668 213326 **119 M4**
southmeadows.co.uk
Total Pitches: 186 (C, CV & T)

Stanmore Hall Touring Park
Stourbridge Road,
Bridgnorth
WV15 6DT
Tel: 01746 761761 **57 N6**
morris-leisure.co.uk
Total Pitches: 129 (C, CV & T)

Stanwix Park Holiday Centre
Greenrow, Silloth
CA7 4HH
Tel: 016973 32666 **109 P10**
stanwix.com
Total Pitches: 337 (C, CV & T)

Stowford Farm Meadows
Berry Down,
Combe Martin
EX34 0PW
Tel: 01271 882476 **17 K3**
stowford.co.uk
Total Pitches: 700 (C, CV & T)

Stroud Hill Park
Fen Road, Pidley,
St Ives
PE28 3DE
Tel: 01487 741333 **62 D5**
stroudhillpark.co.uk
Total Pitches: 60 (C, CV & T)

**Sumners Ponds Fishery
& Campsite**
Chapel Road, Barns Green,
Horsham
RH13 0PR
Tel: 01403 732539 **24 D5**
sumnersponds.co.uk
Total Pitches: 90 (C, CV & T)

Swiss Farm Touring & Camping
Marlow Road,
Henley-on-Thames
RG9 2HY
Tel: 01491 573419 **35 L8**
swissfarmhenley.co.uk
Total Pitches: 148 (C, CV & T)

**Tanner Farm Touring
C & C Park**
Tanner Farm, Goudhurst Road,
Marden
TN12 9ND
Tel: 01622 832399 **26 B3**
tannerfarmpark.co.uk
Total Pitches: 122 (C, CV & T)

Tattershall Lakes Country Park
Sleaford Road,
Tattershall
LN4 4LR
Tel: 01526 348800 **86 H9**
*awayresorts.co.uk/
tattershall-lakes*
Total Pitches: 690 (C, CV & T)

Tehidy Holiday Park
Harris Mill, Illogan, Portreath
TR16 4JQ
Tel: 01209 216489 **2 H5**
tehidy.co.uk
Total Pitches: 52 (C, CV & T)

Tencreek Holiday Park
Polperro Road, Looe
PL13 2JR
Tel: 01503 262447 **5 L11**
dolphinholidays.co.uk
Total Pitches: 355 (C, CV & T)

Teversal C & C Club Site
Silverhill Lane, Teversal
NG17 3JJ
Tel: 01623 551838 **84 G8**
*campingandcaravanning
club.co.uk/teversal*
Total Pitches: 136 (C, CV & T)

The Laurels Holiday Park
Padstow Road, Whitecross,
Wadebridge
PL27 7JQ
Tel: 01208 813341 **4 F7**
thelaurelsholidaypark.co.uk
Total Pitches: 30 (C, CV & T)

The Old Brick Kilns
Little Barney Lane, Barney,
Fakenham
NR21 0NL
Tel: 01328 878305 **76 E5**
old-brick-kilns.co.uk
Total Pitches: 65 (C, CV & T)

**The Orchards Holiday
Caravan Park**
Main Road, Newbridge,
Yarmouth, Isle of Wight
PO41 0TS
Tel: 01983 531331 **14 D9**
orchards-holiday-park.co.uk
Total Pitches: 225 (C, CV & T)

The Quiet Site
Ullswater, Watermillock
CA11 0LS
Tel: 07768 727016 **101 M6**
thequietsite.co.uk
Total Pitches: 151 (C, CV & T)

Thornwick Bay Holiday Village
North Marine Road, Flamborough
YO15 1AU
Tel: 01262 850569 **99 Q6**
*haven.com/parks/yorkshire/
thornwick-bay*
Total Pitches: 225 (C, CV & T)

Thorpe Park Holiday Centre
Cleethorpes
DN35 0PW
Tel: 01472 813395 **93 P9**
haven.com/thorpepark
Total Pitches: 1491 (C, CV & T)

Treago Farm Caravan Site
Crantock, Newquay
TR8 5QS
Tel: 01637 830277 **4 B9**
treagofarm.co.uk
Total Pitches: 100 (C, CV & T)

Treloy Touring Park
Newquay
TR8 4JN
Tel: 01637 872063 **4 D9**
treloy.co.uk
Total Pitches: 223 (C, CV & T)

Trencreek Holiday Park
Hillcrest, Higher Trencreek,
Newquay
TR8 4NS
Tel: 01637 874210 **4 C9**
trencreekholidaypark.co.uk
Total Pitches: 200 (C, CV & T)

Trethem Mill Touring Park
St Just-in-Roseland,
Nr St Mawes, Truro
TR2 5JF
Tel: 01872 580504 **3 M6**
trethem.com
Total Pitches: 84 (C, CV & T)

Trevalgan Touring Park
Trevalgan, St Ives
TR26 3BJ
Tel: 01736 791892 **2 D6**
trevalgantouringpark.co.uk
Total Pitches: 135 (C, CV & T)

Trevarth Holiday Park
Blackwater, Truro
TR4 8HR
Tel: 01872 560266 **3 J4**
trevarth.co.uk
Total Pitches: 50 (C, CV & T)

Trevedra Farm C & C Site
Sennen, Penzance
TR19 7BE
Tel: 01736 871818 **2 B8**
trevedrafarm.co.uk
Total Pitches: 100 (C, CV & T)

Trevella Park
Crantock, Newquay
TR8 5EW
Tel: 01637 830308 **4 C10**
trevella.co.uk
Total Pitches: 290 (C, CV & T)

Trevornick
Holywell Bay, Newquay
TR8 5PW
Tel: 01637 830531 **4 B10**
trevornick.co.uk
Total Pitches: 600 (C, CV & T)

Truro C & C Park
Truro
TR4 8QN
Tel: 01872 560274 **3 K4**
trurocaravanandcampingpark.co.uk
Total Pitches: 100 (C, CV & T)

Tudor C & C
Shepherds Patch, Slimbridge,
Gloucester
GL2 7BP
Tel: 01453 890483 **32 D4**
tudorcaravanpark.com
Total Pitches: 75 (C, CV & T)

Twitchen House Holiday Park
Mortehoe Station Road,
Mortehoe, Woolacombe
EX34 7ES
Tel: 01271 872302 **16 H3**
woolacombe.com
Total Pitches: 569 (C, CV & T)

Two Mills Touring Park
Yarmouth Road, North Walsham
NR28 9NA
Tel: 01692 405829 **77 K6**
twomills.co.uk
Total Pitches: 81 (C, CV & T)

Ulwell Cottage Caravan Park
Ulwell Cottage, Ulwell, Swanage
BH19 3DG
Tel: 01929 422823 **12 H8**
ulwellcottagepark.co.uk
Total Pitches: 219 (C, CV & T)

Upper Lynstone Caravan Park
Lynstone, Bude
EX23 0LP
Tel: 01288 352017 **16 C10**
upperlynstone.co.uk
Total Pitches: 106 (C, CV & T)

Vale of Pickering Caravan Park
Carr House Farm, Allerston,
Pickering
YO18 7PQ
Tel: 01723 859280 **98 H4**
valeofpickering.co.uk
Total Pitches: 120 (C, CV & T)

Waldegraves Holiday Park
Mersea Island, Colchester
CO5 8SE
Tel: 01206 382898 **52 H9**
waldegraves.co.uk
Total Pitches: 30 (C, CV & T)

Waleswood C &C Park
Delves Lane, Waleswood,
Wales Bar, Wales, South
Yorkshire
S26 5RN
Tel: 07825 125328 **84 G4**
waleswood.co.uk
Total Pitches: 163 (C, CV & T)

Warcombe Farm C & C Park
Station Road, Mortehoe,
Woolacombe
EX34 7EJ
Tel: 01271 870690 **16 H2**
warcombefarm.co.uk
Total Pitches: 250 (C, CV & T)

Wareham Forest Tourist Park
North Trigon, Wareham
BH20 7NZ
Tel: 01929 551393 **12 E6**
warehamforest.co.uk
Total Pitches: 200 (C, CV & T)

Waren C & C Park
Waren Mill, Bamburgh
NE70 7EE
Tel: 01668 214366 **119 N4**
meadowhead.co.uk
Total Pitches: 458 (C, CV & T)

Warren Farm Holiday Centre
Brean Sands, Brean,
Burnham-on-Sea
TA8 2RP
Tel: 01278 751227 **19 J3**
warrenfarm.co.uk
Total Pitches: 975 (C, CV & T)

Watergate Bay Touring Park
Watergate Bay, Tregurrian
TR8 4AD
Tel: 01637 860387 **4 D8**
watergatebaytouringpark.co.uk
Total Pitches: 173 (C, CV & T)

Waterrow Touring Park
Wiveliscombe, Taunton
TA4 2AZ
Tel: 01984 623464 **18 E9**
waterrowpark.co.uk
Total Pitches: 44 (C, CV & T)

Wayfarers C & C Park
Relubbus Lane, St Hilary,
Penzance
TR20 9EF
Tel: 01736 763326 **2 F7**
wayfarerspark.co.uk
Total Pitches: 35 (C, CV & T)

Wells Touring Park
Haybridge, Wells
BA5 1AJ
Tel: 01749 676869 **19 P5**
wellstouringpark.co.uk
Total Pitches: 84(C & CV)

Westbrook Park
Little Hereford, Herefordshire
SY8 4AU
Tel: 01584 711280 **57 J11**
westbrookpark.co.uk
Total Pitches: 59 (C, CV & T)

Wheathill Touring Park
Wheathill, Bridgnorth
WV16 6QT
Tel: 01584 823456 — **57 L8**
wheathillpark.co.uk
Total Pitches: 50 (C & CV)

Whitefield Forest Touring Park
Brading Road, Ryde,
Isle of Wight
PO33 1QL
Tel: 01983 617069 — **14 H9**
whitefieldforest.co.uk
Total Pitches: 90 (C, CV & T)

Whitehill Country Park
Stoke Road, Paignton, Devon
TQ4 7PF
Tel: 01803 782338 — **7 M7**
whitehill-park.co.uk
Total Pitches: 325 (C, CV & T)

Whitemead Caravan Park
East Burton Road, Wool
BH20 6HG
Tel: 01929 462241 — **12 D7**
whitemeadcaravanpark.co.uk
Total Pitches: 105 (C, CV & T)

Willowbank Holiday Home & Touring Park
Coastal Road, Ainsdale,
Southport
PR8 3ST
Tel: 01704 571566 — **88 C8**
willowbankcp.co.uk
Total Pitches: 315 (C & CV)

Willow Valley Holiday Park
Bush, Bude, Cornwall
EX23 9LB
Tel: 01288 353104 — **16 C10**
willowvalley.co.uk
Total Pitches: 44 (C, CV & T)

Wilson House Holiday Park
Lancaster Road, Out Rawcliffe,
Preston, Lancashire
PR3 6BN
Tel: 07807 560685 — **88 E2**
whhp.co.uk
Total Pitches: 40 (C & CV)

Wolds View Touring Park
115 Brigg Road, Caistor
LN7 6RX
Tel: 01472 851099 — **93 K10**
woldsviewtouringpark.co.uk
Total Pitches: 60 (C, CV & T)

Wood Farm C & C Park
Axminster Road, Charmouth
DT6 6BT
Tel: 01297 560697 — **10 H6**
woodfarm.co.uk
Total Pitches: 267 (C, CV & T)

Wooda Farm Holiday Park
Poughill, Bude
EX23 9HJ
Tel: 01288 352069 — **16 C10**
wooda.co.uk
Total Pitches: 255 (C, CV & T)

Woodclose Caravan Park
High Casterton,
Kirkby Lonsdale
LA6 2SE
Tel: 01524 271597 — **95 N5**
woodclosepark.com
Total Pitches: 117 (C & CV)

Woodhall Country Park
Stixwold Road, Woodhall Spa
LN10 6UJ
Tel: 01526 353710 — **86 G8**
woodhallcountrypark.co.uk
Total Pitches: 120 (C, CV & T)

Woodland Springs Adult Touring Park
Venton, Drewsteignton
EX6 6PG
Tel: 01647 231695 — **8 G6**
woodlandsprings.co.uk
Total Pitches: 81 (C, CV & T)

Woodlands Grove C & C Park
Blackawton, Dartmouth
TQ9 7DQ
Tel: 01803 712598 — **7 L8**
woodlandsgrove.com
Total Pitches: 350 (C, CV & T)

Woodovis Park
Gulworthy, Tavistock
PL19 8NY
Tel: 01822 832968 — **6 C4**
woodovis.com
Total Pitches: 89 (C, CV & T)

Yeatheridge Farm Caravan Park
East Worlington, Crediton, Devon
EX17 4TN
Tel: 01884 860330 — **9 J2**
yeatheridge.co.uk
Total Pitches: 122 (C, CV & T)

York Meadows Caravan Park
York Road, Sheriff Hutton,
York, North Yorkshire
YO60 6QP
Tel: 01347 878508 — **98 C7**
yorkmeadowscaravanpark.com
Total Pitches: 60 (C, CV & T)

SCOTLAND

Anwoth Caravan Site
Gatehouse of Fleet,
Castle Douglas,
Dumfries & Galloway
DG7 2JU
Tel: 01557 814333 — **108 C9**
swalwellholidaygroup.co.uk
Total Pitches: 72 (C, CV & T)

Auchenlarie Holiday Park
Gatehouse of Fleet
DG7 2EX
Tel: 01556 506200 — **107 P7**
swalwellholidaygroup.co.uk
Total Pitches: 451 (C, CV & T)

Banff Links Caravan Park
Inverboyndie, Banff,
Aberdeenshire
AB45 2JJ
Tel: 01261 812228 — **158 G5**
banfflinkscaravanpark.co.uk
Total Pitches: 93 (C, CV & T)

Beecraigs C & C Site
Beecraigs Country Park,
The Visitor Centre,
Linlithgow
EH49 6PL
Tel: 01506 284516 — **127 J3**
westlothian.gov.uk/
stay-at-beecraigs
Total Pitches: 38 (C, CV & T)

Belhaven Bay C & C Park
Belhaven Bay, Dunbar,
East Lothian
EH42 1TS
Tel: 01368 865956 — **128 H4**
meadowhead.co.uk
Total Pitches: 119 (C, CV & T)

Blair Castle Caravan Park
Blair Atholl, Pitlochry
PH18 5SR
Tel: 01796 481263 — **141 L4**
blaircastlecaravanpark.co.uk
Total Pitches: 325 (C, CV & T)

Brighouse Bay Holiday Park
Brighouse Bay, Borgue,
Kirkcudbright
DG6 4TS
Tel: 01557 870267 — **108 D11**
gillespie-leisure.co.uk
Total Pitches: 418 (C, CV & T)

Cairnsmill Holiday Park
Largo Road, St Andrews
KY16 8NN
Tel: 01334 473604 — **135 M5**
cairnsmill.co.uk
Total Pitches: 256 (C, CV & T)

Craig Tara Holiday Park
Ayr
KA7 4LB
Tel: 0800 975 7579 — **114 F4**
haven.com/craigtara
Total Pitches: 1144 (C & CV)

Craigtoun Meadows Holiday Park
Mount Melville, St Andrews
KY16 8PQ
Tel: 01334 475959 — **135 M4**
craigtounmeadows.co.uk
Total Pitches: 257 (C, CV & T)

Crossburn Caravan Park
Edinburgh Road, Peebles,
Scottish Borders
EH45 8ED
Tel: 01721 720501 — **117 J2**
crossburn-caravans.com
Total Pitches: 132 (C, CV & T)

Faskally Caravan Park
Pitlochry
PH16 5LA
Tel: 01796 472007 — **141 M6**
faskally.co.uk
Total Pitches: 430 (C, CV & T)

Glen Nevis C & C Park
Glen Nevis, Fort William
PH33 6SX
Tel: 01397 702191 — **139 L3**
glen-nevis.co.uk
Total Pitches: 415 (C, CV & T)

Hoddom Castle Caravan Park
Hoddom, Lockerbie
DG11 1AS
Tel: 01576 300251 — **110 C6**
hoddomcastle.co.uk
Total Pitches: 265 (C, CV & T)

Huntly Castle Caravan Park
The Meadow, Huntly
AB54 4UJ
Tel: 01466 794999 — **158 D9**
huntlycastle.co.uk
Total Pitches: 130 (C, CV & T)

Invercoe C & C Park
Ballachulish,
Glencoe
PH49 4HP
Tel: 01855 811210 — **139 K6**
invercoe.co.uk
Total Pitches: 66 (C, CV & T)

Linwater Caravan Park
West Clifton,
East Calder
EH53 0HT
Tel: 0131 333 3326 — **127 L4**
linwater.co.uk
Total Pitches: 64 (C, CV & T)

Loch Ken Holiday Park
Parton, Castle Douglas,
Dumfries & Galloway
DG7 3NE
Tel: 01644 470282 — **108 E6**
lochkenholidaypark.co.uk
Total Pitches: 75 (C, CV & T)

Lomond Woods Holiday Park
Old Luss Road, Balloch,
Loch Lomond
G83 8QP
Tel: 01389 755000 — **132 D11**
woodleisure.co.uk/our-parks/
lomond-woods
Total Pitches: 153 (C & CV)

Milton of Fonab Caravan Park
Bridge Road, Pitlochry
PH16 5NA
Tel: 01796 472882 — **141 M6**
fonab.co.uk
Total Pitches: 188 (C, CV & T)

Sands of Luce Holiday Park
Sands of Luce, Sandhead,
Stranraer
DG9 9JN
Tel: 01776 830456 — **106 F7**
sandsofluce.com
Total Pitches: 350 (C, CV & T)

Seal Shore Camping and Touring Site
Kildonan, Isle of Arran,
North Ayrshire
KA27 8SE
Tel: 01770 820320 — **121 K7**
campingarran.com
Total Pitches: 47 (C, CV & T)

Seaward Holiday Park
Dhoon Bay, Kirkcudbright
DG6 4TJ
Tel: 01557 870267 — **108 E11**
gillespie-leisure.co.uk
Total Pitches: 84 (C, CV & T)

Seton Sands Holiday Village
Longniddry
EH32 0QF
Tel: 01875 813333 — **128 C4**
haven.com/setonsands
Total Pitches: 640 (C & CV)

Shieling Holidays Mull
Craignure,
Isle of Mull,
Argyll & Bute
PA65 6AY
Tel: 01680 812496 — **138 C10**
shielingholidays.co.uk
Total Pitches: 106 (C, CV & T)

Silver Sands Holiday Park
Covesea, West Beach,
Lossiemouth
IV31 6SP
Tel: 01343 813262 — **157 N3**
silver-sands.co.uk
Total Pitches: 340 (C, CV & T)

Skye C & C Club Site
Loch Greshornish, Borve,
Arnisort, Edinbane,
Isle of Skye
IV51 9PS
Tel: 01470 582230 — **152 E7**
campingandcaravanning
club.co.uk/skye
Total Pitches: 107 (C, CV & T)

Thurston Manor Leisure Park
Innerwick, Dunbar
EH42 1SA
Tel: 01368 840643 — **129 J5**
thurstonmanor.co.uk
Total Pitches: 690 (C & CV)

Witches Craig C & C Park
Blairlogie, Stirling
FK9 5PX
Tel: 01786 474947 — **133 N8**
witchescraig.co.uk
Total Pitches: 60 (C, CV & T)

WALES

Bodnant Caravan Park
Nebo Road, Llanrwst,
Conwy Valley, Conwy
LL26 0SD
Tel: 01492 640248 — **67 Q2**
bodnant-caravan-park.co.uk
Total Pitches: 56 (C, CV & T)

Bron Derw Touring Caravan Park
Llanrwst
LL26 0YT
Tel: 01492 640494 — **67 P2**
bronderw-wales.co.uk
Total Pitches: 48 (C & CV)

Bron-Y-Wendon Caravan Park
Wern Road, Llanddulas,
Colwyn Bay
LL22 8HG
Tel: 01492 512903 — **80 C9**
bronywendon.co.uk
Total Pitches: 130 (C & CV)

Bryn Gloch C & C Park
Betws Garmon, Caernarfon
LL54 7YY
Tel: 01286 650216 — **67 J3**
campwales.co.uk
Total Pitches: 177 (C, CV & T)

Caerfai Bay Caravan & Tent Park
Caerfai Bay, St Davids,
Haverfordwest
SA62 6QT
Tel: 01437 720274 — **40 E6**
caerfaibay.co.uk
Total Pitches: 136 (C, CV & T)

Cenarth Falls Holiday Park
Cenarth, Newcastle Emlyn
SA38 9JS
Tel: 01239 710345 — **41 Q2**
cenarth-holipark.co.uk
Total Pitches: 119 (C, CV & T)

Creampots Touring C & C Park
Broadway, Broad Haven,
Haverfordwest,
Pembrokeshire
SA62 3TU
Tel: 01437 781776 — **40 G8**
creampots.co.uk
Total Pitches: 73 (C, CV & T)

Daisy Bank Caravan Park
Snead, Montgomery
SY15 6EB
Tel: 01588 620471 — **56 E6**
daisy-bank.co.uk
Total Pitches: 87 (C, CV & T)

Deucoch Touring & Camping Park
Sarn Bach, Abersoch,
Gwynedd
LL53 7LD
Tel: 01758 713293 — **66 E9**
deucoch.com
Total Pitches: 70 (C, CV & T)

Dinlle Caravan Park
Dinas Dinlle, Caernarfon
LL54 5TW
Tel: 01286 830324 — **66 G3**
thornleyleisure.co.uk
Total Pitches: 349 (C, CV & T)

Eisteddfa
Eisteddfa Lodge, Pentrefelin,
Criccieth
LL52 0PT
Tel: 01766 522696 — **67 J7**
eisteddfapark.co.uk
Total Pitches: 116 (C, CV & T)

Fforest Fields C & C Park
Hundred House,
Builth Wells
LD1 5RT
Tel: 01982 570406 — **44 G4**
fforestfields.co.uk
Total Pitches: 122 (C, CV & T)

Fishguard Bay Resort
Garn Gelli, Fishguard
SA65 9ET
Tel: 01348 811415 — **41 J3**
fishguardbay.com
Total Pitches: 102 (C, CV & T)

Greenacres Holiday Park
Black Rock Sands,
Morfa Bychan, Porthmadog
LL49 9YF
Tel: 01766 512781 — **67 J7**
haven.com/greenacres
Total Pitches: 945 (C & CV)

Hafan y Môr Holiday Park
Pwllheli
LL53 6HJ
Tel: 01758 612112 — **66 G7**
haven.com/hafanymor
Total Pitches: 875 (C & CV)

Hendre Mynach Touring C & C Park
Llanaber Road, Barmouth
LL42 1YR
Tel: 01341 280262 — **67 L11**
hendremynach.co.uk
Total Pitches: 241 (C, CV & T)

Home Farm Caravan Park
Marian-glas,
Isle of Anglesey
LL73 8PH
Tel: 01248 410614 — **78 H8**
homefarm-anglesey.co.uk
Total Pitches: 186 (C, CV & T)

Islawrffordd Caravan Park
Talybont, Barmouth
LL43 2AQ
Tel: 01341 247269 — **67 K10**
islawrffordd.co.uk
Total Pitches: 306 (C & CV)

Kiln Park Holiday Centre
Marsh Road, Tenby
SA70 8RB
Tel: 01834 844121 — **41 M10**
haven.com/kilnpark
Total Pitches: 849 (C, CV & T)

Pencelli Castle C & C Park
Pencelli, Brecon
LD3 7LX
Tel: 01874 665451 — **44 F10**
pencelli-castle.com
Total Pitches: 80 (C, CV & T)

Penisar Mynydd Caravan Park
Caerwys Road, Rhuallt,
St Asaph
LL17 0TY
Tel: 01745 582227 — **80 F9**
penisarmynydd.co.uk
Total Pitches: 71 (C, CV & T)

Plassey Holiday Park
The Plassey, Eyton, Wrexham
LL13 0SP
Tel: 01978 780277 — **69 L5**
plassey.com
Total Pitches: 123 (C, CV & T)

Pont Kemys C & C Park
Chainbridge, Abergavenny
NP7 9DS
Tel: 01873 880688 — **31 K3**
pontkemys.com
Total Pitches: 65 (C, CV & T)

Presthaven Sands Holiday Park
Gronant, Prestatyn
LL19 9TT
Tel: 01745 856471 — **80 F8**
haven.com/presthavensands
Total Pitches: 1102 (C & CV)

Red Kite Touring Park
Van Road, Llanidloes
SY18 6NG
Tel: 01686 412122 — **55 L7**
redkitetouringpark.co.uk
Total Pitches: 66 (C & CV)

Riverside Camping
Seiont Nurseries, Pont Rug,
Caernarfon
LL55 2BB
Tel: 01286 678781 — **67 J2**
riversidecamping.co.uk
Total Pitches: 73 (C, CV & T)

The Trotting Mare Caravan Park
Overton, Wrexham
LL13 0LE
Tel: 01978 711963 — **69 L7**
thetrottingmare.co.uk
Total Pitches: 65 (C, CV & T)

Trawsdir Touring C & C Park
Llanaber, Barmouth
LL42 1RR
Tel: 01341 280999 — **67 K11**
barmouthholidays.co.uk
Total Pitches: 80 (C, CV & T)

Tyddyn Isaf Caravan Park
Lligwy Bay, Dulas,
Isle of Anglesey
LL70 9PQ
Tel: 01248 410203 — **78 H7**
tyddynisaf.co.uk
Total Pitches: 136 (C, CV & T)

White Tower Caravan Park
Llandwrog, Caernarfon
LL54 5UH
Tel: 01286 830649 — **66 H3**
whitetowerpark.co.uk
Total Pitches: 126 (C & CV)

Signs giving orders

**Signs with red circles are mostly prohibitive.
Plates below signs qualify their message**

Entry to 20mph zone

End of 20mph zone

Maximum speed

National speed limit applies

School crossing patrol

Mini-roundabout (roundabout circulation – give way to vehicles from the immediate right)

Route to be used by pedal cycles only

Segregated pedal cycle and pedestrian route

Minimum speed

End of minimum speed

Stop and give way

Give way to traffic on major road

Manually operated temporary STOP and GO signs

No entry for vehicular traffic

Buses and cycles only

Trams only

Pedestrian crossing point over tramway

One-way traffic (note: compare circular 'Ahead only' sign)

No vehicles except bicycles being pushed

No cycling

No motor vehicles

No buses (over 8 passenger seats)

No overtaking

With-flow bus and cycle lane

Contraflow bus lane

With-flow pedal cycle lane

No towed caravans

No vehicles carrying explosives

No vehicle or combination of vehicles over length shown

No vehicles over height shown

No vehicles over width shown

Warning signs

Mostly triangular

Distance to 'STOP' line ahead

Dual carriageway ends

Road narrows on right (left if symbol reversed)

Road narrows on both sides

Give priority to vehicles from opposite direction

No right turn

No left turn

No U-turns

No goods vehicles over maximum gross weight shown (in tonnes) except for loading and unloading

Distance to 'Give Way' line ahead

Crossroads

Junction on bend ahead

T-junction with priority over vehicles from the right

Staggered junction

Traffic merging from left ahead

The priority through route is indicated by the broader line.

No vehicles over maximum gross weight shown (in tonnes)

Parking restricted to permit holders

No stopping during period indicated except for buses

No stopping during times shown except for as long as necessary to set down or pick up passengers

Double bend first to left (symbol may be reversed)

Bend to right (or left if symbol reversed)

Roundabout

Uneven road

Plate below some signs

No waiting

No stopping (Clearway)

Signs with blue circles but no red border mostly give positive instruction.

Two-way traffic crosses one-way road

Two-way traffic straight ahead

Opening or swing bridge ahead

Low-flying aircraft or sudden aircraft noise

Falling or fallen rocks

Ahead only

Turn left ahead (right if symbol reversed)

Turn left (right if symbol reversed)

Keep left (right if symbol reversed)

Vehicles may pass either side to reach same destination

Traffic signals not in use

Traffic signals

Slippery road

Steep hill downwards

Steep hill upwards

Gradients may be shown as a ratio i.e. 20% = 1:5

Tunnel ahead

Trams crossing ahead

Level crossing with barrier or gate ahead

Level crossing without barrier or gate ahead

Level crossing without barrier

Patrol
School crossing patrol ahead (some signs have amber lights which flash when crossings are in use)

Frail (or blind or disabled if shown) pedestrians likely to cross road ahead

No footway for 400 yds
Pedestrians in road ahead

Zebra crossing

Safe height 16'-6"
Overhead electric cable; plate indicates maximum height of vehicles which can pass safely

Available width of headroom indicated

Sharp deviation of route to left (or right if chevrons reversed)

STOP when lights show
Light signals ahead at level crossing, airfield or bridge

Red STOP
Green Clear
IF NO LIGHT - PHONE CROSSING OPERATOR
Miniature warning lights at level crossings

Cattle

Wild animals

Wild horses or ponies

Accompanied horses or ponies

Cycle route ahead

Ice
Risk of ice

Queues likely
Traffic queues likely ahead

Humps for ½ mile
Distance over which road humps extend

Hidden dip
Other danger; plate indicates nature of danger

Soft verges for 2 miles
Soft verges

Side winds

Hump bridge

Ford
Worded warning sign

Quayside or river bank

Risk of grounding

Direction signs

Mostly rectangular

Signs on motorways - blue backgrounds

Nottingham 23 M1
At a junction leading directly into a motorway (junction number may be shown on a black background)

Nottingham A52 25 ½ m
On approaches to junctions (junction number on black background)

M1 The NORTH Sheffield 32 Leeds 59
Route confirmatory sign after junction

A404 Marlow | Birmingham, Oxford M40
4 ½ m
Downward pointing arrows mean 'Get in lane'
The left-hand lane leads to a different destination from the other lanes.

A46 (M69) Leicester, Coventry (E)
2 ½ m | The NORTH WEST, Birmingham, Coventry (N) M6
The panel with the inclined arrow indicates the destinations which can be reached

Signs on primary routes - green backgrounds

PARK STREET ROUNDABOUT
Birmingham
Bourne ✈ 🛣
1 M15 (M1)
(M14)
Penderton A105
Walsham A1183
Nutfield A1183
On approaches to junctions

Lampton Axtley A11
14'-6"
1 mile
At the junction

A46
The SOUTH
Nottingham 17
Leicester 32
(M1 South) 35
Route confirmatory sign after junction

TURPIN'S CROSSROADS
Biggleswick A11
Lampton (M11)
Dorfield A123
Axtley B1991
Steam railway
On approaches to junctions

Swansea Abertawe A483
On approach to a junction in Wales (bilingual)

Blue panels indicate that the motorway starts at the junction ahead.
Motorways shown in brackets can also be reached along the route indicated.
White panels indicate local or non-primary routes leading from the junction ahead.
Brown panels show the route to tourist attractions.
The name of the junction may be shown at the top of the sign.
The aircraft symbol indicates the route to an airport.
A symbol may be included to warn of a hazard or restriction along that route.

Signs on non-primary and local routes - black borders

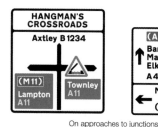
HANGMAN'S CROSSROADS
Axtley B1234
(M11) Lampton A11
Townley A11
On approaches to junctions

(A1(M)) 8
Barnes 10
Mackstone 2½
Elkington 1
A404 (A41)
Millington Green 3
(A4011)

Market Walborough B486 7
At the junction

WC
Direction to toilets with access for the disabled

Green panels indicate that the primary route starts at the junction ahead.
Route numbers on a blue background show the direction to a motorway.
Route numbers on a green background show the direction to a primary route.

Emergency diversion routes

In an emergency it may be necessary to close a section of motorway or other main road to traffic, so a temporary sign may advise drivers to follow a diversion route. To help drivers navigate the route, black symbols on yellow patches may be permanently displayed on existing direction signs, including motorway signs. Symbols may also be used on separate signs with yellow backgrounds.

THE HIGHWAY CODE
KNOW YOUR ROAD SIGNS

Note: The signs shown in this road atlas are those most commonly in use and are not all drawn to the same scale. In Scotland and Wales bilingual versions of some signs are used, showing both English and Gaelic or Welsh spellings. Some older designs of signs may still be seen on the roads. A comprehensive explanation of the signing system illustrating the vast majority of road signs can be found in the AA's handbook *Know Your Road Signs*. Where there is a reference to a rule number, this refers to *The Highway Code*.

Restricted junctions

Motorway and primary route junctions which have access or exit restrictions are shown on the map pages thus:

M1 London - Leeds

Northbound
Access only from A1
(northbound)

Southbound
Exit only to A1
(southbound)

Northbound
Access only from A41
(northbound)

Southbound
Exit only to A41
(southbound)

Northbound
Access only from M25
(no link from A405)

Southbound
Exit only to M25
(no link from A405)

Northbound
Access only from A414

Southbound
Exit only to A414

Northbound
Exit only to M45

Southbound
Access only from M45

Northbound
Exit only to M6
(northbound)

Southbound
Exit only to A14
(southbound)

Northbound
Exit only, no access

Southbound
Access only, no exit

Northbound
No exit, access only

Southbound
Access only from
A50 (eastbound)

Northbound
Exit only, no access

Southbound
Access only, no exit

Northbound
Exit only to M621

Southbound
Access only from M621

Northbound
Exit only to A1(M)
(northbound)

Southbound
Access only from A1(M)
(southbound)

M2 Rochester - Faversham

Westbound
No exit to A2
(eastbound)

Eastbound
No access from A2
(westbound)

M3 Sunbury - Southampton

Northeastbound
Access only from A303,
no exit

Southwestbound
Exit only to A303,
no access

Northbound
Exit only, no access

Southbound
Access only, no exit

Northeastbound
Access from M27 only,
no exit

Southwestbound
No access to M27
(westbound)

M4 London - South Wales

For junctions 1 & 2 see London district map
on pages 178–181

Westbound
Exit only to M48

Eastbound
Access only from M48

Westbound
Access only from M48

Eastbound
Exit only to M48

Westbound
Exit only, no access

Eastbound
Access only, no exit

Westbound
Exit only, no access

Eastbound
Access only, no exit

Westbound
Exit only to A48(M)

Eastbound
Access only from A48(M)

Westbound
Exit only, no access

Eastbound
No restriction

Westbound
Access only, no exit

Eastbound
No access or exit

Westbound
Exit only to A483

Eastbound
Access only from A483

M5 Birmingham - Exeter

Northeastbound
Access only, no exit

Southwestbound
Exit only, no access

Northeastbound
Access only from A417
(westbound)

Southwestbound
Exit only to A417
(eastbound)

Northeastbound
Exit only to M49

Southwestbound
Access only from M49

Northeastbound
No access, exit only

Southwestbound
No exit, access only

M6 Toll Motorway

See M6 Toll motorway map on page *XXIII*

M6 Rugby - Carlisle

Northbound
Exit only to M6 Toll

Southbound
Access only from M6 Toll

Northbound
Exit only to M42
(southbound) and A446

Southbound
Exit only to A446

Northbound
Access only from M42
(southbound)

Southbound
Exit only to M42

Northbound
Exit only, no access

Southbound
Access only, no exit

Northbound
Exit only to M54

Southbound
Access only from M54

Northbound
Access only from M6 Toll

Southbound
Exit only to M6 Toll

Northbound
No restriction

Southbound
Access only from M56
(eastbound)

Northbound
Exit only to M56
(westbound)

Southbound
Access only from M56
(eastbound)

Northbound
Access only, no exit

Southbound
Exit only, no access

Northbound
Exit only, no access

Southbound
Access only, no exit

Northbound
Access only from M61

Southbound
Exit only to M61

Northbound
Exit only, no access

Southbound
Access only, no exit

Northbound
Exit only, no access

Southbound
Access only, no exit

M8 Edinburgh - Bishopton

For junctions 7A to 29A see Glasgow district
map on pages 176–177

Westbound
Exit only, no access

Eastbound
Access only, no exit

Westbound
Access only, no exit

Eastbound
Exit only, no access

Westbound
Access only, no exit

Eastbound
Exit only, no access

M9 Edinburgh - Dunblane

Northwestbound
Access only, no exit

Southeastbound
Exit only, no access

Northwestbound
Exit only, no access

Southeastbound
Access only, no exit

Northwestbound
Access only, no exit

Southeastbound
Exit only to A905

Northwestbound
Exit only to M876
(southwestbound)

Southeastbound
Access only from M876
(northeastbound)

M11 London - Cambridge

Northbound
Access only from A406
(eastbound)

Southbound
Exit only to A406

Northbound
Exit only, no access

Southbound
Access only, no exit

Northbound
Exit only, no access

Southbound
No direct access,
use jct 8

Northbound
Exit only to A11

Southbound
Access only from A11

Northbound
Exit only, no access

Southbound
Access only, no exit

Northbound
Exit only, no access

Southbound
Access only, no exit

M20 Swanley - Folkestone

Northwestbound
Staggered junction; follow
signs - access only

Southeastbound
Staggered junction; follow
signs - exit only

Northwestbound
Exit only to M26
(westbound)

Southeastbound
Access only from M26
(eastbound)

Northwestbound
Access only from A20

Southeastbound
For access follow signs -
exit only to A20

Northwestbound
No restriction

Southeastbound
For exit follow signs

Northwestbound
Access only, no exit

Southeastbound
Exit only, no access

M23 Hooley - Crawley

Northbound
Exit only to A23
(northbound)

Southbound
Access only from A23
(southbound)

Northbound
Access only, no exit

Southbound
Exit only, no access

M25 London Orbital Motorway

See M25 London Orbital motorway map on page XXII

M26 Sevenoaks - Wrotham

Westbound
Exit only to clockwise
M25 (westbound)

Eastbound
Access only from
anticlockwise M25
(eastbound)

Westbound
Access only from M20
(northwestbound)

Eastbound
Exit only to M20
(southeastbound)

M27 Cadnam - Portsmouth

Westbound
Staggered junction; follow
signs - access only from
M3 (southbound). Exit
only to M3 (northbound)

Eastbound
Staggered junction; follow
signs - access only from
M3 (southbound). Exit
only to M3 (northbound)

Westbound
Exit only, no access

Eastbound
Access only, no exit

Westbound
Staggered junction; follow
signs - exit only to M275
(southbound)

Eastbound
Staggered junction; follow
signs - access only from
M275 (northbound)

M40 London - Birmingham

Northwestbound
Exit only, no access

Southeastbound
Access only, no exit

Northwestbound
Exit only, no access

Southeastbound
Access only, no exit

Northwestbound
Exit only to M40/A40

Southeastbound
Access only from
M40/A40

Northwestbound
Exit only, no access

Southeastbound
Access only, no exit

Northwestbound
Access only, no exit

Southeastbound
Exit only, no access

Northwestbound
Access only, no exit

Southeastbound
Exit only, no access

M42 Bromsgrove - Measham

See Birmingham district map on pages 174–175

M45 Coventry - M1

Westbound
Access only from A45
(northbound)

Eastbound
Exit only, no access

Westbound
Access only from M1
(northbound)

Eastbound
Exit only to M1
(southbound)

M48 Chepstow

Westbound
Access only from M4
(westbound)

Eastbound
Exit only to M4
(eastbound)

Westbound
No exit to M4 (eastbound)

Eastbound
No access from M4
(westbound)

M53 Mersey Tunnel - Chester

Northbound
Access only from M56
(westbound). Exit only to
M56 (eastbound)

Southbound
Access only from M56
(westbound). Exit only to
M56 (eastbound)

M54 Telford - Birmingham

Westbound
Access only from M6
(northbound)

Eastbound
Exit only to M6
(southbound)

M56 Chester - Manchester

For junctions 1,2,3,4 & 7 see Manchester district map on pages 182–183

Westbound
Access only, no exit

Eastbound
No access or exit

Westbound
No exit to M6
(southbound)

Eastbound
No access from M6
(northbound)

Westbound
Exit only to M53

Eastbound
Access only from M53

Westbound
No access or exit

Eastbound
No restriction

M57 Liverpool Outer Ring Road

Northwestbound
Access only, no exit

Southeastbound
Exit only, no access

Northwestbound
Access only from A580
(westbound)

Southeastbound
Exit only, no access

M60 Manchester Orbital

See Manchester district map on pages 182–183

M61 Manchester - Preston

Northwestbound
No access or exit

Southeastbound
Exit only, no access

Northwestbound
Exit only to M6
(northbound)

Southeastbound
Access only from M6
(southbound)

M62 Liverpool - Kingston upon Hull

Westbound
Access only, no exit

Eastbound
Exit only, no access

Westbound
No access to A1(M) (southbound)

Eastbound
No restriction

M65 Preston - Colne

Northeastbound
Exit only, no access

Southwestbound
Access only, no exit

Northeastbound
Access only, no exit

Southwestbound
Exit only, no access

M66 Bury

Northbound
Exit only to A56 (northbound)

Southbound
Access only from A56 (southbound)

Northbound
Exit only, no access

Southbound
Access only, no exit

M67 Hyde Bypass

Westbound
Access only, no exit

Eastbound
Exit only, no access

Westbound
Exit only, no access

Eastbound
Access only, no exit

M69 Coventry - Leicester

Northbound
Access only, no exit

Southbound
Exit only, no access

M73 East of Glasgow

Northbound
No exit to A74 and A721

Southbound
No exit to A74 and A721

Northbound
No access from or exit to A89. No access from M8 (eastbound)

Southbound
No access from or exit to A89. No exit to M8 (westbound)

M74 and A74(M) Glasgow - Gretna

Northbound
Exit only, no access

Southbound
Access only, no exit

Northbound
Access only, no exit

Southbound
Exit only, no access

Northbound
No access from A74 and A721

Southbound
Access only, no exit to A74 and A721

Northbound
Access only, no exit

Southbound
Exit only, no access

Northbound
No access or exit

Southbound
Exit only, no access

Northbound
No restriction

Southbound
Access only, no exit

Northbound
Access only, no exit

Southbound
Access only, no exit

Northbound
Exit only, no access

Southbound
Access only, no exit

Northbound
Exit only, no access

Southbound
Access only, no exit

M77 Glasgow - Kilmarnock

Northbound
No exit to M8 (westbound)

Southbound
No access from M8 (eastbound)

Northbound
Access only, no exit

Southbound
Exit only, no access

Northbound
Access only, no exit

Southbound
Exit only, no access

Northbound
Access only, no exit

Southbound
No restriction

Northbound
Exit only, no access

Southbound
Exit only, no access

M80 Glasgow - Stirling

For junctions 1 & 4 see Glasgow district map on pages 176–177

Northbound
Exit only, no access

Southbound
Access only, no exit

Northbound
Access only, no exit

Southbound
Exit only, no access

Northbound
Exit only to M876 (northeastbound)

Southbound
Access only from M876 (southwestbound)

M90 Edinburgh - Perth

Northbound
No exit, access only

Southbound
Exit only to A90 (eastbound)

Northbound
Exit only to A92 (eastbound)

Southbound
Access only from A92 (westbound)

Northbound
Access only, no exit

Southbound
Exit only, no access

Northbound
Exit only, no access

Southbound
Access only, no exit

Northbound
No access from A912 No exit to A912 (southbound)

Southbound
No access from A912 (northbound). No exit to A912

M180 Doncaster - Grimsby

Westbound
Access only, no exit

Eastbound
Exit only, no access

M606 Bradford Spur

Northbound
Exit only, no access

Southbound
No restriction

M621 Leeds - M1

Clockwise
Access only, no exit

Anticlockwise
Exit only, no access

Clockwise
No exit or access

Anticlockwise
No restriction

Clockwise
Access only, no exit

Anticlockwise
Exit only, no access

Clockwise
Exit only, no access

Anticlockwise
Access only, no exit

Clockwise
Exit only to M1 (southbound)

Anticlockwise
Access only from M1 (northbound)

M876 Bonnybridge - Kincardine Bridge

Northeastbound
Access only from M80 (northbound)

Southwestbound
Exit only to M80 (southbound)

Northeastbound
Exit only to M9 (eastbound)

Southwestbound
Access only from M9 (westbound)

A1(M) South Mimms - Baldock

Northbound
Exit only, no access

Southbound
Access only, no exit

Northbound
No restriction

Southbound
Exit only, no access

Northbound
Access only, no exit

Southbound
No access or exit

A1(M) Pontefract - Bedale

Northbound
No access to M62
(eastbound)

Southbound
No restriction

Northbound
Access only from M1
(northbound)

Southbound
Exit only to M1
(southbound)

A1(M) Scotch Corner - Newcastle upon Tyne

Northbound
Exit only to A66(M)
(eastbound)

Southbound
Access only from A66(M)
(westbound)

Northbound
No access. Exit only to
A194(M) & A1
(northbound)

Southbound
No exit. Access only from
A194(M) & A1
(southbound)

A3(M) Horndean - Havant

Northbound
Access only from A3

Southbound
Exit only to A3

Northbound
Exit only, no access

Southbound
Access only, no exit

A38(M) Birmingham Victoria Road (Park Circus)

Northbound
No exit

Southbound
No access

A48(M) Cardiff Spur

Westbound
Access only from M4
(westbound)

Eastbound
Exit only to M4
(eastbound)

Westbound
Exit only to A48
(westbound)

Eastbound
Access only from A48
(eastbound)

A57(M) Manchester Brook Street (A34)

Westbound
No exit

Eastbound
No access

A58(M) Leeds Park Lane and Westgate

Northbound
No restriction

Southbound
No access

A64(M) Leeds Clay Pit Lane (A58)

Westbound
No exit (to Clay Pit Lane)

Eastbound
No access (from Clay Pit
Lane)

A66(M) Darlington Spur

Westbound
Exit only to A1(M)
(southbound)

Eastbound
Access only from A1(M)
(northbound)

A74(M) Gretna - Abington

Northbound
Exit only, no access

Southbound
Access only, no exit

A194(M) Newcastle upon Tyne

Northbound
Access only from A1(M)
(northbound)

Southbound
Exit only to A1(M)
(southbound)

A12 M25 - Ipswich

Northeastbound
Access only, no exit

Southwestbound
No restriction

Northeastbound
Exit only, no access

Southwestbound
Access only, no exit

Northeastbound
Exit only, no access

Southwestbound
Access only, no exit

Northeastbound
Access only, no exit

Southwestbound
Exit only, no access

Northeastbound
No restriction

Southwestbound
Access only, no exit

Northeastbound
Exit only, no access

Southwestbound
Access only, no exit

Northeastbound
Access only, no exit

Southwestbound
Exit only, no access

Northeastbound
Access only, no exit

Southwestbound
Exit only, no access

Northeastbound
Exit only, no access

Southwestbound
Access only, no exit

Northeastbound
Exit only (for Stratford
St Mary and Dedham)

Southwestbound
Access only

A14 M1 - Felixstowe

Westbound
Exit only to M6 & M1
(northbound)

Eastbound
Access only from M6 &
M1 (southbound)

Westbound
Exit only, no access

Eastbound
Access only, no exit

Westbound
Access only, no exit

Eastbound
Exit only, no access

Westbound
Exit only, no access

Eastbound
Access only from A1
(southbound)

Westbound
Access only, no exit

Eastbound
Exit only, no access

Westbound
No restriction

Eastbound
Access only, no exit

Westbound
Access only, no exit

Eastbound
Exit only, no access

Westbound
Exit only to A11
Access only from A1303

Eastbound
Access only from A11

Westbound
Access only from A11

Eastbound
Exit only to A11

Westbound
Exit only, no access

Eastbound
Access only, no exit

Westbound
Access only, no exit

Eastbound
Exit only, no access

A55 Holyhead - Chester

Westbound
Exit only, no access

Eastbound
Access only, no exit

Westbound
Access only, no exit

Eastbound
Exit only, no access

Westbound
No restriction

Eastbound
No access or exit

Westbound
Exit only, no access

Eastbound
No access or exit

Westbound
Exit only, no access

Eastbound
Access only, no exit

Westbound
Exit only to A5104

Eastbound
Access only from A5104

Refer also to atlas pages 36–37 and 50–51

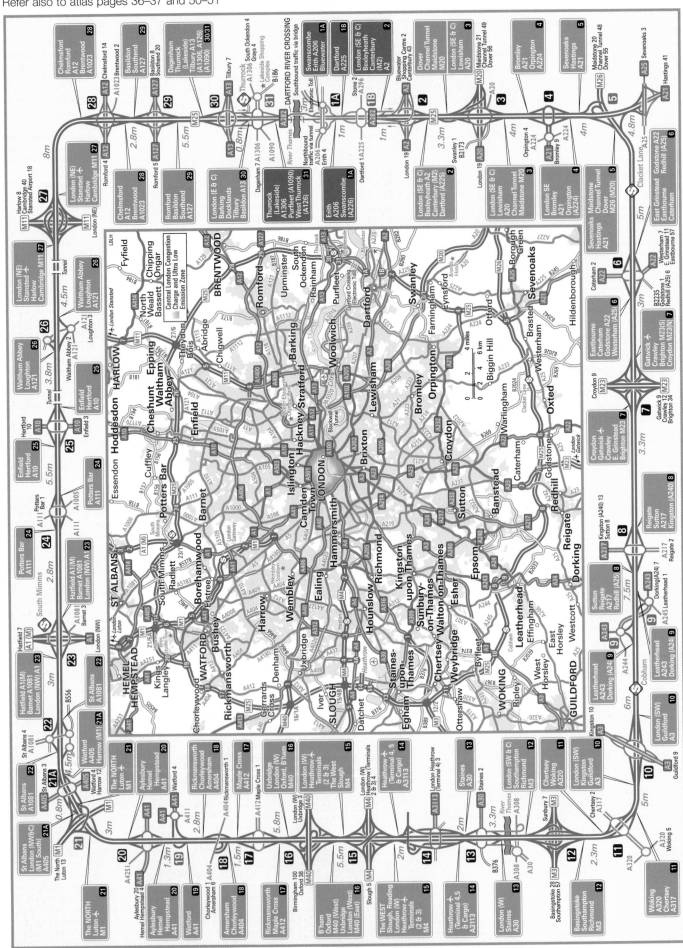

Refer also to atlas pages 58–59

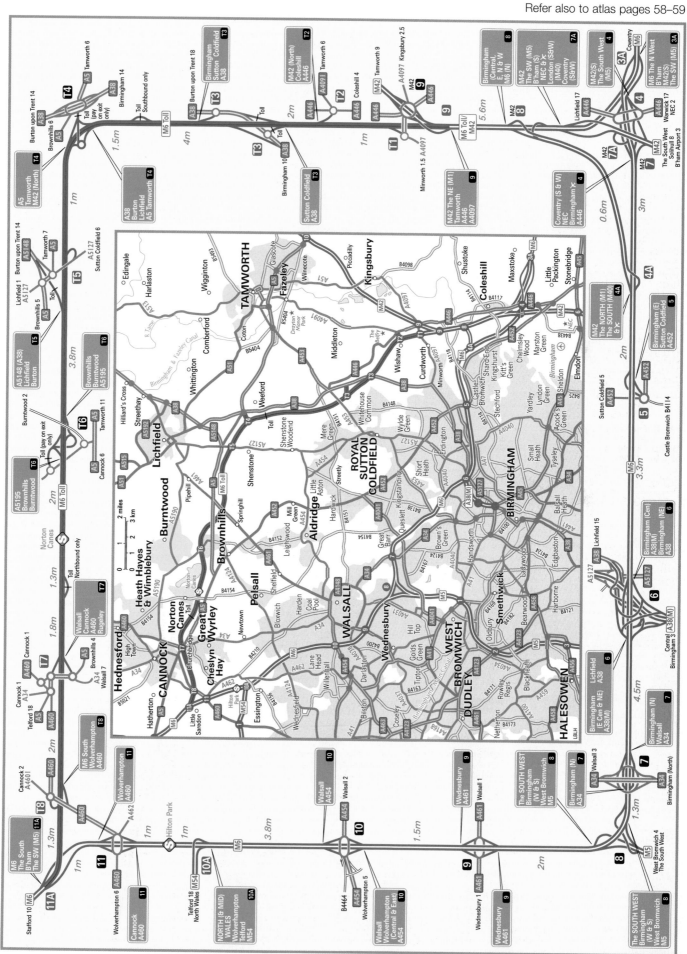

Smart motorways

Since Britain's first motorway (the Preston Bypass) opened in 1958, motorways have changed significantly. A vast increase in car journeys over the last 62 years has meant that motorways quickly filled to capacity. To combat this, the recent development of **smart motorways** uses technology to monitor and actively manage traffic flow and congestion.

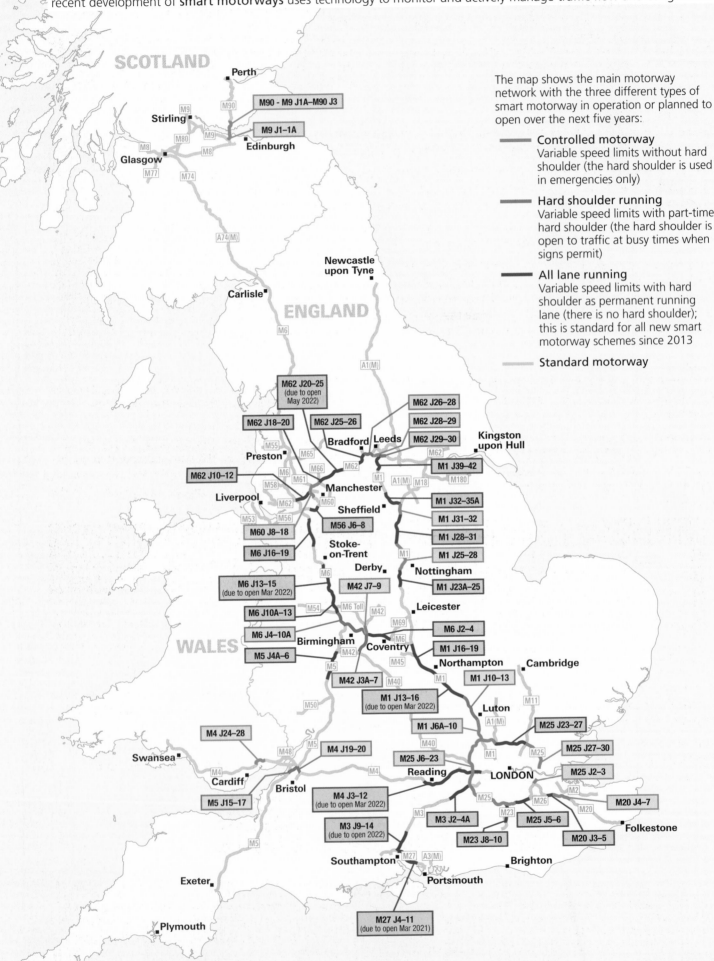

The map shows the main motorway network with the three different types of smart motorway in operation or planned to open over the next five years:

— **Controlled motorway**
Variable speed limits without hard shoulder (the hard shoulder is used in emergencies only)

— **Hard shoulder running**
Variable speed limits with part-time hard shoulder (the hard shoulder is open to traffic at busy times when signs permit)

— **All lane running**
Variable speed limits with hard shoulder as permanent running lane (there is no hard shoulder); this is standard for all new smart motorway schemes since 2013

— **Standard motorway**

Smart motorways (*Intelligent Transport Systems* in Scotland) are the responsibility of Highways England, Transport Scotland and Transport for Wales

How they work

Smart motorways utilise various active traffic management methods, monitored through a regional traffic control centre:

- Traffic flow is monitored using CCTV
- Speed limits are changed to smooth traffic flow and reduce stop-start driving
- Capacity of the motorway can be increased by either temporarily or permanently opening the hard shoulder to traffic

- Warning signs and messages alert drivers to hazards and traffic jams ahead
- Lanes can be closed in the case of an accident or emergency by displaying a red X sign
- Emergency refuge areas are located regularly along the motorway where there is no hard shoulder available

In an emergency

On a smart motorway there is often no hard shoulder so in an emergency you will need to make your way to the nearest **emergency refuge area** or motorway service area.

Emergency refuge areas are lay-bys marked with blue signs featuring an orange SOS telephone symbol. The telephone connects to the regional control centre and pinpoints your location. The control centre will advise you on what to do, send help and assist you in returning to the motorway.

If you are unable to reach an emergency refuge area or hard shoulder (if there is one) move as close to the nearside (left hand) boundary or verge as you can.

If it is not possible to get out of your vehicle safely, or there is no other place of relative safety to wait, stay in your vehicle with your seat-belt on and dial 999 if you have a mobile phone. If you don't have a phone, sit tight and wait to be rescued. Once the regional traffic control centre is aware of your situation, via the police or CCTV, they will use the smart motorway technology to set overhead signs and close the lane to keep traffic away from you. They will also send a traffic officer or the police to help you.

Refuge areas for emergency use only

Sign indicating presence of emergency refuge areas ahead

Emergency refuge area SOS

This sign is located at each emergency refuge area

Signs

Motorway signals and messages advise of abnormal traffic conditions ahead and may indicate speed limits. They may apply to individual lanes when mounted overhead or, when located on the central reservation or at the side of the motorway, to the whole carriageway.

Where traffic is allowed to use the hard shoulder as a traffic lane, each lane will have overhead signals and signs. A red cross (with no signals) displayed above the hard shoulder indicates when it is closed. When the hard shoulder is in use as a traffic lane the red cross will change to a speed limit. Should it be necessary to close any lane, a red cross with red lamps flashing in vertical pairs will be shown above that lane. Prior to this, the signal will show an arrow directing traffic into the adjacent lane.

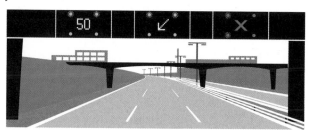

These signals are mounted above the carriageway with a signal for each traffic lane; each signal has two pairs of lamps that flash. You should obey the signal for your lane

Move to adjacent lane (arrow may point downwards to the right)

Leave motorway at next exit

Red lamps flashing from side to side in pairs, together with a red cross, mean 'do not proceed in the traffic lane directly below'. More than one lane may be closed to traffic

Where variable speed limit signs are mounted over individual lanes and the speed limit is shown in a red ring, the limit is mandatory. You will be at risk of a driving offence if you do not keep to the speed limit. Speed limits that do not include the red ring are the maximum speeds advised for the prevailing conditions.

Speed limits of 60, 50 and 40mph are used on all types of smart motorways. When no speed limit is shown the national speed limit of 70mph is in place (this is reduced to 60mph for particular vehicles such as heavy or articulated goods vehicles and vehicles towing caravans or trailers).

Quick tips

- Never drive in a lane closed by a red X
- Keep to the speed limit shown on the gantries
- A solid white line indicates the hard shoulder – do not drive in it unless directed or in the case of an emergency
- A broken white line indicates a normal running lane

- Exit the smart motorway where possible if your vehicle is in difficulty. In an emergency, move onto the hard shoulder where there is one, or the nearest emergency refuge area
- Put on your hazard lights if you break down

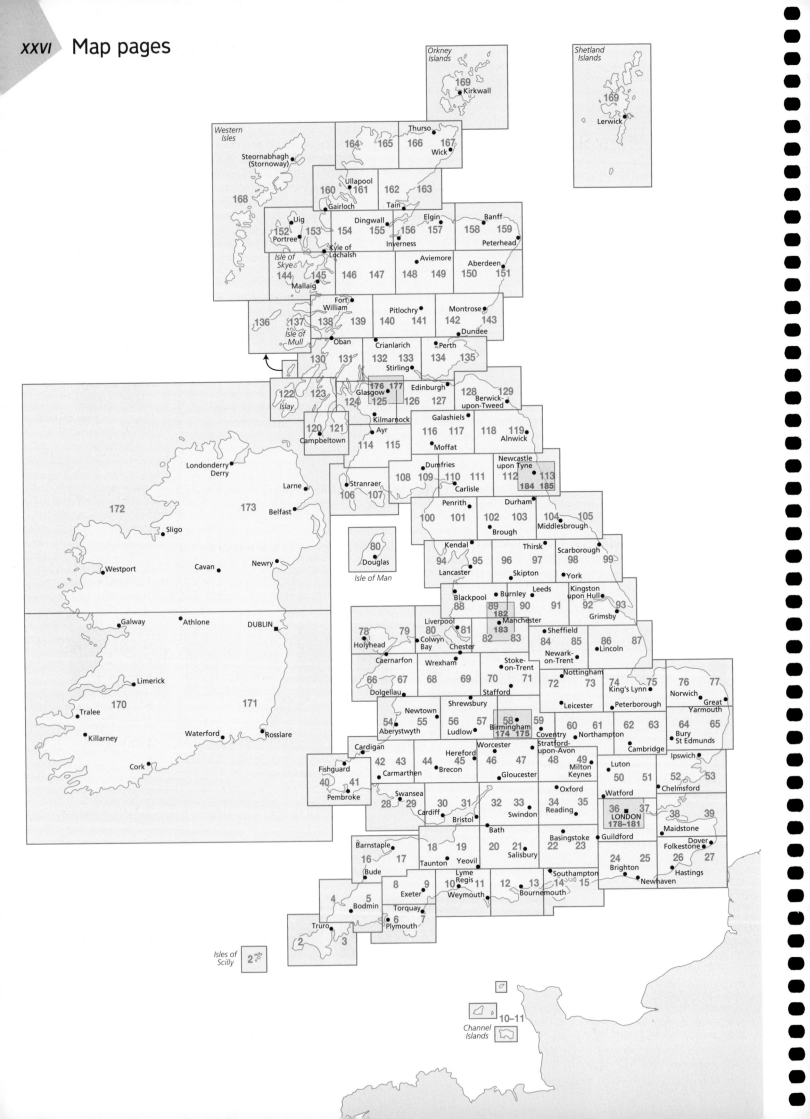

Motoring information

M4 — Motorway with number	S — Primary route service area	Road tunnel	Airport (major/minor), heliport
Toll T4 — Toll motorway with toll station	BATH — Primary route destination	Toll — Road toll, steep gradient (arrows point downhill)	F — International freight terminal
6 — Motorway junction with and without number	A1123 — Other A road single/dual carriageway	5 — Distance in miles between symbols	H — 24-hour Accident & Emergency hospital
5 — Restricted motorway junctions	B2070 — B road single/dual carriageway	Vehicle ferry (all year, seasonal)	C — Crematorium
Fleet S R Todhills — Motorway service area, rest area	Minor road more than 4 metres wide, less than 4 metres wide	Fast vehicle ferry or catamaran	P·R — Park and Ride (at least 6 days per week)
Motorway and junction under construction	Roundabout	Passenger ferry (all year, seasonal)	City, town, village or other built-up area
A3 — Primary route single/dual carriageway	Interchange/junction	Railway line, in tunnel	628 / 637 Lecht Summit — Height in metres, mountain pass
1 — Primary route junction with and without number	Narrow primary/other A/B road with passing places (Scotland)	Railway station, tram stop, level crossing	Snow gates (on main routes)
3 — Restricted primary route junctions	Road under construction	Preserved or tourist railway	National boundary, county or administrative boundary

Touring information
To avoid disappointment, check opening times before visiting

Scenic route	Garden	Waterfall	Motor-racing circuit
Tourist Information Centre	Arboretum	Hill-fort	Air show venue
Tourist Information Centre (seasonal)	Country park	Roman antiquity	Ski slope (natural, artificial)
Visitor or heritage centre	Showground	Prehistoric monument	National Trust site
Picnic site	Theme park	Battle site with year 1066	National Trust for Scotland site
Caravan site (AA inspected)	Farm or animal centre	Preserved or tourist railway	English Heritage site
Camping site (AA inspected)	Zoological or wildlife collection	Cave or cavern	Historic Scotland site
Caravan & camping site (AA inspected)	Bird collection	Windmill, monument or memorial	Cadw (Welsh heritage) site
Abbey, cathedral or priory	Aquarium	Beach (award winning)	Other place of interest
Ruined abbey, cathedral or priory	RSPB site	Lighthouse	Boxed symbols indicate attractions within urban area
Castle	National Nature Reserve (England, Scotland, Wales)	Golf course	World Heritage Site (UNESCO)
Historic house or building	Local nature reserve	Football stadium	National Park and National Scenic Area (Scotland)
Museum or art gallery	Wildlife Trust reserve	County cricket ground	Forest Park
Industrial interest	Forest drive	Rugby Union national stadium	Sandy beach
Aqueduct or viaduct	National trail	International athletics stadium	Heritage coast
Vineyard, brewery or distillery	Viewpoint	Horse racing, show jumping	Major shopping centre

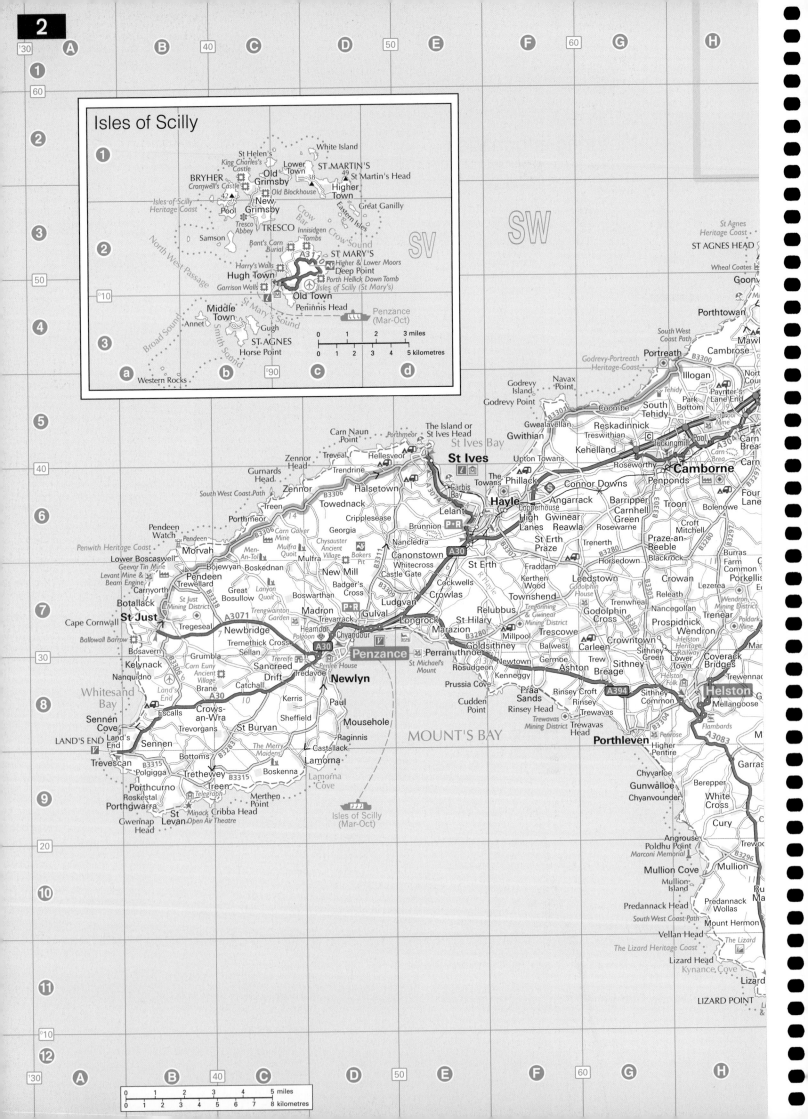

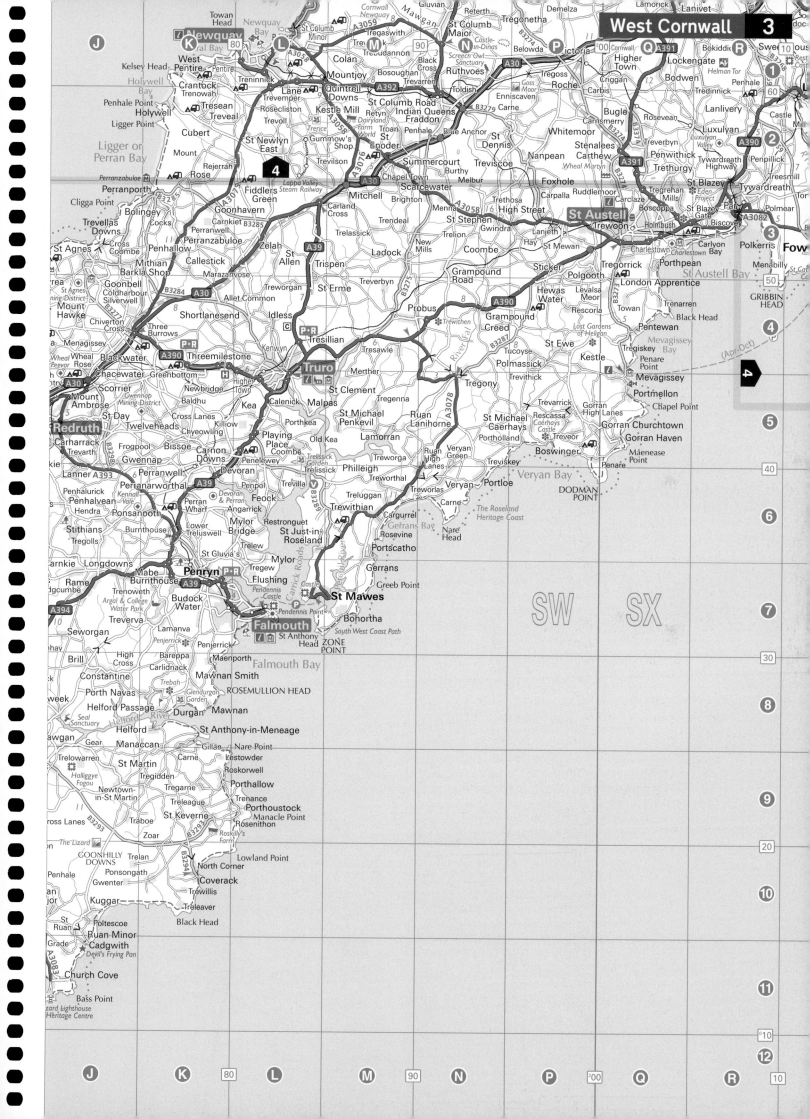

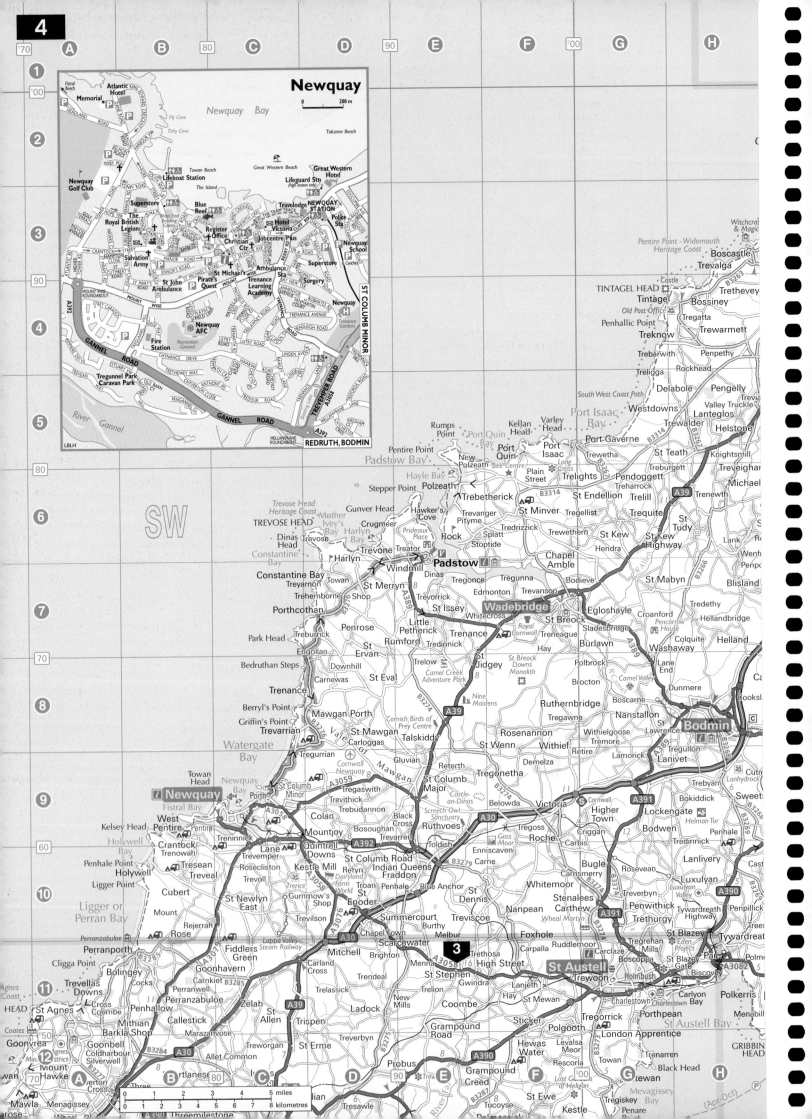

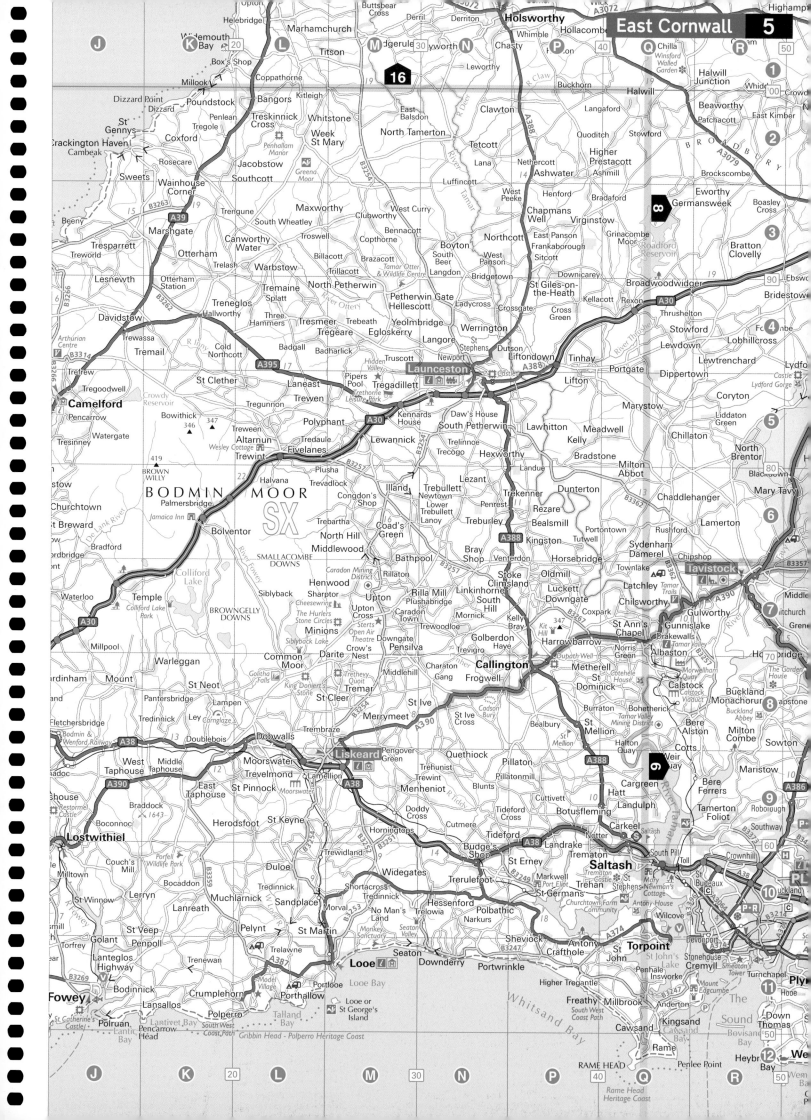

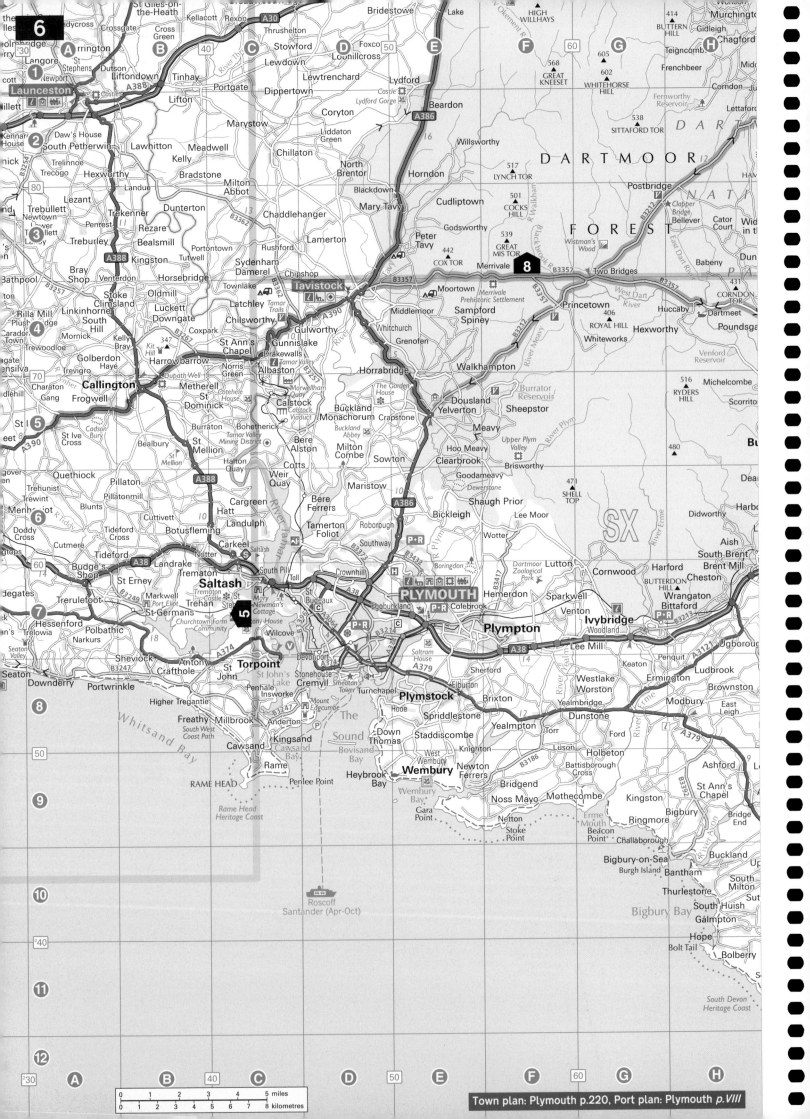

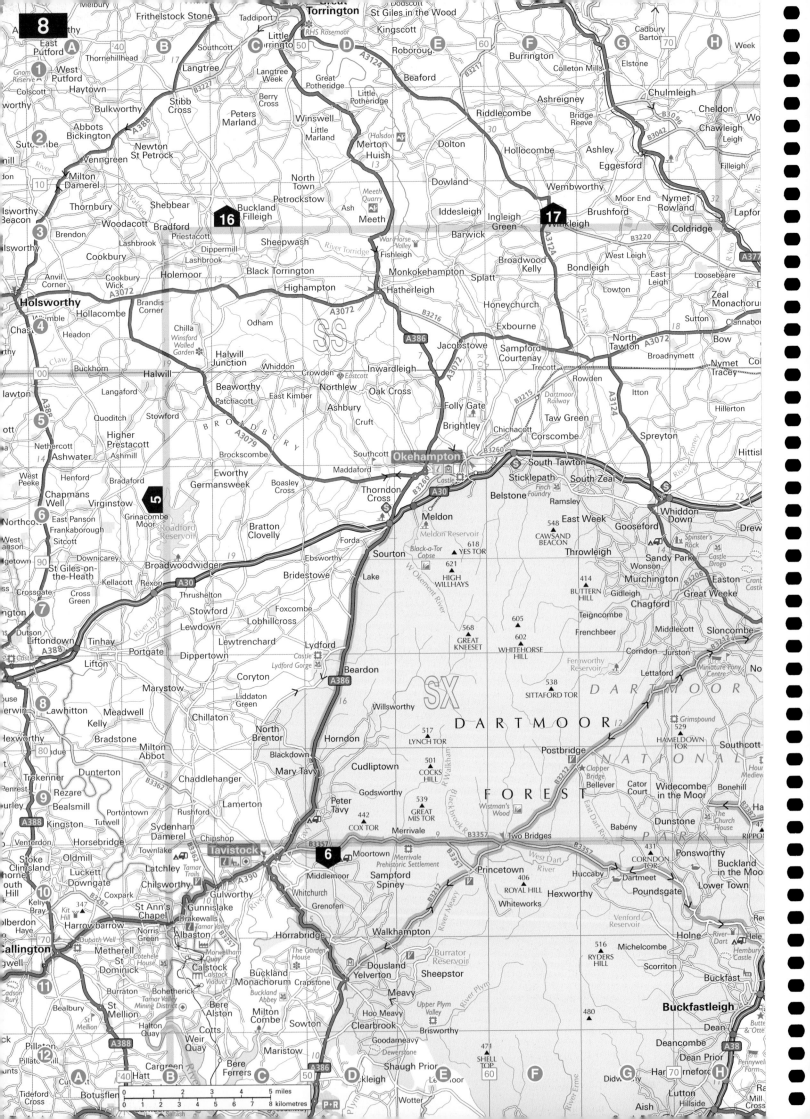

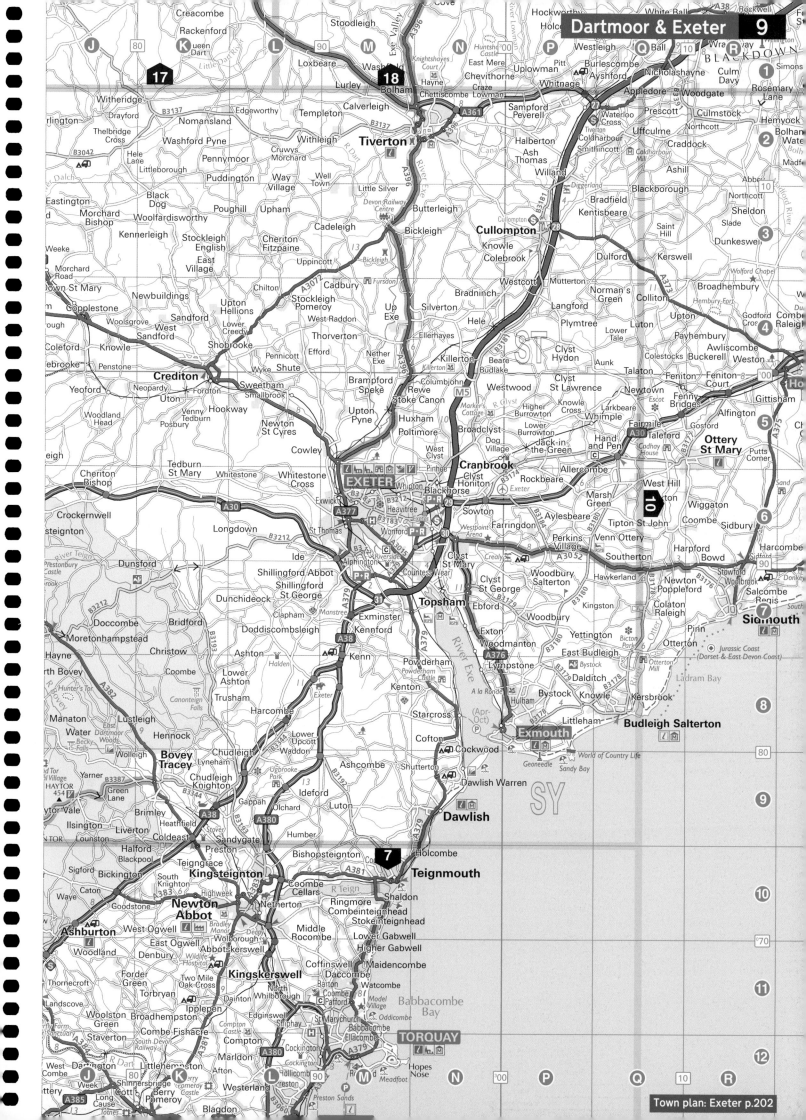

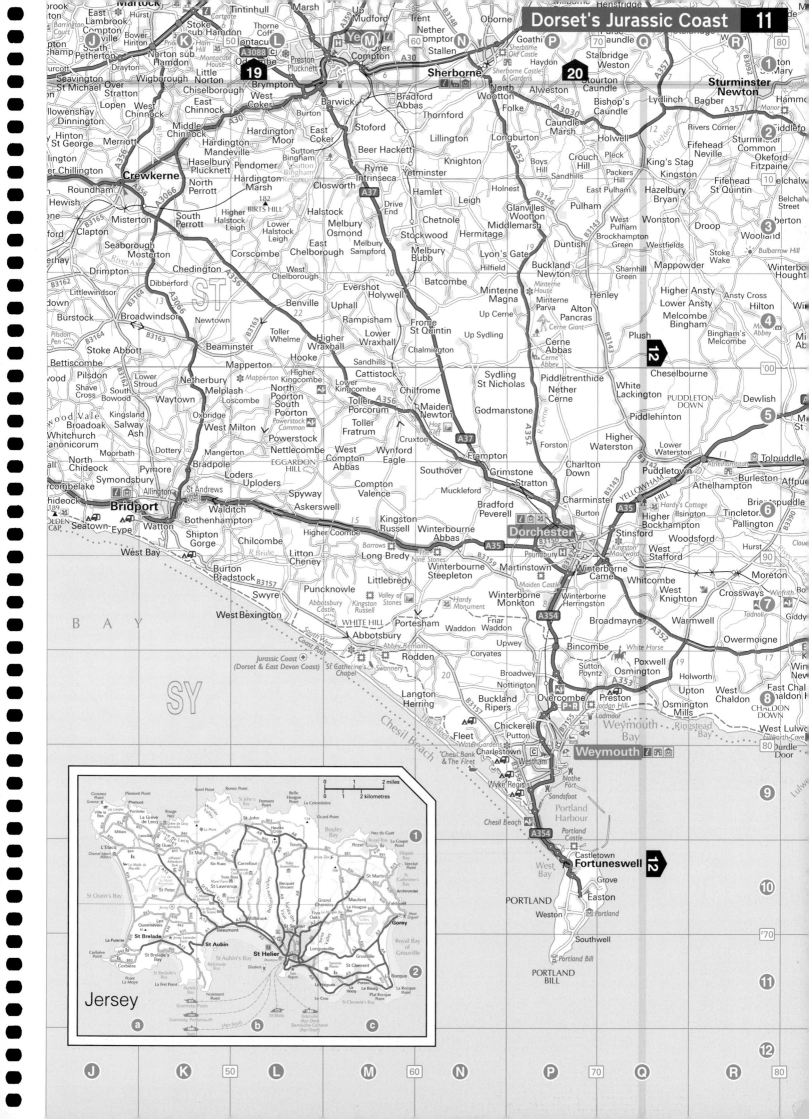

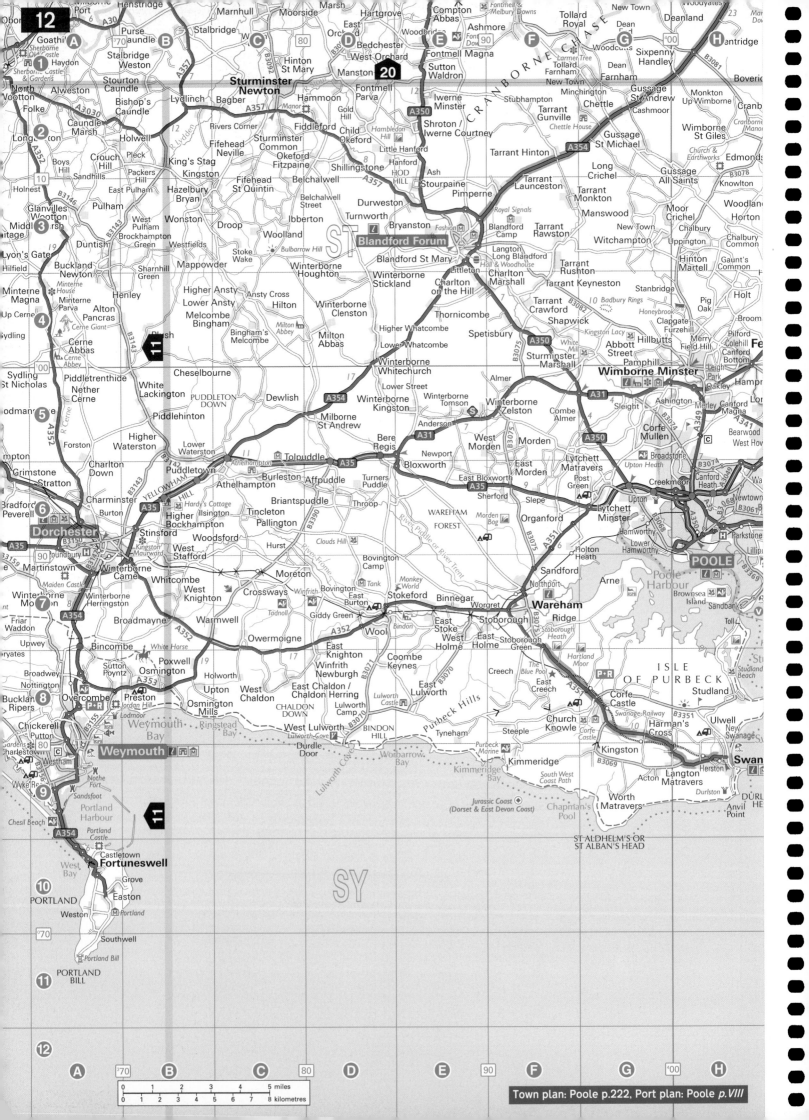

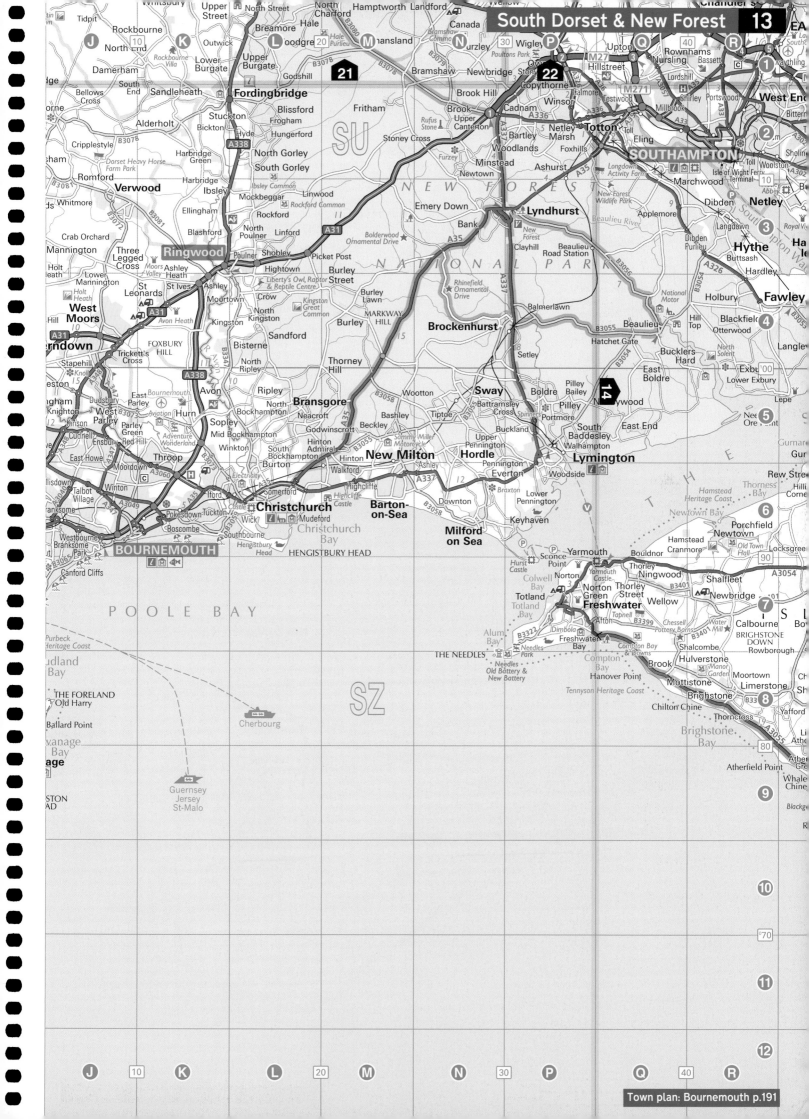

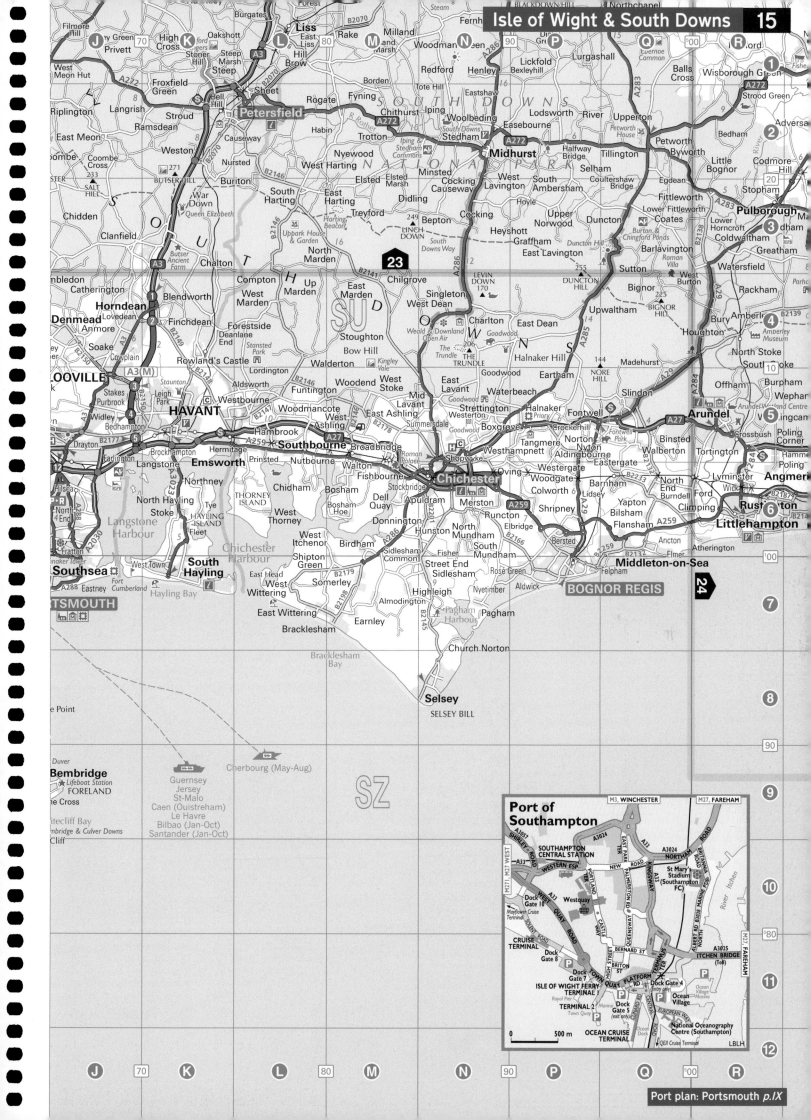

Port plan: Portsmouth p.IX

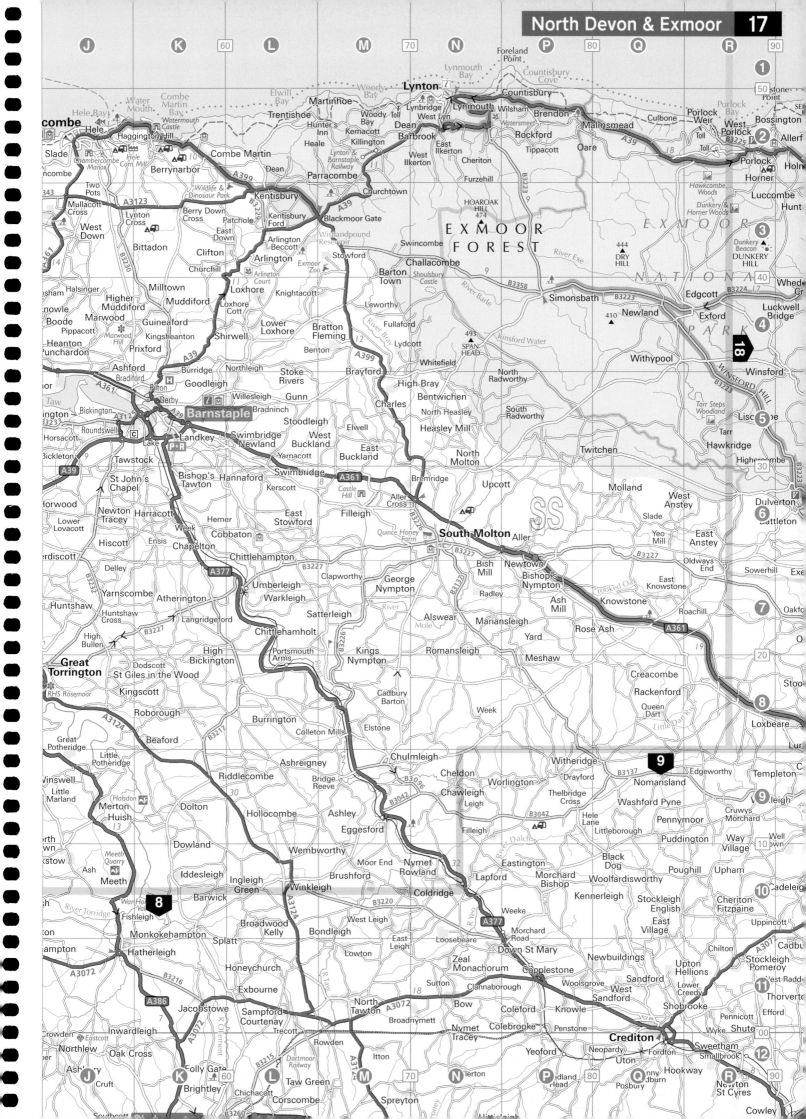

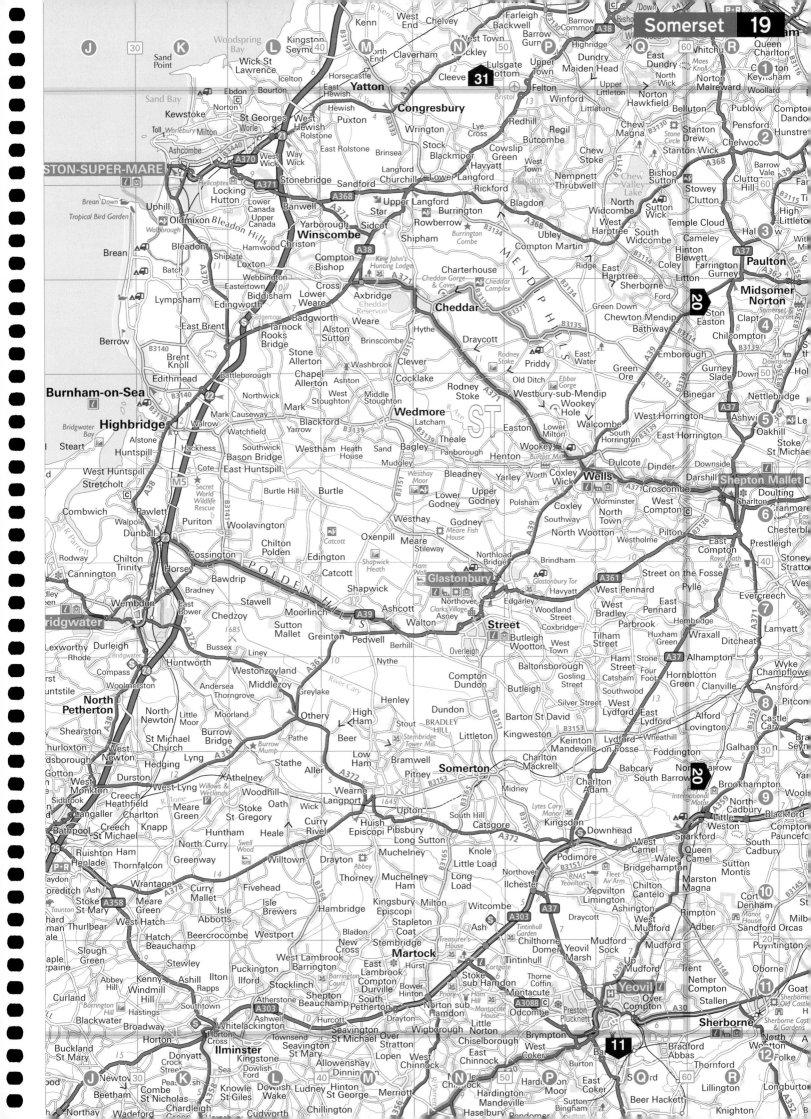

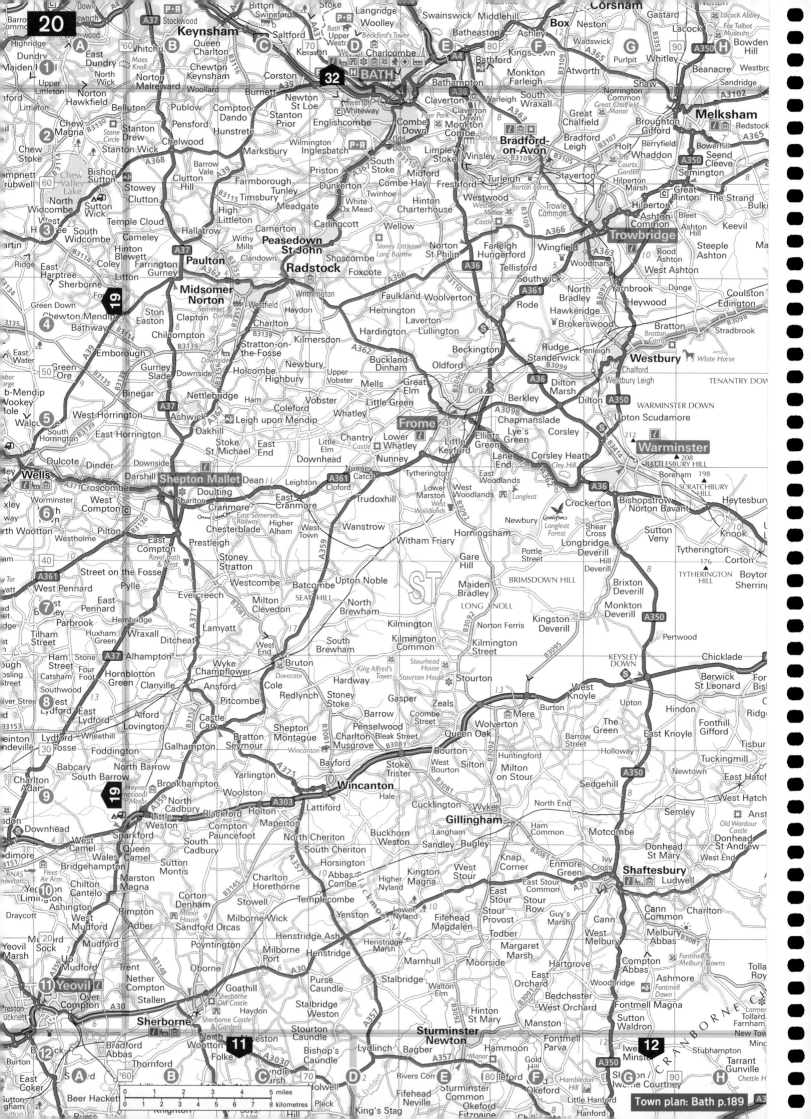

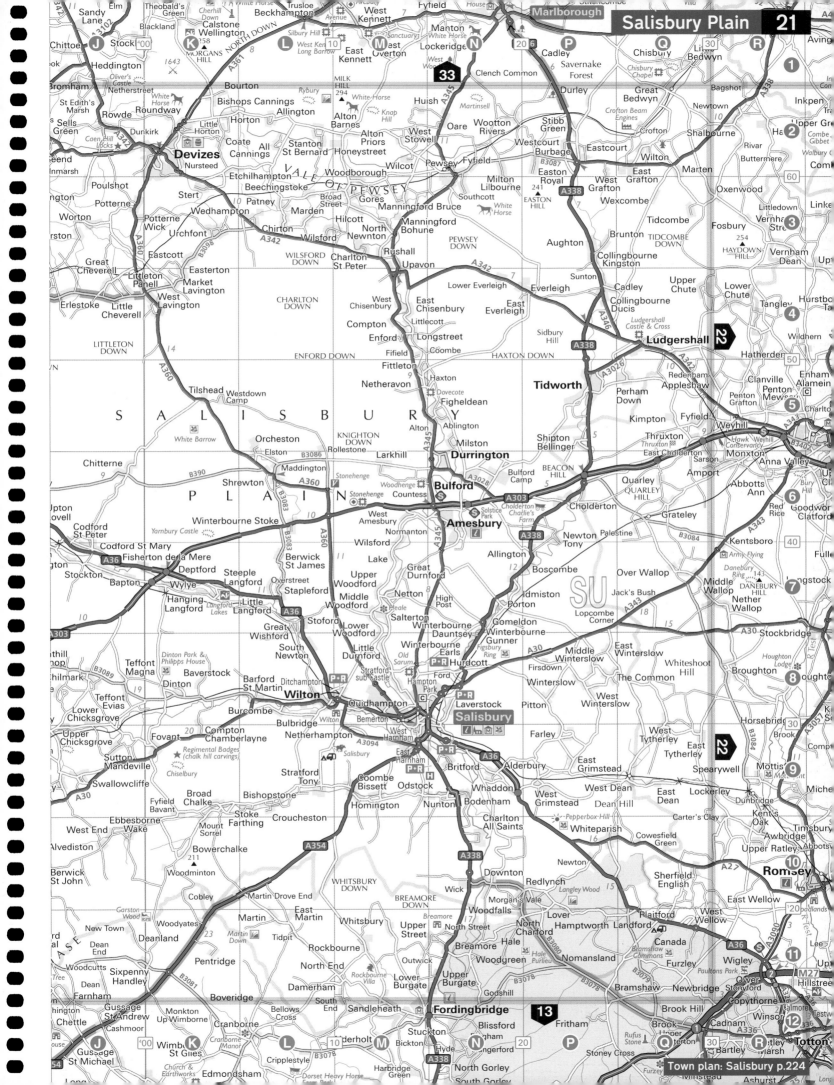

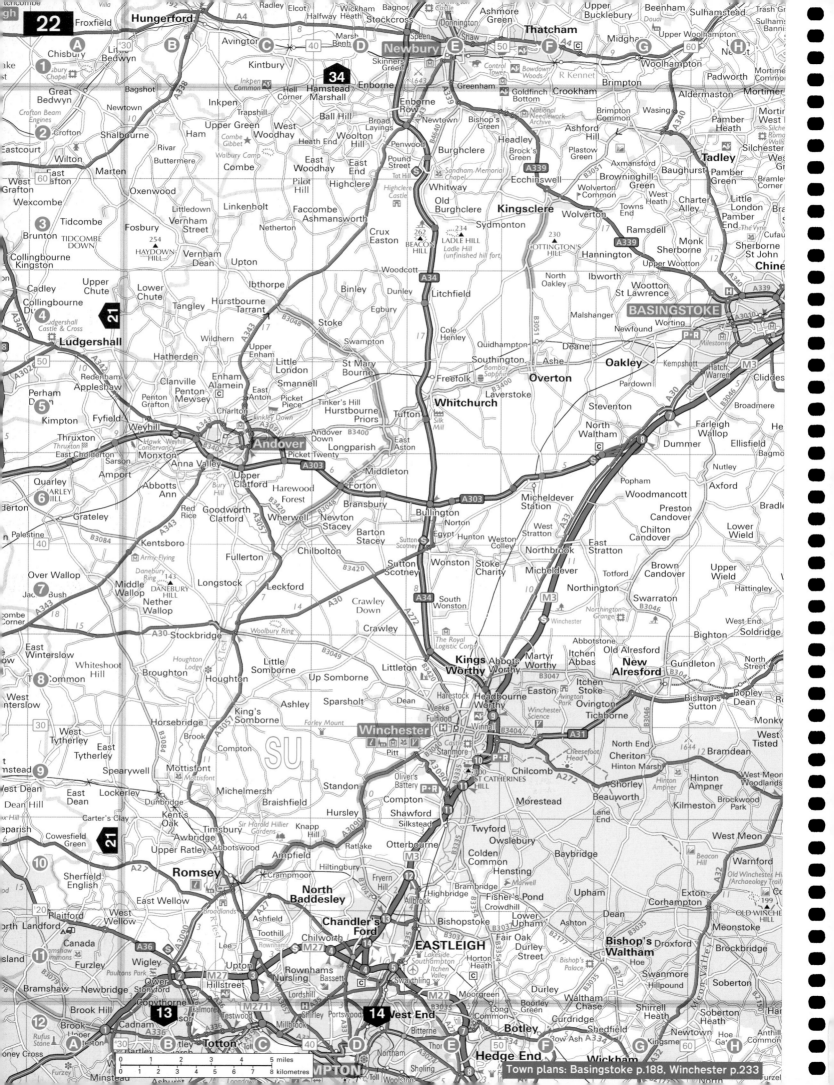

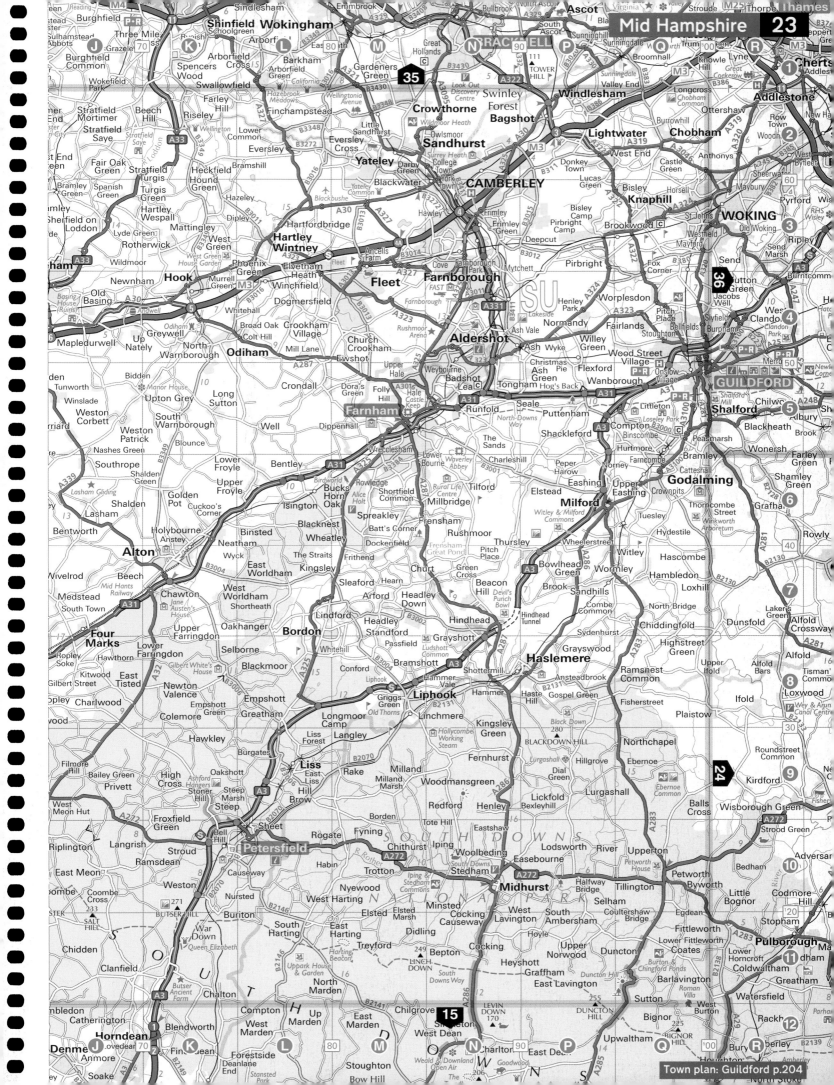

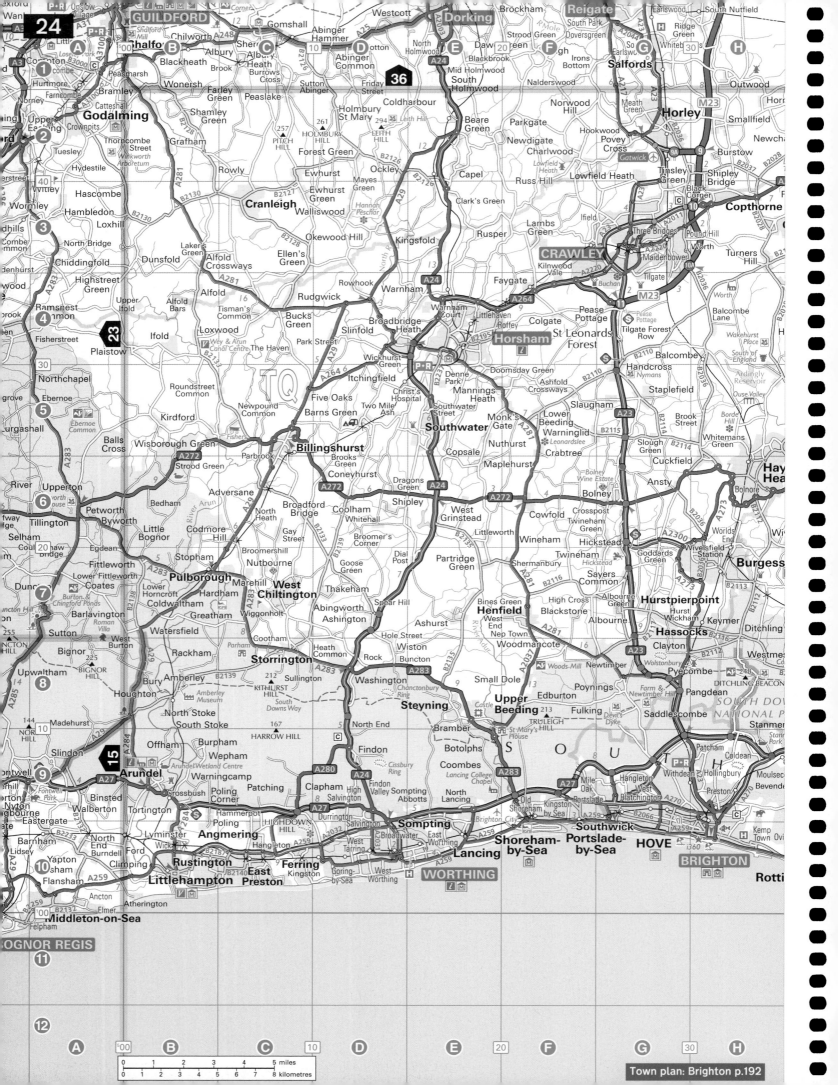

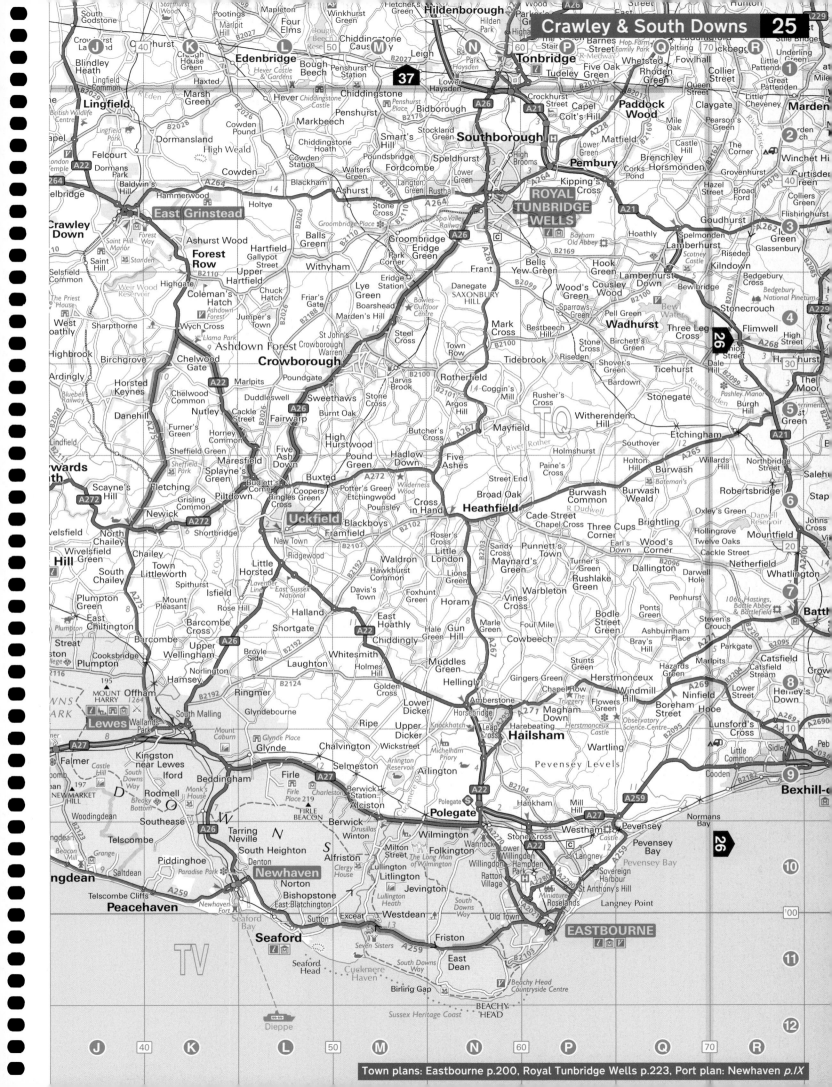

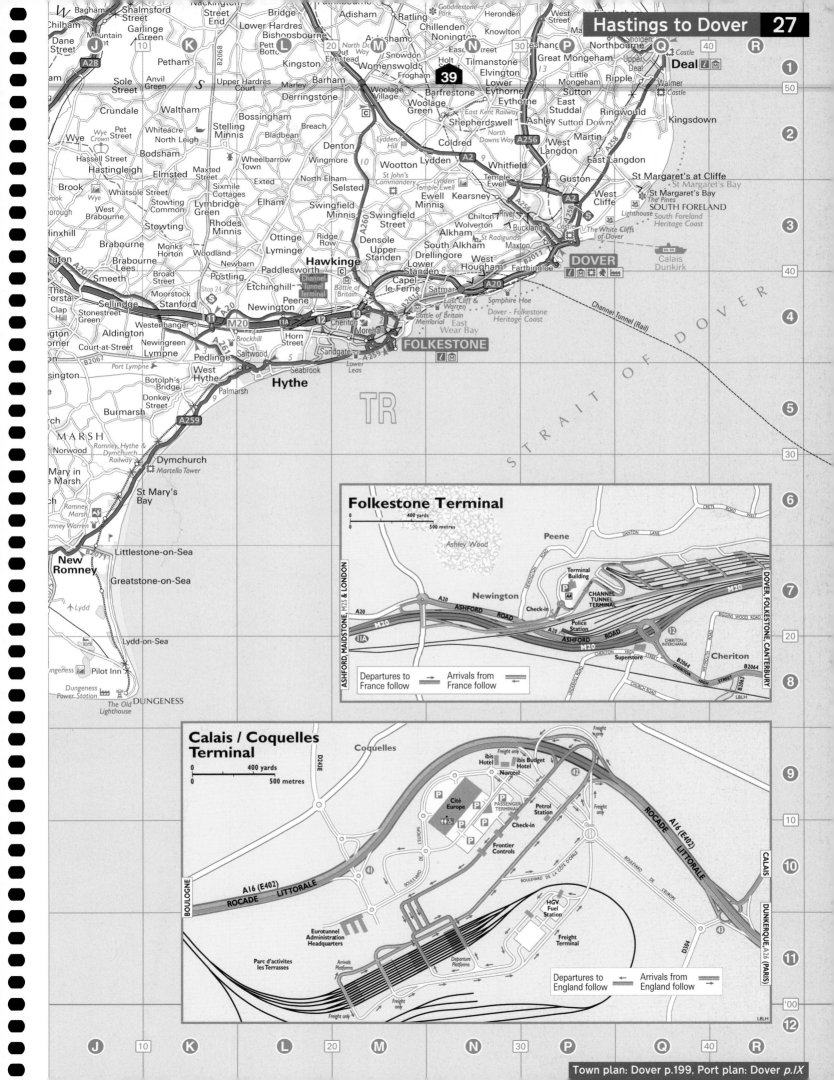

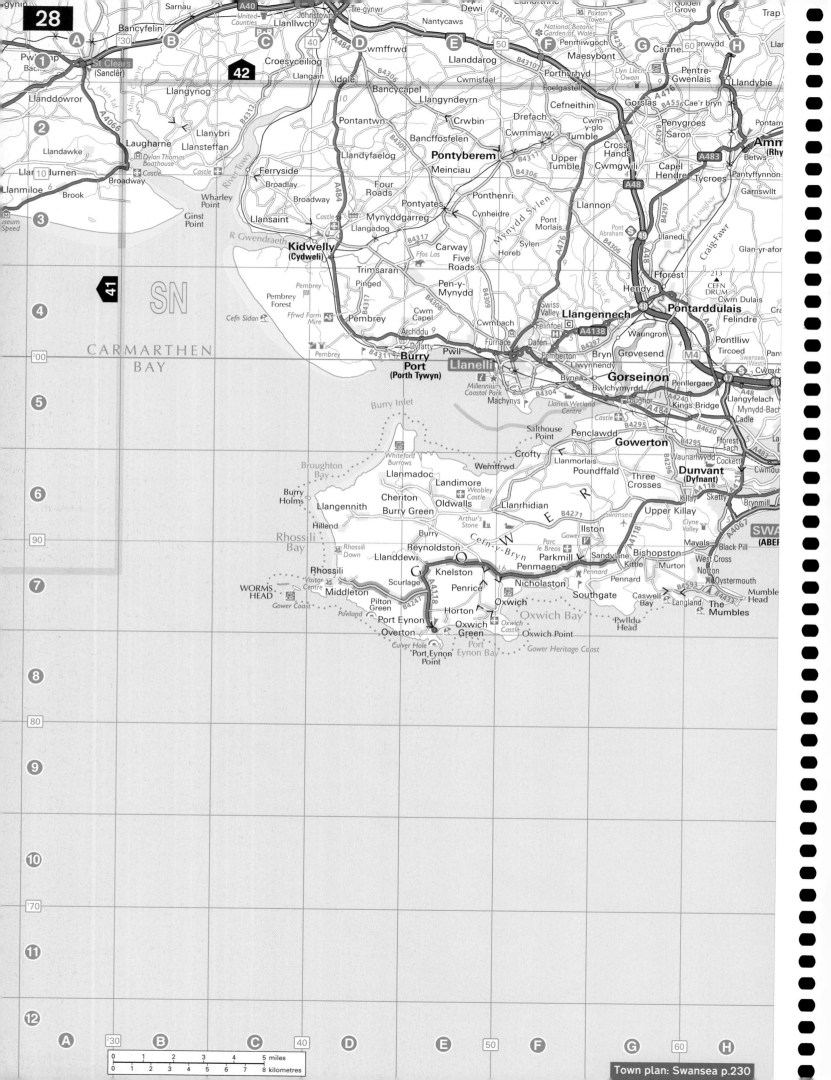

28

42

41

SN

CARMARTHEN
BAY

Town plan: Swansea p.230

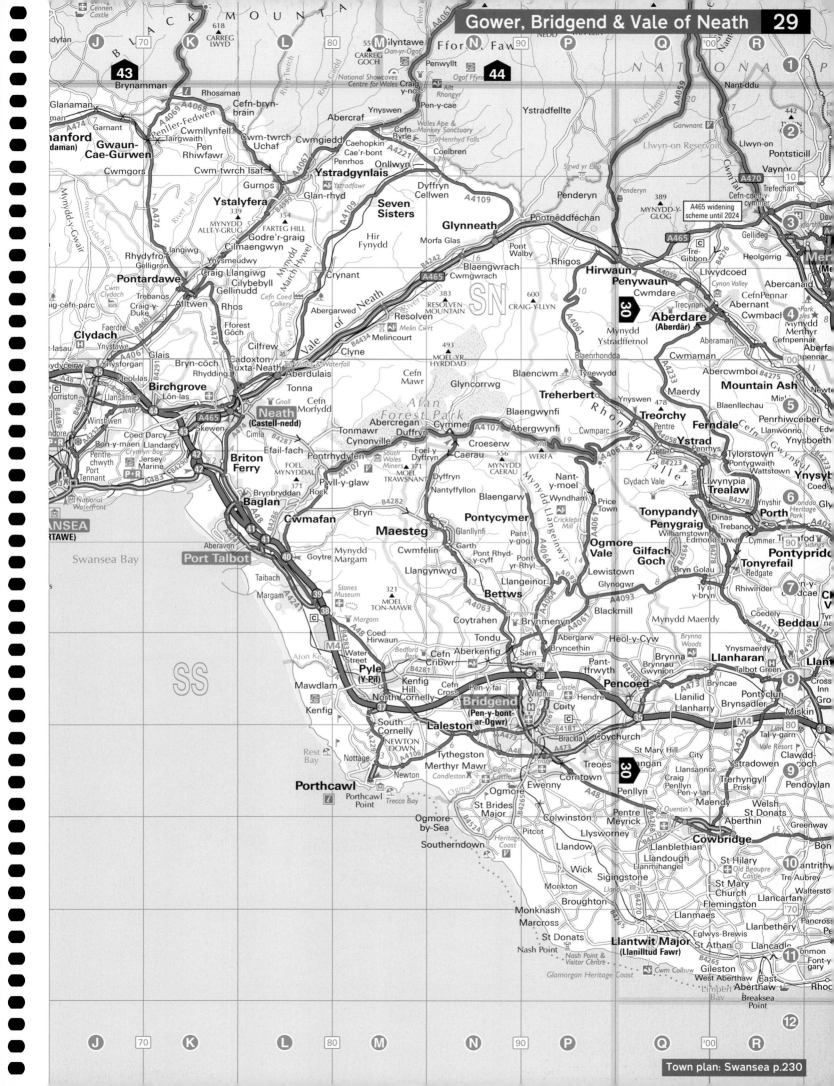

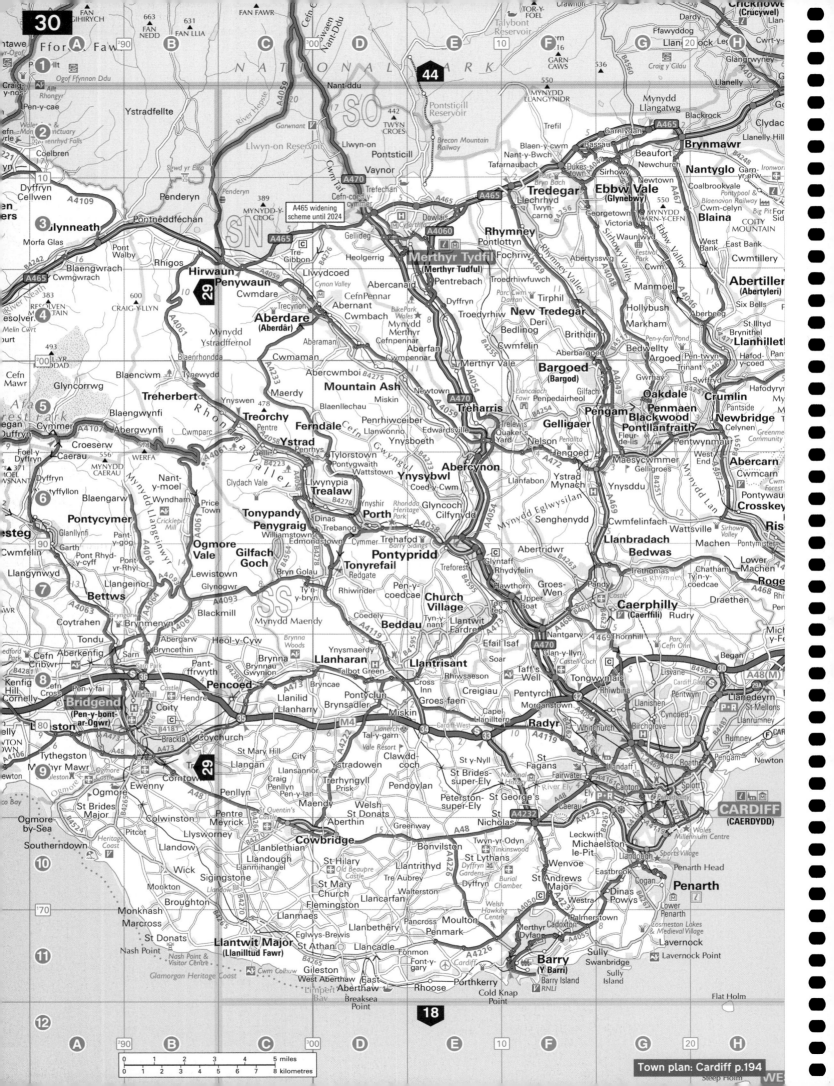

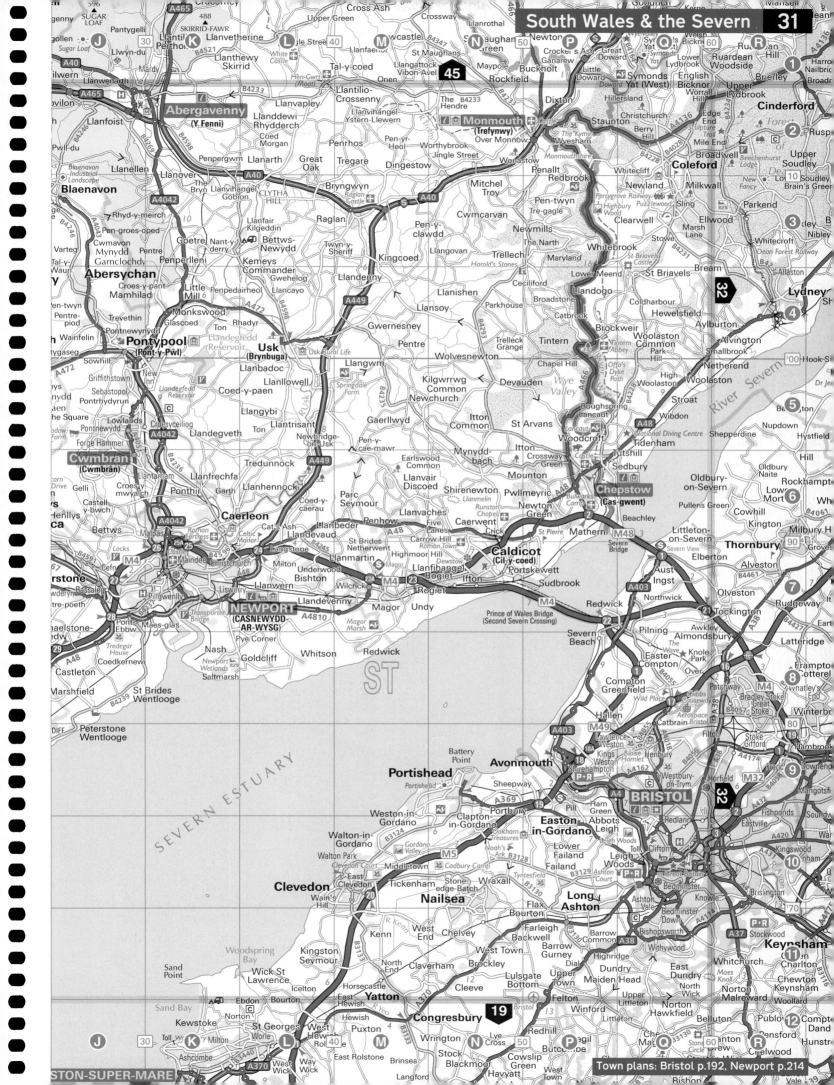

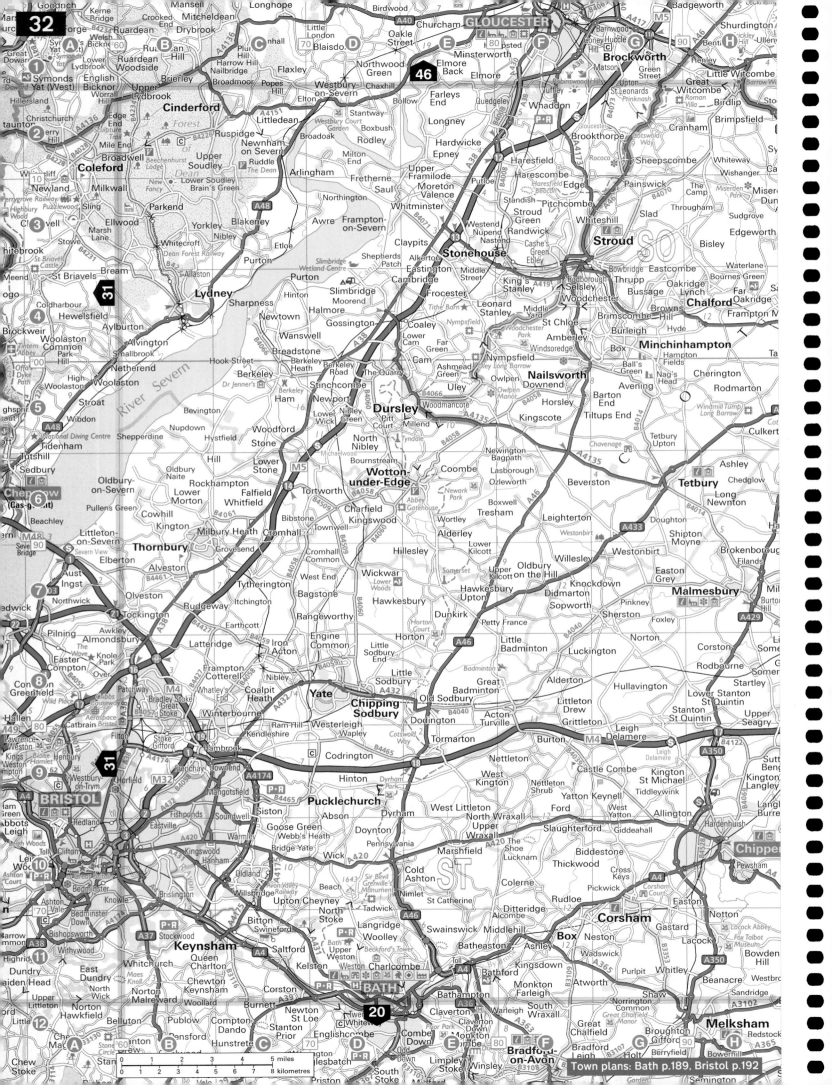

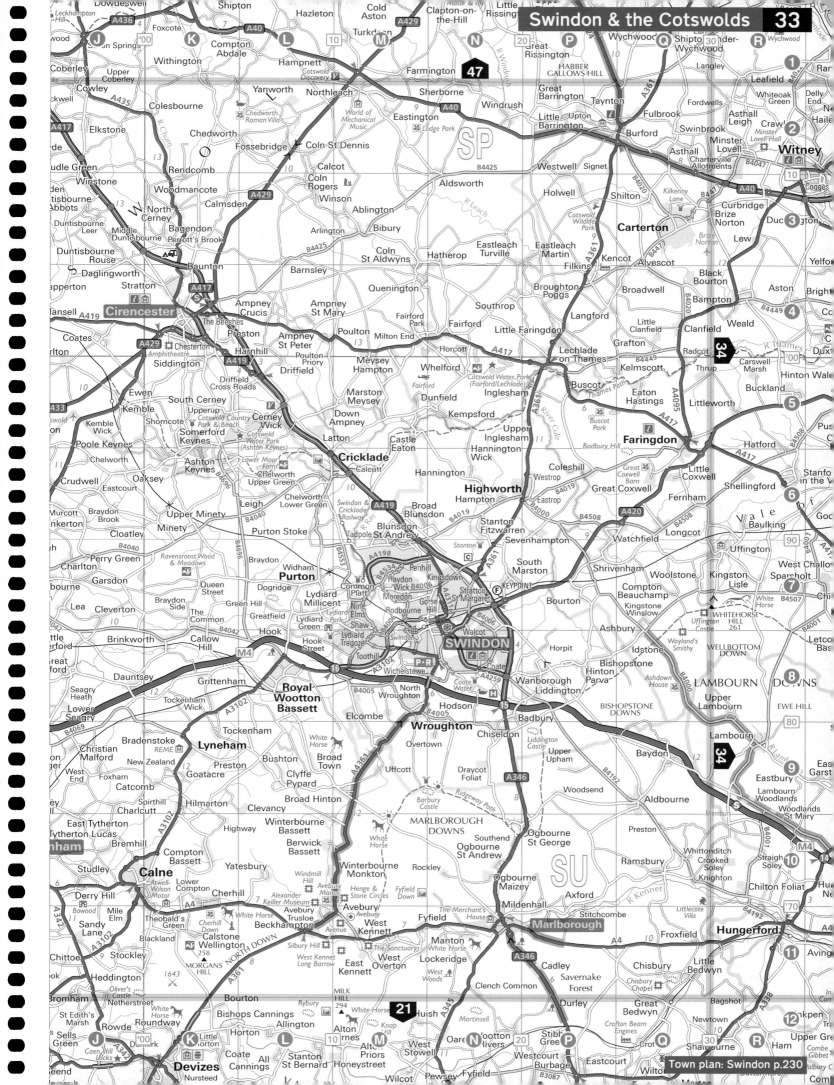

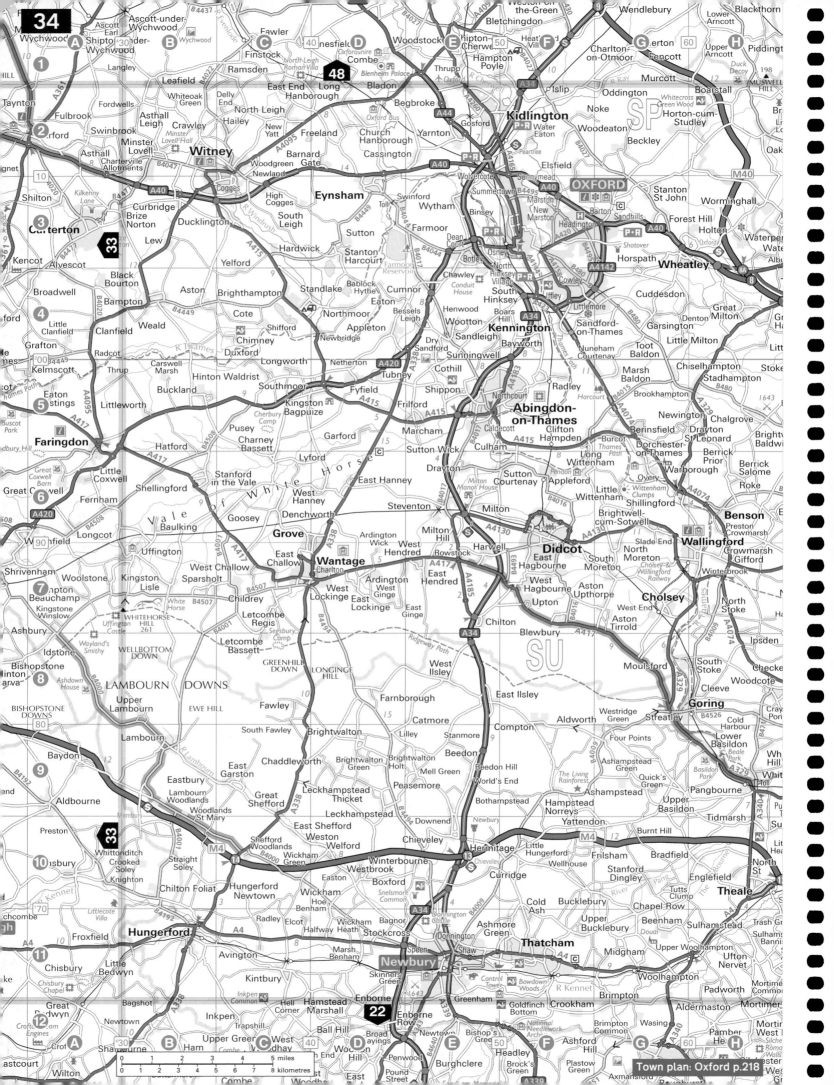

Town plan: Oxford p.218

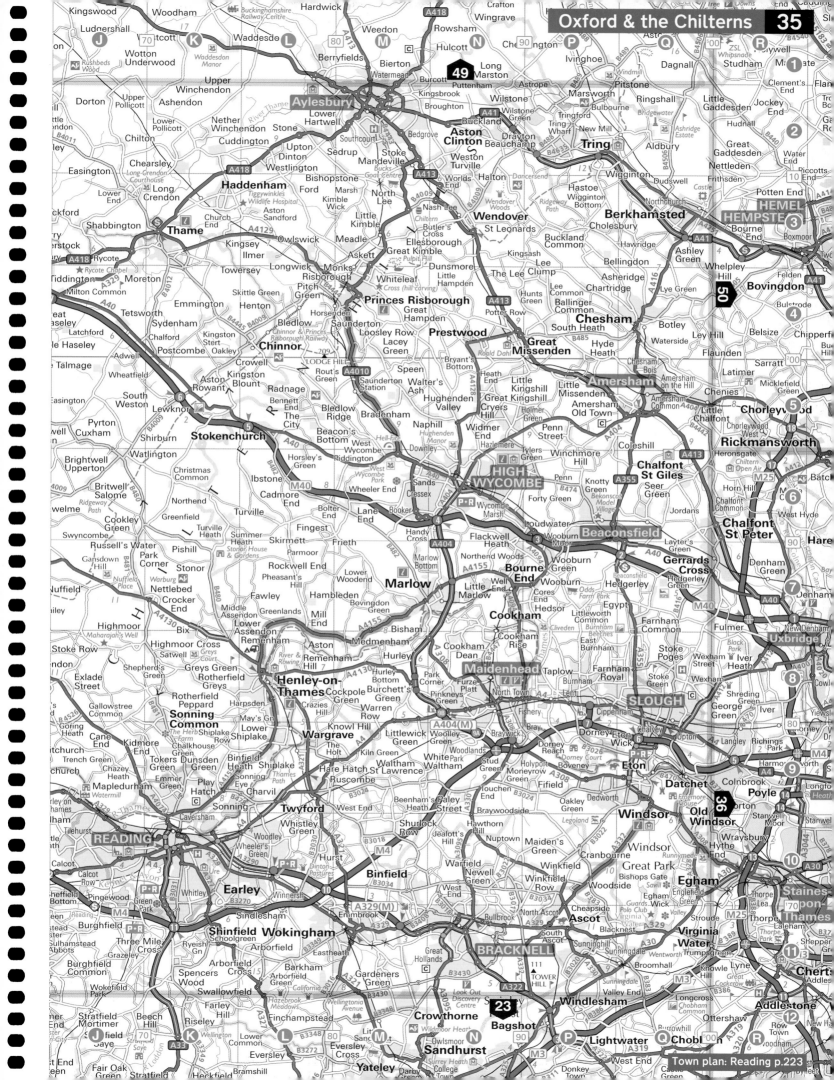

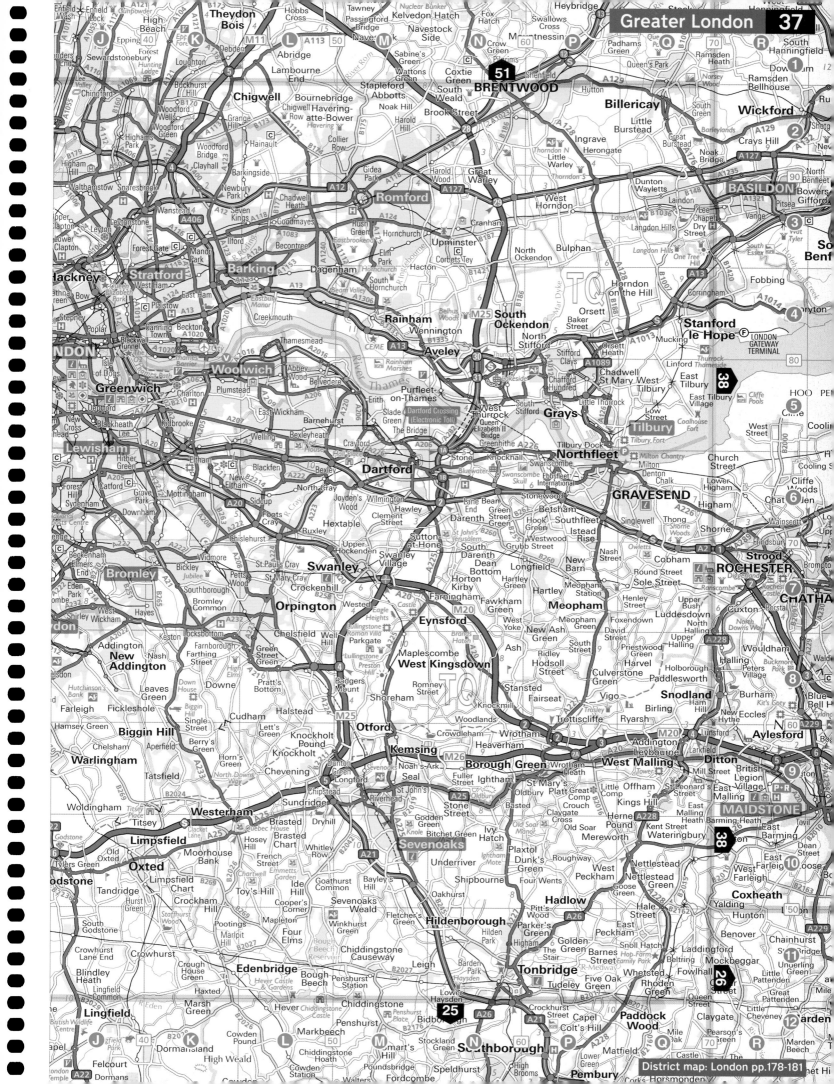

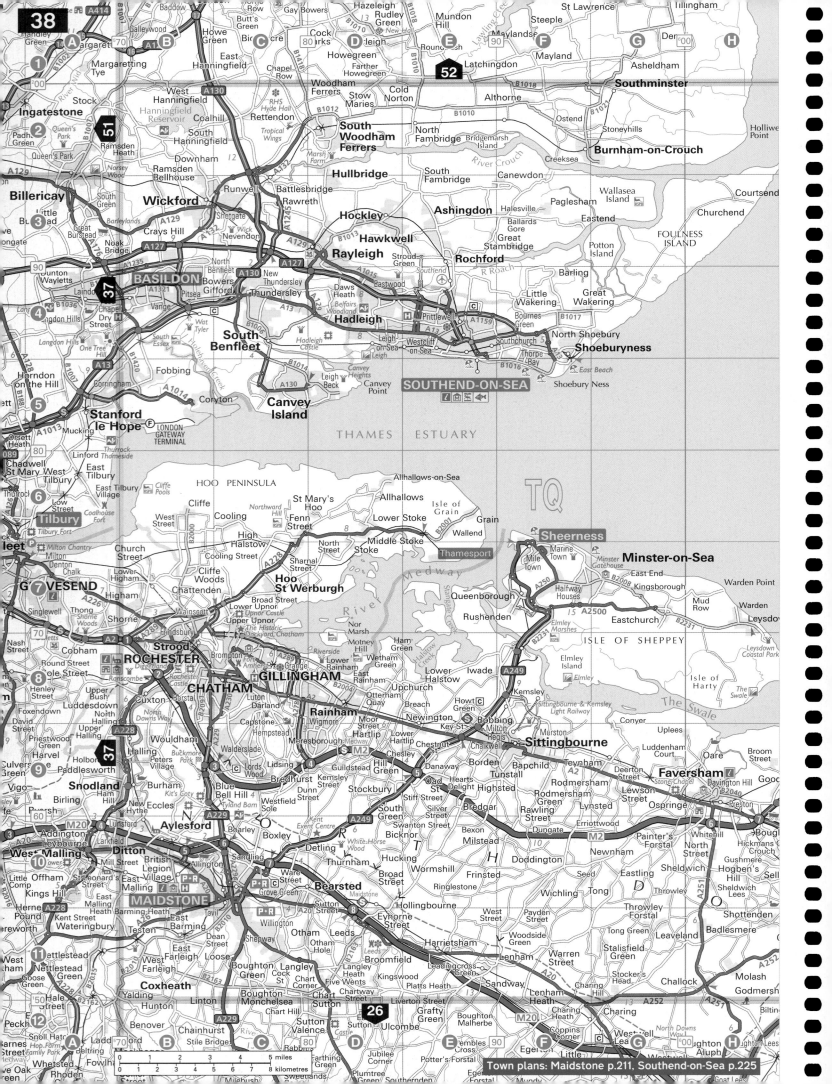

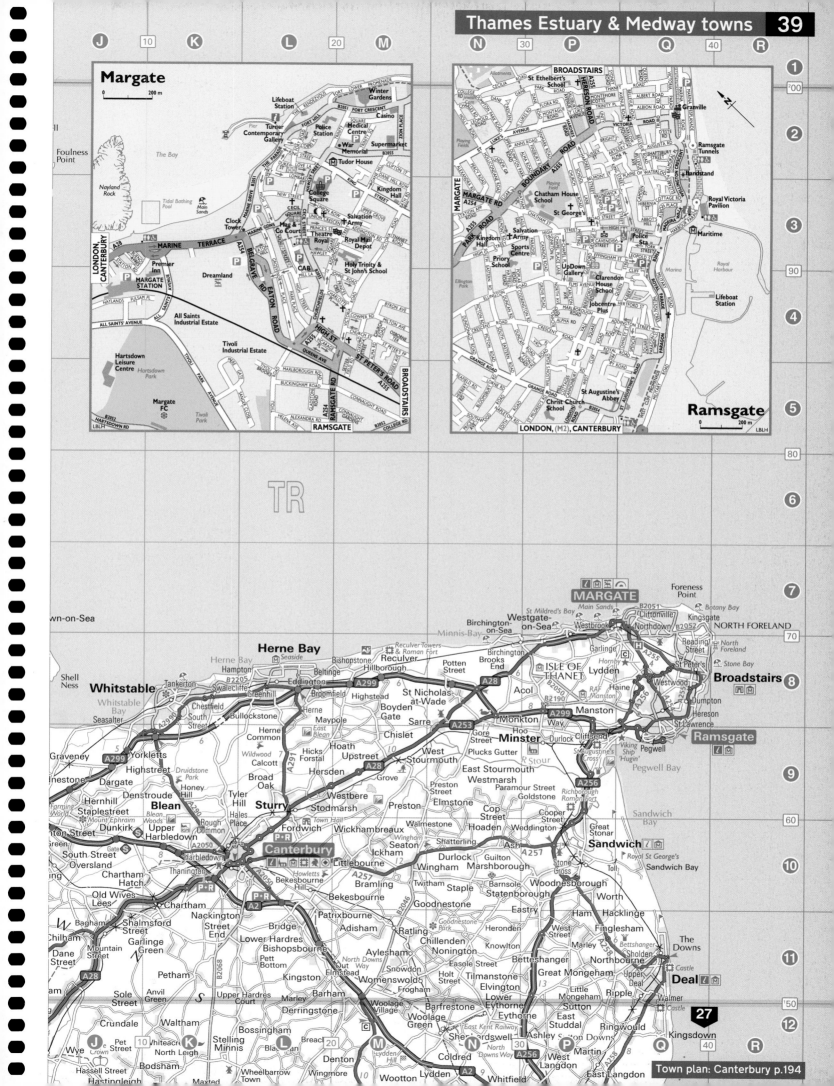

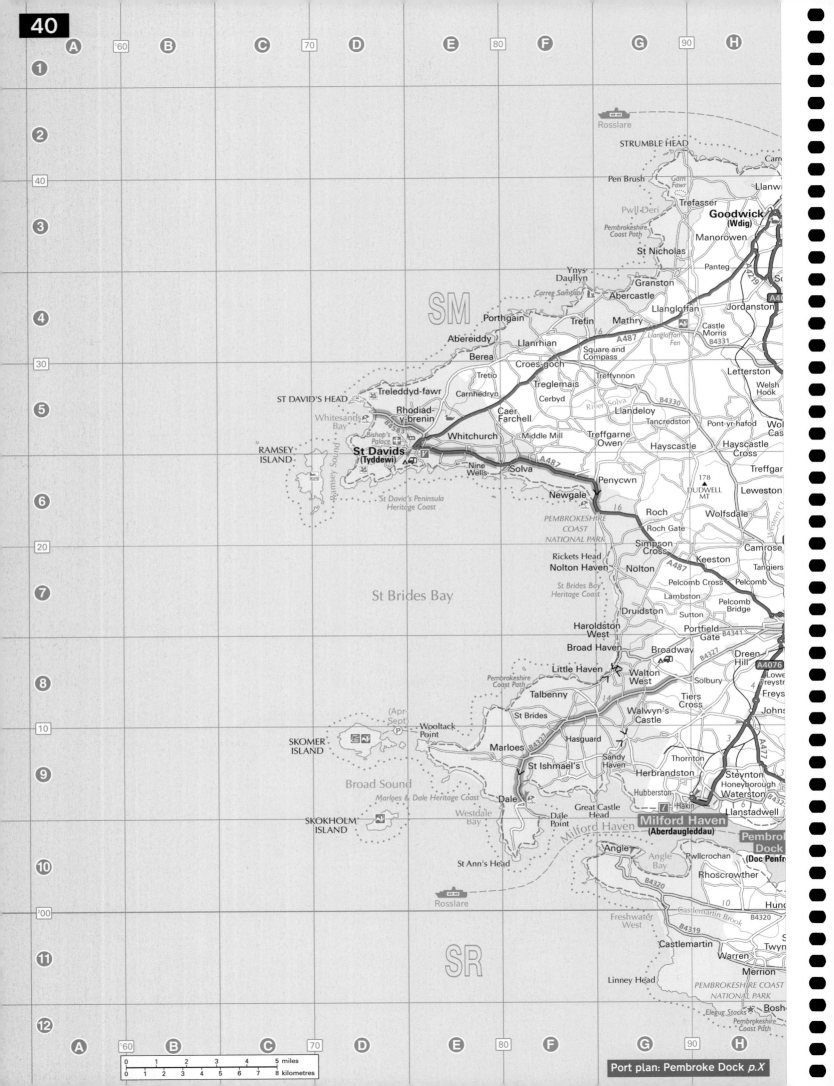

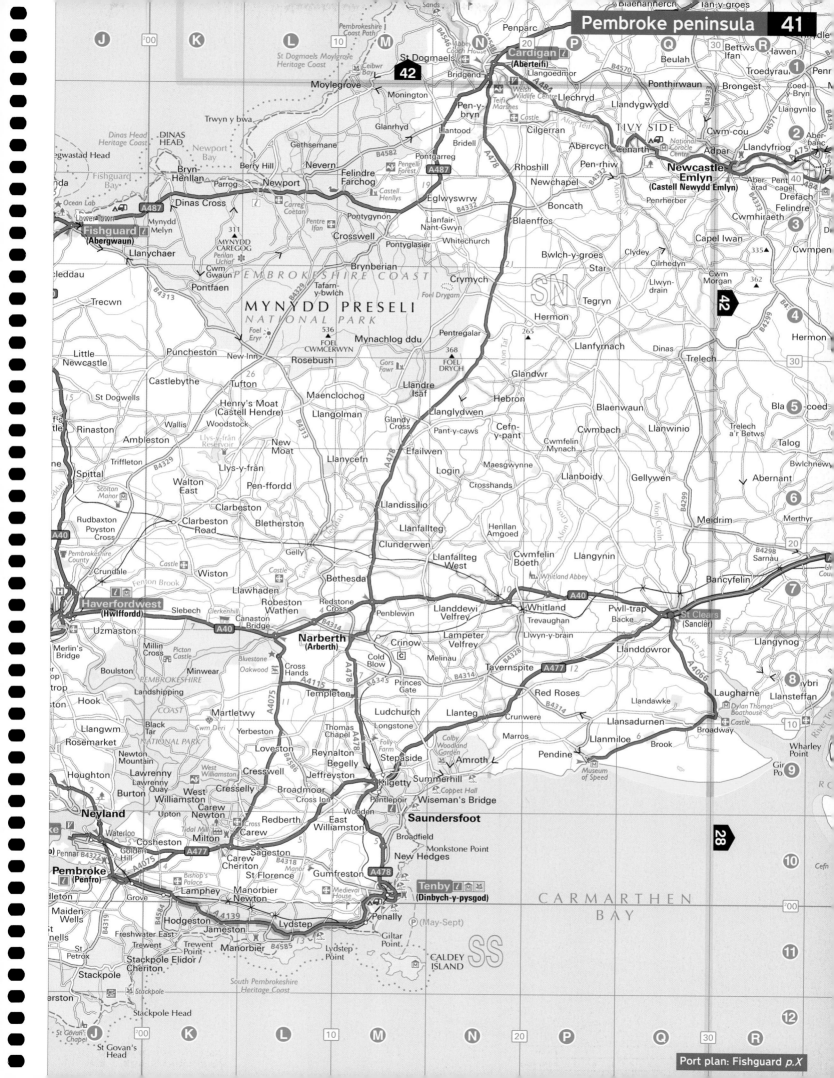

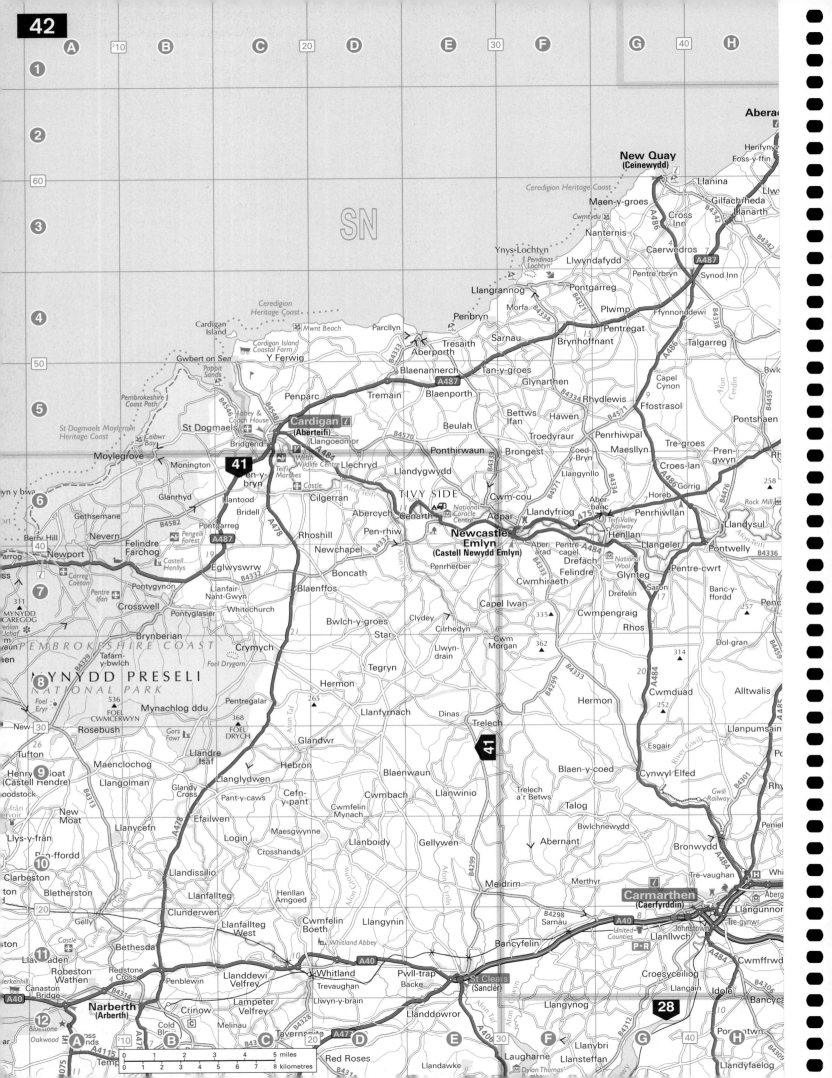

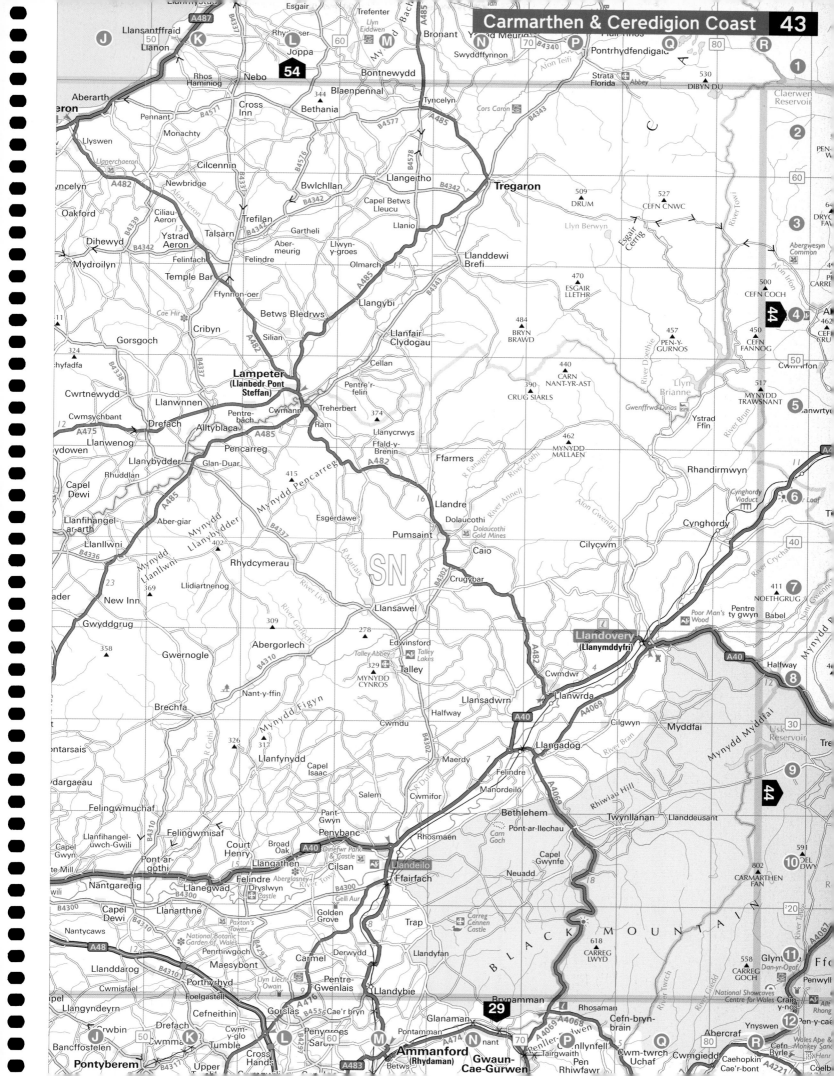

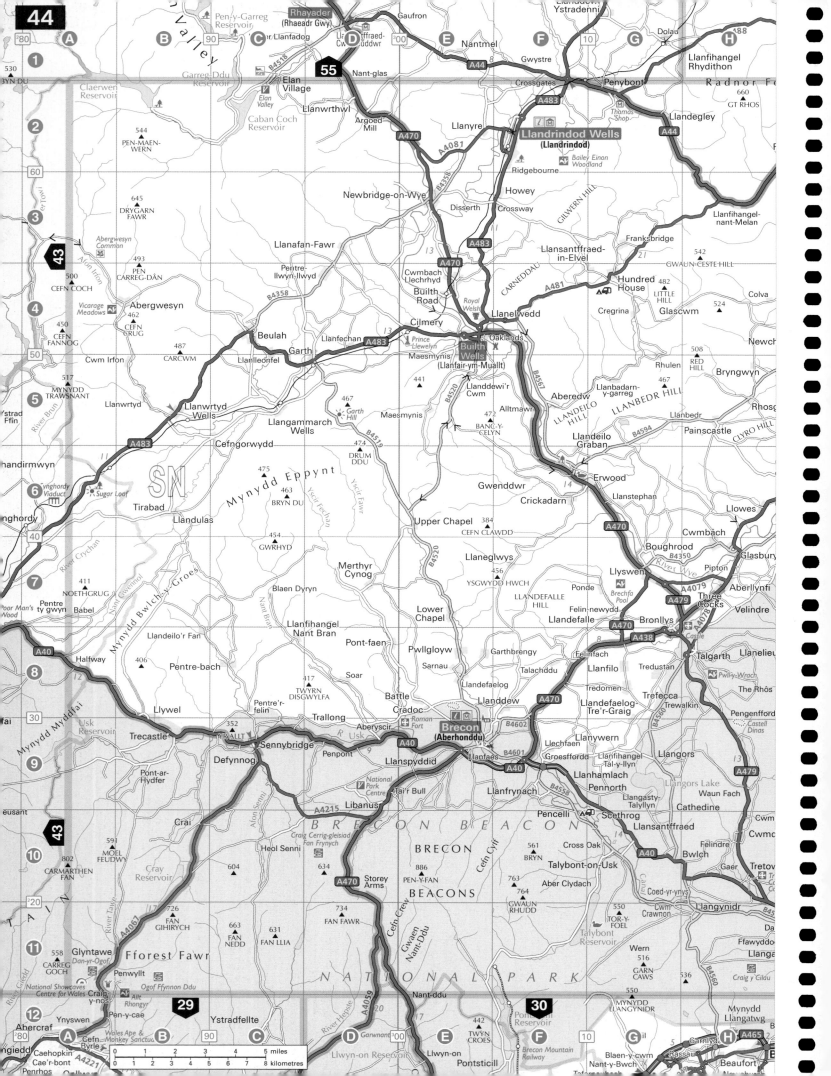

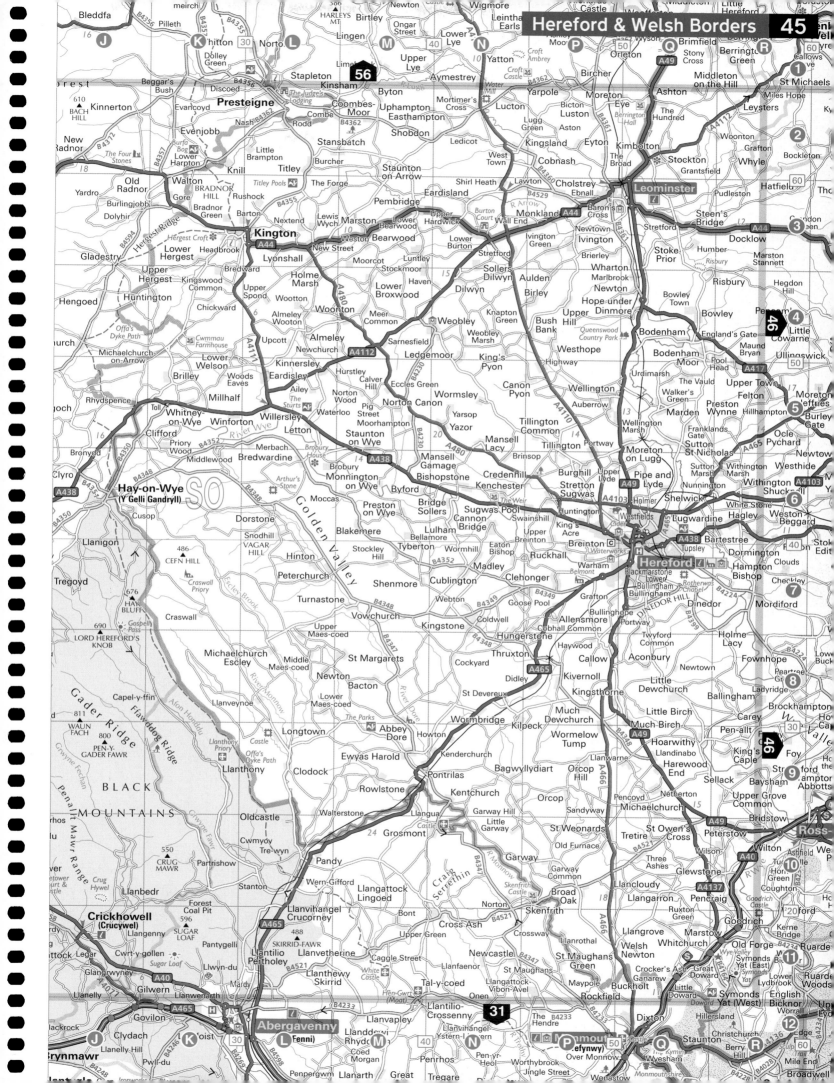

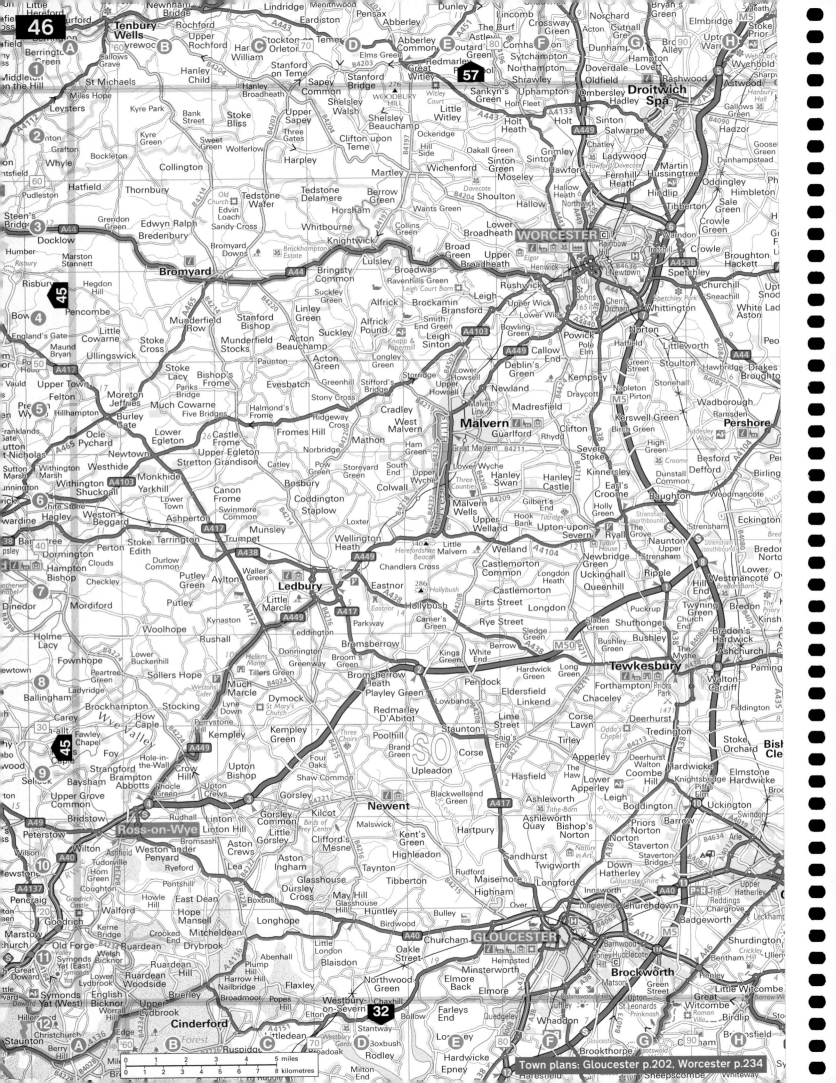

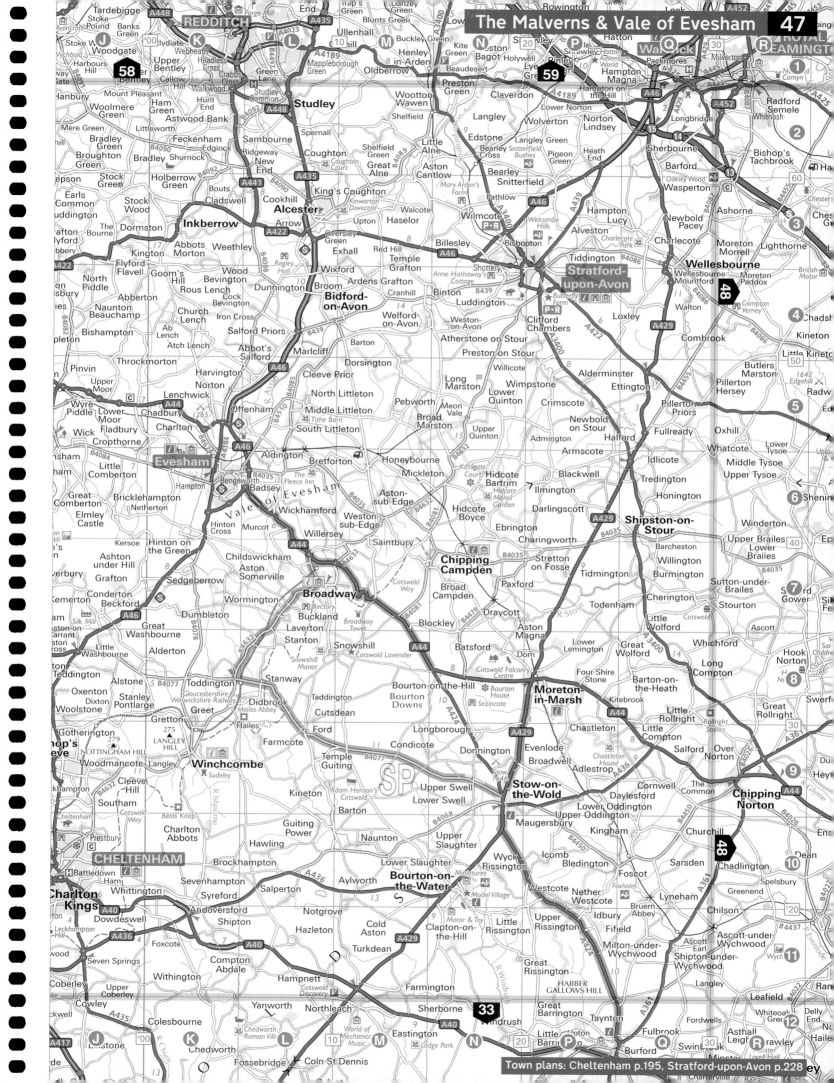

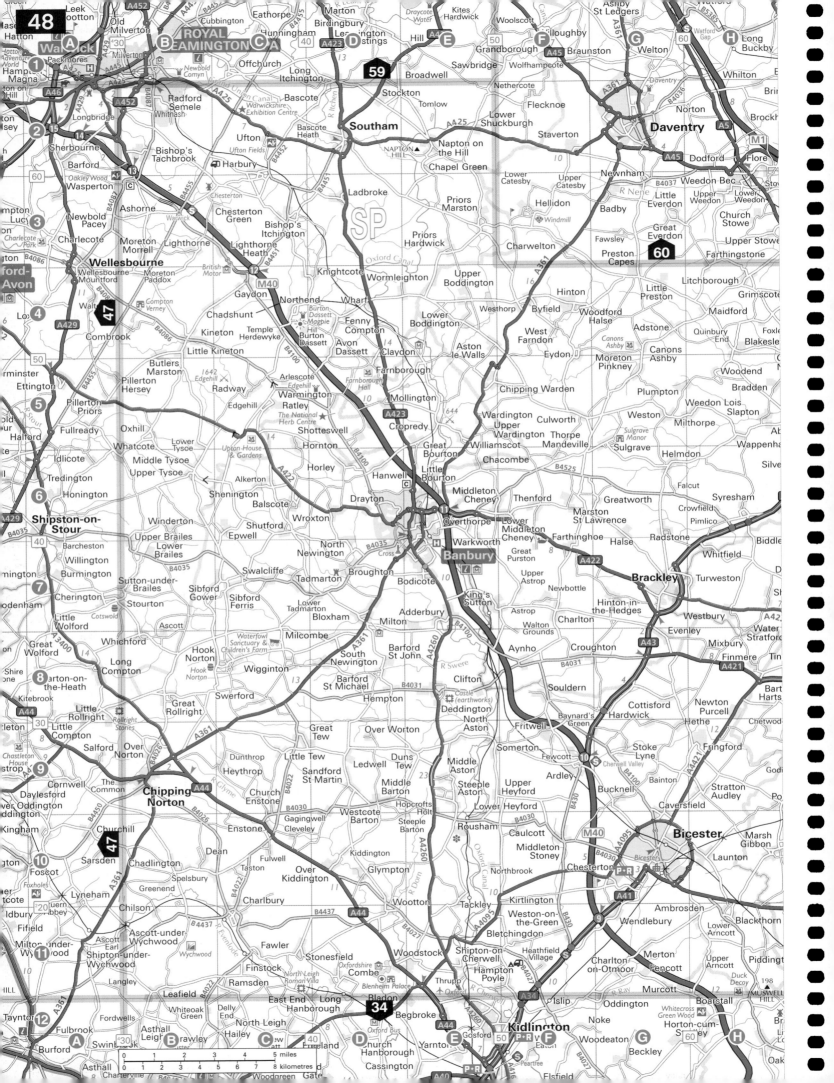

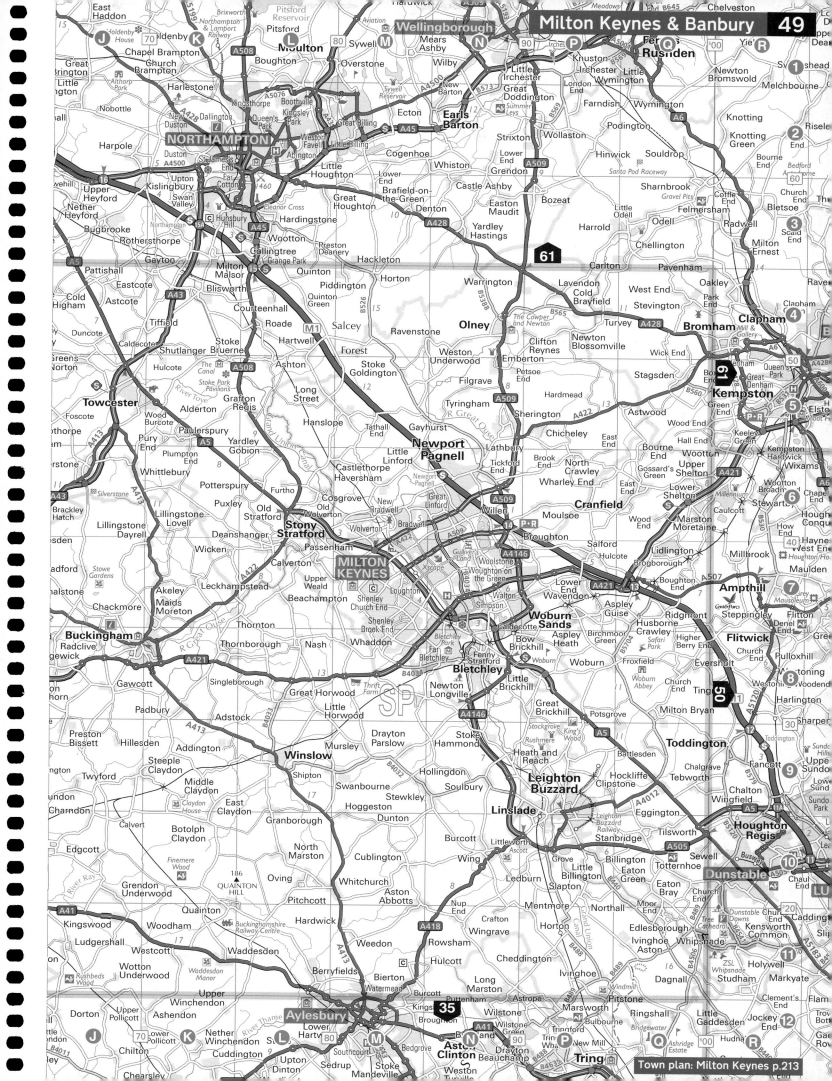

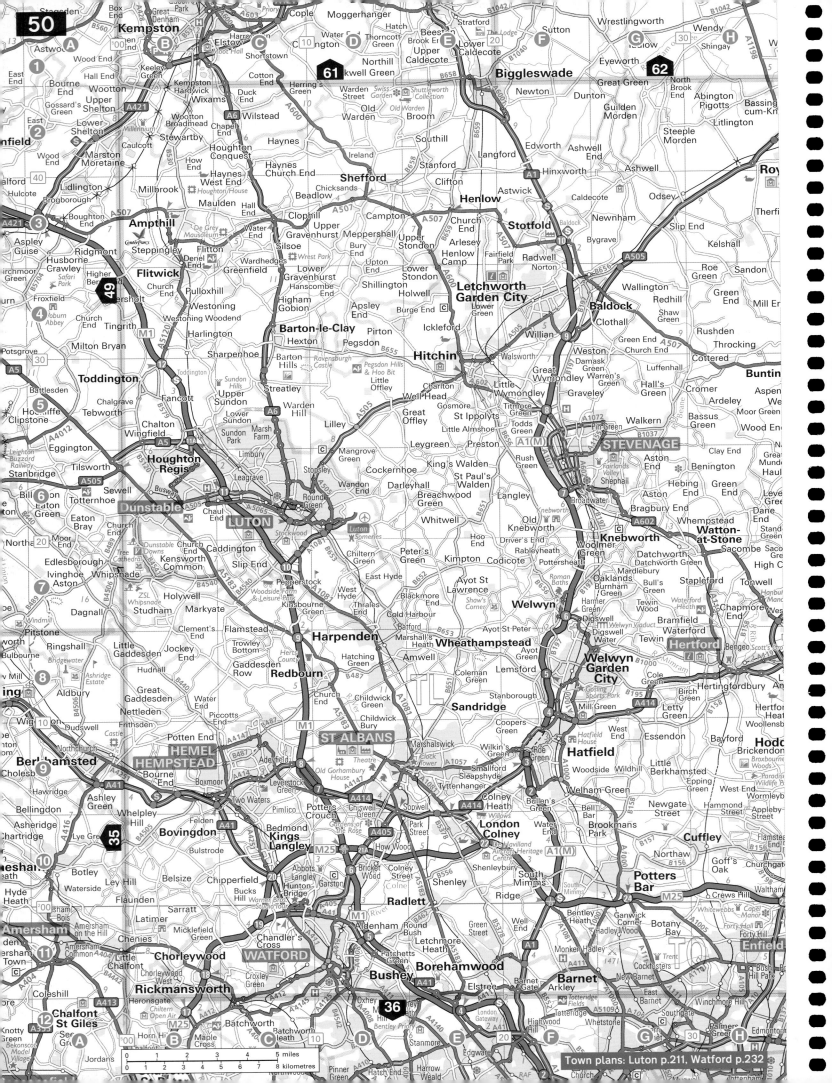

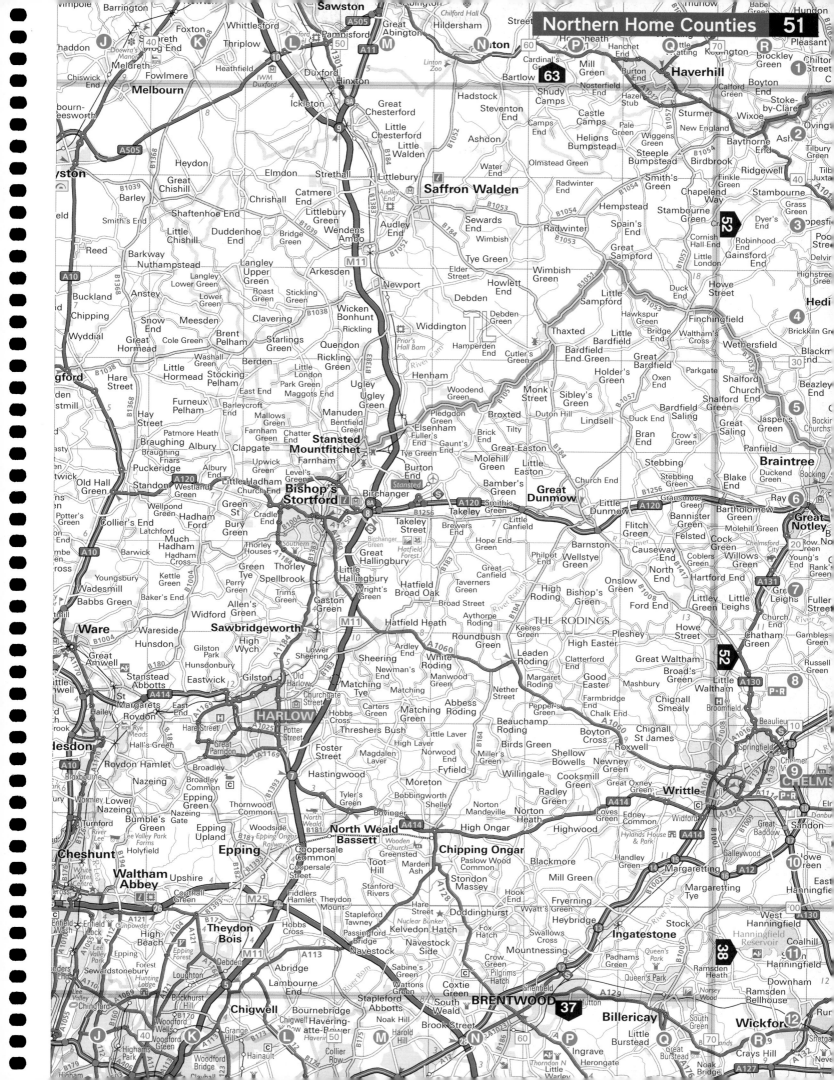

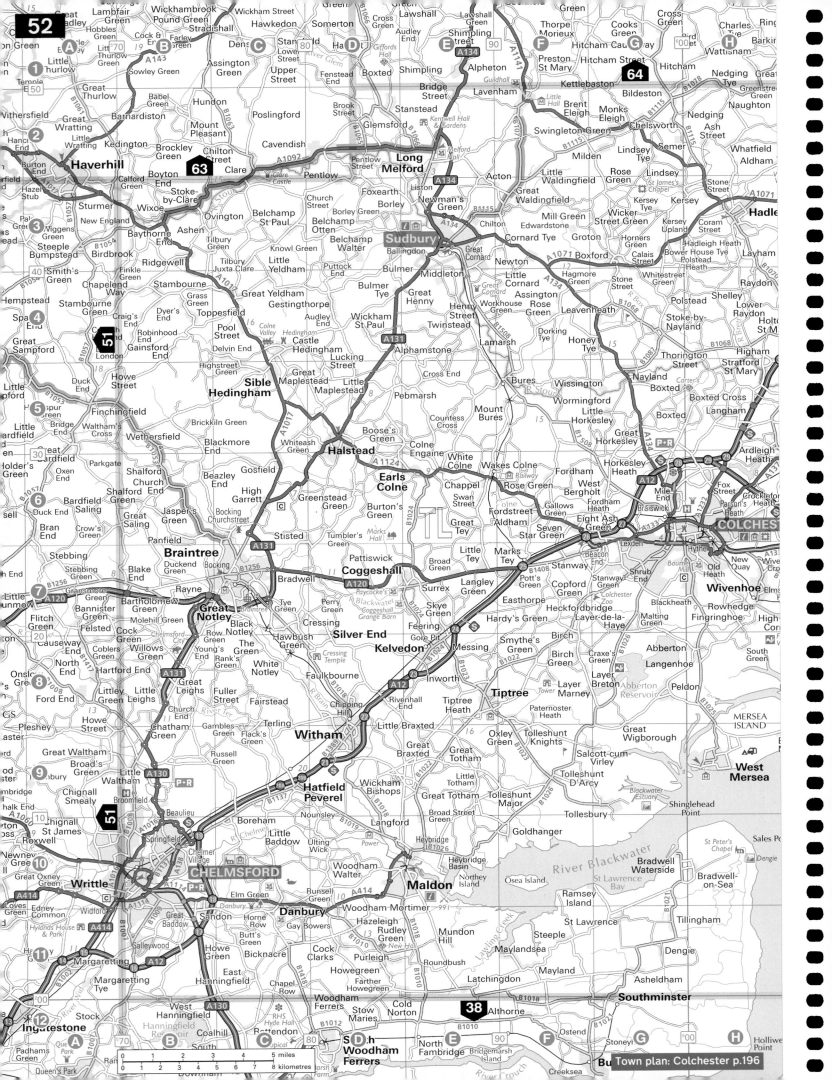

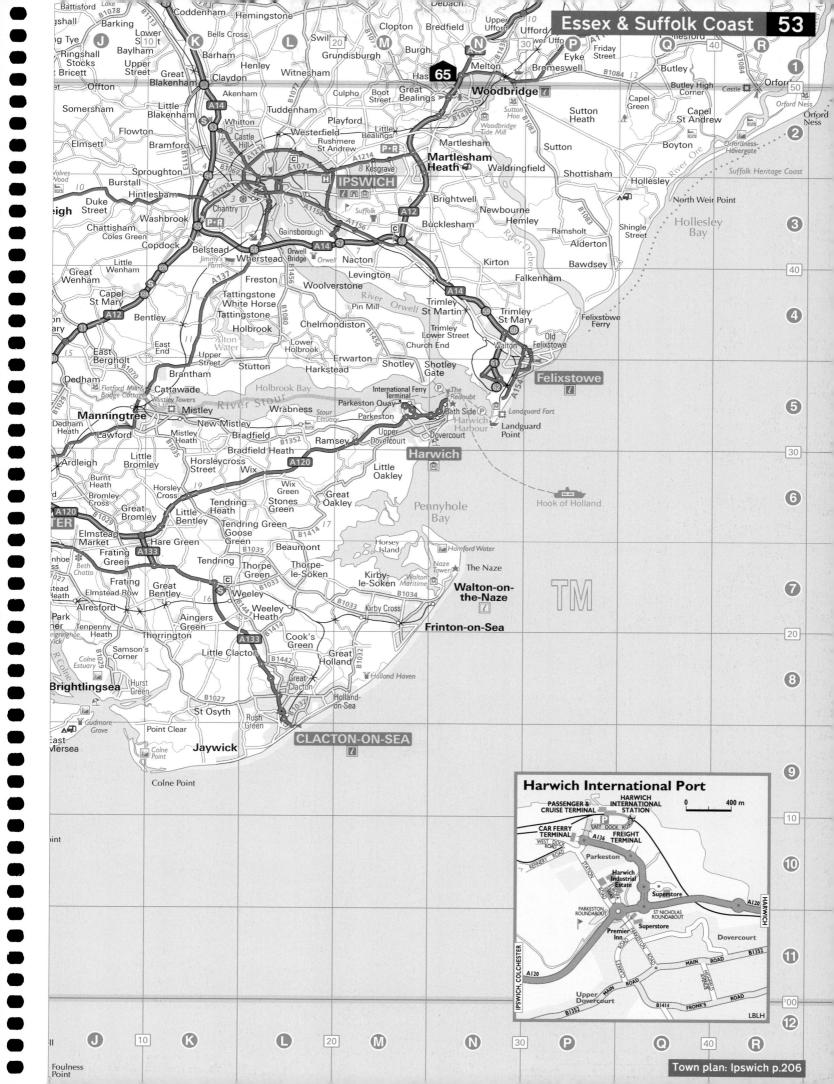

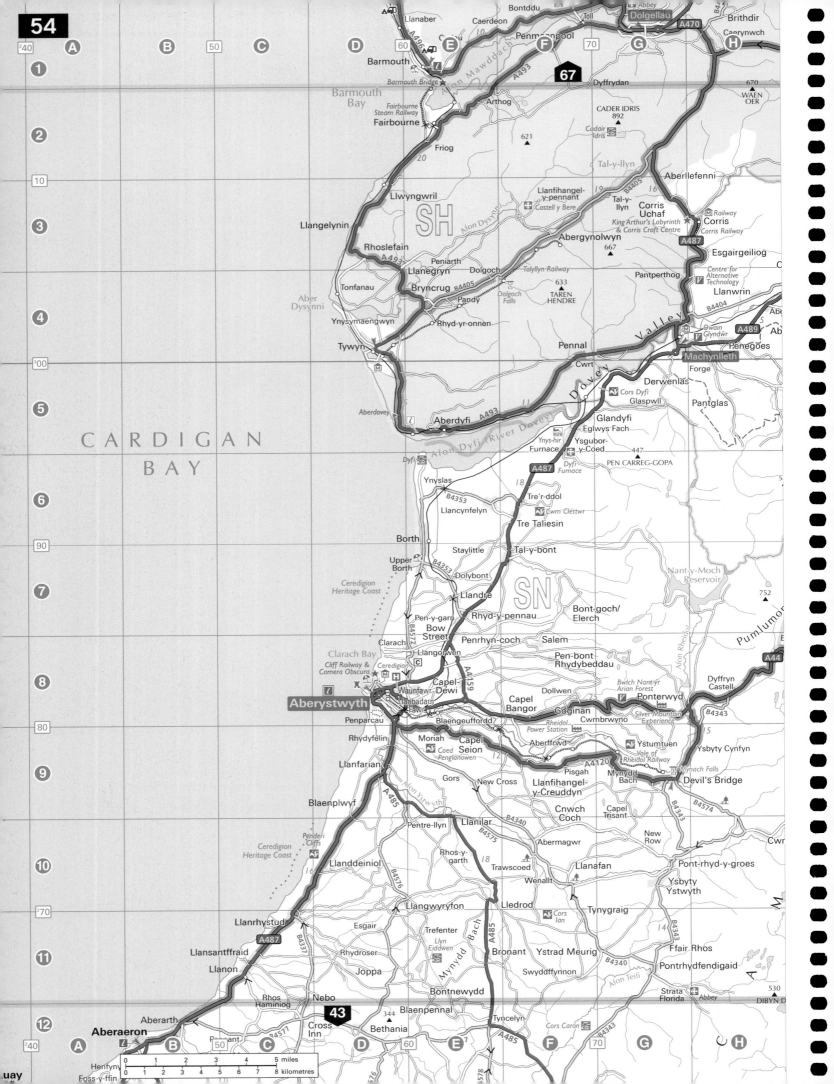

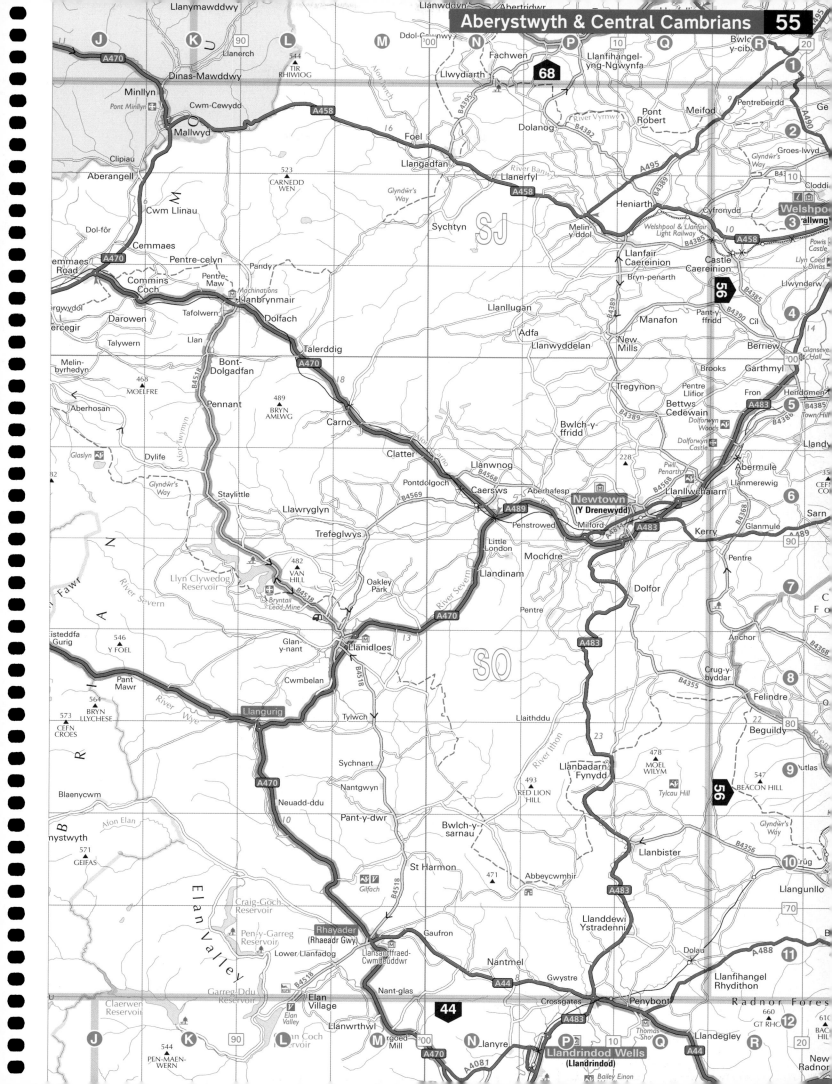

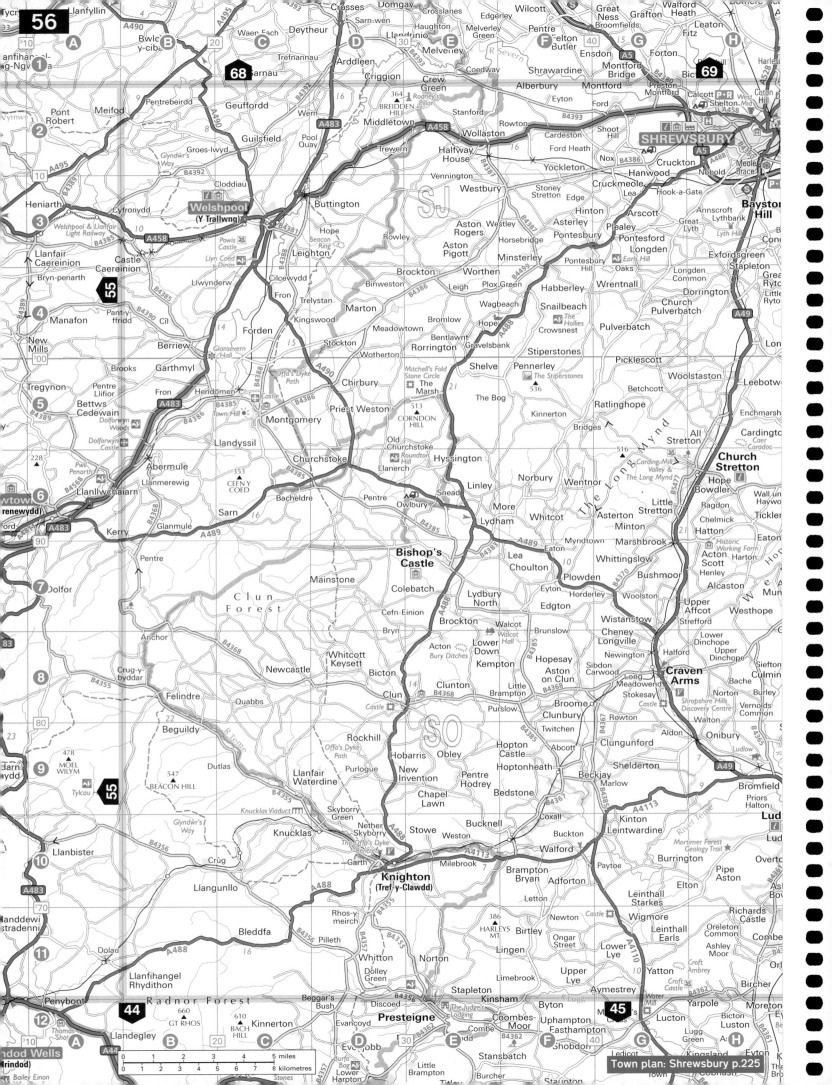

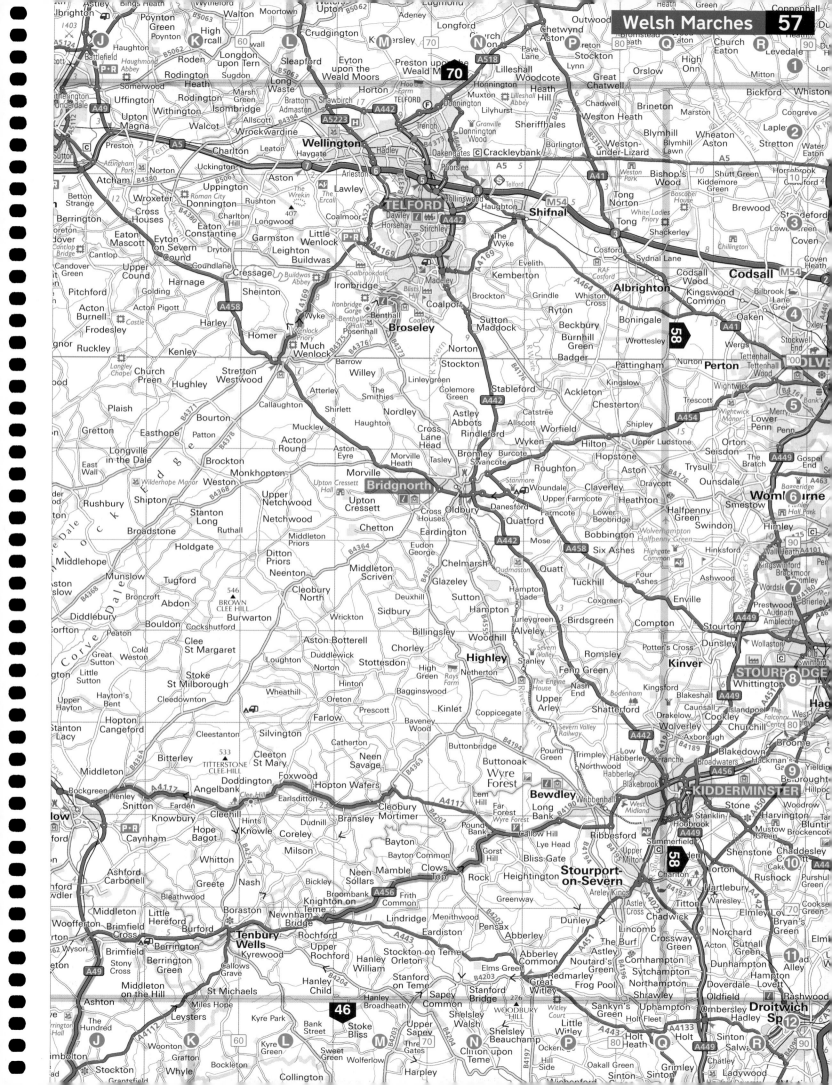

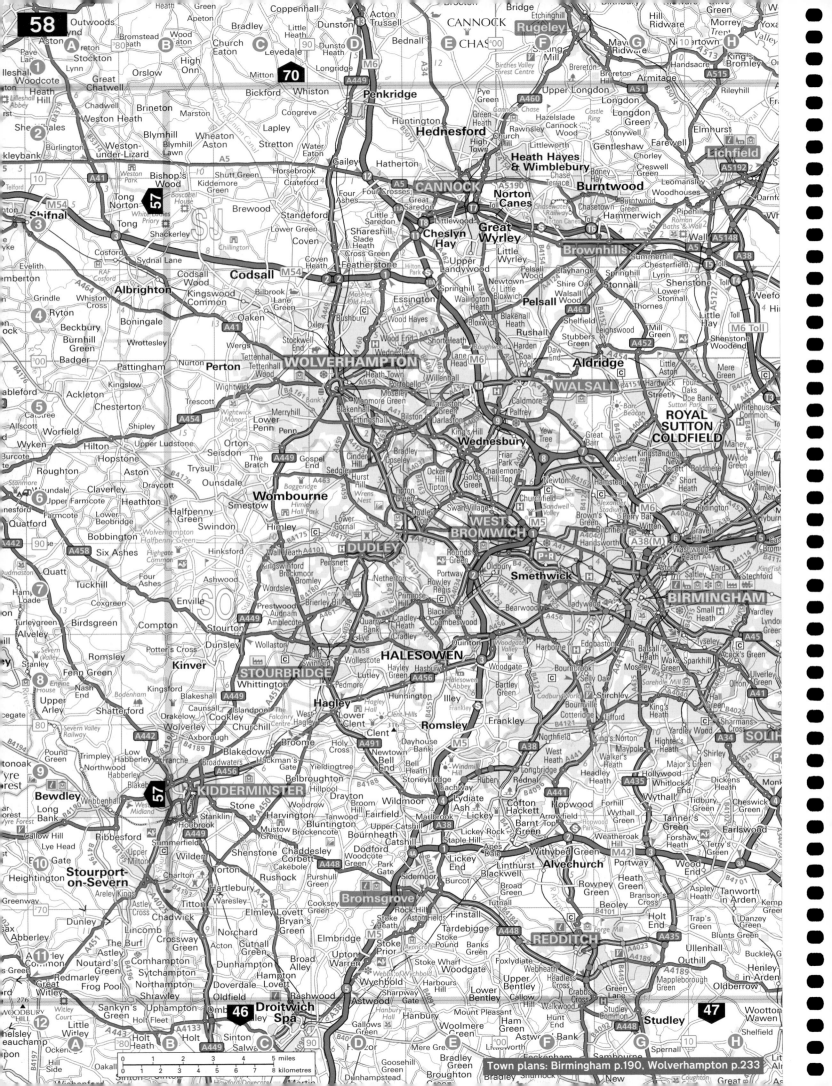

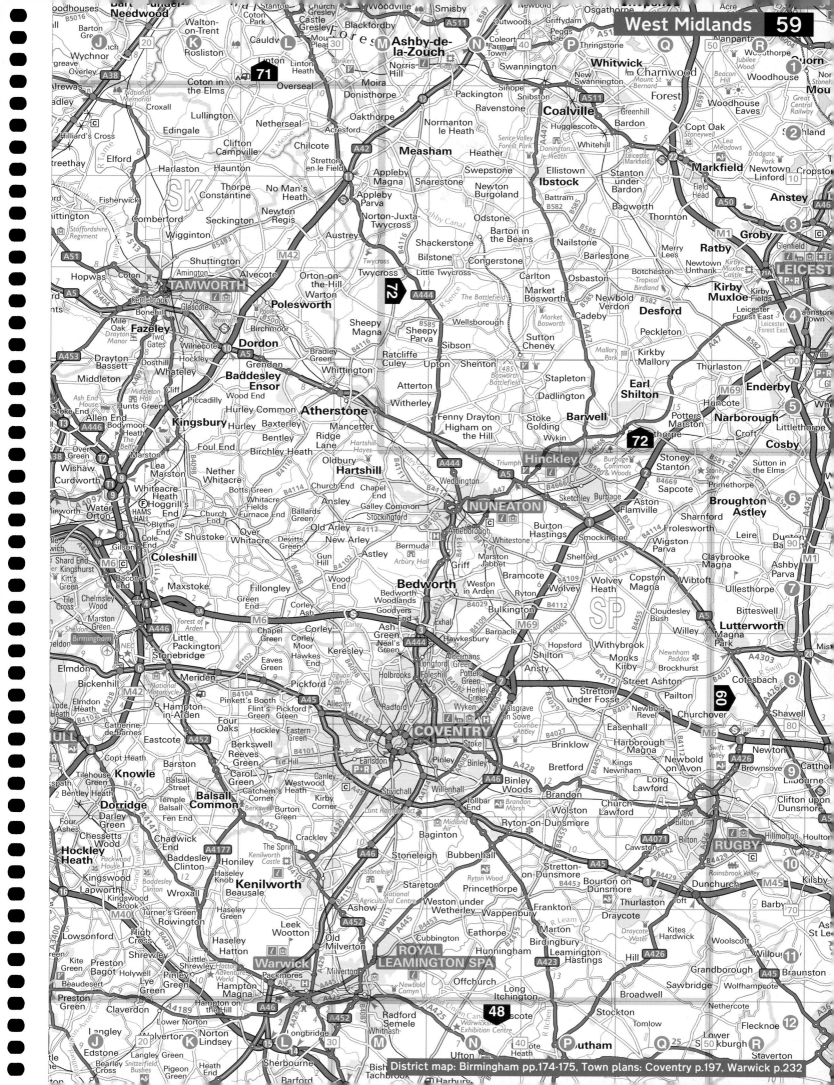

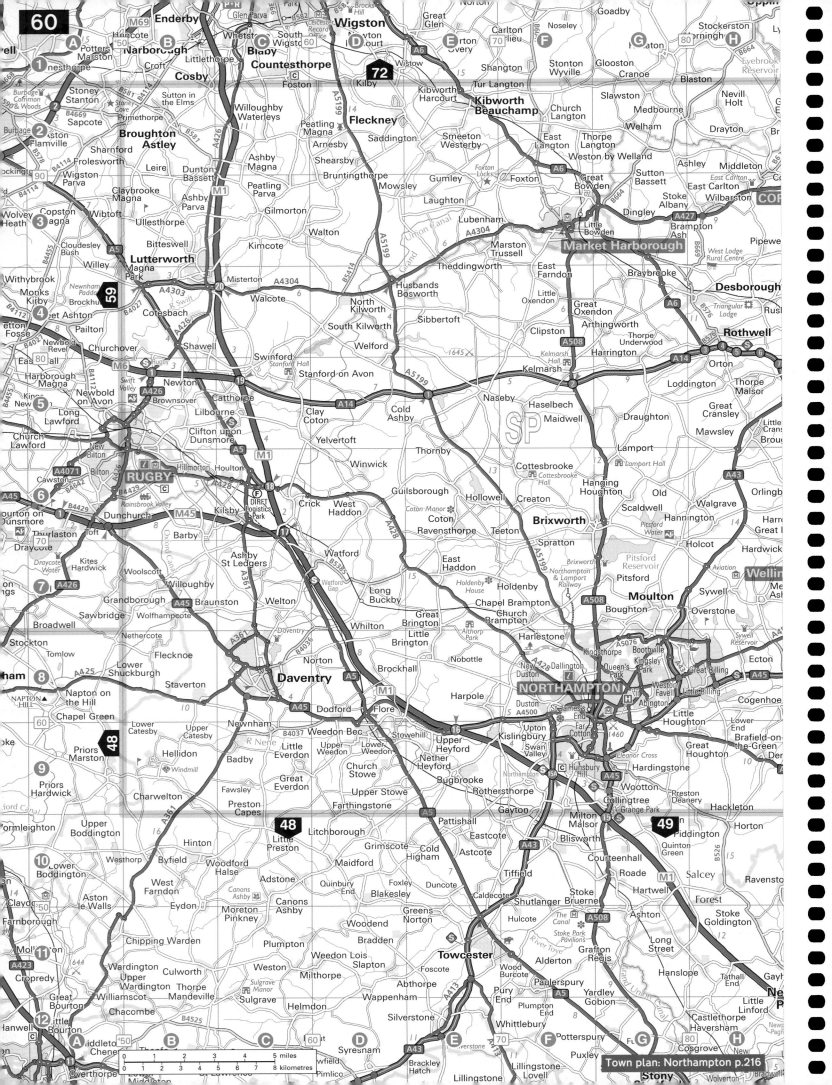

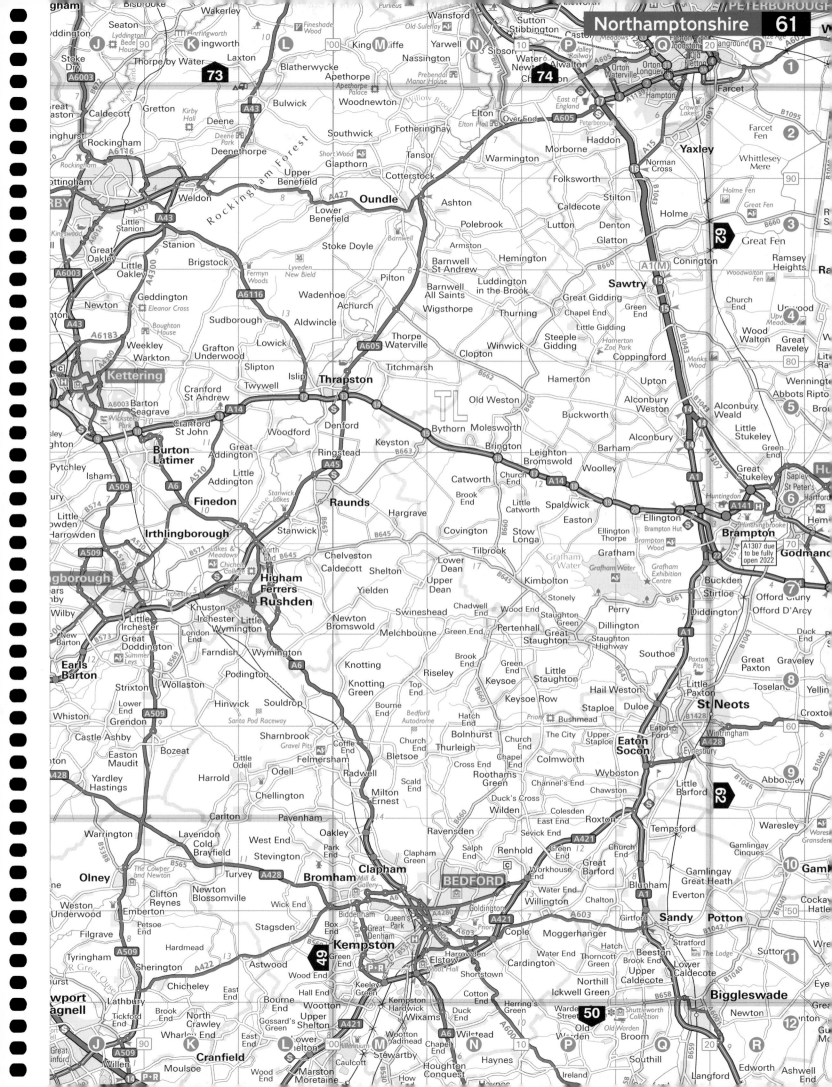

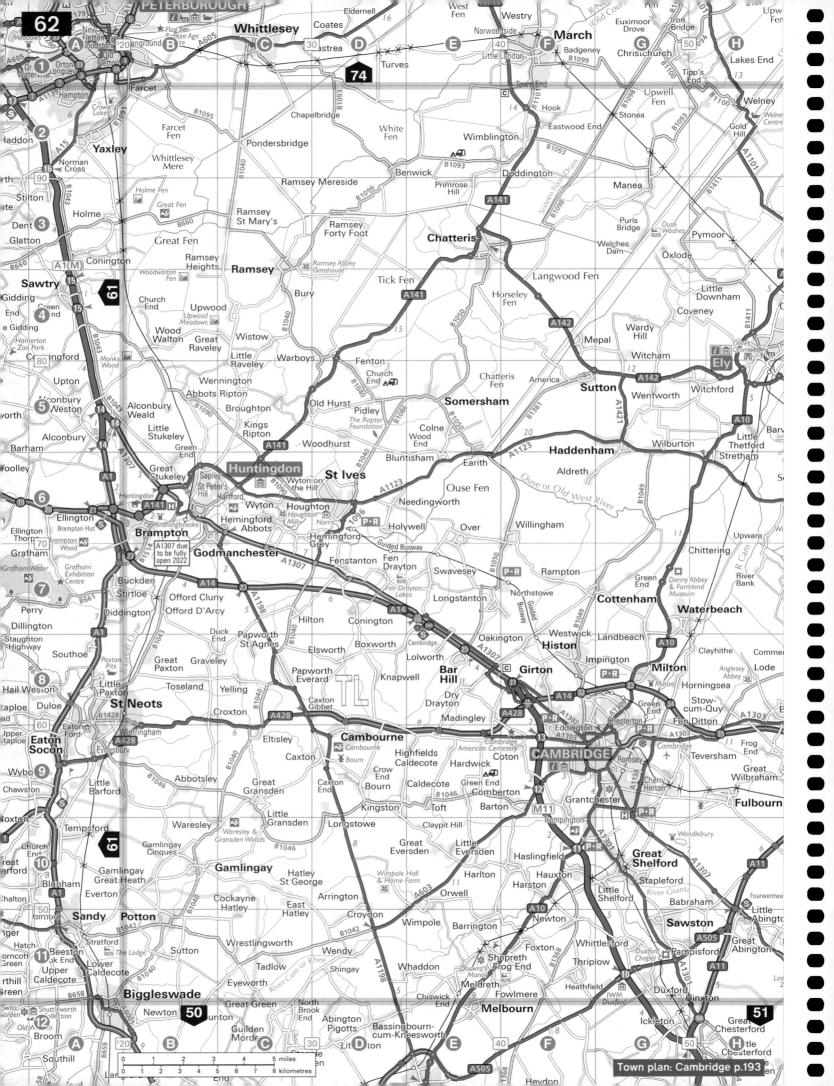

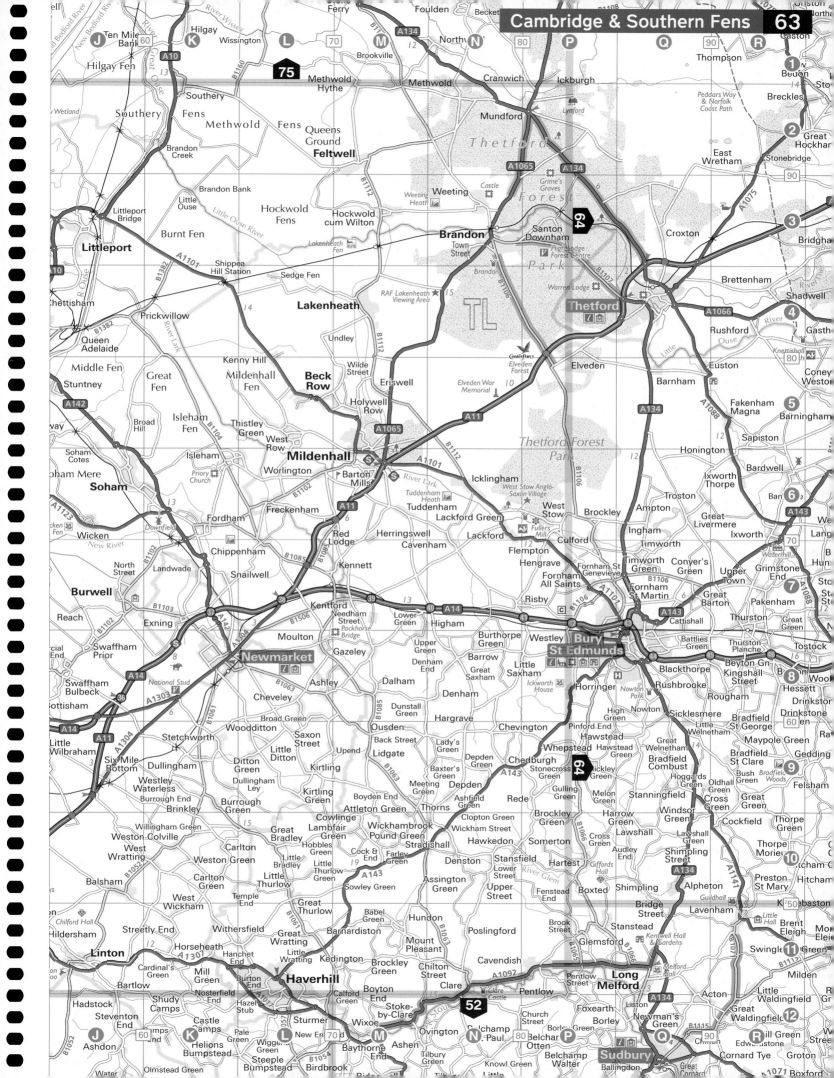

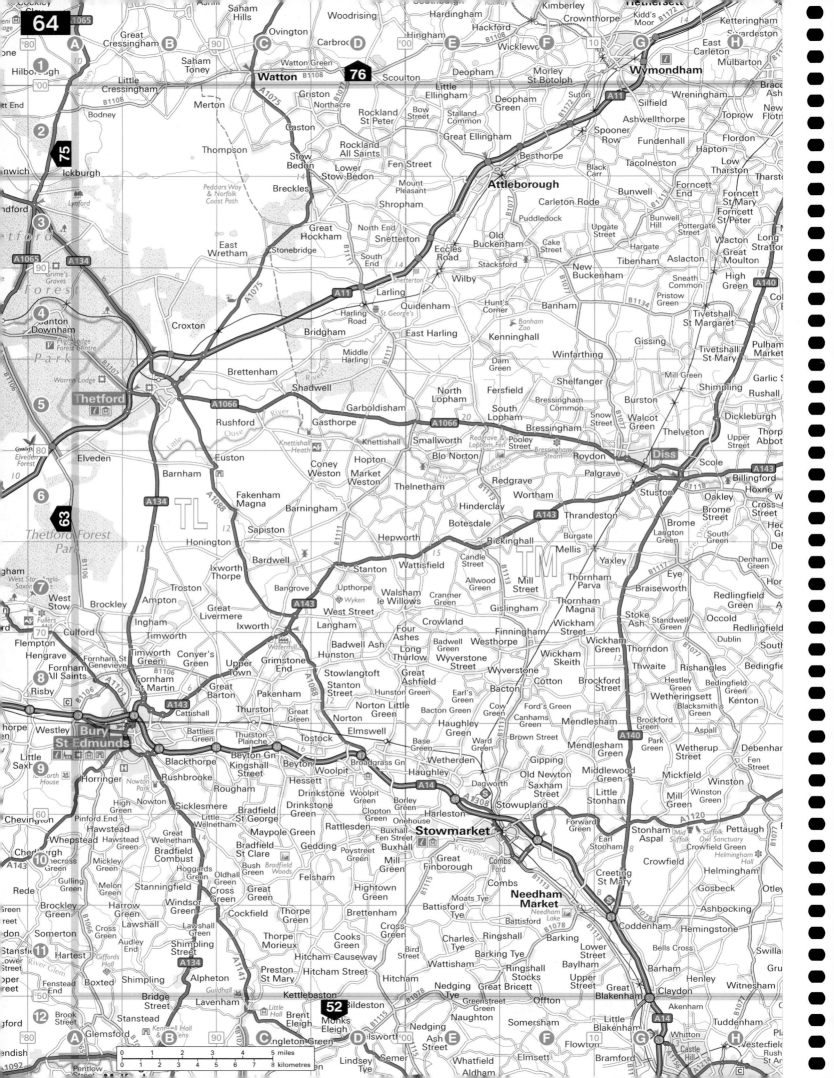

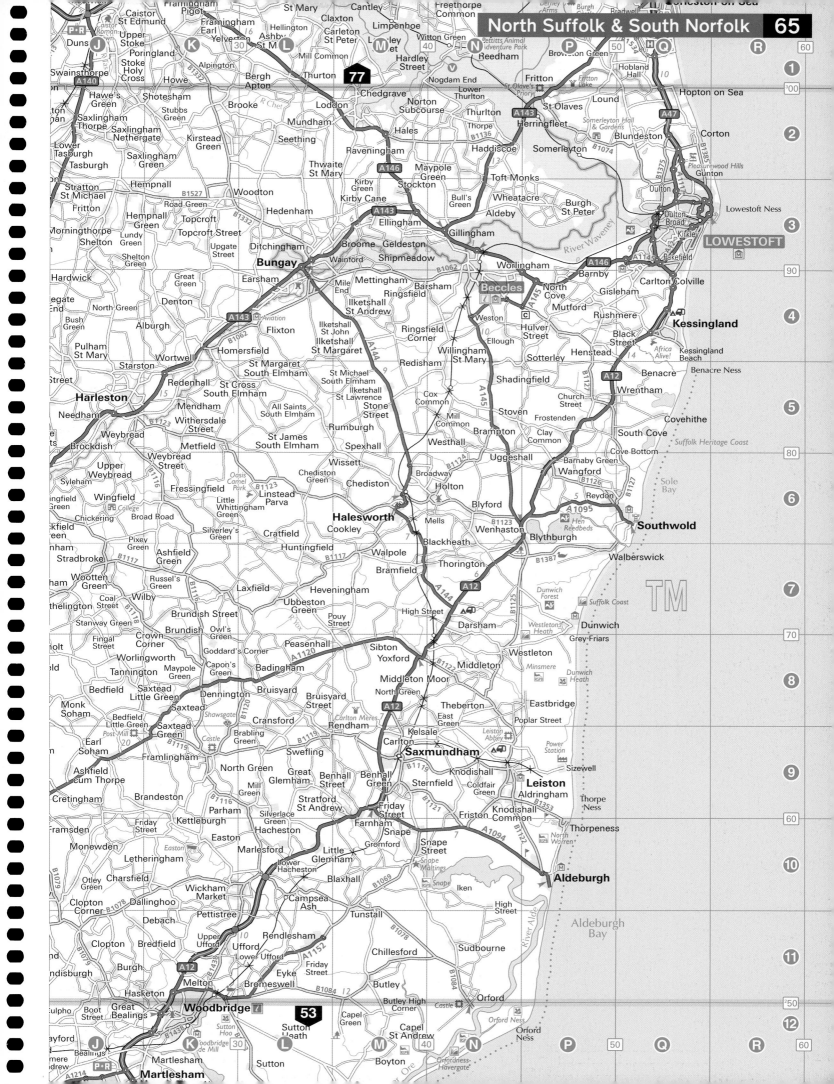

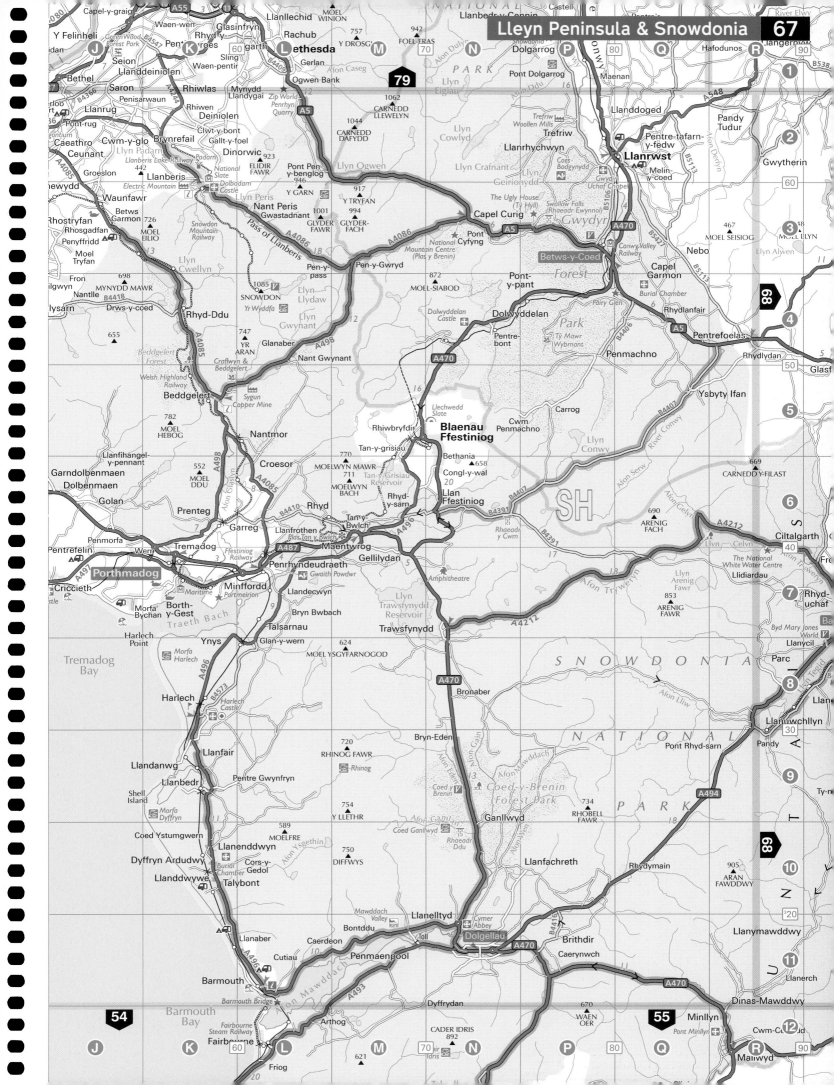

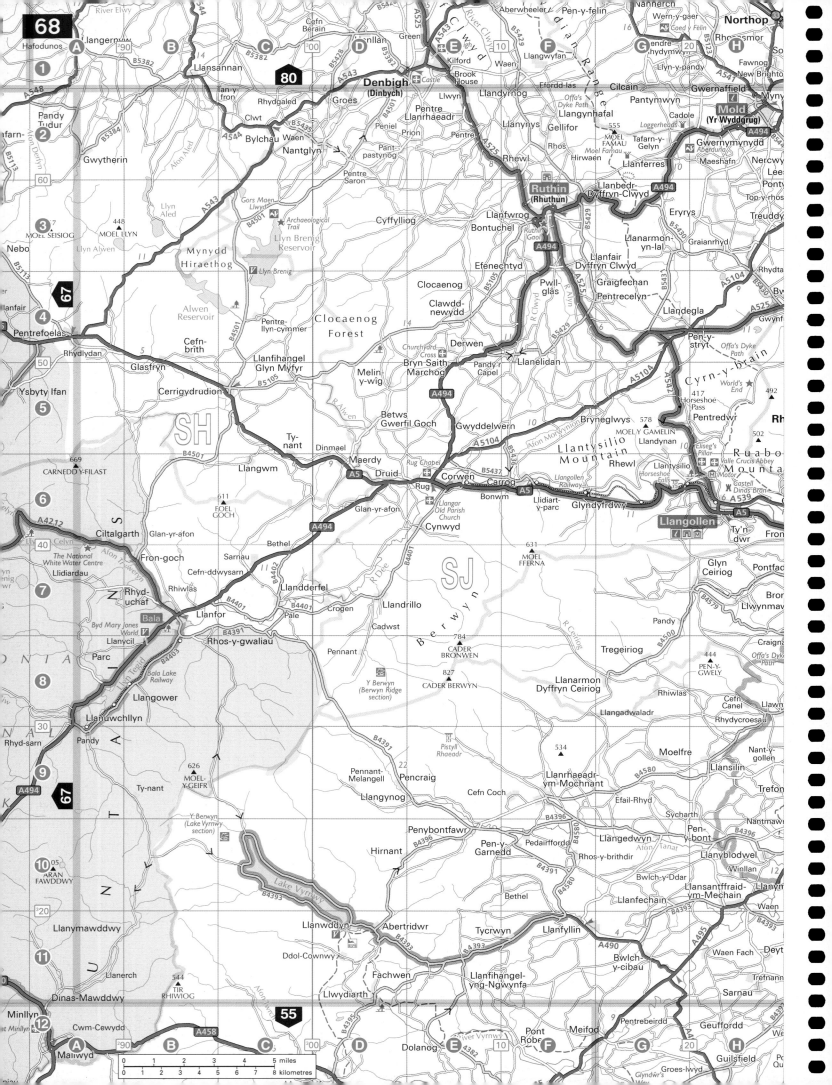

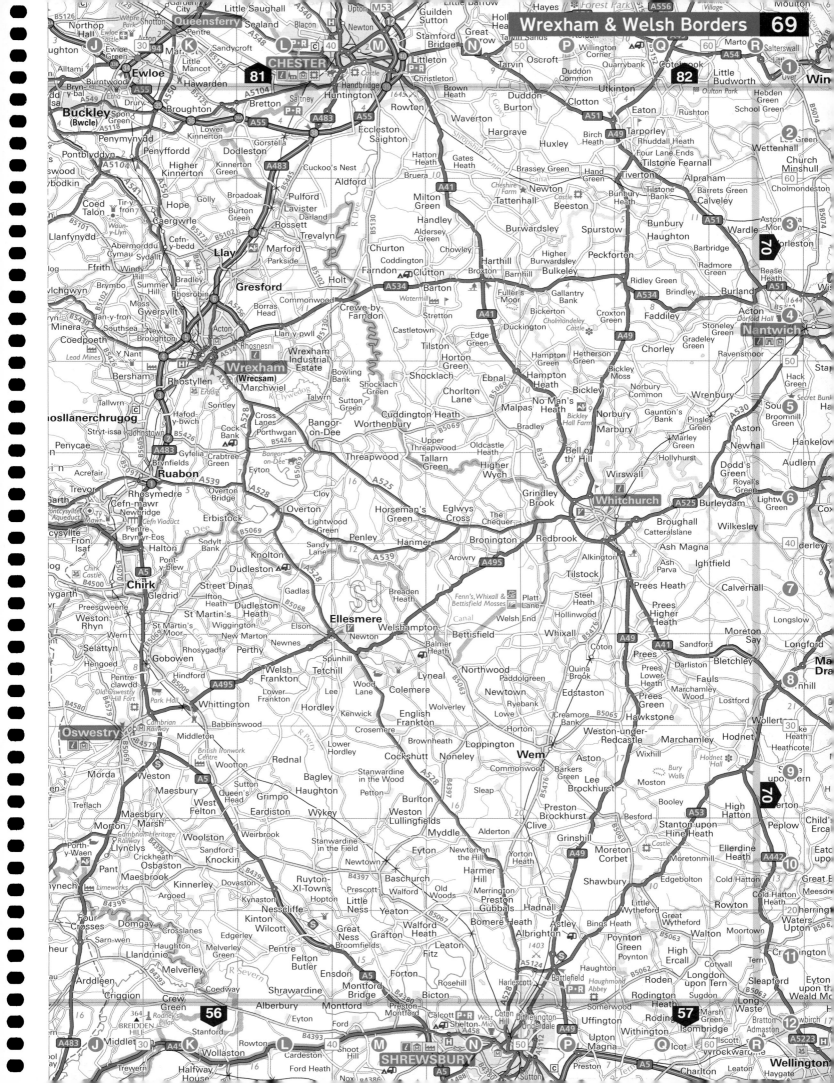

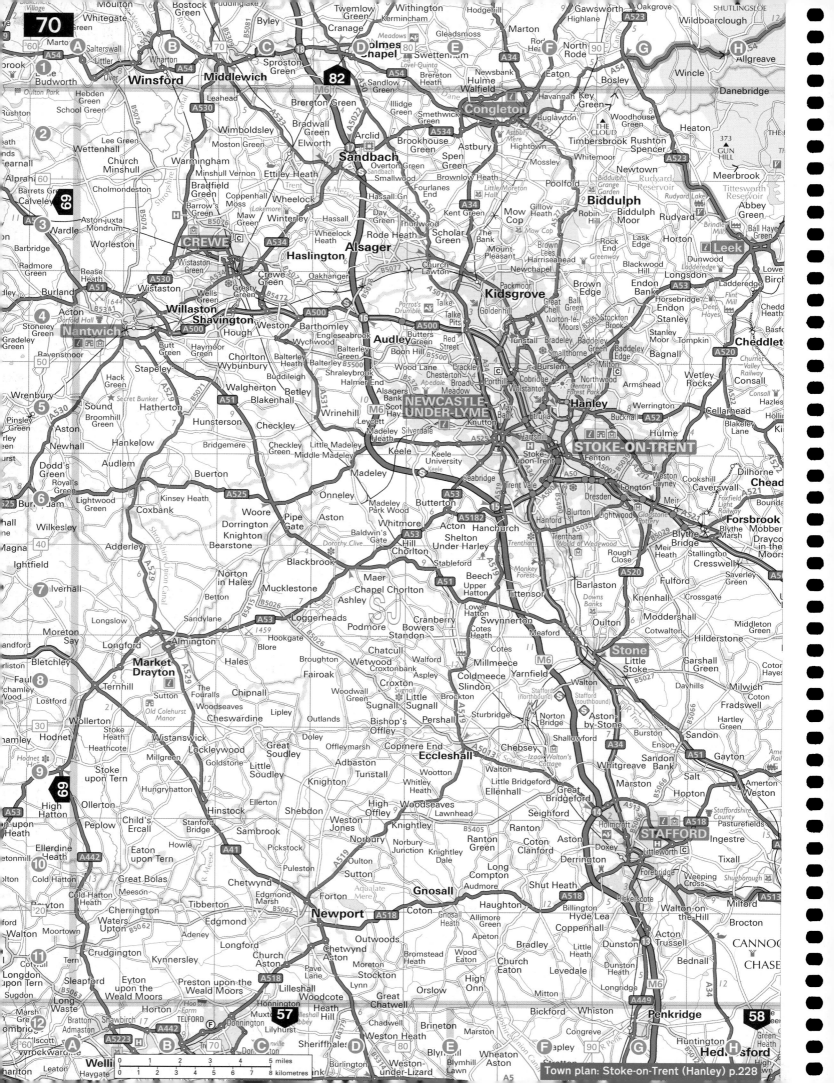

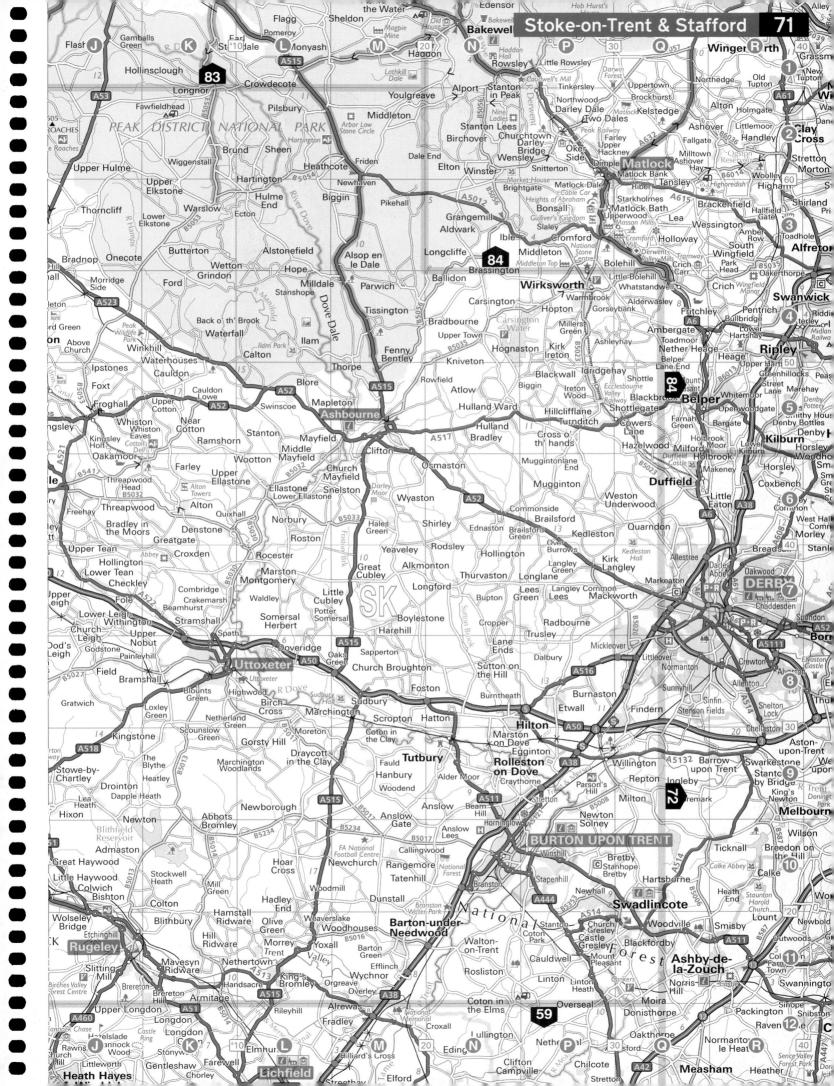

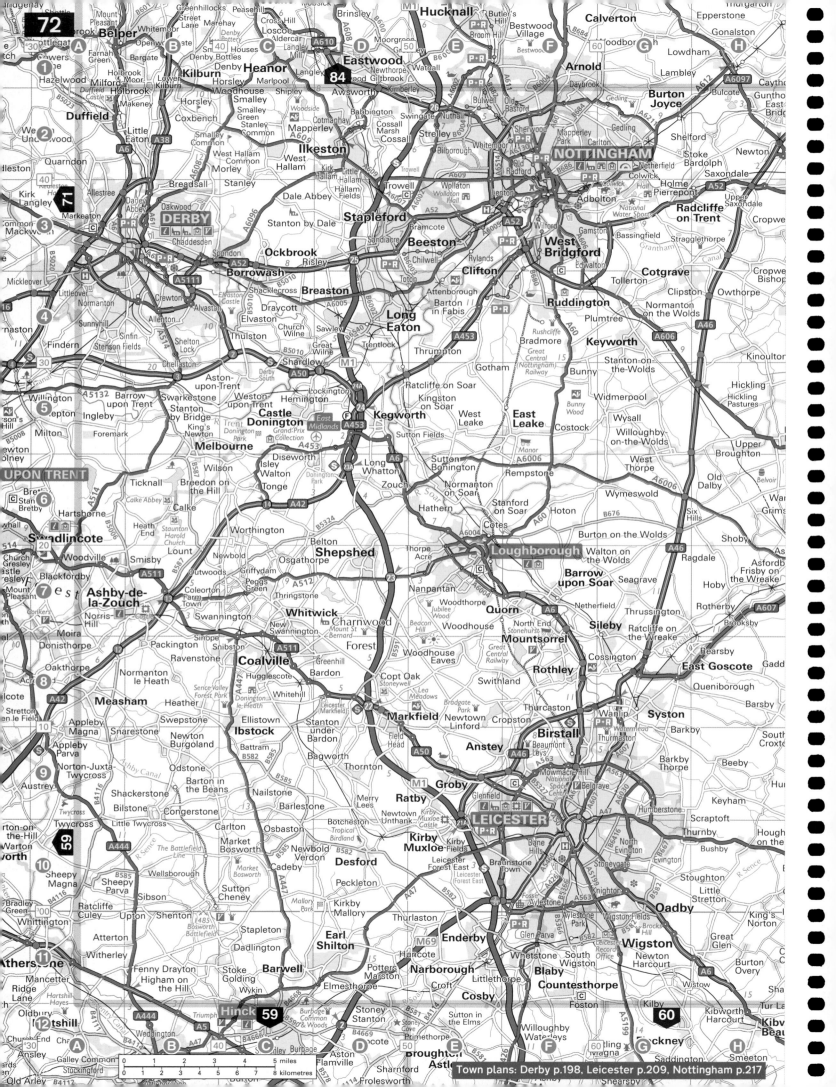

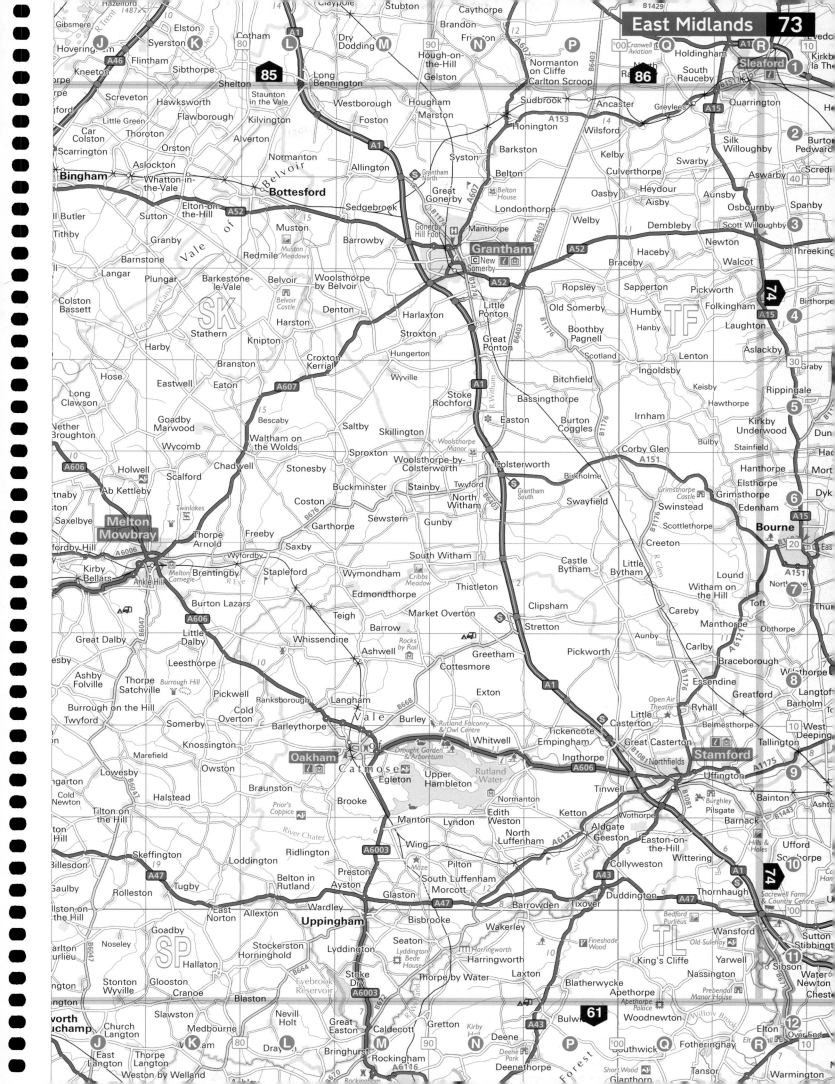

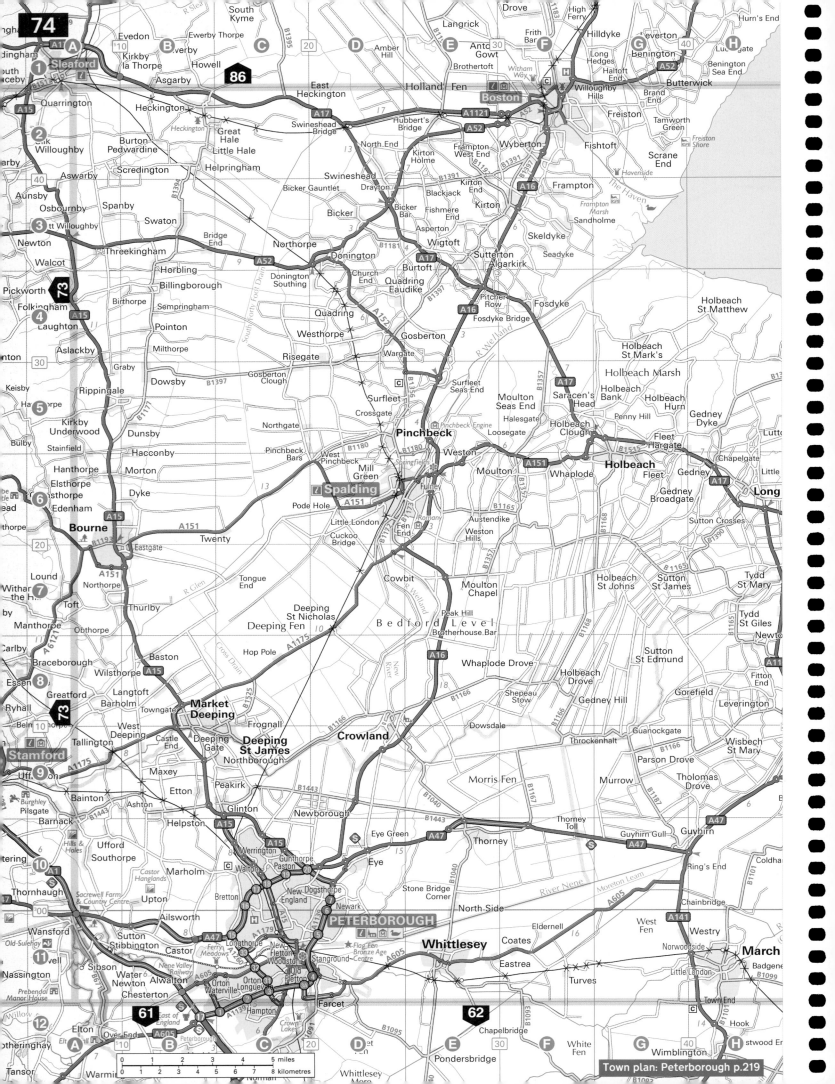

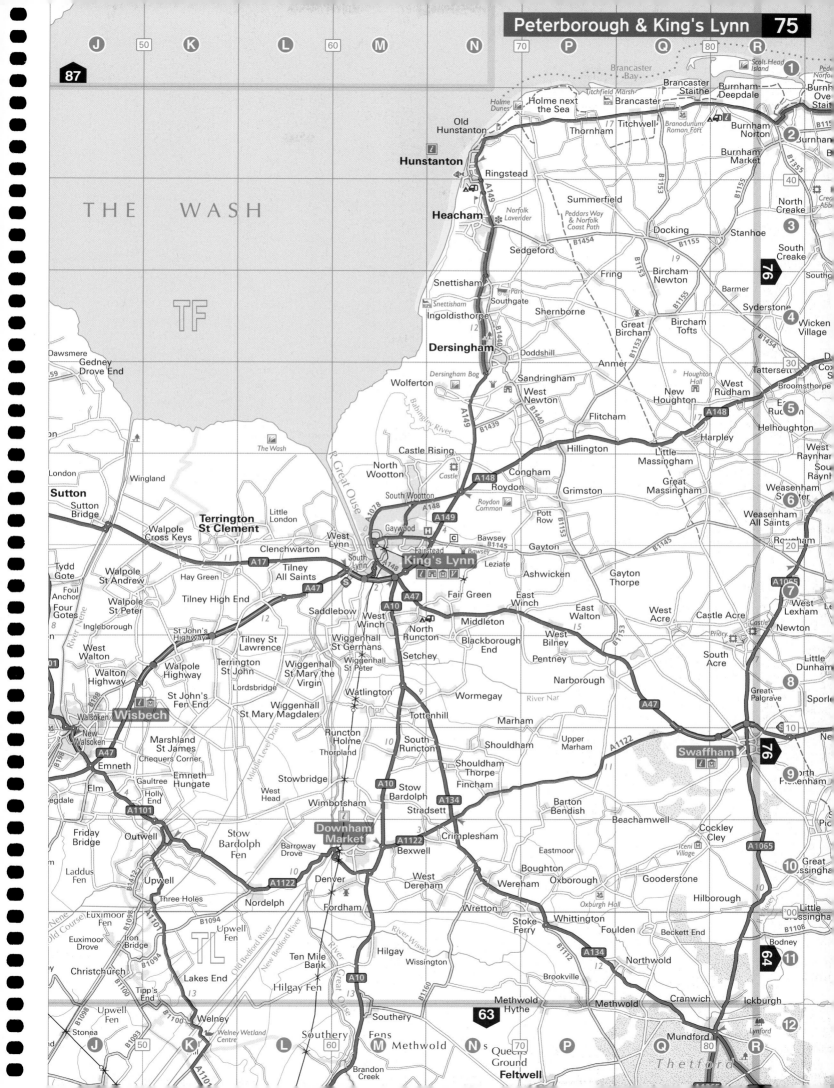

THE WASH

TF

Brancaster Bay

Scolt Head Island

Brancaster Staithe
Brancaster
Burnham Deepdale
Burnham Overy Staithe

Holme Dunes
Holme next the Sea
Titchfield Marsh
Thornham
Titchwell
Branodunum Roman Fort
Burnham Norton
Burnham Market

Old Hunstanton

Summerfield

Hunstanton

Ringstead

North Creake

Stanhoe

Docking

South Creake

Wicken Village

Syderstone

Heacham

Norfolk Lavender

Peddars Way & Norfolk Coast Path

Sedgeford

Fring
Bircham Newton

Snettisham

Southgate
Shernborne

Great Bircham
Bircham Tofts

Barmer

Ingoldisthorpe

Anmer

West Rudham
Broomsthorpe

Dersingham

Doddshill

New Houghton
Houghton Hall

East Rudham

Wolferton
Dersingham Bog

Sandringham
West Newton

Flitcham

Harpley

Helhoughton

Castle Rising

Hillington
Little Massingham

West Raynham
South Raynham

North Wootton

Castle

Congham
Roydon

Grimston
Great Massingham

Weasenham St Peter

South Wootton
Roydon Common

Pott Row

Gayton

Weasenham All Saints

Rougham

West Lynn
Gaywood
King's Lynn
Fairstead
Bawsey

Leziate

Ashwicken

Gayton Thorpe

Sutton

Wingland

Terrington St Clement
Little London

Clenchwarton

South Lynn

Fair Green

East Winch

West Acre

Castle Acre

West Lexham

Sutton Bridge

Walpole Cross Keys

Hay Green

Tilney All Saints

Saddlebow

North Runcton
Middleton

East Walton

South Acre

Newton

Priory

Tydd Gote

Walpole St Andrew

Tilney High End

West Winch

Blackborough End

West Bilney

Little Dunham

Foul Anchor
Four Gotes

Walpole St Peter

Ingleborough

St John's Highway

Tilney St Lawrence

Wiggenhall St Germans

Setchey

Pentney

Narborough

Great Palgrave

Sporle

West Walton

Walpole Highway

Terrington St John

Wiggenhall St Mary the Virgin

Wiggenhall St Peter

Wormegay

River Nar

Walton Highway

Lordsbridge

Watlington

South Acre

Wisbech

Walsoken

St John's Fen End

Wiggenhall St Mary Magdalen

Runcton Holme
Thorpland

South Runcton

Marham

Shouldham

Upper Marham

Swaffham

North Pickenham

New Walsoken

Marshland St James
Chequers Corner

Stowbridge

West Head

Tottenhill

Shouldham Thorpe
Fincham

Barton Bendish

Beachamwell

Emneth

Gaultree
Emneth Hungate

Wimbotsham

Stow Bardolph
Stradsett

Crimplesham

Cockley Cley
Iceni Village

Elm

Holly End

Downham Market
Bexwell

Eastmoor

Boughton
Oxborough

Gooderstone

Great Massingham

Friday Bridge

Outwell

Stow Bardolph Fen

Barroway Drove

Denver

West Dereham

Wereham

Oxburgh Hall

Hilborough

Upwell

Three Holes

Nordelph

Fordham

Wretton

Whittington

Foulden

Beckett End

Bodney

Laddus Fen

Euximoor Fen

Upwell Fen

Stoke Ferry

Northwold

Little Cressingham

Euximoor Drove
Iron Bridge

TL

Old Bedford River
New Bedford River

Ten Mile Bank

Hilgay

Wissington

Brookville

Christchurch

Tipp's End

Lakes End

Hilgay Fen

River Wissey

Methwold Hythe

Methwold

Cranwich

Ickburgh

Stonea

Upwell Fen

Welney

Welney Wetland Centre

Southery
Fens

Southery

Methwold

Queen's Ground

Feltwell

Brandon Creek

Mundford

Lynford

Thetford

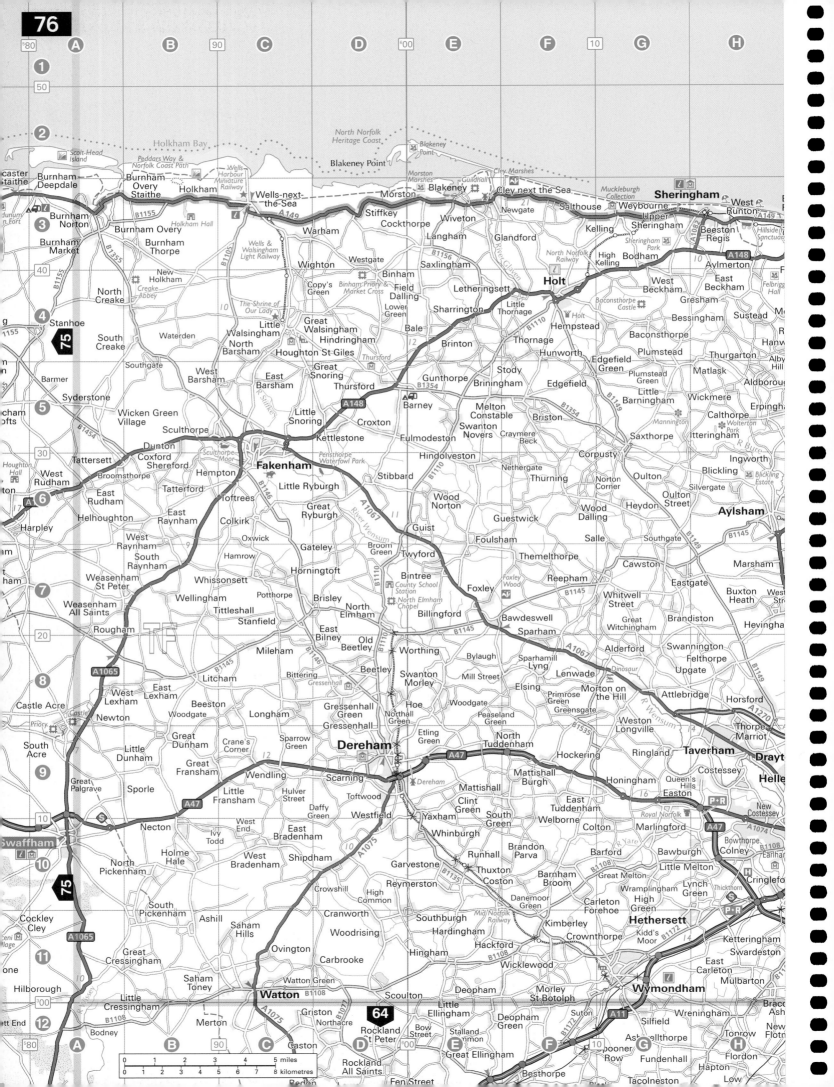

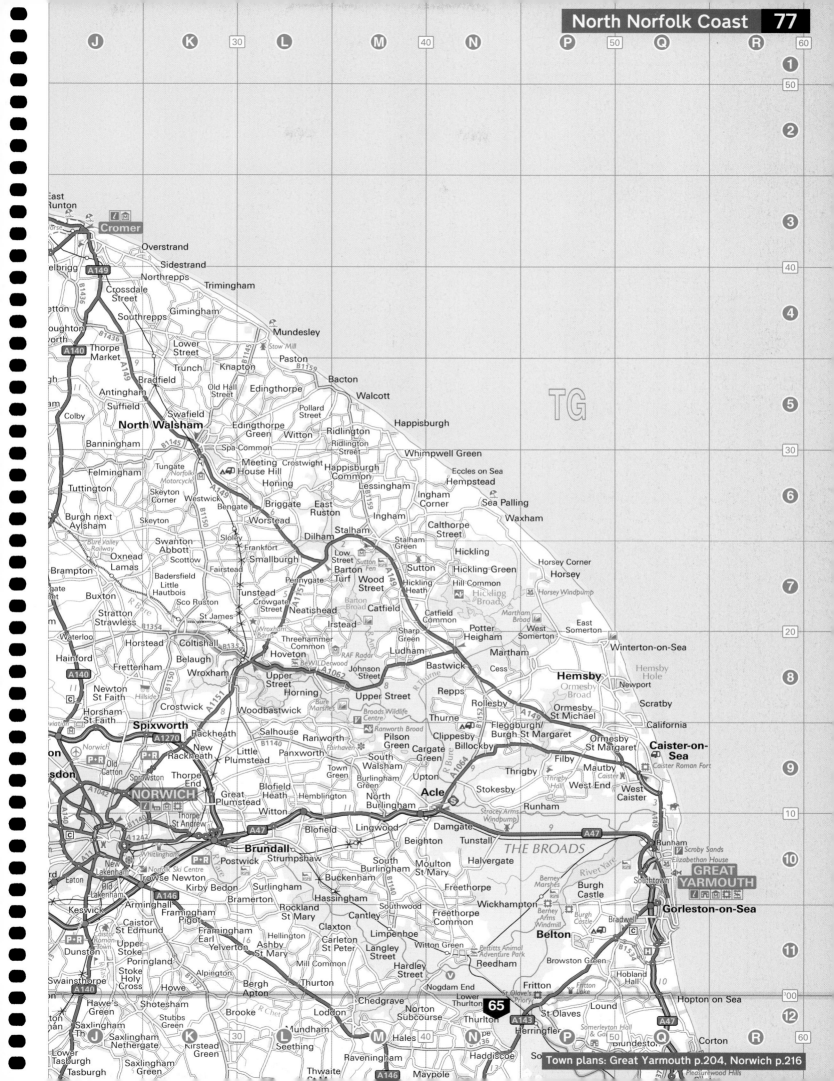

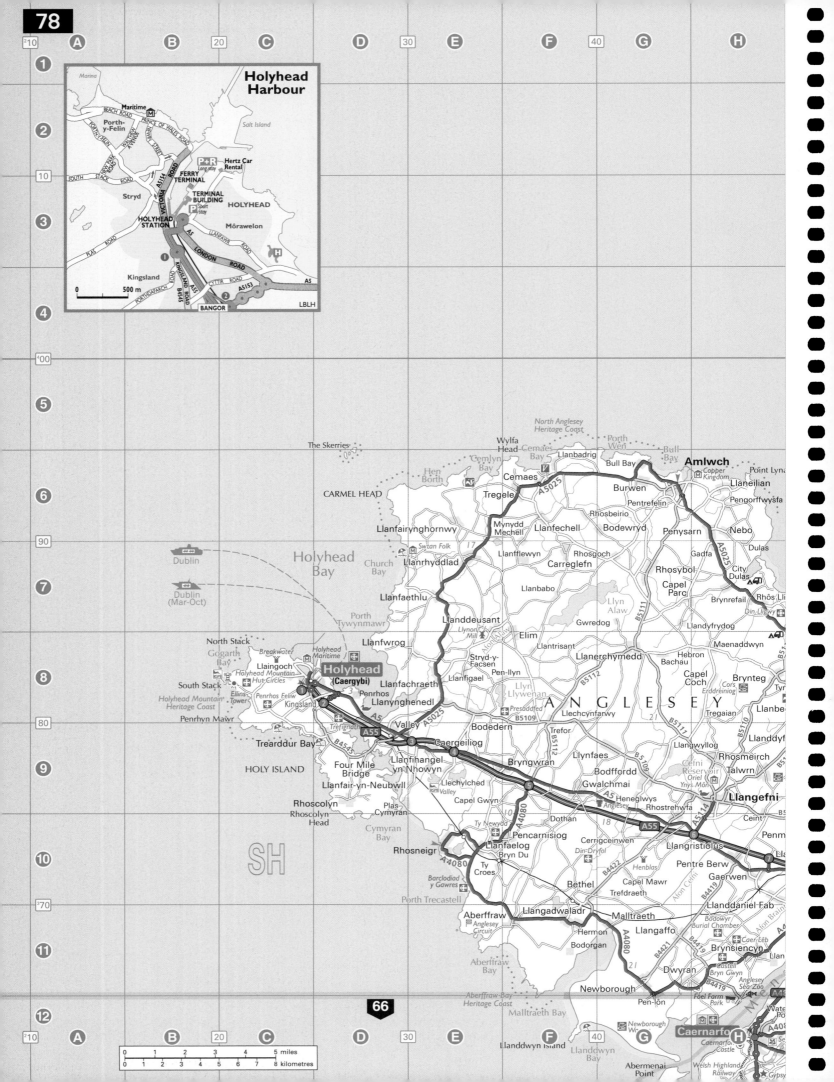

Holyhead Harbour

Marina
Maritime M
BEACH ROAD
Porth-y-Felin
PRINCE OF WALES ROAD
Salt Island
PORTH-Y-FELIN
NEWRY STREET
HENRY STREET
VICTORIA ROAD
WALTHEW AVENUE
STANLEY STREET
P+R Long stay
Hertz Car Rental
SOUTH STACK ROAD
FERRY TERMINAL
TERMINAL BUILDING Short stay
P
HOLYHEAD
Stryd
A5154
A5
LLANFAWR ROAD
HOLYHEAD STATION
Môrawelon
H
LONDON ROAD
PLAS ROAD
KINGSLAND ROAD
A51
CYTTIR ROAD
A5
Kingsland
PORTHDAFARCH ROAD
B4545
A5153
A5
2
BANGOR
LBLH

0   500 m

A 20 B C 20 D 30 E F 40 G H

North Anglesey Heritage Coast
The Skerries
Wylfa Head
Cemaes Bay
Porth Wen
Bull Bay
Amlwch
Point Lynas
Copper Kingdom
Llaneilian
Gemlyn Bay
Llanbadrig
Bull Bay
Hen Borth
Cemaes
A5025
Burwen
Pengorffwysfa
CARMEL HEAD
Tregele
Pentrefelin
Penysarn
Nebo
Llanfairynghornwy
Mynydd Mechell
Llanfechell
Rhosbeirio
Bodewryd
A5025
Dulas
Swtan Folk 17
Llanfflewyn
Rhosgoch
Rhosybol
City Dulas
Church Bay
Llanrhyddlad
Carreglefn
Brynrefail
Rhôs Lli
Llanbabo
Din Lligwy
Holyhead Bay
Llanfaethlu
Llyn Alaw
Capel Parc
B5111
Dublin
Llanddeusant
Gwredog
Llandyfrydog
Dublin (Mar-Oct)
Llynon Mill
Elim
Maenaddwyn
Porth Tywynmawr
Llanfwrog
Llantrisant
Hebron Bachau
North Stack
Llanerchymedd
Capel Coch
Brynteg
Gogarth Bay
Breakwater
Holyhead Maritime
Stryd-y-Facsen
Pen-llyn
Cors Erddreiniog
Tyr
Holyhead Mountain Hut Circles
Holyhead (Caergybi)
Llanfachraeth
Llanfigael
B5112
ANGLESEY
Llanbe
South Stack
Ellins Tower
Penrhos Feilw
Kingsland
Penrhos
Llanynghenedl
Llyn Llywenan
Presaddfed
Llechcynfarwy
Tregaian
Holyhead Mountain Heritage Coast
Trefignath
A5
Valley A5025
Bodedern
B5109
Trefor
Llangwyllog
Rhosmeirch
Penrhyn Mawr
A55
Caergeiliog
Bodffordd
B5110
Llanddy
Trearddur Bay
B4545
Llanfihangel yn Nhowyn
Bryngwran
Gwalchmai
Cefni Reservoir
Oriel Ynys Môn
Rhoscolyn
Four Mile Bridge
Llechylched
Capel Gwyn
A5
Heneglwys
Anglesey
Rhostrehwfa
Llangefni
HOLY ISLAND
Valley
Dothan 18
A55
A5114
Rhoscolyn Head
Llanfair-yn-Neubwll
Plas Cymyran
A4080
Henblas
Llangristiolus
Penm
Cymyran Bay
Ty Newydd
Pencarnisiog
Cerrigceinwen
Din-Dryfol
SH
Rhosneigr
A4080
Llanfaelog
Bryn Du
B4422
Capel Mawr
Pentre Berw
Ty Croes
Bethel
Trefdraeth
Afon Cefni
Gaerwen
Llanddaniel Fab
Barclodiad y Gawres
Aberffraw
B4419
Porth Trecastell
Aberffraw Anglesey Circuit
Llangadwaladr
Malltraeth
Bodowyr Burial Chamber
Caer Lêb
Brynsiencyn
Hermon
Bodorgan
Llangaffo
A4080
B4421
Aberffraw Bay
Dwyran
Castell Bryn Gwyn
Anglesey Sea Zoo
Newborough
Fôel Farm Park
A44
Aberffraw Bay Heritage Coast
Pen-lôn
Caernarfo M
Newborough Wr
Caernarfon
A408
Malltraeth Bay
Llanddwyn Island
Llanddwyn Bay
Caernarfon Castle
Welsh Highland Railway
Gypsy
Abermenai Point

66

0 1 2 3 4 5 miles
0 1 2 3 4 5 6 7 8 kilometres

A B 20 C D 30 E F 40 G H

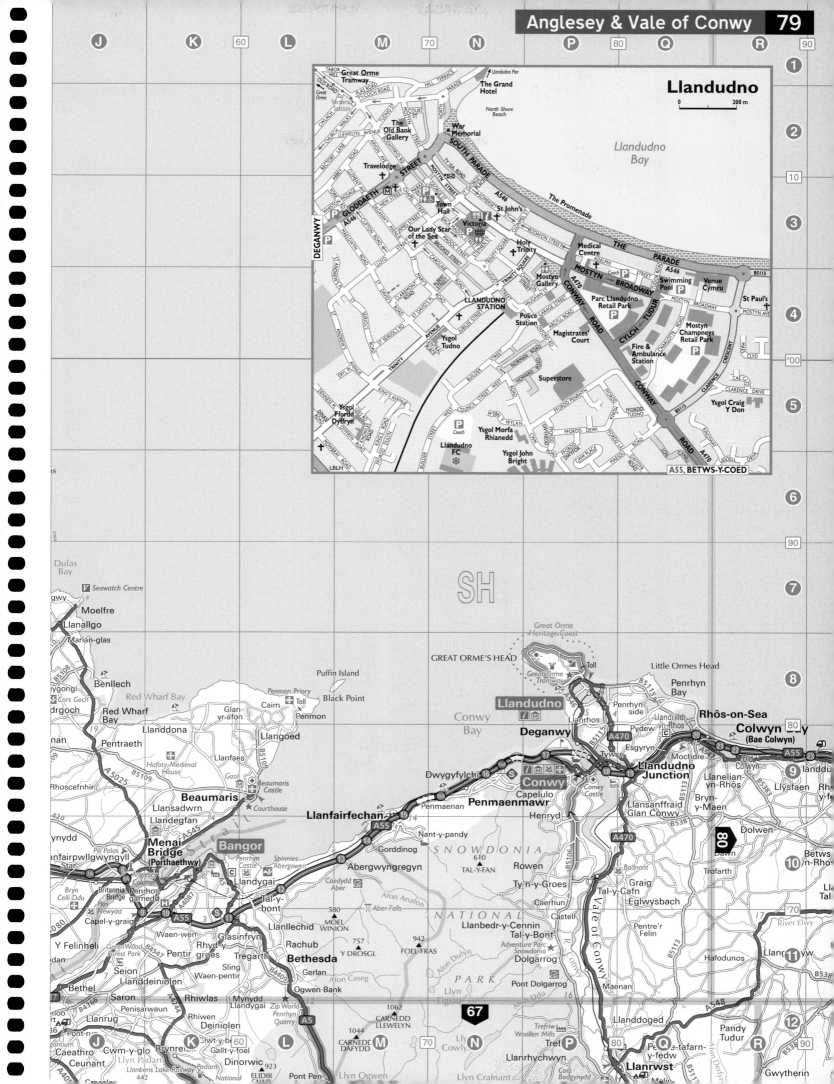

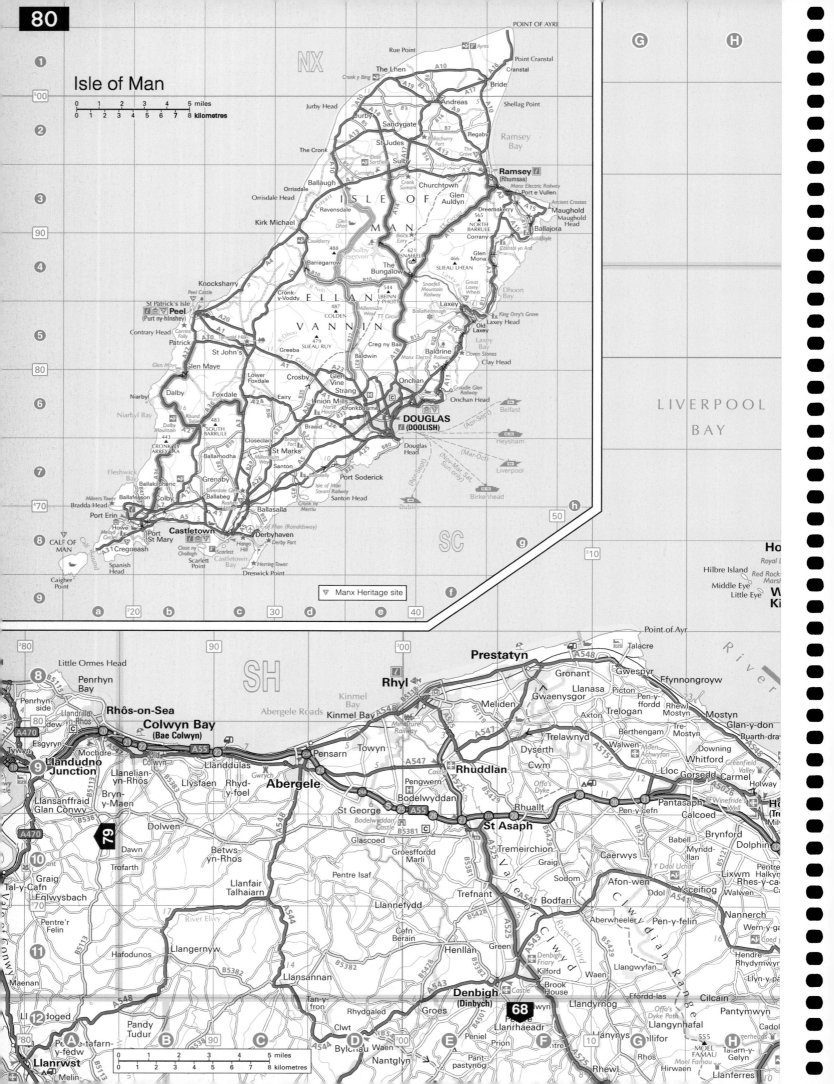

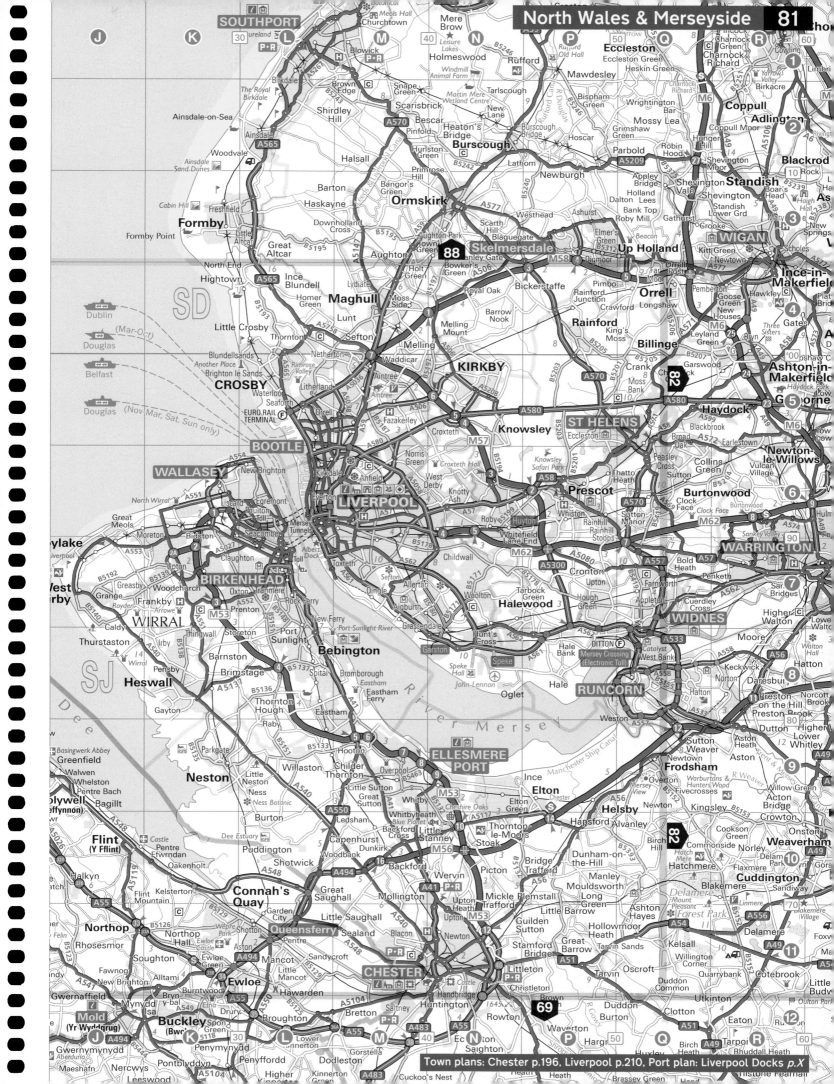

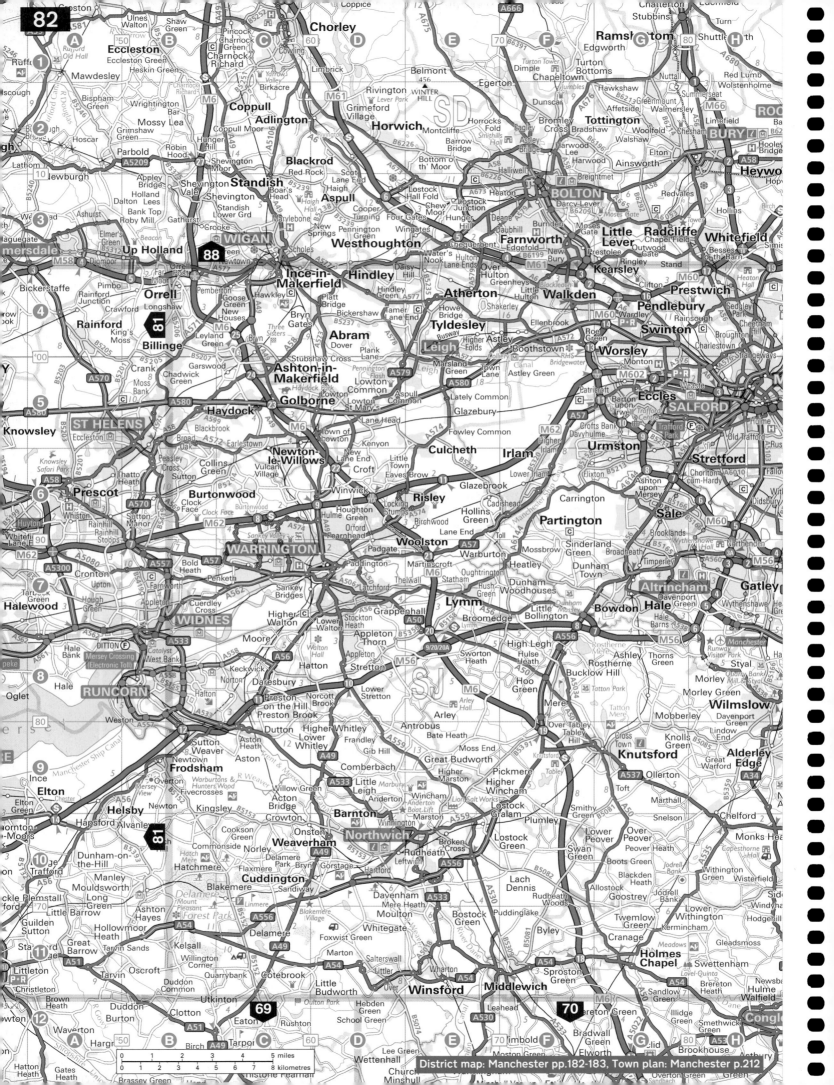

District map: Manchester pp.182-183, Town plan: Manchester p.212

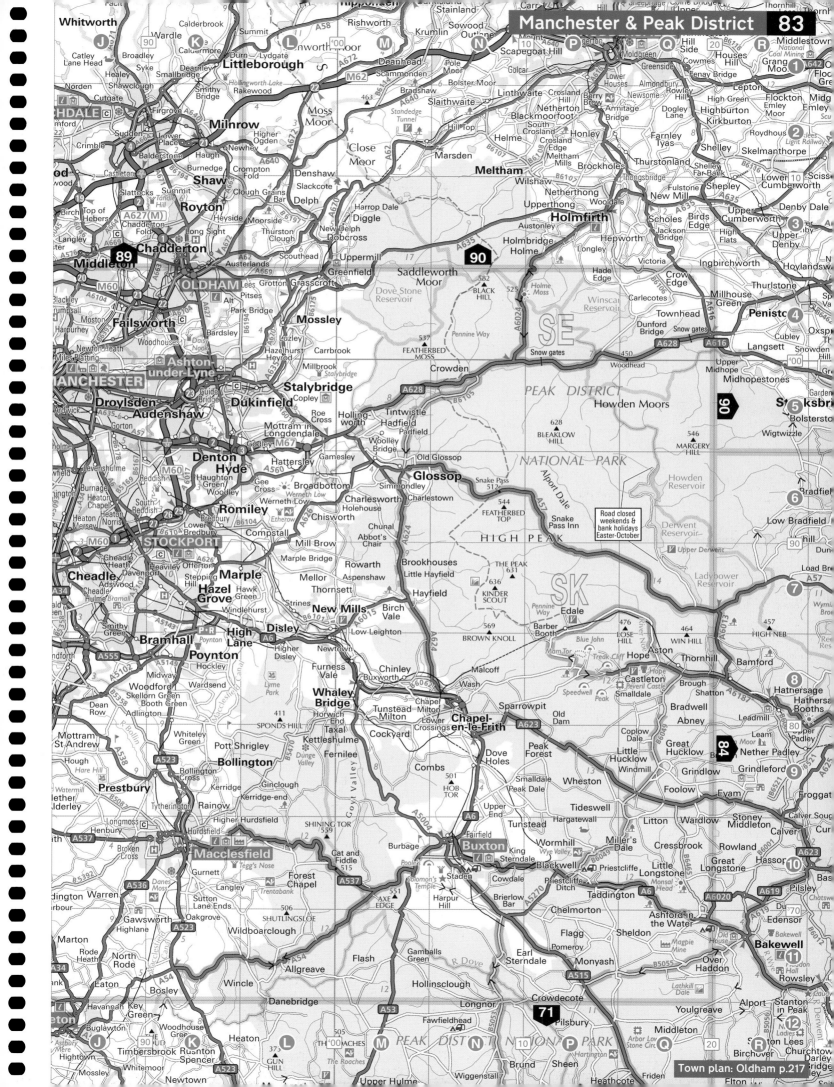

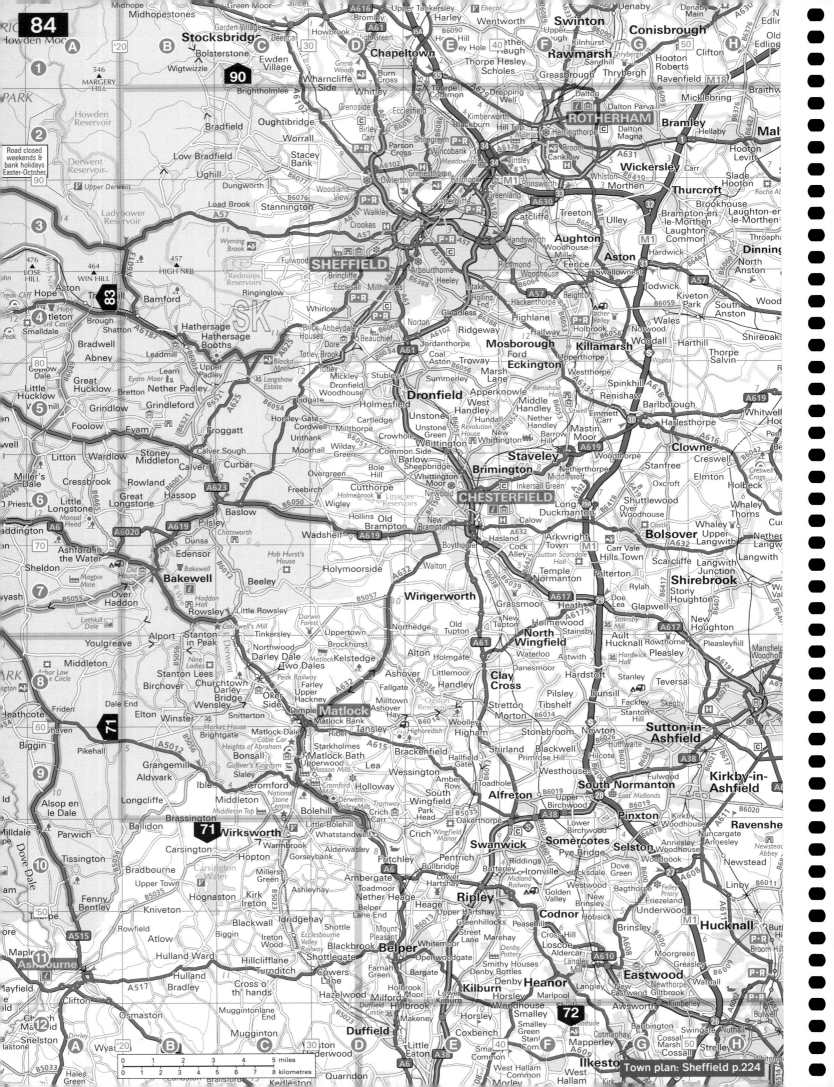

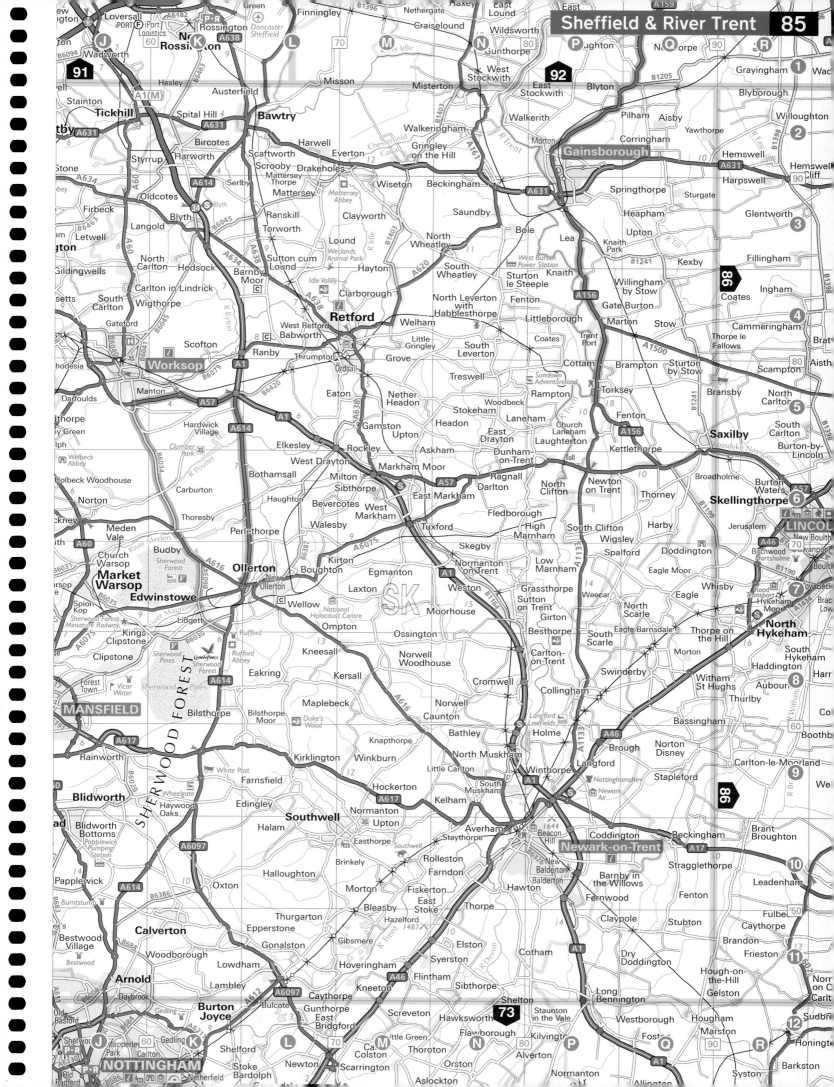

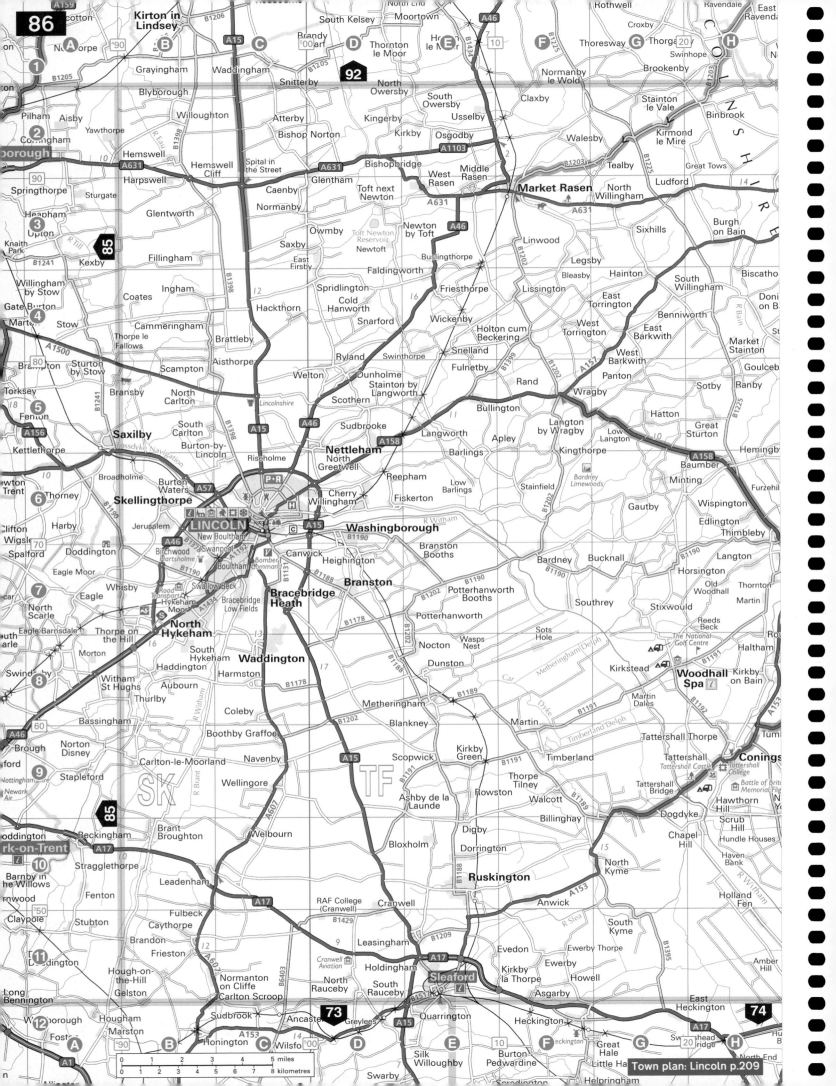

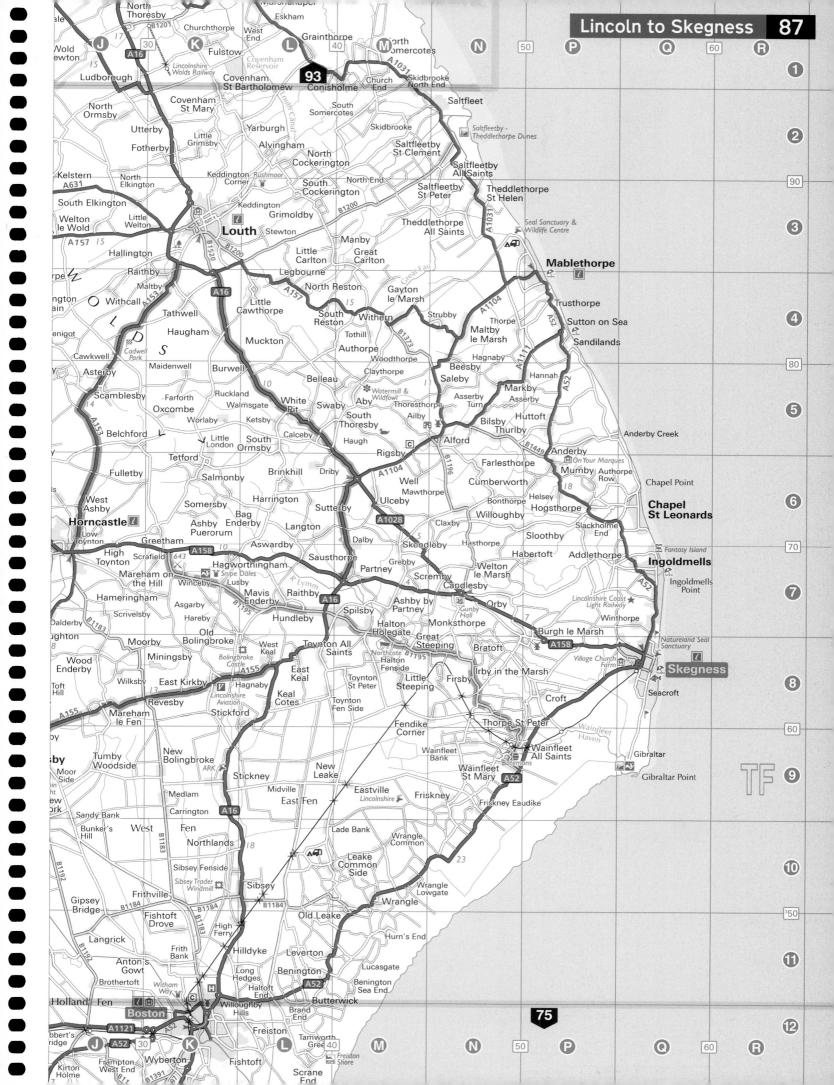

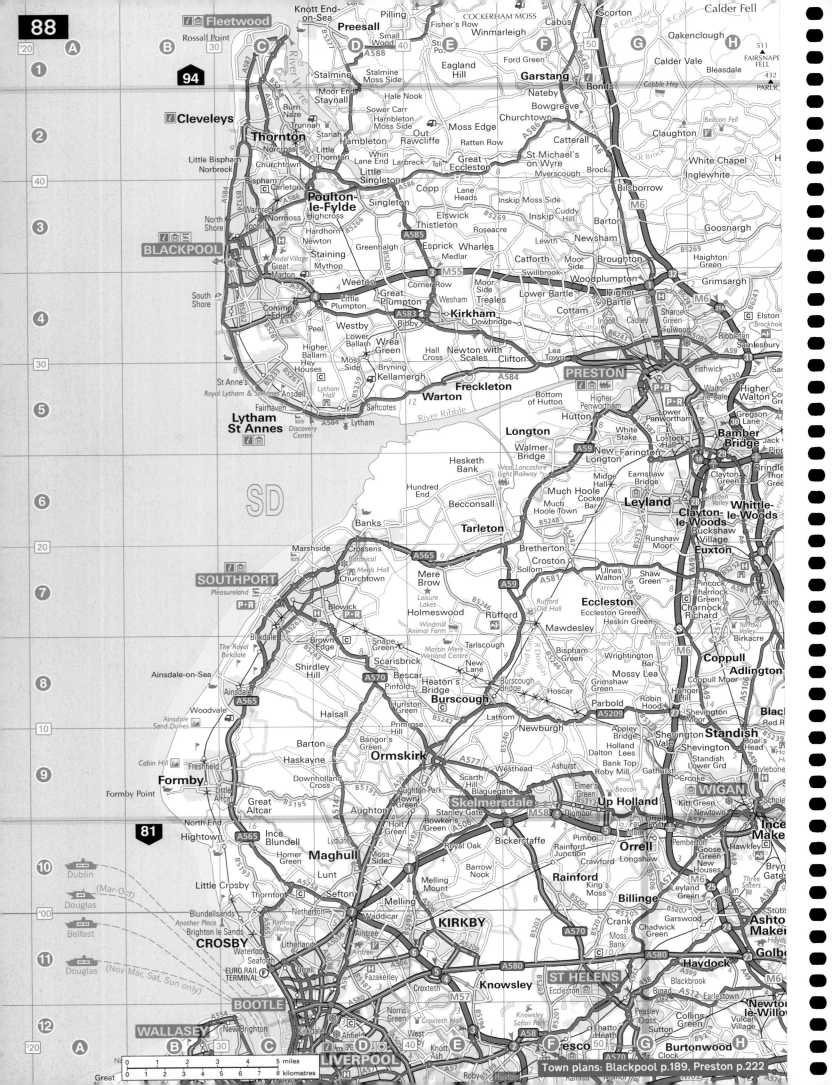

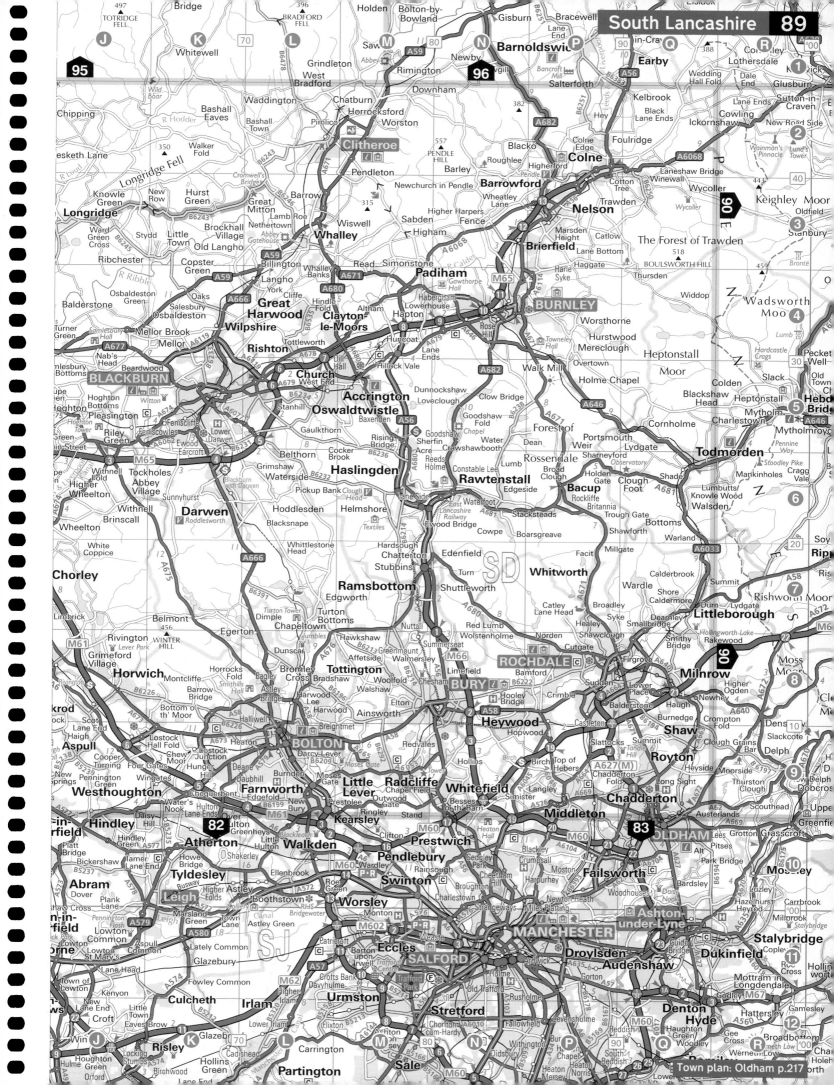

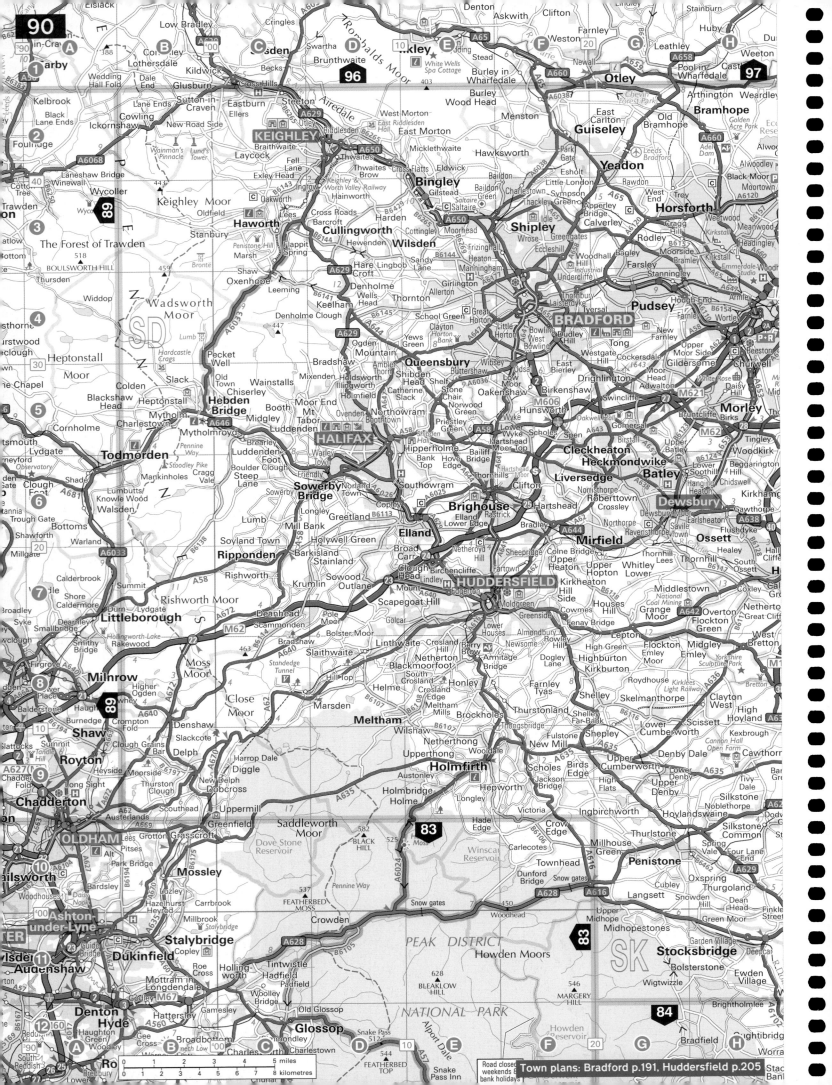

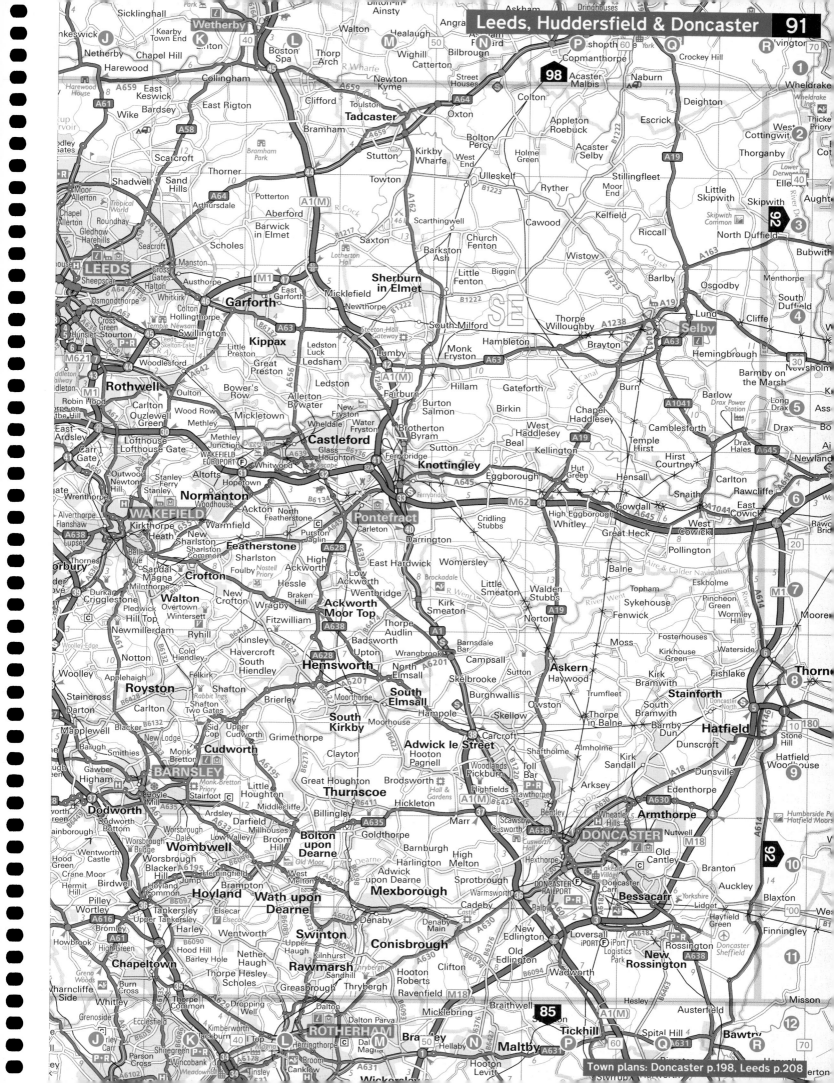

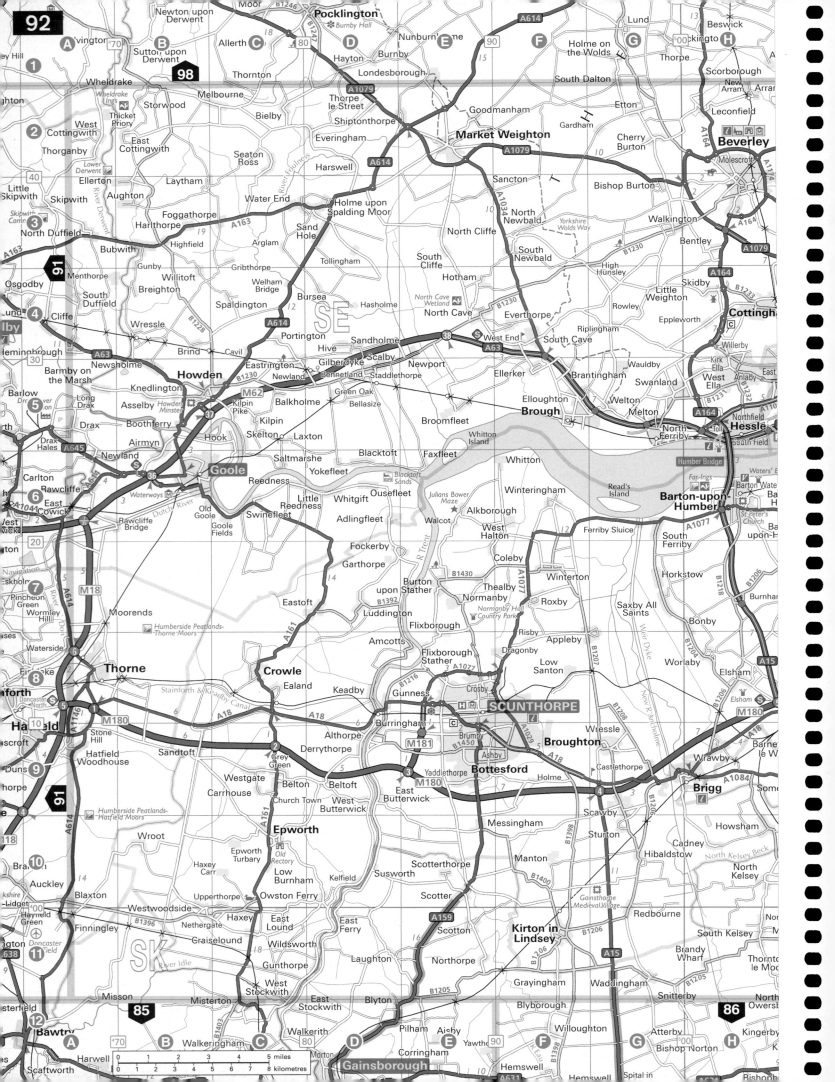

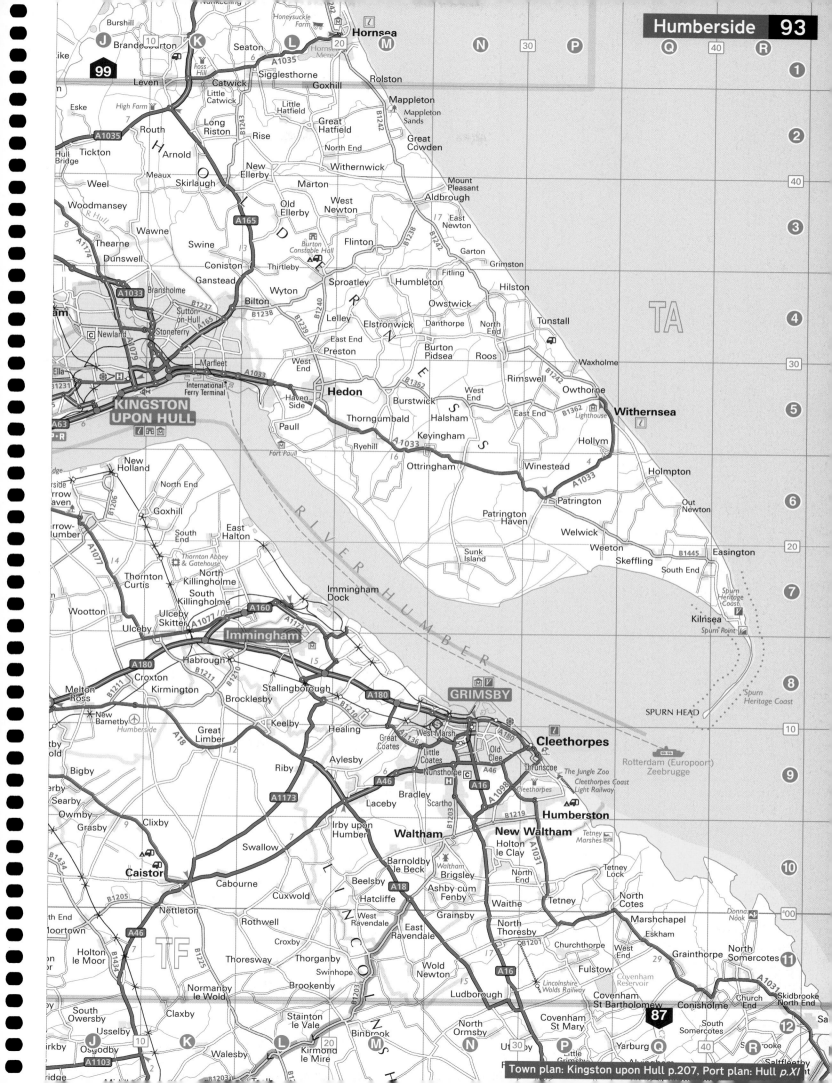

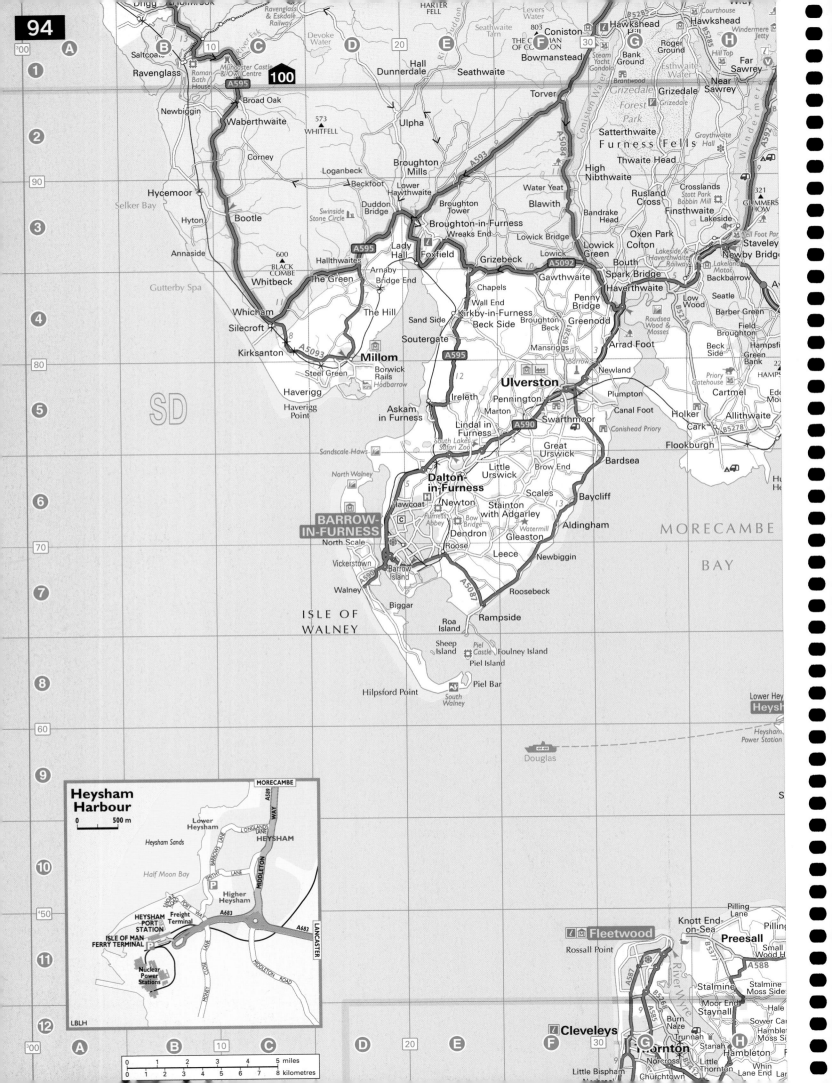

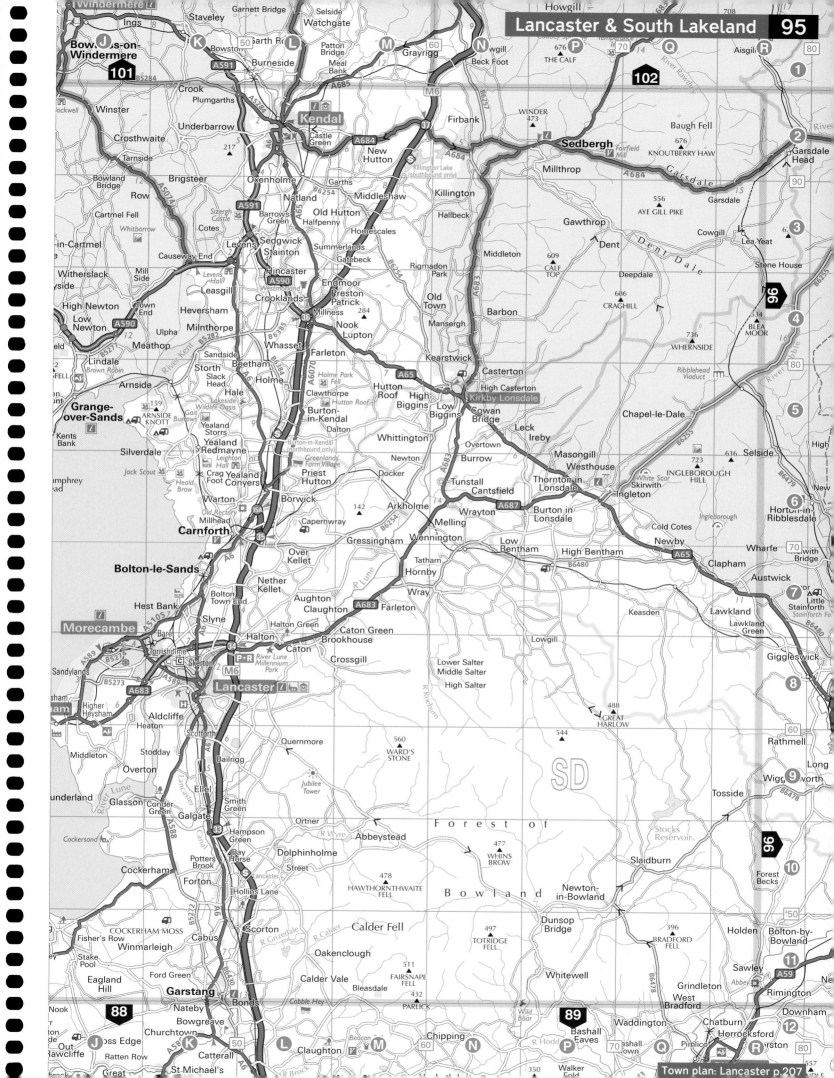

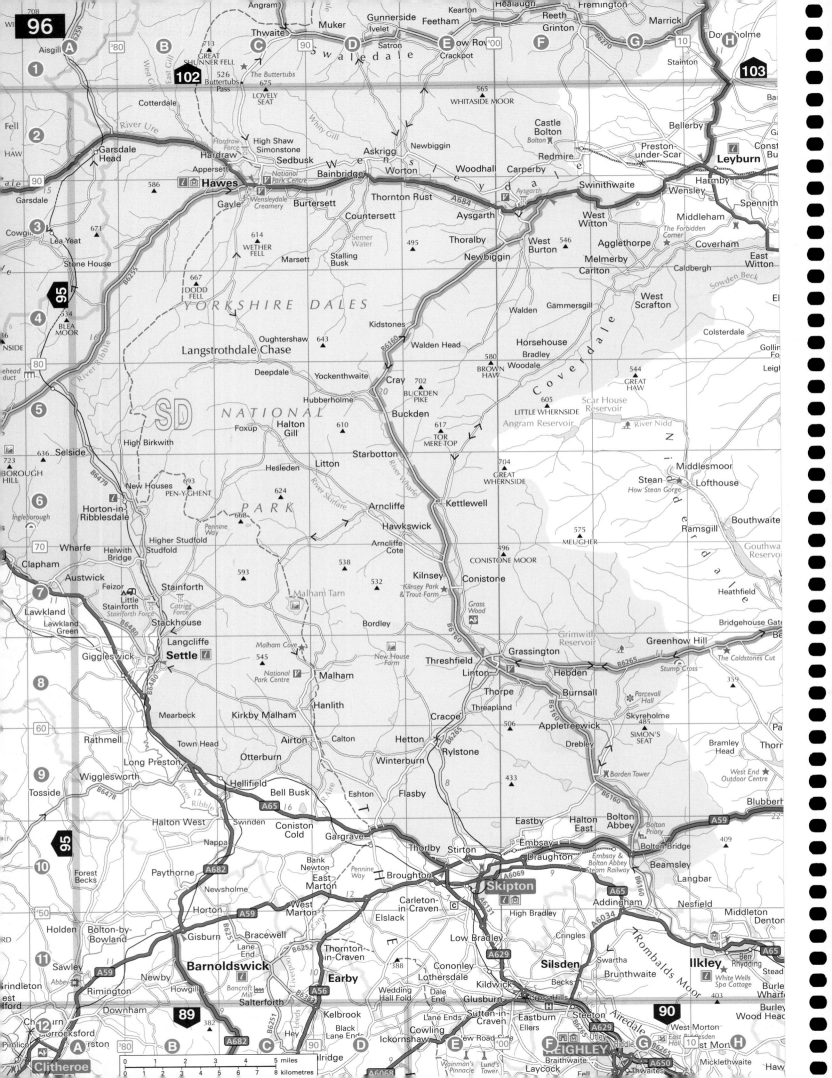

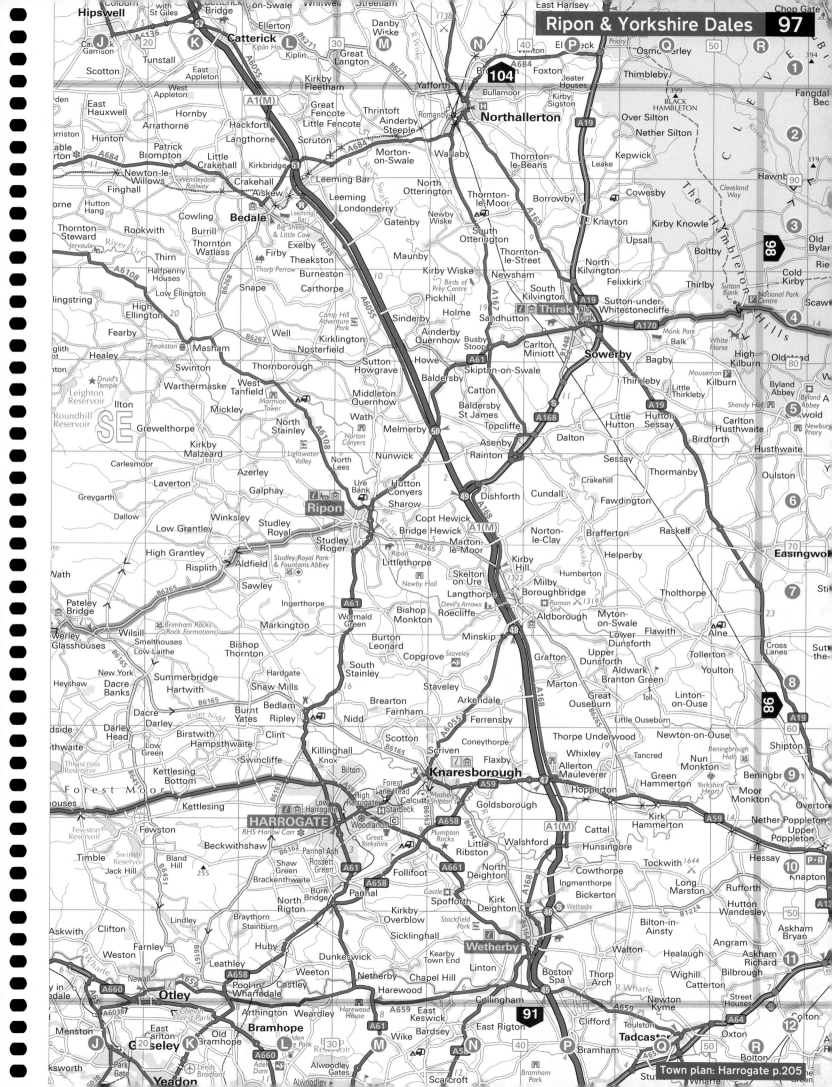

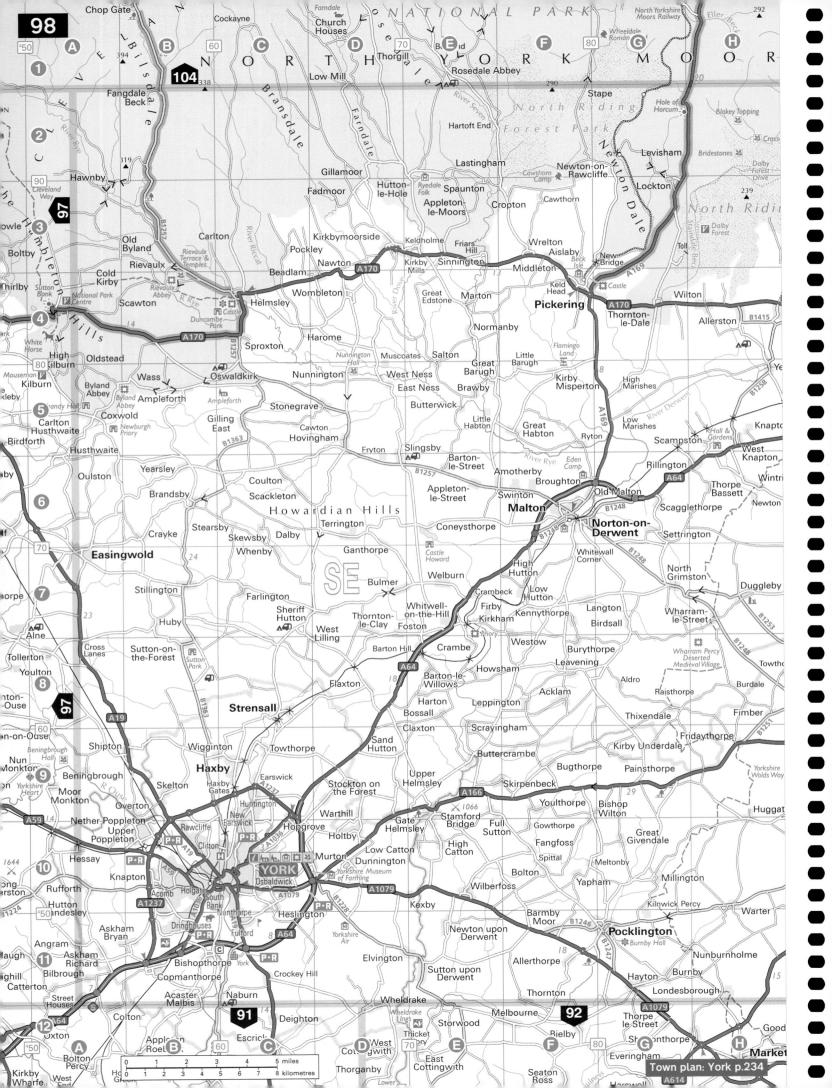

NORTH YORK MOORS NATIONAL PARK

Chop Gate
Cockayne
Farndale
Church Houses
Thorgill
Rosedale Abbey
End
North Yorkshire Moors Railway
292
Eller Beck
Wheeldale Roman
Fangdale Beck
104
Low Mill
Stape
Hole of Horcum
Blakey Topping
Bridestones
Cross
Hawnby
Cleveland Way
Gillamoor
Fadmoor
Hutton-le-Hole
Ryedale Folk
Spaunton
Cawthorn Camp
Newton-on-Rawcliffe
Levisham
Dalby Forest Drive
Lastingham
Hartoft End
North Riding Forest Park
Lockton
North Riding
Boltby
Old Byland
Carlton
Kirkbymoorside
Keldholme
Wrelton
Aislaby
New Bridge
Toll
Dalby Forest
239
Thirlby
Rievaulx Terrace & Temples
Pockley
Nawton
Kirkby Mills
Sinnington
Middleton
Keld Head
Sutton Bank
National Park Centre
Rievaulx
Beadlam
Friars Hill
Isle
Castle
Cold Kirby
Rievaulx Abbey
Scawton
Helmsley
Wombleton
Great Edstone
Marton
Pickering
Thornton-le-Dale
Wilton
Allerston
White Horse
Duncombe Park
Normanby
A170
High Kilburn
Oldstead
Sproxton
Harome
Nunnington Hall
Muscoates
Salton
Little Barugh
Flamingo Land
Mouseman
Kilburn
Wass
Oswaldkirk
Nunnington
West Ness
Great Barugh
Kirby Misperton
High Marishes
Byland Abbey
Ampleforth
East Ness
Brawby
Coxwold
Stonegrave
Butterwick
Little Habton
Great Habton
Low Marishes
Carlton Husthwaite
Newburgh Priory
Gilling East
Cawton
Hovingham
Fryton
Slingsby
Barton-le-Street
Great Habton
Ryton
Scampston
Hall & Gardens
West Knapton
Knapton
Birdforth
Husthwaite
Oulston
Yearsley
Coulton
Scackleton
Amotherby
Broughton
Old Malton
Thorpe Bassett
Newton
Easingwold
Brandsby
Stearsby
Skewsby
Dalby
Terrington
Coneysthorpe
Swinton
Malton
Norton-on-Derwent
Scagglethorpe
Settrington
Crayke
Whenby
Ganthorpe
Castle Howard
Welburn
High Hutton
Whitewall Corner
North Grimston
Duggleby
Stillington
Farlington
Bulmer
Crambeck
Low Hutton
Langton
Birdsall
Wharram-le-Street
Sheriff Hutton
Thornton-le-Clay
Whitwell-on-the-Hill
Firby
Kirkham
Kennythorpe
Huby
West Lilling
Foston
Priory
Westow
Burythorpe
Wharram Percy Deserted Medieval Village
Cross Lanes
Alne
Sutton-on-the-Forest
Sutton Park
Barton Hill
Crambe
Howsham
Leavening
Raisthorpe
Burdale
Tollerton
Youlton
Flaxton
Barton-le-Willows
Harton
Acklam
Aldro
Towthorpe
Strensall
Bossall
Leppington
Thixendale
Fimber
Shipton
Wigginton
Towthorpe
Claxton
Scrayingham
Kirby Underdale
Fridaythorpe
Beningbrough Hall
Sand Hutton
Buttercrambe
Bugthorpe
Painsthorpe
Yorkshire Wolds Way
Nun Monkton
Haxby
Earswick
Stockton on the Forest
Upper Helmsley
Skirpenbeck
A166
Youlthorpe
Bishop Wilton
Huggat
Beningbrough
Skelton
Haxby Gates
Huntington
Warthill
Gate Helmsley
Stamford Bridge
Full Sutton
Gowthorpe
Fangfoss
Great Givendale
Yorkshire Heart
Moor Monkton
Overton
New Earswick
Hopgrove
Holtby
High Catton
Spittal
Meltonby
Nether Poppleton
Upper Poppleton
Rawcliffe
Clifton
Murton
Low Catton
Dunnington
Yorkshire Museum of Farming
Bolton
Yapham
Millington
Hessay
YORK
Osbaldwick
Wilberfoss
Knapton
Acomb
Holgate
South Bank
Nunthorpe
Heslington
Newton upon Derwent
Barmby Moor
Kilnwick Percy
Warter
Rufforth
Ruston
Hutton Wandesley
Dringhouses
York
Kexby
Pocklington
Burnby Hall
Nunburnholme
Askham Bryan
Fulford
Yorkshire Air
Angram
Askham Richard
Bishopthorpe
Elvington
Sutton upon Derwent
Allerthorpe
Hayton
Burnby
Bilbrough
Copmanthorpe
Crockey Hill
Thornton
Londesborough
Catterton
Acaster Malbis
Naburn
Wheldrake
Melbourne
Thorpe le Street
Street Houses
91
Deighton
Escrick
Wheldrake Ings
Storwood
Bielby
92
Everingham
Bolton Percy
Colton
Appleton Roebuck
Thorganby
West Cottingwith
Thornton
Seaton Ross

Scale: 0 1 2 3 4 5 miles / 0 1 2 3 4 5 6 7 8 kilometres

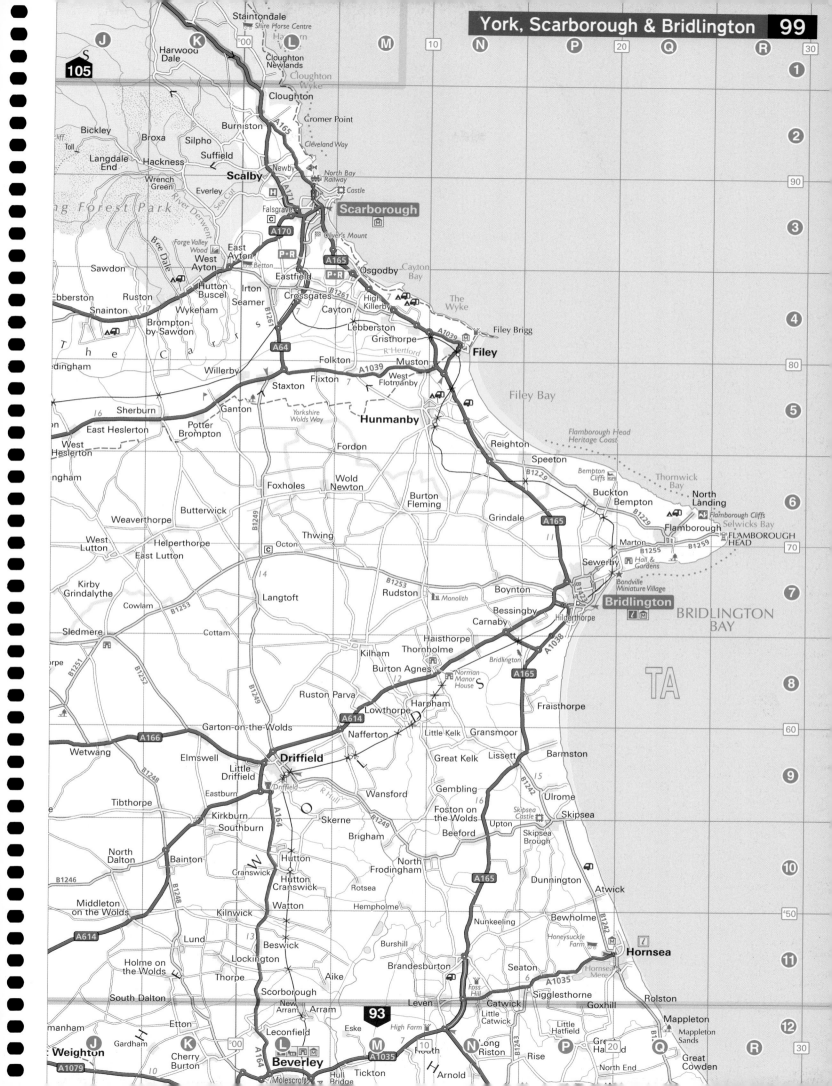

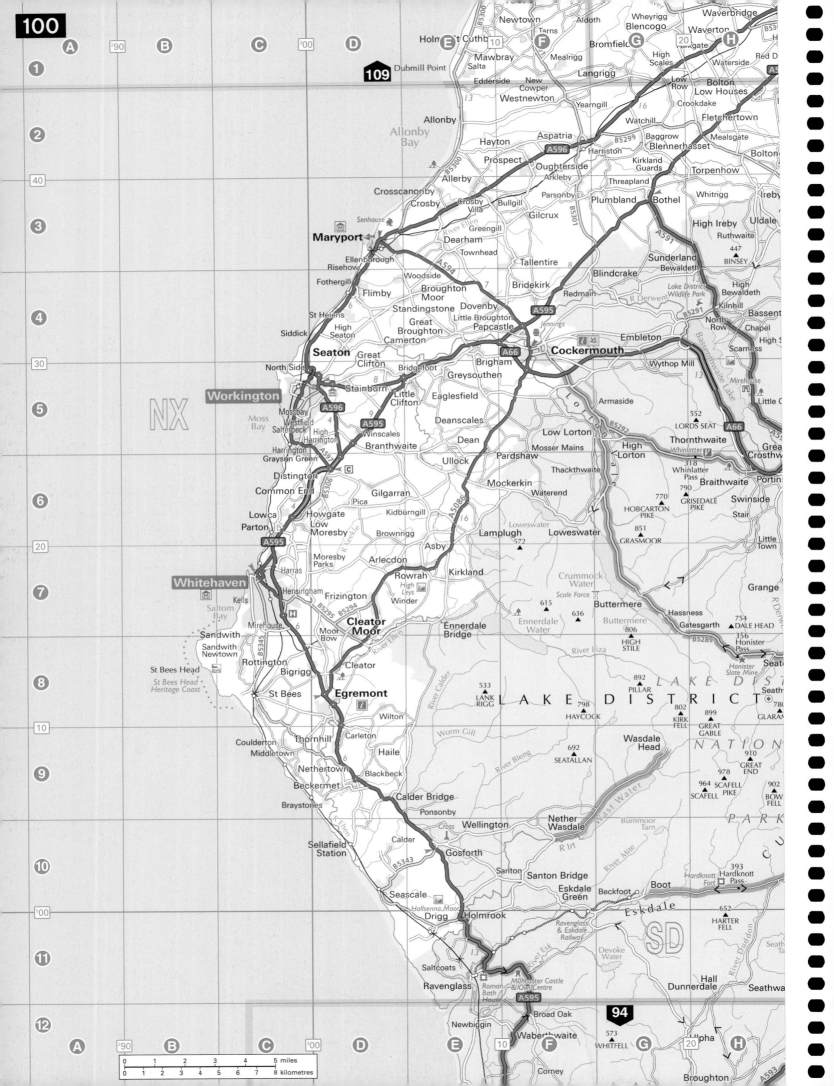

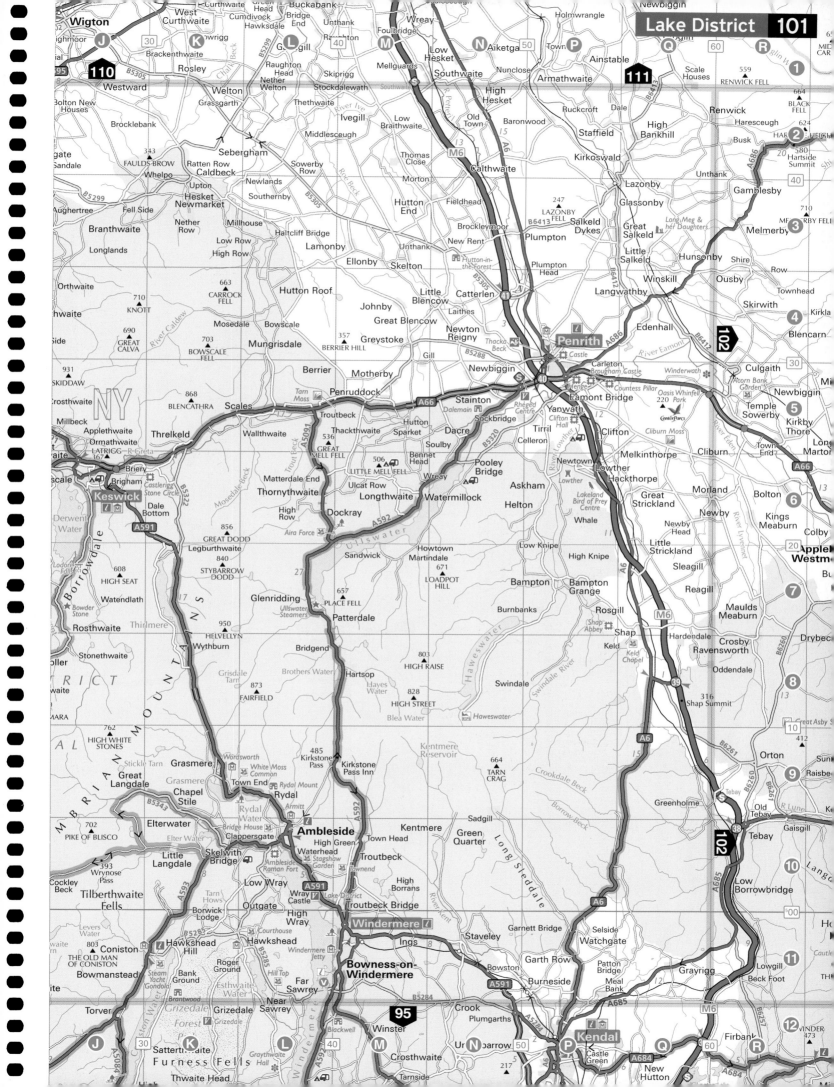

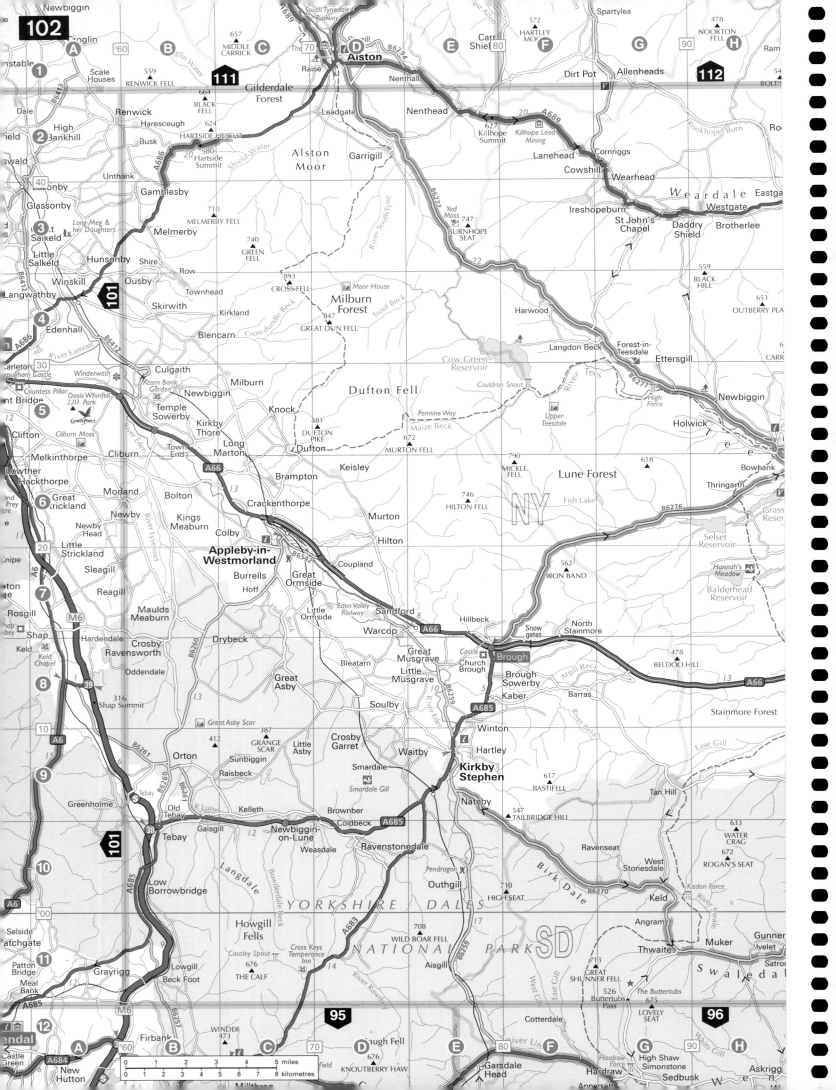

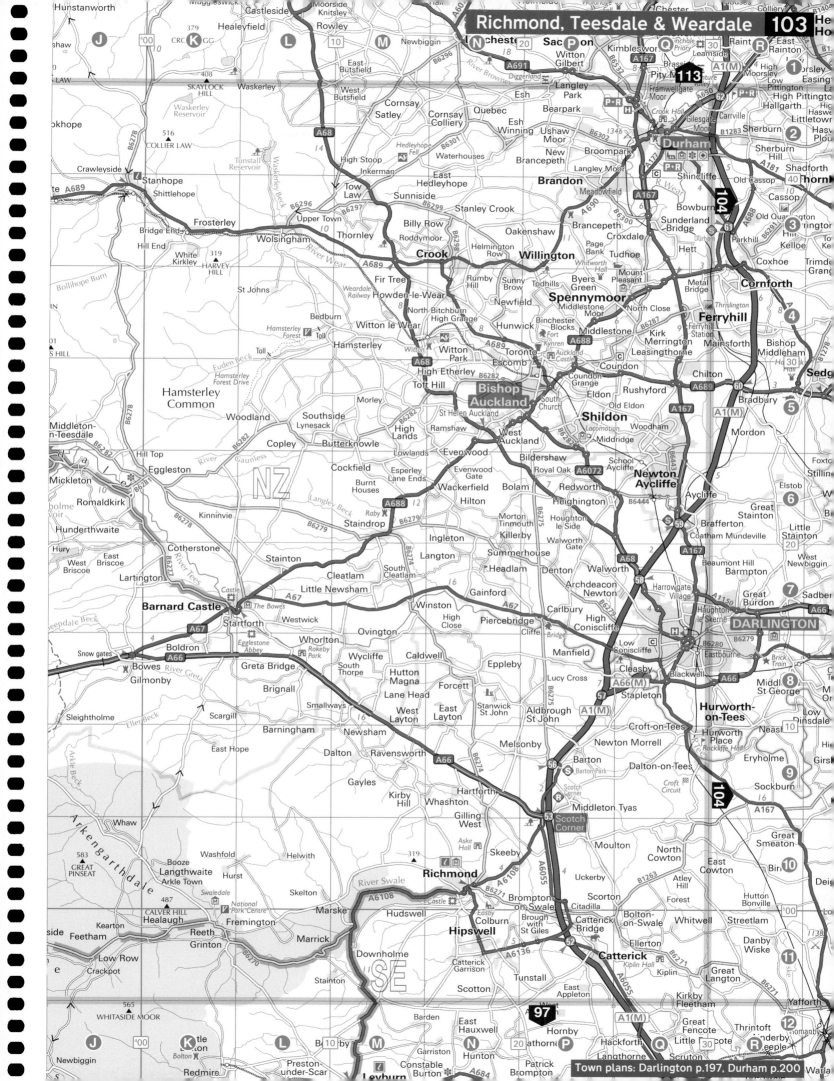

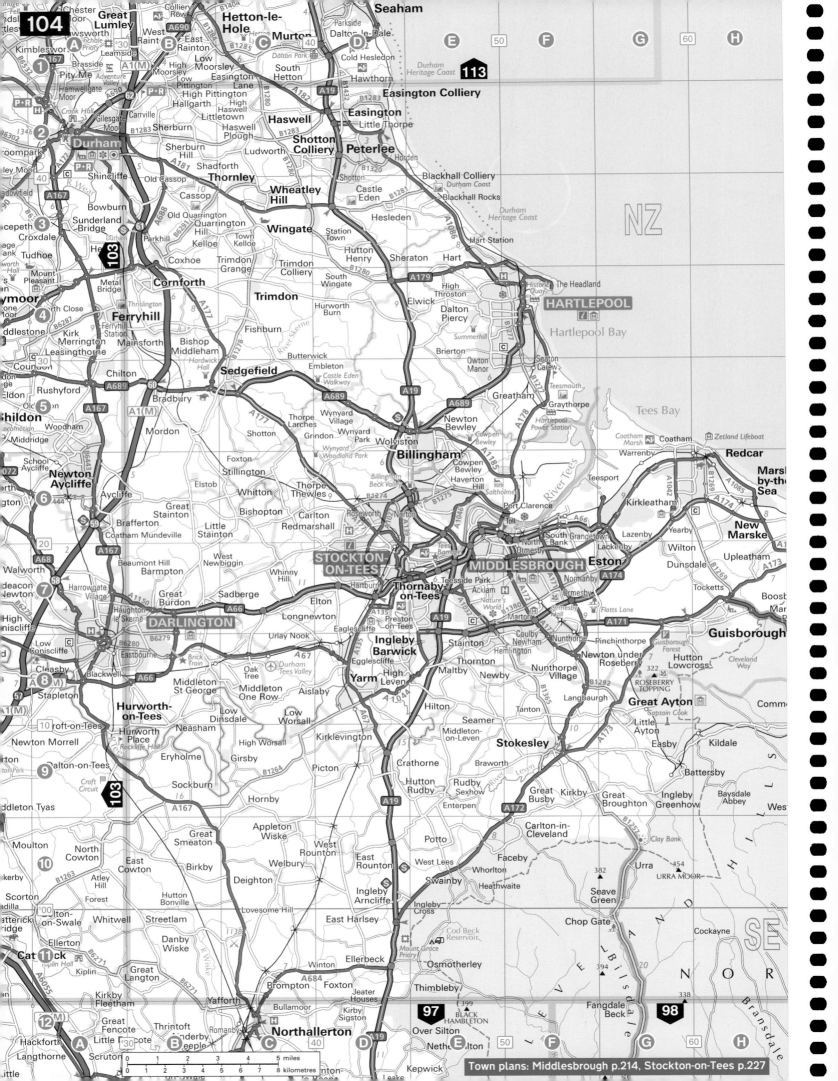

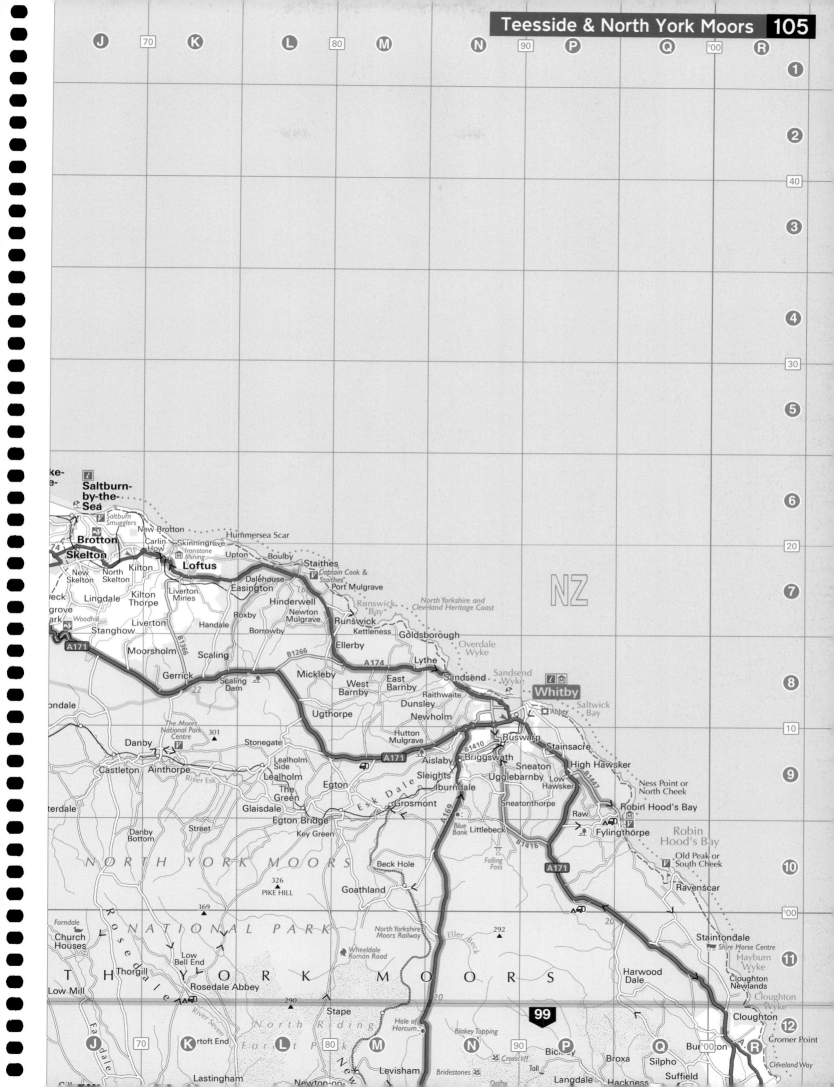

J 70 K L 80 M N 90 P Q 500 R

NZ

North Yorkshire and
Cleveland Heritage Coast

Saltburn-by-the-Sea
Saltburn Smugglers
New Brotton
Brotton
Skelton
Carlin How
Skinningrove
Ironstone Mining
Upton
Boulby
Hummersea Scar
Loftus
New Skelton
North Skelton
Kilton
Kilton Thorpe
Lingdale
Liverton Mines
Dalehouse
Easington
Staithes
Captain Cook & Staithes
Port Mulgrave
Woodhill
Stanghow
Liverton
Handale
Roxby
Hinderwell
Newton Mulgrave
Runswick Bay
Runswick
Kettleness
Goldsborough
Overdale Wyke
Moorsholm
Scaling
B1266
Ellerby
A174
Lythe
Sandsend
Sandsend Wyke
Gerrick
Scaling Dam
Mickleby
West Barnby
East Barnby
Raithwaite
Whitby
Abbey
Saltwick Bay
Ugthorpe
Dunsley
Newholm
Hutton Mulgrave
Ruswarp
Stainsacre
The Moors National Park Centre
301
Danby
Stonegate
B1410
Aislaby
Briggswath
Sneaton
High Hawsker
Castleton
Ainthorpe
Lealholm Side
Lealholm
Egton
Sleights
Iburndale
Ugglebarnby
Low Hawsker
Ness Point or North Cheek
River Esk
The Green
Grosmont
Esk Dale
Sneatonthorpe
Robin Hood's Bay
Glaisdale
Egton Bridge
Key Green
A169
Littlebeck
Raw
Fylingthorpe
Danby Bottom
Street
Blue Bank
Falling Foss
B1416
Old Peak or South Cheek
Robin Hood's Bay
NORTH YORK MOORS
Beck Hole
A171
Farndale
326 PIKE HILL
Goathland
Ravenscar
369
NATIONAL PARK
North Yorkshire Moors Railway
Eller Beck
292
Staintondale
Church Houses
Wheeldale Roman Road
Shire Horse Centre
Hayburn Wyke
Low Bell End
Thorgill
THE YORK MOORS
Harwood Dale
Cloughton Newlands
Low Mill
Rosedale Abbey
River Seven
Cloughton Wyke
290
North Riding
Stape
Hole of Horcum
Cloughton
Forest Park
Cromer Point
J 70 K rtoft End L 80 M N 90 P cy Q Bur on R
Lastingham
Levisham
Blakey Topping
Crosscliff
Bridestones
Dalby
Broxa
Silpho
Suffield
Cleveland Way
Newton-on-
Langdale
Hackness

99

1 2 40 3 30 4 5 20 6 7 8 10 9 500 10 11 12

Barrh

Ballantrae Heronsford Water of Tig

10

114

Currarie Port

Belfast

Larne

BENERAIRD 437

CARLOCK HILL 321

ALTIMEG HILL 387

BENBRAKE HILL 305

Milleur Point

Corsewall Point Lady Bay

Glen App Southern Upland Way

Barnhills Portencalzie Glenwhilly Laggangairn Standing Stones

B738

Kirkcolm Cairnryan

A77 17

Penwhirn Reservoir

Ervie Loch Connell Low Barbeth Low Salchrie

ARTFIELD FELL 271

Braid Fell

Knocknain Leswalt Beoch Burn

New Luce

Loch Ryan

Balgracie Innermessan

Auchnotteroch Castle of St John A751 Black Loch Castle Kennedy Chlenry CRAIG FELL 164

Stranraer Aird White Loch Castle Kennedy

Portslogan A75 10 Glenluce Abbey

Broadsea Bay Glenwhan Dunragit Glenluce

NW Lochans Kildrochet House Whitecrook A747

Black Head CAIRN PAT 181 Piltanton Burn B7084

Dunskey 8 14 B7077 Ringdoo Point Milton

Portpatrick A77 A716 19 B7084 Luce Sands Stairhaven

Stoneykirk Auchenmalg

North Milmain 18 Mull of Sinniness Auchenmalg Bay

Sandhead

Cairngarroch LUCE BA

Money Head Kirkmadrine Stones

High Ardwell Ardwell

Ardwell Bay Chapel Rossan

Drumbreddon Balgowan

Logan

Port Logan Bay A716

Port Logan B7065

Garrochtrie Kilstay

Clanyard Bay Drummore

Laggantalluch Head Kirkmaiden Cailiness Point

Barncorkrie High Drummore

Damnaglaur Maryport

Cardryne B7041

Cardrain West Cairngaan

MULL OF GALLOWAY

0 1 2 3 4 5 miles

0 1 2 3 4 5 6 7 8 kilometres

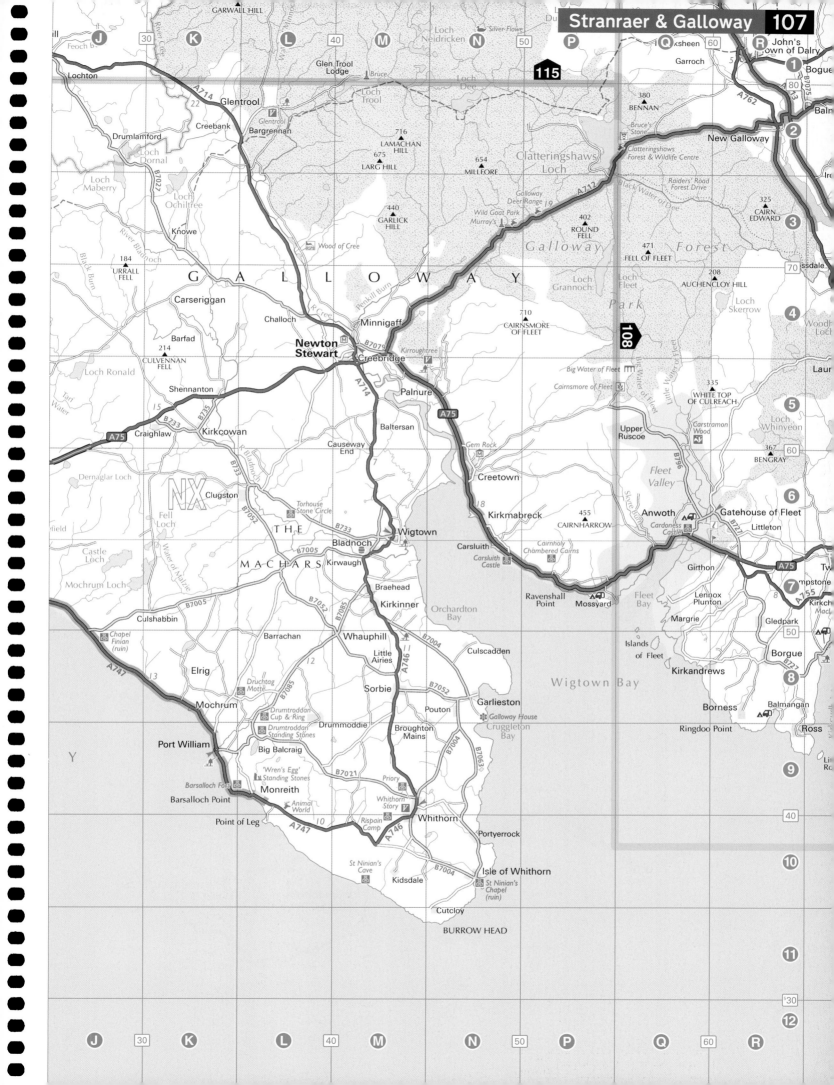

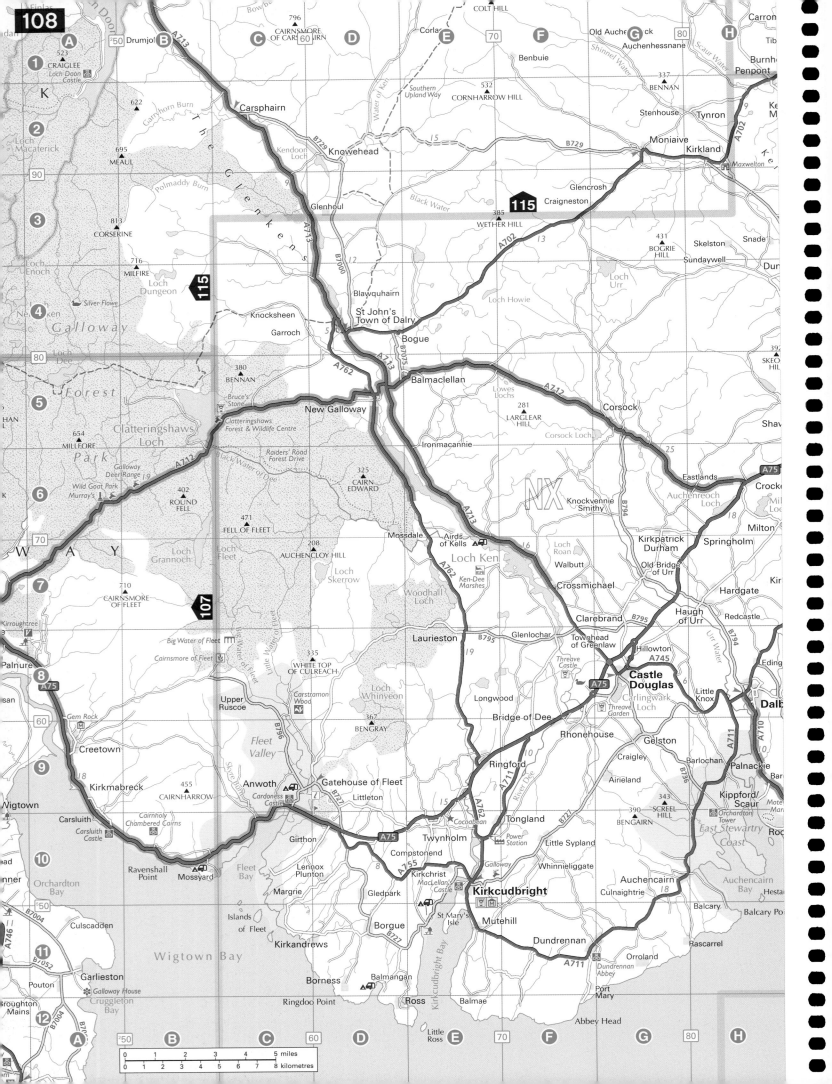

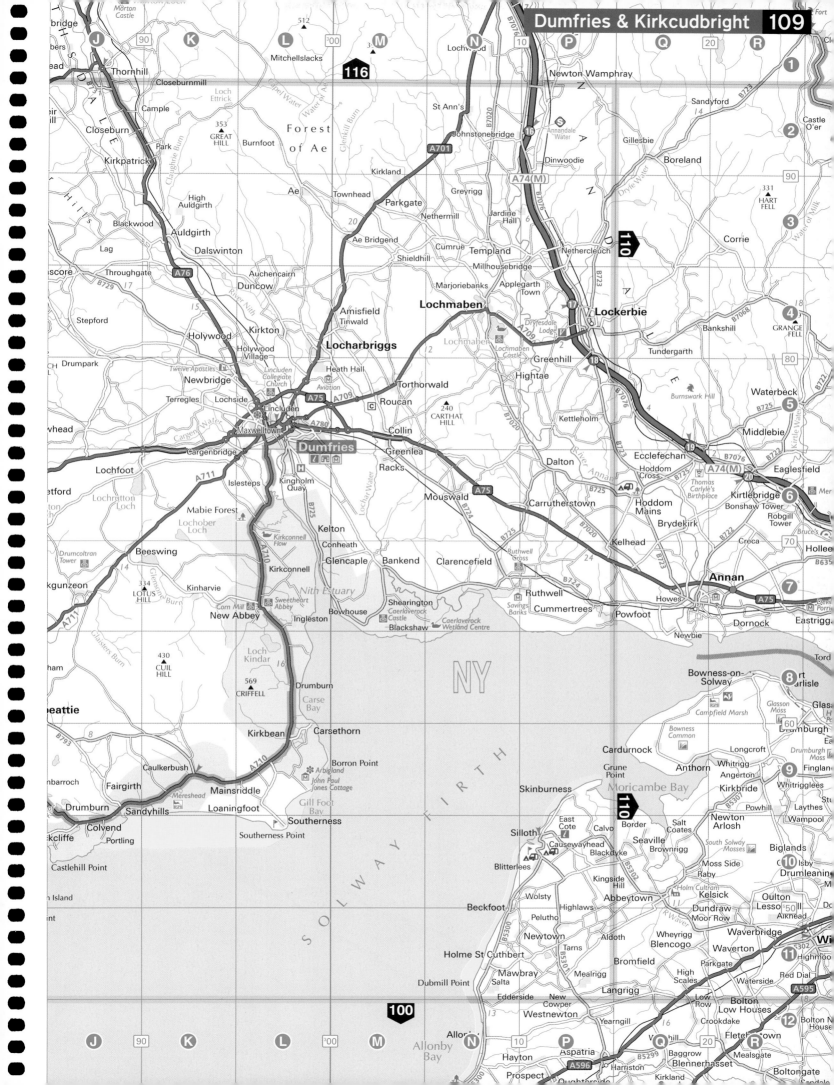

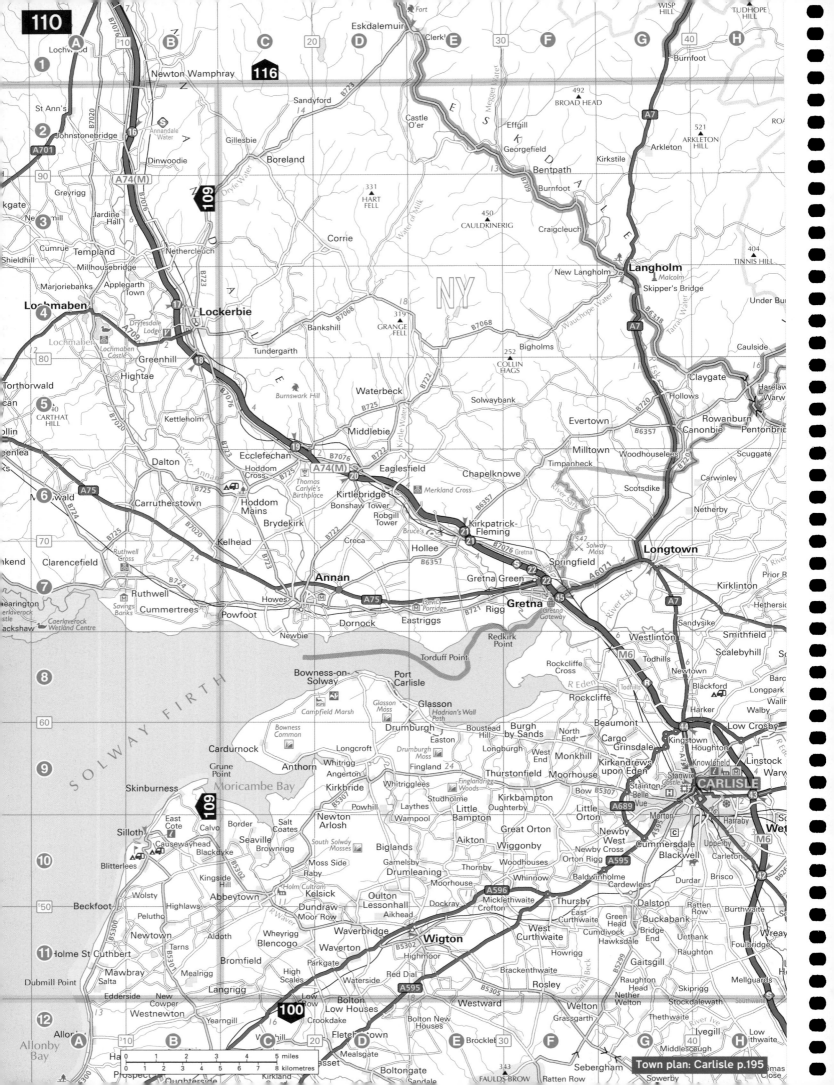

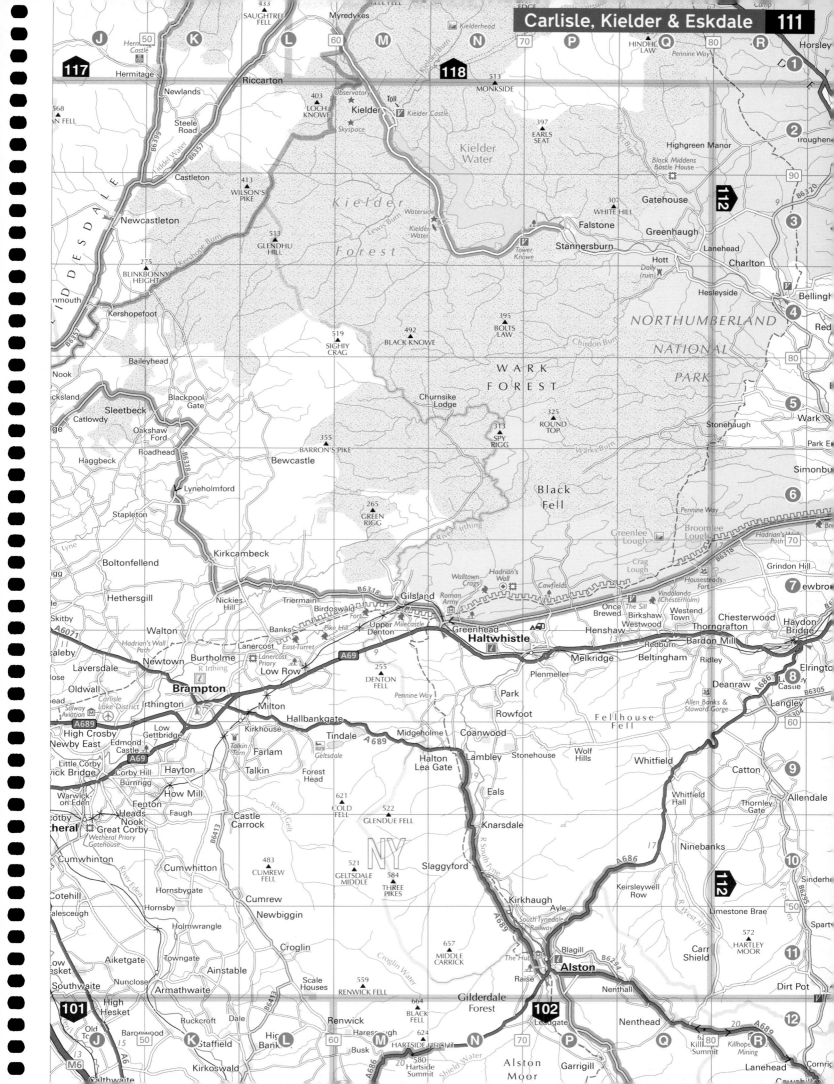

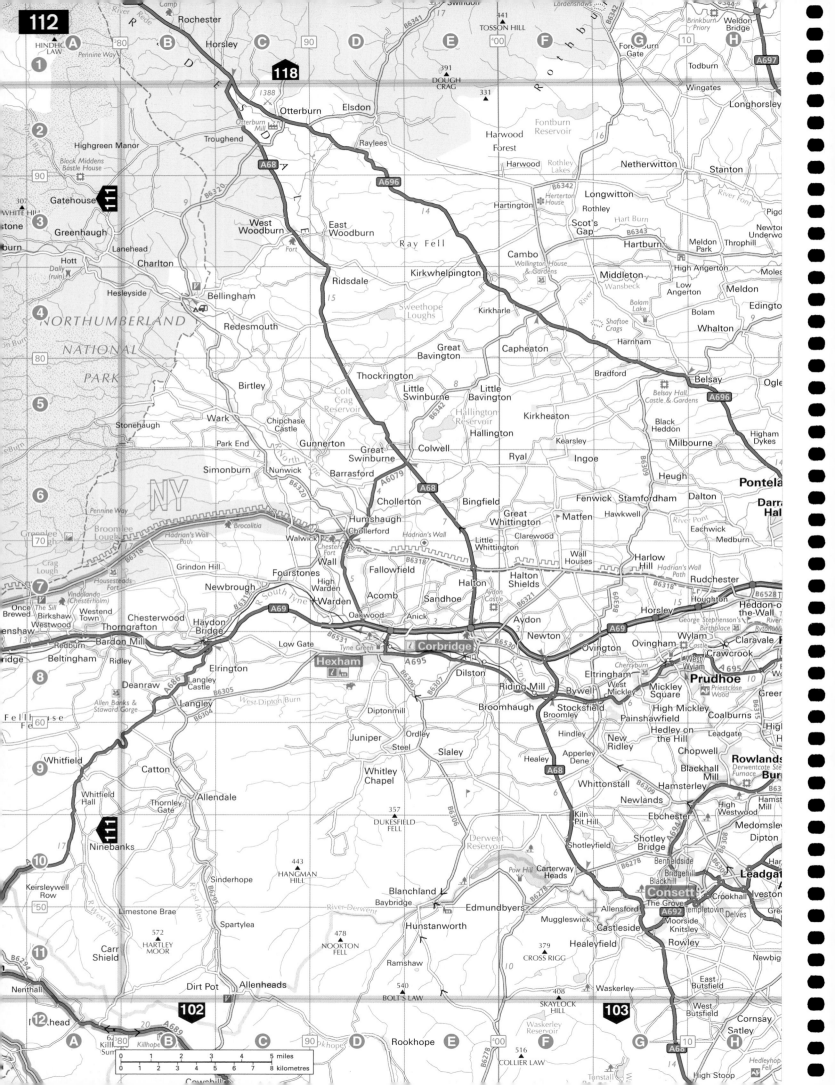

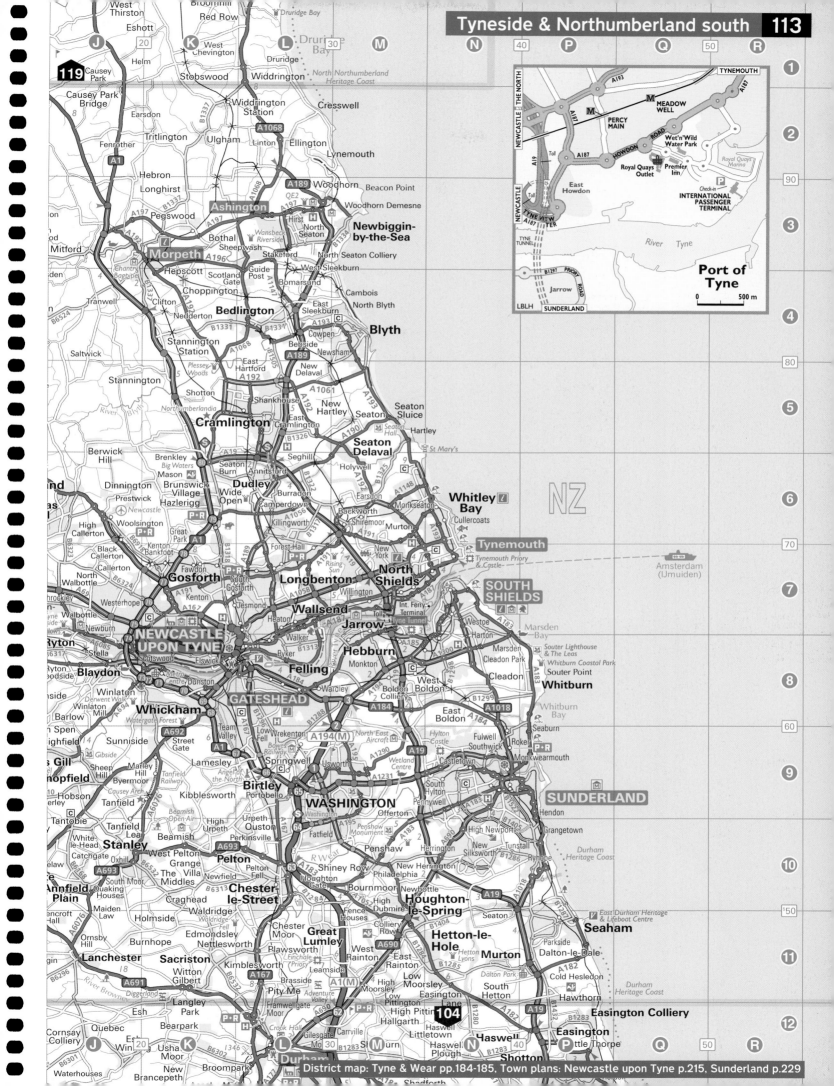

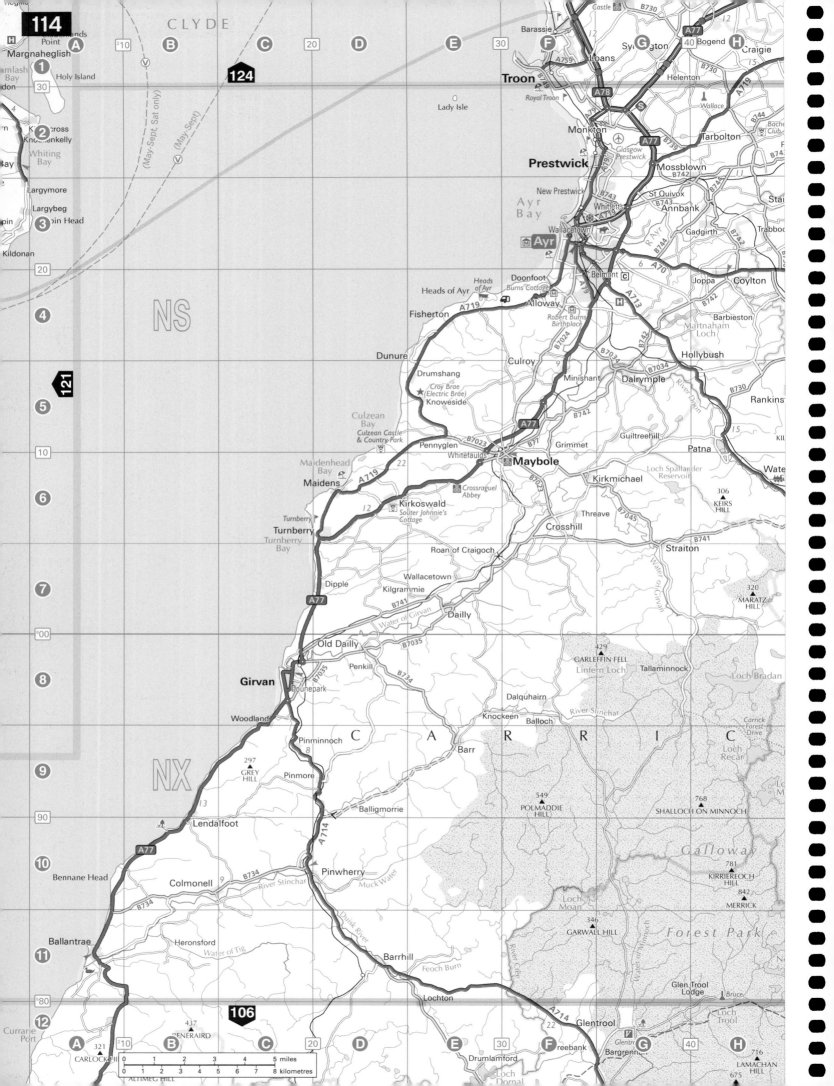

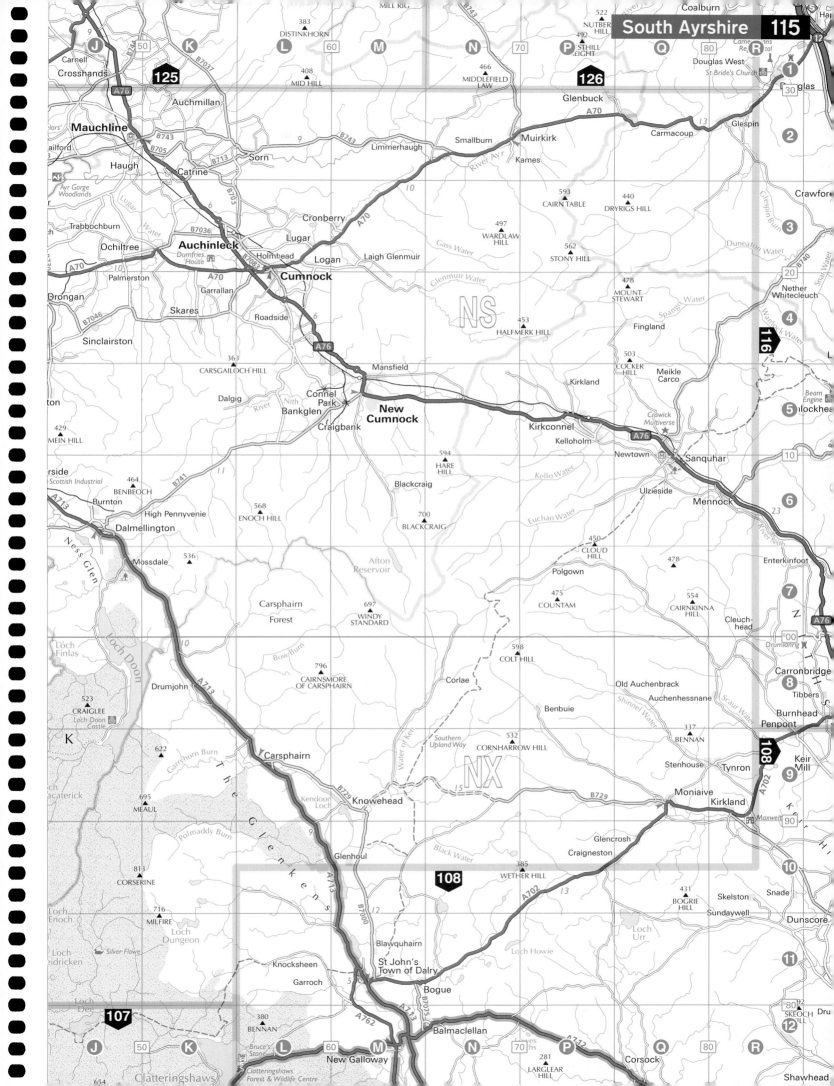

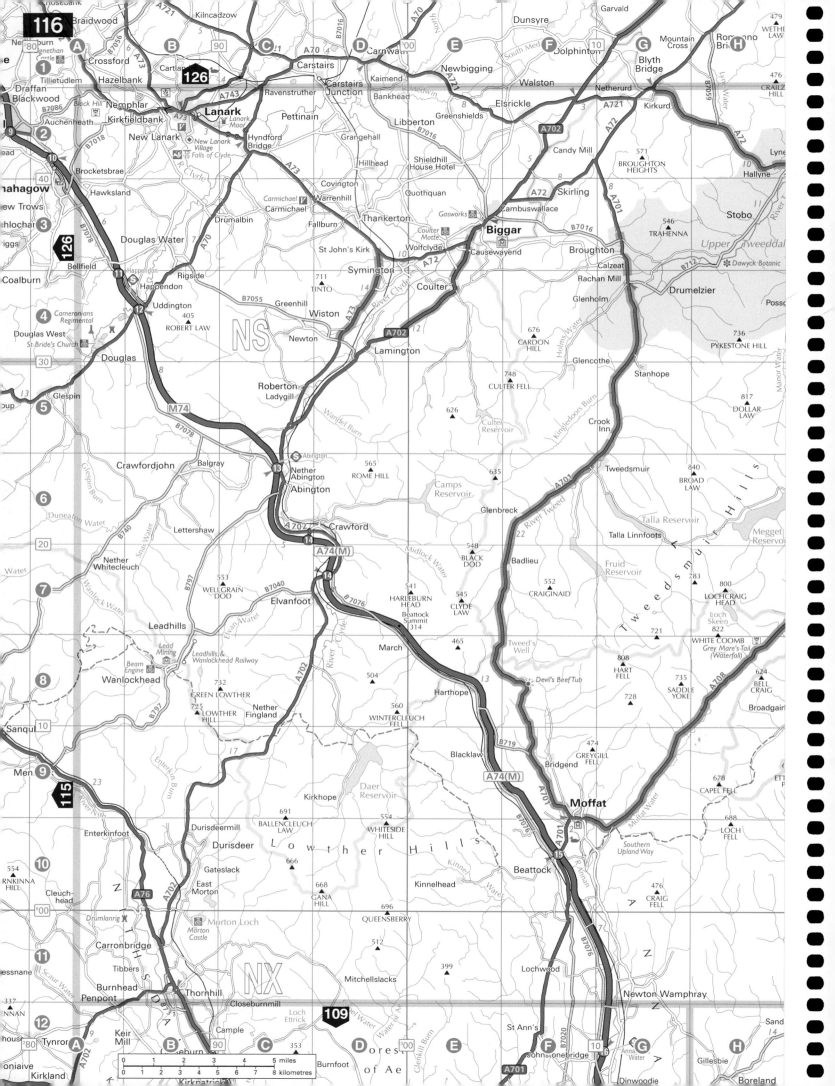

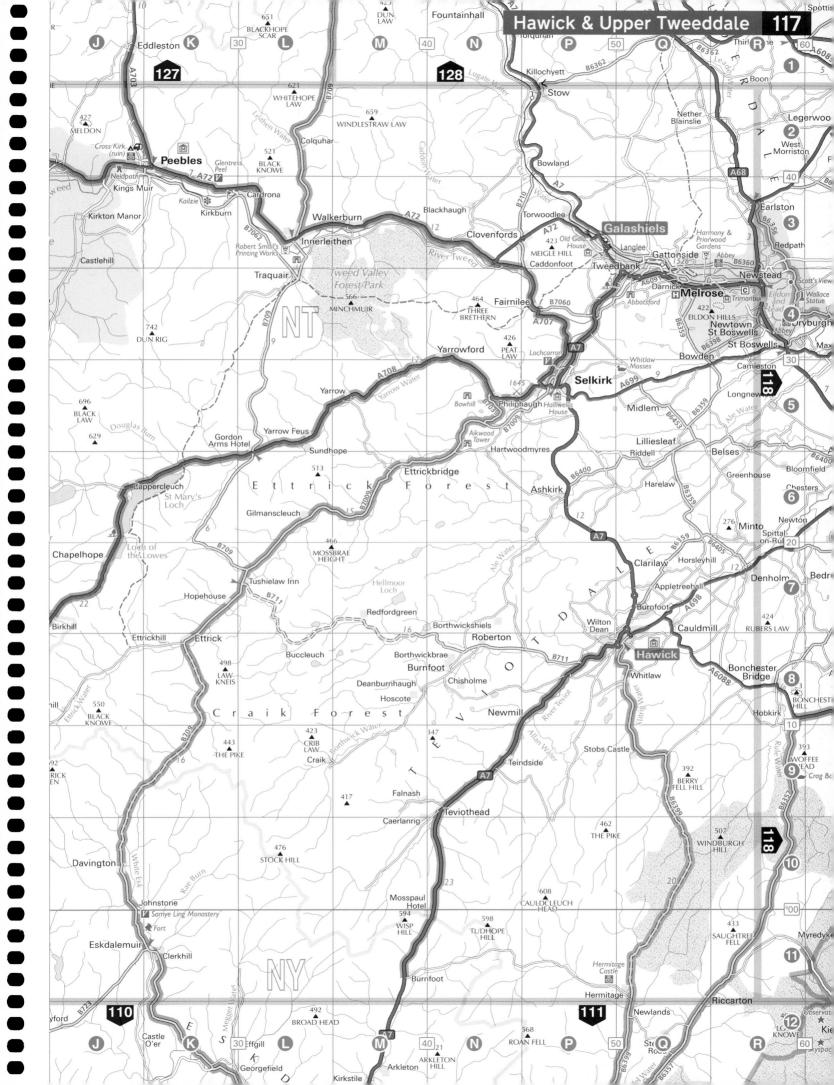

J   K   L   M   N   P   Q   R

127   **128**

1
2
3
4
5
6
7
8
9
10
11
12

Eddleston
651 BLACKHOPE SCAR
427 MELDON
Cross Kirk (ruin)
Peebles
Neidpath
Kings Muir
Kirkton Manor
Castlehill
Glentress Peel
A703
A72
Kailzie
Kirkburn
Cardrona
B7062
Innerleithen
Robert Small's Printing Works
Traquair
NT
566 MINCHMUIR
742 DUN RIG
B709
WHITEHOPE LAW 621
Colquhar
659 WINDLESTRAW LAW
521 BLACK KNOWE
Leithen Water
Caddon Water
Walkerburn
Blackhaugh
A72
Clovenfords
Torwoodlee
River Tweed
464 THREE BRETHREN
Fairnilee
B7060
Yarrowford
426 PEAT LAW
A707
696 BLACK LAW
629
A708
Yarrow
Yarrow Water
Yarrow Feus
Gordon Arms Hotel
Sundhope
Ettrickbridge
513
Cappercleuch
St Mary's Loch
Gilmanscleuch
B7009
466 MOSSBRAE HEIGHT
B709
Loch of the Lowes
Chapelhope
22
Tushielaw Inn
Hopehouse
B711
Hellmoor Loch
Redfordgreen
16
Borthwickshiels
Roberton
Borthwickbrae
Birkhill
Ettrickhill
Ettrick
Buccleuch
498 LAW KNEIS
Burnfoot
Chisholme
Deanburnhaugh
Hoscote
Newmill
550 BLACK KNOWE
Craik Forest
443 THE PIKE
B709
423 CRIB LAW
Craik
417
Falnash
White Esk
Rae Burn
Davington
476 STOCK HILL
Johnstone
Samye Ling Monastery
Fort
Eskdalemuir
Clerkhill
NY
Burnfoot
Megget Water
B723
110
yford
Castle O'er
Effgill
492 BROAD HEAD
Georgefield
Kirkstile
A7
Arkleton
ARKLETON HILL
568 ROAN FELL
111
A7
Mosspaul Hotel
594 WISP HILL
608 CAULDCLEUCH HEAD
598 TUDHOPE HILL
Hermitage Castle
Hermitage
Teviothead
Caerlanrig
462 THE PIKE
Teindside
A7
Stobs Castle
392 BERRY FELL HILL
507 WINDBURGH HILL
433 SAUGHTREE FELL
Riccarton
Newlands
Steele Road

Fountainhall
DUN LAW
A7
Torqunan
Killochyett
B6362
Stow
Lugate Water
Bowland
A7
Nether Blainslie
A68
Earlston
B6356
Redpath
Legerwood
West Morriston
Gala Water
Galashiels
Old Gala House
423 MEIGLE HILL
Caddonfoot
Tweedbank
Langlee
1526
Gattonside
Harmony & Priorwood Gardens
Abbey
B6360
Newstead
Scott's View
A6091
Darnick
Abbotsford
Melrose
422
Trimontium
EILDON HILLS
Newtown St Boswells
B6359
B6398
Dryburgh
Abbey
St Boswells
Bowden
Camieston
Wallace Statue
Max
118
A7
Lochcarron
Whitlaw Mosses
9
Selkirk
A699
Midlem
B6453
Lilliesleaf
Riddell
Longnewton
B6359
Belses
Bloomfield
Greenhouse
Chesters
276 Minto
Newton
Spittal-on-Rule
20
Bowhill
B7039
Philiphaugh
Hartwoodmyres
Aikwood Tower
B7009
Halliwell's House
Ashkirk
B6400
Harelaw
12
A7
Clarilaw
Horsleyhill
12
Denholm
Bedr
424 RUBERS LAW
Appletreehall
A698
Burnfoot
B6359
B6405
Wilton Dean
Cauldmill
B711
Hawick
Whitlaw
A6088
Bonchester Bridge
BONCHESTER HILL
Hobkirk
10
TWOFFEE HEAD
393
Rule Water
B6357
Crag Bo
600
Myredyke
Observa
LOCH KNOWE
Kie

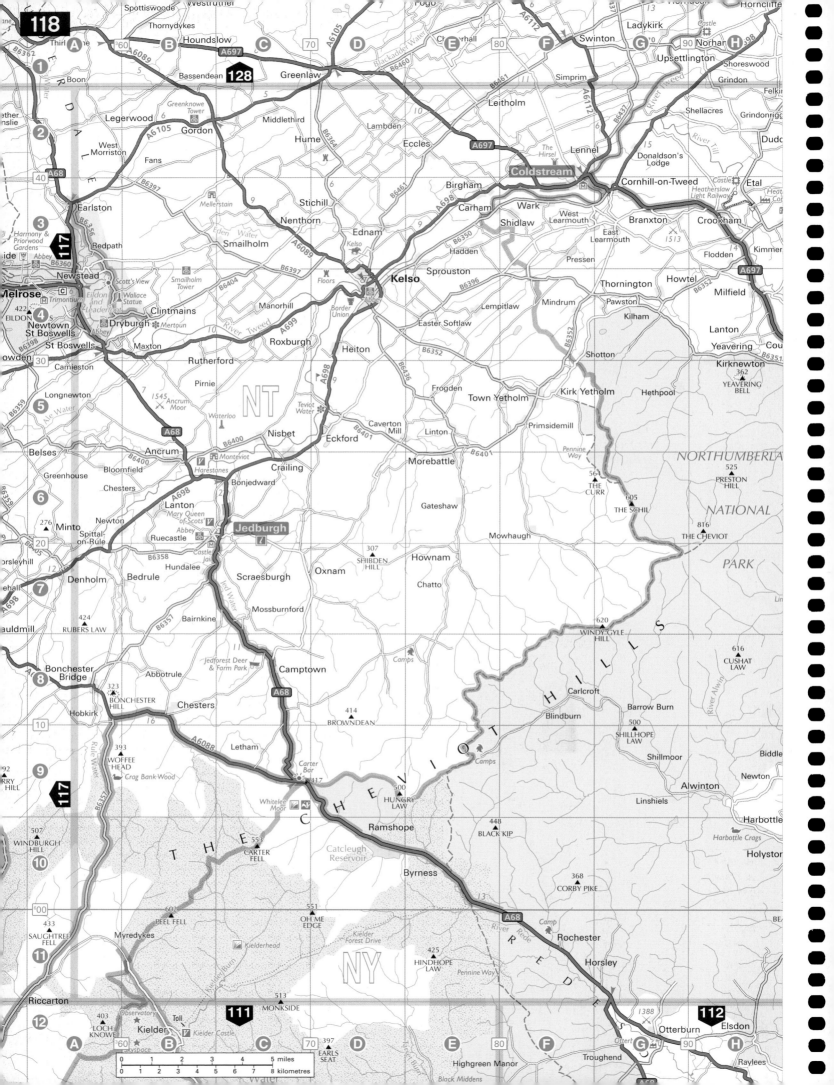

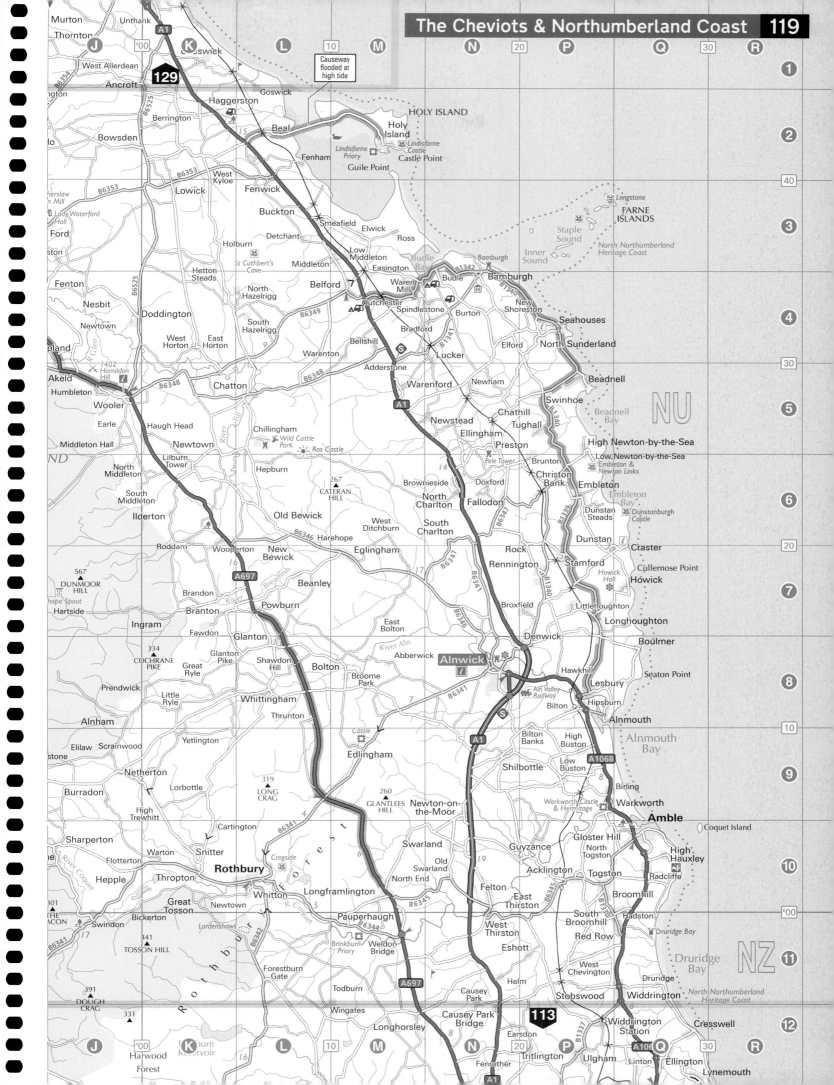

J **K** **L** **M** **N** **P** **Q** **R**

10 20 30

Murton
Unthank
Thornton
A1
West Allerdean
J
K
Goswick
L
10
M
N
20
P
Q
30
R
1

129
Ancroft
Berrington
Haggerston
Goswick
Causeway flooded at high tide
2

Bowsden
Beal
HOLY ISLAND
3

Lowick
Fenham
Lindisfarne Priory
Holy Island
Guile Point
Lindisfarne Castle
Castle Point
40

West Kyloe
Fenwick
Longstone
FARNE ISLANDS
3

Ford
Buckton
Smeafield
Elwick
Ross
Staple Sound
Inner Sound
North Northumberland Heritage Coast

Holburn
Detchant
Low Middleton
Budle Bay
Bamburgh
4

Fenton
St Cuthbert's Cave
Middleton
Easington
Waren Mill
Budle
Bamburgh
B1342
B1340

Nesbit
Belford
Outchester
Spindlestone
Burton
New Shoreston
Seahouses

Doddington
Newtown
North Hazelrigg
South Hazelrigg
Bradford
Elford
North Sunderland

West Horton
East Horton
Bellshill
Lucker
B1341
Seahouses
North Sunderland
4

Homildon Hill
1402
Warenton
Adderstone
Newham
Beadnell
30

Akeld
Humbleton
Chatton
B6348
B6348
Warenford
Swinhoe
Beadnell Bay
NU
5

Wooler
Earle
Haugh Head
Newstead
Chathill
Tughall
Beadnell Bay

Middleton Hall
Chillingham
Wild Cattle Park
Ros Castle
Ellingham
Preston
High Newton-by-the-Sea

Newtown
Lilburn Tower
Hepburn
Brunton
Low Newton-by-the-Sea
Embleton & Newton Links

North Middleton
Brownieside
North Charlton
Doxford
Christon Bank
Embleton
Embleton Bay
6

South Middleton
Ilderton
CATERAN HILL
267
Old Bewick
West Ditchburn
South Charlton
Fallodon
Dunstan Steads
Dunstanburgh Castle

Roddam
Harehope
Eglingham
Rock
Dunstan
Craster
20

DUNMOOR HILL
567
Wooperton
New Bewick
B6346
Rennington
Stamford
Cullernose Point

Hartside
Hope Spout
Brandon
Beanley
Broxfield
Howick Hall
Howick
7

Ingram
Branton
Powburn
East Bolton
Littlehoughton
Longhoughton

Fawdon
Glanton
River Aln
Abberwick
Denwick
Boulmer

Prendwick
COCHRANE PIKE
334
Glanton Pike
Shawdon Hill
Bolton
Broome Park
Alnwick
Hawkhill
Seaton Point
8

Little Ryle
Great Ryle
Whittingham
Aln Valley Railway
Lesbury
Hipsburn

Alnham
Thrunton
Castle
Bilton
Alnmouth
10

Elilaw
Scrainwood
Yetlington
Edlingham
Bilton Banks
High Buston
Alnmouth Bay

Netherton
LONG CRAG
319
Bilton Banks
Shilbottle
Low Buston
A1068
9

Burradon
Lorbottle
GLANTLEES HILL
260
Newton-on-the-Moor
Birling

High Trewhitt
Cartington
B6341
Swarland
Guyzance
Warkworth Castle & Hermitage
Warkworth

Sharperton
Warton
Snitter
Cragside
Old Swarland
North Togston
High Hauxley
10

Flotterton
Hepple
Thropton
Rothbury
North End
Acklington
Togston
Radcliffe
Coquet Island

Great Tosson
Bickerton
Longframlington
Newtown
Felton
East Thirston
Broomhill

THE BEACON
301
Swindon
Whitton
Pauperhaugh
B6345
South Broomhill
Hadston
Druridge Bay
00

TOSSON HILL
441
Lordenshaws
Weldon Bridge
West Thirston
Red Row
NZ
11

DOUGH CRAG
391
331
Brinkburn Priory
Forestburn Gate
Todburn
Eshott
Helm
West Chevington
Druridge
Druridge Bay
North Northumberland Heritage Coast

Harwood Forest
Wingates
Longhorsley
Causey Park
A697
Stobswood
Widdrington
12

113
Causey Park Bridge
Earsdon
Widdrington Station
Cresswell

Harwood Forest
J
K
L
10
M
N
20
P
Q
A106
R
Tritlington
Ulgham
Linton
Ellington

Fenrother
A1
Lynemouth

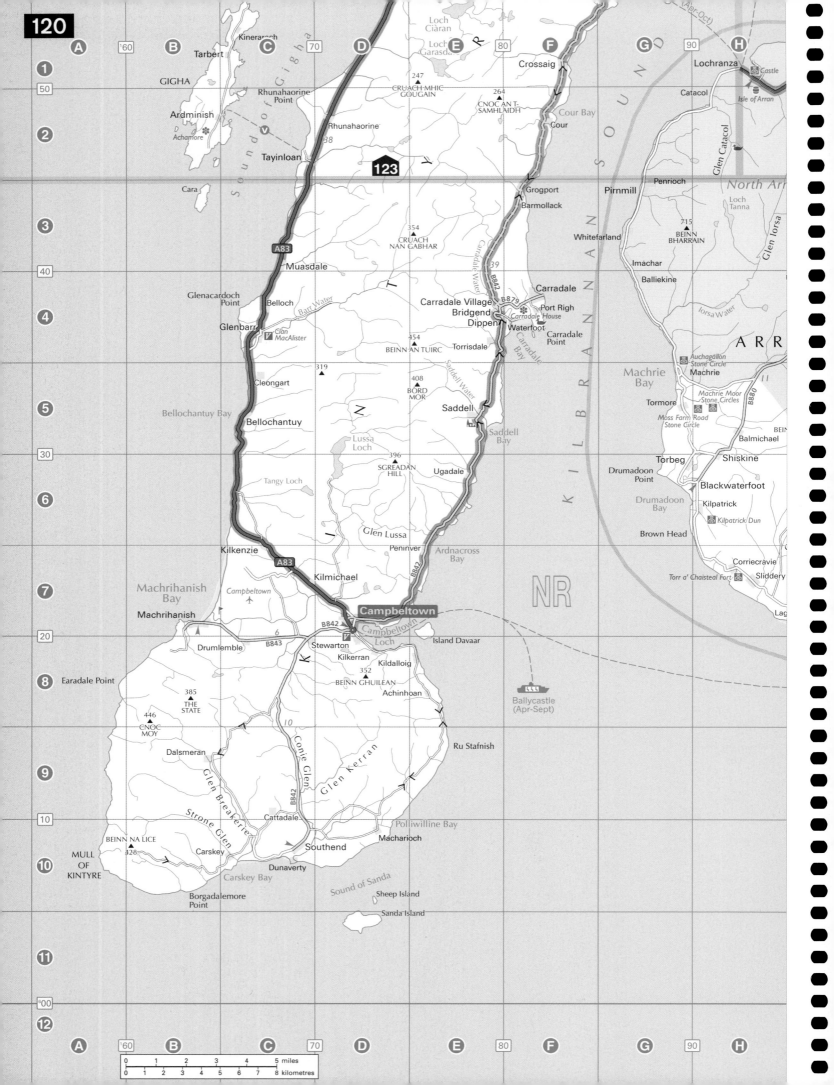

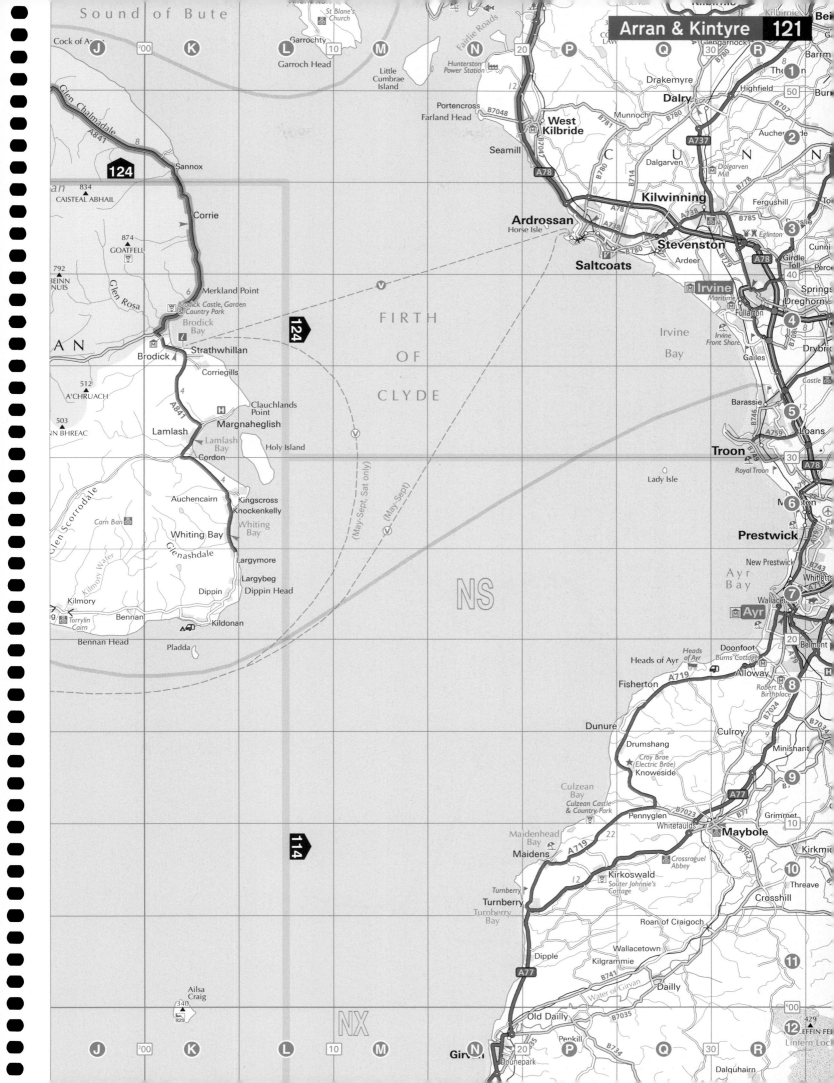

Sound of Bute

Cock of A J

Glen Chalmadale

A841

124

Sannox

834
CAISTEAL ABHAIL

Corrie

874
GOATFELL

792
BEINN NUIS

Glen Rosa

6 Merkland Point

Brodick Castle, Garden & Country Park

Brodick
Bay

124

AN

Brodick

Strathwhillan

Corriegills

512
A'CHRUACH

503
NN BHREAC

A841

4

H

Clauchlands
Point

Margnaheglish

Lamlash

Lamlash
Bay

Cordon

Holy Island

4

Glen Scorrodale

Auchencairn

Kingscross
Knockenkelly

Carn Ban

Whiting Bay

Whiting
Bay

Glenashdale

Largymore

Kilmory Water

Largybeg

Dippin

Dippin Head

Kilmory

Bennan

Kildonan

Torrylin
Cairn

Bennan Head

Pladda

NS

114

Ailsa
Craig

340

NX

Garrochty

Garroch Head

L 10

Little
Cumbrae
Island

St Blane's
Church

Fairlie Roads

M

N

Hunterston
Power Station

20

P

Q

R

Bei

Kilbirnie

Kilbirnie

1

Thornli

Drakemyre

Dalry

Highfield

50

Burn

B780

B707

Portencross
Farland Head

B7048

West
Kilbride

Seamill

A78

B7047

B781

Munnoch

B780

B780

B714

Auchen de

2

Dalgarven

C U N

7

Dalgarven
Mill

Kilwinning

A78

B785

A738

Fergushill

B778

B780

Ardrossan

Horse Isle

A738

A78

Eglinton

3

Stevenston

Saltcoats

B780

Ardeer

A78

B779

Girdle
Toll 40

Cunni

Perc

Irvine

Maritime

Fullarton

Dreghorn

Springs

4

B808

Irvine
Bay

Irvine
Front Shore

Gailes

Drybri

Castle

Barassie

B746

5

12

A759

Loans

Troon

A749

30

A78

Royal Troon

Lady Isle

M ton

6

Prestwick

New Prestwick

B743

Ayr
Bay

Whitletts

A77

7

Wallace

Ayr

20

Belmont

Doonfoot

Heads
of Ayr

Burns Cottage

8

Heads of Ayr

Robert B
Birthplace

Fisherton

A719

Alloway

H

Dunure

B7024

B703

Culroy

Drumshang

Croy Brae
(Electric Brae)

Knoweside

Minishant

9

B

A77

B71

Culzean
Bay

Culzean Castle
& Country Park

Pennyglen

B7023

Whitefaulds

Grimmet

10

Maidenhead
Bay

A719

22

Maybole

Kirkmi

Maidens

Crossraguel
Abbey

10

Threave

Kirkoswald

Souter Johnnie's
Cottage

Roan of Craigoch

Crosshill

Turnberry

Turnberry
Bay

Dipple

Wallacetown

11

A77

Kilgrammie

B741

Dailly

Water of Girvan

B7035

Old Dailly

00

12 EFFIN FEI
429
Linfern Loc

J 00

K 10

L 10

M

N

Girvan

P

Q 30

R

Dounepark

Penkill

B734

20

Dalquhairn

(May-Sept, Sat only)

(May-Sept)

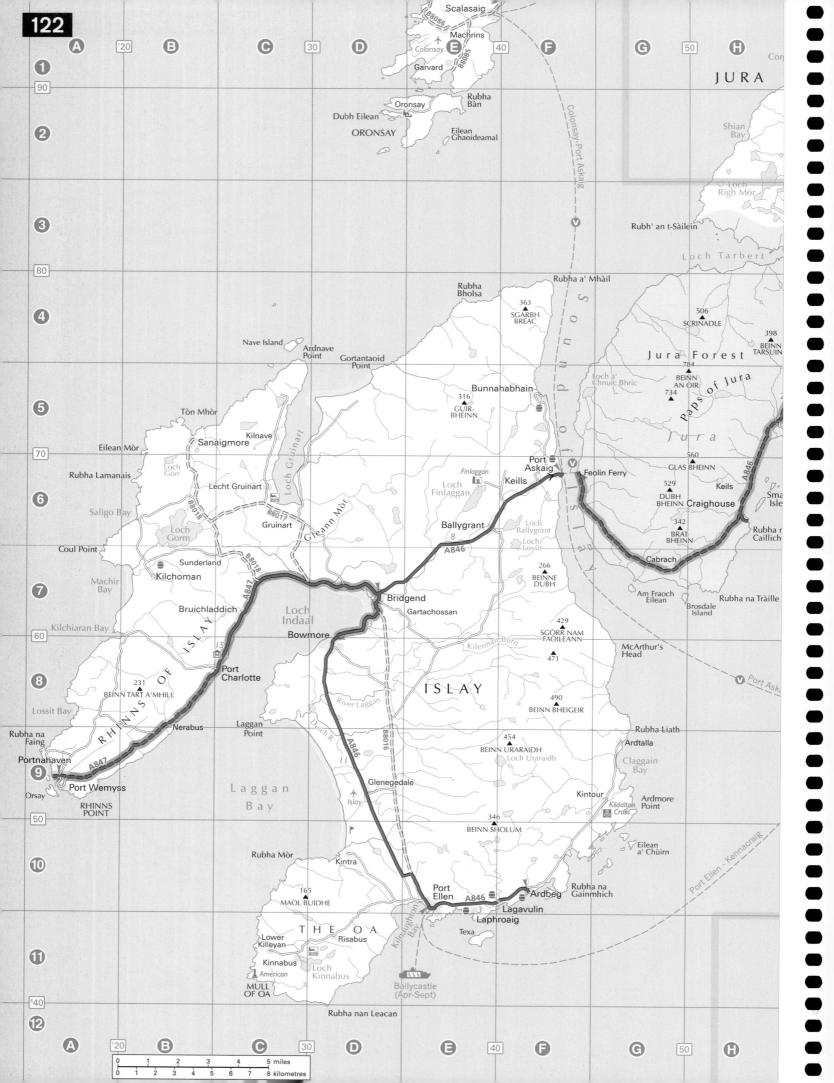

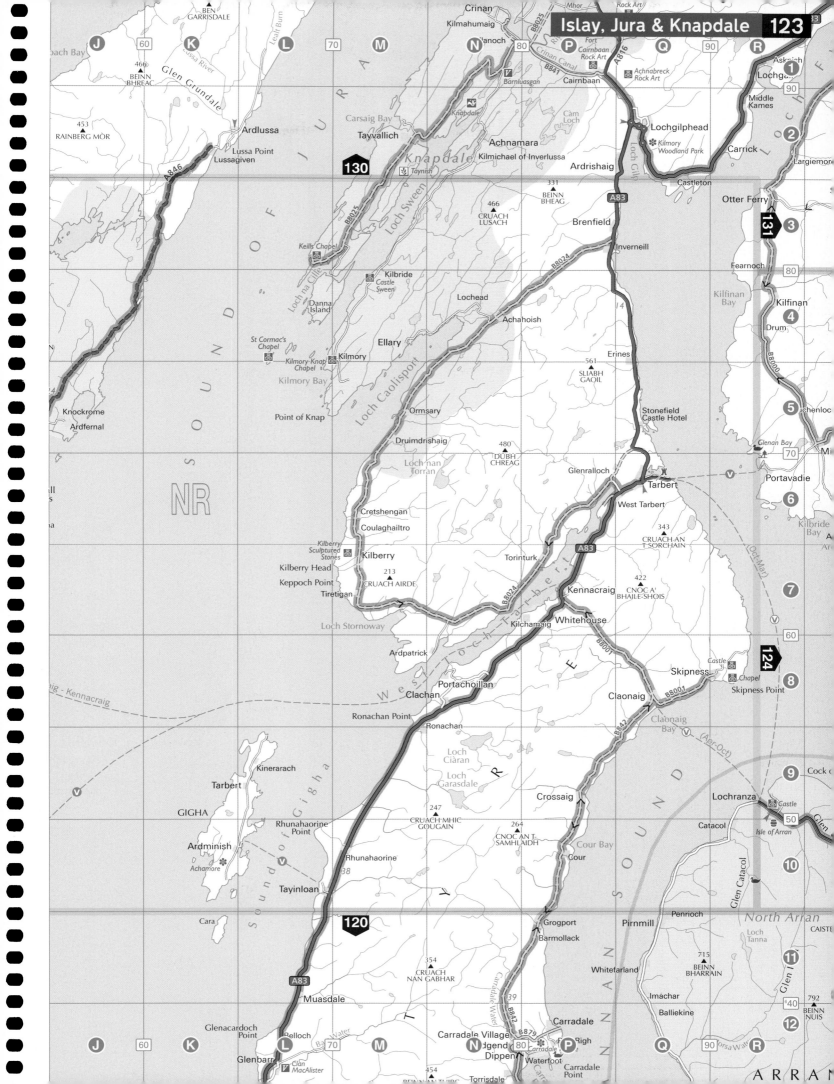

J 60 K L 70 M N P Q 90 R

Crinan
Kilmahumaig
B8025 Mhor
Rock Art

1
Askaig
Lochga...
90

BEN
GARRISDALE

'lanoch
80
Crinan Canal
B841
Fort
Cairnbaan
Rock Art
A816
Achnabreck
Rock Art

Middle
Kames
2
Lochgilphead
Kilmory
Woodland Park
Carrick

466
BEINN
BHREAC

Lealt Burn

Lussa River

Glen Grundale

Barnluasgan
Cairnbaan
Largiemore

453
RAINBERG MÒR

Ardlussa
Carsaig Bay
Knapdale
Càm
Loch

Ardrishaig

Castleton
A83
Otter Ferry

131 3

Lussa Point
Lussagiven

Taynish
130
Knapdale
Achnamara
Kilmichael of Inverlussa

331
BEINN
BHEAG
Brenfield

Fearnoch
80

Keills Chapel
B8025
Loch Sween

466
CRUACH
LUSACH

Inverneill

Kilfinan
Bay
Kilfinan
4

Kilbride
Castle
Sween
Lochead
Achahoish

Drum
B8000

Danna
Island
B8024

561
SLIABH
GAOIL

5
...chenloc

St Cormac's
Chapel
Kilmory
Ellary
Erines

Glenan Bay
70

Kilmory Knap
Chapel
Kilmory Bay
Kilmory

Stonefield
Castle Hotel
M

NR
Point of Knap
Ormsary

Glenralloch
Tarbert
Portavadie

6

480
DUBH
CHREAG
West Tarbert

Kilbride
Bay

Druimdrishaig
Loch nan
Torran

Cretshengan
Coulaghailtro
343
CRUACH AN
T SORCHAIN
(Oct–Mar)

Kilberry
Sculptured
Stones
Kilberry
Torinturk
A83

7

Kilberry Head
213
CRUACH AIRDE
422
CNOC A'
BHAILE-SHOIS
Kennacraig
124
60

Keppoch Point
Tiretigan
B8024
Whitehouse
8

Loch Stornoway
Kilchamaig
B8001
Castle
Skipness
Chapel

...aig - Kennacraig
Ardpatrick
Skipness Point

Claonaig 9
Lochranza
Cock o...

Portachoillan
Clachan
Claonaig
Bay
B842
(Apr–Oct)

Ronachan Point
Ronachan

Loch
Cìaran
Crossaig

Loch
Garasdale
R

Castle
Glen
50

Kinerarach

247
CRUACH MHIC
GOUGAIN

Catacol

Isle of Arran
10

Tarbert
Rhunahaorine
Point

264
CNOC AN T-
SAMHLAIDH
Cour Bay
Cour

Glen Catacol

North Arran

GIGHA
Ardminish
Achamore

Rhunahaorine
38
Tayinloan

Grogport
Barmollack
Pirnmill
Penrioch

Loch
Tanna
CAISTE...

Cara

120
A83
354
CRUACH
NAN GABHAR
715
BEINN
BHARRAIN
11

Muasdale
Whitefarland
Imachar

792
BEINN
NUIS

Glenacardoch
Point
Belloch
Carradale
B879
B842
Carradale Village
Balliekine
12

J 60 K L 70 M N ...dgend P Q 90 R
Glenbarr
Clan
MacAlister
Dippen
Waterfoot
Carradale
Point
A R R A...
454

Carra... Water

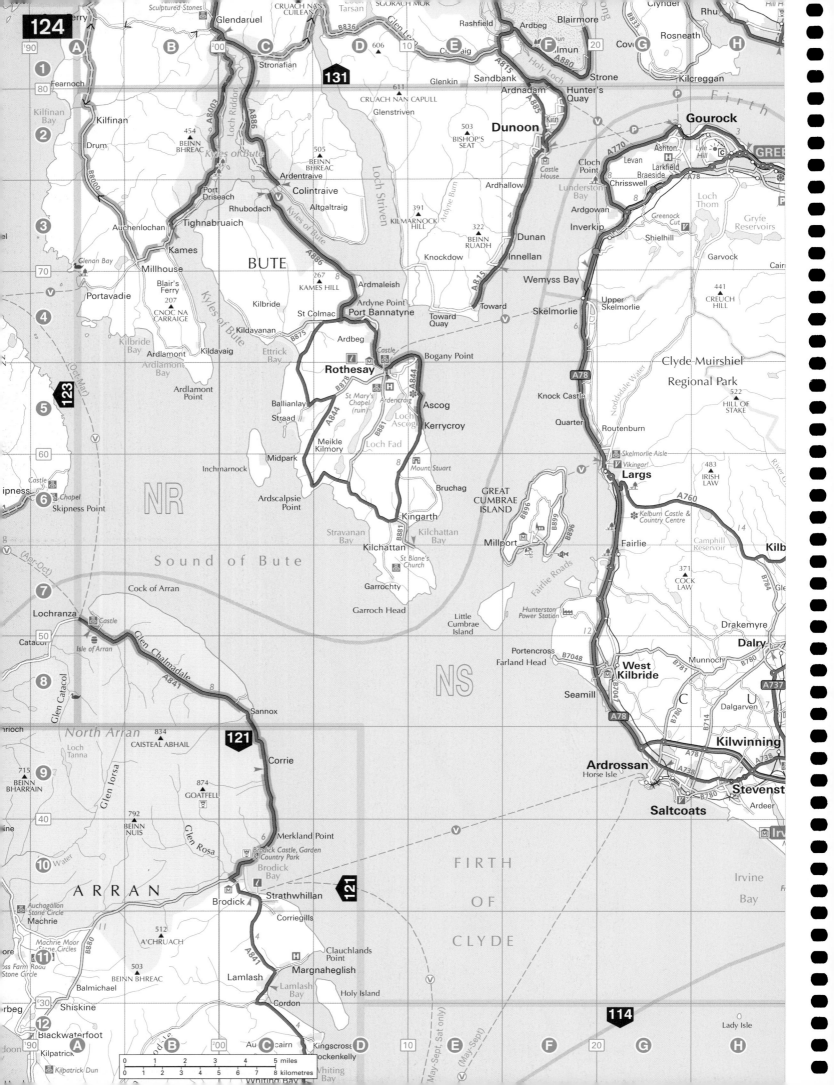

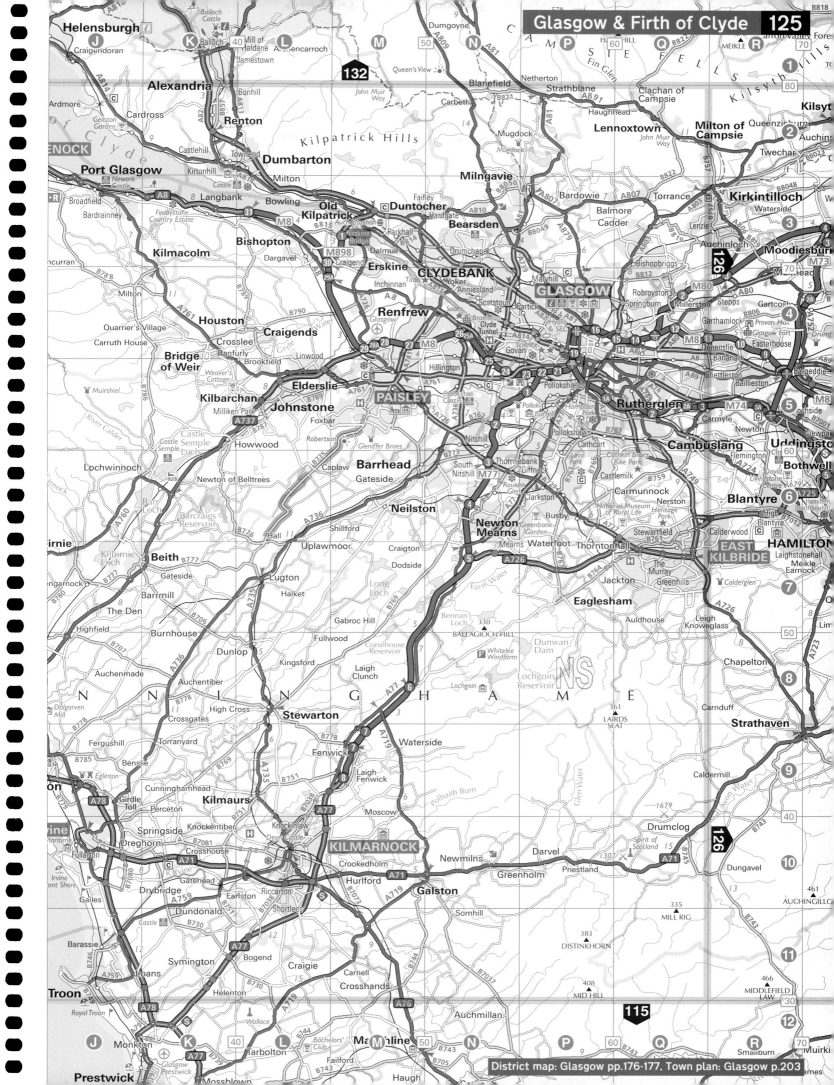

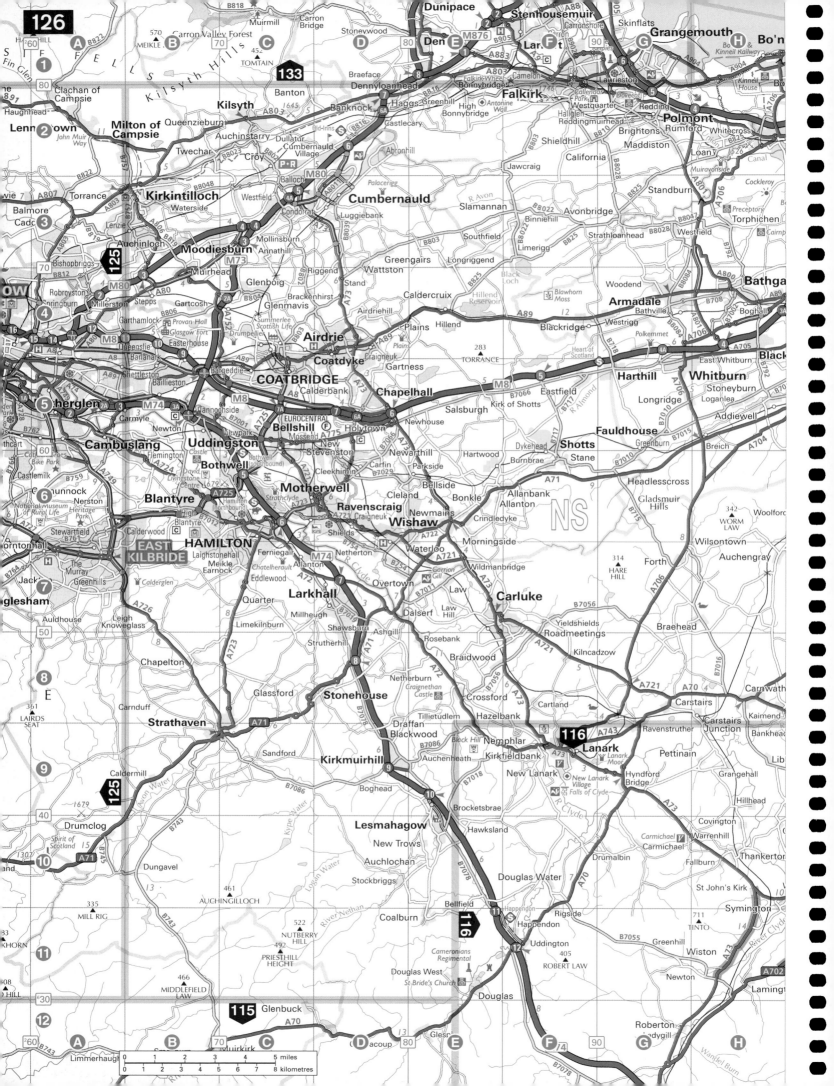

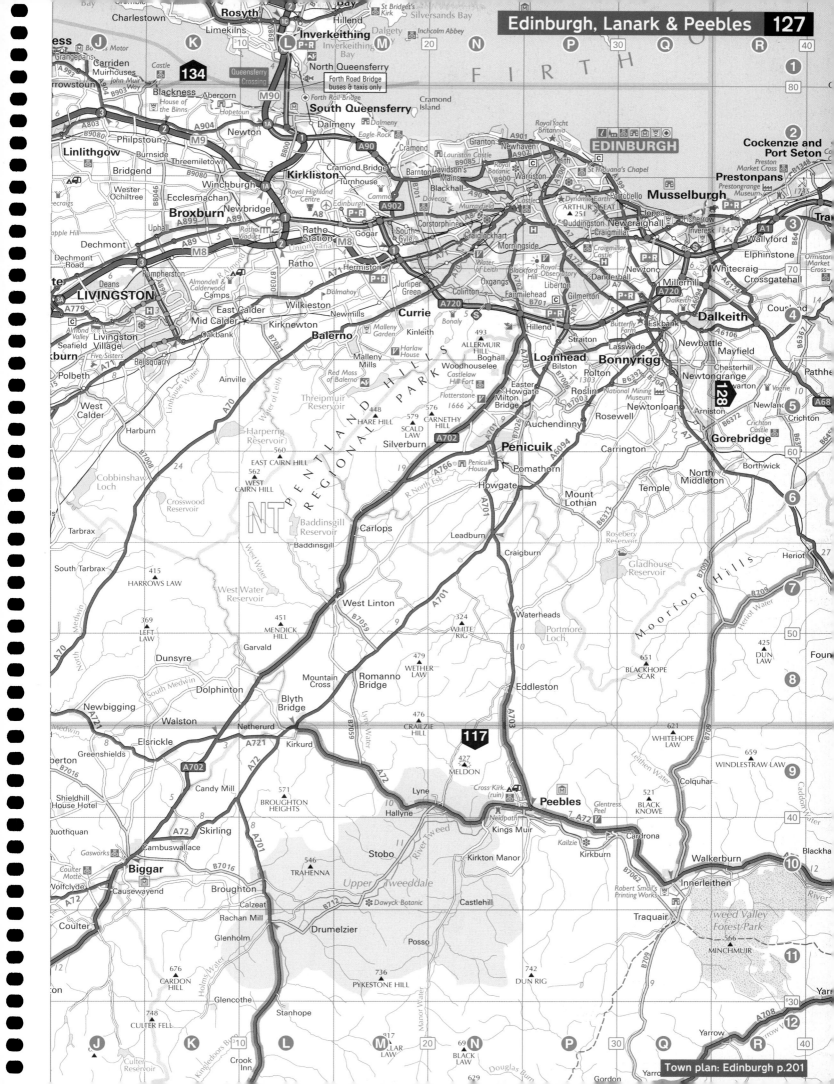

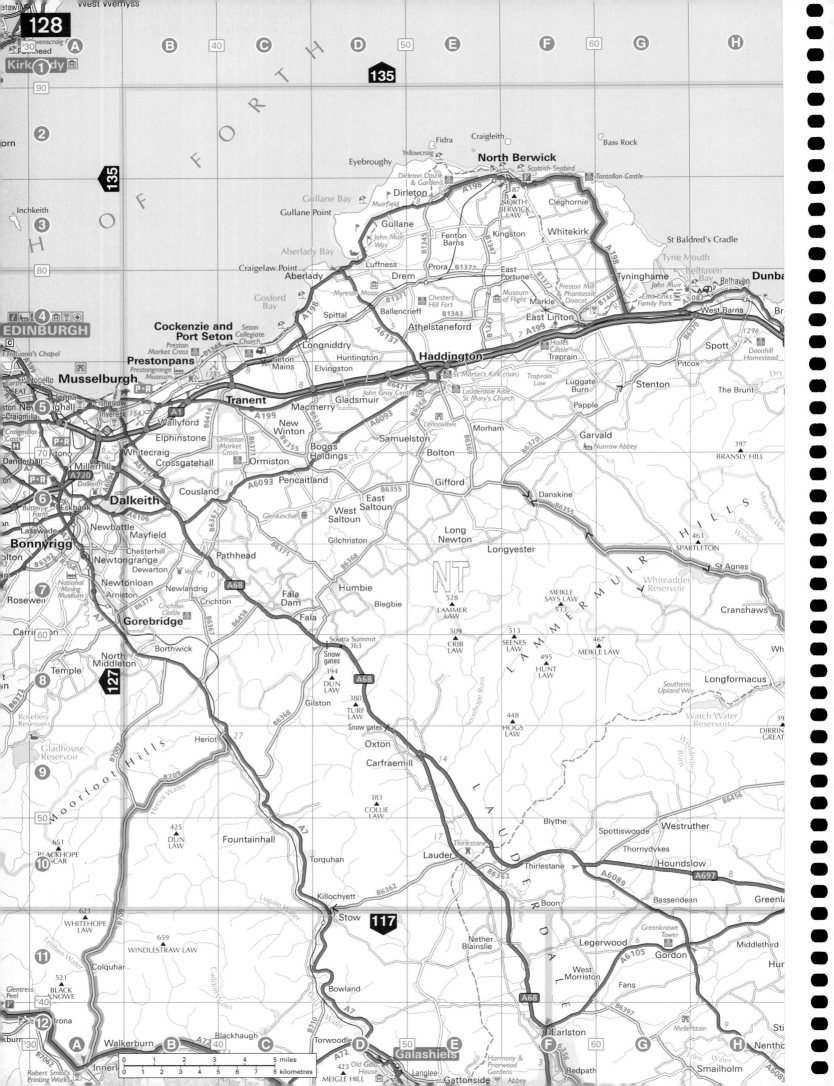

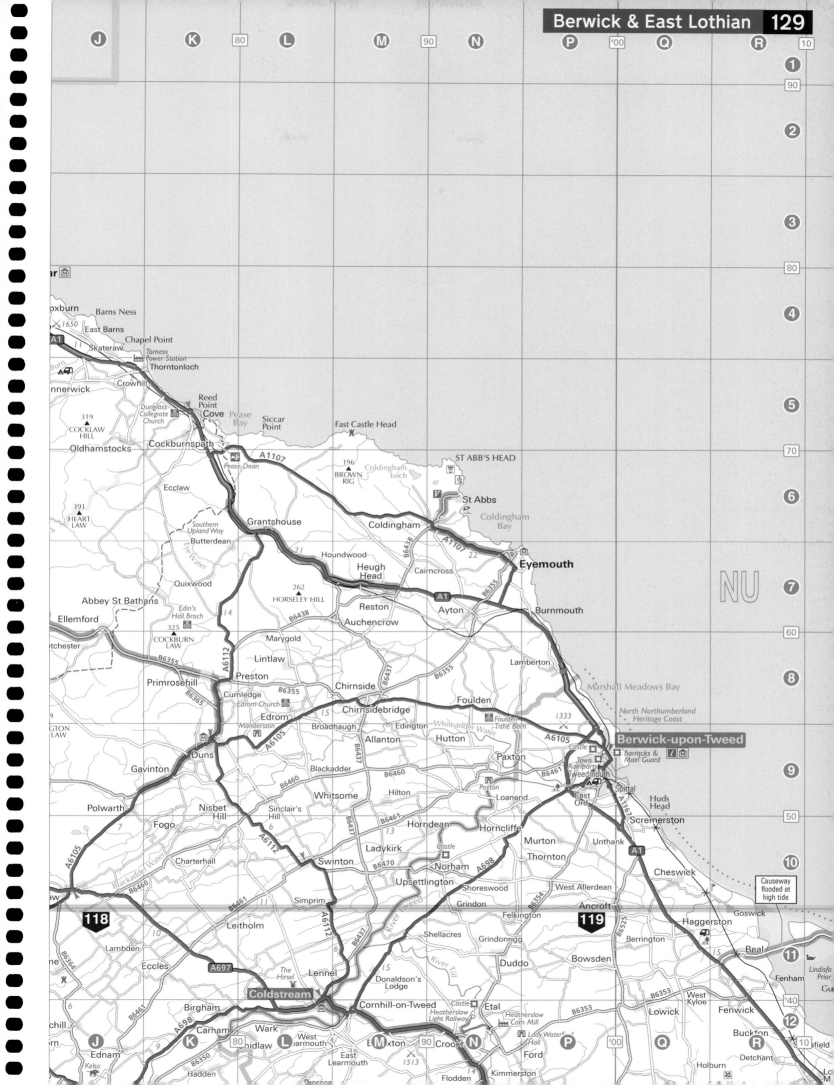

J · K · 80 · L · M · 90 · N · P · 400 · Q · R · 10

1 · 90 · 2 · 3 · 80 · 4 · 5 · 70 · 6 · 7 · 60 · 8 · 9 · 50 · 10 · 11 · 40 · 12 · 10

NU

oxburn · Barns Ness
East Barns · Chapel Point
1650 · Skateraw · *Torness Power Station* · Thorntonloch
nnerwick · Crowhill
Cocklaw Hill · 319 · *Dunglass Collegiate Church* · Reed Point · Cove · Pease Bay · Siccar Point · Fast Castle Head · ST ABB'S HEAD
Oldhamstocks · Cockburnspath · *Pease Dean* · A1107 · 196 · BROWN RIG · *Coldingham Loch*
Ecclaw · St Abbs
391 · HEART LAW · *Southern Upland Way* · Grantshouse · Coldingham · A1107 · Coldingham Bay · Eyemouth
Butterdean · *Eye Water* · Houndwood · Heugh Head · B6438 · 22
Quixwood · 21 · Cairncross
Abbey St Bathans · 262 · HORSELEY HILL · A1 · Burnmouth
Ellemford · *Edin's Hall Broch* · 14 · Reston · Ayton
itchester · 325 · COCKBURN LAW · B6438 · Auchencrow · Lamberton · Marshall Meadows Bay
Marygold · B6437 · B6355
Primrosehill · B6355 · Lintlaw · North Northumberland Heritage Coast
GTON LAW · A6112 · B6365 · Preston · Chirnside · Foulden · 1333 · Berwick-upon-Tweed
Cumledge · *Edrom Church* · Chirnsidebridge · *Foulden Tithe Barn* · *Castle* · *Barracks & Main Guard*
Edrom · 15 · Broadhaugh · Edington · *Whiteadder Water* · A6105 · *Town Ramparts* · Tweedmouth
Duns · *Manderston* · A6105 · Allanton · Hutton · Paxton · B6461
Gavinton · B6437 · Blackadder · B6460 · *Paxton* · East Ord · Spittal · Huds Head
Polwarth · Nisbet Hill · Whitsome · Hilton · Loanend · A1167 · Scremerston
Fogo · Sinclair's Hill · Horndean · Horncliffe · Murton · Unthank · A1
Charterhall · B6437 · 13 · Ladykirk · *Castle* · Thornton · Cheswick
A6105 · B6460 · Swinton · B6470 · Norham · A698 · West Allerdean · Causeway flooded at high tide
118 · *Blackadder Water* · Upsettlington · Shoreswood · 119
10 · Simprim · Grindon · Felkington · Ancroft · Goswick
Leitholm · A6112 · Shellacres · Grindonrigg · Bowsden · B6525 · Haggerston · Beal
Lambden · 6 · Duddo · Berrington · Lindisfarne Priory · Gu
B6364 · Eccles · A697 · *The Hirsel* · Lennel · 15 · *River Till* · Duddo · West Kyloe · Fenwick · Fenham
ne · 6 · Birgham · Coldstream · Donaldson's Lodge · *Castle* · Etal · *Heatherslaw Light Railway* · B6353 · Lowick · Buckton
chill · B6461 · A698 · Carham · Wark · West Learmouth · Crookham · Ford · *Lady Waterford Hall* · Detchant
Ednam · K · 80 · L · M · 90 · Mxton · N · P · 400 · Q · R · field
Kelso · hidlaw · East Learmouth · 1513 · Kimmerston · Holburn · Lc · M
Hadden · Flodden · 14

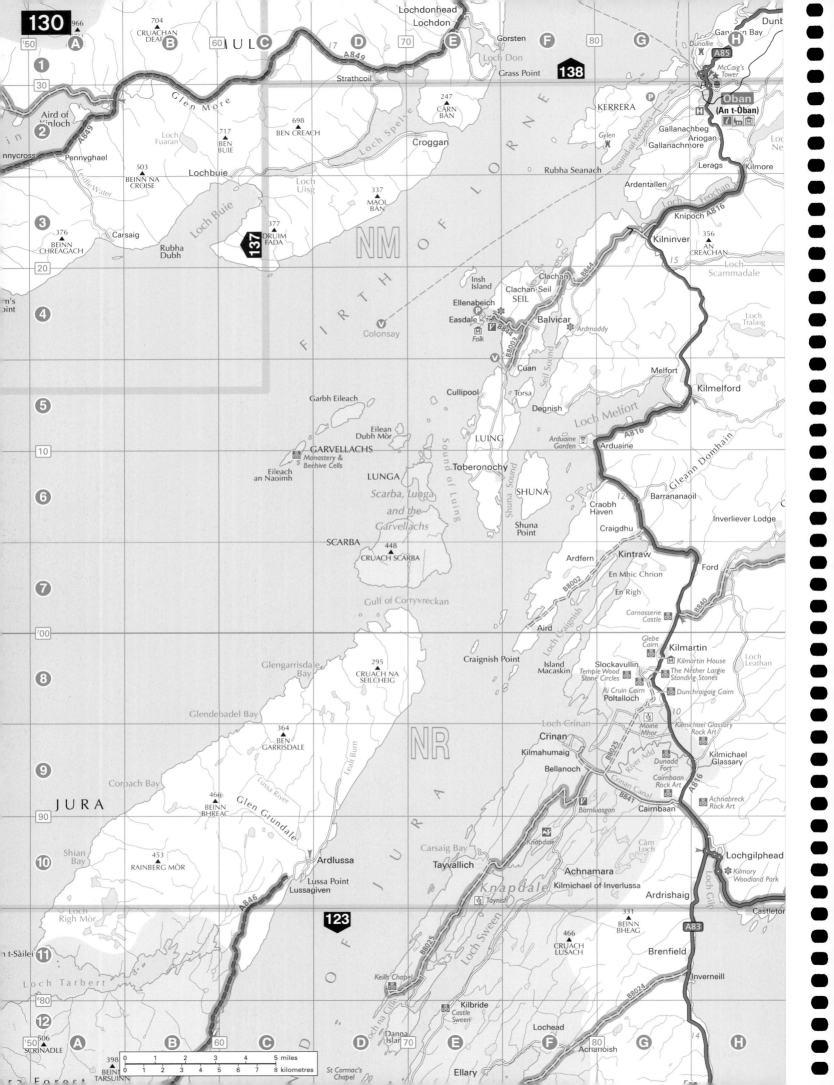

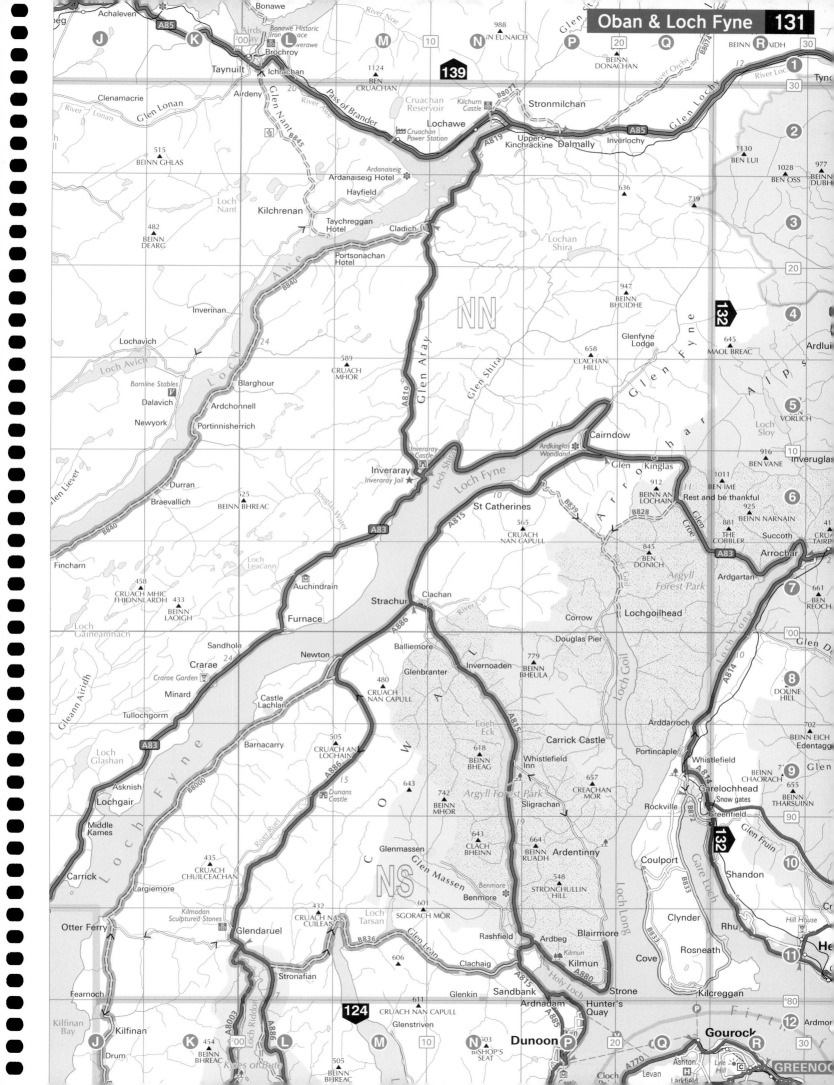

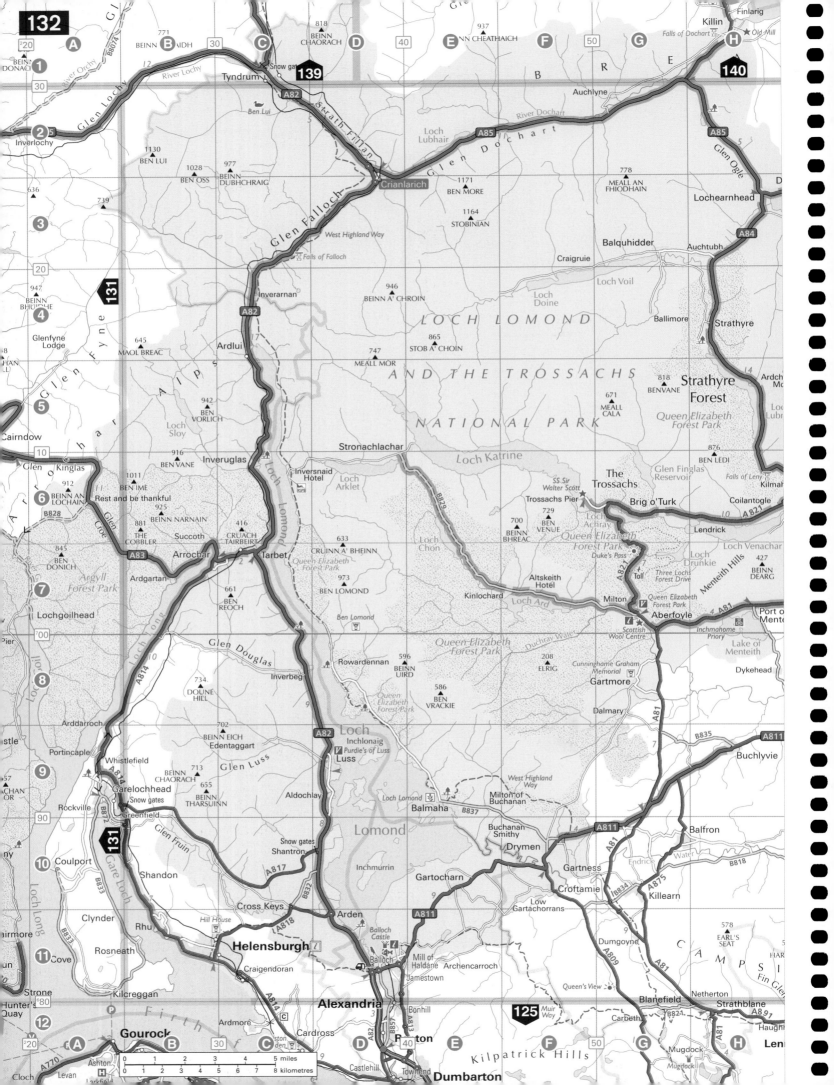

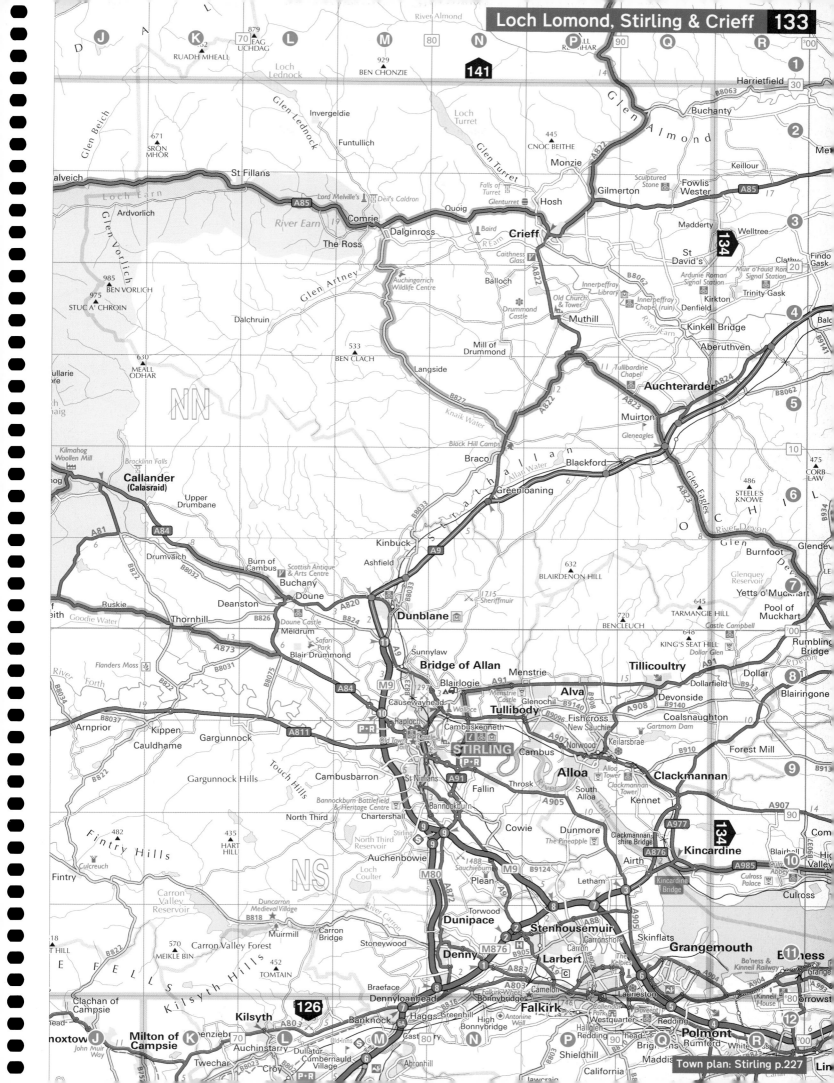

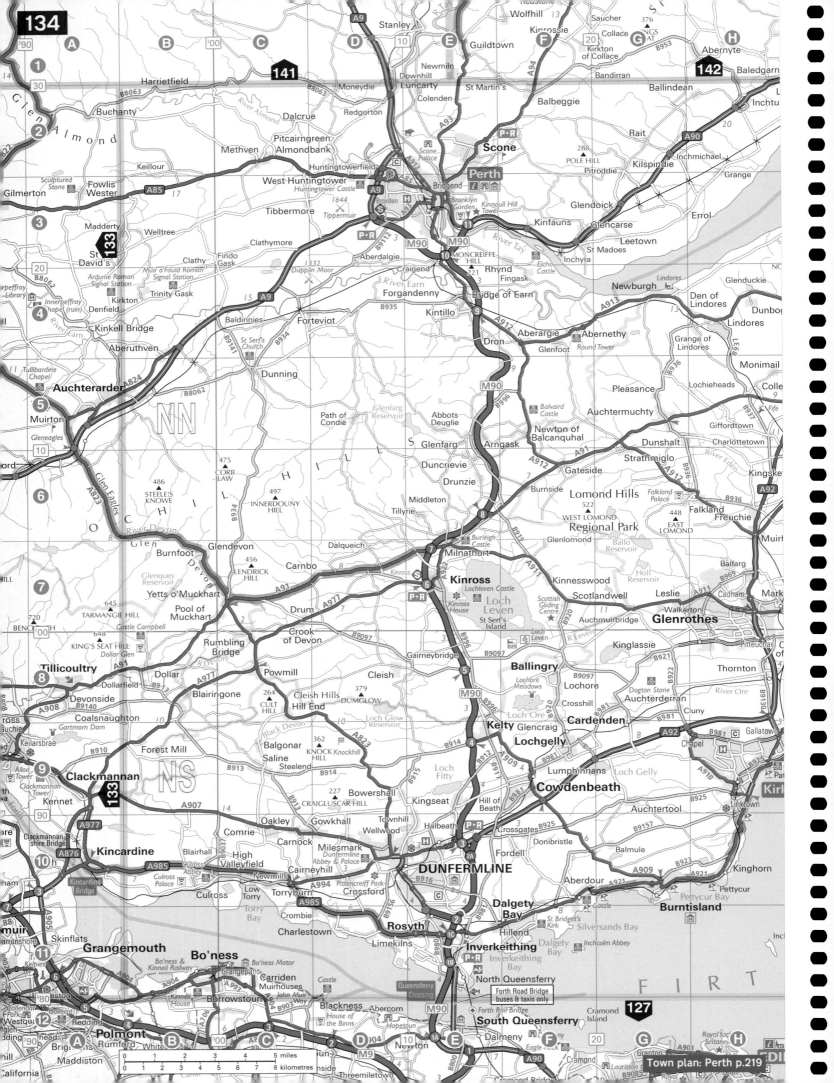

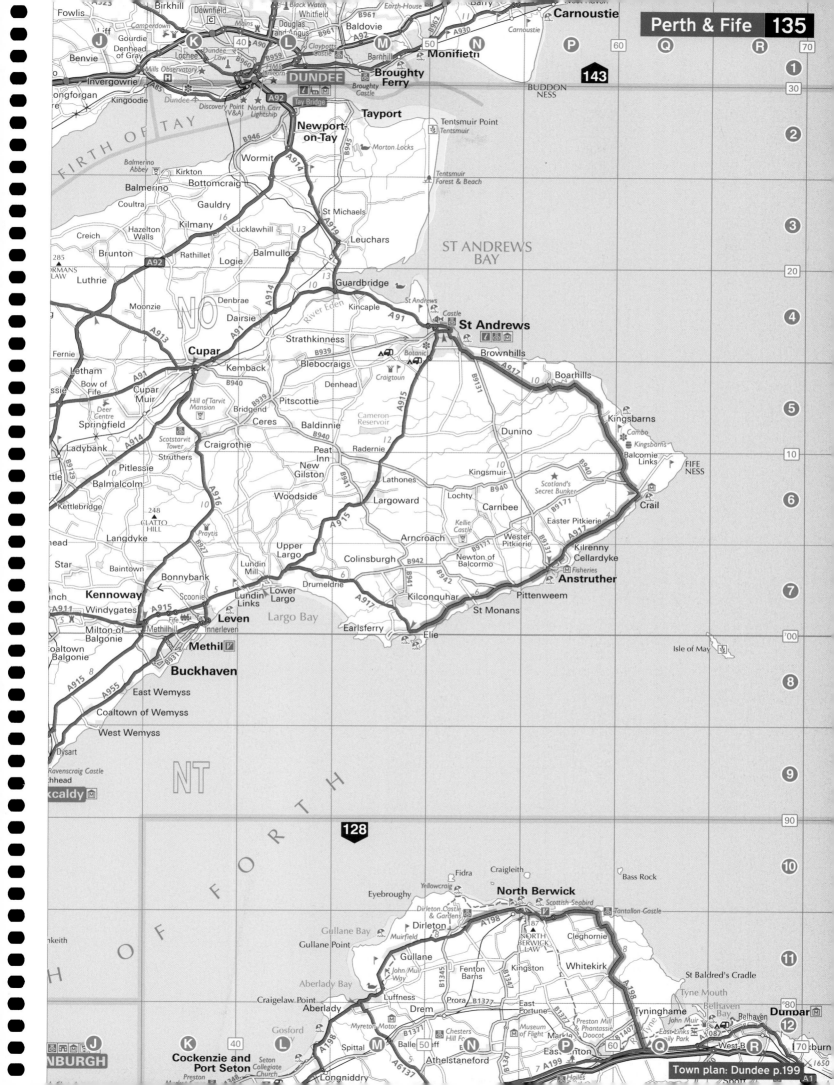

143

128

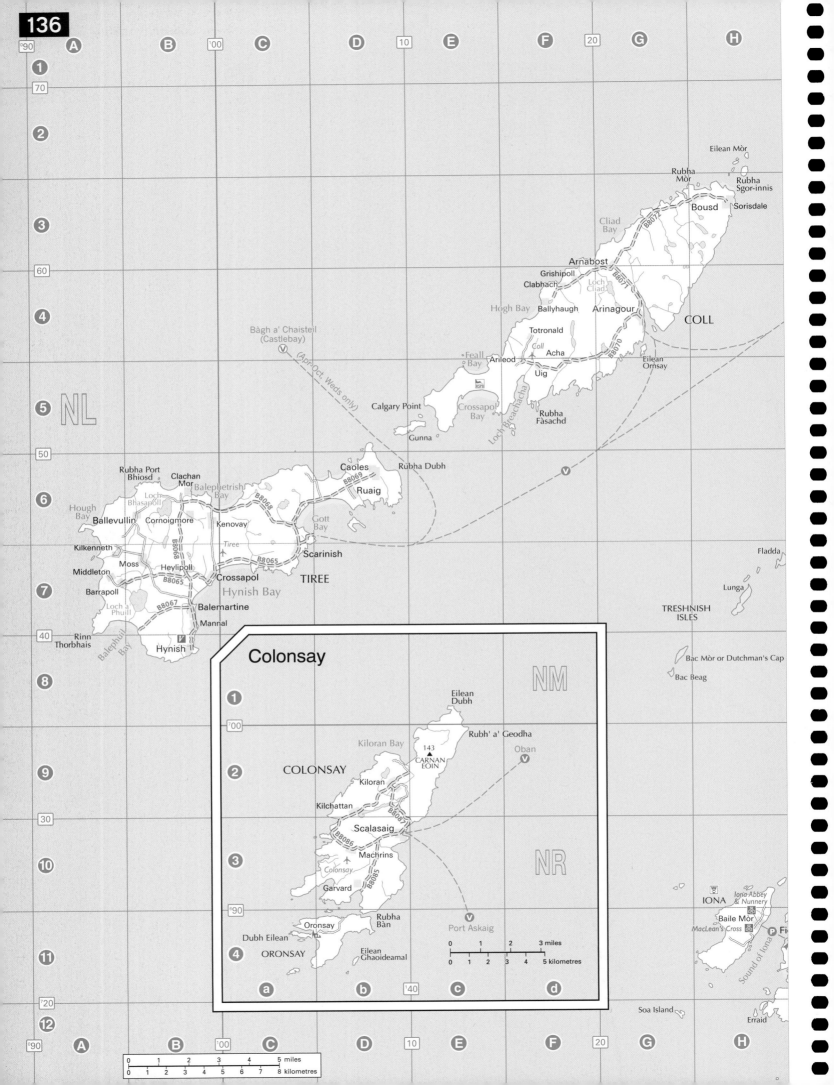

Map labels

COLL area:
Eilean Mòr
Rubha Mòr
Rubha Sgor-innis
Bousd
Sorisdale
Cliad Bay
Arnabost
Grishipoll
Clabhach
Loch Cliad
Ballyhaugh
Arinagour
COLL
Hogh Bay
Totronald
Coll
Acha
Feall Bay
Arileod
Uig
Eilean Ornsay
RSPB
Calgary Point
Crossapol Bay
Loch Breachacha
Rubha Fàsachd
Gunna
Rubha Dubh

TIREE area:
NL
Rubha Port Bhiosd
Clachan Mor
Balephetrish Bay
Caoles
B8069
Ruaig
Loch Bhasapoll
B8058
Hough Bay
Ballevullin
Cornoigmore
Kenovay
Gott Bay
Kilkenneth
B8068
Tiree
Middleton
Moss
Heylipoll
B8065
Scarinish
Barrapoll
B8065
Crossapol
TIREE
Loch a' Phuill
B8067
Balemartine
Hynish Bay
Rinn Thorbhais
Mannal
Balephuil Bay
Hynish

Bàgh a' Chaisteil (Castlebay)
(Apr-Oct, Weds only)

Treshnish area:
Fladda
Lunga
TRESHNISH ISLES
Bac Mòr or Dutchman's Cap
Bac Beag

IONA area:
IONA
Iona Abbey & Nunnery
Baile Mòr
MacLean's Cross
Sound of Iona
Soa Island
Erraid
Fi...

Colonsay

NM
Eilean Dubh
Kiloran Bay
COLONSAY
143
CARNAN EOIN
Rubh' a' Geodha
Oban
Kiloran
Kilchattan
B8087
Scalasaig
NR
B8086
Machrins
Colonsay
B8085
Garvard
Oronsay
Rubha Bàn
Dubh Eilean
Port Askaig
ORONSAY
Eilean Ghaoideamal

| 0 | 1 | 2 | 3 miles |
| 0 | 1 2 3 4 | | 5 kilometres |

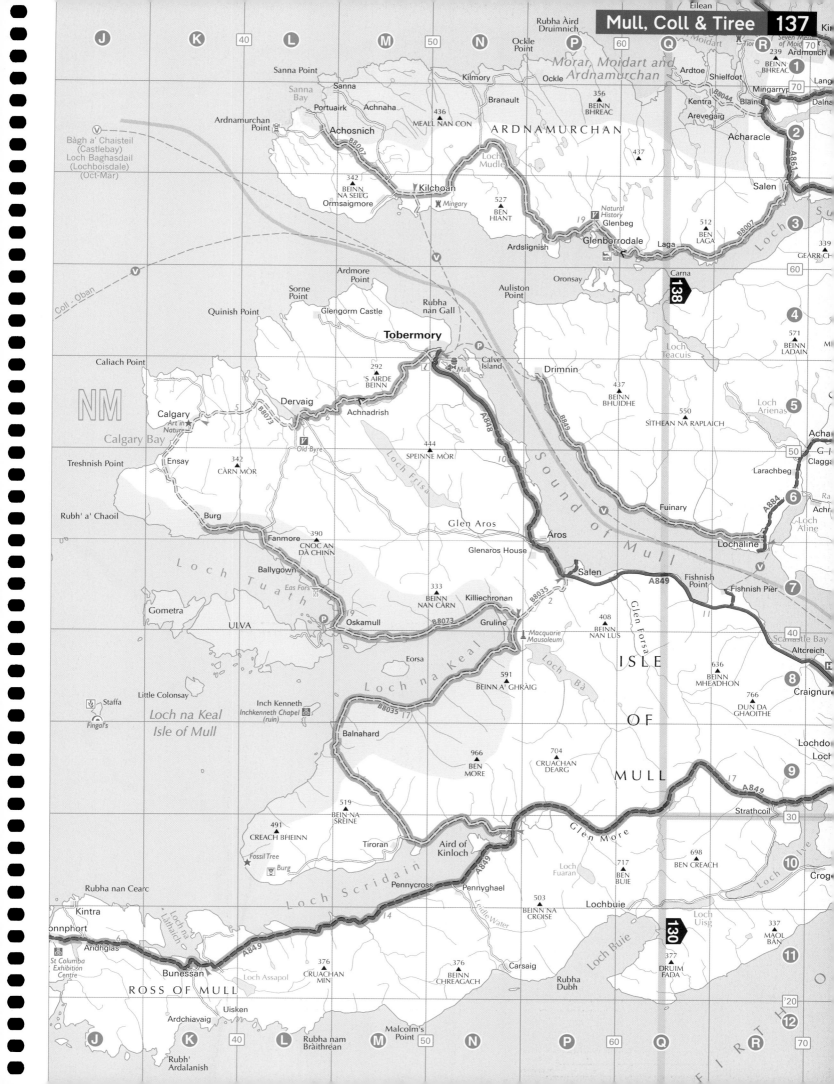

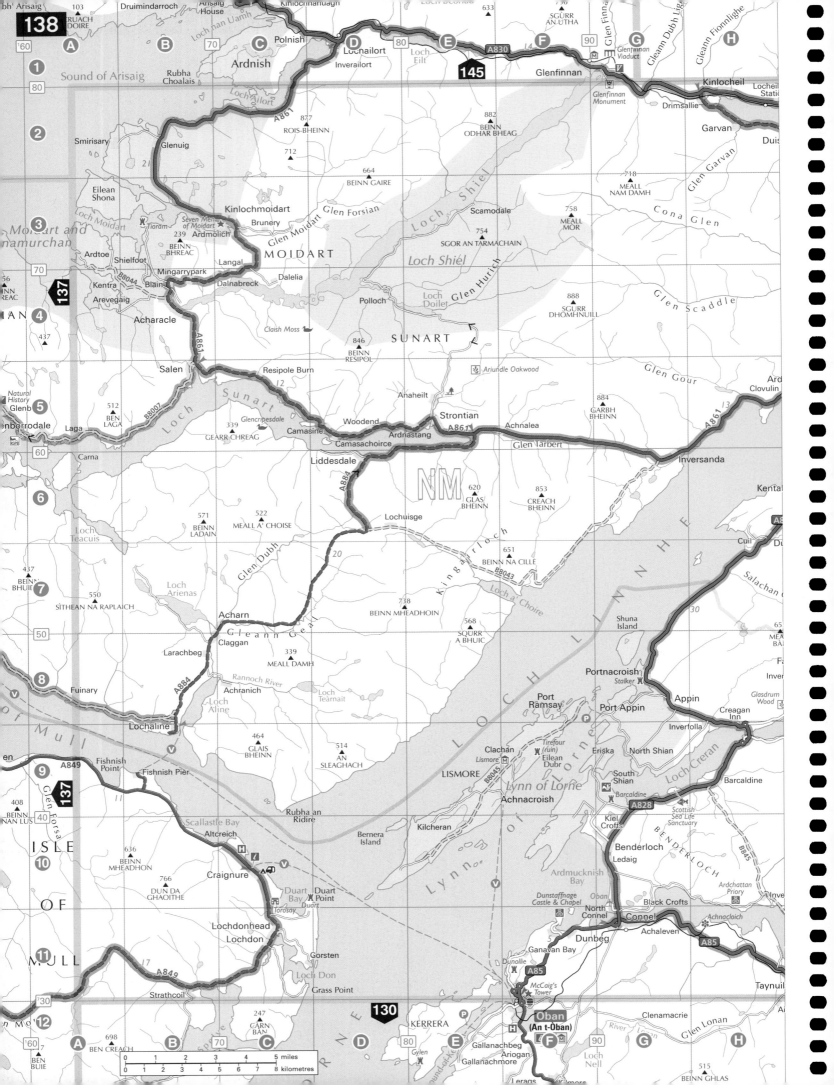

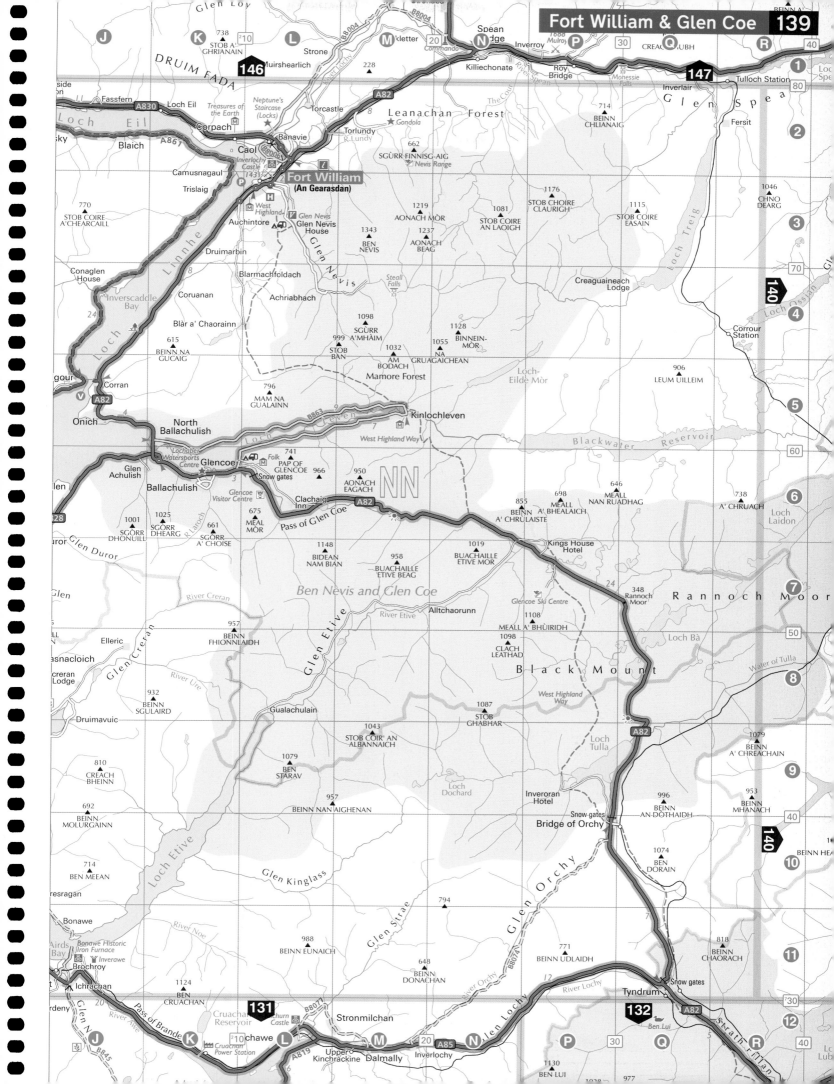

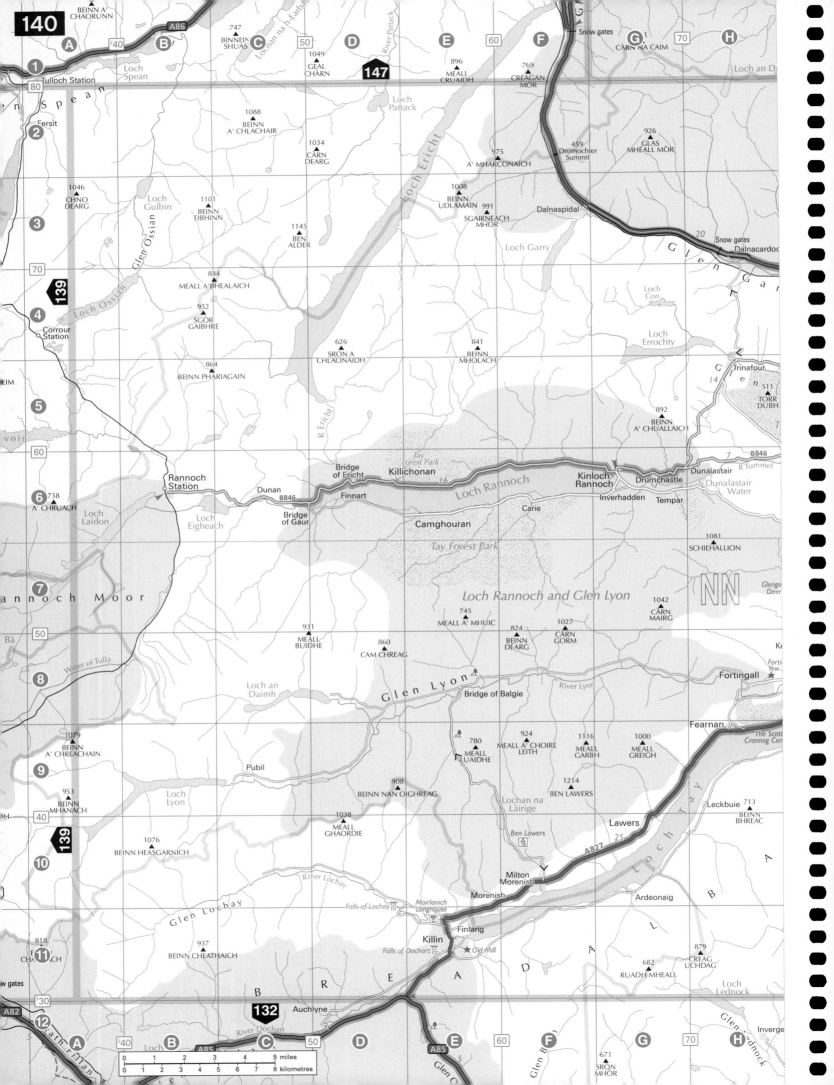

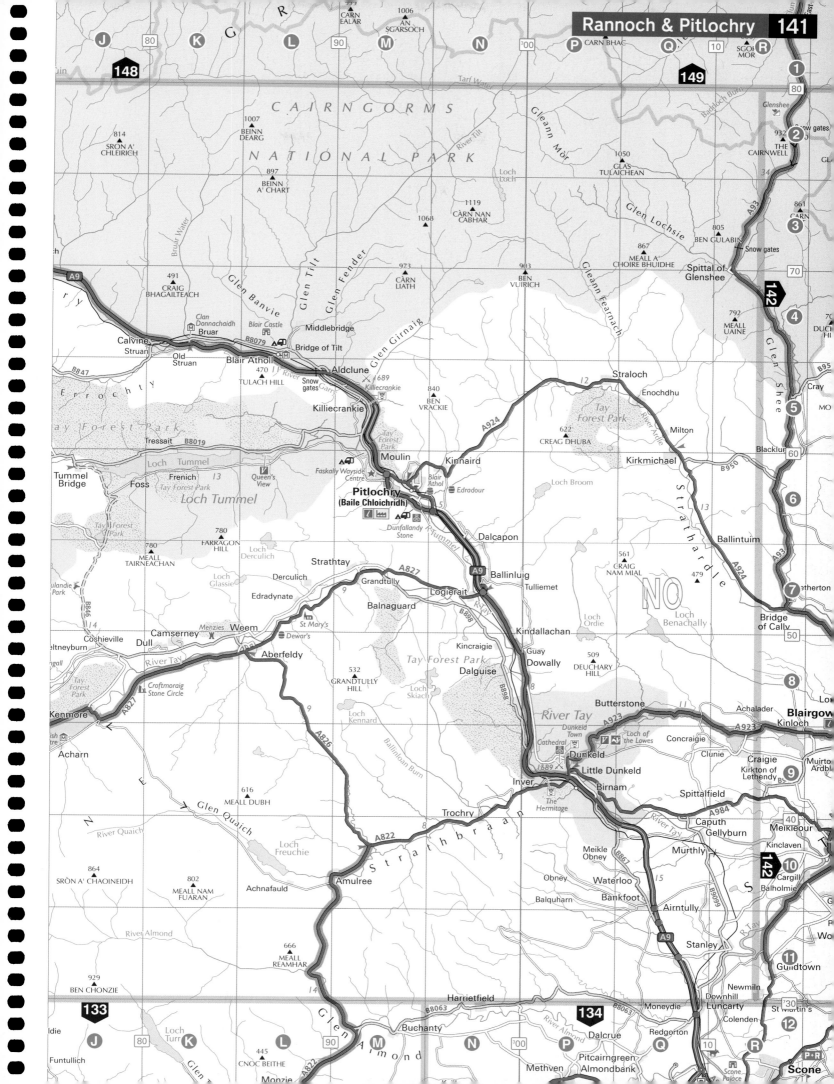

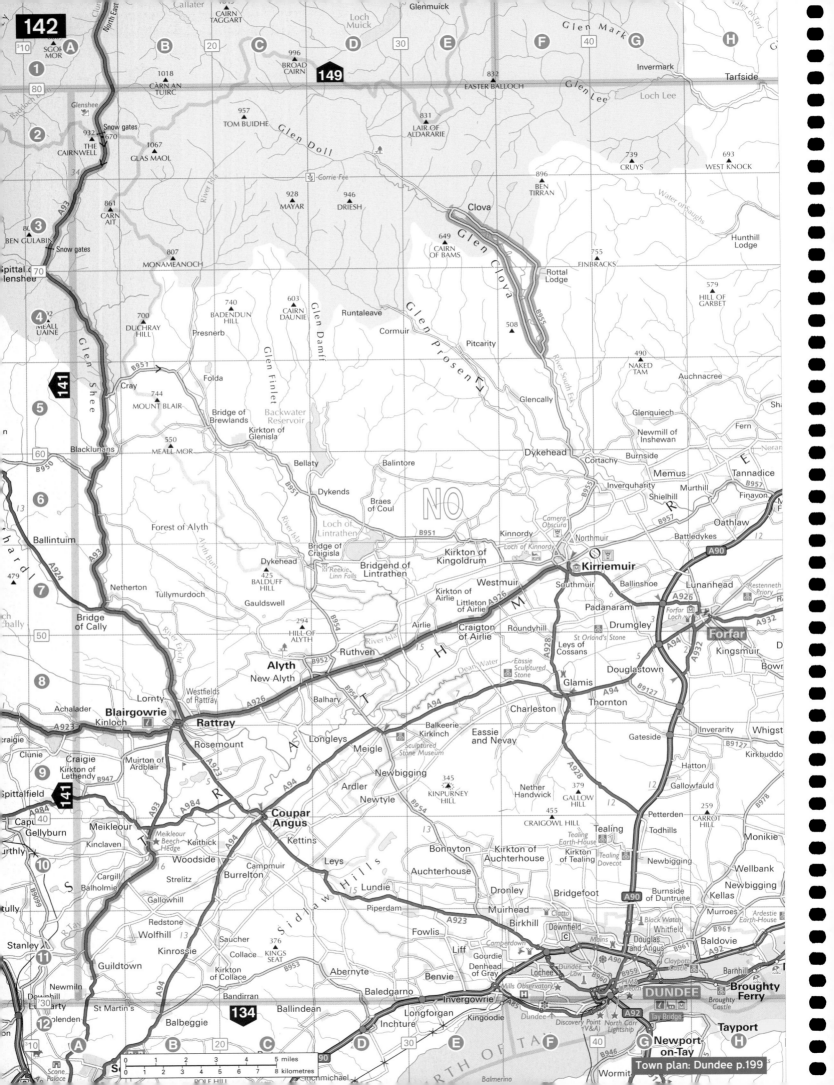

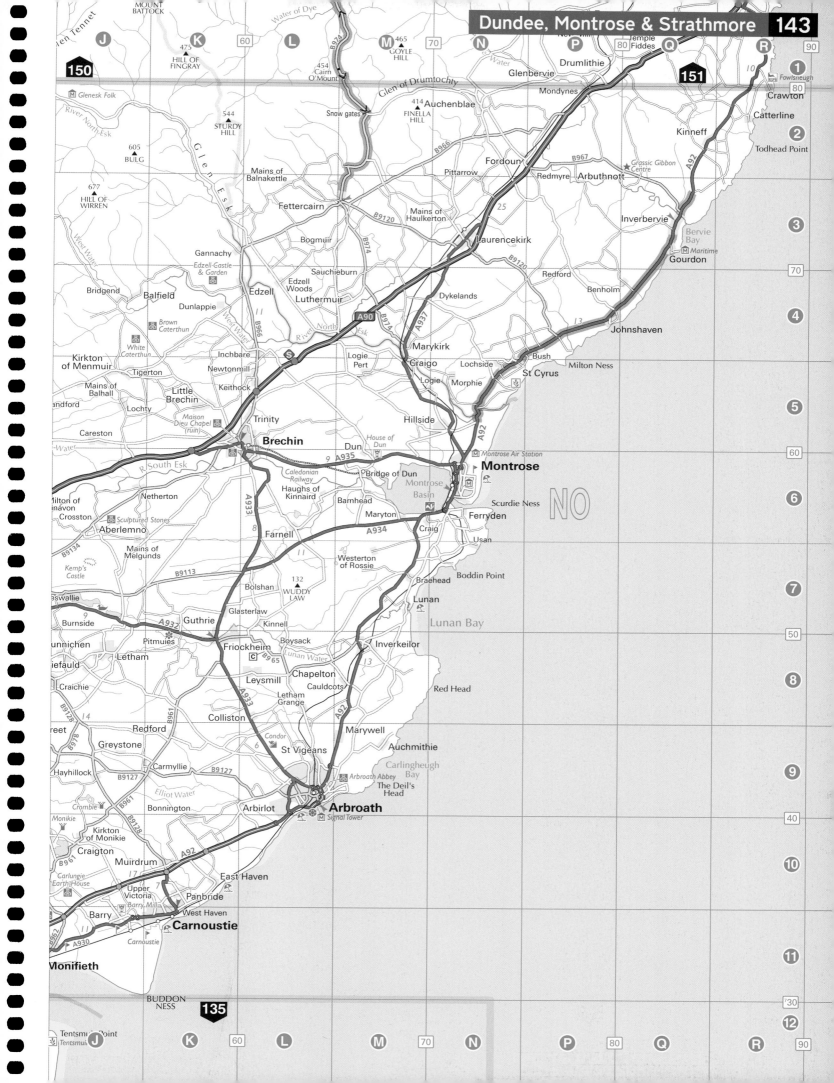

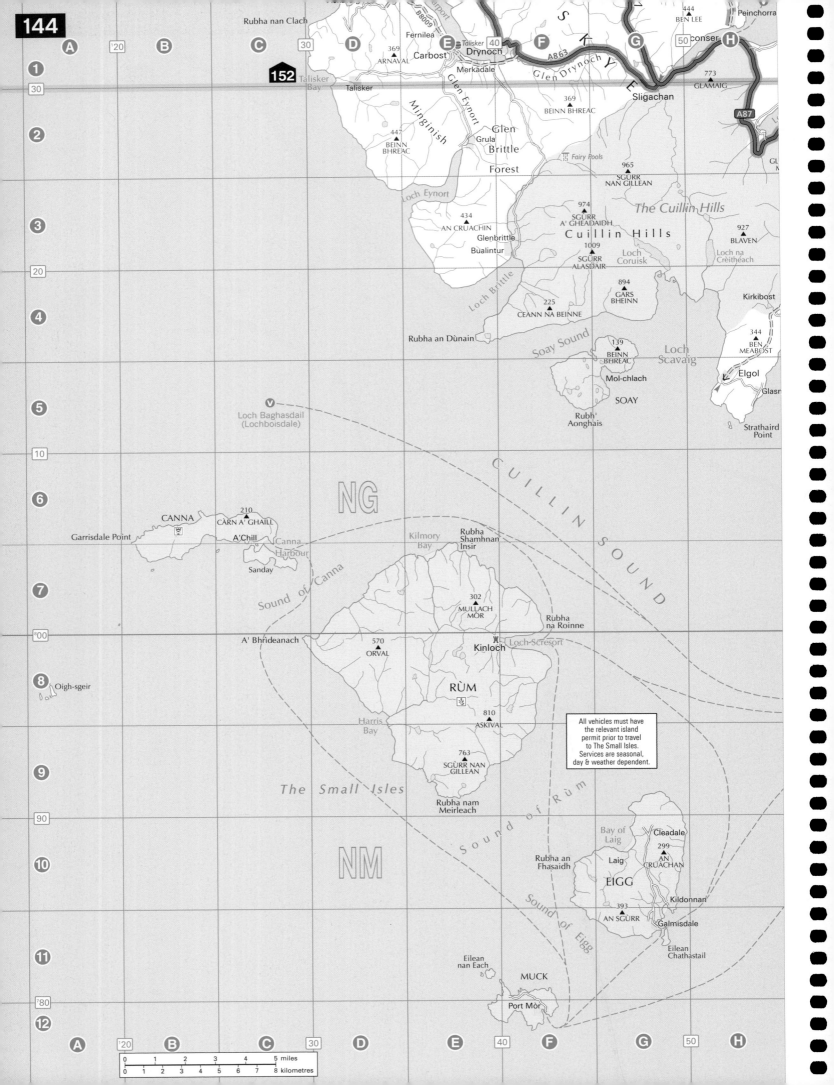

A '20 B 30 C 30 D E Talisker 40 F A863 G 50 conser H

152

1
30

2

3

4

20

5

10

6

7

'00

8

9

90

10

NM

11

'80

12

A '20 B 30 C D E 40 F G 50 H

Rubha nan Clach

Fernilea Talisker SKYE

369 Carbost Drynoch BEN LEE 444 Peinchorra
ARNAVAL Merkadale 773 GLAMAIG

Talisker Glen Drynoch Sligachan A87
Bay Talisker

Minginish Glen Eynort Glen Grula Brittle 369 BEINN BHREAC

447 Brittle Forest Fairy Pools
BEINN 965
BHREAC SGÙRR The Cuillin Hills
NAN GILLEAN

Loch Eynort 974 SGÙRR
A' GHEADAIDH Cuillin Hills 927
434 BLAVEN
AN CRUACHIN Glenbrittle 1009 Loch
Bualintur SGÙRR Coruisk Loch na
ALASDAIR Crèitheach

894 Kirkibost
GARS
BHEINN

225 Rubha an Dùnain CEANN NA BEINNE 344
BEN
Loch Brittle Soay Sound 139 Loch MEABOST
BEINN Scavaig
BHREAC Elgol

Mol-chlach Glasn

SOAY
Rubh' Strathaird
Aonghais Point

Loch Baghasdail
(Lochboisdale) V

CUILLIN SOUND

NG

CANNA 210 Kilmory Rubha
CÀRN A' GHAILL Bay Shamhnan
Garrisdale Point A'Chill Insir
Canna
Harbour 302
Sanday MULLACH
MÒR
Sound of Canna Rubha
na Roinne

A' Bhrideanach 570 Loch Scresort
ORVAL Kinloch

Oigh-sgeir RÙM

810
ASKIVAL

Harris
Bay 763
SGÙRR NAN
GILLEAN

All vehicles must have
the relevant island
permit prior to travel
to The Small Isles.
Services are seasonal,
day & weather dependent.

The Small Isles Rubha nam
Meirleach

Bay of
Laig Cleadale
Rubha an 299
Fhasaidh Laig AN
CRUACHAN

EIGG Kildonnan

393 Galmisdale
AN SGÙRR

Sound of Rùm

Sound of Eigg

Eilean Eilean
nan Each Chathastail

MUCK

Port Mòr

0 1 2 3 4 5 miles
0 1 2 3 4 5 6 7 8 kilometres

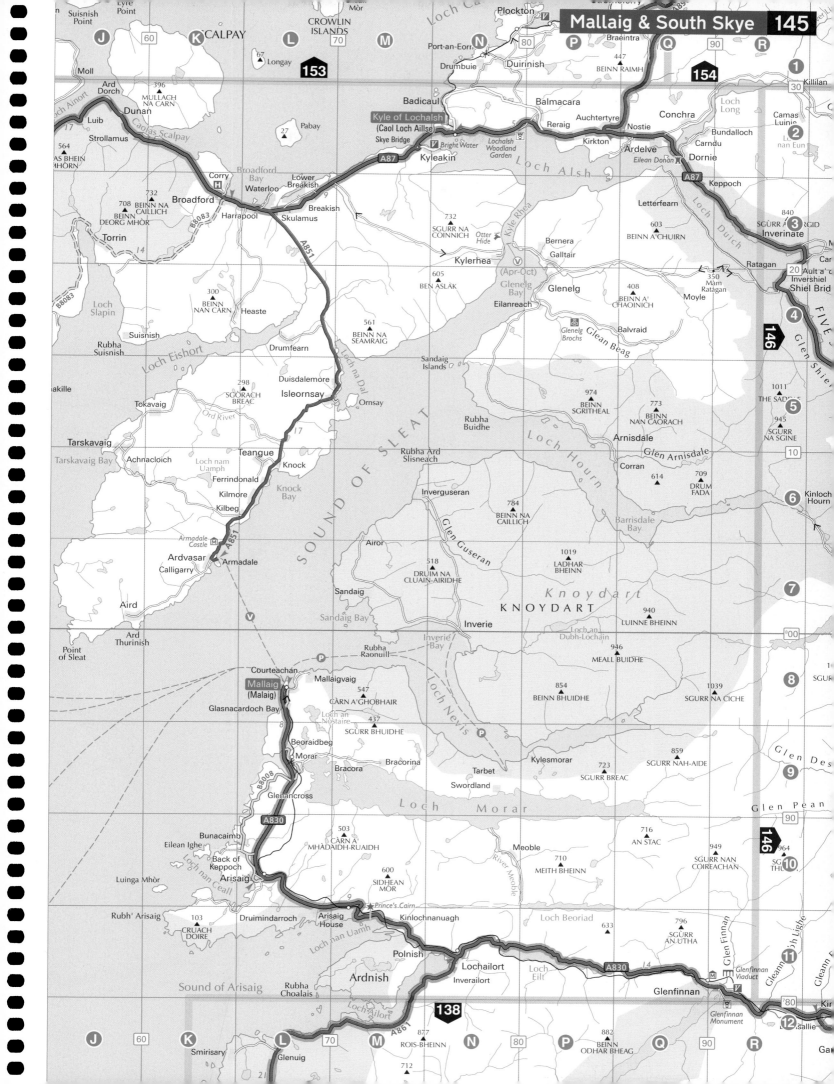

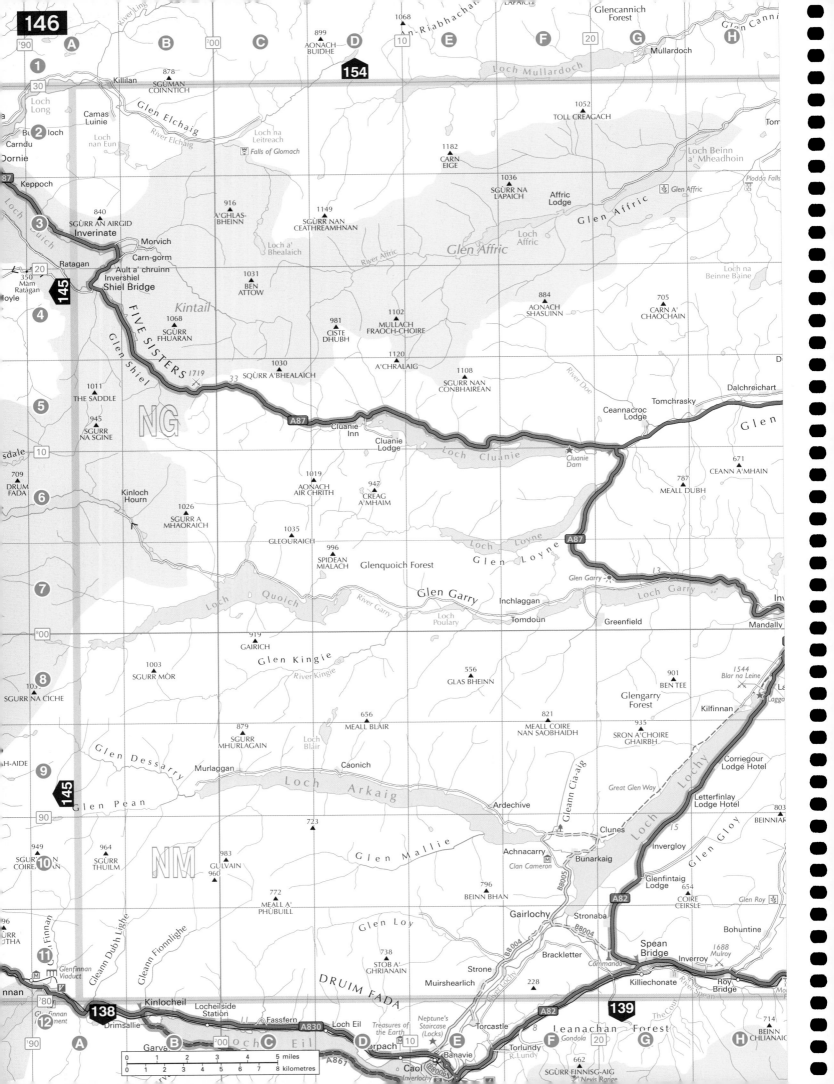

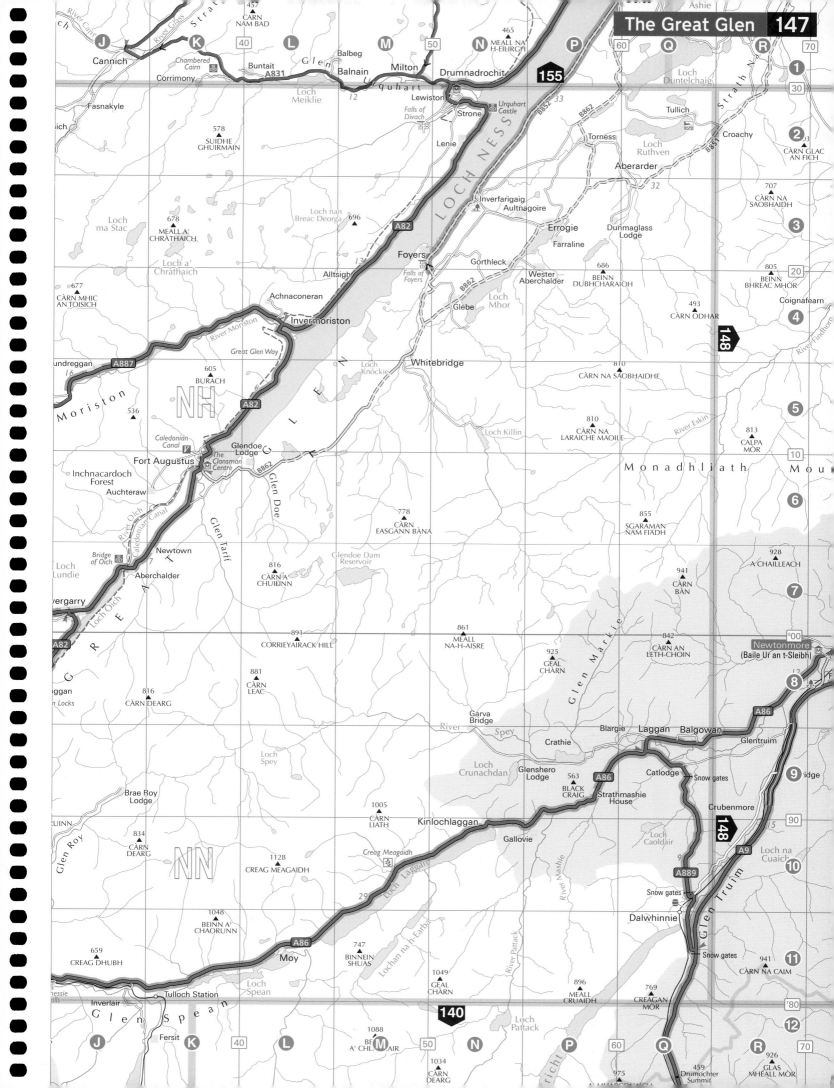

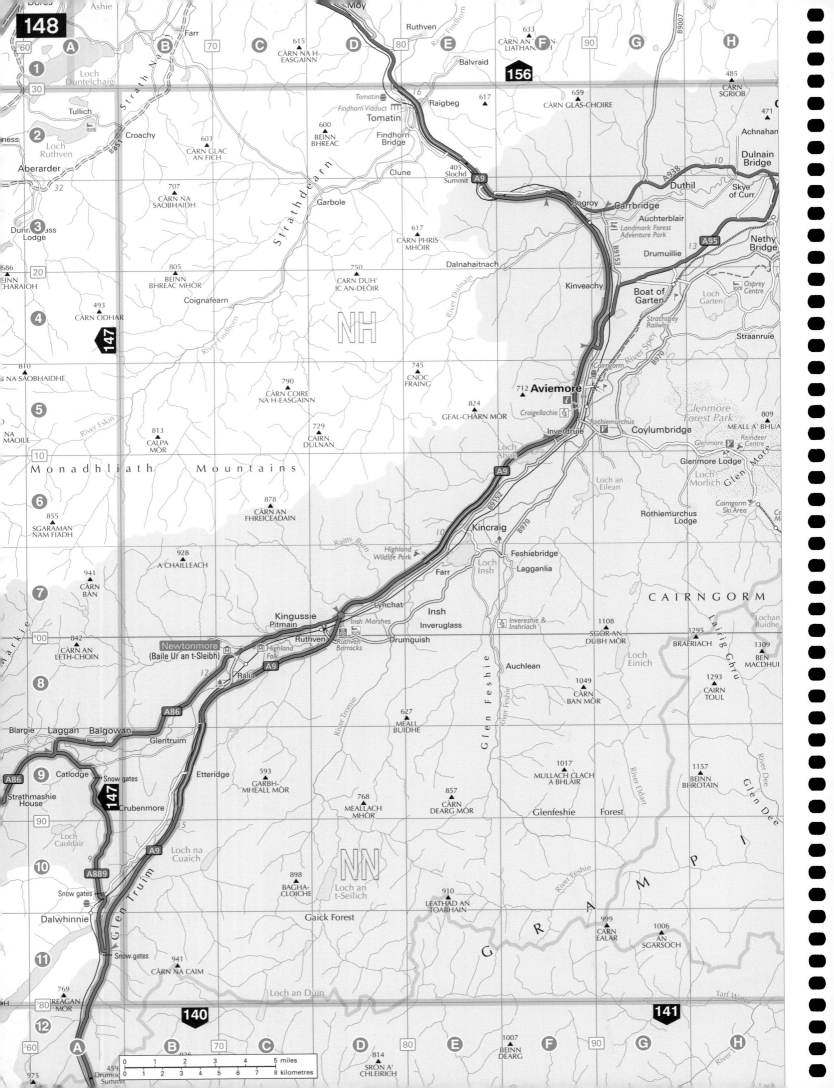

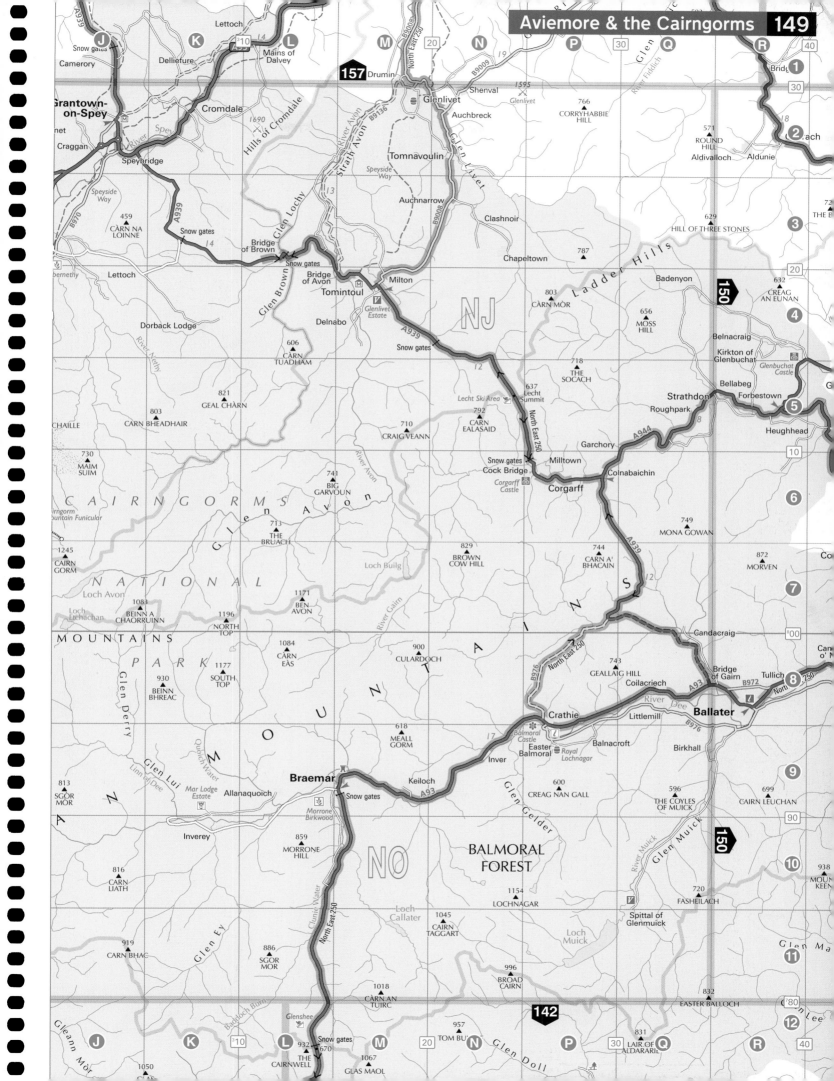

J K L M N P Q R

Lettoch
Snow gates
Camerory
Grantown-on-Spey
Craggan
Speybridge
Delliefure
Mains of Dalvey
157 Drumin
Glenlivet
Shenval
Glenlivet 1595
CORRYHABBIE HILL 766
571 ROUND HILL
Aldivalloch Aldunie

Cromdale
Hills of Cromdale
1690
River Spey
Tomnavoulin
Auchbreck
Auchnarrow
Clashnoir
Chapeltown 787
803 CÀRN MÒR
629 HILL OF THREE STONES
72 THE B

150
632 CREAG AN EUNAN

CÀRN NA LOINNE 459
Speyside Way
B970
Snow gates
Bridge of Brown
Glen Lochy
Lettoch
Glen Brown
Bridge of Avon
Snow gates
Milton
Tomintoul
Glenlivet Estate
Delnabo
A939
NJ
Badenyon
MOSS HILL 656
Belnacraig
Kirkton of Glenbuchat
Glenbuchat Castle
Strathdon
Bellabeg Forbestown
Heughhead

Dorback Lodge
CÀRN TUADHAM 606
Snow gates
12
637 Lecht Summit
THE SOCACH 718
Garchory
A944
Roughpark
8
10

GEAL CHÀRN 821
River Nethy
Lecht Ski Area
792 CÀRN EALASAID
North East 250
Milltown
Colnabaichin
CARN BHEADHAIR 803
CHAILLE
710 CRAIG VEANN
Snow gates
Cock Bridge
Corgarff Castle
Corgarff
MONA GOWAN 749
872 MORVEN

730 MAIM SUIM
CAIRNGORMS
Cairngorm Mountain Funicular
741 BIG GARVOUN
Glen Avon
713 THE BRUACH
Loch Builg
829 BROWN COW HILL
744 CÀRN A' BHACAIN
A939
12

1245 CAIRN GORM
NATIONAL
Loch Avon
Loch Etchachan
1083 BEINN A CHAORRUINN
1171 BEN AVON
1196 NORTH TOP
River Cairn
MOUNTAINS

MOUNTAINS
1084 CÀRN EÀS
900 CULARDOCH
Candacraig
100
Can o' N

PARK
930 BEINN BHREAC
1177 SOUTH TOP
North East 250
743 GEALLAIG HILL
Bridge of Gairn
Tullich
B972

Glen Derry
B976
Coilacriech
A93
River Dee
Ballater
North

Quoich Water
618 MEALL GORM
17
Balmoral Castle
Crathie
Littlemill
B976
Crathie
Easter Balmoral
Royal Lochnagar
Balnacroft
Birkhall

813 SGOR MOR
Glen Lui
Linn of Dee
Mar Lodge Estate
Allanaquoich
Braemar
Snow gates
Keiloch
A93
Inver
Glen Gelder
600 CREAG NAN GALL
596 THE COYLES OF MUICK
699 CAIRN LEUCHAN
90

816 CARN LIATH
Inverey
Morrone Birkwood
859 MORRONE HILL
NO
BALMORAL FOREST
River Muick
Glen Muick
720 FASHEILACH
150
938 MOUN KEEN

919 CARN BHAC
886 SGOR MOR
Clunie Water
1154 LOCHNAGAR
Spittal of Glenmuick
Loch Muick

Glen Ey
North East 250
Loch Callater
1045 CAIRN TAGGART
Glen Ma

1018 CÀRN AN TUIRC
996 BROAD CAIRN
832 EASTER BALLOCH
780
n Lee

Glenshee
142
957 TOM BU
831 LAIR OF ALDARARIL
12

Gleann Mòr
J K L M N P Q R
Snow gates
932 670 THE CAIRNWELL
1067 GLAS MAOL
20
Glen Doll
30 40
1050

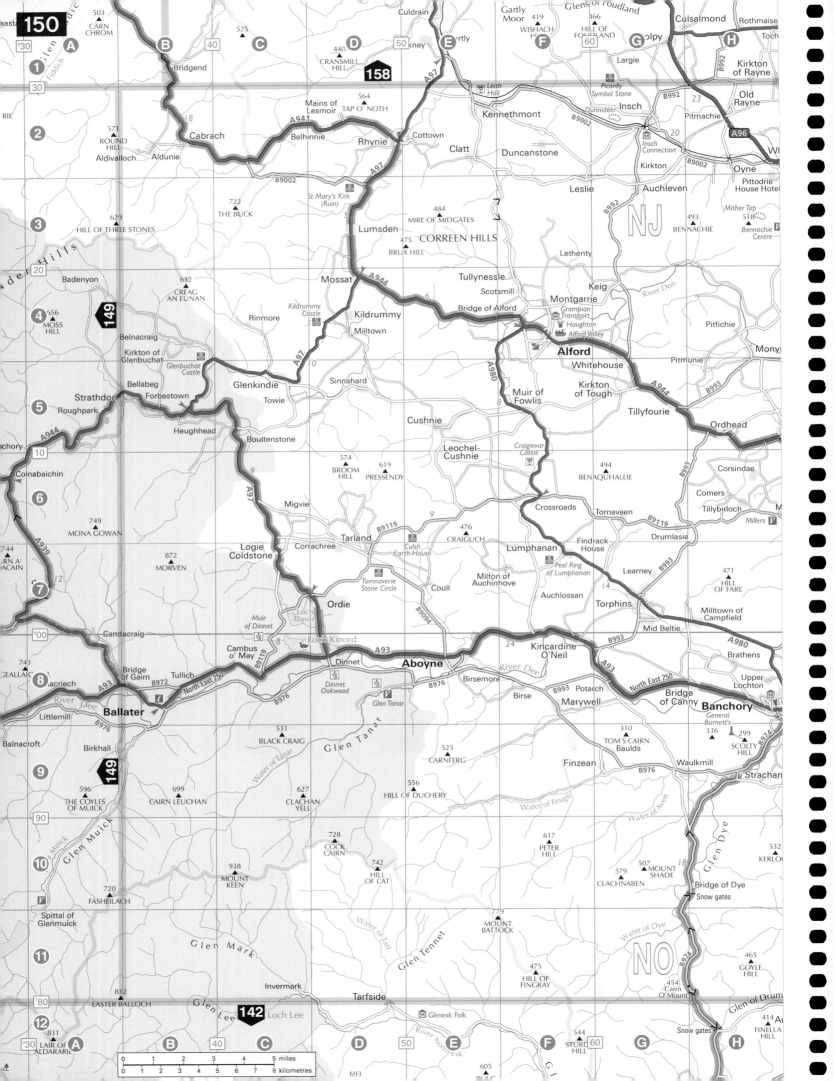

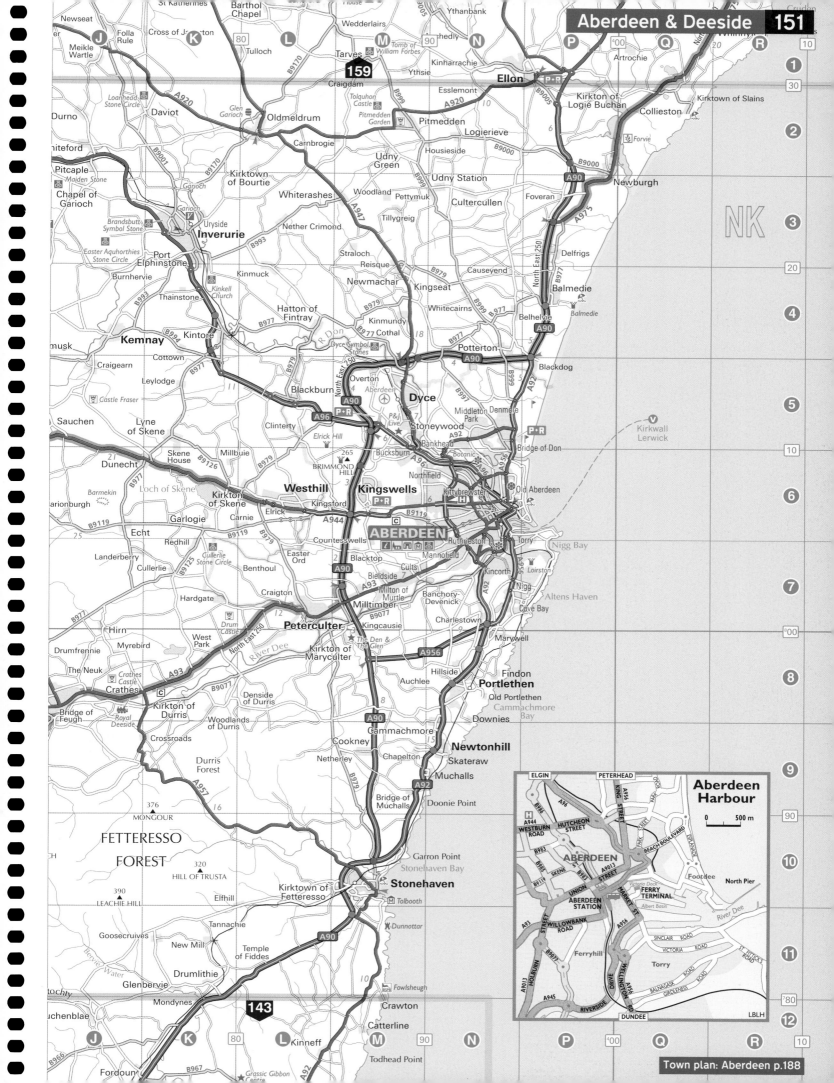

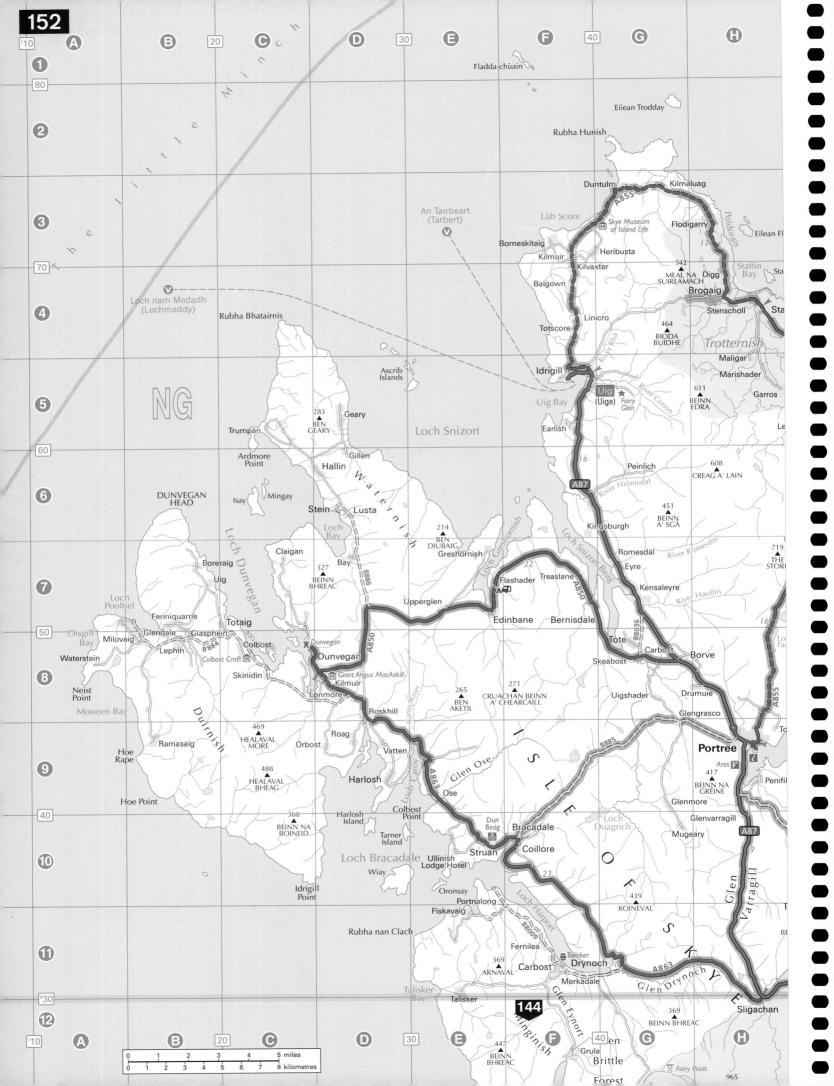

J • K — 60 — L • M — 70 — N • P — 80 — Q • R — 90 —

CNOC
BREAC
Garden

North Erradale • 1
Poolewe
Londubh

Big Sand
160 Strath A832 • 2
Smithstown Heritage
Lonemore Auchtercairn
Longa Gairloch
Island Charlestown
Loch Gairloch & Loch Ewe 421
MEALL AN
Gairloch DOIREIN

Eilean
Horrisdale
Port B8056
Henderson • 3
Badachro River Kerry Loch Bad
Opinan an Sgalaig
Victoria Falls 19
South Erradale Tallad
70

Loch Ghaineamhach • 4
Red Point
Loch a' 875
Ghodhainn BAOSBHEINN 855
BEINN
619 AN EOIN
Red BEINN BHREAC Loch a'
Point Bhealaich • 5

odigarry NG 985
Loch BEINN 914
ffin Island Torridon Rubha ALLIGIN BEINN DEARG
na Fearn 60
Kilt Rock Lower 102
ffin Ellishader Fearnmore Diabaig • 6
Valtos Loch Diabaig
Rubha nam Brathairean Ob Fearnbeg Allligin Shuas Inveralligin
Culnaknock Chuaig Arrina Torridon
alt Tote Kenmore House
A855 Cuaig Ardheslaig Upper Loch Torridon Deer Torrid

Callakille Loch
RONA Shieldaig
Shieldaig Annat
Eilean Weste oss • 7
Tigh Loch
Lonbain 492 Damph
AN GARBH- 902
Eilean MHEALL 493 Glenshieldaig Forest 50
Fladday CROIC- DAMPH
SOUND OF RAASAY Loch BHEINN
Manish Arnish Torran Loch Lundie • 8
312 Point Arnish North Coast 500
Loch Brochel Loch
Leathan River Applecross Coultrie 730
Applecross 895 SGURR A
RAASAY BEINN BHAN GHARAIDH
Applecross Rassal
Bay Ashwood • 9
Milltown 626
Pass of the
412 Camusteel Cattle 774
BEN Bealach na Ba SGURR A' A896
TIANAVAIG INNER SOUND Camusterrach CHAORACHAIN Kishorn Kirkton
Aird Dhubh SGURR A' CHAORACHAIN Lochcarron
444 Culduie Kishorn 154 40
DUN CAAN Ardarroch Slumbay • 10
Rubha na' Leac Loch Kishorn Achintraid 394
Toscaig BAD A
310 Kishorn GHREAMHA
Clachan BEINN NA LEAC River Toscaig Island Strome Ardnarff
Inverarish Ardaneaskan
Eilean Stromeferry Achmore • 11
he Braes Meadhonach Eilean A890
444 Suisnish Eyre Mor Plockton Braeintra
LEE Peinchorran Point CROWLIN Port-an-Eorna 447
Sconser ISLANDS SCALPAY Drumbuie BEINN RAIMH • 12
773 Moll Longay Duirinish Balmacara
GLAMAIG 67 Loch
Ard 396 145 Badicaul Balmacara Conchra Long
J A87 K Dorch L MULLACH Pabay Rera Auchtertyre R
Strollamus NA CARN 70 Nostie Kirkton 90
564 Dunan 80 N Loch Alsh Bright Water
GLAS BHEIN Caolas Scalpay Kyle of Lochalsh P Lochalsh Q Ardelve Carndu
Skye Bridge Woodland Eilean Donan Dornie
A87 Garden Ardvie
Kyleakin

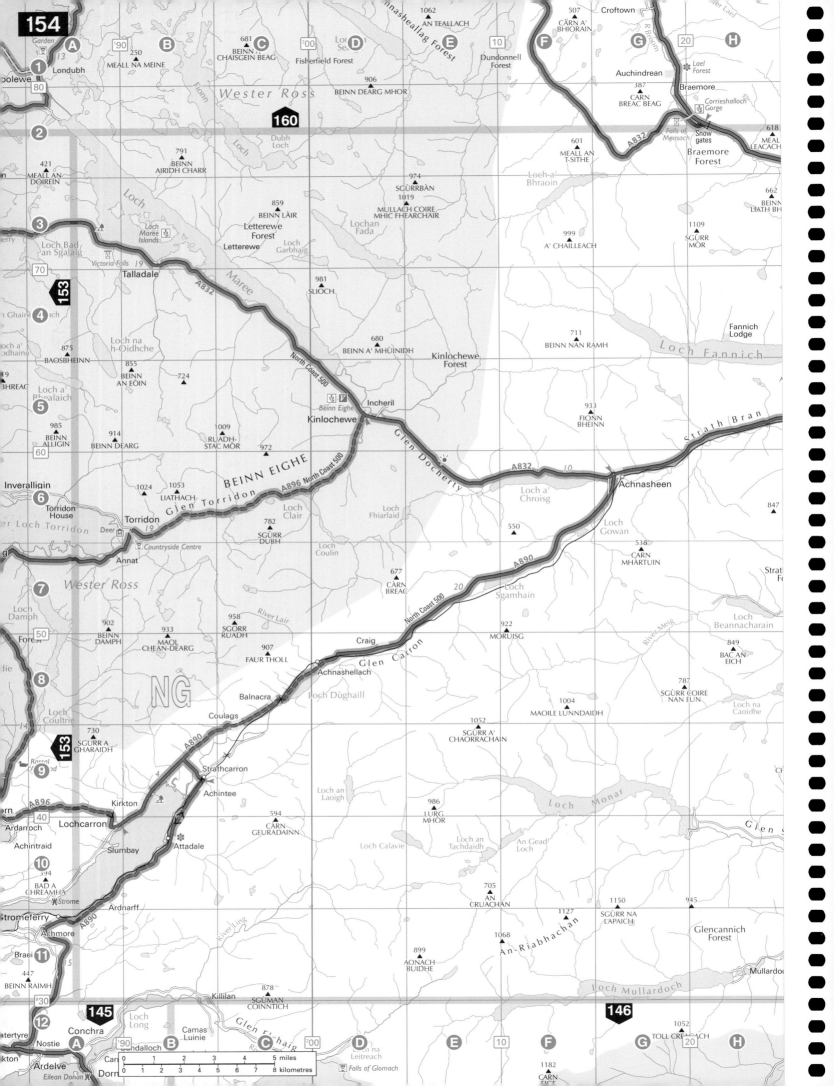

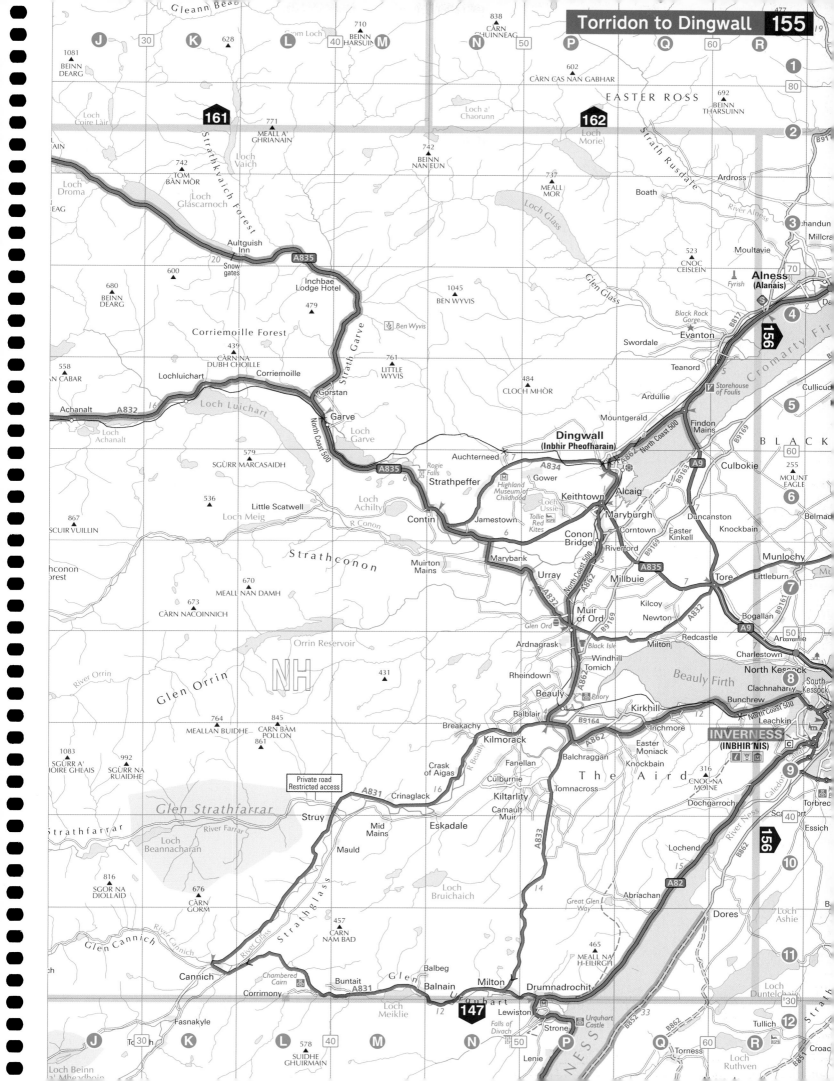

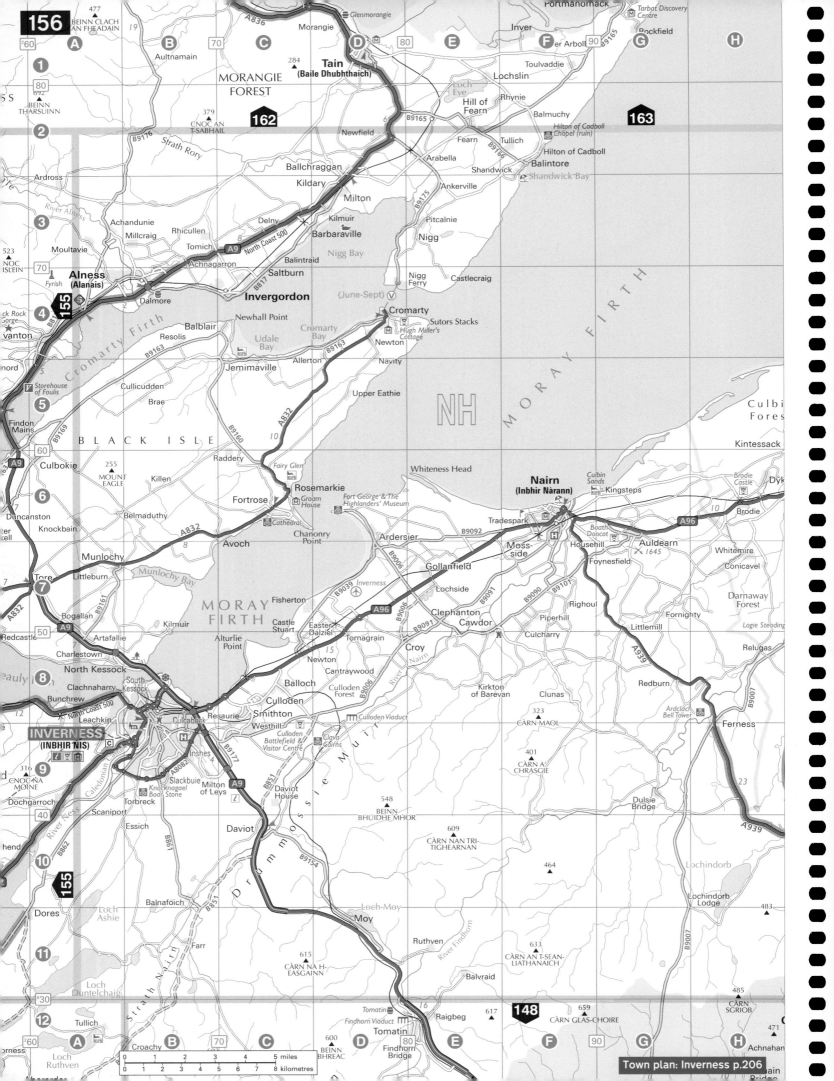

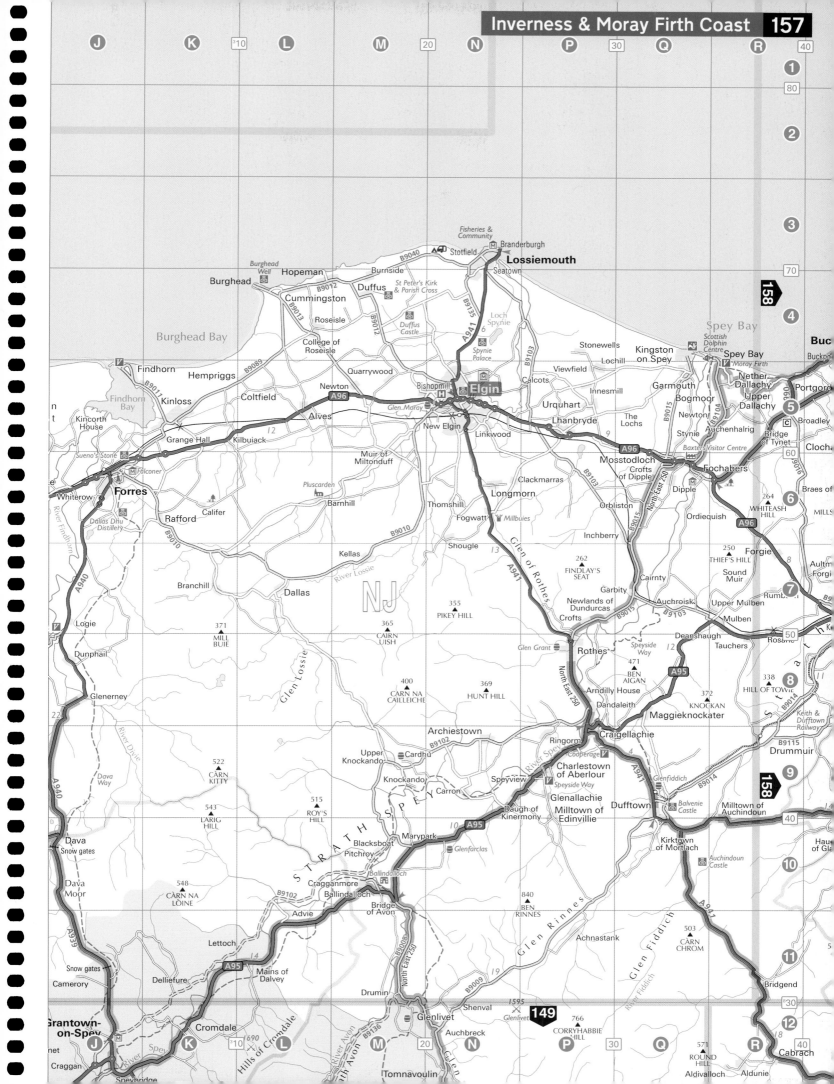

J   K   310   L   M   20   N   P   30   Q   R   40

1
80
2
3
158
70
4

Fisheries & Community
Branderburgh
Stotfield
Lossiemouth
Seatown

Burghead Well
Hopeman   Burnside
Burghead   B9040   St Peter's Kirk & Parish Cross
Cummingston   Duffus
B9012
Roseisle   Duffus Castle
Burghead Bay   B9013   Loch Spynie
B9012   6
College of Roseisle   Spynie Palace
Findhorn   Hempriggs   B9089   Quarrywood   Bishopmill   Elgin   Calcots   Stonewells
Newton   A96   H   Viewfield   Lochill   Kingston on Spey
Kinloss   Coltfield   Alves   Glen Moray   Innesmill   Garmouth   Bogmoor
Findhorn Bay   New Elgin   Urquhart   Lhanbryde   The Lochs   Newton
Kincorth House   Grange Hall   Kilbuiack   12   Muir of Miltonduff   Linkwood   9   Stynie   Auchenhalrig
Sueno's Stone   Falconer   Pluscarden   Thomshill   Clackmarras   B9015   Mosstodloch   North East 250   Fochabers
Forres   Barnhill   Longmorn   Orbliston   Crofts of Dipple   Dipple   Ordiequish
Whiterow   Rafford   Califer   Fogwatt   Millbuies   262   Inchberry   B9015   264
Dallas Dhu Distillery   Kellas   B9010   FINDLAY'S SEAT   Garbity   Cairnty   Auchroisk   Upper Mulben
River Lossie   13   Glen of Rothes   Newlands of Dundurcas   B9015   B9103   Mulben
A940   Branchill   Dallas   NJ   355   Crofts   Deanshaugh   Tauchers
PIKEY HILL   A941   Rothes   Speyside Way   12   50
Logie   365   CAIRN UISH   Glen Grant   Speyside Way   Deanshaugh
Dunphail   371   MILL BUIE   471   A95
400   369   BEN AIGAN
Glenerney   CARN NA CAILLEICHE   HUNT HILL   North East 250   Arndilly House   372   KNOCKAN
22   Archiestown   Dandaleith   Maggieknockater
CARN KITTY   B9102   Ringorm   Craigellachie
522   Upper Knockando   Cardhu   Cooperage   Drummuir
Dava Way   515   Knockando   Charlestown of Aberlour   Glenfiddich   B9014
ROY'S HILL   Carron   Speyview   Speyside Way   158
543   LARIG HILL   Daugh of Kinermony   Glenallachie   Milltown of Edinvillie   Dufftown   Milltown of Auchindoun
Dava   10   A95   Marypark   Balvenie Castle
Snow gates   548   CARN NA LOINE   Blacksboat   Pitchroy   Glenfarclas   Kirktown of Mortlach   40
Dava Moor   Cragganmore   Ballindalloch   840   BEN RINNES   Auchindoun Castle   10
A939   Advie   Ballindalloch   Bridge of Avon   Achnastank   503   CARN CHROM
Snow gates   Lettoch   14   B9102   19   Glen Fiddich   11
Camerory   A95   Mains of Dalvey   North East 250   Bridgend
Grantown-on-Spey   Delliefure   Drumin   B9009   1595   149   766   30
Cromdale   Glenlivet   Glenlivet   CORRYHABBIE HILL   571   ROUND HILL   12
Craggan   J   K   310   690   L   Hills of Cromdale   M   20   N   P   30   Q   R   40   18
Speybridge   Tomnavoulin   Auchbreck   Aldivalloch   Aldunie   Cabrach

Buc
Buckpol
Spey Bay
Scottish Dolphin Centre
Spey Bay   Moray Firth
Nether Dallachy
Upper Dallachy   5
Portgord
Broadley
c
Bridge of Tynet   Clocha
Baxter's Visitor Centre   60
Braes of Glen
6
WHITEASH HILL   MILLS
250   Forgie   8
THIEF'S HILL   Sound Muir   Rumbl
Aultmc Forgi
7
Keith & Dufftown Railway
338   HILL OF TOW   B9014   8
Hau of Gla

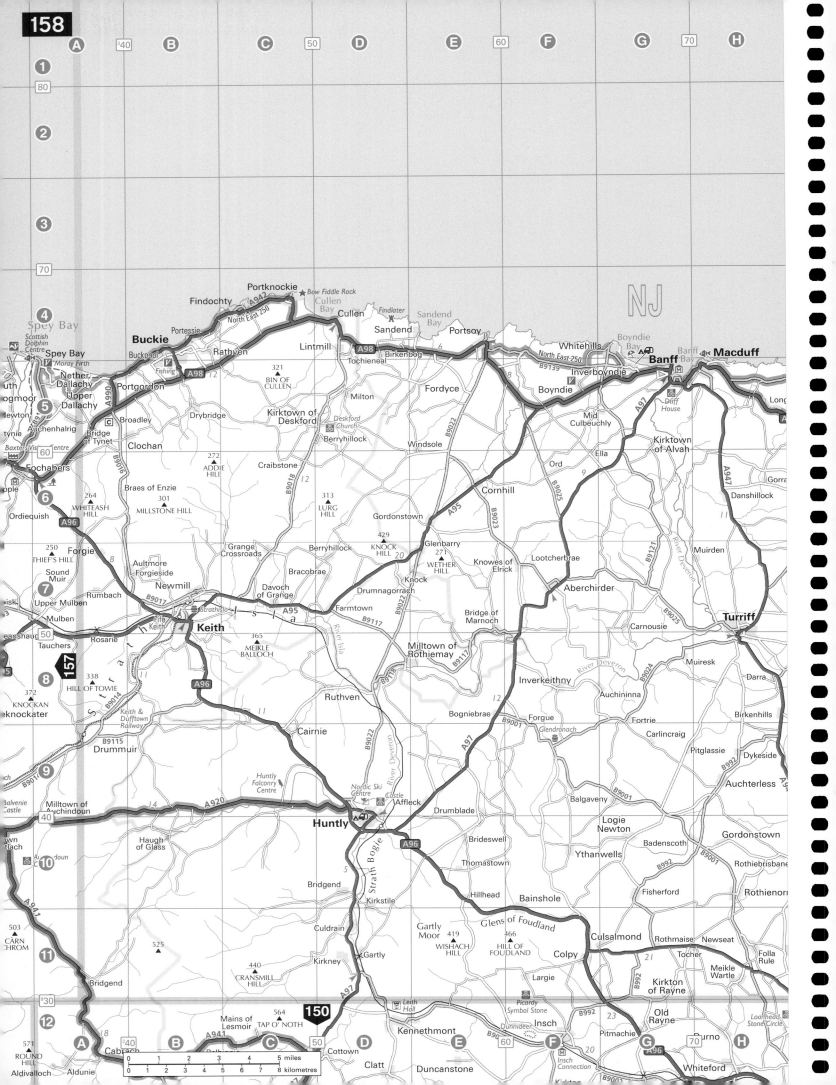

NK

Troup Head
Cullykhan Bay
Gamrie Bay
Gardenstown
Crovie
Silverford
Dubford
Pennan
gmanhill
Gamrie
Protstonhill
Clenerty
Minnonie
Netherbrae
Crudie
chie

Rosehearty
Pittulie
Pitsligo
Sandhaven
Kinnaird Head
Castle, Lighthouse & Museum
Fraserburgh
Fraserburgh Bay
Craigiefold
Peathill
Percyhorner
Coburby
Kirktown
Pitblae
Maggie's Hoosie
Cairnbulg
Inverallochy
Whitelinks Bay
Aberdour Bay
New Aberdour
North East 250
Boyndlie
Mid Ardlaw
Memsie
St Combs
Tyrie
A98
Memsie Cairn
Rathen
Crofts of Savoch
Glasslaw
221
BRACKLAMORE HILL
Newburgh
Lonmay
Rattray Head
B9105
New Pitsligo
B9093
234
WAUGHTON HILL
Strichen
Crimond
Blackhill
18
North East 250
Fintry
New Byth
Bonnykelly
New Leeds
B9093
Loch of Strathbeg
Garmond
B9027
Balthangie
Leys
Kirktown
St Fergus
Scotstown Head
Delgatie
Cuminestown
Denhead
Fetterangus
Backfolds
Rora
A90
13
A981
A950
Deer Abbey
Dunshillock
River Ugie
Peterhead
B9170
Maud
B9106
Old Deer
Mintlaw
Longside
Inverugie
B9170
New Deer
B9029
Railway
B9029
Aden
Aberdeenshire Farming
A950
Peterhead
Buchanhaven
Howe of Teuchar
Blackhill of Clackriach
Inverquhomery
Arbuthnot
Slacks of Cairnbanno
Drymuir
Bulwark
Stuartfield
Peterhead Bay
Prison
Invernettie
A948
B9028
Nethermuir
Millbreck
Nether Kinmundy
Hillhead of Cocklaw
Gourdas
North Millbrex
Knaven
Kinnadie
Clola
Boddam
Lethenty
Cottown of Gight
Cairnorrie
Brownhill
B9030
Blackhill
Stirling
Buchan Ness
Auchnagatt
12
Kinknockie
Lendrum Terrace
Fyvie Castle
Inkhorn
Coldwells
Ardallie
Longhaven
Fyvie
Woodhead
Crofts of Haddo
Methlick
A948
A952
Hatton
A90
Auchiries
Bullers of Buchan
North Haven
St Katherines
Barthol Chapel
Earlsford
Haddo House
Arthrath
Muirtack
Bogbrae
Chapel Hill
North East 250
Cruden Bay
Slains
Cross of Jackston
Wedderlairs
Ythanbank
Birness
Whinnyfold
The Skares
Bay of Cruden
Tulloch
Altar Tomb of William Forbes
Tarves
Auchedly
Kinharrachie
Artrochie
A920
Daviot
Glen Garioch
Old Meldrum
Craigdam
Tolquhon Castle
Pitmedden
Esslemont
Ellon
Kirkton of Logie Buchan
Colliestoun
Kirktown of Slains
B9000
edden
Logierieve
B9005
Forvie
Carnbrogie
Housieside
Udny Green
B9000

151

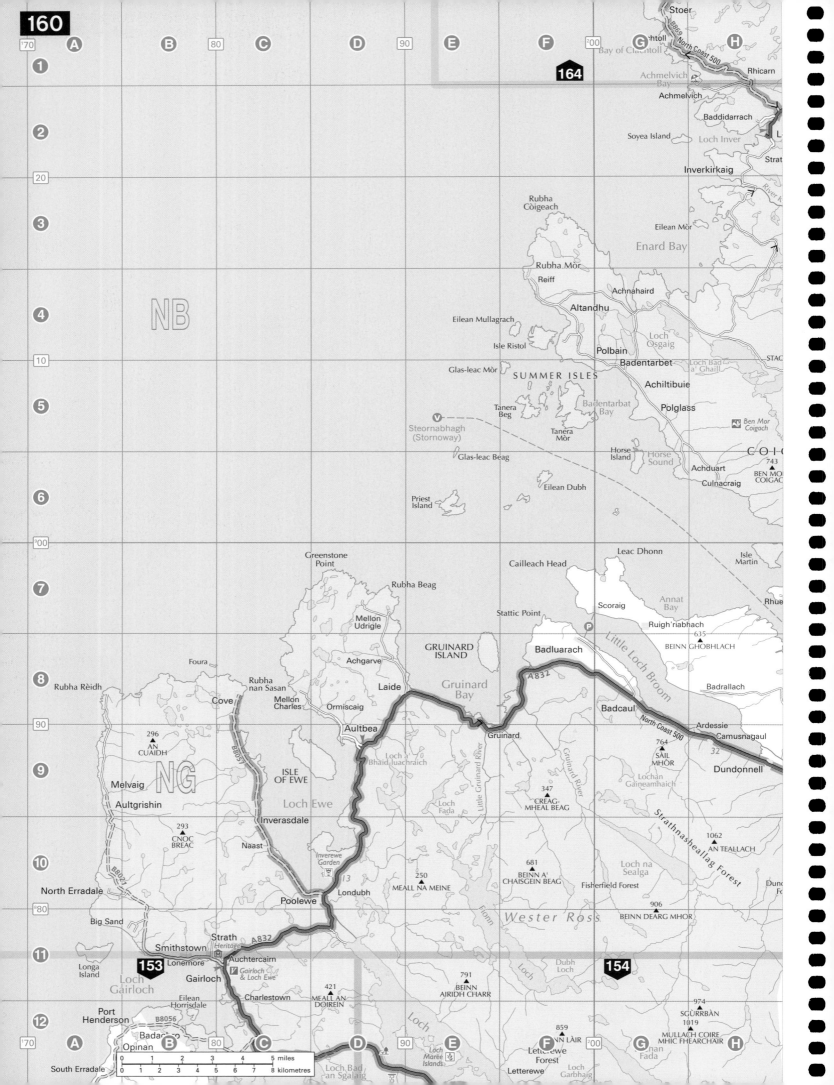

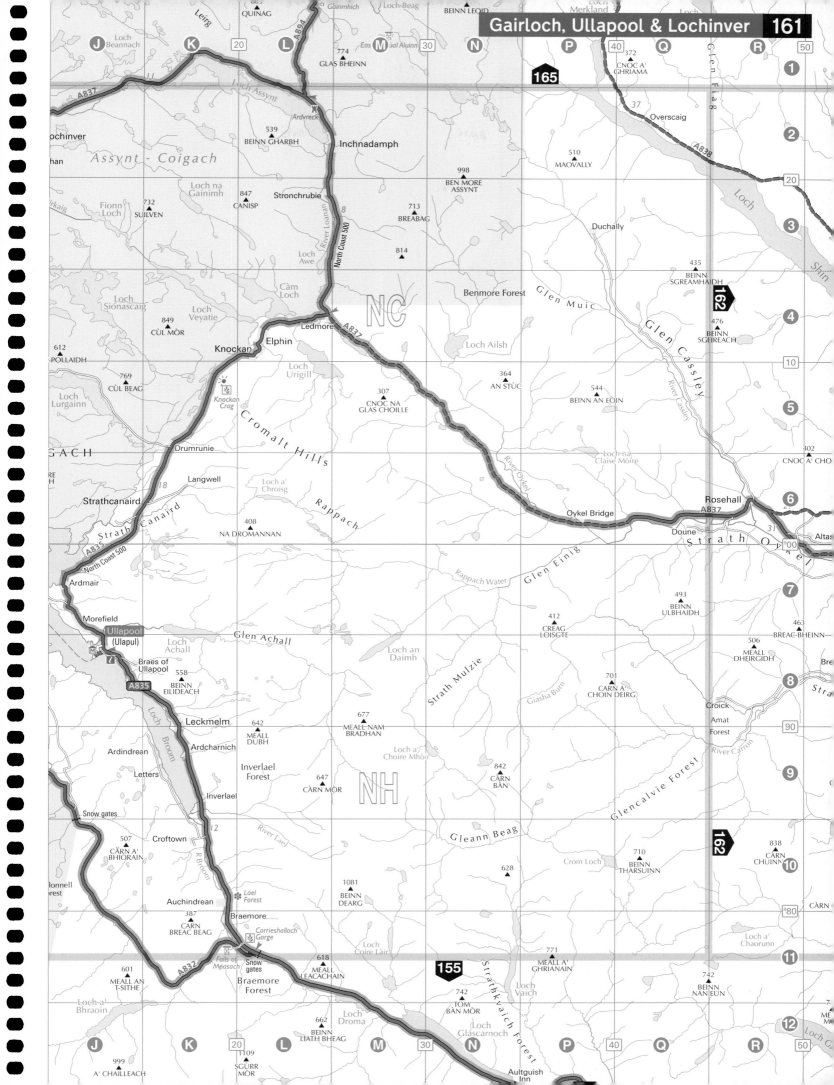

Leirg

QUINAG

Gainmhich Loch Beag BEINN LEOID Loch Merkland Loch

J Loch Beannach K A894 L A837 M *Eas Mùal Aluinn* N P Q Glen Fiag R 50

20 30 40 372 CNOC A' GHRIAMA 1

165 37

774 GLAS BHEINN

A837

Lochinver Ardvreck Inchnadamph Overscaig 2

539 BEINN GHARBH

Assynt - Coigach 510 MAOVALLY A838 20

998 BEN MORE ASSYNT 3

Fionn Loch 847 CANISP Stronchrubie 713 BREABAG Duchally Loch Shin

732 SUILVEN River Loanan 814 435 BEINN SGREAMHAIDH 4

Loch na Gainimh Loch Awe Benmore Forest Glen Muic Glen Cassley

849 CÙL MÒR Càm Loch Ledmore A837 NC 476 BEINN SGEIREACH 10

Loch Veyatie Elphin Knockan Loch Urigill Loch Ailsh River Cassley 5

612 POLLAIDH 307 CNOC NA GLAS CHOILLE 364 AN STÙC 544 BEINN AN EÒIN

Loch Sionascaig Knockan Crag 402 CNOC A' CHO

769 CÙL BEAG Drumrunie Cromalt Hills Loch-na Claise Mòire 6

Loch Lurgainn Langwell Loch a' Chroisg Rappach River Oykel Rosehall A837

GACH Strathcanaird 408 NA DROMANNAN Oykel Bridge Doune Strath Oykel Altas 00

A835 North Coast 500 18 Strath Canaird Glen Einig 493 BEINN ULBHAIDH 7

Ardmair Rappach Water 463 BREAC-BHEINN

Morefield Glen Achall Loch an Daimh 412 CREAG LOISGTE 506 MEALL DHEIRGIDH 8

Ullapool (Ulapul) Loch Achall Strath Mulzie Giasha Burn 701 CARN A' CHOIN DEIRG Stra

Braes of Ullapool 558 BEINN EILIDEACH Croick Amat Forest 90

A835 Leckmelm 642 MEALL DUBH 677 MEALL NAM BRADHAN Loch a' Choire Mhòir River Carron

Ardindrean Ardcharnich Glencalvie Forest 9

Letters Inverlael Forest 647 CÀRN MÒR NH 842 CÀRN BÀN

Inverlael

Snow gates Croftown 507 CÀRN A' BHIORAIN River Lael Gleann Beag 162 838 CÀRN CHUINN 10

12 710 BEINN THARSUINN

nnell Forest Lael Forest Crom Loch 628

Auchindrean 1081 BEINN DEARG 771 MEALL A' GHRIANAIN Loch a' Chaorunn 11

387 CARN BREAC BEAG Braemore Corrieshalloch Gorge 155 742 BEINN NAN EUN

Falls of Measach Snow gates 618 MEALL LEACACHAIN Loch Coire Làir Strathvaich Forest 80

601 MEALL AN T-SITHE A832 Braemore Forest 742 TOM BÀN MÒR Loch Vaich CÀRN

Loch-a' Bhraoin 662 BEINN LIATH BHEAG Loch Droma Loch Glàscarnoch ME

999 A' CHAILLEACH T109 SGURR MÒR Loch

Aultguish Inn

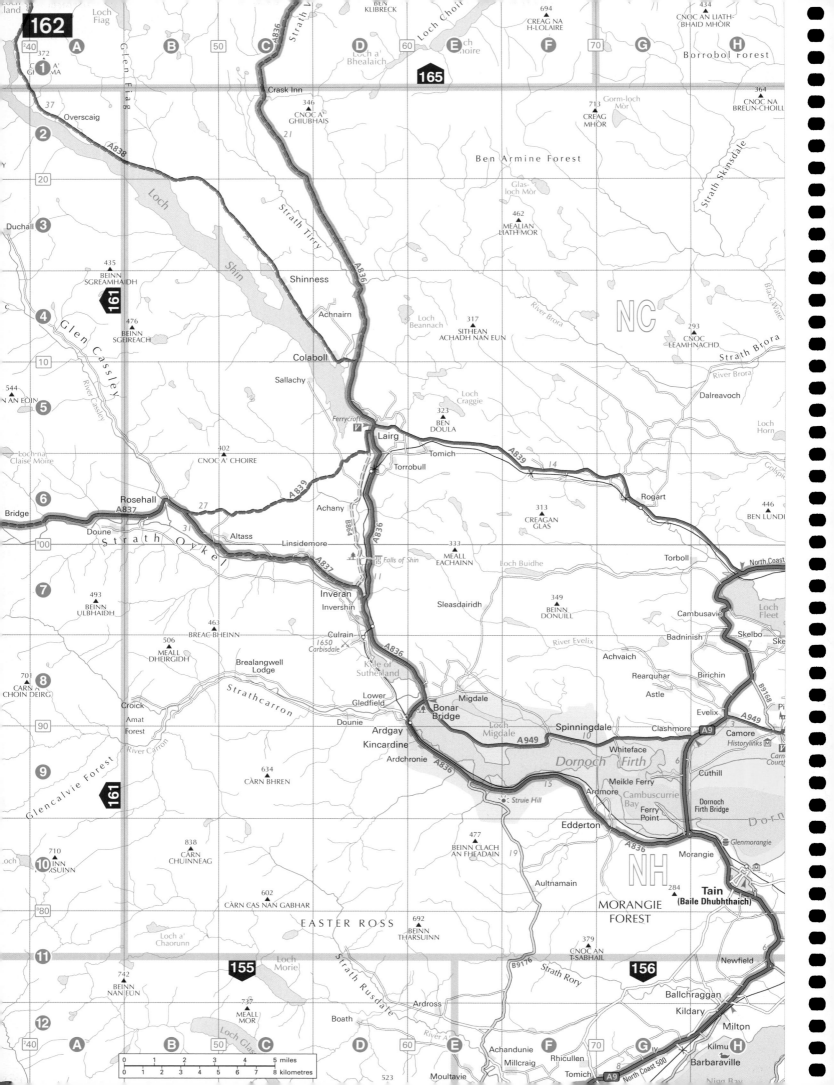

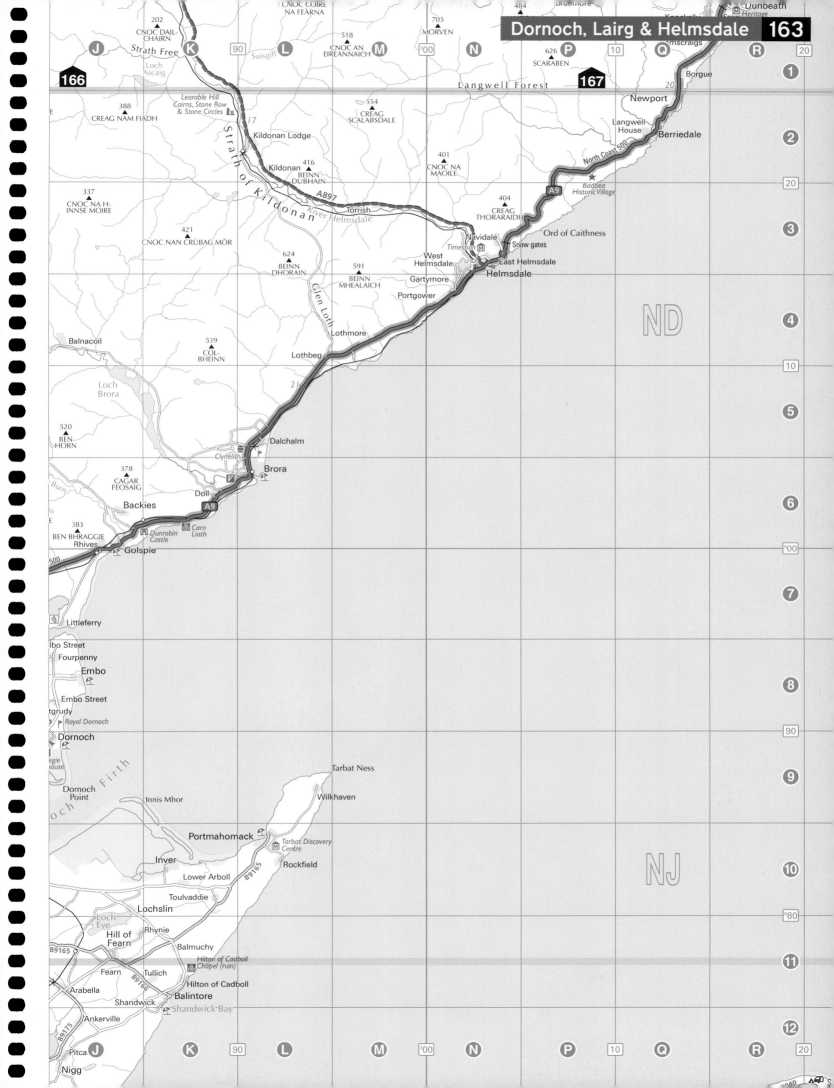

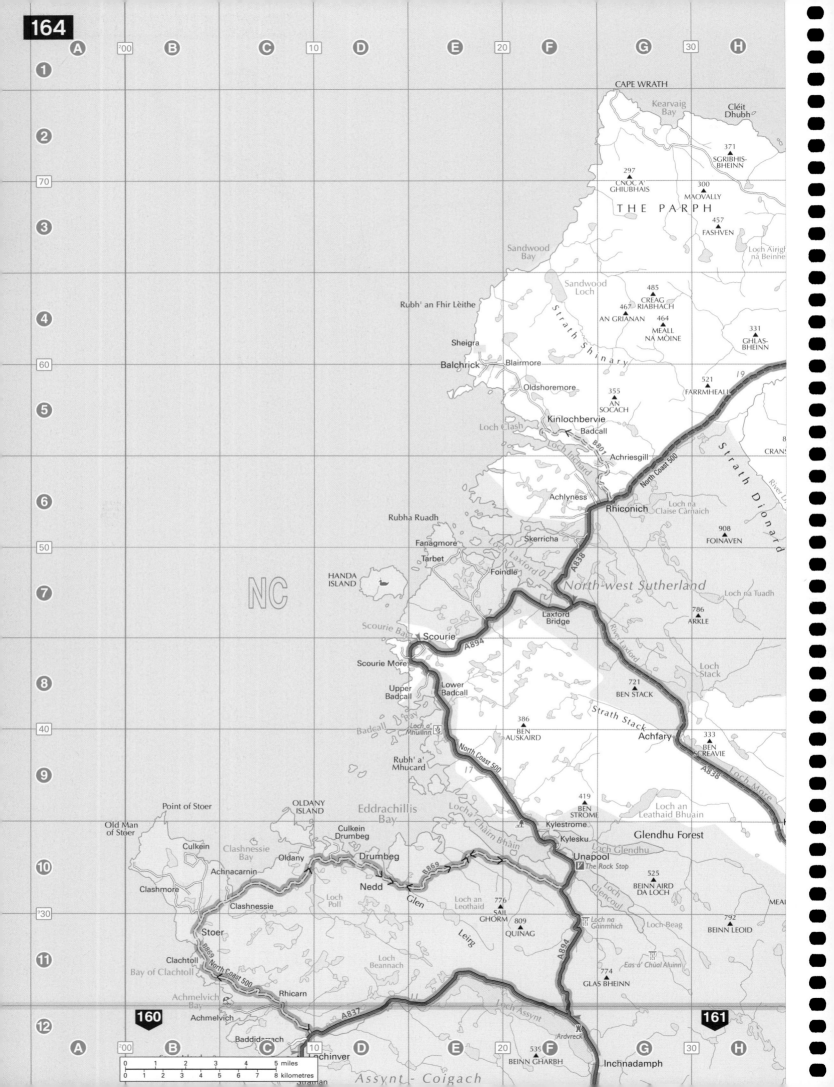

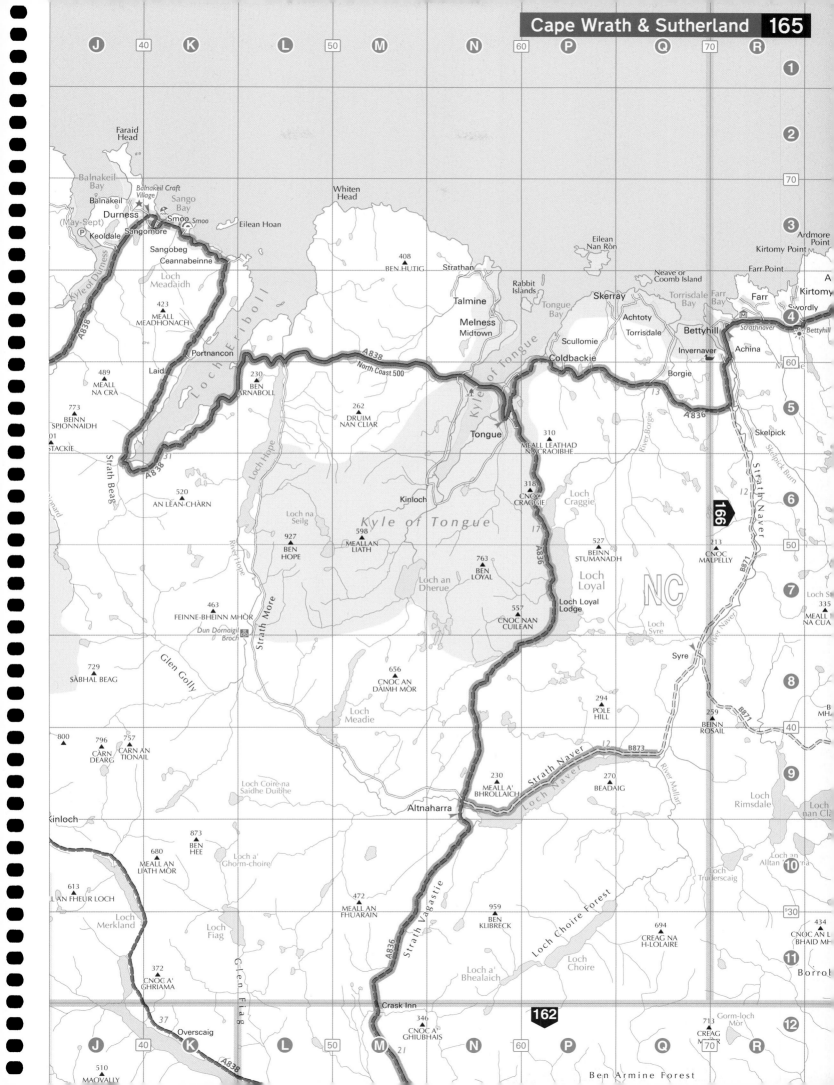

J 40 K L 50 M N 60 P Q 70 R

1
2
70
3

Faraid
Head

Balnakeil
Bay
Balnakeil Craft
Village
Sango
Bay
Balnakeil
Durness
Smoo
Smoo
(May-Sept)
Keoldale
Sangomore
Sangobeg
Ceannabeinne

Whiten
Head

Eilean Hoan

408
BEN HUTIG

Strathan

Eilean
Nan Ròn

Ardmore
Point
Kirtomy Point

Farr Point

Neave or
Coomb Island

Kirtomy

A

Loch
Meadaidh

Loch of Durness

A838

Rabbit
Islands

Talmine

Skerray

Torrisdale
Bay

Farr
Bay

Farr

Swordly

423
MEALL
MEADHONACH

Portnancon

A838

North Coast 500

Kyle of Tongue

Melness
Midtown

Achtoty

Torrisdale

Bettyhill

Invernaver

Strathnaver

Achina

M

Bettyhill

4

Laid

Coldbackie

Scullomie

Borgie

60

489
MEALL
NA CRÀ

230
BEN
ARNABOLL

262
DRUIM
NAN CLIAR

A836

13

River Borgie

Skelpick

5

773
BEINN
SPIONNAIDH

Loch Eriboll

Tongue

310
MEALL LEATHAD
NA CRAOIBHE

Strath Naver

Skelpick Burn

STACKIE

A838

Strath Beag

520
AN LEAN-CHÀRN

Loch na
Seilg

Kyle of Tongue

Kinloch

318
CNOC
CRAGGIE

Loch
Craggie

17

12

6
50

927
BEN
HOPE

463
FEINNE-BHEINN MHÒR

Loch Hope

598
MEALLAN
LIATH

763
BEN
LOYAL

A836

527
BEINN
STUMANADH

Loch
Loyal

NC

213
CNOC
MALPELLY

B871

7

Loch St

335
MEALL
NA CUA

River Hope

Strath More

Dun Dornaigil
Broch

Loch an
Dherue

557
CNOC NAN
CUILEAN

Loch Loyal
Lodge

Loch
Syre

River Naver

Glen Golly

729
SÀBHAL BEAG

656
CNOC AN
DÀIMH MÒR

Syre

8

800

796
CÀRN
DEARG

757
CARN AN
TIONAIL

Loch
Meadie

294
POLE
HILL

259
BEINN
ROSAIL

B871

40

B
MH

Kinloch

Loch Coirè na
Saidhe Duibhe

230
MEALL A'
BHROLLAICH

Strath Naver

12

B873

River Mallart

9

Loch
Rimsdale

Loch
nan Cla

Altnaharra

Loch Naver

270
BEADAIG

10

Loch
Alltan

873
BEN
HEE

Loch a'
Ghorm-choire

Loch
Truderscaig

30

680
MEALL AN
LIATH MÒR

613
L AN FHEUR LOCH

472
MEALL AN
FHUARAIN

Strath Vagastie

959
BEN
KLIBRECK

Loch Choire Forest

694
CREAG NA
H-LOLAIRE

434
CNOC AN L
BHAID MH

11

Borrol

Loch
Merkland

Loch
Fiag

A836

Loch a'
Bhealaich

Loch
Choire

372
CNOC A'
GHRIAMA

Glen Fiag

Crask Inn

162

Gorm-loch
Mòr

713
CREAG
M R

12

Overscaig

37

A838

21

346
CNOC A'
GHIUBHAIS

70

J 40 K 50 L M 60 N P Q R

510
MAOVALLY

Ben Armine Forest

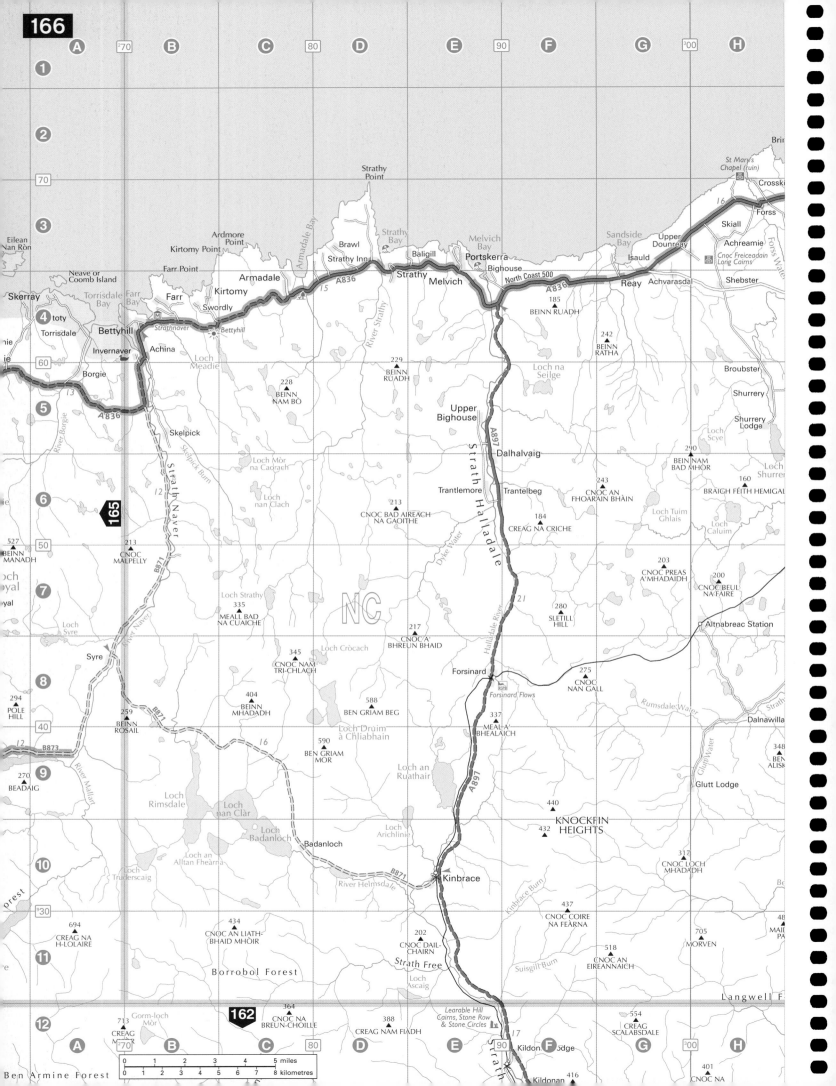

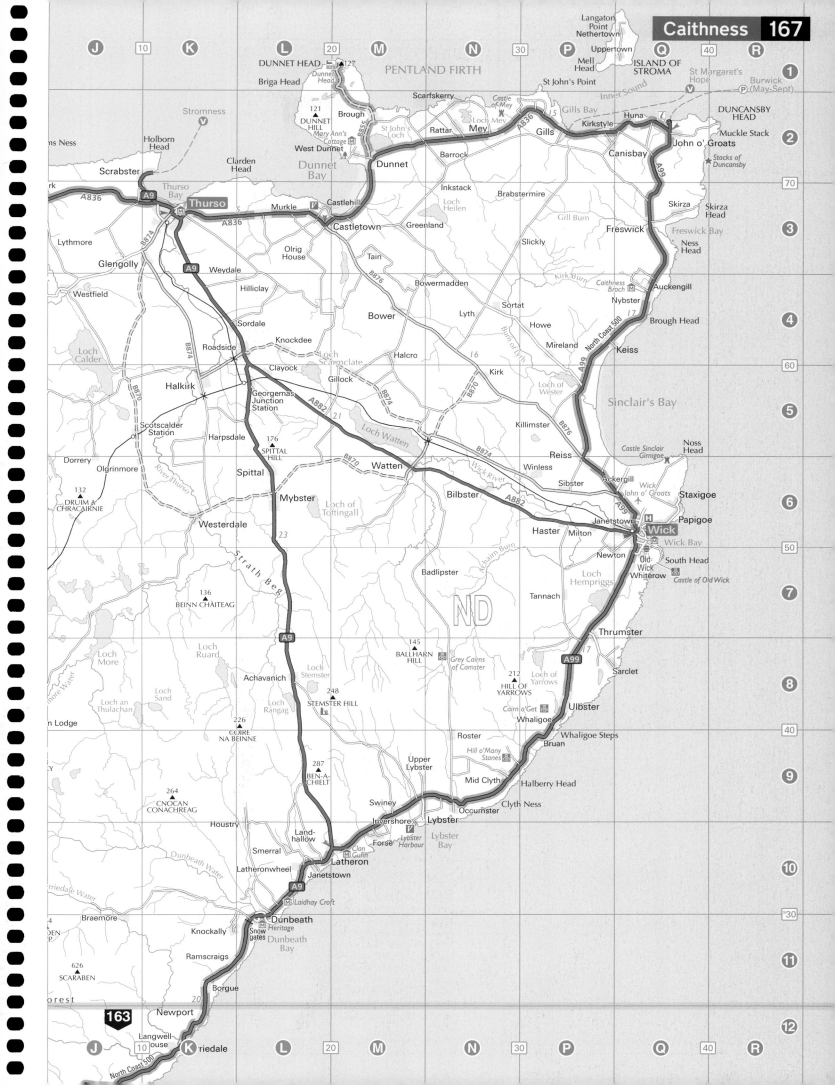

PENTLAND FIRTH

Langaton
Point
Nethertown
Uppertown
Mell
Head
ISLAND OF
STROMA
St Margaret's
Hope
Burwick
(May-Sept)

J
K
L
M
N
P
Q
R

DUNNET HEAD
Dunnet
Head
Briga Head
Brough
DUNNET
HILL
121
Mary Ann's
Cottage
West Dunnet
St John's
Loch
Rattar
Scarfskerry
Castle
of Mey
Loch Mey
Mey
Gills
Gills Bay
Kirkstyle
Huna
Inner Sound
St John's Point
DUNCANSBY
HEAD
John o' Groats
Muckle Stack
Stacks of
Duncansby

Stromness
Holborn
Head
Clarden
Head
Dunnet
Bay
Dunnet
Barrock
Canisbay

Scrabster
Thurso
Bay
Thurso
Murkle
Castlehill
Castletown
Greenland
Inkstack
Brabstermire
Skirza
Skirza
Head
Ness
Head
Freswick
Freswick Bay

Lythmore
Glengolly
Westfield
Weydale
Hilliclay
Olrig
House
Tain
Slickly
Loch
Heilen
Caithness
Broch
Auckengill
Nybster

Loch
Calder
Roadside
Knockdee
Clayock
Bower
Lyth
Howe
Mireland
Brough Head
Keiss

Halkirk
Georgemas
Junction
Station
Gillock
Halcro
Kirk
Loch of
Wester
Sinclair's Bay
Noss
Head

Scotscalder
Station
Harpsdale
176
SPITTAL
HILL
Loch Watten
Killimster
Reiss
Castle Sinclair
Girnigoe

Dorrery
Olgrinmore
Spittal
Watten
Winless
Sibster
Ackergill
Staxigoe

132
DRUIM A'
CHRACAIRNIE
Mybster
Loch of
Toftingall
Bilbster
Wick River
Haster
Milton
Janetstown
Wick
Papigoe

Westerdale
Badlipster
Newton
Old
Wick
Whiterow
South Head
Castle of Old Wick

136
BEINN CHÀITEAG
Strath Beg
ND
Tannach
Loch
Hempriggs

Loch
More
Loch
Ruard
145
BALLHARN
HILL
Grey Cairns
of Camster
Thrumster

Loch an
Thulachan
Loch
Sand
Achavanich
Loch
Stemster
212
HILL OF
YARROWS
Loch of
Yarrows
Sarclet

Lodge
226
COIRE
NA BEINNE
248
STEMSTER HILL
Loch
Rangag
Cairn o'Get
Ulbster

287
BEN-A-
CHIELT
Roster
Whaligoe
Whaligoe Steps
Bruan

264
CNOCAN
CONACHREAG
Upper
Lybster
Hill o'Many
Stanes
Mid Clyth
Halberry Head

Houstry
Swiney
Occumster
Clyth Ness

Smerral
Land-
hallow
Invershore
Forse
Lybster
Harbour
Lybster
Bay

Braemore
Dunbeath Water
Latheronwheel
Latheron
Clan
Gunn
Janetstown

Knockally
Laidhay Croft
Dunbeath
Heritage
Snow
gates
Dunbeath
Bay

626
SCARABEN
Ramscraigs
Borgue

FOREST
Newport
163
Langwell
House
riedale

North Coast 500

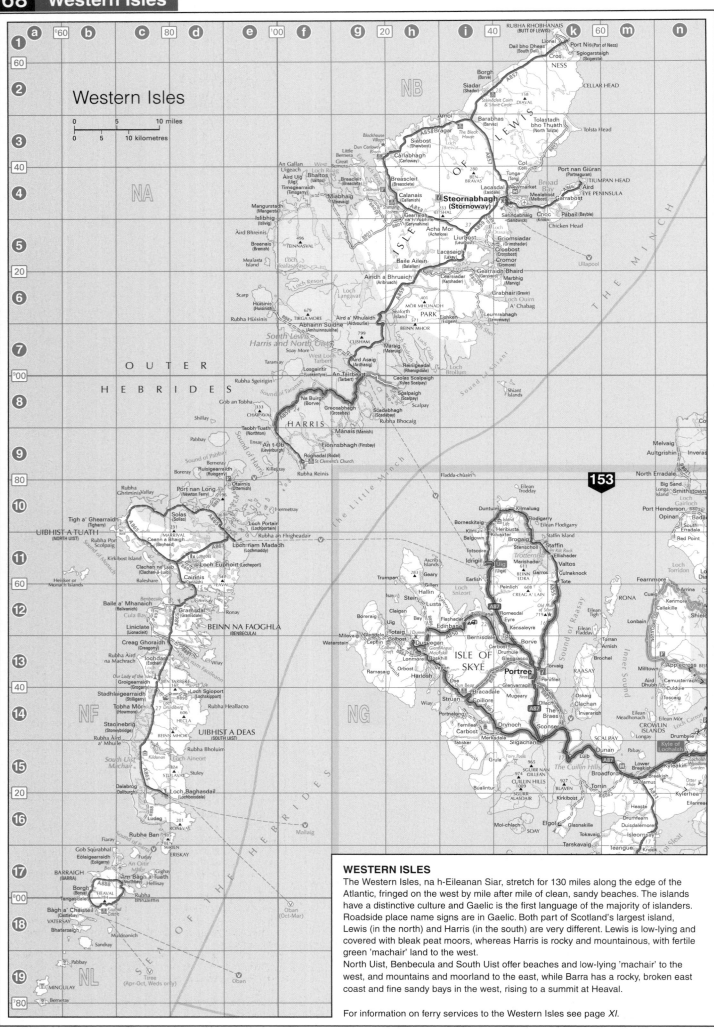

Western Isles

0   5   10 miles
0   5   10 kilometres

WESTERN ISLES

The Western Isles, na h-Eileanan Siar, stretch for 130 miles along the edge of the Atlantic, fringed on the west by mile after mile of clean, sandy beaches. The islands have a distinctive culture and Gaelic is the first language of the majority of islanders. Roadside place name signs are in Gaelic. Both part of Scotland's largest island, Lewis (in the north) and Harris (in the south) are very different. Lewis is low-lying and covered with bleak peat moors, whereas Harris is rocky and mountainous, with fertile green 'machair' land to the west.

North Uist, Benbecula and South Uist offer beaches and low-lying 'machair' to the west, and mountains and moorland to the east, while Barra has a rocky, broken east coast and fine sandy bays in the west, rising to a summit at Heaval.

For information on ferry services to the Western Isles see page *XI*.

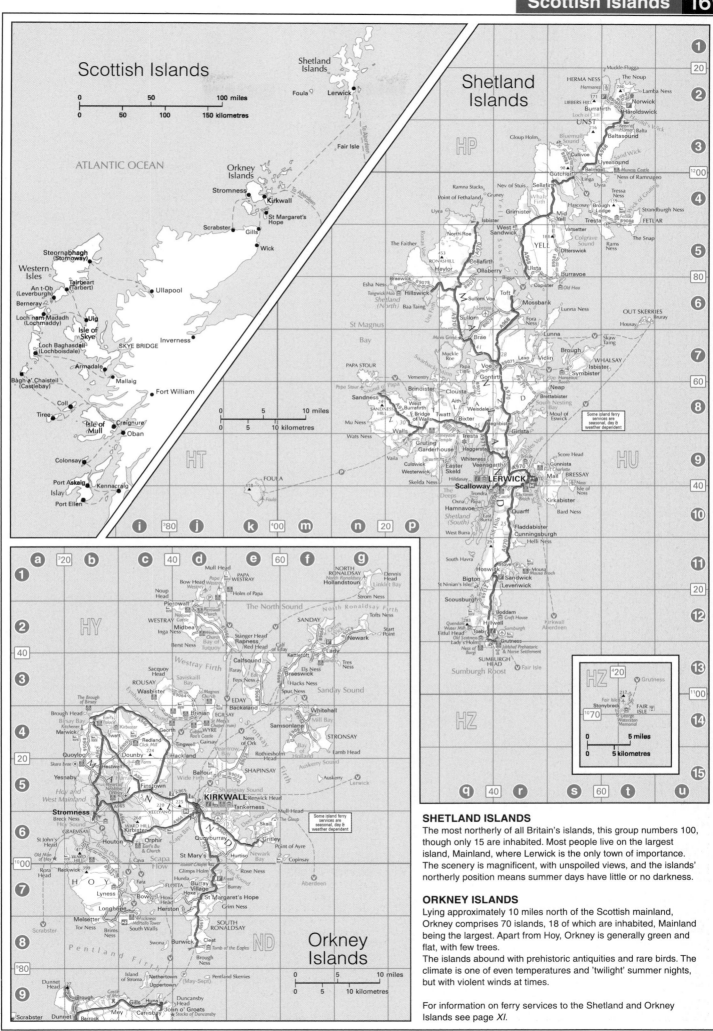

Scottish Islands

ATLANTIC OCEAN

Shetland Islands

Orkney Islands

Western Isles

Shetland Islands

HP

HT

HU

HZ

Orkney Islands

HY

ND

SHETLAND ISLANDS

The most northerly of all Britain's islands, this group numbers 100, though only 15 are inhabited. Most people live on the largest island, Mainland, where Lerwick is the only town of importance. The scenery is magnificent, with unspoiled views, and the islands' northerly position means summer days have little or no darkness.

ORKNEY ISLANDS

Lying approximately 10 miles north of the Scottish mainland, Orkney comprises 70 islands, 18 of which are inhabited, Mainland being the largest. Apart from Hoy, Orkney is generally green and flat, with few trees.
The islands abound with prehistoric antiquities and rare birds. The climate is one of even temperatures and 'twilight' summer nights, but with violent winds at times.

For information on ferry services to the Shetland and Orkney Islands see page XI.

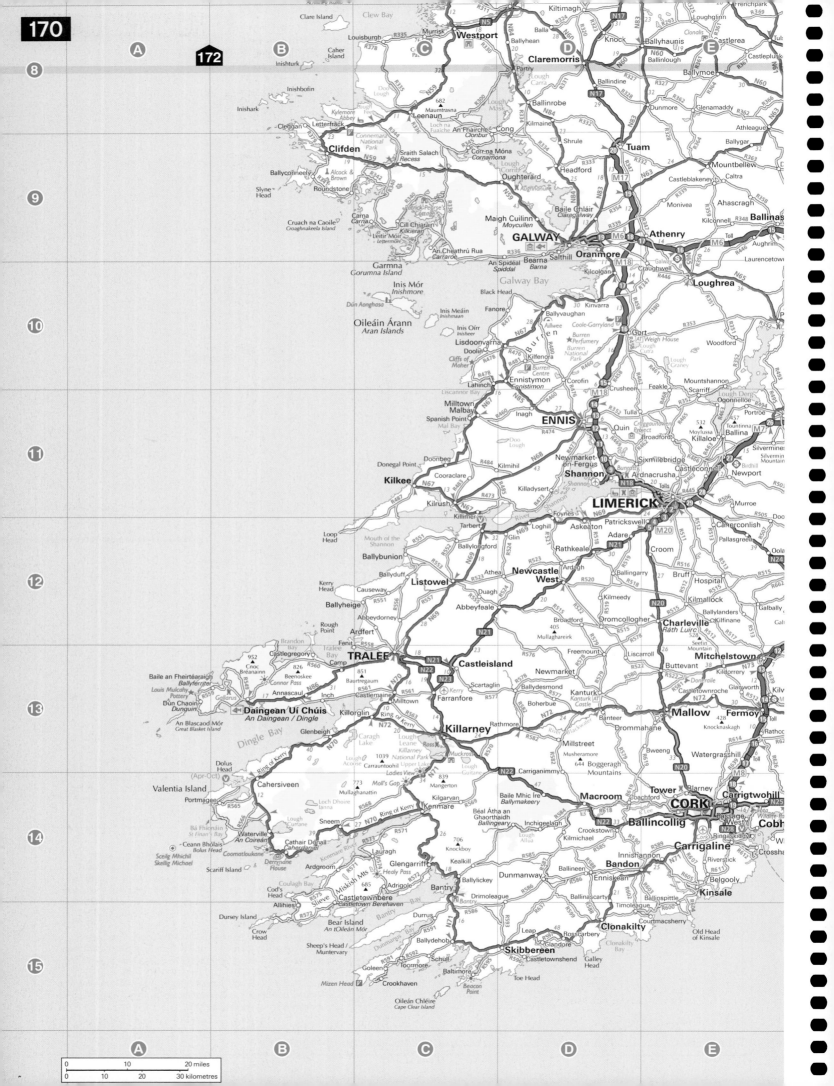

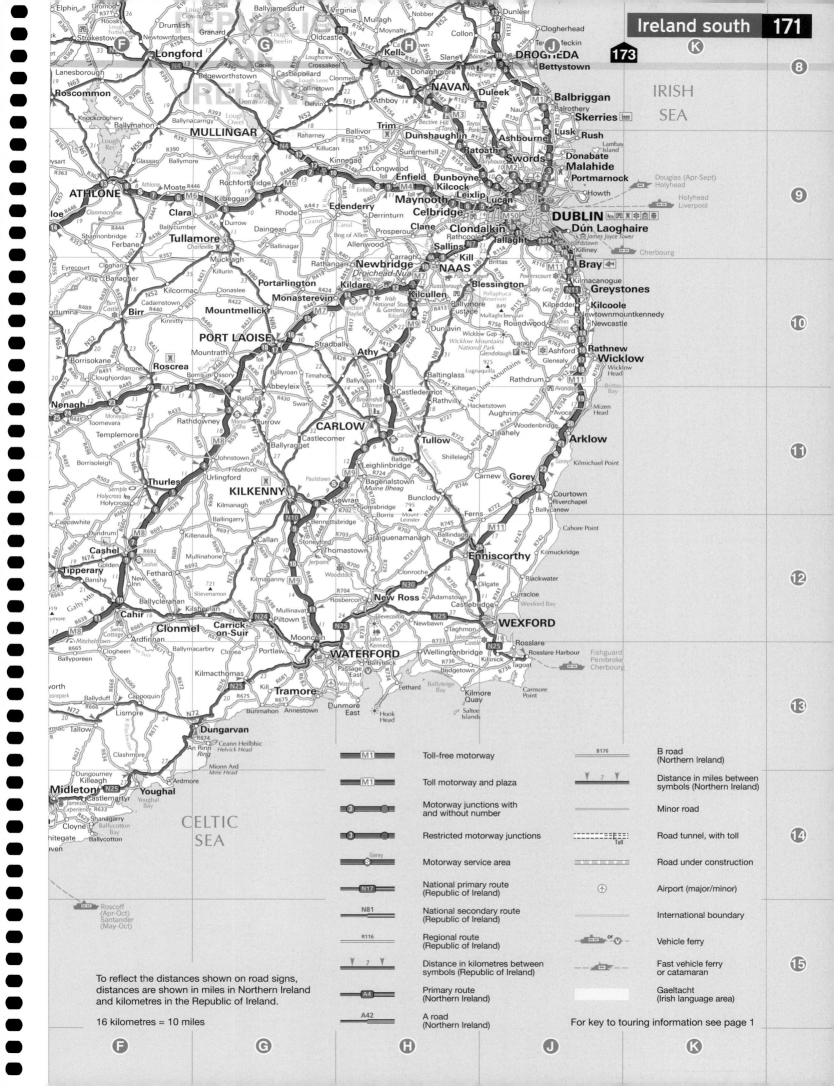

Map legend:

M1	Toll-free motorway
M1	Toll motorway and plaza
①	Motorway junctions with and without number
③	Restricted motorway junctions
S	Motorway service area
N17	National primary route (Republic of Ireland)
N81	National secondary route (Republic of Ireland)
R116	Regional route (Republic of Ireland)
7	Distance in kilometres between symbols (Republic of Ireland)
A4	Primary route (Northern Ireland)
A42	A road (Northern Ireland)
B176	B road (Northern Ireland)
7	Distance in miles between symbols (Northern Ireland)
	Minor road
Toll	Road tunnel, with toll
	Road under construction
⊕	Airport (major/minor)
	International boundary
or V	Vehicle ferry
	Fast vehicle ferry or catamaran
	Gaeltacht (Irish language area)

To reflect the distances shown on road signs, distances are shown in miles in Northern Ireland and kilometres in the Republic of Ireland.

16 kilometres = 10 miles

For key to touring information see page 1

Ireland index

Abbeydorney....C12
Abbeyfeale....D12
Abbeyleix....G11
Adamstown....H12
Adare....D12
Adrigole....C14
Aghalee....J5
Ahascragh....E9
Ahoghill....J4
Allenwood....H9
Allihies....B15
An Bun Beag....E4
An Charraig....E5
An Cheathrú Rua....C9
An Clochán Liath....E4
An Coireán....B14
An Daingean....B13
An Fál Carrach....F3
An Fhairche....C9
Annahilt....J6
Annalong....J7
Annascaul....B13
Annestown....G13
An Rinn....G13
An Spidéal....D9
Antrim....J5
Ardagh....D12
Ardara....E5
Ardee....H8
Ardfert....C12
Ardfinnan....F12
Ardglass....K6
Ardgroom....B14
Ardmore....F14
Ardnacrusha....E11
Arklow....J11
Armagh....H6
Armoy....J3
Arvagh....G7
Ashbourne....J9
Ashford....J10
Askeaton....D12
Athboy....H8
Athea....D12
Athenry....E9
Athleague....E8
Athlone....F9
Athy....H10
Augher....G6
Aughnacloy....H6
Aughrim....E9
Aughrim....J11
Avoca....J11

Bagenalstown....H11
Baile an Fheirtéaraigh....B13
Baile Chláir....D9
Baile Mhic Íre....D14
Baile na Finne....F4
Bailieborough....H7
Balbriggan....J8
Balla....D8
Ballacolla....G11
Ballaghaderreen....E7
Ballina....D7
Ballina....E11
Ballinafad....E7
Ballinagar....G9
Ballinagh....G7
Ballinamallard....F7
Ballinamore....F7
Ballinascarty....D14
Ballinasloe....E9
Ballincollig....E14
Ballindaggan....H12
Ballindine....D8
Ballineen....D14
Ballingarry....D12
Ballingarry....G12
Ballingeary....D14
Ballinlough....E8
Ballinrobe....D8
Ballinspittle....E14
Ballintra....F5
Ballivor....H9
Ballon....H11
Ballybay....H7
Ballybofey....F5
Ballybunion....C12
Ballycanew....J11
Ballycarry....K5

Ballycastle....J3
Ballycastle....C6
Ballyclare....J5
Ballyclerahan....F12
Ballyconneely....B9
Ballyconnell....G7
Ballycotton....F14
Ballycumber....F9
Ballydehob....C15
Ballydesmond....D13
Ballyduff....C12
Ballyduff....F13
Ballyferriter....B13
Ballygally....J4
Ballygar....E9
Ballygawley....H6
Ballygawley....E6
Ballygowan....K5
Ballyhaise....G7
Ballyhalbert....K5
Ballyhaunis....E8
Ballyheige....C12
Ballyhean....D8
Ballyjamesduff....G8
Ballylanders....E12
Ballylickey....C14
Ballyliffin....G3
Ballylongford....C12
Ballylynan....H10
Ballymacarbry....F13
Ballymahon....F8
Ballymakeery....D14
Ballymena....J4
Ballymoney....H4
Ballymore....E9
Ballymore Eustace....H10
Ballymote....G8
Ballynacarrigy....G8
Ballynahinch....J6
Ballynure....J5
Ballyporeen....F13
Ballyragget....G11
Ballyroan....G10
Ballysadare....E6
Ballyshannon....F5
Ballyvaughan....D10
Ballywalter....K5
Balrothery....J8
Baltimore....C15
Baltinglass....H10
Banagher....F10
Banbridge....J6
Bandon....E14
Bangor....K5
Bangor Erris....C7
Bansha....F12
Banteer....D13
Bantry....C14
Barna....D9
Béal an Mhuirthead....B6
Béal Átha an Ghaorthaidh....D14
Bearna....D9
Belcoo....F6
Belfast....J5
Belgooly....E14
Bellaghy....H4
Belleek....F6
Belmullet....B6
Belturbet....G7
Benburb....H6
Bennettsbridge....G12
Beragh....G6
Bessbrook....J6
Bettystown....J8
Birr....F10
Blacklion....F6
Blackwater....J12
Blarney....E14
Blessington....H10
Boherbue....D13
Borris....H12
Borris-in-Ossory....F10
Borrisokane....F10
Borrisoleigh....F11
Boyle....E7
Bray....J10
Bridgetown....H13

Brittas....J9
Broadford....E11
Broadford....D12
Broughshane....J4
Bruff....E12
Bunbeg....E4
Bunclody....H11
Buncrana....G3
Bundoran....E6
Bunmahon....G13
Bunnyconnellan....D7
Bushmills....H3
Buttevant....E13
Bweeng....E13

Cadamstown....F10
Caherconlish....E12
Caherdaniel....B14
Cahersiveen....B14
Cahir....F12
Caledon....H6
Callan....G12
Caltra....E9
Camp....B13
Carndonagh....G3
Cappawhite....F12
Cappoquin....F13
Carlanstown....H8
Carlingford....J7
Carlow....H11
Carna....C9
Carnew....J11
Carnlough....J4
Carragh....H9
Carraig Airt....F3
Carraroe....C9
Carrick....E5
Carrickfergus....K5
Carrickmacross....H7
Carrickmore....G5
Carrick-on-Shannon....F7
Carrigaline....E14
Carrigallen....F7
Carriganimmy....D13
Carrigart....F3
Carrigtwohill....E14
Carryduff....J5
Cashel....F12
Castlebar....D8
Castlebellingham....J7
Castleblakeney....E9
Castleblayney....H7
Castlebridge....J12
Castlecomer....G11
Castleconnell....E11
Castlederg....G5
Castledermot....H11
Castlegregory....B13
Castleisland....C13
Castlemaine....C13
Castlemartyr....F14
Castleplunket....E8
Castlepollard....G8
Castlerea....E8
Castlerock....H3
Castletownbere....B15
Castletownroche....E13
Castletownshend....D15
Castlewellan....J6
Cathair Dónall....B14
Causeway....C12
Cavan....G7
Celbridge....H9
Charlestown....D7
Charleville....E12
Cill Charthaigh....E5
Cill Chiaráin....C9
Clady....H3
Clane....H9
Clara....F9
Claregalway....D9
Claremorris....D8
Clashmore....F13
Claudy....G4
Cleggan....B8
Clifden....B9
Cliffoney....E6
Cloghan....F10
Clogheen....F13
Clogher....G6

Clogherhead....J8
Clogh Mills....J4
Clonakilty....D15
Clonaslee....G10
Clonbur....C9
Clondalkin....J9
Clonea....G13
Clones....G7
Clonmany....G3
Clonmel....F12
Clonmellon....H8
Clonroche....H12
Clough....K6
Cloughjordan....F10
Cloyne....F14
Coachford....D14
Coagh....H5
Coalisland....H5
Cobh....E14
Coleraine....H3
Collinstown....G8
Collon....H8
Collooney....E7
Comber....K5
Cong....D9
Convoy....G4
Cookstown....H5
Coole....G8
Cooraclare....C11
Cootehill....G7
Cork....E14
Cornamona....C9
Corr na Móna....C9
Corrofin....D10
Courtmacsherry....E15
Courtown....J11
Craughwell....E10
Creeslough....F4
Croithlí....E4
Crolly....E4
Crookhaven....C15
Crookstown....D14
Croom....E12
Crossakeel....H8
Crosshaven....E14
Crossmaglen....H7
Crossmolina....D7
Crumlin....J5
Crusheen....D10
Culdaff....G3
Cullybackey....J4
Culmore....G4
Curracloe....J12
Curry....E7
Cushendall....J4
Cushendun....J3

Daingean....G9
Daingean Uí Chúis....B13
Delvin....G8
Derrinturn....H9
Derry....G4
Derrygonnelly....F6
Derrylin....G6
Dervock....H3
Dingle....B13
Doagh....J5
Donabate....J9
Donaghadee....K5
Donaghmore....H5
Donaghmore....H8
Donegal....F5
Donemana....G4
Doolin....C10
Doon....E12
Doonbeg....C11
Downings....F3
Downpatrick....K6
Dowra....F6
Draperstown....H5
Drimoleague....D14
Droichead Nua....H10
Dromahair....E6
Dromara....J6
Dromcolloger....D12
Dromiskin....J7
Drommahane....E13
Dromod....F8
Dromore....G6

Dromore....G5
Dromore West....D6
Drumaness....K6
Drumfries....G3
Drumkeeran....F7
Drumlish....F8
Drumquin....G5
Drumshanbo....F7
Drumsna....F7
Duagh....C12
Dublin....J9
Duleek....J8
Dunboyne....J9
Dún Chaoin....A13
Dundalk....J7
Dundonald....K5
Dundrum....F12
Dunfanaghy....F3
Dungannon....H5
Dungarvan....G13
Dungiven....H4
Dunglow....E4
Dungourney....F14
Dunkineely....E5
Dún Laoghaire....J9
Dunlavin....H10
Dunleer....J8
Dunloy....J4
Dunmanway....D14
Dunmore....E8
Dunmore East....H13
Dunquin....A13
Dunshaughlin....H9
Durrow....G11
Durrow....G9
Durrus....C15
Dysart....E9

Easky....D6
Edenderry....H9
Edgeworthstown....G8
Eglinton....G4
Elphin....F8
Emyvale....H6
Enfield....H9
Ennis....D11
Enniscorthy....H12
Enniscrone....D6
Enniskean....D14
Enniskillen....F6
Ennistymon....D10
Eyrecourt....F10

Fahan....G4
Falcarragh....F3
Fanore....C10
Farranfore....C13
Feakle....E11
Fenagh....F7
Fenit....B13
Ferbane....F9
Fermoy....E13
Ferns....J12
Fethard....F12
Fethard....H13
Fintona....G6
Fintown....F4
Fivemiletown....G6
Foxford....D7
Foynes....D12
Freemount....D13
Frenchpark....E8
Freshford....G11

Galbally....E12
Galway....D9
Garrison....F6
Garvagh....H4
Gilford....J6
Glandore....D15
Glanworth....E13
Glaslough....H6
Gleann Cholm Cille....E5
Glenamaddy....E8
Glenarm....J4
Glenavy....J5
Glenbeigh....B13
Glencolumbkille....E5
Glenealy....J10
Glengarriff....C14
Glenties....E5

Glin....D12
Golden....F12
Goleen....C15
Goresbridge....H11
Gorey....J11
Gort....D10
Gorteen....E7
Gortin....G5
Gowran....H11
Graiguenamanagh....H12
Granard....G8
Grange....E6
Greencastle....H3
Greencastle....G5
Greenore....J7
Greyabbey....K5
Greystones....J10
Gulladuff....H4

Hacketstown....H11
Headford....D9
Hillsborough....J6
Hilltown....J6
Holycross....F11
Holywood....K5
Hospital....E12
Howth....J9

Inagh....D11
Inch....B13
Inchigeelagh....D14
Inishcrone....D6
Innishannon....E14
Irvinestown....F6

Johnstown....G11

Kanturk....D13
Keadue....F7
Keady....H6
Kealkill....C14
Keel....B7
Kells....J4
Kells....H8
Kenmare....C14
Kesh....F5
Kilbeggan....G9
Kilcar....E5
Kilcock....H9
Kilcolgan....D10
Kilconnell....E9
Kilcoole....J10
Kilcormac....F10
Kilcullen....H10
Kildare....H10
Kildorrery....E13
Kilfenora....D10
Kilfinane....E12
Kilgarvan....C14
Kilkee....C11
Kilkeel....J7
Kilkenny....G11
Kilkieran....C9
Kill....H9
Kill....G13
Killadysert....D11
Killala....D6
Killaloe....E11
Killarney....C13
Killashandra....G7
Killeagh....F14
Killeigh....G10
Killenaule....F12
Killimer....C11
Killiney....J9
Killinick....J13
Killorglin....C13
Killough....K6
Killucan....G9
Killurin....G10
Killybegs....E5
Killyleagh....K6
Kilmacanogue....J10
Kilmacrenan....F4
Kilmacthomas....G13
Kilmaganny....G12
Kilmaine....D8
Kilmallock....E12
Kilmanagh....G11
Kilmeedy....D12
Kilmichael....D14
Kilmihil....C11
Kilmore Quay....H13

Kilmuckridge....J12
Kilpedder....J10
Kilrea....H4
Kilrush....C11
Kilsheelan....G12
Kiltegan....H11
Kiltimagh....D8
Kilworth....E13
Kingscourt....H7
Kinlough....E6
Kinnegad....G9
Kinnitty....F10
Kinsale....E14
Kinvarra....D10
Kircubbin....K5
Knock....D8
Knockcroghery....F8

Lahinch....C10
Lanesborough....F8
Laragh....J10
Larne....K4
Lauragh....C14
Laurencetown....F10
Leap....C8
Leenaun....C9
Leighlinbridge....H11
Leitrim....B9
Leitrim....F7
Leixlip....H9
Letterfrack....B8

Letterkenny....F4
Lifford....G4
Limavady....H4
Limerick....E11
Lisbellaw....G6
Lisburn....J5
Liscarroll....D13
Lisdoonvarna....D10
Lismore....F13
Lisnaskea....G6
Listowel....C12
Loghill....D12
Londonderry....G4
Longford....F8
Longwood....H9
Loughbrickland....J6
Loughglinn....E8
Loughrea....E10
Louisburgh....C8
Lucan....J9
Lurgan....J6
Lusk....J9

Macroom....D14
Maghera....H4
Magherafelt....H5
Maguiresbridge....G6
Maigh Cuilinn....D9
Malahide....J9
Málainn Mhóir....E5
Malin....G3

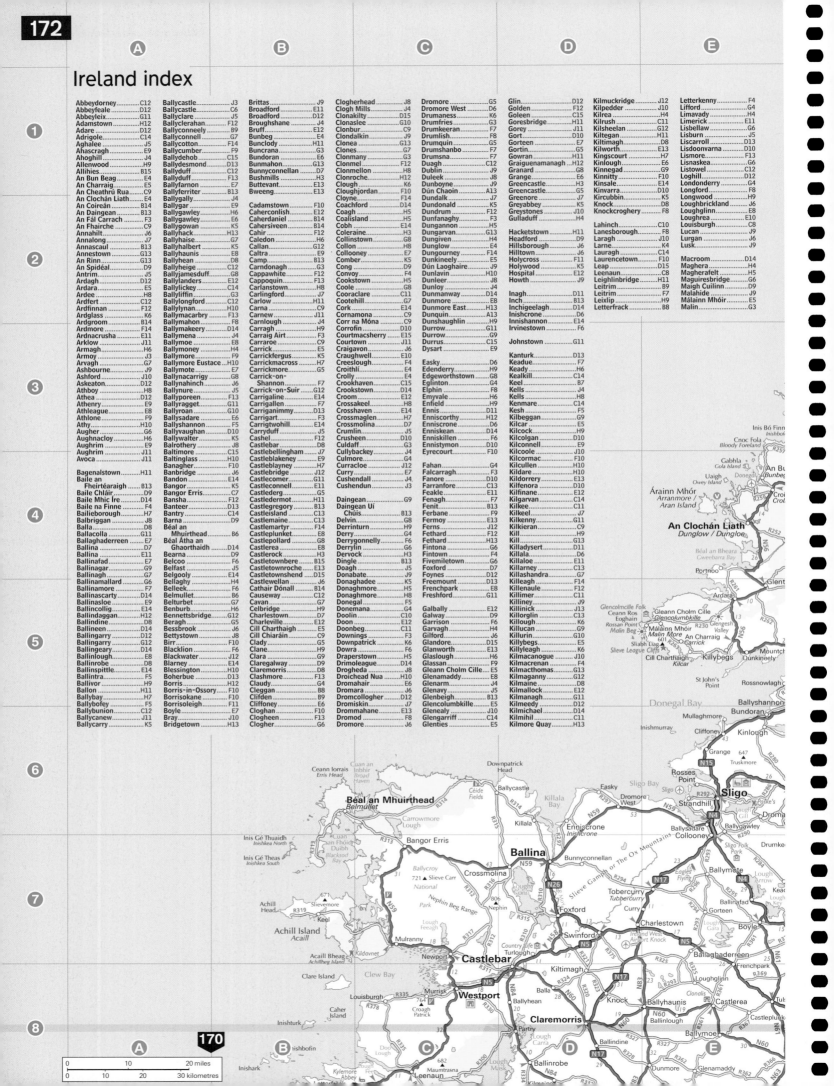

0   10   20 miles
0   10   20   30 kilometres

Malin More E5
Mallow E13
Manorhamilton F6
Markethill H6
Martinstown J4
Maynooth H9
Mayobridge J6
Midleton F14
Milford F4
Millstreet D13
Milltown C13
Milltown Malbay C11
Mitchelstown E13
Moate F9
Mohill F7
Monaghan H6
Monasterevin G10
Moneymore H5
Monivea E9
Mooncoin G13
Mountbellew E9
Mountcharles C11
Mountmellick G10
Mountrath G10
Mountshannon E10
Moville G3
Moy H6
Moycullen D9
Moynalty H8
Mucklagh G9
Muff G4

Muine Bheag H11
Mullagh H8
Mullaghmore E6
Mullinahone G12
Mullinavat G12
Mullingar G9
Mulranny C7
Murrisk C8
Murroe E11
Naas H10
Na Dúnaibh F3
Naul J8
Navan H8
Nenagh E11
Newbawn H12
Newbliss G7
Newbridge H10
Newcastle J6
Newcastle H11
Newcastle West D12
New Inn F12
Newmarket D13
Newmarket-on-Fergus D11
Newport C7
Newport E11
New Ross H12
Newry J6
Newtownabbey J5
Newtownards K5

Newtownbutler G7
Newtown-cunningham G4
Newtownforbes F8
Newtownhamilton H6
Newtownmount-kennedy J10
Newtownstewart G5
Nobber H8
Ogonnelloe E11
Oilgate H12
Oldcastle G8
Omagh G5
Omeath J7
Oola E12
Oranmore D9
Oughterard D9
Pallasgreen E12
Ramelton F4
Randalstown J5
Raphoe G4
Rasharkin H4
Rathangan H10
Rathcormac E13
Rathcoole J9
Rathdowney G11
Rathdrum J10
Rathfriland J6
Rathkeale D12
Ráth Luirc E12

Portavogie K6
Portballintrae H3
Portglenone H4
Port Laoise G10
Portlaw G13
Portmagee B14
Portmarnock J9
Portnablagh F3
Portnoo E4
Portroe E11
Portrush H3
Portstewart H3
Portumna E10
Poyntzpass J6
Prosperous H9
Quin D11
Raharney G9

Rathmore D13
Rathmullan G4
Rathnew J10
Rathvilly H11
Ratoath J9
Recess C9
Rhode G9
Ring G13
Ringaskiddy E14
Riverchapel J11
Riverstick E14
Rochfortbridge G9
Rockcorry H7
Roosky F8
Rosbercon H12
Roscommon E9
Roscrea F10
Rosscarbery D15
Rosses Point E6
Rosslare J13
Rosslare Harbour J13
Rosslea G6
Rossnowlagh E5
Rostrevor J7
Roundstone B9
Roundwood J10
Rush J9

Saintfield K6
St Johnston G4
Sallins H9

Salthill D9
Scarriff E11
Scartaglin C13
Schull C15
Seskinore G5
Shanagarry F14
Shannon D11
Shannonbridge F9
Shercock H7
Shillelagh H11
Shinrone F10
Shrule D9
Silvermines E11
Sion Mills G5
Sixmilebridge D11
Skerries J9
Skibbereen D15
Slane H8
Sligo E6
Smithborough G6
Sneem B14
Spanish Point C11
Spiddal D9
Sraith Salach C9
Stewartstown H5
Stoneyford G12
Strabane G4
Stradbally G10
Stradone G7
Strandhill E6
Strangford K6

Stranorlar F5
Strokestown F8
Summerhill H9
Swan G11
Swanlinbar F7
Swinford D7
Swords J9
Taghmon H12
Tagoat J13
Tallaght J9
Tallow F13
Tandragee J6
Tarbert C12
Templemore F11
Termonfeckin J8
Thomastown G12
Thurles F11
Timahoe G10
Timoleague D15
Tinahely J11
Tipperary F12
Tobercurry E7
Tobermore H4
Toomevara F11
Toomore C15
Tower E14
Tralee C13
Tramore G13
Trim H8
Tuam D9

Tubbercurry E7
Tulla D11
Tullamore G9
Tullow H11
Tulsk E8
Turlough D7
Urlingford G11
Virginia G8
Warrenpoint J7
Waterford G13
Watergrasshill E13
Waterville B14
Wellingtonbridge H13
Westport C8
Wexford J12
Whitegate E14
Whitehead K5
Wicklow J11
Woodenbridge J11
Woodford E10
Youghal F14

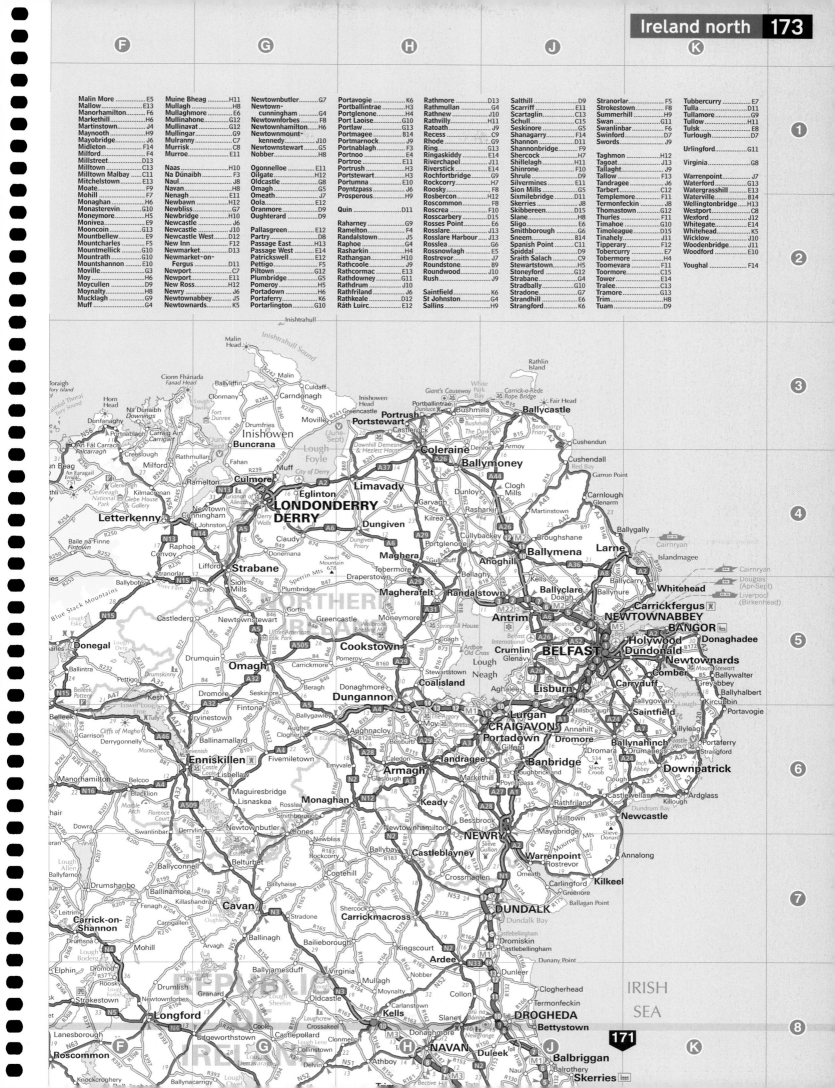

171

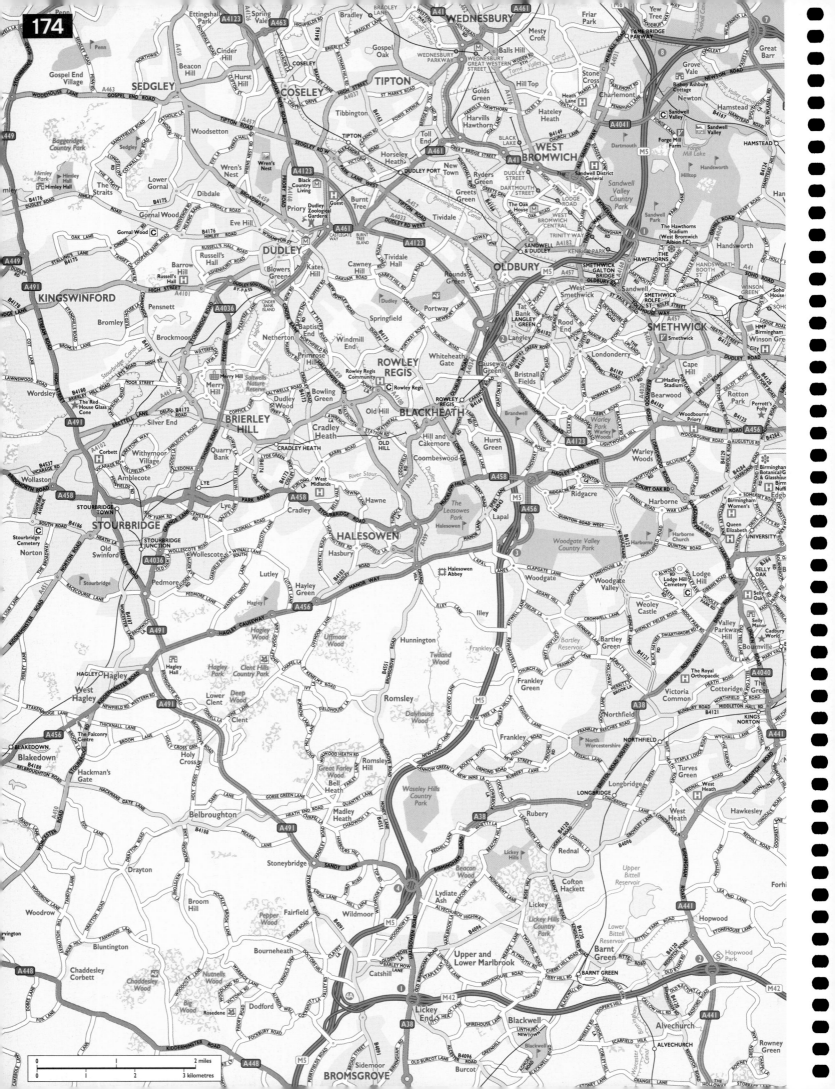

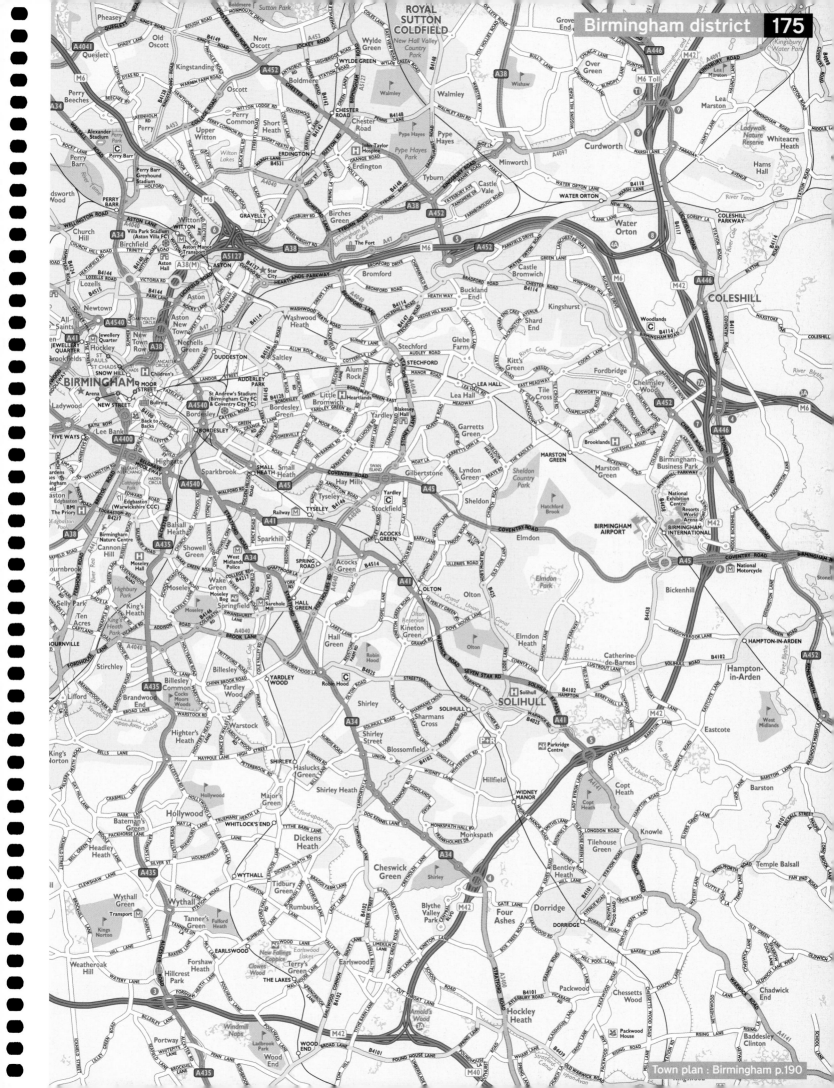

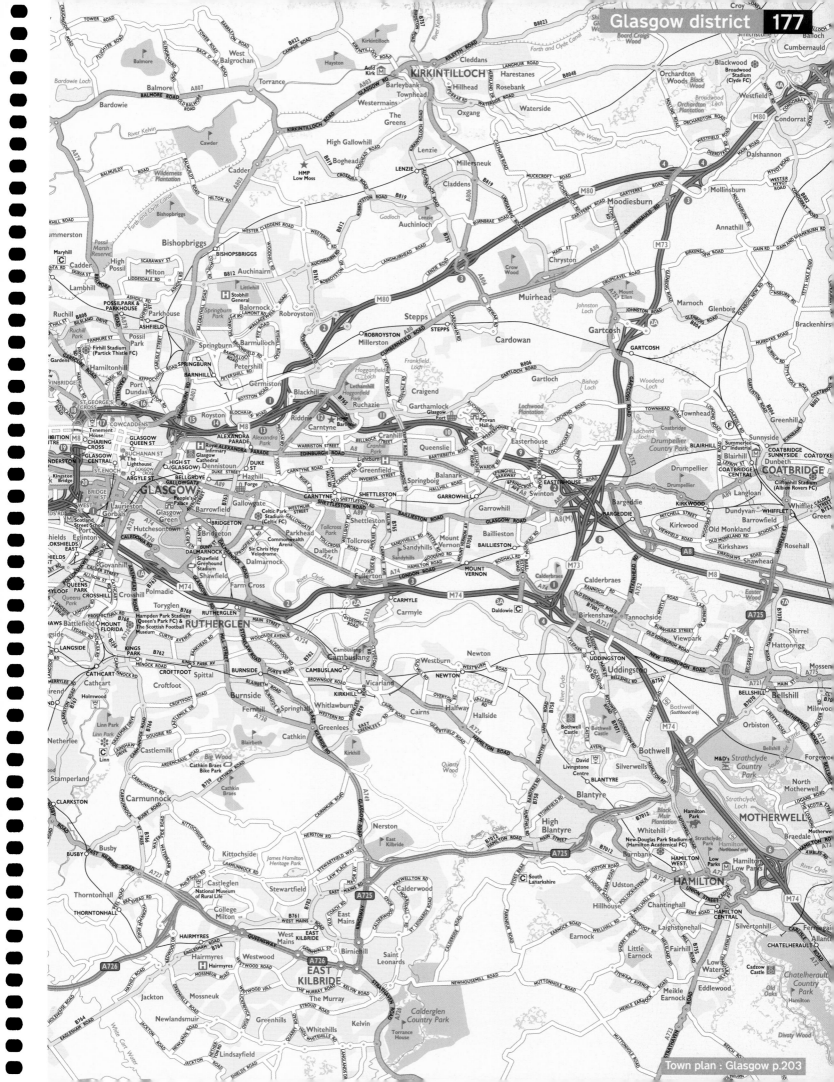

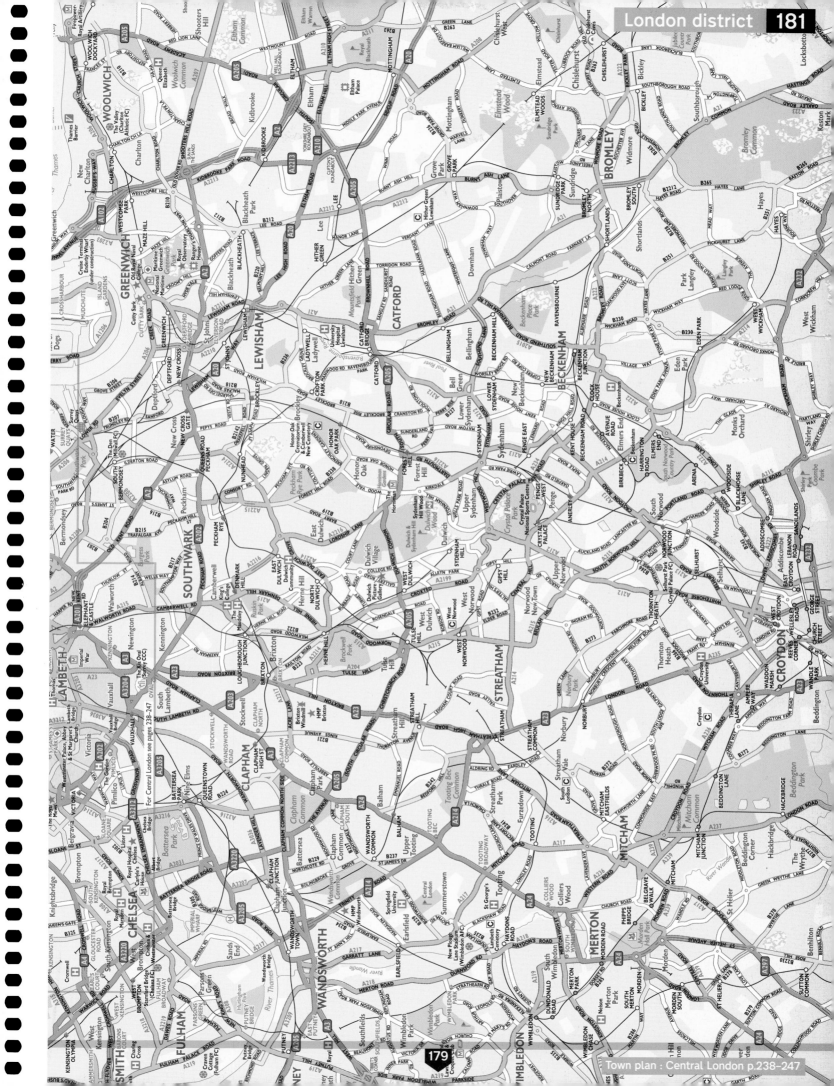

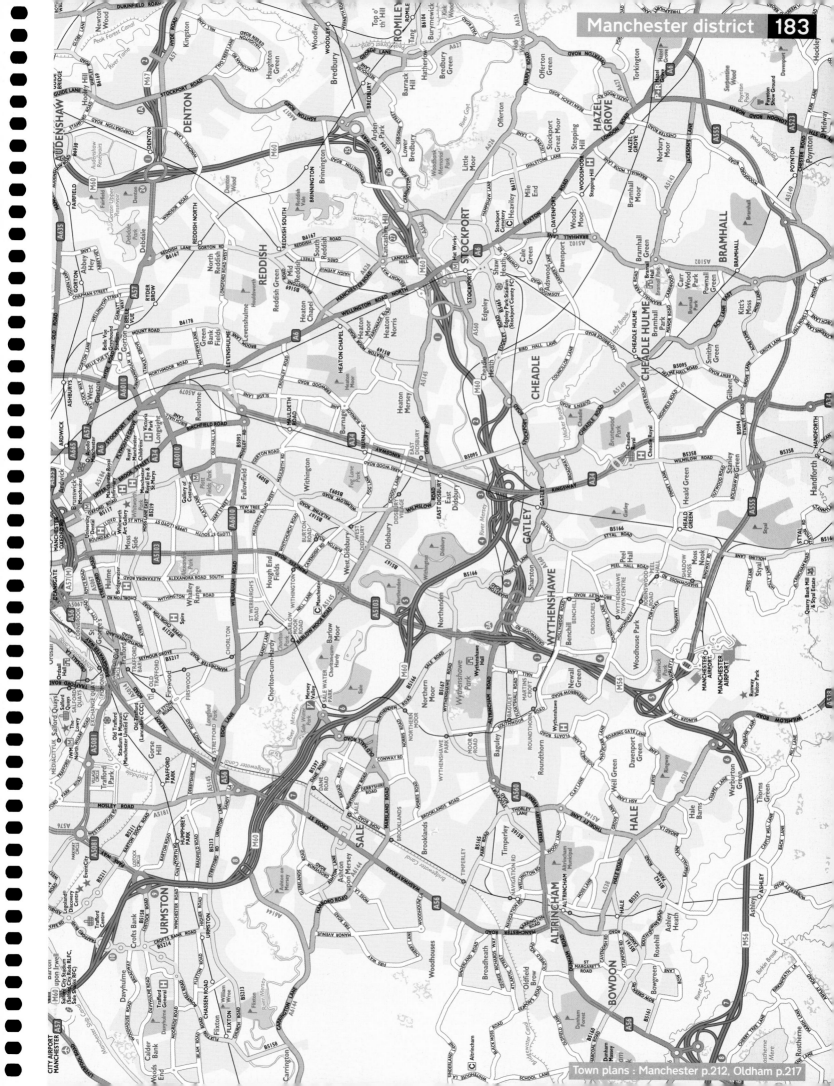

Town plans : Manchester p.212, Oldham p.217

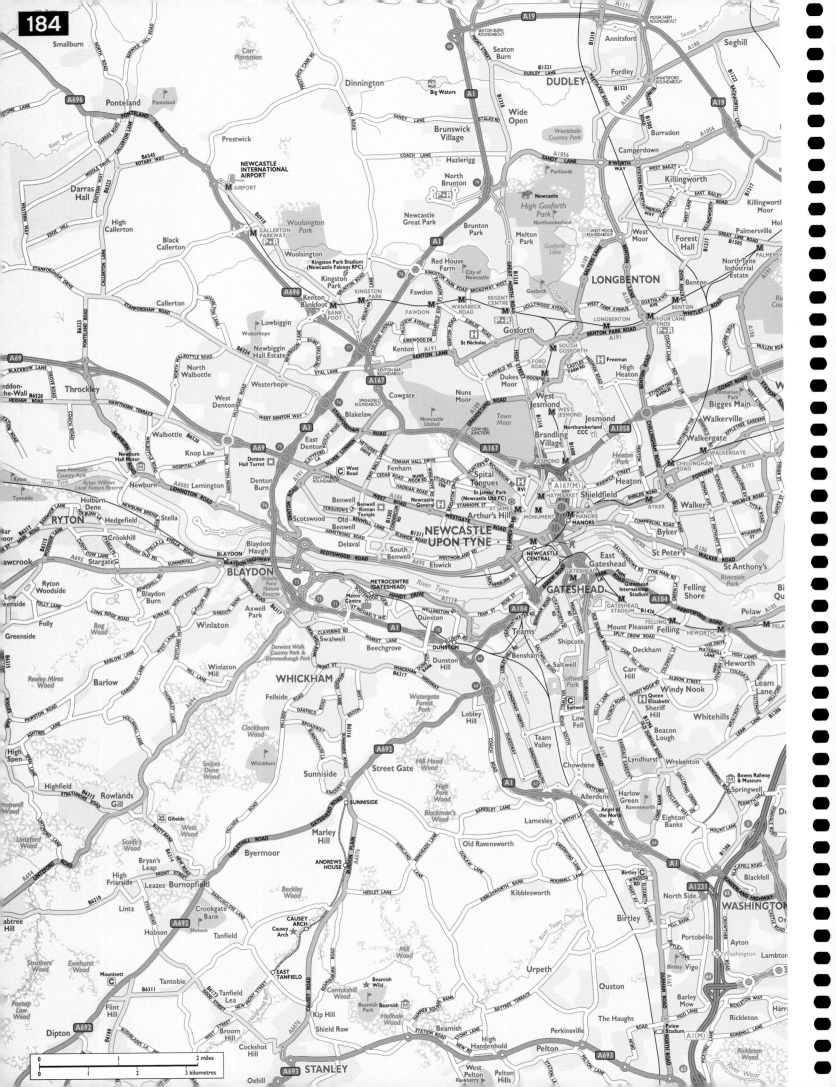

NORTH

SEA

WHITLEY BAY
Whitley Bay
Links Art Gallery
Whitley Bay

St Mary's Island

Bates Cottages
Holywell
East Holywell
Backworth
Backworth Hall
Earsdon
Monkseaton
West Monkseaton
Shiremoor
Murton
New York
West Allotment
Benton Square
Northumberland Park
West Monkseaton
Monkseaton
Marden Park Nature Reserve
Marden
Cullercoats
Blue Reef
Longsands South
King Edwards Bay
TYNEMOUTH
Tynemouth Priory & Castle
Tynemouth
Preston
North Tyneside General
Billy Mill
West Chirton
Stephenson Railway
NORTH SHIELDS
North Shields
Willington Square
Silverlink Roundabout
North Tyneside Steam Railway
Howdon Interchange
Waterville Road
Meadow Well
Percy Main
Holy Cross
Willington
Howdon
WALLSEND
Wallsend
Segedunum Roman Fort & Baths
Hadrian Road
Point Pleasant
Willington Quay
East Howdon
Royal Quays
International Passenger Terminal
Mill Dam
Arbeia Roman Fort & Museum
The Lawe
SOUTH SHIELDS
South Shields
Sandhaven
Chichester
Tyne Dock
Tyne Tunnel
River Tyne
JARROW
Jarrow Hall
St Paul's Monastery
East Jarrow
Hebburn Colliery
Westoe
Cauldwell
Harton
Marsden Rock
Hebburn New Town
HEBBURN
Monkton
Primrose
Simonside
Bede
Temple Park
South Tyneside General
Harton Nook
West Harton
Marsden
Marsden Bay
Souter Lighthouse & The Leas
Riverside Park
Brockley Whins
South Shields
Cleadon Park
Whitburn
Whitburn Coastal Park
Hedworth
Biddick Hall
Whiteleas
Fellgate
Boldon Colliery
Cleadon
Whitburn
Wardley
West Boldon
East Boldon
Folingsby
Testos Roundabout
Downhill
South Bents
George Washington
North East Aircraft
Witherwack
Carley Hill
Whitburn Bay
Usworth
Hylton Castle
Castletown
Marley Pots
High Southwick
Seaburn
Roker
Concord
Sulgrave
Northern Spire Bridge
Low Southwick
Southwick
Monkwearmouth
Stadium of Light
Sunderland Harbour
Albany
Hertburn
Washington Old Hall
Washington Wetland Centre
Pennywell
South Hylton
Ford
Hylton
Deptford
Queen Alexandra Bridge
Ayre's Quay
Pallion
Millfield
Bishopwearmouth
Stadium of Light (Sunderland AFC)
National Glass Centre
St Peter's
Sunderland Royal
University
SUNDERLAND
Washington Village
Barmston
Teal Farm
Columbia
Biddick
Wearside
High Barnes
Barnes Park
Ashbrooke
Humbledon
Hendon
Sunderland Eye Infirmary
Hillview
Grangetown
Fatfield
Mount Pleasant
Penshaw
Herrington Country Park
Hastings Hill
Grindon
Plains Farm
Silksworth Sports Complex & Ski Centre
Shiney Row
New Herrington
Penshaw Monument
Thorney Close
Middle Herrington
East Herrington
New Silksworth
Silksworth
Farringdon
Tunstall
Ryhope
Biddick Gill Wood
The Princess Anne Park

Street map symbols

Town, port and airport plans

Motorway and junction	One-way, gated/ closed road	Railway station
Primary road single/ dual carriageway and numbered junction	Restricted access road	Preserved or tourist railway
A road single/ dual carriageway and numbered junction	Pedestrian area	Light rapid transit system station
B road single/ dual carriageway	Footpath	Level crossing
Local road single/ dual carriageway	Road under construction	Tramway
Other road single/ dual carriageway, minor road	Road tunnel	Airport, heliport
Building of interest	Lighthouse	Railair terminal
Ruined building	Castle	Theatre or performing arts centre
Tourist Information Centre	Castle mound	Cinema
Visitor or heritage centre	Monument, memorial, statue	Abbey, chapel, church
World Heritage Site (UNESCO)	Post Office	Synagogue
Museum	Public library	Mosque
English Heritage site	Shopping centre	Golf course
Historic Scotland site	Shopmobility	Racecourse
Cadw (Welsh heritage) site	Football stadium	Nature reserve
National Trust site	Rugby stadium	Aquarium
National Trust Scotland site	County cricket ground	Showground

Toilet, with facilities for the less able
Car park, with electric charging point
Park and Ride (at least 6 days per week)
Bus/coach station
Hospital, 24-hour Accident & Emergency hospital
Beach (award winning)
City wall
Escarpment
Cliff lift
River/canal, lake
Lock, weir
Viewpoint
Park/sports ground
Cemetery
Woodland
Built-up area
Beach

Central London street map (see pages 238–247)

London Underground station	London Overground station
Docklands Light Railway (DLR) station	Central London Congestion Charge and Ultra Low Emission boundary*

Royal Parks

Green Park	Park open 5am–midnight. Constitution Hill and The Mall closed to traffic Sundays and public holidays 8am–dusk.
Hyde Park	Park open 5am–midnight. Park roads closed to traffic midnight–5am.
Kensington Gardens	Park open 6am–dusk.
Regent's Park	Park open 5am–dusk. Park roads closed to traffic midnight–7am, except for residents.
St James's Park	Park open 5am–midnight. The Mall closed to traffic Sundays and public holidays 8am–dusk.
Victoria Tower Gardens	Park open dawn–dusk.

Traffic regulations in the City of London include security checkpoints and restrict the number of entry and exit points.

Note: Oxford Street is closed to through-traffic (except buses & taxis) 7am–7pm Monday–Saturday.

Central London Congestion Charge Zone (CCZ)
You need to pay a daily charge for driving or parking a vehicle on public roads in this central London area. Payment permits entry, travel within and exit from the CCZ by the vehicle as often as required on that day.

In June 2020, due to the coronavirus pandemic, temporary changes were made to the charges and times of operation and these continue to be under review. At the time of printing you must pay a £15 daily charge if you drive within the zone 07:00-22:00, every day, except Christmas Day (25 December).

For up to date information on the CCZ, exemptions, discounts or ways to pay, visit **tfl.gov.uk/modes/driving/congestion-charge**

Ultra Low Emission Zone (ULEZ)
Most vehicles in Central London, including cars and vans, need to meet minimum exhaust emission standards or drivers must pay a daily charge to drive within the zone. It applies to the same area covered by the Congestion Charge and operates 24 hours a day, every day of the year, except Christmas Day (25 December). The charge is £12.50 for motorcycles, cars and vans and is in addition to the Congestion Charge.

*From 25th October 2021 the ULEZ boundary will be extended from central London to include the area up to, but not including, the North Circular Road (A406) and South Circular Road (A205).

Please note the maps in this atlas show the zone in operation at the time of going to print.

For further information visit **tfl.gov.uk/ULEZ**

In addition the Low Emission Zone (LEZ) operates across Greater London, 24 hours every day of the year and is aimed at the most heavy-polluting vehicles. It does not apply to cars or motorcycles. For details visit **tfl.gov.uk/LEZ**

Town Plans

Aberdeen 188
Basingstoke 188
Bath............................. 189
Birmingham 190
Blackpool 189
Bournemouth 191
Bradford 191
Brighton 192
Bristol 192
Cambridge 193
Canterbury 194
Cardiff 194
Carlisle 195
Cheltenham 195
Chester 196
Colchester.................. 196
Coventry 197
Darlington 197
Derby 198
Doncaster................... 198
Dover 199
Dundee 199
Durham....................... 200
Eastbourne................. 200
Edinburgh 201
Exeter 202
Glasgow 203
Gloucester.................. 202
Great Yarmouth 204

Guildford 204
Harrogate................... 205
Huddersfield 205
Inverness 206
Ipswich 206
Kingston upon Hull 207
Lancaster 207
Leeds 208
Leicester 209
Lincoln 209
Liverpool 210
Llandudno 79
LONDON............... 238-247
Luton.......................... 211
Maidstone 211
Manchester 212
Margate 39
Middlesbrough 214
Milton Keynes 213
Newcastle upon Tyne ... 215
Newport 214
Newquay 4
Northampton 216
Norwich 216
Nottingham................. 217
Oldham 217
Oxford 218
Perth 219
Peterborough............. 219

Plymouth 220
Poole 222
Portsmouth 221
Preston 222
Ramsgate..................... 39
Reading 223
Royal Tunbridge Wells... 223
Salisbury 224
Sheffield..................... 224
Shrewsbury 225
Southampton 226
Southend-on-Sea 225
Stirling 227
Stockton-on-Tees........ 227
Stoke-on-Trent (Hanley) ... 228
Stratford-upon-Avon ... 228
Sunderland................. 229
Swansea 230
Swindon 230
Taunton 231
Torquay 231
Warwick 232
Watford 232
Winchester................. 233
Wolverhampton 233
Worcester 234
York............................ 234

Central London

Ferry Ports

Aberdeen Harbour XI
Calais.......................................IX
Dover, Port of IX
Fishguard Harbour X
Harwich International Port.......... 53
Heysham Harbour......................... X
Holyhead Harbour........................ X
Hull, Port of XI
Liverpool Docks X
Newhaven Harbour IX
Pembroke Dock............................ X
Plymouth, Port of.................... VIII
Poole, Port of VIII
Port of Tyne..............................XI
Portsmouth Harbour IX
Southampton, Port of VIII

Channel Tunnel

Folkestone Terminal 27
Calais / Coquelles Terminal 27

Airports

Aberdeen 237
Birmingham 236
East Midlands 236
Edinburgh 237
Glasgow 237
Leeds Bradford.......................... 237
London City 236
London Gatwick 235
London Heathrow 235
London Luton 235
London Stansted....................... 235
Manchester 236

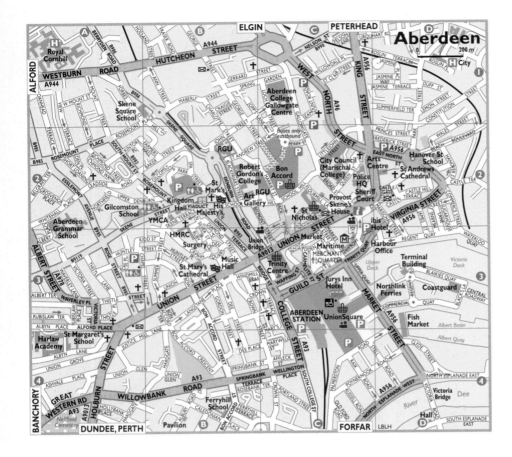

Aberdeen

Aberdeen is found on atlas page **151 N6**

Affleck Street C4	Maberly Street B1
Albert Street A3	Marischal Street.................D2
Albury Road B4	Market Street......................C3
Alford Place A3	Nelson Street......................C1
Ann Street..........................B1	Palmerston Road C4
Beach Boulevard D2	Park Street.........................D1
Belgrave Terrace A2	Portland Street C4
Berryden Road A1	Poynernook Road...............C4
Blackfriars Street B2	Regent Quay......................D3
Blaikies Quay.....................D3	Richmond Street.................A2
Bon Accord Crescent B4	Rose Place.........................A3
Bon Accord Street B3	Rose Street.........................A3
Bridge Street......................C3	Rosemount Place A2
Caledonian Place B4	Rosemount Viaduct............A2
Carmelite Street.................C3	St Andrew Street................B2
Chapel Street......................A3	St Clair Street C1
Charlotte Street..................B1	School Hill..........................C2
College Street.....................C3	Skene Square.....................B2
Constitution Street D1	Skene Street.......................A3
Crimon Place......................B3	Skene Terrace.....................B2
Crown Street.......................B3	South College Street C4
Dee Street..........................B3	South Esplanade East D4
Denburn Road B2	South Mount Street............A2
Diamond Street B3	Spa Street..........................B2
East North Street...............D2	Springbank Street...............B4
Esslemont Avenue A2	Springbank Terrace............B4
Gallowgate.........................C1	Summer Street....................B3
George Street......................B1	Summerfield Terrace..........D1
Gilcomston Park B2	Thistle Lane........................A3
Golden Square....................B3	Thistle Place A3
Gordon Street.....................B3	Thistle Street......................A3
Great Western Road............A4	Trinity Quay........................C3
Guild Street........................C3	Union Bridge B3
Hadden Street.....................C3	Union Grove........................A4
Hanover Street....................D2	Union Street........................B3
Hardgate............................B4	Union Terrace.....................B2
Harriet Street......................C2	Upper Denburn A2
Holburn Street A4	Victoria Road......................D4
Huntley Street A3	Victoria Street.....................A3
Hutcheon Street B1	View Terrace.......................A1
Jasmine Terrace.................D1	Virginia Street D2
John Street.........................B2	Wapping Street C3
Justice Mill Lane................A4	Waverley Place...................A3
King Street..........................C1	Wellington Place.................C4
Langstane Place.................B3	West North Street...............C1
Leadside Road A2	Westburn Road A1
Loanhead Terrace A1	Whitehall Place A2
Loch Street C1	Willowbank Road A4

Basingstoke

Basingstoke is found on atlas page **22 H4**

Alencon Link C1	London Street......................C3
Allnutt Avenue....................D2	Lower Brook Street.............A2
Basing View.......................C1	Lytton Road........................D3
Beaconsfield Road..............C4	Market Place.......................B3
Bounty Rise........................A4	May Place...........................C3
Bounty Road.......................A4	Montague Place C4
Bramblys Close A3	Mortimer Lane....................A2
Bramblys Drive...................A3	New Road B3
Budd's Close A3	New Road C2
Castle Road........................C4	New Street..........................B3
Chapel Hill B1	Penrith Road A3
Chequers Road C2	Rayleigh Road A2
Chester Place A4	Red Lion Lane.....................C3
Churchill Way......................B2	Rochford Road A2
Churchill Way East..............D1	St Mary's Court...................C2
Churchill Way West.............A2	Sarum Hill..........................A3
Church Square B2	Seal Road...........................C2
Church Street......................B2	Solby's Road A2
Church Street......................B3	Southend Road A2
Cliddesden Road.................C4	Southern Road B4
Clifton Terrace....................C1	Stukeley Road.....................A3
Cordale Road......................A4	Sylvia Close B4
Council Road.......................B4	Timberlake Road.................B2
Crossborough Gardens D3	Victoria Street.....................B3
Crossborough Hill................D3	Victory Roundabout A2
Cross Street........................B3	Vyne Road B1
Devonshire Place A4	Winchcombe Road...............A3
Eastfield Avenue D2	Winchester Road A4
Eastrop Lane D2	Winchester Street................B3
Eastrop Roundabout C1	Winterthur Way...................A1
Eastrop Way D2	Worting Road......................A3
Essex Road.........................A2	Wote Street C3
Fairfields Road B4	
Festival Way.......................C2	
Flaxfield Court A2	
Flaxfield Road A3	
Flaxfield Road B3	
Frances Road A4	
Frescade Crescent A4	
Goat Lane...........................C2	
Hackwood Road C4	
Hamelyn Road A4	
Hardy Lane.........................A4	
Hawkfield Lane A4	
Haymarket Yard C3	
Joices Yard B3	
Jubilee Road.......................B4	
London Road.......................D3	

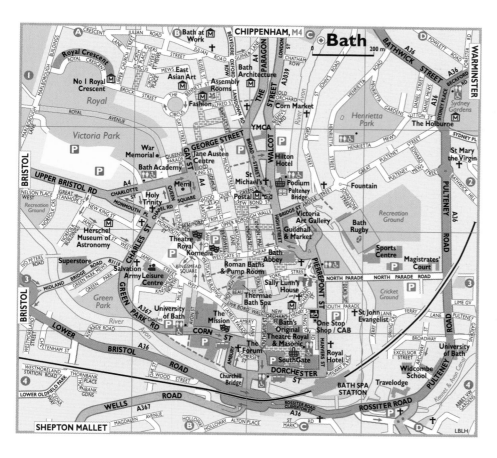

Bath

Bath is found on atlas page **20 D2**

Archway Street D4	Lower Borough Walls............. B3
Argyle Street........................ C2	Lower Bristol Road................ A3
Avon Street B3	Lower Oldfield Park............... A4
Bartlett Street B1	Manvers Street...................... C3
Barton Street B2	Midland Bridge Road A3
Bathwick Street D1	Milk Street............................. B3
Beauford Square B2	Milsom Street........................ B2
Beau Street B3	Monmouth Place.................... A2
Beckford Road...................... D1	Monmouth Street................... B2
Bennett Street B1	New Bond Street.................... B2
Bridge Street........................ C2	New King Street..................... A2
Broad Street B2	New Orchard Street C3
Broadway D4	Norfolk Buildings................... A3
Brock Street......................... A1	North Parade......................... C3
Chapel Road......................... B2	North Parade Road D3
Charles Street A3	Old King Street B2
Charlotte Street A2	Oxford Row B1
Cheap Street......................... C3	Pierrepont Street C3
Cheltenham Street................ A4	Princes Street B2
Circus Mews......................... B1	Pulteney Road D2
Claverton Street................... C4	Queen Square B2
Corn Street B4	Queen Street......................... B2
Daniel Street........................ D1	Railway Place........................ C4
Dorchester Street C4	Rivers Street B1
Edward Street D2	Rossiter Road........................ C4
Ferry Lane D3	Royal Avenue........................ A1
Gay Street B1	Royal Crescent...................... A1
George Street B2	St James's Parade B3
Great Pulteney Street........... C2	St John's Road....................... C1
Great Stanhope Street.......... A2	Saw Close B3
Green Park Road A3	Southgate Street.................... C4
Green Street B2	South Parade......................... C3
Grove Street C2	Stall Street C3
Guinea Lane B1	Sutton Street D1
Henrietta Gardens................ D1	Sydney Place......................... D1
Henrietta Mews.................... C2	The Circus B1
Henrietta Road...................... C1	The Paragon.......................... C1
Henrietta Street.................... C2	Thornbank Place A4
Henry Street C3	Union Street B2
High Street C2	Upper Borough Walls............. B2
Hot Bath Street..................... B3	Upper Bristol Road................ A2
James Street West................ B3	Upper Church Street.............. A1
John Street B2	Walcot Street......................... C2
Julian Road........................... B1	Wells Road A4
Kingsmead North B3	Westgate Buildings B3
Kingston Road...................... C3	Westgate Street..................... B3
Lansdown Road..................... B1	Westmoreland Station Road... A4
London Street........................ C1	York Street............................. C3

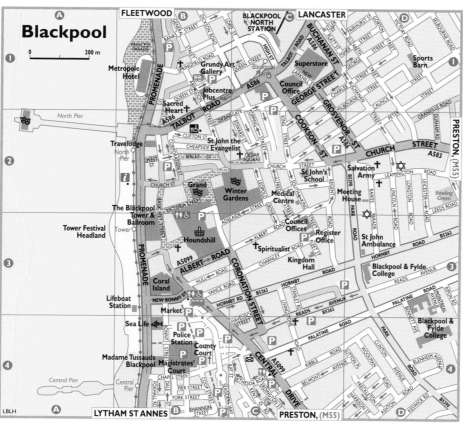

Blackpool

Blackpool is found on atlas page **88 C3**

Abingdon Street.................... B1	Havelock Street...................... C4
Adelaide Street..................... B3	High Street C1
Albert Road........................... B3	Hornby Road.......................... B3
Albert Road........................... C3	Hornby Road.......................... D3
Alfred Street C2	Hull Road B3
Ashton Road......................... D4	Kay Street C4
Bank Hey Street B2	Kent Road C4
Banks Street.......................... B1	King Street C2
Belmont Avenue................... C4	Leamington Road D2
Bennett Avenue D3	Leicester Road D2
Bethesda Road...................... C4	Leopold Grove....................... C2
Birley Street.......................... B2	Lincoln Road D2
Blenheim Avenue.................. D4	Livingstone Road C3
Bonny Street B4	Lord Street B1
Buchanan Street C1	Louise Street.......................... C4
Butler Street C1	Milbourne Street.................... C1
Caunce Street D1	Montreal Avenue D3
Cedar Square C2	New Bonny Street B3
Central Drive......................... C4	New Larkhill Street C1
Chapel Street B4	Palatine Road......................... C4
Charles Street C1	Palatine Road......................... D3
Charnley Road C3	Park Road D2
Cheapside B2	Park Road D4
Church Street B2	Peter Street D2
Church Street C2	Pier Street.............................. B4
Church Street D2	Princess Parade B1
Clifton Street B2	Promenade............................ B1
Clinton Avenue D4	Queen Street......................... B1
Cookson Street...................... C2	Raikes Parade D2
Coop Street........................... B4	Reads Avenue C3
Coronation Street.................. C3	Reads Avenue D3
Corporation Street................. B2	Regent Road C2
Dale Street............................ B4	Ribble Road C4
Deansgate............................. B2	Ripon Road D3
Dickson Road........................ B1	Seasiders Way....................... B4
Edward Street C2	Selbourne Road D1
Elizabeth Street D1	South King Street.................. C2
Fairhurst Street..................... D1	Springfield Road.................... B1
Fisher Street.......................... C1	Stanley Road.......................... C3
Fleet Street C3	Talbot Road........................... B2
Foxhall Road......................... B4	Talbot Road........................... C1
Freckleton Street D4	Topping Street....................... C2
General Street....................... B1	Vance Road B3
George Street C1	Victoria Street........................ B2
Gorton Street D1	Victory Road D1
Granville Road...................... D2	West Street............................ B2
Grosvenor Street................... C1	Woolman Road...................... D4
Harrison Street...................... D4	York Street............................. B4

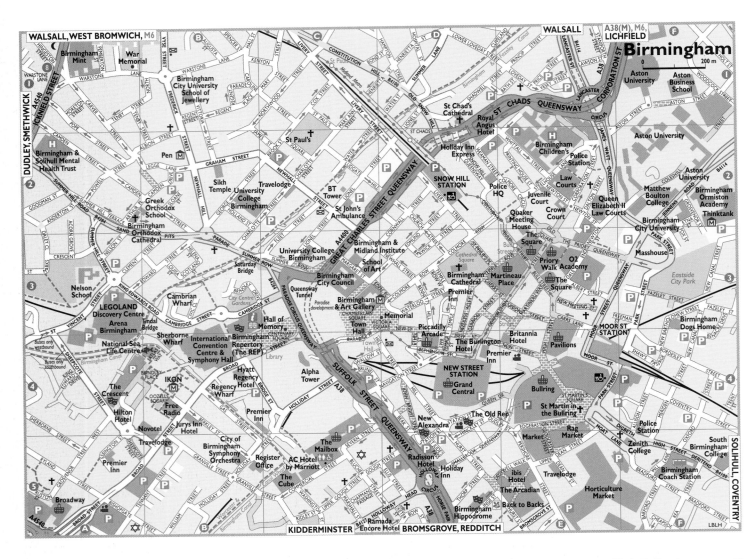

Birmingham

Birmingham is found on atlas page **58 G7**

Acorn Grove	A2
Albert Street	E3
Albert Street	F3
Albion Street	B2
Allison Street	F4
Anderton Street	A2
Arthur Place	A2
Aston Street	F1
Atlas Way	B4
Banbury Street	F3
Barford Street	F5
Bartholomew Street	F3
Barwick Street	D3
Bath Street	E1
Beak Street	D4
Benacre Drive	F4
Bennetts Hill	D3
Berkley Street	B4
Bishopgate Street	A5
Blucher Street	C5
Bond Street	C1
Bordesley Street	F4
Bow Street	D5
Bradford Street	F5
Bridge Street	B4
Brindley Drive	B3
Brindley Place	B4
Broad Street	A5
Bromsgrove Street	E5
Brook Street	C2
Brunel Street	C4
Bull Street	E3
Cambridge Street	B3
Camden Drive	B2
Camden Street	A2
Cannon Street	D3

Caroline Street	B1
Carrs Lane	E3
Carver Street	A1
Chamberlain Square	C3
Chapmans Passage	C5
Charlotte Street	B3
Cheapside	F5
Cherry Street	D3
Church Street	D2
Civic Close	B3
Clement Street	A3
Cleveland Street	D1
Coleshill Street	F2
Colmore Circus Queensway	E2
Colmore Row	D3
Commercial Street	C5
Constitution Hill	C1
Cornwall Street	D3
Corporation Street	E1
Corporation Street	E3
Coventry Street	F4
Cox Street	C1
Dale End	E3
Daley Close	A3
Dalton Street	E2
Dean Street	E5
Digbeth	E4
Dudley Street	D4
Eden Place	C3
Edgbaston Street	E4
Edmund Street	D3
Edward Street	B3
Ellis Street	D5
Essington Street	A5
Ethel Street	D4
Etna Street	F2

Exeter Street	D5
Fazeley Street	F3
Fleet Street	C3
Fox Street	F3
Frederick Street	B1
Freeman Street	E3
Gas Street	B4
George Street	B2
Gloucester Street	E5
Goodman Street	A2
Gough Street	C5
Graham Street	B2
Granville Street	B5
Great Charles Street Queensway	C3
Grosvenor Street	F2
Grosvenor Street West	A5
Hall Street	B1
Hampton Street	D1
Helena Street	B3
Henrietta Street	C1
High Street	E4
High Street Deritend	F5
Hill Street	C4
Hinckley Street	D4
Hingeston Street	A1
Holland Street	B2
Holliday Street	B5
Holloway Circus	D5
Holloway Head	C5
Holt Street	F1
Horse Fair	D5
Hospital Street	D1
Hurst Street	D5
Icknield Street	A1
Inge Street	D5
James Street	B2
James Watt Queensway	E2
Jennens Road	F2
John Bright Street	D4
Kenyon Street	B1

King Edward's Drive	A4
King Edwards Road	A3
Ladywell Walk	D5
Lancaster Circus	E1
Lancaster Street	E1
Lawson Street	E1
Legge Lane	B2
Lighthouse Avenue	A3
Lionel Street	C3
Livery Street	C1
Louisa Street	B3
Loveday Street	E1
Lower Loveday Street	D1
Lower Temple Street	D4
Ludgate Hill	C2
Margaret Street	C3
Marshall Street	C5
Martineau Way	E3
Mary Ann Street	C1
Mary Street	C1
Meriden Street	F4
Mill Lane	F5
Moat Lane	E4
Moor Street	E4
Moor Street Queensway	E4
Moreton Street	A1
Navigation Street	C4
Needless Alley	D3
Nelson Street	A3
New Bartholomew Street	F4
New Canal Street	F4
Newhall Hill	B2
Newhall Street	C2
New Meeting Street	E3
New Street	D3
Newton Street	E2
Northwood Street	C1
Old Snow Hill	D1
Old Square	E3
Oozells Square	B4
Oxford Street	F5

Parade	B3
Paradise Circus Queensway	C3
Paradise Street	C4
Park Street	E4
Pemberton Street	A1
Pershore Street	E5
Pope Street	A1
Powell Street	A2
Price Street	E1
Princip Street	E1
Printing House Street	E2
Queens Drive	D4
Queensway Tunnel	C3
Rea Street	F5
Regent Parade	B1
Regent Place	B1
Regent Street	B1
Ridley Street	C5
Ruston Street	A5
Ryland Street	A5
St Chads Queensway	E1
St Jude's Pass	D5
St Marks Crescent	A3
St Martin's Square	E4
St Paul's Square	C1
St Philip's Place	D3
St Vincent Street	A3
Sand Pitts	A2
Saturday Bridge	B3
Scotland Street	B3
Severn Street	C5
Shadwell Street	D1
Shaw's Passage	F4
Sheepcote Street	A4
Sherborne Street	A4
Sloane Street	B2
Smallbrook Queensway	D5
Snow Hill Queensway	D2
Spencer Street	B1
Staniforth Street	E1
Station Street	D5

Steelhouse Lane	E2
Stephenson Street	D4
Suffolk Street Queensway	C4
Summer Hill Road	A2
Summer Hill Street	A2
Summer Hill Terrace	A2
Summer Lane	D1
Summer Row	B3
Swallow Street	C4
Temple Row	D3
Temple Row West	D3
Temple Street	D3
Tenby Street	A1
Tenby Street North	A1
Tennant Street	A5
The Priory Queensway	E3
Thorp Street	D5
Tindal Bridge	B3
Trent Street	F4
Union Street	E3
Upper Dean Street	E5
Upper Gough Street	C5
Vesey Street	E1
Victoria Square	C3
Vittoria Street	B1
Vyse Street	B1
Warstone Lane	A1
Washington Street	C5
Waterloo Street	D3
Water Street	C2
Weaman Street	D2
Whittall Street	E2
William Street	B5
Woodcock Street	F1

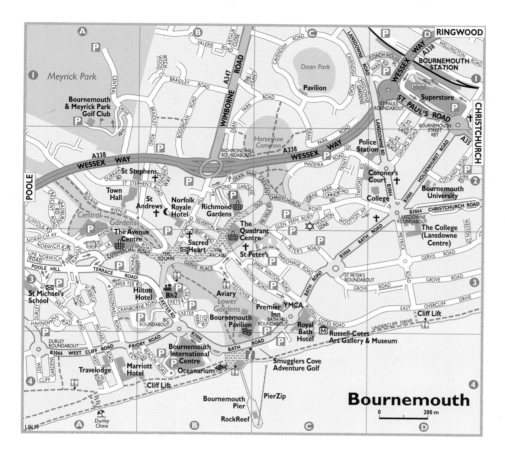

Bournemouth

Bournemouth is found on atlas page **13 J6**

Albert Road	B3	Old Christchurch Road	C2
Avenue Lane	A3	Orchard Street	A3
Avenue Road	A3	Oxford Road	D2
Bath Hill Roundabout	C3	Park Road	D1
Bath Road	B4	Parsonage Road	C3
Beacon Road	B4	Poole Hill	A3
BIC Roundabout	B3	Priory Road	A4
Bodorgan Road	B2	Purbeck Road	A3
Bourne Avenue	A2	Richmond Gardens	B2
Bournemouth Street		Richmond Hill	B3
Roundabout	D1	Richmond Hill Roundabout	B2
Bradburne Road	A2	Russell Cotes Road	C3
Braidley Road	B1	St Michael's Road	A3
Cavendish Road	C1	St Paul's Lane	D1
Central Drive	A1	St Paul's Place	D2
Christchurch Road	D2	St Paul's Road	D1
Coach House Place	D1	St Pauls Roundabout	D1
Commercial Road	A3	St Peter's Road	C3
Cotlands Road	D2	St Peter's Roundabout	C3
Cranborne Road	A3	St Stephen's Road	A2
Crescent Road	A2	St Stephen's Way	B2
Cumnor Road	C2	St Valerie Road	B1
Dean Park Crescent	B2	Stafford Road	C2
Dean Park Road	B2	Suffolk Road	A2
Durley Road	A3	Terrace Road	A3
Durley Roundabout	A4	The Arcade	B3
Durrant Road	A2	The Deans	B1
East Overcliff Drive	D3	The Square	B3
Exeter Crescent	B3	The Triangle	A3
Exeter Park Road	B3	Tregonwell Road	A3
Exeter Road	B3	Trinity Road	C2
Fir Vale Road	C2	Undercliff Drive	D3
Gervis Place	B3	Upper Hinton Road	C3
Gervis Road	D3	Upper Norwich Road	A3
Glen Fern Road	C2	Upper Terrace Road	A3
Grove Road	C3	Wellington Road	D1
Hahnemann Road	A3	Wessex Way	A2
Hinton Road	B3	West Cliff Gardens	A4
Holdenhurst Road	D2	West Cliff Road	A4
Kerley Road	A4	West Hill Road	A3
Lansdowne Gardens	C1	Weston Drive	D2
Lansdowne Road	C1	Westover Road	B3
Lansdowne Roundabout	D2	Wimborne Road	B1
Lorne Park Road	C2	Wootton Gardens	C2
Madeira Road	C2	Wootton Mount	C2
Meyrick Road	D3	Wychwood Close	B1
Norwich Avenue	A3	Yelverton Road	B2
Norwich Road	A3	York Road	D2

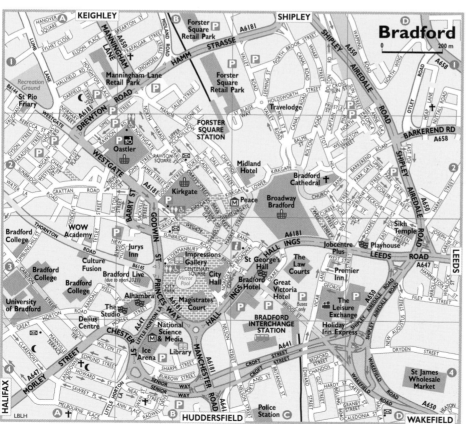

Bradford

Bradford is found on atlas page **90 F4**

Aldermanbury	B3	Lower Kirkgate	C2
Bank Street	B2	Lumb Lane	A1
Barkerend Road	D2	Manchester Road	B4
Barry Street	B2	Manningham Lane	A1
Bolling Road	C4	Manor Row	B1
Bolton Road	C2	Market Street	B3
Bridge Street	C3	Midland Road	B1
Broadway	C3	Morley Street	A4
Burnett Street	D2	Neal Street	B4
Canal Road	C1	Nelson Street	B4
Carlton Street	A3	North Brook Street	C1
Centenary Square	B3	Northgate	B2
Chandos Street	C4	North Parade	B1
Chapel Street	D3	North Street	C2
Cheapside	B2	North Wing	D1
Chester Street	A4	Otley Road	D1
Church Bank	C2	Paradise Street	A2
Claremont	A4	Peckover Street	D2
Croft Street	C4	Piccadilly	B2
Darfield Street	A1	Pine Street	C2
Darley Street	B2	Princes Way	B3
Drewton Road	A2	Randall Well Street	A3
Dryden Street	D4	Rawson Road	A2
Duke Street	B2	Rawson Square	B2
East Parade	D3	Rebecca Street	A2
Edmund Street	A4	St Blaise Way	C1
Edward Street	C4	St Thomas's Road	A2
Eldon Place	A1	Sawrey Place	A4
Filey Street	D3	Senior Way	B4
George Street	C3	Shipley Airedale Road	C1
Godwin Street	B2	Stott Hill	C2
Grattan Road	A2	Sunbridge Road	A2
Great Horton Road	A4	Tetley Street	A3
Grove Terrace	A4	Thornton Road	A3
Hallfield Road	A1	Trafalgar Street	B1
Hall Ings	B4	Tyrrel Street	B3
Hammerton Street	D3	Upper Park Gate	D2
Hamm Strasse	B1	Upper Piccadilly	B2
Holdsworth Street	C1	Valley Road	C1
Houghton Place	A1	Vicar Lane	C3
Howard Street	A4	Wakefield Road	D4
Hustlergate	B3	Wapping Road	D1
Infirmary Street	A1	Water Lane	A2
John Street	B2	Wellington Street	C2
Lansdowne Place	A4	Westgate	A2
Leeds Road	D3	Wharf Street	C1
Little Horton	A4	Wigan Street	A2
Little Horton Lane	B4	Wilton Street	A4

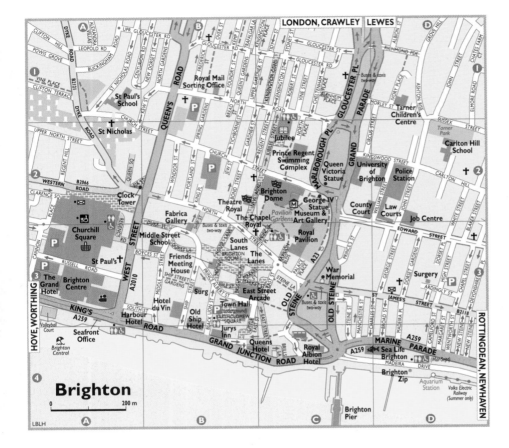

Brighton

Brighton is found on atlas page **24 H10**

Ardingly Street	D3	Madeira Place	D4
Ashton Rise	D1	Manchester Street	C4
Bartholomew Square	B3	Margaret Street	D4
Black Lion Street	B3	Marine Parade	D4
Blaker Street	D3	Market Street	B3
Bond Street	B2	Marlborough Place	C2
Boyces Street	A3	Meeting House Lane	B3
Brighton Place	B3	Middle Street	B3
Broad Street	D4	Morley Street	D1
Buckingham Road	A1	New Dorset Street	B1
Camelford Street	D4	New Road	B2
Cannon Place	A3	New Steine	D4
Carlton Hill	D2	Nile Street	B3
Centurion Road	A1	North Gardens	B1
Chapel Street	D3	North Place	C2
Charles Street	C4	North Road	B1
Cheltenham Place	C1	North Street	B2
Church Street	A1	Old Steine	C3
Church Street	B2	Portland Street	B2
Circus Street	C2	Powis Grove	A1
Clifton Hill	A1	Prince Albert Street	B3
Clifton Terrace	A1	Prince's Street	C3
Devonshire Place	D3	Queen's Gardens	B1
Dukes Lane	B3	Queen Square	A2
Duke Street	B2	Queen's Road	B2
East Street	C3	Regency Road	A2
Edward Street	D3	Regent Hill	A2
Elmore Road	D1	Regent Street	C2
Foundry Street	B1	Robert Street	C1
Frederick Street	B1	St James's Street	D3
Gardner Street	B2	St Nicholas Road	A1
George Street	D3	Ship Street	B3
Gloucester Place	C1	Spring Gardens	B1
Gloucester Road	B1	Steine Street	C4
Gloucester Street	C1	Sussex Street	D2
Grand Junction Road	B4	Sydney Street	C1
Grand Parade	C2	Tichborne Street	B2
High Street	D3	Tidy Street	C1
Ivory Place	D1	Upper Gardner Street	B1
John Street	D2	Upper Gloucester Road	A1
Jubilee Street	C2	Upper North Street	A2
Kensington Gardens	C1	Vine Street	C1
Kensington Street	C1	Wentworth Street	D4
Kew Street	B1	Western Road	A2
King's Road	A3	West Street	A3
Kingswood Street	C2	White Street	D3
Leopold Road	A1	William Street	D2
Little East Street	B4	Windsor Street	B2

Bristol

Bristol is found on atlas page **31 Q10**

Anchor Road	A3	Passage Street	C2
Avon Street	D3	Pembroke Street	C1
Baldwin Street	B2	Penn Street	C1
Bath Bridge	D4	Pero's Bridge	B3
Bond Street	C1	Perry Road	A2
Bond Street	D2	Philadelphia Street	C2
Broadmead	C1	Portwall Lane	C4
Broad Plain	D2	Prewett Street	C4
Broad Quay	B3	Prince Street	B3
Broad Street	B2	Queen Charlotte Street	B3
Broad Weir	C2	Queen Square	B3
Canons Way	A3	Redcliffe Parade West	B4
Canynge Street	C3	Redcliffe Way	C4
Castle Street	C2	Redcliff Hill	C4
College Green	A3	Redcliff Mead Lane	C4
Colston Avenue	B2	Redcliff Street	C3
Colston Street	B2	Royal Fort Road	A1
Commercial Road	B4	Rupert Street	B2
Corn Street	B2	St Augustine's Parade	B3
Counterslip	C3	St George's Road	A3
Cumberland Road	A4	St Matthias Park	D1
Deanery Road	A3	St Michael's Hill	A1
Denmark Street	A3	St Stephen's Street	B2
Explore Lane	A3	St Thomas Street	C3
Fairfax Street	C2	Small Street	B2
Ferry Street	C3	Somerset Street	C4
Friary	D3	Southwell Street	A1
Frogmore Street	A2	Tankards Close	A1
Great George Street	A3	Telephone Avenue	B3
Great George Street	D1	Temple Back	C3
Guinea Street	B4	Temple Back East	D3
Haymarket	C1	Temple Gate	D4
Hill Street	A2	Temple Street	C3
Horfield Road	B1	Temple Way	D3
Jacob Street	D2	The Grove	B4
King Street	B3	The Horsefair	C1
Lewins Mead	B2	The Pithay	C2
Lodge Street	A2	Tower Hill	D2
Lower Castle Street	D2	Trenchard Street	A2
Lower Church Lane	A2	Tyndall Avenue	A1
Lower Maudlin Street	B1	Union Street	C1
Marlborough Hill	B1	Upper Maudlin Street	B1
Marlborough Street	B1	Victoria Street	C2
Marsh Street	B3	Wapping Road	B4
Museum Avenue	A4	Welsh Back	B3
Newgate	C2	Whitson Street	B1
Old Market Street	D2	Wine Street	C2
Park Street	A2	Woodland Road	A1

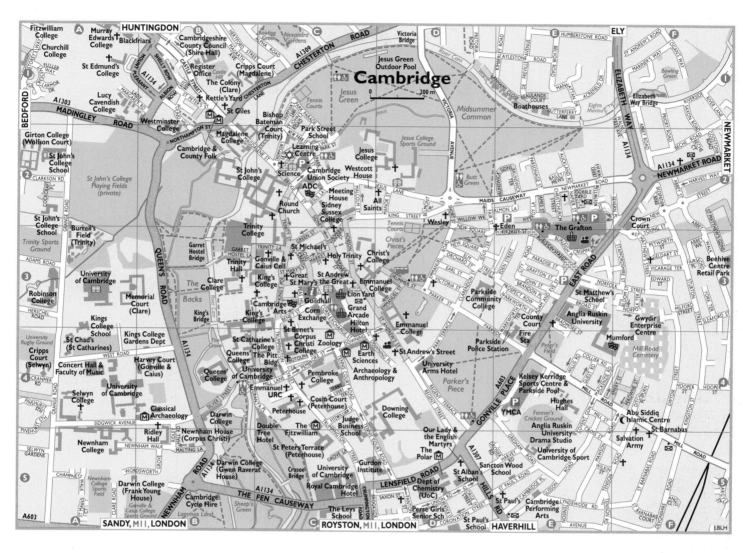

Cambridge

Cambridge is found on atlas page **62 G9**

Abbey Road F1
Abbey Street F2
Abbey Walk F3
Acrefield Drive E1
Adam and Eve Street E3
Albion Row B1
Alpha Road C1
Auckland Road E2
Aylestone Road E1
Bailey Mews E2
Banhams Close D1
Beaulands Court E1
Beche Road F2
Belmont Place D2
Belvoir Road E1
Bene't Street C3
Bloom Street F3
Bradmore Street E3
Brandon Place E3
Bridge Street C2
Broad Street E3
Brookside D5
Brunswick Gardens E2
Brunswick Terrace E2
Burleigh Place E3
Burleigh Street E3
Cambridge Place E5
Castle Row B1
Castle Street B1
Champneys Walk A5
Chesterton Lane B1
Chesterton Road C1
Christchurch Street E2
City Road E3
Clarendon Street D3
Cobble Yard E2

Collier Road E4
Corn Exchange Street C3
Coronation Street D5
Covent Garden E4
Crispin Place E3
Cross Street E4
Crusoe Bridge B5
Cutler Ferry Close E1
Cutterferry Lane E1
De Freville Avenue E1
Devonshire Road F5
Ditchburn Place F4
Downing Place C4
Downing Street C4
Drosier Road D5
Drummer Street D3
Earl Street D3
East Road E3
Eden Street E3
Eden Street Back E3
Edward Street E3
Elizabeth Way F1
Elm Street D3
Emery Street F4
Emmanuel Road D3
Emmanuel Street D3
Evening Court E2
Fairsford Place F3
Fair Street D2
Fitzroy Lane E3
Fitzroy Street E3
Fitzwilliam Street C4
Garret Hostel Bridge B3
Garret Hostel Lane B3
Geldart Street E3
George IV Street D5

Glisson Road E5
Godstone Road F2
Gonville Place D4
Grange Road A3
Grange Road A4
Granta Place B4
Green Street C3
Gresham Road E5
Gwydir Street F4
Harvest Way F2
Harvey Road E5
Hertford Street B1
Hills Road D5
Hobson Street C3
Humberstone Road E1
James Street E2
Jesus Lane C2
Jesus Terrace D3
John Street E3
Kimberley Road E1
King's Bridge B3
King's Parade C3
Kingston Street F4
King Street D2
Lady Margaret Road A1
Lensfield Road D5
Logan's Way F1
Lwr Park Street C2
Lyndewode Road E5
Mackenzie Road E4
Madingley Road A1
Magdalene Street B2
Magrath Avenue B1
Malcolm Street C2
Malting Lane B5
Manhattan Drive E1
Manor Street D2
Mariner's Way F1
Market Street C3
Mawson Road E5

Milford Street F3
Mill Lane C4
Mill Road E4
Mill Street E4
Mortimer Road E4
Mount Pleasant B1
Napier Street E2
Newmarket Road E2
Newnham Road B5
Newnham Walk A5
New Park Street C2
New Square D3
New Street F2
Norfolk Street E3
Norfolk Terrace F3
Northampton Street B2
Occupation Road F2
Orchard Street D3
Panton Street D5
Paradise Street E3
Parker Street D3
Park Parade C1
Park Street C2
Parkside D3
Park Terrace D4
Parsonage Street E2
Peas Hill C3
Pembroke Street C4
Perowne Street F4
Petworth Street F3
Pound Hill B1
Priory Road F1
Prospect Row E3
Queen's Road B3
Regent Street D4
Regent Terrace D4
River Lane F1
Riverside E4
St Andrew's Road F1
St Andrew's Street D3
St Barnabas Road F5

St Mary's Street C3
St Matthew's Gardens F2
St Matthew's Street F3
St Paul's Road E5
St Peter's Street B1
Salmon Lane E2
Saxon Road F1
Saxon Street D5
Severn Place F2
Shelly Row B1
Short Street D2
Sidgwick Avenue A4
Sidney Street C2
Silver Street B4
Staffordshire Street F3
Sturton Street F3
Sussex Street C3
Tenison Avenue E5
Tenison Road E5
Tennis Court Road C4
Tennis Court Terrace C4
The Fen Causeway B5
Thompson's Lane C2
Trinity Lane C3
Trinity Street C2
Trumpington Road C5
Trumpington Street C4
Union Road D5
Vicarage Terrace F3
Victoria Avenue D1
Victoria Bridge D1
Victoria Street D3
Warkworth Street E4
Warkworth Terrace E4
Wellington Street E2
West Road A4
Wilkin Street E5
Willis Road E4
Willow Walk D2
Wordsworth Grove A5
Young Street F3

University Colleges

Christ's College C3
Clare College A3
Clare College B1
Clare College B3
Corpus Christi College C4
Darwin College B4
Downing College D4
Emmanuel College C3
Emmanuel College D3
Fitzwilliam College A1
Girton College
   (Wolfson Court) A2
Gonville & Caius College......... C3
Gonville & Caius College......... B4
Jesus College C2
King's College B3
Lucy Cavendish College A1
Magdalene College B2
Murray Edwards College A1
Newnham College A5
Pembroke College C4
Peterhouse C4
Queens' College B4
Robinson College A3
St Catharine's College C4
St Edmund's College A1
St John's College B2
Selwyn College A4
Sidney Sussex College C2
Trinity College B3
Westminster College B1

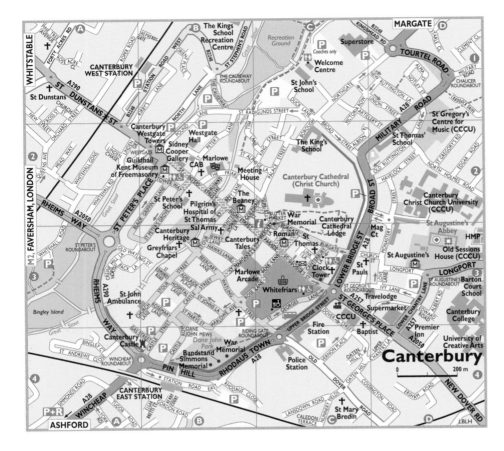

Canterbury

Canterbury is found on atlas page **39 K10**

Adelaide Place	B3	Nunnery Fields	C4
Albion Place	C2	Oaten Hill	C4
Alma Street	D1	Old Dover Road	C4
Artillery Street	C1	Old Ruttington Lane	D2
Beercart Lane	B3	Orchard Street	A2
Best Lane	B2	Palace Street	C2
Black Griffin Lane	A3	Parade	C3
Borough	C2	Pin Hill	B4
Broad Street	D2	Pound Lane	B2
Burgate	C3	Queens Avenue	A2
Butter Market	C2	Rheims Way	A3
Canterbury Lane	C3	Rhodaus Town	B4
Castle Row	B4	Rose Lane	B3
Castle Street	B3	Rosemary Lane	B3
Cossington Road	C4	St Alphege Lane	B2
Dover Street	C3	St Dunstans Street	A1
Duck Lane	C1	St Edmunds Road	B3
Edgar Road	D2	St George's Lane	C3
Edward Road	D3	St George's Place	C3
Ersham Road	D4	St George's Street	C3
Gas Street	A4	St Gregory's Road	D2
Gordon Road	B4	St Johns Lane	B3
Guildhall Street	B2	St Margaret's Street	B3
Havelock Street	D2	St Marys Street	B3
Hawks Lane	B3	St Peter's Grove	B3
High Street	B2	St Peter's Lane	B2
Hospital Lane	B3	St Peter's Place	A3
Ivy Lane	C3	St Peters Street	B2
Jewry Lane	B3	St Radigunds Street	B1
King Street	C2	Station Road East	B4
Kirby's Lane	B1	Station Road West	A1
Lansdown Road	C4	Stour Street	B3
Linden Grove	A2	Sturry Road	D1
Longport	D3	Sun Street	C2
Love Lane	D3	The Causeway	B1
Lower Bridge Street	C3	The Friars	B2
Lower Chantry Lane	D4	Tourtel Road	D1
Marlowe Avenue	B3	Tower Way	B2
Mead Way	A2	Tudor Road	A4
Mercery Lane	C3	Union Street	D1
Military Road	D2	Upper Bridge Street	C4
Mill Lane	B1	Vernon Place	C4
Monastery Street	D3	Victoria Row	C1
New Dover Road	D4	Watling Street	B3
New Ruttington Lane	D1	Whitehall Gardens	A2
North Lane	B1	Whitehall Road	A2
Northgate	C1	Wincheap	A4
Notley Street	D1	York Road	A4

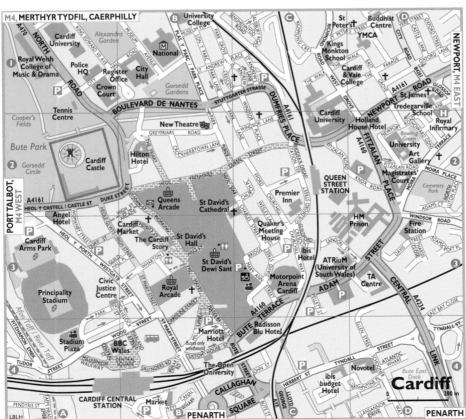

Cardiff

Cardiff is found on atlas page **30 G9**

Adam Street	C3	Museum Avenue	B1
Adams Court	D2	Museum Place	B1
Adamscroft Place	D3	Newport Road	D1
Atlantic Wharf	D4	Newport Road Lane	D2
Boulevard de Nantes	B1	North Luton Place	D2
Bridge Street	C3	North Road	A1
Brigantine Place	D4	Oxford Lane	D1
Bute Street	C4	Oxford Street	D1
Bute Terrace	C3	Park Grove	B1
Callaghan Square	B4	Park Lane	B1
Caroline Street	B3	Park Place	B1
Castle Lane	D1	Park Street	A3
Castle Street	A2	Pellett Street	C3
Central Link	D3	Pendyris Street	A4
Charles Street	B2	Quay Street	A3
Churchill Way	C2	Queen Street	B2
City Hall Road	A1	Richmond Crescent	B1
City Road	D1	Richmond Road	C1
Crockherbtown Lane	B2	St Andrew's Crescent	B1
Custom House Street	B4	St Andrew's Lane	C1
David Street	C3	St Andrew's Place	B1
Davis Street	D3	St John Street	B2
Duke Street	A2	St Mary Street	B3
Dumfries Place	C2	St Peter's Street	C1
East Bay Close	D3	Salisbury Road	C1
East Grove	D1	Sandon Street	C3
Fford Churchill	C2	Saunders Road	B4
Fitzalan Place	D2	Schooner Way	D4
Fitzalan Road	D2	Stuttgarter Strasse	B1
Fitzhamon Embankment	A4	The Friary	B2
Glossop Road	D1	The Hayes	B3
Greyfriars Road	B2	The Parade	C1
Guildford Street	C3	The Walk	C1
Guildhall Place	A3	Trinity Street	B3
Havelock Street	B3	Tudor Street	A4
Hayes Bridge Road	B3	Tyndall Street	D4
Heol Siarl	B2	Vere Street	D1
Herbert Street	C4	Wesley Lane	C2
High Street	B3	West Canal Wharf	B4
High Street Arcade	B2	West Grove	C1
Hills Street	B3	Westgate Street	A3
King Edward VII Avenue	A1	Wharton Street	B3
Knox Road	D2	Windsor Lane	C2
Lloyd George Avenue	C4	Windsor Place	C1
Mary Ann Street	C3	Windsor Road	D3
Mill Lane	B4	Womanby Street	A3
Moira Place	D2	Wood Street	A4
Moira Terrace	D2	Working Street	B3

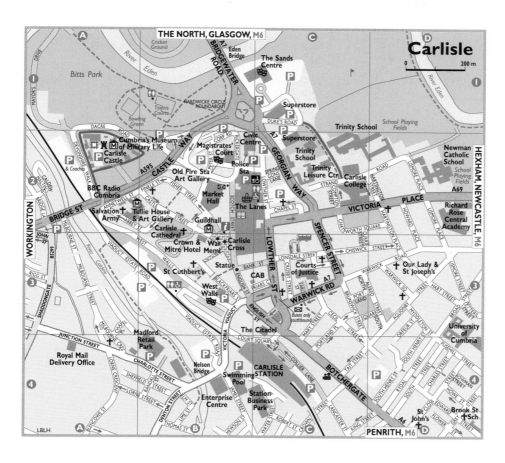

Carlisle

Carlisle is found on atlas page **110 G9**

Abbey Street	A2
Aglionby Street	D3
Annetwell Street	A2
Bank Street	B3
Blackfriars Street	B3
Blencowe Street	A4
Botchergate	C4
Bridge Lane	A2
Bridge Street	A2
Bridgewater Road	B1
Broad Street	D3
Brunswick Street	C3
Caldew Maltings	A2
Castle Street	B2
Castle Way	B2
Cecil Street	C3
Chapel Place	A3
Chapel Street	C2
Charles Street	D4
Charlotte Street	B4
Chatsworth Square	C2
Chiswick Street	C3
Close Street	D4
Collier Lane	C4
Compton Street	C2
Corp Road	B2
Court Square	B4
Crosby Street	C3
Crown Street	C4
Currie Street	C3
Dacre Road	A1
Denton Street	B4
Devonshire Walk	A2
Duke's Road	C1
Edward Street	D4
Elm Street	B4
English Street	B3
Finkle Street	B2
Fisher Street	B2
Flower Street	D4
Friars Court	C3
Fusehill Street	D4
Georgian Way	C2
Grey Street	D4
Hartington Place	D2
Hartington Street	D2
Hart Street	D3
Hewson Street	B4
Howard Place	D2
Howe Street	D4
James Street	B4
John Street	A3
Junction Street	A4
King Street	C4
Lancaster Street	C4
Lime Street	B4
Lismore Place	D2
Lismore Street	D3
Lonsdale Street	C3
Lorne Crescent	A4
Lorne Street	A4
Lowther Street	C3
Mary Street	C3
Mayor's Drive	A1
Milbourne Crescent	A3
Milbourne Street	A3
Myddleton Street	D3
North Alfred Street	D3
Orfeur Street	D3
Peter Street	B2
Petteril Street	D3
Portland Place	C4
Portland Square	C3
Randall Street	B4
Rickergate	B2
Rigg Street	A3
Robert Street	C4
Rydal Street	D4
Scotch Street	B2
Shaddongate	A3
Sheffield Street	A4
South Alfred Street	D3
South Henry Street	D4
Spencer Street	C2
Spring Gardens Lane	C2
Strand Road	C2
Tait Street	C4
Thomas Street	B4
Viaduct Estate Road	A3
Victoria Place	C2
Victoria Viaduct	B4
Warwick Road	D3
Warwick Square	D3
Water Street	C4
West Tower Street	B2
West Walls	B3

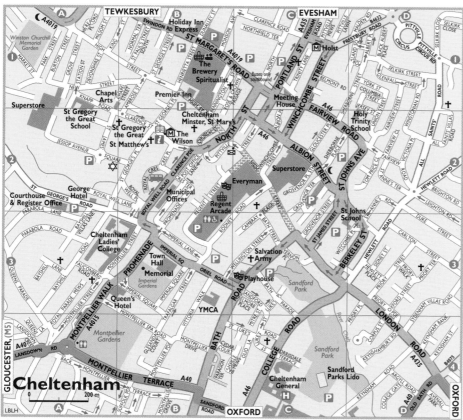

Cheltenham

Cheltenham is found on atlas page **46 H10**

Albion Street	C2
All Saints' Road	D2
Ambrose Street	B1
Argyll Road	D4
Back Montpellier Terrace	A4
Bath Road	B4
Bath Street	C3
Bayshill Road	A3
Bayshill Villas Lane	A3
Bennington Street	B1
Berkeley Street	C3
Burton Street	A1
Carlton Street	D3
Church Street	B2
Clarence Parade	B2
Clarence Road	C1
Clarence Street	B2
College Road	C4
Crescent Terrace	B2
Devonshire Street	A1
Duke Street	D3
Dunalley Street	B1
Evesham Road	C1
Fairview Road	C2
Fairview Street	D2
Fauconberg Road	A3
Glenfall Street	D1
Grosvenor Street	C3
Grove Street	A1
Henrietta Street	B1
Hewlett Road	D3
High Street	A1
High Street	C2
Imperial Lane	B3
Imperial Square	B3
Jersey Street	D1
Jessop Avenue	A2
Keynsham Road	D4
King Street	A1
Knapp Road	A1
Lansdown Road	A4
Leighton Road	D2
London Road	D3
Malden Road	D1
Market Street	A1
Milsom Street	A1
Monson Avenue	B1
Montpellier Grove	B4
Montpellier Parade	B4
Montpellier Spa Road	B4
Montpellier Street	A4
Montpellier Terrace	A4
Montpellier Walk	A4
New Street	A1
North Street	B2
Old Bath Road	D4
Oriel Road	B3
Parabola Lane	A3
Parabola Road	A3
Park Street	A1
Pittville Circus	D1
Pittville Circus Road	D1
Pittville Street	B2
Portland Street	C1
Prestbury Road	C1
Priory Street	D3
Promenade	B3
Queens Parade	A3
Regent Street	B2
Rodney Road	B3
Royal Well Lane	A2
Royal Well Road	B2
St Anne's Road	D2
St Anne's Terrace	D2
St George's Place	B2
St George's Road	A2
St George's Street	B1
St James' Square	A2
St James Street	C3
St Johns Avenue	C2
St Margaret's Road	B1
St Paul's Street South	B1
Sandford Street	C3
Selkirk Street	D1
Sherborne Street	C2
Station Street	A1
Suffolk Parade	B4
Swindon Road	B1
Sydenham Villas Road	D3
Trafalgar Street	B4
Union Street	D2
Wellington Street	C3
Winchcombe Street	C2
Winstonian Road	D2
Witcombe Place	C3
York Street	D1

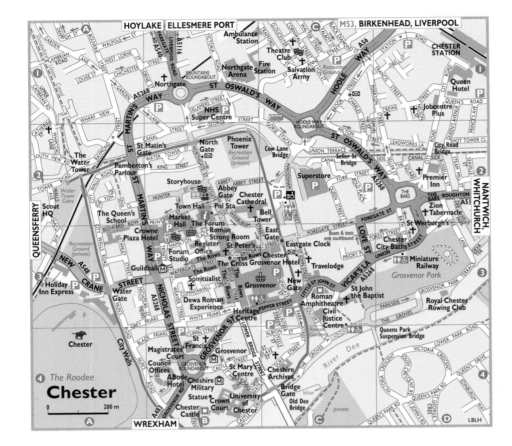

Chester
Chester is found on atlas page **81 N11**

Albion Street	C4	Nicholas Street	B3
Bath Street	D2	Northgate Street	B2
Black Diamond Street	C1	Nun's Road	A3
Boughton	D2	Parkgate Road	B1
Bouverie Street	A1	Park Street	C3
Bridge Street	B3	Pepper Street	C3
Brook Street	C1	Princess Street	B2
Canal Side	C2	Priory Place	C3
Castle Street	B4	Queen's Park Road	C4
Charles Street	C1	Queen's Road	D1
Chichester Street	A1	Queen Street	C2
City Road	D2	Raymond Street	A2
City Walls Road	A2	Russell Street	D2
Commonhall Street	B3	St Anne Street	C1
Cornwall Street	C1	St John's Road	D4
Crewe Street	D1	St John Street	C3
Cuppin Street	B4	St Martin's Way	A2
Dee Hills Park	D2	St Mary's Hill	B4
Dee Lane	D2	St Olave Street	C4
Delamere Street	B1	St Oswald's Way	B1
Duke Street	C4	St Werburgh Street	B2
Eastgate Street	B3	Samuel Street	C2
Egerton Street	C1	Seller Street	D2
Foregate Street	C2	Shipgate Street	B4
Forest Street	C3	Souter's Lane	C3
Francis Street	D1	South View Road	A2
Frodsham Street	C2	Stanley Place	A3
Garden Lane	A1	Station Road	D1
George Street	B2	Steam Mill Street	D2
Gloucester Street	C1	Steele Street	C4
Gorse Stacks	C2	Talbot Street	C1
Grosvenor Park Terrace	D3	Tower Road	A2
Grosvenor Road	B4	Trafford Street	C1
Grosvenor Street	B4	Trinity Street	B3
Hamilton Place	B3	Union Street	D3
Hoole Way	C1	Union Terrace	C2
Hunter Street	B2	Upper Cambrian Road	A1
King Street	B2	Vicar's Lane	C3
Leadworks Lane	D2	Victoria Crescent	D4
Little St John Street	C3	Victoria Road	B1
Liverpool Road	B1	Volunteer Street	C3
Lorne Street	A1	Walpole Street	A1
Love Street	C3	Walter Street	C1
Lower Bridge Street	B4	Watergate Street	B3
Lower Park Road	D4	Water Tower Street	B2
Milton Street	C2	Weaver Street	B3
New Crane Street	A3	White Friars	B3
Newgate Street	C3	York Street	C2

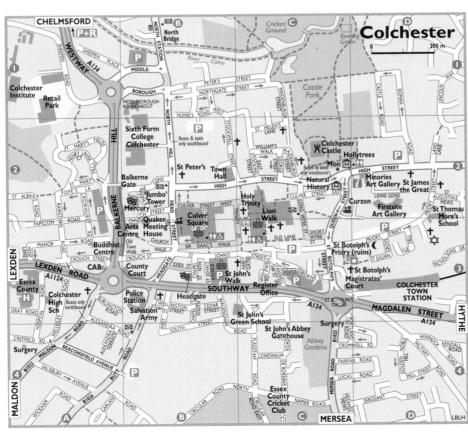

Colchester
Colchester is found on atlas page **52 G6**

Abbey Gates	C3	Middleborough	B1
Alexandra Road	A3	Middleborough Roundabout	A1
Alexandra Terrace	A4	Military Road	D4
Balkerne Hill	A3	Mill Street	D4
Beaconsfield Avenue	A4	Napier Road	C4
Burlington Road	A3	Nicholsons Green	D3
Butt Road	A4	North Bridge	B1
Castle Road	D1	Northgate Street	B1
Cedar Street	B3	North Hill	B1
Chapel Street North	B3	North Station Road	B1
Chapel Street South	B3	Nunn's Road	B1
Church Street	B3	Osborne Street	C3
Church Walk	B3	Papillon Road	A3
Circular Road East	C4	Pope's Lane	A2
Circular Road North	B4	Portland Road	C4
Creffield Road	A4	Priory Street	D3
Cromwell Road	C4	Queen Street	C3
Crouch Street	A3	Rawstorn Road	A2
Crouch Street	B3	Roman Road	D1
Crowhurst Road	A2	St Alban's Road	A2
Culver Street East	C2	St Augustine Mews	D2
Culver Street West	B2	St Botolph's Circus	C3
East Hill	D2	St Botolph's Street	C3
East Stockwell Street	C2	St Helen's Lane	C2
Essex Street	B3	St John's Avenue	B3
Fairfax Road	C4	St John's Street	B3
Flagstaff Road	C4	St Julian Grove	D3
Garland Road	A4	St Mary's Fields	A2
George Street	C2	St Peter's Street	B1
Golden Noble Hill	D4	Salisbury Avenue	A4
Gray Road	A3	Sheepen Place	A1
Headgate	B3	Sheepen Road	A1
Head Street	B2	Short Wyre Street	C3
Henry Laver Court	A2	Sir Isaac's Walk	B3
High Street	B2	South Street	B4
Hospital Road	A4	Southway	B3
Hospital Lane	A3	Stanwell Street	C3
Land Lane	D2	Trinity Street	B2
Lewis Gardens	D2	Walsingham Road	B3
Lexden Road	A3	Wellesley Road	A4
Lincoln Way	D1	Wellington Street	B3
Long Wyre Street	C2	West Stockwell Street	B1
Lucas Road	C4	West Street	B4
Magdalen Street	D3	Westway	A1
Maidenburgh Street	C1	Whitewell Road	C3
Maldon Road	A4	Wickham Road	A4
Manor Road	A3	William's Walk	C2
Mersea Road	C4	Winnock Road	D4

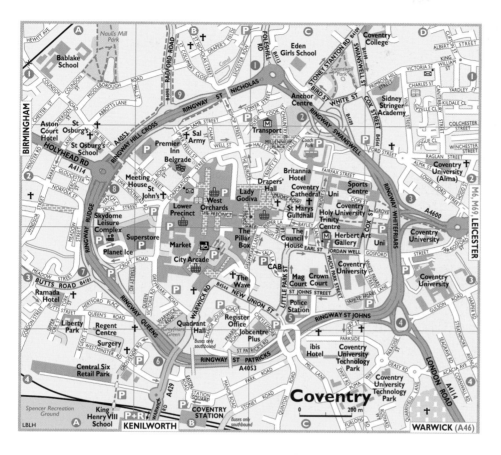

Coventry

Coventry is found on atlas page **59 M9**

Abbotts Lane	A1	Much Park Street	C3
Acacia Avenue	D4	New Union Street	B3
Alma Street	D2	Norfolk Street	A2
Barras Lane	A2	Park Road	B4
Bayley Lane	C2	Parkside	C4
Bird Street	C1	Primrose Hill Street	D1
Bishop Street	B1	Priory Row	C2
Broadgate	B2	Priory Street	C2
Butts Road	A3	Puma Way	C4
Butts Street	A3	Quarryfield Lane	D4
Canterbury Street	D1	Queen's Road	A3
Chester Street	A2	Queen Victoria Road	B3
Cheylesmore	C3	Quinton Road	C4
Cornwall Road	D4	Radford Road	B1
Corporation Street	B2	Raglan Street	D2
Coundon Road	A1	Regent Street	A4
Cox Street	D1	Ringway Hill Cross	A2
Cox Street	D2	Ringway Queens	A3
Croft Road	A3	Ringway Rudge	A3
Earl Street	C3	Ringway St Johns	C3
Eaton Road	B4	Ringway St Nicholas	B1
Fairfax Street	C2	Ringway St Patricks	B4
Foleshill Road	C1	Ringway Swanswell	C1
Gloucester Street	A2	Ringway Whitefriars	D2
Gosford Street	D3	St Johns Street	C3
Greyfriars Lane	B3	St Nicholas Street	B1
Greyfriars Road	B3	Salt Lane	C3
Grosvenor Road	A4	Seagrave Road	D4
Gulson Road	D3	Spon Street	A2
Hales Street	C2	Starley Road	A3
Hertford Place	A3	Stoney Road	B4
High Street	C3	Stoney Stanton Road	C1
Hill Street	B2	Strathmore Avenue	D3
Holyhead Road	A2	Swanswell Street	C1
Jordan Well	C3	The Burges	B2
Lamb Street	B2	Tower Street	B1
Leicester Row	B1	Trinity Street	C2
Little Park Street	C3	Upper Hill Street	B2
London Road	D4	Upper Wells Street	A4
Lower Ford Street	D2	Victoria Street	D1
Lower Holyhead Road	A2	Vine Street	D1
Manor House Road	B4	Warwick Road	B3
Manor Road	B4	Warwick Road	B4
Meadow Street	A3	Westminster Road	A4
Meriden Street	A1	White Friars Street	D3
Middleborough Road	A1	White Street	C1
Mile Lane	C4	Windsor Street	A3
Mill Street	A1	Yardley Street	D1

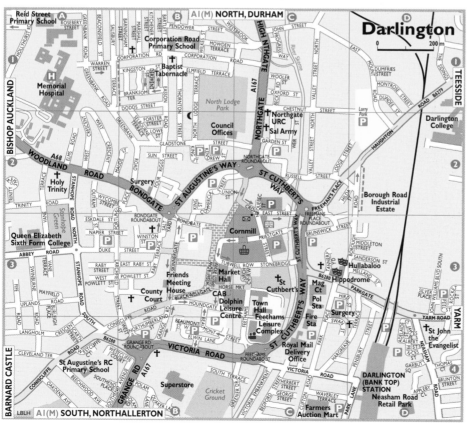

Darlington

Darlington is found on atlas page **103 Q8**

Abbey Road	A3	Maude Street	A2
Albert Street	D4	Melland Street	D3
Appleby Close	D4	Neasham Road	D4
Barningham Street	B1	Northgate	C2
Bartlett Street	B1	North Lodge Terrace	B2
Beaumont Street	B3	Northumberland Street	B4
Bedford Street	C4	Oakdene Avenue	A4
Beechwood Avenue	A4	Outram Street	A2
Blackwellgate	B3	Parkgate	D3
Bondgate	B2	Park Lane	D4
Borough Road	D3	Park Place	C4
Brunswick Street	C3	Pendower Street	B1
Brunton Street	D4	Pensbury Street	D4
Chestnut Street	C1	Polam Lane	B4
Cleveland Terrace	A4	Portland Place	A3
Clifton Road	C4	Powlett Street	B3
Commercial Street	B2	Priestgate	C3
Coniscliffe Road	A4	Raby Terrace	B3
Corporation Road	B1	Russell Street	C2
Crown Street	C2	St Augustine's Way	B2
Dodds Street	B1	St Cuthbert's Way	C2
Duke Street	A3	St Cuthbert's Way	C4
Easson Road	B1	St James Place	D4
East Mount Road	D1	Salisbury Terrace	A1
East Raby Street	B3	Salt Yard	B3
East Street	C3	Scarth Street	A4
Elms Road	A2	Skinnergate	B3
Elwin Lane	B4	Southend Avenue	A4
Feethams	C4	Stanhope Road North	A2
Fife Road	A3	Stanhope Road South	A3
Four Riggs	B2	Stonebridge	C3
Freeman's Place	C2	Sun Street	B2
Gladstone Street	B2	Swan Street	C4
Grange Road	B4	Swinburne Road	A3
Greenbank Road	A1	Trinity Road	A2
Greenbank Road	B2	Tubwell Row	B3
Hargreave Terrace	C4	Uplands Road	A3
Haughton Road	D2	Valley Street North	C2
High Northgate	C1	Vane Terrace	A2
High Row	B3	Victoria Embankment	C4
Hollyhurst Road	A1	Victoria Road	B4
Houndgate	B3	Victoria Road	C4
John Street	C1	West Crescent	A2
John Williams Boulevard	D3	West Powlett Street	A3
Kendrew Street	B2	West Row	B3
Kingston Street	B1	West Street	B4
Langholm Crescent	A4	Woodland Road	A2
Larchfield Street	A3	Yarm Road	D3

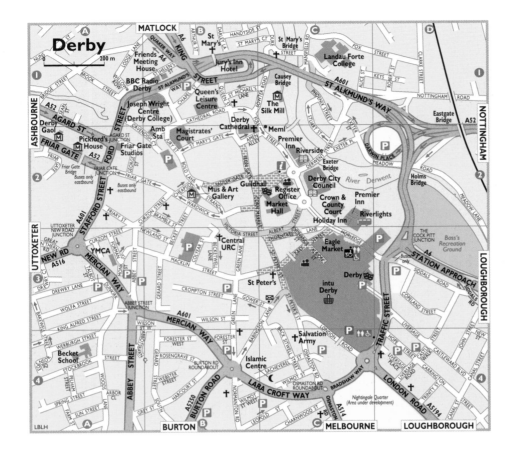

Derby
Derby is found on atlas page **72 B3**

Abbey Street	A4	King Alfred Street	A3
Agard Street	A1	King Street	B1
Albert Street	C3	Lara Croft Way	B4
Babington Lane	B4	Leopold Street	B4
Back Sitwell Street	C4	Liversage Road	D4
Becket Street	B3	Liversage Street	D3
Bold Lane	B2	Lodge Lane	A1
Bradshaw Way	C4	London Road	C3
Bramble Street	B2	Macklin Street	B3
Bridge Street	A1	Mansfield Road	C1
Brook Street	A1	Meadow Lane	D2
Burton Road	B4	Meadow Road	D2
Canal Street	D4	Mercian Way	B3
Carrington Street	D4	Morledge	C3
Cathedral Road	B1	Newland Street	A3
Cavendish Court	A2	New Road	A3
Chapel Street	B1	New Street	D4
Clarke Street	D1	Nottingham Road	D1
Copeland Street	D3	Osmaston Road	C4
Corn Market	B2	Phoenix Street	C1
Crompton Street	B3	Queen Street	B1
Curzon Street	A2	Robert Street	D1
Curzon Street	A3	Rosengrave Street	B4
Darwin Place	C2	Sacheverel Street	C4
Derwent Street	C2	Sadler Gate	B2
Drewry Lane	A3	St Alkmund's Way	C1
Duke Street	C1	St Helen's Street	B1
Dunkirk	A3	St Mary's Gate	B2
East Street	C3	St Peter's Street	C3
Exchange Street	C3	Siddals Road	D3
Exeter Place	C2	Sowter Road	C1
Exeter Street	C2	Spring Street	A4
Ford Street	A2	Stafford Street	A3
Forester Street West	B4	Station Approach	D3
Forman Street	A3	Stockbrook Street	A4
Fox Street	C1	Strand	B2
Friary Street	A2	Stuart Street	C1
Full Street	B1	Sun Street	A4
Gerard Street	B3	The Cock Pitt	D3
Gower Street	B3	Thorntree Lane	C3
Green Lane	B3	Traffic Street	D4
Grey Street	A4	Trinity Street	D4
Handyside Street	B1	Victoria Street	B2
Harcourt Street	B4	Wardwick	B2
Iron Gate	B2	Werburgh Street	A4
John Street	D4	Wilmot Street	C4
Jury Street	B2	Wolfa Street	A3
Keys Street	D1	Woods Lane	A4

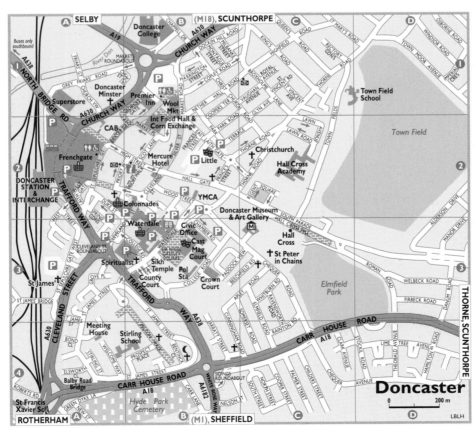

Doncaster
Doncaster is found on atlas page **91 P10**

Alderson Drive	D3	Nelson Street	B4
Apley Road	B3	Nether Hall Road	B1
Balby Road Bridge	A4	North Bridge Road	A1
Beechfield Road	B3	North Street	C4
Broxholme Lane	C1	Osborne Road	D1
Carr House Road	C4	Palmer Street	C4
Carr Lane	B4	Park Road	B2
Chamber Road	B3	Park Terrace	B2
Chequer Avenue	C4	Prince's Street	B2
Chequer Road	C3	Priory Place	A2
Childers Street	C4	Prospect Place	B4
Christ Church Road	B1	Queen's Road	C1
Church View	A1	Rainton Road	C4
Church Way	B1	Ravensworth Road	C3
Clark Avenue	C4	Rectory Gardens	C1
Cleveland Street	A4	Regent Square	C2
College Road	B3	Roman Road	D3
Cooper Street	C4	Royal Avenue	C1
Coopers Terrace	B2	St Georges Gate	B2
Copley Road	B1	St James Street	B4
Cunningham Road	B3	St Mary's Road	C1
Danum Road	D3	St Sepulchre Gate	A2
Dockin Hill Road	B1	St Sepulchre Gate West	A3
Duke Street	A2	St Vincent Avenue	C1
East Laith Gate	B2	St Vincent Road	C1
Elmfield Road	C3	Scot Lane	B2
Firbeck Road	D3	Silver Street	B2
Frances Street	B2	Somerset Road	B3
Glyn Avenue	C1	South Parade	C2
Green Dyke Lane	A4	South Street	C4
Grey Friars' Road	A1	Spring Gardens	A2
Hall Cross Hill	C2	Stirling Street	A4
Hall Gate	B2	Stockil Road	C4
Hamilton Road	D4	Theobald Avenue	D4
Harrington Street	B1	Thorne Road	C1
High Street	A2	Town Fields	C2
Highfield Road	C1	Town Moor Avenue	D1
Jarratt Street	B4	Trafford Way	A2
King's Road	C1	Vaughan Avenue	C1
Lawn Avenue	C2	Waterdale	B3
Lawn Road	C2	Welbeck Road	D3
Lime Tree Avenue	D4	Welcome Way	A4
Manor Drive	D3	West Laith Gate	A2
Market Place	B1	West Street	A3
Market Road	B1	Whitburn Road	C3
Milbanke Street	B1	White Rose Way	B4
Milton Walk	B4	Windsor Road	D1
Montague Street	B1	Wood Street	B2

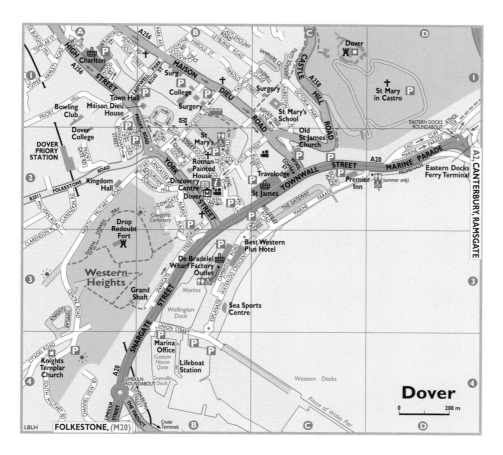

Dover

Dover is found on atlas page **27 P3**

Adrian Street	B3	Marine Parade	D2
Albany Place	B2	Military Road	B2
Ashen Tree Lane	C1	Mill Lane	B2
Athol Terrace	D1	New Street	B2
Biggin Street	B2	Norman Street	A2
Cambridge Road	B3	North Downs Way	A3
Camden Crescent	C2	North Military Road	A3
Castle Hill Road	C1	Park Avenue	B1
Castlemount Road	B1	Park Street	B1
Castle Street	B2	Pencester Road	B2
Centre Road	A3	Peter Street	A1
Channel View Road	A4	Priory Gate Road	A2
Church Street	B2	Priory Hill	A1
Citadel Road	A4	Priory Road	A1
Clarendon Place	A3	Priory Street	B2
Clarendon Road	A2	Promenade	D2
Cowgate Hill	B2	Queen's Gardens	B2
Crafford Street	A1	Queen Street	B2
De Burgh Hill	A1	Russell Street	B2
Douro Place	C2	Samphire Close	C1
Dour Street	A1	Saxon Street	A2
Durham Close	B2	Snargate Street	A4
Durham Hill	B2	South Military Road	A4
East Cliff	D2	Stembrook	B2
Eastern Docks Roundabout	D2	Taswell Close	C1
Effingham Street	A2	Taswell Street	B1
Elizabeth Street	A4	Templar Street	A1
Esplanade	B3	The Viaduct	A4
Folkestone Road	A2	Tower Hamlets Road	A1
Godwyne Close	B1	Townwall Street	C2
Godwyne Road	B1	Union Street	B3
Harold Street	B1	Victoria Park	C1
Harold Street	B1	Waterloo Crescent	B3
Heritage Gardens	C1	Wellesley Road	C2
Hewitt Road	A1	Wood Street	A1
High Street	A1	Woolcomber Street	C2
King Street	B2	York Street	B2
Knights Templar	A3		
Ladywell	A1		
Lancaster Road	B2		
Laureston Place	C1		
Leyburne Road	B1		
Limekiln Roundabout	A4		
Limekiln Street	A4		
Maison Dieu Road	B1		
Malvern Road	A2		
Marine Parade	C2		

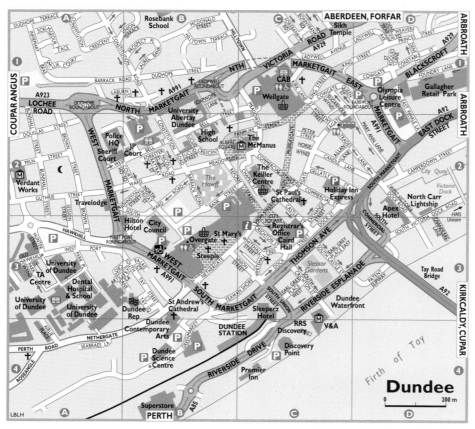

Dundee

Dundee is found on atlas page **142 G11**

Albert Square	B2	Laurel Bank	B1
Bank Street	B2	Lochee Road	A1
Barrack Road	A1	McDonald Street	D2
Barrack Road	B2	Meadowside	B2
Bell Street	B2	Miln Street	A2
Blackscroft	D1	Murraygate	C2
Blinshall Street	A1	Nethergate	A4
Blinshall Street	A2	North Lindsay Street	B2
Bonnybank Road	C1	North Marketgait	B1
Brown Street	A2	North Victoria Road	C1
Candle Lane	C2	Old Hawkhill	A3
Castle Street	C2	Panmure Street	B2
Chapel Street	A2	Perth Road	A4
City Square	C3	Princes Street	D1
Commercial Street	C2	Prospect Place	B1
Constable Street	D1	Queen Street	C1
Constitution Crescent	A1	Reform Street	B2
Constitution Road	A1	Riverside Drive	B4
Constitution Road	B2	Riverside Esplanade	C3
Court House Square	A2	Roseangle	A4
Cowgate	C1	St Andrews Street	C1
Cowgate	D1	Scrimgeour Place	A1
Crichton Street	C3	Seabraes Lane	A4
Dock Street	C3	Seagate	C2
Douglas Street	A2	Session Street	A2
Dudhope Street	B1	South Castle Street	C3
East Dock Street	D2	South Commercial Street	D3
East Marketgait	C1	South Crichton Street	C3
East Whale Lane	D1	South Marketgait	B3
Euclid Crescent	B2	South Tay Street	B3
Euclid Street	B2	South Union Street	C3
Exchange Street	C3	South Victoria Dock Road	D3
Forebank Road	C1	South Ward Road	B2
Foundry Lane	D1	Sugarhouse Wynd	C1
Gellatly Street	C2	Tay Road Bridge	D3
Greenmarket	B4	Tay Square	B3
Guthrie Street	A2	Thomson Avenue	C3
Hawkhill	A3	Trades Lane	C2
High Street	C3	Union Street	B3
Hilltown	B1	Union Terrace	B1
Hilltown Terrace	B1	Ward Road	B2
Hunter Street	A3	Weavers Yard	D1
Infirmary Brae	A1	West Marketgait	A2
Johnston Street	B2	West Port	A3
King Street	C1	West Victoria Dock Road	D2
Kirk Lane	C1	Whitehall Crescent	C3
Laburn Street	A1	Whitehall Street	C3
Ladywell Avenue	C1	Yeaman Shore	B3

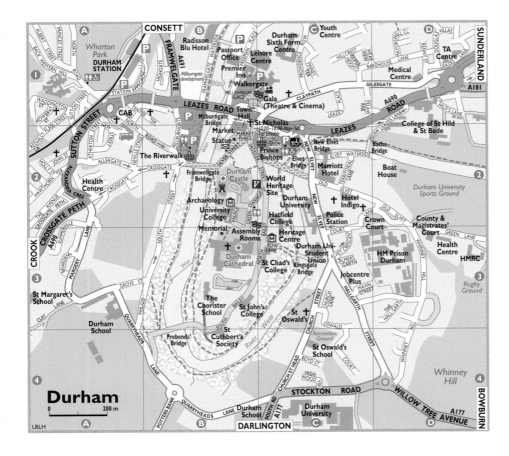

Durham

Durham is found on atlas page **103 Q2**

Albert Street	A1	Millburngate	B2
Alexandria Crescent	A2	Millennium Place	B1
Allergate	A2	Mowbray Street	A1
Atherton Street	A2	Neville Street	A2
Back Western Hill	A1	New Elvet	C2
Bakehouse Lane	C1	New Elvet Bridge	C2
Baths Bridge	C2	New Street	A2
Bow Lane	C3	North Bailey	C3
Boyd Street	C4	North Road	A1
Briardene	A3	Old Elvet	C2
Church Lane	C1	Oswald Court	C3
Church Street	C4	Owengate	B2
Church Street Head	C4	Palace Green	B2
Clay Lane	A3	Palmers Garth	C3
Claypath	C1	Pelaw Leazes Lane	D2
Court Lane	C3	Pelaw Rise	C1
Crossgate	A2	Pimlico	A3
Crossgate Peth	A3	Potters Bank	B4
Douglas Villas	D1	Prebends' Bridge	B4
Elvet Bridge	C2	Princes' Street	A1
Elvet Crescent	C3	Providence Row	C1
Elvet Waterside	C2	Quarryheads Lane	A3
Finney Terrace	C1	Redhills Lane	A2
Flass Street	A2	Renny Street	D1
Framwelgate	B1	Saddler Street	B2
Framwelgate Bridge	B2	St Hild's Lane	D1
Framwelgate Waterside	B1	Silver Street	B2
Freeman Place	B1	South Bailey	B3
Gilesgate	C1	South Road	C4
Green Lane	D3	South Street	B3
Grove Street	A3	Station Approach	A1
Hallgarth Street	C3	Stockton Road	C4
Hawthorn Terrace	A2	Summerville	A3
Highgate	B1	Sutton Street	A2
High Road View	C4	Tenter Terrace	A1
High Street	C2	Territorial Lane	C2
Hillcrest	C1	The Avenue	A2
Holly Street	A2	The Hall Garth	D3
John Street	A2	Waddington Street	A1
Keiper Heights	C1	Wear View	C1
Kingsgate Bridge	C3	Whinney Hill	D3
Leazes Place	C1	Willow Tree Avenue	D4
Leazes Road	B1		
Margery Lane	A3		
Market Square	B2		
Mavin Street	C3		
Mayorswell Close	D1		
Milburngate Bridge	B1		

Eastbourne

Eastbourne is found on atlas page **25 P11**

Arlington Road	A2	Langney Road	D1
Ashford Road	B2	Langney Road	C2
Ashford Road	C1	Lascelles Terrace	B4
Ashford Square	B1	Latimer Road	D1
Avenue Lane	A1	Leaf Road	B1
Belmore Road	C1	Lismore Road	B2
Blackwater Road	A4	Longstone Road	C1
Bolton Road	B3	Lushington Road	B3
Bourne Street	C1	Marine Parade	D2
Burlington Place	B3	Marine Road	D1
Burlington Road	C3	Mark Lane	B2
Camden Road	A3	Meads Road	A3
Carew Road	B1	Melbourne Road	C1
Carlisle Road	A4	Old Orchard Road	A2
Carlisle Road	B4	Old Wish Road	A4
Cavendish Avenue	C1	Pevensey Road	C2
Cavendish Place	C2	Promenade	C3
Ceylon Place	C2	Queen's Gardens	D2
Chiswick Place	B3	Saffrons Road	A2
College Road	B3	St Anne's Road	A1
Colonnade Gardens	D2	St Aubyn's Road	D1
Commercial Road	B1	St Leonard's Road	B1
Compton Street	B4	Seaside	D1
Compton Street	C3	Seaside Road	C2
Cornfield Lane	B3	Southfields Road	A2
Cornfield Road	B2	South Street	A3
Cornfield Terrace	B3	South Street	B3
Devonshire Place	B3	Spencer Road	B3
Dursley Road	C1	Station Parade	A2
Elms Road	C3	Station Street	B2
Enys Road	A1	Susan's Road	C2
Eversfield Road	A1	Sutton Road	B2
Furness Road	A3	Sydney Road	C1
Gildredge Road	B2	Terminus Road	A2
Grand Parade	C3	Terminus Road	C3
Grange Road	A3	The Avenue	A1
Grassington Road	A3	Tideswell Road	C2
Grove Road	A3	Trinity Place	C3
Hardwick Road	B3	Trinity Trees	B3
Hartfield Lane	A1	Upper Avenue	A1
Hartfield Road	A1	Upperton Gardens	A1
Hartington Place	C3	Upperton Road	A1
Howard Square	C4	West Street	A3
Hyde Gardens	B2	West Terrace	A2
Hyde Road	A2	Willowfield Road	D1
Ivy Terrace	A2	Wilmington Square	B4
Jevington Gardens	A4	Wish Road	B3
Junction Road	B2	York Road	A3

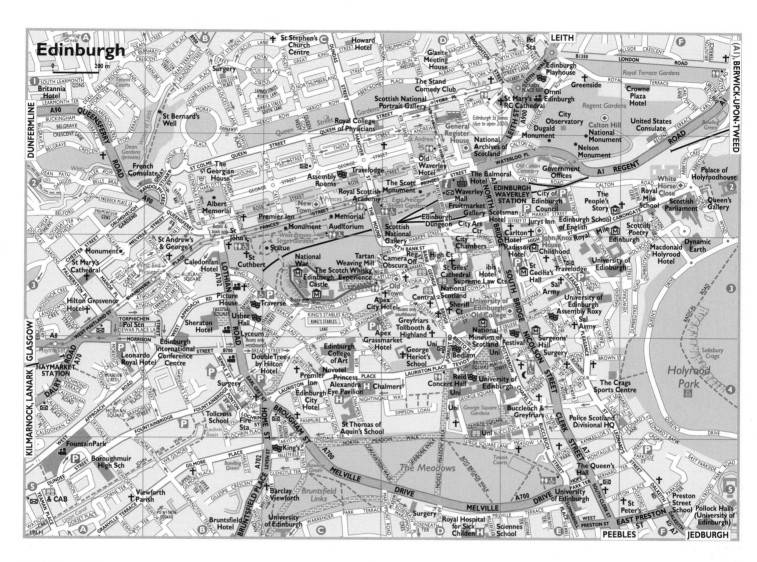

Edinburgh

Edinburgh is found on atlas page **127 P3**

Abbeyhill	F2	
Abercromby Place	C1	
Adam Street	E3	
Albany Street	D1	
Ann Street	A1	
Argyle Place	D5	
Atholl Crescent Lane	A3	
Bank Street	D3	
Barclay Terrace	C5	
Belford Road	A2	
Belgrave Crescent	A2	
Bernard Terrace	E5	
Boys Brigade Walk	D5	
Brandfield Street	A4	
Bread Street	B4	
Bristo Place	D4	
Brougham Street	C4	
Broughton Street	D1	
Broughton Street Lane	E1	
Brunton Terrace	F1	
Bruntsfield Place	B5	
Buccleuch Place	D4	
Buccleuch Street	E4	
Caledonian Place	A4	
Caledonian Road	A4	
Caledonian Street	A4	
Calton Road	E2	
Candlemaker Row	D3	
Canning Street	B3	
Canongate	E2	
Carlton Terrace	F1	
Castle Hill	C3	
Castle Street	C2	
Castle Terrace	B3	
Chalmers Street	C4	
Chambers Street	D3	
Chapel Street	E4	
Charlotte Square	B2	
Chester Street Gardens	A3	
Circus Lane	B1	
Circus Place	B1	
Clarendon Crescent	A1	
Clerk Street	E4	
Cockburn Street	D2	
Coronation Walk	C5	
Cowan's Close	E4	
Cowgate	D3	
Dalkeith Road	F5	
Dalry Road	A4	
Danube Street	B1	
Davie Street	E4	
Dean Park Crescent	A1	
Dean Street	A1	
Dewar Place Lane	A3	
Douglas Gardens	A3	
Doune Terrace	B1	
Drummond Street	E3	
Dublin Street	D1	
Dumbiedykes Road	F3	
Dunbar Street	B4	
Dundas Street	C1	
Dundee Street	A5	
Earl Grey Street	B4	
Easter Road	F1	
East Market Street	E2	
East Parkside	F5	
East Preston Street	F5	
Elder Street	D1	
Forrest Road	D4	
Forth Street	D1	
Fountainbridge	A4	
Frederick Street	C2	
Gardener's Crescent	B4	
George IV Bridge	D3	
George Square	D4	
George Square Lane	D5	
George Street	B2	
George Street	C2	
Gifford Park	E5	
Gillespie Crescent	B5	
Gilmore Park	A5	
Gilmore Place	B5	
Gilmour Street	E4	
Glenfinlas Street	B2	
Gloucester Lane	B1	
Granville Terrace	A5	
Great King Street	C1	
Great Stuart Street	B2	
Greenmarket	C3	
Greenside Row	E1	
Grindlay Street	B3	
Grosvenor Street	A3	
Grove Street	A4	
Haddon's Court	E4	
Hanover Street	C2	
Haymarket Terrace	A4	
Heriot Row	C1	
Hermits Croft	F5	
High Street	D3	
High Street	E3	
Hillside Crescent	E1	
Hill Street	C2	
Holyrood Park Road	F5	
Holyrood Road	E3	
Home Street	C4	
Hope Street	B2	
Horse Wynd	F2	
Howden Street	E4	
Howe Street	C1	
India Place	B1	
India Street	B1	
Jamaica Street South Lane	B1	
Jawbone Walk	D5	
Jeffrey Street	E2	
Johnston Terrace	C3	
Keir Street	C4	
Kerr Street	B1	
King's Stables Road	B3	
Lady Lawson Street	C3	
Lansdowne Crescent	A3	
Lauriston Gardens	C4	
Lauriston Place	C4	
Lauriston Street	C4	
Lawnmarket	D3	
Leamington Terrace	B5	
Leith Street	E1	
Leith Walk	E1	
Lennox Street	A1	
Leven Place	C5	
Lochrin Place	B4	
Lochrin Street	B4	
London Street	D1	
Lothian Road	B3	
Lower Gilmore Place	B5	
Lutton Place	E5	
Lynedoch Place Lane	A2	
Manor Place	A3	
Marchmont Crescent	D5	
Marchmont Road	D5	
Market Street	D2	
Meadow Lane	E5	
Melville Drive	C5	
Melville Street	A3	
Melville Terrace	D5	
Middle Meadow Walk	D5	
Millerfield Place	D5	
Miller Row	A2	
Moncrieff Terrace	E5	
Montague Street	E5	
Moray Place	B1	
Morrison Link	A4	
Morrison Street	A4	
Mound Place	D3	
Nelson Street	C1	
New Street	E2	
Nicolson Square	E4	
Nicolson Street	E4	
Nightingale Way	C4	
North Bridge	D2	
North Castle Street	C2	
North Meadow Walk	C5	
North St Andrew Street	D1	
North St David Street	D1	
Northumberland Street	C1	
Oxford Street	F5	
Palmerston Place	A3	
Panmure Place	C4	
Pleasance	E3	
Ponton Street	B4	
Potterrow	E4	
Princes Street	C2	
Queens Drive	F3	
Queensferry Road	A1	
Queensferry Street	B2	
Queen Street	B2	
Radical Road	F3	
Ramsay Lane	C3	
Randolph Crescent	B2	
Randolph Lane	B2	
Rankeillor Street	E5	
Regent Road	E2	
Richmond Place	E3	
Rose Street	B2	
Roseneath Place	D5	
Rothesay Place	A3	
Royal Circus	B1	
Royal Terrace	E1	
St Andrew Square	D1	
St Bernard's Crescent	A1	
St Colme Street	B2	
St James Place	D1	
St Leonard's Bank	F4	
St Leonard's Hill	E4	
St Leonard's Lane	F4	
St Leonard's Street	E4	
St Patrick Street	E4	
St Stephen Street	B1	
St Vincent Street	C1	
Saunders Street	B1	
Sciennes	E5	
Semple Street	B4	
Shandwick Place	A3	
Simpson Loan	D4	
South Bridge	E3	
South Charlotte Street	B2	
South Clerk Street	E5	
South Learmonth Gardens	A1	
South St Andrew Street	D2	
South St David Street	D2	
Spittal Street	C4	
Stafford Street	B3	
Tarvit Street	C5	
The Mound	C2	
Thistle Street	C2	
Torphichen Street	A3	
Union Street	E1	
Upper Gilmore Place	B5	
Victoria Street	D3	
Viewcraig Gardens	E4	
Viewcraig Street	F3	
Viewforth	A5	
Walker Street	A3	
Warrender Park Terrace	C5	
Waterloo Place	D2	
Waverley Bridge	D2	
West Approach Road	A5	
West Maitland Street	A3	
West Nicolson Street	E4	
West Port	C4	
West Richmond Street	E4	
West Toll Cross	B4	
William Street	A3	
Yeaman Place	A5	
York Lane	D1	
York Place	D1	
Young Street	B2	

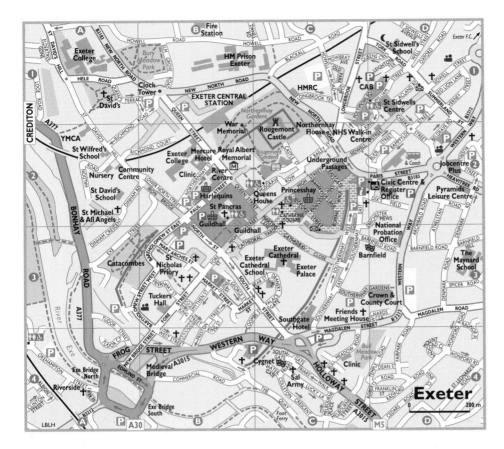

Exeter

Exeter is found on atlas page **9 M6**

Acland Road	D1	King Street	B3
Archibald Road	D3	King William Street	D1
Athelstan Road	D3	Longbrook Street	C1
Bailey Street	C2	Lower North Street	B2
Bampfylde Lane	C2	Magdalen Road	D3
Bampfylde Street	D2	Magdalen Street	C4
Barnfield Road	D3	Market Street	B3
Bartholomew Street East	B3	Martins Lane	C2
Bartholomew Street West	B3	Mary Arches Street	B3
Bear Street	C3	Musgrave Row	C2
Bedford Street	C2	New Bridge Street	A4
Belgrave Road	D2	New North Road	A1
Blackall Road	C1	Northernhay Street	B2
Bonhay Road	A2	North Street	B3
Bude Street	D2	Old Park Road	C1
Bull Meadow Road	C4	Oxford Road	D1
Castle Street	C2	Palace Gate	C3
Cathedral Close	C3	Paris Street	D2
Cathedral Yard	B3	Paul Street	B2
Cedars Road	D4	Preston Street	B4
Cheeke Street	D1	Princesshay	C2
Chichester Mews	C3	Queens Crescent	C1
Commercial Road	B4	Queen's Terrace	A1
Coombe Street	B3	Queen Street	B1
Deanery Place	C3	Radford Road	D4
Dean Street	D4	Richmond Court	B2
Denmark Road	D3	Richmond Road	A2
Dinham Crescent	A3	Roberts Road	C4
Dinham Road	A2	Roman Walk	C2
Dix's Field	D2	St David's Hill	A1
Eastgate	C2	Sidwell Street	C1
Edmund Street	A4	Sidwell Street	D1
Elm Grove Road	B1	Smythen Street	B3
Exe Street	A3	Southernhay East	C3
Fairpark Road	D4	Southernhay Gardens	C3
Fore Street	B3	Southernhay West	C3
Franklin Street	D4	South Street	B3
Friernhay Street	B3	Spicer Road	D3
Frog Street	A4	Summerland Street	D1
George Street	B3	Temple Road	D4
Guinea Street	B3	Tudor Court	A4
Haldon Road	A2	Tudor Street	A3
Heavitree Road	D2	Verney Street	D1
Hele Road	A1	Well Street	D1
High Street	C2	Western Way	B4
Holloway Street	C4	West Street	B4
Howell Road	B1	Wonford Road	D4
Iron Bridge	B2	York Road	D1

Gloucester

Gloucester is found on atlas page **46 F11**

Albert Street	D4	Millbrook Street	D4
Albion Street	B4	Montpellier	B4
All Saints' Road	D4	Napier Street	D4
Alvin Street	C2	Nettleton Road	C3
Archdeacon Street	B2	New Inn Lane	C3
Arthur Street	C4	Norfolk Street	B4
Barbican Road	B3	Northgate Street	C3
Barrack Square	B3	Old Tram Road	B4
Barton Street	D4	Over Causeway	A1
Bedford Street	C3	Oxford Road	D1
Belgrave Road	C4	Oxford Street	D2
Berkeley Street	B3	Park Road	C4
Black Dog Way	C2	Park Street	C2
Blenheim Road	D4	Parliament Street	B3
Brunswick Road	B4	Pembroke Street	C4
Brunswick Square	B4	Pitt Street	B2
Bruton Way	D3	Priory Road	B1
Bull Lane	B3	Quay Street	B2
Castle Meads Way	A2	Royal Oak Road	A2
Clarence Street	C3	Russell Street	C3
Clare Street	B2	St Aldate Street	C2
College Court	B2	St Catherine Street	C1
Commercial Road	B3	St John's Lane	B3
Cromwell Street	C4	St Mark Street	C1
Cross Keys Lane	B3	St Mary's Square	B2
Deans Walk	C1	St Mary's Street	B2
Eastgate Street	C3	St Michael's Square	C4
Gouda Way	B1	St Oswald's Road	B1
Great Western Road	D2	Sebert Street	C1
Greyfriars	B3	Severn Road	A3
Hampden Way	C3	Sherborne Street	D2
Hare Lane	C2	Sinope Street	D4
Heathville Road	D2	Southgate Street	B4
Henry Road	D1	Spa Road	B4
Henry Street	D2	Station Road	C3
High Orchard Street	A4	Swan Road	C1
Honyatt Road	D1	Sweetbriar Street	C1
Kings Barton Street	C4	The Cross	B3
Kingsholm Road	C1	The Oxebode	C3
King's Square	C3	The Quay	A2
Ladybellegate Street	B3	Union Street	C1
Llanthony Road	A4	Upper Quay Street	B2
London Road	D2	Vauxhall Road	D4
Longsmith Street	B3	Wellington Street	C4
Market Parade	C3	Westgate Street	A2
Merchants' Road	A4	Widden Street	D4
Mercia Road	B1	Worcester Parade	C2
Metz Way	D3	Worcester Street	C2

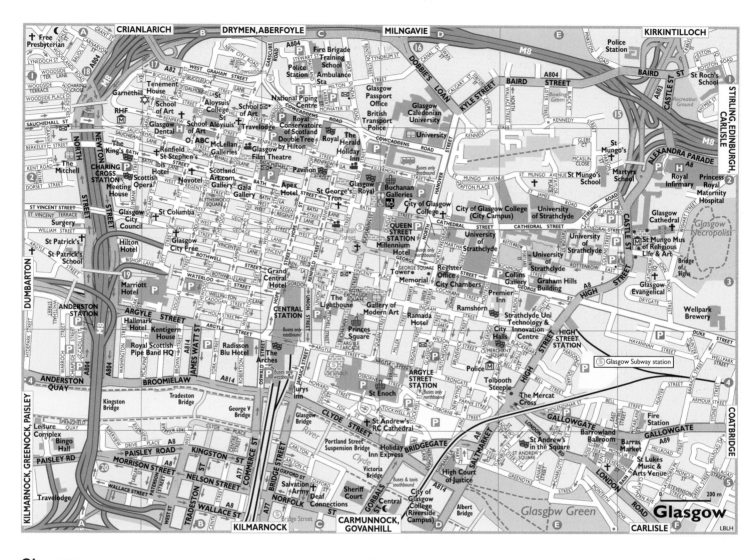

Glasgow

Glasgow is found on atlas page **125 P4**

Street	Ref	Street	Ref	Street	Ref	Street	Ref
Albert Bridge	D5	Candleriggs	D4	Gallowgate	E4	Lanark Street	E5
Albion Street	D4	Carlton Place	C5	Garnethill Street	B1	Larbert Street	C1
Albion Street	E3	Carnarvon Street	A1	Garnet Street	B2	Lister Street	E1
Alexandra Parade	F2	Castle Street	F1	Garscube Road	C1	London Road	E4
Anderston Quay	A4	Castle Street	F2	Garth Street	D3	Maitland Street	C1
Argyle Arcade	C4	Cathedral Square	F3	George Square	D3	Martha Street	D3
Argyle Street	A3	Cathedral Street	D2	George Street	E3	Mart Street	D5
Armour Street	F4	Centre Street	B5	George V Bridge	B4	Maxwell Street	C4
Ashley Street	A1	Chalmer Street	F5	Glasgow Bridge	C5	McAlpine Street	B4
Bain Street	F5	Charing Cross	A1	Glassford Street	D4	McAslin Close	E2
Baird Street	E1	Charles Street	F1	Glebe Court	E2	McFarlane Street	F4
Baliol Street	A1	Charlotte Street	E5	Gorbals Street	C5	McPhater Street	C1
Barrack Street	F4	Cheapside Street	A4	Gordon Street	C3	Merchant Lane	D5
Bath Lane	B2	Claythorn Avenue	F5	Grafton Place	D2	Miller Street	D4
Bath Street	A2	Claythorn Park	F5	Granville Street	A2	Millroad Drive	F5
Bell Street	E4	Clyde Place	B4	Greendyke Street	E5	Millroad Street	F5
Berkeley Street	A2	Clyde Street	C4	Green Street	F5	Milton Street	C1
Blackfriars Street	E4	Cochrane Street	D3	Hanover Street	D3	Mitchell Street	C4
Black Street	E1	Collins Street	E3	High Street	E4	Moir Street	E5
Blythswood Square	B2	Commerce Street	B5	Hill Street	B1	Molendinar Street	E4
Blythswood Street	B3	Couper Street	D1	Holland Street	B2	Moncur Street	E5
Bothwell Lane	B3	Cowcaddens Road	C1	Holm Street	B3	Monteith Row	E5
Bothwell Street	B3	Dalhousie Lane	B1	Hope Street	C3	Montrose Street	D3
Bridgegate	D5	Dixon Street	C4	Howard Street	C4	Morrison Street	A5
Bridge of Sighs	F3	Dobbie's Loan	D1	Hunter Street	F4	Nelson Street	B5
Bridge Street	C5	Dorset Street	A2	Hutcheson Street	D4	New City Road	B1
Broomielaw	B4	Douglas Street	B3	Hydepark Street	A4	Newton Street	A2
Brown Street	B4	Drury Street	C3	Ingram Street	D3	New Wynd	D4
Brunswick Street	D4	Drygate	F3	Jamaica Street	C4	Norfolk Street	C5
Buccleuch Lane	B1	Duke Street	F4	James Watt Street	B4	North Frederick Street	D3
Buccleuch Street	B1	Dundas Street	D3	John Knox Street	F3	North Hanover Street	D3
Buchanan Street	C4	Dunlop Street	D4	John Street	D3	North Portland Street	E3
Cadogan Street	B3	Dyer's Lane	E5	Kennedy Street	D2	North Street	A2
Calgary Street	D1	East Campbell Street	E4	Kennedy Street	E1	North Wallace Street	E1
Cambridge Street	C1	Elmbank Street	A2	Kent Road	A2	Osborne Street	C4
Canal Street	D1	Fox Street	C4	Kent Street	E5	Oswald Street	C4
				Killermont Street	C2	Oxford Street	C5
				Kingston Bridge	A5	Paisley Road	A5
				Kingston Street	B5	Parnie Street	D4
				King Street	D4	Parsonage Square	E4
				Kyle Street	D1	Parson Street	E2

Street	Ref	Street	Ref
Paterson Street	B5	Steel Street	D5
Pinkston Road	E1	Stevenson Street	F5
Pitt Street	B2	Stewart Street	C1
Port Dundas Road	C1	Stirling Road	E2
Portland Street Suspension Bridge	C5	Stockwell Place	D4
Queen Street	C3	Stockwell Street	D4
Renfield Lane	C3	Suffolk Street	E5
Renfield Street	C3	Sydney Street	F4
Renfrew Lane	C2	Taylor Place	E2
Renfrew Street	B1	Taylor Street	E2
Renton Street	C1	Tradeston Bridge	B4
Rhymer Street	F1	Tradeston Street	B5
Richmond Street	E3	Trongate	D4
Riverview Drive	A4	Turnbull Street	D5
Robertson Street	B4	Tyndrum Street	C1
Rose Street	B2	Union Street	C3
Ross Street	E5	Virginia Street	D4
Rottenrow	E3	Wallace Street	A5
Rottenrow East	E3	Walls Street	E4
Royal Exchange Square	C3	Warroch Street	A4
Royston Road	F1	Washington Street	A4
Royston Square	F1	Waterloo Street	B3
St Andrew's Square	E5	Wellington Lane	B3
St Andrew's Street	E4	Wellington Street	B3
St James Road	E2	Wellpark Street	F4
St Mungo Avenue	D2	West Campbell Street	B3
St Vincent Lane	B3	West George Lane	B2
St Vincent Place	C3	West George Street	B2
St Vincent Street	A2	West Graham Street	B1
St Vincent Terrace	A2	West Nile Street	C3
Saltmarket	D5	West Regent Lane	C2
Sauchiehall Lane	A2	West Regent Street	B2
Sauchiehall Street	A1	West Street	B5
Scott Street	B1	William Street	A3
Shipbank Lane	D5	Wilson Street	D4
Shuttle Street	E3	Wishart Street	F3
South Frederick Street	D3	Woodlands Road	A1
Springfield Quay	A4	Woodside Crescent	A1
Stafford Street	D1	Woodside Terrace	A1
		Woodside Terrace Lane	A1
		York Street	B4

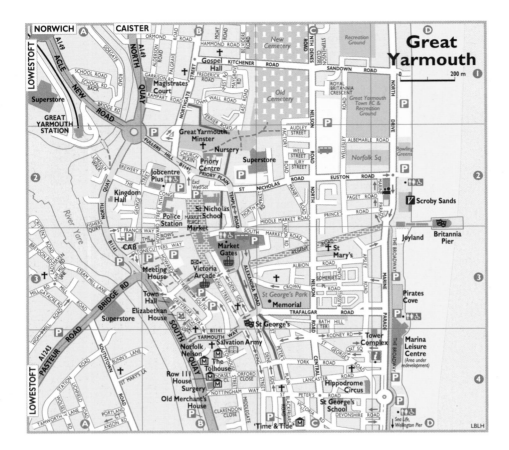

Great Yarmouth

Great Yarmouth is found on atlas page **77 Q10**

Acle New Road	A1	North Drive	D1
Albemarle Road	C2	North Market Road	C2
Albion Road	C3	North Quay	A2
Alderson Road	B1	Northgate Street	B1
Alexandra Road	B3	Nottingham Way	B4
Apsley Road	C3	Ormond Road	B1
Belvidere Road	B1	Paget Road	C2
Blackfriars Road	C4	Palgrave Road	B1
Brewery Street	A2	Pasteur Road	A4
Breydon Road	A3	Prince's Road	C2
Bridge Road	A1	Priory Plain	B2
Bridge Road	A3	Queen Street	B4
Bunn's Lane	A4	Rampart Road	B1
Church Plain	B2	Regent Road	C3
Critten's Road	A3	Rodney Road	C4
Crown Road	C3	Russell Road	C3
Dene Side	B3	St Francis Way	A3
Devonshire Road	C4	St George's Road	C4
East Road	B1	St Nicholas Road	B2
Euston Road	C2	St Peter's Plain	C4
Factory Road	C2	St Peter's Road	C4
Ferrier Road	B1	Sandown Road	C1
Fishers Quay	A2	Saw Mill Lane	A3
Frederick Road	B1	School Road	A1
Fullers Hill	B2	School Road Back	A1
Garrison Road	B1	Sidegate Road	A1
Gatacre Road	A3	South Market Road	C3
George Street	A2	South Quay	B3
Greyfriars Way	B3	Southtown Road	A4
Hammond Road	B1	Station Road	A4
High Mill Road	A3	Steam Mill Lane	A3
Howard Street North	B2	Stephenson Close	C1
Howard Street South	B3	Stonecutters Way	B3
King Street	B3	Tamworth Lane	A4
Kitchener Road	B1	Temple Road	B2
Ladyhaven Road	A3	The Broadway	D3
Lancaster Road	C4	The Conge	A2
Lichfield Road	A4	The Rows	B3
Limekiln Walk	A2	Tolhouse Street	B4
Manby Road	C2	Town Wall Road	B1
Marine Parade	D3	Trafalgar Road	C3
Maygrove Road	B1	Union Road	C3
Middle Market Road	C2	Victoria Road	C4
Middlegate	B4	Wellesley Road	C2
Moat Road	B1	West Road	B1
Nelson Road Central	C3	Wolseley Road	A4
Nelson Road North	C1	Yarmouth Way	B4
North Denes Road	C1	York Road	C4

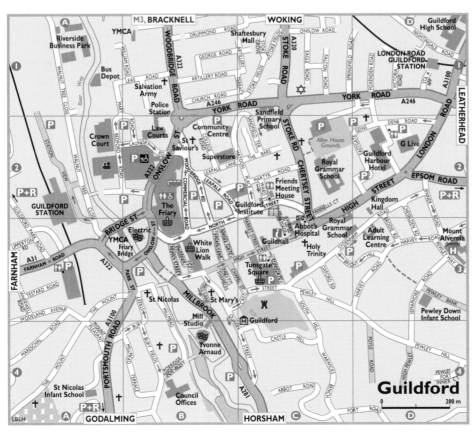

Guildford

Guildford is found on atlas page **23 Q5**

Abbot Road	C4	Millmead	B3
Angel Gate	B3	Millmead Terrace	B4
Artillery Road	B1	Mount Pleasant	A4
Artillery Terrace	C1	Nightingale Road	D1
Bedford Road	A2	North Street	B3
Bridge Street	A3	Onslow Road	C1
Bright Hill	C3	Onslow Street	B2
Brodie Road	D3	Oxford Road	C3
Bury Fields	B4	Pannells Court	C2
Bury Street	B4	Park Street	B3
Castle Hill	C4	Pewley Bank	D3
Castle Street	C3	Pewley Fort Inner Court	D4
Chapel Street	B3	Pewley Hill	C3
Chertsey Street	C2	Pewley Way	D3
Cheselden Road	D2	Phoenix Court	B3
Church Road	B1	Porridge Pot Alley	B4
College Road	B2	Portsmouth Road	A4
Commercial Road	B2	Poyle Road	D4
Dene Road	D2	Quarry Street	B3
Drummond Road	B1	Sandfield Terrace	C2
Eagle Road	C1	Semaphore Road	D3
Eastgate Gardens	D2	South Hill	C3
Epsom Road	D2	Springfield Road	C1
Falcon Road	C1	Station Approach	D1
Farnham Road	A3	Station View	A2
Fort Road	C4	Stoke Fields	C1
Foxenden Road	D1	Stoke Grove	C1
Friary Bridge	A3	Stoke Road	C1
Friary Street	B3	Swan Lane	B3
George Road	B1	Sydenham Road	C3
Guildford Park Road	A2	Testard Road	A3
Harvey Road	D3	The Bars	C2
Haydon Place	C2	The Mount	A4
High Pewley	D4	The Shambles	B3
High Street	C3	Tunsgate	C3
Jeffries Passage	C2	Upperton Road	A3
Jenner Road	D2	Victoria Road	D1
Laundry Road	B2	Walnut Tree Close	A1
Leapale Lane	B2	Ward Street	C2
Leapale Road	B2	Warwicks Bench	C4
Leas Road	B1	Wherwell Road	A3
London Road	D2	William Road	B1
Mareschal Road	A4	Wodeland Avenue	A3
Market Street	C3	Woodbridge Road	B1
Martyr Road	C2	York Road	B1
Mary Road	A1		
Millbrook	B3		
Mill Lane	B3		

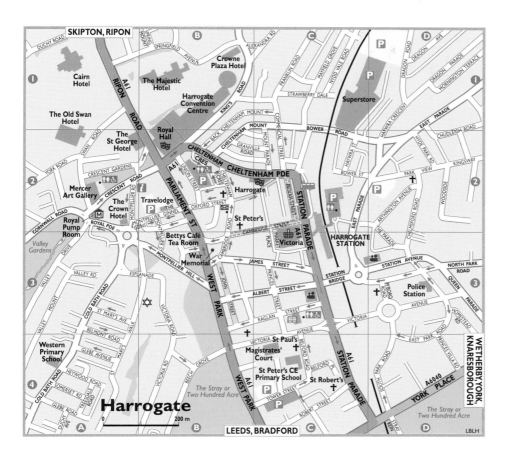

Harrogate

Harrogate is found on atlas page **97 M9**

Albert Street	C3	Montpellier Hill	B3
Alexandra Road	B1	Montpellier Road	A2
Arthington Avenue	D2	Montpellier Street	B2
Back Cheltenham Mount	B2	Mornington Terrace	D1
Beech Grove	B4	Mount Parade	C2
Belford Place	C4	North Park Road	D3
Belford Road	C4	Nydd Vale Road	C1
Belmont Road	A3	Oxford Street	B2
Beulah Street	C2	Park View	D2
Bower Road	C1	Parliament Street	B2
Bower Street	C1	Princes Street	C3
Cambridge Road	B3	Princes Villa Road	D4
Cambridge Street	C2	Queen Parade	D3
Chelmsford Road	D3	Raglan Street	C3
Cheltenham Crescent	B2	Ripon Road	A1
Cheltenham Mount	B2	Robert Street	C4
Cheltenham Parade	B2	Royal Parade	A2
Chudleigh Road	D2	St Mary's Avenue	A3
Cold Bath Road	A3	St Mary's Walk	A4
Commercial Street	C1	Somerset Road	A4
Cornwall Road	A2	South Park Road	D4
Crescent Gardens	A2	Springfield Avenue	B1
Crescent Road	A2	Spring Mount	B1
Dragon Avenue	D1	Station Avenue	D3
Dragon Parade	D1	Station Bridge	C3
Dragon Road	D1	Station Parade	C2
Duchy Avenue	A4	Strawberry Dale	C1
Duchy Road	A1	Stray Rein	D4
East Parade	C2	Swan Road	A2
East Park Road	D4	The Ginnel	B2
Esplanade	A3	The Parade	D2
Franklin Road	C1	Tower Street	C4
Glebe Avenue	A4	Treesdale Road	A4
Glebe Road	A4	Union Street	B2
Granville Road	B2	Valley Drive	A3
Haywra Street	C2	Valley Mount	A3
Heywood Road	A4	Valley Road	A3
Homestead Road	D3	Victoria Avenue	B4
Hyde Park Road	D2	Victoria Road	B3
Hywra Crescent	D2	West Park	B3
James Street	B3	West Park Street	B4
John Street	B3	Woodside	D2
King's Road	B1	York Place	D4
Kingsway	D2	York Road	A2
Market Place	C3		
Marlborough Road	D3		
Mayfield Grove	C1		
Montpellier Gardens	B2		

Huddersfield

Huddersfield is found on atlas page **90 E7**

Albion Street	B4	New North Road	A2
Alfred Street	C4	New Street	B4
Back Union Street	C1	Northgate	C1
Bankfield Road	A4	Northumberland Street	C2
Bath Street	B1	Old Leeds Road	D2
Belmont Street	A1	Old South Street	B3
Brook Street	C2	Outcote Bank	B4
Byram Street	C2	Oxford Street	C1
Cambridge Road	B1	Page Street	C4
Carforth Street	D4	Park Avenue	A2
Castlegate	B2	Park Drive South	A2
Chancery Lane	B3	Peel Street	C4
Chapel Hill	B4	Portland Street	A2
Chapel Street	B4	Princess Street	B4
Church Street	C2	Prospect Street	A4
Clare Hill	B1	Quay Street	D2
Claremont Street	B1	Queen Street	C3
Cloth Hall Street	B3	Queen Street South	C4
Cross Church Street	C3	Queensgate	C4
Dundas Street	B3	Railway Street	B2
Elizabeth Queen Gardens	A2	Ramsden Street	B3
Elmwood Avenue	A1	Rook Street	B1
Firth Street	D4	St Andrew's Road	D2
Fitzwilliam Street	A2	St George's Square	B2
Fitzwilliam Street	B2	St John's Road	B1
Gasworks Street	D1	St Peter's Street	C2
Great Northern Street	C1	Southgate	C2
Greenhead Road	A3	Spring Grove Street	A4
Half Moon Street	B3	Spring Street	A3
High Street	B3	Springwood Avenue	A3
Highfields Road	A1	Stadium Way	D1
John William Street	B2	Station Street	B2
King Street	C3	Trinity Street	A2
King's Mill Lane	D4	Turnbridge Road	D2
Kirkgate	C3	Union Street	C1
Leeds Road	C2	Upper George Street	A3
Lincoln Street	D3	Upperhead Row	B3
Lord Street	C2	Viaduct Street	B2
Lower Fitzwilliam Street	C1	Victoria Lane	C3
Lynton Avenue	A3	Wakefield Road	D3
Manchester Road	A4	Water Street	A3
Market Place	C3	Watergate	D2
Market Street	B3	Waverley Road	A2
Merton Street	A3	Wentworth Street	A2
Milford Street	B4	Westgate	B3
Mountjoy Road	A1	William Street	C1
New North Parade	B2	Wood Street	C2
New North Road	A1	Zetland Street	C3

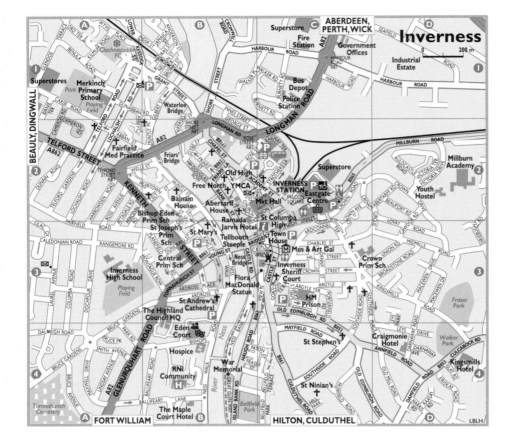

Inverness

Inverness is found on atlas page **156 B8**

Abertaff Road	D2	Glenurquhart Road	A4
Academy Street	B2	Gordon Terrace	C3
Anderson Street	B1	Grant Street	B1
Annfield Road	D4	Great Glen Way	B4
Ardconnel Terrace	C3	Harbour Road	C1
Ardross Street	B3	Harris Road	D4
Argyle Street	C3	Harrowden Road	A2
Argyle Terrace	C3	Haugh Road	B4
Balliefary Lane	A4	High Street	C3
Balliefary Road	B4	Hill Park	C4
Bank Street	B2	Hill Street	C3
Bellfield Terrace	C4	Huntly Street	B2
Benula Road	A1	Innes Street	B1
Birnie Terrace	A1	Kenneth Street	A2
Bishops Road	B4	King Street	B3
Bridge Street	B3	Kingsmills Road	D3
Broadstone Road	D3	Laurel Avenue	A3
Bruce Gardens	A4	Lindsay Avenue	A4
Bruce Park	A4	Lochalsh Road	A2
Burnett Road	C1	Longman Road	C2
Caledonian Road	A3	Lovat Road	D3
Cameron Road	A2	Lower Kessock Street	A1
Cameron Square	A2	Maxwell Drive	A4
Carse Road	A1	Mayfield Road	C4
Castle Road	B3	Midmills Road	D3
Castle Street	C3	Millburn Road	D2
Chapel Street	B2	Mitchell's Lane	C3
Charles Street	C3	Muirfield Road	C4
Columba Road	A3	Ness Bank	B4
Crown Circus	C2	Old Edinburgh Road	C3
Crown Drive	D2	Park Road	A4
Crown Road	C2	Planefield Road	B3
Crown Street	C3	Porterfield Road	C3
Culcabock Road	D4	Raasay Road	D4
Culduthel Road	C4	Rangemore Road	A3
Dalneigh Road	A4	Ross Avenue	A2
Damfield Road	D4	Seafield Road	D1
Darnaway Road	D4	Shore Street	B1
Denny Street	C3	Smith Avenue	A4
Dochfour Drive	A3	Southside Place	C3
Dunabban Road	A1	Southside Road	C4
Dunain Road	A2	Telford Gardens	A2
Duncraig Street	B3	Telford Road	A2
Eriskay Road	D4	Telford Street	A2
Fairfield Road	A3	Tomnahurich Street	B3
Falcon Square	C2	Union Road	D3
Friars' Lane	B2	Walker Road	C1
Glendoe Terrace	A1	Young Street	B3

Ipswich

Ipswich is found on atlas page **53 L3**

Alderman Road	A3	Key Street	C3
Anglesea Road	B1	King Street	B2
Argyle Street	D2	London Road	A2
Austin Street	C4	Lower Brook Street	C3
Barrack Lane	A1	Lower Orwell Street	C3
Belstead Road	B4	Museum Street	B2
Berners Street	B1	Neale Street	C1
Black Horse Lane	B2	Neptune Quay	D3
Blanche Street	D2	New Cardinal Street	B3
Bolton Lane	C1	Newson Street	A1
Bond Street	D3	Northgate Street	C2
Bramford Road	A1	Norwich Road	A1
Bridge Street	C4	Old Foundry Road	C2
Burlington Road	A2	Orchard Street	D2
Burrell Road	B4	Orford Street	A1
Cardigan Street	A1	Orwell Place	C3
Carr Street	C2	Orwell Quay	D4
Cecil Road	B1	Portman Road	A3
Cemetery Road	D1	Princes Street	A3
Chancery Road	A4	Quadling Street	B3
Charles Street	B1	Queen Street	B3
Christchurch Street	D1	Ranelagh Road	A4
Civic Drive	B2	Russell Road	A3
Clarkson Street	A1	St George's Street	B1
Cobbold Street	C2	St Helen's Street	D2
College Street	C3	St Margaret's Street	C2
Commercial Road	A4	St Matthews Street	B2
Constantine Road	A3	St Nicholas Street	B3
Crown Street	B2	St Peter's Street	B3
Cumberland Street	A1	Silent Street	B3
Dalton Road	A2	Sir Alf Ramsey Way	A3
Dock Street	C4	Soane Street	C2
Duke Street	D4	South Street	A1
Eagle Street	C3	Star Lane	C3
Elm Street	B2	Stoke Quay	C4
Falcon Street	B3	Suffolk Road	D1
Fonnereau Road	B1	Tacket Street	C3
Foundation Street	C3	Tavern Street	B3
Franciscan Way	B3	Tower Ramparts	B2
Geneva Road	A1	Tuddenham Avenue	D1
Grafton Way	B3	Turret Lane	C3
Great Gipping Street	A2	Upper Orwell Street	C3
Great Whip Street	C4	Vernon Street	C4
Grey Friars Road	B3	West End Road	A3
Grimwade Street	D3	Westgate Street	B2
Handford Road	A2	Willoughby Road	B4
Hervey Street	D1	Wolsey Street	B3
High Street	B1	Woodbridge Road	D2

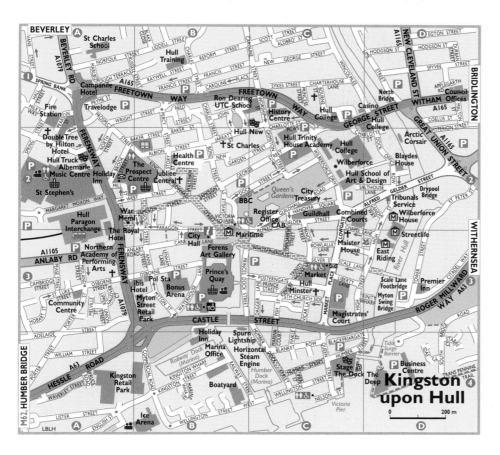

Kingston upon Hull

Kingston upon Hull is found on atlas page **93 J5**

Adelaide Street	A4	Market Place	C3
Albion Street	B2	Mill Street	A2
Alfred Gelder Street	C2	Myton Street	B3
Anlaby Road	A3	New Cleveland Street	D1
Baker Street	B2	New Garden Street	B2
Beverley Road	A1	New George Street	C1
Blackfriargate	C4	Norfolk Street	A1
Blanket Row	C4	Osborne Street	B3
Bond Street	B2	Osborne Street	A3
Brook Street	A2	Paragon Street	B2
Caroline Street	B1	Percy Street	B1
Carr Lane	B3	Porter Street	A3
Castle Street	B3	Portland Place	A2
Chapel Lane	C2	Portland Street	A2
Charles Street	B1	Posterngate	C3
Charterhouse Lane	C1	Princes Dock Street	B3
Citadel Way	D3	Prospect Street	A1
Commercial Road	B4	Queen Street	C4
Dagger Lane	C3	Railway Street	B4
Dock Office Row	D2	Raywell Street	B1
Dock Street	B2	Reform Street	B1
Durban Street	D1	Russell Street	A1
Egginton Street	B1	St Luke's Street	A3
Ferensway	A2	St Peter Street	D2
Freetown Way	A1	Saville Street	B2
Gandhi Way	D2	Scale Lane	C3
Garrison Road	D3	Scott Street	C1
George Street	B2	Silver Street	C3
George Street	D1	South Bridge Road	D4
Great Union Street	D1	South Church Side	C3
Grimston Street	C2	South Street	B2
Guildhall Road	C2	Spring Bank	A1
Hanover Square	C2	Spyvee Street	D1
Hessle Road	A4	Sykes Street	C1
High Street	C3	Tower Street	D3
Hodgson Street	D1	Upper Union Street	A3
Humber Dock Street	C4	Victoria Square	B2
Humber Street	C4	Waterhouse Lane	B3
Hyperion Street	D1	Wellington Street	C4
Jameson Street	B2	Wellington Street West	B4
Jarratt Street	B2	West Street	A2
King Edward Street	B2	Whitefriargate	C3
Kingston Street	B4	Wilberforce Drive	C2
Liddell Street	B1	William Street	A4
Lime Street	C1	Wincolmlee	C1
Lister Street	A4	Witham	D1
Lowgate	C3	Worship Street	C1
Margaret Moxon Way	A2	Wright Street	A1

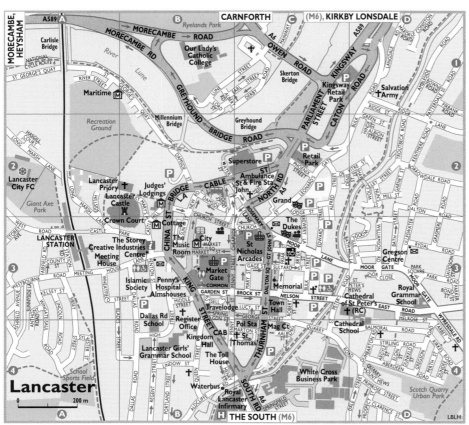

Lancaster

Lancaster is found on atlas page **95 K8**

Aberdeen Road	D4	Lincoln Road	A3
Aldcliffe Road	B4	Lindow Street	B4
Alfred Street	C2	Lodge Street	C2
Ambleside Road	D1	Long Marsh Lane	A2
Balmoral Road	D4	Lune Street	B1
Bath Street	D3	Market Street	B3
Blades Street	A3	Meeting House Lane	A3
Bond Street	D3	Middle Street	B3
Borrowdale Road	D2	Moor Gate	D3
Brewery Lane	C3	Moor Lane	C3
Bridge Lane	B2	Morecambe Road	B1
Brock Street	C3	Nelson Street	C3
Bulk Road	D2	North Road	C2
Bulk Street	C3	Owen Road	C1
Cable Street	B2	Park Road	D3
Castle Hill	B3	Parliament Street	C2
Castle Park	A3	Patterdale Road	D2
Caton Road	C2	Penny Street	B4
Cheapside	C3	Portland Street	B4
China Street	B3	Primrose Street	D4
Church Street	B2	Prospect Street	D4
Common Garden Street	B3	Quarry Road	C4
Dale Street	D4	Queen Street	B4
Dallas Road	B3	Regent Street	B4
Dalton Road	D2	Ridge Lane	D1
Dalton Square	C3	Ridge Street	D1
Damside Street	B2	Robert Street	C3
Derby Road	C1	Rosemary Lane	C2
De Vitre Street	C2	St George's Quay	A1
Dumbarton Road	D4	St Leonard's Gate	C2
East Road	D3	St Peter's Road	C4
Edward Street	C3	Sibsey Street	A3
Fairfield Road	A3	South Road	C4
Fenton Street	B3	Station Road	A3
Gage Street	C3	Stirling Road	D4
Garnet Street	D2	Sulyard Street	C3
George Street	C3	Sun Street	B3
Grasmere Road	D3	Thurnham Street	C4
Great John Street	C3	Troutbeck Road	D2
Gregson Road	D4	Ulleswater Road	D3
Greyhound Bridge Road	B1	West Road	A3
High Street	B4	Westbourne Road	A3
Kelsey Street	A3	Wheatfield Street	A3
Kentmere Road	D2	Williamson Road	D3
King Street	B3	Wingate-Saul Road	A3
Kingsway	C1	Wolseley Street	D2
Kirkes Road	D4	Woodville Street	D3
Langdale Road	D1	Wyresdale Road	D3

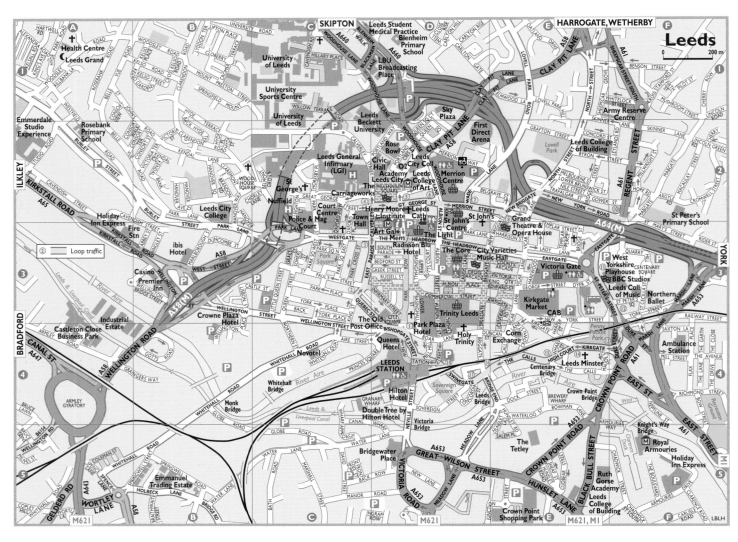

Leeds

Leeds is found on atlas page **90 H4**

Abbey Street	B3
Aire Street	C4
Albion Place	D3
Albion Street	D2
Alexandra Road	A1
Argyle Road	F2
Armley Gyratory	A4
Armley Road	A4
Armouries Drive	F5
Armouries Way	E4
Back Hyde Terrace	B2
Back Row	C5
Bath Road	C5
Bedford Street	D3
Belgrave Street	D2
Belle Vue Road	A1
Belmont Grove	C2
Benson Street	F1
Bingley Street	B3
Bishopgate Street	D4
Black Bull Street	E5
Blackman Lane	C1
Blenheim Walk	C1
Boar Lane	D4
Bowman Lane	E4
Bow Street	F4
Brandon Road	B2
Bridge End	D4
Bridge Road	B5
Bridge Street	E2
Bridge Street	E3
Briggate	D4
Burley Road	A2
Butts Court	D3
Byron Street	E2
Call Lane	E4

Calverley Street	C2
Canal Street	A4
Canal Wharf	C4
Carlton Hill	D1
Carlton Rise	D1
Castle Street	B3
Cavendish Road	C1
Cavendish Street	A2
Centenary Square	F3
Central Road	E3
Chadwick Street	F5
Cherry Row	F1
Chorley Lane	B2
City Square	D3
Claremont	B2
Clarence Road	F5
Clarendon Road	B1
Clay Pit Lane	D2
Cloberry Street	B1
Commercial Street	D3
Concordia Street	D4
Concord Street	E2
Consort Street	B2
Consort View	A1
County Arcade	E3
Cromer Terrace	B1
Cromwell Street	F2
Cross Arcade	D3
Cross Kelso Road	B1
Cross Stamford Street	F1
Crown Point Road	E5
Crown Street	E4
Cudbear Street	E5
David Street	C5
Dock Street	E4
Duke Street	F4

Duke Street	F4
Duncan Street	D4
Duncombe Street	B3
Dyer Street	E3
Eastgate	E3
East Parade	C3
East Street	F4
Elmwood Lane	E1
Flax Place	F4
Front Street	C5
Gelderd Road	A5
George Street	E3
Globe Road	B4
Gotts Road	B4
Gower Street	E2
Grace Street	C3
Grafton Street	E2
Graingers Way	A4
Great George Street	C2
Great Wilson Street	D5
Greek Street	D3
Hanover Avenue	B2
Hanover Lane	B2
Hanover Square	B2
Harewood Street	E3
Harper Street	E4
Harrison Street	E3
Hartwell Road	A1
High Court	E4
Holbeck Lane	B5
Hope Road	F2
Hunslet Road	E4
Hunslet Road	E5
Hyde Park Road	A1
Hyde Street	B2
Hyde Terrace	B1
Infirmary Street	D3
Junction Street	D5
Kelso Road	B1
Kendal Lane	B2
King Edward Street	E3

King's Avenue	A1
King Street	C3
Kirkgate	E3
Kirkstall Road	A2
Lady Lane	E3
Lands Lane	D3
Leighton Street	C2
Leylands Road	F2
Lifton Place	B1
Lincoln Green Road	F2
Lisbon Street	B3
Little Queen Street	C3
Lovell Park Hill	E1
Lovell Park Road	E1
Lower Basinghall Street	D3
Lower Brunswick Street	E2
Lyddon Terrace	B1
Mabgate	F2
Macaulay Street	F2
Manor Road	C5
Mark Lane	D3
Marlborough Street	B3
Marshall Street	C5
Marsh Lane	F4
Maude Street	E4
Meadow Lane	D5
Melbourne Street	E2
Merrion Street	D2
Merrion Way	D2
Millennium Square	D2
Mill Street	F4
Millwright Street	F2
Mount Preston Street	B1
Mushroom Street	F1
Neptune Street	F4
Neville Street	D4
New Briggate	E3
New Lane	D5
New Station Street	D4
New York Road	E2
New York Street	E3

Northern Street	C4
North Street	E2
Oxford Place	C3
Oxford Row	C3
Park Cross Street	C3
Park Lane	B2
Park Place	C3
Park Row	D3
Park Square East	C3
Park Square North	C3
Park Square West	C3
Park Street	C3
Pilot Street	F1
Portland Crescent	D2
Portland Way	D2
Princes Square	C4
Quarry Hill	F3
Quebec Street	C3
Queen Square	D2
Queen Square Court	D2
Queen Street	C3
Railway Street	F3
Regent Street	F2
Richmond Street	F4
Rider Street	F3
Rillbank Lane	A1
Rosebank Road	A1
St Cecilia Street	F3
St John's Road	A1
St Mary's Street	F3
St Paul's Street	C3
St Peter's Square	F3
St Peter's Street	E3
Salem Place	E5
Saxton Lane	F4
Sheepscar Grove	E1
Sheepscar Street South	F1
Skinner Lane	E2
South Parade	D3
Sovereign Street	D4
Spence Lane	A5

Springfield Mount	B1
Springwell Road	B5
Springwell Street	B5
Studio Road	A2
Swinegate	D4
Templar Street	E3
The Avenue	F4
The Boulevard	F5
The Calls	E4
The Headrow	D3
Thoresby Place	C2
Trafalgar Street	E2
Upper Basinghall Street	D3
Vicar Lane	E3
Victoria Road	D5
Victoria Street	B2
Victoria Terrace	B2
Wade Lane	D2
Water Lane	B5
Waterloo Street	E4
Wellington Bridge Street	B3
Wellington Road	A4
Wellington Road	A5
Wellington Street	B3
Westfield Road	A1
Westgate	C3
West Street	B3
Wharf Approach	C4
Wharf Street	E4
Whitehall Quay	C4
Whitehall Road	A5
Whitehall Road	A5
Whitelock Street	F1
Willow Terrace Road	C1
Woodhouse Lane	C1
Woodhouse Square	B2
Woodsley Road	A1
Wortley Lane	A5
Wortley Lane	A5
York Place	C3
York Street	F3

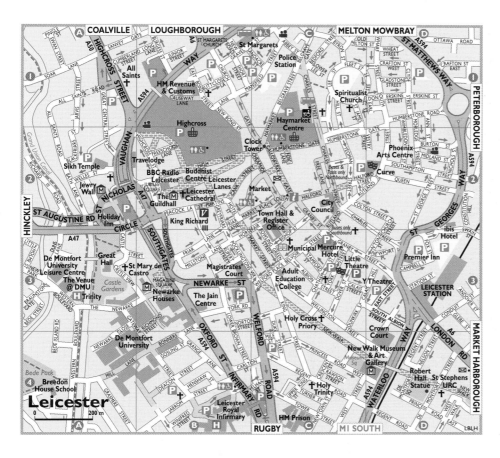

Leicester

Leicester is found on atlas page **72 F10**

Albion Street	C3	Infirmary Road	B4
All Saints Road	A1	Jarrom Street	B4
Bath Lane	A2	Jarvis Street	A1
Bedford Street	C1	King Street	C3
Belgrave Gate	C1	Lee Street	C1
Belvoir Street	C3	London Road	D3
Bishop Street	C3	Lower Brown Street	B3
Bonners Lane	B4	Magazine Square	B3
Bowling Green Street	C3	Mansfield Street	B1
Burgess Street	B1	Market Place South	B2
Burton Street	D2	Market Street	C3
Calais Hill	C3	Mill Lane	A4
Campbell Street	D3	Morledge Street	D1
Cank Street	B2	Newarke Street	B3
Castle Street	A3	New Walk	C3
Charles Street	C1	Oxford Street	B3
Chatham Street	C3	Peacock Lane	B2
Cheapside	C2	Pocklingtons Walk	B3
Church Gate	B1	Princess Road East	D4
Clyde Street	D1	Princess Road West	C4
Colton Street	C2	Queen Street	D2
Conduit Street	D3	Regent Road	C4
Crafton Street West	D1	Regent Street	D4
Deacon Street	B4	Richard III Road	A2
De Montfort Street	D4	Rutland Street	C2
Dover Street	C3	St Augustine Road	A2
Duke Street	C3	St George Street	D2
Duns Lane	A3	St Georges Way	D2
East Bond Street Lane	B1	St James Street	C1
Erskine Street	D1	St Matthews Way	D1
Fleet Street	C1	St Nicholas Circle	A2
Friar Lane	B3	Sanvey Gate	A1
Gallowtree Gate	C2	Soar Lane	A1
Gateway Street	A3	South Albion Street	D3
Granby Street	C2	Southampton Street	D2
Grasmere Street	A4	Southgates	B3
Gravel Street	B1	Station Street	D3
Great Central Street	A1	The Newarke	A3
Greyfriars	B2	Tower Street	C4
Halford Street	C2	Vaughan Way	A2
Haymarket	C2	Waterloo Way	D4
Highcross Street	A1	Welford Road	C3
Highcross Street	B2	Welles Street	A2
High Street	B2	Wellington Street	C3
Hill Street	C1	Western Boulevard	A4
Horsefair Street	B3	West Street	C4
Humberstone Gate	C2	Wharf Street South	D1
Humberstone Road	D1	Yeoman Street	C2

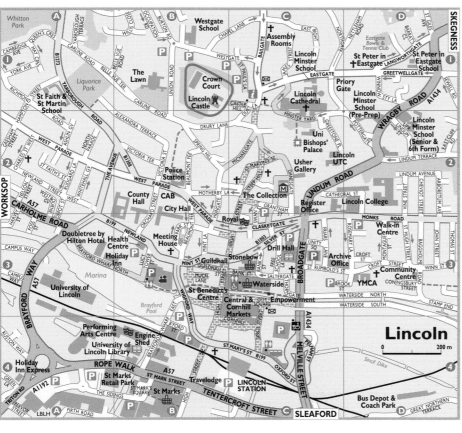

Lincoln

Lincoln is found on atlas page **86 C6**

Alexandra Terrace	B2	Montague Street	D3
Arboretum Avenue	D2	Motherby Lane	B2
Baggholme Road	D3	Nelson Street	A2
Bailgate	C1	Newland	B3
Bank Street	C3	Newland Street West	A2
Beaumont Fee	B3	Northgate	C1
Belle Vue Terrace	A1	Orchard Street	B3
Brayford Way	A4	Oxford Street	C4
Brayford Wharf East	B4	Park Street	B3
Brayford Wharf North	A3	Pelham Street	C4
Broadgate	C3	Pottergate	D2
Burton Road	B1	Queen's Crescent	A1
Carholme Road	A2	Richmond Road	A1
Carline Road	A1	Rope Walk	A4
Cathedral Street	C2	Rosemary Lane	D3
Chapel Lane	B1	Rudgard Lane	A2
Charles Street West	A2	St Hugh Street	D3
Cheviot Street	D2	St Mark Street	B4
City Square	C3	St Martin's Street	C2
Clasketgate	C3	St Mary's Street	B4
Cornhill	B4	St Rumbold's Street	C3
Croft Street	D3	Saltergate	C3
Danesgate	C2	Silver Street	C3
Depot Street	A3	Sincil Street	C4
Drury Lane	B2	Spring Hill	B2
East Bight	C1	Steep Hill	C2
Eastgate	C1	Swan Street	C3
Free School Lane	C3	Tentercroft Street	B4
Friars Lane	C3	The Avenue	A2
Grantham Street	C2	The Sidings	A4
Greetwellgate	D1	Thorngate	C3
Gresham Street	A2	Triton Road	A4
Guildhall Street	B3	Union Road	B1
Hampton Street	A1	Unity Square	C3
High Street	B3	Victoria Street	B2
Hungate	B3	Victoria Terrace	B2
John Street	D3	Vine Street	D2
Langworthgate	D1	Waterside North	C3
Lindum Road	C2	Waterside South	C3
Lindum Terrace	D2	Westgate	B1
Lucy Tower Street	B3	West Parade	A2
May Crescent	A1	Whitehall Grove	A2
Melville Street	C4	Wigford Way	B3
Michaelgate	C2	Winnow Sty Lane	D1
Minster Yard	C2	Winn Street	D3
Mint Lane	B3	Wragby Road	D2
Mint Street	B3	Yarborough Terrace	A1
Monks Road	D3	York Avenue	A1

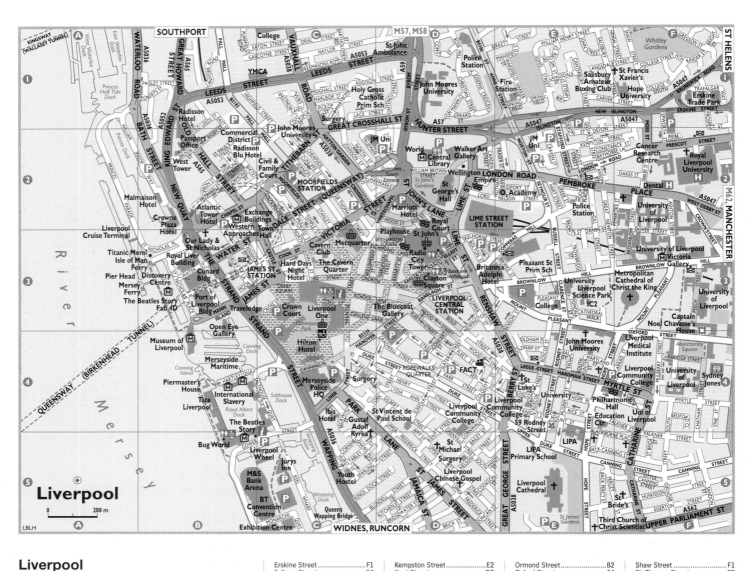

Liverpool

Liverpool is found on atlas page **81 L6**

Addison Street.................C1
Anson Street....................E2
Argyle Street...................C4
Arrad Street.....................F4
Ashton Street...................F2
Audley Street....................E2
Back Canning Street...........E5
Baltimore Street................E4
Bath Street.......................B2
Beckwith Street.................C4
Bedford Street South..........F5
Benson Street...................E3
Berry Street......................E4
Bidder Street....................E1
Birkett Street....................D1
Bixteth Street...................B2
Blackburne Place..............E5
Blundell Street..................C5
Bold Street......................D3
Bosnett Street..................D3
Bridgewater Street............D5
Bridport Street..................E2
Brook Street.....................B2
Brownlow Hill....................E3
Brownlow Street................F3
Brunswick Road................B3
Brunswick Street...............B3
Byrom Street....................D1
Cambridge Street..............F4
Camden Street..................D2
Canning Place..................C4
Canning Street..................E5
Canterbury Street..............E1
Carver Street....................E1
Castle Street.....................C3
Catharine Street................F5

Cathedral Walk.................E3
Chapel Street...................B2
Chatham Street................F4
Cheapside.......................C2
Christian Street.................D1
Churchill Way...................D2
Church Street...................C3
Clarence Street.................E3
Cockspur Street................C1
College Lane....................C3
College Street North...........F1
College Street South...........F1
Colquitt Street..................D4
Constance Street...............E2
Cook Street......................C3
Copperas Hill...................C5
Cornhill...........................C5
Cornwallis Street...............D5
Craven Street....................E2
Cropper Street..................D3
Crosshall Street.................C2
Crown Street....................F2
Dale Street (Queensway).......C2
Dansie Street....................E3
Daulby Street....................F2
Derby Square....................C3
Devon Street.....................E2
Dover Street.....................F3
Drury Lane.......................B3
Duke Street......................D4
East Street........................B1
Eaton Street......................B1
Edmund Street..................B2
Egerton Street...................F5
Elliot Street.......................D3
Epworth Street..................F1

Erskine Street...................F1
Falkner Street...................E4
Fazakerley Street...............B2
Fenwick Street..................B3
Fleet Street.......................D3
Fontenoy Street.................D1
Fraser Street.....................E2
Gascoyne Street................B1
Gilbert Street....................D4
Gildart Street....................E2
Gill Street........................E2
Gower Street.....................B5
Gradwell Street.................D4
Great Crosshall Street.........C1
Great George Street............E5
Great Howard Street...........B1
Great Newton Street...........E2
Greek Street.....................E2
Gregson Street..................F1
Grenville Street South.........D5
Hackins Hey.....................C2
Hanover Street..................C4
Hardman Street.................E4
Harker Street....................E1
Hartley Quay.....................B4
Hart Street.......................C2
Hatton Garden..................C2
Hawke Street....................E3
Henry Street.....................D4
Highfield Street.................B1
Hood Street......................D2
Hope Place.......................E4
Hope Street......................E5
Hotham Street...................E2
Hunter Street....................D1
Huskisson Street................F5
Islington..........................E2
Jamaica Street..................D5
James Street....................B3
Johnson Street..................C2
Keel Wharf.......................C5

Kempston Street................E2
Kent Street.......................D5
Kinder Street....................F1
King Edward Street.............B2
Kingsway (Wallasey Tunnel)....A1
Kitchen Street...................D5
Knight Street.....................E4
Lace Street.......................C1
Langsdale Street...............E1
Leece Street.....................E4
Leeds Street.....................B1
Lime Street......................D2
Liver Street......................C4
London Road....................D2
London Road....................E2
Lord Nelson Street.............D2
Lord Street.......................C3
Lydia Ann Street................D4
Mann Island.....................B3
Mansfield Street................E1
Marybone........................C1
Maryland Street.................E4
Midghall Street.................C1
Moorfields........................C2
Moor Street......................B3
Moss Street......................F1
Mount Pleasant................E3
Mount Street....................E4
Mulberry Street.................F4
Myrtle Street.....................E4
Naylor Street.....................C1
Nelson Street....................D5
Newington........................D4
New Islington....................E1
New Quay........................B2
North John Street...............C3
Norton Street....................E2
Old Hall Street..................B2
Oldham Street...................E4
Old Haymarket..................C2
Old Leeds Street................B1

Ormond Street..................B2
Oxford Street....................F4
Paisley Street....................B1
Pall Mall..........................B1
Paradise Street..................C3
Parker Street.....................D3
Park Lane........................C4
Parr Street........................D4
Peech Street.....................F3
Pembroke Place................E2
Pembroke Street................F2
Percey Street....................E5
Pilgrim Street....................E4
Pleasant Street..................E3
Pomona Street..................E3
Prescot Street...................F2
Princes Parade..................A2
Prospect Street.................F1
Queensway
 (Birkenhead Tunnel)..........A4
Ranelagh Street.................D3
Redcross Street.................C3
Renshaw Street.................D3
Richmond Lane.................C3
Rigby Street......................B2
Rodney Street...................E4
Roscoe Street...................E4
Rose Hill.........................D1
Russell Street....................E3
St Anne Street...................D1
St James Street.................D5
St John's Lane...................D2
St Josephs Crescent...........D1
St Nicholas Place...............B3
St Paul's Street..................B2
Salisbury Street.................E1
Salthouse Quay.................C4
Sandon Street...................F5
School Lane......................C3
Seel Street.......................D4
Seymour Street..................E2

Shaw Street.....................F1
Sir Thomas Street..............C2
Skelhorne Street................D3
Slater Street......................D4
Soho Street.......................E1
Sparling Street..................C5
Springfield........................E1
Stafford Street...................E2
Stanley Street...................C2
Strand Street.....................B3
Suffolk Street....................D4
Tabley Street.....................C5
Tarleton Street...................D3
Temple Street....................C2
The Strand.......................B3
Tithe Barn Street................C2
Trafalgar Way....................F1
Trowbridge Street...............E3
Trueman Street..................C2
Upper Duke Street.............E5
Upper Frederick Street.........D4
Upper Parliament Street.......F5
Upper Pitt Street................D4
Vauxhall Road...................C1
Vernon Street....................C2
Victoria Street...................C3
Wakefield Street................E1
Wall Street.......................C3
Wapping..........................C5
Waterloo Road..................A1
Water Street.....................B3
West Derby Street..............F2
Westmorland Drive.............C1
Whitechapel.....................D2
William Brown Street...........D2
William Henry Street...........E1
William Jessop Way............A2
Williamson Square.............C3
Williamson Street...............C3
Wood Street.....................D3
York Street.......................C4

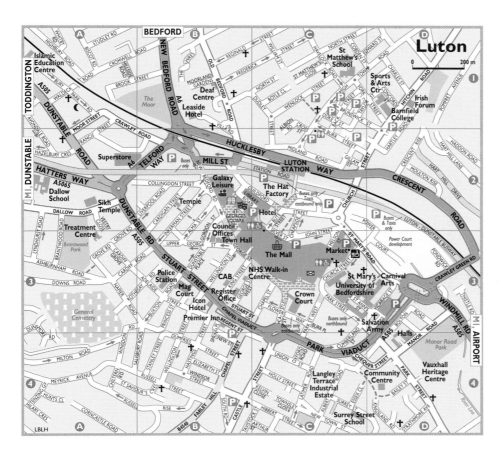

Luton

Luton is found on atlas page **50 C6**

Adelaide Street	B3		Hibbert Street	C4
Albert Road	C4		Highbury Road	A1
Alma Street	B2		High Town Road	C1
Arthur Street	C4		Hitchin Road	D1
Ashburnham Road	A3		Holly Street	C4
Biscot Road	A1		Hucklesby Way	B2
Brantwood Road	A3		Inkerman Street	B3
Brunswick Street	C1		John Street	C3
Burr Street	C2		King Street	B3
Bury Park Road	A1		Latimer Road	C4
Bute Street	C2		Liverpool Road	B2
Buxton Road	B3		Manor Road	D4
Cardiff Road	A3		Meyrick Avenue	A4
Cardigan Street	B2		Midland Road	C2
Castle Street	B4		Mill Street	B2
Chapel Street	B4		Milton Road	A4
Chapel Viaduct	B3		Moor Street	A1
Charles Street	D1		Napier Road	A3
Chequer Street	C4		New Bedford Road	B1
Church Street	C2		New Town Street	C4
Church Street	C3		Old Bedford Road	B1
Cobden Street	C1		Park Street	C3
Collingdon Street	B2		Park Street West	C3
Concorde Street	D1		Park Viaduct	C4
Crawley Green Road	D3		Princess Street	B3
Crawley Road	A1		Regent Street	B3
Crescent Road	D2		Reginald Street	B1
Cromwell Road	A1		Rothesay Road	A3
Cumberland Street	C4		Russell Rise	A4
Dallow Road	A2		Russell Street	B4
Dudley Street	C1		St Mary's Road	C3
Dumfries Street	B4		St Saviour's Crescent	A4
Dunstable Road	A1		Salisbury Road	A4
Farley Hill	B4		Stanley Street	B4
Flowers Way	C3		Station Road	C2
Frederick Street	B1		Strathmore Avenue	D4
George Street	B3		Stuart Street	B3
George Street West	B3		Surrey Street	C4
Gordon Street	B3		Tavistock Street	B4
Grove Road	A3		Telford Way	B2
Guildford Street	B2		Upper George Street	B3
Hart Hill Drive	D2		Vicarage Street	D3
Hart Hill Lane	D2		Waldeck Road	A1
Hartley Road	D2		Wellington Street	B4
Hastings Street	B4		Wenlock Street	C1
Hatters Way	A2		Windmill Road	D3
Havelock Road	C1		Windsor Street	B4
Hazelbury Crescent	A2		Winsdon Road	A4

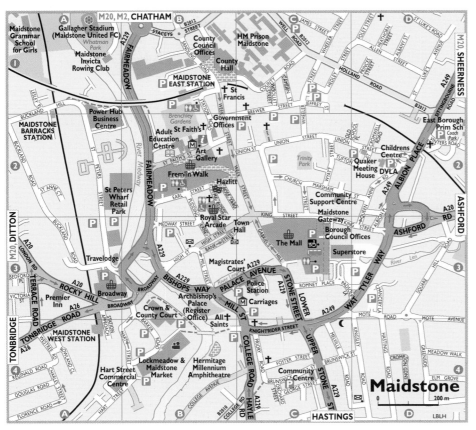

Maidstone

Maidstone is found on atlas page **38 C10**

Albany Street	D1		Market Buildings	B2
Albion Place	D2		Marsham Street	C2
Allen Street	D1		Meadow Walk	D4
Ashford Road	D3		Medway Street	B3
Bank Street	B3		Melville Road	C4
Barker Road	B4		Mill Street	B3
Bedford Place	A3		Mote Avenue	D3
Bishops Way	B3		Mote Road	D3
Brewer Street	C2		Old School Place	D2
Broadway	A3		Orchard Street	C4
Broadway	B3		Padsole Lane	C3
Brunswick Street	C4		Palace Avenue	B3
Buckland Hill	A2		Princess Street	D1
Buckland Road	A2		Priory Road	C4
Camden Street	C1		Pudding Lane	B2
Chancery Lane	D3		Queen Anne Road	D2
Charles Street	A4		Reginald Road	A4
Church Street	C2		Rocky Hill	A3
College Avenue	B4		Romney Place	C3
College Road	C4		Rose Yard	B2
County Road	C1		Rowland Close	A4
Crompton Gardens	D4		St Anne Court	A2
Cromwell Road	D2		St Faith's Street	B2
Douglas Road	A4		St Luke's Avenue	D1
Earl Street	B2		St Luke's Road	D1
Elm Grove	D4		St Peters Street	A2
Fairmeadow	B1		Sandling Road	B1
Florence Road	A4		Sittingbourne Road	D1
Foley Street	D1		Square Hill Road	D3
Foster Street	C4		Staceys Street	B1
Gabriel's Hill	C3		Station Approach	A4
George Street	C4		Station Road	B1
Greenside	D4		Terrace Road	A3
Hart Street	A4		Tonbridge Road	A4
Hastings Road	D4		Tufton Street	C2
Hayle Road	D4		Union Street	C2
Heathorn Street	D1		Upper Stone Street	C4
Hedley Street	C1		Victoria Street	A3
High Street	B3		Vinters Road	D2
Holland Road	D1		Wat Tyler Way	C3
James Street	C1		Week Street	B1
Jeffrey Street	C1		Well Road	C1
King Street	C2		Westree Road	A4
Kingsley Road	D4		Wheeler Street	C1
Knightrider Street	C4		Woollett Street	C1
Lesley Place	A1		Wyatt Street	C2
London Road	A3			
Lower Stone Street	C3			

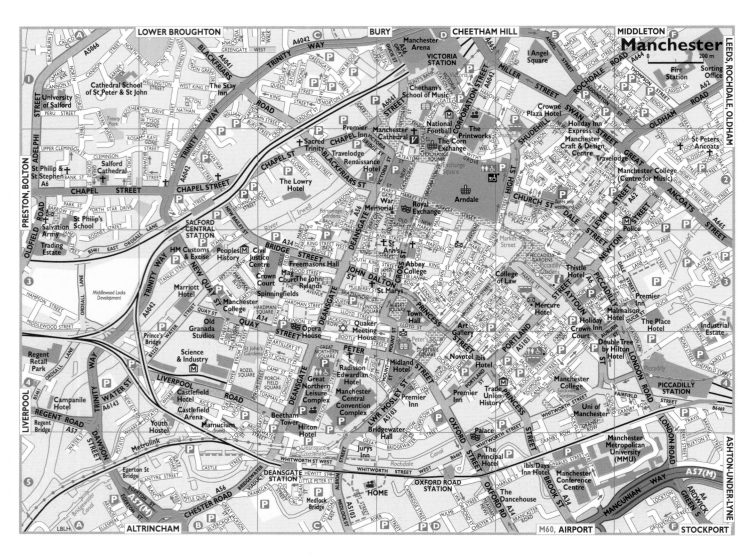

Manchester

Manchester is found on atlas page **82 H5**

Abingdon Street.....................E4	Browning Street......................B2	Dawson Street.....................A5	John Street............................D1	Nathan Drive.........................B1	Sackville Street.....................E4
Addington Street...................E1	Brown Street...........................D3	Deansgate.............................C4	John Street............................E2	New Bailey Street.................B2	St Anns Square....................C2
Adelphi Street.......................A2	Bury Street..............................B1	Dickinson Street....................D4	Joiner Street..........................E2	New Bridge Street................C1	St Ann Street.......................C3
Albion Street.........................C5	Byrom Street...........................B4	Duke Street............................B4	Jutland Street........................F3	New Cathedral Street...........D2	St James Square.................C3
Angel Street..........................E1	Cable Street...........................E1	Dulcie Street..........................F3	Kennedy Street.....................D3	New Elm Road......................A4	St James Street...................D4
Ardwick Green South............F5	Cambridge Street..................D5	East Ordsall Lane.................A3	King Street.............................C1	New George Street...............E2	St Mary's Parsonage...........C3
Artillery Street.......................C4	Camp Street...........................C4	Egerton Street.......................A5	King Street.............................C3	New Quay Street..................B3	St Stephen Street................B2
Atherton Street......................B4	Canal Street...........................E4	Exchange Square..................D2	King Street West...................C3	Newton Street.......................E3	Store Street..........................F3
Atkinson Street.....................C3	Cannon Street........................A1	Fairfield Street.......................F4	Lamb Lane............................B2	New York Street....................E3	Sharp Street.........................E1
Auburn Street.......................E4	Canon Green Drive................B1	Faulkner Street......................D4	Laystall Street.......................F3	Nicholas Street.....................D3	Shudehill..............................E2
Aytoun Street........................E3	Castle Street..........................B5	Fennel Street.........................D1	Left Bank...............................B3	North George Street..............A1	Silk Street............................A1
Back Piccadilly......................E3	Cathedral Street.....................D2	Ford Street.............................A2	Lena Street............................F3	North Hill Street....................A1	Simpson Street.....................E1
Bank Street...........................A2	Chadderton Street.................F1	Fountain Street......................D3	Lever Street...........................E2	North Star Drive....................A2	South King Street.................C3
Baring Street.........................F4	Chapel Street.........................A2	Frederick Street.....................B2	Little Lever Street..................E3	Norton Street.........................C1	Spear Street..........................E3
Barton Street.........................C4	Charles Street........................E5	Garden Lane..........................B1	Little Peter Street..................C5	Oldfield Road.........................A3	Spring Gardens....................D3
Berry Street...........................F4	Charlotte Street......................D3	Gartside Street......................B3	Liverpool Road.......................B4	Oldham Road.........................F1	Station Approach..................F3
Blackfriars Road...................B1	Chatham Street......................E3	George Leigh Street...............F2	Lloyd Street...........................C3	Oldham Street........................E2	Swan Street..........................E1
Blackfriars Street..................C2	Cheapside.............................D3	George Street.........................D4	London Road.........................F4	Ordsall Lane..........................A4	Tariff Street...........................F3
Blantyre Street.......................B5	Chester Road.........................B5	Gore Street............................B2	Long Millgate........................D1	Oxford Road..........................D5	Thomas Street......................E2
Bloom Street..........................B2	China Lane.............................E3	Granby Row............................E5	Longworth Street...................C4	Oxford Street.........................D4	Thompson Street...................F1
Bloom Street..........................E4	Chorlton Street......................E4	Gravel Lane............................C1	Lower Byrom Street...............B4	Pall Mall...............................D3	Tib Lane................................D3
Blossom Street......................F2	Church Street.........................E2	Great Ancoats Street............F2	Lower Mosley Street..............C4	Parker Street.........................E3	Tib Street..............................E2
Boad Street...........................F4	City Road East.......................C5	Great Bridgewater Street.......C5	Lower Ormond Street.............D5	Peru Street............................A1	Todd Street...........................D1
Boond Street.........................C1	Cleminson Street...................A2	Great Ducie Street.................D1	Ludgate Street......................E1	Peter Street...........................C4	Tonman Street......................C4
Booth Street..........................D3	College Land..........................C2	Great George Street...............A2	Major Street...........................E4	Piccadilly..............................E3	Travis Street.........................F4
Bootle Street.........................C4	Collier Street...........................C1	Great Jackson Street.............B5	Mancunian Way.....................E5	Piccadilly Gardens................E3	Trinity Way............................A4
Brancaster Road...................E5	Commercial Street.................C5	Great John Street..................B4	Marble Street.........................D3	Portland Street.......................D4	Turner Street.........................E2
Brazennose Street.................C3	Copperas Street.....................E2	Greengate.............................C1	Market Street.........................D2	Port Street.............................F3	Victoria Bridge Street...........C2
Brewer Street........................F3	Cornell Street.........................F2	Greengate West....................B1	Marsden Street......................D3	Potato Wharf..........................A5	Victoria Station Approach......D1
Bridge Street.........................C3	Corporation Street..................D2	Gun Street.............................F2	Marshall Street......................E1	Princess Street......................D3	Victoria Street........................C2
Bridgewater Place.................E2	Cotton Street.........................F2	Hanover Street......................D2	Mason Street.........................E1	Quay Street............................B3	Warwick Street......................E2
Bridgewater Street................B4	Crosskeys Street...................F1	Hardman Street.....................C3	Mayan Avenue.......................A1	Queen Street.........................C1	Watson Street........................C4
Bridgewater Viaduct..............B5	Cross Street...........................C2	Hewitt Street..........................C5	Medlock Street.......................C5	Queen Street.........................C3	Well Street............................D2
Brook Street..........................E5	Cross Street...........................D3	High Street............................E2	Middlewood Street.................A3	Redhill Street.........................F2	West King Street...................B1
Brotherton Drive....................A1	Dale Street.............................E2	Hood Street...........................F2	Miller Street...........................E1	Regent Road.........................A4	West Mosley Street...............D3
Browncross Street.................B2	Dantzic Street........................D2	Hope Street............................E3	Minshull Street......................E3	Reyner Street........................D4	Whitworth Street....................C4
		Houndsworth Street..............F2	Mirabel Street.........................C1	Rice Street.............................B4	Whitworth Street West...........C5
		Hulme Street..........................D5	Mosley Street.........................D3	Richmond Street....................E3	Windmill Street......................C4
		James Street.........................A3	Mount Street..........................B1	Rochdale Road......................E1	Withy Grove..........................D2
		Jersey Street.........................F2	Mount Street..........................D4	Rodney Street........................A3	Wood Street..........................C3
		John Dalton Street................C3	Museum Street......................C4	Rosamond Drive....................A2	York Street............................D3

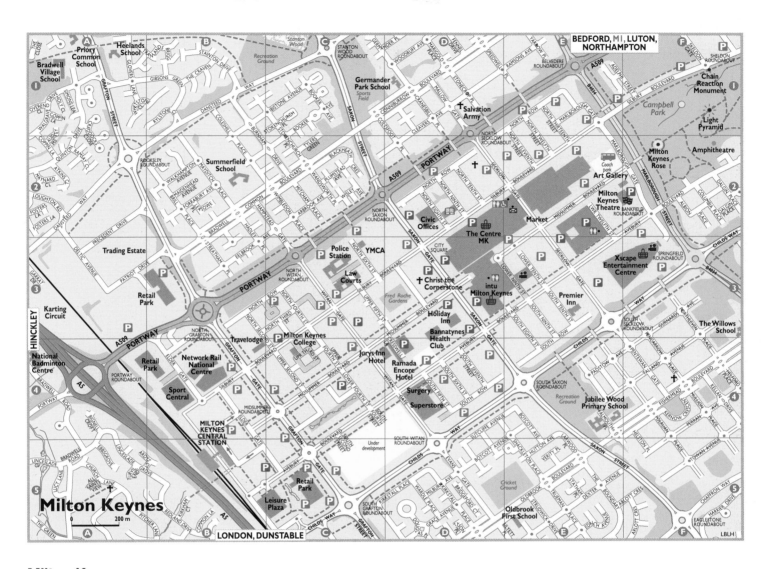

Milton Keynes

Milton Keynes is found on atlas page **49 N7**

Adelphi Street	E1	Cranesbill Place	D1
Albion Place	F2	Cresswell Lane	D3
All Saints View	A5	Dalgin Place	F2
Arbrook Avenue	C2	Dansteed Way	A2
Ardys Court	A5	Dansteed Way	B1
Arlott Crescent	F5	Deltic Avenue	A3
Atkins Close	A2	Dexter Avenue	E5
Audley Mews	A2	Douglas Place	D5
Avebury Boulevard	C5	Eaglestone Roundabout	F5
Bankfield Roundabout	E2	Ebbsgrove	A5
Belvedere Roundabout	E1	Edrich Avenue	E5
Bignell Croft	A4	Eelbrook Avenue	B3
Blackheath Crescent	C2	Elder Gate	B4
Booker Avenue	C1	Evans Gate	D5
Boycott Avenue	D5	Falmouth Place	E4
Boycott Avenue	E4	Fennel Drive	D1
Bradwell Common		Fishermead Boulevard	F4
Boulevard	B2	Forrabury Avenue	B2
Bradwell Road	A4	Fosters Lane	A2
Bradwell Road	A5	Garrat Drive	A3
Bridgeford Court	D5	Germander Place	C1
Brill Place	B2	Gibsons Green	B1
Burnham Drive	B1	Glovers Lane	A1
Chaffron Way	F5	Grace Avenue	D5
Childs Way	C5	Grafton Gate	B4
Childs Way	F3	Grafton Street	A1
Church Lane	A5	Grafton Street	C5
City Square	D3	Gurnards Avenue	F3
Cleavers Avenue	D1	Hadley Place	B2
Coleshill Place	B1	Hampstead Gate	B2
Coltsfoot Place	C1	Harrier Drive	F5
Columbia Place	F2	Helford Place	F4
Common Lane	B5	Helston Place	F4
Conniburrow Boulevard	C1	Holy Close	A1
Coppin Lane	A2	Hutton Avenue	E5
Craddocks Close	A1	Ibistone Avenue	C1

Kellan Drive	F4	North Secklow	
Kernow Crescent	F4	Roundabout	D1
Kirkham Court	B5	North Second Street	B3
Kirkstall Place	C5	North Sixth Street	C3
Larwood Place	E5	North Tenth Street	D2
Leasowe Place	B2	North Third Street	C3
Linceslade Grove	A5	North Thirteenth Street	E1
Loughton Road	A2	North Twelfth Street	E1
Lower Fourth Street	C4	North Witan Roundabout	C3
Lower Ninth Street	E3	Oldbrook Boulevard	E5
Lower Tenth Street	E3	Overend Close	A1
Lower Twelfth Street	E2	Padstow Avenue	E4
Lucy Lane	A5	Patriot Drive	A3
Maidenhead Avenue	B2	Pencarrow Place	F3
Mallow Gate	D1	Pentewan Gate	F4
Marigold Place	D1	Perran Avenue	F4
Marlborough Gate	E1	Pitcher Lane	A5
Marlborough Gate	E2	Plumstead Avenue	C2
Marlborough Street	F2	Polruan Place	F4
Mayditch Place	B2	Porthleven Place	F3
Maynard Close	A2	Portway	A4
Midsummer Boulevard	C4	Portway Roundabout	A4
Midsummer Boulevard	E2	Precedent Drive	A3
Midsummer Roundabout	B4	Quinton Drive	A2
Milburn Avenue	D5	Ramsay Close	A2
Mitcham Place	C2	Ramsons Avenue	E1
Mullion Place	F4	Redland Drive	B5
North Eighth Street	D2	Rooksley Roundabout	A2
North Eleventh Street	E1	Rylstone Close	B1
North Fourth Street	C3	Saxon Gate	D2
North Grafton		Saxon Street	C1
Roundabout	B3	Secklow Gate	D2
North Ninth Street	D2	Shackleton Place	E5
North Row	B3	Sheldon Roundabout	F1
North Row	D2	Silbury Boulevard	B4
North Saxon Roundabout	C2	Silbury Roundabout	B4

North Secklow		Simons Lea	A1
Roundabout	D1	Skeldon Gate	F1
North Second Street	B3	South Eighth Street	E3
North Sixth Street	C3	South Fifth Street	D4
North Tenth Street	D2	South Fourth Street	C4
North Third Street	C3	South Grafton Roundabout	C5
North Thirteenth Street	E1	South Ninth Street	E3
North Twelfth Street	E1	South Row	D4
North Witan Roundabout	C3	South Saxon Roundabout	E4
Oldbrook Boulevard	E5	South Secklow Roundabout	E3
Overend Close	A1	South Second Street	C5
Padstow Avenue	E4	South Seventh Street	D4
Patriot Drive	A3	South Sixth Street	D4
Pencarrow Place	F3	South Tenth Street	E3
Pentewan Gate	F4	South Witan Roundabout	D5
Perran Avenue	F4	Speedwell Place	D1
Pitcher Lane	A5	Springfield Roundabout	F3
Plumstead Avenue	C2	Stainton Drive	B1
Polruan Place	F4	Stanton Wood	
Porthleven Place	F3	Roundabout	C1
Portway	A4	Statham Place	E5
Portway Roundabout	A4	Stokenchurch Place	C1
Precedent Drive	A3	Stonecrop Place	D1
Quinton Drive	A2	Streatham Place	B3
Ramsay Close	A2	Strudwick Drive	E5
Ramsons Avenue	E1	Sutcliffe Avenue	D4
Redland Drive	B5	Talland Avenue	F4
Rooksley Roundabout	A2	The Boundary	E5
Rylstone Close	B1	The Close	A1
Saxon Gate	D2	The Craven	B1
Saxon Street	C1	The Green	A5
Secklow Gate	D2	Towan Avenue	F5
Shackleton Place	E5	Tranlands Brigg	B1
Sheldon Roundabout	F1	Trueman Place	E5
Silbury Boulevard	B4	Turvil End	A5
Silbury Roundabout	B4	Tylers Green	C2

Tyson Place	D5
Ulyett Place	D5
Upper Fifth Street	C3
Upper Fourth Street	C4
Upper Second Street	C4
Upper Third Street	C4
Verity Place	E5
Walgrave Drive	A1
Walkhampton Avenue	B2
Wandsworth Place	C2
Wardle Place	D5
Whetstone Close	A1
Wimbledon Place	C2
Wisely Avenue	C2
Witan Gate	C3
Woodruff Avenue	D1
Yarrow Place	E1

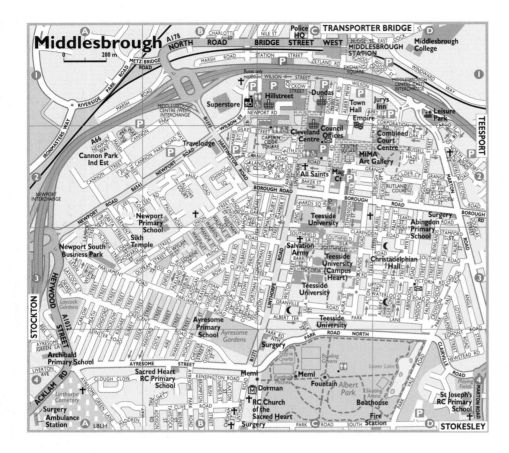

Middlesbrough

Middlesbrough is found on atlas page **104 E7**

Acklam Road	A4	Heywood Street	A3
Acton Street	C3	Ironmasters Way	A2
Aire Street	B4	Kensington Road	B4
Albert Road	C2	Kildare Street	A4
Amber Street	C2	Laurel Street	D3
Athol Street	B3	Lees Road	A2
Aubrey Street	D3	Linthorpe Road	B4
Ayresome Park Road	B4	Longford Street	A4
Ayresome Street	A4	Lorne Street	A3
Borough Road	C2	Lothian Road	D3
Bretnall Street	B2	Marsh Street	A2
Bridge Street East	C1	Marton Road	D2
Bridge Street West	C1	Melrose Street	D2
Bush Street	B4	Metz Bridge Road	A1
Cadogen Street	B3	Myrtle Street	D3
Camden Street	D2	Newlands Road	D3
Cannon Park Road	A2	Newport Road	A2
Cannon Park Way	A2	Palm Street	D3
Cannon Street	A2	Park Lane	C3
Carlow Street	A3	Park Road North	C4
Centre Square	C2	Park Vale Road	D4
Clairville Road	D4	Parliament Road	A3
Clarendon Road	C3	Pearl Street	C2
Clifton Street	B3	Pelham Street	C2
Corporation Road	D1	Portman Street	B3
Costa Street	B4	Princes Road	B3
Craven Street	B3	Riverside Park Road	A1
Crescent Road	A3	Ruby Street	C2
Croydon Road	D3	Russell Street	D2
Derwent Street	A2	St Pauls Road	B2
Diamond Road	B3	Southfield Road	C3
Egmont Road	D4	Station Street	C1
Emily Street	C2	Stowe Street	B3
Errol Street	D3	Tavistock Street	B4
Essex Street	A4	Tennyson Street	B3
Fairbridge Street	C2	Union Street	A3
Falmouth Street	D3	Victoria Road	C3
Finsbury Street	B3	Victoria Street	A3
Fleetham Street	B2	Warren Street	B2
Garnet Street	B2	Waterloo Road	D3
Glebe Road	B3	Waverley Street	B3
Grange Road	B2	Wembley Street	A3
Grange Road	D2	Wilson Street	B2
Granville Road	C3	Wilton Street	C3
Gresham Road	B3	Windsor Street	B2
Harewood Street	B3	Woodlands Road	C3
Harford Street	B4	Worcester Street	B4
Hartington Road	B2	Zetland Road	C1

Newport

Newport is found on atlas page **31 K7**

Albert Terrace	B3	Jones Street	B3
Allt-Yr-Yn Avenue	A2	Keynsham Avenue	C4
Bailey Street	B3	King Street	C4
Bedford Road	D2	Kingsway	C2
Blewitt Street	B3	Kingsway	C4
Bond Street	C1	Llanthewy Road	A3
Bridge Street	B2	Locke Street	B1
Bryngwyn Road	A3	Lower Dock Street	C4
Brynhyfryd Avenue	A4	Lucas Street	B1
Brynhyfryd Road	A4	Market Street	B2
Caerau Crescent	A4	Mellon Street	C4
Caerau Road	A3	Mill Street	B2
Cambrian Road	B2	North Street	B3
Caroline Street	D3	Oakfield Road	A3
Cedar Road	D2	Park Square	C4
Charles Street	C4	Queen's Hill	B1
Chepstow Road	D1	Queen's Hill Crescent	A1
Clarence Place	C1	Queen Street	C4
Clifton Place	B4	Queensway	B2
Clifton Road	B4	Risca Road	A4
Clyffard Crescent	A3	Rodney Road	C2
Clytha Park Road	A2	Rudry Street	D1
Clytha Square	C4	Ruperra Lane	C4
Colts Foot Close	A1	Ruperra Street	D4
Commercial Street	C3	St Edward Street	B3
Corelli Street	D1	St Julian Street	B4
Corn Street	C2	St Mark's Crescent	A2
Corporation Road	D2	St Mary Street	B3
Devon Place	B2	St Vincent Road	C2
Dewsland Park Road	B4	St Woolos Road	B3
Dumfries Place	D4	School Lane	C3
East Street	B3	Serpentine Road	A2
East Usk Road	C1	Skinner Street	C2
Factory Road	B1	Sorrel Drive	A1
Fields Road	A2	Spencer Road	A3
Friars Field	B4	Stow Hill	B3
Friars Road	B4	Stow Hill	B4
Friar Street	C3	Stow Park Avenue	A4
George Street	D4	Talbot Lane	C3
Godfrey Road	A2	Tregare Street	D1
Gold Tops	A2	Tunnel Terrace	A3
Grafton Road	C2	Upper Dock Street	C2
Granville Lane	D4	Upper Dock Street	C3
Granville Street	D4	Usk Way	D3
High Street	B2	Victoria Crescent	B3
Hill Street	C3	West Street	B3
John Frost Square	C3	Wyndham Stret	C1
John Street	D4	York Place	A4

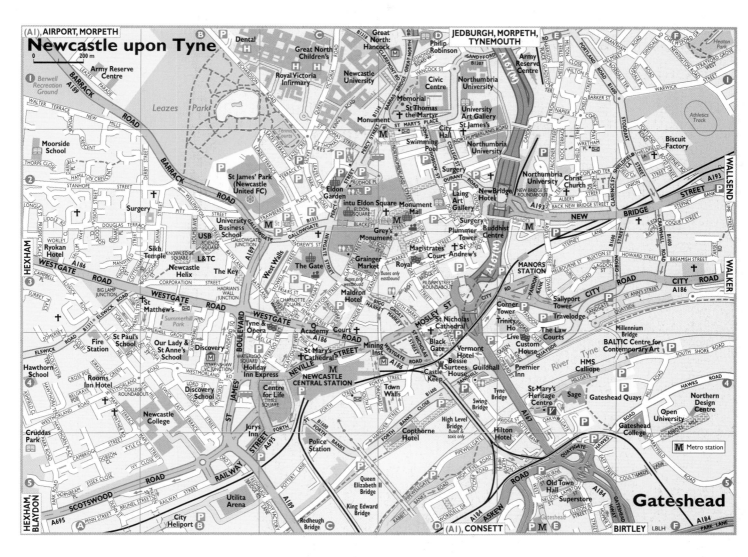

Newcastle upon Tyne

Newcastle upon Tyne is found on atlas page **113 K8**

Abbots Hill F4
Albert Street E2
Argyle Street E2
Askew Road D5
Avision Street A2
Back New Bridge Street E2
Barker Street E1
Barrack Road A1
Barras Bridge D1
Bath Lane B3
Belgrave Parade A4
Big Lamp Junction A3
Blackett Street C2
Blagdon Street E3
Blandford Square B4
Blandford Street B4
Bottle Bank E4
Boyd Street F2
Breamish Street F3
Bridge Street E4
Broad Chare E3
Brunel Street A5
Buckingham Street B3
Buxton Street E3
Byron Street E1
Cambridge Street A5
Camden Street E2
Campbell Place A3
Carliol Square D3
Charlotte Square C3
Chelmsford Grove F1
Chester Street E1
City Road E3
Claremont Road D1
Clarence Street E2
Clayton Street C3

Clayton Street West C4
Cloth Market D3
Colby Court A4
College Roundabout A4
College Street D2
Cookson Close A3
Copland Terrace E2
Coppice Way E1
Coquet Street F2
Corporation Street B3
Cottenham Street A3
Coulthards Lane F5
Crawhall Road F2
Cross Parade A4
Cross Street C3
Darnell Place A2
Dean Street D3
Derby Street B2
Diana Street B3
Dinsdale Place F1
Dinsdale Road F1
Dobson Close A5
Douglas Terrace A2
Duke Street B4
Dunn Street A5
Durant Road D2
East Street E5
Edward Place A3
Eldon Square C2
Ellison Street E5
Elswick East Terrace A4
Elswick Road A3
Elswick Row A5
Essex Close A5
Falconar's Court C3
Falconer Street E2

Fenkle Street C3
Field Close F2
Fletcher Road D5
Forth Banks C4
Forth Banks Close D5
Forth Street C4
Friars Street C3
Gallowgate B2
Gallowgate Junction B3
Gateshead Highway E5
George Street B4
Gibson Street F3
Gladstone Terrace E1
Gloucester Terrace A4
Grainger Street C3
Grantham Road E1
Great North Road D1
Grey Street D3
Groat Market C3
Hamilton Crescent A2
Hanover Street C5
Harrison Place E1
Hawks Road E5
Hawthorn Place A4
Hawthorn Terrace A4
Helmsley Road E1
Henry Square E2
High Bridge D3
High Level Road D5
High Street E5
Hillgate E4
Hood Street D3
Hopper Street E5
Hornbeam Place A5
Houston Street A4
Howard Street F3
Hudson Street E5
Ivy Close A5
Jesmond Road West D1
John Dobson Street D2
Jubilee Road E3

King Edward Bridge C5
King Street E4
Kirkdale Green A4
Kyle Close A5
Lambton Street E5
Leazes Crescent C2
Leazes Lane C2
Leazes Park Road C2
Leazes Terrace C2
Liddle Road A2
Lime Street F2
Lombard Street E4
Longley Street A2
Lord Street B4
Low Friar Street C3
Maiden Street B5
Mansfield Street A3
Maple Street B5
Maple Terrace A4
Market Street D3
Mather Road A4
Melbourne Street E3
Mill Road F4
Milton Close E1
Milton Place E1
Monday Crescent A1
Mosley Street D3
Napier Street E1
Nelson Street C3
Nelson Street E5
Neville Street C4
New Bridge Street E2
Newgate Street C3
Newington Road F1
New Mills A1
Northumberland Road D2
Northumberland Street D2
Nun Street C3
Oakwellgate E4
Orchard Street C4
Ord Street B5

Oxford Street D2
Pandon E3
Pandon Bank E3
Park Lane F5
Park Road A5
Peel Lane B4
Penn Street A5
Percy Street C2
Pilgrim Street D2
Pink Lane C4
Pipewellgate D5
Pitt Street B2
Portland Road E1
Portland Road F1
Pottery Lane C5
Prospect Place A2
Prudhoe Place C2
Quarryfield Road F5
Quayside E5
Quayside F3
Quayside E4
Queen Street E4
Queen Victoria Road C1
Rabbit Banks Road D5
Railway Street B5
Red Barnes F2
Redheugh Bridge Road B5
Richardson Road B1
Rock Terrace E1
Rosedale Terrace E1
Rye Hill A4
St Andrew's Street C3
St Ann's Street F3
St James' Boulevard B4
St Mary's Place D1
St Nicholas Street D4
St Thomas' Crescent C2
St Thomas' Street C1
Sandgate E3
Sandhill D4
Sandyford Road D1

Scotswood Road A5
Shieldfield Lane F2
Shield Street E2
Shot Factory Lane C5
Simpson Terrace E2
Somerset Place A4
South Shore Road F4
South Street C4
Stanhope Street A2
Stepney Bank F2
Stepney Lane E3
Stepney Road F2
Stoddart Street F1
Stowell Street C3
Stratford Grove West F1
Strawberry Place C2
Summerhill Grove B3
Summerhill Street A3
Summerhill Terrace B4
Swinburne Street E5
Tarset Road F3
Terrace Place C2
Tindall Street A3
Tower Street E3
Tyne Bridge E4
Union Street F2
Vallum Way A3
Victoria Street B4
Walter Terrace A1
Warwick Street F1
Waterloo Square B4
Waterloo Street C4
Wellington Street B2
Westgate Road A3
Westmorland Road A4
West Street E5
West Walls C3
Worley Close A3
Worsdell Drive D5
Wretham Place E2
York Street A3

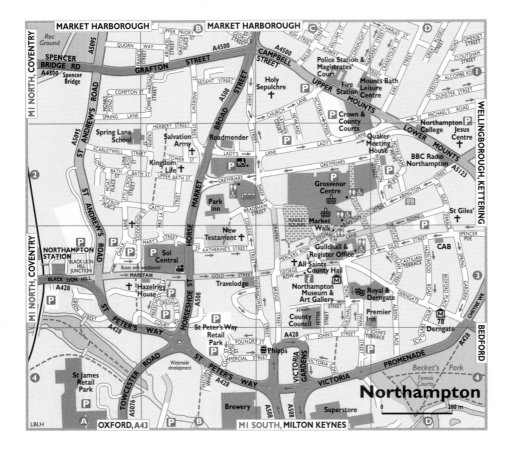

Northampton

Northampton is found on atlas page **60 G8**

Abington Street	C2	Little Cross Street	A2
Albert Place	D2	Lower Bath Street	A2
Albion Place	D3	Lower Cross Street	A2
Angel Street	C3	Lower Harding Street	B1
Arundel Street	B1	Lower Mounts	D2
Ash Street	C1	Marefair	A3
Bailiff Street	C1	Margaret Street	C1
Black Lion Hill	A3	Market Square	C2
Bradshaw Street	B2	Mercers Row	C3
Bridge Street	D3	Moat Place	A2
Broad Street	B1	Monkspond Street	A1
Campbell Street	C1	Newland	C1
Castilian Street	D3	Notredame Mews	D2
Castle Street	B2	Overstone Road	D1
Chalk Lane	A3	Pike Lane	B3
Cheyne Walk	D3	Quorn Way	A1
Church Lane	C1	Regent Street	B1
College Street	B2	Robert Street	C1
Commercial Street	B4	St Andrew's Road	A2
Connaught Street	C1	St Andrew's Street	B1
Court Road	B3	St Giles' Street	D3
Cranstoun Street	D1	St Giles' Terrace	D2
Crispin Street	B2	St John's Street	C4
Derngate	D3	St Katherine's Street	B3
Doddridge Street	A3	St Mary's Street	A3
Drapery	C3	St Michael's Road	D1
Dunster Street	D1	St Peter's Way	B4
Dychurch Lane	C3	Scarletwell Street	A2
Earl Street	D1	Scholars Court	D4
Fetter Street	C3	Sheep Street	B1
Fitzroy Place	A2	Sheep Street	C2
Foundry Street	B4	Spencer Bridge Road	A1
Francis Street	A1	Spencer Parade	D3
Freeschool Lane	B3	Spring Gardens	D3
George Row	C3	Spring Lane	A1
Gold Street	B3	Swan Street	C3
Grafton Street	A1	Tanner Street	A4
Great Russell Street	D1	The Ridings	D2
Green Street	A3	Towcester Road	A4
Gregory Street	B3	Tower Street	B2
Greyfriars	B2	Upper Bath Street	B2
Guildhall Road	C3	Upper Mounts	C1
Hazelwood Road	D3	Upper Priory Street	B1
Herbert Street	B2	Victoria Gardens	C4
Horse Market	B3	Victoria Promenade	C4
Horseshoe Street	B3	Victoria Street	C1
Kingswell Street	C3	Wellington Street	D2
Lady's Lane	B2	Western Wharf	B4

Norwich

Norwich is found on atlas page **77 J10**

All Saints Green	B4	Pottergate	A2
Bank Plain	C2	Prince of Wales Road	C2
Barn Road	A1	Princes Street	C2
Bedding Lane	C1	Quay Side	C1
Bedford Street	B2	Queens Road	B4
Ber Street	C4	Queen Street	C2
Bethel Street	A3	Rampant Horse Street	B3
Bishopgate	D1	Recorder Road	D2
Brigg Street	B3	Red Lion Street	B3
Calvert Street	B1	Riverside Road	D3
Castle Meadow	C3	Riverside Walk	D1
Cathedral Street	D2	Rose Lane	C3
Cattle Market Street	C3	Rouen Road	C3
Chantry Road	B3	Rupert Street	A4
Chapelfield East	A3	St Andrews Street	B2
Chapelfield North	A3	St Benedicts Street	A2
Chapelfield Road	A3	St Faiths Lane	D2
Cleveland Road	A3	St Georges Street	B1
Colegate	B1	St Giles Street	A2
Convent Road	A3	St Julians Alley	C4
Coslany Street	B2	St Marys Plain	B1
Cow Hill	A2	St Peters Street	B3
Davey Place	B3	St Stephens Road	B4
Dove Street	B2	St Stephens Square	A4
Duke Street	B1	St Stephens Street	B4
Elm Hill	C2	St Swithins Road	A2
Exchange Street	B3	St Verdast Street	D2
Farmers Avenue	C3	Surrey Street	B4
Ferry Lane	D2	Ten Bell Lane	A3
Fishergate	C1	Theatre Street	B3
Friars Quay	B1	Thorn Lane	C4
Gaol Hill	B3	Tombland	C2
Gentlemans Walk	B3	Unicorn Yard	A1
Goldenball Street	C3	Union Street	A4
Grapes Hill	A2	Unthank Road	A3
Haymarket	B3	Upper Goat Lane	A2
Heigham Street	A1	Upper King Street	C2
King Street	C2	Upper St Giles Street	A2
London Street	B2	Vauxhall Street	A3
Lower Goat Lane	B2	Walpole Street	A3
Magdalen Street	C1	Wensum Street	C1
Market Avenue	C3	Wessex Street	A4
Mountergate	D3	Westlegate	B3
Music House Lane	D4	Westwick Street	A1
Muspole Street	B1	Wherry Road	D4
New Mills Yard	A1	Whitefriars	C1
Oak Street	A1	White Lion Street	B3
Palace Street	C1	Willow Lane	A2

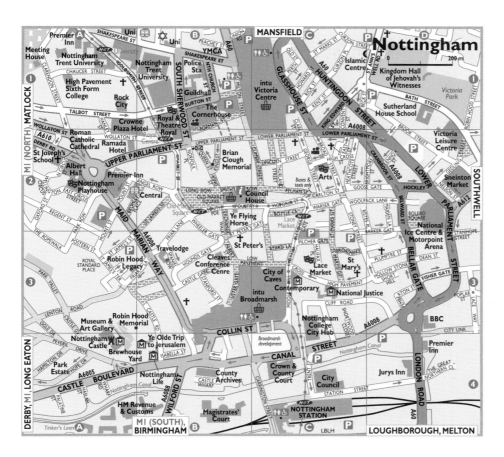

Nottingham

Nottingham is found on atlas page **72 F3**

Albert Street	B3	King Street	B2
Angel Row	B2	Lenton Road	A3
Barker Gate	D2	Lincoln Street	C2
Bath Street	D1	Lister Gate	B3
Bellar Gate	D3	London Road	D4
Belward Street	D2	Long Row	B2
Broad Street	C2	Lower Parliament Street	C2
Broadway	C3	Low Pavement	B3
Bromley Place	A2	Maid Marian Way	A2
Brook Street	D1	Market Street	B2
Burton Street	B1	Middle Hill	C3
Canal Street	C4	Milton Street	B1
Carlton Street	C2	Mount Street	A3
Carrington Street	C4	Norfolk Place	B2
Castle Boulevard	A4	North Circus Street	A2
Castle Gate	B3	Park Row	A3
Castle Road	B3	Pelham Street	C2
Chaucer Street	A1	Peveril Drive	A4
City Link	D3	Pilcher Gate	C3
Clarendon Street	A1	Popham Street	C3
Cliff Road	C3	Poultry	B2
Collin Street	B4	Queen Street	B2
Cranbrook Street	D2	Regent Street	A2
Cumber Street	C2	St Ann's Well Road	D1
Curzon Place	C1	St James's Street	A3
Derby Road	A2	St Marks Gate	C3
Exchange Walk	B2	St Marks Street	C1
Fisher Gate	D3	St Mary's Gate	C3
Fletcher Gate	C3	St Peter's Gate	B3
Forman Street	B1	Shakespeare Street	A1
Friar Lane	A3	Smithy Row	B2
Gedling Street	D2	South Parade	B2
George Street	C2	South Sherwood Street	B1
Glasshouse Street	C1	Spaniel Row	B3
Goldsmith Street	A1	Station Street	C4
Goose Gate	C2	Stoney Street	C2
Halifax Place	C3	Talbot Street	A1
Heathcote Street	C2	Thurland Street	C2
High Cross Street	C3	Trent Street	C4
High Pavement	C3	Upper Parliament Street	A2
Hockley	D2	Victoria Street	C2
Hollow Stone	D3	Warser Gate	C3
Hope Drive	A4	Weekday Cross	C3
Hounds Gate	B3	Wellington Circus	A2
Howard Street	C1	Wheeler Gate	B2
Huntingdon Street	C1	Wilford Street	B4
Kent Street	C1	Wollaton Street	A1
King Edward Street	C1	Woolpack Lane	C2

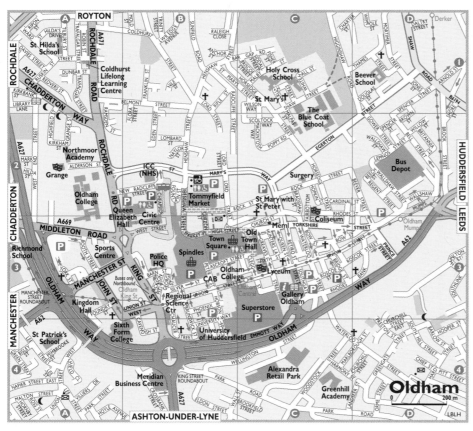

Oldham

Oldham is found on atlas page **83 K4**

Ascroft Street	B3	Napier Street East	A4
Bar Gap Road	B1	New Radcliffe Street	A2
Barlow Street	D4	Oldham Way	A3
Barn Street	B3	Park Road	B4
Beever Street	D2	Park Street	A4
Bell Street	D2	Peter Street	B3
Belmont Street	B1	Prince Street	D3
Booth Street	A3	Queen Street	C3
Bow Street	C3	Radcliffe Street	B1
Brook Street	D2	Ramsden Street	A1
Brunswick Street	B3	Regent Street	D2
Cardinal Street	C2	Rhodes Bank	C3
Chadderton Way	A1	Rhodes Street	C2
Chaucer Street	B3	Rifle Street	B1
Clegg Street	C3	Rochdale Road	A1
Coldhurst Road	B1	Rock Street	B2
Crossbank Street	B4	Roscoe Street	C3
Curzon Street	B2	Ruskin Street	A1
Dunbar Street	A1	St Hilda's Drive	A1
Eden Street	A2	St Marys Street	B1
Egerton Street	C2	St Mary's Way	B2
Emmott Way	C4	Shaw Road	D1
Firth Street	C3	Shaw Street	D1
Fountain Street	B2	Shore Street	D1
Franklin Street	B1	Siddall Street	C1
Gower Street	D2	Silver Street	B3
Grange Street	A2	Southgate Street	C3
Greaves Street	C3	South Hill Street	D4
Greengate Street	D4	Spencer Street	D2
Hardy Street	D4	Sunfield Road	B1
Harmony Street	C4	Thames Street	D1
Henshaw Street	B2	Trafalgar Street	A1
Higginshaw Road	C1	Trinity Street	B1
Highfield Street	A2	Tulbury Street	A1
High Street	B3	Union Street	B3
Hobson Street	B3	Union Street West	A4
Horsedge Street	C1	Union Street West	B3
John Street	A3	University Way	B4
King Street	B3	Wallshaw Street	D2
Lemnos Street	D2	Wall Street	B4
Malby Street	C1	Ward Street	A1
Malton Street	A4	Waterloo Street	C3
Manchester Street	A3	Wellington Street	B4
Market Place	B3	West End Street	A2
Marlborough Street	C4	West Street	B3
Middleton Road	A3	Willow Street	D2
Mortimer Street	D1	Woodstock Street	C4
Mumps	D2	Yorkshire Street	C3

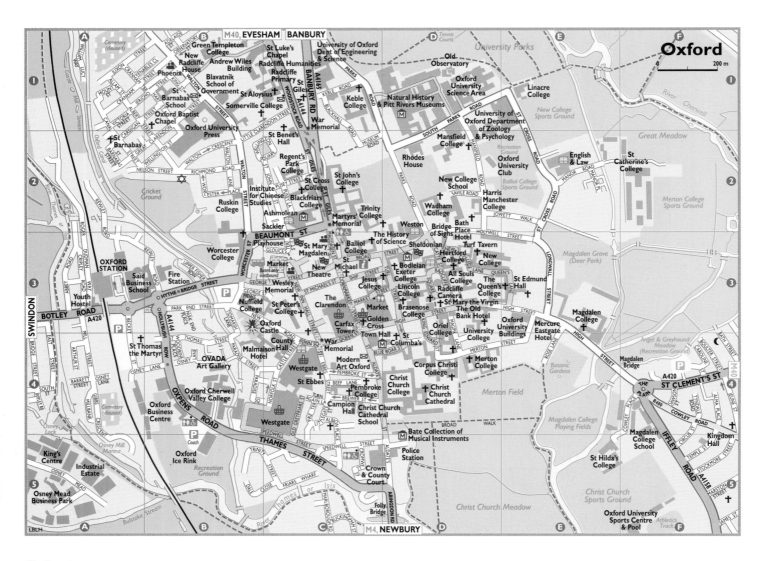

Oxford

Oxford is found on atlas page **34 F3**

Abbey Road A3
Abingdon Road D5
Adelaide Street B1
Albert Street A1
Albion Place C4
Allam Street A1
Alma Place F4
Arthur Street A4
Banbury Road C1
Barrett Street A4
Bath Street F4
Beaumont Street C3
Becket Street A3
Beef Lane C4
Blackhall Road C1
Blue Boar Street C4
Bonn Square C4
Botley Road A3
Boulter Street F4
Brewer Street C4
Bridge Street A4
Broad Street C3
Broad Walk D4
Buckingham Street C5
Canal Street A1
Cardigan Street A2
Caroline Street F4
Castle Street C4
Catte Street D3
Circus Street F5
Cornmarket Street C3
Cowley Place F4
Cowley Road F4
Cranham Street A1
Cranham Terrace A1
Cripley Road A3

Cromwell Street C5
Dale Close B5
Dawson Street F4
East Street A4
Folly Bridge C5
Friars Wharf C5
George Street B3
George Street Mews B3
Gibbs Crescent A4
Gloucester Street C3
Great Clarendon Street......A2
Hart Street B1
High Street D3
High Street E4
Hollybush Row B3
Holywell Street D2
Hythe Bridge Street B3
Iffley Road F4
James Street F5
Jericho Street A1
Jowett Walk D2
Juxon Street A1
Keble Road C1
King Edward Street D3
King Street B1
Little Clarendon Street B2
Littlegate Street C4
Longwall Street E3
Magdalen Bridge E4
Magdalen Street C3
Magpie Lane D3
Manor Place E2
Manor Road E2
Mansfield Road D2
Market Street C3
Marlborough Road C5

Marston Street F5
Merton Street D4
Millbank A4
Mill Street A4
Mount Street A1
Museum Road C2
Nelson Street A2
New College Lane D2
New Inn Hall Street C3
New Road B3
Norfolk Street C4
Observatory Street B1
Old Greyfriars Street.........C4
Osney Lane A4
Osney Lane B4
Osney Mead A5
Oxpens Road B4
Paradise Square B4
Paradise Street B4
Park End Street B3
Parks Road C1
Parks Road D2
Pembroke Street C4
Pike Terrace C4
Pusey Lane C2
Pusey Street C2
Queen's Lane D3
Queen Street C3
Radcliffe Square D3
Rewley Road A2
Rewley Road B3
Richmond Road B2
Roger Dudman Way A3
Rose Lane E4
St Aldate's C4
St Aldate's D5

St Barnabas Street A2
St Clement's Street F4
St Cross Road E1
St Cross Road E2
St Ebbes Street C4
St Giles C2
St John Street C2
St Michael's Street C3
Savile Road D2
Ship Street C3
South Parks Road D2
South Street A4
Speedwell Street C5
Stockmore Street F5
Temple Street F5
Thames Street C5
The Plain F4
Tidmarsh Lane B3
Trinity Street B5
Turl Street D3
Turn Again Lane C4
Tyndale Road F4
Upper Fisher Row B3
Venables Close A1
Victoria Street A1
Walton Crescent B2
Walton Lane B2
Walton Street B1
Wellington Square B2
Wellington Street B2
William Lucy Way A1
Woodbine Place B4
Woodstock Road C1
Worcester Place B2
Worcester Street B3

University Colleges

All Souls College D3
Balliol College C3
Brasenose College D3
Christ Church College..........D4
Corpus Christi College D4
Exeter College...................D3
Harris Manchester College ... D2
Hertford College D3
Jesus College....................C3
Keble College....................C1
Linacre College E1
Lincoln College D3
Magdalen College E3
Mansfield College D2
Merton College D4
New College......................D3
Nuffield College B3
Oriel College D3
Pembroke College..............C4
Ruskin College B2
St Catherine's College F2
St Cross College C2
St Hilda's College E5
St John's College................C2
St Peter's College...............C3
Somerville College B1
The Queen's College D3
Trinity College....................C2
University College D3
Wadham College D2
Worcester College B3

Perth

Perth is found on atlas page **134 E3**

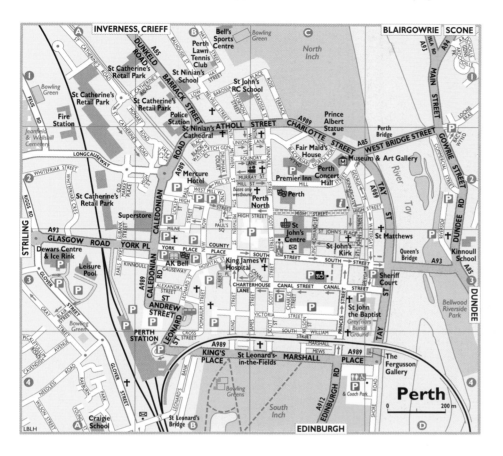

Albert Place	B3	Melville Street	B1
Alexandra Street	B3	Mill Street	B2
Atholl Street	B1	Mill Street	C2
Back Wynd	D2	Milne Street	B2
Balhousie Street	B1	Monart Road	A1
Barossa Place	B1	Murray Street	B2
Barrack Street	B1	Needless Road	A4
Blackfriars Wynd	C2	New Row	B3
Black Watch Garden	B2	North Methven Street	B2
Caledonian Road	B2	North Port	C2
Caledonian Road	B3	North William Street	B2
Canal Street	C3	Old Market Place	A2
Cavendish Avenue	A4	Paul Street	B2
Charles Street	C3	Perth Bridge	D2
Charlotte Street	C2	Pickletullum Road	A4
Charterhouse Lane	B3	Pomarium Street	B3
Commercial Street	D2	Princes Street	C3
County Place	B3	Queen's Bridge	D3
Cross Street	B4	Raeburn Park	A4
Dundee Road	D3	Riggs Road	A2
Dunkeld Road	B1	Riverside	D3
Earls Dykes	A3	Rose Terrace	C1
Edinburgh Road	C4	St Andrew Street	B3
Elibank Street	A3	St Catherine's Road	A1
Feus Road	A1	St John's Place	C3
Foundry Lane	B2	St John Street	C3
George Street	C2	St Leonard's Bank	B4
Glasgow Road	A3	St Paul's Square	B2
Glover Street	A3	Scott Street	C3
Glover Street	A4	Shore Road	D4
Gowrie Street	D2	Skinnergate	C2
Gray Street	A3	South Methven Street	B2
Hay Street	B1	South Street	C3
High Street	B2	South William Street	C4
High Street	C2	Speygate	D3
Hospital Street	B3	Stormont Street	B1
Isla Road	D1	Tay Street	D2
James Street	C3	Tay Street	D4
King Edward Street	C3	Union Lane	B2
King's Place	B4	Victoria Street	C3
King Street	B3	Watergate	D2
Kinnoull Causeway	A3	West Bridge Street	D2
Kinnoull Street	C2	West Mill Wynd	B2
Leonard Street	B3	Whitefriars Crescent	A2
Lochie Brae	D1	Whitefriar Street	A2
Longcauseway	A2	Wilson Street	A4
Main Street	D1	York Place	A3
Marshall Place	C4	York Place	B3

Peterborough

Peterborough is found on atlas page **74 C11**

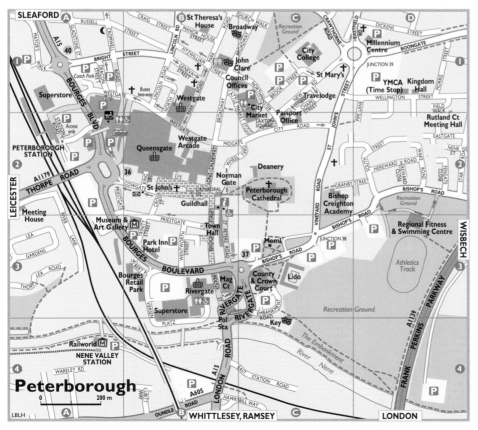

Albert Place	B3	New Road	C1
Bishop's Road	C3	Northminster	C1
Boongate	D1	North Street	B1
Bourges Boulevard	A1	Oundle Road	B4
Bridge Street	B3	Park Road	B1
Bright Street	A1	Pipe Lane	D2
Broadway	B2	Priestgate	A2
Brook Street	C1	Rivergate	B3
Cathedral Square	B2	River Lane	A2
Cattle Market Street	B1	Russell Street	A1
Chapel Street	C1	St John's Street	C2
Church Street	B2	St Peters Road	B3
Church Walk	C1	South Street	D2
City Road	C2	Star Road	D2
Cowgate	B2	Station Road	A2
Craig Street	B1	Thorpe Lea Road	A3
Crawthorne Road	C1	Thorpe Road	A2
Cromwell Road	A1	Trinity Street	B3
Cross Street	B2	Viersen Platz	B3
Cubitt Way	B4	Vineyard Road	C3
Deacon Street	A1	Wake Road	D2
Dickens Street	D1	Wareley Road	A4
Eastfield Road	D1	Wellington Street	D1
Eastgate	D2	Wentworth Street	B3
East Station Road	C4	Westgate	A1
Embankment Road	C3		
Exchange Street	B2		
Fengate Close	D2		
Field Walk	D1		
Fitzwilliam Street	B1		
Frank Perkins Parkway	D4		
Geneva Street	B1		
Gladstone Street	A1		
Granby Street	C2		
Hawksbill Way	B4		
Hereward Close	D2		
Hereward Road	D2		
King Street	B2		
Laxton Square	C2		
Lea Gardens	A3		
Lincoln Road	B1		
London Road	B4		
Long Causeway	B2		
Manor House Street	B1		
Mayor's Walk	A1		
Midgate	B2		
Morris Street	D1		
Nene Street	D2		

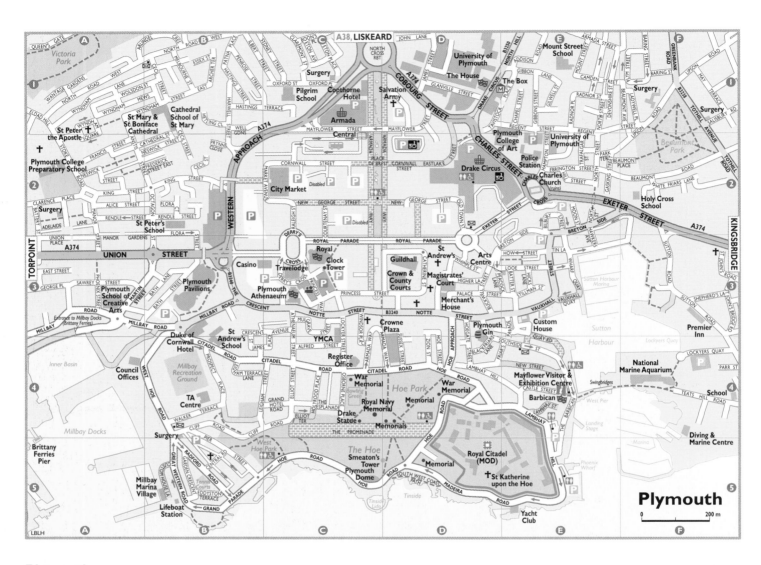

Plymouth

Plymouth is found on atlas page **6 D8**

Addison Road......................E1	Clarence Place......................A2	Great Western Road...............B5	Mayflower Street.................D1	Radnor Place.........................E1	Western Approach...............B2
Adelaide Lane.....................A2	Cliff Road.............................B4	Greenbank Road..................F1	May Terrace.........................F1	Radnor Street........................E1	West Hoe Road.....................A4
Alfred Street........................C4	Cobourg Street.....................D1	Hampton Street....................E2	Melbourne Street.................B1	Raleigh Street.......................C2	Wharf Quay..........................E3
Alice Street..........................A2	Cornwall Street.....................C2	Harwell Street......................B1	Millbay Road.......................A3	Regent Street........................E1	Whimple Street.....................D3
Anstis Street.........................A2	Courtenay Street...................C3	Hastings Street.....................B1	Moon Street.........................E2	Rendle Street........................A2	White Friars Lane..................F2
Archer Terrace......................B1	Crescent Avenue...................B3	Hastings Terrace...................B1	Mount Street........................E1	Royal Parade........................C3	Windsor Place.......................C3
Armada Street.......................E1	Custom House Lane...............B5	Hawkers Avenue...................E2	Mulgrave Street....................C3	St James Place......................B4	Wolsdon Street.....................A1
Armada Way........................C2	Derry's Cross........................C3	Hetling Close........................B1	Neswick Street......................A2	St John's Bridge Road..........F3	Wyndham Lane......................A1
Armada Way........................C4	Devonshire Street..................E1	Hicks Lane............................E3	New George Street................C2	St John's Road......................F3	Wyndham Mews....................A1
Arundel Crescent..................A1	Drake Circus.........................D1	Higher Lane..........................D3	New Street.............................E4	Salisbury Road......................F1	Wyndham Square..................A1
Athenaeum Street..................C3	Eastlake Street......................D2	Hill Street.............................E2	North Cross Roundabout........C1	Sawrey Street........................A3	Wyndham Street East.............A1
Baring Street.........................F1	East Street............................A3	Hoe Approach.......................D4	North Hill.............................E1	Shepherd's Lane....................F3	Zion Street............................D4
Bath Lane.............................B3	Ebrington Street....................E2	Hoegate Street......................D3	North Road West..................A1	Southside Street....................D4	
Bath Street...........................B3	Eddystone Terrace.................B5	Hoe Road.............................C5	North Street..........................E2	South West Coast Path...........D5	
Batter Street.........................E3	Eldad Hill.............................A1	Hoe Street............................D3	Notte Street..........................C3	Stillman Street.......................E3	
Battery Street.......................A2	Elliot Street...........................C4	Holyrood Place.....................C4	Octagon Street.....................B2	Stoke Road...........................A2	
Beaumont Avenue.................F1	Elliot Terrace........................C4	How Street............................E3	Old Town Street...................D2	Sussex Street.........................D3	
Beaumont Place....................E2	Essex Street...........................B1	Ilbert Street..........................B1	Osborne Place......................C4	Sutton Road..........................F3	
Beaumont Road....................F2	Eton Avenue.........................C1	James Street.........................E1	Oxford Street........................C1	Sydney Street........................B1	
Bilbury Street.......................E2	Eton Place............................C1	John Lane.............................D1	Palace Street.........................D3	Tavistock Place......................D1	
Blackfriars Lane....................D4	Exeter Street.........................D2	King Street...........................A2	Park Terrace.........................E2	Teats Hill Road.....................F4	
Boon's Place........................C1	Exeter Street.........................E2	Ladywell Place.....................F1	Parr Street............................F4	The Barbican........................E4	
Breton Side..........................D3	Flora Court...........................B2	Lambhay Hill.......................D4	Patna Place..........................B1	The Crescent........................B3	
Buckwell Street....................D3	Flora Street...........................B2	Lambhay Street.....................E4	Peacock Lane........................D3	The Esplanade......................C4	
Camden Street......................E1	Francis Street........................A2	Leigham Street......................B4	Penrose Street.......................B1	The Promenade.....................C4	
Castle Street.........................E4	Frederick Street East.............B2	Leigham Terrace Lane............B4	Phoenix Street......................A3	Tin Lane...............................E3	
Cathedral Street...................A2	Friar's Parade.......................D4	Lipson Road.........................F1	Pier Street............................B5	Tothill Avenue......................F1	
Catherine Street...................D3	Garden Crescent...................B5	Lockyers Quay......................F4	Place de Brest.......................C2	Tothill Road.........................F2	
Cecil Street..........................B1	Gasking Street......................E2	Lockyer Street......................C3	Plym Street..........................F1	Trafalgar Street.....................E2	
Central Road........................B5	George Street........................A3	Looe Street...........................E3	Princess Street......................C3	Union Place..........................A3	
Chapel Street........................E1	Gibbon Lane.........................E1	Madeira Road.......................D5	Princess Way........................C3	Union Street..........................A3	
Charles Cross.......................E2	Gibbons Street......................E1	Manor Gardens.....................A3	Prospect Place......................B4	Vauxhall Quay......................E3	
Charles Street.......................D2	Gilwell Street........................E1	Manor Street.........................A2	Prynne Close........................B2	Vauxhall Street......................E3	
Citadel Road........................B4	Glanville Street.....................D1	Market Avenue.....................C2	Quay Road...........................E4	Walker Terrace......................B4	
Citadel Road........................C4	Grand Hotel Road.................C4	Martin Street........................A3	Queen's Gate........................A1	Wantage Gardens..................A1	
Claremont Street...................C1	Grand Parade.......................B5	Mayflower Street...................C1	Radford Road.......................B5	Well Gardens........................B1	

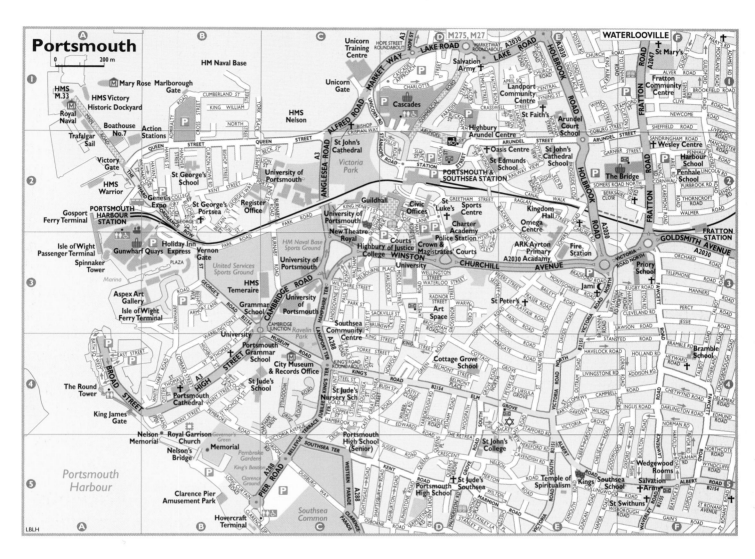

Portsmouth

Portsmouth is found on atlas page **14 H7**

Admiralty Road B2
Albany Road E5
Albert Grove E5
Albert Road E5
Alec Rose Lane D3
Alexandra Road E1
Alfred Road C1
Alver Road F1
Anglesea Road C2
Ariel Road F2
Armory Lane B3
Arundel Street D2
Arundel Street E2
Ashburton Road D5
Bailey's Road E3
Bath Square A4
Bellevue Terrace C5
Belmont Place D4
Bishop Crispian Way C2
Bishop Street B2
Blackfriars Road E2
Blount Road C4
Boulton Road F5
Bramble Road F4
Bridgeside Close E2
Britain Street B2
Broad Street A4
Brookfield Road F1
Brunswick Street C3
Buckingham Street D1
Cambridge Road C3
Campbell Road E4
Canal Walk E2
Carlisle Road E2
Cascades Approach D1
Castle Road C4

Cavendish Road E5
Central Street E1
Charlotte Street D1
Chelsea Road E5
Chester Place E5
Chetwynd Road F4
Church Road E1
Churchill Avenue D3
Claremont Road F2
Clarence Parade C5
Cleveland Road F3
Clive Road F1
Clock Street B2
College Street B2
Collingwood Road E5
Commercial Road D1
Cornwall Road F2
Cottage Grove D4
Cottage View E2
Crasswell Street D1
Cross Street B2
Cumberland Street B1
Curzon Howe Road B2
Darlington Road F4
Drummond Road E1
Duisburg Way C5
Duncan Road E5
Earlsdon Street D3
East Street A4
Eldon Street D4
Elm Grove D4
Elphinstone Road D5
Exmouth Road E5
Fawcett Road F3
Fawcett Road F4
Flint Street C4

Foster Road E1
Fratton Road F2
Gain's Road F5
Garnier Street E2
Goldsmith Avenue F3
Gold Street C4
Goodwood Road E5
Gordon Road C5
Great Southsea Street C4
Green Road D4
Greetham Street D2
Grosvenor Street D3
Grove Road North D4
Grove Road South D5
Guildford Road F1
Guildhall Walk C2
Gunwharf Road B3
Hambrook Street C4
Hampshire Terrace C3
Harold Road F5
Havant Street B2
Havelock Road E4
Hawke Street B2
Hereford Road E5
Highbury Street B4
High Street B4
Holbrook Road E1
Holland Road E4
Hudson Road E3
Hyde Park Road D3
Inglis Road E5
Jessie Road F3
Jubilee Terrace C4
Kent Road D5
Kent Street B2
King Albert Street E1
King Henry I Street C2
King's Road C4
King's Terrace C4
King Street C4
King William Street B1

Lake Road D1
Landport Street E1
Landport Terrace C3
Landsdowne Street C3
Lawrence Road F5
Lawson Road F3
Leopold Street F5
Lincoln Road F2
Little Southsea Street C4
Livingstone Road E4
Lombard Street B4
Londesborough Road F4
Lords Street E1
Lorne Road F4
Main Road A1
Manners Road F3
Margate Road D4
Market Way C1
Marmion Road D5
Mary Rose Street D2
Melbourne Place C3
Merton Road D5
Middle Street D3
Milford Road E2
Montgomerie Road E3
Moorland Road F1
Museum Road C4
Napier Road E5
Nelson Road D5
Newcome Road F1
Nightingale Road C5
Norfolk Street D4
Norman Road F4
Olinda Street F1
Orchard Road F3
Ordnance Row B2
Osborne Road C5
Outram Road E4
Oxford Road F5
Oyster Street B4
Pains Road E3

Palmerston Road D5
Paradise Street D1
Park Road B3
Pelham Road D4
Pembroke Road B4
Penhale Road F2
Penny Street B4
Percy Road F3
Pier Road C5
Playfair Road E3
Portland Road D5
Purbrook Road F2
Queens Crescent D5
Queen Street B2
Raglan Street E2
Railway View E2
Richmond Place D5
Rivers Street D3
Rugby Road F3
Sackville Street C3
St Andrews Road E4
St Bartholomews Gardens ... E4
St Davids Road E4
St Edwards Road D4
St Faith's Road D1
St George's Road B3
St George's Square B2
St George's Way B2
St James's Road D3
St James's Street B2
St Nicholas Street B4
St Paul's Road C3
St Peters Grove E4
St Thomas's Street B4
Sandringham Road E1
Shaftesbury Road C5
Somers Road D4
Somers Road E3
Somers Road North E2
Southsea Terrace C5
Stafford Road E4

Stamford Street E1
Stanhope Road D2
Stansted Road E4
Station Street D2
Steel Street C4
Stone Street C4
Sussex Road D5
Sutherland Road F4
Talbot Road F4
Telephone Road F3
Temple Street D1
The Hard A2
The Retreat D5
The Thicket D4
Thorncroft Road F2
Tottenham Road F1
Trevor Road F4
Unicorn Road C1
Upper Arundel Street D2
Victoria Avenue C5
Victoria Grove E4
Victoria Road North E4
Victoria Road North F3
Victoria Road South E5
Vivash Road F2
Walmer Road F2
Warblington Street B4
Warwick Crescent D3
Waterloo Street D3
Waverley Road F5
Western Parade C5
West Street A4
White Hart Road B4
Wilson Grove E4
Wiltshire Street C3
Winston Churchill Avenue ... D3
Wisborough Road E5
Woodpath D4
Woodville Drive C4
Yarborough Road D4
Yorke Street C4

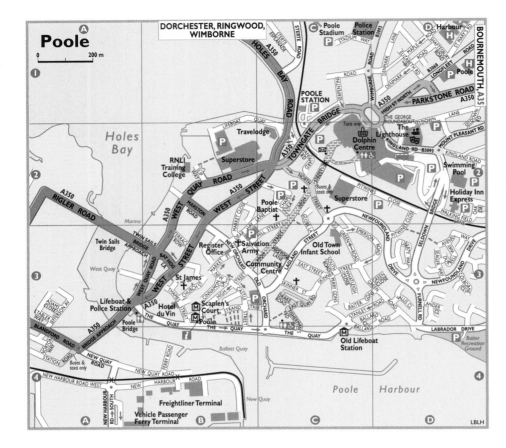

Poole

Poole is found on atlas page **12 H6**

Adams Close	A3	New Harbour Road West	A4
Avenel Way	D3	New Orchard	B3
Baiter Gardens	C3	New Quay Road	A4
Ballard Close	C3	New Street	B3
Ballard Road	C4	North Street	C2
Bay Hog Lane	B3	Norton Way	A4
Blandford Road	A3	Oak Drive	D2
Bridge Approach	A4	Old Orchard	B3
Castle Street	B3	Parkstone Road	D1
Chapel Lane	C2	Perry Gardens	C3
Church Street	B3	Pitwines Close	C2
Cinnamon Lane	B3	Poole Bridge	A3
Colborne Close	D3	Rigler Road	A2
Dear Hay Lane	B3	St Mary's Road	D1
Denmark Lane	D1	Seager Way	D3
Denmark Road	D1	Seldown Bridge	D3
Drake Road	C3	Seldown Lane	D2
Durrell Way	D3	Seldown Road	D2
East Quay Road	C3	Serpentine Road	C1
East Street	C3	Shaftesbury Road	D1
Elizabeth Road	D1	Skinner Street	C3
Emerson Road	C3	Slip Way	B2
Ferry Road	B4	South Road	C3
Fisherman's Road	C3	Stabler Way	A3
Furnell Road	D3	Stadium Way	C1
Globe Lane	C2	Stanley Road	C3
Green Close	D3	Sterte Esplanade	C1
Green Road	C3	Sterte Road	C1
High Street	B3	Strand Street	B3
High Street North	D1	Terrace Row	B3
Hill Street	C3	Thames Street	B3
Holes Bay Road	C1	The Quay	B3
Jefferson Avenue	A3	Towngate Bridge	C2
Kingland Road	D2	Twin Sails Bridge Approach	A3
Labrador Drive	D4	Twin Sails Bridge	A3
Lagland Street	C3	Vallis Close	D3
Lander Close	D3	Vanguard Road	C2
Liberty Way	D3	Walking Field Lane	D2
Lifeboat Quay	B2	Westons Lane	C3
Longfleet Road	D1	West Quay Road	B2
Maple Road	D1	West Street	B3
Market Close	B2	Whatleigh Close	C3
Market Street	B3	Wimborne Road	D1
Marston Road	B2		
Mount Pleasant Road	D2		
Newfoundland Drive	C2		
New Harbour Road	A4		
New Harbour Road South	A4		

Preston

Preston is found on atlas page **88 G5**

Adelphi Street	A1	Holstein Street	D1
Arthur Street	A3	Hopwood Street	D2
Avenham Lane	C4	Jutland Street	D1
Avenham Road	C3	Lancaster Road	C2
Avenham Street	C3	Lancaster Road North	C1
Berwick Road	C4	Latham Street	C4
Birley Street	C2	Lawson Street	B1
Boltons Court	C3	Leighton Street	A2
Bow Lane	A3	Lund Street	C1
Butler Street	B3	Lune Street	B3
Cannon Street	C3	Main Sprit Weind	C3
Carlisle Street	C2	Manchester Road	D3
Chaddock Street	C4	Market Street	C2
Chapel Street	B3	Market Street West	B2
Charlotte Street	D4	Marsh Lane	A2
Cheapside	C3	Maudland Road	A1
Christ Church Street	A3	Meadow Street	C1
Church Street	C3	Moor Lane	B1
Clarendon Street	D4	Mount Street	B3
Corporation Street	B2	North Road	C1
Corporation Street	B3	Oak Street	D3
Craggs Row	B1	Ormskirk Road	C2
Cross Street	C3	Oxford Street	C3
Crown Street	B1	Pedder Street	A1
Deepdale Road	D1	Percy Street	D2
Derby Street	D2	Pitt Street	A3
Earl Street	C2	Pole Street	D2
East Cliff	B4	Pump Street	D1
East Street	D1	Queen Street	D3
Edmund Street	D2	Ribblesdale Place	B4
Edward Street	A2	Ring Way	B2
Elizabeth Street	B1	Rose Street	D3
Fishergate	B3	St Austin's Road	D3
Fishergate Hill	A4	St Paul's Road	D1
Fleet Street	B3	St Paul's Square	D1
Fox Street	B3	St Peter's Street	B1
Friargate	B2	Sedgwick Street	C1
Friargate	C2	Selborne Street	D4
Fylde Road	A1	Shepherd Street	D3
Glover's Court	C3	Snow Hill	B2
Glover Street	C3	Syke Street	C3
Great Avenham Street	C4	Tithebarn Street	C2
Great Shaw Street	B2	Walker Street	B1
Grimshaw Street	D2	Walton's Parade	A3
Guildhall Street	C3	Ward's End	C2
Harrington Street	B1	Warwick Street	B1
Heatley Street	B2	West Cliff	A4
Herschell Street	D4	Winkley Square	B3

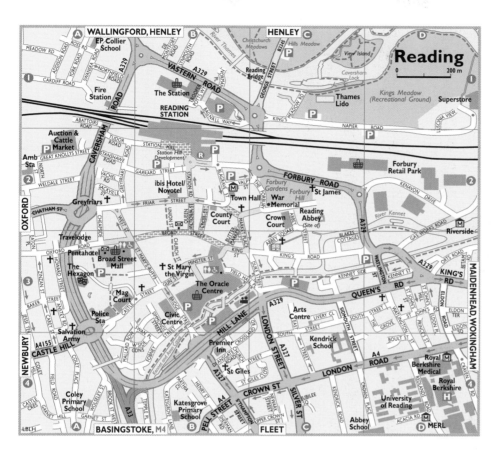

Reading

Reading is found on atlas page **35 K10**

Abbey Square	C3	King's Meadow Road	C1
Abbey Street	C2	King's Road	D3
Addison Road	A1	King Street	B3
Anstey Road	A3	Livery Close	C3
Baker Street	A3	London Road	C4
Blagrave Street	B2	London Street	C3
Blakes Cottages	C3	Mallard Row	A4
Boult Street	D4	Market Place	B2
Bridge Street	B3	Mill Lane	B4
Broad Street	B3	Minster Street	B3
Brook Street West	A4	Napier Road	C1
Buttermarket	B3	Newark Street	C4
Cardiff Road	A1	Northfield Road	A1
Carey Street	A3	Oxford Road	A3
Castle Hill	A4	Parthia Close	B4
Castle Street	A3	Pell Street	B4
Caversham Road	A2	Prince's Street	D3
Chatham Street	A2	Queen's Road	C3
Cheapside	A2	Queen Victoria Street	B2
Church Street	B3	Redlands Road	D4
Church Street	B4	Ross Road	A1
Coley Place	A4	Sackville Street	A2
Craven Road	D4	St Giles Close	B4
Crossland Road	B4	St John's Road	D3
Cross Street	B2	St Mary's Butts	B3
Crown Street	C4	Sidmouth Street	C3
Deansgate Road	B4	Silver Street	C4
Duke Street	C3	Simmonds Street	B3
East Street	C3	Southampton Street	B4
Eldon Road	D3	South Street	C3
Field Road	A4	Station Hill	B2
Fobney Street	B4	Station Road	B2
Forbury Road	C2	Swan Place	B3
Friar Street	B2	Swansea Road	A1
Garnet Street	A4	The Forbury	C2
Garrard Street	B2	Tudor Road	A2
Gas Works Road	D3	Union Street	B2
George Street	C1	Upper Crown Street	C4
Great Knollys Street	A2	Vachel Road	A2
Greyfriars Road	A2	Valpy Street	B2
Gun Street	B3	Vastern Road	B1
Henry Street	B4	Watlington Street	D3
Howard Street	A3	Weldale Street	A2
Katesgrove Lane	B4	West Street	A2
Kenavon Drive	D2	Wolseley Street	A4
Kendrick Road	C4	Yield Hall Place	B3
Kennet Side	C3	York Road	A1
Kennet Street	D3	Zinzan Street	A3

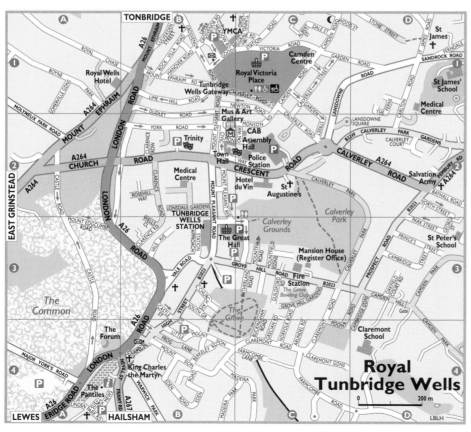

Royal Tunbridge Wells

Royal Tunbridge Wells is found on atlas page **25 N3**

Albert Street	C1	Lansdowne Road	C2
Arundel Road	C4	Lime Hill Road	B1
Bayhall Road	D2	Linden Park Road	A4
Belgrave Road	C1	Little Mount Sion	B4
Berkeley Road	B4	London Road	A2
Boyne Park	A1	Lonsdale Gardens	B2
Buckingham Road	C4	Madeira Park	B4
Calverley Park	C2	Major York's Road	A4
Calverley Park Gardens	D2	Meadow Road	B1
Calverley Road	C2	Molyneux Park Road	A1
Calverley Street	C2	Monson Road	C2
Cambridge Gardens	D4	Monson Way	B2
Cambridge Street	D3	Mount Edgcumbe Road	A3
Camden Hill	D3	Mount Ephraim	A2
Camden Park	D3	Mount Ephraim Road	B1
Camden Road	C1	Mountfield Gardens	C3
Carlton Road	D2	Mountfield Road	C3
Castle Road	A2	Mount Pleasant Avenue	B2
Castle Street	B3	Mount Pleasant Road	B2
Chapel Place	B4	Mount Sion	B4
Christchurch Avenue	B3	Nevill Street	B4
Church Road	A2	Newton Road	B1
Civic Way	B2	Norfolk Road	C4
Claremont Gardens	C4	North Street	D2
Claremont Road	C4	Oakfield Court Road	D3
Clarence Road	B2	Park Street	D3
Crescent Road	C2	Pembury Road	D2
Culverden Street	B1	Poona Road	C4
Dale Street	C1	Prince's Street	D3
Dudley Road	B1	Prospect Road	D3
Eden Road	B4	Rock Villa Road	B1
Eridge Road	A4	Royal Chase	A1
Farmcombe Lane	C4	St James' Road	D1
Farmcombe Road	C4	Sandrock Road	D1
Ferndale	D1	Somerville Gardens	A1
Frant Road	A4	South Green	B3
Frog Lane	B4	Station Approach	B3
Garden Road	C1	Stone Street	D1
Garden Street	C1	Sussex Mews	A4
George Street	C1	Sutherland Road	C3
Goods Station Road	B1	Tunnel Road	C1
Grecian Road	C4	Upper Grosvenor Road	B1
Grosvenor Road	B1	Vale Avenue	B3
Grove Hill Gardens	C3	Vale Road	B3
Grove Hill Road	C3	Victoria Road	C1
Guildford Road	C3	Warwick Park	B4
Hanover Road	B1	Wood Street	C1
High Street	B4	York Road	B2

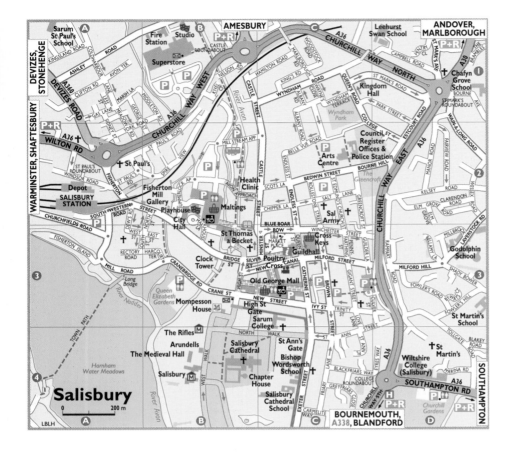

Salisbury

Salisbury is found on atlas page **21 M9**

Albany Road	C1	Kingsland Road	A1
Ashley Road	A1	King's Road	C1
Avon Approach	B2	Laverstock Road	D3
Bedwin Street	C2	Malthouse Lane	B3
Belle Vue Road	C2	Manor Road	D2
Blackfriars Way	C4	Marlborough Road	C1
Blue Boar Row	C3	Meadow Road	A1
Bourne Avenue	D1	Middleton Road	A1
Bourne Hill	C2	Milford Hill	D3
Bridge Street	B3	Milford Street	C3
Brown Street	C3	Mill Road	A3
Campbell Road	D1	Minster Street	C3
Castle Street	B1	Nelson Road	B1
Catherine Street	C3	New Canal	B3
Chipper Lane	C2	New Street	B3
Churchfields Road	A2	North Street	C3
Churchill Way East	D3	Park Street	D1
Churchill Way North	C1	Pennyfarthing Street	C3
Churchill Way South	C4	Queen's Road	C1
Churchill Way West	B2	Queen Street	C3
Clarendon Road	D2	Rampart Road	D3
Clifton Road	A1	Rectory Road	A3
Coldharbour Lane	A1	Rollestone Street	C2
College Street	C1	St Ann Street	C4
Cranebridge Road	B3	St Edmund's Church Street	C2
Crane Street	B3	St Mark's Avenue	D1
Devizes Road	A1	St Mark's Road	D1
Dew's Road	A3	St Paul's Road	B2
East Street	B3	Salt Lane	C2
Elm Grove	D2	Scots Lane	C2
Elm Grove Road	D2	Sidney Street	A1
Endless Street	C2	Silver Street	B3
Estcourt Road	D2	Southampton Road	D4
Exeter Street	C4	South Street	A3
Eyres Way	D4	South Western Road	A2
Fairview Road	D2	Spire View	B2
Fisherton Street	A2	Summerlock Approach	B2
Fowler's Road	D3	Tollgate Road	D4
Friary Lane	C4	Trinity Street	C3
Gas Lane	A1	Wain-A-Long Road	D1
George Street	A1	Wessex Road	D2
Gigant Street	C3	West Street	A3
Greencroft Street	C2	Wilton Road	A2
Guilder Lane	C3	Winchester Street	C3
Hamilton Road	C1	Windsor Road	A2
High Street	B3	Woodstock Road	C1
Ivy Street	C3	Wyndham Road	C1
Kelsey Road	D2	York Road	A2

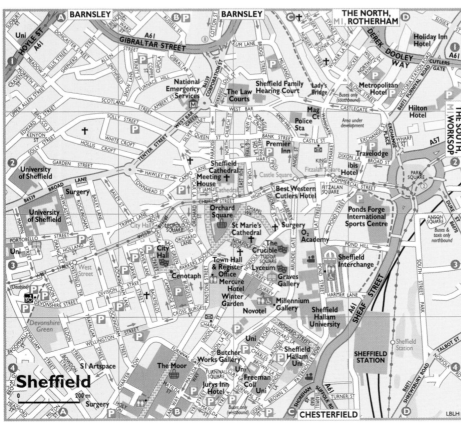

Sheffield

Sheffield is found on atlas page **84 E3**

Angel Street	C2	Howard Street	C4
Arundel Gate	C3	Hoyle Street	A1
Arundel Street	C4	King Street	C2
Backfields	B3	Lambert Street	B1
Bailey Street	A2	Leopold Street	B3
Balm Green	B3	Mappin Street	A3
Bank Street	C2	Meetinghouse Lane	C2
Barkers Pool	B3	Mulberry Street	C2
Broad Lane	A2	Newcastle Street	A2
Broad Street	D2	New Street	C2
Brown Street	C4	Norfolk Street	C3
Cambridge Street	B3	North Church Street	B2
Campo Lane	B2	Orchard Street	B3
Carver Street	B3	Paradise Street	B2
Castlegate	C1	Pinstone Street	B3
Castle Street	C2	Pond Hill	C3
Charles Street	B4	Pond Street	C3
Charter Row	B4	Portobello Street	A3
Church Street	B2	Queen Street	B2
Commercial Street	C2	Rockingham Street	A2
Corporation Street	B1	St James Street	B2
Cross Burgess Street	B3	Scargill Croft	C2
Cutlers Gate	D1	Scotland Street	A1
Derek Dooley Way	D1	Sheaf Street	D4
Devonshire Street	A3	Shoreham Street	C4
Division Street	A3	Shrewsbury Road	D4
Dixon Lane	C2	Silver Street	B2
Duke Street	D2	Smithfield	A1
Exchange Street	D2	Snig Hill	C2
Eyre Street	B4	Solly Street	A2
Fig Tree Lane	C2	South Street Park	D3
Fitzwilliam Street	A4	Suffolk Road	C4
Flat Street	C3	Surrey Street	C3
Furnace Hill	B1	Talbot Street	D4
Furnival Gate	B4	Tenter Street	B2
Furnival Road	D1	Townhead Street	B2
Furnival Street	C4	Trafalgar Street	A4
Garden Street	A2	Trippet Lane	B3
George Street	C2	Union Street	B4
Gibralter Street	B1	Vicar Lane	B2
Harmer Lane	C3	Victoria Station Road	D1
Harts Head	C2	Waingate	C2
Hawley Street	B2	Wellington Street	A4
Haymarket	C2	West Bar	B2
High Street	C2	West Bar Green	B2
Holland Street	A3	West Street	A3
Hollis Croft	A2	White Croft	A2
Holly Street	B3	York Street	C2

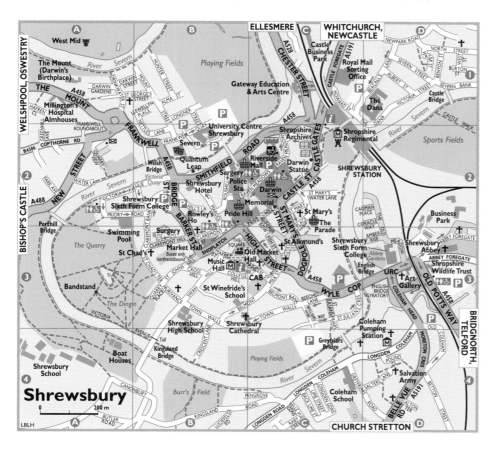

Shrewsbury

Shrewsbury is found on atlas page **56 H2**

Abbey Foregate	D3	Mardol	B2
Albert Street	D1	Market Street	B3
Alma Street	B1	Milk Street	C3
Amber Rise	D3	Moreton Crescent	D4
Barker Street	B2	Mount Street	B1
Beacall's Lane	D1	Murivance	B3
Beeches Lane	C3	Nettles Lane	B1
Belle Vue Gardens	C4	Newpark Road	D1
Belle Vue Road	D4	New Street	A2
Belmont	B3	North Street	D1
Belmont Bank	C3	Old Coleham	D3
Benyon Street	D1	Old Potts Way	D3
Betton Street	D4	Park Avenue	A2
Bridge Street	B2	Pengrove	C4
Burton Street	D1	Pound Close	D4
Butcher Row	C2	Pride Hill	C2
Canonbury	A4	Princess Street	B3
Castle Foregate	C1	Priory Road	A2
Castle Gates	C2	Quarry Place	B3
Castle Street	C2	Quarry View	A2
Chester Street	C1	Raven Meadows	B2
Claremont Bank	B3	Roushill	B2
Claremont Hill	B3	St Chad's Terrace	B3
Claremont Street	B3	St George's Street	A1
Coleham Head	D3	St Johns Hill	B3
College Hill	B3	St Julians Crescent	C3
Copthorne Road	A2	St Julians Friars	C3
Coracle Way	D2	St Mary's Place	C2
Crescent Lane	B4	St Mary's Street	C2
Cross Hill	B3	St Mary's Water Lane	C2
Darwin Gardens	A1	Salters Lane	D4
Darwin Street	A1	Severn Bank	D1
Dogpole	C3	Severn Street	D1
Drinkwater Street	A1	Shoplatch	B3
Fish Street	C3	Smithfield Road	B2
Frankwell	A2	Swan Hill	B3
Frankwell Quay	B2	The Dana	D1
Greenhill Avenue	A2	The Mount	A1
Greyfriars Road	C4	The Old Meadow	D3
High Street	C3	The Square	B3
Hill's Lane	B2	Town Walls	B3
Howard Street	C1	Victoria Avenue	A2
Hunter Street	B1	Victoria Street	D1
Kingsland Road	B4	Water Lane	A2
Lime Street	C4	Water Street	D1
Longden Coleham	C4	West Street	D1
Longden Road	C4	Williams Way	C3
Longner Street	B1	Wyle Cop	C3

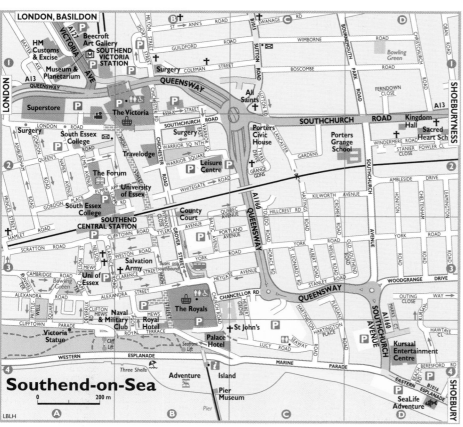

Southend-on-Sea

Southend-on-Sea is found on atlas page **38 E4**

Albert Road	C3	Lancaster Gardens	C2
Alexandra Road	A3	Leamington Road	D2
Alexandra Street	A3	London Road	A2
Ambleside Drive	D2	Lucy Road	C4
Ashburnham Road	A2	Luker Road	A2
Baltic Avenue	B3	Marine Parade	C4
Baxter Avenue	A1	Milton Street	B1
Beach Road	D4	Napier Avenue	A2
Boscombe Road	C1	Nelson Street	A3
Bournemouth Park Road	D1	Oban Road	D1
Cambridge Road	A3	Old Southend Road	D3
Capel Terrace	A3	Outing Close	D3
Chancellor Road	B3	Pitmans Close	B2
Cheltenham Road	D2	Pleasant Road	C3
Chichester Road	B1	Portland Avenue	B3
Christchurch Road	D1	Princes Street	A2
Church Road	B3	Prittlewell Square	A3
Clarence Road	A3	Quebec Avenue	B2
Clarence Street	B3	Queen's Road	A2
Clifftown Parade	A4	Queensway	A1
Clifftown Road	B3	Queensway	C3
Coleman Street	B1	Royal Terrace	B4
Cromer Road	C2	Runwell Terrace	A3
Devereux Road	A4	St Ann's Road	B1
Eastern Esplanade	D4	St Leonard's Road	C3
Elmer Approach	A2	Scratton Road	A3
Elmer Avenue	A2	Short Street	B1
Essex Street	B1	Southchurch Avenue	D2
Ferndown Close	D1	Southchurch Road	B2
Fowler Close	D2	Stanier Close	D2
Gordon Place	A2	Stanley Road	C3
Gordon Road	A2	Sutton Road	C1
Grange Gardens	C2	Swanage Road	C1
Grover Street	B3	Toledo Road	C2
Guildford Road	B1	Tylers Avenue	B3
Hamlet Road	A3	Tyrrel Drive	C2
Hartington Place	C4	Victoria Avenue	A1
Hartington Road	C3	Warrior Square East	B2
Hastings Road	C2	Warrior Square North	B2
Hawtree Close	D4	Warrior Square	B2
Herbert Grove	C3	Wesley Road	C3
Heygate Avenue	B3	Western Esplanade	A4
High Street	B2	Weston Road	B3
Hillcrest Road	C2	Whitegate Road	B2
Honiton Road	D2	Wimborne Road	C1
Horace Road	C3	Windermere Road	D2
Kilworth Avenue	C2	Woodgrange Drive	D3
Kursaal Way	D4	York Road	B3

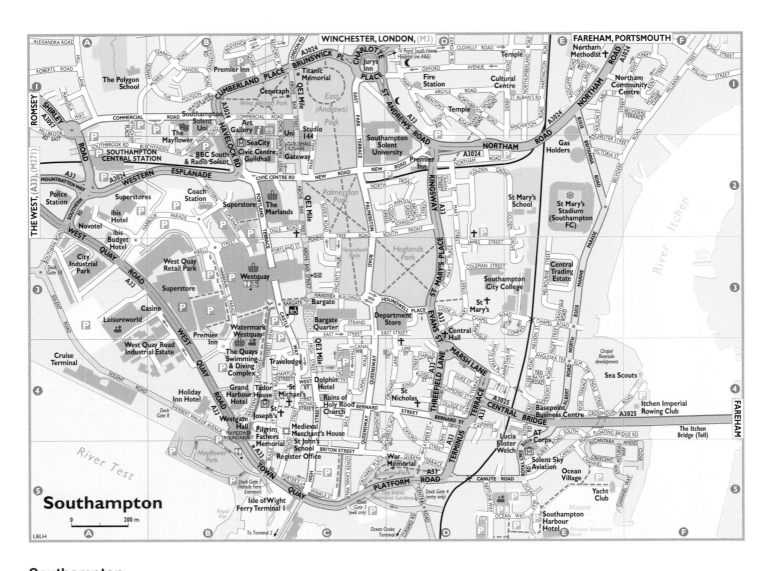

Southampton

Southampton is found on atlas page **14 D4**

Above Bar Street	C1
Albert Road North	E4
Albert Road South	E5
Alcantara Crescent	E5
Alexandra Road	A1
Anderson's Road	E4
Andes Close	F5
Anglesea Terrace	E4
Argyle Road	D1
Asturias Way	E5
Augustine Road	E1
Back Of The Walls	C4
Bargate Street	C3
Bedford Place	C1
Bell Street	D4
Belvidere Road	E2
Belvidere Terrace	F1
Bernard Street	C4
Blechynden Terrace	B2
Bond Street	F1
Brinton's Road	D1
Britannia Road	E1
Briton Street	C5
Broad Green	D2
Brunswick Place	C1
Brunswick Square	C4
Bugle Street	C5
Cable Street	E1
Canal Walk	C4
Canute Road	D5
Captains Place	D4
Carpathia Drive	D4
Castle Way	C3
Central Bridge	D4
Central Road	D5
Challis Court	D4

Channel Way	E5
Chapel Road	D3
Charlotte Place	C1
Civic Centre Road	B2
Clovelly Road	D1
Coleman Street	D3
College Street	D4
Commercial Road	A1
Cook Street	D3
Cossack Green	D2
Craven Street	D2
Crosshouse Road	E4
Cumberland Place	B1
Cunard Road	D5
Derby Road	E1
Devonshire Road	B1
Duke Street	D4
Eastgate Street	C4
East Park Terrace	C1
East Street	C3
Elm Terrace	E4
Endle Street	E4
Evans Street	D3
Exmoor Road	D1
Floating Bridge Road	E4
Forest View	C4
French Street	C5
Glebe Road	E4
Golden Grove	D2
Granville Road	E3
Grosvenor Square	B1
Hamtun Street	C4
Handel Road	B1
Handel Terrace	B1
Hanover Buildings	C3
Harbour Parade	B2

Hartington Road	E1
Havelock Road	B1
Herbert Walker Avenue	B4
High Street	C4
Hill Lane	A1
Houndwell Place	D3
Howell Close	F1
Itchen Bridge	F4
James Street	D3
Johnson Street	D2
John Street	D5
Kent Street	F1
King Street	D4
Kingsway	D2
Latimer Street	D5
Lime Street	D4
London Road	C1
Lower Canal Walk	C5
Lumpy Lane	E1
Mandela Way	A1
Marine Parade	E3
Marsh Lane	D4
Maryfield	D3
Mayflower Roundabout	B4
Melbourne Street	E3
Millbank Street	F1
Morris Road	B1
Mountbatten Way	A2
Nelson Street	E4
Neptune Way	D5
New Road	C2
Nichols Road	D1
Northam Road	D2
Northbrook Road	D1
North Front	C2

Northumberland Road	E1
Ocean Way	D5
Ogle Road	C2
Orchard Place	C5
Oxford Avenue	D1
Oxford Street	D4
Paget Street	E4
Palmerston Road	C2
Park Walk	C2
Peel Street	E1
Pirelli Street	B3
Platform Road	C5
Porter's Lane	C5
Portland Street	C3
Portland Terrace	B2
Pound Tree Road	C3
Queens Terrace	D5
Queensway	C4
Radcliffe Road	E1
Richmond Street	D4
Roberts Road	A1
Rochester Street	E2
Royal Crescent Road	E5
Russell Street	D4
Ryde Terrace	E4
St Alban's Road	E1
St Andrews Road	D1
St Marks Road	D1
St Mary's Place	D3
St Mary's Road	D1
St Mary Street	D2
St Michael Street	C4
Shirley Road	A1
Solent Road	A3
Southbrook Road	A2
Southern Road	A2

South Front	C2
Strand	C3
Sussex Road	C2
Ted Bates Road	E4
Terminus Terrace	D5
The Compass	D3
The Polygon	B1
Threefield Lane	D4
Town Quay	B5
Trinity Road	D1
Upper Bugle Street	C4
Victoria Street	E2
Vincent's Walk	C3
Water Lane	B1
Western Esplanade	A2
Western Esplanade	B4
West Marlands Road	C2
West Park Road	B2
West Quay Road	A2
West Street	C4
White Star Place	D4
William Street	F1
Wilson Street	E1
Winkle Street	C5
Winton Street	D2
Wolverton Road	E1
Wyndham Place	A1

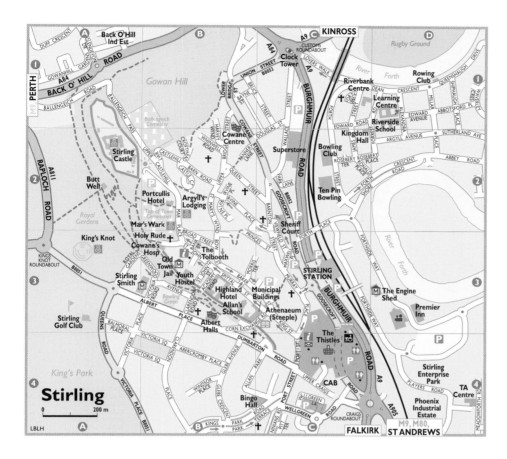

Stirling

Stirling is found on atlas page **133 M9**

Abbey Road	D2	James Street	C2
Abbotsford Place	D1	Kings Knot Roundabout	A3
Abercromby Place	B4	Kings Park Road	B4
Academy Road	B3	King Street	C3
Albert Place	A3	Lovers Walk	C1
Alexandra Place	D1	Lower Bridge Street	B1
Allan Park	B4	Lower Castlehill	B2
Argyll Avenue	D2	Mar Place	B2
Back O' Hill Road	A1	Maxwell Place	C3
Baker Street	B3	Meadowforth Road	D4
Ballengeich Road	A1	Millar Place	D1
Ballengeich Pass	A1	Morris Terrace	B3
Balmoral Place	A3	Murray Place	C3
Bank Street	B3	Ninians Road	C4
Barn Road	B2	Park Lane	C2
Barnton Street	C2	Park Terrace	B4
Bayne Street	B1	Players Road	D4
Bow Street	B3	Port Street	C4
Broad Street	B3	Princes Street	B3
Bruce Street	B1	Queenshaugh Drive	D1
Burghmuir Road	C1	Queens Road	A3
Castle Court	B2	Queen Street	B2
Clarendon Place	B4	Raploch Road	A2
Clarendon Road	B3	Ronald Place	C2
Corn Exchange Road	B3	Rosebery Place	C2
Cowane Street	B1	Rosebery Terrace	C2
Craigs Roundabout	C4	Royal Gardens	A3
Crofthead Court	B2	St John Street	B3
Customs Roundabout	C1	St Mary's Wynd	B2
Dean Crescent	D1	Shiphaugh Place	D1
Douglas Street	C2	Shore Road	C2
Dumbarton Road	B4	Spittal Street	B3
Edward Avenue	D1	Sutherland Avenue	D2
Edward Road	C1	Tannery Lane	B2
Forrest Road	D2	Union Street	B1
Forth Crescent	C2	Upper Bridge Street	B2
Forthside Way	C3	Upper Castlehill	A2
Forth Street	C1	Upper Craigs	C4
Forth Place	C3	Victoria Place	A4
Forth View	C1	Victoria Road	B3
Glebe Avenue	B4	Victoria Square	A4
Glebe Crescent	B4	Viewfield Street	C2
Glendevon Drive	A1	Wallace Street	C2
Goosecroft Road	C2	Waverley Crescent	D1
Gowanhill Gardens	A1	Wellgreen Lane	C4
Greenwood Avenue	A3	Wellgreen Road	C4
Harvey Wynd	B1	Whinwell Road	B2
Irvine Place	B2	Windsor Place	B4

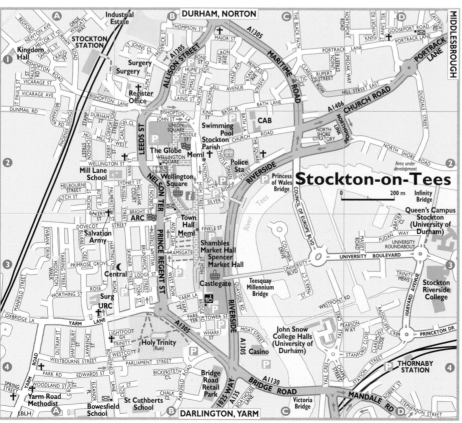

Stockton-on-Tees

Stockton-on-Tees is found on atlas page **104 D7**

1825 Way	B4	Massey Road	D3
Allison Street	B1	Melbourne Street	A2
Alma Street	B1	Middle Street	B2
Bath Lane	C1	Mill Street West	A2
Bedford Street	A1	Nelson Terrace	B2
Bishop Street	B2	North Shore Road	D2
Bishopton Lane	A1	Northport Road	D1
Bishopton Road	A1	Northshore Link	C2
Bowesfield Lane	A4	Norton Road	B1
Bridge Road	B3	Palmerston Street	A2
Bridge Road	C4	Park Road	A4
Bright Street	B2	Park Terrace	C3
Britannia Road	A1	Parkfield Road	B4
Brunswick Street	B3	Parliament Street	B4
Bute Street	A2	Portrack Lane	D1
Church Road	D1	Prince Regent Street	B3
Clarence Row	C1	Princess Avenue	C1
Corportion Street	A2	Princeton Drive	D4
Council of Europe		Quayside Road	C3
Boulevard	C2	Raddcliffe Crescent	D3
Cromwell Avenue	B1	Ramsgate	B3
Dixon Street	A2	Riverside	C3
Dovecot Street	A3	Russell Street	B2
Dugdale Street	D1	St Paul's Street	A1
Durham Road	A1	Silver Street	B2
Durham Street	A2	Skinner Street	B3
Edwards Street	A4	Station Street	D4
Farrer Street	B1	Sydney Street	B2
Finkle Street	B3	The Square	D2
Frederick Street	B1	Thistle Green	C2
Fudan Way	D3	Thomas Street	B1
Gooseport Road	D1	Thompson Street	B1
Hartington Road	A3	Tower Street	B4
Harvard Avenue	D3	Union Street East	C1
High Street	B2	University Boulevard	C3
Hill Street East	D1	Vane Street	B2
Hume Street	B1	Vicarage Street	A1
Hutchinson Street	A2	Wellington Street	A2
John Street	B2	West Row	B3
King Street	B2	Westbourne Street	A4
Knightport Road	D1	Westpoint Road	C3
Knowles Street	C2	Wharf Street	B4
Laing Street	B1	William Street	B3
Leeds Street	B2	Woodland Street	A4
Lobdon Street	B2	Worthing Street	A3
Lodge Street	B3	Yale Crescent	C4
Mandale Road	D4	Yarm Lane	A4
Maritime Road	C1	Yarm Road	A4

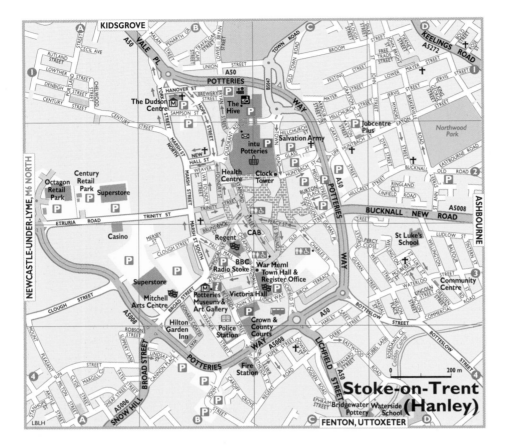

Stoke-on-Trent (Hanley)

Stoke-on-Trent (Hanley) is found on atlas page **70 F5**

Albion Street	B3	Linfield Road	D2
Bagnall Street	B3	Lower Mayer Street	D1
Balfour Street	D3	Lowther Street	A1
Baskerville Road	D1	Ludlow Street	D3
Bathesda Street	B4	Malam Street	B1
Bernard Street	C4	Marsh Street	B2
Bethesda Street	B3	Marsh Street North	B2
Birch Terrace	C3	Marsh Street South	B3
Botteslow Street	C3	Mayer Street	C1
Broad Street	B4	Mersey Street	B3
Broom Street	C1	Milton Street	A4
Brunswick Street	B3	Mount Pleasant	A4
Bryan Street	B1	Mynors Street	D1
Bucknall New Road	C2	New Hall Street	B2
Bucknall Old Road	D2	Ogden Road	C4
Cardiff Grove	B4	Old Hall Street	C3
Century Street	A1	Old Town Road	C1
Charles Street	C3	Pall Mall	B3
Cheapside	B3	Percy Street	C2
Chelwood Street	A1	Piccadilly	B3
Clough Street	A3	Portland Street	A1
Clyde Street	A4	Potteries Way	B1
Commercial Road	D3	Potteries Way	B4
Denbigh Street	A1	Quadrant Road	B2
Derby Street	B3	Regent Road	C4
Dyke Street	D2	Rutland Street	A1
Eastwood Road	C4	St John Street	D1
Eaton Street	D2	St Luke Street	D3
Etruria Road	A2	Sampson Street	B1
Foundry Street	B2	Sheaf Street	A4
Garth Street	C2	Slippery Lane	A4
Gilman Street	C3	Snow Hill	A4
Goodson Street	C2	Stafford Street	B2
Grafton Street	C1	Sun Street	A4
Hanover Street	B1	Tontine Street	C3
Harley Street	C4	Town Road	C2
Hillchurch	C2	Trafalgar Street	B1
Hillcrest Street	C2	Trinity Street	B2
Hinde Street	B4	Union Street	B1
Hope Street	B1	Upper Hillchurch Street	C2
Hordley Street	C3	Upper Huntbach Street	C2
Huntbach Street	C2	Warner Street	B3
Jasper Street	C4	Waterloo Street	D3
Jervis Street	D1	Well Street	D3
John Street	B3	Wellington Road	D3
Keelings Road	D1	Wellington Street	D3
Lichfield Street	C3	Yates Street	A4
Lidice Way	C3	York Street	B1

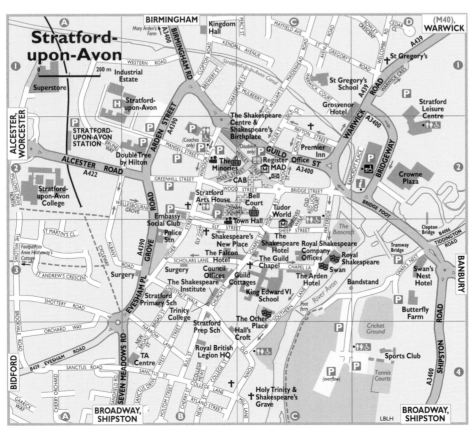

Stratford-upon-Avon

Stratford-upon-Avon is found on atlas page **47 P3**

Albany Road	A3	New Broad Street	B4
Alcester Road	A2	New Street	B4
Arden Street	B2	Old Red Lion Court	C2
Avenue Road	C1	Old Town	C4
Bancroft Place	C2	Orchard Way	A4
Birmingham Road	B1	Payton Street	C2
Brewery Street	B1	Percy Street	C1
Bridge Foot	D2	Rother Street	B3
Bridge Street	C2	Rowley Crescent	D1
Bridgeway	D2	Ryland Street	B4
Broad Street	B4	St Andrew's Crescent	A3
Brookvale Road	A4	St Gregory's Road	C1
Brunel Way	A2	St Martin's Close	A3
Bull Street	B4	Sanctus Drive	B4
Cedar Close	D1	Sanctus Road	A4
Chapel Lane	C3	Sanctus Street	B4
Chapel Street	C3	Sandfield Road	A4
Cherry Orchard	A4	Scholars Lane	B3
Cherry Street	B4	Seven Meadows Road	A4
Chestnut Walk	B3	Shakespeare Street	B1
Church Street	B3	Sheep Street	C3
Clopton Bridge	D3	Shipston Road	D4
Clopton Road	B1	Shottery Road	A3
College Lane	B4	Shrieves Walk	C3
College Mews	B4	Southern Lane	C3
College Street	B4	Swan's Nest	D3
Ely Gardens	B3	The Willows	A3
Ely Street	B3	Tiddington Road	D3
Evesham Place	B3	Town Square	B2
Evesham Road	A4	Tramway Bridge	D3
Garrick Way	A4	Tyler Street	C2
Great William Street	C1	Union Street	C2
Greenhill Street	B2	Warwick Court	C1
Grove Road	B3	Warwick Crescent	D1
Guild Street	C2	Warwick Road	C2
Henley Street	C2	Waterside	C3
High Street	C3	Welcombe Road	D1
Holtom Street	B4	Wellesbourne Grove	B2
John Street	C2	Western Road	B1
Kendall Avenue	B1	West Street	B4
Lock Close	C2	Willows Drive North	A2
Maidenhead Road	C1	Windsor Street	B2
Mansell Street	B2	Wood Street	B2
Mayfield Avenue	C1		
Meer Street	B2		
Mill Lane	C4		
Mulberry Street	C1		
Narrow Lane	B4		

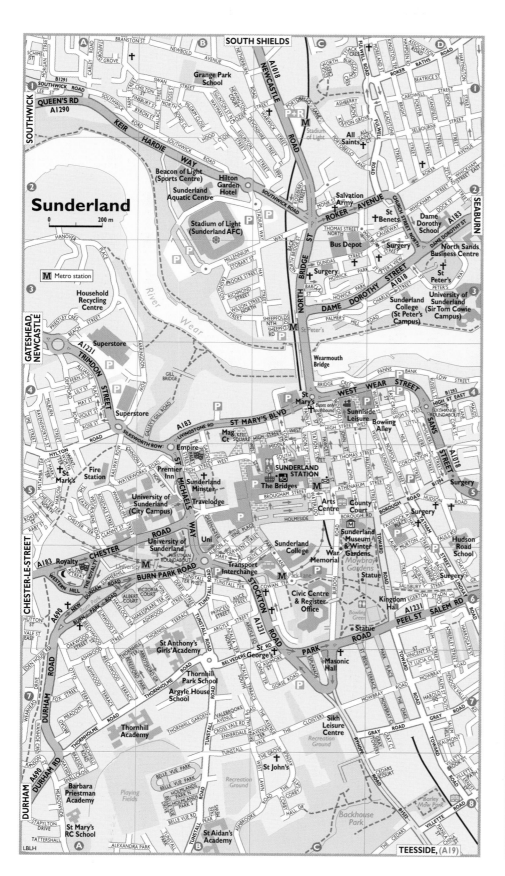

Sunderland

Sunderland is found on atlas page **113 N9**

Abbotsford Green	B7	Milburn Street	A4
Abbs Street	C2	Millennium Way	B3
Albion Place	B6	Monk Street	C2
Alice Street	B6	Moreland Street	D1
Alliance Place	B6	Morgan Street	A1
Amberley Street	D6	Mowbray Road	D7
Argyle Square	B6	Netherburn Road	B1
Argyle Street	B6	Newbold Avenue	B1
Ashbrooke Road	B8	Newcastle Road	C1
Ashmore Street	C7	New Durham Road	A6
Ashwood Street	A7	Nile Street	D4
Ashwood Terrace	A7	Norfolk Street	D5
Association Road	D1	North Bridge Street	C3
Athenaeum Street	C5	Northcote Avenue	D6
Azalea Terrace North	B6	North Street	B1
Azalea Terrace South	B7	Oakwood Street	A6
Back North Bridge Street	C3	Olive Street	B6
Beach Street	A3	Otto Terrace	A7
Bedford Street	C4	Palmer's Hill Road	C3
Beechwood Street	A6	Panns Bank	D4
Beechwood Terrace	A7	Park Lane	C5
Belvedere Road	B7	Park Place	D6
Beresford Park	A7	Park Road	C6
Birchfield Road	A7	Pauls Road	D5
Borough Road	D5	Peel Street	D6
Bridge Crescent	C4	Portobello Lane	C1
Bridge Street	C4	Queen's Road	A1
Briery Vale Road	C7	Railway Row	A5
Bright Street	D1	Ravensworth Street	A4
Brooke Street	B3	Richmond Street	B3
Brougham Street	C5	Ripon Street	D1
Burdon Road	C5	Roker Avenue	C2
Burn Park Road	B6	Roker Baths Road	D1
Cardwell Street	D1	Rosedale Street	A5
Carley Road	A1	Ross Street	B1
Charles Street	D3	Russell Street	D4
Chester Road	A6	Ryhope Road	C7
Churchill Street	D6	St Bede's Terrace	D7
Church Street North	D2	St Mary's Boulevard	B4
Clanny Street	A5	St Michaels Way	B5
Cork Street	D4	St Peter's View	D3
Coronation Street	D5	St Thomas' Street	C5
Cowan Terrace	C6	St Vincent Street	D7
Cross Vale Road	B7	Salem Road	D6
Crozier Street	B1	Salem Street	D6
Dame Dorothy Street	C3	Salem Street South	D7
Deptford Road	A4	Salisbury Street	D6
Derby Street	B6	Sans Street	D4
Derwent Street	B6	Selbourne Street	D1
Devonshire Street	B1	Shakespeare Terrace	A6
Dock Street	D2	Shallcross	A8
Dundas Street	C3	Sheepfolds Road	C3
Durham Road	A7	Silksworth Row	A4
Easington Street	B3	South Street	C5
East Cross Street	D4	Southwick Road	A1
Eden House Road	A7	Southwick Road	C2
Egerton Street	D6	Stadium Way	C2
Eglinton Street	B1	Stansfield Street	D1
Eglinton Street North	B1	Station Street	C4
Elmwood Street	A6	Stobart Street	B3
Ennerdale	B7	Stockton Road	C6
Farm Street	A1	Swan Street	B1
Farringdon Row	B4	Tatham Street	D5
Fawcett Street	C4	Tatham Street Back	D5
Forster Street	D1	The Avenue	C7
Fox Street	A7	The Cloisters	C7
Foyle Street	D5	The Royalty	A6
Frederick Street	D5	Thomas Street North	C2
Fulwell Road	C1	Thornhill Terrace	B6
Galley's Gill Road	B4	Thornholme Road	A7
Gladstone Street	D1	Toward Road	D5
Gorse Road	C7	Trimdon Street	A4
Gray Road	D7	Tunstall Road	B7
Green Terrace	B5	Tunstall Terrace	B6
Hampden Road	D1	Tunstall Terrace West	B6
Hanover Place	A2	Tunstall Vale	B8
Harlow Street	A5	Union Street	C4
Harrogate Street	D6	Valebrooke Avenue	B7
Hartington Street	D1	Villette Road	D8
Havelock Terrace	A6	Villiers Street	D4
Hay Street	C3	Vine Place	B5
Hendon Valley Road	D7	Wallace Street	B1
High Street East	D4	Warwick Street	C1
High Street West	B5	Waterloo Place	C5
Holmeside	C5	Waterworks Road	A5
Hope Street	B5	Wayman Street	B1
Howick Park	C3	Wearhead Drive	A7
Hudson Road	D5	Westbourne Road	A5
Hylton Road	A5	Western Hill	A6
Johnson Street	A5	West Lawn	C8
John Street	C4	West Street	C5
Keir Hardie Way	A1	West Sunniside	D4
Laura Street	D5	West Wear Street	C4
Lindsay Road	D6	Wharncliffe Street	A5
Little Villiers Street	D4	Whickham Street	D2
Livingstone Road	B4	Whickham Street East	D2
Low Street	D4	Whitburn Street	D3
Mary Street	B6	William Street	D4
Mauds Lane	D4	Wilson Street North	B3
Meadowside	A8	York Street	C4
Middle Street	C5	Zetland Street	D2

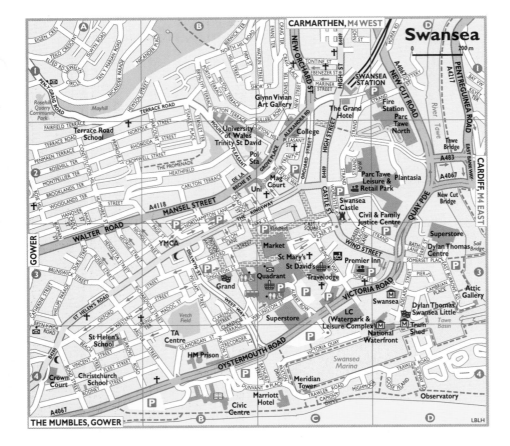

Swansea

Swansea is found on atlas page **29 J6**

Adelaide Street	D3	New Orchard Street	C1
Alexandra Road	C2	New Street	C1
Argyle Street	A4	Nicander Parade	A1
Bath Lane	D3	Nicholl Street	A3
Beach Street	A4	Norfolk Street	A2
Bond Street	A4	North Hill Road	B1
Brunswick Street	A3	Northampton Lane	B2
Burrows Road	A4	Orchard Street	C2
Caer Street	C3	Oxford Street	A3
Carlton Terrace	B2	Oystermouth Road	B4
Castle Street	C2	Page Street	B3
Catherine Street	A3	Park Street	B3
Clarence Street	B3	Paxton Street	B4
Clifton Hill	C2	Pentreguinea Road	D1
Constituion Hill	A2	Pen-Y-Graig Road	A1
Cradock Street	B2	Picton Lane	B3
Craig Place	C1	Pier Street	D3
Cromwell Street	A2	Primrose Street	A2
De La Beche Street	B2	Princess Way	C3
Dillwyn Street	B3	Quay Parade	D2
Duke Street	A3	Recorder Street	B4
Dunvant Place	B4	Rhondda Street	A2
East Bank Way	D2	Richardson Street	A3
East Burrows Road	D3	Rodney Street	A4
Ebenezer Street	C1	Rose Hill	A2
Elfed Road	A1	Russel Street	A3
Ferry Street	D3	St Helen's Road	A3
Firm Street	B1	Short Street	B1
Fleet Street	A4	Singleton Street	B3
George Street	A3	Somerset Place	D3
Glamorgan Street	B4	Strand	C1
Green Dragon Lane	C3	Tan Y Marian Road	A1
Grove Place	C2	Teilo Crescent	A1
Hanover Street	A2	Terrace Road	A2
Harcourt Street	B2	The Kingsway	B2
Heathfield	B2	Tontine Street	C1
Henrietta Street	A3	Trawler Road	C4
Hewson Street	A1	Victoria Quay	C4
High Street	C2	Victoria Road	C3
Hill Street	B1	Vincent Street	A4
Humphrey Street	A2	Walter Road	A3
Islwyn Road	A1	Watkin Street	C1
Llewelyn Circle	A1	Wellington Street	C3
Madoc Street	B3	West Way	B3
Mansel Street	B2	Western Street	A4
Mariner Street	C1	William Street	B3
Mount Pleasant	B2	Wind Street	C3
New Cut Road	D1	York Street	C3

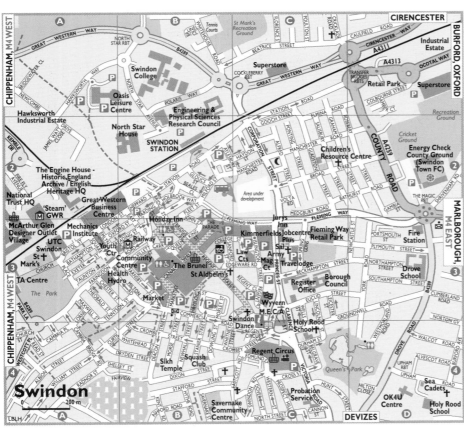

Swindon

Swindon is found on atlas page **33 M8**

Albion Street	A4	Islington Street	C3
Alfred Street	C2	John Street	B3
Ashford Road	B4	King Street	B3
Aylesbury Street	B2	London Street	A3
Bathurst Road	C2	Manchester Road	C2
Beckhampton Street	C3	Market Street	B3
Bridge Street	B2	Maxwell Street	A3
Bristol Street	A3	Medgbury Road	C2
Broad Street	C2	Milford Street	B2
Cambria Bridge Road	A4	Milton Road	B3
Canal Walk	B3	Morley Street	B3
Carr Street	B3	Morse Street	B4
Chester Street	A3	Newcastle Street	D3
Church Place	A3	Newcombe Drive	A1
Cirencester Way	D1	Newhall Street	B4
Clarence Street	C3	Northampton Street	D3
College Street	B3	North Star Avenue	B1
Commercial Road	B3	Ocotal Way	D1
Corporation Street	C2	Park Lane	A3
County Road	D2	Plymouth Street	D3
Crombey Street	B4	Polaris Way	B1
Curtis Street	A4	Ponting Street	C2
Deacon Street	B4	Portsmouth Street	D3
Dixon Street	B4	Princes Street	C3
Dover Street	C4	Prospect Hill	C4
Dowling Street	B4	Queen Street	B3
Drove Road	D4	Radnor Street	A4
Dryden Street	A4	Regent Place	C3
Eastcott Hill	C4	Regent Street	B3
East Street	B2	Rosebery Street	C2
Edgeware Road	B3	Salisbury Street	C2
Elmina Road	C1	Sanford Street	B3
Emlyn Square	A3	Sheppard Street	B2
Euclid Street	C3	Southampton Street	D3
Faringdon Road	A3	Stafford Street	B4
Farnsby Street	B3	Stanier Street	B4
Fire Fly Avenue	A2	Station Road	B2
Fleet Street	B2	Swindon Road	C4
Fleming Way	C3	Tennyson Street	A3
Gladstone Street	C2	Theobald Street	A3
Gooch Street	C2	Victoria Road	C4
Graham Street	B3	Villett Street	B3
Great Western Way	A1	Westcott Place	A4
Groundwell Road	C3	Western Street	C4
Havelock Street	B3	Whitehead Street	B4
Hawksworth Way	A1	Whitney Street	B4
Haydon Street	C2	William Street	A4
Holbrook Way	B2	York Road	D3

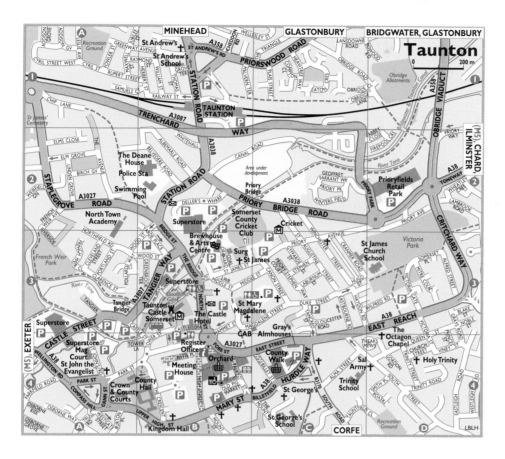

Taunton

Taunton is found on atlas page **18 H10**

Abbey Close	D2	Middle Street	B3
Albemarle Road	B2	Northfield Road	A3
Alfred Street	D3	North Street	B3
Alma Street	C4	Obridge Road	C1
Belvedere Road	B2	Obridge Viaduct	D2
Billetfield	C4	Old Pig Market	B4
Billet Street	C4	Parkfield Road	A4
Bridge Street	B2	Park Street	A4
Canal Road	B2	Paul Street	B4
Cann Street	A4	Plais Street	C1
Canon Street	C3	Portland Street	A3
Castle Street	A4	Priorswood Road	B1
Cheddon Road	B1	Priory Avenue	C3
Chip Lane	A1	Priory Bridge Road	B2
Church Street	D4	Queen Street	D4
Clarence Street	A3	Railway Street	B1
Cleveland Street	A3	Raymond Street	A1
Compass Hill	A4	Rupert Street	A1
Cranmer Road	C3	St Andrew's Road	B1
Critchard Way	D2	St Augustine Street	C3
Cyril Street	A1	St James Street	B3
Deller's Wharf	B2	St John's Road	A4
Duke Street	C3	Samuels Court	A1
Eastbourne Road	C3	South Road	C4
Eastleigh Road	D4	South Street	D4
East Reach	D3	Staplegrove Road	A2
East Street	C4	Station Road	B2
Fore Street	B4	Stephen Street	C3
Fowler Street	A1	Stephen Way	C3
French Weir Avenue	A2	Tancred Street	C3
Gloucester Road	C3	The Avenue	A2
Grays Road	D3	The Bridge	B3
Greenway Avenue	A1	The Crescent	B4
Gyffarde Street	C3	The Triangle	C1
Hammet Street	B4	Thomas Street	B1
Haydon Road	C3	Toneway	D2
Herbert Street	B1	Tower Street	B4
High Street	B4	Trenchard Way	B1
Hugo Street	C3	Trinity Street	D4
Hurdle Way	C4	Upper High Street	B4
Laburnum Street	C3	Victoria Gate	D3
Lansdowne Road	C1	Victoria Street	D3
Leslie Avenue	A1	Viney Street	D4
Linden Grove	A2	Wellington Road	A4
Lower Middle Street	B3	Wilfred Road	C3
Magdalene Street	B3	William Street	B1
Mary Street	B4	Winchester Street	C2
Maxwell Street	A1	Wood Street	B3

Torquay

Torquay is found on atlas page **7 N6**

Abbey Road	B1	Middle Warbury Road	D1
Alexandra Road	C1	Mill Lane	A1
Alpine Road	C2	Montpellier Road	D3
Ash Hill Road	C1	Morgan Avenue	B1
Avenue Road	A1	Palm Road	B1
Bampfylde Road	A2	Parkhill Road	D4
Beacon Hill	D4	Pembroke Road	C1
Belgrave Road	A1	Pennsylvania Road	D1
Braddons Hill Road East	D3	Pimlico	C2
Braddons Hill Road West	C2	Potters Hill	C1
Braddons Street	D2	Princes Road	C1
Bridge Road	A1	Queen Street	C2
Camden Road	D1	Rathmore Road	A2
Cary Parade	C3	Rock Road	C2
Cary Road	C3	Rosehill Road	D1
Castle Lane	C1	St Efride's Road	A1
Castle Road	C1	St Luke's Road	B2
Cavern Road	D1	St Marychurch Road	C1
Chestnut Avenue	A2	Scarborough Road	B2
Church Lane	A1	Seaway Lane	A4
Church Street	A1	Shedden Hill Road	B3
Cleveland Road	A1	Solbro Road	A3
Croft Hill	B2	South Hill Road	D3
Croft Road	B2	South Street	A1
East Street	A1	Stentiford Hill Road	C2
Ellacombe Road	C1	Strand	D3
Falkland Road	A2	Sutherland Road	D1
Fleet Street	C3	Temperance Street	C2
Grafton Road	D2	The King's Drive	A3
Hennapyn Road	A4	The Terrace	D3
Higher Union Lane	B1	Torbay Road	A4
Hillesdon Road	D2	Tor Church Road	A1
Hoxton Road	D1	Tor Hill Road	B1
Hunsdon Road	D3	Torwood Street	D3
Laburnum Street	A1	Trematon Ave	B1
Lime Avenue	A2	Trinity Hill	D3
Lower Ellacombe		Union Street	B1
Church Road	D1	Upper Braddons Hill	D2
Lower Union Lane	C2	Vanehill Road	D4
Lower Warbury Road	D2	Vansittart Road	A1
Lucius Street	A1	Vaughan Parade	C3
Lymington Road	B1	Victoria Parade	D4
Magdalene Road	B1	Victoria Road	C1
Market Street	C2	Vine Road	A1
Marion View	D3	Walnut Road	A2
Meadfoot Lane	D4	Warberry Road West	C1
Melville Lane	C2	Warren Road	B2
Melville Street	C2	Wellington Road	C1

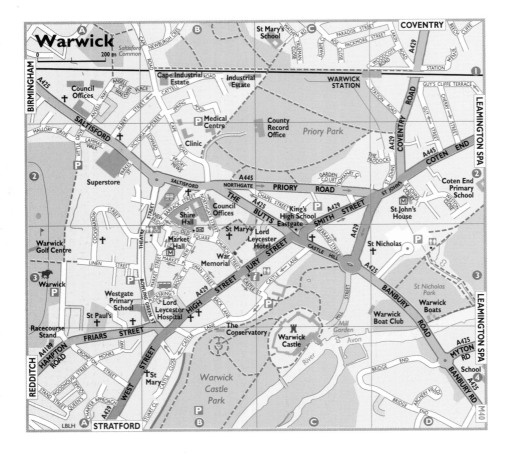

Warwick

Warwick is found on atlas page **59 L11**

Albert Street	A2	Old Square	B3
Ansell Court	A1	Packmore Street	C1
Ansell Way	A1	Paradise Street	C1
Archery Fields	D4	Parkes Street	A2
Back Lane	B3	Priory Mews	B2
Banbury Road	D3	Priory Road	C2
Barrack Street	B2	Puckering's Lane	B3
Beech Cliffe	D1	Queen's Square	A4
Bowling Green Street	B3	Roe Close	C1
Bridge End	D4	St Johns	D2
Brook Street	B3	St Johns Court	D2
Cape Road	B1	Saltisford	A1
Castle Close	B4	Sharpe Close	C1
Castle Hill	C3	Smith Street	C2
Castle Lane	B4	Spring Pool	B1
Castle Street	B3	Stand Street	A4
Cattell Road	B1	Station Avenue	D1
Chapel Street	C2	Station Road	D1
Charter Approach	A4	Stuart Close	B4
Cherry Street	D1	Swan Street	B3
Church Street	B3	Theatre Street	B3
Cocksparrow Street	A3	The Butts	B2
Coten End	D2	The Paddocks	D2
Coventry Road	D2	Trueman Close	C1
Crompton Street	A4	Victoria Street	A2
Edward Street	B2	Vittle Drive	A2
Friars Street	A4	Wallwin Place	A1
Garden Court	C2	Wathen Road	C1
Gerrard Street	C3	Weston Close	D2
Guy's Cliffe Terrace	D1	West Street	A4
Guy Street	D1	Woodcote Road	D1
Hampton Road	A4	Woodhouse Street	A4
High Street	B3	Yeomanry Close	C2
Jury Street	B3		
Lakin Road	D1		
Lammas Walk	A2		
Linen Street	A3		
Mallory Drive	A2		
Market Place	B3		
Market Street	B3		
Mill Street	C3		
Monks Way	A4		
Myton Road	D4		
New Bridge	B2		
Newburgh Crescent	B1		
New Street	B3		
Northgate	B2		
Northgate Street	B2		

Watford

Watford is found on atlas page **50 D11**

Addiscombe Road	B3	Merton Road	B4
Albert Road North	B2	Mildred Avenue	A3
Albert Road South	B2	Monica Close	D1
Alexandra Road	A1	Nascot Street	B1
Anglian Close	D1	New Road	D4
Beechen Grove	C3	New Street	C3
Brocklesbury Close	D2	Orphanage Road	C1
Burton Avenue	A4	Park Avenue	A3
Cassiobury Drive	A2	Peace Drive	A2
Cassio Road	A3	Peace Prospect	A2
Chester Road	A4	Percy Road	B3
Clarendon Road	C1	Pretoria Road	A4
Cross Street	C2	Prince Street	C2
Denmark Street	A1	Queen's Road	C2
Derby Road	C3	Queen Street	C3
Duke Street	C2	Radlett Road	D2
Durban Road East	A4	Raphael Drive	D1
Durban Road West	A4	Reeds Crescent	C1
Earl Street	C3	Rickmansworth Road	A3
Ebury Road	D2	Rosslyn Road	B3
Essex Road	A1	St Albans Road	B1
Estcourt Road	C2	St John's Road	B1
Exchange Road	B3	St Mary's Road	B4
Farraline Road	B4	St Pauls Way	D1
Feranley Street	B4	Shady Lane	B1
Francis Road	B3	Shaftesbury Road	D2
Franklin Road	B1	Smith Street	C4
Gartlet Road	C2	Sotheron Road	C2
Gaumont Approach	B2	Southsea Avenue	A4
George Street	C4	Stanley Road	C3
Gladstone Road	D3	Station Road	B1
Granville Road	C4	Stephenson Way	D3
Grosvenor Road	C3	Sutton Road	C2
Halsey Road	B2	The Avenue	A1
Harwoods Road	A4	The Broadway	C3
Hempstead Road	A1	The Crescent	C4
High Street	C3	The Parade	B2
Hyde Road	A2	Upton Road	B3
Keele Close	C1	Vicarage Road	B4
King Street	C4	Victoria Passage	B4
Lady's Close	C4	Water Lane	D4
Link Road	D1	Wellington Road	B3
Loates Lane	C3	Wellstones	B3
Lord Street	C3	Westland Road	B1
Lower High Street	D4	West Street	B1
Malden Road	A1	Whippendell Road	A4
Market Street	B4	Wiggenhall Road	B4
Marlborough Road	B3	Woodford Road	C1

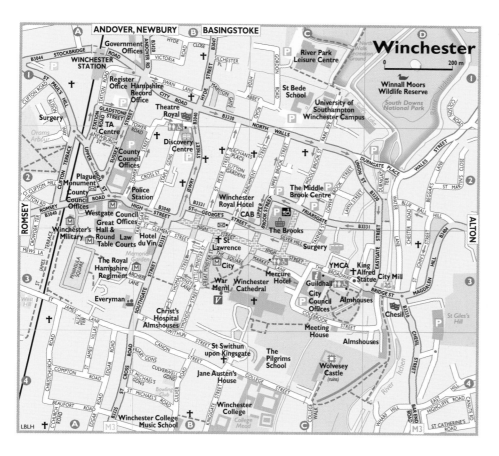

Winchester

Winchester is found on atlas page **22 E9**

Alex Terrace	A3	Market Lane C3
Alison Way	A1	Marston Gate B1
Andover Road	B1	Merchants Place B2
Archery Lane	A3	Mews Lane A3
Bar End Road	D4	Middle Brook Street C2
Beaufort Road	A4	Minster Lane B3
Beggar's Lane	D2	Newburgh Street A2
Blue Ball Hill	D2	North Walls C1
Bridge Street	D3	Parchment Street B2
Canon Street	B4	Park Avenue C2
Canute Road	D4	Romsey Road A2
Chesil Street	D3	St Clement Street B2
Chester Road	D2	St Cross Road A4
Christchurch Road	A4	St George's Street B2
City Road	B1	St James' Lane A3
Clifton Hill	A2	St James Terrace A3
Clifton Road	A1	St James' Villas A4
Clifton Terrace	A2	St John's Street D3
Colebrook Street	C3	St Martin's Close D2
College Street	B4	St Michael's Gardens B4
College Walk	C4	St Michael's Road B4
Colson Road	D1	St Paul's Hill A1
Compton Road	A4	St Peter Street B2
Cross Street	B2	St Swithun Street B3
Crowder Terrace	A3	St Thomas Street B3
Culver Road	B4	Silchester Place B1
Culverwell Gardens	B4	Silver Hill C3
Durngate Place	D2	Southgate Street B3
Durngate Terrace	D2	Staple Gardens B2
Eastgate Street	D3	Station Road A1
East Hill	D4	Stockbridge Road A1
Edgar Road	A4	Sussex Street A2
Friarsgate	C2	Sutton Gardens B2
Friary Gardens	B4	Swan Lane B1
Gladstone Street	A1	Symonds Street B3
Gordon Road	C1	Tanner Street C3
Great Minster Street	B3	The Broadway C3
Highcliffe Road	D4	The Square B3
High Street	B2	Tower Road A1
Hyde Abbey Road	B1	Tower Street A2
Hyde Close	B1	Trafalgar Street B3
Hyde Street	B1	Union Street C2
Jewry Street	B2	Upper Brook Street C2
Kingsgate Street	B4	Upper High Street A2
Lawn Street	C2	Victoria Road B1
Little Minster Street	B3	Wales Street D2
Lower Brook Street	C2	Water Lane D3
Magdalen Hill	D3	Wharf Hill D4

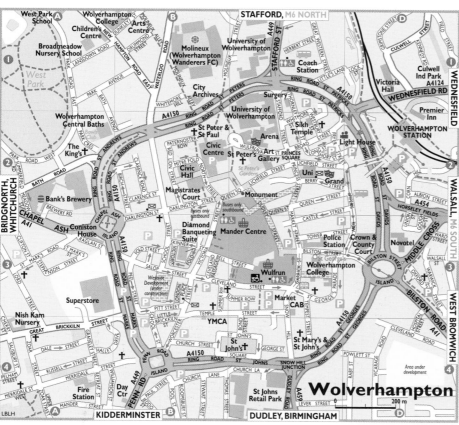

Wolverhampton

Wolverhampton is found on atlas page **58 D5**

Bath Avenue	A1	Peel Street B3
Bath Road	A2	Penn Road B4
Bell Street	B3	Piper's Row D2
Berry Street	C2	Pitt Street B3
Bilston Road	D3	Powlett Street D4
Bilston Street	C3	Princess Street C2
Birch Street	B2	Queen Square B2
Broad Street	C2	Queen Street C2
Castle Street	C3	Raby Street D4
Chapel Ash	A3	Raglan Street A3
Church Lane	B4	Red Lion Street B2
Church Street	B4	Retreat Street A4
Clarence Road	B2	Ring Road St Andrews A2
Clarence Street	B2	Ring Road St Davids D2
Cleveland Road	D4	Ring Road St Georges C4
Cleveland Street	B3	Ring Road St Johns B4
Corn Hill	D2	Ring Road St Marks B3
Culwell Street	D1	Ring Road St Patricks C1
Dale Street	A4	Ring Road St Peters B2
Darlington Street	B3	Russell Street A4
Dudley Road	C4	St George's Parade C3
Dudley Street	C2	St John's Square C4
Fold Street	B3	St Mark's Road A3
Fryer Street	C2	St Mark's Street A3
Garrick Street	C3	Salop Street B3
Graiseley Street	A4	School Street B3
Great Brickkiln Street	A4	Skinner Street B3
Great Western Street	C1	Snow Hill C3
Grimstone Street	D1	Stafford Street C1
Horseley Fields	D2	Stephenson Street A3
Hospital Street	D4	Stewart Street B4
Lansdown Road	A1	Summer Row B3
Lever Street	C4	Tempest Street C3
Lichfield Street	C2	Temple Street B3
Little's Lane	C1	Thomas Street B4
Long Street	C2	Tower Street C3
Lord Street	A3	Vicarage Road D4
Mander Street	A4	Victoria Street B3
Market Street	C3	Walsall Street D3
Merridale Street	A4	Warwick Street D3
Middle Cross	D3	Waterloo Road B1
Mitre Fold	B2	Wednesfield Road D1
Molineux Street	B1	Westbury Street C2
New Hampton Road East	A1	Whitemore Hill B1
North Street	B2	Whitmore Street C2
Park Avenue	A1	Worcester Street B4
Park Road East	B1	Wulfruna Street C2
Park Road West	A2	Zoar Street A4

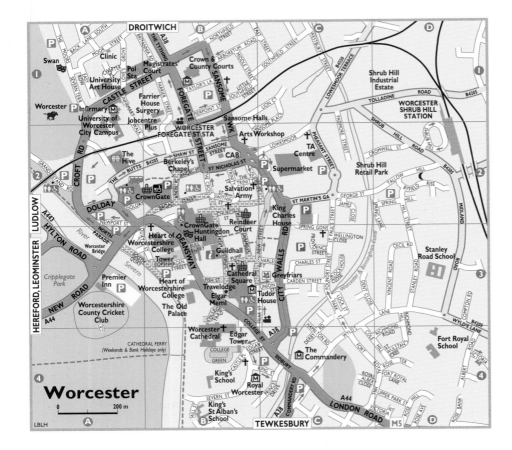

Worcester

Worcester is found on atlas page **46 G4**

Albert Road	D4	Middle Street	B1
Angel Street	B2	Midland Road	D2
Arboretum Road	B1	Mill Street	B4
Back Lane South	A1	Moor Street	A1
Blockhouse Close	C3	Newport Street	A2
Britannia Road	A1	New Road	A3
Broad Street	B2	New Street	C3
Byfield Rise	D2	Northfield Street	B1
Carden Street	C3	North Parade	A3
Castle Street	A1	Padmore Street	C1
Cathedral Ferry	A4	Park Street	C3
Cecil Road	D3	Pheasant Street	C2
Charles Street	C3	Pierpoint Street	B1
Charter Place	A1	Providence Street	C3
Church Street	B2	Pump Street	B3
City Walls Road	C3	Quay Street	A3
Cole Hill	C4	Queen Street	B2
College Street	B3	Richmond Road	D4
Commandery Road	C4	Rose Hill	D4
Compton Road	D3	Rose Terrace	D4
Copenhagen Street	B3	St Martin's Gate	C2
Croft Road	A2	St Nicholas Street	B2
Cromwell Street	D2	St Paul's Street	C3
Deansway	B3	St Swithin Street	B2
Dent Close	C3	Sansome Walk	B1
Derby Road	C4	Severn Street	B4
Dolday	A2	Severn Terrace	A1
East Street	B1	Shaw Street	B2
Edgar Street	B4	Shrub Hill Road	D2
Farrier Street	B1	Sidbury	C4
Fish Street	B3	Southfield Street	C1
Foregate Street	B1	Spring Hill	D2
Fort Royal Hill	C4	Stanley Road	D3
Foundry Street	C3	Tallow Hill	D2
Friar Street	C3	Taylor's Lane	B1
George Street	C2	The Butts	A2
Grandstand Road	A2	The Cross	B2
Hamilton Road	C3	The Moors	A1
High Street	B3	The Shambles	B2
Hill Street	D2	The Tything	B1
Hylton Road	A3	Tolladine Road	C1
King Street	B4	Trinity Street	B2
Little Southfield Street	B1	Union Street	C3
Lock Street	C3	Upper Park Street	D4
London Road	C4	Vincent Road	D3
Love's Grove	A1	Wellington Close	C3
Lowesmoor	C2	Westbury Street	C1
Lowesmoor Terrace	C1	Wyld's Lane	C4

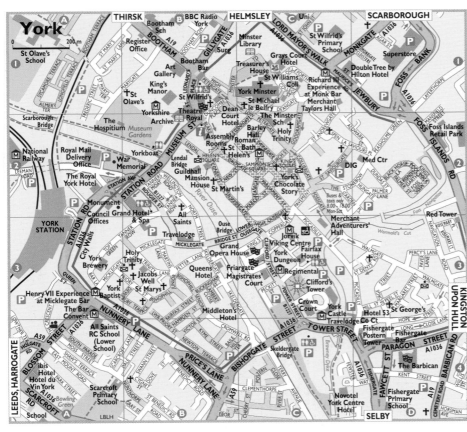

York

York is found on atlas page **98 C10**

Aldwark	C2	Lower Ousegate	C3
Barbican Road	D4	Lower Priory Street	B3
Bishopgate Street	B4	Low Petergate	C2
Bishophill Senior	B3	Margaret Street	D3
Black Horse Lane	D2	Market Street	C2
Blake Street	B2	Micklegate	A3
Blossom Street	A4	Minster Yard	B1
Bootham	B1	Monkgate	C1
Bridge Street	B3	Museum Street	B2
Buckingham Street	B3	Navigation Road	D3
Cemetery Road	D4	New Street	B2
Church Street	C2	North Street	B2
Clifford Street	C3	Nunnery Lane	A3
College Street	C1	Ogleforth	C1
Colliergate	C2	Palmer Lane	D2
Coney Street	B2	Palmer Street	D2
Coppergate	C3	Paragon Street	D4
Cromwell Road	B4	Parliament Street	C2
Davygate	B2	Pavement	C2
Deangate	C1	Peasholme Green	D2
Dove Street	B4	Percy's Lane	D3
Duncombe Place	B2	Piccadilly	C3
Dundas Street	D2	Price's Lane	B4
Fairfax Street	B3	Priory Street	C3
Fawcett Street	D4	Queen Street	A3
Feasegate	C2	Rougier Street	B2
Fetter Lane	B3	St Andrewgate	C2
Finkle Street	C2	St Denys' Road	D3
Fishergate	D4	St Leonard's Place	B1
Foss Bank	D1	St Martins Lane	B3
Fossgate	C2	St Maurice's Road	C1
Foss Islands Road	D2	St Saviourgate	C2
George Street	D3	St Saviours Place	C2
Gillygate	B1	Scarcroft Road	A4
Goodramgate	C2	Shambles	C2
Hampden Street	B4	Skeldergate	B3
High Ousegate	C3	Spen Lane	C2
High Petergate	B1	Spurriergate	B2
Holgate Road	A4	Station Road	A3
Hope Street	D4	Stonegate	B2
Hungate	D2	Swinegate	C2
Jewbury	D1	The Stonebow	C2
Kent Street	D4	Toft Green	A3
King Street	C3	Tower Street	C3
Kyme Street	B4	Trinity Lane	B3
Lendal	B2	Victor Street	B4
Long Close Lane	D4	Walmgate	D3
Lord Mayor's Walk	C1	Wellington Road	B2

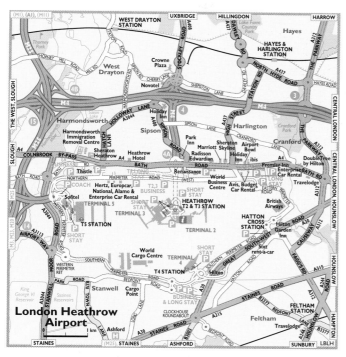

London Heathrow Airport – 17 miles west of central London, M25 junction 14 and M4 junction 4A

Satnav Location: TW6 1EW (Terminal 2), TW6 1QG (T3), TW6 3XA (T4), TW6 2GA (T5)
Information: visit www.heathrow.com
Parking: short-stay, long-stay and business parking is available.
Public Transport: coach, bus, rail and London Underground.
There are several 4-star and 3-star hotels within easy reach of the airport.
Car hire facilities are available.

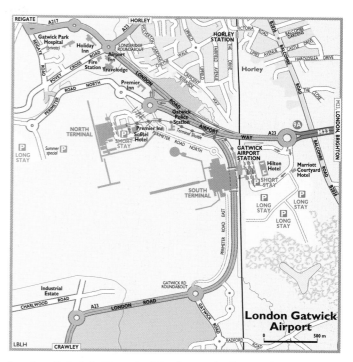

London Gatwick Airport – 29 miles south of central London, M23 junction 9A

Satnav Location: RH6 0NP (South terminal), RH6 0PJ (North terminal)
Information: visit www.gatwickairport.com
Parking: short and long-stay parking is available at both the North and South terminals.
Public Transport: coach, bus and rail.
There are several 4-star and 3-star hotels within easy reach of the airport.
Car hire facilities are available.

London Stansted Airport – 36 miles north-east of central London, M11 junction 8/8A

Satnav Location: CM24 1RW
Information: visit www.stanstedairport.com
Parking: short, mid and long-stay open-air parking is available.
Public Transport: coach, bus and direct rail link to London (Liverpool Street Station) on the Stansted Express.
There are several hotels within easy reach of the airport.
Car hire facilities are available.

London Luton Airport – 34 miles north of central London

Satnav Location: LU2 9QT
Information: visit www.london-luton.co.uk
Parking: short-term, mid-term and long-stay parking is available.
Public Transport: coach, bus and rail.
There are several 3-star hotels within easy reach of the airport.
Car hire facilities are available.

London City Airport – 8 miles east of central London

Satnav Location: E16 2PX
Information: visit *www.londoncityairport.com*
Parking: short and long-stay open-air parking is available.
Public Transport: easy access to the rail network, Docklands Light Railway and the London Underground.
There are 5-star, 4-star and 3-star hotels within easy reach of the airport.
Car hire facilities are available.

Birmingham Airport – 10 miles east of Birmingham, M42 junction 6

Satnav Location: B26 3QJ
Information: visit *www.birminghamairport.co.uk*
Parking: short and long-stay parking is available.
Public Transport: Monorail service (Air-Rail Link) operates to and from Birmingham International Railway Station.
There are several 4-star and 3-star hotels within easy reach of the airport.
Car hire facilities are available.

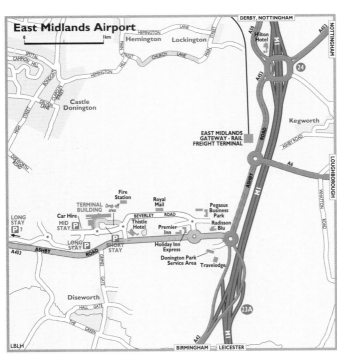

East Midlands Airport – 14 miles south-west of Nottingham, M1 junction 23A/24

Satnav Location: DE74 2SA
Information: visit *www.eastmidlandsairport.com*
Parking: short-term, mid-term and long-stay parking is available.
Public Transport: bus and coach services to major towns and cities in the East Midlands.
There are several 4-star and 3-star hotels within easy reach of the airport.
Car hire facilities are available.

Manchester Airport – 10 miles south of Manchester, M56 junction 5

Satnav Location: M90 1QX
Information visit *www.manchesterairport.co.uk*
Parking: short-term, mid-term and long-stay parking is available.
Public Transport: coach, bus, rail and tram (Metrolink).
There are several 4-star and 3-star hotels within easy reach of the airport.
Car hire facilities are available.

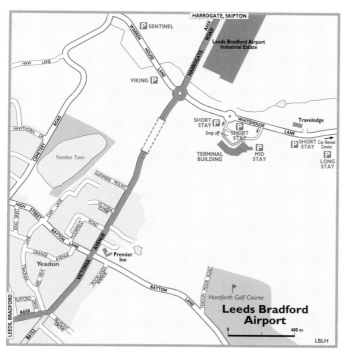

Leeds Bradford Airport – 8 miles north-east of Bradford and 8 miles north-west of Leeds

Satnav Location: LS19 7TU
Information: visit *www.leedsbradfordairport.co.uk*
Parking: short, mid-term and long-stay parking is available.
Public Transport: regular bus services to Bradford, Leeds and Harrogate.
There are several 4-star and 3-star hotels within easy reach of the airport.
Car hire facilities are available.

Aberdeen Airport – 7 miles north-west of Aberdeen

Satnav Location: AB21 7DU
Information: visit *www.aberdeenairport.com*
Parking: short and long-stay parking is available.
Public Transport: regular bus services to central Aberdeen.
There are several 4-star and 3-star hotels within easy reach of the airport.
Car hire facilities are available.

Edinburgh Airport – 9 miles west of Edinburgh

Satnav Location: EH12 9DN
Information: visit *www.edinburghairport.com*
Parking: short and long-stay parking is available.
Public Transport: regular bus services to Scottish cities including central Edinburgh, Glasgow, Dundee and Fife and a tram service to central Edinburgh.
There are several 4-star and 3-star hotels within easy reach of the airport.
Car hire and valet parking facilities are available.

Glasgow Airport – 10 miles west of Glasgow, M8 junction 28/29

Satnav Location: PA3 2SW
Information: visit *www.glasgowairport.com*
Parking: short and long-stay parking is available.
Public Transport: regular direct bus services to central Glasgow.
There are several 3-star hotels within easy reach of the airport.
Car hire facilities are available.

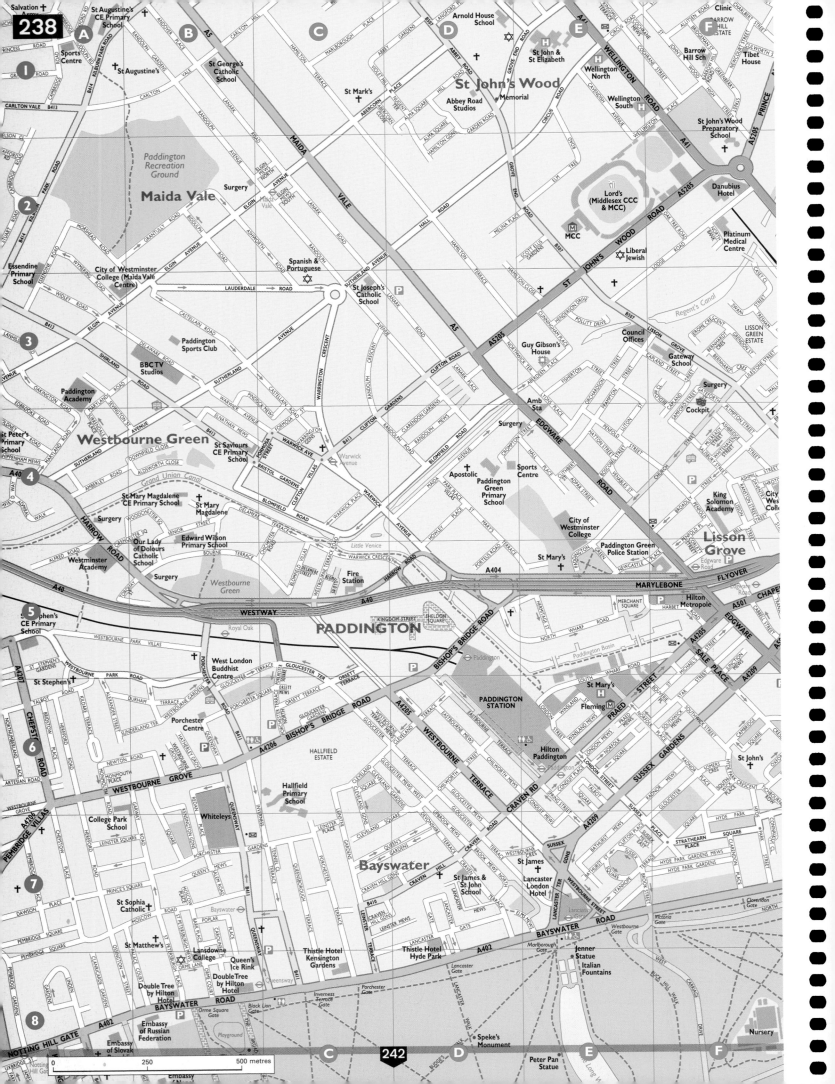

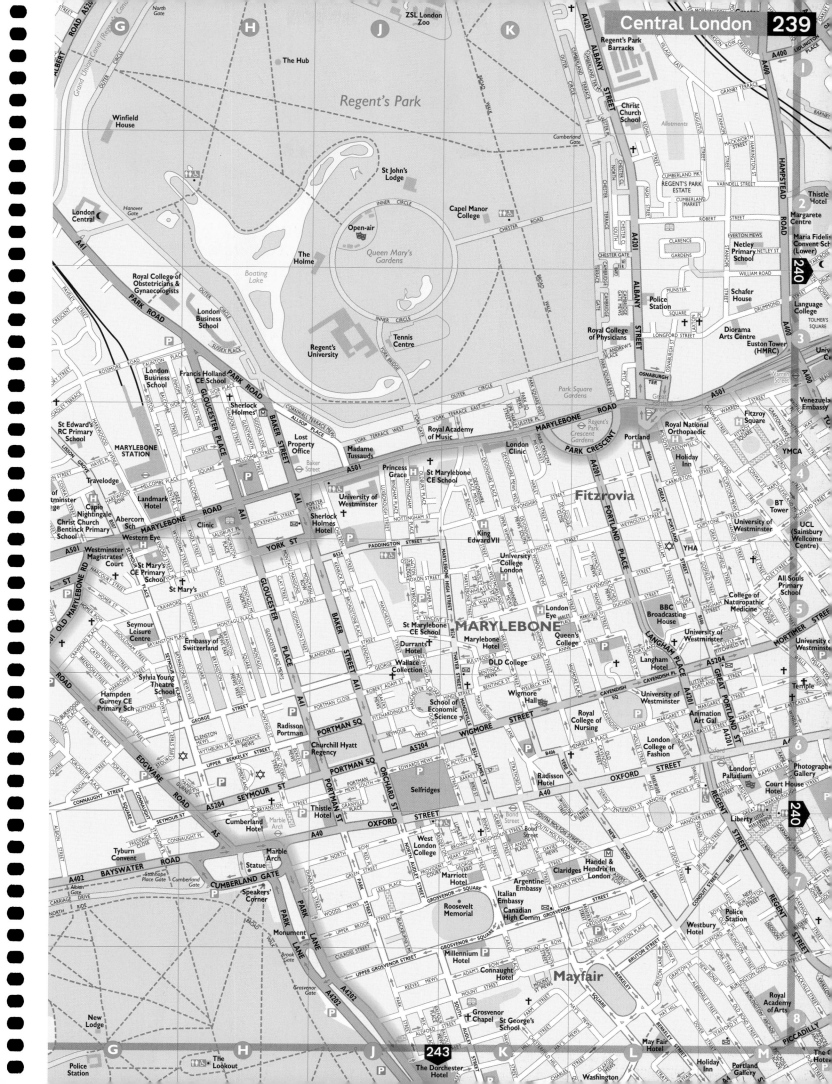

G H J K

Grand Union Canal (Regent's Canal)
North Gate

ZSL London Zoo

Regent's Park Barracks

A4201

A400

The Hub

Regent's Park

Christ Church School

Allotments

Thistle Hotel

2

Winfield House

St John's Lodge

Capel Manor College

CUMBERLAND MKT
REGENT'S PARK ESTATE
CUMBERLAND MARKET

Margarete Centre

London Central

Hanover Gate

INNER CIRCLE

CHESTER ROAD

EVERTON MEWS

Maria Fidelis Convent Sch (Lower)

Open-air

Netley Primary School

The Holme

Queen Mary's Gardens

CLARENCE GARDENS

Schafer House

Language College

Boating Lake

Royal College of Obstetricians & Gynaecologists

PARK ROAD

London Business School

OUTER CIRCLE

Regent's University

INNER CIRCLE

Tennis Centre

YORK BRIDGE

Police Station

Royal College of Physicians

LONGFORD STREET

PETO PL

ST ANDREW'S PL

Diorama Arts Centre

Euston Tower (HMRC)

TOLMER'S SQUARE

3

OSNABURGH TER

OSNABURGH ST

Univ

A501

Warren Street

SUSSEX PLACE

TAUNTON PLACE

London Business School

Francis Holland CE School

IVOR PLACE

OUTER CIRCLE

MARYLEBONE ROAD

Park Square Gardens

Regent's Park Crescent Gardens

PARK CRESCENT

Royal National Orthopaedic

CONWAY ST

Fitzroy Square

H

A501

A4201

A400

A400

Venezuela Embassy

BAKER STREET

Sherlock Holmes'

CORNWALL TERRACE MEWS

ALLSOP PLACE

YORK TERRACE EAST

York Terrace West

Royal Academy of Music

London Clinic

Portland

BOLSOVER ST

GREENWELL'S

Holiday Inn

CLEVELAND ST

Fitzrovia

YMCA

4

St Edward's RC Primary School

MARYLEBONE STATION

DORSET SQUARE

Lost Property Office

Madame Tussauds

A501

Princess Grace

St Marylebone CE School

DEVONSHIRE PLACE

BT Tower

University of Westminster

MARYLEBONE

Travelodge

Sherlock Holmes Hotel

University of Westminster

PORTLAND PLACE

UCL (Sainsbury Wellcome Centre)

Capio Nightingale

Abercorn Sch

Landmark Hotel

Clinic

BICKENHALL STREET

PADDINGTON STREET

B524

King Edward VII

WEYMOUTH

University College London

All Souls Primary School

Western Eye

LISSON GROVE

Christ Church Bentinck Primary School

YORK ST

SALISBURY PL

CHILTERN ST

HARLEY

YHA

College of Naturopathic Medicine

A501

Westminster Magistrates' Court

St Mary's CE Primary School

St Mary's

London Eye

St Marylebone CE School

BBC Broadcasting House

University of Westminster

5

MORTIMER STREET

University of Westminster

OLD MARYLEBONE RD

GLOUCESTER PLACE

BAKER STREET

MARYLEBONE HIGH STREET

Durrants Hotel

Marylebone Hotel

Queen's College

Langham Hotel

Temple

Seymour Leisure Centre

Embassy of Switzerland

DLD College

Wallace Collection

HINDE ST

Wigmore Hall

Royal College of Nursing

University of Westminster

Animation Art Gal

GREAT PORTLAND STREET

A4201

Hampden Gurney CE Primary Sch

Sylvia Young Theatre School

School of Economic Science

WIGMORE STREET

London College of Fashion

6

PORTMAN SQ

A5204

CAVENDISH SQ

London Palladium

Radisson Portman

Churchill Hyatt Regency

PORTMAN SQ

EDWARDS MEWS

Radisson Hotel

OXFORD STREET

A40

Photographers' Gallery

UPPER BERKELEY ST

EDGWARE ROAD

SEYMOUR ST

ORCHARD ST

Selfridges

Bond Street

Liberty

A5204

Cumberland Hotel

Thistle Hotel

OXFORD STREET

Court House Hotel

240

7

Marble Arch

Marble Arch

West London College

Handel & Claridges Hendrix in London

BAYSWATER ROAD

Tyburn Convent

Statue

A402

CUMBERLAND GATE

Marriott Hotel

GROSVENOR SQUARE

Argentine Embassy

Police Station

Speakers' Corner

Roosevelt Memorial

Italian Embassy

Canadian High Comm

Westbury Hotel

Cumberland Gate

PARK LANE

CONNAUGHT

A5

Monument

A4202

Millennium Hotel

Mayfair

Royal Academy of Arts

8

New Lodge

Connaught Hotel

Grosvenor Chapel

St George's School

May Fair Hotel

Holiday Inn

Portland Gallery

Police Station

The Lookout

243

The Dorchester Hotel

Washington

PICCADILLY

G H J K L M

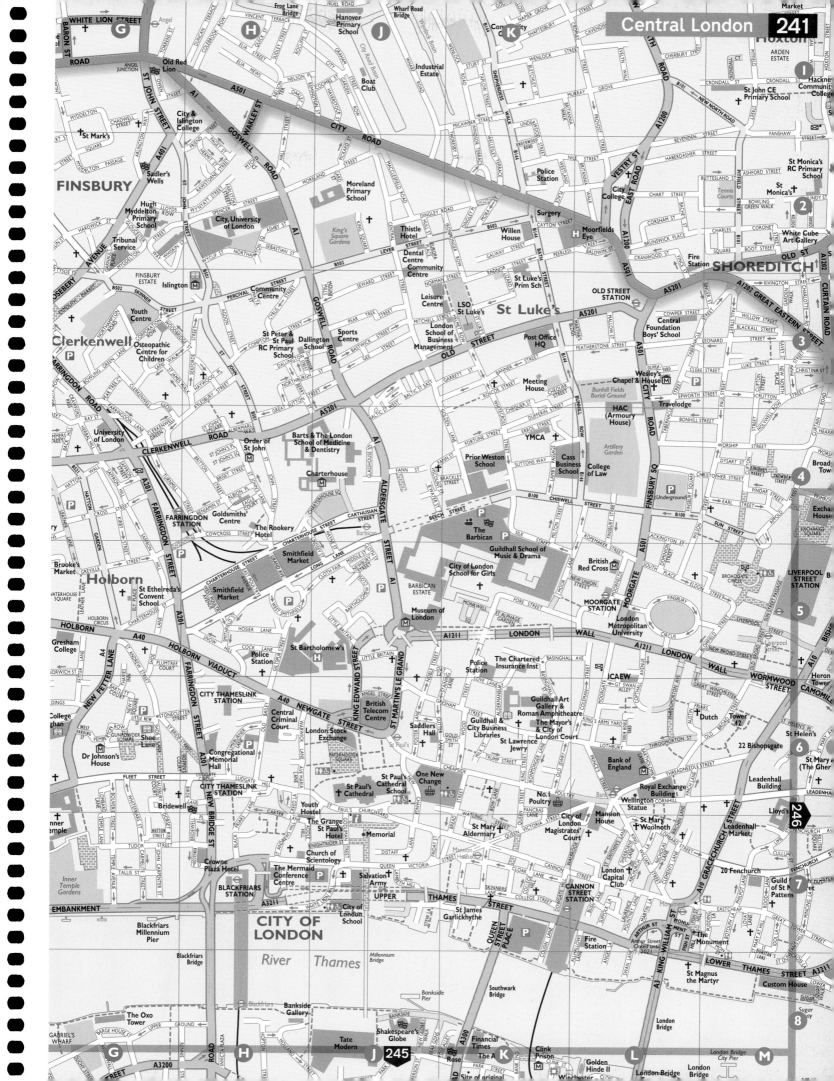

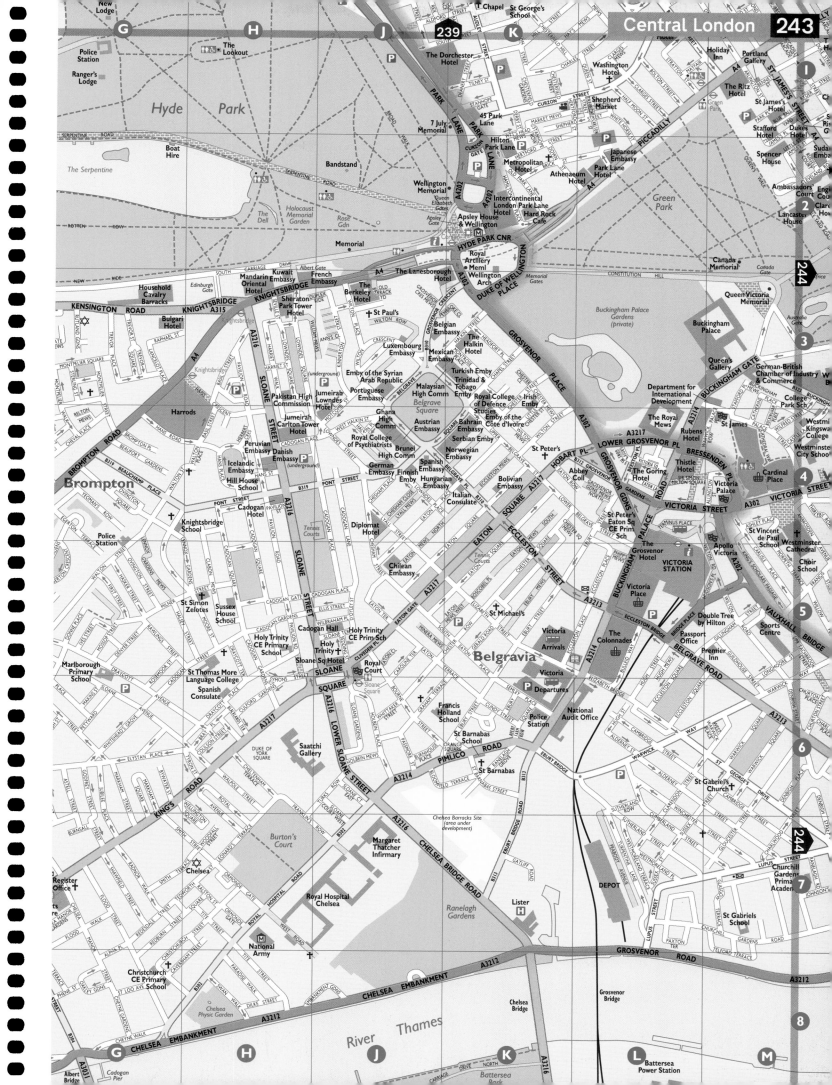

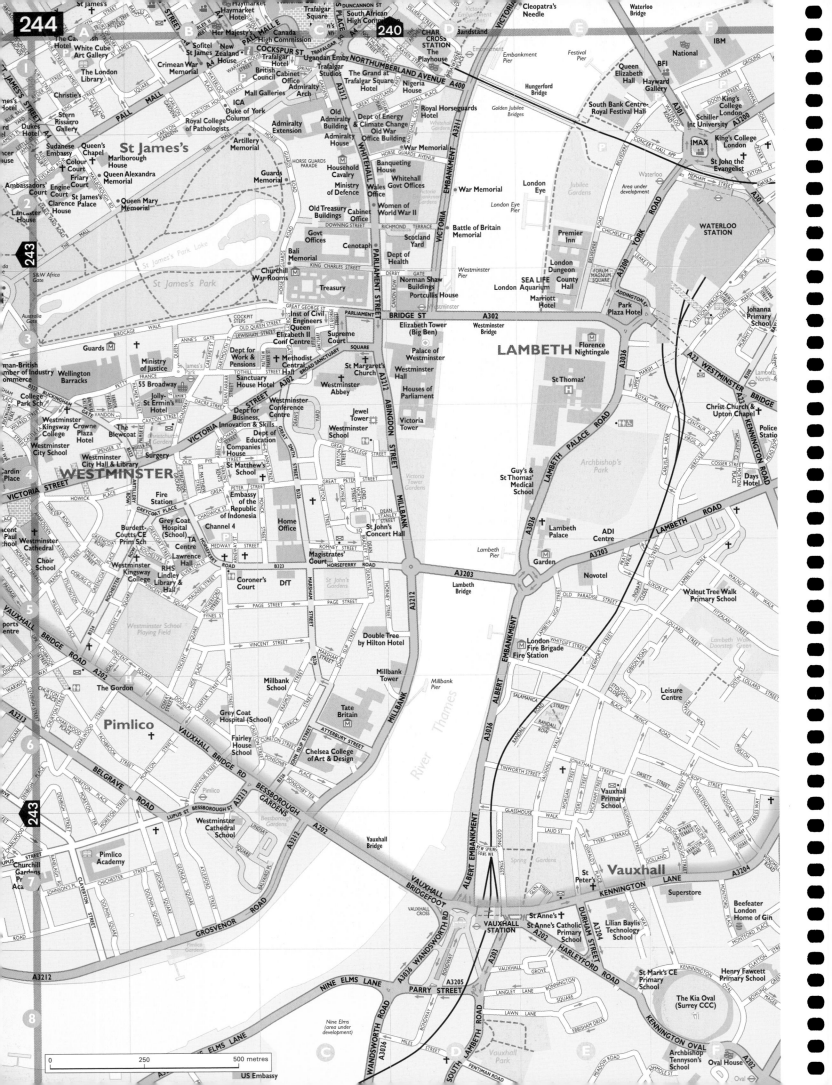

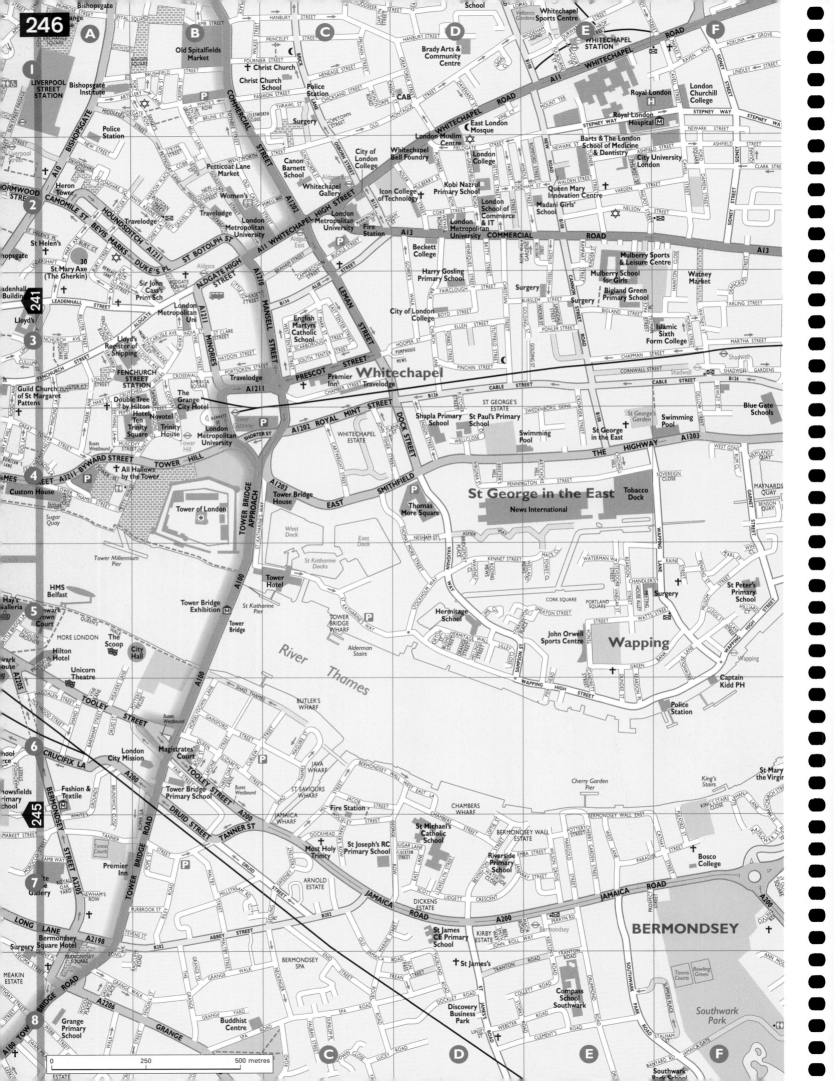

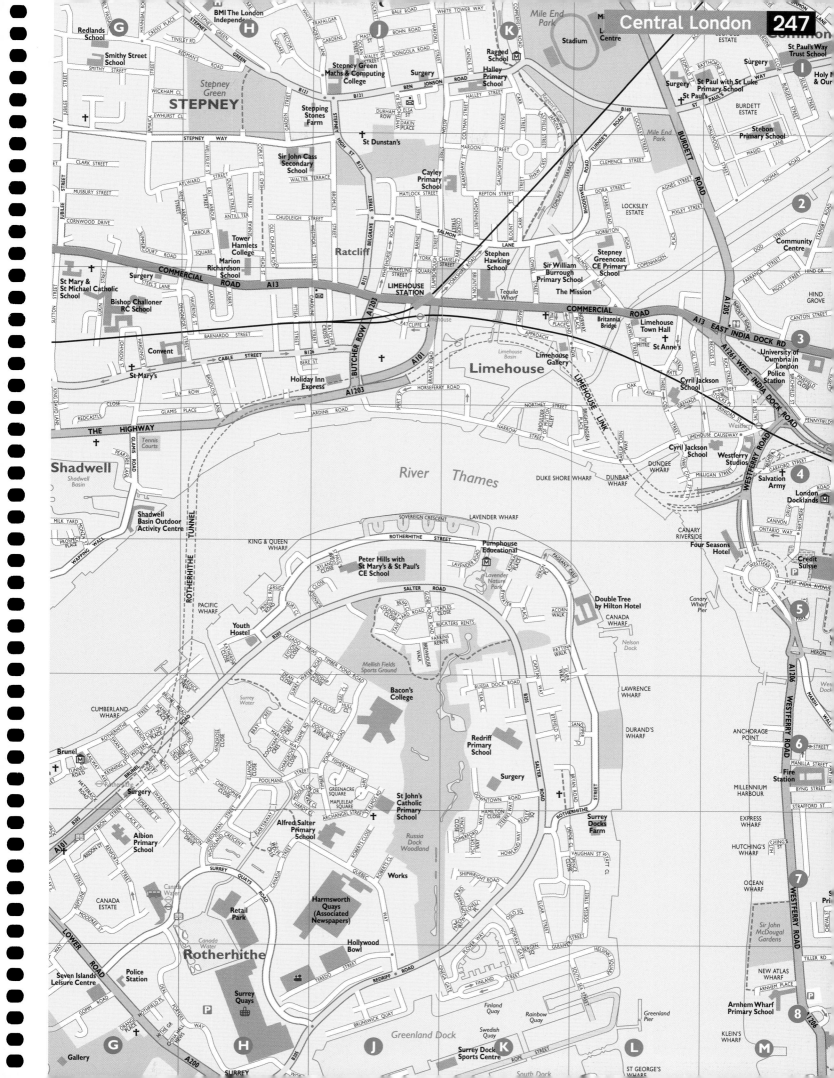

This index lists street and station names, and top places of tourist interest shown in red. Names are listed in alphabetical order and written in full, but may be abbreviated on the map. Each entry is followed by its Postcode District and then the page number and grid reference to the square in which the name is found. Names are asterisked (*) in the index where there is insufficient space to show them on the map.

A

Abbey Gardens NW8 ....238 C1
Abbey Orchard Street SW1P 244 B4
Abbey Road NW8 ....238 D1
Abbey Street SE1 ....246 B7
Abchurch Lane EC4N 241 L7
Abercorn Close NW8 ....238 C1
Abercorn Place NW8 ....238 C1
Aberdeen Place NW8 ....238 E3
Aberdour Street SE1 ....245 M5
Abingdon Road W8 ....242 A4
Abingdon Street SW1P 244 C4
Abingdon Villas W8 ....242 A4
Ackroyd Drive E3 ....247 L1
Acorn Walk SE16 ....247 K5
Acton Street WC1X 240 E2
Adam and Eve Mews W8 ....242 A3
Adam's Row W1K 239 K8
Adam Street WC2N 240 D8
Addington Street SE1 ....244 E3
Addle Hill EC4V 241 H7
Adelina Grove E1 ....246 F1
Adeline Place WC1B 240 B5
Adler Street E1 ....246 D2
Admiral Place SE16 ....247 K5
Admiral Walk W9 ....238 A4
Adpar Street W2 ....238 E4
Agar Street WC2N 240 D8
Agdon Street EC1V 241 H3
Agnes Street E14 ....247 L2
Ainsty Street SE16 ....247 G6
Air Street W1B 240 A8
Alaska Street SE1 ....244 F2
Albany Road SE5 ....245 L8
Albany Street NW1 ....239 L1
Albemarle Street W1S 239 L8
Albemarle Way EC1V 241 H4
Alberta Street SE17 ....245 H6
Albert Bridge SW3 ....243 G8
Albert Embankment SE1 ....244 D7
Albert Gardens E1 ....247 H3
Albert Gate SW1X 243 H2
Albert Place W8 ....242 C3
Albion Gate W2 ....239 G7
Albion Place EC1M 241 H4
Albion Street SE16 ....247 H7
Albion Street W2 ....239 G7
Aldenham Street NW1 ....240 A1
Aldermanbury EC2V 241 K6
Alderney Mews SE1 ....245 K4
Alderney Street SW1V 243 L6
Aldersgate Street EC1A 241 J4
Aldford Street W1K 239 J8
Aldgate EC3M 246 B3
Aldgate ⊖ EC3N 246 B3
Aldgate East ⊖ E1 ....246 C2
Aldgate High Street EC3N 246 B3
Aldgate Square EC3N 246 B3
Aldsworth Close W9 ....238 B4
Aldwych WC2E 240 E7
Alexander Place SW7 ....242 F5
Alexander Street W2 ....238 A6
Alexandra Gate SW7 ....242 E3
Alfred Mews WC1E 240 B4
Alfred Place WC1E 240 B4
Alfred Road W2 ....238 A5
Alice Street SE1 ....245 M4
Alie Street E1 ....246 C3
Allen Street W8 ....242 A4
Allhallows Lane EC4R 241 L8
Allington Street SW1E 243 M4
Allitsen Road NW8 ....238 F1
Allsop Place NW1 ....239 H3
Alma Square NW8 ....238 D1
Alpha Place SW3 ....243 G8
Alsace Road SE17 ....245 M7
Alscot Road * SE1 ....246 C8
Alvey Street SE17 ....245 M6
Ambergate Street SE17 ....245 H7
Amberley Road W9 ....238 A4
Ambrosden Avenue SW1P 244 A4
Amelia Street SE17 ....245 J6
America Square EC3N 246 B3
America Street SE1 ....245 J2
Ampton Street WC1X 240 E2
Amwell Street EC1R 240 F2
Anchorage Point E14 ....247 M6
Andover Place NW6 ....238 B1
Angel ⊖ N1 ....241 G1
Angela Hooper Place * SW1E ...244 A4
Angel Junction N1 ....241 G1
Angel Lane EC4R 241 L8
Angel Street EC1A 241 J6
Ann Moss Way SE16 ....246 F8
Ann's Close SW1X 243 J3
Ansdell Street W8 ....242 B4
Antill Terrace E1 ....247 H2
Antizan Street E1 ....246 B2
Apple Tree Yard SW1Y 240 A8
Appold Street EC2A 241 M4
Apsley Gate W1J 243 J2
Apsley House & Wellington
  Museum W1J 243 K2
Aquinas Street SE1 ....245 G1
Arbour Square E1 ....247 H2
Archangel Street SE16 ....247 H3
Archer Street W1B 240 B7
Arch Street SE1 ....245 J4
Arden Estate N1 ....241 M1
Argyle Square WC1H 240 D2
Argyle Street WC1H 240 D2
Argyll Road W8 ....242 A3
Argyll Street W1F 239 M6
Arlington Street SW1A 243 M1
Arlington Way EC1R 241 G2
Arne Street WC2H 240 D6
Arneway Street SW1P 244 B5
Arnhem Place E14 ....247 M8
Arnold Estate SE1 ....246 C6
Arnside Street SE17 ....245 K8
Artesian Road W11 ....238 A6
Arthur Street EC4R 241 L7
Artichoke Hill E1W 246 E4
Artillery Lane E1 ....246 B1
Artillery Row SW1P 244 B4
Arundel Street WC2R 240 F7

B

Ashbridge Street NW8 ....238 F4
Ashburn Gardens SW7 ....242 C5
Ashburn Place SW7 ....242 C5
Ashby Street EC1V 241 H2
Asher Way E1W 246 D4
Ashfield Street E1 ....246 E2
Ashford Street N1 ....241 M2
Ashley Place SW1P 243 M4
Ashmill Street NW1 ....238 F4
Ashmole Street SW8 ....244 F8
Ashworth Road W9 ....238 B2
Assam Street E1 ....246 C2
Assembly Passage E1 ....247 G1
Astell Street SW3 ....243 G6
Aston Street E14 ....247 K1
Astwood Mews SW7 ....242 C5
Atherstone Mews SW7 ....242 D5
Atterbury Street SW1P 244 C6
Attneave Street WC1X 240 F3
Augustus Street NW1 ....239 L1
Aulton Place SE11 ....245 G7
Austin Friars EC2N 241 L6
Australia Gate SW1A 243 M3
Austral Street SE11 ....245 H5
Aveline Street SE11 ....244 F7
Ave Maria Lane EC1A 241 H6
Avenue Dock Hill SE16 ....247 J6
Avery Farm Row SW1W 243 K6
Avery Row W1K 239 L7
Aybrook Street W1U 239 J5
Aylesbury Road SE17 ....245 L7
Aylesbury Street EC1R 241 H4
Aylesford Street SW1V 244 B7
Aylward Street E1 ....247 G2
Ayres Street SE1 ....245 K2

Babmaes Street SW1Y 240 B8
Bache's Street N1 ....241 L2
Back Church Lane E1 ....246 D3
Back Hill EC1R 241 G4
Bacon Grove SE1 ....246 B8
Bainbridge Street WC1A 240 C6
Bakers Mews W1U 239 J6
Baker's Row EC1R 241 G4
Baker Street NW1 ....239 H4
Baker Street W1U 239 J5
Baker Street ⊖ NW1 ....239 H4
Balcombe Street NW1 ....239 G3
Balderton Street W1K 239 J7
Baldwin's Gardens EC1N 240 F5
Baldwin Street EC1V 241 L2
Bale Road E1 ....247 J1
Balfe Street N1 ....240 D1
Balfour Mews W1K 239 K8
Balfour Place W1K 239 J8
Balfour Street SE17 ....245 K5
Baltic Street East EC1Y 241 J3
Baltic Street West EC1Y 241 J4
Balvaird Place SW1V 244 C7
Bank ⊖ EC2R 241 L6
Bank End SE1 ....245 K1
Bankside SE1 ....241 J8
Banner Street EC1Y 241 K3
Banyard Road SE16 ....246 E8
Barbican EC1A 241 J4
Barbican Estate EC2Y 241 J5
Barge House Street SE1 ......245 G1
Bark Place W2 ....238 B7
Barkston Gardens SW5 ....242 B6
Barley Corn Way E14 ....247 L4
Barlow/Congreve Estate SE17 .245 M5
Barlow Place W1J 239 L7
Barlow Street SE17 ....245 L5
Barnardo Street E1 ....247 H3
Barnby Street NW1 ....240 A1
Barnes Street E14 ....247 J2
Barnham Street SE1 ....246 A6
Baron's Place SE1 ....245 G3
Baron Street N1 ....241 G1
Barrett Street W1U 239 K6
Barrow Hill Estate NW8 ......238 F1
Barrow Hill Road NW8 ....238 F1
Barter Street WC1A 240 D5
Bartholomew Close EC1A 241 J5
Bartholomew Lane EC2R 241 L6
Bartholomew Street SE1 ......245 L5
Bartlett Court EC4A 241 G6
Barton Street SW1P 244 C4
Basil Street SW3 ....243 H4
Basin Approach E14 ....247 K3
Basinghall Avenue EC2V 241 K5
Basinghall Street EC2V 241 K5
Bastwick Street EC1V 241 J3
Bateman's Buildings W1D 240 B6
Bateman Street W1D 240 B6
Bath Street EC1V 241 K2
Bath Terrace SE1 ....245 J4
Bathurst Mews W2 ....238 E7
Bathurst Street W2 ....238 E7
Battle Bridge Lane SE1 ......245 M1
Batty Street E1 ....246 D2
Bayley Street WC1B 240 B5
Baylis Road SE1 ....244 F3
Bayswater ⊖ W2 ....238 B7
Bayswater Road W2 ....238 E7
Baythorne Street E3 ....247 L1
Beaconsfield Road SE17 ......245 M7
Beak Street W1F 240 A7
Bear Gardens SE1 ....241 J8
Bear Lane SE1 ....245 H1
Beauchamp Place SW3 ....243 G4
Beaufort Gardens SW3 ....243 G4
Beaufort Street SW3 ....242 E8
Beaumont Place W1T 240 A3
Beaumont Street W1G 239 K4
Beccles Street E14 ....247 M3
Beckett Street E1 ....245 L3
Beckway Street SE17 ....245 M6
Bedale Street SE1 ....245 L1
Bedford Avenue WC1B 240 C5
Bedford Gardens W8 ....242 A2
Bedford Place WC1N 240 D4

Bedford Row WC1R 240 E4
Bedford Square WC1B 240 B5
Bedford Street WC2E 240 D7
Bedford Way WC1H 240 C3
Bedlow Close NW8 ....238 F3
Beech Street EC2Y 241 J4
Beeston Place SW1W 243 L4
Belgrave Mews North * SW1X .243 J3
Belgrave Mews South * SW1X .243 K4
Belgrave Place SW1X 243 J4
Belgrave Road SW1V 243 L5
Belgrave Road SW1V 244 A6
Belgrave Square SW1X 243 J3
Belgrave Street WC1H 247 J2
Belgrove Street WC1H 240 D2
Bell Lane E1 ....246 B1
Bell Street NW1 ....238 F4
Bell Yard WC2A 240 F6
Belvedere Road SE1 ....244 E2
Benjamin Street EC1M 241 H4
Ben Jonson Road E1 ....247 J1
Bennett Street SW1A 243 M1
Ben Smith Way SE16 ....246 D7
Benson Quay E1W 246 F4
Bentinck Mews W1U 239 K6
Bentinck Street W1U 239 K6
Bere Street E1W 247 H3
Bergen Square SE16 ....247 K8
Berkeley Mews W1H 239 H6
Berkeley Square W1J 239 L8
Berkeley Street W1J 239 L8
Bermondsey ⊖ SE16 ....246 E7
Bermondsey Spa SE16 ....246 C8
Bermondsey Square SE1 ......246 A8
Bermondsey Street SE1 ......246 A6
Bermondsey Wall East SE16 ..246 E7
Bermondsey Wall Estate SE16 246 D7
Bermondsey Wall West SE16 ..246 C6
Bernard Street WC1N 240 D4
Berners Mews W1T 240 A5
Berners Place W1F 240 A6
Berners Street W1T 240 A5
Bernhardt Crescent NW8 .....238 F3
Berryfield Road SE17 ....245 J6
Berry Street EC1V 241 H3
Berwick Street W1F 240 A6
Bessborough Gardens SW1V ...244 C6
Bessborough Street SW1V 244 B6
Betterton Street WC2H 240 D6
Bevenden Street N1 ....241 L2
Bevin Close SE16 ....247 J5
Bevington Street SE16 ......246 D7
Bevin Way WC1X 240 F1
Bevis Marks EC3A 246 A2
Bewley Street E1 ....247 H4
Bickenhall Street W1U 239 H4
Bidborough Street WC1H 240 C2
Biddulph Road W9 ....238 B2
Big Ben (Elizabeth Tower) SW1A ..244 D3
Bigland Street E1 ....246 E3
Billiter Square EC3M 246 A3
Billiter Street EC3M 246 A3
Bina Gardens SW5 ....242 C6
Bingham Place W1U 239 J4
Binney Street W1K 239 K7
Birchfield Street E14 ......247 M3
Birchin Lane EC3V 241 L7
Birdcage Walk SW1H 244 A3
Birde Lane EC4Y 241 H6
Bird Street W1C 239 K6
Birkenhead Street N1 ....240 D1
Bishop's Bridge Road W2 ....238 C6
Bishopsgate EC2M 246 A2
Bishops Square E1 ....246 B1
Bishop's Terrace SE11 ......245 G5
Bittern Street SE1 ....245 J3
Blackall Street EC2A 241 M3
Blackburne's Mews W1K 239 J7
Blackfriars ⊖ EC4V 241 H7
Blackfriars Bridge SE1 .....241 H8
Blacklands Terrace SW3 .....243 H6
Black Friars Lane EC4V 241 H7
Blackfriars Road SE1 ....245 H3
Blackhorse Court SE1 ....245 L4
Black Lion Gate W2 ....238 B8
Black Prince Road SE11 .....244 E6
Blackwood Street SE17 ......245 K6
Blandford Street W1U 239 H5
Blenheim Street W1S 239 L7
Bletchley Street N1 ....241 K1
Blomfield Mews W2 ....238 C5
Blomfield Road W9 ....238 C4
Blomfield Street EC2M 241 M5
Blomfield Villas W2 ....238 C5
Bloomfield Terrace SW1W 243 J6
Bloomsbury Square WC1A 240 D5
Bloomsbury Street WC1B 240 C5
Bloomsbury Way WC1A 240 C5
Blount Street E14 ....247 K2
Blue Ball Yard SW1A 243 M1
Bohn Road E1 ....247 J1
Bolsover Street W1W 239 L4
Bolton Gardens SW5 ....242 B6
Bolton Street W1J 243 L1
Bond Street ⊖ W1C 239 K6
Bondway SW8 ....244 D8
Bonhill Street EC2A 241 L4
Bonnington Square SW8 .....244 E8
Boot Street N1 ....241 M2
Borough ⊖ SE1 ....245 K3
Borough High Street SE1 ....245 K3
Borough Road SE1 ....245 H3
Boscobel Place SW1W 243 K5
Boscobel Street NW8 ....238 E4
Boss Street SE1 ....246 B6
Boston Place NW1 ....239 G3
Botolph Lane EC3R 241 M7
Boundary Lane SE17 ....245 K8
Boundary Row SE1 ....245 G2
Bourdon Street W1K 239 L7
Bourlet Close W1W 239 M5
Bourne Estate EC1N 240 F4
Bourne Street SW1W 243 J6
Bourne Terrace W2 ....238 B5
Bouverie Place W2 ....238 F6
Bouverie Street EC4Y 241 G6
Bowland Yard * SW1X 243 J3
Bow Lane EC4M 241 K6

Bowling Green Lane EC1R 241 G3
Bowling Green Place SE1 ....245 L2
Bowling Green Street SE11 ..244 F8
Bowling Green Walk N1 .....241 M2
Bowsell Street WC1N 240 D4
Bow Street WC2E 240 D7
Boyd Street E1 ....246 D3
Boyfield Street SE1 ....245 H3
Boyle Street W1S 239 M7
Boyson Road SE17 ....245 K8
Brackley Street EC1Y 241 J4
Bradenham Close SE17 ......245 K8
Brad Street SE1 ....245 G2
Braganza Street SE17 ....245 H7
Braham Street E1 ....246 C3
Bramerton Street SW3 ......242 F7
Bramham Gardens SW5 ......242 B6
Brandon Estate SE17 ....245 H8
Brandon Street SE17 ....245 K6
Brangton Road SE11 ....244 F7
Bray Crescent SE16 ....247 H6
Bray Place SW3 ....243 H6
Bread Street EC4M 241 K7
Bream's Buildings EC4A 240 F6
Brechin Place SW7 ....242 D6
Breezer's Hill E1W 246 D4
Brendon Street W1H 239 G5
Bressenden Place SW1W 243 L4
Brettell Street SE17 ....245 L7
Brewers Green SW1H 244 A3
Brewer Street W1F 240 A7
Brewhouse Lane E1W 246 F6
Brewhouse Walk SE16 ....247 J5
Brick Lane E1 ....246 C1
Brick Street W1J 243 K2
Bridewell Place EC4V 241 H7
Bridgeman Street NW8 ......238 F1
Bridge Place SW1V 243 L5
Bridgeport Place E1W 246 D4
Bridge Street SW1A 244 D3
Bridgewater Street EC2Y ...241 J4
Bridgeway Street NW1 ......240 A1
Bridle Lane W1F 240 A7
Bridstow Place W2 ....238 A6
Brightlingsea Place E14 ....247 L4
Brill Place NW1 ....240 C1
Briset Street EC1M 241 H4
Bristol Gardens W9 ....238 B4
Britannia Street WC1X 240 E2
Britannia Walk N1 ....241 L2
Britannia Way N1 ....241 K1
Britten Street SW3 ....242 F7
Britton Street EC1M 241 H4
Broadbent Street W1K 239 L7
Broadgate Circle EC2M 241 M5
Broadley Street NW8 ....238 F4
Broadley Terrace NW1 ......238 F4
Broadstone Place W1U 239 J5
Broadwall SE1 ....245 G1
Broadway SW1H 244 A3
Broadwick Street W1F 240 A7
Brockham Street SE1 ....245 K4
Brodlove Lane E1W 247 H3
Bromley Street E1 ....247 J2
Brompton Place SW3 ....243 G4
Brompton Road SW3 ....243 G4
Brompton Road SW7 ....242 F5
Brompton Square SW3 ......242 F4
Bronti Close SE17 ....245 K7
Brook Drive SE11 ....245 G5
Brooke Street EC1N 240 F5
Brook Gate W2 ....239 H8
Brook Mews North W2 ......238 D7
Brook's Mews W1K 239 K7
Brook Street W1K 239 K7
Brook Street W2 ....238 E7
Brown Heart Gardens W1K ...239 K7
Browning Mews W1G 239 K5
Brownlow Mews WC1N 240 E3
Brownlow Street WC1V 240 E5
Brown Street W1H 239 G6
Brunel Road SE16 ....247 G6
Brune Street E1 ....246 B1
Brunswick Close SE1 ....246 A6
Brunswick Gardens W8 ......242 A1
Brunswick Place N1 ....241 L2
Brunswick Quay SE16 ......247 J8
Brunswick Square WC1N 240 D3
Brunswick Street WC1N 240 D3
Brunton Place E14 ....247 K3
Brushfield Street E1 ......246 B1
Bruton Lane W1J 239 L8
Bruton Place W1J 239 L8
Bruton Street W1J 239 L8
Bryan Road SE16 ....247 K6
Bryanston Mews West W1H ...239 G5
Bryanston Mews East W1H ...239 H5
Bryanston Place W1H 239 H5
Bryanston Square W1H 239 H5
Bryanston Street W1C 239 H7
Buck Hill Walk W2 ....238 E8
Buckingham Gate SW1E 243 L3
Buckingham Mews SW1E 243 M3
Buckingham Palace SW1A 243 L3
Buckingham Palace Road SW1W 243 L5
Buckingham Palace Road SW1E 243 M4
Buckland Street N1 ....241 L1
Buckle Street E1 ....246 C2
Bucknall Street WC2H 240 C6
Buckters Rents SE16 ......247 J5
Budge's Walk W2 ....242 D2
Bulleid Way SW1V 243 L5
Bulstrode Street W1U 239 K5
Bunhill Row EC1Y 241 L3
Burbage Close SE1 ....245 L4
Burdett Estate E14 ....247 M1
Burdett Road E14 ....247 L2
Burdett Street SE1 ....244 F3
Burgess Street E14 ....247 M1
Burge Street SE1 ....245 L4
Burlington Arcade W1J 239 M8
Burlington Gardens W1S 239 M8
Burnhouse Place SW1W 243 J6
Burnsall Street SW3 ....243 G7

Burnside Close SE16 ....247 J5
Burrell Street SE1 ....245 H1
Burslem Street E1 ....246 D3
Burton Grove SE17 ....245 L7
Burton Street WC1H 240 C3
Burwood Place W2 ....239 G6
Bury Close SE16 ....247 H5
Bury Court EC3A 246 A2
Bury Place WC1A 240 D5
Bury Street EC3A 246 A2
Bury Street SW1Y 244 A1
Bury Walk SW3 ....242 F6
Bushell Street E1W 246 D5
Bush Lane EC4V 241 L7
Butcher Row E14 ....247 J3
Bute Street SW7 ....242 E5
Butler Place SW1H 244 B4
Butler's Wharf SE1 ....246 C6
Buttesland Street N1 .....241 L2
Byefield Close SE16 ......247 K6
Bylands Close SE16 ......247 K5
Byng Place WC1E 240 B4
Byng Street E14 ....247 M6
Byward Street EC3R 246 A4
Bywater Place SE16 ......247 K5
Bywater Street SW3 ....243 G6

C

Cabbell Street NW1 ....238 F5
Cable Street E1 ....246 F3
Cadiz Street SE17 ....245 K7
Cadogan Gardens SW3 .....243 H5
Cadogan Gate SW1X 243 H5
Cadogan Lane SW1X 243 J4
Cadogan Place SW1X 243 J4
Cadogan Square SW1X 243 H5
Cadogan Street SW3 ......243 G6
Caledonian Road N1 ......240 D1
Caledonia Street N1 .....240 D1
Cale Street SW3 ....242 F6
Callow Street SW3 ....242 D7
Calshot Street N1 ....240 E1
Calthorpe Street WC1X ...240 E3
Cambridge Circus WC2H ...240 C7
Cambridge Gardens NW6 ...238 A1
Cambridge Gate NW1 ......239 L3
Cambridge Road NW6 ......238 A2
Cambridge Square W2 .....238 F6
Cambridge Terrace NW1 ...239 L2
Cambridge Terrace Mews NW1 239 L3
Camdenhurst Street E14 ..247 K2
Camera Place SW10 ....242 D8
Camomile Street EC3A 246 A2
Campden Grove W8 ....242 A2
Campden Hill Road W8 ....242 A2
Campden Street W8 ....242 A1
Camperdown Street E1 ....246 C3
Canada Estate SE16 ....247 G7
Canada Gate SW1A 243 M3
Canada Street SE16 ......247 H7
Canada Water ⊖ SE16 ....247 G7
Canada Wharf SE16 ....247 L5
Canal Street SE5 ....245 L8
Canary Riverside E14 ....247 L4
Candle Street E1 ....247 K1
Canning Place W8 ....242 C4
Cannon Drive E14 ....247 M4
Cannon Street EC4N 241 K7
Cannon Street ⊖ EC4R ...241 K7
Cannon Street Road E1 ...246 E3
Canon Beck Road SE16 ....247 G6
Canon Row SW1A 244 D3
Canton Street E14 ....247 M3
Capeners Close * SW1X ...243 J3
Capland Street NW8 ......238 E3
Capper Street WC1E 240 A4
Capstan Way SE16 ....247 K5
Carbis Road E14 ....247 L2
Carburton Street W1W 239 L4
Cardigan Street SE11 ....244 F6
Cardington Street NW1 ...240 A2
Carey Street WC2A 240 F6
Carlisle Avenue EC3N 246 B3
Carlisle Lane SE1 ....244 F4
Carlisle Place SW1P 243 M5
Carlisle Street W1D 240 B6
Carlos Place W1K 239 K7
Carlton Gardens SW1Y 244 B2
Carlton Hill NW6 ....238 B1
Carlton House Terrace SW1Y 244 B1
Carlton Vale W1J 243 L1
Carlton Vale NW6 ....238 B1
Carlyle Square SW3 .....242 F7
Carmelite Street EC4Y ...241 G7
Carnaby Street W1F 239 M7
Caroline Place W2 ....238 B7
Caroline Street E1 ......247 H3
Caroline Terrace SW1W ...243 J5
Carpenter Street W1K 239 K7
Carrington Street W1J ...243 L2
Carr Street E14 ....247 K1
Carteret Street SW1H 244 B3
Carter Lane EC4V 241 H7
Carter Place SE17 ....245 K7
Carter Street SE17 ....245 J7
Carthusian Street EC1M ..241 J4
Carting Lane WC2R 240 D8
Cartwright Gardens WC1H ..240 C2
Cartwright Street E1 ....246 C4
Casey Close NW8 ....238 F3
Casson Street E1 ....246 C1
Castellain Road W9 ......238 B3
Castlebrook Close SE11 ..245 G5
Castle Lane SW1E 243 M4
Catesby Street SE17 .....245 L6
Cathay Street SE16 ......246 E7
Cathcart Road SW10 .....242 C8
Cathedral Walk SW1E 243 M4
Catherine Place SW1E 243 M4
Catherine Street WC2E ...240 E7
Cato Street W1H 239 G5
Causton Street SW1P 244 B6

Cavell Street – Farringdon Road 249

Cavell Street E1 246 F1
Cavendish Avenue NW8 238 E1
Cavendish Place W1G 239 L6
Cavendish Square W1G 239 L6
Cavendish Street N1 241 L1
Caversham Street SW3 243 G8
Caxton Street SW1H 244 B4
Cayton Street EC1V 241 K2
Centaur Street SE1 244 F4
Central Street EC1V 241 J2
Chadwell Street EC1R 241 G1
Chadwick Street SW1P 244 B4
Chagford Street NW1 239 H4
Chalton Street NW1 240 B1
Chambers Street SE16 246 D7
Chamber Street E1 246 C3
Chambers Wharf SE16 246 D6
Chancel Street SE1 245 H1
Chancery Lane WC2A 240 F5
Chancery Lane ⊖ WC1V 240 F5
Chandos Place WC2N 240 C8
Chandos Street W1G 239 L5
Chantry Square W8 242 B4
Chapel Market N1 240 F1
Chapel Street NW1 238 F5
Chapel Street SW1X 243 K3
Chaplin Close SE1 245 G3
Chapman Street E1 246 E3
Chapter Road SE17 245 H7
Chapter Street SW1P 244 B6
Chargrove Close SE16 247 H6
Charing Cross ⇌ ⊖ WC2N 244 D1
Charing Cross Road WC2H 240 B6
Charing Cross Road WC2N 240 C7
Charlbert Street NW8 238 F1
Charles II Street SW1Y 240 B8
Charles Square N1 241 M2
Charles Street W1J 243 K1
Charleston Street SE17 245 K6
Charlotte Road EC2A 241 M3
Charlotte Street W1T 240 A4
Charlwood Place SW1V 244 A6
Charlwood Street SW1V 243 M7
Charlwood Street SW1V 244 A6
Charrington Street NW1 240 B1
Charterhouse Square EC1M 241 H4
Charterhouse Street EC1M 241 G5
Chart Street N1 241 L2
Chaseley Street E14 247 J2
Chatham Street SE17 245 L5
Cheapside EC2V 241 K6
Chelsea Bridge SW1W 243 K8
Chelsea Bridge Road SW1W 243 J7
Chelsea Embankment SW3 243 G8
Chelsea Manor Gardens SW3 242 F7
Chelsea Manor Street SW3 243 G7
Chelsea Park Gardens SW3 242 E8
Chelsea Physic Garden SW3 243 H8
Chelsea Square SW3 242 E7
Cheltenham Terrace SW3 243 H6
Chenies Mews WC1E 240 B4
Chenies Street WC1E 240 B4
Cheniston Gardens W8 242 A4
Chepstow Place W2 238 A7
Chepstow Road W2 238 A6
Chequer Street EC1Y 241 K3
Cherbury Street N1 241 L1
Cherry Garden Street SE16 246 E7
Chesham Close SW1X 243 J4
Chesham Place SW1X 243 J4
Chesham Street SW1X 243 J4
Chester Close SW1X 243 K3
Chester Close North NW1 239 L2
Chester Close South NW1 239 L2
Chesterfield Gardens W1J 243 K1
Chesterfield Hill W1J 239 K8
Chesterfield Street W1J 243 K1
Chester Gate NW1 239 L2
Chester Mews SW1X 243 K3
Chester Place NW1 239 L1
Chester Road NW1 239 K2
Chester Row SW1W 243 K5
Chester Square SW1W 243 K5
Chester Square Mews SW1W 243 K4
Chester Street SW1X 243 K4
Chester Terrace NW1 239 L2
Chester Way SE11 245 G6
Cheval Place SW7 243 G4
Cheval Street E14 247 M7
Cheyne Gardens SW3 243 G8
Cheyne Row SW3 242 F8
Cheyne Walk SW3 242 F8
Chicheley Street SE1 244 E2
Chichester Road NW6 238 A1
Chichester Road W2 238 C5
Chichester Street SW1V 244 A7
Chicksand Street E1 246 C1
Chigwell Hill E1W 246 E4
Child's Place SW5 242 A5
Child's Street SW5 242 A5
Chiltern Street W1U 239 J4
Chilworth Mews W2 238 D6
Chilworth Street W2 238 D6
China Hall Mews SE16 247 G8
Chinatown W1D 240 B7
Chippenham Mews W9 238 A4
Chiswell Street EC1Y 241 K4
Chitty Street W1T 240 A4
Christchurch Street SW3 243 G8
Christian Street E1 246 D3
Christina Street EC2A 241 M3
Christopher Close SE16 247 H6
Christopher Street EC2A 241 L4
Chudleigh Street E1 247 H2
Chumleigh Street SE5 245 M8
Churchill Gardens Road SW1V 243 L7
Churchill War Rooms SW1A 244 C3
Church Street NW8 238 F4
Church Way NW1 240 B2
Churchyard Row SE1 245 H5
Churton Place SW1V 244 A6
Churton Street SW1V 244 A6
Circus Road NW8 238 E1
Cirencester Square W2 238 A5
City Garden Row N1 241 J1
City Road EC1V 241 J1
City Road EC1Y 241 L3
City Thameslink ⇌ EC4M 241 H6
Clabon Mews SW1X 243 H5
Clack Street SE16 247 G7
Clanricarde Gardens W2 238 A8
Clarkson Row NW1 239 M1
Claremont Square N1 240 F1
Clarence Gardens NW1 239 L2
Clarence Mews SE16 247 G6
Clarendon Gardens W9 238 D4
Clarendon Gate W2 238 F7
Clarendon Place W2 238 F7
Clarendon Street SW1V 243 L6
Clareville Grove SW7 242 D6
Clareville Street SW7 242 D6
Clarges Mews W1J 243 L1
Clarges Street W1J 243 L1
Clark Street E1 246 F2
Carkson Row NW1 239 M1
Claverton Street SW1V 244 A7
Clave Street E1W 246 F5
Clay Street W1U 239 H5
Clayton Street SE11 244 F8
Cleaver Square SE11 245 G7
Cleaver Street SE11 245 G7
Clegg Street E1W 246 F5
Clemence Street E14 247 L2
Clements Lane EC4N 241 L7
Clement's Road SE16 246 E8
Clenston Mews W1H 239 H6
Clere Street EC2A 241 L3
Clerkenwell Close EC1R 241 G3
Clerkenwell Green EC1R 241 G4
Clerkenwell Road EC1M 241 G4
Cleveland Gardens W2 238 C6
Cleveland Mews W1T 239 M4
Cleveland Place SW1Y 244 A1
Cleveland Row SW1A 244 A2
Cleveland Square W2 238 C6
Cleveland Street W1T 239 M4
Cleveland Terrace W2 238 D6
Clifford Street W1S 239 M7
Clifton Gardens W9 238 C4
Clifton Place SE16 247 G6
Clifton Place W2 238 E7
Clifton Road W9 238 D3
Clifton Street EC2A 241 M3
Clifton Villas W9 238 C4
Clink Street SE1 245 K1
Clipper Close SE16 247 H6
Clipstone Mews W1W 239 M4
Clipstone Street W1W 239 L4
Cliveden Place SW1W 243 J5
Cloak Lane EC4R 241 K7
Cloth Fair EC1A 241 J5
Cloth Street EC1A 241 J5
Cluny Place SE1 246 A8
Cobb Street E1 246 B2
Cobourg Street NW1 240 A2
Coburg Close SW1P 244 A5
Cochrane Mews NW8 238 E1
Cochrane Street NW8 238 E1
Cock Lane EC1A 241 H5
Cockspur Street SW1Y 244 C1
Codling Close * E1W 246 D5
Coin Street SE1 245 G1
Coke Street E1 246 D2
Colbeck Mews SW7 242 C6
Colebrook Row N1 241 H1
Coleherne Road SW10 242 B7
Coleman Street EC2R 241 L6
Cole Street SE1 245 K3
Coley Street WC1X 240 F3
College Hill EC4R 241 K7
College Street EC4R 241 K7
Collett Road SE16 246 D8
Collier Street N1 240 E1
Collingham Gardens SW5 242 B6
Collingham Place SW5 242 B5
Collingham Road SW5 242 B5
Colnbrook Street SE1 245 H4
Colombo Street SE1 245 H1
Colonnade WC1N 240 D4
Coltman Street E14 247 K2
Commercial Road E1 246 D2
Commercial Road E14 247 K3
Commercial Street E1 246 B1
Compton Street EC1V 241 H3
Concert Hall Approach SE1 244 E2
Conder Street E14 247 K2
Conduit Mews W2 238 E6
Conduit Place W2 238 E6
Conduit Street W1S 239 L7
Congreve Street SE17 245 M5
Connaught Close W2 238 F7
Connaught Place W2 239 G7
Connaught Square W2 239 G6
Connaught Street W2 239 G6
Cons Street SE1 245 G2
Constitution Hill SW1A 243 L3
Content Street SE17 245 K5
Conway Street W1T 239 M4
Cookham Crescent SE16 247 H6
Cook's Road SE17 245 H8
Coombs Street N1 241 J1
Cooper's Lane Estate NW1 240 B1
Cooper's Row EC3N 246 B3
Copenhagen Place E14 247 L2
Cope Place W8 242 A4
Copley Court SE17 245 J8
Copley Street E1 247 H2
Copperfield Road E3 247 K1
Copperfield Street SE1 245 J2
Copthall Avenue EC2R 241 L6
Coptic Street WC1A 240 C5
Coral Street SE1 245 G3
Coram Street WC1H 240 C3
Cork Square E1W 246 E5
Cork Street W1S 239 M8
Corlett Street NW1 238 F5
Cornhill EC3V 241 L6
Cornwall Gardens SW7 242 C4
Cornwall Mews South SW7 242 C5
Cornwall Road SE1 244 F1
Cornwall Road SE1 245 G2
Cornwall Street E1 246 E3
Cornwall Terrace Mews NW1 239 H4
Cornwood Drive E1 247 G2
Coronet Street N1 241 M2
Corporation Row EC1R 241 G3
Corsham Street N1 241 L2
Cosser Street SE1 244 F4
Cosway Street NW1 239 G4
Cottage Place SW3 242 F4
Cottesmore Gardens W8 242 B4
Cottons Lane SE1 245 M1
Coulson Street SW3 243 H6
Counter Street SE1 245 M1
County Street SE1 245 K5
Courtenay Square SE11 244 F7
Courtenay Street SE11 244 F6
Courtfield Gardens SW5 242 B5
Courtfield Mews * SW5 242 C5
Courtfield Road SW7 242 C5
Court Street E1 246 E1
Cousin Lane SE1 241 K8
Covent Garden ⊖ WC2E 240 D7
Covent Garden WC2E 240 D7
Coventry Street W1D 240 B8
Cowcross Street EC1M 241 H4
Cowper Street EC2A 241 L3
Crail Row SE17 245 L5
Cramer Street W1U 239 J5
Crampton Street SE17 245 J6
Cranbourn Street WC2H 240 C7
Cranleigh Street NW1 240 A1
Cranley Gardens SW7 242 D6
Cranley Mews SW7 242 D6
Cranley Place SW7 242 E6
Cranston Estate N1 241 L1
Cranwood Street EC1V 241 L2
Craven Hill W2 238 D7
Craven Hill Gardens W2 238 C7
Craven Road W2 238 D7
Craven Street WC2N 244 D1
Craven Terrace W2 238 D7
Crawford Passage EC1R 241 G3
Crawford Place W1H 239 G5
Crawford Street W1H 239 G5
Creechurch Lane EC3A 246 A3
Creed Lane EC4V 241 H7
Cresswell Place SW10 242 D6
Cressy Place E1 247 G1
Crestfield Street WC1H 240 D2
Crimscott Street SE1 246 A8
Crispin Street E1 246 B1
Cromer Street WC1H 240 D2
Crompton Street W2 238 D4
Cromwell Mews * SW7 242 E5
Cromwell Place SW7 242 E5
Cromwell Road SW5 242 B5
Cromwell Road SW7 242 E5
Crondall Court N1 241 M1
Crondall Street N1 241 L1
Cropley Street N1 241 K1
Crosby Row SE1 245 L3
Cross Lane EC3R 246 A4
Crosswall EC3N 246 B3
Crowder Street E1 246 E3
Crucifix Lane SE1 246 A6
Cruikshank Street WC1X 240 F1
Crutched Friars EC3N 246 A3
Cuba Street E14 247 M6
Cubitt Street WC1X 240 E2
Culford Gardens SW3 243 H6
Culling Road SE16 246 F7
Cullum Street EC3M 241 M7
Culross Street W1K 239 J8
Culworth Street NW8 238 F1
Cumberland Gardens WC1X 240 F2
Cumberland Gate W2 239 H7
Cumberland Market NW1 239 L2
Cumberland Street SW1V 243 L6
Cumberland Terrace NW1 239 K1
Cumberland Terrace Mews NW1 239 L1
Cumberland Wharf SE16 247 G6
Cumming Street N1 240 E1
Cundy Street SW1W 243 K6
Cunningham Place NW8 238 E3
Cureton Street SW1P 244 C6
Curlew Street SE1 246 B6
Cursitor Street EC4A 240 F6
Curtain Road EC2A 241 M3
Curtain Road EC2A 241 M4
Curzon Gate W2 243 K2
Curzon Street W1J 243 K1
Cuthbert Street W2 238 E4
Cutler Street EC3A 246 A2
Cynthia Street N1 240 F1
Cypress Place W1T 240 A4
Cyrus Street EC1V 241 H3

D

Dacre Street SW1H 244 B3
Dakin Place E1 247 J1
Dallington Street EC1V 241 H3
Damien Street E1 246 F2
Dane Street WC1R 240 E5
Dansey Place W1D 240 B7
Dante Road SE11 245 H5
Danvers Street SW3 242 F8
D'Arblay Street W1F 240 A6
Dartford Street SE17 245 K8
Dartmouth Street SW1H 244 B3
Darwin Street SE17 245 L5
Date Street SE17 245 K7
Davenant Street E1 246 D1
Daventry Street NW1 238 F4
Davidge Street SE1 245 H3
Davies Mews W1K 239 K7
Davies Street W1K 239 K7
Dawes Street SE17 245 L6
Dawson Place W2 238 A7
Deal Porters Way SE16 247 G8
Deal Street E1 246 D1
Dean Bradley Street SW1P 244 C5
Dean Close SE16 247 H6
Deancross Street E1 246 F3
Deanery Street W1K 243 K1
Dean Farrar Street SW1H 244 B3
Dean Ryle Street SW1P 244 C5
Dean's Buildings SE17 245 L6
Dean Stanley Street SW1P 244 C4
Dean Street W1D 240 B6
Dean's Yard SW1P 244 C4
Decima Street SE1 245 M4
Deck Close SE16 247 J6
Defoe Close SE16 247 K7
Delamere Street W2 238 C5
Delamere Terrace W2 238 B4
De Laune Street SE17 245 H7
Delaware Road W9 238 B3
Dellow Street E1 246 F3
Delverton Road SE17 245 H7
Denbigh Place SW1V 243 M6
Denbigh Street SW1V 243 M6
Denbigh Street SW1V 244 A6
Denman Street W1D 240 B7
Denmark Street WC2H 240 C6
Denny Close SE11 245 G6
Denny Street SE11 245 G6
Denyer Street SW3 243 G5
Derby Gate SW1A 244 D3
Derby Street W1J 243 K1
Dering Street W1S 239 L6
Derry Street W8 242 B3
De Vere Gardens W8 242 C3
Deverell Street SE1 245 L4
Devonport Street E1 247 G3
Devonshire Close W1G 239 K4
Devonshire Mews South W1G 239 K4
Devonshire Mews West W1G 239 K4
Devonshire Place W1G 239 K4
Devonshire Place Mews W1G 239 K4
Devonshire Row EC2M 246 A2
Devonshire Square EC2M 246 A2
Devonshire Street W1G 239 K4
Devonshire Terrace W2 238 D7
De Walden Street W1G 239 K5
Dickens Estate SE16 246 D7
Dickens Square SE1 245 K4
Dilke Street SW3 243 H8
Dingley Place EC1V 241 K2
Dingley Road EC1V 241 J2
Disney Place SE1 245 K2
Distaff Lane EC4V 241 J7
Distin Street SE11 244 F6
Dockhead SE1 246 C7
Dockley Road SE16 246 D8
Dock Street E1 246 D4
Doddington Grove SE17 245 H7
Doddington Place SE17 245 H8
Dodson Street SE1 245 G3
Dod Street E14 247 M2
Dolben Street SE1 245 H2
Dolland Street SE11 244 E7
Dolphin Square SW1V 244 A7
Dolphin Square SW1V 244 B7
Dombey Street WC1N 240 E4
Dominion Drive SE16 247 H7
Dominion Street EC2A 241 L5
Donegal Street N1 240 F1
Dongola Road E1 247 J1
Donne Place SW3 243 G5
Doon Street SE1 244 F1
Dora Street E14 247 L2
Doric Way NW1 240 B2
Dorset Rise EC4Y 241 G7
Dorset Square NW1 239 H4
Dorset Street W1U 239 H5
Doughty Mews WC1N 240 E3
Doughty Street WC1N 240 E3
Douglas Street SW1P 244 B6
Douro Place W8 242 C3
Douthwaite Square * E1W 246 D5
Dovehouse Street SW3 242 E6
Dover Street W1J 243 L1
Dover Street W1S 239 L8
Dowgate Hill EC4R 241 K7
Downfield Close W9 238 B4
Downing Street SW1A 244 C2
Down Street W1J 243 K2
Downtown Road SE16 247 K6
D'Oyley Street SW1X 243 J5
Draco Street SE17 245 J8
Drake Close SE16 247 H6
Draycott Avenue SW3 243 G5
Draycott Place SW3 243 H6
Draycott Terrace SW3 243 H5
Drayson Mews W8 242 A3
Drayton Gardens SW10 242 D6
Druid Street SE1 246 A6
Druid Street SE1 246 B6
Drummond Crescent NW1 240 B2
Drummond Gate * SW1V 244 B6
Drummond Road SE16 246 E8
Drummond Street NW1 240 A3
Drury Lane WC2B 240 D6
Dryden Court SE11 245 G5
Dryden Street WC2B 240 D6
Duchess Mews W1G 239 L5
Duchess Street W1B 239 L5
Duchy Street SE1 245 G1
Duckett Street E1 247 J1
Duck Lane W1F 240 B6
Dufferin Street EC1Y 241 K4
Duke of Wellington Place SW1W 243 K3
Duke of York Square SW3 243 H6
Duke of York Street SW1Y 244 A1
Duke Shore Wharf E14 247 K4
Duke's Lane W8 242 A2
Duke's Place EC3A 246 B2
Duke's Road WC1H 240 C2
Duke Street W1K 239 K7
Duke Street W1U 239 J6
Duke Street Hill SE1 245 L1
Duke Street St James's SW1Y 244 A1
Dunbar Wharf E14 247 L4
Duncannon Street WC2N 240 C8
Duncan Terrace N1 241 H1
Dundee Street E1W 246 E5
Dundee Wharf E14 247 L4
Dunelm Street E1 247 H2
Dunlop Place SE16 246 C8
Dunraven Street W1K 239 H7
Dunster Court EC3R 246 A3
Duplex Ride SW1X 243 H3
Durand's Wharf SE16 247 L6
Durham Row E1 247 J1
Durham Street SE11 244 E7
Durham Terrace W2 238 A6
Dyott Street WC1A 240 C6
Dysart Street EC2A 241 M4

E

Eagle Court EC1M 241 H4
Eagle Street WC1R 240 E5
Eamont Street NW8 239 G1
Eardley Crescent SW5 242 A7
Earlham Street WC2H 240 C7
Earl's Court ⇌ ⊖ SW5 242 A6
Earl's Court Gardens SW5 242 B6
Earl's Court Road SW5 242 A6
Earl's Court Square SW5 242 A6
Earlstoke Street EC1V 241 H2
Earl Street EC2A 241 M4
Earnshaw Street WC2H 240 C6
East Arbour Street E1 247 H2
Eastbourne Mews W2 238 D6
Eastbourne Terrace W2 238 D6
Eastcastle Street W1W 240 A6
Eastcheap EC3M 241 M7
Eastfield Street E14 247 K1
East India Dock Road E14 247 M3
East Lane SE16 246 D6
Easton Street WC1X 240 F3
East Poultry Avenue EC1A 241 H5
East Road N1 241 L2
East Smithfield E1W 246 C4
East Street SE17 245 L6
East Tenter Street E1 246 C3
Eaton Close SW1W 243 J5
Eaton Gate SW1W 243 J5
Eaton Lane SW1W 243 L4
Eaton Mews North SW1W 243 J5
Eaton Mews South SW1W 243 K5
Eaton Mews West SW1W 243 K5
Eaton Place SW1X 243 J4
Eaton Row SW1W 243 K4
Eaton Square SW1W 243 K5
Eaton Terrace SW1W 243 J5
Ebbisham Drive SW8 244 E8
Ebury Bridge SW1W 243 K6
Ebury Bridge Road SW1W 243 K7
Ebury Mews SW1W 243 K5
Ebury Square SW1W 243 K6
Ebury Street SW1W 243 K5
Eccleston Bridge SW1W 243 L5
Eccleston Mews SW1X 243 K4
Eccleston Place SW1W 243 L5
Eccleston Square SW1V 243 L6
Eccleston Street SW1X 243 K4
Edbrooke Road W9 238 A3
Edge Street W8 242 A1
Edgware Road W2 238 F5
Edgware Road ⊖ NW1 238 F5
Edinburgh Gate SW1X 243 H3
Edith Grove SW10 242 C8
Edwards Mews W1H 239 J6
Egerton Crescent SW3 242 F5
Egerton Gardens SW3 242 F5
Egerton Terrace SW3 243 G4
Eglington Court SE17 245 J7
Elba Place SE17 245 K5
Eldon Road W8 242 B4
Eldon Street EC2M 241 L5
Eleanor Close SE16 247 H6
Elephant & Castle SE1 245 J4
Elephant & Castle ⇌ ⊖ SE1 245 J5
Elephant Lane SE16 246 F6
Elephant Road SE17 245 J5
Elf Row E1W 247 G3
Elgar Street SE16 247 K7
Elgin Avenue W9 238 B2
Elgin Mews North W9 238 C2
Elgin Mews South W9 238 C2
Elia Mews N1 241 H1
Elia Street N1 241 H1
Elim Estate SE1 245 M3
Elim Street SE1 245 M3
Elizabeth Bridge SW1V 243 L6
Elizabeth Street SW1W 243 K5
Ellen Street E1 246 D3
Elliott's Row SE11 245 H5
Ellis Street SW1X 243 J5
Elmfield Way W9 238 A4
Elm Park Gardens SW10 242 E7
Elm Park Lane SW3 242 E7
Elm Park Road SW3 242 E8
Elm Place SW7 242 E7
Elms Mews W2 238 D7
Elm Street WC1X 240 F4
Elm Tree Road NW8 238 E2
Elnathan Mews W9 238 B4
Elsa Street E1 247 J1
Elsted Street SE17 245 L6
Elvaston Mews SW7 242 D4
Elvaston Place SW7 242 D4
Elverton Street SW1P 244 B5
Ely Place EC1N 241 G5
Elystan Place SW3 243 G6
Elystan Street SW3 242 F6
Embankment ⊖ WC2N 244 D1
Embankment Gardens SW3 243 H8
Embankment Place WC2N 244 D1
Emba Street SE16 246 D7
Emerald Street WC1N 240 E4
Emerson Street SE1 245 J1
Emery Hill Street SW1P 244 A5
Emery Street SE1 245 G3
Emperor's Gate SW7 242 C5
Empire Square SE1 245 L3
Empress Place SW6 242 A7
Endell Street WC2H 240 C6
Endsleigh Gardens WC1H 240 B3
Endsleigh Place WC1H 240 B3
Endsleigh Street WC1H 240 B3
Enford Street W1H 239 G5
English Grounds SE1 245 M1
Enid Street SE16 246 C8
Ennismore Gardens SW7 242 F3
Ennismore Gardens Mews SW7 242 F3
Ennismore Mews SW7 242 F3
Ennismore Street SW7 242 F4
Ensign Street E1 246 D4
Epworth Street EC2A 241 L3
Erasmus Street SW1P 244 C6
Errol Street EC1Y 241 K4
Essendine Road W9 238 A3
Essex Street WC2R 240 F7
Essex Villas W8 242 A3
Europa Place EC1V 241 J2
Euston ⇌ ⊖ ⊖ NW1 240 B2
Euston Road NW1 240 B3
Euston Square NW1 240 B2
Euston Square ⊖ NW1 240 A3
Euston Street NW1 240 A3
Evelyn Gardens SW7 242 D7
Evelyn Walk N1 241 L1
Eversholt Street NW1 240 A1
Everton Mews NW1 239 M2
Ewer Street SE1 245 J2
Ewhurst Close E1 247 G1
Exchange Square EC2A 241 M4
Exeter Street WC2E 240 D7
Exhibition Road SW7 242 E3
Exmouth Market EC1R 241 G3
Exon Street SE17 245 M6
Exton Street SE1 244 F2
Eyre Street Hill EC1R 240 F4

F

Fairclough Street E1 246 D3
Fair Street SE1 246 B6
Falmouth Road SE1 245 K4
Fann Street EC1M 241 J4
Fanshaw Street N1 241 M1
Farmer Street W8 242 A1
Farm Lane SW6 242 A8
Farm Street W1K 239 K8
Farnham Place SE1 245 J1
Farrance Street E14 247 M3
Farringdon ⇌ ⊖ EC1M 241 G4
Farringdon Lane EC1R 241 G4
Farringdon Road EC1R 240 F3

Farringdon Street EC1M....241 H5
Farrins Rents SE16....247 J5
Farrow Place SE16....247 K7
Farthing Fields * E1W....246 F5
Fashion Street E1....246 B1
Faunce Street SE17....245 H7
Fawcett Street SW10....242 C8
Featherstone Street EC1Y....241 L3
Fenchurch Avenue EC3M....246 A3
Fenchurch Buildings EC3M....246 A3
Fenchurch Place EC3M....246 A3
Fenchurch Street EC3M....246 A3
Fenchurch Street ⇌ EC3M....246 A3
Fendall Street SE1....246 B8
Fenning Street SE1....245 M2
Fentiman Road SW8....245 D8
Fernsbury Street WC1X....240 F2
Fetter Lane EC4A....241 G6
Fieldgate Street E1....246 D2
Fielding Street SE17....245 J7
Field Street WC1X....240 E1
Finborough Road SW10....242 B8
Finch Lane EC3V....241 L6
Finland Street SE16....247 K8
Finsbury Circus EC2M....241 L5
Finsbury Estate EC1R....241 G3
Finsbury Market EC2A....241 M4
Finsbury Square EC2A....241 L4
Finsbury Street EC2Y....241 L4
First Street SW3....243 G5
Fishermans Drive SE16....247 J6
Fisher Street WC1N....240 D5
Fisherton Street NW8....238 E3
Fish Street Hill EC3R....241 L7
Fitzalan Street SE11....244 F5
Fitzhardinge Street W1H....239 J6
Fitzroy Square W1T....239 M4
Fitzroy Street W1T....239 M4
Flamborough Street E14....247 J3
Flank Street E1....246 C4
Flaxman Terrace WC1H....240 C3
Fleet Street EC4A....241 G6
Fleming Road SE17....245 H8
Fletcher Street E1....246 D3
Flint Street SE17....245 L6
Flitcroft Street WC2H....240 C6
Flockton Street SE16....246 D7
Flood Street SW3....243 G7
Flood Walk SW3....243 G7
Floral Street WC2E....240 D7
Foley Street W1W....239 M5
Forbes Street E1....246 D3
Fordham Street E1....246 D2
Ford Square E1....246 F2
Fore Street EC2Y....241 K5
Formosa Street W9....238 C4
Forset Street W1H....239 G6
Forsyth Gardens SE17....245 H8
Fort Street E1....246 B1
Fortune Street EC1Y....241 K4
Forum Magnum Square SE1....244 E3
Foster Lane EC2V....241 J6
Foulis Terrace SW7....242 E6
Foundry Close SE16....247 J5
Fournier Street E1....246 B1
Fowey Close E1W....246 E5
Frampton Street NW8....238 E4
Francis Street SW1P....244 A5
Franklin's Row SW3....243 H6
Frazier Street SE1....245 G3
Frean Street SE16....246 C8
Frederick Close W2....239 G7
Frederick Street WC1X....240 E2
Frederic Mews * SW1X....243 J3
Freemantle Street SE17....245 M6
Friday Street EC4V....241 J7
Friend Street EC1V....241 H2
Frith Street W1D....240 B6
Fulbourne Street E1....246 E1
Fulford Street SE16....246 F7
Fulham Road SW10....242 D8
Fulham Road SW3....242 F6
Furnival Street EC4A....241 F5
Fynes Street SW1P....244 B5

G

Gabriel's Wharf SE1....245 G1
Gainsford Street SE1....246 B6
Galleon Close SE16....247 G6
Galsworthy Avenue E14....247 K2
Galway Street EC1V....241 K2
Gambia Street SE1....245 H2
Garden Road NW8....238 D1
Garden Row SE1....245 H4
Garden Street E1....247 H1
Garden Terrace * SW1V....244 B6
Gard Street EC1V....241 J2
Garford Street E14....247 M4
Garnault Place EC1R....241 G3
Garnet Street E1W....246 F4
Garrett Street EC1Y....241 K3
Garrick Street WC2E....240 C7
Garterway SE16....247 H7
Garway Road W2....238 B6
Gaspar Mews SW7....242 C5
Gataker Street * SE16....246 E8
Gate Mews SW7....242 F3
Gateforth Street NW8....238 F3
Gate Mews NW1....239 L3
Gatesborough Street * EC2A....241 M3
Gate Street WC2A....240 E5
Gatliff Road SW1W....243 K7
Gaunt Street SE1....245 J4
Gayfere Street SW1P....244 C4
Gaywood Street SE1....245 H4
Gaza Street SE17....245 H7
Gedling Place SE1....246 C7
Gee Street EC1V....241 J3
George Mathers Road SE11....245 H5
George Row SE16....246 C7
George Street W1H....239 H6
George Yard W1K....239 K7
Geraldine Street SE11....245 H4
Gerald Road SW1W....243 K5
Gerridge Street SE1....245 G3
Gertrude Street SW10....242 D8
Gibson Road SE11....244 E5
Gilbert Place WC1A....240 C5
Gilbert Road SE11....245 G5
Gilbert Street W1K....239 K7
Gildea Street W1W....239 L5

Gillingham Street SW1V....243 M5
Gill Street E14....247 L3
Gilston Road SW10....242 D7
Giltspur Street EC1A....241 H5
Gladstone Street SE1....245 H4
Glamis Place E1W....247 G4
Glamis Road E1W....247 G4
Glasgow Terrace SW1V....243 M7
Glasshill Street SE1....245 J3
Glasshouse Street W1B....240 A8
Glasshouse Walk SE11....244 D7
Glasshouse Yard EC1....241 J4
Glebe Place SW3....242 F7
Gledhow Road SW5....242 C6
Glentworth Street NW1....239 H4
Globe Pond Road SE16....247 J5
Globe Street SE1....245 K3
Gloucester Court * EC3R....246 A4
Gloucester Gardens W2....238 C6
Gloucester Mews W2....238 D6
Gloucester Mews West W2....238 C6
Gloucester Place NW1....239 H3
Gloucester Place W1U....239 H5
Gloucester Place Mews W1U....239 H5
Gloucester Road SW7....242 C4
Gloucester Road SW7....242 C6
Gloucester Road ⊖ SW7....242 C5
Gloucester Square W2....238 F6
Gloucester Street SW1V....243 M7
Gloucester Terrace W2....238 B5
Gloucester Terrace W2....238 D6
Gloucester Walk W8....242 A2
Gloucester Way EC1R....241 G2
Glyn Street SE11....244 E7
Godfrey Street SW3....243 G6
Goding Street SE11....244 D7
Godliman Street EC4V....241 J7
Godwin Close N1....241 K1
Golden Hinde II SE1....245 L1
Golden Jubilee Bridge WC2N....244 D1
Golden Lane EC1Y....241 J4
Golden Square W1F....240 A7
Golding Street E1....246 E3
Goldney Road W9....238 A4
Goldsmith Street EC2V....241 K6
Gomm Road SE16....247 G8
Goodge Place W1T....240 A5
Goodge Street W1T....240 A5
Goodge Street ⊖ W1T....240 B5
Goodwin Close SE16....246 C8
Gordon Place W8....242 A2
Gordon Square WC1H....240 B3
Gordon Street WC1H....240 B3
Gore Street SW7....242 D4
Goring Street * EC3A....246 A2
Gosfield Street W1W....239 L5
Goslett Yard WC2H....240 B6
Goswell Road EC1V....241 H1
Gough Street WC1X....240 F3
Goulston Street E1....246 B2
Gower Mews WC1E....240 B5
Gower Place NW1....240 A3
Gower Street WC1E....240 B3
Gower's Walk E1....246 D2
Gracechurch Street EC3V....241 M7
Grafton Mews W1T....239 M4
Grafton Place NW1....240 B2
Grafton Street W1S....239 L8
Grafton Way W1T....240 A4
Graham Street N1....241 J1
Graham Terrace SW1W....243 J6
Granby Terrace NW1....239 M1
Grand Avenue EC1A....241 H5
Grange Road SE1....246 B8
Grange Walk SE1....246 A8
Grange Yard SE1....246 B8
Grantully Road W9....238 B2
Granville Place W1H....239 J6
Granville Road NW6....238 A1
Granville Square WC1X....240 F2
Grape Street WC2H....240 C6
Gravel Lane E1....246 B2
Gray's Inn Road WC1X....240 D2
Gray's Inn Square WC1R....240 F5
Gray Street SE1....245 G3
Great Castle Street W1G....239 L6
Great Central Street NW1....239 G4
Great Chapel Street W1D....240 B6
Great College Street SW1P....244 C4
Great Cumberland Place W1H....239 H6
Great Dover Street SE1....245 K3
Great Eastern Street EC2A....241 M3
Great George Street SW1P....244 C3
Great Guildford Street SE1....245 J1
Great James Street WC1N....240 E4
Great Marlborough Street W1F....239 M7
Great Maze Pond SE1....245 L2
Great Newport Street WC2H....240 C7
Greatorex Street E1....246 D1
Great Ormond Street WC1N....240 D4
Great Percy Street WC1X....240 F2
Great Peter Street SW1P....244 B4
Great Portland Street W1W....239 L4
Great Portland Street ⊖ W1W....239 L4
Great Pulteney Street W1F....240 A7
Great Queen Street WC2B....240 D6
Great Russell Street WC1B....240 C5
Great Scotland Yard SW1A....244 C1
Great Smith Street SW1P....244 C4
Great Suffolk Street SE1....245 H2
Great Sutton Street EC1V....241 H4
Great Swan Alley EC2R....241 L6
Great Titchfield Street W1W....239 M4
Great Tower Street EC3M....241 M7
Great Tower Street EC3R....246 A4
Great Winchester Street EC2N....241 L6
Great Windmill Street W1D....240 B7
Greek Street W1D....240 B6
Greenacre Square SE16....247 J6
Green Bank E1W....246 E5
Greenberry Street NW8....238 F1
Greencoat Place SW1P....244 A5
Green Coat Row SW1P....244 A4
Greenfield Road E1....246 D2
Greenham Close SE1....244 F3
Green Park ⊖ W1J....243 M1
Green Street W1K....239 J7
Greenwell Street W1W....239 L4
Greet Street SE1....245 G2
Grenade Street E14....247 L4
Grendon Street NW8....238 F3
Grenville Place SW7....242 C5
Gresham Street EC2V....241 J6
Gresse Street W1T....240 B5
Greville Street EC1N....241 G5

Greycoat Place SW1P....244 B4
Greycoat Street SW1P....244 B4
Grigg's Place SE1....246 A8
Grosvenor Bridge SW8....243 L8
Grosvenor Crescent SW1X....243 J3
Grosvenor Crescent Mews SW1X....243 J3
Grosvenor Gardens SW1W....243 L4
Grosvenor Gardens Mews East SW1W....243 L4
Grosvenor Gardens Mews North SW1W....243 L4
Grosvenor Gardens Mews South * SW1W....243 L4
Grosvenor Gate W2....239 H8
Grosvenor Hill W1K....239 L7
Grosvenor Place SW1X....243 K3
Grosvenor Road SW1V....243 L8
Grosvenor Square W1K....239 J7
Grosvenor Street W1K....239 K7
Grosvenor Terrace SE5....245 K8
Grove End Road NW8....238 D2
Guildhouse Street SW1V....243 M5
Guilford Street WC1N....240 D4
Guinness Square SE1....245 M5
Gulliver Street SE16....247 K8
Gunpowder Square EC4A....241 G6
Gun Street E1....246 B1
Gunthorpe Street E1....246 C2
Gutter Lane EC2V....241 J6
Guy Street SE1....245 L3

H

Haberdasher Street N1....241 L2
Haddonhall Estate SE1....245 M4
Hainton Close E1....246 F3
Halcrow Street * E1....246 F2
Half Moon Street W1J....243 L1
Halford Road SW6....242 A8
Halkin Place SW1X....243 J4
Halkin Street SW1X....243 K3
Hallam Street W1W....239 L5
Halley Street E14....247 K1
Hallfield Estate W2....238 C6
Hall Place W2....238 E4
Hall Road NW8....238 D2
Hall Street EC1V....241 H2
Halpin Place SE17....245 M6
Halsey Street SW3....243 G5
Hamilton Close NW8....238 D2
Hamilton Close SE16....247 K7
Hamilton Gardens NW8....238 D2
Hamilton Place W1J....243 K2
Hamilton Terrace NW8....238 C1
Hamlet Way SE1....245 L3
Hammett Street EC3N....246 B4
Hampden Close NW1....240 B1
Hampden Gurney Street W2....239 H6
Hampstead Road NW1....239 M2
Hampton Street SE17....245 J6
Hanbury Street E1....246 C1
Hand Court WC1V....240 E5
Handel Street WC1N....240 C3
Hankey Place SE1....245 L3
Hannibal Road E1....247 G1
Hanover Square W1S....239 L6
Hanover Street W1S....239 L7
Hans Crescent SW3....243 H3
Hanson Street W1W....239 M4
Hans Place SW1X....243 H4
Hans Road SW3....243 G4
Hans Street SW1X....243 H4
Hanway Place W1T....240 B6
Hanway Street W1T....240 B6
Harbet Road W2....238 F5
Harcourt Street W1H....239 G5
Harcourt Terrace SW10....242 C7
Hardinge Street E1W....247 G3
Hardwick Street EC1R....241 G2
Hardwidge Street SE1....245 M2
Hardy Close SE16....247 H6
Harewood Place W1G....239 L6
Harewood Row NW1....239 G4
Harewoood Avenue NW1....239 G4
Harford Street E1....247 J1
Harleyford Road SE11....244 E8
Harley Gardens SW10....242 D7
Harley Place W1G....239 K5
Harley Street W1G....239 K4
Harmsworth Street SE17....245 G7
Harold Estate SE1....246 A8
Harper Road SE1....245 K4
Harpour Street WC1N....240 E4
Harriet Street SW1X....243 H3
Harriet Walk SW1X....243 H3
Harrington Gardens SW7....242 C6
Harrington Road SW7....242 E5
Harrington Square NW1....239 M1
Harrington Street NW1....239 M2
Harrison Street WC1H....240 D2
Harrods SW1X....243 G4
Harrowby Street W1H....239 G6
Harrow Place E1....246 B2
Harrow Road W2....238 A4
Hart Street EC3R....246 A3
Hasker Street SW3....243 G5
Hastings Street WC1H....240 C2
Hatfields SE1....245 G1
Hatherley Grove W2....238 B6
Hatteraick Road SE16....247 G6
Hatton Garden EC1N....241 G4
Hatton Street W2....238 E4
Hatton Wall EC1N....241 G4
Havering Street E1....247 H3
Haverstock Street N1....241 J1
Hawke Place * SE16....247 H6
Haydon Street EC3N....246 B3
Hayes Place NW1....239 G4
Hay Hill W1J....239 L8
Hayles Street SE11....245 H5
Haymarket SW1Y....240 B8
Hayne Street EC1A....241 J4
Hay's Lane SE1....245 M1
Hay's Mews W1J....239 L8
Haywood Place EC1R....241 H3
Headfort Place SW1X....243 K3
Head Street E1....247 H2
Hearnshaw Street E14....247 K2
Hearn Street EC2A....241 M4
Heathcote Street WC1N....240 E3
Heddon Street W1B....239 M8
Heddon Street W1S....240 A7
Hedger Street SE11....245 H5
Heiron Street SE17....245 J8

Hellings Street E1W....246 D5
Helmet Row EC1V....241 K3
Helsinki Square SE16....247 L8
Henderson Drive NW8....238 E3
Heneage Lane EC3A....246 A3
Heneage Street E1....246 C1
Henrietta Place W1G....239 L6
Henrietta Street WC2E....240 D7
Henriques Street E1....246 D2
Henshaw Street SE17....245 L5
Herbal Hill EC1R....241 G4
Herbert Crescent SW1X....243 H4
Herbrand Street WC1H....240 C3
Hercules Road SE1....244 F4
Hereford Road W2....238 A6
Hereford Square SW7....242 D6
Hermitage Street W2....238 E5
Hermitage Wall E1W....246 D5
Hermit Street EC1V....241 H2
Heron Place SE16....247 K5
Heron Quay E14....247 M5
Herrick Street SW1P....244 C6
Hertford Street W1J....243 K2
Hertsmere Road E14....247 M4
Hesper Mews SW5....242 B6
Hessel Street E1....246 E3
Hewett Street EC2A....241 M3
Heygate Street SE17....245 J5
Hide Place SW1P....244 B6
High Holborn WC1V....240 E5
High Street Kensington ⊖ W8....242 A3
Hildyard Road SW6....242 A8
Hilliards Court E1W....246 F5
Hillingdon Street SE17....245 J8
Hill Road NW8....238 D1
Hills Place W1F....239 M6
Hill Street W1J....239 K8
Hinde Street W1U....239 K6
Hind Grove E14....247 M3
Hindgrove Area E14....247 M3
Hithe Grove SE16....247 G8
HMS Belfast SE1....246 A5
Hobart Place SW1W....243 K4
Hobury Street SW10....242 D8
Hogarth Road SW5....242 B6
Holbein Mews SW1W....243 J6
Holbein Place SW1W....243 J6
Holborn EC1N....241 G5
Holborn ⊖ WC2B....240 E5
Holborn Circus EC1N....241 G5
Holborn Viaduct EC1A....241 G5
Holford Street WC1X....240 F2
Holland Street SE1....245 H1
Holland Street W8....242 A3
Hollen Street W1F....240 A6
Holles Street W1C....239 L6
Hollywood Road SW10....242 C8
Holyoak Road SE11....245 H5
Holyrood Street SE1....245 M2
Holyrood Street SE1....246 A6
Holywell Row EC2A....241 M4
Homefield Street * N1....241 M1
Homer Row W1H....239 G5
Homer Street W1H....239 G5
Hooper Street E1....246 D3
Hopetown Street E1....246 C1
Hopkins Street W1F....240 A7
Hopton Street SE1....245 H1
Hopwood Road SE17....245 L8
Hornton Place W8....242 A3
Hornton Street W8....242 A2
Horse & Dolphin Yard W1D....240 B7
Horseferry Road E14....247 J3
Horseferry Road SW1P....244 B4
Horse Guards Avenue SW1A....244 C2
Horse Guards Parade SW1A....244 C2
Horse Guards Road SW1A....244 C2
Horselydown Lane SE1....246 B6
Horsley Street SE17....245 K8
Hosier Lane EC1A....241 H5
Hothfield Place SE16....247 G8
Hotspur Street SE11....244 F6
Houghton Street WC2A....240 E6
Houndsditch EC3A....246 A2
Houses of Parliament SW1A....244 D3
Howick Place SW1E....244 A4
Howland Street W1T....240 A4
Howland Way SE16....247 K7
Howley Place W2....238 D4
Hoxton Square N1....241 M2
Hoxton Street N1....241 M1
Hudson's Place SW1V....243 M5
Hugh Mews SW1V....243 L6
Hugh Street SW1V....243 L6
Hugh Street SW1V....243 L6
Hull Close SE16....247 J6
Hull Street EC1V....241 J2
Hungerford Bridge SE1....244 E1
Hunter Close SE1....245 M4
Hunter Street WC1N....240 D3
Huntley Street WC1E....240 A4
Huntsman Street SE17....245 M6
Huntsworth Mews NW1....239 H3
Hurley Crescent SE16....247 H6
Hutching's Street E14....247 M7
Hutton Street EC4Y....241 G7
Hyde Park W2....243 G1
Hyde Park Corner W1J....243 K2
Hyde Park Corner ⊖ W1J....243 K2
Hyde Park Court SW7....242 D3
Hyde Park Crescent W2....238 F6
Hyde Park Gardens W2....238 F7
Hyde Park Gardens Mews W2....238 F7
Hyde Park Gate SW7....242 D3
Hyde Park Gate SW7....242 C3
Hyde Park Square W2....238 F7
Hyde Park Street W2....238 F7

I

Idol Lane EC3R....241 M7
Ifield Road SW10....242 B8
Iliffe Street SE17....245 J6
Iliffe Yard SE17....245 J6
Imperial College Road SW7....242 D4
Imperial War Museum SE1....245 G4
India Street EC3N....246 B3
Ingestre Place W1F....240 A7
Inglebert Street EC1R....240 F2
Ingram Close SE11....244 E5
Inner Circle NW1....239 J2
Inverness Terrace W2....238 B6
Inverness Terrace Gate W2....238 C8
Invicta Plaza SE1....245 H1

Inville Road SE17....245 L7
Ironmonger Lane EC2V....241 K6
Ironmonger Row EC1V....241 K2
Irving Street WC2N....240 C8
Isambard Place SE16....247 G6
Island Row E14....247 K3
Iverna Court W8....242 A4
Iverna Gardens W8....242 A4
Ives Street SW3....243 G5
Ivor Place NW1....239 G4
Ixworth Place SW3....242 F6

J

Jacob Street SE1....246 C6
Jamaica Gate SE16....246 F8
Jamaica Road SE1....246 C7
Jamaica Road SE16....246 E7
Jamaica Street E1....247 G2
Jamaica Wharf SE1....246 C6
James Street W1U....239 K6
James Street WC2E....240 D7
Jameson Street W8....238 A1
Jamuna Close E14....247 K1
Janeway Street SE16....246 D7
Jardine Road E1W....247 J4
Java Wharf SE1....246 C6
Jay Mews SW7....242 D3
Jermyn Street SW1Y....240 A8
Jerome Crescent NW8....238 F3
Jewery Street EC3N....246 B3
Joan Street SE1....245 G2
Jockey's Fields WC1R....240 E4
Johanna Street SE1....244 F3
John Adam Street WC2N....240 D8
John Carpenter Street EC4Y....241 G7
John Fisher Street E1....246 C4
John Islip Street SW1P....244 C5
John Prince's Street W1G....239 L6
John Roll Way SE16....246 D7
John Ruskin Street SE5....245 J8
John's Mews WC1N....240 E4
Johnson's Place SW1V....244 A7
Johnson Street E1....247 G3
Johnson Street WC1N....240 E4
Joiner Street SE1....245 L1
Jonathan Street SE11....244 E6
Jubilee Place SW3....243 G6
Jubilee Street E1....247 G2
Jubilee Walk W8....238 B1
Judd Street WC1H....240 C2
Junction Mews W2....238 F5
Juxon Street SE11....244 E5

K

Katherine Close SE16....247 H5
Kean Street WC2B....240 E6
Keel Close SE16....247 J6
Keeley Street WC2B....240 E6
Keeton's Road SE16....246 E7
Kell Street SE1....245 H3
Kelso Place W8....242 B4
Kemble Street WC2B....240 E6
Kempsford Gardens SW5....242 A7
Kempsford Road SE11....245 G6
Kendall Place W1U....239 J5
Kendal Street W2....239 G6
Kennet Street E1W....246 D5
Kenning Street SE16....247 G6
Kennings Way SE11....245 G7
Kennington ⊖ SE11....245 H7
Kennington Lane SE11....244 E7
Kennington Oval SE11....244 E8
Kennington Park Gardens SE11....245 G8
Kennington Park Place SE11....245 G7
Kennington Park Road SE11....245 G7
Kennington Road SE1....244 F4
Kennington Road SE11....245 G5
Kennnington Oval SE11....244 F8
Kenrick Place W1U....239 J5
Kensington Church Street W8....242 A1
Kensington Court W8....242 B3
Kensington Gardens W2....242 C1
Kensington Gardens Square W2....238 B6
Kensington Gate W8....242 C4
Kensington Gore SW7....242 E3
Kensington High Street W8....242 A4
Kensington Palace W8....242 B2
Kensington Palace Gardens W8....242 B1
Kensington Palace Gardens W8....242 B2
Kensington Place W8....242 A1
Kensington Road SW7....243 G3
Kensington Road W8....242 B3
Kensington Square W8....242 B3
Kenton Street WC1H....240 C3
Kenway Road SW5....242 A6
Keystone Close N1....240 D1
Keyworth Street SE1....245 H4
Kia Oval (Surrey County Cricket Ground) SE11....244 F8
Kilburn Park Road NW6....238 A2
Kildare Terrace W2....238 A6
Killick Street N1....240 E1
Kinburn Street SE16....247 H6
Kinder Street E1....246 E2
King & Queen Wharf SE16....247 H5
King and Queen Street SE17....245 K6
King Charles Street SW1A....244 C2
King David Lane E1....247 G3
Kingdom Street W2....238 C5
King Edward Street EC1A....241 J6
King Edward Walk SE1....245 G4
King James Street SE1....245 H3
Kingly Street W1F....239 M7
King's Arms Yard EC2R....241 L6
King's Bench Street SE1....245 H2
Kingscote Street EC4V....241 H7
King's Cross ⇌ N1C....240 D1
King's Cross Road WC1X....240 E2
King's Cross Square N1C....240 D1
King's Cross St Pancras ⊖ N1C....240 D1
Kingsgate Walk * SW1E....244 A4
King's Head Yard SE1....245 L1
King's Mews WC1N....240 F4
Kingsmill Terrace NW8....238 E1
King Square EC1V....241 J2
King's Road SW3....242 E8
King's Scholars Passage SW1P....243 M5
King's Stairs Close SE16....246 F6
King Street WC2E....240 D7
King Street SW1Y....244 A1

King Street EC2V	241	K6
Kingsway WC2B	240	E6
King William Street EC4N	241	L7
Kinnerton Place North * SW1X	243	J3
Kinnerton Place South * SW1X	243	J3
Kinnerton Street SW1X	243	J3
Kinnerton Yard * SW1X	243	J3
Kipling Estate SE1	245	L3
Kipling Street SE1	245	L3
Kirby Estate SE16	246	D7
Kirby Grove SE1	245	M3
Kirby Street EC1N	241	G4
Knaresborough Place SW5	242	B5
Knightrider Street EC4V	241	H7
Knightsbridge SW1X	243	H3
Knightsbridge SW3	243	H3
Knox Street W1H	239	H4
Kynance Mews SW7	242	C4
Kynance Place SW7	242	C4

L

Lackington Street EC2A	241	L4
Lafone Street SE1	246	B6
Lagado Mews SE16	247	H5
Lambeth Bridge SW1P	244	D5
Lambeth High Street SE1	244	E5
Lambeth Hill EC4V	241	J7
Lambeth North ⊖ SE1	244	F3
Lambeth Palace Road SE1	244	E4
Lambeth Road SE1	244	F4
Lambeth Walk SE1	244	F5
Lamb's Conduit Street WC1N	240	E4
Lamb's Passage EC1Y	241	K4
Lamb Street E1	246	B1
Lamb Way SE1	246	A7
Lamlash Street SE11	245	H5
Lanark Place W9	238	D3
Lanark Road W9	238	B1
Lancaster Gate W2	238	D7
Lancaster Gate ⊖ W2	238	E7
Lancaster Mews W2	238	D7
Lancaster Place WC2E	240	E7
Lancaster Street SE1	245	H3
Lancaster Terrace W2	238	E7
Lancaster Walk W2	238	D8
Lancelot Place SW7	243	G3
Lancing Street NW1	240	B2
Lanesborough Place * SW1X	243	J3
Langdale Street E1	246	E3
Langford Place NW8	238	D1
Langham Place W1B	239	L5
Langham Street W1W	239	L5
Langham Street W1W	239	M5
Langley Lane SW8	244	D8
Langley Street WC2H	240	C7
Langton Close WC1X	240	E3
Lanhill Road W9	238	A3
Lansdowne Place SE1	245	L4
Lant Street SE1	245	J3
Larcom Street SE17	245	K6
Lauderdale Road W9	238	B3
Laud Street SE11	244	E7
Launcelot Street SE1	244	F3
Launceston Place W8	242	C4
Laurence Pountney Lane EC4V	241	L7
Lavender Road SE16	247	K5
Lavender Wharf SE16	247	K4
Lavington Street SE1	245	J1
Lawn Lane SW8	244	D8
Lawrence Street SW3	242	F8
Lawrence Wharf SE16	247	L6
Law Street SE1	245	L4
Laxton Place NW1	239	L3
Laystall Street EC1R	240	F4
Leadenhall Street EC3A	246	A3
Leadenhall Street EC3V	241	M6
Leake Street SE1	244	E2
Leather Lane EC1N	241	G4
Leathermarket Street SE1	245	M3
Leeke Street WC1X	240	E2
Lees Place W1K	239	J7
Leicester Square ⊖ WC2H	240	C7
Leicester Square WC2H	240	C7
Leicester Street WC2H	240	B7
Leigh Street WC1H	240	C3
Leinster Gardens W2	238	C6
Leinster Mews W2	238	C7
Leinster Place W2	238	C7
Leinster Square W2	238	A7
Leinster Terrace W2	238	C7
Leman Street E1	246	C3
Lennox Gardens SW1X	243	G4
Lennox Gardens Mews SW1X	243	G5
Leonard Street EC2A	241	L3
Leopold Estate E3	247	M1
Leopold Street E3	247	M1
Leroy Street SE1	245	M5
Lever Street EC1V	241	J2
Lewisham Street SW1H	244	B3
Lexham Gardens W8	242	A5
Lexham Mews W8	242	A5
Lexington Street W1F	240	A7
Leyden Street E1	246	B2
Leydon Close SE16	247	H5
Library Street SE1	245	H3
Lidlington Place NW1	240	A1
Lilestone Street NW8	238	F3
Lilley Close E1W	246	D5
Lilley Street SE1	246	F1
Lillie Road SW6	242	A7
Lillie Yard SW6	242	A7
Limeburner Lane EC4M	241	H6
Lime Close E1W	246	D5
Limehouse Causeway E14	247	L4
Limehouse Link E14	247	L3
Limehouse ⇌ ⊖ E14	247	L3
Limerston Street SW10	242	D8
Lime Street EC3M	241	M7
Lincoln's Inn Fields WC2A	240	E6
Linden Gardens W2	238	A8
Lindley Street E1	246	F1
Lindsay Square SW1V	244	B6
Lindsey Street EC1A	241	H4
Linhope Street NW1	239	G3
Linsey Street SE16	246	D8
Lisle Street WC2H	240	B7
Lisson Green Estate NW8	238	F3
Lisson Grove NW1	239	G4
Lisson Grove NW8	238	F3
Lisson Street NW1	238	F4
Litchfield Street WC2H	240	C7
Little Argyll Street W1F	239	M6
Little Britain EC1A	241	J5

Little Chester Street SW1X	243	K4
Little George Street SW1P	244	C3
Little Marlborough Street W1F	240	A7
Little New Street EC4A	241	G6
Little Portland Street W1G	239	L6
Little Russell Street WC1A	240	C5
Little St James's Street SW1A	243	M2
Little Sanctuary SW1A	244	C3
Little Somerset Street E1	246	B3
Little Titchfield Street W1W	239	M5
Liverpool Grove SE17	245	K7
Liverpool Street EC2M	241	M5
Liverpool Street ⇌ ⊖ EC2M	241	M5
Lizard Street EC1V	241	K3
Llewellyn Street SE16	246	D7
Lloyd Baker Street WC1X	240	F2
Lloyd's Avenue EC3N	246	B3
Lloyd Square WC1X	240	F2
Lloyds Row EC1R	241	G2
Lloyd Street WC1X	240	F2
Locksley Estate E14	247	L2
Locksley Street E14	247	L1
Lockyer Street SE1	245	L3
Lodge Road NW8	238	F3
Loftie Street SE16	246	D7
Logan Place W8	242	A5
Lolesworth Close E1	246	B1
Lollard Street SE11	244	F5
Lollard Street SE11	244	F6
Lomas Street E1	246	D1
Loman Street SE1	245	J2
Lombard Lane EC4Y	241	G6
Lombard Street EC3V	241	L7
London Bridge EC4R	241	L8
London Bridge ⇌ ⊖ SE1	245	L1
London Bridge Street SE1	245	L1
London Dungeon SE1	244	E2
London Eye SE1	244	E2
London Mews W2	238	E6
London Road SE1	245	H4
London Street EC3R	246	A3
London Street W2	238	E6
London Transport Museum WC2E	240	D7
London Wall EC2M	241	K5
London Zoo ZSL NW1	239	J1
Long Acre WC2E	240	D7
Longford Street NW1	239	L3
Long Lane EC1A	241	J5
Long Lane SE1	245	L3
Longmoore Street SW1V	243	M5
Longridge Road SW5	242	A5
Longville Road SE11	245	H5
Long Walk SE1	246	A8
Long Yard WC1N	240	E4
Lord North Street SW1P	244	C4
Lord's Cricket Ground NW8	238	E2
Lorenzo Street WC1X	240	E1
Lorrimore Road SE17	245	J8
Lorrimore Square SE17	245	H8
Lothbury EC2R	241	L6
Loughborough Street SE11	244	F7
Lovat Lane EC3R	241	M7
Love Lane EC2V	241	K6
Lovell Place SE16	247	K7
Lowell Street E14	247	K2
Lower Belgrave Street SW1W	243	K4
Lower Grosvenor Place SW1W	243	L4
Lower James Street W1F	240	A7
Lower John Street W1F	240	A7
Lower Marsh SE1	244	F3
Lower Road SE16	247	G7
Lower Sloane Street SW1W	243	J6
Lower Thames Street EC3R	246	A4
Lower Thames Street EC3R	241	M8
Lowndes Close * SW1X	243	J4
Lowndes Place SW1X	243	J4
Lowndes Square SW1X	243	H3
Lowndes Street SW1X	243	J4
Lucan Place SW3	242	F5
Lucey Road SE16	246	C8
Ludgate Circus EC4M	241	H6
Ludgate Hill EC4M	241	H6
Luke Street EC2A	241	M3
Lukin Street E1	247	G3
Lumley Street W1K	239	K7
Lupus Street SW1V	243	L7
Lupus Street SW1V	244	B7
Luton Street NW8	238	E4
Luxborough Street W1U	239	J4
Lyall Mews SW1X	243	J4
Lyall Street SW1X	243	J4
Lyons Place NW8	238	E3
Lytham Street SE17	245	K7

M

Macclesfield Road EC1V	241	J2
Macclesfield Street * W1D	240	B7
Mace Close E1W	246	E5
Macklin Street WC2B	240	D6
Mackworth Street NW1	239	M2
Macleod Street SE17	245	K7
Madame Tussauds NW1	239	J4
Maddox Street W1S	239	M7
Magdalen Street SE1	245	M2
Magee Street SE11	244	F8
Maguire Street SE1	246	C6
Maida Avenue W9	238	D4
Maida Vale W9	238	C2
Maida Vale ⊖ W9	238	C2
Maiden Lane NW1	240	C1
Maiden Lane WC2E	240	D7
Major Road SE16	246	D7
Makins Street SW3	243	G6
Malet Street WC1E	240	B4
Mallord Street SW3	242	E8
Mallory Street NW8	238	F3
Mallow Street EC1Y	241	L3
Malta Street EC1V	241	H3
Maltby Street SE1	246	B7
Manchester Square W1U	239	J6
Manchester Street W1U	239	J5
Manciple Street SE1	245	L3
Mandeville Place W1U	239	K6
Manette Street W1D	240	B6
Manilla Street E14	247	M6
Manningford Close EC1V	241	H2
Manor Place SE17	245	J7
Manresa Road SW3	242	F7
Mansell Street E1	246	C3
Mansfield Mews W1G	239	L5
Mansfield Street W1G	239	L5
Mansion House ⊖ EC4V	241	K7

Manson Mews SW7	242	D5
Manson Place SW7	242	D6
Mapleleaf Square SE16	247	K6
Maples Place E1	246	F1
Maple Street W1T	239	M4
Marble Arch W1C	239	H7
Marchmont Street WC1H	240	C3
Margaret Street W1W	239	L6
Margaretta Terrace SW3	242	F7
Margery Street WC1X	240	F3
Marigold Street SE16	246	E7
Marine Street SE16	246	C7
Market Mews W1J	243	K1
Market Place W1W	239	M6
Markham Square SW3	243	G6
Markham Street SW3	243	G6
Mark Lane EC3R	246	A4
Marlborough Gate W2	238	E7
Marlborough Place NW8	238	C1
Marlborough Road SW1A	244	A2
Marlborough Street SW3	242	F6
Marloes Road W8	242	B4
Marlow Way SE16	247	H6
Maroon Street E14	247	K2
Marshall Street W1F	240	A7
Marshalsea Road SE1	245	K2
Marsham Street SW1P	244	C5
Marsh Wall E14	247	M5
Martha's Buildings EC1V	241	K3
Martha Street E1	246	F3
Martin Lane EC4V	241	L7
Maryland Road W9	238	A4
Marylands Road W9	238	A4
Marylebone ⊖ W1B	239	G4
Marylebone Flyover W2	238	E5
Marylebone High Street W1U	239	K5
Marylebone Lane W1U	239	K6
Marylebone Road NW1	239	G4
Marylebone Street W1G	239	K5
Marylee Way SE11	244	F6
Masjid Lane E14	247	M2
Mason Street SE17	245	M5
Massinger Street SE17	245	M6
Masters Street E1	247	J1
Matlock Street E14	247	J2
Matthew Parker Street SW1H	244	C3
Maunsel Street SW1P	244	B5
Mayfair Place W1J	243	L1
Mayflower Street SE16	247	F4
Mayford Estate NW1	240	A1
Maynards Quay E1W	246	F4
May's Court WC2N	240	C8
McAuley Close SE1	244	F4
McLeod's Mews SW7	242	C5
Meadcroft Road SE11	245	G8
Meadcroft Road SE11	245	H8
Meadow Road SW8	244	D8
Meadow Row SE1	245	J5
Mead Row SE1	244	F4
Meakin Estate SE1	245	M4
Mecklenburgh Square WC1N	240	E3
Medway Street SW1P	244	B5
Meeting House Alley E1W	246	E5
Melcombe Place NW1	239	G4
Melcombe Street W1U	239	H4
Melina Place NW8	238	D2
Melior Street SE1	245	M2
Melton Street NW1	240	A2
Memorial Gates SW1W	243	K3
Mepham Street SE1	244	F2
Mercer Street WC2H	240	C7
Merchant Square W2	238	E5
Merlin Street EC1R	240	F2
Mermaid Court SE1	245	K2
Merrick Square SE1	245	K4
Merrington Road SW6	242	A8
Merrow Street SE17	245	L7
Methley Street SE11	245	G7
Meymott Street SE1	245	G2
Micawber Street N1	241	K1
Micklethwaite Road SW6	242	A8
Middlesex Street E1	246	A1
Middlesex Street E1	246	B2
Middle Street EC1A	241	J5
Middle Temple WC2R	240	F7
Middle Temple Lane EC4Y	240	F7
Middleton Drive SE16	247	H6
Midland Road NW1	240	C1
Midship Close SE16	247	H6
Milborne Grove SW10	242	D7
Milcote Street SE1	245	H3
Miles Street SW8	244	D8
Milford Lane WC2R	240	F7
Milk Street EC2V	241	K6
Milk Yard E1W	247	G4
Millbank SW1P	244	D4
Millennium Bridge SE1	241	J8
Millennium Harbour E14	247	M6
Milligan Street E14	247	L4
Millman Mews WC1N	240	E4
Millman Street WC1N	240	E4
Mill Place E14	247	K3
Millstream Road SE1	246	B7
Mill Street SE1	246	C6
Mill Street W1S	239	L7
Milner Street SW3	243	G5
Milton Street EC2Y	241	K4
Milverton Street SE11	245	G7
Mincing Lane EC3M	246	A4
Minera Mews SW1W	243	J5
Minories EC3N	246	B3
Mitchell Street EC1V	241	J3
Mitre Road SE1	245	G2
Mitre Street EC3A	246	A3
Molyneux Street W1H	239	G5
Monck Street SW1P	244	C4
Monkton Street SE11	245	G5
Monkwell Square EC2Y	241	K5
Monmouth Place W2	238	A6
Monmouth Road W2	238	A6
Monmouth Street WC2H	240	C6
Montague Close SE1	245	L1
Montague Place EC3R	240	C5
Montague Street WC1B	240	C5
Montagu Mansions W1U	239	H5
Montagu Mews North W1H	239	H5
Montagu Mews West W1H	239	H6
Montagu Place W1H	239	H5
Montagu Row W1U	239	H5
Montagu Square W1H	239	H5
Montagu Street W1H	239	H6
Montford Place SE11	244	F7
Monthorpe Road E1	246	C1
Montpelier Place SW7	243	G3
Montpelier Square SW7	243	G3
Montpelier Street SW7	243	G3
Montpelier Walk SW7	242	G3

Montrose Place SW1X	243	K3
Monument ⊖ EC4R	241	L7
Monument Street EC3R	241	L7
Monument Street EC3R	241	M7
Monza Street E1W	247	G4
Moodkee Street SE16	247	G7
Moore Street SW3	243	H5
Moorfields EC2Y	241	L5
Moorgate EC2R	241	L6
Moorgate ⇌ ⊖ EC2Y	241	L5
Moor Lane EC2Y	241	L5
Moor Street W1D	240	C7
Mora Street EC1V	241	K2
Morecambe Street SE17	245	K6
Moreland Street EC1V	241	H2
Moreton Place SW1V	244	A6
Moreton Street SW1V	244	B6
Moreton Terrace SW1V	244	A6
Morgan's Lane SE1	245	M2
Morgan's Lane SE1	246	A5
Morley Street SE1	245	G3
Mornington Crescent NW1	239	M1
Mornington Place NW1	239	L1
Mornington Terrace NW1	239	L1
Morocco Street SE1	246	A7
Morpeth Terrace SW1P	243	M5
Morris Street E1	246	F3
Morshead Road W9	238	A2
Mortimer Market WC1E	240	A4
Mortimer Street W1T	240	A5
Mortimer Street W1W	239	M5
Morton Place SE1	244	F4
Morwell Street WC1B	240	B5
Moscow Place W2	238	B7
Moscow Road W2	238	B7
Mossop Street SW3	243	G5
Motcomb Street SW1X	243	J4
Mount Gate W2	242	E2
Mount Mills EC1V	241	J3
Mount Pleasant WC1X	240	F4
Mount Row W1K	239	K8
Mount Street W1K	239	K8
Mount Street Mews W1K	239	K8
Mount Terrace E1	246	E1
Moxon Street W1U	239	J5
Mulberry Street E1	246	D2
Mulberry Walk SW3	242	E8
Mulready Street NW8	238	F4
Mundy Street N1	241	M2
Munster Square NW1	239	L3
Munton Road SE17	245	K5
Murphy Street SE1	244	F3
Murray Grove N1	241	K1
Musbury Street E1	247	G2
Muscovy Street EC3N	246	A4
Museum of London EC2Y	241	J5
Museum Street WC1A	240	C5
Myddelton Passage EC1R	241	G2
Myddelton Square EC1R	241	G1
Myddelton Street EC1R	241	G3
Myrdle Street E1	246	D2

N

Naoroji Street WC1X	240	F2
Napier Grove N1	241	K1
Narrow Street E14	247	K4
Nash Street NW1	239	L2
Nassau Street W1W	239	M5
Nathaniel Close * E1	246	C2
National Portrait Gallery WC2H	240	C8
Natural History Museum SW7	242	E4
Neal Street WC2H	240	C6
Neathouse Place * SW1V	243	M5
Neckinger SE1	246	C8
Needleman Street SE16	247	H7
Nelson Close NW6	238	A1
Nelson Place N1	241	H1
Nelson Square SE1	245	H2
Nelson Street E1	246	E2
Nelson Terrace N1	241	H1
Nelson's Column WC2N	240	C8
Neptune Street SE16	247	G7
Nesham Street E1W	246	D4
Netherton Grove SW10	242	D8
Netley Street NW1	239	M2
Nevern Place SW5	242	A6
Nevern Square SW5	242	A6
Neville Street SW7	242	E6
Newark Street E1	246	E2
New Atlas Wharf E14	247	M8
New Bond Street W1S	239	L7
New Bond Street W1S	239	L8
New Bridge Street EC4V	241	H6
New Broad Street EC2M	241	M5
New Burlington Street W1S	239	M7
Newburn Street SE11	244	F7
Newbury Street EC1A	241	J5
Newcastle Place W2	238	E5
New Cavendish Street W1G	239	L5
New Change EC4M	241	J6
New Church Road SE5	245	L8
Newcomen Street SE1	245	K2
New Compton Street WC2H	240	C6
Newcourt Street NW8	238	F1
Newell Street E14	247	L3
New Fetter Lane EC4A	241	G6
Newgate Street EC1A	241	H6
New Globe Walk SE1	241	J8
New Goulston Street E1	246	B2
Newham's Row SE1	246	A7
Newington Butts SE1	245	H5
Newington Causeway SE1	245	J4
New Kent Road SE1	245	K5
Newlands Quay E1W	246	F4
Newman Street W1T	240	A5
New North Place EC2A	241	M3
New North Road N1	241	L1
New North Street WC1N	240	D4
New Oxford Street WC1A	240	C6
Newport Street SE11	244	E5
New Quebec Street W1H	239	H6
New Ride SW7	242	E3
New Road E1	246	E2
New Row WC2N	240	C7
New Spring Gardens Walk SE1	244	D7
New Square WC2A	240	F6
New Street EC2M	246	A2
New Street Square EC4A	241	G6
Newton Road W2	238	A6
Newton Street WC2B	240	D5
New Union Street EC2Y	241	K5

Nicholas Lane EC3V	241	L7
Nicholson Street SE1	245	H1
Nightingale Place SW10	242	D8
Nile Street N1	241	K2
Nine Elms Lane SW8	244	C8
Noble Street EC2V	241	J6
Noel Road N1	241	J1
Noel Street W1F	240	A6
Norbiton Road E14	247	L2
Norfolk Crescent W2	239	G6
Norfolk Place W2	238	E6
Norfolk Square W2	238	E6
Norman Street EC1V	241	J3
Norris Street SW1Y	240	B8
Northampton Road EC1R	241	G3
Northampton Square EC1V	241	H2
North Audley Street W1K	239	J7
North Bank NW8	238	F2
Northburgh Street EC1V	241	H3
North Carriage Drive W2	238	F7
Northdown Street N1	240	D1
Northey Street E14	247	K4
North Gower Street NW1	240	A2
Northington Street WC1N	240	E4
North Mews WC1N	240	E4
North Ride W2	239	G7
North Row W1K	239	J7
North Terrace SW3	242	F5
Northumberland Alley EC3N	246	B3
Northumberland Avenue WC2N	244	C1
Northumberland Place W2	238	A6
Northumberland Street WC2N	244	C1
North Wharf Road W2	238	E5
Northwick Terrace NW8	238	D3
Norway Gate SE16	247	K7
Norway Place E14	247	L3
Norwich Street EC4A	240	F5
Nottingham Place W1U	239	J4
Nottingham Street W1U	239	J4
Notting Hill Gate W11	238	A8
Notting Hill Gate ⊖ W11	242	A1
Nugent Terrace NW8	238	D1
Nutford Place W1H	239	G6

O

Oakden Street SE11	245	G5
Oakington Road W9	238	A3
Oak Lane E14	247	L3
Oakley Close EC1V	241	H1
Oakley Gardens SW3	243	G8
Oakley Square NW1	240	A1
Oakley Street SW3	242	F8
Oak Tree Road NW8	238	F2
Oat Lane EC2V	241	J5
Occupation Road SE17	245	J6
Ocean Square E1	247	J1
Ocean Street E1	247	J1
Odessa Street SE16	247	K7
Ogle Street W1W	239	M5
Old Bailey EC4M	241	H6
Old Barrack Yard SW1X	243	J3
Old Bond Street W1S	239	M8
Old Broad Street EC2N	241	M6
Old Brompton Road SW5	242	B6
Old Brompton Road SW7	242	D6
Old Burlington Street W1S	239	M7
Oldbury Place W1U	239	J4
Old Castle Street E1	246	B2
Old Cavendish Street W1G	239	L6
Old Church Road E1	247	H2
Old Church Street SW3	242	E7
Old Compton Street W1D	240	B7
Old Court Place W8	242	B3
Old Gloucester Street WC1N	240	D4
Old Jamaica Road SE16	246	C7
Old Jewry EC2R	241	K6
Old Kent Road SE1	245	M5
Old Marylebone Road NW1	239	G5
Old Montague Street E1	246	C1
Old North Street WC1X	240	E5
Old Paradise Street SE11	244	E5
Old Park Lane W1J	243	K2
Old Pye Street SW1P	244	B4
Old Queen Street SW1H	244	B3
Old Square WC2A	240	F6
Old Street EC1V	241	K3
Old Street ⇌ ⊖ EC1Y	241	L3
Old Street Junction EC1Y	241	L3
Oliver's Yard EC1Y	241	L3
Olney Road SE17	245	J8
O'Meara Street SE1	245	K2
Omega Place N1	240	D1
Onega Gate SE16	247	K8
Ongar Road SW6	242	A8
Onslow Gardens SW7	242	D6
Onslow Square SW7	242	E5
Onslow Square SW7	242	E6
Ontario Street SE1	245	J4
Ontario Way E14	247	M4
Opal Street SE11	245	H6
Orange Place SE16	247	G8
Orange Square SW1W	243	K6
Orange Street E1W	246	D5
Orange Street WC2H	240	B8
Orb Street SE17	245	L6
Orchardson Street NW8	238	E3
Orchard Street W1H	239	J6
Orde Hall Street WC1N	240	E4
Orient Street SE11	245	H5
Orme Court W2	238	B8
Orme Lane W2	238	B8
Orme Square Gate W2	238	B8
Ormond Close WC1N	240	D4
Ormonde Gate SW3	243	H7
Ormond Yard SW1Y	240	A8
Orsett Mews W2	238	C6
Orsett Street SE11	244	E6
Orsett Terrace W2	238	C5
Orton Street E1W	246	D5
Osbert Street SW1V	244	B6
Osborn Street E1	246	C2
Oslo Square SE16	247	K7
Osnaburgh Street NW1	239	L3
Osnaburgh Terrace NW1	239	L3
Ossington Buildings W1U	239	J5
Ossington Street W2	238	A7
Ossulston Street NW1	240	B1
Oswin Street SE11	245	H5
Othello Close SE11	245	H6
Otto Street SE17	245	H8
Outer Circle NW1	239	H3
Outer Circle NW1	239	K1

252 Oval – South Square

Oval ⊖ SE11 244 F8
Oval Way SE11 244 E7
Ovington Square SW3 243 G4
Ovington Street SW3 243 G5
Owen Street EC1V 241 G1
Oxendon Street SW1Y 240 B8
Oxford Circus ⊖ W1B 239 M6
Oxford Road NW6 238 A1
Oxford Square W2 238 F6
Oxford Street W1C 239 L6
Oxford Street WC1A 240 A6

P

Pace Place E1 246 E3
Pacific Wharf SE16 247 H5
Paddington ⇌ ⊖ W2 238 D6
Paddington Green W2 238 E5
Paddington Street W1U 239 J5
Pageant Crescent SE16 247 K5
Page Street SW1P 244 B5
Paget Street EC1V 241 H2
Pakenham Street WC1X 240 E3
Palace Avenue W8 242 B2
Palace Court W2 238 A7
Palace Gardens Terrace W8 242 A1
Palace Gate W8 242 C3
Palace Green W8 242 B2
Palace of Westminster SW1A 244 D3
Palace Place SW1E 243 M4
Palace Street SW1E 243 M4
Pall Mall SW1Y 244 A1
Pall Mall East SW1Y 244 B1
Palmer Street SW1H 244 B3
Pancras Lane EC4N 241 K6
Pancras Road N1C 240 C1
Panton Street SW1Y 240 B8
Paradise Street SE16 246 E7
Paradise Walk SW3 243 H8
Pardoner Street SE1 245 L4
Pardon Street EC1V 241 H3
Parfett Street E1 246 D2
Paris Garden SE1 245 G1
Park Crescent W1B 239 K4
Park Crescent Mews West W1G 239 K4
Parker's Row SE1 246 C7
Parker Street WC2B 240 D6
Park Lane W1K 239 H7
Park Lane W2 243 J1
Park Place SW1A 243 M1
Park Place Villas W2 238 D4
Park Road NW1 239 H3
Park Square East NW1 239 L3
Park Square Mews NW1 239 K3
Park Square West NW1 239 K3
Park Street SE1 245 K1
Park Street W1K 239 J7
Park Village East NW1 239 L1
Park Walk SW10 242 D8
Park West Place W2 239 G6
Parliament Street SW1A 244 C2
Parry Street SW8 244 D8
Passmore Street SW1W 243 J6
Paternoster Square 241 J6
Pater Street W8 242 A4
Pattina Walk SE16 247 K5
Paul Street EC2A 241 M3
Paultons Square SW3 242 E8
Paveley Street NW1 239 G3
Pavilion Road SW1X 243 H3
Pavilion Street SW1X 243 H4
Paxton Terrace SW1V 243 L7
Peabody Avenue SW1V 243 L7
Peabody Estate SE1 245 J1
Peacock Street SE17 245 J6
Pearl Street E1W 246 F5
Pearman Street SE1 245 G3
Pear Tree Court EC1R 241 G3
Peartree Lane E1W 247 G4
Pear Tree Street EC1V 241 J3
Peel Street W8 242 A1
Peerless Street EC1V 241 K2
Pelham Crescent SW7 242 F6
Pelham Place SW7 242 F5
Pelham Street SW7 242 F5
Pelier Street SE17 245 K8
Pemberton Row EC4A 241 G6
Pembridge Gardens W2 238 A8
Pembridge Place W2 238 A7
Pembridge Square W2 238 A7
Pembridge Villas W11 238 A7
Pembroke Close SW1X 243 J3
Penang Street E1W 246 F5
Penfold Place NW8 238 F5
Penfold Street NW8 238 E4
Pennant Mews W8 242 B5
Pennington Street E1W 246 D4
Pennyfields E14 247 M4
Penrose Grove SE17 245 J7
Penrose Street SE17 245 J7
Penton Place SE17 245 H6
Penton Rise WC1X 240 E2
Penton Street N1 240 F1
Pentonville Road N1 240 E1
Penywern Road SW5 242 A6
Pepper Street SE1 245 J2
Pepys Street EC3N 246 A4
Percival Street EC1V 241 H3
Percy Circus WC1X 240 F2
Percy Street W1T 240 B5
Perkin's Rents SW1P 244 B4
Perryn Road SE16 246 E7
Petersham Mews SW7 242 D4
Petersham Place SW7 242 C4
Peter Street W1F 240 B7
Peto Place NW1 239 L3
Petticoat Lane E1 246 B2
Petty France SW1H 244 A3
Petty Wales EC3R 246 A4
Petyward SW3 243 G6
Phelp Street SE17 245 L7
Phene Street SW3 243 G8
Phillimore Walk W8 242 A3
Philpot Lane EC3M 241 M7
Philpot Street E1 246 E2
Phipp's Mews SW1W 243 L5
Phipp Street EC2A 241 M3
Phoenix Place WC1X 240 F3
Phoenix Road NW1 240 B1
Phoenix Street WC2H 240 C6
Piccadilly W1J 243 L2
Piccadilly Arcade SW1Y 243 M1
Piccadilly Circus W1B 240 A8
Piccadilly Circus ⊖ W1J 240 B8
Pickard Street EC1V 241 J2
Picton Place W1U 239 K6
Pier Head E1W 246 E6
Pigott Street E14 247 M3
Pilgrimage Street SE1 245 L3
Pimlico ⊖ SW1V 244 B6
Pimlico Road SW1W 243 J6
Pinchin Street E1 246 D3
Pindar Street EC2A 241 M4
Pindock Mews W9 238 B3
Pine Street EC1R 240 F3
Pitfield Street N1 241 M1
Pitsea Street E1 247 H3
Pitt's Head Mews W1J 243 K2
Pitt Street W8 242 A2
Pixley Street E14 247 L2
Platina Street * EC2A 241 L3
Plover Way SE16 247 K8
Plumbers Row E1 246 D2
Plumtree Court EC4A 241 G5
Plympton Street NW8 238 F4
Pocock Street SE1 245 H2
Poland Street W1F 240 A6
Pollen Street W1S 239 L7
Pollitt Drive NW8 238 E3
Polperro Mews SE11 245 G5
Polygon Road NW1 240 B1
Pond Place SW3 242 F6
Ponler Street E1 246 E3
Ponsonby Place SW1P 244 C6
Ponsonby Terrace SW1P 244 C6
Ponton Road SW1V 244 B8
Pont Street SW1X 243 H4
Poolmans Street SE16 247 H6
Pope Street SE1 246 B7
Poplar Place W2 238 B7
Poppin's Court EC4A 241 H6
Porchester Gardens W2 238 B7
Porchester Gate W2 238 C8
Porchester Place W2 239 G6
Porchester Road W2 238 B5
Porchester Square W2 238 B6
Porchester Terrace W2 238 C7
Porchester Terrace North W2 238 C6
Porlock Street SE1 245 L3
Porter Street NW1 239 H4
Porteus Road W2 238 D5
Portland Place W1B 239 L4
Portland Place W1B 239 L5
Portland Square E1W 246 E5
Portland Street SE17 245 L7
Portman Close W1H 239 J6
Portman Mews South W1H 239 J6
Portman Square W1H 239 J6
Portman Street W1H 239 J6
Portpool Lane EC1N 240 F4
Portsea Place W2 239 G6
Portsmouth Street WC2A 240 E6
Portsoken Street E1 246 B3
Portugal Street WC2A 240 E6
Potier Street SE1 245 L4
Potters Fields SE1 246 B6
Pottery Street SE16 246 E7
Poultry EC2V 241 K6
Powis Place WC1N 240 D4
Praed Mews W2 238 E6
Praed Street W2 238 E6
Pratt Walk SE1 244 E5
Premier Place E14 247 M4
Prescot Street E1 246 C3
Preston Close SE1 245 M5
Price's Street SE1 245 H1
Prideaux Place WC1X 240 F2
Primrose Street EC2A 246 A1
Prince Albert Road NW8 238 F1
Prince Consort Road SW7 242 D3
Princelet Street E1 246 C1
Prince of Wales Gate SW7 242 F3
Princes Arcade SW1Y 240 A8
Prince's Gardens SW7 242 E3
Prince's Gate Mews SW7 242 E4
Princes Riverside
Road SE16 247 H5
Prince's Square W2 238 A7
Princess Road NW6 238 A1
Princess Street SE1 245 H4
Princes Street W1B 239 L6
Prince's Street EC2R 241 L6
Princeton Street WC1R 240 E5
Prioress Street SE1 245 L4
Priory Green Estate N1 240 E1
Priory Walk SW10 242 D7
Proctor Street WC1V 240 E5
Prospect Place E1W 247 G5
Prospect Street SE16 246 E7
Provident Court W1K 239 J7
Provost Street N1 241 L1
Prusom Street E1W 246 F5
Pudding Lane EC3R 241 M7
Pumphouse Mews E1 246 D3
Purbrook Street SE1 246 A7
Purcell Street N1 241 M1
Purchese Street NW1 240 B1

Q

Quebec Way SE16 247 J7
Queen Anne's Gate SW1H 244 B3
Queen Anne Street W1G 239 K5
Queen Elizabeth Street SE1 246 B6
Queen Mother Gate W2 243 J2
Queensborough Terrace W2 238 C7
Queensbury Place SW7 242 E5
Queen's Gardens W2 238 C7
Queen's Gate SW7 242 D3
Queen's Gate SW7 242 D4
Queen's Gate Gardens SW7 242 D5
Queen's Gate Mews SW7 242 D4
Queen's Gate Place SW7 242 D4
Queen's Gate
Place Mews SW7 242 D4
Queen's Gate Terrace SW7 242 C4
Queen's Mews W2 238 B7
Queen Square WC1N 240 D4
Queen's Row SE17 245 K7
Queen Street EC4N 241 K7
Queen Street W1J 243 L1
Queen Street Place EC4R 241 K7
Queen's Walk SE1 246 A5
Queen's Walk SW1A 243 M2
Queensway W2 238 B6
Queensway ⊖ W2 238 B8
Queen Victoria Street EC4V 241 J7
Quick Street N1 241 H1

R

Raby Street E14 247 K2
Radcliffe Road SE1 246 B8
Radcot Street SE11 245 G7
Radnor Mews W2 238 E6
Radnor Place W2 238 F6
Radnor Street EC1V 241 K3
Radnor Walk SW3 243 G7
Railway Approach SE1 245 L1
Railway Avenue SE16 247 G6
Railway Street N1 240 D1
Raine Street E1W 246 F5
Ralston Street SW3 243 H7
Ramillies Place W1F 239 M6
Ramillies Street W1F 239 M6
Rampart Street E1 246 E2
Rampayne Street SW1V 244 B6
Randall Road SE11 244 D6
Randall Row SE11 244 E6
Randolph Avenue W9 238 B1
Randolph Crescent W9 238 C3
Randolph Gardens NW6 238 B1
Randolph Mews W9 238 D4
Randolph Road W9 238 C4
Ranelagh Grove SW1W 243 K6
Ranelagh Road SW1V 244 A7
Rangoon Street * EC3N 246 B3
Ranston Street NW8 238 F4
Raphael Street SW7 243 G3
Ratcliffe Cross Street E1W 247 J3
Ratcliffe Lane E14 247 J3
Rathbone Place W1T 240 B5
Rathbone Street W1T 240 A5
Raven Row E1 246 F1
Ravensdon Street SE11 245 G7
Ravey Street EC2A 241 M3
Rawlings Street SW3 243 G5
Rawstorne Street EC1V 241 H2
Ray Street EC1R 241 G4
Reardon Place E1W 246 E5
Reardon Street E1W 246 E5
Rectory Square E1 247 H1
Redan Place W2 238 B6
Redburn Street SW3 243 G7
Redcastle Close E1W 247 G4
Redcliffe Gardens SW10 242 B7
Redcliffe Mews SW10 242 C7
Redcliffe Place SW10 242 C8
Redcliffe Road SW10 242 D7
Redcliffe Square SW10 242 B7
Redcliffe Street SW10 242 B8
Redcross Way SE1 245 K2
Redesdale Street SW3 243 G7
Redfield Lane SW5 242 A5
Redhill Street NW1 239 L1
Red Lion Row SE5 245 K8
Red Lion Square WC1R 240 E5
Red Lion Street WC2B 240 E5
Redman's Road E1 247 G1
Red Place W1K 239 J7
Redriff Road SE16 247 J8
Reedworth Street SE11 245 G6
Reeves Mews W1K 239 J8
Regal Close E1 246 D1
Regan Way N1 241 M1
Regency Street SW1P 244 B5
Regent Place W1B 240 A7
Regent's Park ⊖ W1B 239 L4
Regent's Park NW1 239 J1
Regent's Park Estate NW1 239 L2
Regent Square WC1H 240 D2
Regent Street SW1Y 240 B8
Regent Street W1S 239 M7
Relton Mews SW7 243 G4
Remington Street N1 241 H1
Remnant Street WC2A 240 E6
Renforth Street SE16 247 G7
Renfrew Road SE11 245 H5
Rennie Street SE1 245 H1
Rephidim Street SE1 245 M4
Repton Street E14 247 K2
Reveley Square SE16 247 K7
Rex Place W1K 239 J8
Rhodeswell Road E14 247 L2
Rich Street E14 247 M3
Rickett Street SW6 242 A8
Ridgemount Street WC1E 240 B4
Ridgemount Gardens WC1E 240 B4
Riding House Street W1W 239 M5
Riley Road SE1 246 B7
Ripley's Believe It or Not! W1J 240 B8
Risborough Street SE1 245 J2
Risdon Street SE16 247 G7
Rissinghill Street N1 240 F1
River Street EC1R 240 F2
Rivington Street EC2A 241 M3
Robert Adam Street W1U 239 J6
Roberts Close SE16 247 J7
Robert Street NW1 239 L2
Rochester Row SW1P 244 A5
Rochester Street SW1P 244 B5
Rockingham Street SE1 245 J4
Rocliffe Street N1 241 H1
Roding Mews E1W 246 D5
Rodmarton Street W1U 239 H5
Rodney Place SE17 245 K5
Rodney Road SE17 245 K5
Rodney Street N1 240 E1
Roger Street WC1N 240 E4
Roland Gardens SW7 242 D6
Roland Way SE17 245 L7
Romford Street E1 246 E2
Romilly Street W1D 240 B7
Romney Street SW1P 244 C5
Rood Lane EC3M 241 M7
Ropemaker Road SE16 247 K7
Ropemaker Street EC2Y 241 L4
Roper Lane SE1 246 B7
Rope Street SE16 247 K8
Rope Walk Gardens E1 246 E2
Rosary Gardens SW7 242 D6
Roscoe Street EC1Y 241 K3
Rose Alley SE1 241 K8
Rosebery Avenue EC1R 240 F3
Rosemoor Street SW3 243 G6
Rose Street WC2E 240 C7
Rossmore Road NW1 239 G3
Rotary Street SE1 245 H3
Rotherhithe ⊖ SE16 247 G6
Rotherhithe Street SE16 247 G6
Rotherhithe Street SE16 247 J4
Rotherhithe Tunnel SE16 247 H5
Rothsay Street SE1 245 M4
Rotten Row W2 242 F2
Rouel Road SE16 246 C8
Roupell Street SE1 245 G2
Royal Albert Hall SW7 242 E3
Royal Avenue SW3 243 H6
Royal Hospital Road SW3 243 H7
Royal Mint Street E1 246 C4
Royal Oak ⊖ W2 238 B5
Royal Oak Yard SE1 246 A7
Royal Opera House WC2E 240 D7
Royal Road SE17 245 H8
Royal Street SE1 244 E3
Rudolph Road NW6 238 A1
Rugby Street WC1N 240 E4
Rum Close E1W 246 F4
Rupack Street SE16 246 F7
Rupert Street W1D 240 B7
Rushworth Street SE1 245 H2
Russell Court SW1A 244 A2
Russell Square WC1B 240 C4
Russell Square ⊖ WC1B 240 D4
Russell Street WC2B 240 D7
Russia Dock Road SE16 247 K6
Rutherford Street SW1P 244 B5
Rutland Gardens SW7 243 G3
Rutland Gate SW7 242 F3
Rutland Mews SW7 242 F4
Rutland Street SW7 242 F4
Ryder Street SW1Y 244 A1

S

Sackville Street W1S 240 A8
Saffron Hill EC1N 241 G4
Saffron Street EC1N 241 G4
Sail Street SE11 244 F5
St Agnes Place SE11 245 G8
St Alban's Grove W8 242 B4
St Alban's Street SW1Y 240 B8
St Alphage Garden EC2Y 241 K5
St Andrews Hill EC4V 241 H7
St Andrew's Place NW1 239 L3
St Andrew Street EC4A 241 G5
St Anne's Court W1F 240 B6
St Ann's Street SW1P 244 C4
St Anselm's Place W1K 239 K7
St Barnabas Street SW1W 243 K6
St Botolph Street EC3N 246 B2
St Bride Street EC4A 241 G6
St Chad's Street WC1H 240 D2
St Clare Street EC3N 246 B3
St Clements Lane WC2A 240 E6
St Cross Street EC1N 241 G4
St Dunstan's Hill EC3R 241 M8
St Dunstan's Lane EC3R 241 M7
St Elmos Road SE16 247 J7
St Ermin's Hill SW1H 244 B3
St George's Circus SE1 245 H3
St George's Drive SW1V 243 M6
St George's Estate E1 246 D3
St George's Lane * EC3R 241 M7
St George's Road SE1 245 G4
St George's Square SW1V 244 B7
St George Street W1S 239 L7
St Giles High Street WC2H 240 C6
St Helen's Place EC3A 241 M6
St James Market * SW1Y 240 B8
St James's Park ⊖ SW1H 244 B3
St James's Park SW1A 244 B3
St James's Place SW1A 243 M2
St James's Road SE16 246 D8
St James's Square SW1Y 244 A1
St James's Street SW1A 243 M1
St James Walk EC1R 241 G3
St John's Lane EC1M 241 H4
St John's Place EC1M 241 H4
St John's Square EC1V 241 H4
St John Street EC1V 241 H2
St John's Wood High Street NW8 238 F1
St John's Wood Road NW8 238 E3
St Katharine's Way E1W 246 C5
St Leonard's Terrace SW3 243 H7
St Loo Avenue SW3 243 G8
St Luke's Close EC1V 241 K3
St Luke's Street SW3 242 F6
St Manningtree E1 246 C2
St Mark Street E1 246 C3
St Martin's Lane WC2N 240 C7
St Martin's le Grand EC1A 241 J6
St Martin's Place WC2N 240 C8
St Mary at Hill EC3R 241 M8
St Mary Axe EC3A 246 A3
St Marychurch Street SE16 246 F7
St Mary's Gardens SE11 245 G5
St Mary's Terrace W2 238 D4
St Mary's Walk SE11 245 G5
St Matthew Street SW1P 244 B4
St Michael's Street W2 238 F6
St Olav's Square SE16 246 F7
St Oswald's Place SE11 244 E7
St Oswulf Street * SW1P 244 C6
St Pancras International ⇌ N1C 240 C1
St Paul's ⊖ EC1A 241 J6
St Paul's Avenue SE16 247 J5
St Paul's Cathedral EC4M 241 J6
St Paul's Churchyard EC4M 241 J6
St Paul's Way E3 247 L1
St Petersburgh Mews W2 238 B7
St Petersburgh Place W2 238 B7
St Saviours Wharf SE1 246 C6
St Stephen's Gardens W2 238 A5
St Swithin's Lane EC4N 241 L7
St Thomas Street SE1 245 L2
St Vincent Street W1U 239 J5
Salamanca Street SE1 244 D6
Salem Road W2 238 B7
Sale Place W2 238 F5
Salisbury Court EC4Y 241 G6
Salisbury Place W1H 239 H4
Salisbury Street NW8 238 F4
Salmon Lane E14 247 J2
Salter Road SE16 247 J5
Salter Street E14 247 M4
Samford Street NW8 238 F4
Sampson Street E1W 246 D5
Sancroft Street SE11 244 F6
Sandland Street WC1R 240 E5
Sandpiper Close SE16 247 L6
Sandwich Street WC1H 240 C2
Sandy's Row E1 246 B1
Sans Walk EC1R 241 G3
Sardinia Street WC2A 240 E6
Savage Gardens EC3N 246 B3
Savile Row W1S 239 M7
Savoy Hill WC2R 240 E8
Savoy Place WC2R 240 D8
Savoy Street WC2E 240 E7
Sawyer Street SE1 245 J2
Scala Street W1T 240 A5
Scandrett Street E1W 246 E5
Scarborough Street E1 246 C3
Scarsdale Villas W8 242 A4
Schooner Close * SE16 247 H6
Science Museum SW7 242 E4
Scoresby Street SE1 245 H2
Scotch House Junction SW1X 243 H3
Scotland Place SW1A 244 C1
Scott Ellis Gardens NW8 238 E2
Scott Lidgett Crescent SE16 246 D7
Scrutton Street EC2A 241 M3
Seaford Street WC1H 240 D2
Seagrave Road SW6 242 A8
Sea Life London Aquarium SE1 244 E3
Searles Road SE1 245 L5
Sebastian Street EC1V 241 H2
Secker Street SE1 244 F2
Sedan Way SE17 245 M6
Sedding Street SW1X 243 J5
Seddon Street WC1X 240 E3
Seething Lane EC3N 246 A4
Sekforde Street EC1R 241 H3
Selfridges W1A 239 J6
Selsey Street E14 247 M1
Selwood Place SW7 242 E6
Semley Place SW1W 243 K6
Senior Street W2 238 B4
Senrab Street E1 247 H2
Serle Street WC2A 240 F6
Serpentine Bridge W2 242 E1
Serpentine Road W2 242 F2
Seth Street SE16 247 G7
Settles Street E1 246 D2
Seven Dials WC2H 240 C6
Seville Street SW1X 243 H3
Sevington Street W9 238 A3
Seward Street EC1V 241 J3
Seymour Mews W1H 239 J6
Seymour Place W1H 239 G5
Seymour Street W1H 239 H6
Seymour Street W2 239 G7
Seymour Walk SW10 242 C7
Shad Thames SE1 246 B6
Shad Thames SE1 246 C6
Shadwell ⊖ ⊖ E1 246 F3
Shadwell Gardens E1 246 F3
Shaftesbury Avenue W1D 240 B7
Shaftesbury Avenue WC2H 240 C6
Shaftesbury Street N1 241 K1
Shakespeare's Globe SE1 241 J8
Shand Street SE1 246 A6
Sharsted Street SE17 245 H7
Shaw Crescent E14 247 K2
Shawfield Street SW3 243 G7
Sheffield Terrace W8 242 A2
Sheldon Square W2 238 D5
Shelmerdine Close E3 247 M1
Shelton Street WC2H 240 D6
Shepherdess Walk N1 241 K1
Shepherd Street W1J 243 K1
Sheraton Street W1F 240 B6
Sherborne Lane EC4N 241 L7
Sherwood Street W1D 240 A7
Ship and Mermaid Row SE1 245 M2
Shipwright Road SE16 247 K7
Shirland Road W9 238 A3
Shoe Lane EC4A 241 G5
Shorter Street EC3N 246 B4
Shorts Gardens WC2H 240 C6
Short Street SE1 245 G2
Shoulder of Mutton Alley E14 247 K4
Shouldham Street W1H 239 G5
Shroton Street NW1 238 F4
Siddons Lane W1H 239 H4
Sidmouth Street WC1N 240 D3
Sidney Square E1 246 F2
Sidney Street E1 246 F1
Silex Street SE1 245 H3
Silk Street EC2Y 241 K4
Silver Walk SE16 247 K5
Silvester Street SE1 245 K3
Singer Street EC2A 241 L3
Sir John Soane's Museum WC2A 240 E5
Sir Simon Milton Square SW1V 243 L4
Skinner Place * SW1W 243 J6
Skinners Lane EC4V 241 K7
Skinner Street EC1R 241 G3
Slippers Place SE16 246 F8
Sloane Avenue SW3 243 G6
Sloane Court East SW3 243 J6
Sloane Court West SW3 243 J6
Sloane Gardens SW1W 243 J6
Sloane Square SW1W 243 J5
Sloane Square ⊖ SW1W 243 J6
Sloane Street SW1X 243 H3
Sloane Terrace SW1X 243 J5
Smeaton Street E1W 246 E5
Smithfield Street EC1A 241 H5
Smith Square SW1P 244 C4
Smith Street SW3 243 G7
Smith Terrace SW3 243 G7
Smithy Street E1 247 G1
Snowden Street EC2A 241 M4
Snow Hill EC1A 241 H5
Snowsfields SE1 245 L2
Soho Square W1D 240 B6
Soho Street W1D 240 B6
Somerford Way SE16 247 K7
Somers Crescent W2 238 F6
Somerset House WC2R 240 E7
Somerstown Estate NW1 240 A1
Sondes Street SE17 245 L7
South & West Africa Gate SW1A 244 A3
Southall Place SE1 245 L3
Southampton Buildings WC2A 240 F5
Southampton Place WC1A 240 D5
Southampton Row WC1B 240 D4
Southampton Street WC2E 240 D7
South Audley Street W1K 239 K8
South Carriage Drive SW1X 243 H3
South Carriage Drive SW7 242 F3
South Eaton Place SW1W 243 J5
Southern Street N1 240 E1
South Kensington ⊖ SW7 242 E4
South Kensington ⊖ SW7 242 E5
South Lambeth Road SW8 244 D8
South Molton Lane W1K 239 K7
South Molton Street W1K 239 K7
South Parade SW3 242 E7
South Place EC2M 241 L5
South Sea Street SE16 247 L8
South Square WC1R 240 F5

South Street W1K 243 J1
South Tenter Street E1 .... 246 C3
South Terrace SW7 .... 242 F5
Southwark ⊖ SE1 .... 245 H2
Southwark Bridge SE1 .... 241 K8
Southwark Bridge Road SE1 .... 245 J3
Southwark Park Road SE16 .... 246 E8
Southwark Street SE1 .... 245 H1
Southwell Gardens SW7 .... 242 C5
South Wharf Road W2 .... 238 E6
Southwick Mews W2 .... 238 F6
Southwick Place W2 .... 238 F6
Southwick Street W2 .... 238 F6
Sovereign Close E1W 246 F4
Sovereign Crescent SE16 .... 247 J4
Spanish Place W1U 239 J5
Spa Road SE16 .... 246 C8
Spear Mews SW5 .... 242 C4
Spelman Street E1 .... 246 C1
Spence Close SE16 .... 247 K7
Spencer Street EC1V 241 H2
Spenser Street SW1E 244 A4
Spert Street E14 .... 247 J4
Spital Square E1 .... 246 A1
Spring Gardens SW1A 244 C1
Spring Street W2 .... 238 E6
Spurgeon Street SE1 .... 245 L4
Spur Road SE1 .... 244 F3
Stables Way SE11 .... 244 F7
Stable Yard Road SW1A 244 A2
Stacey Street WC2H 240 C6
Stafford Place SW1E 243 M3
Stafford Road NW6 .... 238 A2
Stafford Street W1S 239 M8
Stafford Terrace W8 .... 242 A3
Stainer Street SE1 .... 245 L2
Staining Lane EC2V 241 K6
Stainsby Road E14 .... 247 M2
Stalham Street SE16 .... 246 D8
Stamford Street SE1 .... 245 G1
Stanford Street SE1 .... 245 M6
Stanford Road W8 .... 242 C4
Stanford Street * SW1V 244 B6
Stanhope Close * SE16 .... 247 H6
Stanhope Gardens SW7 .... 242 D5
Stanhope Gate W1K 243 K1
Stanhope Mews SW7 .... 242 D5
Stanhope Mews East SW7 .... 242 D5
Stanhope Mews West SW7 .... 242 D5
Stanhope Place W2 .... 239 G7
Stanhope Place Gate W2 .... 239 G7
Stanhope Row W1J 243 K1
Stanhope Street NW1 .... 239 M1
Stanhope Terrace W2 .... 238 E7
Stannary Street SE11 .... 245 G7
Staples Close SE16 .... 247 J5
Staple Street SE1 .... 245 L3
Starcross Street NW1 .... 240 A2
Star Street W2 .... 238 F6
Station Approach SE1 .... 244 F3
Stave Yard Road SE16 .... 247 J3
Stead Street SE17 .... 245 K6
Steedman Street SE17 .... 245 J5
Steel's Lane E1 .... 247 G3
Steeres Way SE16 .... 247 K7
Stephenson Way NW1 .... 240 A3
Stephen Street W1T 240 B5
Stepney Green E1 .... 247 H1
Stepney High Street E1 .... 247 J1
Stepney Way E1 .... 246 E1
Sterling Street SW7 .... 243 G3
Stevedore Street E1W 246 E5
Stevens Street SE1 .... 246 A7
Steward Street * E1 .... 246 B1
Stewart's Grove SW3 .... 242 F6
Stew Lane EC4V 241 J7
Stillington Street SW1P 244 A5
Stockholm Way E1W 246 D5
Stocks Place E14 .... 247 M3
Stone Buildings WC2A 240 F5
Stonecutter Street EC4A 241 G6
Stoney Lane E1 .... 246 B2
Stoney Street SE1 .... 245 K1
Stopford Road SE17 .... 245 J7
Store Street WC1E 240 B5
Storey's Gate SW1H 244 C3
Storks Road SE16 .... 246 D8
Stoughton Close SE11 .... 244 E6
Stourcliffe Street W1H 239 G6
Strafford Street E14 .... 247 M6
Strand WC2R 240 D8
Stratford Place W1C 239 K6
Stratford Road W8 .... 242 A5
Strathearn Place W2 .... 238 F7
Stratton Street W1J 243 L1
Strutton Ground SW1P 244 B4
Strype Street E1 .... 246 B2
Stuart Road NW6 .... 238 A2
Stukeley Street WC2B 240 D6
Sturgeon Road SE17 .... 245 J7
Sturge Street SE1 .... 245 J3
Sturt Street N1 .... 241 K1
Stutfield Street E1 .... 246 D3
Sudley Street N1 .... 241 H1
Sudrey Street SE1 .... 245 J3
Suffolk Lane EC4V 241 L7
Suffolk Street SW1Y 240 B8
Sugar Lane SE16 .... 246 D7
Sugar Quay Walk EC3R 246 A4
Sullivan Road SE11 .... 245 G5
Summercourt Road E1 .... 247 G2
Summers Street EC1R 240 F4
Sumner Place SW7 .... 242 E6
Sumner Street SE1 .... 245 J1
Sunderland Terrace W2 .... 238 A6
Sun Passage SE16 .... 246 D8
Sun Street EC2M 241 M4
Sun Street Passage EC2M 241 M5
Surrendale Place W9 .... 238 A4
Surrey Quays Road SE16 .... 247 H7
Surrey Row SE1 .... 245 H2
Surrey Square SE17 .... 245 M6
Surrey Street WC2E 240 E7
Surrey Water Road SE16 .... 247 H6
Sussex Gardens W2 .... 238 E6
Sussex Mews East W2 .... 238 E7
Sussex Place NW1 .... 239 H3
Sussex Place W2 .... 238 E6
Sussex Square W2 .... 238 E7
Sussex Street SW1V 243 L7
Sutherland Avenue W9 .... 238 A4
Sutherland Row SW1V 243 L6
Sutherland Square SE17 .... 245 J7
Sutherland Street SW1V 243 L7
Sutton Row W1D 240 B6
Sutton Street E1 .... 247 G3

Suttons Way EC1Y 241 K4
Swain Street NW8 .... 238 F3
Swallow Place W1B 239 L6
Swallow Street W1B 240 A8
Swan Lane EC4R 241 L8
Swan Mead SE1 .... 245 M4
Swan Road SE16 .... 247 G6
Swan Street SE1 .... 245 K3
Swan Walk SW3 .... 243 H8
Swedenborg Gardens E1 .... 246 E4
Sweeney Crescent SE1 .... 246 C7
Swinton Street WC1X 240 E2
Sydney Place SW7 .... 242 F6
Sydney Street SW3 .... 242 F6
Symons Street SW3 .... 243 H6

T

Tabard Gardens Estate SE1 .... 245 L3
Tabard Street SE1 .... 245 L3
Tabernacle Street EC2A 241 L3
Tachbrook Street SW1V 244 A6
Talbot Road W2 .... 238 A6
Talbot Square W2 .... 238 E6
Talbot Yard SE1 .... 245 L2
Tallis Street EC4Y 241 G7
Tamworth Street SW6 .... 242 A8
Tanner Street SE1 .... 246 A7
Taplow Street N1 .... 241 K1
Tarling Street E1 .... 246 F3
Tarver Road SE17 .... 245 H7
Tatum Street SE1 .... 245 M6
Taunton Place NW1 .... 239 G3
Tavistock Place WC1H 240 C3
Tavistock Square WC1H 240 C3
Tavistock Street WC2E 240 D7
Taviton Street WC1H 240 B3
Teak Close SE16 .... 247 K6
Tedworth Square SW3 .... 243 G7
Telford Terrace SW1V 243 M7
Temeraire Street SE16 .... 247 G6
Temple ⊖ WC2R 240 F7
Temple Avenue EC4Y 241 G7
Temple Lane EC4Y 241 G7
Temple Place WC2R 240 F7
Templeton Place SW5 .... 242 A5
Tench Street E1W 246 E5
Tenniel Close W2 .... 238 C7
Tennis Street SE1 .... 245 L2
Tenterden Street W1S 239 L6
Tenterground E1 .... 246 B1
Teredo Street SE16 .... 247 J8
Terminus Place SW1V 243 L4
Thame Road SE16 .... 247 H6
Thanet Street WC1H 240 C2
Thavies Inn EC4A 241 G6
Thayer Street W1U 239 K5
The Arches WC2N 240 D8
The Boltons SW10 .... 242 C7
The British Library NW1 .... 240 C2
The British Museum WC1B 240 C5
The Broad Walk W2 .... 238 B8
The Broad Walk W8 .... 242 C2
The Cut SE1 .... 245 G2
The Flower Walk W2 .... 242 D3
The Grange SE1 .... 246 B8
The Highway E1 .... 246 E4
The Little Boltons SW10 .... 242 C7
The Mall SW1A 244 B2
The Mitre E14 .... 247 L3
The Monument EC3R 241 L7
The National Gallery WC2N 240 C8
Theobald's Road WC1X 240 E4
Theobald Street SE1 .... 245 L5
The Oval (Surrey County
Cricket Ground) SE11 .... 244 F8
The Shard SE1 .... 245 L2
The Vale SW3 .... 242 E8
Thirleby Road SW1P 244 A4
Thomas More Street E1W 245 D4
Thomas Road E14 .... 247 M2
Thoresby Street N1 .... 241 K1
Thorney Street SW1P 244 C5
Thornton Place W1H 239 H4
Thrale Street SE1 .... 245 K1
Thrawl Street E1 .... 245 C1
Threadneedle Street EC2R 241 L6
Three Colt Street E14 .... 247 L3
Three Oak Lane SE1 .... 245 B6
Throgmorton Avenue EC2N 241 L6
Throgmorton Street EC2N 241 L6
Thurland Road SE16 .... 245 D8
Thurloe Place SW7 .... 242 F5
Thurloe Square SW7 .... 242 F5
Thurloe Street SW7 .... 242 E5
Thurlow Street SE17 .... 245 M7
Tichbourne Row W2 .... 238 F6
Tiller Road E14 .... 247 M8
Tillman Street E1 .... 246 E3
Tilney Street W1J 243 K1
Timber Pond Road SE16 .... 247 G6
Tinsley Road E1 .... 247 G1
Tinworth Street SE11 .... 244 D6
Tisdall Place SE17 .... 245 L6
Tite Street SW3 .... 243 H8
Tiverton Street SE1 .... 245 J4
Token House Yard EC2R 241 L6
Tolmer's Square NW1 .... 240 A3
Tomlin's Terrace E14 .... 247 K2
Tonbridge Street WC1H 240 D2
Tooley Street SE1 .... 245 L1
Tooley Street SE1 .... 246 B6
Tor Gardens W8 .... 242 A2
Torquay Street W2 .... 238 A5
Torrens Street EC1V 241 G1
Torrington Place E1W 246 D5
Torrington Place WC1E 240 B4
Torrington Square WC1E 240 B4
Tothill Street SW1H 244 B3
Tottenham Court Road W1T 240 A4
Tottenham Court Road ⊖ W1D 240 B6
Tottenham Street W1T 240 A5
Toulmin Street SE1 .... 245 J3
Tower Bridge SE1 .... 246 B5
Tower Bridge Approach EC3N 246 B5
Tower Bridge Road SE1 .... 246 A7
Tower Bridge Wharf E1W 246 C5
Tower Gateway ⊖ EC3N 246 B4
Tower Hill EC3N 246 B4
Tower Hill ⊖ EC3N 246 B4
Tower of London EC3N 246 B4

Tower Place EC3R 246 A4
Tower Street WC2H 240 C7
Townsend Street SE17 .... 245 M5
Toynbee Street E1 .... 246 B1
Trafalgar Gardens E1 .... 247 H1
Trafalgar Square WC2N 240 C8
Trafalgar Street SE17 .... 245 L7
Transept Street NW1 .... 238 F5
Trebeck Street W1J 243 L1
Trebovir Road SW5 .... 242 A6
Tregunter Road SW10 .... 242 C7
Trenton Road SE16 .... 246 E8
Tresham Crescent NW8 .... 238 F3
Trevor Place SW7 .... 243 G3
Trevor Square SW7 .... 243 G3
Trevor Street SW7 .... 243 G3
Trinidad Street E14 .... 247 M4
Trinity Church Square SE1 .... 245 K3
Trinity Square EC3N 246 B4
Trinity Street SE1 .... 245 K3
Trump Street EC2V 241 K6
Tudor Street EC4Y 241 G7
Tufton Street SW1P 244 C4
Tunnel Road SE16 .... 247 G6
Turks Row SW3 .... 243 J6
Turner's Road E3 .... 247 L2
Turner Street E1 .... 246 E2
Turnmill Street EC1N 241 G4
Turpentine Lane SW1V 243 L7
Turquand Street SE17 .... 245 K6
Tyers Gate SE1 .... 245 M3
Tyers Street SE11 .... 244 E7
Tyers Terrace SE11 .... 244 E7
Tyron Street SW3 .... 243 H6
Tysoe Street EC1R 241 G3

U

Udall Street SW1P 244 A5
Ufford Street SE1 .... 245 G2
Ulster Place NW1 .... 239 K4
Umberston Street E1 .... 246 E2
Undershaft EC3A 246 A2
Underwood Road N1 .... 241 K2
Underwood Street N1 .... 241 K1
Union Street SE1 .... 245 H2
University Street WC1E 240 A4
Upbrook Mews W2 .... 238 D6
Upper Belgrave Street SW1X 243 K4
Upper Berkeley Street W1H 239 H6
Upper Brook Street W1K 239 J7
Upper Cheyne Row SW3 .... 242 F8
Upper Grosvenor Street W1K 239 J8
Upper Ground SE1 .... 244 F1
Upper Harley Street NW1 .... 239 K3
Upper James Street W1F 240 A7
Upper John Street W1F 240 A7
Upper Marsh SE1 .... 244 E3
Upper Montagu Street W1H 239 H5
Upper St Martin's WC2H 240 C7
Upper Tachbrook Street SW1V 244 A5
Upper Thames Street EC4V 241 J7
Upper Wimpole Street W1G 239 K4
Upper Woburn Place WC1H 240 B2
Urlwin Street SE5 .... 245 J8
Uxbridge Street W8 .... 242 A1

V

Valentine Place SE1 .... 245 G3
Vandon Passage SW1H 244 A3
Vandon Street SW1H 244 A4
Varden Street E1 .... 246 E2
Varndell Street NW1 .... 239 M2
Vauban Street SE16 .... 246 C8
Vaughan Street SE16 .... 247 L7
Vaughan Way E1W 246 D5
Vauxhall ⊖ ≥ SW8 .... 244 D7
Vauxhall Bridge SW1V 244 C7
Vauxhall Bridgefoot SE1 .... 244 D7
Vauxhall Bridge Road SW1V 243 M5
Vauxhall Cross SE1 .... 244 D7
Vauxhall Grove SW8 .... 244 D8
Vauxhall Street SE11 .... 244 E6
Vauxhall Walk SE11 .... 244 E6
Venables Street W2 .... 238 E4
Vere Street W1G 239 K6
Vernon Place WC1A 240 D5
Vernon Rise WC1X 240 E2
Verulam Street WC1X 240 F4
Vestry Street N1 .... 241 L2
Victoria ⊖ ≥ SW1V 243 L5
Victoria & Albert Museum SW7 .... 242 F4
Victoria Embankment SW1A 244 D2
Victoria Embankment WC2R 240 F7
Victoria Gate W2 .... 238 F7
Victoria Road W8 .... 242 C4
Victoria Square SW1W 243 L4
Victoria Street SW1E 243 L4
Victory Place SE17 .... 245 K5
Victory Way SE16 .... 247 K7
Vigo Street W1S 239 M8
Villa Street SE17 .... 245 L7
Villiers Street WC2N 240 D8
Vincent Close SE16 .... 247 K7
Vincent Square SW1P 244 B5
Vincent Street SW1P 244 B5
Vincent Terrace N1 .... 241 H1
Vince Street EC1V 241 L2
Vine Court E1 .... 246 D1
Vinegar Street E1W 246 E5
Vine Hill EC1R 240 F4
Vine Lane SE1 .... 246 A6
Vine Street EC3N 246 B3
Violet Hill NW8 .... 238 C1
Virgil Street SE1 .... 244 F4
Virginia Street E1W 246 D4
Viscount Street EC2Y 241 J4

W

Wadding Street SE17 .... 245 K6
Wakefield Street WC1H 240 D3
Wakeling Street E14 .... 247 J3
Wakley Street EC1V 241 H2
Walbrook EC4N 241 L7
Walcorde Avenue SE17 .... 245 K6
Walcot Square SE11 .... 245 G5
Walden Street E1 .... 246 E2
Waley Street E1 .... 247 J1

Wallwood Street E14 .... 247 M1
Walnut Tree Walk SE11 .... 244 F5
Walpole Street SW3 .... 243 H6
Walter Terrace E1 .... 247 H2
Walton Place SW3 .... 243 H4
Walton Street SW3 .... 243 G4
Walworth Place SE17 .... 245 K7
Walworth Road SE17 .... 245 J5
Wansey Street SE17 .... 245 J6
Wapping ⊖ E1W 246 F5
Wapping High Street E1W 246 E6
Wapping Lane E1W 246 F4
Wapping Wall E1W 247 G5
Warden's Grove SE1 .... 245 J2
Wardour Street W1F 240 B6
Warner Street EC1R 240 F4
Warren Street W1T 239 M4
Warren Street ⊖ NW1 .... 239 M3
Warrington Crescent W9 .... 238 C3
Warrington Gardens W9 .... 238 C4
Warwick Avenue W9 .... 238 B3
Warwick Avenue ⊖ W9 .... 238 C4
Warwick Crescent W2 .... 238 C5
Warwick House Street SW1Y 244 B1
Warwick Lane EC4M 241 H6
Warwick Place W9 .... 238 C4
Warwick Road SW5 .... 242 A6
Warwick Row SW1E 243 L4
Warwick Square SW1V 243 M6
Warwick Street W1B 240 A7
Warwick Way SW1V 243 L6
Waterhouse Square EC1N 241 G5
Waterloo ⊖ ≥ SE1 .... 244 F2
Waterloo Bridge SE1 .... 244 E1
Waterloo Bridge WC2R 240 E8
Waterloo East ≥ SE1 .... 245 G2
Waterloo Place SW1Y 244 B1
Waterloo Road SE1 .... 244 F1
Waterloo Road SE1 .... 245 G2
Waterman Way E1W 246 E5
Waterside Close SE16 .... 246 D7
Watling Street EC4N 241 K7
Watney Street E1 .... 246 E3
Watts Street E1W 246 E5
Waveney Close E1W 246 D5
Waverton Street W1J 239 K8
Weavers Lane SE1 .... 246 A6
Webber Row SE1 .... 245 G3
Webber Street SE1 .... 245 H3
Webb Street SE1 .... 246 A8
Webster Road SE16 .... 246 D8
Weighhouse Street W1K 239 K7
Welbeck Street W1G 239 K5
Welbeck Way W1G 239 K6
Welland Mews E1W 246 E5
Wellclose Square E1 .... 246 D4
Wellesley Street E1 .... 247 H2
Wellesley Terrace N1 .... 241 K2
Wellington Arch W1J 243 K2
Wellington Square SW3 .... 243 H6
Wellington Place NW8 .... 238 E2
Wellington Road NW8 .... 238 D1
Wellington Street WC2E 240 D7
Wells Mews W1T 240 A5
Wells Street W1T 240 A5
Wells Way SE5 .... 245 M8
Wenlock Road N1 .... 241 K1
Wenlock Street N1 .... 241 K1
Wentworth Street E1 .... 246 B2
Werrington Street NW1 .... 240 A1
Wesley Street W1G 239 K5
West Arbour Street E1 .... 247 G2
Westbourne Crescent W2 .... 238 D7
Westbourne Gardens W2 .... 238 B6
Westbourne Gate W2 .... 238 E7
Westbourne Grove W2 .... 238 A6
Westbourne Grove Terrace W2 .... 238 B6
Westbourne Park Road W2 .... 238 A5
Westbourne Park Villas W2 .... 238 A5
Westbourne Street W2 .... 238 E7
Westbourne Terrace W2 .... 238 D6
Westbourne Terrace Mews W2 .... 238 C6
Westbourne Terrace Road W2 .... 238 C5
West Brompton ⊖ ≥ SW5 .... 242 A7
West Carriage Drive W2 .... 242 E2
Westcott Road SE17 .... 245 H8
West Cromwell Road SW5 .... 242 A5
Western Place SE16 .... 247 G6
Westferry ⊖ E14 .... 247 M4
Westferry Circus E14 .... 247 M5
Westferry Road E14 .... 247 M5
West Gardens E1W 246 F4
Westgate Terrace SW10 .... 242 B7
West Halkin Street SW1X 243 J4
West Harding Street EC4A 241 G6
West India Avenue E14 .... 247 M5
West India Dock Road E14 .... 247 M3
Westland Place N1 .... 241 K2
West Lane SE16 .... 246 E7
Westminster ⊖ SW1A 244 D3
Westminster Abbey SW1P 244 C3
Westminster Bridge SE1 .... 244 D3
Westminster Bridge Road SE1 .... 244 F3
Westmoreland Place SW1V 243 L7
Westmoreland Road SE17 .... 245 K8
Westmoreland Street W1G 239 K5
Westmoreland Terrace SW1V 243 L7
Weston Rise WC1X 240 E1
Weston Street SE1 .... 245 M2
Weston Street SE1 .... 245 M3
Westport Street E1 .... 247 H2
West Poultry Avenue EC1A 241 H5
West Road SW3 .... 243 H7
West Smithfield EC1A 241 H5
West Square SE11 .... 245 H4
West Street WC2H 240 C7
West Tenter Street E1 .... 246 C3
West Warwick Place SW1V 243 M6
Westway W2 .... 238 B5
Wetherby Gardens SW5 .... 242 C6
Weyhill Road E1 .... 246 D2
Weymouth Mews W1G 239 L5
Weymouth Street W1G 239 K5
Wharfdale Road N1 .... 240 D1
Wharfedale Street SW10 .... 242 B7
Wharf Road N1 .... 241 J1

Whitechapel Road E1 .... 246 D1
Whitecross Street EC1Y 241 K3
Whitefriars Street EC4Y 241 G6
Whitehall SW1A 244 C2
Whitehall Court SW1A 244 D2
Whitehall Place SW1A 244 D1
White Hart Street SE11 .... 245 G6
White Hart Yard SE1 .... 245 L2
Whitehaven Street NW8 .... 238 F4
Whitehead's Grove SW3 .... 243 G6
White Horse Lane E1 .... 247 H1
Whitehorse Road E1 .... 247 J1
Whitehorse Road E1 .... 247 J3
White Horse Street W1J 243 L1
White Kennett Street E1 .... 246 B2
White Lion Hill EC4V 241 H7
White Lion Street N1 .... 240 F1
White's Grounds SE1 .... 246 A7
White's Row E1 .... 246 B1
White Tower Way E1 .... 247 J1
Whitfield Place W1T 240 A4
Whitfield Street W1T 240 A4
Whitgift Street SE11 .... 244 E5
Whittaker Street SW1W 243 J6
Whittlesey Street SE1 .... 245 G2
Wicker Street E1 .... 246 E3
Wickham Close E1 .... 247 G1
Wickham Street SE11 .... 244 E7
Wicklow Street WC1X 240 E2
Widegate Street E1 .... 246 A1
Widley Road W9 .... 238 A3
Wigmore Place W1G 239 K5
Wigmore Street W1U 239 K6
Wigton Place SE11 .... 245 G7
Wilbraham Place SW1X 243 J5
Wilcox Place * SW1E 244 A4
Wild Court WC2B 240 E6
Wild's Rents SE1 .... 245 M4
Wild Street WC2B 240 D6
Wilfred Street SW1E 243 M4
Wilkes Street E1 .... 246 B1
William IV Street WC2N 240 C8
William Mews SW1X 243 H3
William Road NW1 .... 239 M3
Willow Place SW1P 244 A5
Willow Street EC2A 241 M3
Wilmington Square WC1X 240 F3
Wilmington Street WC1X 240 F2
Wilson Grove SE16 .... 246 E7
Wilson Street EC2A 241 L4
Wilton Crescent SW1X 243 J3
Wilton Mews SW1X 243 K4
Wilton Place SW1X 243 J3
Wilton Road SW1V 243 M5
Wilton Row SW1X 243 J3
Wilton Street SW1X 243 K4
Wimpole Mews W1G 239 K5
Wimpole Street W1G 239 K5
Winchester Street SW1V 243 L6
Winchester Walk SE1 .... 245 K1
Wincott Street SE11 .... 245 G5
Windmill Road SE11 .... 244 F7
Windmill Street W1T 240 B5
Windrose Close SE16 .... 247 H6
Windsor Terrace N1 .... 241 K1
Wine Close E1W 246 F5
Winnett Street W1D 240 B7
Winsland Mews W2 .... 238 E6
Winsland Street W2 .... 238 E6
Winsley Street W1W 240 A6
Winthrop Street E1 .... 246 E1
Woburn Place WC1H 240 C3
Woburn Square WC1H 240 C4
Wodeham Gardens E1 .... 246 E1
Wolfe Crescent SE16 .... 247 H7
Wolseley Street SE1 .... 246 C6
Woodbridge Street EC1R 241 G3
Woodchester Square W9 .... 238 A4
Woodfall Street SW3 .... 243 H7
Woodland Crescent SE16 .... 247 H7
Woodseer Street E1 .... 246 C1
Woods Mews W1K 239 J7
Woods Place SE1 .... 246 A8
Woodstock Street W1C 239 K6
Wood Street EC2V 241 K6
Woolaston Close SE1 .... 245 J5
Wooler Street SE17 .... 245 L7
Wootton Street SE1 .... 245 G2
Worgan Street SE11 .... 244 E6
Worgan Street SE16 .... 247 H8
Wormwood Street EC2M 241 M5
Worship Street EC2A 241 M4
Wren Street WC1X 240 E3
Wright's Lane W8 .... 242 A3
Wyatt Close SE16 .... 247 L7
Wyclif Street EC1V 241 H2
Wymering Road W9 .... 238 A2
Wynard Terrace SE11 .... 244 F7
Wyndham Place W1H 239 H5
Wyndham Street W1H 239 G4
Wynnstay Gardens W8 .... 242 A4
Wynyatt Street EC1V 241 H2
Wythburn Place W1H 239 H6

Y

Yalding Road * SE16 .... 246 C8
Yardley Street WC1X 240 F2
Yeoman's Row SW3 .... 243 G4
York Boulevard WC2N 240 D8
York Bridge NW1 .... 239 J3
York Gate NW1 .... 239 J4
York Road SE1 .... 244 E2
Yorkshire Road E14 .... 247 K3
York Square E14 .... 247 J2
York Street W1U 239 G5
York Street W1U 239 H5
York Terrace East NW1 .... 239 J4
York Terrace West NW1 .... 239 J4
York Way N1 .... 240 D1
Young Street W8 .... 242 B3

Z

Zoar Street SE1 .... 245 J1
ZSL London Zoo NW1 .... 239 J1

This index lists places appearing in the main map section of the atlas in alphabetical order. The reference following each name gives the atlas page number and grid reference of the square in which the place appears. The map shows counties, unitary authorities and administrative areas, together with a list of the abbreviated name forms used in the index. The top 100 places of tourist interest are indexed in **red**, World Heritage sites in **green**, motorway service areas in **blue**, airports in blue *italic* and National Parks in green *italic*.

Scotland

Abers	Aberdeenshire
Ag & B	Argyll and Bute
Angus	Angus
Border	Scottish Borders
C Aber	City of Aberdeen
C Dund	City of Dundee
C Edin	City of Edinburgh
C Glas	City of Glasgow
Clacks	Clackmannanshire (1)
D & G	Dumfries & Galloway
E Ayrs	East Ayrshire
E Duns	East Dunbartonshire (2)
E Loth	East Lothian
E Rens	East Renfrewshire (3)
Falk	Falkirk
Fife	Fife
Highld	Highland
Inver	Inverclyde (4)
Mdloth	Midlothian (5)
Moray	Moray
N Ayrs	North Ayrshire
N Lans	North Lanarkshire (6)
Ork	Orkney Islands
P & K	Perth & Kinross
Rens	Renfrewshire (7)
S Ayrs	South Ayrshire
S Lans	South Lanarkshire
Shet	Shetland Islands
Stirlg	Stirling
W Duns	West Dunbartonshire (8)
W Isls	Western Isles (Na h-Eileanan an Iar)
W Loth	West Lothian

Wales

Blae G	Blaenau Gwent (9)
Brdgnd	Bridgend (10)
Caerph	Caerphilly (11)
Cardif	Cardiff
Carmth	Carmarthenshire
Cerdgn	Ceredigion
Conwy	Conwy
Denbgs	Denbighshire
Flints	Flintshire
Gwynd	Gwynedd
IoA	Isle of Anglesey
Mons	Monmouthshire
Myr Td	Merthyr Tydfil (12)
Neath	Neath Port Talbot (13)
Newpt	Newport (14)
Pembks	Pembrokeshire
Powys	Powys
Rhondd	Rhondda Cynon Taf (15)
Swans	Swansea
Torfn	Torfaen (16)
V Glam	Vale of Glamorgan (17)
Wrexhm	Wrexham

Channel Islands & Isle of Man

Guern	Guernsey
Jersey	Jersey
IoM	Isle of Man

England

BaNES	Bath & N E Somerset (18)
Barns	Barnsley (19)
BCP	Bournemouth, Christchurch and Poole (20)
Bed	Bedford
Birm	Birmingham
Bl w D	Blackburn with Darwen (21)
Bolton	Bolton (22)
Bpool	Blackpool
Br & H	Brighton & Hove (23)
Br For	Bracknell Forest (24)
Bristl	City of Bristol
Bucks	Buckinghamshire
Bury	Bury (25)
C Beds	Central Bedfordshire
C Brad	City of Bradford
C Derb	City of Derby
C KuH	City of Kingston upon Hull
C Leic	City of Leicester
C Nott	City of Nottingham

C Pete	City of Peterborough
C Plym	City of Plymouth
C Port	City of Portsmouth
C Sotn	City of Southampton
C Stke	City of Stoke-on-Trent
C York	City of York
Calder	Calderdale (26)
Cambs	Cambridgeshire
Ches E	Cheshire East
Ches W	Cheshire West and Chester
Cnwll	Cornwall
Covtry	Coventry
Cumb	Cumbria
Darltn	Darlington (27)
Derbys	Derbyshire
Devon	Devon
Donc	Doncaster (28)
Dorset	Dorset
Dudley	Dudley (29)
Dur	Durham
E R Yk	East Riding of Yorkshire
E Susx	East Sussex
Essex	Essex
Gatesd	Gateshead (30)
Gloucs	Gloucestershire
Gt Lon	Greater London
Halton	Halton (31)
Hants	Hampshire
Hartpl	Hartlepool (32)
Herefs	Herefordshire
Herts	Hertfordshire
IoS	Isles of Scilly
IoW	Isle of Wight
Kent	Kent
Kirk	Kirklees (33)
Knows	Knowsley (34)
Lancs	Lancashire
Leeds	Leeds
Leics	Leicestershire
Lincs	Lincolnshire
Lpool	Liverpool
Luton	Luton

M Keyn	Milton Keynes
Manch	Manchester
Medway	Medway
Middsb	Middlesbrough
N Linc	North Lincolnshire
N Som	North Somerset
N Tyne	North Tyneside (35)
N u Ty	Newcastle upon Tyne
N York	North Yorkshire
NE Lin	North East Lincolnshire
Nhants	Northamptonshire
Norfk	Norfolk
Notts	Nottinghamshire
Nthumb	Northumberland
Oldham	Oldham (36)
Oxon	Oxfordshire
R & Cl	Redcar & Cleveland
Readg	Reading
Rochdl	Rochdale (37)
Rothm	Rotherham (38)
Rutlnd	Rutland
S Glos	South Gloucestershire (39)
S on T	Stockton-on-Tees (40)
S Tyne	South Tyneside (41)
Salfd	Salford (42)
Sandw	Sandwell (43)
Sefton	Sefton (44)
Sheff	Sheffield
Shrops	Shropshire
Slough	Slough (45)
Solhll	Solihull (46)
Somset	Somerset
St Hel	St Helens (47)
Staffs	Staffordshire
Sthend	Southend-on-Sea
Stockp	Stockport (48)
Suffk	Suffolk
Sundld	Sunderland
Surrey	Surrey
Swindn	Swindon
Tamesd	Tameside (49)
Thurr	Thurrock (50)
Torbay	Torbay
Traffd	Trafford (51)
W & M	Windsor & Maidenhead (52)
W Berk	West Berkshire
W Susx	West Sussex
Wakefd	Wakefield (53)
Warrtn	Warrington (54)
Warwks	Warwickshire
Wigan	Wigan (55)
Wilts	Wiltshire
Wirral	Wirral (56)
Wokham	Wokingham (57)
Wolves	Wolverhampton (58)
Worcs	Worcestershire
Wrekin	Telford & Wrekin (59)
Wsall	Walsall (60)

Abbas Combe – Ansley 255

A

Abbas Combe Somset 20 D10
Abberley Worcs 57 P11
Abberley Common Worcs 57 N11
Abberton Essex 52 H8
Abberton Worcs 47 J4
Abberwick Nthumb 119 M8
Abbess Roding Essex 51 N8
Abbey Devon 10 C2
Abbeycwmhir Powys 55 P10
Abbeydale Sheff 84 D4
Abbey Dore Herefs 45 M8
Abbey Green Staffs 70 H3
Abbey Hill Somset 19 J11
Abbey St Bathans Border 129 K7
Abbeystead Lancs 95 M10
Abbeytown Cumb 110 C10
Abbey Village Lancs 89 J6
Abbey Wood Gt Lon 37 L5
Abbotrule Border 118 B8
Abbots Bickington Devon 16 F9
Abbots Bromley Staffs 71 K10
Abbotsbury Dorset 11 M7
Abbot's Chair Derbys 83 M6
Abbots Deuglie P & K 134 E5
Abbotsham Devon 16 G6
Abbotskerswell Devon 7 M5
Abbots Langley Herts 50 C10
Abbotsleigh Devon 7 L9
Abbots Leigh N Som 31 P10
Abbotsley Cambs 62 B9
Abbots Morton Worcs 47 K3
Abbots Ripton Cambs 62 B5
Abbot's Salford Warwks 47 L4
Abbotstone Hants 22 G8
Abbotswood Hants 22 C10
Abbots Worthy Hants 22 E8
Abbotts Ann Hants 22 B6
Abbott Street Dorset 12 G4
Abcott Shrops 56 F9
Abdon Shrops 57 K7
Abenhall Gloucs 46 C11
Aberaeron Cerdgn 43 J2
Aberaman Rhondd 30 D4
Aberangell Gwynd 55 J2
Aber-arad Carmth 42 F6
Aberarder Highld 147 Q2
Aberargie P & K 134 F4
Aberarth Cerdgn 43 J2
Aberavon Neath 29 K7
Aber-banc Cerdgn 42 G6
Aberbargoed Caerph 30 G4
Aberbeeg Blae G 30 H4
Abercanaid Myr Td 30 E4
Abercarn Caerph 30 H6
Abercastle Pembks 40 G4
Abercegir Powys 55 J4
Aberchalder Highld 147 J7
Aberchirder Abers 158 F7
Aber Clydach Powys 44 G10
Abercorn W Loth 127 K2
Abercraf Powys 29 M2
Abercregan Neath 29 M5
Abercwmboi Rhondd 30 D5
Abercych Pembks 41 P2
Abercynon Rhondd 30 E6
Aberdalgie P & K 134 D3
Aberdare Rhondd 30 D4
Aberdaron Gwynd 66 B9
Aberdeen C Aber 151 N6
Aberdeen Airport C Aber 151 M5
Aberdesach Gwynd 66 G4
Aberdour Fife 134 F10
Aberdulais Neath 29 L5
Aberdyfi Gwynd 54 E5
Aberedw Powys 44 F5
Abereiddy Pembks 40 E4
Abererch Gwynd 66 F7
Aberfan Myr Td 30 E4
Aberfeldy P & K 141 L8
Aberffraw IoA 78 F11
Aberffrwd Cerdgn 54 F9
Aberford Leeds 91 L3
Aberfoyle Stirlg 132 G7
Abergarw Brdgnd 29 P8
Abergarwed Neath 29 M4
Abergavenny Mons 31 J2
Abergele Conwy 80 C9
Aber-giar Carmth 43 K6
Abergorlech Carmth 43 L8
Abergwesyn Powys 44 B4
Abergwili Carmth 42 H10
Abergwydol Powys 54 H4
Abergwynfi Neath 29 N5
Abergwyngregyn Gwynd 79 M10
Abergynolwyn Gwynd 54 F3
Aberhafesp Powys 55 P6
Aberhosan Powys 55 J5
Aberkenfig Brdgnd 29 N8
Aberlady E Loth 128 D4
Aberlemno Angus 143 J6
Aberllefenni Gwynd 54 H3
Aberllynfi Powys 44 H7
Aberlour, Charlestown of Moray 157 P9
Abermagwr Cerdgn 54 F10
Aber-meurig Cerdgn 43 L3
Abermorddu Flints 69 K3
Abermule Powys 56 B6
Abernant Carmth 42 F10
Abernant Rhondd 30 D4
Abernethy P & K 134 F4
Abernyte P & K 142 D11
Aberporth Cerdgn 42 E4
Abersoch Gwynd 66 E9
Abersychan Torfn 31 J4
Aberthin V Glam 30 D10
Abertillery Blae G 30 H4
Abertridwr Caerph 30 F7
Abertridwr Powys 68 D11
Abertysswg Caerph 30 F3
Aberuthven P & K 134 B4
Aberwheeler Denbgs 80 F11
Aberyscir Powys 44 D9
Aberystwyth Cerdgn 54 D8
Abingdon-on-Thames Oxon 34 E5
Abinger Common Surrey 36 D11
Abinger Hammer Surrey 36 C11
Abington Nhants 60 G8
Abington S Lans 116 C6
Abington Pigotts Cambs 50 H2
Abington Services S Lans 116 C6
Abingworth W Susx 24 D7
Ab Kettleby Leics 73 J6
Ab Lench Worcs 47 K4
Ablington Gloucs 33 M3
Ablington Wilts 21 N5
Abney Derbys 83 Q8
Above Church Staffs 71 J4
Aboyne Abers 150 E8
Abhainn Suidhe W Isls 168 f7
Abram Wigan 82 D4
Abriachan Highld 155 Q10
Abridge Essex 51 L11
Abronhill N Lans 126 D2
Abson S Glos 32 D10
Abthorpe Nhants 48 H5
Aby Lincs 87 M5
Acaster Malbis C York 98 B11
Acaster Selby N York 91 P2
Accrington Lancs 89 M5
Acha Ag & B 136 F5
Achahoish Ag & B 123 N4
Achalader P & K 141 R8
Achaleven Ag & B 138 G11
Acha Mor W Isls 168 i5
Achanalt Highld 155 J5
Achandunie Highld 156 A3
Achany Highld 162 D6
Acharacle Highld 138 B4
Acharn Highld 138 C7
Acharn P & K 141 J9
Achavanich Highld 167 L8
Achduart Highld 160 G6
Achfary Highld 164 G9
Achgarve Highld 160 D8
A'Chill Highld 144 C6
Achiltibuie Highld 160 G5
Achina Highld 166 B4
Achinhoan Ag & B 120 E8
Achintee Highld 154 B9
Achintraid Highld 153 Q10
Achlyness Highld 164 F6
Achmelvich Highld 160 H2
Achmore Highld 153 R11
Achmore W Isls 168 i5
Achnacarnin Highld 164 B10
Achnacarry Highld 146 F10
Achnacloich Highld 145 J6
Achnaconeran Highld 147 L4
Achnacroish Ag & B 138 F9
Achnadrish Ag & B 137 M5
Achnafauld P & K 141 L10
Achnagarron Highld 156 B3
Achnaha Highld 137 M2
Achnahaird Highld 160 G4
Achnahannet Highld 148 H2
Achnairn Highld 162 D4
Achnalea Highld 138 F5
Achnamara Ag & B 130 F10
Achnasheen Highld 154 G6
Achnashellach Highld 154 D8
Achnastank Moray 157 P11
Achosnich Highld 137 L2
Achranich Highld 138 C8
Achreamie Highld 166 H3
Achriabhach Highld 139 L4
Achriesgill Highld 164 G6
Achtoty Highld 165 Q4
Achurch Nhants 61 M4
Achvaich Highld 162 G8
Achvarasdal Highld 166 G4
Ackergill Highld 167 Q6
Acklam Middsb 104 E7
Acklam N York 98 F8
Ackleton Shrops 57 P5
Acklington Nthumb 119 P10
Ackton Wakefd 91 L6
Ackworth Moor Top Wakefd 91 L7
Acle Norfk 77 N9
Acock's Green Birm 58 H8
Acol Kent 39 P8
Acomb C York 98 B10
Acomb Nthumb 112 D7
Acombe Somset 10 D2
Aconbury Herefs 45 Q8
Acre Lancs 89 M6
Acrefair Wrexhm 69 J6
Acresford Derbys 59 L2
Acton Ches E 70 A4
Acton Dorset 12 G9
Acton Gt Lon 36 F4
Acton Shrops 56 E8
Acton Staffs 70 E6
Acton Suffk 52 E2
Acton Worcs 58 B11
Acton Wrexhm 69 K4
Acton Beauchamp Herefs 46 C4
Acton Bridge Ches W 82 C9
Acton Burnell Shrops 57 J4
Acton Green Herefs 46 C4
Acton Pigott Shrops 57 J4
Acton Round Shrops 57 L5
Acton Scott Shrops 56 H7
Acton Trussell Staffs 70 G11
Acton Turville S Glos 32 F8
Adbaston Staffs 70 D9
Adber Dorset 19 Q10
Adbolton Notts 72 F3
Adderbury Oxon 48 E7
Adderley Shrops 70 B7
Adderstone Nthumb 119 M4
Addiewell W Loth 126 H5
Addingham C Brad 96 G11
Addington Bucks 49 K9
Addington Gt Lon 37 J8
Addington Kent 37 Q9
Addiscombe Gt Lon 36 H7
Addlestone Surrey 36 C8
Addlestonemoor Surrey 36 C7
Addlethorpe Lincs 87 P7
Adeney Wrekin 70 B11
Adeyfield Herts 50 C9
Adfa Powys 55 P4
Adforton Herefs 56 G10
Adisham Kent 39 M11
Adlestrop Gloucs 47 P9
Adlingfleet E R Yk 92 D6
Adlington Ches E 83 K8
Adlington Lancs 89 J8
Admaston Staffs 71 J10
Admaston Wrekin 57 L2
Admington Warwks 47 P5
Adpar Cerdgn 42 F6
Adsborough Somset 19 J9
Adscombe Somset 18 G7
Adstock Bucks 49 K9
Adstone Nhants 48 G4
Adswood Stockp 83 J7
Adversane W Susx 24 C6
Advie Highld 157 L11
Adwalton Leeds 90 G5
Adwell Oxon 35 J5
Adwick le Street Donc 91 N9
Adwick upon Dearne Donc 91 M10
Ae D & G 109 L3
Ae Bridgend D & G 109 M3
Afan Forest Park Neath 29 N5
Affetside Bury 89 M8
Affleck Abers 158 E9
Affpuddle Dorset 12 D6
Affric Lodge Highld 146 F3
Afon-wen Flints 80 G10
Afon Wen Gwynd 66 G7
Afton Devon 7 L6
Afton IoW 13 P7
Agglethorpe N York 96 G3
Aigburth Lpool 81 M7
Aike E R Yk 99 L11
Aiketgate Cumb 111 J11
Aikhead Cumb 110 D11
Aikton Cumb 110 E10
Ailby Lincs 87 M5
Ailey Herefs 45 L5
Ailsworth C Pete 74 B11
Ainderby Quernhow N York 97 M4
Ainderby Steeple N York 97 M2
Aingers Green Essex 53 K7
Ainsdale Sefton 88 C8
Ainsdale-on-Sea Sefton 88 B8
Ainstable Cumb 111 K11
Ainsworth Bury 89 M8
Ainthorpe N York 105 K9
Aintree Sefton 81 M5
Ainville W Loth 127 L5
Aird Ag & B 130 F7
Aird D & G 106 E5
Aird Highld 145 J7
Aird W Isls 168 k4
Àird a' Mhulaidh W Isls 168 g6
Aird Asaig W Isls 168 g7
Aird Dhubh Highld 153 N9
Airdeny Ag & B 131 K2
Airdrie N Lans 126 D4
Airdriehill N Lans 126 D4
Airds of Kells D & G 108 E6
Àird Uig W Isls 168 f4
Airidh a bhruaich W Isls 168 h6
Airieland D & G 108 G9
Airlie Angus 142 E7
Airmyn E R Yk 92 B6
Airntully P & K 141 Q10
Airor Highld 145 M6
Airth Falk 133 Q10
Airton N York 96 D9
Aisby Lincs 73 Q3
Aisby Lincs 85 Q2
Aisgill Cumb 102 E11
Aish Devon 6 H6
Aish Devon 7 L7
Aisholt Somset 18 G7
Aiskew N York 97 L3
Aislaby N York 98 F3
Aislaby N York 105 N9
Aislaby S on T 104 D8
Aisthorpe Lincs 86 B4
Aith Shet 169 q8
Akeld Nthumb 119 J5
Akeley Bucks 49 K7
Akenham Suffk 53 L2
Albaston Cnwll 5 Q7
Alberbury Shrops 56 F2
Albourne W Susx 24 G7
Albourne Green W Susx 24 G7
Albrighton Shrops 57 Q4
Albrighton Shrops 69 N11
Alburgh Norfk 65 K4
Albury Herts 51 K6
Albury Oxon 35 J3
Albury Surrey 36 B11
Albury End Herts 51 K6
Albury Heath Surrey 36 C11
Alby Hill Norfk 76 H5
Alcaig Highld 155 Q6
Alcaston Shrops 56 H7
Alcester Warwks 47 L3
Alciston E Susx 25 M9
Alcombe Somset 18 C5
Alcombe Wilts 32 F11
Alconbury Cambs 61 Q5
Alconbury Weald Cambs 62 B5
Alconbury Weston Cambs 61 Q5
Aldborough N York 97 P7
Aldborough Norfk 76 H5
Aldbourne Wilts 33 Q9
Aldbrough E R Yk 93 M3
Aldbrough St John N York 103 P8
Aldbury Herts 35 Q2
Aldcliffe Lancs 95 K8
Aldclune P & K 141 L5
Aldeburgh Suffk 65 P10
Aldeby Norfk 65 N3
Aldenham Herts 50 D11
Alderbury Wilts 21 N9
Aldercar Derbys 84 F11
Alderford Norfk 76 G8
Alderholt Dorset 13 K2
Alderley Gloucs 32 E6
Alderley Edge Ches E 82 H9
Aldermans Green Covtry 59 N8
Aldermaston W Berk 34 G11
Alderminster Warwks 47 P5
Alder Moor Staffs 71 N9
Aldersey Green Ches W 69 N3
Aldershot Hants 23 N4
Alderton Gloucs 47 K8
Alderton Nhants 49 K5
Alderton Shrops 69 N10
Alderton Suffk 53 P3
Alderton Wilts 32 F8
Alderwasley Derbys 71 Q4
Aldfield N York 97 L7
Aldford Ches W 69 M3
Aldgate Rutlnd 73 P10
Aldham Essex 52 F6
Aldham Suffk 52 J2
Aldingbourne W Susx 15 P5
Aldingham Cumb 94 F6
Aldington Kent 27 J4
Aldington Worcs 47 L6
Aldington Corner Kent 27 J4
Aldivalloch Moray 150 B2
Aldochlay Ag & B 132 D9
Aldon Shrops 56 G9
Aldoth Cumb 109 P11
Aldreth Cambs 62 F6
Aldridge Wsall 58 G4
Aldringham Suffk 65 N9
Aldro N York 98 G8
Aldsworth Gloucs 33 N3
Aldsworth W Susx 15 L5
Aldunie Moray 150 B2
Aldwark Derbys 84 B9
Aldwark N York 97 Q8
Aldwick W Susx 15 P7
Aldwincle Nhants 61 M4
Aldworth W Berk 34 G9
Alexandria W Duns 125 K2
Aley Somset 18 G7
Alfardisworthy Devon 16 D9
Alfington Devon 10 C5
Alfold Surrey 24 B4
Alfold Bars W Susx 24 B4
Alfold Crossways Surrey 24 B3
Alford Abers 150 F4
Alford Lincs 87 N5
Alford Somset 20 B8
Alfreton Derbys 84 F9
Alfrick Worcs 46 D4
Alfrick Pound Worcs 46 D4
Alfriston E Susx 25 M10
Algarkirk Lincs 74 E3
Alhampton Somset 20 B8
Alkborough N Linc 92 E6
Alkerton Gloucs 32 E3
Alkerton Oxon 48 C6
Alkham Kent 27 N3
Alkington Shrops 69 P7
Alkmonton Derbys 71 M7
Allaleigh Devon 7 L8
Allanaquoich Abers 149 L9
Allanbank N Lans 126 E6
Allanton Border 129 M9
Allanton N Lans 126 E6
Allanton S Lans 126 C7
Allaston Gloucs 32 B4
Allbrook Hants 22 E10
All Cannings Wilts 21 L2
Allendale Nthumb 112 B9
Allen End Warwks 59 J5
Allenheads Nthumb 112 C11
Allensford Dur 112 G10
Allen's Green Herts 51 L7
Allensmore Herefs 45 P7
Allenton C Derb 72 B4
Aller Devon 17 P6
Aller Somset 19 M9
Allerby Cumb 100 E3
Allercombe Devon 9 P6
Aller Cross Devon 17 N6
Allerford Somset 18 B5
Allerston N York 98 H4
Allerthorpe E R Yk 98 F11
Allerton C Brad 90 E4
Allerton Highld 156 D4
Allerton Lpool 81 M7
Allerton Bywater Leeds 91 L5
Allerton Mauleverer N York 97 P9
Allesley Covtry 59 M8
Allestree C Derb 72 A3
Allet Common Cnwll 3 K4
Allexton Leics 73 L10
Allgreave Ches E 83 L11
Allhallows Medway 38 D6
Allhallows-on-Sea Medway 38 D6
Alligin Shuas Highld 153 Q6
Allimore Green Staffs 70 F11
Allington Dorset 11 K6
Allington Kent 38 C10
Allington Lincs 73 M2
Allington Wilts 21 L2
Allington Wilts 21 P7
Allington Wilts 32 G9
Allithwaite Cumb 94 H5
Alloa Clacks 133 P9
Allonby Cumb 100 E2
Allostock Ches W 82 F10
Alloway S Ayrs 114 F4
Allowenshay Somset 10 H2
All Saints South Elmham Suffk 65 L5
Allscott Shrops 57 N5
Allscott Wrekin 57 L2
All Stretton Shrops 56 H5
Alltami Flints 81 K11
Alltchaorunn Highld 139 M7
Alltmawr Powys 44 F5
Alltsigh Highld 147 M4
Alltwalis Carmth 42 H8
Alltwen Neath 29 K5
Alltyblaca Cerdgn 43 K5
Allwood Green Suffk 64 E7
Almeley Herefs 45 L4
Almeley Wooton Herefs 45 L4
Almer Dorset 12 F5
Almholme Donc 91 P9
Almington Staffs 70 C8
Almodington W Susx 15 M7
Almondbank P & K 134 D2
Almondbury Kirk 90 F8
Almondsbury S Glos 32 B8
Alne N York 97 Q7
Alness Highld 156 B4
Alnham Nthumb 119 J8
Alnmouth Nthumb 119 P8
Alnwick Nthumb 119 N8
Alperton Gt Lon 36 E4
Alphamstone Essex 52 E4
Alpheton Suffk 64 B11
Alphington Devon 9 M6
Alpington Norfk 77 K11
Alport Derbys 84 B8
Alpraham Ches E 69 Q3
Alresford Essex 53 J7
Alrewas Staffs 59 J2
Alsager Ches E 70 D3
Alsagers Bank Staffs 70 D5
Alsop en le Dale Derbys 71 M4
Alston Cumb 111 P11
Alston Devon 10 G4
Alstone Gloucs 47 J8
Alstone Somset 19 K5
Alstonefield Staffs 71 L3
Alston Sutton Somset 19 M4
Alswear Devon 17 N7
Alt Oldham 83 K4
Altandhu Highld 160 F4
Altarnun Cnwll 5 L5
Altass Highld 162 C6
Altcreich Ag & B 138 B10
Altgaltraig Ag & B 124 C3
Altham Lancs 89 M4
Althorne Essex 38 F2
Althorpe N Linc 92 D9
Altnabreac Station Highld 166 H7
Altnaharra Highld 165 N9
Altofts Wakefd 91 K6
Alton Derbys 84 E8
Alton Hants 23 K7
Alton Staffs 71 K6
Alton Wilts 21 N5
Alton Barnes Wilts 21 M2
Alton Pancras Dorset 11 Q4
Alton Priors Wilts 21 M2
Alton Towers Staffs 71 K6
Altrincham Traffd 82 G7
Altskeith Hotel Stirlg 132 F7
Alva Clacks 133 P8
Alvanley Ches W 81 P10
Alvaston C Derb 72 B4
Alvechurch Worcs 58 F10
Alvecote Warwks 59 K4
Alvediston Wilts 21 J10
Alveley Shrops 57 P8
Alverdiscott Devon 17 J6
Alverstoke Hants 14 H7
Alverstone IoW 14 G9
Alverthorpe Wakefd 91 J6
Alverton Notts 73 K2
Alves Moray 157 L5
Alvescot Oxon 33 Q4
Alveston S Glos 32 B7
Alveston Warwks 47 P3
Alvingham Lincs 87 L2
Alvington Gloucs 32 B4
Alwalton C Pete 74 B11
Alweston Dorset 11 P2
Alwinton Nthumb 118 H9
Alwoodley Leeds 90 H2
Alwoodley Gates Leeds 91 J2
Alyth P & K 142 C8
Am Bàgh a Tuath W Isls 168 c17
Ambergate Derbys 84 D10
Amber Hill Lincs 86 H11
Amberley Gloucs 32 G4
Amberley W Susx 24 B8
Amber Row Derbys 84 E9
Amberstone E Susx 25 N8
Amble Nthumb 119 Q10
Amblecote Dudley 58 C7
Ambler Thorn C Brad 90 D5
Ambleside Cumb 101 L10
Ambleston Pembks 41 K5
Ambrosden Oxon 48 H11
Amcotts N Linc 92 E8
America Cambs 62 F5
Amersham Bucks 35 Q5
Amersham Common Bucks 35 Q5
Amersham Old Town Bucks 35 Q5
Amersham on the Hill Bucks 35 Q5
Amerton Staffs 70 H9
Amesbury Wilts 21 N6
Amhuinnsuidhe W Isls 168 f7
Amington Staffs 59 K4
Amisfield D & G 109 M4
Amlwch IoA 78 G6
Ammanford Carmth 28 H2
Amotherby N York 98 E6
Ampfield Hants 22 D10
Ampleforth N York 98 B5
Ampney Crucis Gloucs 33 L4
Ampney St Mary Gloucs 33 L4
Ampney St Peter Gloucs 33 L4
Amport Hants 22 B6
Ampthill C Beds 50 B3
Ampton Suffk 64 B7
Amroth Pembks 41 N9
Amulree P & K 141 L10
Amwell Herts 50 E8
Anaheilt Highld 138 E5
Ancaster Lincs 73 P2
Ancells Farm Hants 23 M3
Anchor Shrops 56 B7
Ancroft Nthumb 129 P11
Ancrum Border 118 B6
Ancton W Susx 15 Q6
Anderby Lincs 87 P5
Anderby Creek Lincs 87 Q5
Andersea Somset 19 K8
Andersfield Somset 18 H8
Anderson Dorset 12 E5
Anderton Ches W 82 D9
Anderton Cnwll 6 C8
Andover Hants 22 C5
Andover Down Hants 22 C5
Andoversford Gloucs 47 K11
Andreas IoM 80 f2
Anelog Gwynd 66 B9
Anerley Gt Lon 36 H7
Anfield Lpool 81 M6
Angarrack Cnwll 2 F6
Angarrick Cnwll 3 K6
Angelbank Shrops 57 K9
Angersleigh Somset 18 G11
Angerton Cumb 110 D9
Angle Pembks 40 G10
Anglesey IoA 78 G8
Anglesey Abbey Cambs 62 H8
Angmering W Susx 24 C10
Angram N York 97 R11
Angram N York 102 G11
Angrouse Cnwll 2 H10
Anick Nthumb 112 D7
Ankerville Highld 156 E3
Ankle Hill Leics 73 K7
Anlaby E R Yk 92 H5
Anmer Norfk 75 P5
Anmore Hants 15 J4
Annan D & G 110 C7
Annandale Water Services D & G 109 P2
Annaside Cumb 94 B3
Annat Highld 154 A7
Annathill N Lans 126 C3
Anna Valley Hants 22 C6
Annbank S Ayrs 114 H3
Anne Hathaway's Cottage Warwks 47 N4
Annesley Notts 84 H10
Annesley Woodhouse Notts 84 G10
Annfield Plain Dur 113 J10
Anniesland C Glas 125 N4
Annitsford N Tyne 113 L6
Annscroft Shrops 56 H3
Ansdell Lancs 88 C5
Ansford Somset 20 B8
Ansley Warwks 59 M6

Anslow Staffs 71 N9
Anslow Gate Staffs 71 M10
Anslow Lees Staffs 71 N10
Ansteadbrook Surrey 23 P8
Anstey Hants 23 K6
Anstey Herts 51 K4
Anstey Leics 72 F9
Anstruther Fife 135 P7
Ansty W Susx 24 G6
Ansty Warwks 59 P8
Ansty Wilts 21 J9
Ansty Cross Dorset 12 C4
An Tairbeart W Isls 168 h7
Anthill Common Hants 14 H4
Anthonys Surrey 36 B8
Anthorn Cumb 110 C9
Antingham Norfk 77 K5
An t-Òb W Isls 168 f9
Antonine Wall 126 E2
Anton's Gowt Lincs 87 K11
Antony Cnwll 5 Q11
Antrobus Ches W 82 D9
Anvil Corner Devon 16 F11
Anvil Green Kent 27 K2
Anwick Lincs 86 F10
Anwoth D & G 108 C9
Aperfield Gt Lon 37 K9
Apes Dale Worcs 58 E10
Apethorpe Nhants 73 Q11
Apeton Staffs 70 F11
Apley Lincs 86 F5
Apperknowle Derbys 84 E5
Apperley Gloucs 46 G9
Apperley Bridge C Brad 90 F3
Apperley Dene Nthumb 112 G9
Appersett N York 96 C2
Appin Ag & B 138 G8
Appleby N Linc 92 G8
Appleby-in-Westmorland Cumb 102 C6
Appleby Magna Leics 59 M3
Appleby Parva Leics 59 M3
Appleby Street Herts 50 H10
Applecross Highld 153 N9
Appledore Devon 9 Q2
Appledore Devon 16 H5
Appledore Kent 26 G6
Appledore Heath Kent 26 G5
Appleford Oxon 34 F6
Applegarth Town D & G 109 P4
Applehaigh Wakefd 91 K8
Applemore Hants 14 C5
Appleshaw Hants 22 B5
Applethwaite Cumb 101 J5
Appleton Halton 81 Q7
Appleton Oxon 34 D4
Appleton Warrtn 82 D8
Appleton-le-Moors N York 98 E3
Appleton-le-Street N York 98 E6
Appleton Roebuck N York 91 P2
Appleton Thorn Warrtn 82 D8
Appleton Wiske N York 104 C10
Appletreehall Border 117 Q7
Appletreewick N York 96 G8
Appley Somset 18 E10
Appley Bridge Lancs 88 G9
Apse Heath IoW 14 G10
Apsley End C Beds 50 D4
Apuldram W Susx 15 M6
Arabella Highld 156 E2
Arborfield Wokham 35 L11
Arborfield Cross Wokham 35 L11
Arborfield Green Wokham 35 L11
Arbourthorne Sheff 84 E3
Arbroath Angus 143 L9
Arbuthnott Abers 143 P2
Arcadia Kent 26 E4
Archddu Carmth 28 D4
Archdeacon Newton Darltn 103 Q7
Archencarroch W Duns 132 E11
Archiestown Moray 157 N9
Archirondel Jersey 11 c1
Arclid Ches E 70 D2
Ardallie Abers 159 P10
Ardanaiseig Hotel Ag & B 131 M3
Ardaneaskan Highld 153 Q10
Ardarroch Highld 153 Q10
Ardbeg Ag & B 122 F10
Ardbeg Ag & B 131 D4
Ardbeg Ag & B 131 P11
Ardcharnich Highld 161 K9
Ardchiavaig Ag & B 137 K12
Ardchonnell Ag & B 131 K5
Ardchronie Highld 162 E9
Ardchullarie More Stirlg 132 H5
Arddarroch Ag & B 131 Q9
Arddleen Powys 69 J11
Ard Dorch Highld 145 J2
Ardechive Highld 146 E9
Ardeer N Ayrs 124 H9
Ardeley Herts 50 H5
Ardelve Highld 145 Q2
Arden Ag & B 132 D11
Ardens Grafton Warwks 47 M4
Ardentallen Ag & B 130 G3
Ardentinny Ag & B 131 P10
Ardentraive Ag & B 124 C3
Ardeonaig Stirlg 140 G10
Ardersier Highld 156 D7
Ardessie Highld 160 H9
Ardfern Ag & B 130 G7
Ardfernal Ag & B 123 J5
Ardgartan Ag & B 132 B7
Ardgay Highld 162 D8
Ardgour Highld 139 J5
Ardgowan Inver 124 G3
Ardhallow Ag & B 124 F3
Ardhasig W Isls 168 g7
Ardheslaig Highld 153 P6
Ardindrean Highld 161 K9
Ardingly W Susx 24 H5
Ardington Oxon 34 D7
Ardington Wick Oxon 34 D7
Ardlamont Ag & B 124 B4
Ardleigh Essex 53 J6
Ardleigh Heath Essex 52 H5
Ardler P & K 142 D9
Ardley Oxon 48 F9
Ardley End Essex 51 M8
Ardlui Ag & B 132 C4
Ardlussa Ag & B 130 C10
Ardmair Highld 161 J7
Ardmaleish Ag & B 124 D4
Ardminish Ag & B 123 K10
Ardmolich Highld 138 C3
Ardmore Ag & B 125 J2
Ardmore Highld 162 G9
Ardnadam Ag & B 131 P11
Ardnagrask Highld 155 P8
Ardnamurchan Highld 137 P2
Ardnarff Highld 154 A10
Ardnastang Highld 138 E5
Ardpatrick Ag & B 123 N8
Ardrishaig Ag & B 130 H10
Ardross Highld 155 R3
Ardrossan N Ayrs 124 G9
Ardsley Barns 91 K9
Ardslignish Highld 137 P3
Ardtalla Ag & B 122 G9
Ardtoe Highld 138 A3
Arduaine Ag & B 130 F5
Ardullie Highld 155 Q5
Ardvasar Highld 145 K7
Ardvorlich P & K 133 J3
Ardvourlie W Isls 168 g6
Ardwell D & G 106 F8
Ardwick Manch 83 J5
Areley Kings Worcs 57 P10
Arevegaig Highld 138 B4
Arford Hants 23 M7
Arglam E R Yk 92 C3
Argoed Caerph 30 G5
Argoed Shrops 69 K10
Argoed Mill Powys 44 D2
Argos Hill E Susx 25 N5
Argyll Forest Park Ag & B 131 Q7
Aribruach W Isls 168 h6
Aridhglas Ag & B 137 J11
Arileod Ag & B 136 F5
Arinagour Ag & B 136 G4
Ariogan Ag & B 130 H2
Arisaig Highld 145 L10
Arisaig House Highld 145 L11
Arkendale N York 97 N8
Arkesden Essex 51 L4
Arkleby Cumb 100 F3
Arkleton D & G 110 G2
Arkle Town N York 103 K10
Arkley Gt Lon 50 F11
Arksey Donc 91 P9
Arkwright Town Derbys 84 F6
Arle Gloucs 46 H10
Arlecdon Cumb 100 D7
Arlescote Warwks 48 C5
Arlesey C Beds 50 E3
Arleston Wrekin 57 M2
Arley Ches E 82 E8
Arlingham Gloucs 32 D2
Arlington Devon 17 L3
Arlington E Susx 25 M9
Arlington Gloucs 33 M3
Arlington Beccott Devon 17 L3
Armadale Highld 145 K7
Armadale Highld 166 C4
Armadale W Loth 126 G4
Armaside Cumb 100 G5
Armathwaite Cumb 111 K11
Arminghall Norfk 77 K11
Armitage Staffs 71 K11
Armitage Bridge Kirk 90 E7
Armley Leeds 90 H4
Armscote Warwks 47 P6
Armshead Staffs 70 G5
Armston Nhants 61 N3
Armthorpe Donc 91 Q10
Arnabost Ag & B 136 G3
Arnaby Cumb 94 D4
Arncliffe N York 96 D6
Arncliffe Cote N York 96 D6
Arncroach Fife 135 N6
Arndilly House Moray 157 P8
Arne Dorset 12 G7
Arnesby Leics 60 D2
Arngask P & K 134 E5
Arnisdale Highld 145 P5
Arnish Highld 153 K8
Arniston Mdloth 127 Q5
Arnol W Isls 168 i3
Arnold E R Yk 93 K2
Arnold Notts 85 J11
Arnprior Stirlg 133 J9
Arnside Cumb 95 K5
Aros Ag & B 137 P6
Arowry Wrexhm 69 N7
Arrad Foot Cumb 94 G4
Arram E R Yk 92 H2
Arran N Ayrs 120 H4
Arrathorne N York 97 K2
Arreton IoW 14 F9
Arrina Highld 153 N6
Arrington Cambs 62 D10
Arrochar Stirlg 132 B7
Arrow Warwks 47 L3
Arrowfield Top Worcs 58 F10
Arscott Shrops 56 G3
Artafallie Highld 156 A8
Arthington Leeds 90 H2
Arthingworth Nhants 60 G4
Arthog Gwynd 54 G2
Arthrath Abers 159 N10
Arthursdale Leeds 91 K3
Arundel W Susx 24 B9
Asby Cumb 100 E6
Ascog Ag & B 124 E5
Ascot W & M 35 P11
Ascott Warwks 48 B8
Ascott Earl Oxon 48 B11
Ascott-under-Wychwood Oxon 48 B11
Asenby N York 97 N5
Asfordby Leics 73 J7
Asfordby Hill Leics 73 J7
Asgarby Lincs 86 F11
Asgarby Lincs 87 K7
Ash Devon 7 L9
Ash Devon 17 J10
Ash Dorset 12 E2
Ash Kent 37 P8
Ash Kent 39 N10
Ash Somset 19 N10
Ash Somset 19 N10
Ash Surrey 23 P4
Ashampstead W Berk 34 G9
Ashampstead Green W Berk 34 G9
Ashbocking Suffk 64 H11
Ashbourne Derbys 71 M5
Ashbrittle Somset 18 E10
Ashburnham Place E Susx 25 Q8
Ashburton Devon 7 K4
Ashbury Devon 8 D5
Ashbury Oxon 33 Q7
Ashby N Linc 92 F9
Ashby by Partney Lincs 87 M7
Ashby cum Fenby NE Lin 93 N10
Ashby de la Launde Lincs 86 E9
Ashby-de-la-Zouch Leics 72 B7
Ashby Folville Leics 73 J8
Ashby Magna Leics 60 C2
Ashby Parva Leics 60 B3
Ashby Puerorum Lincs 87 K6
Ashby St Ledgers Nhants 60 C7
Ashby St Mary Norfk 77 L11
Ashchurch Gloucs 46 H8
Ashcombe Devon 9 M9
Ashcombe N Som 19 K2
Ashcott Somset 19 M7
Ashdon Essex 51 N2
Ashdown Forest E Susx 25 L4
Ashe Hants 22 F4
Asheldham Essex 52 G11
Ashen Essex 52 B3
Ashendon Bucks 35 K2
Asheridge Bucks 35 P4
Ashfield Hants 22 C11
Ashfield Herefs 46 A10
Ashfield Stirlg 133 M7
Ashfield cum Thorpe Suffk 65 J9
Ashfield Green Suffk 63 N9
Ashfield Green Suffk 65 K7
Ashfold Crossways W Susx 24 F5
Ashford Devon 6 H9
Ashford Devon 17 J4
Ashford Kent 26 H3
Ashford Surrey 36 C6
Ashford Bowdler Shrops 57 J10
Ashford Carbonell Shrops 57 J10
Ashford Hill Hants 22 G2
Ashford in the Water Derbys 83 Q11
Ashgill S Lans 126 D7
Ash Green Surrey 23 P5
Ash Green Warwks 59 M8
Ashill Devon 10 B2
Ashill Norfk 76 B11
Ashill Somset 19 K11
Ashingdon Essex 38 E3
Ashington BCP 12 H5
Ashington Nthumb 113 L3
Ashington Somset 19 Q10
Ashington W Susx 24 D7
Ashkirk Border 117 P6
Ashlett Hants 14 E6
Ashleworth Gloucs 46 F9
Ashleworth Quay Gloucs 46 F9
Ashley Cambs 63 L8
Ashley Ches E 82 G8
Ashley Devon 17 M9
Ashley Dorset 13 K4
Ashley Gloucs 32 H6
Ashley Hants 13 N5
Ashley Hants 22 C8
Ashley Kent 27 P2
Ashley Nhants 60 G2
Ashley Staffs 70 D7
Ashley Wilts 32 F11
Ashley Green Bucks 35 Q3
Ashleyhay Derbys 71 P4
Ashley Heath Dorset 13 K4
Ashley Moor Herefs 56 H11
Ash Magna Shrops 69 Q7
Ashmansworth Hants 22 D3
Ashmansworthy Devon 16 E8
Ashmead Green Gloucs 32 E5
Ashmill Devon 5 P2
Ash Mill Devon 17 P7
Ashmore Dorset 20 H11
Ashmore Green W Berk 34 F11
Ashorne Warwks 48 B3
Ashover Derbys 84 D8
Ashover Hay Derbys 84 D8
Ashow Warwks 59 M10
Ash Parva Shrops 69 Q7
Ashperton Herefs 46 B6
Ashprington Devon 7 L7
Ash Priors Somset 18 G9
Ashreigney Devon 17 L9
Ash Street Suffk 52 H2
Ashtead Surrey 36 E9
Ash Thomas Devon 9 P2
Ashton Cnwll 2 G8
Ashton Devon 9 L8
Ashton Hants 22 F11
Ashton Herefs 45 Q2
Ashton Inver 124 G2
Ashton Nhants 49 L5
Ashton Nhants 61 N3
Ashton Somset 19 M5
Ashton Common Wilts 20 G3
Ashton Hayes Ches W 81 Q11
Ashton Hill Wilts 20 H3
Ashton-in-Makerfield Wigan 82 C5
Ashton Keynes Wilts 33 K6
Ashton under Hill Worcs 47 J7
Ashton-under-Lyne Tamesd 83 K5
Ashton upon Mersey Traffd 82 G6
Ashton Vale Bristl 31 Q10
Ashurst Hants 13 P2
Ashurst Kent 25 M3
Ashurst Lancs 88 F9
Ashurst W Susx 24 E7
Ashurst Wood W Susx 25 K3
Ash Vale Surrey 23 N4
Ashwater Devon 5 P2
Ashwell Herts 50 G3
Ashwell Rutlnd 73 M8
Ashwell End Herts 50 G2
Ashwellthorpe Norfk 64 G2
Ashwick Somset 19 L11
Ashwicken Norfk 75 P7
Ashwood Staffs 58 C7
Askam in Furness Cumb 94 E5
Askern Donc 91 P8
Askerswell Dorset 11 L6
Askett Bucks 35 M3
Askham Cumb 101 P6
Askham Notts 85 M6
Askham Bryan C York 98 B11
Askham Richard C York 98 A11
Asknish Ag & B 131 J9
Askrigg N York 96 D2
Askwith N York 97 J11
Aslackby Lincs 74 A4
Aslacton Norfk 64 H3
Aslockton Notts 73 J3
Asney Somset 19 N7
Aspall Suffk 64 H9
Aspatria Cumb 100 F2
Aspenden Herts 51 J5
Aspenshaw Derbys 83 M7
Asperton Lincs 74 E3
Aspley Staffs 70 E8
Aspley Guise C Beds 49 P7
Aspley Heath C Beds 49 P8
Aspley Heath Warwks 58 G10
Aspull Wigan 89 J9
Aspull Common Wigan 82 D5
Asselby E R Yk 92 B5
Asserby Lincs 87 N5
Asserby Turn Lincs 87 N5
Assington Suffk 52 F4
Assington Green Suffk 63 N10
Astbury Ches E 70 E2
Astcote Nhants 49 J4
Asterley Shrops 56 F3
Asterton Shrops 56 F6
Asthall Oxon 33 Q2
Asthall Leigh Oxon 34 B2
Astle Highld 162 G8
Astley Shrops 69 P11
Astley Warwks 59 M7
Astley Worcs 57 P11
Astley Abbots Shrops 57 N5
Astley Bridge Bolton 89 L8
Astley Cross Worcs 57 Q11
Astley Green Wigan 82 F5
Aston Birm 58 G7
Aston Ches E 69 R5
Aston Ches W 82 C9
Aston Derbys 83 Q8
Aston Flints 81 L11
Aston Herefs 45 P2
Aston Herefs 56 H6
Aston Oxon 34 B4
Aston Rothm 84 G3
Aston Shrops 57 Q6
Aston Shrops 69 P9
Aston Staffs 70 D6
Aston Staffs 70 F10
Aston Wokham 35 L8
Aston Wrekin 57 L3
Aston Abbotts Bucks 49 M10
Aston Botterell Shrops 57 L8
Aston-by-Stone Staffs 70 G8
Aston Cantlow Warwks 47 M2
Aston Clinton Bucks 35 N2
Aston Crews Herefs 46 C10
Aston Cross Gloucs 46 H8
Aston End Herts 50 G6
Aston-Eyre Shrops 57 M6
Aston Fields Worcs 58 E11
Aston Flamville Leics 59 Q6
Aston Heath Ches W 82 C9
Aston Ingham Herefs 46 C10
Aston juxta Mondrum Ches E 70 A3
Aston le Walls Nhants 48 E4
Aston Magna Gloucs 47 N7
Aston Munslow Shrops 57 J7
Aston-on-Carrant Gloucs 46 H8
Aston on Clun Shrops 56 F8
Aston Pigott Shrops 56 E3
Aston Rogers Shrops 56 E3
Aston Rowant Oxon 35 K5
Aston Sandford Bucks 35 L3
Aston Somerville Worcs 47 K7
Aston-sub-Edge Gloucs 47 M6
Aston Tirrold Oxon 34 G7
Aston-upon-Trent Derbys 72 C5
Aston Upthorpe Oxon 34 G7
Astrop Nhants 48 F7
Astrope Herts 35 N2
Astwick C Beds 50 F3
Astwith Derbys 84 F8
Astwood M Keyn 49 Q5
Astwood Worcs 58 D11
Astwood Bank Worcs 47 K2
Aswarby Lincs 73 R3
Aswardby Lincs 87 L6
Atcham Shrops 57 J3
Atch Lench Worcs 47 K4
Athelhampton Dorset 12 C6
Athelington Suffk 65 J7
Athelney Somset 19 K9
Athelstaneford E Loth 128 E4
Atherfield Green IoW 14 E11
Atherington Devon 17 K7
Atherington W Susx 24 B10
Atherstone Somset 19 M5
Atherstone Warwks 59 M5
Atherstone on Stour Warwks 47 P4
Atherton Wigan 82 E4
Atley Hill N York 103 Q10
Atlow Derbys 71 N5
Attadale Highld 154 B10
Attenborough Notts 72 E4
Atterby Lincs 85 R3
Attercliffe Sheff 84 E3
Atterley Shrops 57 L5
Atterton Leics 72 B11
Attingham Park Shrops 57 J2
Attleborough Norfk 64 E2
Attleborough Warwks 59 N6
Attlebridge Norfk 76 G8
Attleton Green Suffk 63 M10
Atwick E R Yk 99 P10
Atworth Wilts 32 G11
Auberrow Herefs 45 P5
Aubourn Lincs 86 B8
Auchbreck Moray 149 N2
Auchedly Abers 159 L11
Auchenblae Abers 143 N2
Auchenbowie Stirlg 133 M10
Auchencairn D & G 108 G10
Auchencairn D & G 109 L4
Auchencairn N Ayrs 121 K6
Auchencrow Border 129 M7
Auchendinny Mdloth 127 P5
Auchengray S Lans 126 H7
Auchenhalrig Moray 157 R5
Auchenheath S Lans 126 E9
Auchenhessnane D & G 115 R8
Auchenlochan Ag & B 124 B3
Auchenmade N Ayrs 125 K7
Auchenmalg D & G 106 H7
Auchentiber N Ayrs 125 K8
Auchindrain Ag & B 131 L7
Auchindrean Highld 161 K10
Auchininna Abers 158 G8
Auchinleck E Ayrs 115 L3
Auchinloch N Lans 126 B3
Auchintore Highld 139 K3
Auchiries Abers 159 Q10
Auchlean Highld 148 F8
Auchlee Abers 151 M8
Auchleven Abers 150 G3
Auchlochan S Lans 126 E10
Auchlossan Abers 150 F7
Auchlyne Stirlg 132 G2
Auchmillan E Ayrs 115 K2
Auchmithie Angus 143 M9
Auchmuirbridge Fife 134 G7
Auchnacree Angus 142 H5
Auchnagatt Abers 159 M9
Auchnarrow Moray 149 N3
Auchnotteroch D & G 106 C5
Auchroisk Moray 157 Q7
Auchterarder P & K 133 Q5
Auchteraw Highld 147 K6
Auchterblair Highld 148 G3
Auchtercairn Highld 153 Q2
Auchterderran Fife 134 G8
Auchterhouse Angus 142 E10
Auchterless Abers 158 H9
Auchtermuchty Fife 134 G5
Auchterneed Highld 155 N6
Auchtertool Fife 134 G9
Auchtertyre Highld 145 P2
Auchtubh Stirlg 132 H3
Auckengill Highld 167 Q4
Auckley Donc 91 Q10
Audenshaw Tamesd 83 K5
Audlem Ches E 70 B6
Audley Staffs 70 D4
Audley End Essex 51 M3
Audley End Essex 52 D4
Audley End Suffk 64 B11
Audley End House & Gardens Essex 51 M3
Audmore Staffs 70 E10
Audnam Dudley 58 C7
Aughertree Cumb 101 J3
Aughton E R Yk 92 B3
Aughton Lancs 88 D9
Aughton Lancs 95 M7
Aughton Rothm 84 G3
Aughton Wilts 21 P3
Aughton Park Lancs 88 E9
Auldearn Highld 156 G6
Aulden Herefs 45 P4
Auldgirth D & G 109 K3
Auldhouse S Lans 125 Q7
Ault a' chruinn Highld 146 A3
Aultbea Highld 160 D9
Aultgrishin Highld 160 A9
Aultguish Inn Highld 155 L3
Ault Hucknall Derbys 84 G7
Aultmore Moray 158 B7
Aultnagoire Highld 147 N3
Aultnamain Highld 162 F10
Aunby Lincs 73 Q8
Aunk Devon 9 P4
Aunsby Lincs 73 Q3
Aust S Glos 31 Q7
Austendike Lincs 74 E6
Austerfield Donc 85 L2
Austerlands Oldham 90 B9
Austhorpe Leeds 91 K4
Austonley Kirk 90 E9
Austrey Warwks 59 L3
Austwick N York 95 M7
Authorpe Lincs 87 L4
Authorpe Row Lincs 87 P6
Avebury Wilts 33 M11
Avebury Wilts 33 M11
Avebury Trusloe Wilts 33 L11
Aveley Thurr 37 N4
Avening Gloucs 32 G5
Averham Notts 85 M10
Aveton Gifford Devon 6 H9
Aviemore Highld 148 F5
Avington W Berk 34 C11
Avoch Highld 156 C6
Avon Hants 13 K5
Avonbridge Falk 126 G3
Avon Dassett Warwks 48 D4
Avonmouth Bristl 31 P9
Avonwick Devon 7 J7
Awbridge Hants 22 B10
Awkley S Glos 31 Q7
Awliscombe Devon 10 C4
Awre Gloucs 32 D3
Awsworth Notts 72 D2
Axborough Worcs 58 C9
Axbridge Somset 19 M4
Axford Hants 22 H6
Axford Wilts 33 P10
Axmansford Hants 22 G2
Axminster Devon 10 F5
Axmouth Devon 10 F6
Axton Flints 80 G8
Aycliffe Dur 103 Q6
Aydon Nthumb 112 F7
Aylburton Gloucs 32 B4
Ayle Nthumb 111 P11
Aylesbeare Devon 9 P6
Aylesbury Bucks 35 M2
Aylesby NE Lin 93 M9
Aylesford Kent 38 B10
Aylesham Kent 39 M11
Aylestone C Leic 72 F10
Aylestone Park C Leic 72 F10
Aylmerton Norfk 76 H4
Aylsham Norfk 76 H6
Aylton Herefs 46 C7
Aylworth Gloucs 47 M10
Aymestrey Herefs 56 H11
Aynho Nhants 48 F8
Ayot Green Herts 50 E7
Ayot St Lawrence Herts 50 E7
Ayot St Peter Herts 50 E7
Ayr S Ayrs 114 F3
Aysgarth N York 96 F3
Ayshford Devon 18 D11
Ayside Cumb 94 H4
Ayston Rutlnd 73 M10
Aythorpe Roding Essex 51 N7
Ayton Border 129 N7
Azerley N York 97 L6

Babbacombe - Beam Hill 257

B

Babbacombe Torbay 7 N5
Babbington Notts 72 D2
Babbinswood Shrops 69 K9
Babbs Green Herts 51 J7
Babcary Somset 19 Q9
Babel Carmth 44 A7
Babel Green Suffk 63 M11
Babell Flints 80 H10
Babeny Devon 8 G9
Bablock Hythe Oxon 34 D4
Babraham Cambs 62 H10
Babworth Notts 85 L4
Bachau IoA 78 G8
Bache Shrops 56 H8
Bacheldre Powys 56 C6
Bachelor's Bump E Susx 26 D9
Backaland Ork 169 e3
Backbarrow Cumb 94 H4
Backe Carmth 41 Q7
Backfolds Abers 159 P7
Backford Ches W 81 M10
Backford Cross Ches W 81 M10
Backies Highld 163 J6
Back of Keppoch Highld 145 L10
Back o' th' Brook Staffs 71 K4
Back Street Suffk 63 M9
Backwell N Som 31 N11
Backworth N Tyne 113 M6
Bacon's End Solhll 59 J7
Baconsthorpe Norfk 76 G4
Bacton Herefs 45 M8
Bacton Norfk 77 L5
Bacton Suffk 64 F8
Bacton Green Suffk 64 E8
Bacup Lancs 89 P6
Badachro Highld 153 P3
Badanloch Highld 166 C10
Badbury Swindn 33 N8
Badby Nhants 60 C9
Badcall Highld 164 F5
Badcaul Highld 160 G8
Baddeley Edge C Stke 70 G4
Baddeley Green C Stke 70 G4
Baddesley Clinton Warwks 59 K10
Baddesley Ensor Warwks 59 L5
Baddidarrach Highld 160 H2
Baddinsgill Border 127 L7
Badenscoth Abers 158 G10
Badentarbet Highld 160 G5
Badenyon Abers 149 Q4
Badersfield Norfk 77 K7
Badgall Cnwll 5 L4
Badgeney Cambs 74 H11
Badger Shrops 57 P5
Badger's Cross Cnwll 2 D7
Badgers Mount Kent 37 L8
Badgeworth Gloucs 46 H11
Badgworth Somset 19 L4
Badharlick Cnwll 5 M4
Badicaul Highld 145 N2
Badingham Suffk 65 L8
Badlesmere Kent 38 H11
Badlieu Border 116 F7
Badlipster Highld 167 M7
Badluarach Highld 160 F8
Badninish Highld 162 H8
Badrallach Highld 160 H8
Badsey Worcs 47 L6
Badshot Lea Surrey 23 N5
Badsworth Wakefd 91 M8
Badwell Ash Suffk 64 D8
Badwell Green Suffk 64 E8
Bagber Dorset 12 C2
Bagby N York 97 Q4
Bag Enderby Lincs 87 L6
Bagendon Gloucs 33 K3
Bagginswood Shrops 57 M8
Baggrow Cumb 100 G2
Bàgh a' Chaisteil W Isls 168 b18
Bagham Kent 39 J11
Bagillt Flints 81 J9
Baginton Warwks 59 M10
Baglan Neath 29 K6
Bagley Leeds 90 G3
Bagley Shrops 69 M9
Bagley Somset 19 N5
Bagmore Hants 23 J6
Bagnall Staffs 70 G4
Bagnor W Berk 34 E11
Bagshot Surrey 23 P2
Bagshot Wilts 34 B11
Bagstone S Glos 32 C7
Bagthorpe Notts 84 G10
Bagworth Leics 72 C9
Bagwyllydiart Herefs 45 N9
Baildon C Brad 90 F3
Baildon Green C Brad 90 E3
Baile Ailein W Isls 168 h5
Baile a' Mhanaich W Isls 168 c12
Baile Mòr Ag & B 136 H11
Bailey Green Hants 23 J9
Baileyhead Cumb 111 K5
Bailiff Bridge Calder 90 E5
Baillieston C Glas 126 B5
Bailrigg Lancs 95 K9
Bainbridge N York 96 D2
Bainshole Abers 158 F10
Bainton C Pete 74 A9
Bainton E R Yk 99 K10
Bainton Oxon 48 G9
Baintown Fife 135 K7
Bairnkine Border 118 C7
Baker's End Herts 51 J7
Baker Street Thurr 37 P4
Bakewell Derbys 84 B7
Bala Gwynd 68 B7
Balallan W Isls 168 h5
Balbeg Highld 155 M11
Balbeggie P & K 134 F2
Balblair Highld 155 P8
Balblair Highld 156 C4
Balby Donc 91 P10
Balcary D & G 108 H11
Balchraggan Highld 155 P9
Balchrick Highld 164 E4
Balcombe W Susx 24 H4
Balcombe Lane W Susx 24 H4
Balcomie Links Fife 135 Q6
Baldersby N York 97 N5
Baldersby St James N York 97 N5
Balderstone Lancs 89 J4
Balderstone Rochdl 89 Q8
Balderton Notts 85 P10
Baldhu Cnwll 3 K5
Baldinnie Fife 135 L5
Baldinnies P & K 134 C4
Baldock Herts 50 F4
Baldock Services Herts 50 F3
Baldovie C Dund 142 H11
Baldrine IoM 80 f5
Baldslow E Susx 26 D9
Baldwin IoM 80 e5
Baldwinholme Cumb 110 F10
Baldwin's Gate Staffs 70 D7
Baldwin's Hill W Susx 25 J3
Bale Norfk 76 E4
Baledgarno P & K 142 D11
Balemartine Ag & B 136 B7
Balerno C Edin 127 M4
Balfarg Fife 134 H7
Balfield Angus 143 J4
Balfour Ork 169 d5
Balfron Stirlg 132 G10
Balgaveny Abers 158 G9
Balgonar Fife 134 C9
Balgowan D & G 106 F9
Balgowan Highld 147 Q9
Balgown Highld 152 F4
Balgracie D & G 106 C5
Balgray S Lans 116 B6
Balham Gt Lon 36 G6
Balhary P & K 142 D8
Balholmie P & K 142 A10
Baligill Highld 166 E3
Balintore Angus 142 D6
Balintore Highld 156 F2
Balintraid Highld 156 C3
Balivanich W Isls 168 c12
Balk N York 97 Q4
Balkeerie Angus 142 E9
Balkholme E R Yk 92 C5
Ballabeg IoM 80 c7
Ballachulish Highld 139 K6
Ballafesson IoM 80 b7
Ballajora IoM 80 g3
Ballakilpheric IoM 80 b7
Ballamodha IoM 80 c7
Ballantrae S Ayrs 114 A11
Ballards Gore Essex 38 F3
Ballards Green Warwks 59 L6
Ballasalla IoM 80 c7
Ballater Abers 150 B8
Ballaugh IoM 80 d3
Ballchraggan Highld 156 D2
Ballencrieff E Loth 128 D4
Ballevullin Ag & B 136 B6
Ball Green C Stke 70 F4
Ball Haye Green Staffs 70 H3
Ball Hill Hants 22 D2
Ballianlay Ag & B 124 C5
Ballidon Derbys 71 N4
Balliekine N Ayrs 120 G4
Balliemore Ag & B 131 N8
Balligmorrie S Ayrs 114 D9
Ballimore Stirlg 132 G4
Ballindalloch Moray 157 M10
Ballindean P & K 134 H2
Ballingdon Suffk 52 E3
Ballinger Common Bucks 35 P4
Ballingham Herefs 46 A8
Ballingry Fife 134 F8
Ballinluig P & K 141 N7
Ballinshoe Angus 142 G7
Ballintuim P & K 141 R6
Balloch Highld 156 C8
Balloch N Lans 126 C3
Balloch P & K 133 N4
Balloch S Ayrs 114 F8
Balloch W Duns 132 D11
Balls Cross W Susx 23 Q9
Balls Green E Susx 25 L3
Ball's Green Gloucs 32 G5
Ballygown Ag & B 137 L7
Ballygrant Ag & B 122 E6
Ballyhaugh Ag & B 136 F4
Balmacara Highld 145 P2
Balmaclellan D & G 108 E5
Balmae D & G 108 E12
Balmaha Stirlg 132 E9
Balmalcolm Fife 135 J6
Balmangan D & G 108 D11
Balmedie Abers 151 P4
Balmer Heath Shrops 69 M8
Balmerino Fife 135 K3
Balmerlawn Hants 13 P4
Balmichael N Ayrs 120 H5
Balmore E Duns 125 P3
Balmuchy Highld 163 K11
Balmule Fife 134 G10
Balmullo Fife 135 L3
Balnacoil Highld 163 J4
Balnacra Highld 154 C8
Balnacroft Abers 149 P9
Balnafoich Highld 156 B10
Balnaguard P & K 141 M7
Balnahard Ag & B 137 M9
Balnain Highld 155 M11
Balnakeil Highld 165 J3
Balne N York 91 P7
Balquharn P & K 141 P10
Balquhidder Stirlg 132 G3
Balsall Common Solhll 59 K9
Balsall Heath Birm 58 G8
Balsall Street Solhll 59 K9
Balscote Oxon 48 C6
Balsham Cambs 63 J10
Baltasound Shet 169 t3
Balterley Staffs 70 D4
Balterley Green Staffs 70 D4
Balterley Heath Staffs 70 C4
Baltersan D & G 107 M5
Balthangie Abers 159 K7
Baltonsborough Somset 19 P8
Balvicar Ag & B 130 F4
Balvraid Highld 145 P4
Balvraid Highld 156 E11
Balwest Cnwll 2 F7
Bamber Bridge Lancs 88 H5
Bamber's Green Essex 51 N6
Bamburgh Nthumb 119 N4
Bamburgh Castle Nthumb 119 N3
Bamford Derbys 84 B4
Bamford Rochdl 89 P8
Bampton Cumb 101 P7
Bampton Devon 18 C10
Bampton Oxon 34 B4
Bampton Grange Cumb 101 P7
Banavie Highld 139 L2
Banbury Oxon 48 E6
Bancffosfelen Carmth 28 E2
Banchory Abers 150 H8
Banchory-Devenick Abers 151 N7
Bancycapel Carmth 28 D2
Bancyfelin Carmth 42 F11
Banc-y-ffordd Carmth 42 H7
Bandirran P & K 142 C11
Bandrake Head Cumb 94 G3
Banff Abers 158 G5
Bangor Gwynd 79 K10
Bangor-on-Dee Wrexhm 69 L5
Bangors Cnwll 5 L2
Bangor's Green Lancs 88 D9
Bangrove Suffk 64 C7
Banham Norfk 64 F4
Bank Hants 13 N3
Bankend D & G 109 M7
Bankfoot P & K 141 Q10
Bankglen E Ayrs 115 L5
Bank Ground Cumb 101 K11
Bankhead C Aber 151 N6
Bankhead S Lans 116 D2
Bank Newton N York 96 D10
Banknock Falk 126 D2
Banks Cumb 111 L8
Banks Lancs 88 D6
Banks Green Worcs 58 E11
Bankshill D & G 110 C4
Bank Street Worcs 46 B2
Bank Top Calder 90 E6
Bank Top Lancs 88 G9
Banningham Norfk 77 J6
Bannister Green Essex 51 Q6
Bannockburn Stirlg 133 N9
Banstead Surrey 36 G9
Bantham Devon 6 H10
Banton N Lans 126 C2
Banwell N Som 19 L3
Bapchild Kent 38 F9
Bapton Wilts 21 J7
Barabhas W Isls 168 i3
Barassie S Ayrs 125 J11
Barbaraville Highld 156 C3
Barber Booth Derbys 83 P8
Barber Green Cumb 94 H4
Barbieston S Ayrs 114 H4
Barbon Cumb 95 N4
Barbridge Ches E 69 R3
Barbrook Devon 17 N2
Barby Nhants 60 B6
Barcaldine Ag & B 138 H9
Barcheston Warwks 47 Q7
Barclose Cumb 110 H8
Barcombe E Susx 25 K8
Barcombe Cross E Susx 25 K7
Barcroft C Brad 90 C3
Barden N York 96 H2
Barden Park Kent 37 N11
Bardfield End Green Essex 51 P4
Bardfield Saling Essex 51 Q5
Bardney Lincs 86 F7
Bardon Leics 72 C8
Bardon Mill Nthumb 111 Q8
Bardowie E Duns 125 P3
Bardown E Susx 25 Q5
Bardrainney Inver 125 J3
Bardsea Cumb 94 G6
Bardsey Leeds 91 K2
Bardsey Island Gwynd 66 A10
Bardsley Oldham 83 K4
Bardwell Suffk 64 C7
Bare Lancs 95 K8
Bareppa Cnwll 3 K8
Barfad D & G 107 K4
Barford Norfk 76 G10
Barford Warwks 47 Q2
Barford St John Oxon 48 D8
Barford St Martin Wilts 21 L8
Barford St Michael Oxon 48 D8
Barfrestone Kent 39 N11
Bargate Derbys 84 E11
Bargeddie N Lans 126 B5
Bargoed Caerph 30 G5
Bargrennan D & G 107 L2
Barham Cambs 61 P5
Barham Kent 39 M11
Barham Suffk 64 G11
Bar Hill Cambs 62 E8
Barholm Lincs 74 A8
Barkby Leics 72 G9
Barkby Thorpe Leics 72 G9
Barkers Green Shrops 69 P9
Barkestone-le-Vale Leics 73 K4
Barkham Wokham 35 L11
Barking Gt Lon 37 K4
Barking Suffk 64 F11
Barkingside Gt Lon 37 K3
Barking Tye Suffk 64 F11
Barkisland Calder 90 D7
Barkla Shop Cnwll 3 J3
Barkston Lincs 73 N2
Barkston Ash N York 91 M3
Barkway Herts 51 J3
Barlanark C Glas 126 B5
Barlaston Staffs 70 F7
Barlavington W Susx 23 Q11
Barlborough Derbys 84 G5
Barlby N York 91 Q4
Barlestone Leics 72 C9
Barley Herts 51 K3
Barley Lancs 89 N2
Barleycroft End Herts 51 K5
Barley Hole Rothm 91 K11
Barleythorpe Rutlnd 73 L9
Barling Essex 38 F4
Barlings Lincs 86 E6
Barlochan D & G 108 H9
Barlow Derbys 84 D6
Barlow Gatesd 113 J8
Barlow N York 91 Q5
Barmby Moor E R Yk 98 F11
Barmby on the Marsh E R Yk 92 A5
Barmer Norfk 75 R4
Barming Heath Kent 38 B10
Barmollack Ag & B 120 F3
Barmouth Gwynd 67 L11
Barmpton Darltn 104 B7
Barmston E R Yk 99 P9
Barnaby Green Suffk 65 P5
Barnacarry Ag & B 131 L9
Barnack C Pete 74 A9
Barnacle Warwks 59 N8
Barnard Castle Dur 103 L7
Barnard Gate Oxon 34 D2
Barnardiston Suffk 63 M11
Barnbarroch D & G 108 H9
Barnburgh Donc 91 M10
Barnby Suffk 65 P4
Barnby Dun Donc 91 Q9
Barnby in the Willows Notts 85 Q10
Barnby Moor Notts 85 L4
Barncorkrie D & G 106 E10
Barnehurst Gt Lon 37 L5
Barnes Gt Lon 36 F5
Barnes Street Kent 37 P11
Barnet Gt Lon 50 F11
Barnetby le Wold N Linc 93 J9
Barnet Gate Gt Lon 50 F11
Barney Norfk 76 D5
Barnham Suffk 64 B6
Barnham W Susx 15 Q6
Barnham Broom Norfk 76 F10
Barnhead Angus 143 M6
Barnhill C Dund 142 H11
Barnhill Ches W 69 N4
Barnhill Moray 157 L6
Barnhills D & G 106 C3
Barningham Dur 103 L8
Barningham Suffk 64 D6
Barnoldby le Beck NE Lin 93 M10
Barnoldswick Lancs 96 C11
Barnsdale Bar Donc 91 N8
Barns Green W Susx 24 D5
Barnsley Barns 91 J9
Barnsley Gloucs 33 L4
Barnsole Kent 39 N10
Barnstaple Devon 17 K5
Barnston Essex 51 P7
Barnston Wirral 81 K8
Barnstone Notts 73 J3
Barnt Green Worcs 58 F10
Barnton C Edin 127 M3
Barnton Ches W 82 D10
Barnwell All Saints Nhants 61 N4
Barnwell St Andrew Nhants 61 N4
Barnwood Gloucs 46 G11
Baron's Cross Herefs 45 P3
Baronwood Cumb 101 P2
Barr S Ayrs 114 E9
Barra W Isls 168 b17
Barra Airport W Isls 168 c17
Barrachan D & G 107 L8
Barraigh W Isls 168 b17
Barrananaoil Ag & B 130 G6
Barrapoll Ag & B 136 A7
Barras Cumb 102 F8
Barrasford Nthumb 112 D6
Barregarrow IoM 80 d4
Barrets Green Ches E 69 Q3
Barrhead E Rens 125 M6
Barrhill S Ayrs 114 D11
Barrington Cambs 62 E11
Barrington Somset 19 L11
Barripper Cnwll 2 G6
Barrmill N Ayrs 125 K7
Barrock Highld 167 N2
Barrow Gloucs 46 G10
Barrow Lancs 89 L3
Barrow Rutlnd 73 M7
Barrow Shrops 57 M4
Barrow Somset 20 D8
Barrow Suffk 63 N8
Barroway Drove Norfk 75 L10
Barrow Bridge Bolton 89 K8
Barrow Burn Nthumb 118 G8
Barrowby Lincs 73 M3
Barrow Common N Som 31 P11
Barrowden Rutlnd 73 N10
Barrowford Lancs 89 P3
Barrow Gurney N Som 31 P11
Barrow Haven N Linc 93 J6
Barrow Hill Derbys 84 F5
Barrow-in-Furness Cumb 94 E7
Barrow Island Cumb 94 D7
Barrow Nook Lancs 81 N4
Barrow's Green Ches E 70 B3
Barrows Green Cumb 95 L3
Barrow Street Wilts 20 F8
Barrow-upon-Humber N Linc 93 J6
Barrow upon Soar Leics 72 F7
Barrow upon Trent Derbys 72 B5
Barrow Vale BaNES 20 B2
Barry Angus 143 J11
Barry V Glam 30 F11
Barry Island V Glam 30 F11
Barsby Leics 72 H8
Barsham Suffk 65 M4
Barston Solhll 59 K9
Bartestree Herefs 45 R6
Barthol Chapel Abers 159 K11
Bartholomew Green Essex 52 B7
Barthomley Ches E 70 D4
Bartley Hants 13 P2
Bartley Green Birm 58 F8
Bartlow Cambs 63 J11
Barton Cambs 62 F9
Barton Ches W 69 M4
Barton Gloucs 47 L9
Barton Herefs 45 K3
Barton Lancs 88 D9
Barton Lancs 88 G3
Barton N York 103 P9
Barton Oxon 34 G3
Barton Torbay 7 N5
Barton Warwks 47 M4
Barton Bendish Norfk 75 P9
Barton End Gloucs 32 F5
Barton Green Staffs 71 M11
Barton Hartshorn Bucks 48 H8
Barton Hill N York 98 E8
Barton in Fabis Notts 72 E4
Barton in the Beans Leics 72 B9
Barton-le-Clay C Beds 50 C4
Barton-le-Street N York 98 E6
Barton-le-Willows N York 98 E8
Barton Mills Suffk 63 M6
Barton-on-Sea Hants 13 M6
Barton-on-the-Heath Warwks 47 Q8
Barton Park Services N York 103 P9
Barton St David Somset 19 P8
Barton Seagrave Nhants 61 J5
Barton Stacey Hants 22 D6
Barton Town Devon 17 M3
Barton Turf Norfk 77 M7
Barton-under-Needwood Staffs 71 M11
Barton-upon-Humber N Linc 92 H6
Barton upon Irwell Salfd 82 G5
Barton Waterside N Linc 92 H6
Barugh Barns 91 J9
Barugh Green Barns 91 J9
Barvas W Isls 168 i3
Barway Cambs 63 J5
Barwell Leics 72 C11
Barwick Devon 17 K10
Barwick Herts 51 J7
Barwick Somset 11 M2
Barwick in Elmet Leeds 91 L3
Baschurch Shrops 69 M10
Bascote Warwks 48 D2
Bascote Heath Warwks 48 C2
Base Green Suffk 64 E9
Basford Green Staffs 70 H4
Bashall Eaves Lancs 89 K2
Bashall Town Lancs 89 L2
Bashley Hants 13 M5
Basildon Essex 38 B4
Basingstoke Hants 22 H4
Baslow Derbys 84 C6
Bason Bridge Somset 19 K5
Bassaleg Newpt 31 J7
Bassendean Border 128 G10
Bassenthwaite Cumb 100 H4
Bassett C Sotn 22 D11
Bassingbourn-cum-Kneesworth Cambs 50 H2
Bassingfield Notts 72 G3
Bassingham Lincs 86 B9
Bassingthorpe Lincs 73 P5
Bassus Green Herts 50 H5
Basted Kent 37 P9
Baston Lincs 74 B8
Bastwick Norfk 77 N8
Batch Somset 19 K3
Batchworth Herts 36 C2
Batchworth Heath Herts 36 C2
Batcombe Dorset 11 N4
Batcombe Somset 20 C7
Bate Heath Ches E 82 E9
Batford Herts 50 D7
Bath BaNES 20 D2
Bath BaNES 20 E2
Bathampton BaNES 32 E11
Bathealton Somset 18 E10
Batheaston BaNES 32 E11
Bathford BaNES 32 E11
Bathgate W Loth 126 H4
Bathley Notts 85 N9
Bathpool Cnwll 5 M7
Bathpool Somset 19 J9
Bath Side Essex 53 N5
Bathville W Loth 126 G4
Bathway Somset 19 Q4
Batley Kirk 90 G6
Batsford Gloucs 47 N8
Batson Devon 7 J11
Battersby N York 104 G9
Battersea Gt Lon 36 G5
Battisborough Cross Devon 6 F9
Battisford Suffk 64 F11
Battisford Tye Suffk 64 E11
Battle E Susx 26 C8
Battle Powys 44 E8
Battleborough Somset 19 K4
Battledown Gloucs 47 J10
Battledykes Angus 142 H6
Battlefield Shrops 69 P11
Battlesbridge Essex 38 C3
Battlesden C Beds 49 Q9
Battleton Somset 18 B9
Battlies Green Suffk 64 C9
Battram Leics 72 C9
Battramsley Cross Hants 13 P5
Batt's Corner Hants 23 M6
Baughton Worcs 46 G6
Baughurst Hants 22 G2
Baulds Abers 150 G9
Baulking Oxon 34 B6
Baumber Lincs 86 H6
Baunton Gloucs 33 K4
Baveney Wood Shrops 57 M9
Baverstock Wilts 21 K8
Bawburgh Norfk 76 H10
Bawdeswell Norfk 76 E7
Bawdrip Somset 19 K7
Bawdsey Suffk 53 P3
Bawsey Norfk 75 N6
Bawtry Donc 85 K2
Baxenden Lancs 89 M5
Baxterley Warwks 59 L5
Baxter's Green Suffk 63 N9
Bay Highld 152 D7
Bayble W Isls 168 k4
Baybridge Hants 22 F10
Baybridge Nthumb 112 E10
Baycliff Cumb 94 F6
Baydon Wilts 33 Q9
Bayford Herts 50 H9
Bayford Somset 20 D9
Bayhead W Isls 168 c11
Bay Horse Lancs 95 K10
Bayley's Hill Kent 37 M10
Baylham Suffk 64 G11
Baynard's Green Oxon 48 F9
Baysdale Abbey N York 104 H9
Baysham Herefs 45 R9
Bayston Hill Shrops 56 H3
Baythorne End Essex 52 B3
Bayton Worcs 57 M10
Bayton Common Worcs 57 N10
Bayworth Oxon 34 E4
Beach S Glos 32 D10
Beachampton Bucks 49 L7
Beachamwell Norfk 75 Q9
Beachley Gloucs 31 Q6
Beachy Head E Susx 25 N11
Beacon Devon 10 D3
Beacon End Essex 52 G7
Beacon Hill Kent 26 D5
Beacon Hill Notts 85 P10
Beacon Hill Surrey 23 N7
Beacon's Bottom Bucks 35 L5
Beaconsfield Bucks 35 P6
Beaconsfield Services Bucks 35 Q7
Beadlam N York 98 D4
Beadlow C Beds 50 D3
Beadnell Nthumb 119 P5
Beaford Devon 17 K8
Beal N York 91 N5
Beal Nthumb 119 L2
Bealbury Cnwll 5 P8
Bealsmill Cnwll 5 P6
Beam Hill Staffs 71 N9

Beamhurst Staffs	71	K7
Beaminster Dorset	11	K4
Beamish Dur	113	K10
Beamish Open Air		
Museum Dur	113	K10
Beamsley N York	96	G10
Bean Kent	37	N6
Beanacre Wilts	32	H11
Beanley Nthumb	119	L7
Beardon Devon	8	D8
Beardwood Bl w D	89	K5
Beare Devon	9	N4
Beare Green Surrey	24	E2
Bearley Warwks	47	N2
Bearley Cross Warwks	47	N2
Bearpark Dur	103	P2
Bearsden E Duns	125	N3
Bearsted Kent	38	D10
Bearstone Shrops	70	C7
Bearwood BCP	12	H5
Bearwood Birm	58	F7
Bearwood Herefs	45	M3
Beattock D & G	116	F10
Beauchamp Roding Essex	51	N9
Beauchief Sheff	84	D4
Beaudesert Warwks	59	J11
Beaufort Blae G	30	G2
Beaulieu Essex	52	B10
Beaulieu Hants	14	C6
Beaulieu Road Station		
Hants	13	P3
Beauly Highld	155	P8
Beaumaris IoA	79	L9
Beaumaris Castle IoA	79	L9
Beaumont Cumb	110	F9
Beaumont Essex	53	L7
Beaumont Jersey	11	b2
Beaumont Hill Darltn	103	Q7
Beaumont Leys C Leic	72	F9
Beausale Warwks	59	K10
Beauworth Hants	22	G9
Beaworthy Devon	8	C5
Beazley End Essex	52	B6
Bebington Wirral	81	L6
Bebside Nthumb	113	L4
Beccles Suffk	65	N4
Becconsall Lancs	88	F6
Beckbury Shrops	57	P4
Beckenham Gt Lon	37	J7
Beckermet Cumb	100	D9
Beckett End Norfk	75	Q11
Beckfoot Cumb	94	D3
Beckfoot Cumb	100	G10
Beck Foot Cumb	102	B11
Beckfoot Cumb	109	N11
Beckford Worcs	47	J7
Beckhampton Wilts	33	L11
Beck Hole N York	105	M10
Beckingham Lincs	85	Q10
Beckingham Notts	85	N3
Beckington Somset	20	F4
Beckjay Shrops	56	F9
Beckley E Susx	26	E7
Beckley Hants	13	M5
Beckley Oxon	34	G2
Beck Row Suffk	63	L5
Becks C Brad	96	F11
Beck Side Cumb	94	E4
Beck Side Cumb	94	H4
Beckton Gt Lon	37	K4
Beckwithshaw N York	97	L10
Becontree Gt Lon	37	L3
Becquet Vincent Jersey	11	b1
Bedale N York	97	L3
Bedburn Dur	103	L4
Bedchester Dorset	20	G11
Beddau Rhondd	30	E7
Beddgelert Gwynd	67	K5
Beddingham E Susx	25	K9
Beddington Gt Lon	36	H7
Beddington Corner Gt Lon	36	G7
Bedfield Suffk	65	J8
Bedfield Little Green Suffk	65	J8
Bedford Bed	61	M11
Bedgebury Cross Kent	26	B5
Bedgrove Bucks	35	M2
Bedham W Susx	24	B6
Bedhampton Hants	15	K5
Bedingfield Suffk	64	H8
Bedingfield Green Suffk	64	H8
Bedlam N York	97	L8
Bedlington Nthumb	113	L4
Bedlinog Myr Td	30	E4
Bedminster Bristl	31	Q10
Bedminster Down Bristl	31	Q10
Bedmond Herts	50	C10
Bednall Staffs	70	H11
Bedrule Border	118	B7
Bedstone Shrops	56	F9
Bedwas Caerph	30	G7
Bedwellty Caerph	30	G4
Bedworth Warwks	59	N7
Bedworth Woodlands		
Warwks	59	M7
Beeby Leics	72	H9
Beech Hants	23	J7
Beech Staffs	70	F7
Beech Hill W Berk	23	J2
Beechingstoke Wilts	21	L3
Beedon W Berk	34	E9
Beedon Hill W Berk	34	E9
Beeford E R Yk	99	N10
Beeley Derbys	84	C7
Beelsby NE Lin	93	M10
Beenham W Berk	34	G11
Beenham's Heath W & M	35	M9
Beeny Cnwll	5	J3
Beer Devon	10	E7
Beer Somset	19	M8
Beercrocombe Somset	19	K10
Beer Hackett Dorset	11	N2
Beesands Devon	7	L10
Beesby Lincs	87	N4
Beeson Devon	7	L10
Beeston C Beds	61	Q11
Beeston Ches W	69	P3
Beeston Leeds	90	H4
Beeston Norfk	76	C8
Beeston Notts	72	E3
Beeston Regis Norfk	76	H3
Beeswing D & G	109	J7
Beetham Cumb	95	K5
Beetham Somset	10	F2
Beetley Norfk	76	D8
Began Cardif	30	H8
Begbroke Oxon	34	E2
Begdale Cambs	75	J9
Begelly Pembks	41	M9
Beggarington Hill Leeds	90	H6
Beggar's Bush Powys	45	K2
Beguildy Powys	56	B9
Beighton Norfk	77	M10
Beighton Sheff	84	F4
Beinn Na Faoghla W Isls	168	d12
Beith N Ayrs	125	K7
Bekesbourne Kent	39	L10
Bekesbourne Hill Kent	39	L10
Belaugh Norfk	77	K8
Belbroughton Worcs	58	D9
Belchalwell Dorset	12	C3
Belchalwell Street Dorset	12	C3
Belchamp Otten Essex	52	D3
Belchamp St Paul Essex	52	C3
Belchamp Walter Essex	52	D3
Belchford Lincs	87	J5
Belford Nthumb	119	M4
Belgrave C Leic	72	F9
Belhaven E Loth	128	H4
Belhelvie Abers	151	N4
Belhinnie Abers	150	D2
Bellabeg Abers	150	B5
Bellamore Herefs	45	M6
Bellanoch Ag & B	130	F9
Bellasize E R Yk	92	D5
Bellaty Angus	142	C6
Bell Bar Herts	50	D9
Bell Busk N York	96	D9
Belleau Lincs	87	M5
Bell End Worcs	58	D9
Bellerby N York	96	H1
Bellever Devon	8	G9
Belle Vue Cumb	110	G9
Belle Vue Wakefd	91	J7
Bellfield S Lans	126	E11
Bellfields Surrey	23	Q4
Bell Heath Worcs	58	D9
Bell Hill Hants	23	K10
Bellingdon Bucks	35	P3
Bellingham Nthumb	112	B4
Belloch Ag & B	120	C4
Bellochantuy Ag & B	120	C5
Bell o' th' Hill Ches W	69	P5
Bellows Cross Dorset	13	J2
Bells Cross Suffk	64	H11
Bellshill N Lans	126	C5
Bellshill Nthumb	119	M4
Bellside N Lans	126	E6
Bellsquarry W Loth	127	K4
Bells Yew Green E Susx	25	P3
Belluton BaNES	20	B2
Belmaduthy Highld	156	A6
Belmesthorpe Rutlnd	73	Q8
Belmont Bl w D	89	K7
Belmont Gt Lon	36	G8
Belmont S Ayrs	114	F4
Belmont Shet	169	s3
Belnacraig Abers	150	B4
Belowda Cnwll	4	F9
Belper Derbys	84	D11
Belper Lane End Derbys	84	D11
Belph Derbys	84	H5
Belsay Nthumb	112	G5
Belses Border	117	R5
Belsford Devon	7	K7
Belsize Herts	50	B10
Belstead Suffk	53	K3
Belstone Devon	8	F6
Belthorn Bl w D	89	L6
Beltinge Kent	39	L8
Beltingham Nthumb	111	Q8
Beltoft N Linc	92	D9
Belton Leics	72	C6
Belton Lincs	73	N3
Belton Lincs	92	C9
Belton Norfk	77	P11
Belton House Lincs	73	N3
Belton in Rutland Rutlnd	73	L10
Beltring Kent	37	Q11
Belvedere Gt Lon	37	L5
Belvoir Leics	73	L4
Bembridge IoW	14	H9
Bemerton Wilts	21	M8
Bempton E R Yk	99	P6
Benacre Suffk	65	Q5
Benbecula W Isls	168	d12
Benbecula Airport W Isls	168	c12
Benbuie D & G	115	P8
Benderloch Ag & B	138	G10
Benenden Kent	26	D5
Benfieldside Dur	112	G10
Bengate Norfk	77	L6
Bengeo Herts	50	H8
Bengeworth Worcs	47	K6
Benhall Green Suffk	65	M9
Benhall Street Suffk	65	M9
Benholm Abers	143	Q4
Beningbrough N York	98	A9
Benington Herts	50	G6
Benington Lincs	87	L11
Benington Sea End Lincs	87	M11
Benllech IoA	79	J8
Benmore Ag & B	131	N10
Bennacott Cnwll	5	M3
Bennan N Ayrs	121	J7
Bennet Head Cumb	101	M6
Bennetland E R Yk	92	D5
Bennett End Bucks	35	L5
Benniworth Lincs	86	H4
Benover Kent	26	B2
Ben Rhydding C Brad	96	H11
Benslie N Ayrs	125	J9
Benson Oxon	34	H6
Benthall Shrops	57	M4
Bentham Gloucs	46	H11
Benthoul C Aber	151	L7
Bentlawnt Shrops	56	E4
Bentley Donc	91	P9
Bentley E R Yk	92	H3
Bentley Hants	23	L6
Bentley Suffk	53	K4
Bentley Warwks	59	L5
Bentley Heath Herts	50	G11
Bentley Heath Solhll	59	J9
Benton Devon	17	M4
Bentpath D & G	110	F2
Bentwichen Devon	17	N5
Bentworth Hants	23	J6
Benvie Angus	142	E11
Benville Dorset	11	L4
Benwick Cambs	62	D2
Beoley Worcs	58	G11
Beoraidbeg Highld	145	L9
Bepton W Susx	23	N11
Berden Essex	51	L5
Berea Pembks	40	E4
Bere Alston Devon	6	C5
Bere Ferrers Devon	6	D6
Berepper Cnwll	2	H9
Bere Regis Dorset	12	D6
Bergh Apton Norfk	77	L11
Berhill Somset	19	M7
Berinsfield Oxon	34	G5
Berkeley Gloucs	32	C5
Berkeley Heath Gloucs	32	C5
Berkeley Road Gloucs	32	D4
Berkhamsted Herts	35	Q3
Berkley Somset	20	F5
Berkswell Solhll	59	K9
Bermondsey Gt Lon	36	H5
Bermuda Warwks	59	N7
Bernera Highld	145	P3
Bernisdale Highld	152	G7
Berrick Prior Oxon	34	H6
Berrick Salome Oxon	34	H6
Berriedale Highld	163	Q2
Berrier Cumb	101	L5
Berriew Powys	56	B4
Berrington Nthumb	119	K2
Berrington Shrops	57	J3
Berrington Worcs	57	K11
Berrington Green Worcs	57	K11
Berrow Somset	19	J4
Berrow Worcs	46	E8
Berrow Green Worcs	46	D3
Berry Brow Kirk	90	E7
Berry Cross Devon	16	H9
Berry Down Cross Devon	17	K3
Berryfields Bucks	49	L11
Berry Hill Gloucs	31	Q2
Berry Hill Pembks	41	L1
Berryhillock Moray	158	D5
Berryhillock Moray	158	F4
Berrynarbor Devon	17	K2
Berry Pomeroy Devon	7	L5
Berry's Green Gt Lon	37	K9
Bersham Wrexhm	69	K5
Bersted W Susx	15	P6
Berthengam Flints	80	G9
Berwick E Susx	25	M9
Berwick Bassett Wilts	33	L10
Berwick Hill Nthumb	113	J5
Berwick St James Wilts	21	L7
Berwick St John Wilts	20	H10
Berwick St Leonard Wilts	20	H8
Berwick Station E Susx	25	M9
Berwick-upon-Tweed		
Nthumb	129	P9
Bescaby Leics	73	L5
Bescar Lancs	88	D8
Besford Shrops	69	Q9
Besford Worcs	46	H6
Bessacarr Donc	91	Q10
Bessels Leigh Oxon	34	E4
Besses o' th' Barn Bury	89	N9
Bessingby E R Yk	99	P7
Bessingham Norfk	76	H4
Bestbeech Hill E Susx	25	P4
Besthorpe Norfk	64	F2
Besthorpe Notts	85	P8
Bestwood Village Notts	85	J11
Beswick E R Yk	99	L11
Betchcott Shrops	56	G5
Betchworth Surrey	36	F10
Bethania Cerdgn	43	L2
Bethania Gwynd	67	N6
Bethel Gwynd	68	C7
Bethel Gwynd	79	J11
Bethel IoA	78	F10
Bethel Powys	68	F10
Bethersden Kent	26	F3
Bethesda Gwynd	79	L11
Bethesda Pembks	41	L7
Bethlehem Carmth	43	N9
Bethnal Green Gt Lon	36	H4
Betley Staffs	70	D5
Betsham Kent	37	P6
Betteshanger Kent	39	P11
Bettiscombe Dorset	10	H4
Betton Shrops	70	B7
Betton Strange Shrops	57	J3
Bettws Brdgnd	29	P7
Bettws Newpt	31	J6
Bettws Cedewain Powys	55	Q5
Bettws Ifan Cerdgn	42	F5
Bettws-Newydd Mons	31	L3
Bettyhill Highld	166	B4
Betws Carmth	28	H2
Betws Bledrws Cerdgn	43	L4
Betws Garmon Gwynd	67	J3
Betws Gwerfil Goch Denbgs	68	D5
Betws-y-Coed Conwy	67	P3
Betws-yn-Rhos Conwy	80	C10
Beulah Cerdgn	42	E5
Beulah Powys	44	D4
Bevendean Br & H	24	H9
Bevercotes Notts	85	L6
Beverley E R Yk	92	H3
Beverston Gloucs	32	G5
Bevington Gloucs	32	C5
Bewaldeth Cumb	100	H4
Bewcastle Cumb	111	L6
Bewdley Worcs	57	P9
Bewerley N York	97	J7
Bewholme E R Yk	99	P11
Bewlbridge Kent	25	Q4
Bexhill-on-Sea E Susx	26	B10
Bexley Gt Lon	37	L5
Bexleyheath Gt Lon	37	L5
Bexleyhill W Susx	23	P9
Bexon Kent	38	E10
Bexwell Norfk	75	M10
Beyton Suffk	64	C9
Beyton Green Suffk	64	C9
Bhaltos W Isls	168	f4
Bhatarsaigh W Isls	168	b18
Bibstone S Glos	32	C6
Bibury Gloucs	33	M3
Bicester Oxon	48	G10
Bickenhill Solhll	59	J8
Bicker Lincs	74	D4
Bicker Bar Lincs	74	D3
Bicker Gauntlet Lincs	74	D3
Bickershaw Wigan	82	D4
Bickerstaffe Lancs	81	N4
Bickerton Ches E	69	P4
Bickerton Devon	7	L11
Bickerton N York	97	Q10
Bickerton Nthumb	119	J10
Bickford Staffs	58	C2
Bickington Devon	7	L4
Bickington Devon	17	J5
Bickleigh Devon	6	E6
Bickleigh Devon	9	M3
Bickleton Devon	17	J5
Bickley Ches W	69	P5
Bickley Gt Lon	37	K7
Bickley N York	99	J2
Bickley Worcs	57	L10
Bickley Moss Ches W	69	P5
Bicknacre Essex	52	C11
Bicknoller Somset	18	F7
Bicknor Kent	38	E10
Bickton Hants	13	K2
Bicton Herefs	45	P2
Bicton Shrops	56	G9
Bicton Shrops	69	M11
Bidborough Kent	25	N2
Bidden Hants	23	K5
Biddenden Kent	26	E4
Biddenden Green Kent	26	E3
Biddenham Bed	61	M10
Biddestone Wilts	32	G10
Biddisham Somset	19	L4
Biddlesden Bucks	48	H7
Biddlestone Nthumb	119	J9
Biddulph Staffs	70	F3
Biddulph Moor Staffs	70	G3
Bideford Devon	16	H6
Bidford-on-Avon Warwks	47	M4
Bidston Wirral	81	K6
Bielby E R Yk	92	C2
Bieldside C Aber	151	M7
Bierley IoW	14	F11
Bierton Bucks	49	M11
Big Balcraig D & G	107	L9
Bigbury Devon	6	H9
Bigbury-on-Sea Devon	6	H10
Bigby Lincs	93	J9
Biggar Cumb	94	D7
Biggar S Lans	116	E3
Biggin Derbys	71	M3
Biggin Derbys	71	P5
Biggin N York	91	N4
Biggin Hill Gt Lon	37	K9
Biggleswade C Beds	50	E2
Bigholms D & G	110	F4
Bighouse Highld	166	E4
Bighton Hants	22	H8
Biglands Cumb	110	E10
Bignor W Susx	15	Q4
Big Sand Highld	160	B11
Bigrigg Cumb	100	D8
Bigton Shet	169	q11
Bilborough C Nott	72	E2
Bilbrook Somset	18	D6
Bilbrook Staffs	58	C4
Bilbrough N York	98	A11
Bilbster Highld	167	N6
Bildershaw Dur	103	P6
Bildeston Suffk	52	G2
Billacott Cnwll	5	M3
Billericay Essex	37	Q2
Billesdon Leics	73	J10
Billesley Warwks	47	M3
Billingborough Lincs	74	B4
Billinge St Hel	82	B4
Billingford Norfk	64	H6
Billingford Norfk	76	E7
Billingham S on T	104	E6
Billinghay Lincs	86	G10
Billingley Barns	91	L10
Billingshurst W Susx	24	C5
Billingsley Shrops	57	N8
Billington C Beds	49	P10
Billington Lancs	89	L3
Billington Staffs	70	F10
Billockby Norfk	77	N9
Billy Row Dur	103	N3
Bilsborrow Lancs	88	G3
Bilsby Lincs	87	N5
Bilsham W Susx	15	Q6
Bilsington Kent	26	H5
Bilson Green Gloucs	32	B2
Bilsthorpe Notts	85	K8
Bilsthorpe Moor Notts	85	L8
Bilston Mdloth	127	P5
Bilston Wolves	58	E5
Bilstone Leics	72	B9
Bilting Kent	26	H2
Bilton E R Yk	93	L4
Bilton N York	97	M9
Bilton Nthumb	119	P8
Bilton Warwks	59	Q10
Bilton Banks Nthumb	119	P8
Bilton-in-Ainsty N York	97	Q11
Binbrook Lincs	86	H2
Binchester Blocks Dur	103	P4
Bincombe Dorset	11	P8
Binegar Somset	20	B5
Bines Green W Susx	24	E7
Binfield Br For	35	M10
Binfield Heath Oxon	35	K9
Bingfield Nthumb	112	E6
Bingham Notts	73	J2
Bingham's Melcombe		
Dorset	12	C4
Bingley C Brad	90	E3
Bings Heath Shrops	69	P11
Binham Norfk	76	D4
Binley Covtry	59	N9
Binley Hants	22	D4
Binley Woods Warwks	59	N9
Binnegar Dorset	12	E7
Binniehill Falk	126	F3
Binscombe Surrey	23	Q5
Binsey Oxon	34	E3
Binstead IoW	14	G8
Binsted Hants	23	L6
Binsted W Susx	15	Q5
Binton Warwks	47	M4
Bintree Norfk	76	E7
Binweston Shrops	56	E4
Birch Essex	52	F8
Birch Rochdl	89	P9
Birchall Staffs	70	H4
Bircham Newton Norfk	75	Q4
Bircham Tofts Norfk	75	Q4
Birchanger Essex	51	M6
Birchanger Green Services		
Essex	51	M6
Birch Cross Staffs	71	L8
Birchencliffe Kirk	90	E7
Bircher Herefs	56	H11
Birchett's Green E Susx	25	Q4
Birchfield Birm	58	G6
Birch Green Essex	52	F8
Birch Green Herts	50	G8
Birch Green Worcs	46	G5
Birchgrove Cardif	30	G9
Birchgrove Swans	29	K5
Birchgrove W Susx	25	K5
Birch Heath Ches W	69	P2
Birch Hill Ches W	81	Q10
Birchington Kent	39	P8
Birchington-on-Sea Kent	39	N8
Birchley Heath Warwks	59	L6
Birchmoor Warwks	59	L4
Birchmoor Green C Beds	49	Q8
Birchover Derbys	84	B8
Birch Services Rochdl	89	N9
Birch Vale Derbys	83	M7
Birchwood Lincs	86	B7
Birch Wood Somset	10	E2
Birchwood Warrtn	82	E6
Bircotes Notts	85	K2
Birdbrook Essex	52	B3
Birdforth N York	97	Q5
Birdham W Susx	15	M6
Birdingbury Warwks	59	P11
Birdlip Gloucs	32	H2
Birdoswald Cumb	111	M7
Birdsall N York	98	G7
Birds Edge Kirk	90	G9
Birds Green Essex	51	N9
Birdsgreen Shrops	57	P7
Birdsmoorgate Dorset	10	H4
Bird Street Suffk	64	E11
Birdwell Barns	91	J10
Birdwood Gloucs	46	D11
Birgham Border	118	E3
Birichin Highld	162	H8
Birkacre Lancs	88	H8
Birkby N York	104	B10
Birkdale Sefton	88	C8
Birkenbog Abers	158	D4
Birkenhead Wirral	81	L7
Birkenhead (Queensway)		
Tunnel Lpool	81	L7
Birkenhills Abers	158	H8
Birkenshaw Kirk	90	G5
Birkhall Abers	149	Q9
Birkhill Angus	142	F11
Birkhill D & G	117	J7
Birkholme Lincs	73	P6
Birkin N York	91	N5
Birks Leeds	90	H5
Birkshaw Nthumb	111	Q7
Birley Herefs	45	P4
Birley Carr Sheff	84	D2
Birling Kent	37	Q8
Birling Nthumb	119	P9
Birling Gap E Susx	25	N11
Birlingham Worcs	46	H6
Birmingham Birm	58	G7
Birmingham Airport Solhll	59	J8
Birnam P & K	141	P9
Birness Abers	159	N11
Birse Abers	150	F8
Birsemore Abers	150	E8
Birstall Kirk	90	G5
Birstall Leics	72	F9
Birstwith N York	97	K9
Birthorpe Lincs	74	B4
Birtley Gatesd	113	L9
Birtley Herefs	56	F11
Birtley Nthumb	112	C5
Birts Street Worcs	46	E7
Bisbrooke Rutlnd	73	M11
Biscathorpe Lincs	86	H4
Biscovey Cnwll	3	R3
Bisham W & M	35	M7
Bishampton Worcs	47	J4
Bish Mill Devon	17	N6
Bishop Auckland Dur	103	P5
Bishopbridge Lincs	86	D2
Bishopbriggs E Duns	125	Q3
Bishop Burton E R Yk	92	G3
Bishop Middleham Dur	104	B4
Bishopmill Moray	157	N5
Bishop Monkton N York	97	M7
Bishop Norton Lincs	86	C2
Bishopsbourne Kent	39	L11
Bishops Cannings Wilts	21	K2
Bishop's Castle Shrops	56	E7
Bishop's Caundle Dorset	11	P2
Bishop's Cleeve Gloucs	47	J9
Bishop's Frome Herefs	46	C5
Bishops Gate Surrey	35	Q10
Bishop's Green Essex	51	P7
Bishop's Green Hants	22	F2
Bishop's Hull Somset	18	H10
Bishop's Itchington Warwks	48	C3
Bishops Lydeard Somset	18	G9
Bishop's Norton Gloucs	46	F10
Bishop's Nympton Devon	17	P7
Bishop's Offley Staffs	70	D9
Bishop's Stortford Herts	51	L6
Bishop's Sutton Hants	22	H8
Bishop's Tachbrook Warwks	48	B2
Bishop's Tawton Devon	17	K6
Bishopsteignton Devon	7	N4
Bishopstoke Hants	22	E11
Bishopston Swans	28	G7
Bishopstone Bucks	35	M2
Bishopstone E Susx	25	L10
Bishopstone Herefs	45	N6
Bishopstone Kent	39	M8
Bishopstone Swindn	33	P8
Bishopstone Wilts	21	L9
Bishopstrow Wilts	20	G6
Bishop Sutton BaNES	19	Q3
Bishop's Waltham Hants	22	G11
Bishopswood Somset	10	F2
Bishop's Wood Staffs	58	B3
Bishopsworth Bristl	31	Q11
Bishop Thornton N York	97	L8
Bishopthorpe C York	98	B11
Bishopton Darltn	104	C6
Bishopton Rens	125	N3
Bishopton Warwks	47	N3
Bishop Wilton E R Yk	98	F9
Bishton Newpt	31	L7
Bishton Staffs	71	J10
Bisley Gloucs	32	H3
Bisley Surrey	23	Q3
Bisley Camp Surrey	23	P3
Bispham Bpool	88	C2

Bispham Green Lancs....88 F8
Bissoe Cnwll....3 K5
Bisterne Hants....13 K4
Bitchet Green Kent....37 N10
Bitchfield Lincs....73 P5
Bittaford Devon....17 J3
Bittaford Devon....6 H7
Bittering Norfk....76 C8
Bitterley Shrops....57 K9
Bitterne C Sotn....14 E4
Bitteswell Leics....60 B3
Bitton S Glos....32 C11
Bix Oxon....35 K8
Bixter Shet....169 q8
Blaby Leics....72 F11
Blackadder Border....129 L9
Blackawton Devon....7 L8
Blackbeck Cumb....100 D9
Blackborough Devon....10 B3
Blackborough End Norfk....75 N7
Black Bourton Oxon....33 Q4
Blackboys E Susx....25 M6
Blackbrook Derbys....84 D11
Blackbrook St Hel....82 B5
Blackbrook Staffs....70 D7
Blackbrook Surrey....36 E11
Blackburn Abers....151 L5
Blackburn Bl w D....89 K5
Blackburn Rothm....84 E2
Blackburn W Loth....126 H4
Blackburn with Darwen Services Bl w D....89 K6
Black Callerton N u Ty....113 J7
Black Carr Norfk....64 F2
Black Corner W Susx....24 G3
Blackcraig E Ayrs....115 M6
Black Crofts Ag & B....138 G11
Black Cross Cnwll....4 E9
Blackden Heath Ches E....82 G10
Blackdog Abers....151 P5
Black Dog Devon....9 K3
Blackdown Devon....8 D9
Blackdown Dorset....10 H4
Blackdyke Cumb....109 P10
Blacker Barns....91 J9
Blacker Hill Barns....91 K10
Blackfen Gt Lon....37 L6
Blackfield Hants....14 D6
Blackford Cumb....110 G8
Blackford P & K....133 P6
Blackford Somset....19 M5
Blackford Somset....20 C9
Blackfordby Leics....72 A7
Blackgang IoW....14 E11
Blackhall C Edin....127 N3
Blackhall Colliery Dur....104 E3
Blackhall Mill Gatesd....112 H9
Blackhall Rocks Dur....104 E3
Blackham E Susx....25 L2
Blackhaugh Border....117 N3
Blackheath Essex....52 H7
Blackheath Gt Lon....37 J5
Blackheath Sandw....58 E7
Blackheath Suffk....65 N7
Blackheath Surrey....36 B11
Black Heddon Nthumb....112 G5
Blackhill Abers....159 Q6
Blackhill Abers....159 Q9
Blackhill Dur....112 G10
Blackhill of Clackriach Abers....159 M8
Blackhorse Devon....9 N6
Blackjack Lincs....74 E3
Blackland Wilts....33 K11
Black Lane Ends Lancs....89 Q2
Blacklaw D & G....116 E9
Blackley Manch....83 J4
Blacklunans P & K....142 A5
Blackmarstone Herefs....45 Q7
Blackmill Brdgnd....29 P7
Blackmoor Hants....23 L8
Black Moor Leeds....90 H3
Blackmoor N Som....19 N2
Blackmoorfoot Kirk....90 D8
Blackmoor Gate Devon....17 L3
Blackmore Essex....51 P10
Blackmore End Essex....52 B5
Blackmore End Herts....50 E7
Black Mountains....45 K9
Blackness Falk....127 K2
Blacknest Hants....23 L6
Blacknest W & M....35 Q11
Black Notley Essex....52 C7
Blacko Lancs....89 P2
Black Pill Swans....28 H6
Blackpool Bpool....88 C3
Blackpool Devon....7 L4
Blackpool Devon....7 M9
Blackpool Gate Cumb....111 K5
Blackpool Zoo Bpool....88 C3
Blackridge W Loth....126 F4
Blackrock Cnwll....2 H7
Blackrock Mons....30 H2
Blackrod Bolton....89 J8
Blacksboat Moray....157 M10
Blackshaw D & G....109 M7
Blackshaw Head Calder....90 B5
Blacksmith's Green Suffk....64 G8
Blacksnape Bl w D....89 L6
Blackstone W Susx....24 F7
Black Street Suffk....65 Q4
Black Tar Pembks....41 J9
Blackthorn Oxon....48 H11
Blackthorpe Suffk....64 C9
Blacktoft E R Yk....92 D6
Blacktop C Aber....151 M7
Black Torrington Devon....8 C3
Blackwall Derbys....71 P5
Blackwall Tunnel Gt Lon....37 J4
Blackwater Cnwll....3 J4
Blackwater Hants....23 M3
Blackwater IoW....14 F9
Blackwater Somset....19 J11
Blackwaterfoot N Ayrs....120 H6
Blackwell Cumb....110 H10
Blackwell Darltn....103 Q8
Blackwell Derbys....83 P10
Blackwell Derbys....84 F9
Blackwell Warwks....47 N6
Blackwell Worcs....58 E10
Blackwellsend Green Gloucs....46 F9
Blackwood Caerph....30 G5
Blackwood D & G....109 K3
Blackwood S Lans....126 D9
Blackwood Hill Staffs....70 G3
Blacon Ches W....81 M11

Bladbean Kent....27 L2
Bladnoch D & G....107 M7
Bladon Oxon....34 E2
Bladon Somset....19 M10
Blaenannerch Cerdgn....42 D5
Blaenau Ffestiniog Gwynd....67 N5
Blaenavon Torfn....31 J3
Blaenavon Industrial Landscape Torfn....30 H3
Blaencwm Rhondd....29 P5
Blaen Dyryn Powys....44 C7
Blaenffos Pembks....41 N3
Blaengarw Brdgnd....29 P6
Blaengeuffordd Cerdgn....54 E8
Blaengwrach Neath....29 N3
Blaengwynfi Neath....29 N5
Blaenllechau Rhondd....30 D5
Blaenpennal Cerdgn....43 M2
Blaenplwyf Cerdgn....54 D9
Blaenporth Cerdgn....42 E5
Blaenrhondda Rhondd....29 P5
Blaenwaun Carmth....41 P5
Blaen-y-coed Carmth....42 F9
Blaen-y-cwm Blae G....30 F2
Blaenycwm Cerdgn....55 J9
Blagdon N Som....19 P3
Blagdon Somset....18 H11
Blagdon Torbay....7 M6
Blagdon Hill Somset....18 H11
Blagill Cumb....111 P11
Blaguegate Lancs....88 F9
Blaich Highld....139 J2
Blain Highld....138 B4
Blaina Blae G....30 H3
Blair Atholl P & K....141 L4
Blair Drummond Stirlg....133 L8
Blairgowrie P & K....142 B8
Blairhall Fife....134 B10
Blairingone P & K....134 B8
Blairlogie Stirlg....133 N8
Blairmore Ag & B....131 P11
Blairmore Highld....164 E5
Blair's Ferry Ag & B....124 B4
Blaisdon Gloucs....46 D11
Blakebrook Worcs....57 Q9
Blakedown Worcs....58 C9
Blake End Essex....52 B7
Blakeley Lane Staffs....70 H5
Blakemere Ches W....82 C10
Blakemere Herefs....45 M6
Blakemore Devon....7 K6
Blakenall Heath Wsall....58 F4
Blakeney Gloucs....32 C3
Blakeney Norfk....76 E3
Blakenhall Ches E....70 C5
Blakenhall Wolves....58 D5
Blakeshall Worcs....58 B8
Blakesley Nhants....48 H4
Blanchland Nthumb....112 E10
Blandford Camp Dorset....12 F3
Blandford Forum Dorset....12 E3
Blandford St Mary Dorset....12 E3
Bland Hill N York....97 K10
Blanefield Stirlg....125 N2
Blankney Lincs....86 E8
Blantyre S Lans....126 B6
Blàr a' Chaorainn Highld....139 L4
Blarghour Ag & B....131 K5
Blargie Highld....147 Q9
Blarmachfoldach Highld....139 K4
Blashford Hants....13 L3
Blaston Leics....73 L11
Blatherwycke Nhants....73 P11
Blawith Cumb....94 F3
Blawquhairn D & G....108 D4
Blaxhall Suffk....65 M10
Blaxton Donc....91 R10
Blaydon Gatesd....113 J8
Bleadney Somset....19 N5
Bleadon N Som....19 K3
Bleak Street Somset....20 E8
Blean Kent....39 K9
Bleasby Lincs....86 F4
Bleasby Notts....85 M11
Bleasdale Lancs....95 M11
Bleatarn Cumb....102 D8
Bleathwood Herefs....57 K10
Blebocraigs Fife....135 L4
Bleddfa Powys....56 C11
Bledington Gloucs....47 P10
Bledlow Bucks....35 L4
Bledlow Ridge Bucks....35 L5
Bleet Wilts....20 G3
Blegbie E Loth....128 D7
Blencarn Cumb....102 B4
Blencogo Cumb....110 C11
Blendworth Hants....15 K4
Blenheim Palace Oxon....48 D11
Blennerhasset Cumb....100 G2
Bletchingdon Oxon....48 F11
Bletchingley Surrey....36 H10
Bletchley M Keyn....49 N8
Bletchley Shrops....69 R8
Bletchley Park Museum M Keyn....49 N8
Bletherston Pembks....41 L6
Bletsoe Bed....61 M9
Blewbury Oxon....34 F7
Blickling Norfk....76 H6
Blidworth Notts....85 J9
Blidworth Bottoms Notts....85 J10
Blindburn Nthumb....118 F6
Blindcrake Cumb....100 F4
Blindley Heath Surrey....37 J11
Blisland Cnwll....5 J7
Blissford Hants....13 L2
Bliss Gate Worcs....57 N10
Blisworth Nhants....49 K4
Blithbury Staffs....71 K11
Blitterlees Cumb....109 P10
Blockley Gloucs....47 N7
Blofield Norfk....77 L10
Blofield Heath Norfk....77 L9
Blo Norton Norfk....64 E6
Bloomfield Border....118 A6
Blore Staffs....71 L5
Blounce Hants....23 K5
Blount's Green Staffs....71 K8
Blowick Sefton....88 D7
Bloxham Oxon....48 D7
Bloxholm Lincs....86 E10
Bloxwich Wsall....58 E4
Bloxworth Dorset....12 E6
Blubberhouses N York....97 J9
Blue Anchor Cnwll....4 E10

Blue Anchor Somset....18 D6
Blue Bell Hill Kent....38 B9
Blue John Cavern Derbys....83 P8
Blundellsands Sefton....81 L5
Blundeston Suffk....65 Q2
Blunham C Beds....61 Q10
Blunsdon St Andrew Swindn....33 M7
Bluntington Worcs....58 D10
Bluntisham Cambs....62 E6
Blunts Cnwll....5 N9
Blunts Green Warwks....58 H11
Blurton C Stke....70 F6
Blyborough Lincs....86 B2
Blyford Suffk....65 N6
Blymhill Staffs....57 Q2
Blymhill Lawn Staffs....57 Q2
Blyth Notts....85 K3
Blyth Nthumb....113 M4
Blyth Bridge Border....127 L8
Blythburgh Suffk....65 N6
Blythe Border....128 F10
Blythe Bridge Staffs....70 H6
Blythe End Warwks....59 K6
Blythe Marsh Staffs....70 H6
Blyth Services Notts....85 K3
Blyton Lincs....85 Q2
Boarhills Fife....135 P5
Boarhunt Hants....14 H5
Boarley Kent....38 C10
Boarsgreave Lancs....89 N6
Boarshead E Susx....25 M4
Boar's Head Wigan....88 H9
Boars Hill Oxon....34 E4
Boarstall Bucks....34 H2
Boasley Cross Devon....8 E7
Boath Highld....155 Q3
Boat of Garten Highld....148 G4
Bobbing Kent....38 E8
Bobbington Staffs....57 Q6
Bobbingworth Essex....51 M9
Bocaddon Cnwll....5 K10
Bocking Essex....52 C7
Bocking Churchstreet Essex....52 C6
Bockleton Worcs....46 A2
Boconnoc Cnwll....5 J9
Boddam Abers....159 R9
Boddam Shet....169 q12
Boddington Gloucs....46 G9
Bodedern IoA....78 E8
Bodelwyddan Denbgs....80 E9
Bodenham Herefs....45 Q4
Bodenham Wilts....21 N9
Bodenham Moor Herefs....45 Q4
Bodewryd IoA....78 G6
Bodfari Denbgs....80 F10
Bodffordd IoA....78 G9
Bodham Norfk....76 H4
Bodiam E Susx....26 C6
Bodicote Oxon....48 E7
Bodieve Cnwll....4 F7
Bodinnick Cnwll....5 J11
Bodle Street Green E Susx....25 Q8
Bodmin Cnwll....4 H8
Bodmin Moor Cnwll....5 K6
Bodney Norfk....64 A2
Bodorgan IoA....78 F11
Boduan Gwynd....66 E7
Bodymoor Heath Warwks....59 J5
Bogallan Highld....156 A7
Bogbrae Abers....159 R9
Bogend S Ayrs....125 L11
Boggs Holdings E Loth....128 C5
Boghall Mdloth....127 N4
Boghall W Loth....126 H4
Boghead S Lans....126 D9
Bogmoor Moray....157 R5
Bogmuir Abers....143 L3
Bogniebrae Abers....158 E8
Bognor Regis W Susx....15 P7
Bogroy Highld....148 G3
Bogue D & G....108 D4
Bohetherick Cnwll....5 Q8
Bohortha Cnwll....3 M7
Bohuntine Highld....146 H11
Bojewyan Cnwll....2 B7
Bokiddick Cnwll....4 H9
Bolam Dur....103 N6
Bolam Nthumb....112 H4
Bolberry Devon....6 H11
Bold Heath St Hel....82 B7
Boldmere Birm....58 H6
Boldon Colliery S Tyne....113 M8
Boldre Hants....13 P5
Boldron Dur....103 K8
Bole Notts....85 N3
Bolehill Derbys....84 C9
Bole Hill Derbys....84 D6
Bolenowe Cnwll....2 H6
Bolham Devon....18 C11
Bolham Water Devon....10 D2
Bolingey Cnwll....3 K3
Bollington Ches E....83 K9
Bollington Cross Ches E....83 K9
Bollow Gloucs....32 D2
Bolney W Susx....24 G6
Bolnhurst Bed....61 N9
Bolnore W Susx....24 H6
Bolshan Angus....143 L7
Bolsover Derbys....84 G6
Bolsterstone Sheff....90 H11
Boltby N York....97 Q3
Bolter End Bucks....35 L6
Bolton Bolton....89 L9
Bolton Cumb....102 B6
Bolton E Loth....128 E6
Bolton E R Yk....98 E10
Bolton Nthumb....119 M8
Bolton Abbey N York....96 G10
Bolton Bridge N York....96 G10
Bolton-by-Bowland Lancs....96 A11
Boltonfellend Cumb....111 J7
Boltongate Cumb....100 H2
Bolton-le-Sands Lancs....95 K7
Bolton Low Houses Cumb....100 H2
Bolton New Houses Cumb....100 H2
Bolton-on-Swale N York....103 Q4
Bolton Percy N York....91 N2
Bolton Town End Lancs....95 K7
Bolton upon Dearne Barns....91 M10
Bolventor Cnwll....5 K6
Bomarsund Nthumb....113 L4
Bomere Heath Shrops....69 N11

Bonar Bridge Highld....162 E8
Bonawe Ag & B....139 J11
Bonby N Linc....92 H7
Boncath Pembks....41 P3
Bonchester Bridge Border....118 A8
Bonchurch IoW....14 G11
Bondleigh Devon....8 G4
Bonds Lancs....88 F2
Bonehill Devon....8 H9
Bonehill Staffs....59 J4
Bo'ness Falk....134 C11
Boney Hay Staffs....58 F2
Bonhill W Duns....125 K2
Boningale Shrops....57 Q4
Bonjedward Border....118 C6
Bonkle N Lans....126 E6
Bonnington Angus....143 K10
Bonnington Kent....27 J4
Bonnybank Fife....135 K7
Bonnybridge Falk....126 E2
Bonnykelly Abers....159 L7
Bonnyrigg Mdloth....127 Q4
Bonnyton Angus....142 E10
Bonsall Derbys....84 C9
Bonshaw Tower D & G....110 D6
Bont Mons....45 M11
Bontddu Gwynd....67 M11
Bont-Dolgadfan Powys....55 K4
Bont-goch Cerdgn....54 F7
Bonthorpe Lincs....87 N6
Bontnewydd Cerdgn....54 E11
Bontnewydd Gwynd....66 H3
Bontuchel Denbgs....68 E3
Bonvilston V Glam....30 E10
Bonwm Denbgs....68 F6
Bon-y-maen Swans....29 J5
Boode Devon....17 J4
Booker Bucks....35 M6
Booley Shrops....69 Q9
Boon Border....128 F10
Boon Hill Staffs....70 E4
Boorley Green Hants....14 F4
Boosbeck R & Cl....105 J7
Boose's Green Essex....52 D5
Boot Cumb....100 G10
Boothby Graffoe Lincs....86 C9
Boothby Pagnell Lincs....73 P4
Boothferry E R Yk....92 B5
Booth Green Ches E....83 K8
Boothstown Salfd....82 F4
Boothtown Calder....90 D5
Boothville Nhants....60 G8
Bootle Cumb....94 C3
Bootle Sefton....81 L5
Boots Green Ches W....82 G10
Boot Street Suffk....53 M2
Booze N York....103 K10
Boraston Shrops....57 L11
Bordeaux Guern....10 c1
Borden Kent....38 E9
Borden W Susx....23 M10
Border Cumb....110 C10
Bordley N York....96 D7
Bordon Hants....23 L7
Boreham Essex....52 C10
Boreham Wilts....20 G6
Boreham Street E Susx....25 Q8
Borehamwood Herts....50 E11
Boreland D & G....110 C2
Boreraig Highld....152 B7
Boreton Shrops....57 J3
Borgh W Isls....168 b17
Borgh W Isls....168 j2
Borgie Highld....165 Q5
Borgue D & G....108 D11
Borgue Highld....167 K11
Borley Essex....52 D3
Borley Green Essex....52 D3
Borley Green Suffk....64 D9
Borneskitaig Highld....152 F3
Borness D & G....108 D11
Boroughbridge N York....97 N7
Borough Green Kent....37 P9
Borras Head Wrexhm....69 L4
Borreraig Derbys....72 C4
Borrowby N York....97 P3
Borrowby N York....105 L7
Borrowdale Cumb....101 J7
Borrowstoun Falk....134 B11
Borstal Medway....38 B8
Borth Cerdgn....54 E6
Borthwick Mdloth....128 B8
Borthwickbrae Border....117 N8
Borthwickshiels Border....117 N7
Borth-y-Gest Gwynd....67 K7
Borve Highld....152 G8
Borve W Isls....168 b17
Borve W Isls....168 f8
Borve W Isls....168 j2
Borwick Lancs....95 L6
Borwick Lodge Cumb....101 K11
Borwick Rails Cumb....94 D5
Bosavern Cnwll....2 B7
Bosbury Herefs....46 C6
Boscarne Cnwll....4 G8
Boscastle Cnwll....4 H3
Boscombe BCP....13 K6
Boscombe Wilts....21 P7
Boscoppa Cnwll....3 Q3
Bosham W Susx....15 M6
Bosham Hoe W Susx....15 M6
Bosherston Pembks....41 J12
Boskednan Cnwll....2 C7
Boskenna Cnwll....2 C9
Bosley Ches E....83 K11
Bosoughan Cnwll....4 D9
Bossall N York....98 E8
Bossiney Cnwll....4 H4
Bossingham Kent....27 L2
Bossington Somset....18 A5
Bostock Green Ches W....82 E11
Boston Lincs....74 F2
Boston Spa Leeds....97 P11
Boswarthan Cnwll....2 C7
Boswinger Cnwll....3 P5
Botallack Cnwll....2 B7
Botany Bay Gt Lon....50 G11
Botcheston Leics....72 D10
Botesdale Suffk....64 E6
Bothal Nthumb....113 K3
Bothampstead W Berk....34 F9
Bothamsall Notts....85 L6
Bothel Cumb....100 G3
Bothenhampton Dorset....11 K6
Bothwell S Lans....126 C6

Bothwell Services (southbound) S Lans....126 C6
Botley Bucks....35 Q4
Botley Hants....14 F4
Botley Oxon....34 E3
Botolph Claydon Bucks....49 K10
Botolphs W Susx....24 E9
Botolph's Bridge Kent....27 K5
Bottesford Leics....73 L3
Bottesford N Linc....92 E9
Bottisham Cambs....62 H8
Bottomcraig Fife....135 K3
Bottom of Hutton Lancs....88 F5
Bottom o' th' Moor Bolton....89 K8
Bottoms Calder....89 Q6
Bottoms Cnwll....2 B9
Botts Green Warwks....59 K6
Botusfleming Cnwll....5 Q9
Botwnnog Gwynd....66 D8
Bough Beech Kent....37 L11
Boughrood Powys....44 G7
Boughspring Gloucs....31 Q5
Boughton Nhants....60 G7
Boughton Norfk....75 P10
Boughton Notts....85 L7
Boughton Aluph Kent....26 H2
Boughton End C Beds....49 Q7
Boughton Green Kent....38 C11
Boughton Lees Kent....26 H2
Boughton Malherbe Kent....26 E2
Boughton Monchelsea Kent....38 C11
Boughton Street Kent....39 J10
Boulby R & Cl....105 L7
Boulder Clough Calder....90 C6
Bouldnor IoW....14 C9
Bouldon Shrops....57 J7
Boulmer Nthumb....119 Q8
Boulston Pembks....41 J8
Boultenstone Abers....150 C5
Boultham Lincs....86 C7
Boundary Staffs....70 H6
Bourn Cambs....62 D9
Bournbrook Birm....58 F8
Bourne Lincs....74 A6
Bournebridge Essex....37 M2
Bourne End Bed....61 M8
Bourne End Bucks....35 N7
Bourne End C Beds....49 Q6
Bourne End Herts....50 B9
Bournemouth BCP....13 J6
Bournemouth Airport BCP....13 K5
Bournes Green Gloucs....32 H4
Bournes Green Sthend....38 F4
Bournheath Worcs....58 E10
Bournmoor Dur....113 M10
Bournstream Gloucs....32 D6
Bournville Birm....58 F8
Bourton Dorset....20 E8
Bourton N Som....19 L2
Bourton Oxon....33 P7
Bourton Shrops....57 K5
Bourton Wilts....21 K2
Bourton on Dunsmore Warwks....59 P10
Bourton-on-the-Hill Gloucs....47 N8
Bourton-on-the-Water Gloucs....47 N10
Bousd Ag & B....136 H3
Boustead Hill Cumb....110 E9
Bouth Cumb....94 G3
Bouthwaite N York....96 H6
Bouts Worcs....47 K3
Boveney Bucks....35 P9
Boveridge Dorset....13 J2
Bovey Tracey Devon....9 K9
Bovingdon Herts....50 B9
Bovingdon Green Bucks....35 M7
Bovinger Essex....51 M9
Bovington Dorset....12 D7
Bovington Camp Dorset....12 D7
Bow Cumb....110 F9
Bow Devon....7 L7
Bow Devon....8 H4
Bow Gt Lon....37 J4
Bow Ork....169 c7
Bowbank Dur....102 H6
Bow Brickhill M Keyn....49 P8
Bowbridge Gloucs....32 G3
Bowburn Dur....104 B3
Bowcombe IoW....14 E9
Bowd Devon....10 C6
Bowden Border....117 R4
Bowden Devon....7 L9
Bowden Hill Wilts....32 H11
Bowdon Traffd....82 G7
Bower Highld....167 M4
Bowerchalke Wilts....21 K10
Bowerhill Wilts....20 H2
Bower Hinton Somset....19 N11
Bower House Tye Suffk....52 G3
Bowermadden Highld....167 M4
Bowers Staffs....70 E7
Bowers Gifford Essex....38 C4
Bowershall Fife....134 D9
Bower's Row Leeds....91 L5
Bowes Dur....103 J8
Bowgreave Lancs....88 F2
Bowhouse D & G....109 M7
Bowithick Cnwll....5 K5
Bowker's Green Lancs....81 N4
Bowland Border....117 P2
Bowland Bridge Cumb....95 J3
Bowley Herefs....45 Q4
Bowley Town Herefs....45 Q4
Bowlhead Green Surrey....23 P7
Bowling C Brad....90 F4
Bowling W Duns....125 L3
Bowling Bank Wrexhm....69 L5
Bowling Green Worcs....46 F4
Bowmanstead Cumb....101 K11
Bowmore Ag & B....122 D8
Bowness-on-Solway Cumb....110 D8
Bowness-on-Windermere Cumb....101 M11
Bow of Fife Fife....135 J5
Bowriefauld Angus....143 J8
Bowscale Cumb....101 L4
Bowsden Nthumb....119 L2
Bowston Cumb....101 M11
Bow Street Cerdgn....54 E7
Bow Street Norfk....64 E2
Bowthorpe Norfk....76 H10
Box Gloucs....32 G3
Box Wilts....32 F11
Boxbush Gloucs....32 D2
Boxbush Gloucs....46 C10

260 Box End – Brocton

Box End Bed 61 M11
Boxford Suffk 52 G3
Boxford W Berk 34 D10
Boxgrove W Susx 15 P5
Box Hill Surrey 36 E10
Boxley Kent 38 C10
Boxmoor Herts 50 B9
Box's Shop Cnwll 16 C11
Boxted Essex 52 G5
Boxted Essex 52 H5
Boxted Suffk 64 A11
Boxted Cross Essex 52 H5
Boxwell Gloucs 32 F6
Boxworth Cambs 62 D8
Boyden End Suffk 63 M9
Boyden Gate Kent 39 M8
Boylestone Derbys 71 M7
Boyndie Abers 158 F5
Boyndlie Abers 159 M5
Boynton E R Yk 99 N7
Boysack Angus 143 L8
Boys Hill Dorset 11 P2
Boythorpe Derbys 84 E7
Boyton Cnwll 5 N3
Boyton Suffk 53 Q2
Boyton Wilts 21 J7
Boyton Cross Essex 51 P9
Boyton End Suffk 52 B3
Bozeat Nhants 61 K9
Braaid IoM 80 d6
Brabling Green Suffk 65 K9
Brabourne Kent 27 K3
Brabourne Lees Kent 27 J3
Brabstermire Highld 167 P3
Bracadale Highld 152 F10
Braceborough Lincs 74 A8
Bracebridge Heath Lincs 86 C7
Bracebridge Low Fields Lincs 86 C7
Braceby Lincs 73 Q3
Bracewell Lancs 96 C11
Brackenfield Derbys 84 E9
Brackenhirst N Lans 126 C4
Brackenthwaite Cumb 110 E11
Brackenthwaite N York 97 L10
Brackla Brdgnd 29 P9
Bracklesham W Susx 15 M7
Brackletter Highld 146 F11
Brackley Nhants 48 G7
Brackley Hatch Nhants 48 H6
Bracknell Br For 35 N11
Braco P & K 133 N6
Bracobrae Moray 158 D7
Bracon Ash Norfk 64 H2
Bracora Highld 145 M9
Bracorina Highld 145 M9
Bradaford Devon 5 P3
Bradbourne Derbys 71 N4
Bradbury Dur 104 B5
Bradden Nhants 48 H5
Braddock Cnwll 5 K9
Bradeley C Stke 70 F4
Bradenham Bucks 35 M5
Bradenstoke Wilts 33 K9
Bradfield Devon 9 Q3
Bradfield Essex 53 K5
Bradfield Norfk 77 K5
Bradfield Sheff 84 C2
Bradfield W Berk 34 H10
Bradfield Combust Suffk 64 B10
Bradfield Green Ches E 70 B3
Bradfield Heath Essex 53 K5
Bradfield St Clare Suffk 64 C10
Bradfield St George Suffk 64 C10
Bradford C Brad 90 F4
Bradford Cnwll 5 J6
Bradford Devon 16 G10
Bradford Nthumb 112 G5
Bradford Nthumb 119 N4
Bradford Abbas Dorset 11 M2
Bradford Leigh Wilts 20 F2
Bradford-on-Avon Wilts 20 F2
Bradford-on-Tone Somset 18 G10
Bradford Peverell Dorset 11 P6
Bradiford Devon 17 K5
Brading IoW 14 H9
Bradley Ches W 69 P5
Bradley Derbys 71 N5
Bradley Hants 22 H6
Bradley Kirk 90 F6
Bradley N York 96 F4
Bradley NE Lin 93 M9
Bradley Staffs 70 F11
Bradley Wolves 58 E5
Bradley Worcs 47 J2
Bradley Wrexhm 69 K4
Bradley Green Somset 19 J7
Bradley Green Warwks 59 L4
Bradley Green Worcs 47 J2
Bradley in the Moors Staffs 71 K6
Bradley Stoke S Glos 32 B8
Bradmore Notts 72 F4
Bradney Somset 19 K7
Bradninch Devon 9 N4
Bradninch Devon 17 L5
Bradnop Staffs 71 J3
Bradnor Green Herefs 45 K3
Bradpole Dorset 11 K6
Bradshaw Bolton 89 L8
Bradshaw Calder 90 D5
Bradshaw Kirk 90 D8
Bradstone Devon 5 P5
Bradwall Green Ches E 70 D2
Bradwell Derbys 83 Q8
Bradwell Devon 17 J3
Bradwell Essex 52 D7
Bradwell M Keyn 49 M6
Bradwell Norfk 77 Q11
Bradwell-on-Sea Essex 52 H10
Bradwell Waterside Essex 52 G10
Bradworthy Devon 16 E9
Brae Highld 156 B5
Brae Shet 169 q7
Braeface Falk 133 M11
Braehead Angus 143 M7
Braehead D & G 107 M7
Braehead S Lans 126 H7
Braeintra Highld 153 R11
Braemar Abers 149 M9
Braemore Highld 161 K11
Braemore Highld 167 J11
Brae Roy Lodge Highld 147 J9
Braeside Inver 124 G3
Braes of Coul Angus 142 D6
Braes of Enzie Moray 158 A6
Braes of Ullapool Highld 161 J8
Braeswick Ork 169 f3
Braevallich Ag & B 131 K6
Braewick Shet 169 p6
Brafferton Darltn 103 Q6
Brafferton N York 97 P6
Brafield-on-the-Green Nhants 60 H9
Bragar W Isls 168 h3
Bragbury End Herts 50 G6
Braidwood S Lans 126 E8
Brailsford Derbys 71 P6
Brailsford Green Derbys 71 P6
Brain's Green Gloucs 32 C3
Braintree Essex 52 C7
Braiseworth Suffk 64 G7
Braishfield Hants 22 C9
Braiswick Essex 52 G6
Braithwaite C Brad 90 C2
Braithwaite Cumb 100 H6
Braithwell Donc 84 H2
Braken Hill Wakefd 91 L7
Bramber W Susx 24 E8
Brambridge Hants 22 E10
Bramcote Notts 72 E3
Bramcote Warwks 59 P7
Bramdean Hants 22 H9
Bramerton Norfk 77 K11
Bramfield Herts 50 G7
Bramfield Suffk 65 M7
Bramford Suffk 53 K2
Bramhall Stockp 83 J8
Bramham Leeds 91 L2
Bramhope Leeds 90 H2
Bramley Hants 23 J3
Bramley Leeds 90 G3
Bramley Rothm 84 G2
Bramley Surrey 24 B2
Bramley Corner Hants 22 H3
Bramley Green Hants 23 J3
Bramley Head N York 96 H9
Bramling Kent 39 M10
Brampford Speke Devon 9 M5
Brampton Cambs 62 B6
Brampton Cumb 102 C6
Brampton Cumb 111 K8
Brampton Lincs 85 P5
Brampton Norfk 77 J7
Brampton Rothm 91 L10
Brampton Suffk 65 N5
Brampton Abbotts Herefs 46 B9
Brampton Ash Nhants 60 G3
Brampton Bryan Herefs 56 F10
Brampton-en-le-Morthen Rothm 84 G3
Bramshall Staffs 71 K8
Bramshaw Hants 21 Q11
Bramshill Hants 23 K2
Bramshott Hants 23 M8
Bramwell Somset 19 M9
Branault Highld 137 N2
Brancaster Norfk 75 Q2
Brancaster Staithe Norfk 75 Q2
Brancepeth Dur 103 P3
Branchill Moray 157 K7
Brand End Lincs 87 L11
Branderburgh Moray 157 N3
Brandesburton E R Yk 99 N11
Brandeston Suffk 65 J9
Brand Green Gloucs 46 D9
Brandis Corner Devon 16 G11
Brandiston Norfk 76 G7
Brandon Dur 103 P2
Brandon Lincs 86 B11
Brandon Nthumb 119 K7
Brandon Suffk 63 N3
Brandon Warwks 59 P9
Brandon Bank Norfk 63 K3
Brandon Creek Norfk 63 K2
Brandon Parva Norfk 76 F10
Brandsby N York 98 B6
Brandy Wharf Lincs 92 H11
Brane Cnwll 2 C8
Bran End Essex 51 Q5
Branksome BCP 12 H6
Branksome Park BCP 13 J6
Bransbury Hants 22 D6
Bransby Lincs 85 Q5
Branscombe Devon 10 D7
Bransford Worcs 46 E4
Bransgore Hants 13 L5
Bransholme C KuH 93 K4
Bransley Shrops 57 M9
Branson's Cross Worcs 58 G10
Branston Leics 73 L5
Branston Lincs 86 D7
Branston Staffs 71 N10
Branston Booths Lincs 86 E7
Branstone IoW 14 G10
Brant Broughton Lincs 86 B10
Brantham Suffk 53 K5
Branthwaite Cumb 100 E6
Branthwaite Cumb 101 J3
Brantingham E R Yk 92 F5
Branton Donc 91 Q10
Branton Nthumb 119 K7
Branton Green N York 97 P8
Branxton Nthumb 118 G3
Brassey Green Ches W 69 P2
Brasside Dur 113 L11
Brassington Derbys 71 N4
Brasted Kent 37 L9
Brasted Chart Kent 37 L10
Brathens Abers 150 H8
Bratoft Lincs 87 N8
Brattleby Lincs 86 B4
Bratton Somset 18 B5
Bratton Wilts 20 H4
Bratton Wrekin 57 L2
Bratton Clovelly Devon 8 C6
Bratton Fleming Devon 17 L4
Bratton Seymour Somset 20 C9
Braughing Herts 51 J5
Braughing Friars Herts 51 K6
Braunston Nhants 60 B7
Braunston Rutlnd 73 L9
Braunstone Town Leics 72 F10
Braunton Devon 16 H4
Brawby N York 98 E5
Brawl Highld 166 D3
Braworth N York 104 F9
Bray W & M 35 P9
Braybrooke Nhants 60 G4
Braydon Wilts 33 L7
Braydon Brook Wilts 33 J6
Braydon Side Wilts 33 K7
Brayford Devon 17 M5
Bray's Hill E Susx 25 Q8
Bray Shop Cnwll 5 N7
Braystones Cumb 100 D9
Braythorn N York 97 K11
Brayton N York 91 Q4
Braywick W & M 35 N9
Braywoodside W & M 35 N9
Brazacott Cnwll 5 M3
Breach Kent 27 L2
Breach Kent 38 D8
Breachwood Green Herts 50 E6
Breacleit W Isls 168 g4
Breaclete W Isls 168 g4
Breaden Heath Shrops 69 M7
Breadsall Derbys 72 B3
Breadstone Gloucs 32 D4
Breage Cnwll 2 G8
Breakachy Highld 155 N9
Breakish Highld 145 L3
Brealangwell Lodge Highld 162 C8
Bream Gloucs 32 B3
Breamore Hants 21 N11
Brean Somset 19 J3
Breanais W Isls 168 e5
Brearley Calder 90 C5
Brearton N York 97 M8
Breascleit W Isls 168 h4
Breasclete W Isls 168 h4
Breaston Derbys 72 D4
Brechfa Carmth 43 K8
Brechin Angus 143 L5
Breckles Norfk 64 D3
Brecon Powys 44 E9
Brecon Beacons National Park 44 E10
Bredbury Stockp 83 K6
Brede E Susx 26 D8
Bredenbury Herefs 46 B3
Bredfield Suffk 65 K11
Bredgar Kent 38 E9
Bredhurst Kent 38 C9
Bredon Worcs 46 H7
Bredon's Hardwick Worcs 46 H7
Bredon's Norton Worcs 46 H7
Bredward Herefs 45 K4
Bredwardine Herefs 45 L6
Breedon on the Hill Leics 72 C6
Breich W Loth 126 H5
Breightmet Bolton 89 L9
Breighton E R Yk 92 B4
Breinton Herefs 45 P7
Bremhill Wilts 33 J10
Bremridge Devon 17 M6
Brenchley Kent 25 Q2
Brendon Devon 16 F10
Brendon Devon 17 P2
Brendon Hill Somset 18 D8
Brenfield Ag & B 123 P3
Brenish W Isls 168 e5
Brenkley N u Ty 113 K5
Brent Cross Gt Lon 36 F3
Brent Eleigh Suffk 52 F2
Brentford Gt Lon 36 E5
Brentingby Leics 73 K7
Brent Knoll Somset 19 K4
Brent Mill Devon 6 H7
Brent Pelham Herts 51 K4
Brentwood Essex 37 N2
Brenzett Kent 26 H6
Brenzett Green Kent 26 H6
Brereton Staffs 71 K11
Brereton Green Ches E 70 D2
Brereton Heath Ches E 82 H11
Brereton Hill Staffs 71 K11
Bressay Shet 169 s9
Bressingham Norfk 64 F5
Bressingham Common Norfk 64 F5
Bretby Derbys 71 P10
Bretford Warwks 59 P9
Bretforton Worcs 47 L6
Bretherton Lancs 88 F6
Brettabister Shet 169 r8
Brettenham Norfk 64 C5
Brettenham Suffk 64 D11
Bretton C Pete 74 C10
Bretton Derbys 84 B5
Bretton Flints 69 L2
Brewers End Essex 51 N6
Brewer Street Surrey 36 H10
Brewood Staffs 58 C3
Briantspuddle Dorset 12 D6
Brick End Essex 51 N5
Brickendon Herts 50 H9
Bricket Wood Herts 50 D10
Brick Houses Sheff 84 D4
Brickkiln Green Essex 52 B5
Bricklehampton Worcs 47 J6
Bride IoM 80 f1
Bridekirk Cumb 100 F4
Bridell Pembks 41 N2
Bridestowe Devon 8 D7
Brideswell Abers 158 E10
Bridford Devon 9 K7
Bridge Kent 39 L11
Bridge End Cumb 94 D4
Bridge End Cumb 110 G11
Bridge End Devon 6 H9
Bridge End Dur 103 K3
Bridge End Essex 51 Q4
Bridge End Lincs 74 B3
Bridgefoot Angus 142 F10
Bridgefoot Cumb 100 E5
Bridge Green Essex 51 L3
Bridgehampton Somset 19 Q10
Bridge Hewick N York 97 M6
Bridgehill Dur 112 G10
Bridgehouse Gate N York 97 J7
Bridgemary Hants 14 G6
Bridgemere Ches E 70 C5
Bridgend Abers 158 D10
Bridgend Ag & B 120 E4
Bridgend Ag & B 122 D7
Bridgend Angus 143 J4
Bridgend Brdgnd 29 P9
Bridgend Cerdgn 42 C5
Bridgend Cumb 101 M8
Bridgend D & G 116 F9
Bridgend Devon 6 F9
Bridgend Fife 135 K5
Bridgend Moray 158 A11
Bridgend P & K 134 E3
Bridgend W Loth 127 J2
Bridgend of Lintrathen Angus 142 D7
Bridge of Alford Abers 150 F4
Bridge of Allan Stirlg 133 M8
Bridge of Avon Moray 149 M4
Bridge of Avon Moray 157 M10
Bridge of Balgie P & K 140 E8
Bridge of Brewlands Angus 142 B5
Bridge of Brown Highld 149 L3
Bridge of Cally P & K 142 A7
Bridge of Canny Abers 150 H8
Bridge of Craigisla Angus 142 D7
Bridge of Dee D & G 108 F9
Bridge of Don C Aber 151 N6
Bridge of Dun Angus 143 M6
Bridge of Dye Abers 150 H10
Bridge of Earn P & K 134 E4
Bridge of Ericht P & K 140 D6
Bridge of Feugh Abers 151 J8
Bridge of Gairn Abers 150 B8
Bridge of Gaur P & K 140 D6
Bridge of Marnoch Abers 158 E7
Bridge of Muchalls Abers 151 M9
Bridge of Orchy Ag & B 139 P10
Bridge of Tilt P & K 141 L4
Bridge of Tynet Moray 158 A5
Bridge of Walls Shet 169 p8
Bridge of Weir Rens 125 K4
Bridge Reeve Devon 17 M9
Bridgerule Devon 16 D11
Bridges Shrops 56 F5
Bridge Sollers Herefs 45 N6
Bridge Street Suffk 52 E2
Bridgetown Cnwll 5 N4
Bridgetown Somset 18 B8
Bridge Trafford Ches W 81 P10
Bridge Yate S Glos 32 C10
Bridgham Norfk 64 D4
Bridgnorth Shrops 57 N6
Bridgwater Somset 19 J7
Bridgwater Services Somset 19 K8
Bridlington E R Yk 99 P7
Bridport Dorset 11 K6
Bridstow Herefs 46 A10
Brierfield Lancs 89 N3
Brierley Barns 91 L8
Brierley Gloucs 46 B11
Brierley Herefs 45 P3
Brierley Hill Dudley 58 D7
Brierlow Bar Derbys 83 N11
Brierton Hartpl 104 E4
Briery Cumb 101 J6
Brigg N Linc 92 H9
Briggate Norfk 77 L6
Briggswath N York 105 N9
Brigham Cumb 100 E4
Brigham Cumb 101 J6
Brigham E R Yk 99 M10
Brighouse Calder 90 E6
Brighstone IoW 14 D10
Brightgate Derbys 84 C9
Brighthampton Oxon 34 C4
Brightholmlee Sheff 90 H11
Brightley Devon 8 F5
Brightling E Susx 25 Q6
Brightlingsea Essex 53 J8
Brighton Br & H 24 H10
Brighton Cnwll 3 N3
Brighton City Airport W Susx 24 E9
Brighton le Sands Sefton 81 L5
Brightons Falk 126 G2
Brightwalton W Berk 34 D9
Brightwalton Green W Berk 34 D9
Brightwalton Holt W Berk 34 D9
Brightwell Suffk 53 N3
Brightwell Baldwin Oxon 35 J5
Brightwell-cum-Sotwell Oxon 34 G6
Brightwell Upperton Oxon 35 J6
Brignall Dur 103 L8
Brig o'Turk Stirlg 132 G6
Brigsley NE Lin 93 N10
Brigsteer Cumb 95 K3
Brigstock Nhants 61 K3
Brill Bucks 35 J2
Brill Cnwll 3 J8
Brilley Herefs 45 K5
Brimfield Herefs 57 J11
Brimfield Cross Herefs 57 J11
Brimington Derbys 84 F6
Brimley Devon 9 K9
Brimpsfield Gloucs 32 H2
Brimpton W Berk 22 G2
Brimpton Common W Berk 22 G2
Brimscombe Gloucs 32 G4
Brimstage Wirral 81 L8
Brincliffe Sheff 84 D4
Brind E R Yk 92 B4
Brindham Somset 19 P7
Brindister Shet 169 p8
Brindle Lancs 88 H6
Brindley Ches E 69 Q4
Brineton Staffs 57 Q2
Bringhurst Leics 60 H2
Bringsty Common Herefs 46 D3
Brington Cambs 61 N5
Brinian Ork 169 d4
Briningham Norfk 76 E5
Brinkely Notts 85 M10
Brinkhill Lincs 87 L6
Brinkley Cambs 63 K10
Brinklow Warwks 59 P9
Brinkworth Wilts 33 K8
Brinscall Lancs 89 J6
Brinscombe Somset 19 M4
Brinsea N Som 19 M2
Brinsley Notts 84 G11
Brinsop Herefs 45 N6
Brinsworth Rothm 84 F3
Brinton Norfk 76 E4
Brisco Cumb 110 H10
Brisley Norfk 76 C7
Brislington Bristl 32 B10
Brissenden Green Kent 26 F4
Bristol Bristl 31 Q10
Bristol Airport N Som 31 P11
Bristol Zoo Gardens Bristl 31 Q10
Briston Norfk 76 F5
Brisworthy Devon 6 F5
Britannia Lancs 89 P6
Britford Wilts 21 N9
Brithdir Caerph 30 F4
Brithdir Gwynd 67 P11
British Legion Village Kent 38 B10
Briton Ferry Neath 29 K6
Britwell Salome Oxon 35 J6
Brixham Torbay 7 N7
Brixton Devon 6 F8
Brixton Gt Lon 36 H5
Brixton Deverill Wilts 20 G7
Brixworth Nhants 60 F6
Brize Norton Oxon 33 Q3
Brize Norton Airport Oxon 33 Q3
Broad Alley Worcs 58 C11
Broad Blunsdon Swindn 33 M6
Broadbottom Tamesd 83 L6
Broadbridge W Susx 15 M5
Broadbridge Heath W Susx 24 D4
Broad Campden Gloucs 47 N7
Broad Carr Calder 90 D7
Broad Chalke Wilts 21 K9
Broad Clough Lancs 89 P6
Broadclyst Devon 9 N5
Broadfield Inver 125 J3
Broadfield Pembks 41 M10
Broadford Highld 145 K3
Broad Ford Kent 26 B4
Broadford Bridge W Susx 24 C6
Broadgairhill Border 117 J8
Broadgrass Green Suffk 64 D9
Broad Green Cambs 63 L8
Broad Green Essex 52 E7
Broad Green Worcs 46 E3
Broad Green Worcs 58 E10
Broadhaugh Border 129 M9
Broad Haven Pembks 40 G8
Broadheath Traffd 82 G7
Broadhembury Devon 10 C4
Broadhempston Devon 7 L5
Broad Hill Cambs 63 J5
Broad Hinton Wilts 33 M9
Broadholme Lincs 85 Q6
Broadland Row E Susx 26 D8
Broadlay Carmth 28 C3
Broad Layings Hants 22 D2
Broadley Essex 51 K9
Broadley Lancs 89 P7
Broadley Moray 158 A5
Broadley Common Essex 51 K9
Broad Marston Worcs 47 M5
Broadmayne Dorset 12 B7
Broad Meadow Staffs 70 E5
Broadmere Hants 22 H5
Broadmoor Gloucs 46 B11
Broadmoor Pembks 41 L9
Broadnymett Devon 8 H4
Broad Oak Carmth 43 L10
Broad Oak Cumb 94 C2
Broadoak Dorset 11 J5
Broad Oak E Susx 25 P6
Broad Oak E Susx 26 D8
Broadoak Gloucs 32 C2
Broad Oak Hants 23 L4
Broad Oak Herefs 45 P10
Broad Oak Kent 39 L9
Broad Oak St Hel 82 B5
Broadoak Wrexhm 69 L3
Broad Road Suffk 65 K6
Broadsands Torbay 7 M7
Broad's Green Essex 51 Q8
Broadstairs Kent 39 Q8
Broadstone BCP 12 H5
Broadstone Mons 31 P4
Broadstone Shrops 57 J7
Broad Street E Susx 26 E8
Broad Street Essex 51 N7
Broad Street Kent 27 K3
Broad Street Kent 38 D10
Broad Street Medway 38 C7
Broad Street Wilts 21 M3
Broad Street Green Essex 52 E10
Broad Town Wilts 33 L9
Broadwas Worcs 46 E3
Broadwater Herts 50 F6
Broadwater W Susx 24 D10
Broadwaters Worcs 58 B9
Broadway Carmth 28 C3
Broadway Carmth 41 Q8
Broadway Pembks 40 G8
Broadway Somset 19 K11
Broadway Suffk 65 M6
Broadway Worcs 47 L7
Broadwell Gloucs 31 Q2
Broadwell Gloucs 47 P9
Broadwell Oxon 33 Q4
Broadwell Warwks 59 Q11
Broadwey Dorset 11 P8
Broadwindsor Dorset 11 J4
Broadwood Kelly Devon 8 F3
Broadwoodwidger Devon 5 Q4
Brobury Herefs 45 L6
Brochel Highld 153 K8
Brochroy Ag & B 139 J11
Brock Lancs 88 G2
Brockamin Worcs 46 E4
Brockbridge Hants 22 H11
Brockdish Norfk 65 J6
Brockencote Worcs 58 C10
Brockenhurst Hants 13 P4
Brocketsbrae S Lans 126 E10
Brockford Green Suffk 64 G8
Brockford Street Suffk 64 G8
Brockhall Nhants 60 D8
Brockhall Village Lancs 89 L3
Brockham Surrey 36 E11
Brockhampton Gloucs 46 H9
Brockhampton Gloucs 47 K10
Brockhampton Hants 15 K5
Brockhampton Herefs 46 A8
Brockhampton Green Dorset 11 Q3
Brockholes Kirk 90 F8
Brockhurst Derbys 84 D8
Brockhurst Warwks 59 Q8
Brocklebank Cumb 101 K2
Brocklesby Lincs 93 K8
Brockley N Som 31 N11
Brockley Suffk 64 A7
Brockley Green Suffk 63 M11
Brockley Green Suffk 64 A11
Brockleymoor Cumb 101 N3
Brockmoor Dudley 58 D7
Brockscombe Devon 8 C5
Brock's Green Hants 22 F2
Brockton Shrops 56 E4
Brockton Shrops 56 E7
Brockton Shrops 57 K6
Brockton Shrops 57 N4
Brockton Staffs 70 E8
Brockweir Gloucs 31 P4
Brockwood Park Hants 22 H9
Brockworth Gloucs 46 G11
Brocton Cnwll 4 G8
Brocton Staffs 70 H11

Brodick – Buttercrambe 261

Brodick N Ayrs 121 K4
Brodie Moray 156 H6
Brodsworth Donc 91 N9
Brogaig Highld 152 H4
Brogborough C Beds 49 Q7
Brokenborough Wilts 32 H7
Broken Cross Ches E 83 J10
Broken Cross Ches W 82 E10
Brokerswood Wilts 20 F4
Bromborough Wirral 81 M8
Brome Suffk 64 G6
Brome Street Suffk 64 H6
Bromeswell Suffk 65 L11
Bromfield Cumb 110 C11
Bromfield Shrops 56 H9
Bromham Bed 61 M10
Bromham Wilts 33 J11
Bromley Barns 91 J11
Bromley Dudley 58 D7
Bromley Gt Lon 37 K7
Bromley Shrops 57 N5
Bromley Common Gt Lon 37 K7
Bromley Cross Bolton 89 L8
Bromley Cross Essex 53 J6
Bromley Green Kent 26 G4
Bromlow Shrops 56 E4
Brompton Medway 38 C8
Brompton N York 104 C11
Brompton-by-Sawdon N York 99 J4
Brompton-on-Swale N York 103 P11
Brompton Ralph Somset 18 E8
Brompton Regis Somset 18 C8
Bromsash Herefs 46 C10
Bromsberrow Gloucs 46 D8
Bromsberrow Heath Gloucs 46 D8
Bromsgrove Worcs 58 E10
Bromstead Heath Staffs 70 D11
Bromyard Herefs 46 C4
Bromyard Downs Herefs 46 C3
Bronaber Gwynd 67 N8
Bronant Cerdgn 54 E11
Broncroft Shrops 57 J7
Brongest Cerdgn 42 F5
Bronington Wrexhm 69 N7
Bronllys Powys 44 G8
Bronwydd Carmth 42 H10
Bronydd Powys 45 J5
Bronygarth Shrops 69 J7
Brook Carmth 41 Q9
Brook Hants 13 N2
Brook Hants 22 B9
Brook IoW 14 C10
Brook Kent 27 J3
Brook Surrey 23 P7
Brook Surrey 36 C11
Brooke Norfk 65 K2
Brooke Rutlnd 73 L9
Brookenby Lincs 93 M11
Brook End Bed 61 N8
Brook End C Beds 61 Q11
Brook End Cambs 61 N6
Brook End M Keyn 49 P6
Brookfield Rens 125 L5
Brookhampton Oxon 34 H5
Brookhampton Somset 20 B9
Brook Hill Hants 13 N2
Brook House Denbgs 80 F11
Brookhouse Lancs 95 L8
Brookhouse Rothm 84 H3
Brookhouse Green Ches E 70 E2
Brookhouses Derbys 83 M7
Brookland Kent 26 G6
Brooklands Traffd 82 G6
Brookmans Park Herts 50 F10
Brooks Powys 55 Q5
Brooksby Leics 72 H7
Brooks End Kent 39 N8
Brooks Green W Susx 24 D6
Brook Street Essex 37 N2
Brook Street Kent 26 F5
Brook Street Suffk 52 D2
Brook Street W Susx 24 H5
Brookthorpe Gloucs 32 F2
Brookville Norfk 75 P11
Brookwood Surrey 23 Q3
Broom C Beds 50 E2
Broom Rothm 84 F2
Broom Warwks 47 L4
Broombank Worcs 57 M10
Broome Norfk 65 M3
Broome Shrops 56 G8
Broome Worcs 58 D9
Broomedge Warrtn 82 F7
Broome Park Nthumb 119 M8
Broomer's Corner W Susx 24 D6
Broomershill W Susx 24 C7
Broomfield Essex 52 B9
Broomfield Kent 38 D11
Broomfield Kent 39 L8
Broomfield Somset 18 H8
Broomfields Shrops 69 M11
Broomfleet E R Yk 92 E5
Broom Green Norfk 76 D7
Broomhall W & M 35 Q11
Broomhaugh Nthumb 112 F8
Broom Hill Barns 91 L10
Broom Hill Dorset 12 H4
Broom Hill Notts 84 H11
Broomhill Nthumb 119 P10
Broom Hill Worcs 58 D9
Broomhill Green Ches E 70 A5
Broomley Nthumb 112 F8
Broompark Dur 103 P2
Broom's Green Gloucs 46 D8
Broomsthorpe Norfk 76 A6
Broom Street Kent 38 H9
Brora Highld 163 L6
Broseley Shrops 57 M4
Brotherhouse Bar Lincs 74 E8
Brotherlee Dur 102 H3
Brothertoft Lincs 87 J11
Brotherton N York 91 M5
Brotton R & Cl 105 J7
Broubster Highld 166 H5
Brough Cumb 102 E8
Brough Derbys 83 Q8
Brough E R Yk 92 F5
Brough Highld 167 M2
Brough Notts 85 P9
Brough Shet 169 s7
Broughall Shrops 69 Q6
Brough Lodge Shet 169 s4
Brough Sowerby Cumb 102 E8
Broughton Border 116 G3
Broughton Bucks 35 M2
Broughton Cambs 62 C5
Broughton Flints 69 K2
Broughton Hants 22 B8
Broughton Lancs 88 G4
Broughton M Keyn 49 N7
Broughton N Linc 92 G9
Broughton N York 96 D10
Broughton N York 98 F6
Broughton Nhants 60 H5
Broughton Oxon 48 D7
Broughton Salfd 82 H4
Broughton Staffs 70 D8
Broughton V Glam 29 P10
Broughton Astley Leics 60 B2
Broughton Beck Cumb 94 F4
Broughton Gifford Wilts 20 G2
Broughton Green Worcs 47 J2
Broughton Hackett Worcs 46 H4
Broughton-in-Furness Cumb 94 E3
Broughton Mains D & G 107 N8
Broughton Mills Cumb 94 E2
Broughton Moor Cumb 100 E4
Broughton Poggs Oxon 33 P4
Broughton Tower Cumb 94 E3
Broughty Ferry C Dund 142 H11
Brough with St Giles N York 103 P11
Brow End Cumb 94 F6
Brownber Cumb 102 D9
Brown Candover Hants 22 G7
Brown Edge Lancs 88 D8
Brown Edge Staffs 70 G4
Brown Heath Ches W 69 N2
Brownheath Shrops 69 N9
Brownhill Abers 159 L9
Brownhills Fife 135 N4
Brownhills Wsall 58 F3
Brownieside Nthumb 119 N6
Browninghill Green Hants 22 G3
Brown Lees Staffs 70 F3
Brownlow Heath Ches E 70 E2
Brownrigg Cumb 100 D6
Brownrigg Cumb 110 C10
Brownsea Island Dorset 12 H7
Brown's Green Birm 58 G6
Brownsham Devon 16 D6
Browns Hill Gloucs 32 G4
Brownsover Warwks 60 B5
Brownston Devon 6 H8
Brown Street Suffk 64 F9
Browston Green Norfk 77 P11
Broxa N York 99 J2
Broxbourne Herts 51 J9
Broxburn E Loth 128 H4
Broxburn W Loth 127 K3
Broxfield Nthumb 119 P7
Broxted Essex 51 N5
Broxton Ches W 69 N4
Broyle Side E Susx 25 L8
Bruan Highld 167 P9
Bruar P & K 141 K4
Bruchag Ag & B 124 E6
Bruera Ches W 69 M2
Bruern Abbey Oxon 47 Q10
Bruichladdich Ag & B 122 C7
Bruisyard Suffk 65 L8
Bruisyard Street Suffk 65 L8
Brumby N Linc 92 E9
Brund Staffs 71 L2
Brundall Norfk 77 L10
Brundish Suffk 65 K8
Brundish Street Suffk 65 K7
Brunery Highld 138 C3
Brunnion Cnwll 2 E6
Brunslow Shrops 56 F8
Brunswick Village N u Ty 113 K6
Bruntcliffe Leeds 90 H5
Brunthwaite C Brad 96 G11
Bruntingthorpe Leics 60 D3
Brunton Fife 135 J3
Brunton Nthumb 119 P6
Brunton Wilts 21 P3
Brushford Devon 17 M10
Brushford Somset 18 B9
Bruton Somset 20 C7
Bryan's Green Worcs 58 C11
Bryanston Dorset 12 E3
Bryant's Bottom Bucks 35 N5
Brydekirk D & G 110 C6
Bryher IoS 2 b2
Brymbo Wrexhm 69 J4
Brympton Somset 19 P11
Bryn Carmth 28 F4
Bryn Ches W 82 D10
Bryn Neath 29 M6
Bryn Shrops 56 D7
Bryn Wigan 82 C4
Brynamman Carmth 29 K2
Brynberian Pembks 41 M3
Brynbryddan Neath 29 L6
Bryn Bwbach Gwynd 67 L7
Bryncae Rhondd 30 C8
Bryncethin Brdgnd 29 P8
Bryncir Gwynd 66 H6
Bryn-côch Neath 29 K5
Bryncroes Gwynd 66 C8
Bryncrug Gwynd 54 E4
Bryn Du IoA 78 E10
Bryn-Eden Gwynd 67 N9
Bryneglwys Denbgs 68 F5
Brynfields Wrexhm 69 K6
Brynford Flints 80 H10
Bryn Gates Wigan 82 C4
Bryn Golau Rhondd 30 D7
Bryngwran IoA 78 F9
Bryngwyn Mons 31 L3
Bryngwyn Powys 44 H5
Bryn-Henllan Pembks 41 K3
Brynhoffnant Cerdgn 42 F4
Bryning Lancs 88 E5
Brynithel Blae G 30 H4
Brynmawr Blae G 30 G2
Bryn-mawr Gwynd 66 C8
Brynmenyn Brdgnd 29 P8
Brynmill Swans 28 H6
Brynna Rhondd 30 C8
Brynnau Gwynion Rhondd 30 C8
Bryn-penarth Powys 55 Q4
Brynrefail Gwynd 67 K2
Brynrefail IoA 78 H7
Brynsadler Rhondd 30 D8
Bryn Saith Marchog Denbgs 68 E4
Brynsiencyn IoA 78 H11
Brynteg IoA 78 H8
Bryn-y-bal Flints 69 J2
Bryn-y-Maen Conwy 79 Q9
Bryn-yr-Eos Wrexhm 69 J6
Bualintur Highld 144 F3
Buarth-draw Flints 80 H9
Bubbenhall Warwks 59 N10
Bubwith E R Yk 92 B3
Buccleuch Border 117 L8
Buchanan Smithy Stirlg 132 F10
Buchanhaven Abers 159 R8
Buchanty P & K 133 Q2
Buchany Stirlg 133 L7
Buchlyvie Stirlg 132 H9
Buckabank Cumb 110 G11
Buckden Cambs 61 Q7
Buckden N York 96 D5
Buckenham Norfk 77 M10
Buckerell Devon 10 C4
Buckfast Devon 7 J5
Buckfastleigh Devon 7 J5
Buckhaven Fife 135 K8
Buckholt Mons 45 Q11
Buckhorn Devon 5 P2
Buckhorn Weston Dorset 20 E10
Buckhurst Hill Essex 37 K2
Buckie Moray 158 B4
Buckingham Bucks 49 J8
Buckland Bucks 35 N2
Buckland Devon 6 H10
Buckland Gloucs 47 L7
Buckland Hants 13 P5
Buckland Herts 51 J4
Buckland Kent 27 P3
Buckland Oxon 34 B5
Buckland Surrey 36 F10
Buckland Brewer Devon 16 G7
Buckland Common Bucks 35 P3
Buckland Dinham Somset 20 E4
Buckland Filleigh Devon 16 H10
Buckland in the Moor Devon 7 J4
Buckland Monachorum Devon 6 D5
Buckland Newton Dorset 11 P3
Buckland Ripers Dorset 11 P8
Buckland St Mary Somset 10 F2
Buckland-Tout-Saints Devon 7 K9
Bucklebury W Berk 34 G10
Bucklers Hard Hants 14 D6
Bucklesham Suffk 53 M3
Buckley Flints 69 J2
Buckley Green Warwks 59 J11
Bucklow Hill Ches E 82 F8
Buckminster Leics 73 M6
Bucknall C Stke 70 G5
Bucknall Lincs 86 G7
Bucknell Oxon 48 G9
Bucknell Shrops 56 F10
Buckpool Moray 158 B4
Bucksburn C Aber 151 M6
Buck's Cross Devon 16 F7
Bucks Green W Susx 24 C4
Buckshaw Village Lancs 88 H6
Bucks Hill Herts 50 C10
Bucks Horn Oak Hants 23 M6
Buck's Mills Devon 16 F7
Buckton E R Yk 99 P6
Buckton Herefs 56 F10
Buckton Nthumb 119 L3
Buckworth Cambs 61 P5
Budby Notts 85 K7
Buddileigh Staffs 70 C5
Bude Cnwll 16 C10
Budge's Shop Cnwll 5 N10
Budlake Devon 9 N4
Budle Nthumb 119 N3
Budleigh Salterton Devon 9 Q8
Budlett's Common E Susx 25 L6
Budock Water Cnwll 3 K7
Buerton Ches E 70 B6
Bugbrooke Nhants 60 E9
Bugford Devon 7 L8
Buglawton Ches E 70 F2
Bugle Cnwll 4 G10
Bugley Dorset 20 E10
Bugthorpe E R Yk 98 F9
Buildwas Shrops 57 L4
Builth Road Powys 44 E4
Builth Wells Powys 44 E4
Bulbourne Herts 35 P2
Bulbridge Wilts 21 L8
Bulby Lincs 73 R5
Bulcote Notts 72 H2
Bulford Wilts 21 N6
Bulford Camp Wilts 21 N6
Bulkeley Ches E 69 P4
Bulkington Warwks 59 N7
Bulkington Wilts 20 H3
Bulkworthy Devon 16 F9
Bullamoor N York 97 N2
Bull Bay IoA 78 G6
Bullbridge Derbys 84 E10
Bullbrook Br For 35 N11
Bullen's Green Herts 50 F9
Bulley Gloucs 46 E11
Bullgill Cumb 100 E3
Bullingham Herefs 45 Q7
Bullinghope Herefs 45 Q7
Bullington Hants 22 E6
Bullington Lincs 86 E5
Bullockstone Kent 39 L8
Bull's Green Herts 50 G7
Bull's Green Norfk 65 N3
Bulmer Essex 52 D3
Bulmer N York 98 D7
Bulmer Tye Essex 52 D4
Bulphan Thurr 37 P3
Bulstone Devon 10 D7
Bulstrode Herts 50 B10
Bulverhythe E Susx 26 C10
Bulwark Abers 159 M8
Bulwell C Nott 72 E2
Bulwick Nhants 61 L2
Bumble's Green Essex 51 K9
Bunacaimb Highld 145 L10
Bunarkaig Highld 146 F10
Bunbury Ches E 69 Q3
Bunbury Heath Ches E 69 Q3
Bunchrew Highld 155 R8
Buncton W Susx 24 D8
Bundalloch Highld 145 Q2
Bunessan Ag & B 137 K11
Bungay Suffk 65 L4
Bunker's Hill Lincs 87 J10
Bunnahabhain Ag & B 122 F5
Bunny Notts 72 F5
Buntait Highld 155 M11
Buntingford Herts 51 J5
Bunwell Norfk 64 G3
Bunwell Hill Norfk 64 G3
Bupton Derbys 71 N7
Burbage Derbys 83 M10
Burbage Leics 59 P6
Burbage Wilts 21 P2
Burcher Herefs 45 L2
Burchett's Green W & M 35 M8
Burcombe Wilts 21 L8
Burcot Oxon 34 G5
Burcot Worcs 58 E10
Burcote Shrops 57 N5
Burcott Bucks 49 M11
Burcott Bucks 49 N10
Burdale N York 98 H8
Bures Essex 52 F5
Burford Oxon 33 Q2
Burford Shrops 57 K11
Burg Ag & B 137 K6
Burgate Suffk 64 F6
Burgates Hants 23 L9
Burge End Herts 50 D4
Burgess Hill W Susx 24 H7
Burgh Suffk 65 J11
Burgh by Sands Cumb 110 F9
Burgh Castle Norfk 77 P10
Burghclere Hants 22 E2
Burghead Moray 157 L4
Burghfield W Berk 35 J11
Burghfield Common W Berk 35 J11
Burgh Heath Surrey 36 F9
Burgh Hill E Susx 26 B6
Burghill Herefs 45 P6
Burgh Island Devon 6 G10
Burgh le Marsh Lincs 87 P7
Burgh next Aylsham Norfk 77 J6
Burgh on Bain Lincs 86 H3
Burgh St Margaret Norfk 77 N9
Burgh St Peter Norfk 65 P3
Burghwallis Donc 91 N8
Burham Kent 38 B9
Buriton Hants 23 K11
Burland Ches E 69 R4
Burlawn Cnwll 4 F7
Burleigh Gloucs 32 G4
Burlescombe Devon 18 E11
Burleston Dorset 12 C6
Burlestone Devon 7 L9
Burley Hants 13 M4
Burley Rutlnd 73 M8
Burley Shrops 56 H8
Burleydam Ches E 69 R6
Burley Gate Herefs 46 A5
Burley in Wharfedale C Brad 97 J11
Burley Lawn Hants 13 M4
Burley Street Hants 13 M4
Burley Wood Head C Brad 90 F2
Burlingham Green Norfk 77 M9
Burlingjobb Powys 45 K3
Burlington Shrops 57 P2
Burlton Shrops 69 N9
Burmarsh Kent 27 K5
Burmington Warwks 47 Q7
Burn N York 91 P5
Burnage Manch 83 J6
Burnaston Derbys 71 P8
Burnbanks Cumb 101 P7
Burnbrae N Lans 126 F6
Burn Bridge N York 97 L10
Burnby E R Yk 98 G11
Burn Cross Sheff 91 J11
Burndell W Susx 15 Q6
Burnden Bolton 89 L9
Burnedge Rochdl 89 Q8
Burneside Cumb 101 P11
Burneston N York 97 M4
Burnett BaNES 32 C11
Burnfoot Border 117 N8
Burnfoot Border 117 Q7
Burnfoot D & G 109 L2
Burnfoot D & G 110 F3
Burnfoot D & G 117 M11
Burnfoot P & K 134 B7
Burnham Bucks 35 P8
Burnham N Linc 93 J7
Burnham Deepdale Norfk 75 R2
Burnham Green Herts 50 G7
Burnham Market Norfk 76 A3
Burnham Norton Norfk 76 A3
Burnham-on-Crouch Essex 38 F2
Burnham-on-Sea Somset 19 K5
Burnham Overy Norfk 76 A3
Burnham Overy Staithe Norfk 76 A3
Burnham Thorpe Norfk 76 B3
Burnhead D & G 116 B11
Burnhervie Abers 151 J4
Burnhill Green Staffs 57 P4
Burnhope Dur 113 J11
Burnhouse N Ayrs 125 K7
Burniston N York 99 L2
Burnley Lancs 89 N4
Burnmouth Border 129 P7
Burn Naze Lancs 88 C2
Burn of Cambus Stirlg 133 L7
Burnopfield Dur 113 J9
Burnrigg Cumb 111 J9
Burnsall N York 96 F8
Burnside Angus 142 G6
Burnside Angus 143 J7
Burnside Fife 134 F6
Burnside Moray 157 M4
Burnside W Loth 127 K2
Burnside of Duntrune Angus 142 G11
Burntcommon Surrey 36 B10
Burntheath Derbys 71 N8
Burnt Heath Essex 53 J6
Burnt Hill W Berk 34 G10
Burnthouse Cnwll 3 K6
Burnt Houses Dur 103 M6
Burntisland Fife 134 G10
Burnt Oak E Susx 25 M5
Burnton E Ayrs 115 J6
Burntwood Staffs 58 G3
Burntwood Flints 69 J2
Burntwood Green Staffs 58 G3
Burnt Yates N York 97 L8
Burnworthy Somset 18 G11
Burpham Surrey 36 B10
Burpham W Susx 24 B9
Burradon N Tyne 113 L6
Burradon Nthumb 119 J9
Burrafirth Shet 169 t2
Burras Cnwll 2 H7
Burraton Cnwll 5 Q8
Burravoe Shet 169 s5
Burray Village Ork 169 d7
Burrells Cumb 102 C7
Burrelton P & K 142 C10
Burridge Devon 10 G3
Burridge Devon 17 K4
Burridge Hants 14 F4
Burrill N York 97 K3
Burringham N Linc 92 D9
Burrington Devon 17 L8
Burrington Herefs 56 G10
Burrington N Som 19 N3
Burrough End Cambs 63 K9
Burrough Green Cambs 63 K9
Burrough on the Hill Leics 73 K8
Burrow Lancs 95 N6
Burrow Somset 18 B6
Burrow Bridge Somset 19 L8
Burrowhill Surrey 23 Q2
Burrows Cross Surrey 36 C11
Burry Swans 28 E6
Burry Green Swans 28 E6
Burry Port Carmth 28 D4
Burscough Lancs 88 E8
Burscough Bridge Lancs 88 E8
Bursea E R Yk 92 D4
Burshill E R Yk 99 M11
Bursledon Hants 14 E5
Burslem C Stke 70 F5
Burstall Suffk 53 J3
Burstock Dorset 11 J4
Burston Norfk 64 G5
Burston Staffs 70 G8
Burstow Surrey 24 H2
Burstwick E R Yk 93 M5
Burtersett N York 96 C3
Burtholme Cumb 111 K8
Burthorpe Green Suffk 63 N8
Burthwaite Cumb 110 H11
Burthy Cnwll 4 E10
Burtle Somset 19 L6
Burtle Hill Somset 19 L6
Burtoft Lincs 74 E3
Burton BCP 13 L6
Burton Ches W 69 P2
Burton Ches W 81 L10
Burton Dorset 11 P6
Burton Nthumb 119 N4
Burton Pembks 41 J9
Burton Somset 11 L2
Burton Somset 18 G6
Burton Wilts 20 F8
Burton Wilts 32 F9
Burton Agnes E R Yk 99 N8
Burton Bradstock Dorset 11 K7
Burton-by-Lincoln Lincs 86 C6
Burton Coggles Lincs 73 P5
Burton Dassett Warwks 48 C4
Burton End Essex 51 M6
Burton End Suffk 63 L11
Burton Fleming E R Yk 99 M6
Burton Green Warwks 59 L9
Burton Green Wrexhm 69 K3
Burton Hastings Warwks 59 P7
Burton Hill Wilts 32 H7
Burton-in-Kendal Cumb 95 L5
Burton-in-Kendal Services Cumb 95 L5
Burton in Lonsdale N York 95 P6
Burton Joyce Notts 72 G2
Burton Latimer Nhants 61 K6
Burton Lazars Leics 73 K7
Burton Leonard N York 97 M8
Burton on the Wolds Leics 72 F6
Burton Overy Leics 72 H11
Burton Pedwardine Lincs 74 B2
Burton Pidsea E R Yk 93 M4
Burton Salmon N York 91 M5
Burton's Green Essex 52 D6
Burton upon Stather N Linc 92 E7
Burton upon Trent Staffs 71 N10
Burton Waters Lincs 86 B6
Burtonwood Warrtn 82 C6
Burtonwood Services Warrtn 82 C6
Burwardsley Ches W 69 P3
Burwarton Shrops 57 L7
Burwash E Susx 25 Q6
Burwash Common E Susx 25 P6
Burwash Weald E Susx 25 Q6
Burwell Cambs 63 J7
Burwell Lincs 87 L5
Burwen IoA 78 G6
Burwick Ork 169 d8
Bury Bury 89 N8
Bury Cambs 62 C4
Bury Somset 18 B9
Bury W Susx 24 B8
Bury End C Beds 50 D3
Bury Green Herts 51 L6
Bury St Edmunds Suffk 64 B9
Burythorpe N York 98 F8
Busby E Rens 125 P6
Busby Stoop N York 97 N4
Buscot Oxon 33 P5
Bush Abers 143 P4
Bush Cnwll 16 C10
Bush Bank Herefs 45 P4
Bushbury Wolves 58 D4
Bushby Leics 72 H10
Bushey Herts 50 D11
Bushey Heath Herts 36 D2
Bush Green Norfk 65 J4
Bush Green Suffk 64 C10
Bush Hill Park Gt Lon 50 H11
Bushley Worcs 46 G8
Bushley Green Worcs 46 G8
Bushmead Bed 61 P8
Bushmoor Shrops 56 G7
Bushton Wilts 33 L9
Busk Cumb 102 B2
Buslingthorpe Lincs 86 E3
Bussage Gloucs 32 G4
Bussex Somset 19 L7
Butcher's Cross E Susx 25 N5
Butcombe N Som 19 P2
Bute Ag & B 124 C4
Butleigh Somset 19 P8
Butleigh Wootton Somset 19 P7
Butler's Cross Bucks 35 M3
Butler's Hill Notts 84 H11
Butlers Marston Warwks 48 B4
Butley Suffk 65 M11
Butley High Corner Suffk 53 Q2
Buttercrambe N York 98 E9

Butterdean Border 129 K7
Butterknowle Dur 103 M5
Butterleigh Devon 9 L3
Butterley Derbys 84 F10
Buttermere Cumb 100 G7
Buttermere Wilts 22 B2
Butters Green Staffs 70 E4
Buttershaw C Brad 90 E5
Butterstone P & K 141 Q8
Butterton Staffs 70 E6
Butterton Staffs 71 K3
Butterwick Dur 104 C4
Butterwick Lincs 87 L11
Butterwick N York 98 E5
Butterwick N York 99 K6
Butt Green Ches E 70 B4
Buttington Powys 56 C3
Buttonbridge Shrops 57 N9
Buttonoak Shrops 57 P9
Buttsash Hants 14 D5
Buttsbear Cross Cnwll 16 D11
Butt's Green Essex 52 C11
Buxhall Suffk 64 E10
Buxhall Fen Street Suffk 64 E10
Buxted E Susx 25 L6
Buxton Derbys 83 N10
Buxton Norfk 77 J7
Buxton Heath Norfk 76 H7
Buxworth Derbys 83 M8
Bwlch Powys 44 H10
Bwlchgwyn Wrexhm 69 J4
Bwlchllan Cerdgn 43 L3
Bwlchnewydd Carmth 42 G10
Bwlchtocyn Gwynd 66 E9
Bwlch-y-cibau Powys 68 G11
Bwlch-y-Ddar Powys 68 G10
Bwlchyfadfa Cerdgn 42 H5
Bwlch-y-ffridd Powys 55 P5
Bwlch-y-groes Pembks 41 P3
Bwlchymyrdd Swans 28 G5
Bwlch-y-sarnau Powys 55 N10
Byermoor Gatesd 113 J9
Byers Green Dur 103 P4
Byfield Nhants 48 F4
Byfleet Surrey 36 C8
Byford Herefs 45 M6
Bygrave Herts 50 G3
Byker N u Ty 113 L8
Byland Abbey N York 98 A5
Bylaugh Norfk 76 E8
Bylchau Conwy 68 C2
Byley Ches W 82 F11
Bynea Carmth 28 F5
Byram N York 91 M5
Byrness Nthumb 118 C10
Bystock Devon 9 P8
Bythorn Cambs 61 N5
Byton Herefs 45 M2
Bywell Nthumb 112 F8
Byworth W Susx 23 Q10

C

Cabbacott Devon 16 G7
Cabourne Lincs 93 K10
Cabrach Ag & B 122 G2
Cabrach Moray 150 B2
Cabus Lancs 95 K11
Cackle Street E Susx 25 L5
Cackle Street E Susx 25 Q7
Cackle Street E Susx 26 D8
Cadbury Devon 9 M3
Cadbury Barton Devon 17 M8
Cadbury World Birm 58 F8
Cadder E Duns 125 Q3
Caddington C Beds 50 C7
Caddonfoot Border 117 P3
Cadeby Donc 91 N10
Cadeby Leics 72 C10
Cadeleigh Devon 9 M3
Cade Street E Susx 25 P6
Cadgwith Cnwll 3 J11
Cadham Fife 134 H7
Cadishead Salfd 82 F6
Cadle Swans 28 H5
Cadley Lancs 88 G4
Cadley Wilts 21 P4
Cadley Wilts 33 P11
Cadmore End Bucks 35 L6
Cadnam Hants 13 P2
Cadney N Linc 92 H10
Cadole Flints 68 H2
Cadoxton V Glam 30 F11
Cadoxton Juxta-Neath
Neath 29 L5
Cadwst Denbgs 68 D7
Caeathro Gwynd 67 J2
Caehopkin Powys 29 M2
Caenby Lincs 86 C3
Caerau Brdgnd 29 N6
Caerau Cardif 30 F9
Cae'r-bont Powys 29 M2
Cae'r bryn Carmth 28 G2
Caerdeon Gwynd 67 M11
Caer Farchell Pembks 40 E5
Caergeiliog IoA 78 E9
Caergwrle Flints 69 K3
Caerhun Conwy 79 P10
Caerlanrig Border 117 M10
Caerleon Newpt 31 K6
Caernarfon Gwynd 66 H2
Caernarfon Castle Gwynd 66 H2
Caerphilly Caerph 30 G7
Caersws Powys 55 N6
Caerwedros Cerdgn 42 G3
Caerwent Mons 31 N6
Caerwys Flints 80 G10
Caerynwch Gwynd 67 P11
Caggle Street Mons 45 M11
Caim IoA 79 L8
Caio Carmth 43 N7
Cairinis W Isls 168 d11
Cairnbaan Ag & B 130 G9
Cairnbulg Abers 159 P4
Cairncross Border 129 M7
Cairncurran Inver 125 J3
Cairndow Ag & B 131 P5
Cairneyhill Fife 134 C10
Cairngarroch D & G 106 E8
Cairngorms National Park 149 K7
Cairnie Abers 158 C9
Cairnorrie Abers 159 L9
Cairnryan D & G 106 K4
Cairnty Moray 157 Q7

Caister-on-Sea Norfk 77 Q9
Caistor Lincs 93 K10
Caistor St Edmund Norfk 77 J11
Cakebole Worcs 58 C10
Cake Street Norfk 64 F3
Calais Street Suffk 52 G4
Calanais W Isls 168 h4
Calbourne IoW 14 D9
Calceby Lincs 87 L5
Calcoed Flints 80 H10
Calcot Gloucs 33 L2
Calcot W Berk 35 J10
Calcot Row W Berk 35 J10
Calcots Moray 157 P5
Calcott Kent 39 L9
Calcott Shrops 56 G2
Calcutt Wilts 33 M6
Calcutt N York 97 M9
Caldbeck Cumb 101 K2
Caldbergh N York 96 G3
Caldecote Cambs 61 P3
Caldecote Cambs 62 D9
Caldecote Herts 50 F3
Caldecote Nhants 49 J4
Caldecott Nhants 61 L7
Caldecott Oxon 34 E5
Caldecott Rutlnd 61 J2
Caldecotte M Keyn 49 N7
Calder Cumb 100 D10
Calderbank N Lans 126 D5
Calder Bridge Cumb 100 D9
Calderbrook Rochdl 89 Q7
Caldercruix N Lans 126 E4
Calder Grove Wakefd 91 J7
Caldermill S Lans 126 B9
Calder Vale Lancs 95 L11
Calderwood S Lans 126 B6
Caldey Island Pembks 41 M11
Caldicot Mons 31 N7
Caldmore Wsall 58 F5
Caldwell N York 103 N8
Caldy Wirral 81 J7
Calenick Cnwll 3 L5
Calf of Man IoM 80 a8
Calford Green Suffk 63 M11
Calfsound Ork 169 e3
Calgary Ag & B 137 K5
Califer Moray 157 K6
California Falk 126 G2
California Norfk 77 Q8
California Cross Devon 7 J6
Calke Derbys 72 B6
Calke Abbey Derbys 72 B6
Callakille Highld 153 M6
Callander Stirlg 133 J6
Callanish W Isls 168 h4
Callaughton Shrops 57 M4
Callerton N u Ty 113 J7
Callestick Cnwll 3 K3
Calligarry Highld 145 K7
Callington Cnwll 5 P8
Callingwood Staffs 71 M10
Callow Herefs 45 P8
Callow End Worcs 46 F4
Callow Hill Wilts 33 K8
Callow Hill Worcs 47 K2
Callow Hill Worcs 57 N10
Callows Grave Worcs 57 K11
Calmore Hants 13 P2
Calmsden Gloucs 33 K3
Calne Wilts 33 J10
Calow Derbys 84 F6
Calshot Hants 14 E6
Calstock Cnwll 6 C5
Calstone Wellington
Wilts 33 K11
Calthorpe Norfk 76 H5
Calthorpe Street Norfk 77 N6
Calthwaite Cumb 101 N2
Calton N York 96 D9
Calton Staffs 71 L5
Calveley Ches E 69 Q3
Calver Derbys 84 B6
Calverhall Shrops 69 R7
Calver Hill Herefs 45 M5
Calverleigh Devon 9 M2
Calverley Leeds 90 G3
Calver Sough Derbys 84 B6
Calvert Bucks 49 J10
Calverton M Keyn 49 L7
Calverton Notts 85 K11
Calvine P & K 141 K4
Calvo Cumb 109 P10
Calzeat Border 116 G2
Cam Gloucs 32 E5
Camasachoirce Highld 138 D5
Camasine Highld 138 D5
Camas Luinie Highld 146 A2
Camastianavaig Highld 153 J10
Camault Muir Highld 155 P9
Camber E Susx 26 G8
Camberley Surrey 23 N2
Camberwell Gt Lon 36 H5
Camblesforth N York 91 Q5
Cambo Nthumb 112 H3
Cambois Nthumb 113 M4
Camborne Cnwll 2 G5
Camborne & Redruth
Mining District Cnwll 2 G5
Cambourne Cambs 62 D9
Cambridge Cambs 62 G9
Cambridge Gloucs 32 D4
Cambridge Airport Cambs 62 G9
Cambrose Cnwll 2 H4
Cambus Clacks 133 P9
Cambusavie Highld 162 H7
Cambusbarron Stirlg 133 M9
Cambuskenneth Stirlg 133 N9
Cambuslang S Lans 125 Q5
Cambus o' May Abers 150 C8
Cambuswallace S Lans 116 E3
Camden Town Gt Lon 36 G4
Cameley BaNES 20 B3
Camelford Cnwll 5 J3
Camelon Falk 133 P10
Camer's Green Worcs 46 E7
Camerton BaNES 20 C3
Camerton Cumb 100 D4
Camghouran P & K 140 E6
Camieston Border 117 R4
Cammachmore Abers 151 N8
Cammeringham Lincs 86 B4
Camore Highld 162 H7
Campbeltown Ag & B 120 D7

Campbeltown Airport
Ag & B 120 C7
Camperdown N Tyne 113 L6
Cample D & G 109 J2
Campmuir P & K 142 C10
Camps W Loth 127 K4
Campsall Donc 91 N8
Campsea Ash Suffk 65 L10
Camps End Cambs 51 P2
Campton C Beds 50 D3
Camptown Border 118 C8
Camrose Pembks 40 H6
Camserney P & K 141 K8
Camusnagaul Highld 139 K3
Camusnagaul Highld 160 H9
Camusteel Highld 153 N9
Camusterrach Highld 153 N9
Canada Hants 21 Q11
Canal Foot Cumb 94 G5
Canaston Bridge Pembks 41 L7
Candacraig Abers 149 Q8
Candlesby Lincs 87 N7
Candle Street Suffk 64 E7
Candover Green Shrops 57 J3
Candy Mill Border 116 F2
Cane End Oxon 35 J9
Canewdon Essex 38 F3
Canford Bottom Dorset 12 H4
Canford Cliffs BCP 13 J7
Canford Heath BCP 12 H6
Canford Magna BCP 12 H5
Canhams Green Suffk 64 F8
Canisbay Highld 167 P2
Canklow Rothm 84 F2
Canley Covtry 59 M9
Cann Dorset 20 G10
Canna Highld 144 B6
Cann Common Dorset 20 G10
Cannich Highld 155 K11
Cannington Somset 19 J7
Canning Town Gt Lon 37 K4
Cannock Staffs 58 E2
Cannock Chase Staffs 70 H11
Cannock Wood Staffs 58 F2
Cannon Bridge Herefs 45 N6
Canon Frome Herefs 46 B6
Canon Pyon Herefs 45 P5
Canons Ashby Nhants 48 G4
Canonstown Cnwll 2 E6
Canterbury Kent 39 L10
Canterbury Cathedral Kent 39 L10
Cantley Norfk 77 M11
Cantlop Shrops 57 J3
Canton Cardif 30 G9
Cantraywood Highld 156 D8
Cantsfield Lancs 95 N6
Canvey Island Essex 38 C5
Canwick Lincs 86 C7
Canworthy Water Cnwll 5 L3
Caol Highld 139 L2
Caolas Scalpaigh W Isls 168 h8
Caoles Ag & B 136 D6
Caonich Highld 146 D9
Capel Kent 25 P2
Capel Surrey 24 E2
Capel Bangor Cerdgn 54 F8
Capel Betws Lleucu Cerdgn 43 M3
Capel Coch IoA 78 H8
Capel Curig Conwy 67 N3
Capel Cynon Cerdgn 42 G5
Capel Dewi Carmth 43 J10
Capel Dewi Cerdgn 43 J6
Capel-Dewi Cerdgn 54 E8
Capel Garmon Conwy 67 Q3
Capel Green Suffk 53 Q2
Capel Gwyn Carmth 43 J10
Capel Gwyn IoA 78 E9
Capel Gwynfe Carmth 43 P10
Capel Hendre Carmth 28 G2
Capel Isaac Carmth 43 L9
Capel Iwan Carmth 41 Q3
Capel-le-Ferne Kent 27 N4
Capelles Guern 10 c1
Capel Llanilltern Cardif 30 E9
Capel Mawr IoA 78 G10
Capel Parc IoA 78 G7
Capel St Andrew Suffk 53 Q2
Capel St Mary Suffk 53 J4
Capel Seion Cerdgn 54 E9
Capel Trisant Cerdgn 54 G9
Capeluchaf Gwynd 66 G5
Capelulo Conwy 79 N9
Capel-y-ffin Powys 45 K8
Capel-y-graig Gwynd 79 J11
Capenhurst Ches W 81 M10
Capernwray Lancs 95 L6
Cape Wrath Highld 164 G1
Capheaton Nthumb 112 H4
Caplaw E Rens 125 L6
Capon's Green Suffk 65 K8
Cappercleuch Border 117 J6
Capstone Medway 38 C8
Capton Devon 7 L8
Capton Somset 18 E7
Caputh P & K 141 Q9
Caradon Mining District
Cnwll 5 M7
Caradon Town Cnwll 5 M7
Carbeth Stirlg 125 N2
Carbis Cnwll 4 G10
Carbis Bay Cnwll 2 E6
Carbost Highld 152 F11
Carbost Highld 152 G8
Carbrook Sheff 84 E3
Carbrooke Norfk 76 C11
Carburton Notts 85 K6
Carclaze Cnwll 3 Q3
Car Colston Notts 73 J2
Carcroft Donc 91 N9
Cardenden Fife 134 G8
Cardeston Shrops 56 F2
Cardewlees Cumb 110 G10
Cardiff Cardif 30 G9
Cardiff Airport V Glam 30 E11
Cardiff Gate Services Cardif 30 H8
Cardiff West Services Cardif 30 E9
Cardigan Cerdgn 42 C5
Cardinal's Green Cambs 63 K11
Cardington Bed 61 N11
Cardington Shrops 57 J5
Cardinham Cnwll 5 J8
Cardrain D & G 106 F11
Cardrona Border 117 L3
Cardross Ag & B 125 J2

Cardryne D & G 106 F11
Cardurnock Cumb 110 C9
Careby Lincs 73 Q7
Careston Angus 143 J5
Carew Pembks 41 K10
Carew Cheriton Pembks 41 K10
Carew Newton Pembks 41 K10
Carey Herefs 45 R8
Carfin N Lans 126 D6
Carfraemill Border 128 E9
Cargate Green Norfk 77 M9
Cargenbridge D & G 109 L6
Cargill P & K 142 B10
Cargo Cumb 110 G9
Cargreen Cnwll 6 C6
Cargurrel Cnwll 3 M6
Carham Nthumb 118 E3
Carhampton Somset 18 E6
Carharrack Cnwll 3 J5
Carie P & K 140 F6
Carinish W Isls 168 d11
Carisbrooke IoW 14 E9
Cark Cumb 94 H5
Carkeel Cnwll 5 Q9
Càrlabhagh W Isls 168 h3
Carland Cross Cnwll 3 M3
Carlbury Darltn 103 P7
Carlby Lincs 73 Q8
Carlcroft Nthumb 118 F8
Carlecotes Barns 83 Q4
Carleen Cnwll 2 G7
Carlesmoor N York 97 K6
Carleton Cumb 100 D9
Carleton Cumb 101 P5
Carleton Cumb 110 H10
Carleton Lancs 88 C3
Carleton Wakefd 91 M6
Carleton Forehoe Norfk 76 F10
Carleton-in-Craven N York 96 E11
Carleton Rode Norfk 64 G3
Carleton St Peter Norfk 77 L11
Carlidnack Cnwll 3 K8
Carlincraig Abers 158 G9
Carlingcott BaNES 20 C3
Carlin How R & Cl 105 K7
Carlisle Cumb 110 H9
Carlisle Lake District
Airport Cumb 111 J8
Carloggas Cnwll 4 D8
Carlops Border 127 M6
Carloway W Isls 168 h3
Carlton Barns 91 K8
Carlton Bed 61 L9
Carlton Cambs 63 K10
Carlton Leeds 91 J5
Carlton N York 91 M6
Carlton N York 96 G4
Carlton N York 98 C3
Carlton Notts 72 G2
Carlton S on T 104 C6
Carlton Suffk 65 M9
Carlton Colville Suffk 65 Q4
Carlton Curlieu Leics 72 H11
Carlton Green Cambs 63 K10
Carlton Husthwaite N York 97 Q5
Carlton-in-Cleveland
N York 104 F10
Carlton in Lindrick Notts 85 J4
Carlton-le-Moorland Lincs 86 B9
Carlton Miniott N York 97 N4
Carlton-on-Trent Notts 85 N8
Carlton Scroop Lincs 86 B11
Carluke S Lans 126 E7
Carlyon Bay Cnwll 3 R3
Carmacoup S Lans 115 Q2
Carmarthen Carmth 42 H10
Carmel Carmth 43 L11
Carmel Flints 80 H9
Carmel Gwynd 66 H4
Carmichael S Lans 116 C3
Carmunnock C Glas 125 P6
Carmyle C Glas 125 Q5
Carmyllie Angus 143 J9
Carnaby E R Yk 99 N7
Carnbee Fife 135 N6
Carnbo P & K 134 D7
Carn Brea Cnwll 2 H5
Carnbrogie Abers 151 M2
Carndu Highld 145 Q2
Carnduff S Lans 126 B8
Carne Cnwll 3 K9
Carne Cnwll 3 L7
Carne Cnwll 4 F10
Carnell E Ayrs 125 M11
Carnewas Cnwll 4 D8
Carnforth Lancs 95 K6
Carn-gorm Highld 146 B3
Carnhedryn Pembks 40 F5
Carnhell Green Cnwll 2 G6
Carnie Abers 151 L6
Carnkie Cnwll 2 H5
Carnkie Cnwll 3 J7
Carnkiet Cnwll 3 K3
Carno Powys 55 M5
Carnock Fife 134 C10
Carnon Downs Cnwll 3 K5
Carnousie Abers 158 G7
Carnoustie Angus 143 K11
Carnsmerry Cnwll 4 G10
Carnwath S Lans 126 H8
Carnyorth Cnwll 2 B7
Carol Green Solhll 59 L9
Carpalla Cnwll 3 P3
Carperby N York 96 F3
Carr Rothm 84 H2
Carradale Ag & B 120 F4
Carradale Village Ag & B 120 E4
Carrbridge Highld 148 G3
Carrbrook Tamesd 83 L4
Carrefour Jersey 11 b1
Carreglefn IoA 78 F7
Carr Gate Wakefd 91 J6
Carrhouse N Linc 92 C9
Carrick Ag & B 131 J10
Carrick Castle Ag & B 131 P9
Carriden Falk 134 C11
Carrington Lincs 87 K9
Carrington Mdloth 127 Q5
Carrington Traffd 82 F6
Carrog Conwy 67 P5
Carrog Denbgs 68 F6
Carron Falk 133 P11
Carron Moray 157 N9
Carronbridge D & G 109 B11
Carron Bridge Stirlg 133 L11

Carronshore Falk 133 P11
Carrow Hill Mons 31 M6
Carr Shield Nthumb 112 B11
Carrutherstown D & G 109 P6
Carruth House Inver 125 K4
Carr Vale Derbys 84 G7
Carrville Dur 104 B2
Carsaig Ag & B 137 N11
Carseriggan D & G 107 K4
Carsethorn D & G 109 L9
Carshalton Gt Lon 36 G8
Carsington Derbys 71 P4
Carskey Ag & B 120 C10
Carsluith D & G 107 N7
Carsphairn D & G 115 L9
Carstairs S Lans 126 G8
Carstairs Junction S Lans 126 H8
Carswell Marsh Oxon 34 B5
Carters Green Essex 51 M8
Carterton Oxon 33 Q3
Carterway Heads Nthumb 112 F10
Carthew Cnwll 4 G10
Carthorpe N York 97 M4
Cartington Nthumb 119 K10
Cartland S Lans 126 F8
Cartledge Derbys 84 D5
Cartmel Cumb 94 H5
Cartmel Fell Cumb 95 J3
Carway Carmth 28 E3
Carwinley Cumb 110 H6
Cashe's Green Gloucs 32 F3
Cashmoor Dorset 12 G2
Cassington Oxon 34 E2
Cassop Dur 104 B3
Castallack Cnwll 2 D8
Castel Guern 10 b2
Castell Conwy 79 P11
Castell-y-bwch Torfn 31 J6
Casterton Cumb 95 N5
Castle Cnwll 4 H10
Castle Acre Norfk 75 R7
Castle Ashby Nhants 61 J9
Castlebay W Isls 168 b18
Castle Bolton N York 96 F2
Castle Bromwich Solhll 58 H7
Castle Bytham Lincs 73 P7
Castlebythe Pembks 41 K5
Castle Caereinion Powys 56 B3
Castle Camps Cambs 51 P2
Castle Carrock Cumb 111 K9
Castlecary Falk 126 D2
Castle Cary Somset 20 B8
Castle Combe Wilts 32 F9
Castlecraig Highld 156 E4
Castle Donington Leics 72 C5
Castle Douglas D & G 108 G8
Castle Eaton Swindn 33 M5
Castle Eden Dur 104 D3
Castle End C Pete 74 B9
Castleford Wakefd 91 L5
Castle Frome Herefs 46 C5
Castle Gate Cnwll 2 D7
Castle Green Cumb 95 L2
Castle Green Surrey 23 Q2
Castle Gresley Derbys 71 N11
Castle Hedingham Essex 52 C4
Castlehill Border 117 J3
Castlehill Highld 167 L3
Castle Hill Kent 25 Q2
Castle Hill Suffk 53 K2
Castlehill W Duns 125 K2
Castle Howard N York 98 E6
Castle Kennedy D & G 106 F6
Castle Lachlan Ag & B 131 L8
Castlemartin Pembks 40 H11
Castlemilk C Glas 125 P6
Castle Morris Pembks 40 H4
Castlemorton Worcs 46 E7
Castlemorton Common
Worcs 46 E7
Castle O'er D & G 110 D2
Castle Rising Norfk 75 N6
Castleside Dur 112 G11
Castle Stuart Highld 156 C8
Castlethorpe M Keyn 49 M6
Castlethorpe N Linc 92 G9
Castleton Ag & B 130 H11
Castleton Border 111 K3
Castleton Derbys 83 Q8
Castleton N York 105 J9
Castleton Newpt 31 J8
Castleton Rochdl 89 P8
Castletown Ches W 69 M4
Castletown Dorset 11 P10
Castletown Highld 167 L3
Castletown IoM 80 c8
Castletown Sundld 113 N9
Castley N York 97 L11
Caston Norfk 64 D2
Castor C Pete 74 B11
Caswell Bay Swans 28 G7
Catacol N Ayrs 123 R10
Cat and Fiddle Derbys 83 M10
Catbrain S Glos 31 Q8
Catbrook Mons 31 P4
Catch Flints 81 J10
Catchall Cnwll 2 C8
Catchem's Corner Solhll 59 L9
Catchgate Dur 113 J10
Catcliffe Rothm 84 F3
Catcomb Wilts 33 K9
Catcott Somset 19 L7
Caterham Surrey 36 H9
Catfield Norfk 77 M7
Catfield Common Norfk 77 N7
Catford Gt Lon 37 J6
Catforth Lancs 88 F3
Cathcart C Glas 125 P5
Cathedine Powys 44 G9
Catherine-de-Barnes Solhll 59 J8
Catherine Slack C Brad 90 D5
Catherington Hants 15 J4
Catherston Leweston
Dorset 10 H6
Catherton Shrops 57 M9
Catisfield Hants 14 G5
Catley Herefs 46 C6
Catley Lane Head Rochdl 89 P7
Catlodge Highld 147 Q9
Catlow Lancs 89 P3
Catlowdy Cumb 111 J5
Catmere End Essex 51 L3
Catmore W Berk 34 E8
Caton Devon 7 K4
Caton Lancs 95 L8

Caton Green – Church End 263

Caton Green Lancs 95 M7
Cator Court Devon 8 G9
Catrine E Ayrs 115 K2
Cat's Ash Newpt 31 L6
Catsfield E Susx 26 B9
Catsfield Stream E Susx 26 B9
Catsgore Somset 19 P9
Catsham Somset 19 Q8
Catshill Worcs 58 E10
Catstree Shrops 57 N5
Cattadale Ag & B 120 C9
Cattal N York 97 P10
Cattawade Suffk 53 K5
Catterall Lancs 88 F2
Catteralslane Shrops 69 Q6
Catterick N York 103 P11
Catterick Bridge N York 103 P11
Catterick Garrison N York 103 N11
Catterlen Cumb 101 N4
Catterline Abers 143 R2
Catterton N York 97 R11
Catteshall Surrey 23 Q6
Catthorpe Leics 60 C5
Cattishall Suffk 64 B8
Cattistock Dorset 11 M5
Catton N York 97 N5
Catton Nthumb 112 B9
Catwick E R Yk 99 N11
Catworth Cambs 61 N6
Caudle Green Gloucs 32 H2
Caulcott C Beds 50 B2
Caulcott Oxon 48 F10
Cauldcots Angus 143 M8
Cauldhame Stirlg 133 J9
Cauldmill Border 117 Q7
Cauldon Staffs 71 K5
Cauldon Lowe Staffs 71 K5
Cauldwell Derbys 71 P11
Caulkerbush D & G 109 K9
Caulside D & G 110 H4
Caundle Marsh Dorset 11 P2
Caunsall Worcs 58 C8
Caunton Notts 85 M8
Causeway Hants 23 K10
Causeway End Cumb 95 K3
Causeway End D & G 107 M6
Causeway End Essex 51 Q7
Causewayend S Lans 116 E3
Causewayhead Cumb 109 P10
Causewayhead Stirlg 133 N8
Causeyend Abers 151 N4
Causey Park Nthumb 113 J2
Causey Park Bridge Nthumb 113 J2
Cavendish Suffk 63 P11
Cavenham Suffk 63 N6
Caversfield Oxon 48 G9
Caversham Readg 35 K10
Caverswall Staffs 70 H6
Caverton Mill Border 118 D5
Cavil E R Yk 92 C4
Cawdor Highld 156 E7
Cawkwell Lincs 87 J5
Cawood N York 91 P3
Cawsand Cnwll 6 C8
Cawston Norfk 76 G7
Cawston Warwks 59 Q10
Cawthorn N York 98 F3
Cawthorne Barns 90 H9
Cawton N York 98 C5
Caxton Cambs 62 D9
Caxton End Cambs 62 D9
Caxton Gibbet Cambs 62 C8
Caynham Shrops 57 K10
Caythorpe Lincs 86 B11
Caythorpe Notts 85 L11
Cayton N York 99 M4
Ceannabeinne Highld 165 K3
Ceann a Bhaigh W Isls 168 c11
Ceannacroc Lodge Highld 146 G5
Cearsiadar W Isls 168 i6
Ceciliford Mons 31 P4
Cefn Newpt 31 J7
Cefn Berain Conwy 80 D11
Cefn-brîth Conwy 68 B4
Cefn-bryn-brain Carmth 29 K2
Cefn Byrle Powys 29 M2
Cefn Canel Powys 68 H8
Cefn Coch Powys 68 F9
Cefn-coed-y-cymmer Myr Td 30 D3
Cefn Cribwr Brdgnd 29 N8
Cefn Cross Brdgnd 29 N8
Cefn-ddwysarn Gwynd 68 C7
Cefn-Einion Shrops 56 D7
Cefneithin Carmth 28 G2
Cefngorwydd Powys 44 C5
Cefn-mawr Wrexhm 69 J6
Cefnpennar Rhondd 30 D4
Cefn-y-bedd Flints 69 K3
Cefn-y-pant Carmth 41 N5
Ceint IoA 78 H9
Cellan Cerdgn 43 M5
Cellardyke Fife 135 P7
Cellarhead Staffs 70 H5
Celleron Cumb 101 N5
Celynen Caerph 30 H5
Cemaes IoA 78 F6
Cemmaes Powys 55 J3
Cemmaes Road Powys 55 J4
Cenarth Cerdgn 41 Q2
Cerbyd Pembks 40 F5
Ceres Fife 135 L5
Cerne Abbas Dorset 11 P4
Cerney Wick Gloucs 33 L5
Cerrigceinwen IoA 78 G10
Cerrigydrudion Conwy 68 C5
Cess Norfk 77 N8
Ceunant Gwynd 67 J2
Chaceley Gloucs 46 G8
Chacewater Cnwll 3 K5
Chackmore Bucks 49 J7
Chacombe Nhants 48 E6
Chadbury Worcs 47 K5
Chadderton Oldham 89 Q9
Chadderton Fold Oldham 89 Q9
Chaddesden C Derb 72 B3
Chaddesley Corbett Worcs 58 C10
Chaddlehanger Devon 8 C9
Chaddleworth W Berk 34 D9
Chadlington Oxon 48 B10
Chadshunt Warwks 48 B4
Chadwell Leics 73 K6
Chadwell Shrops 57 P2
Chadwell End Bed 61 N7
Chadwell Heath Gt Lon 37 L3
Chadwell St Mary Thurr 37 P5
Chadwick Worcs 58 B11
Chadwick End Solhll 59 K10
Chadwick Green St Hel 82 B5
Chaffcombe Somset 10 H2
Chafford Hundred Thurr 37 P5
Chagford Devon 8 H7
Chailey E Susx 25 J7
Chainbridge Cambs 74 H10
Chainhurst Kent 26 B2
Chalbury Dorset 12 H3
Chalbury Common Dorset 12 H3
Chaldon Surrey 36 H9
Chaldon Herring Dorset 12 C8
Chale IoW 14 E11
Chale Green IoW 14 E11
Chalfont Common Bucks 36 B2
Chalfont St Giles Bucks 35 Q6
Chalfont St Peter Bucks 36 B2
Chalford Gloucs 32 G4
Chalford Oxon 35 K4
Chalford Wilts 20 G4
Chalgrave C Beds 50 B5
Chalgrove Oxon 34 H5
Chalk Kent 37 Q6
Chalk End Essex 51 P8
Chalkhouse Green Oxon 35 K9
Chalkway Somset 10 H3
Chalkwell Kent 38 E9
Challaborough Devon 6 H10
Challacombe Devon 17 M3
Challoch D & G 107 L4
Challock Kent 38 H11
Chalmington Dorset 11 M4
Chalton C Beds 50 B5
Chalton C Beds 61 P10
Chalton Hants 23 K11
Chalvey Slough 35 Q9
Chalvington E Susx 25 M9
Chambers Green Kent 26 F3
Chandler's Cross Herts 50 C11
Chandlers Cross Worcs 46 E7
Chandler's Ford Hants 22 D11
Channel's End Bed 61 P9
Channel Tunnel Terminal Kent 27 L4
Chantry Somset 20 D5
Chantry Suffk 53 K3
Chapel Cumb 100 H4
Chapel Fife 134 H9
Chapel Allerton Leeds 91 J3
Chapel Allerton Somset 19 M4
Chapel Amble Cnwll 4 F6
Chapel Brampton Nhants 60 F7
Chapelbridge Cambs 62 C2
Chapel Chorlton Staffs 70 E7
Chapel Cross E Susx 25 P6
Chapel End Bed 61 P9
Chapel End C Beds 50 C2
Chapel End Cambs 61 P4
Chapel End Warwks 59 M6
Chapelend Way Essex 52 B4
Chapel-en-le-Frith Derbys 83 N8
Chapel Field Bury 89 M9
Chapelgate Lincs 74 H6
Chapel Green Warwks 48 E2
Chapel Green Warwks 59 L7
Chapel Haddlesey N York 91 P5
Chapelhall N Lans 126 D5
Chapel Hill Abers 159 Q10
Chapel Hill Lincs 86 H10
Chapel Hill Mons 31 P5
Chapel Hill N York 97 M11
Chapelhope Border 117 J7
Chapelknowe D & G 110 F6
Chapel Lawn Shrops 56 E9
Chapel-le-Dale N York 95 Q5
Chapel Leigh Somset 18 F9
Chapel Milton Derbys 83 N8
Chapel of Garioch Abers 151 J3
Chapel Rossan D & G 106 F9
Chapel Row E Susx 25 P8
Chapel Row Essex 52 C11
Chapel Row W Berk 34 G11
Chapels Cumb 94 E4
Chapel St Leonards Lincs 87 Q6
Chapel Stile Cumb 101 K9
Chapelton Abers 151 M9
Chapelton Angus 143 L8
Chapelton Devon 17 K6
Chapelton S Lans 126 B8
Chapeltown Bl w D 89 L7
Chapel Town Cnwll 4 D10
Chapeltown Moray 149 N3
Chapeltown Sheff 91 K11
Chapmanslade Wilts 20 F5
Chapmans Well Devon 5 P3
Chapmore End Herts 50 H7
Chappel Essex 52 E6
Charaton Cnwll 5 N8
Chard Somset 10 G3
Chard Junction Somset 10 G4
Chardleigh Green Somset 10 G2
Chardstock Devon 10 G4
Charfield S Glos 32 D6
Chargrove Gloucs 46 H11
Charing Kent 26 G2
Charing Heath Kent 26 F2
Charing Hill Kent 38 G11
Charingworth Gloucs 47 N7
Charlbury Oxon 48 C11
Charlcombe BaNES 32 D11
Charlcutt Wilts 33 J9
Charlecote Warwks 47 Q3
Charlemont Sandw 58 F6
Charles Devon 17 M5
Charleshill Surrey 23 N6
Charleston Angus 142 F8
Charlestown C Aber 151 N7
Charlestown C Brad 90 F3
Charlestown Calder 90 B5
Charlestown Cnwll 3 Q3
Charlestown Cnwll 3 Q3
Charlestown Derbys 83 M6
Charlestown Dorset 11 P9
Charlestown Fife 134 D11
Charlestown Highld 153 Q3
Charlestown Highld 156 A8
Charlestown Salfd 82 H4
Charlestown of Aberlour Moray 157 P9
Charles Tye Suffk 64 E11
Charlesworth Derbys 83 M6
Charlinch Somset 18 H7
Charlottetown Fife 134 H5
Charlton Gt Lon 37 K5
Charlton Hants 22 C5
Charlton Herts 50 E5
Charlton Nhants 48 F7
Charlton Nthumb 112 B4
Charlton Oxon 34 D7
Charlton Somset 19 J9
Charlton Somset 20 B6
Charlton Somset 20 C4
Charlton Surrey 36 C7
Charlton W Susx 15 N4
Charlton Wilts 20 H10
Charlton Wilts 33 J7
Charlton Worcs 47 K5
Charlton Worcs 58 B10
Charlton Wrekin 57 K2
Charlton Abbots Gloucs 47 K10
Charlton Adam Somset 19 P9
Charlton All Saints Wilts 21 N10
Charlton Down Dorset 11 P5
Charlton Hill Shrops 57 K3
Charlton Horethorne Somset 20 C10
Charlton Kings Gloucs 47 J10
Charlton Mackrell Somset 19 P9
Charlton Marshall Dorset 12 F4
Charlton Musgrove Somset 20 D9
Charlton-on-Otmoor Oxon 48 G11
Charlton on the Hill Dorset 12 E4
Charlton St Peter Wilts 21 M3
Charlwood Hants 23 J8
Charlwood Surrey 24 F2
Charminster Dorset 11 P6
Charmouth Dorset 10 H6
Charndon Bucks 49 J10
Charney Bassett Oxon 34 C6
Charnock Green Lancs 88 H7
Charnock Richard Lancs 88 H7
Charnock Richard Services Lancs 88 G7
Charsfield Suffk 65 K10
Chart Corner Kent 38 C11
Charter Alley Hants 22 G3
Charterhall Border 129 K10
Charterhouse Somset 19 N3
Chartershall Stirlg 133 M9
Charterville Allotments Oxon 34 B2
Chartham Kent 39 K11
Chartham Hatch Kent 39 K10
Chart Hill Kent 26 C2
Chartridge Bucks 35 P4
Chart Sutton Kent 26 D2
Chartway Street Kent 38 D11
Charvil Wokham 35 L9
Charwelton Nhants 60 B9
Chase Terrace Staffs 58 F3
Chasetown Staffs 58 F3
Chastleton Oxon 47 P9
Chasty Devon 16 E11
Chatburn Lancs 89 M2
Chatcull Staffs 70 D8
Chatham Caerph 30 H7
Chatham Medway 38 C8
Chatham Green Essex 52 B8
Chathill Nthumb 119 N5
Chatley Worcs 46 G2
Chatsworth House Derbys 84 C6
Chattenden Medway 38 C7
Chatter End Essex 51 L5
Chatteris Cambs 62 E3
Chatterton Lancs 89 M7
Chattisham Suffk 53 J3
Chatto Border 118 E7
Chatton Nthumb 119 L5
Chaul End C Beds 50 C6
Chawleigh Devon 17 N9
Chawley Oxon 34 E4
Chawston Bed 61 Q9
Chawton Hants 23 K7
Chaxhill Gloucs 32 D2
Chazey Heath Oxon 35 J9
Cheadle Staffs 71 J6
Cheadle Stockp 83 J7
Cheadle Heath Stockp 83 J7
Cheadle Hulme Stockp 83 J7
Cheam Gt Lon 36 F8
Cheapside W & M 35 P11
Chearsley Bucks 35 K2
Chebsey Staffs 70 F9
Checkendon Oxon 35 J8
Checkley Ches E 70 C5
Checkley Herefs 46 A7
Checkley Staffs 71 J7
Checkley Green Ches E 70 C5
Chedburgh Suffk 63 N9
Cheddar Somset 19 N4
Cheddington Bucks 49 P11
Cheddleton Staffs 70 H4
Cheddleton Heath Staffs 70 H4
Cheddon Fitzpaine Somset 18 H9
Chedglow Wilts 32 H6
Chedgrave Norfk 65 M2
Chedington Dorset 11 K3
Chediston Suffk 65 M6
Chediston Green Suffk 65 M6
Chedworth Gloucs 33 L2
Chedzoy Somset 19 K7
Cheeseman's Green Kent 26 H4
Cheetham Hill Manch 82 H4
Cheldon Devon 8 H2
Chelford Ches E 82 H10
Chellaston C Derb 72 B4
Chellington Bed 61 L9
Chelmarsh Shrops 57 N7
Chelmer Village Essex 52 B10
Chelmick Shrops 56 H6
Chelmondiston Suffk 53 M4
Chelmorton Derbys 83 P11
Chelmsford Essex 52 B10
Chelmsley Wood Solhll 59 J7
Chelsea Gt Lon 36 G5
Chelsfield Gt Lon 37 L8
Chelsham Surrey 37 J9
Chelston Somset 18 G10
Chelsworth Suffk 52 G2
Cheltenham Gloucs 46 H10
Chelveston Nhants 61 L7
Chelvey N Som 31 N11
Chelwood BaNES 20 B2
Chelwood Common E Susx 25 K5
Chelwood Gate E Susx 25 K4
Chelworth Wilts 33 J6
Chelworth Lower Green Wilts 33 L6
Chelworth Upper Green Wilts 33 L6
Cheney Longville Shrops 56 G8
Chenies Bucks 50 B11
Chepstow Mons 31 P6
Chequerbent Bolton 89 K9
Chequers Corner Norfk 75 J9
Cherhill Wilts 33 K10
Cherington Gloucs 32 H5
Cherington Warwks 47 Q7
Cheriton Devon 17 N2
Cheriton Hants 22 G9
Cheriton Kent 27 M4
Cheriton Pembks 41 J11
Cheriton Swans 28 E6
Cheriton Bishop Devon 9 J6
Cheriton Fitzpaine Devon 9 L3
Cherrington Wrekin 70 B11
Cherry Burton E R Yk 92 G2
Cherry Hinton Cambs 62 G9
Cherry Orchard Worcs 46 G4
Cherry Willingham Lincs 86 D6
Chertsey Surrey 36 B7
Cherwell Valley Services Oxon 48 F9
Cheselbourne Dorset 12 C5
Chesham Bucks 35 Q4
Chesham Bury 89 N8
Chesham Bois Bucks 35 Q5
Cheshunt Herts 51 J10
Chesil Beach Dorset 11 N9
Chesley Kent 38 E9
Cheslyn Hay Staffs 58 E3
Chessetts Wood Warwks 59 J10
Chessington Gt Lon 36 E8
Chessington World of Adventures Gt Lon 36 E8
Chester Ches W 81 N11
Chesterblade Somset 20 C6
Chesterfield Derbys 84 E6
Chesterfield Staffs 58 G3
Chesterhill Mdloth 128 B7
Chester-le-Street Dur 113 L10
Chester Moor Dur 113 L11
Chesters Border 118 B6
Chesters Border 118 B8
Chester Services Ches W 81 P9
Chesterton Cambs 62 G8
Chesterton Cambs 74 B11
Chesterton Gloucs 33 K4
Chesterton Oxon 48 G10
Chesterton Shrops 57 P5
Chesterton Staffs 70 E5
Chesterton Green Warwks 48 C3
Chesterwood Nthumb 112 B7
Chester Zoo Ches W 81 N10
Chestfield Kent 39 K8
Chestnut Street Kent 38 E9
Cheston Devon 6 H7
Cheswardine Shrops 70 C8
Cheswick Nthumb 129 Q10
Cheswick Green Solhll 58 H9
Chetnole Dorset 11 N3
Chettiscombe Devon 9 N2
Chettisham Cambs 62 H4
Chettle Dorset 12 G2
Chetton Shrops 57 M6
Chetwode Bucks 48 H9
Chetwynd Wrekin 70 C10
Chetwynd Aston Wrekin 70 D11
Cheveley Cambs 63 L8
Chevening Kent 37 L9
Cheverton IoW 14 E10
Chevington Suffk 63 N9
Cheviot Hills 118 E9
Chevithorne Devon 18 C11
Chew Magna BaNES 19 Q2
Chew Moor Bolton 89 K9
Chew Stoke BaNES 19 Q2
Chewton Keynsham BaNES 32 C11
Chewton Mendip Somset 19 Q4
Chichacott Devon 8 F5
Chicheley M Keyn 49 P5
Chichester W Susx 15 N6
Chickerell Dorset 11 N8
Chickering Suffk 65 J6
Chicklade Wilts 20 H8
Chicksands C Beds 50 D3
Chickward Herefs 45 K4
Chidden Hants 23 J11
Chiddingfold Surrey 23 Q7
Chiddingly E Susx 25 M8
Chiddingstone Kent 25 M2
Chiddingstone Causeway Kent 37 M11
Chiddingstone Hoath Kent 25 L2
Chideock Dorset 11 J6
Chidham W Susx 15 L6
Chidswell Kirk 90 H6
Chieveley W Berk 34 E10
Chieveley Services W Berk 34 E10
Chignall St James Essex 51 Q8
Chignall Smealy Essex 51 Q8
Chigwell Essex 37 K2
Chigwell Row Essex 37 L2
Chilbolton Hants 22 C6
Chilcomb Hants 22 F9
Chilcombe Dorset 11 L6
Chilcompton Somset 20 B4
Chilcote Leics 59 L2
Childer Thornton Ches W 81 M9
Child Okeford Dorset 12 D2
Childrey Oxon 34 C7
Child's Ercall Shrops 70 B9
Childswickham Worcs 47 L7
Childwall Lpool 81 N7
Childwick Bury Herts 50 D8
Childwick Green Herts 50 D8
Chilfrome Dorset 11 M5
Chilgrove W Susx 15 M4
Chilham Kent 39 J11
Chilla Devon 8 B4
Chillaton Devon 8 B8
Chillenden Kent 39 N11
Chillerton IoW 14 E10
Chillesford Suffk 65 M11
Chillingham Nthumb 119 L5
Chillington Devon 7 K10
Chillington Somset 10 H2
Chilmark Wilts 21 J8
Chilmington Green Kent 26 G3
Chilson Oxon 48 B11
Chilsworthy Cnwll 5 Q7
Chilsworthy Devon 16 E10
Chiltern Green C Beds 50 D7
Chiltern Hills 35 L5
Chilthorne Domer Somset 19 P11
Chilton Bucks 35 J2
Chilton Devon 9 L4
Chilton Dur 103 Q5
Chilton Kent 27 N3
Chilton Oxon 34 E7
Chilton Suffk 52 E3
Chilton Candover Hants 22 G6
Chilton Cantelo Somset 19 Q10
Chilton Foliat Wilts 34 B10
Chilton Polden Somset 19 L6
Chilton Street Suffk 63 N11
Chilton Trinity Somset 19 J7
Chilwell Notts 72 E3
Chilworth Hants 22 D11
Chilworth Surrey 36 B11
Chimney Oxon 34 C4
Chineham Hants 23 J3
Chingford Gt Lon 37 J2
Chinley Derbys 83 M8
Chinnor Oxon 35 L4
Chipchase Castle Nthumb 112 C5
Chipnall Shrops 70 C8
Chippenham Cambs 63 L7
Chippenham Wilts 32 H10
Chipperfield Herts 50 B10
Chipping Herts 51 J4
Chipping Lancs 89 J2
Chipping Campden Gloucs 47 N7
Chipping Hill Essex 52 D8
Chipping Norton Oxon 48 B9
Chipping Ongar Essex 51 N10
Chipping Sodbury S Glos 32 D8
Chipping Warden Nhants 48 E5
Chipshop Devon 8 B9
Chipstable Somset 18 D9
Chipstead Kent 37 M9
Chipstead Surrey 36 G9
Chirbury Shrops 56 D5
Chirk Wrexhm 69 J7
Chirnside Border 129 M8
Chirnsidebridge Border 129 M8
Chirton Wilts 21 L3
Chisbury Wilts 33 Q11
Chiselborough Somset 11 K2
Chiseldon Swindn 33 N8
Chiselhampton Oxon 34 G5
Chiserley Calder 90 C5
Chisholme Border 117 N8
Chislehurst Gt Lon 37 K6
Chislet Kent 39 M9
Chiswell Green Herts 50 D10
Chiswick Gt Lon 36 F5
Chiswick End Cambs 62 E11
Chisworth Derbys 83 L6
Chitcombe E Susx 26 D7
Chithurst W Susx 23 M10
Chittering Cambs 62 G7
Chitterne Wilts 21 J6
Chittlehamholt Devon 17 M7
Chittlehampton Devon 17 L6
Chittoe Wilts 33 J11
Chivelstone Devon 7 K11
Chivenor Devon 17 J5
Chiverton Cross Cnwll 3 J4
Chlenry D & G 106 F5
Chobham Surrey 23 Q2
Cholderton Wilts 21 P6
Cholesbury Bucks 35 P3
Chollerford Nthumb 112 D6
Chollerton Nthumb 112 D6
Cholmondeston Ches E 70 A3
Cholsey Oxon 34 G7
Cholstrey Herefs 45 P3
Chop Gate N York 104 G11
Choppington Nthumb 113 L4
Chopwell Gatesd 112 H9
Chorley Ches E 69 Q4
Chorley Lancs 88 H7
Chorley Shrops 57 M8
Chorley Staffs 58 G2
Chorleywood Herts 50 B11
Chorleywood West Herts 50 B11
Chorlton Ches E 70 C4
Chorlton-cum-Hardy Manch 82 H6
Chorlton Lane Ches W 69 N5
Choulton Shrops 56 F7
Chowley Ches W 69 N3
Chrishall Essex 51 K3
Chrisswell Inver 124 G3
Christchurch BCP 13 L6
Christchurch Cambs 75 J11
Christchurch Gloucs 31 Q2
Christchurch Newpt 31 K7
Christian Malford Wilts 33 J9
Christleton Ches W 81 N11
Christmas Common Oxon 35 K6
Christmas Pie Surrey 23 P5
Christon N Som 19 L3
Christon Bank Nthumb 119 P6
Christow Devon 9 K7
Christ's Hospital W Susx 24 D5
Chuck Hatch E Susx 25 L4
Chudleigh Devon 9 L9
Chudleigh Knighton Devon 9 K9
Chulmleigh Devon 17 M9
Chunal Derbys 83 M6
Church Lancs 89 L5
Churcham Gloucs 46 E11
Church Aston Wrekin 70 C11
Church Brampton Nhants 60 F7
Church Brough Cumb 102 E8
Church Broughton Derbys 71 N8
Church Cove Cnwll 3 J11
Church Crookham Hants 23 M4
Churchdown Gloucs 46 G11
Church Eaton Staffs 70 E11
Church End Bed 61 N9
Church End Bed 61 P9
Church End Bucks 35 K3
Church End C Beds 49 Q10
Church End C Beds 49 Q8
Church End C Beds 50 B4
Church End C Beds 50 B7
Church End C Beds 50 E3
Church End C Beds 61 Q10
Church End Cambs 61 N6
Church End Cambs 62 B4
Church End Cambs 62 D5
Churchend Essex 38 H3
Church End Essex 51 P6
Church End Essex 52 B6
Church End Essex 52 B8
Church End Gloucs 46 G7
Church End Gt Lon 36 F2
Church End Herts 50 D8
Church End Herts 50 G4
Church End Herts 51 K6
Church End Lincs 74 D4

Church End Lincs 93 R11
Church End Suff 53 M4
Church End Warwks 59 K6
Church End Warwks 59 L6
Church Enstone Oxon 48 C9
Church Fenton N York 91 N3
Churchfield Sandw 58 F6
Churchgate Herts 50 H10
Churchgate Street Essex 51 L8
Church Green Devon 10 D5
Church Gresley Derbys 71 P11
Church Hanborough Oxon 34 D2
Church Hill Staffs 58 F2
Church Houses N York 105 J11
Churchill Devon 10 H4
Churchill Devon 17 K3
Churchill N Som 19 M3
Churchill Oxon 47 Q10
Churchill Worcs 46 H4
Churchill Worcs 58 C9
Churchinford Somset 10 E2
Church Knowle Dorset 12 F8
Church Laneham Notts 85 P5
Church Langton Leics 60 F2
Church Lawford Warwks 59 Q9
Church Lawton Ches E 70 E3
Church Leigh Staffs 71 J7
Church Lench Worcs 47 K4
Church Mayfield Staffs 71 M6
Church Minshull Ches E 70 B2
Church Norton W Susx 15 N7
Churchover Warwks 60 B4
Church Preen Shrops 57 J5
Church Pulverbatch Shrops 56 G4
Churchstanton Somset 10 D2
Churchstoke Powys 56 D6
Churchstow Devon 7 J9
Church Stowe Nhants 60 D9
Church Street Essex 52 C3
Church Street Kent 38 B7
Church Street Suff 65 P5
Church Stretton Shrops 56 H6
Churchthorpe Lincs 93 P11
Churchtown Bpool 88 C2
Churchtown Cnwll 4 H6
Churchtown Derbys 84 C8
Churchtown Devon 17 M3
Churchtown IoM 80 f3
Churchtown Lancs 88 F2
Church Town N Linc 92 C9
Churchtown Sefton 88 D7
Church Village Rhondd 30 E8
Church Warsop Notts 85 J7
Church Wilne Derbys 72 C4
Churnsike Lodge Nthumb 111 N5
Churston Ferrers Torbay 7 N7
Churt Surrey 23 N7
Churton Ches W 69 M3
Churwell Leeds 90 H5
Chyandour Cnwll 2 D7
Chyanvounder Cnwll 2 H9
Chyeowling Cnwll 3 K5
Chyvarloe Cnwll 2 H9
Cil Powys 56 B4
Cilcain Flints 80 H11
Cilcennin Cerdgn 43 K2
Cilcewydd Powys 56 C4
Cilfrew Neath 29 L4
Cilfynydd Rhondd 30 E6
Cilgerran Pembks 41 N2
Cilgwyn Carmth 43 P9
Cilgwyn Gwynd 66 H4
Ciliau-Aeron Cerdgn 43 K3
Cilmaengwyn Neath 29 K3
Cilmery Powys 44 E4
Cilrhedyn Pembks 41 Q4
Cilsan Carmth 43 L10
Ciltalgarth Gwynd 68 A6
Cilycwm Carmth 43 Q7
Cimla Neath 29 L5
Cinderford Gloucs 32 C2
Cinder Hill Wolves 58 D6
Cippenham Slough 35 Q8
Cirencester Gloucs 33 K4
Citadilla N York 103 P11
City Gt Lon 36 H4
City V Glam 30 C9
City Airport Gt Lon 37 K4
City Dulas IoA 78 H7
Clabhach Ag & B 136 F4
Clachaig Ag & B 131 N11
Clachaig Inn Highld 139 L6
Clachan Ag & B 123 N8
Clachan Ag & B 130 F4
Clachan Ag & B 131 M7
Clachan Ag & B 138 F9
Clachan Highld 153 J10
Clachan-a-Luib W Isls 168 d11
Clachan Mor Ag & B 136 B6
Clachan na Luib W Isls 168 d11
Clachan of Campsie E Duns 125 Q2
Clachan-Seil Ag & B 130 F4
Clachnaharry Highld 156 A8
Clachtoll Highld 164 B11
Clacket Lane Services
　Surrey 37 K10
Clackmannan Clacks 133 Q9
Clackmannanshire Bridge
　Fife 133 Q10
Clackmarras Moray 157 N6
Clacton-on-Sea Essex 53 L8
Cladich Ag & B 131 M3
Cladswell Worcs 47 L3
Claggan Highld 138 C8
Claigan Highld 152 C7
Clandown BaNES 20 C3
Clanfield Hants 23 J11
Clanfield Oxon 33 Q4
Clannaborough Devon 8 H4
Clanville Hants 22 B5
Clanville Somset 20 B8
Claonaig Ag & B 123 Q8
Clapgate Dorset 12 H4
Clapgate Herts 51 K6
Clapham Bed 61 M10
Clapham Devon 9 L7
Clapham Gt Lon 36 G5
Clapham N York 95 Q7
Clapham W Susx 24 C9
Clapham Green Bed 61 M10
Clap Hill Kent 27 J4
Clappersgate Cumb 101 L10
Clapton Somset 11 J3
Clapton Somset 20 B4
Clapton-in-Gordano N Som 31 N10

Clapton-on-the-Hill Gloucs 47 N11
Clapworthy Devon 17 M7
Clarach Cerdgn 54 E8
Claravale Gatesd 112 H8
Clarbeston Pembks 41 L6
Clarbeston Road Pembks 41 K6
Clarborough Notts 85 M4
Clare Suff 63 N11
Clarebrand D & G 108 G7
Clarencefield D & G 109 N7
Clarewood Nthumb 112 F7
Clarilaw Border 117 Q7
Clark's Green Surrey 24 E2
Clarkston E Rens 125 P6
Clashmore Highld 162 G9
Clashmore Highld 164 B10
Clashnessie Highld 164 C10
Clashnoir Moray 149 N3
Clathy P & K 134 B3
Clathymore P & K 134 C3
Clatt Abers 150 E2
Clatter Powys 55 M6
Clatterford End Essex 51 P8
Clatworthy Somset 18 E8
Claughton Lancs 88 G2
Claughton Lancs 95 M7
Claughton Wirral 81 L7
Clavelshay Somset 19 J8
Claverdon Warwks 59 J11
Claverham N Som 31 N11
Clavering Essex 51 L4
Claverley Shrops 57 P6
Claverton BaNES 20 E2
Claverton Down BaNES 20 E2
Clawdd-coch V Glam 30 E9
Clawdd-newydd Denbgs 68 E4
Clawthorpe Cumb 95 L5
Clawton Devon 5 P2
Claxby Lincs 86 F2
Claxby Lincs 87 N4
Claxton N York 98 D9
Claxton Norfk 77 L11
Claybrooke Magna Leics 59 Q7
Clay Common Suff 65 P5
Clay Coton Nhants 60 C5
Clay Cross Derbys 84 E8
Claydon Oxon 48 E5
Claydon Suff 53 K2
Clay End Herts 50 H6
Claygate D & G 110 G5
Claygate Kent 26 B3
Claygate Surrey 36 E8
Claygate Cross Kent 37 P9
Clayhall Gt Lon 37 K2
Clayhanger Devon 18 D10
Clayhanger Wsall 58 F4
Clayhidon Devon 18 G11
Clayhill E Susx 26 D7
Clayhill Hants 13 P3
Clayhithe Cambs 62 H8
Clayock Highld 167 L5
Claypit Hill Cambs 62 E10
Claypits Gloucs 32 E3
Claypole Lincs 85 P11
Claythorpe Lincs 87 M5
Clayton C Brad 90 E4
Clayton Donc 91 M9
Clayton W Susx 24 G8
Clayton Green Lancs 88 H4
Clayton-le-Moors Lancs 89 M4
Clayton-le-Woods Lancs 88 H4
Clayton West Kirk 90 H8
Clayworth Notts 85 M3
Cleadale Highld 144 G10
Cleadon S Tyne 113 N8
Cleadon Park S Tyne 113 N8
Clearbrook Devon 6 E5
Clearwell Gloucs 31 Q3
Cleasby N York 103 Q8
Cleat Ork 169 d8
Cleatlam Dur 103 M7
Cleator Cumb 100 D8
Cleator Moor Cumb 100 D7
Cleckheaton Kirk 90 F5
Cleedownton Shrops 57 K8
Cleehill Shrops 57 K9
Clee St Margaret Shrops 57 K8
Cleestanton Shrops 57 K9
Cleethorpes NE Lin 93 P9
Cleeton St Mary Shrops 57 L9
Cleeve N Som 31 N11
Cleeve Oxon 34 H8
Cleeve Hill Gloucs 47 J9
Cleeve Prior Worcs 47 L5
Cleghornie E Loth 128 F3
Clehonger Herefs 45 N7
Cleish P & K 134 D8
Cleland N Lans 126 D6
Clement's End C Beds 50 B8
Clement Street Kent 37 M6
Clenamacrie Ag & B 131 J2
Clench Common Wilts 33 N11
Clenchwarton Norfk 75 L6
Clenerty Abers 159 J5
Clent Worcs 58 D9
Cleobury Mortimer Shrops 57 M9
Cleobury North Shrops 57 L7
Cleongart Ag & B 120 C5
Clephanton Highld 156 E7
Clerkhill D & G 117 K11
Cleuch-head D & G 115 R7
Clevancy Wilts 33 L9
Clevedon N Som 31 M10
Cleveley Gloucs 48 C10
Cleveleys Lancs 88 C2
Cleverton Wilts 33 J7
Clewer Somset 19 M4
Cley next the Sea Norfk 76 E3
Cliburn Cumb 101 Q6
Cliddesden Hants 22 H5
Cliff Warwks 59 K5
Cliffe Lancs 89 L4
Cliffe Medway 38 B6
Cliffe N York 91 R4
Cliffe N York 103 P7
Cliff End E Susx 26 E9
Cliffe Woods Medway 38 B7
Clifford Herefs 45 J5
Clifford Leeds 91 L2
Clifford Chambers Warwks 47 N4
Clifford's Mesne Gloucs 46 D10
Cliffsend Kent 39 P9
Clifton Bristl 31 Q10
Clifton C Beds 50 E3
Clifton C Nott 72 E4

Clifton C York 98 B10
Clifton Calder 90 F6
Clifton Cumb 101 P5
Clifton Derbys 71 M6
Clifton Devon 17 L3
Clifton Donc 91 N11
Clifton Lancs 88 F4
Clifton N York 97 J11
Clifton Nthumb 113 K4
Clifton Oxon 48 E8
Clifton Salfd 82 G4
Clifton Worcs 46 F5
Clifton Campville Staffs 59 L2
Clifton Hampden Oxon 34 F5
Clifton Reynes M Keyn 49 P4
Clifton upon Dunsmore
　Warwks 60 B5
Clifton upon Teme Worcs 46 D2
Cliftonville Kent 39 Q7
Climping W Susx 15 Q6
Clink Somset 20 E5
Clint N York 97 L9
Clint Green Norfk 76 E9
Clintmains Border 118 B4
Clipiau Gwynd 55 J2
Clippesby Norfk 77 N9
Clipsham Rutlnd 73 P7
Clipston Nhants 60 F4
Clipston Notts 72 G4
Clipstone C Beds 49 P9
Clipstone Notts 85 J8
Clitheroe Lancs 89 L2
Clive Shrops 69 P10
Clixby Lincs 93 J10
Cloatley Wilts 33 J6
Clocaenog Denbgs 68 E4
Clochan Moray 158 B5
Clock Face St Hel 82 B6
Cloddiau Powys 56 C3
Clodock Herefs 45 L9
Cloford Somset 20 D6
Clola Abers 159 P9
Clophill C Beds 50 C3
Clopton Nhants 61 N4
Clopton Suff 65 J11
Clopton Corner Suff 65 J11
Clopton Green Suff 63 N10
Clopton Green Suff 64 D10
Clos du Valle Guern 10 c1
Closeburn D & G 109 J2
Closeburnmill D & G 109 K2
Closeclark IoM 80 c6
Closworth Somset 11 M2
Clothall Herts 50 G4
Clotton Ches W 69 P2
Cloudesley Bush Warwks 59 Q7
Clouds Herefs 46 A7
Clough Oldham 89 Q9
Clough Foot Calder 89 Q6
Clough Head Calder 90 D7
Cloughton N York 99 L2
Cloughton Newlands N York 105 R11
Clousta Shet 169 q8
Clova Angus 142 E3
Clovelly Devon 16 E7
Clovenfords Border 117 P3
Clovulin Highld 139 J5
Clow Bridge Lancs 89 N5
Clowne Derbys 84 G5
Clows Top Worcs 57 N10
Cloy Wrexhm 69 L6
Cluanie Inn Highld 146 D5
Cluanie Lodge Highld 146 D5
Clubworthy Cnwll 5 M3
Clugston D & G 107 L6
Clun Shrops 56 E8
Clunas Highld 156 F8
Clunbury Shrops 56 F8
Clunderwen Carmth 41 M7
Clune Highld 148 D2
Clunes Highld 146 F10
Clungunford Shrops 56 F9
Clunie P & K 141 R9
Clunton Shrops 56 E8
Cluny Fife 134 G8
Clutton BaNES 20 B3
Clutton Ches W 69 N4
Clutton Hill BaNES 20 B3
Clwt Conwy 68 C2
Clwt-y-bont Gwynd 67 K2
Clydach Mons 30 H2
Clydach Swans 29 J4
Clydach Vale Rhondd 30 C6
Clydebank W Duns 125 M3
Clydey Pembks 41 Q3
Clyffe Pypard Wilts 33 L9
Clynder Ag & B 131 Q11
Clyne Neath 29 M4
Clynnog Fawr Gwynd 66 G5
Clyro Powys 45 J6
Clyst Honiton Devon 9 N6
Clyst Hydon Devon 9 P5
Clyst St George Devon 9 N7
Clyst St Lawrence Devon 9 P5
Clyst St Mary Devon 9 N6
Cnoc W Isls 168 j4
Cnwch Coch Cerdgn 54 F10
Coad's Green Cnwll 5 M6
Coal Aston Derbys 84 E5
Coalbrookvale Blae G 30 G3
Coalburn S Lans 126 E11
Coalburns Gatesd 112 H8
Coaley Gloucs 32 E4
Coalhill Essex 38 C2
Coalmoor Wrekin 57 M3
Coalpit Heath S Glos 32 C8
Coal Pool Wsall 58 F5
Coalport Wrekin 57 M4
Coalsnaughton Clacks 133 Q8
Coal Street Suff 65 J7
Coaltown of Balgonie Fife 134 H8
Coaltown of Wemyss Fife 135 J8
Coalville Leics 72 C8
Coanwood Nthumb 111 N9
Coat Somset 19 N10
Coatbridge N Lans 126 C4
Coatdyke N Lans 126 C4
Coate Swindn 33 N8
Coate Wilts 21 K2
Coates Cambs 74 F11
Coates Gloucs 33 J4
Coates Lincs 86 B4
Coates Notts 85 P4
Coates W Susx 23 Q11

Coatham R & Cl 104 G5
Coatham Mundeville Darltn 103 Q6
Cobbaton Devon 17 L6
Coberley Gloucs 47 J11
Cobhall Common Herefs 45 P7
Cobham Kent 37 Q7
Cobham Surrey 36 D8
Coblers Green Essex 51 Q7
Cobley Dorset 21 K10
Cobnash Herefs 45 P2
Cobo Guern 10 b1
Cobridge C Stke 70 F5
Coburby Abers 159 M5
Cock Alley Derbys 84 F6
Cock Bank Wrexhm 69 L5
Cock Bevington Warwks 47 L4
Cock Bridge Abers 149 P6
Cockburnspath Border 129 K5
Cock Clarks Essex 52 D11
Cock & End Suff 63 M10
Cockenzie and Port Seton
　E Loth 128 C4
Cocker Bar Lancs 88 G6
Cocker Brook Lancs 89 L5
Cockerham Lancs 95 K10
Cockermouth Cumb 100 F4
Cockernhoe Herts 50 D6
Cockersdale Leeds 90 G5
Cockett Swans 28 H6
Cockfield Dur 103 M6
Cockfield Suff 64 C11
Cockfosters Gt Lon 50 G11
Cock Green Essex 51 Q7
Cocking W Susx 23 N11
Cocking Causeway W Susx 23 N11
Cockington Torbay 7 M6
Cocklake Somset 19 M5
Cockley Beck Cumb 100 H10
Cockley Cley Norfk 75 Q10
Cock Marling E Susx 26 E8
Cockpole Green Wokham 35 L8
Cocks Cnwll 3 K3
Cockshutford Shrops 57 K7
Cockshutt Shrops 69 M9
Cock Street Kent 38 C11
Cockthorpe Norfk 76 D3
Cockwells Cnwll 2 E7
Cockwood Devon 9 N8
Cockwood Somset 18 H6
Cockyard Derbys 83 M9
Cockyard Herefs 45 N8
Coddenham Suff 64 G11
Coddington Ches W 69 N3
Coddington Herefs 46 D6
Coddington Notts 85 P10
Codford St Mary Wilts 21 J7
Codford St Peter Wilts 21 J7
Codicote Herts 50 F7
Codmore Hill W Susx 24 C6
Codnor Derbys 84 F11
Codrington S Glos 32 D9
Codsall Staffs 58 C4
Codsall Wood Staffs 58 B4
Coed Darcy Neath 29 K5
Coedely Rhondd 30 D7
Coed Hirwaun Neath 29 M8
Coedkernew Newpt 31 J8
Coed Morgan Mons 31 L2
Coedpoeth Wrexhm 69 J4
Coed Talon Flints 69 J3
Coedway Powys 69 K11
Coed-y-Bryn Cerdgn 42 G5
Coed-y-caerau Newpt 31 L6
Coed-y-Cwm Rhondd 30 E6
Coed-y-paen Mons 31 K5
Coed-yr-ynys Powys 44 H10
Coed Ystumgwern Gwynd 67 K10
Coelbren Powys 29 N2
Coffinswell Devon 7 M5
Coffle End Bed 61 M9
Cofton Devon 9 N8
Cofton Hackett Worcs 58 F9
Cogan V Glam 30 G10
Cogenhoe Nhants 60 H8
Cogges Oxon 34 C3
Coggeshall Essex 52 E7
Coggin's Mill E Susx 25 N5
Coignafearn Highld 148 C4
Coilacriech Abers 149 Q8
Coilantogle Stirlg 132 H6
Coillore Highld 152 F10
Coity Brdgnd 29 P8
Col W Isls 168 j4
Colaboll Highld 162 D4
Colan Cnwll 4 D9
Colaton Raleigh Devon 10 B7
Colbost Highld 152 C10
Colburn N York 103 N11
Colby Cumb 102 C6
Colby IoM 80 b7
Colby Norfk 77 J5
Colchester Essex 52 G6
Colchester Zoo Essex 52 G7
Cold Ash W Berk 34 F11
Cold Ashby Nhants 60 E5
Cold Ashton S Glos 32 E10
Cold Aston Gloucs 47 M11
Coldbackie Highld 165 P4
Coldbeck Cumb 102 D10
Cold Blow Pembks 41 M8
Cold Brayfield M Keyn 49 P4
Cold Cotes N York 95 Q6
Coldean Br & H 24 H9
Coldeast Devon 7 L4
Colden Calder 90 B5
Colden Common Hants 22 E10
Coldfair Green Suff 65 N9
Coldham Cambs 74 H10
Cold Hanworth Lincs 86 D4
Coldharbour Cnwll 3 K4
Coldharbour Surrey 24 D2
Coldharbour Gloucs 31 Q4
Cold Harbour Herts 50 D7
Cold Harbour Oxon 34 H9
Cold Hatton Wrekin 70 A10
Cold Hatton Heath Wrekin 70 A10
Cold Hesledon Dur 113 P11
Cold Hiendley Wakefd 91 K8
Cold Higham Nhants 49 J4
Coldingham Border 129 N6
Cold Kirby N York 98 B7
Coldmeece Staffs 70 F8

Cold Newton Leics 73 J9
Cold Northcott Cnwll 5 L4
Cold Norton Essex 52 E11
Cold Overton Leics 73 L8
Coldred Kent 27 N2
Coldridge Devon 17 M10
Coldstream Border 118 F3
Coldwaltham W Susx 24 B7
Coldwell Herefs 45 N7
Coldwells Abers 159 N10
Cold Weston Shrops 57 K8
Cole Somset 20 C8
Colebatch Shrops 56 E7
Colebrook C Plym 6 E7
Colebrook Devon 9 P3
Colebrooke Devon 9 J5
Coleby Lincs 86 C8
Coleby N Linc 92 E7
Cole End Warwks 59 K7
Coleford Devon 9 J4
Coleford Gloucs 31 Q2
Coleford Somset 20 C5
Coleford Water Somset 18 F8
Colegate End Norfk 64 H4
Cole Green Herts 50 G8
Cole Green Herts 51 K4
Cole Henley Hants 22 E4
Colehill Dorset 12 H4
Coleman Green Herts 50 E8
Coleman's Hatch E Susx 25 K4
Colemere Shrops 69 M8
Colemore Hants 23 K8
Colemore Green Shrops 57 N5
Colenden P & K 134 E2
Coleorton Leics 72 C7
Colerne Wilts 32 F10
Colesbourne Gloucs 33 K2
Cole's Cross Devon 7 K9
Coles Cross Dorset 10 H4
Colesden Bed 61 P9
Coles Green Suff 53 K3
Coleshill Bucks 35 P5
Coleshill Oxon 33 P6
Coleshill Warwks 59 K7
Colestocks Devon 10 B4
Coley BaNES 19 Q3
Colgate W Susx 24 F4
Colinsburgh Fife 135 M7
Colinton C Edin 127 N4
Colintraive Ag & B 124 C3
Colkirk Norfk 76 C6
Coll Ag & B 136 G4
Coll W Isls 168 j4
Collace P & K 142 C11
Collafirth Shet 169 q5
Coll Airport Ag & B 136 F4
Collaton Devon 7 J11
Collaton St Mary Torbay 7 M6
College of Roseisle Moray 157 L2
College Town Br For 23 N2
Collessie Fife 134 H5
Colleton Mills Devon 17 M8
Collier Row Gt Lon 37 M2
Collier's End Herts 51 J6
Collier's Green E Susx 26 C7
Colliers Green Kent 26 C4
Collier Street Kent 26 B2
Colliery Row Sundld 113 M11
Collieston Abers 151 Q2
Collin D & G 109 M5
Collingbourne Ducis Wilts 21 P4
Collingbourne Kingston
　Wilts 21 P3
Collingham Leeds 97 N11
Collingham Notts 85 P8
Collington Herefs 46 B2
Collingtree Nhants 60 G9
Collins Green Warrtn 82 C6
Collins Green Worcs 46 D3
Colliston Angus 143 L8
Colliton Devon 10 B4
Collyweston Nhants 73 P10
Colmonell S Ayrs 114 B10
Colmworth Bed 61 P9
Colnabaichin Abers 149 P6
Colnbrook Slough 36 B5
Colne Cambs 62 E5
Colne Lancs 89 P3
Colne Bridge Kirk 90 F6
Colne Edge Lancs 89 P2
Colne Engaine Essex 52 D5
Colney Norfk 76 H10
Colney Heath Herts 50 F9
Colney Street Herts 50 E10
Coln Rogers Gloucs 33 L3
Coln St Aldwyns Gloucs 33 M3
Coln St Dennis Gloucs 33 L2
Colonsay Ag & B 136 b2
Colonsay Airport Ag & B 136 b3
Colpy Abers 158 F11
Colquhar Border 117 L2
Colquite Cnwll 4 H7
Colscott Devon 16 H9
Colsterdale N York 96 H4
Colsterworth Lincs 73 N6
Colston Bassett Notts 73 J4
Coltfield Moray 157 L5
Colt Hill Hants 23 L4
Coltishall Norfk 77 K8
Colton Cumb 94 G3
Colton Leeds 91 K4
Colton N York 91 N2
Colton Norfk 76 G10
Colton Staffs 71 J10
Colt's Hill Kent 25 P2
Columbjohn Devon 9 N5
Colva Powys 44 H4
Colvend D & G 109 J10
Colwall Herefs 46 E6
Colwell Nthumb 112 E5
Colwich Staffs 71 J10
Colwick Notts 72 G3
Colwinston V Glam 29 P9
Colworth W Susx 15 P6
Colwyn Bay Conwy 80 B9
Colyford Devon 10 F6
Colyton Devon 10 E6
Combe Devon 7 J11
Combe Herefs 45 L2
Combe Oxon 34 D2
Combe Oxon 48 D11
Combe W Berk 22 C2
Combe Almer Dorset 12 G5
Combe Common Surrey 23 P7
Combe Down BaNES 20 E2
Combe Fishacre Devon 7 L5
Combe Florey Somset 18 G8

Place	County	Page	Grid
Combe Hay	BaNES	20	D3
Combeinteignhead	Devon	7	N4
Combe Martin	Devon	17	K2
Combe Raleigh	Devon	10	D4
Comberbach	Ches W	82	D9
Comberford	Staffs	59	J3
Comberton	Cambs	62	E9
Comberton	Herefs	56	H11
Combe St Nicholas	Somset	10	G2
Combpyne	Devon	10	F6
Combridge	Staffs	71	K7
Combrook	Warwks	48	B3
Combs	Derbys	83	M9
Combs	Suffk	64	E10
Combs Ford	Suffk	64	E10
Combwich	Somset	19	J6
Comers	Abers	150	H6
Comeytrowe	Somset	18	H10
Comhampton	Worcs	58	B11
Commercial End	Cambs	63	J8
Commins Coch	Powys	55	J4
Commondale	N York	105	J8
Common Edge	Bpool	88	C4
Common End	Cumb	100	D6
Common Moor	Cnwll	5	L8
Common Platt	Wilts	33	M7
Commonside	Ches W	82	B10
Commonside	Derbys	71	N6
Common Side	Derbys	84	D5
Commonwood	Shrops	69	N9
Commonwood	Wrexhm	69	L4
Compass	Somset	19	J8
Compstall	Stockp	83	L6
Compstonend	D & G	108	E10
Compton	Devon	7	M6
Compton	Hants	22	C9
Compton	Hants	22	E9
Compton	Staffs	57	Q8
Compton	Surrey	23	Q5
Compton	W Berk	34	F8
Compton	W Susx	15	L4
Compton	Wilts	21	M4
Compton Abbas	Dorset	20	G11
Compton Abdale	Gloucs	47	L11
Compton Bassett	Wilts	33	K10
Compton Beauchamp	Oxon	33	Q3
Compton Bishop	Somset	19	L3
Compton Chamberlayne	Wilts	21	K9
Compton Dando	BaNES	20	B2
Compton Dundon	Somset	19	N8
Compton Durville	Somset	19	M11
Compton Greenfield	S Glos	31	Q8
Compton Martin	BaNES	19	P3
Compton Pauncefoot	Somset	20	B9
Compton Valence	Dorset	11	M6
Comrie	Fife	134	C10
Comrie	P & K	133	M3
Conaglen House	Highld	139	J4
Concha	Highld	145	Q2
Concraigie	P & K	141	Q9
Conder Green	Lancs	95	K9
Conderton	Worcs	47	J7
Condicote	Gloucs	47	N9
Condorrat	N Lans	126	C3
Condover	Shrops	56	H3
Coney Hill	Gloucs	46	G11
Coneyhurst	W Susx	24	D6
Coneysthorpe	N York	98	E6
Coneythorpe	N York	97	N9
Coney Weston	Suffk	64	D6
Conford	Hants	23	M8
Congdon's Shop	Cnwll	5	M6
Congerstone	Leics	72	B9
Congham	Norfk	75	P6
Congleton	Ches E	70	F2
Congl-y-wal	Gwynd	67	N6
Congresbury	N Som	19	M2
Congreve	Staffs	58	D2
Conheath	D & G	109	L7
Conicavel	Moray	156	H7
Coningsby	Lincs	86	H9
Conington	Cambs	61	Q3
Conington	Cambs	62	D7
Conisbrough	Donc	91	N11
Conisholme	Lincs	93	R11
Coniston	Cumb	101	K11
Coniston	E R Yk	93	L9
Coniston Cold	N York	96	D10
Conistone	N York	96	E7
Connah's Quay	Flints	81	K11
Connel	Ag & B	138	G11
Connel Park	E Ayrs	115	M5
Connor Downs	Cnwll	2	F6
Conon Bridge	Highld	155	P6
Cononley	N York	96	E11
Consall	Staffs	70	H5
Consett	Dur	112	H10
Constable Burton	N York	97	J2
Constable Lee	Lancs	89	N6
Constantine	Cnwll	3	J8
Constantine Bay	Cnwll	4	D7
Contin	Highld	155	N6
Conwy	Conwy	79	P9
Conwy Castle	Conwy	79	P9
Conyer	Kent	38	G9
Conyer's Green	Suffk	64	B8
Cooden	E Susx	26	B10
Cookbury	Devon	16	G10
Cookbury Wick	Devon	16	F10
Cookham	W & M	35	N7
Cookham Dean	W & M	35	N7
Cookham Rise	W & M	35	N7
Cookhill	Worcs	47	L3
Cookley	Suffk	65	L6
Cookley	Worcs	58	B8
Cookley Green	Oxon	35	J6
Cookney	Abers	151	M9
Cooksbridge	E Susx	25	K8
Cooksey Green	Worcs	58	D11
Cook's Green	Essex	53	L8
Cooks Green	Suffk	64	D11
Cookshill	Staffs	70	G6
Cooksmill Green	Essex	51	P9
Coolham	W Susx	24	D6
Cooling	Medway	38	C7
Cooling Street	Medway	38	B7
Coombe	Cnwll	2	G5
Coombe	Cnwll	3	L5
Coombe	Cnwll	3	N5
Coombe	Devon	7	N4
Coombe	Devon	9	K8
Coombe	Devon	10	C6
Coombe	Gloucs	32	E6
Coombe	Hants	23	J10
Coombe	Wilts	21	M4
Coombe Bissett	Wilts	21	M9
Coombe Cellars	Devon	7	N4
Coombe Cross	Hants	23	J10
Coombe Hill	Gloucs	46	G9
Coombe Keynes	Dorset	12	D8
Coombe Pafford	Torbay	7	N5
Coombes	W Susx	24	E9
Coombes-Moor	Herefs	45	M2
Coombe Street	Somset	20	E8
Coombeswood	Dudley	58	E7
Coopersale Common	Essex	51	L10
Coopersale Street	Essex	51	L10
Cooper's Corner	Kent	37	L11
Coopers Green	E Susx	25	L6
Coopers Green	Herts	50	E9
Cooper Street	Kent	39	P9
Cootham	W Susx	24	C8
Copdock	Suffk	53	K3
Copford Green	Essex	52	F7
Copgrove	N York	97	M8
Copister	Shet	169	r6
Cople	Bed	61	P11
Copley	Calder	90	D6
Copley	Dur	103	L5
Copley	Tamesd	83	L5
Coplow Dale	Derbys	83	Q9
Copmanthorpe	C York	98	B11
Copmere End	Staffs	70	E9
Copp	Lancs	88	E3
Coppathorne	Cnwll	16	C11
Coppenhall	Staffs	70	G11
Coppenhall Moss	Ches E	70	C3
Copperhouse	Cnwll	2	F6
Coppicegate	Shrops	57	N8
Coppingford	Cambs	61	Q5
Coppins Corner	Kent	26	F2
Copplestone	Devon	9	J4
Coppull	Lancs	88	H8
Coppull Moor	Lancs	88	H8
Copsale	W Susx	24	E6
Copster Green	Lancs	89	K4
Copston Magna	Warwks	59	Q7
Cop Street	Kent	39	N9
Copthall Green	Essex	51	K10
Copt Heath	Solhll	59	J9
Copt Hewick	N York	97	M6
Copthorne	Cnwll	5	M3
Copthorne	W Susx	24	H3
Copt Oak	Leics	72	D8
Copy's Green	Norfk	76	C4
Coram Street	Suffk	52	H3
Corbets Tey	Gt Lon	37	N3
Corbière	Jersey	11	a2
Corbridge	Nthumb	112	E8
Corby	Nhants	61	J3
Corby Glen	Lincs	73	Q6
Corby Hill	Cumb	111	J9
Cordwell	Derbys	84	D5
Coreley	Shrops	57	L10
Cores End	Bucks	35	P7
Corfe	Somset	18	H11
Corfe Castle	Dorset	12	G8
Corfe Mullen	Dorset	12	G5
Corfton	Shrops	56	H7
Corgarff	Abers	149	P6
Corhampton	Hants	22	H10
Corks Pond	Kent	25	Q2
Corlae	D & G	115	N8
Corley	Warwks	59	M7
Corley Ash	Warwks	59	L7
Corley Moor	Warwks	59	L8
Corley Services	Warwks	59	M7
Cormuir	Angus	142	E4
Cornard Tye	Suffk	52	F3
Corndon	Devon	8	G7
Corney	Cumb	94	C2
Cornforth	Dur	104	B4
Cornhill	Abers	158	E6
Cornhill-on-Tweed	Nthumb	118	G3
Cornholme	Calder	89	Q5
Cornish Hall End	Essex	51	Q3
Cornoigmore	Ag & B	136	B6
Cornriggs	Dur	102	F2
Cornsay	Dur	103	M2
Cornsay Colliery	Dur	103	N2
Corntown	Highld	155	Q6
Corntown	V Glam	29	P9
Cornwall Airport Newquay	Cnwll	4	D9
Cornwell	Oxon	47	Q9
Cornwood	Devon	6	G7
Cornworthy	Devon	7	L7
Corpach	Highld	139	K2
Corpusty	Norfk	76	G6
Corrachree	Abers	150	D7
Corran	Highld	139	J5
Corran	Highld	145	P6
Corrany	IoM	80	g4
Corrie	D & G	110	D3
Corrie	N Ayrs	121	K3
Corriecravie	N Ayrs	120	H7
Corriegills	N Ayrs	121	K4
Corriegour Lodge Hotel	Highld	146	H9
Corriemoille	Highld	155	L5
Corrimony	Highld	155	L11
Corringham	Lincs	85	Q2
Corringham	Thurr	38	B5
Corris	Gwynd	54	H3
Corris Uchaf	Gwynd	54	G3
Corrow	Ag & B	131	P7
Corry	Highld	145	K3
Corscombe	Devon	8	F5
Corscombe	Dorset	11	L3
Corse	Gloucs	46	E9
Corse Lawn	Gloucs	46	F8
Corsham	Wilts	32	G10
Corsindae	Abers	150	H6
Corsley	Wilts	20	F5
Corsley Heath	Wilts	20	F5
Corsock	D & G	108	G5
Corston	BaNES	32	C11
Corston	Wilts	32	H8
Corstorphine	C Edin	127	M3
Cors-y-Gedol	Gwynd	67	L10
Cortachy	Angus	142	F6
Corton	Suffk	65	Q2
Corton	Wilts	20	H6
Corton Denham	Somset	20	B10
Coruanan	Highld	139	K4
Corwen	Denbgs	68	E6
Coryates	Dorset	11	N7
Coryton	Devon	8	C8
Coryton	Thurr	38	B5
Cosby	Leics	72	E11
Coseley	Dudley	58	D6
Cosford	Shrops	57	Q3
Cosgrove	Nhants	49	L6
Cosham	C Port	15	J5
Cosheston	Pembks	41	K10
Coshieville	P & K	141	J8
Cossall	Notts	72	D2
Cossall Marsh	Notts	72	D2
Cossington	Leics	72	G8
Cossington	Somset	19	L6
Costessey	Norfk	76	H9
Costock	Notts	72	F5
Coston	Leics	73	L6
Coston	Norfk	76	F10
Cote	Oxon	34	C4
Cote	Somset	19	K6
Cotebrook	Ches W	82	C11
Cotehill	Cumb	111	J10
Cotes	Cumb	95	K3
Cotes	Leics	72	F6
Cotes	Staffs	70	E8
Cotesbach	Leics	60	B4
Cotes Heath	Staffs	70	E8
Cotford St Luke	Somset	18	G9
Cotgrave	Notts	72	G3
Cothal	Abers	151	M4
Cotham	Notts	85	N11
Cothelstone	Somset	18	G8
Cotherstone	Dur	103	K7
Cothill	Oxon	34	E5
Cotleigh	Devon	10	E4
Cotmanhay	Derbys	72	D2
Coton	Cambs	62	F9
Coton	Nhants	60	E6
Coton	Shrops	69	P8
Coton	Staffs	59	J4
Coton	Staffs	70	E10
Coton	Staffs	70	H8
Coton Clanford	Staffs	70	F10
Coton Hayes	Staffs	70	H8
Coton Hill	Shrops	56	H2
Coton in the Clay	Staffs	71	M9
Coton in the Elms	Derbys	71	N11
Coton Park	Derbys	71	P11
Cott	Devon	7	K6
Cottam	E R Yk	99	K7
Cottam	Lancs	88	G4
Cottam	Notts	85	P5
Cottenham	Cambs	62	F7
Cotterdale	N York	96	B2
Cottered	Herts	50	H5
Cotteridge	Birm	58	F8
Cotterstock	Nhants	61	M2
Cottesbrooke	Nhants	60	F6
Cottesmore	RutInd	73	N8
Cottingham	E R Yk	92	H4
Cottingham	Nhants	60	H2
Cottingley	C Brad	90	E3
Cottisford	Oxon	48	G8
Cotton	Suffk	64	F8
Cotton End	Bed	61	N11
Cotton Tree	Lancs	89	Q3
Cottown	Abers	150	E2
Cottown	Abers	151	K4
Cottown of Gight	Abers	159	K9
Cotts	Devon	6	C5
Cotwall	Wrekin	69	R11
Cotwalton	Staffs	70	G8
Couch's Mill	Cnwll	5	J10
Coughton	Herefs	46	A10
Coughton	Warwks	47	L2
Coulaghailtro	Ag & B	123	M6
Coulags	Highld	154	C9
Coulby Newham	Middsb	104	F8
Coulderton	Cumb	100	C9
Coull	Abers	150	E7
Coulport	Ag & B	131	Q10
Coulsdon	Gt Lon	36	G9
Coulston	Wilts	21	J4
Coulter	S Lans	116	E4
Coultershaw Bridge	W Susx	23	Q11
Coultings	Somset	18	H6
Coulton	N York	98	C6
Coultra	Fife	135	K3
Cound	Shrops	57	K3
Coundlane	Shrops	57	K4
Coundon	Dur	103	P5
Coundon Grange	Dur	103	P5
Countersett	N York	96	D3
Countess	Wilts	21	N6
Countess Cross	Essex	52	E5
Countess Wear	Devon	9	M7
Countesswells	C Aber	151	M7
Countesthorpe	Leics	72	F11
Countisbury	Devon	17	N2
Coupar Angus	P & K	142	C10
Coupe Green	Lancs	88	H5
Coupland	Cumb	102	D7
Coupland	Nthumb	118	H4
Cour	Ag & B	123	P10
Court-at-Street	Kent	27	J4
Courteachan	Highld	145	L8
Courtenhall	Nhants	49	L4
Court Henry	Carmth	43	L10
Courtsend	Essex	38	H3
Courtway	Somset	18	H8
Cousland	Mdloth	128	B6
Cousley Wood	E Susx	25	Q4
Cove	Ag & B	131	Q11
Cove	Border	129	K5
Cove	Devon	18	C11
Cove	Hants	23	N3
Cove	Highld	160	C8
Cove Bay	C Aber	151	P7
Cove Bottom	Suffk	65	P6
Covehithe	Suffk	65	Q5
Coven	Staffs	58	D3
Coveney	Cambs	62	G4
Covenham St Bartholomew	Lincs	87	K2
Covenham St Mary	Lincs	87	K2
Coven Heath	Staffs	58	D3
Coventry	Covtry	59	M9
Coverack	Cnwll	3	K10
Coverack Bridges	Cnwll	2	H7
Coverham	N York	96	H3
Covington	Cambs	61	N6
Covington	S Lans	116	D3
Cowan Bridge	Lancs	95	N5
Cowbeech	E Susx	25	P8
Cowbit	Lincs	74	E7
Cowbridge	V Glam	30	C10
Cowdale	Derbys	83	N10
Cowden	Kent	25	L2
Cowdenbeath	Fife	134	F9
Cowden Pound	Kent	25	L2
Cowden Station	Kent	25	L2
Cowers Lane	Derbys	71	Q5
Cowes	IoW	14	E7
Cowesby	N York	97	Q3
Cowesfield Green	Wilts	21	Q10
Cowfold	W Susx	24	F6
Cowgill	Cumb	95	R3
Cow Green	Suffk	64	F8
Cowhill	S Glos	32	B6
Cowie	Stirlg	133	N10
Cowlam	E R Yk	99	K7
Cowley	Devon	9	M5
Cowley	Gloucs	33	J3
Cowley	Gt Lon	36	C4
Cowley	Oxon	34	F4
Cowling	Lancs	88	H7
Cowling	N York	90	B2
Cowling	N York	97	K3
Cowlinge	Suffk	63	M10
Cowmes	Kirk	90	F7
Cowpe	Lancs	89	N6
Cowpen	Nthumb	113	L5
Cowpen Bewley	S on T	104	E6
Cowplain	Hants	15	J4
Cowshill	Dur	102	G2
Cowslip Green	N Som	19	N2
Cowthorpe	N York	97	P10
Coxall	Herefs	56	F10
Coxbank	Ches E	70	B6
Coxbench	Derbys	72	B2
Coxbridge	Somset	19	P7
Cox Common	Suffk	65	N5
Coxford	Cnwll	5	K2
Coxford	Norfk	76	B6
Coxgreen	Staffs	57	Q7
Coxheath	Kent	38	B11
Coxhoe	Dur	104	B3
Coxley	Somset	19	P6
Coxley	Wakefd	90	H7
Coxley Wick	Somset	19	P6
Coxpark	Cnwll	5	Q7
Coxtie Green	Essex	51	N11
Coxwold	N York	98	A5
Coychurch	Brdgnd	29	P9
Coylton	S Ayrs	114	H4
Coylumbridge	Highld	148	G5
Coytrahen	Brdgnd	29	N7
Crabbs Cross	Worcs	58	F11
Crab Orchard	Dorset	13	J3
Crabtree	W Susx	24	F5
Crabtree Green	Wrexhm	69	K6
Crackenthorpe	Cumb	102	C6
Crackington Haven	Cnwll	5	J2
Crackley	Staffs	70	E4
Crackley	Warwks	59	L10
Crackleybank	Shrops	57	P2
Crackpot	N York	103	J11
Cracoe	N York	96	E8
Craddock	Devon	10	B2
Cradle End	Herts	51	L6
Cradley	Dudley	58	D7
Cradley	Herefs	46	D5
Cradley Heath	Sandw	58	D7
Cradoc	Powys	44	E8
Crafthole	Cnwll	5	P11
Crafton	Bucks	49	N11
Crag Foot	Lancs	95	K6
Craggan	Highld	149	J2
Cragganmore	Moray	157	M10
Cragg Hill	Leeds	90	G3
Cragg Vale	Calder	90	C6
Craghead	Dur	113	K10
Crai	Powys	44	B10
Craibstone	Moray	158	C6
Craichie	Angus	143	J8
Craig	Angus	143	M6
Craig	Highld	154	D8
Craigbank	E Ayrs	115	L5
Craigburn	Border	127	N7
Craigcleuch	D & G	110	F3
Craigdam	Abers	159	K11
Craigdhu	Ag & B	131	G6
Craigearn	Abers	151	J5
Craigellachie	Moray	157	P9
Craigend	P & K	134	E3
Craigend	Rens	125	M3
Craigendoran	Ag & B	132	C11
Craigends	Rens	125	L4
Craighlaw	D & G	107	K5
Craighouse	Ag & B	122	H6
Craigie	P & K	141	R9
Craigie	S Ayrs	125	L11
Craigiefold	Abers	159	M4
Craigley	D & G	108	G9
Craig Llangiwg	Neath	29	K4
Craiglockhart	C Edin	127	N3
Craigmillar	C Edin	127	Q3
Craignant	Shrops	69	J7
Craigneston	D & G	115	Q10
Craigneuk	N Lans	126	D4
Craigneuk	N Lans	126	D6
Craignure	Ag & B	138	C10
Craigo	Angus	143	M5
Craig Penllyn	V Glam	30	C9
Craigrothie	Fife	135	K5
Craigruie	Stirlg	132	F3
Craig's End	Essex	52	B4
Craigton	Angus	143	J4
Craigton	C Aber	151	L7
Craigton	E Rens	125	M7
Craigton of Airlie	Angus	142	F8
Craig-y-Duke	Neath	29	K4
Craig-y-nos	Powys	44	A11
Craik	Border	117	L9
Crail	Fife	135	Q6
Crailing	Border	118	C6
Craiselound	N Linc	92	C11
Crakehall	N York	97	K3
Crakehill	N York	97	P6
Crakemarsh	Staffs	71	K7
Crambe	N York	98	E8
Crambeck	N York	98	E7
Cramlington	Nthumb	113	L5
Cramond	C Edin	127	M2
Cramond Bridge	C Edin	127	M2
Crampmoor	Hants	22	C10
Cranage	Ches E	82	G11
Cranberry	Staffs	70	E7
Cranbourne	Br For	35	P10
Cranbrook	Devon	9	N6
Cranbrook	Kent	26	C4
Cranbrook Common	Kent	26	C4
Crane Moor	Barns	91	J10
Crane's Corner	Norfk	76	C9
Cranfield	C Beds	49	Q6
Cranford	Devon	16	E7
Cranford	Gt Lon	36	D5
Cranford St Andrew	Nhants	61	K5
Cranford St John	Nhants	61	K5
Cranham	Gloucs	32	G2
Cranham	Gt Lon	37	N3
Cranhill	Warwks	47	M4
Crank	St Hel	81	Q5
Cranleigh	Surrey	24	C3
Cranmer Green	Suffk	64	E7
Cranmore	IoW	14	C8
Cranmore	Somset	20	C6
Cranoe	Leics	73	K11
Cransford	Suffk	65	L9
Cranshaws	Border	128	H7
Cranstal	IoM	80	g1
Cranswick	E R Yk	99	L10
Crantock	Cnwll	4	B9
Cranwell	Lincs	86	D11
Cranwich	Norfk	63	N2
Cranworth	Norfk	76	D11
Craobh Haven	Ag & B	130	D2
Crapstone	Devon	6	E5
Crarae	Ag & B	131	K8
Crask Inn	Highld	162	C2
Crask of Aigas	Highld	155	N9
Craster	Nthumb	119	Q8
Craswall	Herefs	45	K7
Crateford	Staffs	58	D3
Cratfield	Suffk	65	L6
Crathes	Abers	151	K8
Crathie	Abers	149	P8
Crathie	Highld	147	P9
Crathorne	N York	104	D9
Craven Arms	Shrops	56	G8
Crawcrook	Gatesd	112	H8
Crawford	Lancs	81	P4
Crawford	S Lans	116	E7
Crawfordjohn	S Lans	116	B6
Crawley	Hants	22	D8
Crawley	Oxon	34	B2
Crawley	W Susx	24	G3
Crawley Down	W Susx	24	H3
Crawleyside	Dur	103	J2
Crawshawbooth	Lancs	89	N5
Crawton	Abers	143	R2
Craxe's Green	Essex	52	F3
Cray	N York	96	D5
Cray	P & K	142	A5
Crayford	Gt Lon	37	M5
Crayke	N York	98	B6
Craymere Beck	Norfk	76	F5
Crays Hill	Essex	38	B3
Cray's Pond	Oxon	34	H8
Craythorne	Staffs	71	N9
Craze Lowman	Devon	9	N2
Crazies Hill	Wokam	35	L8
Creacombe	Devon	17	Q8
Creagan Inn	Ag & B	138	H9
Creag Ghoraidh	W Isls	168	c13
Creagorry	W Isls	168	c13
Creaguaineach Lodge	Highld	139	Q4
Creamore Bank	Shrops	69	P8
Creaton	Nhants	60	F6
Creca	D & G	110	D6
Credenhill	Herefs	45	P6
Crediton	Devon	9	K4
Creebank	D & G	107	K3
Creebridge	D & G	107	M4
Creech	Dorset	12	F8
Creech Heathfield	Somset	19	J9
Creech St Michael	Somset	19	J9
Creed	Cnwll	3	N4
Creekmoor	BCP	12	H6
Creekmouth	Gt Lon	37	L4
Creeksea	Essex	38	F2
Creeting St Mary	Suffk	64	F10
Creeton	Lincs	73	Q6
Creetown	D & G	107	M6
Cregneash	IoM	80	a8
Creg ny Baa	IoM	80	e5
Cregrina	Powys	44	G4
Creich	Fife	135	J3
Creigiau	Cardif	30	D7
Cremyll	Cnwll	6	D8
Cressage	Shrops	57	K4
Cressbrook	Derbys	83	Q10
Cresselly	Pembks	41	L9
Cressex	Bucks	35	M6
Cressing	Essex	52	C7
Cresswell	Nthumb	113	L2
Cresswell	Pembks	41	L9
Cresswell	Staffs	70	H6
Creswell	Derbys	84	H6
Creswell Green	Staffs	58	G2
Cretingham	Suffk	65	J9
Cretshengan	Ag & B	123	M6
Crewe	Ches E	70	C3
Crewe-by-Farndon	Ches W	69	M4
Crewe Green	Ches E	70	C3
Crew Green	Powys	69	K11
Crewkerne	Somset	11	J3
Crews Hill	Gt Lon	50	H11
Crewton	C Derb	72	B4
Crianlarich	Stirlg	132	D2
Cribyn	Cerdgn	43	K4
Criccieth	Gwynd	66	H7
Crich	Derbys	84	D10
Crich Carr	Derbys	84	D10
Crichton	Mdloth	128	B7
Crick	Mons	31	N6
Crick	Nhants	60	C6
Crickadarn	Powys	44	F6
Cricket St Thomas	Somset	10	H3
Crickheath	Shrops	69	J10
Crickhowell	Powys	45	J11
Cricklade	Wilts	33	L6
Cricklewood	Gt Lon	36	F3
Cridling Stubbs	N York	91	N6
Crieff	P & K	133	Q3
Criggan	Cnwll	4	G9
Criggion	Powys	69	J11

266 Crigglestone – Davington

Crigglestone Wakefd 91 J7
Crimble Rochdl 89 P8
Crimond Abers 159 Q6
Crimplesham Norfk 75 N10
Crimscote Warwks 47 P5
Crinaglack Highld 155 M9
Crinan Ag & B 130 F9
Crindledyke N Lans 126 E6
Cringleford Norfk 76 H10
Cringles C Brad 96 F11
Crinow Pembks 41 M8
Cripplesease Cnwll 2 E6
Cripplestyle Dorset 13 J2
Cripp's Corner E Susx 26 C7
Croachy Highld 148 B2
Croanford Cnwll 4 G7
Crockenhill Kent 37 M7
Crocker End Oxon 35 K7
Crockerhill W Susx 15 P5
Crockernwell Devon 9 J6
Crocker's Ash Herefs 45 Q11
Crockerton Wilts 20 G6
Crocketford D & G 108 H6
Crockey Hill C York 98 C11
Crockham Hill Kent 37 K10
Crockhurst Street Kent 37 P11
Crockleford Heath Essex 52 H6
Crock Street Somset 10 G2
Croeserw Neath 29 N5
Croes-goch Pembks 40 F4
Croes-lan Cerdgn 42 G6
Croesor Gwynd 67 L6
Croesyceiliog Carmth 42 H11
Croesyceiliog Torfn 31 K5
Croes-y-mwyalch Torfn 31 K6
Croes-y-pant Mons 31 K4
Croft Leics 72 E11
Croft Lincs 87 P8
Croft Warrtn 82 D6
Croftamie Stirlg 132 F10
Croft Mitchell Cnwll 2 H6
Crofton Cumb 110 F10
Crofton Wakefd 91 K7
Crofton Wilts 21 Q2
Croft-on-Tees N York 103 Q9
Croftown Highld 161 K10
Crofts Moray 157 P7
Crofts Bank Traffd 82 G5
Crofts of Dipple Moray 157 Q6
Crofts of Haddo Abers 159 K10
Crofts of Savoch Abers 159 P5
Crofty Swans 28 F6
Crogen Gwynd 68 D7
Croggan Ag & B 130 E2
Croglin Cumb 111 L11
Croick Highld 162 B8
Cromarty Highld 156 D4
Crombie Fife 134 D11
Cromdale Highld 149 K2
Cromer Herts 50 G5
Cromer Norfk 77 J3
Cromford Derbys 84 C9
Cromhall S Glos 32 C6
Cromhall Common S Glos 32 C7
Cromor W Isls 168 j5
Cromore W Isls 168 j5
Crompton Fold Oldham 89 Q9
Cromwell Notts 85 N8
Cronberry E Ayrs 115 M3
Crondall Hants 23 L5
Cronkbourne IoM 80 e6
Cronk-y-Voddy IoM 80 d4
Cronton Knows 81 P7
Crook Cumb 101 N11
Crook Dur 103 N3
Crookdake Cumb 100 G2
Crooke Wigan 88 H9
Crooked End Gloucs 46 B11
Crookedholm E Ayrs 125 M10
Crooked Soley Wilts 34 B10
Crookes Sheff 84 D3
Crookhall Dur 112 H10
Crookham Nthumb 118 H3
Crookham W Berk 22 F2
Crookham Village Hants 23 L4
Crook Inn Border 116 G5
Crooklands Cumb 95 L4
Crook of Devon P & K 134 C7
Cropper Derbys 71 N7
Cropredy Oxon 48 E5
Cropston Leics 72 F8
Cropthorne Worcs 47 J5
Cropton N York 98 F3
Cropwell Bishop Notts 72 H3
Cropwell Butler Notts 72 H3
Cros W Isls 168 k1
Crosbost W Isls 168 i5
Crosby Cumb 100 E3
Crosby IoM 80 d6
Crosby N Linc 92 E8
Crosby Sefton 81 L5
Crosby Garret Cumb 102 D9
Crosby Ravensworth Cumb 102 B8
Crosby Villa Cumb 100 E3
Croscombe Somset 19 Q6
Crosemere Shrops 69 M9
Crosland Edge Kirk 90 E8
Crosland Hill Kirk 90 E8
Cross Somset 19 M4
Crossaig Ag & B 123 P9
Crossapol Ag & B 136 B7
Cross Ash Mons 45 N11
Cross-at-Hand Kent 26 C2
Crossbost W Isls 168 i5
Crossbush W Susx 24 B9
Crosscanonby Cumb 100 E3
Cross Coombe Cnwll 3 J3
Crossdale Street Norfk 77 J4
Cross End Bed 61 N9
Cross End Essex 52 E5
Crossens Sefton 88 D6
Cross Flatts C Brad 90 E2
Crossford Fife 134 D10
Crossford S Lans 126 E8
Crossgate Cnwll 5 N4
Crossgate Lincs 74 D5
Crossgate Staffs 70 G7
Crossgatehall E Loth 128 B6
Crossgates E Ayrs 125 K9
Crossgates Fife 134 E10
Cross Gates Leeds 91 K4
Crossgates N York 99 L4
Crossgates Powys 44 F2
Crossgill Lancs 95 M8
Cross Green Devon 5 P4
Cross Green Leeds 91 J4
Cross Green Staffs 58 D3
Cross Green Suffk 64 A11
Cross Green Suffk 64 B10
Cross Green Suffk 64 D11
Cross Hands Carmth 28 G2
Crosshands Carmth 41 N6
Crosshands E Ayrs 125 M11
Cross Hands Pembks 41 L8
Cross Hill Derbys 84 F11
Crosshill Fife 134 F8
Crosshill S Ayrs 114 F6
Cross Hills N York 96 F11
Crosshouse E Ayrs 125 K10
Cross Houses Shrops 57 J3
Cross Houses Shrops 57 M6
Cross in Hand E Susx 25 N6
Cross Inn Cerdgn 42 G3
Cross Inn Cerdgn 43 K2
Cross Inn Pembks 41 M9
Cross Inn Rhondd 30 E8
Cross Keys Ag & B 132 C10
Crosskeys Caerph 30 H6
Cross Keys Wilts 32 G10
Crosskirk Highld 166 H3
Crosslands Cumb 94 G3
Cross Lane IoW 14 F9
Cross Lane Head Shrops 57 N5
Cross Lanes Cnwll 2 H9
Cross Lanes Cnwll 3 K5
Cross Lanes N York 98 A8
Crosslanes Shrops 69 K11
Cross Lanes Wrexhm 69 L5
Crosslee Rens 125 L4
Crossley Kirk 90 G6
Crossmichael D & G 108 F7
Cross Oak Powys 44 G10
Cross of Jackston Abers 158 H11
Cross o' th' hands Derbys 71 P5
Crosspost W Susx 24 G6
Crossroads Abers 150 F6
Crossroads Abers 151 K9
Cross Roads C Brad 90 D3
Cross Street Suffk 64 H6
Crosston Angus 143 J6
Cross Town Ches E 82 G9
Crossway Mons 45 N11
Crossway Powys 44 F3
Crossway Green Mons 31 P6
Crossway Green Worcs 58 B11
Crossways Dorset 12 C7
Crosswell Pembks 41 M3
Crosthwaite Cumb 95 J2
Croston Lancs 88 F7
Crostwick Norfk 77 K8
Crostwight Norfk 77 L6
Crouch Kent 37 P9
Crouch Kent 39 J10
Crouch End Gt Lon 36 H3
Croucheston Wilts 21 L9
Crouch Hill Dorset 11 Q2
Crough House Green Kent 37 K11
Croughton Nhants 48 F8
Crovie Abers 159 K4
Crow Hants 13 L4
Crowan Cnwll 2 G7
Crowborough E Susx 25 M4
Crowborough Warren E Susx 25 M4
Crowcombe Somset 18 F7
Crowdecote Derbys 83 P11
Crowden Derbys 83 N5
Crowden Devon 8 C5
Crowdhill Hants 22 E10
Crowdleham Kent 37 N9
Crow Edge Barns 83 Q4
Crowell Oxon 35 K5
Crow End Cambs 62 D9
Crowfield Nhants 48 H6
Crowfield Suffk 64 G10
Crowfield Green Suffk 64 G10
Crowgate Street Norfk 77 L7
Crow Green Essex 51 N11
Crowhill E Loth 129 J5
Crow Hill Herefs 46 B9
Crowhole Derbys 84 D5
Crowhurst E Susx 26 C9
Crowhurst Surrey 37 J11
Crowhurst Lane End Surrey 37 J11
Crowland Lincs 74 D8
Crowland Suffk 64 E7
Crowlas Cnwll 2 E7
Crowle N Linc 92 C8
Crowle Worcs 46 H3
Crowle Green Worcs 46 H3
Crowmarsh Gifford Oxon 34 H7
Crown Corner Suffk 65 K7
Crownhill C Plym 6 D7
Crownpits Surrey 23 Q6
Crownthorpe Norfk 76 F11
Crowntown Cnwll 2 G7
Crows-an-Wra Cnwll 2 B8
Crow's Green Essex 51 Q5
Crowshill Norfk 76 D10
Crow's Nest Cnwll 5 M8
Crowsnest Shrops 56 F4
Crowthorne Wokham 23 M2
Crowton Ches W 82 C10
Croxall Staffs 59 J2
Croxby Lincs 93 L11
Croxdale Dur 103 Q3
Croxden Staffs 71 K7
Croxley Green Herts 50 C11
Croxteth Lpool 81 N5
Croxton Cambs 62 B8
Croxton N Linc 93 J8
Croxton Norfk 64 B4
Croxton Norfk 76 D5
Croxton Staffs 70 D8
Croxtonbank Staffs 70 D8
Croxton Green Ches E 69 Q4
Croxton Kerrial Leics 73 L5
Croy Highld 156 D8
Croy N Lans 126 C2
Croyde Devon 16 G4
Croyde Bay Devon 16 G4
Croydon Cambs 62 D11
Croydon Gt Lon 36 H7
Crubenmore Highld 148 B9
Cruckmeole Shrops 56 G3
Cruckton Shrops 56 G2
Cruden Bay Abers 159 Q10
Crudgington Wrekin 70 A11
Crudie Abers 159 J6
Crudwell Wilts 33 J6
Cruft Devon 8 D5
Crûg Powys 56 B10
Crugmeer Cnwll 4 E6
Crugybar Carmth 43 N7
Crug-y-byddar Powys 56 B8
Crumlin Caerph 30 H5
Crumplehorn Cnwll 5 L11
Crumpsall Manch 82 H4
Crundale Kent 27 J2
Crundale Pembks 41 J7
Crunwere Pembks 41 N8
Cruwys Morchard Devon 9 L2
Crux Easton Hants 22 D3
Cruxton Dorset 11 N5
Crwbin Carmth 28 E2
Cryers Hill Bucks 35 N5
Crymych Pembks 41 N4
Crynant Neath 29 L4
Crystal Palace Gt Lon 36 H6
Cuaig Highld 153 N6
Cuan Ag & B 130 F5
Cubbington Warwks 59 M11
Cubert Cnwll 4 B10
Cubley Barns 90 G10
Cublington Bucks 49 M10
Cublington Herefs 45 N7
Cuckfield W Susx 24 H5
Cucklington Somset 20 E9
Cuckney Notts 85 J6
Cuckoo Bridge Lincs 74 D6
Cuckoo's Corner Hants 23 K6
Cuckoo's Nest Ches W 69 L2
Cuddesdon Oxon 34 G4
Cuddington Bucks 35 K2
Cuddington Ches W 82 C10
Cuddington Heath Ches W 69 N5
Cuddy Hill Lancs 88 F3
Cudham Gt Lon 37 K9
Cudliptown Devon 8 D9
Cudnell BCP 13 J5
Cudworth Barns 91 K9
Cudworth Somset 10 H2
Cuerdley Cross Warrtn 82 B7
Cufaude Hants 23 J3
Cuffley Herts 50 H10
Cuil Highld 138 H6
Culbokie Highld 155 R6
Culbone Somset 17 Q2
Culburnie Highld 155 N9
Culcabock Highld 156 B9
Culcharry Highld 156 F7
Culcheth Warrtn 82 E6
Culdrain Abers 158 D11
Culduie Highld 153 N9
Culford Suffk 64 A7
Culgaith Cumb 102 B5
Culham Oxon 34 F5
Culkein Highld 164 B10
Culkein Drumbeg Highld 164 D10
Culkerton Gloucs 32 H5
Cullen Moray 158 D4
Cullercoats N Tyne 113 N6
Cullerlie Abers 151 K7
Cullicudden Highld 156 A5
Cullingworth C Brad 90 D3
Cuillin Hills Highld 144 G3
Cullipool Ag & B 130 E5
Cullivoe Shet 169 s3
Culloden Highld 156 C8
Cullompton Devon 9 P3
Cullompton Services Devon 9 P3
Culm Davy Devon 18 F11
Culmington Shrops 56 H8
Culmstock Devon 10 C2
Culnacraig Highld 160 H6
Culnaightrie D & G 108 G10
Culnaknock Highld 153 J5
Culpho Suffk 53 M2
Culrain Highld 162 D8
Culross Fife 134 B10
Culroy S Ayrs 114 F5
Culsalmond Abers 158 G11
Culscadden D & G 107 N8
Culshabbin D & G 107 K7
Culswick Shet 169 p9
Cultercullen Abers 151 N3
Cults C Aber 151 M7
Culverstone Green Kent 37 P8
Culverthorpe Lincs 73 Q2
Culworth Nhants 48 F5
Culzean Castle & Country Park S Ayrs 114 D5
Cumbernauld N Lans 126 D3
Cumbernauld Village N Lans 126 D2
Cumberworth Lincs 87 P6
Cumdivock Cumb 110 F11
Cuminestown Abers 159 K7
Cumledge Border 129 K8
Cummersdale Cumb 110 G10
Cummertrees D & G 109 P7
Cummingston Moray 157 L4
Cumnock E Ayrs 115 L3
Cumnor Oxon 34 E4
Cumrew Cumb 111 L10
Cumrue D & G 109 N3
Cumwhinton Cumb 111 J10
Cumwhitton Cumb 111 K10
Cundall N York 97 P6
Cunninghamhead N Ayrs 125 K9
Cunningsburgh Shet 169 r10
Cupar Fife 135 K5
Cupar Muir Fife 135 K5
Curbar Derbys 84 C6
Curbridge Hants 14 F4
Curbridge Oxon 34 B3
Curdridge Hants 14 F4
Curdworth Warwks 59 J6
Curland Somset 19 J11
Curridge W Berk 34 E10
Currie C Edin 127 M4
Curry Mallet Somset 19 K10
Curry Rivel Somset 19 L9
Curteis Corner Kent 26 E4
Curtisden Green Kent 26 B3
Curtisknowle Devon 7 J8
Cury Cnwll 2 H9
Cushnie Abers 150 E5
Cushuish Somset 18 G8
Cusop Herefs 45 J6
Cusworth Donc 91 N10
Cutcloy D & G 107 N11
Cutcombe Somset 18 B7
Cutgate Rochdl 89 P8
Cuthill Highld 162 H9
Cutiau Gwynd 67 L11
Cutler's Green Essex 51 N4
Cutmadoc Cnwll 4 H9
Cutmere Cnwll 5 N9
Cutnall Green Worcs 58 C11
Cutsdean Gloucs 47 L8
Cutthorpe Derbys 84 D6
Cuttivett Cnwll 5 P9
Cuxham Oxon 35 J5
Cuxton Medway 38 B8
Cuxwold Lincs 93 L10
Cwm Blae G 30 G3
Cwm Denbgs 80 F9
Cwmafan Neath 29 L6
Cwmaman Rhondd 30 D5
Cwmann Carmth 43 L5
Cwmavon Torfn 31 J3
Cwmbach Carmth 28 E4
Cwmbach Carmth 41 Q5
Cwmbâch Powys 44 H7
Cwmbach Rhondd 30 D4
Cwmbach Llechrhyd Powys 44 E4
Cwmbelan Powys 55 L8
Cwmbran Torfn 31 J6
Cwmbrwyno Cerdgn 54 G8
Cwm Capel Carmth 28 E4
Cwmcarn Caerph 30 H6
Cwmcarvan Mons 31 N3
Cwm-celyn Blae G 30 H3
Cwm-Cewydd Gwynd 55 K2
Cwm-cou Cerdgn 41 Q2
Cwm Crawnon Powys 44 G11
Cwmdare Rhondd 30 C4
Cwmdu Carmth 43 M8
Cwmdu Powys 44 H10
Cwmdu Swans 28 H6
Cwmduad Carmth 42 G8
Cwm Dulais Swans 28 H4
Cwmdwr Carmth 43 P8
Cwmfelin Brdgnd 29 N7
Cwmfelin Myr Td 30 E4
Cwmfelin Boeth Carmth 41 N7
Cwmfelinfach Caerph 30 G6
Cwmfelin Mynach Carmth 41 P6
Cwmffrwd Carmth 42 H11
Cwmgiedd Powys 29 L2
Cwmgorse Carmth 29 K2
Cwm Gwaun Pembks 41 K4
Cwmgwili Carmth 28 G2
Cwmgwrach Neath 29 N4
Cwmhiraeth Carmth 42 F7
Cwmifor Carmth 43 N9
Cwm Irfon Powys 44 B5
Cwmisfael Carmth 43 J11
Cwm Llinau Powys 55 J3
Cwmllynfell Neath 29 K2
Cwmmawr Carmth 28 F2
Cwm Morgan Carmth 41 Q4
Cwmparc Rhondd 29 P5
Cwmpengraig Carmth 42 G7
Cwm Penmachno Conwy 67 P5
Cwmpennar Rhondd 30 D4
Cwmrhos Powys 44 H10
Cwmrhydyceirw Swans 29 J5
Cwmsychbant Cerdgn 43 J5
Cwmtillery Blae G 30 H3
Cwm-twrch Isaf Powys 29 L2
Cwm-twrch Uchaf Powys 29 L2
Cwm-y-glo Carmth 28 G2
Cwm-y-glo Gwynd 67 K2
Cwmyoy Mons 45 K10
Cwmystwyth Cerdgn 54 H10
Cwrt Gwynd 54 F5
Cwrtnewydd Cerdgn 43 J5
Cwrt-y-gollen Powys 45 J11
Cyfarthfa Castle Museum Myr Td 30 D3
Cyffylliog Denbgs 68 E3
Cyfronydd Powys 55 Q3
Cylibebyll Neath 29 K4
Cymau Flints 69 J3
Cymmer Neath 29 N5
Cymmer Rhondd 30 D6
Cyncoed Cardif 30 G8
Cynghordy Carmth 43 R6
Cynheidre Carmth 28 E3
Cynonville Neath 29 M5
Cynwyd Denbgs 68 E6
Cynwyl Elfed Carmth 42 G9

D

Daccombe Devon 7 N5
Dacre Cumb 101 N5
Dacre N York 97 J8
Dacre Banks N York 97 J8
Daddry Shield Dur 102 G3
Dadford Bucks 49 J7
Dadlington Leics 72 C11
Dafen Carmth 28 F4
Daffy Green Norfk 76 D10
Dagenham Gt Lon 37 M4
Daglingworth Gloucs 33 J3
Dagnall Bucks 49 Q11
Dagworth Suffk 64 E9
Dail bho Dheas W Isls 168 j1
Dailly S Ayrs 114 E7
Dainton Devon 7 M5
Dairsie Fife 135 L4
Daisy Hill Bolton 82 E4
Daisy Hill Leeds 90 H5
Dalabrog W Isls 168 c15
Dalavich Ag & B 131 K5
Dalbeattie D & G 108 H8
Dalbury Derbys 71 P8
Dalby IoM 80 b6
Dalby Lincs 87 M7
Dalby N York 98 C6
Dalcapon P & K 141 N7
Dalchalm Highld 163 L5
Dalchreichart Highld 146 H5
Dalchruin P & K 133 L4
Dalcrue P & K 134 C2
Dalderby Lincs 87 J7
Daldith Devon 9 P8
Dale Cumb 101 P2
Dale Pembks 40 F9
Dale Abbey Derbys 72 C3
Dale Bottom Cumb 101 J6
Dale End Derbys 84 B8
Dale End N York 96 E11
Dale Hill E Susx 26 B5
Dalehouse N York 105 L7
Dalelia Highld 138 C4
Dalgarven N Ayrs 124 H8
Dalgety Bay Fife 134 F11
Dalgig E Ayrs 115 L5
Dalginross P & K 133 M3
Dalguise P & K 141 N8
Dalhalvaig Highld 166 E6
Dalham Suffk 63 M8
Daliburgh W Isls 168 c15
Dalkeith Mdloth 127 Q4
Dallas Moray 157 L7
Dallinghoo Suffk 65 K10
Dallington E Susx 25 Q7
Dallington Nhants 60 F8
Dallow N York 97 J6
Dalmally Ag & B 131 P2
Dalmary Stirlg 132 G8
Dalmellington E Ayrs 115 J6
Dalmeny C Edin 127 L2
Dalmore Highld 156 B4
Dalmuir W Duns 125 M3
Dalnabreck Highld 138 C4
Dalnacardoch P & K 140 H3
Dalnahaitnach Highld 148 F4
Dalnaspidal P & K 140 F3
Dalnawillan Lodge Highld 166 H8
Dalqueich P & K 134 D7
Dalquhairn S Ayrs 114 F8
Dalreavoch Highld 162 H5
Dalry N Ayrs 124 H8
Dalrymple E Ayrs 114 G5
Dalserf S Lans 126 D7
Dalsmeran Ag & B 120 B9
Dalston Cumb 110 G10
Dalston Gt Lon 36 H4
Dalswinton D & G 109 K3
Dalton Cumb 95 L5
Dalton D & G 109 P6
Dalton Lancs 88 F9
Dalton N York 97 P5
Dalton N York 103 M9
Dalton Nthumb 112 H6
Dalton Rothm 84 G2
Dalton-in-Furness Cumb 94 E6
Dalton-le-Dale Dur 113 P11
Dalton Magna Rothm 84 G2
Dalton-on-Tees N York 103 Q9
Dalton Parva Rothm 84 G2
Dalton Piercy Hartpl 104 E4
Dalveich Stirlg 133 J3
Dalwhinnie Highld 147 Q11
Dalwood Devon 10 E4
Damask Green Herts 50 G5
Damerham Hants 21 M11
Damgate Norfk 77 N10
Dam Green Norfk 64 E4
Damnaglaur D & G 106 F10
Danaway Kent 38 E9
Danbury Essex 52 C10
Danby N York 105 K9
Danby Bottom N York 105 J10
Danby Wiske N York 104 B11
Dandaleith Moray 157 P8
Danderhall Mdloth 127 Q4
Danebridge Ches E 83 L11
Dane End Herts 50 H6
Danegate E Susx 25 N4
Danehill E Susx 25 K5
Dane Hills C Leic 72 F10
Danemoor Green Norfk 76 F10
Danesford Shrops 57 N6
Danesmoor Derbys 84 F8
Dane Street Kent 39 J11
Daniel's Water Kent 26 G3
Danshillock Abers 158 H6
Danskine E Loth 128 F6
Danthorpe E R Yk 93 N4
Danzey Green Warwks 58 H11
Dapple Heath Staffs 71 J9
Darby Green Hants 23 M2
Darcy Lever Bolton 89 L9
Dardy Powys 45 J11
Darenth Kent 37 N6
Daresbury Halton 82 C8
Darfield Barns 91 L10
Darfoulds Notts 85 J5
Dargate Kent 39 J9
Dargavel Rens 125 L3
Darite Cnwll 5 M8
Darland Medway 38 C8
Darland Wrexhm 69 L3
Darlaston Wsall 58 E5
Darlaston Green Wsall 58 E5
Darley N York 97 K9
Darley Abbey C Derb 72 B3
Darley Bridge Derbys 84 C8
Darley Dale Derbys 84 C8
Darley Green Solhll 59 J10
Darleyhall Herts 50 D6
Darley Head N York 97 J9
Darlingscott Warwks 47 P6
Darlington Darltn 103 Q8
Darliston Shrops 69 Q8
Darlton Notts 85 N6
Darnford Staffs 58 H3
Darnick Border 117 Q4
Darowen Powys 55 J4
Darra Abers 158 H8
Darracott Devon 16 C8
Darracott Devon 16 H4
Darras Hall Nthumb 113 J6
Darrington Wakefd 91 M7
Darsham Suffk 65 N8
Darshill Somset 20 B6
Dartford Kent 37 M6
Dartford Crossing Kent 37 N5
Dartington Devon 7 K6
Dartmeet Devon 6 H4
Dartmoor National Park Devon 8 G9
Dartmouth Devon 7 M8
Darton Barns 91 J8
Darvel E Ayrs 125 P10
Darwell Hole E Susx 25 Q7
Darwen Bl w D 89 K6
Datchet W & M 35 Q9
Datchworth Herts 50 G7
Datchworth Green Herts 50 G7
Daubhill Bolton 89 L9
Daugh of Kinermony Moray 157 N9
Dauntsey Wilts 33 J8
Dava Highld 157 J10
Davenham Ches W 82 E10
Davenport Stockp 83 K7
Davenport Green Ches E 82 H9
Davenport Green Traffd 82 H7
Daventry Nhants 60 C8
Davidson's Mains C Edin 127 N2
Davidstow Cnwll 5 K4
David Street Kent 37 P8
Davington D & G 117 J10

Davington Hill Kent....38 H9
Daviot Abers....151 J2
Daviot Highld....156 C10
Daviot House Highld....156 C9
Davis's Town E Susx....25 M7
Davoch of Grange Moray....158 C7
Davyhulme Traffd....82 G5
Daw End Wsall....58 F4
Dawesgreen Surrey....36 F11
Dawley Wrekin....57 M3
Dawlish Devon....9 N9
Dawlish Warren Devon....9 N9
Dawn Conwy....80 B10
Daws Green Somset....18 G10
Daws Heath Essex....38 D4
Daw's House Cnwll....5 N5
Dawsmere Lincs....74 H4
Daybrook Notts....85 J11
Day Green Ches E....70 D3
Dayhills Staffs....70 H8
Dayhouse Bank Worcs....58 E9
Daylesford Gloucs....47 P9
Ddol Flints....80 G10
Ddol-Cownwy Powys....68 D11
Deal Kent....39 Q11
Dean Cumb....100 E5
Dean Devon....7 J6
Dean Devon....17 L2
Dean Devon....17 N2
Dean Dorset....21 J11
Dean Hants....22 D8
Dean Hants....22 G11
Dean Lancs....89 P5
Dean Oxon....48 B10
Dean Somset....20 C6
Dean Bottom Kent....37 N7
Deanburnhaugh Border....117 M8
Deancombe Devon....7 J6
Dean Court Oxon....34 E3
Deane Bolton....89 K9
Deane Hants....22 F4
Dean End Dorset....21 J11
Dean Head Barns....90 H10
Deanhead Kirk....90 C7
Deanland Dorset....21 J11
Deanlane End W Susx....15 K4
Dean Prior Devon....7 J6
Deanraw Nthumb....112 B8
Dean Row Ches E....83 J8
Deans W Loth....127 J4
Deanscales Cumb....100 E5
Deanshanger Nhants....49 L7
Deanshaugh Moray....157 R7
Deanston Stirlg....133 L7
Dean Street Kent....38 B11
Dearham Cumb....100 E5
Dearnley Rochdl....89 Q7
Debach Suffk....65 J11
Debden Essex....51 K11
Debden Essex....51 N4
Debden Green Essex....51 N4
Debenham Suffk....64 H9
Deblin's Green Worcs....46 F5
Dechmont W Loth....127 J3
Dechmont Road W Loth....127 J4
Deddington Oxon....48 E8
Dedham Essex....53 J5
Dedham Heath Essex....53 J5
Dedworth W & M....35 P9
Deene Nhants....61 K2
Deenethorpe Nhants....61 L2
Deepcar Sheff....90 H11
Deepcut Surrey....23 P3
Deepdale Cumb....95 Q4
Deepdale N York....96 C5
Deeping Gate C Pete....74 B9
Deeping St James Lincs....74 C9
Deeping St Nicholas Lincs....74 D7
Deerhurst Gloucs....46 G8
Deerhurst Walton Gloucs....46 G9
Deerton Street Kent....38 G9
Defford Worcs....46 H6
Defynnog Powys....44 D9
Deganwy Conwy....79 P9
Degnish Ag & B....130 F5
Deighton C York....91 Q2
Deighton N York....104 C10
Deiniolen Gwynd....67 K2
Delabole Cnwll....4 H5
Delamere Ches W....82 C11
Delamere Park Ches W....82 C10
Delfrigs Abers....151 P3
Delley Devon....17 J7
Delliefure Highld....157 K11
Dell Quay W Susx....15 M6
Delly End Oxon....34 C2
Delnabo Moray....149 M4
Delny Highld....156 C3
Delph Oldham....90 B9
Delves Dur....112 H11
Delvin End Essex....52 C4
Dembleby Lincs....73 Q3
Demelza Cnwll....4 F9
Denaby Donc....91 M11
Denaby Main Donc....91 M11
Denbies Surrey....36 D10
Denbigh Denbgs....80 F11
Denbrae Fife....135 K4
Denbury Devon....7 L5
Denby Derbys....84 E11
Denby Bottles Derbys....84 E11
Denby Dale Kirk....90 G9
Denchworth Oxon....34 C6
Dendron Cumb....94 E6
Denel End C Beds....50 B3
Denfield P & K....134 B4
Denford Nhants....61 L5
Dengie Essex....52 G11
Denham Bucks....36 B3
Denham Suffk....63 N8
Denham Suffk....64 H7
Denham End Suffk....63 N8
Denham Green Bucks....36 B3
Denham Green Suffk....64 H7
Denhead Abers....159 N9
Denhead Fife....135 M5
Denhead of Gray C Dund....142 F11
Denholm Border....117 R7
Denholme C Brad....90 D4
Denholme Clough C Brad....90 D4
Denio Gwynd....66 F7
Denmead Hants....15 J4
Denmore C Aber....151 N5
Denne Park W Susx....24 E5
Dennington Suffk....65 K8
Denny Falk....133 N11

Dennyloanhead Falk....133 N11
Den of Lindores Fife....134 H4
Denshaw Oldham....90 B8
Denside of Durris Abers....151 L8
Densole Kent....27 M3
Denston Suffk....63 N10
Denstone Staffs....71 K6
Denstroude Kent....39 K9
Dent Cumb....95 Q3
Denton Cambs....61 Q3
Denton Darltn....103 P7
Denton E Susx....25 L10
Denton Kent....27 M2
Denton Kent....37 Q6
Denton Lincs....73 M4
Denton N York....96 H11
Denton Nhants....60 H9
Denton Norfk....65 K4
Denton Oxon....34 G4
Denton Tamesd....83 K5
Denver Norfk....75 M10
Denwick Nthumb....119 P8
Deopham Norfk....76 E11
Deopham Green Norfk....64 E2
Depden Suffk....63 N9
Depden Green Suffk....63 N9
Deptford Gt Lon....37 J5
Deptford Wilts....21 K7
Derby C Derb....72 B3
Derby Devon....17 K5
Derbyhaven IoM....80 c8
Derculich P & K....141 L7
Dereham Norfk....76 D9
Deri Caerph....30 F4
Derril Devon....16 E11
Derringstone Kent....27 M2
Derrington Staffs....70 F10
Derriton Devon....16 E11
Derry Hill Wilts....33 J10
Derrythorpe N Linc....92 D9
Dersingham Norfk....75 N4
Dervaig Ag & B....137 L5
Derwen Denbgs....68 E4
Derwenlas Powys....54 G5
Derwent Valley Mills Derbys....84 D9
Derwent Water Cumb....101 J6
Derwydd Carmth....43 M11
Desborough Nhants....60 H4
Desford Leics....72 D10
Detchant Nthumb....119 L3
Detling Kent....38 C10
Deuxhill Shrops....57 M7
Devauden Mons....31 N5
Devil's Bridge Cerdgn....54 G9
Devitts Green Warwks....59 L6
Devizes Wilts....21 K2
Devonport C Plym....6 D8
Devonside Clacks....133 Q8
Devoran Cnwll....3 K6
Devoran & Perran Cnwll....3 K6
Dewarton Mdloth....128 B7
Dewlish Dorset....12 C5
Dewsbury Kirk....90 G6
Dewsbury Moor Kirk....90 G6
Deytheur Powys....68 H11
Dial N Som....31 P11
Dial Green W Susx....23 P9
Dial Post W Susx....24 E7
Dibberford Dorset....11 K4
Dibden Hants....14 D5
Dibden Purlieu Hants....14 D5
Dickens Heath Solhl....58 H9
Dickleburgh Norfk....64 H5
Didbrook Gloucs....47 L8
Didcot Oxon....34 F6
Diddington Cambs....61 Q7
Diddlebury Shrops....57 J7
Didley Herefs....45 P8
Didling W Susx....23 M11
Didmarton Gloucs....32 F7
Didsbury Manch....82 H6
Didworthy Devon....6 H7
Digby Lincs....86 E10
Digg Highld....152 H4
Diggle Oldham....90 C9
Digmoor Lancs....88 F9
Digswell Herts....50 F7
Digswell Water Herts....50 G8
Dihewyd Cerdgn....43 J3
Dilham Norfk....77 L6
Dilhorne Staffs....70 H6
Dill Hall Lancs....89 M5
Dillington Cambs....61 P7
Dilston Nthumb....112 H8
Dilton Wilts....20 G5
Dilton Marsh Wilts....20 F5
Dilwyn Herefs....45 N4
Dimple Bolton....89 L7
Dimple Derbys....84 C8
Dinas Carmth....41 Q4
Dinas Cnwll....4 E7
Dinas Gwynd....66 D7
Dinas Gwynd....66 H3
Dinas Rhondd....30 D6
Dinas Cross Pembks....41 K3
Dinas Dinlle Gwynd....66 G3
Dinas-Mawddwy Gwynd....67 R11
Dinas Powys V Glam....30 G10
Dinder Somset....19 Q6
Dinedor Herefs....45 Q7
Dingestow Mons....31 N2
Dingle Lpool....81 M7
Dingleden Kent....26 D5
Dingley Nhants....60 G3
Dingwall Highld....155 P6
Dinmael Conwy....68 D6
Dinnet Abers....150 D8
Dinnington N u Ty....113 K6
Dinnington Rothm....84 H3
Dinnington Somset....11 J2
Dinorwic Gwynd....67 K2
Dinton Bucks....35 L2
Dinton Wilts....21 K8
Dinwoodie D & G....109 P2
Dinworthy Devon....16 E8
Dipford Somset....18 H10
Dipley Hants....23 K3
Dippen Ag & B....120 F4
Dippenhall Surrey....23 M5
Dippermill Devon....8 B3
Dippertown Devon....8 B8
Dippin N Ayrs....121 K7
Dipple Moray....157 Q6
Dipple S Ayrs....114 D7
Diptford Devon....7 J7
Dipton Dur....113 J10

Diptonmill Nthumb....112 D8
Dirleton E Loth....128 E3
Dirt Pot Nthumb....112 C11
Discoed Powys....45 K2
Diseworth Leics....72 D6
Dishforth N York....97 N6
Disley Ches E....83 L8
Diss Norfk....64 G5
Disserth Powys....44 E3
Distington Cumb....100 D6
Ditchampton Wilts....21 L8
Ditcheat Somset....20 B7
Ditchingham Norfk....65 L3
Ditchling E Susx....24 H7
Ditherington Shrops....57 J2
Ditteridge Wilts....32 F11
Dittisham Devon....7 M7
Ditton Kent....38 B10
Ditton Green Cambs....63 L9
Ditton Priors Shrops....57 L7
Dixton Gloucs....47 J8
Dixton Mons....31 P2
Dizzard Cnwll....5 K2
Dobcross Oldham....90 B9
Dobwalls Cnwll....5 L8
Doccombe Devon....9 J7
Dochgarroch Highld....155 R9
Dockenfield Surrey....23 M6
Docker Lancs....95 M6
Docking Norfk....75 Q3
Docklow Herefs....45 R3
Dockray Cumb....101 L6
Dockray Cumb....110 E11
Dodbrooke Devon....7 J10
Doddinghurst Essex....51 N11
Doddington Cambs....62 F2
Doddington Kent....38 F10
Doddington Lincs....85 Q6
Doddington Nthumb....119 J4
Doddington Shrops....57 L9
Doddiscombsleigh Devon....9 L7
Dodd's Green Ches E....69 R6
Doddshill Norfk....75 N4
Doddy Cross Cnwll....5 N9
Dodford Nhants....60 D8
Dodford Worcs....58 D10
Dodington S Glos....32 E8
Dodington Somset....18 G6
Dodleston Ches W....69 L2
Dodscott Devon....17 J8
Dod's Leigh Staffs....71 J8
Dodworth Barns....91 J9
Dodworth Bottom Barns....91 J10
Dodworth Green Barns....91 J10
Doe Bank Birm....58 H5
Doe Lea Derbys....84 G7
Dogdyke Lincs....86 H9
Dogley Lane Kirk....90 F8
Dogmersfield Hants....23 L4
Dogridge Wilts....33 L7
Dogsthorpe C Pete....74 C10
Dog Village Devon....9 N5
Dolanog Powys....55 P2
Dolau Powys....55 Q11
Dolaucothi Carmth....43 N6
Dolbenmaen Gwynd....67 J6
Doley Staffs....70 C9
Dolfach Powys....55 L4
Dol-fôr Powys....55 J3
Dolfor Powys....55 Q7
Dolgarrog Conwy....79 P11
Dolgellau Gwynd....67 N11
Dolgoch Gwynd....54 F4
Dol-gran Carmth....42 H8
Doll Highld....163 K6
Dollar Clacks....134 B8
Dollarfield Clacks....134 B8
Dolley Green Powys....56 D11
Dollwen Cerdgn....54 F8
Dolphin Flints....80 H10
Dolphinholme Lancs....95 L10
Dolphinton S Lans....127 L8
Dolton Devon....17 K9
Dolwen Conwy....80 B10
Dolwyddelan Conwy....67 N4
Dolybont Cerdgn....54 E7
Dolyhir Powys....45 J3
Domgay Powys....69 J11
Donaldson's Lodge Nthumb....118 G2
Doncaster Donc....91 P10
Doncaster Carr Donc....91 P10
Doncaster North Services
Donc....91 R8
Doncaster Sheffield Airport Donc....91 R11
Donhead St Andrew Wilts....20 H10
Donhead St Mary Wilts....20 H10
Donibristle Fife....134 E10
Doniford Somset....18 E6
Donington Lincs....74 D3
Donington on Bain Lincs....86 H4
Donington Park Services Leics....72 D5
Donington Southing Lincs....74 D4
Donisthorpe Leics....59 M2
Donkey Street Kent....27 K5
Donkey Town Surrey....23 P2
Donnington Gloucs....47 N9
Donnington Herefs....46 D8
Donnington Shrops....57 K3
Donnington W Berk....34 E11
Donnington W Susx....15 N6
Donnington Wrekin....57 N2
Donnington Wood Wrekin....57 N2
Donyatt Somset....10 G2
Doomsday Green W Susx....24 E5
Doonfoot S Ayrs....114 F4
Dora's Green Hants....23 M5
Dorback Lodge Highld....149 K4
Dorchester-on-Thames Oxon....34 G6
Dordon Warwks....59 L4
Dore Sheff....84 D4
Dores Highld....155 Q10
Dorking Surrey....36 E11
Dorking Tye Suffk....52 F4
Dormansland Surrey....25 K2
Dormans Park Surrey....25 J2
Dormington Herefs....46 A6
Dormston Worcs....47 J3
Dorn Gloucs....47 P8
Dorney Bucks....35 P9
Dorney Reach Bucks....35 P9
Dornie Highld....145 Q2

Dornoch Highld....162 H9
Dornock D & G....110 D7
Dorrery Highld....167 J6
Dorridge Solhll....59 J10
Dorrington Lincs....86 E10
Dorrington Shrops....56 H4
Dorrington Shrops....70 C6
Dorsington Warwks....47 M5
Dorstone Herefs....45 L6
Dorton Bucks....35 J2
Dosthill Staffs....59 K5
Dothan IoA....78 F10
Dottery Dorset....11 K5
Doublebois Cnwll....5 K9
Doughton Gloucs....32 G6
Douglas IoM....80 e6
Douglas S Lans....116 A4
Douglas and Angus C Dund....142 G11
Douglas Pier Ag & B....131 P8
Douglastown Angus....142 G8
Douglas Water S Lans....116 B3
Douglas West S Lans....126 E11
Doulting Somset....20 B6
Dounby Ork....169 b4
Doune Highld....161 Q6
Doune Stirlg....133 L7
Dounepark S Ayrs....114 C8
Dounie Highld....162 D8
Dousland Devon....6 E5
Dovaston Shrops....69 L10
Dove Dale Derbys....71 L4
Dove Green Notts....84 G10
Dove Holes Derbys....83 N9
Dovenby Cumb....100 E4
Dover Kent....27 P3
Dover Wigan....82 D4
Dover Castle Kent....27 P3
Dovercourt Essex....53 M5
Doverdale Worcs....58 C11
Doveridge Derbys....71 L8
Doversgreen Surrey....36 G11
Dowally P & K....141 P8
Dowbridge Lancs....88 E4
Dowdeswell Gloucs....47 K11
Dowlais Myr Td....30 E3
Dowland Devon....17 K9
Dowlish Ford Somset....10 H2
Dowlish Wake Somset....10 H2
Down Ampney Gloucs....33 L5
Downderry Cnwll....5 N11
Downe Gt Lon....37 K8
Downend Gloucs....32 F5
Downend IoW....14 F9
Downend S Glos....32 C9
Downend W Berk....34 E9
Downfield C Dund....142 F11
Downgate Cnwll....5 M7
Downgate Cnwll....5 P7
Downham Essex....38 B2
Downham Gt Lon....37 J6
Downham Lancs....89 M2
Downham Market Norfk....75 M10
Down Hatherley Gloucs....46 G10
Downhead Somset....19 Q9
Downhead Somset....20 C5
Downhill Cnwll....4 D8
Downhill P & K....134 D2
Downholland Cross Lancs....88 D9
Downholme N York....103 M11
Downicarey Devon....5 P3
Downies Abers....151 N9
Downing Flints....80 H9
Downley Bucks....35 M5
Down St Mary Devon....8 H4
Downside Somset....20 B4
Downside Somset....20 B6
Downside Surrey....36 D9
Down Thomas Devon....6 E8
Downton Hants....13 N6
Downton Wilts....21 N10
Dowsby Lincs....74 B5
Dowsdale Lincs....74 E8
Doxey Staffs....70 F10
Doxford Nthumb....119 N6
Doynton S Glos....32 D10
Draethen Caerph....30 H7
Draffan S Lans....126 D8
Dragonby N Linc....92 F8
Dragons Green W Susx....24 D6
Drakeholes Notts....85 M2
Drakelow Worcs....57 Q8
Drakemyre N Ayrs....124 H7
Drakes Broughton Worcs....46 H5
Drakewalls Cnwll....6 C4
Draughton N York....96 F10
Draughton Nhants....60 G5
Drax N York....92 A5
Drax Hales N York....91 R5
Draycote Warwks....59 P10
Draycot Foliat Swindn....33 N9
Draycott Derbys....72 C4
Draycott Gloucs....47 N7
Draycott Shrops....57 Q6
Draycott Somset....19 N4
Draycott Somset....19 Q10
Draycott Worcs....46 G5
Draycott in the Clay Staffs....71 M9
Draycott in the Moors Staffs....70 H6
Drayford Devon....9 J2
Drayton C Port....15 J5
Drayton Leics....60 H2
Drayton Lincs....74 D3
Drayton Norfk....76 H9
Drayton Oxon....34 E6
Drayton Oxon....48 D6
Drayton Somset....19 M10
Drayton Somset....19 N11
Drayton Worcs....58 D9
Drayton Bassett Staffs....59 J4
Drayton Beauchamp Bucks....35 P2
Drayton Manor Park Staffs....59 J4
Drayton Parslow Bucks....49 M8
Drayton St Leonard Oxon....34 G5
Drebley N York....96 G9
Dreemskerry IoM....80 g3
Dreen Hill Pembks....40 H8
Drefach Carmth....42 F2
Drefach Carmth....42 G7
Drefach Cerdgn....43 J5
Drefelin Carmth....42 G7
Dreghorn N Ayrs....125 K10
Drellingore Kent....27 M3
Drem E Loth....128 E4
Dresden C Stke....70 G6
Drewsteignton Devon....8 H6

Driby Lincs....87 L6
Driffield E R Yk....99 L9
Driffield Gloucs....33 L5
Driffield Cross Roads Gloucs....33 L5
Drift Cnwll....2 C8
Drigg Cumb....100 E11
Drighlington Leeds....90 G5
Drimnin Highld....137 P5
Drimpton Dorset....11 J4
Drimsallie Highld....138 H2
Dringhouses C York....98 B11
Drinkstone Suffk....64 D9
Drinkstone Green Suffk....64 D9
Drive End Dorset....11 M3
Driver's End Herts....50 F6
Drointon Staffs....71 J9
Droitwich Spa Worcs....46 G2
Dron P & K....134 E4
Dronfield Derbys....84 E5
Dronfield Woodhouse Derbys....84 D5
Drongan E Ayrs....114 H4
Dronley Angus....142 E10
Droop Dorset....12 C3
Dropping Well Rothm....84 E2
Droxford Hants....22 H11
Droylsden Tamesd....83 K5
Druid Denbgs....68 D6
Druidston Pembks....40 G7
Druimarbin Highld....139 K3
Druimavuic Ag & B....139 J8
Druimdrishaig Ag & B....123 M5
Druimindarroch Highld....145 L11
Drum Ag & B....123 A2
Drum P & K....134 C7
Drumalbin S Lans....116 C3
Drumbeg Highld....164 D10
Drumblade Abers....158 E9
Drumbreddon D & G....106 E9
Drumbuie Highld....153 P11
Drumburgh Cumb....110 E9
Drumburn D & G....109 J10
Drumburn D & G....109 L8
Drumchapel C Glas....125 N3
Drumchastle P & K....140 G6
Drumclog S Lans....125 Q10
Drumeldrie Fife....135 L7
Drumelzier Border....116 G4
Drumfearn Highld....145 L4
Drumfrennie Abers....151 J8
Drumgley Angus....142 G7
Drumguish Highld....148 D7
Drumin Moray....157 M11
Drumjohn D & G....115 K8
Drumlamford S Ayrs....107 J2
Drumlasie Abers....150 G6
Drumleaning Cumb....110 E10
Drumlemble Ag & B....120 C8
Drumlithie Abers....151 K11
Drummoddie D & G....107 L8
Drummore D & G....106 F10
Drumnadrochit Highld....155 P11
Drumnagorrach Moray....158 D7
Drumpark D & G....109 J5
Drumrunie Highld....161 K5
Drumshang S Ayrs....114 E5
Drumuie Highld....152 H8
Drumuillie Highld....148 G3
Drumvaich Stirlg....133 K7
Drunzie P & K....134 E6
Druridge Nthumb....119 Q11
Drury Flints....69 J2
Drws-y-coed Gwynd....67 J4
Drybeck Cumb....102 C7
Drybridge Moray....158 B5
Drybridge N Ayrs....125 K10
Drybrook Gloucs....46 B11
Dryburgh Border....118 A4
Dry Doddington Lincs....85 Q13
Dry Drayton Cambs....62 E8
Dryhill Kent....37 L10
Drymen Stirlg....132 F10
Drymuir Abers....159 M8
Drynoch Highld....152 G11
Dry Sandford Oxon....34 E4
Dryslwyn Carmth....43 L10
Dry Street Essex....37 Q3
Dryton Shrops....57 K3
Dubford Abers....159 J5
Dublin Suffk....64 H8
Duchally Highld....161 P3
Duck End Bed....50 C2
Duck End Cambs....62 B8
Duck End Essex....51 Q4
Duck End Essex....51 Q5
Duckend Green Essex....52 B7
Duckington Ches W....69 N4
Ducklington Oxon....34 C3
Duck's Cross Bed....61 P9
Duddenhoe End Essex....51 L3
Duddingston C Edin....127 P3
Duddington Nhants....73 P10
Duddlestone Somset....18 H10
Duddleswell E Susx....25 L5
Duddlewick Shrops....57 M8
Duddo Nthumb....118 H2
Duddon Ches W....69 P2
Duddon Bridge Cumb....94 D3
Duddon Common Ches W....81 Q11
Dudleston Shrops....69 K7
Dudleston Heath Shrops....69 L7
Dudley Dudley....58 D6
Dudley N Tyne....113 L6
Dudley Hill C Brad....90 F4
Dudley Port Sandw....58 E6
Dudnill Shrops....57 L10
Dudsbury Dorset....13 J5
Dudswell Herts....35 Q3
Duffield Derbys....72 A2
Duffryn Neath....29 M5
Dufftown Moray....157 Q9
Duffus Moray....157 M4
Dufton Cumb....102 C5
Duggleby N York....98 H7
Duirinish Highld....153 P11
Duisdalemore Highld....145 M5
Duisky Highld....139 J2
Dukestown Blae G....30 F2
Duke Street Suffk....53 J3
Dukinfield Tamesd....83 K5
Dulas IoA....78 H7
Dulcote Somset....19 Q6
Dulford Devon....9 Q3
Dull P & K....141 K8

Dullatur N Lans 126 C2
Dullingham Cambs 63 K9
Dullingham Ley Cambs 63 K9
Dulnain Bridge Highld 148 H3
Duloe Bed 61 Q8
Duloe Cnwll 5 L10
Dulsie Bridge Highld 156 G9
Dulverton Somset 18 B9
Dulwich Gt Lon 36 H6
Dumbarton W Duns 125 L2
Dumbleton Gloucs 47 K7
Dumfries D & G 109 L5
Dumgoyne Stirlg 132 G11
Dummer Hants 22 G5
Dumpton Kent 39 Q8
Dun Angus 143 M6
Dunalastair P & K 140 H6
Dunan Ag & B 124 F3
Dunan Highld 145 J2
Dunan P & K 140 C6
Dunaverty Ag & B 120 C10
Dunball Somset 19 K6
Dunbar E Loth 128 H4
Dunbeath Highld 167 L11
Dunbeg Ag & B 138 F11
Dunblane Stirlg 133 M7
Dunbog Fife 134 H4
Dunbridge Hants 22 B9
Duncanston Highld 155 Q6
Duncanstone Abers 150 F2
Dunchideock Devon 9 L7
Dunchurch Warwks 59 Q10
Duncote Nhants 49 J4
Duncow D & G 109 L4
Duncrievie P & K 134 E6
Duncton W Susx 23 Q11
Dundee C Dund 142 G11
Dundee Airport C Dund 135 K2
Dundon Somset 19 N8
Dundonald S Ayrs 125 K11
Dundonnell Highld 160 H9
Dundraw Cumb 110 D11
Dundreggan Highld 147 J5
Dundrennan D & G 108 F11
Dundry N Som 31 Q11
Dunecht Abers 151 K6
Dunfermline Fife 134 D10
Dunfield Gloucs 33 M5
Dunford Bridge Barns 83 Q4
Dungate Kent 38 F10
Dungavel S Lans 126 B10
Dunge Wilts 20 G4
Dungeness Kent 27 J8
Dungworth Sheff 84 C3
Dunham Massey Traffd 82 F7
Dunham-on-the-Hill Ches W 81 P10
Dunham-on-Trent Notts 85 P6
Dunhampstead Worcs 46 H2
Dunhampton Worcs 58 B11
Dunham Town Traffd 82 F7
Dunham Woodhouses Traffd 82 F7
Dunholme Lincs 86 D5
Dunino Fife 135 N5
Dunipace Falk 133 N11
Dunkeld P & K 141 P9
Dunkerton BaNES 20 D3
Dunkeswell Devon 10 C3
Dunkeswick N York 97 M11
Dunkirk Ches W 81 M10
Dunkirk Kent 39 J10
Dunkirk S Glos 32 E7
Dunkirk Wilts 21 J2
Dunk's Green Kent 37 P10
Dunlappie Angus 143 K4
Dunley Hants 22 E4
Dunley Worcs 57 P11
Dunlop E Ayrs 125 L8
Dunmaglass Highld 147 P9
Dunmere Cnwll 4 G8
Dunmore Falk 133 P10
Dunnet Highld 167 M2
Dunnichen Angus 143 J8
Dunning P & K 134 C5
Dunnington C York 98 D10
Dunnington E R Yk 99 P10
Dunnington Warwks 47 L4
Dunnockshaw Lancs 89 N5
Dunn Street Kent 38 C9
Dunoon Ag & B 124 F2
Dunphail Moray 157 J8
Dunragit D & G 106 G6
Duns Border 129 K9
Dunsa Derbys 84 B6
Dunsby Lincs 74 B5
Dunscar Bolton 89 L8
Dunscore D & G 109 J4
Dunscroft Donc 91 Q9
Dunsdale R & Cl 104 H7
Dunsden Green Oxon 35 K9
Dunsdon Devon 16 E10
Dunsfold Surrey 24 B3
Dunsford Devon 9 K7
Dunshalt Fife 134 G5
Dunshillock Abers 159 N8
Dunsill Notts 84 G8
Dunsley N York 105 N8
Dunsley Staffs 58 C8
Dunsmore Bucks 35 N3
Dunsop Bridge Lancs 95 P11
Dunstable C Beds 50 B6
Dunstall Staffs 71 M10
Dunstall Common Worcs 46 G6
Dunstall Green Suffk 63 M8
Dunstan Nthumb 119 P7
Dunstan Steads Nthumb 119 P6
Dunster Somset 18 C6
Duns Tew Oxon 48 E9
Dunston Gatesd 113 K8
Dunston Lincs 86 E8
Dunston Norfk 77 J11
Dunston Staffs 70 G11
Dunstone Devon 6 F8
Dunstone Devon 8 H9
Dunston Heath Staffs 70 G11
Dunsville Donc 91 Q9
Dunswell E R Yk 93 J3
Dunsyre S Lans 127 K8
Dunterton Devon 5 P6
Dunthrop Oxon 48 C9
Duntisbourne Abbots Gloucs 33 J3
Duntisbourne Leer Gloucs 33 J3
Duntisbourne Rouse Gloucs 33 J3
Duntish Dorset 11 P3
Duntocher W Duns 125 M3

Dunton Bucks 49 M10
Dunton C Beds 50 F2
Dunton Norfk 76 B5
Dunton Bassett Leics 60 B2
Dunton Green Kent 37 M9
Dunton Wayletts Essex 37 Q2
Duntulm Highld 152 G3
Dunure S Ayrs 114 E4
Dunvant Swans 28 G6
Dunvegan Highld 152 D8
Dunwich Suffk 65 P7
Dunwood Staffs 70 G3
Durdar Cumb 110 H10
Durgan Cnwll 3 K8
Durham Dur 103 Q2
Durham Cathedral Dur 103 Q2
Durham Services Dur 104 B3
Durham Tees Valley Airport S on T 104 C8
Durisdeer D & G 116 B10
Durisdeermill D & G 116 B10
Durkar Wakefd 91 J7
Durleigh Somset 19 J7
Durley Hants 22 F11
Durley Wilts 21 P2
Durley Street Hants 22 F11
Durlock Kent 39 N10
Durlock Kent 39 P9
Durlow Common Herefs 46 B7
Durn Rochdl 89 Q7
Durness Highld 165 K3
Durno Abers 151 J2
Duror Highld 138 H6
Durran Ag & B 131 K6
Durrington W Susx 24 D9
Durrington Wilts 21 N6
Dursley Gloucs 32 E5
Dursley Cross Gloucs 46 C10
Durston Somset 19 J9
Durweston Dorset 12 E3
Duston Nhants 60 F8
Duthil Highld 148 G3
Dutlas Powys 56 C9
Duton Hill Essex 51 P5
Dutson Cnwll 5 N4
Dutton Ches W 82 C9
Duxford Cambs 62 G11
Duxford Oxon 34 C5
Duxford IWM Cambs 62 G11
Dwygyfylchi Conwy 79 N9
Dwyran IoA 78 G11
Dyce C Aber 151 M5
Dyer's End Essex 52 B4
Dyfatty Carmth 28 E4
Dyffryn Brdgnd 29 N6
Dyffryn Myr Td 30 D4
Dyffryn V Glam 30 E10
Dyffryn Ardudwy Gwynd 67 K10
Dyffryn Castell Cerdgn 54 H8
Dyffryn Cellwen Neath 29 N2
Dyke Lincs 74 B6
Dyke Moray 156 H6
Dykehead Angus 142 C7
Dykehead Angus 142 F6
Dykehead N Lans 126 F6
Dykehead Stirlg 132 M8
Dykelands Abers 143 N4
Dykends Angus 142 D6
Dykeside Abers 158 H9
Dylife Powys 55 K6
Dymchurch Kent 27 K6
Dymock Gloucs 46 D8
Dyrham S Glos 32 D9
Dysart Fife 135 J9
Dyserth Denbgs 80 F9

E

Eachway Worcs 58 E9
Eachwick Nthumb 112 H6
Eagland Hill Lancs 95 J11
Eagle Lincs 85 Q7
Eagle Barnsdale Lincs 85 Q7
Eagle Moor Lincs 85 Q7
Eaglescliffe S on T 104 D7
Eaglesfield Cumb 100 E5
Eaglesfield D & G 110 D6
Eaglesham E Rens 125 P7
Eagley Bolton 89 L8
Eairy IoM 80 c6
Eakring Notts 85 L8
Ealand N Linc 92 C8
Ealing Gt Lon 36 E4
Eals Nthumb 111 N9
Eamont Bridge Cumb 101 P5
Earby Lancs 96 D11
Earcroft Bl w D 89 K6
Eardington Shrops 57 N6
Eardisland Herefs 45 N3
Eardisley Herefs 45 L5
Eardiston Shrops 69 L9
Eardiston Worcs 57 M11
Earith Cambs 62 E5
Earle Nthumb 119 J5
Earlestown St Hel 82 C5
Earley Wokham 35 K10
Earlham Norfk 76 H10
Earlish Highld 152 F5
Earls Barton Nhants 61 J8
Earls Colne Essex 52 E6
Earls Common Worcs 47 J3
Earl's Croome Worcs 46 G6
Earlsditton Shrops 57 L9
Earlsdon Covtry 59 M9
Earl's Down E Susx 25 P7
Earlsferry Fife 135 M7
Earlsfield Gt Lon 36 G6
Earlsford Abers 159 K11
Earl's Green Suffk 64 E8
Earlsheaton Kirk 90 H6
Earl Shilton Leics 72 D11
Earl Soham Suffk 65 J9
Earl Sterndale Derbys 83 N11
Earlston Border 117 R3
Earlston E Ayrs 125 L10
Earl Stonham Suffk 64 G10
Earlswood Surrey 36 G11
Earlswood Warwks 58 H10
Earlswood Common Mons 31 N6
Earnley W Susx 15 M7
Earnshaw Bridge Lancs 88 G5
Earsdon N Tyne 113 M6
Earsdon Nthumb 113 J2

Earsham Norfk 65 L4
Earswick C York 98 C9
Eartham W Susx 15 P5
Earthcott S Glos 32 C7
Easby N York 104 G9
Easdale Ag & B 130 E4
Easebourne W Susx 23 N10
Easenhall Warwks 59 Q9
Eashing Surrey 23 P6
Easington Bucks 35 J2
Easington Dur 104 D2
Easington E R Yk 93 Q7
Easington Nthumb 119 M4
Easington Oxon 35 J2
Easington R & Cl 105 K7
Easington Colliery Dur 104 D2
Easington Lane Sundld 113 N11
Easingwold N York 98 A7
Easole Street Kent 39 N11
Eassie and Nevay Angus 142 E9
East Aberthaw V Glam 30 D11
East Allington Devon 7 K9
East Anstey Devon 17 R6
East Anton Hants 22 C5
East Appleton N York 103 P11
East Ardsley Leeds 91 J5
East Ashey IoW 14 G9
East Ashling W Susx 15 M5
East Aston Hants 22 D5
East Ayton N York 99 J3
East Balsdon Cnwll 5 M2
East Bank Blae G 30 H3
East Barkwith Lincs 86 G4
East Barming Kent 38 B11
East Barnby N York 105 M8
East Barnet Gt Lon 50 G11
East Barns E Loth 129 J4
East Barsham Norfk 76 C5
East Beckham Norfk 76 H4
East Bedfont Gt Lon 36 C6
East Bergholt Suffk 53 J5
East Bierley Kirk 90 F5
East Bilney Norfk 76 D8
East Blatchington E Susx 25 L10
East Bloxworth Dorset 12 E6
East Boldon S Tyne 113 N8
East Boldre Hants 14 C6
East Bolton Nthumb 119 M7
Eastbourne Darltn 104 B8
Eastbourne E Susx 25 P11
East Bower Somset 19 K7
East Bradenham Norfk 76 C10
East Brent Somset 19 K4
Eastbridge Suffk 65 P8
East Bridgford Notts 72 H2
East Briscoe Dur 103 J7
Eastbrook V Glam 30 G10
East Buckland Devon 17 M5
East Budleigh Devon 9 Q8
Eastburn C Brad 90 C2
Eastburn E R Yk 99 K9
East Burnham Bucks 35 Q8
East Burton Dorset 12 D7
Eastbury W Berk 34 B9
Eastby N York 96 F10
East Butsfield Dur 112 H11
East Butterwick N Linc 92 D9
Eastby N York 96 F10
East Calder W Loth 127 K4
East Carleton Norfk 76 H11
East Carlton Leeds 90 G2
East Carlton Nhants 60 H3
East Chaldon Dorset 12 C8
East Challow Oxon 34 C7
East Charleton Devon 7 K10
East Chelborough Dorset 11 M3
East Chiltington E Susx 25 J7
East Chinnock Somset 11 M2
East Chisenbury Wilts 21 M4
East Cholderton Hants 21 Q5
Eastchurch Kent 38 G7
East Clandon Surrey 36 C10
East Claydon Bucks 49 K9
East Clevedon N Som 31 M10
East Coker Somset 11 L2
Eastcombe Gloucs 32 G4
Eastcombe Somset 18 G8
East Compton Somset 20 B6
East Cornworthy Devon 7 L7
East Cote Cumb 109 P9
Eastcote Gt Lon 36 D3
Eastcote Nhants 49 J4
Eastcote Solhll 59 J9
Eastcott Cnwll 16 D8
Eastcott Wilts 21 K3
East Cottingwith E R Yk 92 B2
Eastcourt Wilts 21 P2
Eastcourt Wilts 33 J6
East Cowes IoW 14 F7
East Cowick E R Yk 91 R6
East Cowton N York 104 B10
East Cramlington Nthumb 113 L5
East Cranmore Somset 20 C6
East Creech Dorset 12 F8
East Curthwaite Cumb 110 F11
East Dean E Susx 25 N11
East Dean Gloucs 46 C10
East Dean Hants 21 Q9
East Dean W Susx 15 P4
Eastdown Devon 7 L9
East Down Devon 17 L3
East Drayton Notts 85 N5
East Dulwich Gt Lon 36 H5
East Dundry N Som 31 Q11
East Ella C KuH 93 J5
East End Bed 61 P9
East End C Beds 49 Q6
East End E R Yk 93 L4
East End E R Yk 93 N4
Eastend Devon 7 L9
East End Essex 38 D7
East End Essex 51 K8
East End Hants 14 C7
East End Hants 22 D4
East End Herts 51 L5
East End Kent 26 D4
East End Kent 38 G7
East End M Keyn 49 N7
East End Oxon 48 C11
East End Somset 20 C5
East End Suffk 53 K4
Eastoft N Linc 92 D7
East Ogwell Devon 7 L4
Easton Cambs 61 P6
Easton Cumb 110 C10
Easton Cumb 110 H7
Easton Devon 8 H7
Easton Dorset 11 P10
Easton Hants 22 F8
Easton Lincs 73 M6
Easton Norfk 76 G9

Easter Moniack Highld 155 Q9
Eastern Green Covtry 59 L9
Easter Ord Abers 151 L7
Easter Pitkierie Fife 135 P6
Easter Skeld Shet 169 q9
Easter Softlaw Border 118 E4
Easterton Wilts 21 K4
Eastertown Somset 19 K4
East Everleigh Wilts 21 P4
East Farleigh Kent 38 B11
East Farndon Nhants 60 F4
East Ferry Lincs 92 D11
Eastfield N Lans 126 F5
Eastfield N York 99 L4
East Firsby Lincs 86 D3
East Fortune E Loth 128 E4
East Garforth Leeds 91 L4
East Garston W Berk 34 C9
Eastgate Dur 103 J3
Eastgate Lincs 74 B7
Eastgate Norfk 76 G7
East Ginge Oxon 34 D7
East Goscote Leics 72 G8
East Grafton Wilts 21 Q2
East Green Suffk 65 N8
East Grimstead Wilts 21 P9
East Grinstead W Susx 25 J3
East Guldeford E Susx 26 F7
East Haddon Nhants 60 E7
East Hagbourne Oxon 34 F7
East Halton N Linc 93 K7
East Ham Gt Lon 37 K4
Eastham Wirral 81 M8
Eastham Ferry Wirral 81 M8
Easthampton Herefs 45 N2
East Hanney Oxon 34 D6
East Hanningfield Essex 52 C11
East Hardwick Wakefd 91 M7
East Harling Norfk 64 D4
East Harlsey N York 104 D11
East Harnham Wilts 21 M9
East Harptree BaNES 19 Q3
East Hartford Nthumb 113 L5
East Harting W Susx 23 L11
East Hatch Wilts 20 H9
East Hatley Cambs 62 C10
East Hauxwell N York 97 J2
East Haven Angus 143 K10
Eastheath Wokam 35 L11
East Heckington Lincs 74 C2
East Hedleyhope Dur 103 N2
East Helmsdale Highld 163 N3
East Hendred Oxon 34 E7
East Hesleron N York 99 J5
East Hewish N Som 31 M2
East Hoathly E Susx 25 M7
East Holme Dorset 12 E7
East Hope Dur 103 K9
Easthope Shrops 57 K5
Easthorpe Essex 52 F7
Easthorpe Notts 85 M10
East Horrington Somset 19 Q5
East Horsley Surrey 36 C10
East Horton Nthumb 119 K4
East Howe BCP 13 J5
East Huntspill Somset 19 K5
East Ilkerton Devon 17 N2
East Ilsley W Berk 34 E8
East Keal Lincs 87 L8
East Kennett Wilts 33 M11
East Keswick Leeds 91 K2
East Kilbride S Lans 125 Q7
East Kimber Devon 8 C5
East Kirkby Lincs 87 K8
East Knighton Dorset 12 D7
East Knowstone Devon 17 Q7
East Knoyle Wilts 20 G8
East Lambrook Somset 19 M11
East Langdon Kent 27 P2
East Langton Leics 60 F2
East Lavant W Susx 15 N5
East Lavington W Susx 23 P11
East Layton N York 103 N9
Eastleach Martin Gloucs 33 P4
Eastleach Turville Gloucs 33 N3
East Leake Notts 72 F5
East Learmouth Nthumb 118 G3
East Leigh Devon 6 H8
East Leigh Devon 7 K7
East Leigh Devon 8 G3
Eastleigh Devon 16 H6
Eastleigh Hants 22 E11
East Lexham Norfk 76 B8
East Linton E Loth 128 F4
East Liss Hants 23 L9
East Lockinge Oxon 34 D7
East Lound N Linc 92 C11
East Lulworth Dorset 12 E8
East Lutton N York 99 J7
East Lydeard Somset 18 G9
East Lydford Somset 19 Q8
East Malling Kent 38 B10
East Malling Heath Kent 37 Q9
East Marden W Susx 15 M4
East Markham Notts 85 N5
East Martin Hants 21 L11
East Marton N York 96 D10
East Meon Hants 23 J10
East Mere Devon 18 C11
East Mersea Essex 52 H9
East Midlands Airport Leics 72 D5
East Molesey Surrey 36 D7
Eastmoor Norfk 75 P10
East Morden Dorset 12 F6
East Morton C Brad 90 D2
East Morton D & G 116 B10
East Ness N York 98 D5
East Newton E R Yk 93 N3
Eastney C Port 15 J7
Eastnor Herefs 46 D7
East Norton Leics 73 K10
Eastoft N Linc 92 D7
East Ogwell Devon 7 L4
Easton Cambs 61 P6
Easton Cumb 110 C10
Easton Cumb 110 H7
Easton Devon 8 H7
Easton Dorset 11 P10
Easton Hants 22 F8
Easton Lincs 73 M6
Easton Norfk 76 G9

Easton Somset 19 P5
Easton Suffk 65 K10
Easton W Berk 34 D10
Easton Wilts 32 G7
Easton Grey Wilts 32 G7
Easton-in-Gordano N Som 31 P9
Easton Maudit Nhants 61 J9
Easton-on-the-Hill Nhants 73 Q10
Easton Royal Wilts 21 P2
East Orchard Dorset 20 F11
East Ord Nthumb 129 P9
East Panson Devon 5 P3
East Parley BCP 13 J5
East Peckham Kent 37 Q11
East Pennard Somset 19 Q7
East Portlemouth Devon 7 K11
East Prawle Devon 7 K11
East Preston W Susx 24 C10
East Pulham Dorset 11 Q3
East Putford Devon 16 F8
East Quantoxhead Somset 18 F6
East Rainham Medway 38 D8
East Rainton Sundld 113 M11
East Ravendale NE Lin 93 M11
East Raynham Norfk 76 B6
Eastrea Cambs 74 E11
Eastriggs D & G 110 D7
East Rigton Leeds 91 K2
Eastrington E R Yk 92 C5
East Rolstone N Som 19 L2
Eastrop Swindn 33 P6
East Rounton N York 104 D10
East Rudham Norfk 76 A6
East Runton Norfk 76 H3
East Ruston Norfk 77 L6
Eastry Kent 39 P11
East Saltoun E Loth 128 D6
Eastshaw W Susx 23 N10
East Sheen Gt Lon 36 F6
East Shefford W Berk 34 C10
East Sleekburn Nthumb 113 L4
East Somerton Norfk 77 P8
East Stockwith Lincs 85 N2
East Stoke Dorset 12 E7
East Stoke Notts 85 N11
East Stour Dorset 20 F10
East Stour Common Dorset 20 F10
East Stourmouth Kent 39 N9
East Stowford Devon 17 L6
East Stratton Hants 22 F6
East Studdal Kent 27 P2
East Sutton Kent 26 D2
East Taphouse Cnwll 5 K9
East-the-Water Devon 16 H6
East Thirston Nthumb 119 N10
East Tilbury Thurr 37 Q5
East Tilbury Village Thurr 37 Q5
East Tisted Hants 23 K8
East Torrington Lincs 86 F4
East Tuddenham Norfk 76 F9
East Tytherley Hants 21 Q9
East Tytherton Wilts 33 J10
East Village Devon 9 K3
Eastville Bristl 31 B10
Eastville Lincs 87 M9
East Wall Shrops 57 J6
East Walton Norfk 75 P7
East Water Somset 19 P4
East Week Devon 8 G6
Eastwell Leics 73 K5
East Wellow Hants 22 B10
East Wemyss Fife 135 J8
East Whitburn W Loth 126 H4
Eastwick Herts 51 K8
East Wickham Gt Lon 37 L5
East Williamston Pembks 41 L10
East Winch Norfk 75 N7
East Winterslow Wilts 21 P8
East Wittering W Susx 15 L7
East Witton N York 96 H3
Eastwood Notts 84 G11
Eastwood Sthend 38 D4
East Woodburn Nthumb 112 D3
Eastwood End Cambs 62 F2
East Woodhay Hants 22 D2
East Woodlands Somset 20 E6
East Worldham Hants 23 L7
East Worthing W Susx 24 E10
East Wretham Norfk 64 C3
East Youlstone Devon 16 D8
Eathorpe Warwks 59 N11
Eaton Ches E 83 J11
Eaton Ches W 82 C11
Eaton Leics 73 K5
Eaton Norfk 77 J10
Eaton Notts 85 M5
Eaton Oxon 34 D4
Eaton Shrops 56 F7
Eaton Shrops 57 J7
Eaton Bishop Herefs 45 N7
Eaton Bray C Beds 49 Q10
Eaton Constantine Shrops 57 K3
Eaton Ford C Beds 61 Q9
Eaton Green C Beds 49 Q10
Eaton Hastings Oxon 33 Q5
Eaton Mascott Shrops 57 J3
Eaton Socon Cambs 61 Q9
Eaton upon Tern Shrops 70 B10
Eaves Brow Warrtn 82 D6
Eaves Green Solhll 59 L8
Ebberston N York 98 H4
Ebbesborne Wake Wilts 21 J10
Ebbw Vale Blae G 30 G3
Ebchester Dur 112 H9
Ebdon N Som 19 L2
Ebernoe W Susx 23 Q9
Ebford Devon 9 N7
Ebley Gloucs 32 F3
Ebnal Ches W 69 N5
Ebnall Herefs 45 P3
Ebrington Gloucs 47 N6
Ebsworthy Devon 8 D6
Ecchinswell Hants 22 E3
Ecclaw Border 129 K6
Ecclefechan D & G 110 C6
Eccles Border 118 E2
Eccles Kent 38 B9
Eccles Salfd 82 G5
Ecclesall Sheff 84 D4
Ecclesfield Sheff 84 E2
Eccles Green Herefs 45 M5
Eccleshall Staffs 70 E9
Eccleshill C Brad 90 F3
Ecclesmachan W Loth 127 K3
Eccles on Sea Norfk 77 N6
Eccles Road Norfk 64 E4

Eccleston Ches W 69 M2
Eccleston Lancs 88 G7
Eccleston St Hel 81 P5
Eccleston Green Lancs 88 G7
Echt Abers 151 J6
Eckford Border 118 D5
Eckington Derbys 84 F5
Eckington Worcs 46 H6
Ecton Nhants 60 H8
Ecton Staffs 71 K3
Edale Derbys 83 P7
Eday Ork 169 e3
Eday Airport Ork 169 e3
Edburton W Susx 24 F8
Edderside Cumb 109 P11
Edderton Highld 162 G10
Eddington Cambs 62 F9
Eddington Kent 39 L8
Eddleston Border 127 N8
Eddlewood S Lans 126 C7
Edenbridge Kent 37 K11
Edenfield Lancs 89 N7
Edenhall Cumb 101 Q4
Edenham Lincs 73 R6
Eden Mount Cumb 95 J5
Eden Park Gt Lon 37 J7
Eden Project Cnwll 3 Q3
Edensor Derbys 84 B7
Edentaggart Ag & B 132 C9
Edenthorpe Donc 91 Q9
Edern Gwynd 66 D7
Edgarley Somset 19 P7
Edgbaston Birm 58 G8
Edgcott Bucks 49 J10
Edgcott Somset 17 Q4
Edgcumbe Cnwll 3 J7
Edge Gloucs 32 F3
Edge Shrops 56 F3
Edgebolton Shrops 69 Q10
Edge End Gloucs 31 Q2
Edgefield Norfk 76 F5
Edgefield Green Norfk 76 F5
Edgefold Bolton 89 L9
Edge Green Ches W 69 N4
Edgehill Warwks 48 C5
Edgerley Shrops 69 L11
Edgerton Kirk 90 E7
Edgeside Lancs 89 N6
Edgeworth Gloucs 32 H3
Edgeworthy Devon 9 K2
Edginswell Torbay 7 M5
Edgiock Worcs 47 K2
Edgmond Wrekin 70 C11
Edgmond Marsh Wrekin 70 C10
Edgton Shrops 56 F7
Edgware Gt Lon 36 E2
Edgworth Bl w D 89 L7
Edinbane Highld 152 E7
Edinburgh C Edin 127 P3
Edinburgh Airport C Edin 127 L3
Edinburgh Castle C Edin 127 P3
Edinburgh Old & New
 Town C Edin 127 P3
Edinburgh Royal Botanic
 Gardens C Edin 127 N2
Edinburgh Zoo RZSS C Edin 127 N3
Edingale Staffs 59 K2
Edingham D & G 108 H8
Edingley Notts 85 L9
Edingthorpe Norfk 77 L5
Edingthorpe Green Norfk 77 L5
Edington Border 129 M9
Edington Nthumb 113 J4
Edington Somset 19 L7
Edington Wilts 20 H4
Edingworth Somset 19 L4
Edistone Devon 16 D7
Edithmead Somset 19 K5
Edith Weston Rutlnd 73 N9
Edlesborough Bucks 49 Q11
Edlingham Nthumb 119 M9
Edlington Lincs 86 H6
Edmond Castle Cumb 111 J9
Edmondsham Dorset 13 J2
Edmondsley Dur 113 K11
Edmondstown Rhondd 30 D6
Edmondthorpe Leics 73 M7
Edmonton Cnwll 4 F7
Edmonton Gt Lon 36 H2
Edmundbyers Dur 112 F10
Ednam Border 118 D3
Ednaston Derbys 71 N6
Edney Common Essex 51 Q10
Edradynate P & K 141 L7
Edrom Border 129 L8
Edstaston Shrops 69 P8
Edstone Warwks 47 N2
Edvin Loach Herefs 46 C3
Edwalton Notts 72 F3
Edwardstone Suffk 52 F3
Edwardsville M Td 30 L6
Edwinsford Carmth 43 M8
Edwinstowe Notts 85 K7
Edworth C Beds 50 F2
Edwyn Ralph Herefs 46 B3
Edzell Angus 143 L4
Edzell Woods Abers 143 L4
Efail-fach Neath 29 L5
Efail Isaf Rhondd 30 L8
Efailnewydd Gwynd 66 F7
Efail-Rhyd Powys 68 L3
Efailwen Carmth 41 M5
Efenechtyd Denbgs 68 F3
Effgill D & G 110 F2
Effingham Surrey 36 D10
Effingham Junction Surrey 36 D9
Efflinch Staffs 71 M11
Efford Devon 9 L4
Egbury Hants 22 D4
Egdean W Susx 23 Q10
Egerton Bolton 89 L8
Egerton Kent 26 F2
Egerton Forstal Kent 26 E2
Eggborough N York 91 P6
Eggbuckland C Plym 6 E7
Eggesford Devon 17 M9
Eggington C Beds 49 Q9
Egginton Derbys 71 P9
Egglescliffe S on T 104 D8
Eggleston Dur 103 J6
Egham Surrey 36 B6
Egham Wick Surrey 35 Q10
Egleton Rutlnd 73 M9
Eglingham Nthumb 119 M6
Egloshayle Cnwll 4 G7
Egloskerry Cnwll 5 M4

Eglwysbach Conwy 79 Q10
Eglwys-Brewis V Glam 30 D11
Eglwys Cross Wrexhm 69 N6
Eglwys Fach Cerdgn 54 F5
Eglwyswrw Pembks 41 M3
Egmanton Notts 85 M7
Egremont Cumb 100 D8
Egremont Wirral 81 L6
Egton N York 105 M9
Egton Bridge N York 105 M10
Egypt Bucks 35 Q7
Egypt Hants 22 E6
Eigg Highld 144 G10
Eight Ash Green Essex 52 F6
Eilanreach Highld 145 P4
Eilean Donan Castle Highld 145 Q2
Eisgein W Isls 168 i6
Eishken W Isls 168 i6
Eisteddfa Gurig Cerdgn 54 H8
Elan Valley Powys 55 K11
Elan Village Powys 44 C2
Elberton S Glos 32 B7
Elbridge W Susx 15 P6
Elburton C Plym 6 E7
Elcombe Swindn 33 M8
Elcot W Berk 34 C11
Eldernell Cambs 74 F11
Eldersfield Worcs 46 E8
Elderslie Rens 125 L5
Elder Street Essex 51 N4
Eldon Dur 103 P5
Eldwick C Brad 90 E2
Elerch Cerdgn 54 F7
Elfhill Abers 151 L10
Elford Nthumb 119 N4
Elford Staffs 59 J2
Elgin Moray 157 N5
Elgol Highld 144 H5
Elham Kent 27 L3
Elie Fife 135 M7
Elilaw Nthumb 119 J9
Elim IoA 78 F8
Eling Hants 14 C4
Elkesley Notts 85 L5
Elkstone Gloucs 33 J2
Ella Abers 158 F6
Ellacombe Torbay 7 N6
Elland Calder 90 E6
Elland Lower Edge Calder 90 E6
Ellary Ag & B 123 M4
Ellastone Staffs 71 L6
Ellel Lancs 95 K9
Ellemford Border 129 J7
Ellenabeich Ag & B 130 E4
Ellenborough Cumb 100 D3
Ellenbrook Salfd 82 F4
Ellenhall Staffs 70 E9
Ellen's Green Surrey 24 C3
Ellerbeck N York 104 D11
Ellerby N York 105 L8
Ellerdine Heath Wrekin 69 R10
Ellerhayes Devon 9 N4
Elleric Ag & B 139 J8
Ellerker E R Yk 92 F5
Ellers N York 90 C2
Ellerton E R Yk 92 B3
Ellerton N York 103 Q11
Ellerton Shrops 70 C9
Ellesborough Bucks 35 M3
Ellesmere Shrops 69 L8
Ellesmere Port Ches W 81 N9
Ellingham Hants 13 K3
Ellingham Norfk 65 M3
Ellingham Nthumb 119 N5
Ellingstring N York 97 J4
Ellington Cambs 61 Q6
Ellington Nthumb 113 L2
Ellington Thorpe Cambs 61 Q6
Elliots Green Somset 20 E5
Ellisfield Hants 22 H5
Ellishader Highld 153 J4
Ellistown Leics 72 C8
Ellon Abers 159 N11
Ellonby Cumb 101 M3
Ellough Suffk 65 N3
Elloughton E R Yk 92 F5
Ellwood Gloucs 31 Q3
Elm Cambs 75 J9
Elmbridge Worcs 58 D11
Elmdon Essex 51 L3
Elmdon Solhll 59 J8
Elmdon Heath Solhll 59 J8
Elmer W Susx 15 Q6
Elmers End Gt Lon 37 J7
Elmer's Green Lancs 88 G9
Elmesthorpe Leics 72 D11
Elm Green Essex 52 C10
Elmhurst Staffs 58 H2
Elmley Castle Worcs 47 J6
Elmley Lovett Worcs 58 C11
Elmore Gloucs 46 E11
Elmore Back Gloucs 46 E11
Elm Park Gt Lon 37 M3
Elmscott Devon 16 C7
Elmsett Suffk 53 J2
Elms Green Worcs 57 N11
Elmstead Heath Essex 53 J7
Elmstead Market Essex 53 J7
Elmstead Row Essex 53 J7
Elmsted Kent 27 K3
Elmstone Kent 39 N9
Elmstone Hardwicke Gloucs 46 H9
Elmswell E R Yk 99 K9
Elmswell Suffk 64 D9
Elmton Derbys 84 H6
Elphin Highld 161 L4
Elphinstone E Loth 128 B6
Elrick Abers 151 L6
Elrig D & G 107 K8
Elrington Nthumb 112 C8
Elsdon Nthumb 112 H2
Elsecar Barns 91 K11
Elsenham Essex 51 M5
Elsham N Linc 92 H8
Elsing Norfk 76 F8
Elslack N York 96 D11
Elson Hants 14 H6
Elson Shrops 69 L7
Elsrickle S Lans 116 F2
Elstead Surrey 23 P6
Elsted W Susx 23 M11
Elsted Marsh W Susx 23 M10
Elsthorpe Lincs 73 R6
Elstob Dur 104 B4
Elston Lancs 88 H4

Elston Notts 85 N11
Elston Wilts 21 L6
Elstone Devon 17 M8
Elstow Bed 61 N11
Elstree Herts 50 E11
Elstronwick E R Yk 93 M4
Elswick Lancs 88 E3
Elswick N u Ty 113 K8
Elsworth Cambs 62 D8
Elterwater Cumb 101 K10
Eltham Gt Lon 37 K6
Eltisley Cambs 62 C9
Elton Bury 89 M8
Elton Cambs 61 N2
Elton Ches W 81 P9
Elton Derbys 84 B8
Elton Gloucs 32 D2
Elton Herefs 56 H10
Elton S on T 104 D7
Elton Green Ches W 81 P10
Elton-on-the-Hill Notts 73 K3
Eltringham Nthumb 112 G8
Elvanfoot S Lans 116 D7
Elvaston Derbys 72 C4
Elveden Suffk 63 P4
Elvetham Heath Hants 23 M3
Elvingston E Loth 128 D5
Elvington C York 98 E11
Elvington Kent 39 N11
Elwell Devon 17 M5
Elwick Hartpl 104 E4
Elwick Nthumb 119 M3
Elworth Ches E 70 C2
Elworthy Somset 18 E8
Ely Cambs 62 H4
Ely Cardif 30 F9
Emberton M Keyn 49 N5
Embleton Cumb 100 G4
Embleton Dur 104 D5
Embleton Nthumb 119 P6
Embo Highld 163 J8
Emborough Somset 20 B4
Embo Street Highld 163 J8
Embsay N York 96 F10
Emery Down Hants 13 N3
Emley Kirk 90 G8
Emley Moor Kirk 90 G8
Emmbrook Wokham 35 M11
Emmer Green Readg 35 K9
Emmett Carr Derbys 84 G5
Emmington Oxon 35 K4
Emneth Norfk 75 J9
Emneth Hungate Norfk 75 K9
Empingham Rutlnd 73 N9
Empshott Hants 23 L8
Empshott Green Hants 23 K8
Emsworth Hants 15 M5
Enborne W Berk 34 D11
Enborne Row W Berk 22 D2
Enchmarsh Shrops 57 J5
Enderby Leics 72 E11
Endmoor Cumb 95 L4
Endon Staffs 70 G4
Endon Bank Staffs 70 G4
Enfield Gt Lon 51 J11
Enfield Lock Gt Lon 51 J11
Enfield Wash Gt Lon 51 J11
Enford Wilts 21 M4
Engine Common S Glos 32 C8
England's Gate Herefs 45 Q4
Englefield W Berk 34 H10
Englefield Green Surrey 35 Q10
Engleseabrook Ches E 70 D4
English Bicknor Gloucs 46 A11
Englishcombe BaNES 20 D2
English Frankton Shrops 69 N9
Engollan Cnwll 4 D7
Enham Alamein Hants 22 C5
Enmore Somset 18 H7
Enmore Green Dorset 20 G10
Ennerdale Bridge Cumb 100 E7
Enniscaven Cnwll 4 F10
Enochdhu P & K 141 Q5
Ensay Ag & B 137 K6
Ensbury BCP 13 J5
Ensdon Shrops 69 M11
Enson Devon 17 K6
Enson Staffs 70 G9
Enstone Oxon 48 C10
Enterkinfoot D & G 116 B10
Enterpen N York 104 E9
Enville Staffs 58 B7
Eochar W Isls 168 c13
Eòlaigearraidh W Isls 168 c17
Eoligarry W Isls 168 c17
Epney Gloucs 32 E2
Epperstone Notts 85 L11
Epping Essex 51 L10
Epping Green Essex 51 K9
Epping Green Herts 50 G9
Epping Upland Essex 51 K10
Eppleby N York 103 N8
Eppleworth E R Yk 92 H4
Epsom Surrey 36 F8
Epwell Oxon 48 C6
Epworth N Linc 92 C10
Epworth Turbary N Linc 92 C10
Erbistock Wrexhm 69 L6
Erbusaig Highld 145 N2
Erchless Castle Highld 155 P8
Erdington Birm 58 H6
Eridge Green E Susx 25 N3
Eridge Station E Susx 25 M4
Erines Ag & B 123 Q4
Eriska Ag & B 138 G9
Eriskay W Isls 168 c17
Eriswell Suffk 63 M5
Erith Gt Lon 37 M5
Erlestoke Wilts 21 J4
Ermington Devon 6 G8
Erpingham Norfk 76 H5
Erriottwood Kent 38 F10
Errogie Highld 147 P3
Errol P & K 134 G3
Erskine Rens 125 M3
Erskine Bridge Rens 125 M3
Ervie D & G 106 D4
Erwarton Suffk 53 M5
Erwood Powys 44 F6
Eryholme N York 104 B9
Eryrys Denbgs 68 H3
Escalls Cnwll 2 B8
Escomb Dur 103 N4
Escott Somset 18 E7
Escrick N York 91 Q2
Esgair Carmth 42 G9
Esgair Cerdgn 54 D11
Esgairgeiliog Powys 54 H3

Esgerdawe Carmth 43 M6
Esgyryn Conwy 79 Q9
Esh Dur 103 N2
Esher Surrey 36 D8
Esholt C Brad 90 F2
Eshott Nthumb 119 P11
Eshton N York 96 D9
Esh Winning Dur 103 N2
Eskadale Highld 155 N9
Eskbank Mdloth 127 Q4
Eskdale Green Cumb 100 F10
Eskdalemuir D & G 117 K11
Eske E R Yk 93 J2
Eskham Lincs 93 Q11
Esknish Ag & B 122 D7
Esperley Lane Ends Dur 103 M6
Esprick Lancs 88 E3
Essendine Rutlnd 73 Q8
Essendon Herts 50 G9
Essich Highld 156 A10
Essington Staffs 58 E4
Esslemont Abers 151 N2
Eston R & Cl 104 F7
Etal Nthumb 118 H3
Etchilhampton Wilts 21 K2
Etchingham E Susx 26 B6
Etchinghill Kent 27 L4
Etchinghill Staffs 71 J11
Etchingwood E Susx 25 M6
Etling Green Norfk 76 E9
Etloe Gloucs 32 C3
Eton W & M 35 Q9
Eton Wick W & M 35 P9
Etruria C Stke 70 F5
Etteridge Highld 148 B9
Ettersgill Dur 102 H5
Ettiley Heath Ches E 70 C2
Ettingshall Wolves 58 D5
Ettington Warwks 47 Q5
Etton C Pete 74 B9
Etton E R Yk 92 G2
Ettrick Border 117 K8
Ettrickbridge Border 117 M6
Ettrickhill Border 117 K8
Etwall Derbys 71 P8
Eudon George Shrops 57 M7
Euston Suffk 64 B6
Euximoor Drove Cambs 75 J11
Euxton Lancs 88 H7
Evancoyd Powys 45 K2
Evanton Highld 155 R4
Evedon Lincs 86 E11
Evelith Shrops 57 N3
Evelix Highld 162 H8
Evenjobb Powys 45 K2
Evenley Nhants 48 G8
Evenlode Gloucs 47 P9
Evenwood Dur 103 N6
Evenwood Gate Dur 103 N6
Evercreech Somset 20 B7
Everingham E R Yk 92 D2
Everleigh Wilts 21 P4
Everley N York 99 K3
Eversholt C Beds 49 Q8
Evershot Dorset 11 M4
Eversley Hants 23 L2
Eversley Cross Hants 23 L2
Everthorpe E R Yk 92 F4
Everton C Beds 62 B10
Everton Hants 13 N6
Everton Lpool 81 L6
Everton Notts 85 L2
Evertown D & G 110 G5
Evesbatch Herefs 46 C5
Evesham Worcs 47 K6
Evington C Leic 72 G10
Ewden Village Sheff 90 H11
Ewell Surrey 36 F8
Ewell Minnis Kent 27 N3
Ewelme Oxon 34 H6
Ewen Gloucs 33 K5
Ewenny V Glam 29 P9
Ewerby Lincs 86 F11
Ewerby Thorpe Lincs 86 F11
Ewhurst Surrey 24 C2
Ewhurst Green E Susx 26 C7
Ewhurst Green Surrey 24 C3
Ewloe Flints 81 L11
Ewloe Green Flints 81 K11
Ewood Bl w D 89 K5
Ewood Bridge Lancs 89 M6
Eworthy Devon 8 B5
Ewshot Hants 23 M5
Ewyas Harold Herefs 45 M9
Exbourne Devon 8 F4
Exbury Hants 14 D6
Exceat E Susx 25 M11
Exebridge Somset 18 B10
Exelby N York 97 L3
Exeter Devon 9 M6
Exeter Airport Devon 9 N6
Exeter Services Devon 9 N6
Exford Somset 17 R4
Exfordsgreen Shrops 56 H3
Exhall Warwks 47 M3
Exhall Warwks 59 N7
Exlade Street Oxon 35 J8
Exley Head C Brad 90 C2
Exminster Devon 9 M7
Exmoor National Park 17 R4
Exmouth Devon 9 P8
Exning Suffk 63 K7
Exted Kent 27 L3
Exton Devon 9 N7
Exton Hants 22 H10
Exton Rutlnd 73 N8
Exton Somset 18 B8
Exwick Devon 9 M6
Eyam Derbys 84 B5
Eydon Nhants 48 F5
Eye C Pete 74 D10
Eye Herefs 45 P2
Eye Suffk 64 G7
Eye Green C Pete 74 D10
Eyemouth Border 129 N7
Eyeworth C Beds 62 C11
Eyhorne Street Kent 38 D11
Eyke Suffk 65 L11
Eynesbury Cambs 61 Q9
Eynsford Kent 37 M7
Eynsham Oxon 34 D3
Eype Dorset 11 J6
Eyre Highld 152 G7
Eythorne Kent 27 N2
Eyton Herefs 45 P2
Eyton Shrops 56 F6

Eyton Shrops 56 F7
Eyton Shrops 69 M10
Eyton Wrexhm 69 L6
Eyton on Severn Shrops 57 K3
Eyton upon the Weald
 Moors Wrekin 57 M2

F

Faccombe Hants 22 C3
Faceby N York 104 E10
Fachwen Powys 68 D11
Facit Lancs 89 P7
Fackley Notts 84 G8
Faddiley Ches E 69 Q4
Fadmoor N York 98 D3
Faerdre Swans 29 J4
Faifley W Duns 125 M3
Failand N Som 31 P10
Failford S Ayrs 115 J2
Failsworth Oldham 83 J4
Fairbourne Gwynd 54 E2
Fairburn N York 91 M5
Fairfield Derbys 83 N10
Fairfield Kent 26 G6
Fairfield Worcs 58 D9
Fairfield Park Herts 50 F4
Fairford Gloucs 33 N4
Fairford Park Gloucs 33 N4
Fairgirth D & G 109 J3
Fair Green Norfk 75 N7
Fairhaven Lancs 88 C5
Fair Isle Shet 169 t14
Fair Isle Airport Shet 169 t14
Fairlands Surrey 23 Q4
Fairlie N Ayrs 124 G3
Fairlight E Susx 26 E9
Fairlight Cove E Susx 26 E9
Fairmile Devon 10 B5
Fairmile Surrey 36 D8
Fairmilehead C Edin 127 N4
Fairnilee Border 117 P4
Fair Oak Hants 22 E11
Fair Oak Hants 23 J2
Fair Oak Green Hants 23 J2
Fairseat Kent 37 P8
Fairstead Essex 52 C8
Fairstead Norfk 75 M6
Fairstead Norfk 77 K7
Fairwarp E Susx 25 L5
Fairwater Cardif 30 F9
Fairy Cross Devon 16 G7
Fakenham Norfk 76 C6
Fakenham Magna Suffk 64 C6
Fala Mdloth 128 C7
Fala Dam Mdloth 128 C7
Falcut Nhants 48 G6
Faldingworth Lincs 86 E4
Faldouët Jersey 11 c2
Falfield S Glos 32 C6
Falkenham Suffk 53 N4
Falkirk Falk 133 P11
Falkirk Wheel Falk 133 P11
Falkland Fife 134 H6
Fallburn S Lans 116 D3
Fallgate Derbys 84 E8
Fallin Stirlg 133 N9
Fallodon Nthumb 119 N6
Fallowfield Manch 83 J6
Fallowfield Nthumb 112 D7
Falmer E Susx 25 J9
Falmouth Cnwll 3 L7
Falnash Border 117 M9
Falsgrave N York 99 L3
Falstone Nthumb 111 P3
Fanagmore Highld 164 E7
Fancott C Beds 49 R8
Fanellan Highld 155 N9
Fangdale Beck N York 98 B2
Fangfoss E R Yk 98 F10
Fanmore Ag & B 137 L2
Fannich Lodge Highld 154 H4
Fans Border 118 B2
Far Bletchley M Keyn 49 N8
Farcet Cambs 62 B2
Far Cotton Nhants 60 G9
Farden Shrops 57 K9
Fareham Hants 14 G5
Farewell Staffs 58 G2
Far Forest Worcs 57 N9
Farforth Lincs 87 K5
Far Green Gloucs 32 E4
Faringdon Oxon 33 Q5
Farington Lancs 88 G5
Farlam Cumb 111 L9
Farleigh N Som 31 P11
Farleigh Surrey 37 J8
Farleigh Hungerford Somset 20 F3
Farleigh Wallop Hants 22 H5
Farlesthorpe Lincs 87 N6
Farleton Cumb 95 L4
Farleton Lancs 95 M7
Farley Derbys 84 C8
Farley Staffs 71 K6
Farley Wilts 21 P9
Farley Green Suffk 63 M10
Farley Green Surrey 36 C11
Farley Hill Wokham 23 K2
Farleys End Gloucs 32 E2
Farlington C Port 15 J5
Farlington N York 98 C7
Farlow Shrops 57 L8
Farmborough BaNES 20 C2
Farmbridge End Essex 51 P8
Farmcote Gloucs 47 L9
Farmcote Shrops 57 P6
Farmington Gloucs 47 M11
Farmoor Oxon 34 E3
Far Moor Wigan 82 B4
Farms Common Cnwll 2 H7
Farm Town Leics 72 B7
Farmtown Moray 158 D7
Farnah Green Derbys 84 D11
Farnborough Gt Lon 37 K8
Farnborough Hants 23 N4
Farnborough W Berk 34 D8
Farnborough Warwks 48 D5
Farnborough Park Hants 23 N4
Farncombe Surrey 23 Q6
Farndish Bed 61 M8
Farndon Ches W 69 M4
Farndon Notts 85 N10
Farne Islands Nthumb 119 P3
Farnell Angus 143 L6

Farnham Dorset 21 J11
Farnham Essex 51 L6
Farnham N York 97 M8
Farnham Suffk 65 M9
Farnham Surrey 23 M5
Farnham Common Bucks 35 Q7
Farnham Green Essex 51 L5
Farnham Royal Bucks 35 Q8
Farningham Kent 37 M7
Farnley Leeds 90 H4
Farnley N York 97 K11
Farnley Tyas Kirk 90 F8
Farnsfield Notts 85 K9
Farnworth Bolton 89 L9
Farnworth Halton 81 Q7
Far Oakridge Gloucs 32 H4
Farr Highld 148 E7
Farr Highld 156 B11
Farr Highld 166 B4
Farraline Highld 147 P3
Farringdon Devon 9 P6
Farrington Gurney BaNES 20 B3
Far Sawrey Cumb 101 L11
Farsley Leeds 90 G3
Farther Howegreen Essex 52 D11
Farthing Green Kent 26 D2
Farthinghoe Nhants 48 F7
Farthingloe Kent 27 N3
Farthingstone Nhants 48 H4
Farthing Street Gt Lon 37 K8
Fartown Kirk 90 F7
Farway Devon 10 D5
Fasnacloich Ag & B 139 J8
Fasnakyle Highld 147 J2
Fassfern Highld 139 J2
Fatfield Sundld 113 M10
Faugh Cumb 111 K10
Fauld Staffs 71 M9
Fauldhouse W Loth 126 G5
Faulkbourne Essex 52 C8
Faulkland Somset 20 D4
Fauls Shrops 69 Q8
Faversham Kent 38 H9
Fawdington N York 97 P6
Fawdon N u Ty 113 K7
Fawdon Nthumb 119 K7
Fawfieldhead Staffs 71 K2
Fawkham Green Kent 37 N7
Fawler Oxon 48 C11
Fawley Bucks 35 L7
Fawley Hants 14 E6
Fawley W Berk 34 C8
Fawley Chapel Herefs 46 A9
Fawnog Flints 81 J11
Fawsley Nhants 60 C9
Faxfleet E R Yk 92 E6
Faygate W Susx 24 F4
Fazakerley Lpool 81 M5
Fazeley Staffs 59 K4
Fearby N York 97 J4
Fearn Highld 156 E2
Fearnan P & K 140 H9
Fearnbeg Highld 153 N6
Fearnhead Warrtn 82 D6
Fearnmore Highld 153 N5
Fearnoch Ag & B 124 A2
Featherstone Staffs 58 D3
Featherstone Wakefd 91 L7
Feckenham Worcs 47 K2
Feering Essex 52 E7
Feetham N York 103 J11
Feizor N York 96 A7
Felbridge Surrey 25 J3
Felbrigg Norfk 77 J4
Felcourt Surrey 25 J2
Felden Herts 50 B10
Felindre Carmth 42 G7
Felindre Carmth 43 L10
Felindre Carmth 43 P9
Felindre Cerdgn 43 L3
Felindre Powys 44 H10
Felindre Powys 56 B8
Felindre Swans 28 H4
Felindre Farchog Pembks 41 M3
Felinfach Cerdgn 43 K3
Felinfach Powys 44 F8
Felinfoel Carmth 28 F4
Felingwmisaf Carmth 43 K10
Felingwmuchaf Carmth 43 K10
Felin-newydd Powys 44 G7
Felixkirk N York 97 Q4
Felixstowe Suffk 53 P5
Felixstowe Ferry Suffk 53 P4
Felkington Nthumb 118 H2
Felkirk Wakefd 91 K8
Felling Gatesd 113 L8
Fell Lane C Brad 90 C2
Fell Side Cumb 101 K3
Felmersham Bed 61 L9
Felmingham Norfk 77 K6
Felpham W Susx 15 P7
Felsham Suffk 64 C10
Felsted Essex 51 Q6
Feltham Gt Lon 36 D6
Felthamhill Surrey 36 C6
Felthorpe Norfk 76 H8
Felton Herefs 46 A5
Felton N Som 31 P11
Felton Nthumb 119 N10
Felton Butler Shrops 69 L11
Feltwell Norfk 63 M2
Fenay Bridge Kirk 90 F7
Fence Lancs 89 N3
Fence Rothm 84 F3
Fence Houses Sundld 113 M11
Fencott Oxon 48 G11
Fendike Corner Lincs 87 N8
Fen Ditton Cambs 62 G8
Fen Drayton Cambs 62 D7
Fen End Lincs 74 D6
Fen End Solhll 59 K10
Fenham Nthumb 119 L2
Feniscliffe Bl w D 89 K5
Feniscowles Bl w D 89 J5
Feniton Devon 10 B5
Feniton Court Devon 10 C5
Fenn Green Shrops 57 P8
Fenn Street Medway 38 C6
Fenny Bentley Derbys 71 M5
Fenny Bridges Devon 10 C5
Fenny Compton Warwks 48 D4
Fenny Drayton Leics 72 B11
Fenny Stratford M Keyn 49 N8
Fenrother Nthumb 113 J2
Fenstanton Cambs 62 D7
Fenstead End Suffk 63 P10

Fen Street Norfk 64 D2
Fen Street Suffk 64 H9
Fenton C Stke 70 F6
Fenton Cambs 62 D5
Fenton Cumb 111 K9
Fenton Lincs 85 P5
Fenton Lincs 85 Q10
Fenton Notts 85 N4
Fenton Nthumb 119 J4
Fenton Barns E Loth 128 E3
Fenwick Donc 91 P7
Fenwick E Ayrs 125 M9
Fenwick Nthumb 112 G6
Fenwick Nthumb 119 L2
Feock Cnwll 3 L6
Feolin Ferry Ag & B 122 F6
Fergushill N Ayrs 125 J9
Feriniquarrie Highld 152 B7
Fermain Bay Guern 10 c2
Fern Angus 142 H5
Ferndale Rhondd 30 C5
Ferndown Dorset 13 J4
Ferness Highld 156 H8
Fernham Oxon 33 Q6
Fernhill Heath Worcs 46 G3
Fernhurst W Susx 23 N9
Fernie Fife 135 J4
Ferniegair S Lans 126 C7
Fernilea Highld 152 F11
Fernilee Derbys 83 M9
Fernwood Notts 85 P10
Ferrensby N York 97 N8
Ferriby Sluice N Linc 92 G6
Ferrindonald Highld 145 L6
Ferring W Susx 24 C10
Ferrybridge Wakefd 91 M6
Ferrybridge Services Wakefd 91 M6
Ferryden Angus 143 N6
Ferryhill Dur 103 Q4
Ferryhill Station Dur 103 Q4
Ferry Point Highld 162 G9
Ferryside Carmth 28 C2
Fersfield Norfk 64 F5
Fersit Highld 139 R2
Feshiebridge Highld 148 F7
Fetcham Surrey 36 D9
Fetlar Shet 169 t4
Fetterangus Abers 159 N7
Fettercairn Abers 143 M3
Fewcott Oxon 48 F9
Fewston N York 97 J10
Ffairfach Carmth 43 M10
Ffair Rhos Cerdgn 54 G11
Ffald-y-Brenin Carmth 43 M6
Ffarmers Carmth 43 N6
Ffawyddog Powys 45 J11
Ffestiniog Railway Gwynd 67 L7
Ffordd-las Denbgs 68 F2
Fforest Carmth 28 G4
Fforest Gôch Neath 29 K4
Ffostrasol Cerdgn 42 G5
Ffrith Flints 69 J3
Ffynnonddewi Cerdgn 42 G4
Ffynnongroyw Flints 80 G8
Ffynnon-oer Cerdgn 43 K4
Fickleshole Surrey 37 J8
Fiddington Gloucs 46 H8
Fiddington Somset 18 H6
Fiddleford Dorset 12 D2
Fiddlers Green Cnwll 4 C10
Fiddlers Hamlet Essex 51 L10
Field Staffs 71 J8
Field Broughton Cumb 94 H4
Field Dalling Norfk 76 E4
Fieldhead Cumb 101 N3
Field Head Leics 72 D9
Fifehead Magdalen Dorset 20 E10
Fifehead Neville Dorset 12 C2
Fifehead St Quintin Dorset 12 C2
Fife Keith Moray 158 B7
Fifield Oxon 47 P11
Fifield W & M 35 P9
Fifield Wilts 21 M4
Figheldean Wilts 21 N5
Filands Wilts 32 H1
Filby Norfk 77 P9
Filey N York 99 N4
Filgrave M Keyn 49 N5
Filkins Oxon 33 P4
Filleigh Devon 8 H2
Filleigh Devon 17 M6
Fillingham Lincs 86 B3
Fillongley Warwks 59 L7
Filmore Hill Hants 23 J9
Filton S Glos 32 B9
Fimber E R Yk 98 H8
Finavon Angus 142 H6
Finberry Kent 26 H4
Fincham Norfk 75 N9
Finchampstead Wokham 23 L2
Fincharn Ag & B 131 J7
Finchdean Hants 15 K4
Finchingfield Essex 51 Q4
Finchley Gt Lon 36 G2
Findern Derbys 71 Q8
Findhorn Moray 157 J5
Findhorn Bridge Highld 148 E2
Findochty Moray 158 C4
Findo Gask P & K 134 C4
Findon Abers 151 N8
Findon W Susx 24 D9
Findon Mains Highld 155 R5
Findon Valley W Susx 24 D9
Findrack House Abers 150 G7
Finedon Nhants 61 K6
Fingal Street Suffk 65 J8
Fingask P & K 134 F3
Fingest Bucks 35 L6
Finghall N York 97 J3
Fingland Cumb 110 E9
Fingland D & G 116 B3
Finglesham Kent 39 P11
Fingringhoe Essex 52 H7
Finkle Green Essex 52 B3
Finkle Street Barns 91 J11
Finlarig Stirlg 140 E11
Finmere Oxon 48 H8
Finnart P & K 140 D6
Finningham Suffk 64 F8
Finningley Donc 91 R11
Finsbay W Isls 168 f9
Finstall Worcs 58 E10
Finsthwaite Cumb 94 H3
Finstock Oxon 48 C11
Finstown Ork 169 c5

Fintry Abers 159 J7
Fintry Stirlg 133 J10
Finzean Abers 150 G9
Fionnphort Ag & B 137 J11
Fionnsbhagh W Isls 168 f9
Firbank Cumb 95 N2
Firbeck Rothm 85 J3
Firby N York 97 L3
Firby N York 98 F2
Firgrove Rochdl 89 Q8
Firle E Susx 25 L9
Firsby Lincs 87 N8
Firsdown Wilts 21 P8
Fir Tree Dur 103 M4
Fishbourne IoW 14 G8
Fishbourne W Susx 15 M6
Fishbourne Roman Palace W Susx 15 M6
Fishburn Dur 104 C4
Fishcross Clacks 133 P8
Fisher W Susx 15 N6
Fisherford Abers 158 G10
Fisherrow E Loth 127 Q3
Fisher's Pond Hants 22 E10
Fisher's Row Lancs 95 J11
Fisherstreet W Susx 23 N8
Fisherton Highld 156 C7
Fisherton S Ayrs 114 E4
Fisherton de la Mere Wilts 21 K7
Fisherwick Staffs 59 J3
Fishery W & M 35 N8
Fishguard Pembks 41 J3
Fishlake Donc 91 R8
Fishleigh Devon 8 D3
Fishmere End Lincs 74 E3
Fishnish Pier Ag & B 138 B9
Fishpond Bottom Dorset 10 H5
Fishponds Bristl 32 B9
Fishtoft Lincs 74 G2
Fishtoft Drove Lincs 87 K11
Fishwick Lancs 88 H5
Fiskavaig Highld 152 E11
Fiskerton Lincs 86 D6
Fiskerton Notts 85 M10
Fitling E R Yk 93 N4
Fittleton Wilts 21 M5
Fittleworth W Susx 24 B7
Fitton End Cambs 74 H8
Fitz Shrops 69 M11
Fitzhead Somset 18 F9
Fitzroy Somset 18 G9
Fitzwilliam Wakefd 91 L7
Five Ash Down E Susx 25 L6
Five Ashes E Susx 25 N5
Five Bells Somset 18 E6
Five Bridges Herefs 46 B5
Fivecrosses Ches W 82 B9
Fivehead Somset 19 L10
Fivelanes Cnwll 5 L2
Five Lanes Mons 31 M6
Five Oak Green Kent 37 P11
Five Oaks Jersey 11 c2
Five Oaks W Susx 24 C5
Five Roads Carmth 28 E3
Five Wents Kent 38 D11
Flack's Green Essex 52 C9
Flackwell Heath Bucks 35 N7
Fladbury Worcs 47 J5
Fladdabister Shet 169 r10
Flagg Derbys 83 P11
Flamborough E R Yk 99 Q6
Flamborough Head E R Yk 99 R6
Flamingo Land Theme Park N York 98 F5
Flamstead Herts 50 C8
Flamstead End Herts 50 H10
Flansham W Susx 15 Q6
Flanshaw Wakefd 91 J6
Flappit Spring C Brad 90 D3
Flasby N York 96 D9
Flash Staffs 83 M11
Flashader Highld 152 E7
Flaunden Herts 50 B10
Flawborough Notts 73 K2
Flawith N York 97 Q7
Flax Bourton N Som 31 P11
Flaxby N York 97 N9
Flaxley Gloucs 46 C11
Flaxmere Ches W 82 C10
Flaxpool Somset 18 F7
Flaxton N York 98 D8
Fleckney Leics 60 D2
Flecknoe Warwks 60 B8
Fledborough Notts 85 P6
Fleet Dorset 11 N8
Fleet Hants 15 K6
Fleet Hants 23 M4
Fleet Lincs 74 G6
Fleetend Hants 14 F5
Fleet Hargate Lincs 74 G6
Fleet Services Hants 23 L3
Fleetwood Lancs 94 G11
Fleggburgh Norfk 77 N9
Flemingston V Glam 30 D11
Flemington S Lans 126 B6
Flempton Suffk 63 P7
Fletchersbridge Cnwll 5 J8
Fletcher's Green Kent 37 M11
Fletchertown Cumb 100 H2
Fletching E Susx 25 K6
Fleur-de-lis Caerph 30 G6
Flexbury Cnwll 16 C10
Flexford Surrey 23 P4
Flimby Cumb 100 D4
Flimwell E Susx 26 B5
Flint Flints 81 J10
Flintham Notts 85 M11
Flint Mountain Flints 81 J10
Flinton E R Yk 93 M3
Flint's Green Solhll 59 L8
Flishinghurst Kent 26 C4
Flitcham Norfk 75 P5
Flitch Green Essex 51 Q6
Flitton C Beds 50 C3
Flitwick C Beds 50 B4
Flixborough N Linc 92 E8
Flixborough Stather N Linc 92 E8
Flixton N York 99 L5
Flixton Suffk 65 L4
Flixton Traffd 82 F6
Flockton Kirk 90 G8
Flockton Green Kirk 90 H7
Flodden Nthumb 118 H3
Flodigarry Highld 152 H3
Flookburgh Cumb 94 H5
Flordon Norfk 64 H2

Flore Nhants 60 D8
Flotterton Nthumb 119 J10
Flowers Green E Susx 25 P8
Flowton Suffk 53 J2
Flushdyke Wakefd 90 H6
Flushing Cnwll 3 L7
Fluxton Devon 10 B6
Flyford Flavell Worcs 47 J3
Fobbing Thurr 38 B5
Fochabers Moray 157 Q6
Fochriw Caerph 30 F3
Fockerby N Linc 92 D7
Foddington Somset 19 Q9
Foel Powys 55 M2
Foelgastell Carmth 28 F2
Foel y Dyffryn Brdgnd 29 N6
Foggathorpe E R Yk 92 C3
Fogo Border 129 K10
Fogwatt Moray 157 N6
Foindle Highld 164 E7
Folda Angus 142 B5
Fole Staffs 71 J7
Foleshill Covtry 59 N8
Folksworth Cambs 61 P3
Folkestone Kent 27 M4
Folkingham Lincs 73 R4
Folkington E Susx 25 N10
Folksworth Cambs 61 P3
Folkton N York 99 M5
Folla Rule Abers 158 H11
Follifoot N York 97 M10
Folly Gate Devon 8 E5
Folly Hill Surrey 23 M5
Fonmon V Glam 30 D11
Fonthill Bishop Wilts 20 H8
Fonthill Gifford Wilts 20 H8
Fontmell Magna Dorset 20 G11
Fontmell Parva Dorset 12 D2
Fontwell W Susx 15 P5
Font-y-gary V Glam 30 E11
Foolow Derbys 83 Q9
Foots Cray Gt Lon 37 L6
Forbestown Abers 150 B5
Forcett N York 103 N8
Ford Ag & B 130 H7
Ford Bucks 35 L3
Ford Derbys 84 F4
Ford Devon 6 G8
Ford Devon 7 K10
Ford Devon 16 G7
Ford Gloucs 47 L9
Ford Nthumb 118 H3
Ford Shrops 56 G2
Ford Somset 18 E9
Ford Somset 19 Q4
Ford Staffs 71 K4
Ford W Susx 15 Q6
Ford Wilts 21 N8
Ford Wilts 32 F9
Forda Devon 8 D6
Fordcombe Kent 25 M2
Fordell Fife 134 F10
Forden Powys 56 C4
Ford End Essex 51 Q7
Forder Green Devon 7 K5
Ford Green Lancs 95 K11
Fordham Cambs 63 K6
Fordham Essex 52 F6
Fordham Norfk 75 M11
Fordham Heath Essex 52 F6
Ford Heath Shrops 56 G2
Fordingbridge Hants 13 K2
Fordon E R Yk 99 L5
Fordoun Abers 143 N2
Ford's Green Suffk 64 F8
Fordstreet Essex 52 F6
Ford Street Somset 18 G11
Fordton Devon 9 K5
Fordwells Oxon 34 B2
Fordwich Kent 39 L10
Fordyce Abers 158 E5
Forebridge Staffs 70 G10
Foremark Derbys 72 A5
Forest Guern 10 b2
Forest N York 103 N8
Forest Becks Lancs 96 B1
Forestburn Gate Nthumb 119 L11
Forest Chapel Ches E 83 L10
Forest Coal Pit Mons 45 K10
Forest Gate Gt Lon 37 K3
Forest Green Surrey 24 D2
Forest Hall N Tyne 113 L7
Forest Head Cumb 111 L9
Forest Hill Gt Lon 37 J5
Forest Hill Oxon 34 G3
Forest-in-Teesdale Dur 102 G4
Forest Lane Head N York 97 M9
Forest Mill Clacks 134 B9
Forest of Bowland Lancs 95 N10
Forest of Dean Gloucs 32 B2
Forest Row E Susx 25 K4
Forest Side IoW 14 E9
Forestside W Susx 15 L4
Forest Town Notts 85 J8
Forfar Angus 142 H7
Forgandenny P & K 134 C4
Forge Powys 54 H5
Forge Hammer Torfn 31 J5
Forge Side Torfn 30 H3
Forgie Moray 158 A7
Forgieside Moray 158 B7
Forgue Abers 158 F8
Forhill Worcs 58 G9
Formby Sefton 88 C9
Forncett End Norfk 64 G3
Forncett St Mary Norfk 64 H3
Forncett St Peter Norfk 64 H3
Fornham All Saints Suffk 64 B8
Fornham St Martin Suffk 64 B8
Fornham St Genevieve Suffk 64 A8
Fornighty Highld 156 G7
Forres Moray 157 J6
Forsbrook Staffs 70 H5
Forse Highld 167 M10
Forshaw Heath Warwks 58 G10
Forsinard Highld 166 E8
Forss Highld 166 H3
Forston Dorset 11 P5
Fort Augustus Highld 147 K6
Forteviot P & K 134 C4
Forth S Lans 126 G7
Forthampton Gloucs 46 G8
Fort Hommet Guern 10 b1
Forth Rail Bridge C Edin 127 L2
Forth Road Bridge Fife 127 L2

Fortingall P & K 140 H8
Forton Hants 22 D6
Forton Lancs 95 K10
Forton Shrops 69 M11
Forton Somset 10 G3
Forton Staffs 70 D10
Fort Richmond Guern 10 b2
Fortrie Abers 158 G8
Fortrose Highld 156 C6
Fortuneswell Dorset 11 P10
Fort William Highld 139 L3
Forty Green Bucks 35 P6
Forty Hill Gt Lon 50 H11
Forward Green Suffk 64 G10
Fosbury Wilts 22 B3
Foscot Oxon 47 P10
Foscote Nhants 49 J5
Fosdyke Lincs 74 F4
Fosdyke Bridge Lincs 74 F4
Foss P & K 141 J6
Fossebridge Gloucs 33 L2
Foss-y-ffin Cerdgn 42 H2
Fosterhouses Donc 91 R8
Foster Street Essex 51 L9
Foston Derbys 71 M8
Foston Leics 60 D2
Foston Lincs 73 M2
Foston N York 98 D7
Foston on the Wolds E R Yk 99 N9
Fotherby Lincs 87 K2
Fothergill Cumb 100 D4
Fotheringhay Nhants 61 N2
Foula Shet 169 k10
Foula Airport Shet 169 k10
Foul Anchor Cambs 75 J7
Foulbridge Cumb 110 H11
Foulby Wakefd 91 K7
Foulden Border 129 N8
Foulden Norfk 63 Q11
Foul End Warwks 59 K6
Foul Mile E Susx 25 P7
Foulness Island Essex 38 G3
Foulridge Lancs 89 P2
Foulsham Norfk 76 E7
Fountainhall Border 128 C10
Four Ashes Solhll 59 J9
Four Ashes Staffs 57 Q7
Four Ashes Staffs 58 D3
Four Ashes Suffk 64 E7
Four Cabots Guern 10 b2
Four Crosses Powys 69 J11
Four Crosses Staffs 58 E3
Four Elms Kent 37 L11
Four Foot Somset 19 Q8
Four Forks Somset 18 H7
Four Gates Bolton 89 J9
Four Gotes Cambs 75 J7
Four Lane End Barns 90 H10
Four Lane Ends Ches W 69 Q2
Four Lanes Cnwll 2 H6
Fourlanes End Ches E 70 E3
Four Marks Hants 23 J7
Four Mile Bridge IoA 78 D9
Four Oaks Birm 58 H5
Four Oaks E Susx 26 E7
Four Oaks Gloucs 46 C9
Four Oaks Solhll 59 K8
Fourpenny Highld 163 J8
Four Points W Berk 34 G9
Four Roads Carmth 28 D3
Four Shire Stone Warwks 47 P8
Fourstones Nthumb 112 C7
Four Throws Kent 26 C6
Four Wents Kent 37 P10
Fovant Wilts 21 K9
Foveran Abers 151 P3
Fowey Cnwll 5 J11
Fowley Common Warrtn 82 E5
Fowlhall Kent 37 Q11
Fowlis Angus 142 E11
Fowlis Wester P & K 133 Q3
Fowlmere Cambs 62 F11
Fownhope Herefs 46 A8
Foxbar Rens 125 M5
Foxcombe Devon 8 C7
Fox Corner Surrey 23 Q4
Foxcote Gloucs 47 K11
Foxcote Somset 20 D3
Foxdale IoM 80 c6
Foxearth Essex 52 D3
Foxendown Kent 37 P7
Foxfield Cumb 94 E3
Foxham Wilts 33 J9
Fox Hatch Essex 51 N11
Foxhills Hants 13 P2
Foxhole Cnwll 3 P3
Foxholes N York 99 L6
Foxhunt Green E Susx 25 M7
Foxley Nhants 48 H4
Foxley Norfk 76 E7
Foxley Wilts 32 G7
Foxlydiate Worcs 58 F11
Fox Street Essex 53 J6
Foxt Staffs 71 J5
Foxton Cambs 62 F11
Foxton Dur 104 C6
Foxton Leics 60 F3
Foxton N York 104 D11
Foxup N York 96 C5
Foxwist Green Ches W 82 D11
Foxwood Shrops 57 L9
Foy Herefs 46 A9
Foyers Highld 147 M3
Foynesfield Highld 156 F7
Fraddam Cnwll 2 F7
Fraddon Cnwll 4 E10
Fradley Staffs 59 J2
Fradswell Staffs 70 H8
Fraisthorpe E R Yk 99 P8
Framfield E Susx 25 L6
Framingham Earl Norfk 77 K11
Framingham Pigot Norfk 77 K11
Framlingham Suffk 65 K9
Frampton Dorset 11 N5
Frampton Lincs 74 F3
Frampton Cotterell S Glos 32 C8
Frampton Mansell Gloucs 32 H4
Frampton-on-Severn Gloucs 32 D3
Frampton West End Lincs 74 F2
Framsden Suffk 64 H10
Framwellgate Moor Dur 103 Q2
Franche Worcs 57 Q9
Frandley Ches W 82 D9
Frankaborough Devon 5 P3
Frankby Wirral 81 J7

Frankfort – Glewstone 271

Frankfort Norfk 77 L7
Franklands Gate Herefs 45 Q5
Frankley Worcs 58 E8
Frankley Services Worcs 58 E8
Franksbridge Powys 44 G3
Frankton Warwks 59 P10
Frant E Susx 25 N3
Fraserburgh Abers 159 N4
Frating Essex 53 J7
Frating Green Essex 53 J7
Fratton C Port 15 J6
Freathy Cnwll 5 P11
Freckenham Suffk 63 L6
Freckleton Lancs 88 E5
Freebirch Derbys 84 D6
Freeby Leics 73 L6
Freefolk Hants 22 E5
Freehay Staffs 71 J6
Freeland Oxon 34 D2
Freethorpe Norfk 77 N10
Freethorpe Common Norfk 77 N11
Freiston Lincs 74 G2
Fremington Devon 17 J5
Fremington N York 103 K11
Frenchay S Glos 32 B9
Frenchbeer Devon 8 G7
French Street Kent 37 L10
Frenich P & K 141 K6
Frensham Surrey 23 M6
Freshfield Sefton 88 B9
Freshford Wilts 20 E2
Freshwater IoW 13 P7
Freshwater Bay IoW 13 P7
Freshwater East Pembks 41 K11
Fressingfield Suffk 65 K6
Freston Suffk 53 L4
Freswick Highld 167 Q3
Fretherne Gloucs 32 D2
Frettenham Norfk 77 J8
Freuchie Fife 134 H6
Freystrop Pembks 41 J8
Friar Park Sandw 58 F6
Friar's Gate E Susx 25 L4
Friars' Hill N York 98 E3
Friar Waddon Dorset 11 N7
Friday Bridge Cambs 75 J10
Friday Street Suffk 65 J10
Friday Street Suffk 65 L11
Friday Street Suffk 65 M9
Friday Street Surrey 36 D11
Fridaythorpe E R Yk 98 H9
Friden Derbys 71 M2
Friendly Calder 90 D6
Friern Barnet Gt Lon 36 G2
Friesthorpe Lincs 86 E4
Frieston Lincs 86 B11
Frieth Bucks 35 L6
Friezeland Notts 84 G10
Frilford Oxon 34 D5
Frilsham W Berk 34 F10
Frimley Surrey 23 N3
Frimley Green Surrey 23 N3
Frindsbury Medway 38 B8
Fring Norfk 75 P4
Fringford Oxon 48 H9
Frinsted Kent 38 E10
Frinton-on-Sea Essex 53 M7
Friockheim Angus 143 K8
Friog Gwynd 54 E2
Frisby on the Wreake Leics 72 H7
Friskney Lincs 87 N9
Friskney Eaudike Lincs 87 N9
Friston E Susx 25 N11
Friston Suffk 65 N9
Fritchley Derbys 84 E10
Fritham Hants 13 M2
Frith Bank Lincs 87 K11
Frith Common Worcs 57 M11
Frithelstock Devon 16 H8
Frithelstock Stone Devon 16 H8
Frithend Hants 23 M7
Frithsden Herts 50 B9
Frithville Lincs 87 K10
Frittenden Kent 26 D3
Frittiscombe Devon 7 L10
Fritton Norfk 65 J3
Fritton Norfk 77 P11
Fritwell Oxon 48 F9
Frizinghall C Brad 90 E3
Frizington Cumb 100 D7
Frocester Gloucs 32 E4
Frodesley Shrops 57 J4
Frodsham Ches W 81 Q9
Frogden Border 118 E5
Frog End Cambs 62 E11
Frog End Cambs 62 H9
Froggatt Derbys 84 B5
Froghall Staffs 71 J5
Frogham Hants 13 L2
Frogham Kent 39 N11
Frogmore Devon 7 K10
Frognall Lincs 74 C8
Frogpool Cnwll 3 K5
Frog Pool Worcs 57 Q11
Frogwell Cnwll 5 N8
Frolesworth Leics 60 B2
Frome Somset 20 E5
Frome St Quintin Dorset 11 M4
Fromes Hill Herefs 46 C5
Fron Gwynd 66 F7
Fron Gwynd 67 J4
Fron Powys 56 B5
Fron Powys 56 C4
Froncysyllte Wrexhm 69 J6
Fron-goch Gwynd 68 B7
Fron Isaf Wrexhm 69 J6
Frostenden Suffk 65 P5
Frosterley Dur 103 K3
Froxfield C Beds 49 Q8
Froxfield Wilts 33 Q11
Froxfield Green Hants 23 K9
Fryern Hill Hants 22 D10
Fryerning Essex 51 P10
Fryton N York 98 D6
Fuinary Highld 137 Q6
Fulbeck Lincs 86 B10
Fulbourn Cambs 62 H9
Fulbrook Oxon 33 Q2
Fulflood Hants 22 E8
Fulford C York 98 C11
Fulford Somset 18 H9
Fulford Staffs 70 H7
Fulham Gt Lon 36 G5
Fulking W Susx 24 F8
Fullaford Devon 17 M4
Fullarton N Ayrs 125 J10
Fuller's End Essex 51 M5
Fuller's Moor Ches W 69 N4
Fuller Street Essex 52 B8
Fuller Street Kent 37 N9
Fullerton Hants 22 C7
Fulletby Lincs 87 J6
Fullready Warwks 47 Q5
Full Sutton E R Yk 98 E9
Fullwood E Ayrs 125 L7
Fulmer Bucks 35 Q7
Fulmodeston Norfk 76 D5
Fulnetby Lincs 86 E5
Fulney Lincs 74 E6
Fulstone Kirk 90 F9
Fulstow Lincs 93 P11
Fulwell Oxon 48 C10
Fulwell Sundld 113 N9
Fulwood Lancs 88 G4
Fulwood Notts 84 G9
Fulwood Sheff 84 D3
Fulwood Somset 18 H10
Fundenhall Norfk 64 H2
Funtington W Susx 15 M5
Funtley Hants 14 G5
Funtullich P & K 133 M2
Furley Devon 10 F4
Furnace Ag & B 131 L7
Furnace Carmth 28 F4
Furnace Cerdgn 54 F5
Furnace End Warwks 59 K6
Furner's Green E Susx 25 K5
Furness Vale Derbys 83 M8
Furneux Pelham Herts 51 K5
Further Quarter Kent 26 E4
Furtho Nhants 49 L6
Furzehill Devon 17 N2
Furzehill Dorset 12 H4
Furzehills Lincs 87 J6
Furzeley Corner Hants 15 J4
Furze Platt W & M 35 N8
Furzley Hants 21 Q11
Fyfett Somset 10 E2
Fyfield Essex 51 N9
Fyfield Hants 21 Q5
Fyfield Oxon 34 D5
Fyfield Wilts 21 N2
Fyfield Wilts 33 M11
Fyfield Bavant Wilts 21 K9
Fylingthorpe N York 105 P10
Fyning W Susx 23 M10
Fyvie Abers 159 J10

G

Gabroc Hill E Ayrs 125 M7
Gaddesby Leics 72 H8
Gaddesden Row Herts 50 C8
Gadfa IoA 78 H7
Gadgirth S Ayrs 114 H3
Gadlas Shrops 69 L7
Gaer Powys 44 H10
Gaerllwyd Mons 31 M5
Gaerwen IoA 78 H10
Gagingwell Oxon 48 D9
Gailes N Ayrs 125 J10
Gailey Staffs 58 D2
Gainford Dur 103 N7
Gainsborough Lincs 85 P3
Gainsborough Suffk 53 L3
Gainsford End Essex 52 B4
Gairloch Highld 153 Q2
Gairlochy Highld 146 F11
Gairneybridge P & K 134 E8
Gaisgill Cumb 102 B9
Gaitsgill Cumb 110 G11
Galashiels Border 117 P3
Galgate Lancs 95 K9
Galhampton Somset 20 B9
Gallanachbeg Ag & B 130 G2
Gallanachmore Ag & B 130 G2
Gallantry Bank Ches E 69 P4
Gallatown Fife 134 H9
Galley Common Warwks 59 M6
Galleywood Essex 52 B11
Gallovie Highld 147 P10
Galloway Forest Park 114 H10
Gallowfauld Angus 142 G9
Gallowhill P & K 142 B10
Gallows Green Essex 52 F6
Gallows Green Worcs 46 H2
Gallowstree Common Oxon 35 J8
Galltair Highld 145 P3
Gallt-y-foel Gwynd 67 K2
Gallypot Street E Susx 25 L3
Galmisdale Highld 144 G11
Galmpton Devon 6 H10
Galmpton Torbay 7 M7
Galphay N York 97 L6
Galston E Ayrs 125 N10
Gamballs Green Staffs 83 M11
Gamblesby Cumb 102 B3
Gambles Green Essex 52 C9
Gamelsby Cumb 110 E10
Gamesley Derbys 83 M6
Gamlingay Cambs 62 B10
Gamlingay Cinques Cambs 62 B10
Gamlingay Great Heath Cambs 62 B10
Gammersgill N York 96 G4
Gamrie Abers 159 J5
Gamston Notts 72 F3
Gamston Notts 85 M5
Ganarew Herefs 45 Q11
Ganavan Bay Ag & B 138 F11
Gang Cnwll 5 N8
Ganllwyd Gwynd 67 N10
Gannachy Angus 143 K3
Ganstead E R Yk 93 K4
Ganthorpe N York 98 D6
Ganton N York 99 K5
Ganwick Corner Herts 50 G11
Gappah Devon 9 L9
Garbity Moray 157 Q7
Garboldisham Norfk 64 E5
Garbole Highld 148 D3
Garchory Abers 149 Q5
Garden City Flints 81 L11
Gardeners Green Wokham 35 M11
Gardenstown Abers 159 K5
Garden Village Sheff 90 H11
Garderhouse Shet 169 q9
Gardham E R Yk 92 G2
Gare Hill Somset 20 E6
Garelochhead Ag & B 131 Q9
Garford Oxon 34 D5
Garforth Leeds 91 L4
Gargrave N York 96 D10
Gargunnock Stirlg 133 L9
Garlic Street Norfk 65 J5
Garlieston D & G 107 N8
Garlinge Kent 39 P8
Garlinge Green Kent 39 K11
Garlogie Abers 151 K6
Garmond Abers 159 K7
Garmouth Moray 157 Q5
Garmston Shrops 57 L3
Garnant Carmth 29 J2
Garndolbenmaen Gwynd 66 H6
Garnett Bridge Cumb 101 P11
Garnfadryn Gwynd 66 D8
Garnlydan Blae G 30 G2
Garnswllt Swans 28 H3
Garn-yr-erw Torfn 30 H3
Garrabost W Isls 168 k4
Garrallan E Ayrs 115 K4
Garras Cnwll 3 J9
Garreg Gwynd 67 L6
Garrigill Cumb 102 D2
Garriston N York 97 J2
Garroch D & G 108 C4
Garrochtrie D & G 106 F10
Garrochty Ag & B 124 D7
Garros Highld 152 H5
Garsdale Cumb 95 Q3
Garsdale Head Cumb 96 A2
Garsdon Wilts 33 J7
Garshall Green Staffs 70 H8
Garsington Oxon 34 G4
Garstang Lancs 95 K11
Garston Herts 50 D10
Garston Lpool 81 N8
Garswood St Hel 82 C5
Gartachossan Ag & B 122 D7
Gartcosh N Lans 126 B4
Garth Brdgnd 29 N6
Garth Mons 31 K6
Garth Powys 44 D5
Garth Powys 56 D10
Garth Wrexhm 69 J6
Garthamlock C Glas 126 B4
Garthbrengy Powys 44 E8
Gartheli Cerdgn 43 L3
Garthmyl Powys 56 B5
Garthorpe Leics 73 L6
Garthorpe N Linc 92 D7
Garth Row Cumb 101 P11
Garths Cumb 95 L3
Gartly Abers 158 D11
Gartmore Stirlg 132 G8
Gartness N Lans 126 D5
Gartness Stirlg 132 G10
Gartocharn W Duns 132 E10
Garton E R Yk 93 N3
Garton-on-the-Wolds E R Yk 99 K9
Gartymore Highld 163 N4
Garva Bridge Highld 147 N9
Garvald Border 127 L8
Garvald E Loth 128 F5
Garvan Highld 138 H2
Garvard Ag & B 136 b3
Garve Highld 155 L5
Garvellachs Ag & B 130 D5
Garvestone Norfk 76 E10
Garvock Inver 124 H3
Garway Herefs 45 P10
Garway Common Herefs 45 P10
Garway Hill Herefs 45 N9
Garynahine W Isls 168 h4
Garyvard W Isls 168 i6
Gasper Wilts 20 E8
Gastard Wilts 32 G11
Gasthorpe Norfk 64 D5
Gaston Green Essex 51 L7
Gatcombe IoW 14 E9
Gatebeck Cumb 95 L3
Gate Burton Lincs 85 P4
Gateford Notts 85 J4
Gateforth N York 91 P5
Gatehead E Ayrs 125 K10
Gate Helmsley N York 98 D9
Gatehouse Nthumb 111 Q3
Gatehouse of Fleet D & G 108 C9
Gateley Norfk 76 D7
Gatenby N York 97 M3
Gatesgarth Cumb 100 G7
Gateshaw Border 118 E6
Gateshead Gatesd 113 L8
Gates Heath Ches W 69 N2
Gateside Angus 142 G9
Gateside E Rens 125 M6
Gateside Fife 134 F6
Gateside N Ayrs 125 K7
Gateslack D & G 116 B10
Gathurst Wigan 88 G9
Gatley Stockp 82 H7
Gatton Surrey 36 G10
Gattonside Border 117 Q3
Gatwick Airport W Susx 24 G2
Gaufron Powys 55 M11
Gaulby Leics 72 H10
Gauldry Fife 135 K3
Gauldswell P & K 142 C7
Gaulkthorn Lancs 89 M5
Gaultree Norfk 75 J9
Gaunton's Bank Ches E 69 Q5
Gaunt's Common Dorset 12 H3
Gaunt's End Essex 51 N5
Gautby Lincs 86 G6
Gavinton Border 129 K9
Gawber Barns 91 J9
Gawcott Bucks 49 J8
Gawsworth Ches E 83 J11
Gawthorpe Wakefd 90 H6
Gawthrop Cumb 95 P3
Gawthwaite Cumb 94 F4
Gay Bowers Essex 52 C11
Gaydon Warwks 48 C4
Gayhurst M Keyn 49 M5
Gayle N York 96 C3
Gayles N York 103 M9
Gay Street W Susx 24 C6
Gayton Nhants 49 K4
Gayton Norfk 75 P7
Gayton Staffs 70 H9
Gayton Wirral 81 K8
Gayton le Marsh Lincs 87 M4
Gayton Thorpe Norfk 75 P7
Gaywood Norfk 75 M6
Gazeley Suffk 63 M8
Gear Cnwll 3 J9
Gearraidh Bhaird W Isls 168 i6
Gearraidh na h-Aibhne W Isls 168 h4
Geary Highld 152 D5
Gedding Suffk 64 C10
Geddington Nhants 61 J4
Gedling Notts 72 G2
Gedney Lincs 74 H6
Gedney Broadgate Lincs 74 H6
Gedney Drove End Lincs 75 J5
Gedney Dyke Lincs 74 H5
Gedney Hill Lincs 74 F8
Gee Cross Tamesd 83 L6
Geeston Rutlnd 73 P10
Geirinis W Isls 168 c13
Geldeston Norfk 65 M3
Gelli Rhondd 30 C6
Gelli Torfn 31 J6
Gellideg Myr Td 30 D3
Gellifor Denbgs 68 F2
Gelligaer Caerph 30 F5
Gelligroes Caerph 30 G6
Gelligron Neath 29 K4
Gellilydan Gwynd 67 M7
Gellinudd Neath 29 K4
Gelly Pembks 41 L7
Gellyburn P & K 141 Q10
Gellywen Carmth 41 Q6
Gelston D & G 108 G9
Gelston Lincs 86 B11
Gembling E R Yk 99 N9
Gentleshaw Staffs 58 G2
Georgefield D & G 110 E2
George Green Bucks 35 Q8
Georgeham Devon 16 H4
Georgemas Junction Station Highld 167 L5
George Nympton Devon 17 N7
Georgetown Blae G 30 G3
Georgia Cnwll 2 D6
Georth Ork 169 c4
Gerinish W Isls 168 c13
Gerlan Gwynd 79 L11
Germansweek Devon 8 B6
Germoe Cnwll 2 F8
Gerrans Cnwll 3 M6
Gerrards Cross Bucks 36 B3
Gerrick R & Cl 105 K8
Gestingthorpe Essex 52 D4
Gethsemane Pembks 41 L2
Geuffordd Powys 56 C2
Gib Hill Ches W 82 D9
Gibraltar Lincs 87 Q9
Gibsmere Notts 85 M11
Giddeahall Wilts 32 G10
Giddy Green Dorset 12 D7
Gidea Park Gt Lon 37 M2
Gidleigh Devon 8 G7
Giffnock E Rens 125 P6
Gifford E Loth 128 E6
Giffordtown Fife 134 H5
Giggleswick N York 96 B8
Gigha Ag & B 123 K10
Gilberdyke E R Yk 92 D5
Gilbert's End Worcs 46 F6
Gilbert Street Hants 22 H8
Gilchriston E Loth 128 D6
Gilcrux Cumb 100 F3
Gildersome Leeds 90 G5
Gildingwells Rothm 85 J3
Gilesgate Moor Dur 103 Q2
Gileston V Glam 30 D11
Gilfach Caerph 30 G5
Gilfach Goch Brdgnd 30 C6
Gilfachrheda Cerdgn 42 H3
Gilgarran Cumb 100 D6
Gill Cumb 101 M5
Gillamoor N York 98 D3
Gillan Cnwll 3 K8
Gillen Highld 152 D6
Gillesbie D & G 110 C2
Gilling East N York 98 C5
Gillingham Dorset 20 F9
Gillingham Medway 38 C8
Gillingham Norfk 65 N3
Gilling West N York 103 N9
Gillock Highld 167 M5
Gillow Heath Staffs 70 F3
Gills Highld 167 P2
Gill's Green Kent 26 C5
Gilmanscleuch Border 117 L6
Gilmerton C Edin 127 P4
Gilmerton P & K 133 P3
Gilmonby Dur 103 J8
Gilmorton Leics 60 C3
Gilsland Nthumb 111 M7
Gilson Warwks 59 J7
Gilstead C Brad 90 E3
Gilston Border 128 C8
Gilston Herts 51 K8
Gilston Park Herts 51 K8
Giltbrook Notts 84 G11
Gilwern Mons 30 H2
Gimingham Norfk 77 K4
Ginclough Ches E 83 L9
Gingers Green E Susx 25 P8
Gipping Suffk 64 F9
Gipsey Bridge Lincs 87 J11
Girdle Toll N Ayrs 125 J9
Girlington C Brad 90 E4
Girlsta Shet 169 r8
Girsby N York 104 C9
Girtford C Beds 61 Q11
Girthon D & G 108 D10
Girton Cambs 62 F8
Girton Notts 85 P7
Girvan S Ayrs 114 C8
Gisburn Lancs 96 B11
Gisleham Suffk 65 Q4
Gislingham Suffk 64 F7
Gissing Norfk 64 G4
Gittisham Devon 10 C5
Givons Grove Surrey 36 E10
Gladestry Powys 45 J3
Gladsmuir E Loth 128 D5
Glais Swans 29 K4
Glaisdale N York 105 L9
Glamis Angus 142 F8
Glanaber Gwynd 67 L4
Glanaman Carmth 29 J2
Glandford Norfk 76 E3
Glan-Duar Carmth 43 K6
Glandwr Pembks 41 N5
Glan-Dwyfach Gwynd 66 H6
Glandy Cross Carmth 41 M5
Glandyfi Cerdgn 54 F5
Glangrwyney Powys 45 J11
Glanllynfi Brdgnd 29 N6
Glanmule Powys 56 B6
Glanrhyd Pembks 41 M2
Glan-rhyd Powys 29 L3
Glanton Nthumb 119 L8
Glanton Pike Nthumb 119 L8
Glanvilles Wootton Dorset 11 P3
Glan-y-don Flints 80 H9
Glan-y-llyn Rhondd 30 F8
Glan-y-nant Powys 55 L8
Glan-yr-afon Gwynd 68 B6
Glan-yr-afon Gwynd 68 D6
Glan-yr-afon IoA 79 L8
Glan-yr-afon Swans 28 H3
Glan-y-wern Gwynd 67 L8
Glapthorn Nhants 61 M2
Glapwell Derbys 84 G7
Glasbury Powys 44 H7
Glascoed Denbgs 80 D10
Glascoed Mons 31 K4
Glascote Staffs 59 K4
Glascwm Powys 44 H4
Glasfryn Conwy 68 B4
Glasgow C Glas 125 P4
Glasgow Airport Rens 125 M4
Glasgow Prestwick Airport S Ayrs 114 G2
Glasgow Science Centre C Glas 125 P4
Glasinfryn Gwynd 79 K11
Glasnacardoch Bay Highld 145 L8
Glasnakille Highld 144 H5
Glasphein Highld 152 B8
Glaspwll Powys 54 G5
Glassenbury Kent 26 C4
Glassford S Lans 126 C8
Glass Houghton Wakefd 91 L6
Glasshouse Gloucs 46 D10
Glasshouse Hill Gloucs 46 D10
Glasshouses N York 97 J8
Glasslaw Abers 159 L6
Glasson Cumb 110 E8
Glasson Lancs 95 J9
Glassonby Cumb 101 Q3
Glasterlaw Angus 143 K7
Glaston Rutlnd 73 M10
Glastonbury Somset 19 P7
Glatton Cambs 61 Q3
Glazebrook Warrtn 82 E6
Glazebury Warrtn 82 E5
Glazeley Shrops 57 N7
Gleadless Sheff 84 E4
Gleadsmoss Ches E 82 H11
Gleaston Cumb 94 F6
Glebe Highld 147 N4
Gledhow Leeds 91 J3
Gledpark D & G 108 D10
Gledrid Shrops 69 K7
Glemsford Suffk 52 D2
Glen Achulish Highld 139 K6
Glenallachie Moray 157 P9
Glenancross Highld 145 L9
Glenaros House Ag & B 137 P7
Glen Auldyn IoM 80 f3
Glenbarr Ag & B 120 C4
Glenbarry Abers 158 E7
Glenbeg Highld 137 P3
Glenbervie Abers 151 K11
Glenboig N Lans 126 C4
Glenborrodale Highld 137 Q3
Glenbranter Ag & B 131 N8
Glenbreck Border 116 F6
Glenbrittle Highld 144 F3
Glenbuck E Ayrs 115 P2
Glencally Angus 142 F5
Glencaple D & G 109 L7
Glencarse P & K 134 F3
Glencoe Highld 139 L6
Glencothe Border 116 F5
Glencraig Fife 134 F9
Glencrosh D & G 115 Q10
Glendale Highld 152 B8
Glendaruel Ag & B 131 K11
Glendevon P & K 134 B7
Glendoe Lodge Highld 147 L6
Glendoick P & K 134 G3
Glenduckie Fife 134 H4
Glenegedale Ag & B 122 D9
Glenelg Highld 145 P4
Glenerney Moray 157 J8
Glenfarg P & K 134 E5
Glenfield Leics 72 E9
Glenfinnan Highld 145 R11
Glenfintaig Lodge Highld 146 G10
Glenfoot P & K 134 F4
Glenfyne Lodge Ag & B 131 Q4
Glengarnock N Ayrs 125 J7
Glengolly Highld 167 K3
Glengorm Castle Ag & B 137 L4
Glengrasco Highld 152 G9
Glenholm Border 116 G4
Glenhoul D & G 115 M10
Glenkin Ag & B 131 N11
Glenkindie Abers 150 C5
Glenlivet Moray 149 M2
Glenlochar D & G 108 F8
Glenlomond P & K 134 F7
Glenluce D & G 106 G6
Glenmassen Ag & B 131 N10
Glenmavis N Lans 126 D4
Glen Maye IoM 80 b6
Glen Mona IoM 80 g4
Glenmore Highld 152 G9
Glenmore Lodge Highld 148 H6
Glen Nevis House Highld 139 L3
Glenochil Clacks 133 P8
Glen Parva Leics 72 F11
Glenquiech Angus 142 G5
Glenralloch Ag & B 123 Q6
Glenridding Cumb 101 L7
Glenrothes Fife 134 H7
Glenshero Lodge Highld 147 P9
Glenstriven Ag & B 124 D2
Glentham Lincs 86 D2
Glentrool D & G 107 L2
Glen Trool Lodge D & G 114 H11
Glentruim Highld 148 B9
Glentworth Lincs 86 B3
Glenuig Highld 138 B2
Glenvarragill Highld 152 H10
Glen Vine IoM 80 d6
Glenwhilly D & G 106 G3
Glespin S Lans 115 R2
Glewstone Herefs 45 R10

Place	Region	Page	Grid
Glinton	C Pete	74	C9
Glooston	Leics	73	K11
Glossop	Derbys	83	M6
Gloster Hill	Nthumb	119	Q10
Gloucester	Gloucs	46	F11
Gloucester Services	Gloucs	32	F2
Gloucestershire Airport	Gloucs	46	G10
Glusburn	N York	96	F11
Glutt Lodge	Highld	166	H9
Gluvian	Cnwll	4	E9
Glympton	Oxon	48	D10
Glynarthen	Cerdgn	42	F5
Glyn Ceiriog	Wrexhm	68	H7
Glyncoch	Rhondd	30	E6
Glyncorrwg	Neath	29	N5
Glynde	E Susx	25	L9
Glyndebourne	E Susx	25	L8
Glyndyfrdwy	Denbgs	68	F6
Glynneath	Neath	29	N3
Glynogwr	Brdgnd	30	C7
Glyntaff	Rhondd	30	L7
Glyntawe	Powys	44	A11
Glynteg	Carmth	42	G7
Gnosall	Staffs	70	E10
Gnosall Heath	Staffs	70	E10
Goadby	Leics	73	K11
Goadby Marwood	Leics	73	K5
Goatacre	Wilts	33	K9
Goatham Green	E Susx	26	D7
Goathill	Dorset	20	C11
Goathland	N York	105	M10
Goathurst	Somset	19	J8
Goathurst Common	Kent	37	L10
Goat Lees	Kent	26	H2
Gobowen	Shrops	69	K8
Godalming	Surrey	23	Q6
Goddard's Corner	Suffk	65	K8
Goddard's Green	Kent	26	D5
Goddards Green	W Susx	24	G6
Godden Green	Kent	37	N9
Godford Cross	Devon	10	C4
Godington	Oxon	48	H9
Godley	Tamesd	83	L5
Godmanchester	Cambs	62	B6
Godmanstone	Dorset	11	P5
Godmersham	Kent	39	J11
Godney	Somset	19	N6
Godolphin Cross	Cnwll	2	G7
Godre'r-graig	Neath	29	L3
Godshill	Hants	21	N11
Godshill	IoW	14	F10
Godstone	Staffs	71	J8
Godstone	Surrey	37	J10
Godsworthy	Devon	8	D9
Godwinscroft	Hants	13	L5
Goetre	Mons	31	K3
Goff's Oak	Herts	50	H10
Gogar	C Edin	127	M3
Goginan	Cerdgn	54	F8
Golan	Gwynd	67	J6
Golant	Cnwll	5	J11
Golberdon	Cnwll	5	N7
Golborne	Wigan	82	D5
Golcar	Kirk	90	D7
Goldcliff	Newpt	31	L8
Golden Cross	E Susx	25	M8
Golden Green	Kent	37	P11
Golden Grove	Carmth	43	L11
Goldenhill	C Stke	70	F4
Golden Hill	Pembks	41	J10
Golden Pot	Hants	23	K6
Golden Valley	Derbys	84	F10
Golders Green	Gt Lon	36	F3
Goldfinch Bottom	W Berk	22	F2
Goldhanger	Essex	52	F10
Gold Hill	Cambs	62	H2
Gold Hill	Dorset	12	D2
Golding	Shrops	57	J4
Goldington	Bed	61	N10
Goldsborough	N York	97	N9
Goldsborough	N York	105	M8
Golds Green	Sandw	58	E6
Goldsithney	Cnwll	2	E7
Goldstone	Kent	39	N9
Goldstone	Shrops	70	C9
Goldthorpe	Barns	91	M10
Goldworthy	Devon	16	F7
Golford	Kent	26	C4
Golford Green	Kent	26	C4
Gollanfield	Highld	156	E7
Gollinglith Foot	N York	96	H4
Golly	Wrexhm	69	K3
Golsoncott	Somset	18	D7
Golspie	Highld	163	J6
Gomeldon	Wilts	21	N7
Gomersal	Kirk	90	G5
Gomshall	Surrey	36	C11
Gonalston	Notts	85	L11
Gonerby Hill Foot	Lincs	73	N3
Gonfirth	Shet	169	q7
Goodameavy	Devon	6	E6
Good Easter	Essex	51	P8
Gooderstone	Norfk	75	Q10
Goodleigh	Devon	17	L5
Goodmanham	E R Yk	92	E2
Goodmayes	Gt Lon	37	L3
Goodnestone	Kent	38	H9
Goodnestone	Kent	39	N11
Goodrich	Herefs	45	R11
Goodrington	Torbay	7	M7
Goodshaw	Lancs	89	N5
Goodshaw Fold	Lancs	89	N5
Goodstone	Devon	7	K4
Goodwick	Pembks	40	H3
Goodwood	W Susx	15	N5
Goodworth Clatford	Hants	22	C6
Goodyers End	Warwks	59	M7
Goole	E R Yk	92	B6
Goole Fields	E R Yk	92	C6
Goom's Hill	Worcs	47	K4
Goonbell	Cnwll	3	J4
Goonhavern	Cnwll	3	K3
Goonvrea	Cnwll	3	J4
Goosecruives	Abers	151	K11
Gooseford	Devon	8	G6
Goose Green	Essex	53	K6
Goose Green	Kent	26	D4
Goose Green	Kent	37	P10
Goose Green	S Glos	32	C10
Goose Green	W Susx	24	D7
Goose Green	Wigan	82	C4
Gooseham	Cnwll	16	C8
Gooseham Mill	Cnwll	16	C8
Goosehill Green	Worcs	47	H2
Goose Pool	Herefs	45	P7
Goosey	Oxon	34	C6
Goosnargh	Lancs	88	H3
Goostrey	Ches E	82	G10
Gordano Services	N Som	31	P9
Gorddinog	Conwy	79	M10
Gordon	Border	118	B2
Gordon Arms Hotel	Border	117	L5
Gordonstown	Abers	158	E6
Gordonstown	Abers	158	H10
Gore	Powys	45	K3
Gorebridge	Mdloth	127	Q5
Gorefield	Cambs	74	H8
Gore Pit	Essex	52	E8
Gores	Wilts	21	M3
Gore Street	Kent	39	N8
Gorey	Jersey	11	c2
Goring	Oxon	34	H8
Goring-by-Sea	W Susx	24	D10
Goring Heath	Oxon	35	J9
Gorleston-on-Sea	Norfk	77	Q11
Gorrachie	Abers	158	H6
Gorran Churchtown	Cnwll	3	P5
Gorran Haven	Cnwll	3	Q5
Gorran High Lanes	Cnwll	3	P5
Gorrig	Cerdgn	42	H6
Gors	Cerdgn	54	E9
Gorsedd	Flints	80	H9
Gorse Hill	Swindn	33	N7
Gorseinon	Swans	28	G5
Gorseybank	Derbys	71	P4
Gorsgoch	Cerdgn	43	J4
Gorslas	Carmth	28	G2
Gorsley	Gloucs	46	C9
Gorsley Common	Herefs	46	C9
Gorstage	Ches W	82	D10
Gorstan	Highld	155	L5
Gorstella	Ches W	69	L2
Gorsten	Ag & B	138	C11
Gorst Hill	Worcs	57	N10
Gorsty Hill	Staffs	71	L9
Gorthleck	Highld	147	N3
Gorton	Manch	83	J5
Gosbeck	Suffk	64	H10
Gosberton	Lincs	74	D4
Gosberton Clough	Lincs	74	C5
Gosfield	Essex	52	C6
Gosford	Devon	10	C5
Gosford	Oxon	34	E2
Gosforth	Cumb	100	E10
Gosforth	N u Ty	113	K7
Gosling Street	Somset	19	P8
Gosmore	Herts	50	E5
Gospel End	Staffs	58	C6
Gospel Green	W Susx	23	P8
Gosport	Hants	14	H7
Gossard's Green	C Beds	49	Q6
Gossington	Gloucs	32	D4
Goswick	Nthumb	119	L2
Gotham	Notts	72	E4
Gotherington	Gloucs	47	J9
Gotton	Somset	18	H9
Goudhurst	Kent	26	B4
Goulceby	Lincs	87	J5
Gourdas	Abers	159	J9
Gourdie	C Dund	142	F11
Gourdon	Abers	143	Q3
Gourock	Inver	124	G2
Govan	C Glas	125	N4
Goveton	Devon	7	K9
Govilon	Mons	31	J2
Gowdall	E R Yk	91	Q6
Gower	Highld	155	P6
Gower	Swans	28	F6
Gowerton	Swans	28	G5
Gowkhall	Fife	134	D10
Gowthorpe	E R Yk	98	F10
Goxhill	E R Yk	93	L2
Goxhill	N Linc	93	K6
Goytre	Neath	29	L7
Grabhair	W Isls	168	i6
Graby	Lincs	74	A5
Grade	Cnwll	3	J11
Gradeley Green	Ches E	69	Q4
Graffham	W Susx	23	P11
Grafham	Cambs	61	Q7
Grafham	Surrey	24	B2
Grafton	Herefs	45	P7
Grafton	N York	97	P8
Grafton	Oxon	33	Q4
Grafton	Shrops	69	M11
Grafton	Worcs	46	A2
Grafton	Worcs	47	J7
Grafton Flyford	Worcs	47	J3
Grafton Regis	Nhants	49	L5
Grafton Underwood	Nhants	61	K2
Grafty Green	Kent	26	E2
Graianrhyd	Denbgs	68	H3
Graig	Conwy	79	Q10
Graig	Denbgs	80	F10
Graigfechan	Denbgs	68	F4
Grain	Medway	38	E6
Grains Bar	Oldham	89	B9
Grainsby	Lincs	93	N11
Grainthorpe	Lincs	93	Q11
Grampound	Cnwll	3	N4
Grampound Road	Cnwll	3	N3
Gramsdal	W Isls	168	d12
Gramsdale	W Isls	168	d12
Granborough	Bucks	49	L9
Granby	Notts	73	K3
Grandborough	Warwks	59	Q11
Grand Chemins	Jersey	11	c2
Grandes Rocques	Guern	10	b1
Grandtully	P & K	141	M7
Grange	Cumb	101	J7
Grange	Medway	38	C8
Grange	P & K	134	H2
Grange	Wirral	81	J7
Grange Crossroads	Moray	158	C7
Grange Hall	Moray	157	J4
Grangehall	S Lans	116	D2
Grange Hill	Essex	37	K2
Grangemill	Derbys	84	B9
Grange Moor	Kirk	90	G7
Grangemouth	Falk	133	Q11
Grange of Lindores	Fife	134	H4
Grange-over-Sands	Cumb	95	J5
Grangepans	Falk	134	C11
Grange Park	Nhants	60	G9
Grangetown	R & Cl	104	F6
Grangetown	Sundld	113	P10
Grange Villa	Dur	113	K10
Gransmoor	E R Yk	99	N9
Gransmore Green	Essex	51	Q6
Granston	Pembks	40	G4
Grantchester	Cambs	62	F9
Grantham	Lincs	73	N3
Granton	C Edin	127	N2
Grantown-on-Spey	Highld	149	Q2
Grantsfield	Herefs	45	Q2
Grantshouse	Border	129	L6
Grappenhall	Warrtn	82	D7
Grasby	Lincs	93	J10
Grasmere	Cumb	101	K9
Grasscroft	Oldham	83	L4
Grassendale	Lpool	81	M7
Grassgarth	Cumb	101	K2
Grass Green	Essex	52	B4
Grassington	N York	96	F7
Grassmoor	Derbys	84	F7
Grassthorpe	Notts	85	N7
Grateley	Hants	21	Q6
Gratwich	Staffs	71	J8
Graveley	Cambs	62	C8
Graveley	Herts	50	F5
Gravelly Hill	Birm	58	H6
Gravelsbank	Shrops	56	E4
Graveney	Kent	39	J9
Gravesend	Kent	37	Q6
Gravir	W Isls	168	i6
Grayingham	Lincs	92	F11
Grayrigg	Cumb	101	Q11
Grays	Thurr	37	P5
Grayshott	Hants	23	N7
Grayson Green	Cumb	100	C5
Grayswood	Surrey	23	P8
Graythorpe	Hartpl	104	F5
Grazeley	Wokham	35	J11
Greasbrough	Rothm	91	L11
Greasby	Wirral	81	K7
Greasley	Notts	84	G11
Great Abington	Cambs	62	H11
Great Addington	Nhants	61	L5
Great Alne	Warwks	47	M3
Great Altcar	Lancs	88	C9
Great Amwell	Herts	51	J8
Great Asby	Cumb	102	C8
Great Ashfield	Suffk	64	D8
Great Ayton	N York	104	G8
Great Baddow	Essex	52	B11
Great Badminton	S Glos	32	F8
Great Bardfield	Essex	51	Q4
Great Barford	Bed	61	P10
Great Barr	Sandw	58	F5
Great Barrington	Gloucs	33	P2
Great Barrow	Ches W	81	P11
Great Barton	Suffk	64	B8
Great Barugh	N York	98	E5
Great Bavington	Nthumb	112	G4
Great Bealings	Suffk	53	M2
Great Bedwyn	Wilts	21	Q2
Great Bentley	Essex	53	K7
Great Billing	Nhants	60	H8
Great Bircham	Norfk	75	Q4
Great Blakenham	Suffk	64	G11
Great Blencow	Cumb	101	N4
Great Bolas	Wrekin	70	A10
Great Bookham	Surrey	36	D10
Great Bosullow	Cnwll	2	C7
Great Bourton	Oxon	48	E5
Great Bowden	Leics	60	F3
Great Bradley	Suffk	63	L10
Great Braxted	Essex	52	E9
Great Bricett	Suffk	64	E11
Great Brickhill	Bucks	49	P8
Great Bridgeford	Staffs	70	F9
Great Brington	Nhants	60	E7
Great Bromley	Essex	53	J6
Great Broughton	Cumb	100	E4
Great Broughton	N York	104	G9
Great Budworth	Ches W	82	E9
Great Burdon	Darltn	104	B7
Great Burstead	Essex	37	Q2
Great Busby	N York	104	F9
Great Canfield	Essex	51	N7
Great Carlton	Lincs	87	M3
Great Casterton	Rutlnd	73	Q9
Great Chalfield	Wilts	20	G2
Great Chart	Kent	26	G3
Great Chatwell	Staffs	57	P2
Great Chell	C Stke	70	F4
Great Chesterford	Essex	51	M2
Great Cheverell	Wilts	21	J4
Great Chishill	Cambs	51	K3
Great Clacton	Essex	53	L8
Great Cliffe	Wakefd	91	J7
Great Clifton	Cumb	100	D5
Great Coates	NE Lin	93	M9
Great Comberton	Worcs	47	J6
Great Comp	Kent	37	P9
Great Corby	Cumb	111	J10
Great Cornard	Suffk	52	E3
Great Cowden	E R Yk	93	M2
Great Coxwell	Oxon	33	Q6
Great Cransley	Nhants	60	H5
Great Cressingham	Norfk	76	B11
Great Crosthwaite	Cumb	101	J6
Great Cubley	Derbys	71	M7
Great Cumbrae Island	N Ayrs	124	F6
Great Dalby	Leics	73	J8
Great Denham	Bed	61	M11
Great Doddington	Nhants	61	J8
Great Doward	Herefs	45	Q11
Great Dunham	Norfk	76	B9
Great Dunmow	Essex	51	P6
Great Durnford	Wilts	21	M7
Great Easton	Essex	51	P5
Great Easton	Leics	60	H2
Great Eccleston	Lancs	88	E2
Great Edstone	N York	98	E4
Great Ellingham	Norfk	64	E2
Great Elm	Somset	20	D5
Great Everdon	Nhants	60	C9
Great Eversden	Cambs	62	E10
Great Fencote	N York	97	L2
Greatfield	Wilts	33	L7
Great Finborough	Suffk	64	E10
Greatford	Lincs	74	A8
Great Fransham	Norfk	76	B9
Great Gaddesden	Herts	50	B8
Greatgate	Staffs	71	K7
Great Gidding	Cambs	61	P4
Great Givendale	E R Yk	98	G10
Great Glemham	Suffk	65	L9
Great Glen	Leics	72	H11
Great Gonerby	Lincs	73	M3
Great Gransden	Cambs	62	C9
Great Green	Cambs	50	G2
Great Green	Norfk	65	K4
Great Green	Norfk	64	G1
Great Green	Suffk	64	C10
Great Green	Suffk	64	C8
Great Habton	N York	98	F5
Great Hale	Lincs	74	B2
Great Hallingbury	Essex	51	M7
Greatham	Hants	23	L8
Greatham	Hartpl	104	E5
Greatham	W Susx	24	B7
Great Hampden	Bucks	35	M4
Great Harrowden	Nhants	61	J6
Great Harwood	Lancs	89	L4
Great Haseley	Oxon	34	H4
Great Hatfield	E R Yk	93	L2
Great Haywood	Staffs	70	H10
Great Heck	N York	91	P6
Great Henny	Essex	52	E4
Great Hinton	Wilts	20	H3
Great Hockham	Norfk	64	D3
Great Holland	Essex	53	M8
Great Hollands	Br For	35	N11
Great Horkesley	Essex	52	F5
Great Hormead	Herts	51	K5
Great Horton	C Brad	90	E4
Great Horwood	Bucks	49	L8
Great Houghton	Barns	91	L9
Great Houghton	Nhants	60	G9
Great Hucklow	Derbys	83	Q9
Great Kelk	E R Yk	99	N9
Great Kimble	Bucks	35	M3
Great Kingshill	Bucks	35	N5
Great Langdale	Cumb	101	J9
Great Langton	N York	103	Q11
Great Leighs	Essex	52	B8
Great Limber	Lincs	93	K9
Great Linford	M Keyn	49	N6
Great Livermere	Suffk	64	B7
Great Longstone	Derbys	84	B6
Great Lumley	Dur	113	L11
Great Lyth	Shrops	56	H3
Great Malvern	Worcs	46	E5
Great Maplestead	Essex	52	D5
Great Marton	Bpool	88	C3
Great Massingham	Norfk	75	Q6
Great Melton	Norfk	76	G10
Great Meols	Wirral	81	J6
Great Milton	Oxon	34	H4
Great Missenden	Bucks	35	N4
Great Mitton	Lancs	89	L3
Great Mongeham	Kent	39	Q11
Great Moulton	Norfk	64	H3
Great Munden	Herts	51	J6
Great Musgrave	Cumb	102	E8
Great Ness	Shrops	69	L11
Great Notley	Essex	52	B7
Great Oak	Mons	31	L2
Great Oakley	Essex	53	L6
Great Oakley	Nhants	61	J3
Great Offley	Herts	50	D5
Great Ormside	Cumb	102	D7
Great Orton	Cumb	110	F10
Great Ouseburn	N York	97	P8
Great Oxendon	Nhants	60	G4
Great Oxney Green	Essex	51	Q9
Great Palgrave	Norfk	76	A9
Great Park	N u Ty	113	K6
Great Parndon	Essex	51	K9
Great Pattenden	Kent	26	B3
Great Paxton	Cambs	62	B8
Great Plumpton	Lancs	88	D4
Great Plumstead	Norfk	77	L9
Great Ponton	Lincs	73	N4
Great Potheridge	Devon	17	J9
Great Preston	Leeds	91	L5
Great Purston	Nhants	48	F7
Great Raveley	Cambs	62	C4
Great Rissington	Gloucs	47	N11
Great Rollright	Oxon	48	B8
Great Ryburgh	Norfk	76	D6
Great Ryle	Nthumb	119	K8
Great Ryton	Shrops	56	H4
Great Saling	Essex	51	Q5
Great Salkeld	Cumb	101	Q3
Great Sampford	Essex	51	P3
Great Saredon	Staffs	58	D3
Great Saughall	Ches W	81	M11
Great Saxham	Suffk	63	N8
Great Shefford	W Berk	34	C9
Great Shelford	Cambs	62	G10
Great Smeaton	N York	104	B10
Great Snoring	Norfk	76	C5
Great Somerford	Wilts	33	J8
Great Soudley	Shrops	70	C9
Great Stainton	Darltn	104	B6
Great Stambridge	Essex	38	E3
Great Staughton	Cambs	61	P8
Great Steeping	Lincs	87	M8
Great Stoke	S Glos	32	B8
Great Stonar	Kent	39	P10
Greatstone-on-Sea	Kent	27	J7
Great Strickland	Cumb	101	Q6
Great Stukeley	Cambs	62	B6
Great Sturton	Lincs	86	H5
Great Sutton	Ches W	81	M9
Great Sutton	Shrops	57	J8
Great Swinburne	Nthumb	112	D5
Great Tew	Oxon	48	D9
Great Tey	Essex	52	E6
Great Thurlow	Suffk	63	L10
Great Torrington	Devon	16	H8
Great Tosson	Nthumb	119	K10
Great Totham	Essex	52	E9
Great Totham	Essex	52	E9
Great Tows	Lincs	86	H2
Great Urswick	Cumb	94	F6
Great Wakering	Essex	38	F4
Great Waldingfield	Suffk	52	F3
Great Walsingham	Norfk	76	C4
Great Waltham	Essex	51	Q8
Great Warford	Ches E	82	H9
Great Warley	Essex	37	N2
Great Washbourne	Gloucs	47	J8
Great Weeke	Devon	8	G8
Great Welnetham	Suffk	64	B10
Great Wenham	Suffk	53	J4
Great Whittington	Nthumb	112	F6
Great Wigborough	Essex	52	G8
Great Wilbraham	Cambs	63	J9
Great Wilne	Derbys	72	C4
Great Wishford	Wilts	21	L7
Great Witchingham	Norfk	76	G7
Great Witcombe	Gloucs	32	H2
Great Witley	Worcs	57	P11
Great Wolford	Warwks	47	Q8
Greatworth	Nhants	48	G6
Great Wratting	Suffk	63	L11
Great Wymondley	Herts	50	F5
Great Wyrley	Staffs	58	E3
Great Wytheford	Shrops	69	Q11
Great Yarmouth	Norfk	77	Q10
Great Yeldham	Essex	52	C4
Grebby	Lincs	87	M7
Greeba	IoM	80	d5
Green Bank	Cumb	94	H4
Greenbottom	Cnwll	3	K4
Greenburn	W Loth	126	G5
Greencroft Hall	Dur	113	J11
Green Cross	Surrey	23	N7
Green Down	Somset	19	Q4
Green End	Bed	61	M11
Green End	Bed	61	N8
Green End	Bed	61	P10
Green End	Bed	61	P8
Green End	Cambs	61	Q4
Green End	Cambs	62	B6
Green End	Cambs	62	E9
Green End	Cambs	62	G7
Green End	Cambs	62	G8
Green End	Herts	50	G4
Green End	Herts	50	H4
Green End	Herts	50	H6
Greenend	Oxon	48	B10
Green End	Warwks	59	L7
Greenfield	Ag & B	131	Q9
Greenfield	C Beds	50	C4
Greenfield	Flints	80	H9
Greenfield	Highld	146	G7
Greenfield	Oldham	83	L4
Greenfield	Oxon	35	K6
Greenford	Gt Lon	36	D4
Greengairs	N Lans	126	D3
Greengates	C Brad	90	F3
Greengill	Cumb	100	F3
Greenhalgh	Lancs	88	E3
Greenham	Somset	18	E10
Greenham	W Berk	34	E11
Green Hammerton	N York	97	Q9
Greenhaugh	Nthumb	111	Q3
Green Head	Cumb	110	G11
Greenhead	Nthumb	111	N7
Green Heath	Staffs	58	E2
Greenheys	Salfd	82	F4
Greenhill	D & G	109	P5
Greenhill	Falk	126	E2
Greenhill	Herefs	46	D5
Greenhill	Kent	39	L8
Greenhill	Leics	72	C8
Greenhill	S Lans	116	C4
Green Hill	Wilts	33	L7
Greenhillocks	Derbys	84	F11
Greenhills	S Lans	125	Q7
Greenhithe	Kent	37	N5
Greenholm	E Ayrs	125	N10
Greenholme	Cumb	101	Q9
Greenhouse	Border	117	R6
Greenhow Hill	N York	96	H8
Greenland	Highld	167	M3
Greenland	Sheff	84	E3
Greenlands	Bucks	35	L7
Green Lane	Devon	9	J9
Green Lane	Worcs	47	L2
Greenlaw	Border	129	J10
Greenlea	D & G	109	M5
Greenloaning	P & K	133	N6
Green Moor	Barns	90	H11
Greenmount	Bury	89	M8
Green Oak	E R Yk	92	D5
Greenock	Inver	124	H2
Greenodd	Cumb	94	G4
Green Ore	Somset	19	Q4
Green Park	Readg	35	K10
Green Quarter	Cumb	101	N10
Greensgate	Norfk	76	G8
Greenshields	S Lans	116	E2
Greenside	Gatesd	112	H8
Greenside	Kirk	90	F7
Greens Norton	Nhants	49	J5
Greenstead Green	Essex	52	D6
Greensted	Essex	51	M10
Green Street	E Susx	26	C9
Green Street	Gloucs	46	G11
Green Street	Herts	50	E11
Green Street	Herts	51	L6
Green Street	Worcs	46	G5
Green Street Green	Gt Lon	37	L8
Green Street Green	Kent	37	N6
Greenstreet Green	Suffk	52	H2
Green Tye	Herts	51	K7
Greenway	Gloucs	46	D8
Greenway	Somset	19	K10
Greenway	V Glam	30	E10
Greenway	Worcs	57	N10
Greenwich	Gt Lon	37	J5
Greenwich Maritime	Gt Lon	37	J5
Greet	Gloucs	47	K8
Greete	Shrops	57	K10
Greetham	Lincs	87	K6
Greetham	Rutlnd	73	N8
Greetland	Calder	90	D6
Gregson Lane	Lancs	88	H5
Greinton	Somset	19	M7
Grenaby	IoM	80	c7
Grendon	Nhants	61	J8
Grendon	Warwks	59	L5
Grendon Green	Herefs	46	A3
Grendon Underwood	Bucks	49	J10
Grenofen	Devon	6	D4
Grenoside	Sheff	84	D2
Greosabhagh	W Isls	168	g8
Gresford	Wrexhm	69	K4
Gresham	Norfk	76	H4
Greshornish	Highld	152	E7
Gressenhall	Norfk	76	D8
Gressenhall Green	Norfk	76	D8
Gressingham	Lancs	95	M7
Gresty Green	Ches E	70	C4
Greta Bridge	Dur	103	L8
Gretna	D & G	110	F7
Gretna Green	D & G	110	F7
Gretna Services	D & G	110	F7
Gretton	Gloucs	47	K8
Gretton	Nhants	61	J2
Gretton	Shrops	57	J5
Grewelthorpe	N York	97	K5
Grey Friars	Suffk	65	P7
Greygarth	N York	97	J6
Grey Green	N Linc	92	C9
Greylake	Somset	19	L8
Greylees	Lincs	73	Q2
Greyrigg	D & G	109	N3
Greys Green	Oxon	35	K8
Greysouthen	Cumb	100	E5
Greystoke	Cumb	101	M4
Greystone	Angus	143	J9

Greywell Hants 23 K4
Gribb Dorset 10 H4
Gribthorpe E R Yk 92 C3
Griff Warwks 59 N7
Griffithstown Torfn 31 J5
Griffydam Leics 72 C7
Griggs Green Hants 23 M8
Grimeford Village Lancs 89 J8
Grimesthorpe Sheff 84 E3
Grimethorpe Barns 91 L9
Grimister Shet 169 r4
Grimley Worcs 46 F2
Grimmet S Ayrs 114 F5
Grimoldby Lincs 87 L3
Grimpo Shrops 69 L9
Grimsargh Lancs 88 H4
Grimsby NE Lin 93 N8
Grimscote Nhants 49 J4
Grimscott Cnwll 16 D10
Grimshader W Isls 168 j5
Grimshaw Bl w D 89 L6
Grimshaw Green Lancs 88 F8
Grimsthorpe Lincs 73 Q6
Grimston E R Yk 93 N3
Grimston Leics 72 H6
Grimston Norfk 75 P6
Grimstone Dorset 11 N6
Grimstone End Suffk 64 C8
Grinacombe Moor Devon 5 Q3
Grindale E R Yk 99 N6
Grindle Shrops 57 P4
Grindleford Derbys 84 B5
Grindleton Lancs 95 R11
Grindley Brook Shrops 69 P6
Grindlow Derbys 83 Q9
Grindon S on T 104 C5
Grindon Staffs 71 K4
Grindon Hill Nthumb 112 B7
Grindonrigg Nthumb 118 H2
Gringley on the Hill Notts 85 M2
Grinsdale Cumb 110 G9
Grinshill Shrops 69 P10
Grinton N York 103 K11
Griomsiadar W Isls 168 j5
Grishipoll Ag & B 136 F4
Grisling Common E Susx 25 K6
Gristhorpe N York 99 M4
Griston Norfk 64 C2
Gritley Ork 169 e6
Grittenham Wilts 33 K8
Grittleton Wilts 32 G8
Grizebeck Cumb 94 E4
Grizedale Cumb 94 G2
Groby Leics 72 E9
Groes Conwy 68 D2
Groes-faen Rhondd 30 E8
Groesffordd Gwynd 66 D7
Groesffordd Powys 44 F9
Groesffordd Marli Denbgs 80 E10
Groeslon Gwynd 66 H3
Groeslon Gwynd 67 J2
Groes-lwyd Powys 56 C2
Groes-Wen Caerph 30 F7
Grogarry W Isls 168 c14
Grogport Ag & B 120 F3
Groigearraidh W Isls 168 c14
Gromford Suffk 65 M10
Gronant Flints 80 F8
Groombridge E Susx 25 M3
Grosebay W Isls 168 g8
Grosmont Mons 45 N10
Grosmont N York 105 M9
Groton Suffk 52 G3
Grotton Oldham 83 L4
Grouville Jersey 11 c2
Grove Bucks 49 P10
Grove Dorset 11 P10
Grove Kent 39 M9
Grove Notts 85 M5
Grove Oxon 34 D6
Grove Pembks 41 J10
Grove Green Kent 38 C10
Grovenhurst Kent 26 B3
Grove Park Gt Lon 37 K6
Grovesend S Glos 32 C7
Grovesend Swans 28 G4
Grubb Street Kent 37 N7
Gruinard Highld 160 E9
Gruinart Ag & B 122 C6
Grula Highld 144 E2
Gruline Ag & B 137 N7
Grumbla Cnwll 2 C8
Grundisburgh Suffk 65 J11
Gruting Shet 169 p9
Grutness Shet 169 r12
Gualachulain Highld 139 L8
Guanockgate Lincs 74 G8
Guardbridge Fife 135 M4
Guarlford Worcs 46 F5
Guay P & K 141 P8
Guernsey Guern 10 b2
Guernsey Airport Guern 10 b2
Guestling Green E Susx 26 E9
Guestling Thorn E Susx 26 E8
Guestwick Norfk 76 F6
Guide Bridge Tamesd 83 K5
Guide Post Nthumb 113 L3
Guilden Morden Cambs 50 G2
Guilden Sutton Ches W 81 N11
Guildford Surrey 23 Q5
Guildstead Kent 38 D9
Guildtown P & K 142 A11
Guilsborough Nhants 60 E6
Guilsfield Powys 56 C2
Guilton Kent 39 N10
Guiltreehill S Ayrs 114 G5
Guineaford Devon 17 K4
Guisborough R & Cl 104 H7
Guiseley Leeds 90 F2
Guist Norfk 76 E6
Guiting Power Gloucs 47 L10
Gullane E Loth 128 D3
Gulling Green Suffk 64 A10
Gulval Cnwll 2 D7
Gulworthy Devon 6 D4
Gumfreston Pembks 41 M10
Gumley Leics 60 E3
Gummow's Shop Cnwll 4 D10
Gunby E R Yk 92 B3
Gunby Lincs 73 N6
Gundleton Hants 22 H8
Gun Green Kent 26 C5
Gun Hill E Susx 25 N8
Gun Hill Warwks 59 L7
Gunn Devon 17 L5

Gunnerside N York 103 J11
Gunnerton Nthumb 112 D6
Gunness N Linc 92 D8
Gunnislake Cnwll 6 C4
Gunnista Shet 169 s9
Gunthorpe C Pete 74 C10
Gunthorpe N Linc 92 D11
Gunthorpe Norfk 76 E5
Gunthorpe Notts 72 H2
Gunton Suffk 65 Q2
Gunwalloe Cnwll 2 H9
Gupworthy Somset 18 C8
Gurnard IoW 14 E7
Gurnett Ches E 83 K10
Gurney Slade Somset 20 B5
Gurnos Powys 29 L3
Gushmere Kent 38 H10
Gussage All Saints Dorset 12 H2
Gussage St Andrew Dorset 12 G2
Gussage St Michael Dorset 12 G2
Guston Kent 27 P3
Gutcher Shet 169 s4
Guthrie Angus 143 K7
Guyhirn Cambs 74 H10
Guyhirn Gull Cambs 74 G10
Guy's Marsh Dorset 20 F10
Guyzance Nthumb 119 P10
Gwaenysgor Flints 80 F8
Gwalchmai IoA 78 F9
Gwastadnant Gwynd 67 L3
Gwaun-Cae-Gurwen
  Carmth 29 J2
Gwbert on Sea Cerdgn 42 C4
Gwealavellan Cnwll 2 G5
Gweek Cnwll 3 J8
Gwehelog Mons 31 L4
Gwenddwr Powys 44 F6
Gwennap Cnwll 3 J5
Gwennap Mining District
  Cnwll 3 K5
Gwenter Cnwll 3 J10
Gwernaffield Flints 81 J11
Gwernesney Mons 31 M4
Gwernogle Carmth 43 K8
Gwernymynydd Flints 68 H2
Gwersyllt Wrexhm 69 K4
Gwespyr Flints 80 G8
Gwindra Cnwll 3 P3
Gwinear Cnwll 2 F6
Gwithian Cnwll 2 F5
Gwredog IoA 78 G7
Gwrhay Caerph 30 G5
Gwyddelwern Denbgs 68 E5
Gwyddgrug Carmth 43 J7
Gwynfryn Wrexhm 69 J4
Gwystre Powys 55 P11
Gwytherin Conwy 68 A2
Gyfelia Wrexhm 69 K5
Gyrn Goch Gwynd 66 G5

H

Habberley Shrops 56 F4
Habberley Worcs 57 Q9
Habergham Lancs 89 N4
Habertoft Lincs 87 P7
Habin W Susx 23 M10
Habrough NE Lin 93 K8
Hacconby Lincs 74 B5
Haceby Lincs 73 Q3
Hacheston Suffk 65 L10
Hackbridge Gt Lon 36 G7
Hackenthorpe Sheff 84 F4
Hackford Norfk 76 F11
Hackforth N York 97 K2
Hack Green Ches E 70 A5
Hackland Ork 169 c4
Hackleton Nhants 60 H9
Hacklinge Kent 39 P11
Hackman's Gate Worcs 58 C9
Hackness N York 99 K2
Hackness Somset 19 K5
Hackney Gt Lon 36 H4
Hackthorn Lincs 86 C4
Hackthorpe Cumb 101 P6
Hacton Gt Lon 37 N3
Hadden Border 118 E3
Haddenham Bucks 35 K3
Haddenham Cambs 62 G5
Haddington E Loth 128 E5
Haddington Lincs 86 B8
Haddiscoe Norfk 65 N2
Haddon Cambs 61 P2
Hade Edge Kirk 83 P4
Hadfield Derbys 83 M5
Hadham Cross Herts 51 K7
Hadham Ford Herts 51 K6
Hadleigh Essex 38 D4
Hadleigh Suffk 52 H3
Hadleigh Heath Suffk 52 G3
Hadley Worcs 46 G2
Hadley Wrekin 57 M2
Hadley End Staffs 71 L10
Hadley Wood Gt Lon 50 G11
Hadlow Kent 37 P10
Hadlow Down E Susx 25 M6
Hadnall Shrops 69 P10
Hadrian's Wall 112 E7
Hadstock Essex 51 N2
Hadston Nthumb 119 Q11
Hadzor Worcs 46 H2
Haffenden Quarter Kent 26 E3
Hafodunos Conwy 80 B11
Hafod-y-bwch Wrexhm 69 K5
Hafod-y-coed Blae G 30 H4
Hafodyrynys Caerph 30 H5
Haggate Lancs 89 P3
Haggbeck Cumb 111 J6
Haggersta Shet 169 q9
Haggington Hill Devon 17 K2
Haigh Wigan 89 J9
Haighton Green Lancs 88 H4
Haile Cumb 100 D9
Hailes Gloucs 47 K8
Hailey Herts 51 J8
Hailey Oxon 34 C2

Hailey Oxon 34 H7
Hailsham E Susx 25 N9
Hail Weston Cambs 61 Q8
Hainault Gt Lon 37 L2
Haine Kent 39 Q8
Hainford Norfk 77 J8
Hainton Lincs 86 G4
Hainworth C Brad 90 D3
Haisthorpe E R Yk 99 N8
Hakin Pembks 40 G9
Halam Notts 85 L10
Halbeath Fife 134 E10
Halberton Devon 9 P2
Halcro Highld 167 M4
Hale Cumb 95 L5
Hale Halton 81 P8
Hale Hants 21 N11
Hale Somset 20 D9
Hale Surrey 23 M5
Hale Traffd 82 G7
Hale Bank Halton 81 P8
Hale Barns Traffd 82 G7
Hale Green E Susx 25 N8
Hale Nook Lancs 88 D2
Hales Norfk 65 M2
Hales Staffs 70 C8
Halesgate Lincs 74 F5
Hales Green Derbys 71 M6
Halesowen Dudley 58 E8
Hales Place Kent 39 K10
Halesville Essex 38 F3
Halesworth Suffk 65 M6
Halewood Knows 81 P7
Halford Devon 7 L4
Halford Shrops 56 G8
Halford Warwks 47 Q5
Halfpenny Cumb 95 L3
Halfpenny Green Staffs 58 B6
Halfpenny Houses N York 97 K4
Halfway Carmth 43 M8
Halfway Carmth 44 A8
Halfway Sheff 84 F4
Halfway W Berk 34 D11
Halfway Bridge W Susx 23 P10
Halfway House Shrops 56 E2
Halfway Houses Kent 38 F7
Halifax Calder 90 D5
Halket E Ayrs 125 L7
Halkirk Highld 167 K5
Halkyn Flints 81 J10
Hall E Rens 125 L7
Hallam Fields Derbys 72 D3
Halland E Susx 25 L7
Hallaton Leics 73 K11
Hallatrow BaNES 20 B3
Hallbankgate Cumb 111 J9
Hallbeck Cumb 95 N3
Hall Cliffe Wakefd 90 H7
Hall Cross Lancs 88 E4
Hall Dunnerdale Cumb 100 H11
Hallen S Glos 31 Q8
Hall End Bed 61 M11
Hall End C Beds 50 C3
Hallfield Gate Derbys 84 E9
Hallgarth Dur 104 B2
Hallglen Falk 126 F2
Hall Green Birm 58 H8
Hallin Highld 152 D6
Halling Medway 38 B9
Hallington Lincs 87 K3
Hallington Nthumb 112 E5
Halliwell Bolton 89 K8
Halloughton Notts 85 L10
Hallow Worcs 46 F3
Hallow Heath Worcs 46 F3
Hallsands Devon 7 L11
Hall's Green Essex 51 K9
Hall's Green Herts 50 G5
Hallthwaites Cumb 94 D3
Hallworthy Cnwll 5 K4
Hallyne Border 116 H2
Halmer End Staffs 70 D5
Halmond's Frome Herefs 46 C5
Halmore Gloucs 32 D4
Halnaker W Susx 15 N5
Halsall Lancs 88 D8
Halse Nhants 48 G6
Halse Somset 18 F9
Halsetown Cnwll 2 E6
Halsham E R Yk 93 N5
Halsinger Devon 17 J4
Halstead Essex 52 D5
Halstead Kent 37 L8
Halstead Leics 73 K9
Halstock Dorset 11 L3
Halsway Somset 18 F7
Haltcliff Bridge Cumb 101 L3
Haltham Lincs 86 H8
Haltoft End Lincs 87 L11
Halton Bucks 35 N3
Halton Halton 82 B8
Halton Lancs 95 L8
Halton Leeds 91 K4
Halton Nthumb 112 E7
Halton Wrexhm 69 K7
Halton East N York 96 F10
Halton Fenside Lincs 87 M8
Halton Gill N York 96 C5
Halton Green Lancs 95 L7
Halton Holegate Lincs 87 M7
Halton Lea Gate Nthumb 111 M9
Halton Quay Cnwll 5 Q8
Halton Shields Nthumb 112 F7
Halton West N York 96 B10
Haltwhistle Nthumb 111 P8
Halvana Cnwll 5 L6
Halvergate Norfk 77 N10
Halwell Devon 7 K8
Halwill Devon 8 B5
Halwill Junction Devon 8 B4
Ham Devon 10 E4
Ham Gloucs 32 C5
Ham Gloucs 46 B11
Ham Gt Lon 36 E6
Ham Kent 39 P11
Ham Somset 19 J9
Ham Somset 20 C5
Ham Wilts 22 B2
Hambleden Bucks 35 L7
Hambledon Hants 14 H4
Hambledon Surrey 23 Q7
Hamble-le-Rice Hants 14 E5
Hambleton Lancs 88 D2
Hambleton N York 91 P4
Hambleton Moss Side Lancs 88 D2

Hambridge Somset 19 L10
Hambrook S Glos 32 B9
Hambrook W Susx 15 L5
Ham Common Dorset 20 F9
Hameringham Lincs 87 K7
Hamerton Cambs 61 P5
Ham Green Herefs 46 E6
Ham Green Kent 26 E6
Ham Green Kent 38 D8
Ham Green N Som 31 P9
Ham Green Worcs 47 K2
Ham Hill Kent 37 Q8
Hamilton S Lans 126 C6
Hamilton Services
  (northbound) S Lans 126 C6
Hamlet Dorset 11 M3
Hammer W Susx 23 N8
Hammerpot W Susx 24 C9
Hammersmith Gt Lon 36 F5
Hammer Vale Hants 23 N8
Hammerwich Staffs 58 G3
Hammerwood E Susx 25 K3
Hammond Street Herts 50 H10
Hammoon Dorset 12 D2
Hamnavoe Shet 169 q10
Hampden Park E Susx 25 P10
Hamperden End Essex 51 N4
Hampnett Gloucs 47 L11
Hampole Donc 91 N8
Hampreston Dorset 13 J5
Hampsfield Cumb 95 J4
Hampson Green Lancs 95 K10
Hampstead Gt Lon 36 G3
Hampstead Norreys W Berk 34 F9
Hampsthwaite N York 97 L9
Hampton C Pete 61 Q2
Hampton Devon 10 F5
Hampton Gt Lon 36 D7
Hampton Kent 39 L8
Hampton Shrops 57 N7
Hampton Swindn 33 N6
Hampton Worcs 47 K6
Hampton Bishop Herefs 45 R7
Hampton Court Palace
  Gt Lon 36 E7
Hampton Fields Gloucs 32 G5
Hampton Green Ches W 69 P5
Hampton Heath Ches W 69 P5
Hampton-in-Arden Solhll 59 K8
Hampton Loade Shrops 57 N7
Hampton Lovett Worcs 58 C11
Hampton Lucy Warwks 47 Q3
Hampton Magna Warwks 59 L11
Hampton on the Hill
  Warwks 47 Q2
Hampton Park Wilts 21 N8
Hampton Poyle Oxon 48 F11
Hampton Wick Gt Lon 36 E7
Hamptworth Wilts 21 P11
Hamrow Norfk 76 C7
Hamsey E Susx 25 K8
Hamsey Green Surrey 37 J9
Hamstall Ridware Staffs 71 L11
Hamstead Birm 58 G6
Hamstead IoW 14 D8
Hamstead Marshall W Berk 34 D11
Hamsterley Dur 103 M4
Hamsterley Dur 112 H9
Hamsterley Mill Dur 112 H9
Hamstreet Kent 26 H5
Ham Street Somset 19 Q8
Hamwood N Som 19 L3
Hamworthy BCP 12 G6
Hanbury Staffs 71 M9
Hanbury Worcs 47 J2
Hanby Lincs 73 Q4
Hanchet End Suffk 63 K11
Hanchurch Staffs 70 E6
Handa Island Highld 164 D7
Handale R & Cl 105 K7
Hand and Pen Devon 9 P5
Handbridge Ches W 81 N11
Handcross W Susx 24 G5
Handforth Ches E 83 J8
Hand Green Ches W 69 P2
Handley Ches W 69 N3
Handley Derbys 84 E8
Handley Green Essex 51 Q10
Handsacre Staffs 71 K11
Handsworth Birm 58 F7
Handsworth Sheff 84 F3
Handy Cross Bucks 35 N6
Hanford C Stke 70 F6
Hanford Dorset 12 D2
Hanging Heaton Kirk 90 H6
Hanging Houghton Nhants 60 G6
Hanging Langford Wilts 21 K7
Hangleton Br & H 24 G9
Hangleton W Susx 24 C10
Hanham S Glos 32 B10
Hankelow Ches E 70 B5
Hankerton Wilts 33 J6
Hankham E Susx 25 P9
Hanley C Stke 70 F5
Hanley Broadheath Worcs 57 M11
Hanley Castle Worcs 46 F6
Hanley Child Worcs 57 M11
Hanley Swan Worcs 46 F6
Hanley William Worcs 57 M11
Hanlith N York 96 C8
Hanmer Wrexhm 69 N7
Hannaford Devon 17 L6
Hannah Lincs 87 N5
Hannington Hants 22 F3
Hannington Nhants 60 H6
Hannington Swindn 33 N6
Hannington Wick Swindn 33 N5
Hanscombe End C Beds 50 D4
Hanslope M Keyn 49 M5
Hanthorpe Lincs 74 A6
Hanwell Gt Lon 36 E5
Hanwell Oxon 48 D6
Hanwood Shrops 56 G3
Hanworth Gt Lon 36 D6
Hanworth Norfk 76 H4
Happendon Services S Lans 116 B4
Happisburgh Norfk 77 M5
Happisburgh Common
  Norfk 77 M6
Hapsford Ches W 81 P10
Hapton Lancs 89 M4
Hapton Norfk 64 H2
Harberton Devon 7 K7
Harbertonford Devon 7 K7
Harbledown Kent 39 K10

Harborne Birm 58 F8
Harborough Magna Warwks 59 Q9
Harbottle Nthumb 118 H10
Harbourneford Devon 7 J6
Harbours Hill Worcs 58 E11
Harbridge Hants 13 K2
Harbridge Green Hants 13 K2
Harburn W Loth 127 J5
Harbury Warwks 48 C3
Harby Leics 73 J4
Harby Notts 85 Q6
Harcombe Devon 9
Harcombe Devon 10 D4
Harcombe Bottom Devon 10 G4
Harden C Brad 90 D3
Harden Wsall 58 F4
Hardendale Cumb 101 Q8
Hardenhuish Wilts 32 H10
Hardgate Abers 151 K7
Hardgate D & G 108 H7
Hardgate N York 97 L8
Hardgate W Duns 125 N3
Hardham W Susx 24 B7
Hardhorn Lancs 88 D3
Hardingham Norfk 76 E11
Hardingstone Nhants 60 G9
Hardington Somset 20 D4
Hardington Mandeville
  Somset 11 L2
Hardington Marsh Somset 11 L3
Hardington Moor Somset 11 L2
Hardisworthy Devon 16 C7
Hardley Hants 14 D6
Hardley Street Norfk 77 M11
Hardmead M Keyn 49 P5
Hardraw N York 96 C2
Hardsough Lancs 89 M6
Hardstoft Derbys 84 F8
Hardway Hants 14 H6
Hardway Somset 20 D8
Hardwick Bucks 49 M11
Hardwick Cambs 62 E9
Hardwick Nhants 60 H7
Hardwick Norfk 65 J4
Hardwick Oxon 34 C3
Hardwick Oxon 48 G9
Hardwick Rothm 84 G3
Hardwick Wsall 58 G5
Hardwicke Gloucs 32 E2
Hardwicke Gloucs 46 H9
Hardwick Hall Derbys 84 G8
Hardwick Village Notts 85 K5
Hardy's Green Essex 52 F7
Harebeating E Susx 25 N8
Hareby Lincs 87 K7
Hare Croft C Brad 90 D3
Harefield Gt Lon 36 C2
Hare Green Essex 53 K6
Hare Hatch Wokham 35 M9
Harehill Derbys 71 M7
Harehills Leeds 91 J4
Harehope Nthumb 119 L6
Harelaw Border 117 Q6
Harelaw D & G 110 H5
Harelaw Dur 113 J10
Hareplain Kent 26 D4
Haresceugh Cumb 102 B2
Harescombe Gloucs 32 F2
Haresfield Gloucs 32 F2
Harestock Hants 22 E8
Hare Street Essex 51 K9
Hare Street Essex 51 M10
Hare Street Herts 51 J5
Harewood Leeds 97 M11
Harewood End Herefs 45 Q7
Harford Devon 6 G7
Hargate Norfk 64 G3
Hargatewall Derbys 83 P9
Hargrave Ches W 69 N2
Hargrave Nhants 61 N6
Hargrave Suffk 63 N9
Harker Cumb 110 G8
Harkstead Suffk 53 L5
Harlaston Staffs 59 K2
Harlaxton Lincs 73 M4
Harlech Gwynd 67 K8
Harlech Castle Gwynd 67 K8
Harlescott Shrops 69 N11
Harlesden Gt Lon 36 F4
Harlesthorpe Derbys 84 G5
Harleston Devon 7 K9
Harleston Norfk 65 J5
Harleston Suffk 64 E9
Harlestone Nhants 60 F8
Harle Syke Lancs 89 P3
Harley Rothm 91 K11
Harley Shrops 57 K4
Harling Road Norfk 64 D4
Harlington C Beds 50 B4
Harlington Donc 91 M10
Harlington Gt Lon 36 C5
Harlosh Highld 152 D9
Harlow Essex 51 K8
Harlow Carr RHS N York 97 L10
Harlow Hill Nthumb 112 G7
Harlthorpe E R Yk 92 B3
Harlton Cambs 62 E10
Harlyn Cnwll 4 D6
Harman's Cross Dorset 12 G8
Harmby N York 96 H3
Harmer Green Herts 50 G7
Harmer Hill Shrops 69 N10
Harmondsworth Gt Lon 36 C5
Harmston Lincs 86 C8
Harnage Shrops 57 K4
Harnham Nthumb 112 G4
Harnhill Gloucs 33 L4
Harold Hill Gt Lon 37 M2
Haroldston West Pembks 40 G7
Haroldswick Shet 169 t1
Harold Wood Gt Lon 37 N2
Harome N York 98 C4
Harpenden Herts 50 D8
Harpford Devon 10 B6
Harpham E R Yk 99 M8
Harpley Norfk 75 Q5
Harpley Worcs 46 B4
Harpole Nhants 60 F8
Harpsdale Highld 167 K5
Harpsden Oxon 35 L8
Harpswell Lincs 86 B4
Harpurhey Manch 83 J4
Harpur Hill Derbys 83 N10
Harraby Cumb 110 H10
Harracott Devon 17 K6
Harrapool Highld 145 L3

274 Harras – Heydour

Harras Cumb 100 C7
Harrietfield P & K 134 B2
Harrietsham Kent 38 E11
Harringay Gt Lon 36 H3
Harrington Cumb 100 C5
Harrington Lincs 87 L6
Harrington Nhants 60 G4
Harringworth Nhants 73 N11
Harris W Isls 168 f8
Harriseahead Staffs 70 F3
Harriston Cumb 100 G2
Harrogate N York 97 M9
Harrold Bed 61 K9
Harrop Dale Oldham 90 C9
Harrow Gt Lon 36 E3
Harrowbarrow Cnwll 5 Q7
Harrowden Bed 61 N11
Harrowgate Village Darltn 103 Q7
Harrow Green Suffk 64 B11
Harrow Hill Gloucs 46 C11
Harrow on the Hill Gt Lon 36 E3
Harrow Weald Gt Lon 36 E2
Harston Cambs 62 F10
Harston Leics 73 L4
Harswell E R Yk 92 D2
Hart Hartpl 104 E3
Hartburn Nthumb 112 G3
Hartburn S on T 104 D7
Hartest Suffk 64 A11
Hartfield E Susx 25 L3
Hartford Cambs 62 C6
Hartford Ches W 82 D10
Hartford Somset 18 C9
Hartfordbridge Hants 23 L3
Hartford End Essex 51 Q7
Hartforth N York 103 N9
Hartgrove Dorset 20 F11
Harthill Ches W 69 N3
Harthill N Lans 126 G5
Harthill Rothm 84 G4
Harthope D & G 116 E8
Hartington Derbys 71 L2
Hartington Nthumb 112 F3
Hartland Devon 16 D7
Hartland Quay Devon 16 C7
Hartlebury Worcs 58 B10
Hartlepool Hartpl 104 F4
Hartley Cumb 102 E9
Hartley Kent 26 C5
Hartley Kent 37 P7
Hartley Nthumb 113 M5
Hartley Green Kent 37 P7
Hartley Green Staffs 70 H9
Hartley Wespall Hants 23 J3
Hartley Wintney Hants 23 L3
Hartlip Kent 38 D9
Hartoft End N York 98 E2
Harton N York 98 E8
Harton S Tyne 113 N7
Harton Shrops 56 H7
Hartpury Gloucs 46 E10
Hartshead Kirk 90 F6
Hartshead Moor Services Calder 90 F6
Hartshead Moor Top Kirk 90 F5
Hartshill C Stke 70 F5
Hartshill Warwks 59 M6
Hartshorne Derbys 71 Q10
Hartside Nthumb 119 J7
Hartsop Cumb 101 M8
Hart Station Hartpl 104 E3
Hartswell Somset 18 E9
Hartwell Nhants 49 L4
Hartwith N York 97 K8
Hartwood N Lans 126 E6
Hartwoodmyres Border 117 N6
Harvel Kent 37 Q8
Harvington Worcs 47 L5
Harvington Worcs 58 C10
Harwell Notts 85 L2
Harwell Oxon 34 E7
Harwich Essex 53 N5
Harwood Bolton 89 L8
Harwood Dur 102 F4
Harwood Nthumb 112 F2
Harwood Dale N York 105 Q11
Harwood Lee Bolton 89 L8
Harworth Notts 85 K2
Hasbury Dudley 58 E8
Hascombe Surrey 24 B3
Haselbech Nhants 60 F5
Haselbury Plucknett Somset 11 K2
Haseley Warwks 59 K11
Haseley Green Warwks 59 K11
Haseley Knob Warwks 59 K10
Haselor Warwks 47 M3
Hasfield Gloucs 46 F9
Hasguard Pembks 40 G9
Hasholme E R Yk 92 D4
Haskayne Lancs 88 D9
Hasketon Suffk 65 J11
Hasland Derbys 84 E7
Haslemere Surrey 23 P8
Haslingden Lancs 89 M6
Haslingfield Cambs 62 F10
Haslington Ches E 70 C3
Hassall Ches E 70 D3
Hassall Green Ches E 70 D3
Hassell Street Kent 27 J2
Hassingham Norfk 77 M10
Hassness Cumb 100 G7
Hassocks W Susx 24 H7
Hassop Derbys 84 B6
Haste Hill Surrey 23 P8
Haster Highld 167 P6
Hasthorpe Lincs 87 N7
Hastingleigh Kent 27 J2
Hastings E Susx 26 D10
Hastings Somset 19 K11
Hastingwood Essex 51 L9
Hastoe Herts 35 P3
Haswell Dur 104 C2
Haswell Plough Dur 104 C2
Hatch C Beds 61 Q11
Hatch Beauchamp Somset 19 K10
Hatch End Bed 61 N8
Hatch End Gt Lon 36 D2
Hatchet Gate Hants 14 C6
Hatching Green Herts 50 D8
Hatchmere Ches W 82 C10
Hatch Warren Hants 22 H5
Hatcliffe NE Lin 93 M10
Hatfield Donc 91 R9
Hatfield Herefs 46 A3
Hatfield Herts 50 F9
Hatfield Worcs 46 G4
Hatfield Broad Oak Essex 51 M7
Hatfield Heath Essex 51 M7
Hatfield Peverel Essex 52 C9
Hatfield Woodhouse Donc 92 A9
Hatford Oxon 34 B6
Hatherden Hants 22 B4
Hatherleigh Devon 8 D4
Hathern Leics 72 E6
Hatherop Gloucs 33 N3
Hathersage Derbys 84 B4
Hathersage Booths Derbys 84 B4
Hatherton Ches E 70 B5
Hatherton Staffs 58 E2
Hatley St George Cambs 62 C10
Hatt Cnwll 5 Q9
Hattersley Tamesd 83 L6
Hattingley Hants 22 H7
Hatton Abers 159 Q10
Hatton Angus 142 H9
Hatton Derbys 71 N8
Hatton Gt Lon 36 C5
Hatton Lincs 86 G5
Hatton Shrops 56 H6
Hatton Warrtn 82 C8
Hatton Warwks 59 K11
Hatton Heath Ches W 69 N2
Hatton of Fintray Abers 151 L4
Haugh E Ayrs 115 J2
Haugh Lincs 87 M5
Haugh Rochdl 89 Q8
Haugham Lincs 87 K4
Haughhead E Duns 125 Q2
Haugh Head Nthumb 119 K5
Haughley Suffk 64 E9
Haughley Green Suffk 64 E9
Haugh of Glass Moray 158 B10
Haugh of Urr D & G 108 H7
Haughs of Kinnaird Angus 143 L6
Haughton Ches E 69 Q3
Haughton Notts 85 L6
Haughton Powys 69 K11
Haughton Shrops 57 M5
Haughton Shrops 57 N3
Haughton Shrops 69 L9
Haughton Shrops 69 Q11
Haughton Staffs 70 F10
Haughton Green Tamesd 83 K6
Haughton le Skerne Darltn 104 B7
Haultwick Herts 50 H6
Haunton Staffs 59 K2
Hautes Croix Jersey 11 b1
Hauxton Cambs 62 F10
Havannah Ches E 70 F2
Havant Hants 15 K5
Haven Herefs 45 N4
Haven Bank Lincs 86 H10
Haven Side E R Yk 93 L5
Havenstreet IoW 14 G8
Havercroft Wakefd 91 K8
Haverfordwest Pembks 41 J7
Haverhill Suffk 63 L11
Haverigg Cumb 94 D5
Havering-atte-Bower Gt Lon 37 M2
Haversham M Keyn 49 M6
Haverthwaite Cumb 94 G4
Haverton Hill S on T 104 E6
Havyatt N Som 19 N2
Havyatt Somset 19 P7
Hawarden Flints 81 L11
Hawbridge Worcs 46 H5
Hawbush Green Essex 52 C7
Hawcoat Cumb 94 E6
Hawen Cerdgn 42 F5
Hawes N York 96 C3
Hawe's Green Norfk 65 J2
Hawford Worcs 46 F2
Hawick Border 117 Q8
Hawkchurch Devon 10 G4
Hawkedon Suffk 63 N10
Hawkenbury Kent 26 D2
Hawkeridge Wilts 20 G4
Hawkerland Devon 9 Q7
Hawker's Cove Cnwll 4 E6
Hawkesbury S Glos 32 E7
Hawkesbury Warwks 59 N8
Hawkesbury Upton S Glos 32 E7
Hawkes End Covtry 59 L8
Hawk Green Stockp 83 L7
Hawkhill Nthumb 119 P8
Hawkhurst Kent 26 C5
Hawkhurst Common E Susx 25 M7
Hawkinge Kent 27 M4
Hawkley Hants 23 K9
Hawkley Wigan 82 C4
Hawkridge Somset 17 R5
Hawksdale Cumb 110 G11
Hawkshaw Bury 89 M7
Hawkshead Cumb 101 L11
Hawkshead Hill Cumb 101 K11
Hawksland S Lans 116 A3
Hawkspur Green Essex 51 Q4
Hawkstone Shrops 69 Q8
Hawkswick N York 96 E6
Hawksworth Leeds 90 F2
Hawksworth Notts 73 K2
Hawkwell Essex 38 E3
Hawkwell Nthumb 112 G6
Hawley Hants 23 N3
Hawley Kent 37 M6
Hawling Gloucs 47 L10
Hawnby N York 98 A3
Haworth C Brad 90 C3
Hawridge Bucks 35 P3
Hawstead Suffk 64 B10
Hawstead Green Suffk 64 B10
Hawthorn Dur 113 P11
Hawthorn Hants 23 J8
Hawthorn Rhondd 30 E7
Hawthorn Hill Br For 35 N10
Hawthorn Hill Lincs 86 H9
Hawthorpe Lincs 73 Q5
Hawton Notts 85 N10
Haxby C York 98 C9
Haxby Gates C York 98 C9
Haxey N Linc 92 C11
Haxey Carr N Linc 92 C10
Haxted Surrey 37 K11
Haxton Wilts 21 M5
Hay Cnwll 3 P3
Hay Cnwll 4 F7
Haydock St Hel 82 C5
Haydon BaNES 20 C4
Haydon Dorset 20 C11
Haydon Somset 19 J10
Haydon Bridge Nthumb 112 B8
Haydon Wick Swindn 33 M7
Haye Cnwll 5 P7
Hayes Gt Lon 36 C4
Hayes Gt Lon 37 K7
Hayes End Gt Lon 36 C4
Hayfield Ag & B 131 M3
Hayfield Derbys 83 M7
Hayfield Green Donc 91 R11
Haygate Wrekin 57 L2
Hay Green Norfk 75 K7
Hayhillock Angus 143 J9
Hayle Cnwll 2 F6
Hayle Port Cnwll 2 F6
Hayley Green Dudley 58 E8
Hayling Island Hants 15 K6
Haymoor Green Ches E 70 B4
Hayne Devon 9 J7
Hayne Devon 18 C11
Haynes C Beds 50 C2
Haynes Church End C Beds 50 C2
Haynes West End C Beds 50 C2
Hay-on-Wye Powys 45 J6
Hayscastle Pembks 40 G5
Hayscastle Cross Pembks 40 H5
Hay Street Herts 51 J5
Hayton Cumb 100 F2
Hayton Cumb 111 K9
Hayton E R Yk 98 G11
Hayton Notts 85 M4
Hayton's Bent Shrops 57 J8
Haytor Vale Devon 9 J9
Haytown Devon 16 F9
Haywards Heath W Susx 24 H6
Haywood Donc 91 P8
Haywood Herefs 45 P8
Haywood Oaks Notts 85 K9
Hazards Green E Susx 25 Q8
Hazelbank S Lans 126 E8
Hazelbury Bryan Dorset 12 B3
Hazeleigh Essex 52 D11
Hazeley Hants 23 K3
Hazelford Notts 85 M11
Hazel Grove Stockp 83 K7
Hazelhurst Tamesd 83 L4
Hazelslade Staffs 58 F2
Hazel Street Kent 25 Q3
Hazel Stub Suffk 51 Q2
Hazelton Walls Fife 135 J3
Hazelwood Derbys 84 D11
Hazlemere Bucks 35 N5
Hazlerigg N u Ty 113 K6
Hazles Staffs 71 J5
Hazleton Gloucs 47 L11
Heacham Norfk 75 N3
Headbourne Worthy Hants 22 E8
Headbrook Herefs 45 K3
Headcorn Kent 26 D3
Headingley Leeds 90 H3
Headington Oxon 34 F3
Headlam Dur 103 N7
Headlesscross N Lans 126 G6
Headless Cross Worcs 58 F11
Headley Hants 22 F2
Headley Hants 23 M7
Headley Surrey 36 F10
Headley Down Hants 23 M7
Headley Heath Worcs 58 G9
Headon Devon 16 F11
Headon Notts 85 M5
Heads Nook Cumb 111 K10
Heage Derbys 84 E10
Healaugh N York 97 R11
Healaugh N York 103 K11
Heald Green Stockp 82 H7
Heale Devon 17 L2
Heale Somset 18 H10
Heale Somset 19 L9
Healey N York 97 J4
Healey Nthumb 112 F9
Healey Rochdl 89 P7
Healey Wakefd 90 H7
Healeyfield Dur 112 G11
Healing NE Lin 93 M8
Heamoor Cnwll 2 D7
Heanor Derbys 84 F11
Heanton Punchardon Devon 17 J4
Heapham Lincs 85 Q3
Hearn Hants 23 M7
Heart of Scotland Services N Lans 126 G5
Hearts Delight Kent 38 E9
Heasley Mill Devon 17 N5
Heaste Highld 145 K4
Heath Derbys 84 F7
Heath Wakefd 91 K6
Heath and Reach C Beds 49 P9
Heath Common W Susx 24 D7
Heathcote Derbys 71 L2
Heathcote Shrops 70 B9
Heath End Bucks 35 N5
Heath End Hants 22 D2
Heath End Leics 72 B6
Heath End Warwks 47 P2
Heather Leics 72 B8
Heathfield Cambs 62 G11
Heathfield Devon 9 K9
Heathfield E Susx 25 N6
Heathfield N York 96 H7
Heathfield Somset 18 G9
Heathfield Village Oxon 48 F11
Heath Green Worcs 58 G10
Heath Hall D & G 109 L5
Heath Hayes & Wimblebury Staffs 58 F2
Heath Hill Shrops 57 P2
Heath House Somset 19 M5
Heathrow Airport Gt Lon 36 C5
Heathstock Devon 10 E4
Heathton Shrops 57 Q6
Heath Town Wolves 58 D5
Heathwaite N York 104 E10
Heatley Staffs 71 K9
Heatley Warrtn 82 F7
Heaton Bolton 89 K9
Heaton C Brad 90 E3
Heaton Lancs 95 J8
Heaton N u Ty 113 L7
Heaton Staffs 70 H2
Heaton Chapel Stockp 83 J6
Heaton Mersey Stockp 83 J6
Heaton Norris Stockp 83 J6
Heaton's Bridge Lancs 88 E8
Heaverham Kent 37 N9
Heaviley Stockp 83 K7
Heavitree Devon 9 M6
Hebburn S Tyne 113 M8
Hebden N York 96 F8
Hebden Bridge Calder 90 B5
Hebden Green Ches W 82 D11
Hebing End Herts 50 H6
Hebron Carmth 41 N5
Hebron IoA 78 H8
Hebron Nthumb 113 J3
Heckfield Hants 23 K2
Heckfield Green Suffk 64 H6
Heckfordbridge Essex 52 F7
Heckington Lincs 74 B2
Heckmondwike Kirk 90 G6
Heddington Wilts 33 J11
Heddon-on-the-Wall Nthumb 112 H7
Hedenham Norfk 65 L3
Hedge End Hants 14 E4
Hedgerley Bucks 35 Q7
Hedgerley Green Bucks 35 Q7
Hedging Somset 19 K9
Hedley on the Hill Nthumb 112 G9
Hednesford Staffs 58 E2
Hedon E R Yk 93 L5
Hedsor Bucks 35 P7
Heeley Sheff 84 E4
Hegdon Hill Herefs 46 A4
Heglibister Shet 169 q8
Heighington Darltn 103 P6
Heighington Lincs 86 D7
Heightington Worcs 57 P10
Heiton Border 118 D4
Hele Devon 7 J4
Hele Devon 9 N4
Hele Devon 17 J2
Hele Somset 18 G10
Helebridge Cnwll 16 C11
Hele Lane Devon 9 J2
Helensburgh Ag & B 132 B11
Helenton S Ayrs 125 K11
Helford Cnwll 3 K8
Helford Passage Cnwll 3 K8
Helhoughton Norfk 76 B6
Helions Bumpstead Essex 51 Q2
Hellaby Rothm 84 H2
Helland Cnwll 4 H7
Hellandbridge Cnwll 4 H7
Hell Corner W Berk 22 C2
Hellescott Cnwll 5 M4
Hellesdon Norfk 77 J9
Hellesveor Cnwll 2 E5
Hellidon Nhants 60 B9
Hellifield N York 96 C9
Hellingly E Susx 25 N8
Hellington Norfk 77 L11
Helm Nthumb 119 N11
Helmdon Nhants 48 G6
Helme Kirk 90 D8
Helmingham Suffk 64 H10
Helmington Row Dur 103 N3
Helmsdale Highld 163 N3
Helmshore Lancs 89 M6
Helmsley N York 98 C4
Helperby N York 97 P7
Helperthorpe N York 99 K6
Helpringham Lincs 74 B2
Helpston C Pete 74 B9
Helsby Ches W 81 P9
Helsey Lincs 87 P6
Helston Cnwll 2 H8
Helstone Cnwll 4 H5
Helton Cumb 101 P6
Helwith N York 103 L10
Helwith Bridge N York 96 B7
Hemblington Norfk 77 L9
Hembridge Somset 19 Q7
Hemel Hempstead Herts 50 C9
Hemerdon Devon 6 F7
Hemingbrough N York 91 R4
Hemingby Lincs 86 H6
Hemingfield Barns 91 K10
Hemingford Abbots Cambs 62 C6
Hemingford Grey Cambs 62 C6
Hemingstone Suffk 64 G11
Hemington Leics 72 D5
Hemington Nhants 61 N3
Hemington Somset 20 D4
Hemley Suffk 53 N3
Hemlington Middsb 104 F8
Hempholme E R Yk 99 M10
Hempnall Norfk 65 J3
Hempnall Green Norfk 65 J3
Hempriggs Moray 157 L5
Hempstead Essex 51 P3
Hempstead Medway 38 C9
Hempstead Norfk 76 G4
Hempstead Norfk 77 N6
Hempsted Gloucs 46 F11
Hempton Norfk 76 C6
Hempton Oxon 48 D8
Hemsby Norfk 77 P8
Hemswell Lincs 86 B2
Hemswell Cliff Lincs 86 B3
Hemsworth Wakefd 91 L8
Hemyock Devon 10 C2
Henbury Bristl 31 Q9
Henbury Ches E 83 J10
Hendham Devon 7 J8
Hendomen Powys 56 C5
Hendon Gt Lon 36 F3
Hendon Sundld 113 P9
Hendra Cnwll 3 J6
Hendra Cnwll 4 G6
Hendre Brdgnd 29 P8
Hendre Flints 80 H11
Hendy Carmth 28 G4
Heneglwys IoA 78 G9
Henfield W Susx 24 F7
Henford Devon 5 P3
Henfynyw Cerdgn 43 J2
Henghurst Kent 26 G4
Hengoed Caerph 30 G5
Hengoed Powys 45 J4
Hengoed Shrops 69 J8
Hengrave Suffk 63 P7
Henham Essex 51 M5
Heniarth Powys 55 Q3
Henlade Somset 19 J10
Henley Dorset 11 P4
Henley Gloucs 46 H11
Henley Shrops 56 H7
Henley Shrops 57 J9
Henley Somset 19 M8
Henley Suffk 64 H11
Henley W Susx 23 N9
Henley Green Covtry 59 N8
Henley-in-Arden Warwks 59 J11
Henley-on-Thames Oxon 35 L8
Henley Park Surrey 23 P4
Henley's Down E Susx 26 B9
Henley Street Kent 37 Q7
Henllan Cerdgn 42 G6
Henllan Denbgs 80 E11
Henllan Amgoed Carmth 41 N7
Henllys Torfn 31 J6
Henlow C Beds 50 E3
Henlow Camp C Beds 50 E3
Hennock Devon 9 K8
Henny Street Essex 52 E4
Henryd Conwy 79 P10
Henry's Moat (Castell Hendre) Pembks 41 K5
Hensall N York 91 P6
Henshaw Nthumb 111 Q8
Hensingham Cumb 100 C7
Henstead Suffk 65 P4
Hensting Hants 22 E10
Henstridge Somset 20 D11
Henstridge Ash Somset 20 D10
Henstridge Marsh Somset 20 D10
Henton Oxon 35 L4
Henton Somset 19 N5
Henwick Worcs 46 F3
Henwood Cnwll 5 M7
Henwood Oxon 34 E4
Heolgerrig Myr Td 30 D3
Heol-las Swans 29 J5
Heol Senni Powys 44 C10
Heol-y-Cyw Brdgnd 29 P8
Hepburn Nthumb 119 L6
Hepple Nthumb 119 J10
Hepscott Nthumb 113 K4
Heptonstall Calder 90 B5
Hepworth Kirk 90 F9
Hepworth Suffk 64 D7
Herbrandston Pembks 40 G9
Hereford Herefs 45 Q7
Hereson Kent 39 Q8
Heribusta Highld 152 F3
Heriot Border 128 C9
Hermiston C Edin 127 M3
Hermitage Border 117 Q11
Hermitage Dorset 11 P3
Hermitage W Berk 34 F10
Hermitage W Susx 15 L5
Hermit Hill Barns 91 J10
Hermon Carmth 42 G8
Hermon IoA 78 F11
Hermon Pembks 41 P4
Herne Kent 39 L8
Herne Bay Kent 39 L8
Herne Common Kent 39 L8
Herne Hill Gt Lon 36 H6
Herne Pound Kent 37 Q10
Herner Devon 17 K6
Hernhill Kent 39 J9
Herodsfoot Cnwll 5 L9
Heronden Kent 39 N11
Herongate Essex 37 P2
Heronsford S Ayrs 114 B11
Heronsgate Herts 36 B2
Herriard Hants 23 J5
Herringfleet Suffk 65 P2
Herring's Green Bed 50 C2
Herringswell Suffk 63 M6
Herringthorpe Rothm 84 F2
Herrington Sundld 113 N10
Hersden Kent 39 M9
Hersham Cnwll 16 D10
Hersham Surrey 36 D8
Herstmonceux E Susx 25 P8
Herston Dorset 12 H9
Herston Ork 169 d7
Hertford Herts 50 H8
Hertford Heath Herts 51 J8
Hertingfordbury Herts 50 H8
Hesketh Bank Lancs 88 E6
Hesketh Lane Lancs 89 J2
Hesket Newmarket Cumb 101 K3
Heskin Green Lancs 88 G7
Hesleden Dur 104 D3
Hesleden N York 96 C6
Hesley Donc 85 K2
Hesleyside Nthumb 112 B4
Heslington C York 98 C10
Hessay C York 97 R10
Hessenford Cnwll 5 N10
Hessett Suffk 64 C9
Hessle E R Yk 92 H5
Hessle Wakefd 91 L7
Hest Bank Lancs 95 K7
Hestley Green Suffk 64 H8
Heston Gt Lon 36 D5
Heston Services Gt Lon 36 D5
Hestwall Ork 169 b5
Heswall Wirral 81 K8
Hethe Oxon 48 G9
Hethersett Norfk 76 G11
Hethersgill Cumb 111 J7
Hetherside Cumb 110 H7
Hetherson Green Ches W 69 P4
Hethpool Nthumb 118 G5
Hett Dur 103 Q3
Hetton N York 96 E9
Hetton-le-Hole Sundld 113 N11
Hetton Steads Nthumb 119 K3
Heugh Nthumb 112 G6
Heughhead Abers 150 B5
Heugh Head Border 129 M7
Heveningham Suffk 65 L7
Hever Kent 37 L11
Heversham Cumb 95 K4
Hevingham Norfk 76 H7
Hewas Water Cnwll 3 P4
Hewelsfield Gloucs 31 Q4
Hewenden C Brad 90 D3
Hewish N Som 19 M2
Hewish Somset 11 J3
Hewood Dorset 10 H4
Hexham Nthumb 112 D8
Hextable Kent 37 M6
Hexthorpe Donc 91 P10
Hexton Herts 50 D4
Hexworthy Cnwll 5 P5
Hexworthy Devon 6 H4
Hey Lancs 89 P2
Heybridge Essex 51 P11
Heybridge Essex 52 E10
Heybridge Basin Essex 52 E10
Heybrook Bay Devon 6 D9
Heydon Cambs 51 K3
Heydon Norfk 76 G6
Heydour Lincs 73 Q3

Hey Houses Lancs 88 C5
Heyliphall Ag & B 136 B7
Heylor Shet 169 p5
Heyrod Tamesd 83 L5
Heysham Lancs 95 J8
Heyshaw N York 97 J8
Heyshott W Susx 23 N11
Heyside Oldham 89 Q9
Heytesbury Wilts 20 H6
Heythrop Oxon 48 C9
Heywood Rochdl 89 P8
Heywood Wilts 20 G4
Hibaldstow N Linc 92 G10
Hickleton Donc 91 M9
Hickling Norfk 77 N7
Hickling Notts 72 H5
Hickling Green Norfk 77 N7
Hickling Heath Norfk 77 N7
Hickling Pastures Notts 72 H5
Hickmans Green Kent 39 J10
Hicks Forstal Kent 39 L9
Hickstead W Susx 24 G6
Hidcote Bartrim Gloucs 47 N6
Hidcote Boyce Gloucs 47 N6
High Ackworth Wakefd 91 L7
Higham Barns 91 J9
Higham Derbys 84 E9
Higham Kent 37 P11
Higham Kent 38 B7
Higham Lancs 89 N3
Higham Suffk 52 H4
Higham Suffk 63 M7
Higham Dykes Nthumb 112 H5
Higham Ferrers Nhants 61 L7
Higham Gobion C Beds 50 D4
Higham Hill Gt Lon 37 J2
Higham on the Hill Leics 72 B11
Highampton Devon 8 C4
Highams Park Gt Lon 37 J2
High Angerton Nthumb 112 G3
High Ardwell D & G 106 E8
High Auldgirth D & G 109 K3
High Bankhill Cumb 101 Q2
High Beach Essex 51 K11
High Bentham N York 95 P7
High Bewaldeth Cumb 100 H4
High Bickington Devon 17 L7
High Biggins Cumb 95 N5
High Birkwith N York 96 B5
High Blantyre S Lans 126 B6
High Bonnybridge Falk 126 G2
High Borrans Cumb 101 M10
High Bradley N York 96 F11
High Bray Devon 17 M5
Highbridge Hants 22 E10
Highbridge Somset 19 K5
Highbrook W Susx 25 J4
High Brooms Kent 25 N2
High Bullen Devon 17 J7
Highburton Kirk 90 F8
Highbury Gt Lon 36 H3
Highbury Somset 20 C5
High Buston Nthumb 119 P9
High Callerton Nthumb 113 J6
High Casterton Cumb 95 N5
High Catton E R Yk 98 E10
Highclere Hants 22 D3
Highcliffe BCP 13 M6
High Close Dur 103 N7
High Cogges Oxon 34 C3
High Common Norfk 76 D10
High Coniscliffe Darltn 103 P7
High Crosby Cumb 111 J9
High Cross Cnwll 3 J8
High Cross E Ayrs 125 L8
High Cross Hants 23 K9
High Cross Herts 51 J7
Highcross Lancs 88 C3
High Cross W Susx 24 F7
High Cross Warwks 59 K11
High Drummore D & G 106 F10
High Dubmire Sundld 113 M11
High Easter Essex 51 P8
High Eggborough N York 91 P6
High Ellington N York 97 J4
Higher Alham Somset 20 C6
Higher Ansty Dorset 12 C4
Higher Ballam Lancs 88 D4
Higher Bartle Lancs 88 G4
Higher Berry End C Beds 49 Q8
Higher Bockhampton
  Dorset 12 B6
Higher Brixham Torbay 7 N8
Higher Burrowton Devon 9 P5
Higher Burwardsley Ches W 69 P3
High Ercall Wrekin 69 Q11
Higher Chillington Somset 10 H2
Higher Clovelly Devon 16 E7
Highercombe Somset 18 B8
Higher Coombe Dorset 11 L6
Higher Disley Ches E 83 L8
Higher Folds Wigan 82 E4
Higherford Lancs 89 P2
Higher Gabwell Devon 7 N5
Higher Halstock Leigh
  Dorset 11 L3
Higher Harpers Lancs 89 N3
Higher Heysham Lancs 95 J8
Higher Hurdsfield Ches E 83 K10
Higher Irlam Salfd 82 F5
Higher Kingcombe Dorset 11 L5
Higher Kinnerton Flints 69 K2
Higher Marston Ches W 82 E9
Higher Muddiford Devon 17 K4
Higher Nyland Dorset 20 D10
Higher Ogden Rochdl 90 B8
Higher Pentire Cnwll 2 H8
Higher Penwortham Lancs 88 G5
Higher Prestacott Devon 5 P2
Higher Studfold N York 96 B6
Higher Town Cnwll 3 L5
Higher Town Cnwll 4 G9
Higher Town IoS 2 c1
Higher Tregantle Cnwll 5 Q11
Higher Walton Lancs 88 H5
Higher Walton Warrtn 82 C7
Higher Wambrook Somset 10 F3
Higher Waterston Dorset 11 Q5
Higher Whatcombe Dorset 12 D4
Higher Wheelton Lancs 89 J6
Higher Whitley Ches W 82 D8
Higher Wincham Ches W 82 E9
Higher Wraxhall Dorset 11 M4
Higher Wych Ches W 69 N6
High Etherley Dur 103 N5
High Ferry Lincs 87 L11

Highfield E R Yk 92 B3
Highfield Gatesd 112 H9
Highfield N Ayrs 125 J7
Highfields Caldecote Cambs 62 E9
High Flats Kirk 90 G9
High Garrett Essex 52 C6
Highgate E Susx 25 K4
Highgate Gt Lon 36 G3
Highgate Kent 26 C5
High Grange Dur 103 N4
High Grantley N York 97 K7
High Green Cumb 101 M10
High Green Kirk 90 G8
High Green Norfk 64 H4
High Green Norfk 76 G10
High Green Sheff 91 J11
High Green Shrops 57 N8
High Green Suffk 64 B9
High Green Worcs 46 G5
Highgreen Manor Nthumb 112 B2
High Halden Kent 26 E4
High Halstow Medway 38 C6
High Ham Somset 19 M8
High Harrington Cumb 100 D5
High Harrogate N York 97 M9
High Haswell Dur 104 C2
High Hatton Shrops 69 R10
High Hauxley Nthumb 119 Q10
High Hawsker N York 105 P9
High Hesket Cumb 101 N3
High Hoyland Barns 90 H9
High Hunsley E R Yk 92 G3
High Hurstwood E Susx 25 L5
High Hutton N York 98 F7
High Ireby Cumb 100 H3
High Kelling Norfk 76 G3
High Kilburn N York 97 R5
High Killerby N York 99 M4
High Knipe Cumb 101 P7
High Lands Dur 103 M5
Highlane Ches E 83 J11
Highlane Derbys 84 F4
High Lane Stockp 83 L7
High Lanes Cnwll 2 F6
High Laver Essex 51 M9
Highlaws Cumb 109 P11
Highleadon Gloucs 46 E10
High Legh Ches E 82 F8
Highleigh W Susx 15 M7
Highley Shrops 57 N8
High Littleton BaNES 20 B3
High Lorton Cumb 100 G5
High Marishes N York 98 G5
High Marnham Notts 85 P6
High Melton Donc 91 N10
High Mickley Nthumb 112 G8
Highmoor Cumb 110 E11
Highmoor Oxon 35 K8
Highmoor Cross Oxon 35 K8
Highmoor Hill Mons 31 N7
High Moorsley Sundld 113 M11
Highnam Gloucs 46 E10
High Newport Sundld 113 N10
High Newton Cumb 95 J4
High Newton-by-the-Sea
  Nthumb 119 P5
High Nibthwaite Cumb 94 F3
High Offley Staffs 70 D9
High Ongar Essex 51 N10
High Onn Staffs 70 E11
High Park Corner Essex 52 H7
High Pennyvenie E Ayrs 115 J6
High Pittington Dur 104 B2
High Post Wilts 21 N7
Highridge N Som 31 Q11
High Roding Essex 51 P7
High Row Cumb 101 L3
High Row Cumb 101 L6
High Salter Lancs 95 N8
High Salvington W Susx 24 D9
High Scales Cumb 110 C11
High Seaton Cumb 100 D4
High Shaw N York 96 C2
High Side Cumb 100 H4
High Spen Gatesd 112 H9
Highstead Kent 39 M8
Highsted Kent 38 F9
High Stoop Dur 103 M2
High Street Cnwll 3 P3
High Street Kent 26 B5
Highstreet Kent 39 J9
High Street Suffk 65 N10
High Street Suffk 65 N7
Highstreet Green Essex 52 C5
Highstreet Green Surrey 23 Q7
Hightae D & G 109 N5
Highter's Heath Birm 58 G9
High Throston Hartpl 104 E4
Hightown Ches E 70 F2
Hightown Hants 13 L4
Hightown Sefton 81 L4
High Town Staffs 58 D7
Hightown Green Suffk 64 D10
High Toynton Lincs 87 J7
High Trewhitt Nthumb 119 K9
High Urpeth Dur 113 K10
High Valleyfield Fife 134 C10
High Warden Nthumb 112 D7
Highway Herefs 45 P5
Highway Wilts 33 L9
Highweek Devon 7 L4
High Westwood Dur 112 H9
Highwood Essex 51 P10
Highwood Staffs 71 K8
Highwood Hill Gt Lon 36 F2
High Woolaston Gloucs 31 Q5
High Worsall N York 104 C9
Highworth Swindn 33 P6
High Wray Cumb 101 L11
High Wych Herts 51 L8
High Wycombe Bucks 35 N6
Hilborough Norfk 75 R10
Hilcote Derbys 84 G9
Hilcott Wilts 21 M3
Hildenborough Kent 37 N11
Hilden Park Kent 37 N11
Hildersham Cambs 62 H11
Hilderstone Staffs 70 H8
Hilderthorpe E R Yk 99 P7
Hilfield Dorset 11 N3
Hilgay Norfk 75 M11
Hill S Glos 32 B5
Hill Warwks 59 N11
Hillam N York 91 N5

Hillbeck Cumb 102 E7
Hillborough Kent 39 M8
Hill Brow Hants 23 L9
Hillbutts Dorset 12 G4
Hill Chorlton Staffs 70 D7
Hillclifflane Derbys 71 P5
Hill Common Norfk 77 N7
Hill Common Somset 18 F9
Hill Deverill Wilts 20 G6
Hilldyke Lincs 87 K11
Hill End Dur 103 K3
Hill End Fife 134 C8
Hill End Fife 134 E11
Hill End Gloucs 46 H7
Hillend Mdloth 127 P4
Hillend N Lans 126 E4
Hillend Swans 28 D6
Hillersland Gloucs 31 Q2
Hillerton Devon 8 H5
Hillesden Bucks 49 J9
Hillesley Gloucs 32 E7
Hillfarrance Somset 18 G10
Hill Green Kent 38 D9
Hillgrove W Susx 23 P9
Hillhampton Herefs 46 A5
Hillhead Abers 158 E10
Hillhead Devon 7 N8
Hill Head Hants 14 F6
Hillhead S Lans 116 D2
Hillhead of Cocklaw Abers 159 Q9
Hilliard's Cross Staffs 59 J2
Hilliclay Highld 167 L4
Hillingdon Gt Lon 36 C4
Hillington C Glas 125 N5
Hillington Norfk 75 P5
Hillis Corner IoW 14 E8
Hillmorton Warwks 60 B6
Hillock Vale Lancs 89 M5
Hill of Beath Fife 134 F9
Hill of Fearn Highld 163 J11
Hillowton D & G 108 G8
Hillpool Worcs 58 C9
Hillpound Hants 22 G11
Hill Ridware Staffs 71 K11
Hillside Abers 151 N8
Hillside Angus 143 N5
Hill Side Devon 7 J6
Hill Side Kirk 90 F7
Hill Side Worcs 46 E2
Hills Town Derbys 84 G7
Hillstreet Hants 22 B11
Hillswick Shet 169 p6
Hill Top Dur 103 J6
Hill Top Hants 14 D6
Hill Top Kirk 90 D8
Hill Top Rothm 84 E2
Hill Top Sandw 58 E6
Hill Top Wakefd 91 J7
Hillwell Shet 169 q12
Hilmarton Wilts 33 K9
Hilperton Wilts 20 G3
Hilperton Marsh Wilts 20 G3
Hilsea C Port 15 J6
Hilston E R Yk 93 N4
Hiltingbury Hants 22 D10
Hilton Border 129 M9
Hilton Cambs 62 C7
Hilton Cumb 102 D6
Hilton Derbys 71 N8
Hilton Dorset 12 C4
Hilton Dur 103 N6
Hilton S on T 104 E8
Hilton Shrops 57 P5
Hilton of Cadboll Highld 156 F2
Hilton Park Services Staffs 58 E4
Himbleton Worcs 46 H3
Himley Staffs 58 C6
Hincaster Cumb 95 L4
Hinchley Wood Surrey 36 E7
Hinckley Leics 59 P6
Hinderclay Suffk 64 E6
Hinderwell N York 105 L7
Hindford Shrops 69 K8
Hindhead Surrey 23 N7
Hindhead Tunnel Surrey 23 N7
Hindle Fold Lancs 89 L4
Hindley Nthumb 112 F9
Hindley Wigan 82 D4
Hindley Green Wigan 82 D4
Hindlip Worcs 46 G3
Hindolveston Norfk 76 E6
Hindon Wilts 20 H8
Hindringham Norfk 76 D4
Hingham Norfk 76 E11
Hinksford Staffs 58 C7
Hinstock Shrops 70 B9
Hintlesham Suffk 53 J3
Hinton Gloucs 32 C4
Hinton Hants 13 M5
Hinton Herefs 45 L7
Hinton Nhants 48 F4
Hinton S Glos 32 D4
Hinton Shrops 56 G3
Hinton Shrops 57 M5
Hinton Admiral Hants 13 M5
Hinton Ampner Hants 22 H9
Hinton Blewett BaNES 19 Q3
Hinton Charterhouse BaNES 20 E3
Hinton Cross Worcs 47 K3
Hinton-in-the-Hedges
  Nhants 48 G7
Hinton Marsh Hants 22 G9
Hinton Martell Dorset 12 H3
Hinton on the Green Worcs 47 K6
Hinton Parva Swindn 33 P8
Hinton St George Somset 11 J2
Hinton St Mary Dorset 20 E11
Hinton Waldrist Oxon 34 C5
Hints Shrops 57 M5
Hints Staffs 59 J4
Hinwick Bed 61 K8
Hinxhill Kent 26 H3
Hinxton Cambs 62 G11
Hinxworth Herts 51 F2
Hipperholme Calder 90 E5
Hipswell N York 103 N11
Hirn Abers 151 J7
Hirnant Powys 68 D10
Hirst Nthumb 113 L3
Hirst Courtney N York 91 Q6
Hirwaen Denbgs 68 F2
Hirwaun Rhondd 30 C3
Hiscott Devon 17 J6
Histon Cambs 62 F8
Hitcham Suffk 64 D11

Hitcham Causeway Suffk 64 D11
Hitcham Street Suffk 64 D11
Hitchin Herts 50 E5
Hittisleigh Devon 8 H5
Hive E R Yk 92 D4
Hixon Staffs 71 J9
Hoaden Kent 39 N10
Hoar Cross Staffs 71 L10
Hoarwithy Herefs 45 Q9
Hoath Kent 39 M9
Hoathly Kent 25 Q3
Hobarris Shrops 56 F9
Hobbles Green Suffk 63 M10
Hobbs Cross Essex 51 L11
Hobbs Cross Essex 51 L8
Hobkirk Border 118 A8
Hobland Hall Norfk 77 Q11
Hobsick Notts 84 G11
Hobson Dur 113 J9
Hoby Leics 72 H7
Hoccombe Somset 18 F9
Hockering Norfk 76 F9
Hockerton Notts 85 M9
Hockley Ches E 83 K8
Hockley Covtry 59 L9
Hockley Essex 38 D3
Hockley Staffs 59 K4
Hockley Heath Solhll 59 J10
Hockliffe C Beds 49 Q9
Hockwold cum Wilton Norfk 63 M3
Hockworthy Devon 18 D11
Hoddesdon Herts 51 J9
Hoddlesden Bl w D 89 L6
Hoddom Cross D & G 110 C6
Hoddom Mains D & G 110 C6
Hodgehill Ches E 82 H11
Hodgeston Pembks 41 K11
Hodnet Shrops 69 R9
Hodsock Notts 85 K3
Hodsoll Street Kent 37 P8
Hodson Swindn 33 N8
Hodthorpe Derbys 84 H5
Hoe Hants 22 G11
Hoe Norfk 76 D8
Hoe Benham W Berk 34 D11
Hoe Gate Hants 14 H4
Hoff Cumb 102 C7
Hogben's Hill Kent 38 H10
Hoggards Green Suffk 64 B10
Hoggeston Bucks 49 M10
Hoggrill's End Warwks 59 K6
Hog Hill E Susx 26 E8
Hoghton Lancs 89 J5
Hoghton Bottoms Lancs 89 J5
Hognaston Derbys 71 N4
Hogsthorpe Lincs 87 P6
Holbeach Lincs 74 G6
Holbeach Bank Lincs 74 G5
Holbeach Clough Lincs 74 G5
Holbeach Drove Lincs 74 F8
Holbeach Hurn Lincs 74 G5
Holbeach St Johns Lincs 74 G7
Holbeach St Mark's Lincs 74 G4
Holbeach St Matthew Lincs 74 H4
Holbeck Notts 84 H6
Holbeck Woodhouse Notts 84 H6
Holberrow Green Worcs 47 K3
Holbeton Devon 6 G8
Holborn Gt Lon 36 H4
Holborough Kent 37 Q8
Holbrook Derbys 72 B2
Holbrook Sheff 84 F4
Holbrook Suffk 53 L4
Holbrook Moor Derbys 84 E11
Holbrooks Covtry 59 M8
Holburn Nthumb 119 K3
Holbury Hants 14 D6
Holcombe Devon 7 P4
Holcombe Somset 20 C5
Holcombe Rogus Devon 18 E11
Holcot Nhants 60 G7
Holden Lancs 96 A11
Holdenby Nhants 60 E7
Holden Gate Calder 89 P6
Holder's Green Essex 51 P5
Holdgate Shrops 57 K7
Holdingham Lincs 86 E11
Holditch Dorset 10 G4
Holdsworth Calder 90 D5
Holehouse Derbys 83 M6
Hole-in-the-Wall Herefs 46 B9
Holemoor Devon 16 G10
Hole Street W Susx 24 D8
Holford Somset 18 G6
Holgate C York 98 B10
Holker Cumb 94 H5
Holkham Norfk 76 B3
Hollacombe Devon 16 F11
Holland Fen Lincs 86 H11
Holland Lees Lancs 88 G4
Holland-on-Sea Essex 53 L8
Hollandstoun Ork 169 g1
Hollee D & G 110 E7
Hollesley Suffk 53 Q3
Hollicombe Torbay 7 M6
Hollingbourne Kent 38 D10
Hollingbury Br & H 24 H9
Hollingdon Bucks 49 N9
Hollingrove E Susx 25 Q6
Hollingthorpe Leeds 91 K4
Hollington Derbys 71 N7
Hollington Staffs 71 K7
Hollingworth Tamesd 83 M5
Hollins Bury 89 N9
Hollins Derbys 84 D6
Hollins Staffs 70 H5
Hollinsclough Staffs 83 N11
Hollins End Sheff 84 E4
Hollins Green Warrtn 82 E6
Hollins Lane Lancs 95 K10
Hollinswood Wrekin 57 N3
Hollinwood Shrops 69 P7
Hollocombe Devon 17 L9
Holloway Derbys 84 D9
Holloway Gt Lon 36 H3
Holloway Wilts 20 G8
Hollowell Nhants 60 E6
Hollowmoor Heath Ches W 81 P11
Hollows D & G 110 G5
Hollybush Caerph 30 G4
Hollybush E Ayrs 114 G4
Hollybush Herefs 46 E7
Holly End Norfk 75 J9
Holly Green Worcs 46 G6
Hollyhurst Ches E 69 Q6

Hollym E R Yk 93 P5
Hollywood Worcs 58 G9
Holmbridge Kirk 90 E9
Holmbury St Mary Surrey 24 D2
Holmbush Cnwll 3 Q3
Holmcroft Staffs 70 G10
Holme Cambs 61 Q3
Holme Cumb 95 L5
Holme Kirk 90 E9
Holme N Linc 92 F9
Holme N York 97 N4
Holme Notts 85 P9
Holme Chapel Lancs 89 P5
Holme Green N York 91 P2
Holme Hale Norfk 76 B10
Holme Lacy Herefs 45 R7
Holme Marsh Herefs 45 L4
Holme next the Sea Norfk 75 P2
Holme on the Wolds E R Yk 99 K11
Holme Pierrepont Notts 72 G3
Holmer Herefs 45 Q6
Holmer Green Bucks 35 P5
Holme St Cuthbert Cumb 109 P11
Holmes Chapel Ches E 82 G11
Holmesfield Derbys 84 D5
Holmes Hill E Susx 25 M8
Holmeswood Lancs 88 E7
Holmethorpe Surrey 36 G10
Holme upon Spalding
  Moor E R Yk 92 D3
Holmewood Derbys 84 F7
Holmfield Calder 90 D5
Holmfirth Kirk 90 E9
Holmgate Derbys 84 E8
Holmhead E Ayrs 115 L3
Holmpton E R Yk 93 Q6
Holmrook Cumb 100 E11
Holmshurst E Susx 25 P5
Holmside Dur 113 K11
Holmwrangle Cumb 111 K11
Holne Devon 7 J5
Holnest Dorset 11 P3
Holnicote Somset 18 B5
Holsworthy Devon 16 E11
Holsworthy Beacon Devon 16 F10
Holt Dorset 12 H4
Holt Norfk 76 F4
Holt Wilts 20 G2
Holt Worcs 46 F2
Holt Wrexhm 69 M4
Holtby C York 98 D10
Holt End Worcs 58 G11
Holt Fleet Worcs 46 F2
Holt Green Lancs 88 D9
Holt Heath Dorset 13 J4
Holt Heath Worcs 46 F2
Holton Oxon 34 H3
Holton Somset 20 C9
Holton Suffk 65 N6
Holton cum Beckering Lincs 86 F4
Holton Heath Dorset 12 F6
Holton le Clay Lincs 93 N10
Holton le Moor Lincs 93 J11
Holton St Mary Suffk 53 J4
Holt Street Kent 39 N11
Holtye E Susx 25 L3
Holway Flints 80 H9
Holwell Dorset 11 P2
Holwell Herts 50 E4
Holwell Leics 73 J6
Holwell Oxon 33 P3
Holwick Dur 102 H5
Holworth Dorset 12 C8
Holybourne Hants 23 K6
Holy Cross Worcs 58 D9
Holyfield Essex 51 J10
Holyhead IoA 78 C8
Holy Island IoA 78 D8
Holy Island Nthumb 119 M2
Holy Island Nthumb 119 M2
Holymoorside Derbys 84 D7
Holyport W & M 35 N9
Holystone Nthumb 119 J10
Holytown N Lans 126 D5
Holywell C Beds 50 B7
Holywell Cambs 62 D6
Holywell Cnwll 4 B10
Holywell Dorset 11 M4
Holywell Flints 80 H9
Holywell Nthumb 113 M6
Holywell Warwks 59 K11
Holywell Green Calder 90 D7
Holywell Lake Somset 18 F10
Holywell Row Suffk 63 M5
Holywood D & G 109 K3
Holywood Village D & G 109 L5
Homer Shrops 57 L4
Homer Green Sefton 81 L4
Homersfield Suffk 65 K4
Homescales Cumb 95 M3
Hom Green Herefs 46 A10
Homington Wilts 21 M9
Honeyborough Pembks 40 H9
Honeybourne Worcs 47 M6
Honeychurch Devon 8 F4
Honey Hill Kent 39 M9
Honeystreet Wilts 21 M2
Honey Tye Suffk 52 G4
Honiley Warwks 59 K10
Honing Norfk 77 L6
Honingham Norfk 76 G9
Honington Lincs 73 N2
Honington Suffk 64 C7
Honington Warwks 47 Q6
Honiton Devon 10 D4
Honley Kirk 90 E8
Honnington Wrekin 70 C11
Hoo Kent 39 N9
Hoobrook Worcs 58 B10
Hood Green Barns 91 J10
Hood Hill Rothm 91 K11
Hooe C Plym 6 E8
Hooe E Susx 25 Q8
Hoo End Herts 50 E6
Hoo Green Ches E 82 F8
Hoohill Bpool 88 C3
Hook Cambs 62 F2
Hook Devon 10 G3
Hook E R Yk 92 C5
Hook Gt Lon 36 E7
Hook Hants 14 F6
Hook Hants 23 K4
Hook Pembks 41 J8
Hook Wilts 33 L8
Hook-a-Gate Shrops 56 H3

Hook Bank Worcs....46 F6
Hooke Dorset....11 L4
Hook End Essex....51 N10
Hookgate Staffs....70 C7
Hook Green Kent....25 G3
Hook Green Kent....37 P6
Hook Norton Oxon....48 C8
Hook Street Gloucs....32 C5
Hook Street Wilts....33 L8
Hookway Devon....9 L5
Hookwood Surrey....24 G2
Hooley Surrey....36 G9
Hooley Bridge Rochdl....89 P8
Hoo Meavy Devon....6 E5
Hoo St Werburgh Medway....38 C7
Hooton Ches W....81 M9
Hooton Levitt Rothm....84 H2
Hooton Pagnell Donc....91 M9
Hooton Roberts Rothm....91 M11
Hopcrofts Holt Oxon....48 E9
Hope Derbys....83 Q8
Hope Devon....6 H10
Hope Flints....69 K3
Hope Powys....56 D3
Hope Shrops....56 E4
Hope Staffs....71 L4
Hope Bagot Shrops....57 K10
Hope Bowdler Shrops....56 H6
Hope End Green Essex....51 N6
Hopehouse Border....117 K7
Hopeman Moray....157 L4
Hope Mansell Herefs....46 B11
Hopesay Shrops....56 F8
Hopetown Wakefd....91 K6
Hope under Dinmore Herefs....45 Q4
Hopgrove C York....98 C10
Hopperton N York....97 P9
Hop Pole Lincs....74 C8
Hopsford Warwks....59 P8
Hopstone Shrops....57 P6
Hopton Derbys....71 P4
Hopton Shrops....69 L10
Hopton Staffs....70 G9
Hopton Suffk....64 D6
Hopton Cangeford Shrops....57 J9
Hopton Castle Shrops....56 F9
Hoptonheath Shrops....56 F9
Hopton on Sea Norfk....65 Q2
Hopton Wafers Shrops....57 L9
Hopwas Staffs....59 J4
Hopwood Rochdl....89 P9
Hopwood Worcs....58 F9
Hopwood Park Services
  Worcs....58 F10
Horam E Susx....25 N7
Horbling Lincs....74 B3
Horbury Wakefd....90 H7
Horcott Gloucs....33 N4
Horden Dur....104 D2
Horderley Shrops....56 G7
Hordle Hants....13 N5
Hordley Shrops....69 L8
Horeb Carmth....28 E3
Horeb Cerdgn....42 G6
Horfield Bristl....31 Q9
Horham Suffk....65 J7
Horkesley Heath Essex....52 G6
Horkstow N Linc....92 G7
Horley Oxon....48 D6
Horley Surrey....24 G2
Hornblotton Green Somset....19 Q8
Hornby Lancs....95 M4
Hornby N York....97 K2
Hornby N York....104 C9
Horncastle Lincs....87 J7
Hornchurch Gt Lon....37 M3
Horncliffe Nthumb....129 N10
Horndean Border....129 N10
Horndean Hants....15 K4
Horndon Devon....8 D8
Horndon on the Hill Thurr....37 Q4
Horne Surrey....24 H2
Horner Somset....18 B5
Horne Row Essex....52 C11
Horners Green Suffk....52 G3
Horney Common E Susx....25 L5
Horn Hill Bucks....36 B2
Horning Norfk....77 L8
Horninghold Leics....73 L11
Horninglow Staffs....71 N9
Horningsea Cambs....62 G8
Horningsham Wilts....20 F6
Horningtoft Norfk....76 C7
Horningtops Cnwll....5 M9
Hornsbury Somset....10 G2
Hornsby Cumb....111 K10
Hornsbygate Cumb....111 K10
Horns Cross Devon....16 F7
Horns Cross E Susx....26 D7
Hornsea E R Yk....99 P11
Hornsey Gt Lon....36 H3
Horn's Green Gt Lon....37 L9
Horn Street Kent....27 L4
Hornton Oxon....48 C5
Horpit Swindn....33 P8
Horrabridge Devon....6 E5
Horringer Suffk....64 A9
Horringford IoW....14 F9
Horrocks Fold Bolton....89 L8
Horrocksford Lancs....89 M2
Horsacott Devon....17 J5
Horsebridge Devon....5 Q6
Horsebridge E Susx....25 N8
Horsebridge Hants....22 B8
Horsebridge Shrops....56 F3
Horsebridge Staffs....70 H4
Horsebrook Staffs....58 C2
Horsecastle N Som....31 M11
Horsedown Cnwll....2 G7
Horsehay Wrekin....57 M3
Horseheath Cambs....63 K11
Horsehouse N York....96 F4
Horsell Surrey....23 Q3
Horseman's Green Wrexhm....69 M6
Horsenden Bucks....35 L4
Horsey Norfk....77 P7
Horsey Somset....19 K7
Horsey Corner Norfk....77 P7
Horsford Norfk....76 H8
Horsforth Leeds....90 G3
Horsham W Susx....24 E4
Horsham Worcs....46 D3
Horsham St Faith Norfk....77 J8
Horsington Lincs....86 G7
Horsington Somset....20 D10
Horsley Derbys....72 B2

Horsley Gloucs....32 F5
Horsley Nthumb....112 G7
Horsley Nthumb....118 F11
Horsley Cross Essex....53 K6
Horsleycross Street Essex....53 K6
Horsley-Gate Derbys....84 D5
Horsleyhill Border....117 Q7
Horsley's Green Bucks....35 L6
Horsley Woodhouse Derbys....72 B2
Horsmonden Kent....26 B3
Horspath Oxon....34 G3
Horstead Norfk....77 K8
Horsted Keynes W Susx....25 J5
Horton Bucks....49 P11
Horton Dorset....12 H3
Horton Lancs....96 C6
Horton Nhants....49 M4
Horton S Glos....32 E8
Horton Shrops....69 N9
Horton Somset....10 G2
Horton Staffs....70 G3
Horton Surrey....36 E8
Horton Swans....28 E7
Horton W & M....36 B5
Horton Wilts....21 K2
Horton Wrekin....57 M2
Horton Cross Somset....19 K11
Horton-cum-Studley Oxon....34 G2
Horton Green Ches W....69 N5
Horton Heath Hants....22 E11
Horton-in-Ribblesdale
  N York....96 B6
Horton Kirby Kent....37 N7
Horwich Bolton....89 J8
Horwich End Derbys....83 M8
Horwood Devon....17 J6
Hoscar Lancs....88 F8
Hoscote Border....117 M8
Hose Leics....73 J5
Hosey Hill Kent....37 L10
Hosh P & K....133 P3
Hoswick Shet....169 r11
Hotham E R Yk....92 E4
Hothfield Kent....26 G3
Hoton Leics....72 F6
Hott Nthumb....111 Q3
Hough Ches E....70 C4
Hough Ches E....83 J9
Hougham Lincs....73 M2
Hough End Leeds....90 G4
Hough Green Halton....81 P7
Hough-on-the-Hill Lincs....86 B11
Houghton Cambs....62 C6
Houghton Cumb....110 H9
Houghton Hants....22 B8
Houghton Nthumb....112 H7
Houghton Pembks....41 J9
Houghton W Susx....24 B8
Houghton Conquest C Beds....50 B2
Houghton Gate Dur....113 M10
Houghton Green E Susx....26 F7
Houghton Green Warrtn....82 D6
Houghton le Side Darltn....103 P6
Houghton-le-Spring Sundld....113 M11
Houghton on the Hill Leics....72 H10
Houghton Regis C Beds....50 B6
Houghton St Giles Norfk....76 C4
Houlton Warwks....60 C6
Hound Green Hants....23 K3
Houndslow Border....128 G10
Houndsmoor Somset....18 F9
Houndwood Border....129 L7
Hounslow Gt Lon....36 D5
Househill Highld....156 F6
Houses Hill Kirk....90 F7
Housieside Abers....151 M2
Houston Rens....125 L4
Houstry Highld....167 L10
Houton Ork....169 c6
Hove Br & H....24 G10
Hove Edge Calder....90 E6
Hoveringham Notts....85 L11
Hoveton Norfk....77 L8
Hovingham N York....98 D5
Howbrook Barns....91 J11
How Caple Herefs....46 B8
Howden E R Yk....92 B5
Howden-le-Wear Dur....103 N4
Howe Highld....167 P4
Howe IoM....80 a8
Howe N York....97 M4
Howe Norfk....65 K2
Howe Bridge Wigan....82 E4
Howe Green Essex....52 B11
Howegreen Essex....52 D11
Howell Lincs....86 F11
How End C Beds....50 B2
Howe of Teuchar Abers....159 J8
Howes D & G....110 C7
Howe Street Essex....51 Q4
Howe Street Essex....51 L8
Howey Powys....44 F3
Howgate Cumb....100 C6
Howgate Mdloth....127 N6
Howgill Lancs....96 B11
Howick Nthumb....119 Q7
Howle Wrekin....70 B10
Howle Hill Herefs....46 B10
Howlett End Essex....51 N4
Howley Somset....10 F3
How Mill Cumb....111 K9
Howmore W Isls....168 c14
Hownam Border....118 E7
Howrigg Cumb....110 F11
Howsham N Linc....92 H10
Howsham N York....98 E8
Howtel Nthumb....118 G4
Howt Green Kent....38 E8
Howton Herefs....45 N9
Howtown Cumb....101 M7
How Wood Herts....50 D10
Howwood Rens....125 K5
Hoxa Ork....169 d7
Hoxne Suffk....64 H6
Hoy Ork....169 b7
Hoylake Wirral....81 J7
Hoyland Barns....91 K10
Hoyland Common Barns....91 K10
Hoylandswaine Barns....90 H10
Hoyle W Susx....23 P11
Hoyle Mill Barns....91 K9
Hubberholme N York....96 E5
Hubberston Pembks....40 G9
Hubbert's Bridge Lincs....74 E2
Huby N York....97 L11
Huby N York....98 B7

Huccaby Devon....6 H4
Hucclecote Gloucs....46 G11
Hucking Kent....38 D10
Hucknall Notts....84 H11
Huddersfield Kirk....90 E7
Huddington Worcs....46 H3
Hudnall Herts....50 B8
Hudswell N York....103 M10
Huggate E R Yk....98 H9
Hugglescote Leics....72 C8
Hughenden Valley Bucks....35 N5
Hughley Shrops....57 K5
Hugh Town IoS....2 c2
Huish Devon....17 J9
Huish Wilts....21 M2
Huish Champflower Somset....18 D5
Huish Episcopi Somset....19 M9
Hüisinis W Isls....168 e6
Huisinish W Isls....168 e6
Hulcote C Beds....49 P7
Hulcote Nhants....49 K5
Hulcott Bucks....49 N11
Hulham Devon....9 P8
Hulland Derbys....71 N5
Hulland Ward Derbys....71 P5
Hullavington Wilts....32 G8
Hull Bridge E R Yk....93 J2
Hullbridge Essex....38 D2
Hull, Kingston upon C KuH....93 J5
Hulme Manch....82 H5
Hulme Staffs....70 G5
Hulme Warrtn....82 D6
Hulme End Staffs....71 L3
Hulme Walfield Ches E....82 H11
Hulse Heath Ches E....82 F6
Hulton Lane Ends Bolton....89 K9
Hulverstone IoW....14 C10
Hulver Street Norfk....76 C9
Hulver Street Suffk....65 P4
Humber Devon....9 L2
Humber Herefs....45 Q3
Humber Bridge N Linc....92 H6
Humberside Airport N Linc....93 J8
Humberston NE Lin....93 P9
Humberstone C Leic....72 G9
Humberton N York....97 P7
Humbie E Loth....128 C7
Humbleton E R Yk....93 M4
Humbleton Nthumb....119 J5
Humby Lincs....73 Q4
Hume Border....118 D2
Humshaugh Nthumb....112 D6
Huna Highld....167 Q2
Huncoat Lancs....89 M4
Huncote Leics....72 E11
Hundalee Border....118 B7
Hundall Derbys....84 E5
Hunderthwaite Dur....103 J6
Hundleby Lincs....87 L7
Hundle Houses Lincs....86 H10
Hundleton Pembks....41 J10
Hundon Suffk....63 M11
Hundred End Lancs....88 E6
Hundred House Powys....44 G4
Hungarton Leics....72 H9
Hungerford Hants....13 L2
Hungerford Somset....18 D5
Hungerford W Berk....34 B11
Hungerford Newtown
  W Berk....34 C10
Hunger Hill Bolton....89 K9
Hunger Hill Lancs....88 G8
Hungerstone Herefs....45 N7
Hungerton Lincs....73 M5
Hungryhatton Shrops....70 B9
Hunmanby N York....99 M5
Hunningham Warwks....59 N11
Hunnington Worcs....58 E8
Hunsbury Hill Nhants....60 F9
Hunsdon Herts....51 K8
Hunsdonbury Herts....51 K8
Hunsingore N York....97 P10
Hunslet Leeds....91 J4
Hunsonby Cumb....101 Q3
Hunstanton Norfk....75 N2
Hunstanworth Dur....112 D11
Hunsterson Ches E....70 B5
Hunston Suffk....64 D8
Hunston W Susx....15 N6
Hunston Green Suffk....64 D8
Hunstrete BaNES....20 B2
Hunsworth Kirk....90 F5
Hunt End Worcs....47 K2
Hunter's Inn Devon....17 M2
Hunter's Quay Ag & B....124 F2
Huntham Somset....19 K9
Hunthill Lodge Angus....142 H3
Huntingdon Cambs....62 B6
Huntingfield Suffk....65 L7
Huntingford Dorset....20 F7
Huntington C York....98 C9
Huntington Ches W....69 M2
Huntington E Loth....128 D5
Huntington Herefs....45 K4
Huntington Herefs....45 P6
Huntington Staffs....58 E2
Huntingtowerfield P & K....134 D2
Huntley Gloucs....46 D11
Huntly Abers....158 D10
Hunton Hants....22 E6
Hunton Kent....26 B2
Hunton N York....97 J2
Hunton Bridge Herts....50 C10
Hunt's Corner Norfk....64 E4
Huntscott Somset....18 B6
Hunt's Cross Lpool....81 N7
Hunts Green Bucks....35 N4
Hunts Green Warwks....59 J3
Huntsham Devon....18 D10
Huntshaw Devon....17 J7
Huntshaw Cross Devon....17 J7
Huntspill Somset....19 K5
Huntstile Somset....19 J8
Huntworth Somset....19 K8
Hunwick Dur....103 N4
Hunworth Norfk....76 F4
Hurcott Somset....19 L11
Hurdcott Wilts....21 N8
Hurdsfield Ches E....83 K10
Hurley W & M....35 M8
Hurley Warwks....59 K5
Hurley Bottom W & M....35 M8
Hurley Common Warwks....59 K5
Hurlford E Ayrs....125 M10
Hurlston Green Lancs....88 D7
Hurn BCP....13 K5

Hurn's End Lincs....87 M11
Hursley Hants....22 D9
Hurst Dorset....12 C6
Hurst N York....103 K10
Hurst Somset....19 N11
Hurst Wokham....35 L10
Hurstbourne Priors Hants....22 D5
Hurstbourne Tarrant Hants....22 C4
Hurst Green E Susx....26 B6
Hurst Green Essex....53 J8
Hurst Green Lancs....89 K3
Hurst Green Surrey....37 K10
Hurst Hill Dudley....58 D6
Hurstley Herefs....45 M5
Hurstpierpoint W Susx....24 G7
Hurst Wickham W Susx....24 G7
Hurstwood Lancs....89 P4
Hurtiso Ork....169 e6
Hurtmore Surrey....23 P5
Hurworth Burn Dur....104 D4
Hurworth-on-Tees Darltn....104 B9
Hurworth Place Darltn....103 Q9
Hury Dur....103 J7
Husbands Bosworth Leics....60 D4
Husborne Crawley C Beds....49 Q7
Husthwaite N York....97 R6
Hutcherleigh Devon....7 K8
Hut Green N York....91 P6
Huthwaite Notts....84 G9
Huttoft Lincs....87 P5
Hutton Border....129 N9
Hutton Cumb....101 M5
Hutton E R Yk....99 L10
Hutton Essex....37 P2
Hutton Lancs....88 F5
Hutton N Som....19 L3
Hutton Bonville N York....104 B10
Hutton Buscel N York....99 K4
Hutton Conyers N York....97 M6
Hutton Cranswick E R Yk....99 L10
Hutton End Cumb....101 N3
Hutton Hang N York....97 J3
Hutton Henry Dur....104 D3
Hutton-le-Hole N York....98 E2
Hutton Lowcross R & Cl....104 G8
Hutton Magna Dur....103 M8
Hutton Mulgrave N York....105 M9
Hutton Roof Cumb....95 M5
Hutton Roof Cumb....101 L4
Hutton Rudby N York....104 E9
Hutton Sessay N York....97 Q5
Hutton Wandesley N York....97 R10
Huxham Devon....9 M5
Huxham Green Somset....19 Q7
Huxley Ches W....69 P2
Huyton Knows....81 N6
Hycemoor Cumb....94 B3
Hyde Gloucs....32 G4
Hyde Hants....13 L2
Hyde Tamesd....83 K6
Hyde Heath Bucks....35 P4
Hyde Lea Staffs....70 G11
Hydestile Surrey....23 Q6
Hykeham Moor Lincs....86 B7
Hylands House & Park
  Essex....51 Q10
Hyndford Bridge S Lans....116 C2
Hynish Ag & B....136 B8
Hyssington Powys....56 E6
Hystfield Gloucs....32 C5
Hythe Essex....52 H6
Hythe Hants....14 D5
Hythe Kent....27 L5
Hythe Somset....19 M4
Hythe End W & M....36 B6
Hyton Cumb....94 B3

I

Ibberton Dorset....12 C3
Ible Derbys....84 B9
Ibsley Hants....13 L3
Ibstock Leics....72 C9
Ibstone Bucks....35 L6
Ibthorpe Hants....22 C4
Iburndale N York....105 N9
Ibworth Hants....22 G4
Icelton N Som....31 L11
Ichrachan Ag & B....139 J4
Ickburgh Norfk....75 R11
Ickenham Gt Lon....36 C3
Ickford Bucks....34 H3
Ickham Kent....39 M10
Ickleford Herts....50 E4
Icklesham E Susx....26 E8
Ickleton Cambs....51 L2
Icklingham Suffk....63 N6
Ickornshaw N York....90 B2
Ickwell Green C Beds....61 Q11
Icomb Gloucs....47 P10
Idbury Oxon....47 P11
Iddesleigh Devon....17 K10
Ide Devon....9 L6
Ideford Devon....9 L9
Ide Hill Kent....37 L10
Iden E Susx....26 F7
Iden Green Kent....26 B4
Iden Green Kent....26 D5
Idle C Brad....90 F3
Idless Cnwll....3 L4
Idlicote Warwks....47 Q6
Idmiston Wilts....21 N7
Idole Carmth....42 H11
Idridgehay Derbys....71 P5
Idrigill Highld....152 F5
Idstone Oxon....33 Q8
Iffley Oxon....34 F4
Ifield W Susx....24 G3
Ifold W Susx....24 B4
Iford BCP....13 K6
Iford E Susx....25 K9
Ifton Mons....31 N7
Ifton Heath Shrops....69 K7
Ightfield Shrops....69 Q7
Ightham Kent....37 N9
Iken Suffk....65 N10
Ilam Staffs....71 L4
Ilchester Somset....19 P10
Ilderton Nthumb....119 K6
Ilford Gt Lon....37 K3
Ilford Somset....19 L11
Ilfracombe Devon....17 J2
Ilkeston Derbys....72 D2
Ilketshall St Andrew Suffk....65 M4

Ilketshall St John Suffk....65 M4
Ilketshall St Lawrence Suffk....65 M5
Ilketshall St Margaret Suffk....65 L4
Ilkley C Brad....96 H11
Illand Cnwll....5 M6
Illey Dudley....58 E8
Illidge Green Ches E....70 D2
Illingworth Calder....90 D5
Illogan Cnwll....2 H5
Illston on the Hill Leics....73 J11
Ilmer Bucks....35 L3
Ilmington Warwks....47 P6
Ilminster Somset....10 H2
Ilsington Devon....9 J9
Ilsington Dorset....12 C6
Ilston Swans....28 G6
Ilton N York....97 J5
Ilton Somset....19 L11
Imachar N Ayrs....120 G3
Immingham NE Lin....93 L8
Immingham Dock NE Lin....93 L7
Impington Cambs....62 F8
Ince Ches W....81 P9
Ince Blundell Sefton....81 L4
Ince-in-Makerfield Wigan....82 C4
Inchbae Lodge Hotel Highld....155 M4
Inchbare Angus....143 L4
Inchberry Moray....157 Q6
Incheril Highld....154 D5
Inchinnan Rens....125 M4
Inchlaggan Highld....146 F7
Inchmichael P & K....134 G2
Inchmore Highld....155 Q8
Inchnadamph Highld....161 M2
Inchture P & K....134 H2
Inchyra P & K....134 F3
Indian Queens Cnwll....4 E10
Ingatestone Essex....51 P11
Ingbirchworth Barns....90 G9
Ingerthorpe N York....97 L7
Ingestre Staffs....70 H10
Ingham Lincs....86 B4
Ingham Norfk....77 M6
Ingham Suffk....64 B7
Ingham Corner Norfk....77 M6
Ingleborough Norfk....75 J7
Ingleby Derbys....72 A5
Ingleby Arncliffe N York....104 D10
Ingleby Barwick S on T....104 D8
Ingleby Cross N York....104 E10
Ingleby Greenhow N York....104 G9
Ingleigh Green Devon....8 F3
Inglesbatch BaNES....20 D2
Inglesham Swindn....33 P5
Ingleton D & G....109 L7
Ingleton Dur....103 N6
Ingleton N York....95 N5
Inglewhite Lancs....88 G3
Ingmanthorpe N York....97 P10
Ingoe Nthumb....112 F6
Ingol Lancs....88 G4
Ingoldisthorpe Norfk....75 N4
Ingoldmells Lincs....87 Q7
Ingoldsby Lincs....73 Q5
Ingram Nthumb....119 K7
Ingrave Essex....37 P2
Ingrow C Brad....90 D3
Ings Cumb....101 M11
Ingst S Glos....31 Q7
Ingthorpe Rutlnd....73 P9
Ingworth Norfk....76 H6
Inkberrow Worcs....47 K3
Inkerman Dur....103 M3
Inkersall Green Derbys....84 F6
Inkhorn Abers....159 M10
Inkpen W Berk....22 C2
Inkstack Highld....167 N2
Inmarsh Wilts....20 H2
Innellan Ag & B....124 F3
Innerleithen Border....117 L3
Innerleven Fife....135 K7
Innermessan D & G....106 E5
Innerwick E Loth....129 J5
Innesmill Moray....157 P5
Innsworth Gloucs....46 G10
Insch Abers....150 G2
Insh Highld....148 E7
Inshes Highld....156 B9
Inskip Lancs....88 F3
Inskip Moss Side Lancs....88 F3
Instow Devon....16 H5
Insworke Cnwll....6 C8
Intake Sheff....84 E4
Inver Abers....149 N9
Inver Highld....163 K10
Inver P & K....141 P9
Inveralligin Highld....145 N11
Inverallochy Abers....159 P4
Inveran Highld....162 D7
Inveraray Ag & B....131 M6
Inverarish Highld....153 K10
Inverarity Angus....142 H9
Inverarnan Stirlg....132 C4
Inverasdale Highld....160 C10
Inverbeg Ag & B....132 C8
Inverbervie Abers....143 Q3
Inverboyndie Abers....158 G5
Invercreran Lodge Ag & B....139 J4
Inverdruie Highld....148 F5
Inveresk E Loth....127 Q3
Inveresragan Ag & B....138 H10
Inverey Abers....149 K10
Inverfarigaig Highld....147 N3
Inverfolla Ag & B....138 H9
Invergarry Highld....147 J7
Invergeldie P & K....133 L2
Invergloy Highld....146 G10
Invergordon Highld....156 C4
Invergowrie P & K....142 E11
Inverguseran Highld....145 M6
Inverhadden P & K....140 G6
Inverie Highld....145 N7
Inverinan Ag & B....131 K4
Inverinate Highld....145 R3
Inverkeilor Angus....143 M8
Inverkeithing Fife....134 E11
Inverkeithny Abers....158 F8
Inverkip Inver....124 G3
Inverkirkaig Highld....160 H3
Inverlael Highld....161 K9
Inverlair Highld....139 Q2
Inverliever Lodge Ag & B....130 H6
Inverlochy Ag & B....131 P2
Invermark Angus....150 C11
Invermoriston Highld....147 L4

Invernaver Highld 166 B4
Inverneill Ag & B 123 P3
Inverness Highld 156 B8
Inverness Airport Highld 156 D7
Invernettie Abers 159 R9
Invernoaden Ag & B 131 N8
Inveroran Hotel Ag & B 139 P9
Inverquharity Angus 142 G6
Inverquhomery Abers 159 P8
Inverroy Highld 146 H11
Inversanda Highld 138 G6
Invershiel Highld 146 A4
Invershin Highld 162 D7
Invershore Highld 167 M9
Inversnaid Hotel Stirlg 132 C6
Inveruglas Abers 159 Q8
Inveruglas Ag & B 132 C6
Inveruglass Highld 148 E7
Inverurie Abers 151 K3
Inwardleigh Devon 8 L5
Inworth Essex 52 E8
Iochdar W Isls 168 c13
Iona Ag & B 136 H10
Iping W Susx 23 N10
iPort Logistics Park Donc 91 Q11
Ipplepen Devon 7 L5
Ipsden Oxon 34 H7
Ipstones Staffs 71 J5
Ipswich Suffk 53 L3
Irby Wirral 81 K8
Irby in the Marsh Lincs 87 N8
Irby upon Humber NE Lin 93 L10
Irchester Nhants 61 K7
Ireby Cumb 100 H3
Ireby Lancs 95 P5
Ireland C Beds 50 D2
Ireleth Cumb 94 E5
Ireshopeburn Dur 102 G3
Ireton Wood Derbys 71 P5
Irlam Salfd 82 F6
Irnham Lincs 73 Q5
Iron Acton S Glos 32 C8
Iron Bridge Cambs 75 J11
Ironbridge Wrekin 57 M4
Ironbridge Gorge Wrekin 57 M4
Iron Cross Warwks 47 L4
Ironmacannie D & G 108 E5
Ironville Derbys 84 F10
Irstead Norfk 77 M7
Irthington Cumb 111 J8
Irthlingborough Nhants 61 K6
Irton N York 99 L4
Irvine N Ayrs 125 J10
Isauld Highld 166 G3
Isbister Shet 169 q4
Isbister Shet 169 s7
Isfield E Susx 25 K7
Isham Nhants 61 J6
Isington Hants 23 L6
Islandpool Worcs 58 C8
Islay Ag & B 122 E8
Islay Airport Ag & B 122 D9
Isle Abbotts Somset 19 L10
Isle Brewers Somset 19 L10
Isleham Cambs 63 K6
Isle of Dogs Gt Lon 37 J5
Isle of Grain Medway 38 E6
Isle of Lewis W Isls 168 i4
Isle of Man IoM 80 e4
Isle of Man Ronaldsway Airport IoM 80 c8
Isle of Mull Ag & B 137 Q8
Isle of Purbeck Dorset 12 H8
Isle of Sheppey Kent 38 G8
Isle of Skye Highld 152 L10
Isle of Thanet Kent 39 P8
Isle of Walney Cumb 94 D7
Isle of Whithorn D & G 107 N10
Isle of Wight IoW 14 F9
Isleornsay Highld 145 M5
Isles of Scilly IoS 2 c2
Isles of Scilly St Mary's Airport IoS 2 c2
Islesteps D & G 109 L6
Islet Village Guern 10 c1
Isleworth Gt Lon 36 E5
Isley Walton Leics 72 C6
Islibhig W Isls 168 f5
Islington Gt Lon 36 H4
Islip Nhants 61 L5
Islip Oxon 34 F2
Isliveig W Isls 168 f5
Isombridge Wrekin 57 L2
Istead Rise Kent 37 P6
Itchen Abbas Hants 22 F8
Itchen Stoke Hants 22 G8
Itchingfield W Susx 24 D5
Itchington S Glos 32 C7
Itteringham Norfk 76 G5
Itton Devon 8 G5
Itton Mons 31 N5
Itton Common Mons 31 N5
Ivegill Cumb 101 M2
Ivelet N York 102 H11
Iver Bucks 36 B4
Iver Heath Bucks 36 B4
Iveston Dur 112 H10
Ivinghoe Bucks 49 P11
Ivinghoe Aston Bucks 49 Q11
Ivington Herefs 45 P3
Ivington Green Herefs 45 P3
Ivybridge Devon 6 G7
Ivychurch Kent 26 H6
Ivy Cross Dorset 20 G10
Ivy Hatch Kent 37 N10
Ivy Todd Norfk 76 B10
Iwade Kent 38 F8
Iwerne Courtney Dorset 12 E2
Iwerne Minster Dorset 12 E2
Ixworth Suffk 64 C7
Ixworth Thorpe Suffk 64 C7

J

Jack Green Lancs 88 H5
Jack Hill N York 97 J10
Jack-in-the-Green Devon 9 P5
Jack's Bush Hants 21 Q7
Jacksdale Notts 84 F10
Jackson Bridge Kirk 90 F9
Jackton S Lans 125 P7
Jacobstow Cnwll 5 K2
Jacobstowe Devon 8 E4

Jacobs Well Surrey 23 Q4
Jameston Pembks 41 L11
Jamestown Highld 155 N6
Jamestown W Duns 132 D11
Janetstown Highld 167 L10
Janetstown Highld 167 Q6
Jardine Hall D & G 109 P3
Jarrow S Tyne 113 M8
Jarvis Brook E Susx 25 M5
Jasper's Green Essex 52 B6
Jawcraig Falk 126 E2
Jaywick Essex 53 L9
Jealott's Hill Br For 35 N10
Jeater Houses N York 97 P2
Jedburgh Border 118 B6
Jeffreyston Pembks 41 L9
Jemimaville Highld 156 C4
Jerbourg Guern 10 c2
Jersey Jersey 11 b1
Jersey Airport Jersey 11 a2
Jersey Marine Neath 29 K6
Jerusalem Lincs 86 B6
Jesmond N u Ty 113 L7
Jevington E Susx 25 N10
Jingle Street Mons 31 N2
Jockey End Herts 50 B8
Jodrell Bank Ches E 82 G10
Jodrell Bank Ches E 82 G10
Johnby Cumb 101 M4
John Lennon Airport Lpool 81 N8
John o' Groats Highld 167 Q2
Johns Cross E Susx 26 B7
Johnshaven Abers 143 P4
Johnson Street Norfk 77 M8
Johnston Pembks 40 H8
Johnstone D & G 117 J10
Johnstone Rens 125 L5
Johnstonebridge D & G 109 P2
Johnstown Carmth 42 G11
Johnstown Wrexhm 69 K5
Joppa C Edin 127 Q3
Joppa Cerdgn 54 D11
Joppa S Ayrs 114 H4
Jordans Bucks 35 Q6
Jordanston Pembks 40 H4
Jordanthorpe Sheff 84 E4
Joyden's Wood Kent 37 M6
Jubilee Corner Kent 26 D2
Jump Barns 91 K10
Jumper's Town E Susx 25 L4
Juniper Nthumb 112 D9
Juniper Green C Edin 127 M4
Jura Ag & B 122 H3
Jurassic Coast Devon 10 G7
Jurby IoM 80 e2
Jurston Devon 8 G8

K

Kaber Cumb 102 E8
Kaimend S Lans 126 H8
Kames Ag & B 124 B3
Kames E Ayrs 115 N2
Kea Cnwll 3 L5
Keadby N Linc 92 D8
Keal Cotes Lincs 87 L8
Kearby Town End N York 97 M11
Kearsley Bolton 82 G4
Kearsley Nthumb 112 F5
Kearsney Kent 27 N3
Kearstwick Cumb 95 N5
Kearton N York 103 J11
Keasden N York 95 Q7
Keaton Devon 6 G8
Keckwick Halton 82 C8
Keddington Lincs 87 K3
Keddington Corner Lincs 87 L3
Kedington Suffk 63 M11
Kedleston Derbys 71 Q6
Keelby Lincs 93 L8
Keele Staffs 70 E5
Keele Services Staffs 70 E6
Keele University Staffs 70 E5
Keeley Green Bed 61 M11
Keelham C Brad 90 D4
Keeres Green Essex 51 N8
Keeston Pembks 40 H7
Keevil Wilts 20 H3
Kegworth Leics 72 C5
Kehelland Cnwll 2 G5
Keig Abers 150 G4
Keighley C Brad 90 D2
Keilarsbrae Clacks 133 P9
Keillour P & K 134 B2
Keiloch Abers 149 M9
Keils Ag & B 122 H6
Keinton Mandeville Somset 19 P8
Keir Mill D & G 109 J2
Keirsleywell Row Nthumb 111 J10
Keisby Lincs 73 Q5
Keisley Cumb 102 D6
Keiss Highld 167 Q4
Keith Moray 158 B7
Keithick P & K 142 C10
Keithock Angus 143 L5
Keithtown Highld 155 P6
Kelbrook Lancs 89 Q2
Kelby Lincs 73 Q2
Keld Cumb 101 Q8
Keld N York 102 G11
Keld Head N York 98 F4
Keldholme N York 98 E3
Kelfield N Linc 92 D10
Kelfield N York 91 P3
Kelham Notts 85 N9
Kelhead D & G 109 P7
Kellacott Devon 5 P4
Kellamergh Lancs 88 E5
Kellas Angus 142 H10
Kellas Moray 157 M7
Kellaton Devon 7 L11
Kelleth Cumb 102 C9
Kelling Norfk 76 F3
Kellington N York 91 P6
Kelloe Dur 104 B3
Kelloholm D & G 115 P5
Kells Cumb 100 C7
Kelly Devon 5 P5
Kelly Bray Cnwll 5 P5
Kelmarsh Nhants 60 F5
Kelmscott Oxon 33 P5
Kelsale Suffk 65 M8
Kelsall Ches W 81 Q11
Kelshall Herts 50 H3

Kelsick Cumb 110 C10
Kelso Border 118 D4
Kelstedge Derbys 84 D8
Kelstern Lincs 86 H3
Kelsterton Flints 81 K10
Kelston BaNES 32 D11
Keltneyburn P & K 141 J8
Kelton D & G 109 L6
Kelty Fife 134 E9
Kelvedon Essex 52 E8
Kelvedon Hatch Essex 51 N11
Kelynack Cnwll 2 B8
Kemacott Devon 17 M2
Kemback Fife 135 L5
Kemberton Shrops 57 N4
Kemble Gloucs 33 J5
Kemble Wick Gloucs 33 J5
Kemerton Worcs 47 J7
Kemeys Commander Mons 31 K4
Kemnay Abers 151 J4
Kempe's Corner Kent 26 H2
Kempley Gloucs 46 C9
Kempley Green Gloucs 46 C9
Kempsey Worcs 46 F5
Kempsford Gloucs 33 N5
Kemps Green Warwks 58 H10
Kempshott Hants 22 H4
Kempston Bed 61 M11
Kempston Hardwick Bed 50 B2
Kempton Shrops 56 F8
Kemp Town Br & H 24 H10
Kemsing Kent 37 N9
Kemsley Kent 38 F8
Kemsley Street Kent 38 D9
Kenardington Kent 26 G5
Kenchester Herefs 45 N6
Kencot Oxon 33 Q4
Kendal Cumb 95 L2
Kenderchurch Herefs 45 N9
Kendleshire S Glos 32 C9
Kenfig Brdgnd 29 M8
Kenfig Hill Brdgnd 29 M8
Kenilworth Warwks 59 L10
Kenley Gt Lon 36 H8
Kenley Shrops 57 K4
Kenmore Highld 153 P6
Kenmore P & K 141 J8
Kenn Devon 9 M7
Kenn N Som 31 M11
Kennacraig Ag & B 123 P7
Kennall Vale Cnwll 3 J6
Kennards House Cnwll 5 M5
Kenneggy Cnwll 2 F8
Kennerleigh Devon 9 K3
Kennet Clacks 133 Q9
Kennethmont Abers 150 E2
Kennett Cambs 63 L8
Kennford Devon 9 M7
Kenninghall Norfk 64 E4
Kennington Kent 26 H2
Kennington Oxon 34 F4
Kennoway Fife 135 K7
Kenny Somset 19 K11
Kenny Hill Suffk 63 L5
Kennythorpe N York 98 F7
Kenovay Ag & B 136 B6
Kensaleyre Highld 152 G7
Kensington Gt Lon 36 G5
Kensington Palace Gt Lon 36 G4
Kensworth Common C Beds 50 B7
Kentallen Highld 139 J6
Kentchurch Herefs 45 N9
Kentford Suffk 63 M7
Kent Green Ches E 70 E3
Kentisbeare Devon 9 Q3
Kentisbury Devon 17 L3
Kentisbury Ford Devon 17 L3
Kentish Town Gt Lon 36 G4
Kentmere Cumb 101 N10
Kenton Devon 9 N8
Kenton Gt Lon 36 E3
Kenton N u Ty 113 K7
Kenton Suffk 64 H8
Kenton Bankfoot N u Ty 113 K7
Kentra Highld 138 B4
Kents Bank Cumb 94 H5
Kentsboro Hants 22 B7
Kent's Green Gloucs 46 D10
Kent's Oak Hants 22 B10
Kent Street E Susx 26 C8
Kent Street Kent 37 Q10
Kenwick Shrops 69 M8
Kenwyn Cnwll 3 L4
Kenyon Warrtn 82 D5
Keoldale Highld 165 J3
Keppoch Highld 145 Q3
Kepwick N York 97 Q2
Keresley Covtry 59 M8
Kermincham Ches E 82 H11
Kernborough Devon 7 K10
Kerne Bridge Herefs 46 A11
Kerridge Ches E 83 K9
Kerridge-end Ches E 83 K9
Kerris Cnwll 2 C8
Kerry Powys 55 Q6
Kerrycroy Ag & B 124 E5
Kersall Notts 85 M8
Kersbrook Devon 9 Q8
Kerscott Devon 17 L6
Kersey Suffk 52 H3
Kersey Tye Suffk 52 G3
Kersey Upland Suffk 52 G3
Kershader W Isls 168 i6
Kershopefoot Cumb 111 J4
Kersoe Worcs 47 J6
Kerswell Devon 10 B3
Kerswell Green Worcs 46 G5
Kerthen Wood Cnwll 2 F7
Kesgrave Suffk 53 M2
Kessingland Suffk 65 Q4
Kessingland Beach Suffk 65 Q4
Kestle Cnwll 3 P4
Kestle Mill Cnwll 4 C10
Keston Gt Lon 37 K8
Keswick Cumb 101 J6
Keswick Norfk 77 J11
Ketsby Lincs 87 L5
Kettering Nhants 61 J5
Ketteringham Norfk 76 H11
Kettins P & K 142 C10
Kettlebaston Suffk 64 D11
Kettlebridge Fife 135 J6
Kettlebrook Staffs 59 K4
Kettleburgh Suffk 65 K9
Kettle Green Herts 51 K7

Kettleholm D & G 109 P5
Kettleness N York 105 M7
Kettleshulme Ches E 83 L9
Kettlesing N York 97 K9
Kettlesing Bottom N York 97 K9
Kettlestone Norfk 76 D5
Kettlethorpe Lincs 85 P5
Kettletoft Ork 169 f3
Kettlewell N York 96 E6
Ketton Rutlnd 73 P10
Kew Gt Lon 36 E5
Kew Royal Botanic Gardens Gt Lon 36 E5
Kewstoke N Som 19 K2
Kexbrough Barns 91 J9
Kexby C York 98 E10
Kexby Lincs 85 Q3
Key Green Ches E 70 F2
Key Green N York 105 M10
Keyham Leics 72 H9
Keyhaven Hants 13 P6
Keyingham E R Yk 93 M5
Keymer W Susx 24 H7
Keynsham BaNES 32 C11
Keysoe Bed 61 N8
Keysoe Row Bed 61 N8
Keyston Cambs 61 M5
Key Street Kent 38 E9
Keyworth Notts 72 G4
Kibbear Somset 18 H10
Kibblesworth Gatesd 113 K9
Kibworth Beauchamp Leics 60 E2
Kibworth Harcourt Leics 60 E2
Kidbrooke Gt Lon 37 K5
Kidburngill Cumb 100 E6
Kiddemore Green Staffs 58 C3
Kidderminster Worcs 58 B9
Kiddington Oxon 48 D10
Kidd's Moor Norfk 76 G11
Kidlington Oxon 34 E2
Kidmore End Oxon 35 J9
Kidsdale D & G 107 M10
Kidsgrove Staffs 70 E4
Kidstones N York 96 E4
Kidwelly Carmth 28 D3
Kiel Crofts Ag & B 138 G10
Kielder Nthumb 111 M2
Kielder Forest 111 M3
Kiells Ag & B 122 F6
Kilbagie Fife 133 Q9
Kilberry Ag & B 123 M7
Kilbirnie N Ayrs 125 J7
Kilbride Ag & B 123 M4
Kilbride Ag & B 124 C4
Kilbuiack Moray 157 K5
Kilburn Derbys 84 E11
Kilburn Gt Lon 36 F4
Kilburn N York 97 R5
Kilby Leics 72 G11
Kilchamaig Ag & B 123 P7
Kilchattan Ag & B 124 E7
Kilchattan Ag & B 136 b2
Kilcheran Ag & B 138 E10
Kilchoan Highld 137 M3
Kilchoman Ag & B 122 B7
Kilchrenan Ag & B 131 L3
Kilconquhar Fife 135 M7
Kilcot Gloucs 46 C9
Kilcoy Highld 155 Q7
Kilcreggan Ag & B 131 Q11
Kildale N York 104 H9
Kildalloig Ag & B 120 E8
Kildary Highld 156 D3
Kildavaig Ag & B 124 B4
Kildavanan Ag & B 124 C4
Kildonan Highld 163 L2
Kildonan N Ayrs 121 K7
Kildonan Lodge Highld 163 L2
Kildonnan Highld 144 G10
Kildrochet House D & G 106 E6
Kildrummy Abers 150 D4
Kildwick N York 96 F11
Kilfinan Ag & B 124 A2
Kilfinnan Highld 146 H8
Kilford Denbgs 80 F11
Kilgetty Pembks 41 M9
Kilgrammie S Ayrs 114 E7
Kilgwrrwg Common Mons 31 N5
Kilham E R Yk 99 M8
Kilham Nthumb 118 G4
Kilkenneth Ag & B 136 A7
Kilkenzie Ag & B 120 C7
Kilkerran Ag & B 120 D8
Kilkhampton Cnwll 16 D9
Killamarsh Derbys 84 G4
Killay Swans 28 H6
Killean Stirlg 132 G10
Killen Highld 156 B6
Killerby Darltn 103 N7
Killerton Devon 9 N4
Killichonan P & K 140 D6
Killiechonate Highld 146 G11
Killiechronan Highld 137 N7
Killiecrankie P & K 141 M5
Killilan Highld 154 B11
Killimster Highld 167 P5
Killin Stirlg 140 E11
Killinghall N York 97 L9
Killington Cumb 95 N3
Killington Devon 17 M2
Killingworth N Tyne 113 L6
Killiow Cnwll 3 L5
Killochyett Border 128 D10
Kilmacolm Inver 125 K3
Kilmahog Stirlg 133 J6
Kilmahumaig Ag & B 130 F9
Kilmaluag Highld 152 G3
Kilmany Fife 135 K3
Kilmarnock E Ayrs 125 L10
Kilmaurs E Ayrs 125 L9
Kilmelford Ag & B 130 H5
Kilmersdon Somset 20 C4
Kilmeston Hants 22 G9
Kilmichael Ag & B 120 C7
Kilmichael Glassary Ag & B 130 H9
Kilmichael of Inverlussa Ag & B 130 F10
Kilmington Devon 10 F5
Kilmington Wilts 20 E7
Kilmington Common Wilts 20 E7
Kilmington Street Wilts 20 E7
Kilmorack Highld 155 N9

Kilmore Ag & B 130 H2
Kilmore Highld 145 L6
Kilmory Ag & B 123 M5
Kilmory Highld 137 N2
Kilmory N Ayrs 121 J7
Kilmuir Highld 152 D8
Kilmuir Highld 152 F3
Kilmuir Highld 156 B8
Kilmuir Highld 156 D3
Kilmun Ag & B 131 P11
Kilnave Ag & B 122 C5
Kilncadzow S Lans 126 F8
Kilndown Kent 26 B4
Kiln Green Wokham 35 M9
Kilnhill Cumb 100 H4
Kilnhurst Rothm 91 M11
Kilninver Ag & B 130 G3
Kiln Pit Hill Nthumb 112 F9
Kilnsea E R Yk 93 R7
Kilnsey N York 96 E7
Kilnwick E R Yk 99 K11
Kilnwick Percy E R Yk 98 G11
Kilnwood Vale W Susx 24 F4
Kiloran Ag & B 136 b2
Kilpatrick N Ayrs 120 H6
Kilpeck Herefs 45 N8
Kilpin E R Yk 92 C5
Kilpin Pike E R Yk 92 C5
Kilrenny Fife 135 P7
Kilsby Nhants 60 C6
Kilspindie P & K 134 G2
Kilstay D & G 106 F10
Kilsyth N Lans 126 C2
Kiltarlity Highld 155 P9
Kilton R & Cl 105 K7
Kilton Somset 18 G6
Kilton Thorpe R & Cl 105 J7
Kilvaxter Highld 152 F4
Kilve Somset 18 F6
Kilvington Notts 73 L2
Kilwinning N Ayrs 125 J9
Kimberley Norfk 76 F11
Kimberley Notts 72 D2
Kimberworth Rothm 84 F2
Kimblesworth Dur 113 L11
Kimble Wick Bucks 35 M3
Kimbolton Cambs 61 P7
Kimbolton Herefs 45 Q2
Kimcote Leics 60 C3
Kimmeridge Dorset 12 F9
Kimmerston Nthumb 119 J3
Kimpton Hants 21 Q5
Kimpton Herts 50 E7
Kimworthy Devon 16 E9
Kinbrace Highld 166 E10
Kinbuck Stirlg 133 M6
Kincaple Fife 135 M4
Kincardine Fife 133 Q10
Kincardine Highld 162 E9
Kincardine Bridge Fife 133 Q10
Kincardine O'Neil Abers 150 F8
Kinclaven P & K 142 B10
Kincorth C Aber 151 N7
Kincorth House Moray 157 J5
Kincraig Highld 148 E6
Kincraigie P & K 141 N8
Kindallachan P & K 141 N8
Kinerarach Ag & B 123 L9
Kineton Gloucs 47 L9
Kineton Warwks 48 B4
Kinfauns P & K 134 F3
Kingarth Ag & B 124 D6
Kingcausie Abers 151 M8
Kingcoed Mons 31 M3
Kingerby Lincs 86 E2
Kingford Devon 16 D10
Kingham Oxon 47 Q10
Kingholm Quay D & G 109 L6
Kinghorn Fife 134 H10
Kinglassie Fife 134 G8
Kingoodie P & K 135 J2
King's Acre Herefs 45 P6
Kingsand Cnwll 6 C8
Kingsash Bucks 35 N3
Kingsbarns Fife 135 P5
Kingsborough Kent 38 G7
Kingsbridge Devon 7 J10
Kingsbridge Somset 18 C7
Kings Bridge Swans 28 G5
King's Bromley Staffs 71 L11
Kingsbrook Bucks 35 M2
Kingsburgh Highld 152 F6
Kingsbury Gt Lon 36 E3
Kingsbury Warwks 59 K5
Kingsbury Episcopi Somset 19 M10
King's Caple Herefs 45 R9
Kingsclere Hants 22 F3
King's Cliffe Nhants 73 Q11
Kings Clipstone Notts 85 K8
Kingscote Gloucs 32 F5
Kingscott Devon 17 J8
King's Coughton Warwks 47 L3
Kingscross N Ayrs 121 K6
Kingsdon Somset 19 P9
Kingsdown Kent 27 Q2
Kingsdown Swindn 33 N7
Kingsdown Wilts 32 F11
Kingseat Abers 151 N4
Kingseat Fife 134 E9
Kingsey Bucks 35 K3
Kingsfold W Susx 24 E3
Kingsford C Aber 151 M6
Kingsford E Ayrs 125 L8
Kingsford Worcs 57 Q8
Kingsgate Kent 39 Q7
Kings Green Gloucs 46 E8
Kingshall Street Suffk 64 C9
Kingsheanton Devon 17 K4
King's Heath Birm 58 G8
Kings Hill Kent 37 Q9
King's Hill Wsall 58 E5
Kings House Hotel Highld 139 N7
Kingshurst Solhll 59 J7
Kingside Hill Cumb 110 C10
Kingskerswell Devon 7 M5
Kingskettle Fife 135 J6
Kingsland Dorset 11 K5
Kingsland Herefs 45 N2
Kingsland IoA 78 D8
Kings Langley Herts 50 C10
Kingsley Ches W 82 C10
Kingsley Hants 23 L7
Kingsley Staffs 71 J5
Kingsley Green W Susx 23 N8
Kingsley Holt Staffs 71 J5
Kingsley Park Nhants 60 G8

Kingslow Shrops 57 P5
King's Lynn Norfk 75 M6
Kings Meaburn Cumb 102 B6
Kingsmead Hants 14 G4
King's Mills Guern 10 b2
King's Moss St Hel 81 Q4
Kingsmuir Angus 142 H8
Kings Muir Border 117 K3
Kingsmuir Fife 135 N6
Kings Newnham Warwks 59 Q9
King's Newton Derbys 72 B5
King's Norton Birm 58 G9
King's Norton Leics 72 H10
Kings Nympton Devon 17 M8
King's Pyon Herefs 45 N4
Kings Ripton Cambs 62 C5
King's Somborne Hants 22 C8
King's Stag Dorset 11 Q2
King's Stanley Gloucs 32 F4
King's Sutton Nhants 48 E7
Kingstanding Birm 58 G6
Kingsteignton Devon 7 M4
Kingsteps Highld 156 G6
King Sterndale Derbys 83 N10
Kingsthorne Herefs 45 P8
Kingsthorpe Nhants 60 G8
Kingston Cambs 62 D9
Kingston Cnwll 5 P6
Kingston Devon 6 G9
Kingston Devon 9 Q7
Kingston Dorset 12 C3
Kingston Dorset 12 G9
Kingston E Loth 128 E3
Kingston Hants 13 K4
Kingston IoW 14 E10
Kingston Kent 39 L11
Kingston W Susx 24 C10
Kingston Bagpuize Oxon 34 D5
Kingston Blount Oxon 35 K5
Kingston by Sea W Susx 24 F9
Kingston Deverill Wilts 20 F7
Kingstone Herefs 45 N7
Kingstone Somset 10 H2
Kingstone Staffs 71 K9
Kingstone Winslow Oxon 33 Q7
Kingston Lacy House &
   Gardens Dorset 12 G4
Kingston Lisle Oxon 34 B7
Kingston near Lewes E Susx 25 J9
Kingston on Soar Notts 72 E5
Kingston on Spey Moray 157 Q4
Kingston Russell Dorset 11 M6
Kingston St Mary Somset 18 H9
Kingston Seymour N Som 31 M11
Kingston Stert Oxon 35 K4
Kingston upon Hull C KuH 93 J5
Kingston upon Thames
   Gt Lon 36 E7
Kingstown Cumb 110 G9
King's Walden Herts 50 E6
Kingswear Devon 7 M8
Kingswells C Aber 151 M6
Kings Weston Bristl 31 P9
Kingswinford Dudley 58 C7
Kingswood Bucks 49 J11
Kingswood Gloucs 32 D6
Kingswood Kent 38 D11
Kingswood Powys 56 C4
Kingswood S Glos 32 B10
Kingswood Somset 18 F7
Kingswood Surrey 36 F9
Kingswood Warwks 59 J10
Kingswood Brook Warwks 59 J10
Kingswood Common Herefs 45 K4
Kingswood Common Staffs 58 B4
Kings Worthy Hants 22 E8
Kingthorpe Lincs 86 F5
Kington Herefs 45 K3
Kington S Glos 32 B6
Kington Worcs 47 J3
Kington Langley Wilts 32 H9
Kington Magna Dorset 20 E10
Kington St Michael Wilts 32 H9
Kingussie Highld 148 D7
Kingweston Somset 19 P8
Kinharrachie Abers 159 M11
Kinharvie D & G 109 K7
Kinkell Bridge P & K 133 Q4
Kinknockie Abers 159 P9
Kinleith C Edin 127 M4
Kinlet Shrops 57 N8
Kinloch Highld 144 F8
Kinloch Highld 164 H10
Kinloch Highld 165 N6
Kinloch P & K 142 A9
Kinlochard Stirlg 132 F7
Kinlochbervie Highld 164 F5
Kinlocheil Highld 138 H2
Kinlochewe Highld 154 D5
Kinloch Hourn Highld 146 B6
Kinlochlaggan Highld 147 N10
Kinlochleven Highld 139 M5
Kinlochmoidart Highld 138 C3
Kinlochnanuagh Highld 145 M11
Kinloch Rannoch P & K 140 G6
Kinloss Moray 157 K5
Kinmel Bay Conwy 80 D8
Kinmuck Abers 151 L4
Kinmundy Abers 151 M4
Kinnabus Ag & B 122 C11
Kinnadie Abers 159 N9
Kinnaird P & K 141 N6
Kinneff Abers 143 Q2
Kinnelhead D & G 116 E10
Kinnell Angus 143 L7
Kinnerley Shrops 69 K10
Kinnersley Herefs 45 L5
Kinnersley Worcs 46 G6
Kinnerton Powys 45 J2
Kinnerton Shrops 56 F5
Kinnerton Green Flints 69 K2
Kinnesswood P & K 134 F7
Kinninvie Dur 103 L6
Kinnordy Angus 142 F6
Kinoulton Notts 72 H4
Kinross P & K 134 E7
Kinrossie P & K 142 B11
Kinross Services P & K 134 E7
Kinsbourne Green Herts 50 D7
Kinsey Heath Ches E 70 B6
Kinsham Herefs 56 F11
Kinsham Worcs 46 H7
Kinsley Wakefd 91 L8
Kinson BCP 13 J5
Kintail Highld 146 B4

Kintbury W Berk 34 C11
Kintessack Moray 157 J5
Kintillo P & K 134 E4
Kinton Herefs 56 G10
Kinton Shrops 69 L11
Kintore Abers 151 K4
Kintour Ag & B 122 G9
Kintra Ag & B 122 D10
Kintra Ag & B 137 J10
Kintraw Ag & B 130 G7
Kintyre Ag & B 120 D4
Kinveachy Highld 148 G4
Kinver Staffs 58 B8
Kiplin N York 103 Q11
Kippax Leeds 91 L4
Kippen Stirlg 133 J9
Kippford D & G 108 H10
Kipping's Cross Kent 25 Q7
Kirbister Ork 169 c6
Kirby Bedon Norfk 77 K10
Kirby Bellars Leics 73 J7
Kirby Cane Norfk 65 M3
Kirby Corner Covtry 59 L9
Kirby Cross Essex 53 M7
Kirby Fields Leics 72 E10
Kirby Green Norfk 65 M3
Kirby Grindalythe N York 99 J7
Kirby Hill N York 97 N7
Kirby Hill N York 103 M9
Kirby Knowle N York 97 Q3
Kirby-le-Soken Essex 53 M7
Kirby Misperton N York 98 F5
Kirby Muxloe Leics 72 E10
Kirby Sigston N York 97 P2
Kirby Underdale E R Yk 98 G9
Kirby Wiske N York 97 N4
Kirdford W Susx 24 B5
Kirk Highld 167 N5
Kirkabister Shet 169 r10
Kirkandrews D & G 108 D11
Kirkandrews upon Eden
   Cumb 110 G9
Kirkbampton Cumb 110 F9
Kirkbean D & G 109 L9
Kirk Bramwith Donc 91 Q8
Kirkbride Cumb 110 D9
Kirkbridge N York 97 L2
Kirkbuddo Angus 143 J9
Kirkburn Border 117 K3
Kirkburn E R Yk 99 K9
Kirkburton Kirk 90 F8
Kirkby Knows 81 N5
Kirkby Lincs 86 F2
Kirkby N York 104 F9
Kirkby Fleetham N York 97 L2
Kirkby Green Lincs 86 E9
Kirkby-in-Ashfield Notts 84 H9
Kirkby-in-Furness Cumb 94 E4
Kirkby la Thorpe Lincs 86 E11
Kirkby Lonsdale Cumb 95 N5
Kirkby Malham N York 96 C8
Kirkby Mallory Leics 72 D10
Kirkby Malzeard N York 97 K6
Kirkby Mills N York 98 E3
Kirkbymoorside N York 98 D3
Kirkby on Bain Lincs 86 H8
Kirkby Overblow N York 97 M11
Kirkby Stephen Cumb 102 E9
Kirkby Thore Cumb 102 B5
Kirkby Underwood Lincs 73 R5
Kirkby Wharf N York 91 N2
Kirkby Woodhouse Notts 84 G10
Kirkcaldy Fife 134 H9
Kirkcambeck Cumb 111 L7
Kirkchrist D & G 108 E10
Kirkcolm D & G 106 D4
Kirkconnel D & G 115 P5
Kirkconnell D & G 109 L7
Kirkcowan D & G 107 K5
Kirkcudbright D & G 108 E10
Kirkdale Lpool 81 L6
Kirk Deighton N York 97 N10
Kirk Ella E R Yk 92 H5
Kirkfieldbank S Lans 116 B2
Kirkgunzeon D & G 109 J7
Kirk Hallam Derbys 72 D2
Kirkham Lancs 88 E4
Kirkham N York 98 E7
Kirkhamgate Wakefd 90 H6
Kirk Hammerton N York 97 Q9
Kirkharle Nthumb 112 F4
Kirkhaugh Nthumb 111 N11
Kirkheaton Kirk 90 F7
Kirkheaton Nthumb 112 F5
Kirkhill Highld 155 Q8
Kirkhope S Lans 116 D9
Kirkhouse Cumb 111 L9
Kirkhouse Green Donc 91 Q8
Kirkibost Highld 145 J4
Kirkinch P & K 142 E9
Kirkinner D & G 107 M7
Kirkintilloch E Duns 126 B3
Kirk Ireton Derbys 71 P4
Kirkland Cumb 100 E7
Kirkland Cumb 102 B4
Kirkland D & G 109 M3
Kirkland D & G 115 P5
Kirkland D & G 115 R9
Kirkland Guards Cumb 100 G2
Kirk Langley Derbys 71 P7
Kirkleatham R & Cl 104 G6
Kirklevington S on T 104 D9
Kirkley Suffk 65 Q3
Kirklington N York 97 M4
Kirklington Notts 85 L9
Kirklinton Cumb 110 H7
Kirkliston C Edin 127 L3
Kirkmabreck D & G 107 N6
Kirkmaiden D & G 106 F10
Kirk Merrington Dur 103 Q4
Kirk Michael IoM 80 d3
Kirkmichael P & K 141 Q6
Kirkmichael S Ayrs 114 F6
Kirkmuirhill S Lans 126 D9
Kirknewton Nthumb 118 H4
Kirknewton W Loth 127 L4
Kirkney Abers 158 D11
Kirk of Shotts N Lans 126 E5
Kirkoswald Cumb 101 Q2
Kirkoswald S Ayrs 114 E4
Kirkpatrick Durham D & G 108 G6
Kirkpatrick-Fleming D & G 110 E6
Kirk Sandall Donc 91 Q9
Kirksanton Cumb 94 C4
Kirk Smeaton N York 91 N7

Kirkstall Leeds 90 H3
Kirkstead Lincs 86 G8
Kirkstile Abers 158 D10
Kirkstile D & G 110 G2
Kirkstone Pass Inn Cumb 101 M9
Kirkstyle Highld 167 P2
Kirkthorpe Wakefd 91 K6
Kirkton Abers 150 G2
Kirkton D & G 109 L4
Kirkton Fife 135 K2
Kirkton Highld 145 P2
Kirkton Highld 154 B9
Kirkton P & K 134 B4
Kirkton Manor Border 117 J3
Kirkton of Airlie Angus 142 E7
Kirkton of Auchterhouse
   Angus 142 E10
Kirkton of Barevan Highld 156 E8
Kirkton of Collace P & K 142 B11
Kirkton of Durris Abers 151 K8
Kirkton of Glenbuchat
   Abers 150 B4
Kirkton of Glenisla Angus 142 C5
Kirkton of Kingoldrum
   Angus 142 E6
Kirkton of Lethendy P & K 142 A9
Kirkton of Logie Buchan
   Abers 151 P2
Kirkton of Maryculter
   Abers 151 M8
Kirkton of Menmuir Angus 143 J5
Kirkton of Monikie Angus 143 J10
Kirkton of Rayne Abers 158 G11
Kirkton of Skene Abers 151 L6
Kirkton of Tealing Angus 142 G10
Kirkton of Tough Abers 150 G5
Kirktown Abers 159 N4
Kirktown Abers 159 Q7
Kirktown of Alvah Abers 158 G5
Kirktown of Bourtie Abers 151 L2
Kirktown of Deskford Moray 158 D5
Kirktown of Fetteresso
   Abers 151 M10
Kirktown of Mortlach Moray 157 Q10
Kirktown of Slains Abers 151 Q2
Kirkurd Border 116 G2
Kirkwall Ork 169 d5
Kirkwall Airport Ork 169 d6
Kirkwhelpington Nthumb 112 E4
Kirk Yetholm Border 118 F5
Kirmington N Linc 93 K8
Kirmond le Mire Lincs 86 G2
Kirn Ag & B 124 F2
Kirriemuir Angus 142 F7
Kirstead Green Norfk 65 K2
Kirtlebridge D & G 110 D6
Kirtling Cambs 63 L9
Kirtling Green Cambs 63 L9
Kirtlington Oxon 48 E11
Kirtomy Highld 166 B4
Kirton Lincs 74 F3
Kirton Notts 85 L7
Kirton Suffk 53 N3
Kirton End Lincs 74 E2
Kirtonhill W Duns 125 K2
Kirton Holme Lincs 74 E2
Kirton in Lindsey N Linc 92 F11
Kirwaugh D & G 107 M7
Kishorn Highld 153 Q10
Kislingbury Nhants 60 E9
Kitebrook Warwks 47 P8
Kite Green Warwks 59 J11
Kites Hardwick Warwks 59 Q11
Kitleigh Cnwll 5 L2
Kitt Green Wigan 88 G9
Kittisford Somset 18 E10
Kittle Swans 28 G7
Kitt's Green Birm 59 J7
Kittybrewster C Aber 151 N6
Kitwood Hants 23 J8
Kivernoll Herefs 45 P8
Kiveton Park Rothm 84 G4
Knaith Lincs 85 P4
Knaith Park Lincs 85 P3
Knap Corner Dorset 20 F10
Knaphill Surrey 23 Q3
Knapp Somset 19 K11
Knapp Hill Hants 22 D10
Knapthorpe Notts 85 M9
Knapton C York 98 B10
Knapton N York 98 H5
Knapton Norfk 77 L5
Knapton Green Herefs 45 N4
Knapwell Cambs 62 D8
Knaresborough N York 97 N9
Knarsdale Nthumb 111 N10
Knaven Abers 159 L9
Knayton N York 97 P3
Knebworth Herts 50 G6
Knedlington E R Yk 92 B5
Kneesall Notts 85 M8
Kneeton Notts 85 M11
Knelston Swans 28 E7
Knenhall Staffs 70 G7
Knettishall Suffk 64 D5
Knightacott Devon 17 M4
Knightcote Warwks 48 D4
Knightley Staffs 70 E10
Knightley Dale Staffs 70 E10
Knighton BCP 13 J5
Knighton C Leic 72 G10
Knighton Devon 6 E9
Knighton Dorset 11 N2
Knighton Powys 56 D10
Knighton Somset 18 G6
Knighton Staffs 70 C6
Knighton Staffs 70 D9
Knighton Wilts 33 Q10
Knighton on Teme Worcs 57 L11
Knightsbridge Gloucs 46 G9
Knightsmill Cnwll 4 H5
Knightwick Worcs 46 D3
Knill Herefs 45 K2
Knipoch Ag & B 130 G3
Knipton Leics 73 L4
Kniveton Derbys 71 N4
Knock Cumb 102 C5
Knock Highld 145 L6
Knock Moray 158 D7
Knock W Isls 168 j4
Knockally Highld 167 K11
Knockan Highld 161 L4
Knockando Moray 157 M9
Knockbain Highld 155 Q9
Knockbain Highld 156 A6

Knock Castle N Ayrs 124 F5
Knockdee Highld 167 L4
Knockdow Ag & B 124 E3
Knockdown Wilts 32 F7
Knockeen S Ayrs 114 F8
Knockenkelly N Ayrs 121 K6
Knockentiber E Ayrs 125 L10
Knockhall Kent 37 N6
Knockholt Kent 37 L9
Knockholt Pound Kent 37 L9
Knockin Shrops 69 K10
Knockinlaw E Ayrs 125 L10
Knockmill Kent 37 N8
Knocknain D & G 106 C5
Knockrome Ag & B 123 J5
Knocksharry IoM 80 c4
Knocksheen D & G 108 C4
Knockvennie Smithy D & G 108 G6
Knodishall Suffk 65 N9
Knodishall Common Suffk 65 N9
Knole Somset 19 N9
Knole Park S Glos 31 Q8
Knolls Green Ches E 82 H9
Knolton Wrexhm 69 L7
Knook Wilts 20 H6
Knossington Leics 73 L9
Knott End-on-Sea Lancs 94 H11
Knotting Bed 61 M8
Knotting Green Bed 61 M8
Knottingley Wakefd 91 N6
Knotty Ash Lpool 81 N6
Knotty Green Bucks 35 P6
Knowbury Shrops 57 K9
Knowe D & G 107 K3
Knowehead D & G 115 M9
Knoweside S Ayrs 114 E5
Knowes of Elrick Abers 158 F7
Knowle Bristl 32 B10
Knowle Devon 9 J4
Knowle Devon 9 P3
Knowle Devon 9 Q8
Knowle Devon 9 H4
Knowle Shrops 57 K10
Knowle Solhll 59 J9
Knowle Somset 18 C6
Knowle Cross Devon 9 P5
Knowlefield Cumb 110 H9
Knowle Green Lancs 89 J3
Knowle Hill Surrey 35 Q11
Knowle St Giles Somset 10 G2
Knowle Village Hants 14 G5
Knowle Wood Calder 89 Q6
Knowl Green Essex 52 C3
Knowl Hill W & M 35 M9
Knowlton Dorset 12 H3
Knowlton Kent 39 N11
Knowsley Knows 81 N5
Knowsley Safari Park
   Knows 81 P6
Knowstone Devon 17 Q7
Knox N York 97 L9
Knox Bridge Kent 26 C3
Knoydart Highld 145 P7
Knucklas Powys 56 D10
Knuston Nhants 61 K7
Knutsford Ches E 82 G9
Knutsford Services Ches E 82 F9
Knutton Staffs 70 E5
Krumlin Calder 90 D7
Kuggar Cnwll 3 J10
Kyleakin Highld 145 N2
Kyle of Lochalsh Highld 145 N2
Kylerhea Highld 145 N3
Kylesku Highld 164 F10
Kylesmorar Highld 145 P9
Kyles Scalpay W Isls 168 h8
Kylestrome Highld 164 F10
Kynaston Herefs 46 B7
Kynaston Shrops 69 L10
Kynnersley Wrekin 70 B11
Kyre Green Worcs 46 B2
Kyre Park Worcs 46 B2
Kyrewood Worcs 57 K11
Kyrle Somset 18 E10

L

La Bellieuse Guern 10 b2
Lacasaigh W Isls 168 i5
Lacasdal W Isls 168 j4
Laceby NE Lin 93 M9
Lacey Green Bucks 35 M4
Lach Dennis Ches W 82 F10
Lackenby R & Cl 104 G7
Lackford Suffk 63 N6
Lackford Green Suffk 63 N6
Lacock Wilts 32 H11
Ladbroke Warwks 48 D3
Ladderedge Staffs 70 H4
Laddingford Kent 37 Q11
Lade Bank Lincs 87 L10
Ladock Cnwll 3 M3
Lady Ork 169 f2
Ladybank Fife 135 J6
Ladycross Cnwll 5 N4
Ladygill S Lans 116 C5
Lady Hall Cumb 94 D3
Ladykirk Border 129 M10
Ladyridge Herefs 46 A8
Lady's Green Suffk 63 N9
Ladywood Birm 58 G7
Ladywood Worcs 46 G2
La Fontenelle Guern 10 c1
La Fosse Guern 10 b2
Lag D & G 109 J3
Lagavulin Ag & B 122 F10
Lagg N Ayrs 121 J7
Laggan Highld 146 H8
Laggan Highld 147 Q9
Lagganlia Highld 148 F7
La Grève de Lecq Jersey 11 a1
La Hougue Bie Jersey 11 c2
La Houguette Guern 10 b2
Laid Highld 165 K5
Laide Highld 160 E8
Laig Highld 144 G10
Laigh Clunch E Ayrs 125 M8
Laigh Fenwick E Ayrs 125 M9
Laigh Glenmuir E Ayrs 115 M3
Laighstonehall S Lans 126 C7
Laindon Essex 37 Q3
Lairg Highld 162 D5

Laisterdyke C Brad 90 F4
Laithes Cumb 101 N4
Lake Devon 8 D7
Lake Devon 17 K5
Lake IoW 14 G10
Lake Wilts 21 M7
Lake District Cumb 100 H8
Lake District National Park
   Cumb 100 H8
Lakenheath Suffk 63 M4
Laker's Green Surrey 24 B3
Lakes End Norfk 75 K11
Lakeside Cumb 94 H3
Laleham Surrey 36 C7
Laleston Brdgnd 29 N9
Lamanva Cnwll 3 K7
Lamarsh Essex 52 E4
Lamas Norfk 77 J7
Lambden Border 118 D2
Lamberhurst Kent 25 Q3
Lamberhurst Down Kent 25 Q3
Lamberton Border 129 P8
Lambeth Gt Lon 36 H5
Lambfair Green Suffk 63 M10
Lambley Notts 85 K11
Lambley Nthumb 111 N9
Lambourn W Berk 34 B9
Lambourne End Essex 37 L2
Lambourn Woodlands
   W Berk 34 B9
Lamb Roe Lancs 89 L3
Lambs Green W Susx 24 F3
Lambston Pembks 40 H7
Lamellion Cnwll 5 L9
Lamerton Devon 8 C9
Lamesley Gatesd 113 L9
Lamington S Lans 116 D4
Lamlash N Ayrs 121 K5
Lamonby Cumb 101 M3
Lamorick Cnwll 4 G9
Lamorna Cnwll 2 C9
Lamorran Cnwll 3 M5
Lampen Cnwll 5 K8
Lampeter Cerdgn 43 L5
Lampeter Velfrey Pembks 41 N8
Lamphey Pembks 41 K10
Lamplugh Cumb 100 E6
Lamport Nhants 60 G6
Lamyatt Somset 20 C7
Lana Devon 5 N2
Lana Devon 16 E10
Lanark S Lans 116 B2
Lancaster Lancs 95 K8
Lancaster Services Lancs 95 L10
Lancaut Gloucs 31 P5
Lanchester Dur 113 J11
Lancing W Susx 24 E10
L'Ancresse Guern 10 c1
Landbeach Cambs 62 G7
Landcross Devon 16 H7
Landerberry Abers 151 J7
Landford Wilts 21 Q11
Land-hallow Highld 167 L10
Landimore Swans 28 E6
Landkey Devon 17 K5
Landore Swans 29 J5
Landrake Cnwll 5 P9
Landscove Devon 7 K5
Land's End Cnwll 2 A8
Land's End Airport Cnwll 2 B8
Landshipping Pembks 41 K8
Landue Cnwll 5 P6
Landulph Cnwll 6 C6
Landwade Suffk 63 K7
Lane Cnwll 4 C9
Laneast Cnwll 5 L5
Lane Bottom Lancs 89 P3
Lane End Bucks 35 M4
Lane End Cnwll 4 G8
Lane End Hants 22 G9
Lane End Kent 37 N6
Lane End Lancs 96 C11
Lane End Warrtn 82 E6
Lane End Wilts 20 F5
Lane Ends Derbys 71 N8
Lane Ends Lancs 89 M4
Lane Ends N York 90 B2
Lane Green Staffs 58 C4
Laneham Notts 85 P5
Lanehead Dur 102 F2
Lane Head Dur 103 M8
Lanehead Nthumb 111 Q3
Lane Head Wigan 82 D5
Lane Head Wsall 58 E4
Lane Heads Lancs 88 E3
Lanercost Cumb 111 L8
Laneshaw Bridge Lancs 89 Q2
Lane Side Lancs 89 M6
Langaford Devon 5 Q2
Langal Highld 138 C4
Langaller Somset 19 J9
Langar Notts 73 J4
Langbank Rens 125 K3
Langbar N York 96 G10
Langbaurgh N York 104 G8
Langcliffe N York 96 B8
Langdale End N York 99 J2
Langdon Cnwll 5 N4
Langdon Beck Dur 102 G4
Langdon Hills Essex 37 Q3
Langdown Hants 14 D5
Langdyke Fife 135 J7
Langenhoe Essex 52 H8
Langford C Beds 50 E2
Langford Devon 9 P4
Langford Essex 52 D10
Langford N Som 19 N2
Langford Notts 85 P9
Langford Oxon 33 P4
Langford Budville Somset 18 F10
Langham Dorset 20 E9
Langham Essex 52 H5
Langham Norfk 76 E3
Langham Rutlnd 73 L8
Langham Suffk 64 D8
Langho Lancs 89 L4
Langholm D & G 110 G4
Langland Swans 28 H7
Langlee Border 117 Q3
Langley Ches E 83 K10
Langley Derbys 84 F11
Langley Gloucs 47 K9
Langley Hants 14 D6
Langley Herts 50 F6
Langley Kent 38 D11
Langley Nthumb 112 B8

Langley – Little Braxted 279

Langley Oxon 47 Q11
Langley Rochdl 89 P9
Langley Slough 36 B5
Langley Somset 18 E9
Langley W Susx 23 M9
Langley Warwks 47 N2
Langley Burrell Wilts 32 H9
Langley Castle Nthumb 112 B8
Langley Common Derbys 71 P7
Langley Green Derbys 71 P7
Langley Green Essex 52 E7
Langley Green Warwks 47 N2
Langley Heath Kent 38 D11
Langley Lower Green Essex 51 K4
Langley Marsh Somset 18 E9
Langley Mill Derbys 84 F11
Langley Moor Dur 103 Q2
Langley Park Dur 113 K11
Langley Street Norfk 77 M11
Langley Upper Green Essex 51 K4
Langley Vale Surrey 36 F9
Langney E Susx 25 P10
Langold Notts 85 J3
Langore Cnwll 5 M4
Langport Somset 19 M9
Langrick Lincs 87 J11
Langridge BaNES 32 D11
Langridgeford Devon 17 K7
Langrigg Cumb 110 C11
Langrish Hants 23 K10
Langsett Barns 90 G10
Langside P & K 133 M5
Langstone Hants 15 K6
Langstone Newpt 31 L7
Langthorne N York 97 K2
Langthorpe N York 97 N7
Langthwaite N York 103 K10
Langtoft E R Yk 99 L7
Langtoft Lincs 74 B8
Langton Dur 103 N7
Langton Lincs 86 H7
Langton Lincs 87 L6
Langton N York 98 F7
Langton by Wragby Lincs 86 F5
Langton Green Kent 25 M3
Langton Green Suffk 64 G7
Langton Herring Dorset 11 N8
Langton Long Blandford
Dorset 12 F3
Langton Matravers Dorset 12 H9
Langtree Devon 16 H8
Langtree Week Devon 16 H8
Langwathby Cumb 101 Q4
Langwell Highld 161 K6
Langwell House Highld 163 Q2
Langwith Derbys 84 H7
Langwith Junction Derbys 84 H7
Langworth Lincs 86 E5
Lanhydrock House &
Gardens Cnwll 4 H9
Lanivet Cnwll 4 G9
Lanjeth Cnwll 3 P3
Lank Cnwll 4 H6
Lanlivery Cnwll 4 H10
Lanner Cnwll 3 J6
Lanoy Cnwll 5 M6
Lanreath Cnwll 5 K10
Lansallos Cnwll 5 K11
Lanteglos Cnwll 4 H5
Lanteglos Highway Cnwll 5 J11
Lanton Border 118 B6
Lanton Nthumb 118 H4
La Passee Guern 10 b1
Lapford Devon 8 H3
Laphroaig Ag & B 122 E10
Lapley Staffs 58 C2
La Pulente Jersey 11 a2
Lapworth Warwks 59 J10
Larachbeg Highld 138 B8
Larbert Falk 133 P11
Larbreck Lancs 88 E2
Largie Abers 158 F11
Largiemore Ag & B 131 J10
Largoward Fife 135 M6
Largs N Ayrs 124 G6
Largybeg N Ayrs 121 K7
Largymore N Ayrs 121 K7
Larkbeare Devon 9 Q5
Larkfield Inver 124 G2
Larkfield Kent 38 B10
Larkhall S Lans 126 D7
Larkhill Wilts 21 M6
Larling Norfk 64 D4
La Rocque Jersey 11 c2
La Rousaillerie Guern 10 b1
Lartington Dur 103 K7
Lasborough Gloucs 32 F6
Lasham Hants 23 J6
Lashbrook Devon 8 B3
Lashbrook Devon 16 G10
Lashenden Kent 26 D3
Lask Edge Staffs 70 G3
Lasswade Mdloth 127 Q4
Lastingham N York 98 E2
Latcham Somset 19 M5
Latchford Herts 51 J6
Latchford Oxon 35 J4
Latchford Warrtn 82 D7
Latchingdon Essex 52 E11
Latchley Cnwll 5 Q7
Lately Common Warrtn 82 E5
Lathbury M Keyn 49 N6
Latheron Highld 167 M10
Latheronwheel Highld 167 L10
Lathom Lancs 88 F8
Lathones Fife 135 M6
Latimer Bucks 50 B11
Latteridge S Glos 32 C8
Lattiford Somset 20 C9
Latton Wilts 33 L5
Lauder Border 128 E10
Laugharne Carmth 28 B2
Laughterton Lincs 85 P5
Laughton E Susx 25 L8
Laughton Leics 60 E3
Laughton Lincs 74 A4
Laughton Lincs 92 D11
Laughton Common Rothm 84 H3
Laughton-en-le-Morthen
Rothm 84 H3
Launcells Cnwll 16 C10
Launcells Cross Cnwll 16 D10
Launceston Cnwll 5 N5
Launton Oxon 48 H10
Laurencekirk Abers 143 N3
Laurieston D & G 108 E8
Laurieston Falk 126 G2
Lavendon M Keyn 49 P4
Lavenham Suffk 52 F2
Lavernock V Glam 30 G11
Laversdale Cumb 111 J8
Laverstock Wilts 21 N8
Laverstoke Hants 22 E5
Laverton Gloucs 47 L7
Laverton N York 97 K6
Laverton Somset 20 E4
La Villette Guern 10 b2
Lavister Wrexhm 69 L3
Law S Lans 126 E7
Lawers P & K 140 G10
Lawford Essex 53 J5
Lawford Somset 18 F7
Law Hill S Lans 126 E7
Lawhitton Cnwll 5 P5
Lawkland N York 95 R7
Lawkland Green N York 96 A7
Lawley Wrekin 57 M3
Lawnhead Staffs 70 E9
Lawrence Weston Bristl 31 P9
Lawrenny Pembks 41 K9
Lawrenny Quay Pembks 41 K9
Lawshall Suffk 64 B11
Lawshall Green Suffk 64 B11
Lawton Herefs 45 N3
Laxay W Isls 168 i5
Laxdale W Isls 168 j4
Laxey IoM 80 f5
Laxfield Suffk 65 K7
Laxford Bridge Highld 164 F7
Laxo Shet 169 r7
Laxton E R Yk 92 C5
Laxton Nhants 73 P11
Laxton Notts 85 M7
Laycock C Brad 90 C2
Layer Breton Essex 52 F8
Layer-de-la-Haye Essex 52 G7
Layer Marney Essex 52 F8
Layham Suffk 52 H3
Laymore Dorset 10 H4
Layter's Green Bucks 35 Q6
Laytham E R Yk 92 B3
Laythes Cumb 110 D9
Lazenby R & Cl 104 G7
Lazonby Cumb 101 P3
Lea Derbys 84 D9
Lea Herefs 46 C10
Lea Lincs 85 P3
Lea Shrops 56 F7
Lea Shrops 56 G3
Lea Wilts 33 J7
Leachkin Highld 156 A8
Leadburn Border 127 N6
Leadenham Lincs 86 B10
Leaden Roding Essex 51 N8
Leadgate Cumb 102 D2
Leadgate Dur 112 H10
Leadgate Nthumb 112 H9
Leadhills S Lans 116 B7
Leadingcross Green Kent 38 E11
Leadmill Derbys 84 B4
Leafield Oxon 48 B11
Leagrave Luton 50 C6
Leahead Ches W 70 B2
Lea Heath Staffs 71 J9
Leake N York 97 P2
Leake Common Side Lincs 87 L10
Lealholm N York 105 L9
Lealholm Side N York 105 L9
Lealt Highld 153 J5
Leam Derbys 84 B5
Lea Marston Warwks 59 K6
Leamington Hastings
Warwks 59 P11
Leamington Spa Warwks 59 M11
Leamside Dur 113 M11
Leap Cross E Susx 25 N8
Learney Abers 150 G7
Leasgill Cumb 95 K4
Leasingham Lincs 86 E11
Leasingthorne Dur 103 Q4
Leatherhead Surrey 36 E9
Leathley N York 97 K11
Leaton Shrops 69 N11
Leaton Wrekin 57 L2
Lea Town Lancs 88 F4
Leaveland Kent 38 H11
Leavenheath Suffk 52 G4
Leavening N York 98 F8
Leaves Green Gt Lon 37 K8
Lea Yeat Cumb 95 R3
Lebberston N York 99 M4
Le Bigard Guern 10 b2
Le Bourg Guern 10 b2
Le Bourg Jersey 11 c2
Lechlade on Thames
Gloucs 33 P5
Lecht Gruinart Ag & B 122 C6
Leck Lancs 95 N5
Leckbuie P & K 140 H9
Leckford Hants 22 C7
Leckhampstead Bucks 49 K7
Leckhampstead W Berk 34 D9
Leckhampstead Thicket
W Berk 34 D9
Leckhampton Gloucs 46 H11
Leckmelm Highld 161 K9
Leckwith V Glam 30 G10
Leconfield E R Yk 92 H2
Ledaig Ag & B 138 G10
Ledburn Bucks 49 P10
Ledbury Herefs 46 D7
Leddington Gloucs 46 C8
Ledgemoor Herefs 45 N4
Ledicot Herefs 45 N2
Ledmore Highld 161 L4
Ledsham Ches W 81 M10
Ledsham Leeds 91 M5
Ledston Leeds 91 L5
Ledstone Devon 7 J9
Ledston Luck Leeds 91 L4
Ledwell Oxon 48 D9
Lee Devon 16 H2
Lee Gt Lon 37 J5
Lee Hants 22 C11
Lee Shrops 69 M8
Leebotwood Shrops 56 H5
Lee Brockhurst Shrops 69 P9
Leece Cumb 94 E7
Lee Chapel Essex 37 Q3
Lee Clump Bucks 35 P4
Lee Common Bucks 35 P4
Leeds Kent 38 D11
Leeds Leeds 90 H4
Leeds Bradford Airport
Leeds 90 G2
Leeds Castle Kent 38 D11
Leeds Skelton Lake
Services Leeds 91 K4
Leedstown Cnwll 2 G7
Lee Green Ches E 70 B2
Leek Staffs 70 H3
Leek Wootton Warwks 59 L11
Lee Mill Devon 6 F7
Leeming C Brad 90 C4
Leeming N York 97 L3
Leeming Bar N York 97 L3
Leeming Bar Rest Area
N York 97 L3
Lee Moor Devon 6 F6
Lee-on-the-Solent Hants 14 G6
Lees C Brad 90 C3
Lees Derbys 71 P7
Lees Oldham 83 L4
Lees Green Derbys 71 P7
Leesthorpe Leics 73 K8
Leeswood Flints 69 J2
Leetown P & K 134 G3
Leftwich Ches W 82 E10
Legar Powys 45 J11
Legbourne Lincs 87 L4
Legburthwaite Cumb 101 K7
Legerwood Border 118 A2
Legoland W & M 35 P10
Le Gron Guern 10 b2
Legsby Lincs 86 F3
Le Haguais Jersey 11 c2
Le Hocq Jersey 11 c2
Leicester C Leic 72 F10
Leicester Forest East Leics 72 E10
Leicester Forest East
Services Leics 72 E10
Leigh Devon 17 N9
Leigh Dorset 11 N3
Leigh Gloucs 46 G9
Leigh Kent 37 M11
Leigh Shrops 56 E4
Leigh Surrey 36 F11
Leigh Wigan 82 E5
Leigh Wilts 33 L6
Leigh Worcs 46 E4
Leigh Beck Essex 38 D5
Leigh Delamere Wilts 32 G9
Leigh Delamere Services
Wilts 32 G9
Leigh Green Kent 26 F5
Leigh Knoweglass S Lans 125 Q7
Leighland Chapel Somset 18 D7
Leigh-on-Sea Sthend 38 D4
Leigh Park Dorset 12 H5
Leigh Park Hants 15 K5
Leigh Sinton Worcs 46 E4
Leighswood Wsall 58 G4
Leighterton Gloucs 32 F6
Leighton N York 97 J5
Leighton Powys 56 C3
Leighton Shrops 57 L3
Leighton Somset 20 D6
Leighton Bromswold Cambs 61 P5
Leighton Buzzard C Beds 49 P9
Leigh upon Mendip Somset 20 C5
Leigh Woods N Som 31 Q10
Leinthall Earls Herefs 56 G11
Leinthall Starkes Herefs 56 G11
Leintwardine Herefs 56 G10
Leire Leics 60 B3
Leiston Suffk 65 N9
Leith C Edin 127 P2
Leitholm Border 118 E2
Lelant Cnwll 2 E6
Lelley E R Yk 93 M4
Lem Hill Worcs 57 N9
Lempitlaw Border 118 E4
Lemreway W Isls 168 i6
Lemsford Herts 50 F8
Lenchwick Worcs 47 K5
Lendalfoot S Ayrs 114 B9
Lendrick Stirlg 132 H6
Lendrum Terrace Abers 159 R9
Lenham Kent 38 E11
Lenham Heath Kent 26 F2
Lenie Highld 147 N2
Lennel Border 118 G2
Lennox Plunton D & G 108 D10
Lennoxtown E Duns 125 Q2
Lent Bucks 35 P8
Lenton C Nott 72 F3
Lenton Lincs 73 Q4
Lenwade Norfk 76 F8
Lenzie E Duns 126 B3
Leochel-Cushnie Abers 150 E5
Leomansley Staffs 58 H3
Leominster Herefs 45 P3
Leonard Stanley Gloucs 32 F4
Leoville Jersey 11 a1
Lepe Hants 14 D7
Lephin Highld 152 B8
Leppington N York 98 F8
Lepton Kirk 90 G7
Lerags Ag & B 130 H2
L'Erée Guern 10 a2
Lerryn Cnwll 5 J10
Lerwick Shet 169 r9
Les Arquêts Guern 10 b2
Lesbury Nthumb 119 P8
Les Hubits Guern 10 c2
Leslie Abers 150 F3
Leslie Fife 134 H7
Les Lohiers Guern 10 b2
Lesmahagow S Lans 126 E10
Les Murchez Guern 10 b2
Lesnewth Cnwll 5 J3
Les Nicolles Guern 10 b2
Les Quartiers Guern 10 c1
Les Quennevais Jersey 11 a2
Les Sages Guern 10 b2
Lessingham Norfk 77 M6
Lessonhall Cumb 110 D10
Lestowder Cnwll 3 K9
Les Villets Guern 10 b2
Leswalt D & G 106 D5
L'Etacq Jersey 11 a1
Letchmore Heath Herts 50 E11
Letchworth Garden City
Herts 50 F4
Letcombe Bassett Oxon 34 C8
Letcombe Regis Oxon 34 C7
Letham Angus 143 J8
Letham Border 118 C9
Letham Falk 133 P10
Letham Fife 135 J5
Letham Grange Angus 143 L8
Lethenty Abers 150 F3
Lethenty Abers 159 K9
Letheringham Suffk 65 K10
Letheringsett Norfk 76 F4
Lettaford Devon 8 H8
Letterewe Highld 154 C3
Letterfearn Highld 145 Q3
Letterfinlay Lodge Hotel
Highld 146 H9
Letters Highld 161 K9
Lettershaw S Lans 116 B6
Letterston Pembks 40 H5
Lettoch Highld 149 J4
Lettoch Highld 157 L11
Letton Herefs 45 L5
Letton Herefs 56 F10
Lett's Green Kent 37 L9
Letty Green Herts 50 G8
Letwell Rothm 85 J3
Leuchars Fife 135 M3
Leumrabhagh W Isls 168 i6
Leurbost W Isls 168 i5
Levalsa Meor Cnwll 3 Q4
Levan Inver 124 G2
Levedale Staffs 70 F11
Level's Green Essex 51 L6
Leven E R Yk 99 N11
Leven Fife 135 K7
Levens Cumb 95 K3
Levens Green Herts 51 J6
Levenshulme Manch 83 J6
Levenwick Shet 169 r11
Leverburgh W Isls 168 f9
Leverington Cambs 74 H8
Leverstock Green Herts 50 C9
Leverton Lincs 87 M11
Le Villocq Guern 10 b1
Levington Suffk 53 M4
Levisham N York 98 G2
Lew Oxon 34 B3
Lewannick Cnwll 5 M5
Lewdown Devon 8 C7
Lewes E Susx 25 K8
Leweston Pembks 40 H6
Lewisham Gt Lon 37 J6
Lewiston Highld 147 N2
Lewistown Brdgnd 29 P7
Lewis Wych Herefs 45 L3
Lewknor Oxon 35 K5
Leworthy Devon 16 E11
Leworthy Devon 17 M4
Lewson Street Kent 38 G9
Lewth Lancs 88 F3
Lewtrenchard Devon 8 C7
Lexden Essex 52 G6
Lexworthy Somset 19 J7
Ley Cnwll 5 K8
Leybourne Kent 37 Q9
Leyburn N York 96 H2
Leycett Staffs 70 D5
Leygreen Herts 50 E6
Ley Hill Bucks 35 Q4
Leyland Lancs 88 G6
Leyland Green St Hel 82 C4
Leylodge Abers 151 K5
Leys Abers 159 P7
Leys P & K 142 D10
Leysdown-on-Sea Kent 38 H7
Leysmill Angus 143 L8
Leys of Cossans Angus 142 F8
Leysters Herefs 45 R2
Leyton Gt Lon 37 J3
Leytonstone Gt Lon 37 J3
Lezant Cnwll 5 N6
Lezerea Cnwll 2 H7
Leziate Norfk 75 N7
Lhanbryde Moray 157 P5
Libanus Powys 44 D9
Libberton S Lans 116 D2
Libbery Worcs 47 J3
Liberton C Edin 127 P4
Lichfield Staffs 58 H3
Lickey Worcs 58 E9
Lickey End Worcs 58 E10
Lickey Rock Worcs 58 E10
Lickfold W Susx 23 P9
Liddaton Green Devon 8 C8
Liddesdale Highld 138 D6
Liddington Swindn 33 P8
Lidgate Derbys 84 D5
Lidgate Suffk 63 M9
Lidget Donc 91 R10
Lidgett Notts 85 K7
Lidham Hill E Susx 26 D8
Lidlington C Beds 49 Q7
Lidsey W Susx 15 P6
Lidsing Kent 38 C9
Liff Angus 142 E11
Lifford Birm 58 G8
Lifton Devon 5 P4
Liftondown Devon 5 P4
Lighthorne Warwks 48 B3
Lighthorne Heath Warwks 48 C3
Lightwater Surrey 23 P2
Lightwater Valley Theme
Park N York 97 L5
Lightwood C Stke 70 G6
Lightwood Green Ches E 70 A6
Lightwood Green Wrexhm 69 L6
Lilbourne Nhants 60 C5
Lilburn Tower Nthumb 119 K6
Lilleshall Wrekin 70 C11
Lilley Herts 50 D5
Lilley W Berk 34 D9
Lilliesleaf Border 117 Q5
Lillingstone Dayrell Bucks 49 K7
Lillingstone Lovell Bucks 49 K6
Lillington Dorset 11 N2
Lilliput BCP 12 H7
Lilstock Somset 18 G5
Lilyhurst Shrops 57 N2
Limbrick Lancs 89 J7
Limbury Luton 50 C6
Limebrook Herefs 56 F11
Limefield Bury 89 N8
Limekilnburn S Lans 126 C7
Limekilns Fife 134 D11
Limerigg Falk 126 F3
Limerstone IoW 14 D10
Limestone Brae Nthumb 111 Q11
Lime Street Worcs 46 F8
Limington Somset 19 P10
Limmerhaugh E Ayrs 115 M2
Limpenhoe Norfk 77 M11
Limpley Stoke Wilts 20 E2
Limpsfield Surrey 37 K10
Limpsfield Chart Surrey 37 K10
Linby Notts 84 H10
Linchmere W Susx 23 N8
Lincluden D & G 109 L5
Lincoln Lincs 86 C6
Lincomb Worcs 57 Q11
Lincombe Devon 7 J10
Lincombe Devon 16 H2
Lindale Cumb 95 J4
Lindal in Furness Cumb 94 E5
Lindfield W Susx 24 H5
Lindford Hants 23 M7
Lindley Kirk 90 E7
Lindley N York 97 K11
Lindores Fife 134 H4
Lindow End Ches E 82 H9
Lindridge Worcs 57 M11
Lindsell Essex 51 P5
Lindsey Suffk 52 G2
Lindsey Tye Suffk 52 G2
Liney Somset 19 L7
Linford Hants 13 L3
Linford Thurr 37 Q5
Lingbob C Brad 90 D3
Lingdale R & Cl 105 J7
Lingen Herefs 56 F11
Lingfield Surrey 25 J2
Lingfield Common Surrey 25 J2
Lingwood Norfk 77 M10
Liniclate W Isls 168 c13
Linicro Highld 152 F4
Linkend Worcs 46 F8
Linkenholt Hants 22 C3
Linkhill Kent 26 D6
Linkinhorne Cnwll 5 N7
Linktown Fife 134 H9
Linkwood Moray 157 N5
Linley Shrops 56 F6
Linley Green Herefs 46 C4
Linleygreen Shrops 57 M5
Linlithgow W Loth 126 H2
Linshiels Nthumb 118 G9
Linsidemore Highld 162 C7
Linslade C Beds 49 P9
Linstead Parva Suffk 65 L6
Linstock Cumb 110 H9
Linthurst Worcs 58 E10
Linthwaite Kirk 90 E8
Lintlaw Border 129 L8
Lintmill Moray 158 D4
Linton Border 118 E5
Linton Cambs 63 J11
Linton Derbys 71 P11
Linton Herefs 46 C9
Linton Kent 38 C11
Linton Leeds 97 N11
Linton N York 96 E8
Linton Nthumb 113 L2
Linton Heath Derbys 71 P11
Linton Hill Herefs 46 C10
Linton-on-Ouse N York 97 Q8
Linwood Hants 13 L3
Linwood Lincs 86 F3
Linwood Rens 125 L5
Lionacleit W Isls 168 c13
Lional W Isls 168 k1
Lions Green E Susx 25 N7
Liphook Hants 23 M8
Lipley Shrops 70 C8
Liscard Wirral 81 K6
Liscombe Somset 18 A8
Liskeard Cnwll 5 M9
Lismore Ag & B 138 E9
Liss Hants 23 L9
Lissett E R Yk 99 N9
Liss Forest Hants 23 L9
Lissington Lincs 86 F4
Liston Essex 52 E3
Lisvane Cardif 30 G8
Liswerry Newpt 31 K7
Litcham Norfk 76 B8
Litchborough Nhants 48 H4
Litchfield Hants 22 E4
Litherland Sefton 81 L5
Litlington Cambs 50 H2
Litlington E Susx 25 M10
Little Abington Cambs 62 H11
Little Addington Nhants 61 L6
Little Airies D & G 107 M8
Little Almshoe Herts 50 F5
Little Alne Warwks 47 M2
Little Altcar Sefton 88 C9
Little Amwell Herts 51 J8
Little Asby Cumb 102 C9
Little Aston Staffs 58 G5
Little Atherfield IoW 14 E11
Little Ayton N York 104 G8
Little Baddow Essex 52 C10
Little Badminton S Glos 32 F8
Little Bampton Cumb 110 E9
Little Bardfield Essex 51 Q4
Little Barford Bed 61 Q9
Little Barningham Norfk 76 G5
Little Barrington Gloucs 33 P2
Little Barrow Ches W 81 P11
Little Barugh N York 98 F5
Little Bavington Nthumb 112 E5
Little Bealings Suffk 53 M2
Littlebeck N York 105 N10
Little Bedwyn Wilts 33 Q11
Little Bentley Essex 53 K6
Little Berkhamsted Herts 50 G9
Little Billing Nhants 60 H8
Little Billington C Beds 49 P10
Little Birch Herefs 45 Q8
Little Bispham Bpool 88 C2
Little Blakenham Suffk 53 K2
Little Blencow Cumb 101 N4
Little Bloxwich Wsall 58 F4
Little Bognor W Susx 24 B6
Little Bolehill Derbys 71 P4
Little Bollington Ches E 82 F7
Little Bookham Surrey 36 D10
Littleborough Devon 9 K2
Littleborough Notts 85 P4
Littleborough Rochdl 89 Q7
Littlebourne Kent 39 M10
Little Bourton Oxon 48 E6
Little Bowden Leics 60 F3
Little Bradley Suffk 63 L10
Little Brampton Herefs 45 L2
Little Brampton Shrops 56 F8
Little Braxted Essex 52 D9

Little Brechin Angus 143 K5
Littlebredy Dorset 11 M7
Little Brickhill M Keyn 49 P8
Little Bridgeford Staffs 70 F9
Little Brington Nhants 60 E8
Little Bromley Essex 53 J6
Little Broughton Ches W 100 E4
Little Budworth Ches W 82 C11
Littleburn Highld 156 A7
Littlebury Essex 37 Q2
Littlebury Essex 51 M3
Littlebury Green Essex 51 L3
Little Bytham Lincs 73 Q7
Little Canfield Essex 51 N6
Little Carlton Lincs 87 L3
Little Carlton Notts 85 N9
Little Casterton Rutlnd 73 Q9
Little Catwick E R Yk 93 K2
Little Catworth Cambs 61 P6
Little Cawthorpe Lincs 87 L4
Little Chalfont Bucks 35 Q5
Little Chart Kent 26 F2
Little Chesterford Essex 51 M2
Little Cheveney Kent 26 B3
Little Cheverell Wilts 21 J4
Little Chishill Cambs 51 K3
Little Clacton Essex 53 L8
Little Clanfield Oxon 33 Q4
Little Clifton Cumb 100 E5
Little Coates NE Lin 93 M9
Little Comberton Worcs 47 J6
Little Common E Susx 26 B10
Little Comp Kent 37 P9
Little Compton Warwks 47 Q8
Little Corby Cumb 111 J9
Little Cornard Suffk 52 F4
Littlecott Wilts 21 M4
Little Cowarne Herefs 46 B4
Little Coxwell Oxon 33 Q6
Little Crakehall N York 97 K2
Little Cransley Nhants 60 H5
Little Cressingham Norfk 76 B11
Little Crosby Sefton 81 L4
Little Crosthwaite Cumb 100 H5
Little Cubley Derbys 71 M7
Little Dalby Leics 73 K8
Littledean Gloucs 32 C2
Little Dewchurch Herefs 45 Q8
Little Ditton Cambs 63 L9
Little Doward Herefs 45 Q11
Littledown Hants 22 B3
Little Downham Cambs 62 H4
Little Driffield E R Yk 99 L9
Little Dunham Norfk 76 B9
Little Dunkeld P & K 141 P9
Little Dunmow Essex 51 Q6
Little Durnford Wilts 21 M8
Little Easton Essex 51 P6
Little Eaton Derbys 72 B2
Little Ellingham Norfk 64 E2
Little Elm Somset 20 D5
Little Everdon Nhants 60 C9
Little Eversden Cambs 62 E10
Little Faringdon Oxon 33 P4
Little Fencote N York 97 L2
Little Fenton N York 91 N3
Littleferry Highld 163 J7
Little Fransham Norfk 76 C9
Little Gaddesden Herts 35 Q2
Little Garway Herefs 45 N10
Little Gidding Cambs 61 P4
Little Glemham Suffk 65 L10
Little Gorsley Herefs 46 C10
Little Gransden Cambs 62 C9
Little Green Notts 73 J2
Little Green Somset 20 D5
Little Grimsby Lincs 87 K2
Little Gringley Notts 85 M4
Little Habton N York 98 E5
Little Hadham Herts 51 K6
Little Hale Lincs 74 B2
Little Hallam Derbys 72 D2
Little Hallingbury Essex 51 M7
Littleham Devon 9 P8
Littleham Devon 16 G7
Little Hampden Bucks 35 N4
Littlehampton W Susx 24 B10
Little Hanford Dorset 12 D2
Little Harrowden Nhants 61 J6
Little Haseley Oxon 34 H4
Little Hatfield E R Yk 93 L2
Little Hautbois Norfk 77 K7
Little Haven Pembks 40 G8
Littlehaven W Susx 24 E4
Little Hay Staffs 58 H4
Little Hayfield Derbys 83 M7
Little Haywood Staffs 71 J10
Little Heath Staffs 70 F11
Little Heath W Berk 35 J10
Littlehempston Devon 7 L6
Little Hereford Herefs 57 K11
Little Horkesley Essex 52 G5
Little Hormead Herts 51 K5
Little Horsted E Susx 25 L7
Little Horton C Brad 90 F4
Little Horton Wilts 21 K2
Little Horwood Bucks 49 L8
Little Houghton Barns 91 L9
Little Houghton Nhants 60 H9
Littlehoughton Nthumb 119 P7
Little Hucklow Derbys 83 Q9
Little Hulton Salfd 82 F4
Little Hungerford W Berk 34 F10
Little Hutton N York 97 Q5
Little Irchester Nhants 61 K7
Little Kelk E R Yk 99 M9
Little Keyford Somset 20 E5
Little Kimble Bucks 35 M3
Little Kineton Warwks 48 B4
Little Knill Bucks 35 N5
Little Knox D & G 108 H8
Little Langdale Cumb 101 K10
Little Langford Wilts 21 K7
Little Laver Essex 51 M9
Little Leigh Ches W 82 D9
Little Leighs Essex 52 B8
Little Lever Bolton 89 M9
Little Linford M Keyn 49 M6
Little Load Somset 19 N10
Little London Bucks 34 H2
Little London Cambs 74 H11
Little London E Susx 25 N6
Little London Essex 51 L5
Little London Essex 51 Q3
Little London Gloucs 46 D11
Little London Hants 22 C5

Little London Hants 22 H3
Little London Leeds 90 G3
Little London Lincs 74 D6
Little London Lincs 74 H6
Little London Lincs 87 K6
Little London Norfk 75 L6
Little London Powys 55 N7
Little Longstone Derbys 83 Q10
Little Madeley Staffs 70 D5
Little Malvern Worcs 46 E6
Little Maplestead Essex 52 D5
Little Marcle Herefs 46 C7
Little Marland Devon 17 J9
Little Marlow Bucks 35 N7
Little Massingham Norfk 75 Q6
Little Melton Norfk 76 H10
Littlemill Abers 149 Q8
Littlemill Highld 156 G7
Little Mill Mons 31 K4
Little Milton Oxon 34 H4
Little Missenden Bucks 35 P5
Littlemoor Derbys 84 E8
Little Moor Somset 19 K8
Littlemore Oxon 34 F4
Little Musgrave Cumb 102 E8
Little Ness Shrops 69 M11
Little Neston Ches W 81 K9
Little Newcastle Pembks 41 J5
Little Newsham Dur 103 M7
Little Norton Somset 19 N11
Little Oakley Essex 53 M6
Little Oakley Nhants 61 J3
Little Odell Bed 61 L9
Little Offley Herts 50 D5
Little Ormside Cumb 102 D7
Little Orton Cumb 110 G9
Little Ouse Cambs 63 K3
Little Ouseburn N York 97 P8
Littleover C Derb 72 A4
Little Oxendon Nhants 60 F4
Little Packington Warwks 59 K8
Little Pattenden Kent 26 B2
Little Paxton Cambs 61 Q8
Little Petherick Cnwll 4 E7
Little Plumpton Lancs 88 D4
Little Plumstead Norfk 77 L9
Little Ponton Lincs 73 N4
Littleport Cambs 63 J3
Littleport Bridge Cambs 63 J3
Little Posbrook Hants 14 F6
Little Potheridge Devon 17 J9
Little Preston Leeds 91 K4
Little Preston Nhants 48 G4
Littler Ches W 82 D11
Little Raveley Cambs 62 C5
Little Reedness E R Yk 92 D6
Little Ribston N York 97 N10
Little Rissington Gloucs 47 N11
Little Rollright Oxon 47 Q8
Little Rowsley Derbys 84 C7
Little Ryburgh Norfk 76 D6
Little Ryle Nthumb 119 K8
Little Ryton Shrops 56 H4
Little Salkeld Cumb 101 Q3
Little Sampford Essex 51 Q4
Little Sandhurst Br For 23 M2
Little Saredon Staffs 58 D3
Little Saughall Ches W 81 M11
Little Saxham Suffk 63 P8
Little Scatwell Highld 155 L6
Little Shelford Cambs 62 G10
Little Shrewley Warwks 59 K11
Little Silver Devon 9 M3
Little Singleton Lancs 88 D3
Little Skipwith N York 91 R3
Little Smeaton N York 91 N7
Little Snoring Norfk 76 D5
Little Sodbury S Glos 32 E8
Little Sodbury End S Glos 32 D8
Little Somborne Hants 22 C8
Little Somerford Wilts 33 J8
Little Soudley Shrops 70 C9
Little Stainforth N York 96 B7
Little Stainton Darltn 104 B6
Little Stanion Nhants 61 J3
Little Stanney Ches W 81 N10
Little Staughton Bed 61 P8
Little Steeping Lincs 87 M8
Littlestone-on-Sea Kent 27 J7
Little Stonham Suffk 64 G9
Little Stretton Leics 72 H10
Little Stretton Shrops 56 G6
Little Strickland Cumb 101 Q7
Little Stukeley Cambs 62 B5
Little Sugnall Staffs 70 E8
Little Sutton Ches W 81 M9
Little Sutton Shrops 57 J8
Little Swinburne Nthumb 112 D5
Little Sypland D & G 108 F10
Little Tew Oxon 48 C9
Little Tey Essex 52 E7
Little Thetford Cambs 62 H5
Little Thirkleby N York 97 Q5
Little Thornage Norfk 76 F4
Little Thornton Lancs 88 D2
Little Thorpe Dur 104 D2
Littlethorpe Leics 72 E11
Littlethorpe N York 97 M7
Little Thurlow Suffk 63 L10
Little Thurlow Green Suffk 63 L10
Little Thurrock Thurr 37 P5
Littleton BaNES 19 Q2
Littleton Ches W 81 N11
Littleton D & G 108 D9
Littleton Dorset 12 E4
Littleton Hants 22 E8
Littleton Somset 19 N9
Littleton Surrey 23 Q5
Littleton Surrey 36 C7
Littleton Drew Wilts 32 F8
Littleton of Airlie Angus 142 F7
Littleton-on-Severn S Glos 31 Q7
Littleton Panell Wilts 21 J4
Little Torrington Devon 16 H8
Little Totham Essex 52 E9
Little Town Cumb 100 H7
Littletown Dur 104 B2
Little Town Lancs 89 K3
Little Town Warrtn 82 D6
Little Twycross Leics 72 A9
Little Urswick Cumb 94 F6
Little Wakering Essex 38 F4
Little Walden Essex 51 M2

Little Waldingfield Suffk 52 F2
Little Walsingham Norfk 76 C4
Little Waltham Essex 52 B9
Little Warley Essex 37 P2
Little Washbourne Gloucs 47 J8
Little Weighton E R Yk 92 G4
Little Welnetham Suffk 64 B10
Little Welton Lincs 87 K3
Little Wenham Suffk 53 J4
Little Wenlock Wrekin 57 L3
Little Weston Somset 20 B9
Little Whitefield IoW 14 G9
Little Whittingham Green Suffk 65 K6
Little Whittington Nthumb 112 E7
Littlewick Green W & M 35 M9
Little Wilbraham Cambs 62 H9
Littlewindsor Dorset 11 J4
Little Witcombe Gloucs 46 H11
Little Witley Worcs 46 E2
Little Wittenham Oxon 34 G6
Little Wolford Warwks 47 Q7
Littlewood Staffs 58 E3
Little Woodcote Gt Lon 36 G8
Littleworth Bucks 49 N10
Littleworth Oxon 34 B5
Littleworth Staffs 58 F2
Littleworth Staffs 70 G10
Littleworth W Susx 24 E6
Littleworth Worcs 46 G4
Littleworth Worcs 47 J2
Littleworth Common Bucks 35 P7
Little Wratting Suffk 63 L11
Little Wymington Bed 61 L8
Little Wymondley Herts 50 F5
Little Wyrley Staffs 58 F3
Little Wytheford Shrops 69 Q11
Little Yeldham Essex 52 C4
Littley Green Essex 51 Q7
Litton Derbys 83 Q9
Litton N York 96 D6
Litton Somset 19 Q4
Litton Cheney Dorset 11 L6
Liurbost W Isls 168 i5
Liverpool Lpool 81 L6
Liverpool Maritime Mercantile City Lpool 81 L7
Liversedge Kirk 90 F6
Liverton Devon 9 K9
Liverton R & Cl 105 K7
Liverton Mines R & Cl 105 K7
Liverton Street Kent 38 E11
Livingston W Loth 127 K4
Livingston Village W Loth 127 J4
Lixwm Flints 80 H10
Lizard Cnwll 3 J11
Llaingoch IoA 78 C8
Llaithddu Powys 55 P8
Llan Powys 55 K4
Llanaber Gwynd 67 L11
Llanaelhaearn Gwynd 66 F6
Llanafan Cerdgn 54 F10
Llanafan-Fawr Powys 44 D3
Llanallgo IoA 79 J7
Llanarmon Gwynd 66 G7
Llanarmon Dyffryn Ceiriog Wrexhm 68 G8
Llanarmon-yn-Ial Denbgs 68 G3
Llanarth Cerdgn 42 H3
Llanarth Mons 31 L2
Llanarthne Carmth 43 K11
Llanasa Flints 80 G8
Llanbabo IoA 78 F7
Llanbadarn Fawr Cerdgn 54 E8
Llanbadarn Fynydd Powys 55 P9
Llanbadarn-y-garreg Powys 44 G5
Llanbadoc Mons 31 L5
Llanbadrig IoA 78 F6
Llanbeder Newpt 31 L6
Llanbedr Gwynd 67 K9
Llanbedr Powys 44 G5
Llanbedr Powys 45 J10
Llanbedr-Dyffryn-Clwyd Denbgs 68 F3
Llanbedrgoch IoA 79 J8
Llanbedrog Gwynd 66 E8
Llanbedr-y-Cennin Conwy 79 P11
Llanberis Gwynd 67 K2
Llanbethèry V Glam 30 D11
Llanbister Powys 55 N9
Llanblethian V Glam 30 C10
Llanboidy Carmth 41 P6
Llanbradach Caerph 30 F6
Llanbrynmair Powys 55 K4
Llancadle V Glam 30 D11
Llancarfan V Glam 30 D10
Llancayo Mons 31 L4
Llancloudy Herefs 45 P10
Llancynfelyn Cerdgn 54 E6
Llandaff Cardif 30 G9
Llandanwg Gwynd 67 K9
Llandarcy Neath 29 K5
Llandawke Carmth 41 Q8
Llanddaniel Fab IoA 78 H10
Llanddarog Carmth 43 K11
Llanddeiniol Cerdgn 54 D10
Llanddeiniolen Gwynd 79 J11
Llanderfel Gwynd 68 C7
Llanddeusant Carmth 43 Q10
Llanddeusant IoA 78 E7
Llanddew Powys 44 F8
Llanddewi Swans 28 C7
Llanddewi Brefi Cerdgn 43 N3
Llanddewi'r Cwm Powys 44 E5
Llanddewi Rhydderch Mons 31 L2
Llanddewi Velfrey Pembks 41 M7
Llanddewi Ystradenni Powys 55 N9
Llanddoged Conwy 67 Q2
Llanddona IoA 79 K9
Llanddowror Carmth 41 Q8
Llanddulas Conwy 80 C9
Llanddwywe Gwynd 67 K10
Llanddyfnan IoA 79 J9
Llandecwyn Gwynd 67 L7
Llandefaelog Powys 44 E8
Llandefaelog-Tre'r-Graig Powys 44 G9
Llandefalle Powys 44 G7
Llandegfan IoA 79 J10
Llandegla Denbgs 68 G4
Llandegley Powys 44 G2
Llandegveth Mons 31 K5
Llandegwning Gwynd 66 D9
Llandeilo Carmth 43 M10
Llandeilo Graban Powys 44 F6

Llandeilo'r Fan Powys 44 B8
Llandeloy Pembks 40 G5
Llandenny Mons 31 M4
Llandevaud Newpt 31 M6
Llandevenny Mons 31 M7
Llandinabo Herefs 45 Q9
Llandinam Powys 55 N7
Llandissilio Pembks 41 M6
Llandogo Mons 31 P4
Llandough V Glam 30 C10
Llandough V Glam 30 G10
Llandovery Carmth 43 Q8
Llandow V Glam 29 P10
Llandre Carmth 43 N6
Llandre Cerdgn 54 E7
Llandre Isaf Pembks 41 M5
Llandrillo Denbgs 68 D7
Llandrillo-yn-Rhos Conwy 79 Q8
Llandrindod Wells Powys 44 F2
Llandrinio Powys 69 J11
Llandudno Conwy 79 P8
Llandudno Junction Conwy 79 P9
Llandulas Powys 44 B6
Llandwrog Gwynd 66 H3
Llandybie Carmth 43 M11
Llandyfaelog Carmth 28 D2
Llandyfan Carmth 43 M11
Llandyfriog Cerdgn 42 F6
Llandyfrydog IoA 78 G7
Llandygai Gwynd 79 K10
Llandygwydd Cerdgn 41 P2
Llandynan Denbgs 68 G5
Llandyrnog Denbgs 80 G11
Llandyssil Powys 56 B5
Llandysul Cerdgn 42 H6
Llanedeyrn Cardif 30 H8
Llanedi Carmth 28 G3
Llaneglwys Powys 44 F7
Llanegryn Gwynd 54 E3
Llanegwad Carmth 43 K10
Llaneilian IoA 78 H6
Llanelian-yn-Rhôs Conwy 80 B9
Llanelidan Denbgs 68 F4
Llanelieu Powys 44 H8
Llanellen Mons 31 K2
Llanelli Carmth 28 F4
Llanelltyd Gwynd 67 N11
Llanelly Mons 30 H2
Llanelly Hill Mons 30 H2
Llanelwedd Powys 44 E4
Llanenddwyn Gwynd 67 K10
Llanengan Gwynd 66 D9
Llanerch Gwynd 68 A11
Llanerch Powys 56 E6
Llanerchymedd IoA 78 G8
Llanerfyl Powys 55 N3
Llanfabon Caerph 30 F6
Llanfachraeth IoA 78 E8
Llanfachreth Gwynd 67 P10
Llanfaelog IoA 78 E10
Llanfaelrhys Gwynd 66 C9
Llanfaenor Mons 45 N11
Llanfaes IoA 79 L9
Llanfaes Powys 44 E9
Llanfaethlu IoA 78 E7
Llanfair Gwynd 67 K9
Llanfair Caereinion Powys 55 Q3
Llanfair Clydogau Cerdgn 43 M4
Llanfair Dyffryn Clwyd Denbgs 68 F3
Llanfairfechan Conwy 79 M10
Llanfair Kilgeddin Mons 31 L3
Llanfair-Nant-Gwyn Pembks 41 N3
Llanfairpwllgwyngyll IoA 79 J10
Llanfair Talhaiarn Conwy 80 C10
Llanfair Waterdine Shrops 56 C9
Llanfairynghornwy IoA 78 E6
Llanfair-yn-Neubwll IoA 78 E10
Llanfallteg Carmth 41 N6
Llanfallteg West Carmth 41 M7
Llanfarian Cerdgn 54 D9
Llanfechain Powys 68 G10
Llanfechan Powys 44 D4
Llanfechell IoA 78 F6
Llanferres Denbgs 68 G2
Llan Ffestiniog Gwynd 67 N6
Llanfflewyn IoA 78 F7
Llanfigael IoA 78 E8
Llanfihangel-ar-arth Carmth 43 J7
Llanfihangel Glyn Myfyr Conwy 68 C5
Llanfihangel Nant Bran Powys 44 C8
Llanfihangel-nant-Melan Powys 44 H3
Llanfihangel Rhydithon Powys 56 B11
Llanfihangel Rogiet Mons 31 N7
Llanfihangel Tal-y-llyn Powys 44 G9
Llanfihangel-uwch-Gwili Carmth 43 J10
Llanfihangel-y-Creuddyn Cerdgn 54 F9
Llanfihangel-yng-Ngwynfa Powys 68 E11
Llanfihangel yn Nhowyn IoA 78 E9
Llanfihangel-y-pennant Gwynd 54 F3
Llanfihangel-y-pennant Gwynd 67 J6
Llanfilo Powys 44 G8
Llanfoist Mons 31 J2
Llanfor Gwynd 68 B7
Llanfrechfa Torfn 31 K6
Llanfrothen Gwynd 67 L6
Llanfrynach Powys 44 F9
Llanfwrog Denbgs 68 F3
Llanfwrog IoA 78 E8
Llanfyllin Powys 68 F11
Llanfynydd Carmth 43 L9
Llanfynydd Flints 69 J3
Llanfyrnach Pembks 41 P4
Llangadfan Powys 55 N2
Llangadog Carmth 43 P9
Llangadwaladr IoA 78 F11
Llangadwaladr Powys 68 G8
Llangaffo IoA 78 G11
Llangain Carmth 42 G11
Llangammarch Wells Powys 44 C6
Llangan V Glam 30 C9
Llangarron Herefs 45 Q10
Llangasty-Talyllyn Powys 44 G9

Llangathen Carmth 43 L10
Llangattock Powys 45 J11
Llangattock Lingoed Mons 45 M10
Llangattock-Vibon-Avel Mons 45 P11
Llangedwyn Powys 68 G10
Llangefni IoA 78 H9
Llangeinor Brdgnd 29 P7
Llangeitho Cerdgn 43 M3
Llangeler Carmth 42 G7
Llangelynin Gwynd 54 D3
Llangennech Carmth 28 G4
Llangennith Swans 28 D6
Llangenny Powys 45 J11
Llangernyw Conwy 80 B11
Llangian Gwynd 66 D9
Llangiwg Neath 29 K3
Llangloffan Pembks 40 H4
Llanglydwen Carmth 41 N5
Llangoed IoA 79 L9
Llangoedmor Cerdgn 42 D5
Llangollen Denbgs 68 H6
Llangolman Pembks 41 M5
Llangors Powys 44 G9
Llangorwen Cerdgn 54 E8
Llangovan Mons 31 N3
Llangower Gwynd 68 B8
Llangrannog Cerdgn 42 F4
Llangristiolus IoA 78 G10
Llangrove Herefs 45 Q11
Llangua Mons 45 M9
Llangunllo Powys 56 C10
Llangunnor Carmth 42 H10
Llangurig Powys 55 L9
Llangwm Conwy 68 C6
Llangwm Mons 31 M5
Llangwm Pembks 41 J9
Llangwnnadl Gwynd 66 C8
Llangwyfan Denbgs 80 G11
Llangwyllog IoA 78 G9
Llangwyryfon Cerdgn 54 D10
Llangybi Gwynd 66 G6
Llangybi Mons 31 L5
Llangyfelach Swans 28 H5
Llangyndeyrn Carmth 28 E2
Llangynhafal Denbgs 80 G11
Llangynidr Powys 44 H11
Llangynin Carmth 41 Q7
Llangynllo Cerdgn 42 G6
Llangynog Carmth 28 B2
Llangynog Powys 68 E9
Llangynwyd Brdgnd 29 N7
Llanhamlach Powys 44 F9
Llanharan Rhondd 30 D8
Llanharry Rhondd 30 D8
Llanhennock Mons 31 L6
Llanhilleth Blae G 30 H4
Llanidan IoA 78 H11
Llanidloes Powys 55 M8
Llaniestyn Gwynd 66 D8
Llanigon Powys 45 J7
Llanilar Cerdgn 54 E9
Llanilid Rhondd 30 C8
Llanina Cerdgn 42 H3
Llanio Cerdgn 43 M3
Llanishen Cardif 30 G8
Llanishen Mons 31 N4
Llanllechid Gwynd 79 L11
Llanllowell Mons 31 L5
Llanllugan Powys 55 P4
Llanllwch Carmth 42 G11
Llanllwchaiarn Powys 56 Q6
Llanllwni Carmth 43 J7
Llanllyfni Gwynd 66 H4
Llanmadoc Swans 28 D6
Llanmaes V Glam 30 C11
Llanmartin Newpt 31 L7
Llanmerewig Powys 56 B6
Llanmihangel V Glam 30 C10
Llanmiloe Carmth 41 P9
Llanmorlais Swans 28 F6
Llannefydd Conwy 80 D10
Llannon Carmth 28 F3
Llannor Gwynd 66 F7
Llanon Cerdgn 54 C11
Llanover Mons 31 K3
Llanpumsaint Carmth 42 H9
Llanrhaeadr-ym-Mochnant Powys 68 F9
Llanrhian Pembks 40 F4
Llanrhidian Swans 28 E6
Llanrhos Conwy 79 P8
Llanrhychwyn Conwy 67 P2
Llanrhyddlad IoA 78 E7
Llanrhystud Cerdgn 54 C11
Llanrothal Herefs 45 P11
Llanrug Gwynd 67 J2
Llanrumney Cardif 30 H8
Llanrwst Conwy 67 Q2
Llansadurnen Carmth 41 Q8
Llansadwrn Carmth 43 N8
Llansadwrn IoA 79 K9
Llansaint Carmth 28 C3
Llansamlet Swans 29 J5
Llansanffraid Glan Conwy Conwy 79 Q9
Llansannan Conwy 80 C11
Llansannor V Glam 30 C9
Llansantffraed Powys 44 G10
Llansantffraed-Cwmdeuddwr Powys 55 M11
Llansantffraed-in-Elvel Powys 44 F4
Llansantffraid Cerdgn 54 C11
Llansantffraid-ym-Mechain Powys 68 H10
Llansawel Carmth 43 M7
Llansilin Powys 68 H9
Llansoy Mons 31 M4
Llanspyddid Powys 44 E9
Llanstadwell Pembks 40 H10
Llansteffan Carmth 28 C2
Llanstephan Powys 44 G6
Llantarnam Torfn 31 K6
Llanteg Pembks 41 N8
Llanthewy Skirrid Mons 45 K9
Llanthony Mons 45 K9
Llantilio-Crossenny Mons 31 L2
Llantilio Pertholey Mons 45 L11
Llantood Pembks 41 N2
Llantrisant IoA 78 F8
Llantrisant Mons 31 L5
Llantrisant Rhondd 30 D8
Llantrithyd V Glam 30 D10

Llantwit Fardre Rhondd 30 E7
Llantwit Major V Glam 30 C11
Llantysilio Denbgs 68 G6
Llanuwchllyn Gwynd 68 A8
Llanvaches Newpt 31 M6
Llanvair Discoed Mons 31 M6
Llanvapley Mons 31 L2
Llanvetherine Mons 45 M11
Llanveynoe Herefs 45 L8
Llanvihangel Crucorney Mons 45 L10
Llanvihangel Gobion Mons 31 K3
Llanvihangel-Ystern-Llewern Mons 31 M2
Llanwarne Herefs 45 Q9
Llanwddyn Powys 68 D11
Llanwenarth Mons 31 J2
Llanwenog Cerdgn 43 J5
Llanwern Newpt 31 L7
Llanwinio Carmth 41 Q5
Llanwnda Gwynd 66 H3
Llanwnda Pembks 40 H3
Llanwnnen Cerdgn 43 K5
Llanwnog Powys 55 N6
Llanwonno Rhondd 30 D5
Llanwrda Carmth 43 P8
Llanwrin Powys 54 H4
Llanwrthwl Powys 44 D2
Llanwrtyd Powys 44 B5
Llanwrtyd Wells Powys 44 B5
Llanwyddelan Powys 55 P4
Llanyblodwel Shrops 68 H10
Llanybri Carmth 28 B2
Llanybydder Carmth 43 K6
Llanycefn Pembks 41 L6
Llanychaer Pembks 41 J3
Llanycil Gwynd 68 B8
Llanycrwys Carmth 43 M5
Llanymawddwy Gwynd 68 B11
Llanymynech Powys 69 J10
Llanynghenedl IoA 78 E8
Llanynys Denbgs 68 F2
Llan-y-pwll Wrexhm 69 L4
Llanyre Powys 44 E2
Llanystumdwy Gwynd 66 H7
Llanywern Powys 44 G9
Llawhaden Pembks 41 L7
Llawnt Shrops 68 H8
Llawryglyn Powys 55 L6
Llay Wrexhm 69 K3
Llechcynfarwy IoA 78 F8
Llechfaen Powys 44 F9
Llechrhyd Caerph 30 F3
Llechryd Cerdgn 41 P2
Llechylched IoA 78 E9
Lledrod Cerdgn 54 E10
Lleyn Peninsula Gwynd 66 E7
Llidiardau Gwynd 68 A7
Llidiartnenog Carmth 43 K7
Llidiart-y-parc Denbgs 68 F6
Llithfaen Gwynd 66 F6
Lloc Flints 80 G9
Llowes Powys 44 H6
Llwydcoed Rhondd 30 C4
Llwydiarth Powys 68 D11
Llwyn Denbgs 68 E2
Llwyncelyn Cerdgn 42 H3
Llwyndafydd Cerdgn 42 G3
Llwynderw Powys 56 C4
Llwyn-drain Pembks 41 Q4
Llwyn-du Mons 45 K11
Llwyndyrys Gwynd 66 F6
Llwyngwril Gwynd 54 D3
Llwynhendy Carmth 28 F5
Llwynmawr Wrexhm 68 H7
Llwyn-on Myr Td 30 D2
Llwyn-y-brain Carmth 41 N8
Llwyn-y-groes Cerdgn 43 L3
Llwynypia Rhondd 30 C6
Llynclys Shrops 69 J10
Llynfaes IoA 78 G9
Llyn-y-pandy Flints 81 J11
Llysfaen Conwy 80 B9
Llyswen Cerdgn 43 J2
Llyswen Powys 44 G7
Llysworney V Glam 30 C10
Llys-y-frân Pembks 41 K6
Llywel Powys 44 B8
Load Brook Sheff 84 C3
Loan C Edin 126 H2
Loanend Nthumb 129 N9
Loanhead Mdloth 127 P4
Loaningfoot D & G 109 L9
Loans S Ayrs 125 J11
Lobb Devon 16 H4
Lobhillcross Devon 8 C7
Lochailort Highld 145 N11
Lochaline Highld 138 B9
Lochans D & G 106 E6
Locharbriggs D & G 109 L4
Lochavich Ag & B 131 J4
Lochawe Ag & B 131 N2
Loch Baghasdail W Isls 168 c16
Lochboisdale W Isls 168 c16
Lochbuie Ag & B 137 Q10
Lochcarron Highld 154 A10
Lochdon Ag & B 138 C11
Lochdonhead Ag & B 138 C11
Lochead Ag & B 123 N4
Lochearnhead Stirlg 132 H3
Lochee C Dund 142 F11
Loch Eil Highld 139 K2
Locheilside Station Highld 138 H2
Lochend Highld 155 Q10
Locheport W Isls 168 d11
Loch Euphoirt W Isls 168 d11
Lochfoot D & G 109 J6
Lochgair Ag & B 131 J9
Lochgelly Fife 134 F7
Lochgilphead Ag & B 130 H10
Lochgoilhead Ag & B 131 Q7
Lochieheads Fife 134 H5
Lochill Moray 157 P5
Lochindorb Lodge Highld 156 H10
Lochinver Highld 160 H2
Loch Lomond and The Trossachs National Park 132 E5
Loch Loyal Lodge Highld 165 P7
Lochluichart Highld 155 K5
Lochmaben D & G 109 N4
Lochmaddy W Isls 168 e11
Loch nam Madadh W Isls 168 e11
Loch Ness Highld 147 N2
Lochore Fife 134 F8
Loch Portain W Isls 168 e10

Lochportain W Isls 168 e10
Lochranza N Ayrs 124 A7
Loch Sgioport W Isls 168 d14
Lochside Abers 143 N5
Lochside D & G 109 L5
Lochside Highld 156 E7
Lochskipport W Isls 168 d14
Lochslin Highld 163 J10
Lochty Angus 143 J5
Lochty Fife 135 N6
Lochuisge Highld 138 D6
Lochwinnoch Rens 125 K6
Lochwood D & G 116 F11
Lockengate Cnwll 4 G9
Lockerbie D & G 109 P4
Lockeridge Wilts 33 M11
Lockerley Hants 22 B9
Locking N Som 19 L3
Locking Stumps Warrtn 82 D6
Lockington E R Yk 99 K11
Lockington Leics 72 D5
Lockleywood Shrops 70 B9
Locksbottom Gt Lon 37 K7
Locksgreen IoW 14 D8
Locks Heath Hants 14 F5
Lockton N York 98 G3
Loddington Leics 73 K10
Loddington Nhants 60 H5
Loddiswell Devon 7 J9
Loddon Norfk 65 M2
Lode Cambs 62 H8
Lode Heath Solhll 59 J8
Loders Dorset 11 K6
Lodsworth W Susx 23 P10
Lofthouse Leeds 91 J5
Lofthouse N York 96 H6
Lofthouse Gate Wakefd 91 J6
Loftus R & Cl 105 K7
Logan E Ayrs 115 L3
Loganbeck Cumb 94 D2
Loganlea W Loth 126 H5
Loggerheads Staffs 70 C7
Logie Angus 143 M5
Logie Fife 135 L3
Logie Moray 157 J7
Logie Coldstone Abers 150 C7
Logie Newton Abers 158 G10
Logie Pert Angus 143 M5
Logierait P & K 141 N7
Logierieve Abers 151 N2
Login Carmth 41 N6
Lolworth Cambs 62 E8
Lonbain Highld 153 M7
Londesborough E R Yk 98 H11
London Gt Lon 36 H4
London Apprentice Cnwll 3 Q4
London Beach Kent 26 E4
London City Airport Gt Lon 37 K4
London Colney Herts 50 E10
Londonderry N York 97 M3
London End Nhants 61 K7
London Gateway Services Gt Lon 36 E2
London Gatwick Airport W Susx 24 G2
London Heathrow Airport Gt Lon 36 C5
London Luton Airport Luton 50 D6
London Oxford Airport Oxon 48 E11
London Southend Airport Essex 38 E4
London Stansted Airport Essex 51 N6
Londonthorpe Lincs 73 P3
London Zoo ZSL Gt Lon 36 G4
Londubh Highld 160 D10
Lonemore Highld 153 P2
Long Ashton N Som 31 P10
Long Bank Worcs 57 P10
Long Bennington Lincs 73 L2
Longbenton N Tyne 113 L7
Longborough Gloucs 47 N9
Long Bredy Dorset 11 M6
Longbridge Birm 58 F9
Longbridge Warwks 47 Q2
Longbridge Deverill Wilts 20 G6
Long Buckby Nhants 60 D7
Longburgh Cumb 110 F9
Longburton Dorset 11 N2
Long Cause Devon 7 K6
Long Clawson Leics 73 J5
Longcliffe Derbys 84 B9
Longcombe Devon 7 L7
Long Common Hants 14 F4
Long Compton Staffs 70 F10
Long Compton Warwks 47 Q8
Longcot Oxon 33 Q6
Long Crendon Bucks 35 J3
Long Crichel Dorset 12 G2
Longcroft Cumb 110 D9
Longcross Surrey 35 Q11
Longden Shrops 56 G3
Longden Common Shrops 56 G3
Long Ditton Surrey 36 E7
Longdon Staffs 58 G2
Longdon Worcs 46 F7
Longdon Green Staffs 58 G2
Longdon Heath Worcs 46 F7
Longdon upon Tern Wrekin 69 R11
Longdown Devon 9 L6
Longdowns Cnwll 3 J7
Long Drax N York 92 A5
Long Duckmanton Derbys 84 F6
Long Eaton Derbys 72 D4
Longfield Kent 37 P7
Longford Covtry 59 N8
Longford Derbys 71 N7
Longford Gloucs 46 F10
Longford Gt Lon 36 C5
Longford Kent 37 M9
Longford Shrops 70 A8
Longford Wrekin 70 C11
Longforgan P & K 134 H2
Longformacus Border 128 H8
Longframlington Nthumb 119 M10
Long Green Ches W 81 P10
Long Green Worcs 46 F8
Longham Dorset 13 J5
Longham Norfk 76 C8
Long Hanborough Oxon 34 D2
Longhaven Abers 159 R10
Long Hedges Lincs 87 L11
Longhirst Nthumb 113 K3
Longhope Gloucs 46 C11

Longhope Ork 169 c7
Longhorsley Nthumb 112 H2
Longhoughton Nthumb 119 P7
Long Itchington Warwks 59 P11
Longlands Cumb 101 J3
Longlane Derbys 71 N7
Long Lawford Warwks 59 Q9
Longleat Safari & Adventure Park Wilts 20 F6
Longlevens Gloucs 46 G11
Longley Calder 90 D6
Longley Kirk 90 E9
Longley Green Worcs 46 D4
Longleys P & K 142 D9
Long Load Somset 19 N10
Longmanhill Abers 158 H5
Long Marston Herts 49 N11
Long Marston N York 97 R10
Long Marston Warwks 47 N5
Long Marton Cumb 102 C6
Long Meadowend Shrops 56 G8
Long Melford Suffk 52 E2
Longmoor Camp Hants 23 L8
Longmorn Moray 157 N6
Longmoss Ches E 83 J10
Long Newnton Gloucs 32 H6
Longnewton Border 118 A5
Long Newton E Loth 128 E7
Longnewton S on T 104 C7
Longney Gloucs 32 E2
Longniddry E Loth 128 C4
Longnor Shrops 56 H4
Longnor Staffs 71 K2
Longparish Hants 22 D5
Longpark Cumb 110 H8
Long Preston N York 96 B9
Longridge Lancs 89 J3
Longridge Staffs 70 G11
Longridge W Loth 126 G5
Longriggend N Lans 126 E3
Long Riston E R Yk 93 K2
Longrock Cnwll 2 E7
Longsdon Staffs 70 H4
Longshaw Wigan 82 B4
Longside Abers 159 P8
Long Sight Oldham 89 Q9
Longslow Shrops 70 B7
Longstanton Cambs 62 E7
Longstock Hants 22 C7
Longstone Pembks 41 M9
Longstowe Cambs 62 D10
Long Stratton Norfk 65 H3
Long Street M Keyn 49 L5
Longstreet Wilts 21 M4
Long Sutton Hants 23 K5
Long Sutton Lincs 74 H6
Long Sutton Somset 19 N9
Longthorpe C Pete 74 C11
Long Thurlow Suffk 64 E8
Longthwaite Cumb 101 M6
Longton C Stke 70 G6
Longton Lancs 88 F5
Longtown Cumb 110 G7
Longtown Herefs 45 L9
Longueville Jersey 11 c2
Longville in the Dale Shrops 57 J6
Long Waste Wrekin 69 R11
Long Whatton Leics 72 D6
Longwick Bucks 35 L3
Long Wittenham Oxon 34 F6
Longwitton Nthumb 112 G3
Longwood D & G 108 F8
Longworth Oxon 34 C5
Longyester E Loth 128 E7
Lôn-las Swans 29 K5
Lonmay Abers 159 P6
Lonmore Highld 152 D8
Looe Cnwll 5 M11
Loose Kent 38 C11
Loosebeare Devon 8 H3
Loosegate Lincs 74 F5
Loosley Row Bucks 35 M4
Lootcherbrae Abers 158 F7
Lopcombe Corner Wilts 21 Q7
Lopen Somset 11 J2
Loppington Shrops 69 N9
Lorbottle Nthumb 119 K9
Lordington W Susx 15 L5
Lordsbridge Norfk 75 L8
Lordshill C Sotn 22 C11
Lords Wood Medway 38 C9
Lornty P & K 142 B8
Loscoe Derbys 84 F11
Loscombe Dorset 11 K5
Losgaintir W Isls 168 f8
Lossiemouth Moray 157 N3
Lostford Shrops 69 R8
Lostock Gralam Ches W 82 E10
Lostock Green Ches W 82 E10
Lostock Hall Lancs 88 G5
Lostock Hall Fold Bolton 89 K9
Lostock Junction Bolton 89 K9
Lostwithiel Cnwll 5 J10
Lothbeg Highld 163 L4
Lothersdale N York 96 E11
Lothmore Highld 163 M4
Loudwater Bucks 35 P6
Loughborough Leics 72 E7
Loughor Swans 28 G5
Loughton Essex 51 K11
Loughton M Keyn 49 M7
Loughton Shrops 57 L8
Lound Lincs 73 R7
Lound Notts 85 L3
Lound Suffk 65 Q2
Lounston Devon 9 J9
Lount Leics 72 B7
Louth Lincs 87 K3
Loveclough Lancs 89 N5
Lovedean Hants 15 J4
Lover Wilts 21 P10
Loversall Donc 91 P11
Loves Green Essex 51 P10
Lovesome Hill N York 104 C11
Loveston Pembks 41 L9
Lovington Somset 19 Q8
Low Ackworth Wakefd 91 M7
Low Angerton Nthumb 112 G4
Lowbands Gloucs 46 E8
Low Barbeth D & G 106 D4
Low Barlings Lincs 86 E6
Low Bell End N York 105 K11
Low Bentham N York 95 N7
Low Biggins Cumb 95 N5
Low Borrowbridge Cumb 102 B10

Low Bradfield Sheff 84 C2
Low Bradley N York 96 F11
Low Braithwaite Cumb 101 M2
Low Burnham N Linc 92 C10
Low Buston Nthumb 119 P9
Lowca Cumb 100 C6
Low Catton E R Yk 98 E10
Low Coniscliffe Darltn 103 Q8
Low Crosby Cumb 110 H9
Lowdham Notts 85 L11
Low Dinsdale Darltn 104 B8
Lowe Shrops 69 N8
Lowe Hill Staffs 70 H3
Low Ellington N York 97 K4
Lower Aisholt Somset 18 H7
Lower Ansty Dorset 12 C4
Lower Apperley Gloucs 46 G9
Lower Arboll Highld 163 K10
Lower Arncott Oxon 48 H11
Lower Ashton Devon 9 K8
Lower Assendon Oxon 35 K8
Lower Ballam Lancs 88 D4
Lower Bartle Lancs 88 F4
Lower Basildon W Berk 34 H9
Lower Bearwood Herefs 45 M3
Lower Beeding W Susx 24 F5
Lower Benefield Nhants 61 L3
Lower Bentley Worcs 58 E11
Lower Beobridge Shrops 57 P6
Lower Birchwood Derbys 84 F10
Lower Boddington Nhants 48 E4
Lower Boscaswell Cnwll 2 B7
Lower Bourne Surrey 23 M6
Lower Brailes Warwks 48 B7
Lower Breakish Highld 145 L3
Lower Bredbury Stockp 83 K6
Lower Broadheath Worcs 46 F3
Lower Broxwood Herefs 45 M4
Lower Buckenhill Herefs 46 B8
Lower Bullingham Herefs 45 Q7
Lower Burgate Hants 21 N11
Lower Burrowton Devon 9 P5
Lower Burton Herefs 45 N3
Lower Caldecote C Beds 61 Q11
Lower Cam Gloucs 32 D4
Lower Canada N Som 19 L3
Lower Catesby Nhants 60 B9
Lower Chapel Powys 44 E7
Lower Chicksgrove Wilts 21 J9
Lower Chute Wilts 22 B4
Lower Clapton Gt Lon 36 H3
Lower Clent Worcs 58 D9
Lower Common Hants 23 L2
Lower Compton Wilts 33 K10
Lower Creedy Devon 9 K4
Lower Crossings Derbys 83 M8
Lower Cumberworth Kirk 90 G9
Lower Darwen Bl w D 89 K5
Lower Dean Bed 61 N7
Lower Denby Kirk 90 G9
Lower Diabaig Highld 153 P5
Lower Dicker E Susx 25 N8
Lower Dinchope Shrops 56 H8
Lower Down Shrops 56 E8
Lower Dunsforth N York 97 P8
Lower Egleton Herefs 46 B5
Lower Elkstone Staffs 71 K3
Lower Ellastone Staffs 71 L6
Lower End Bucks 35 J3
Lower End M Keyn 49 P7
Lower End Nhants 61 H9
Lower End Nhants 61 J8
Lower Everleigh Wilts 21 N4
Lower Exbury Hants 14 D7
Lower Eythorne Kent 27 N2
Lower Failand N Som 31 N10
Lower Farringdon Hants 23 K7
Lower Feltham Gt Lon 36 C6
Lower Fittleworth W Susx 24 B7
Lower Foxdale IoM 80 c6
Lower Frankton Shrops 69 L8
Lower Freystrop Pembks 41 J8
Lower Froyle Hants 23 L4
Lower Gabwell Devon 7 N5
Lower Gledfield Highld 162 E6
Lower Godney Somset 19 N6
Lower Gornal Dudley 58 D6
Lower Gravenhurst C Beds 50 D3
Lower Green Herts 50 E4
Lower Green Herts 51 K4
Lower Green Kent 25 N2
Lower Green Kent 25 P2
Lower Green Norfk 76 D4
Lower Green Staffs 58 D3
Lower Green Suffk 63 M7
Lower Hacheston Suffk 65 L10
Lower Halstock Leigh Dorset 11 L3
Lower Halstow Kent 38 E8
Lower Hamworthy BCP 12 G6
Lower Hardres Kent 39 L11
Lower Harpton Herefs 45 K2
Lower Hartlip Kent 38 D9
Lower Hartshay Derbys 84 E10
Lower Hartwell Bucks 35 L2
Lower Hatton Staffs 70 E7
Lower Hawthwaite Cumb 94 E3
Lower Haysden Kent 37 N11
Lower Hergest Herefs 45 K3
Lower Heyford Oxon 48 E10
Lower Heysham Lancs 95 J8
Lower Higham Kent 38 B7
Lower Holbrook Suffk 53 L4
Lower Hordley Shrops 69 L9
Lower Horncroft W Susx 24 B7
Lowerhouse Lancs 89 N4
Lower Houses Kirk 90 F7
Lower Howsell Worcs 46 E5
Lower Irlam Salfd 82 F6
Lower Kilburn Derbys 72 B2
Lower Kilcot Gloucs 32 E7
Lower Killeyan Ag & B 122 C11
Lower Kingscombe Dorset 11 M5
Lower Kingswood Surrey 36 F10
Lower Kinnerton Ches W 69 K2
Lower Langford N Som 19 N2
Lower Largo Fife 135 L7
Lower Leigh Staffs 71 J7
Lower Lemington Gloucs 47 P8
Lower Llanfadog Powys 44 M11
Lower Lovacott Devon 17 J6
Lower Loxhore Devon 17 L4
Lower Lydbrook Gloucs 46 A11
Lower Lye Herefs 56 G11
Lower Machen Newpt 30 H7

Lower Maes-coed Herefs 45 L8
Lower Mannington Dorset 13 J4
Lower Marston Somset 20 E6
Lower Meend Gloucs 31 Q4
Lower Merridge Somset 18 H8
Lower Middleton Cheney Nhants 48 F6
Lower Milton Somset 19 P5
Lower Moor Worcs 47 J5
Lower Morton S Glos 32 B6
Lower Nazeing Essex 51 J9
Lower Norton Warwks 47 P2
Lower Nyland Dorset 20 E10
Lower Oddington Gloucs 47 P9
Lower Penarth V Glam 30 G11
Lower Penn Staffs 58 C5
Lower Pennington Hants 13 P6
Lower Penwortham Lancs 88 G5
Lower Peover Ches E 82 F10
Lower Place Rochdl 89 Q8
Lower Pollicott Bucks 35 K2
Lower Quinton Warwks 47 N5
Lower Rainham Medway 38 D8
Lower Raydon Suffk 52 H4
Lower Roadwater Somset 18 D7
Lower Salter Lancs 95 N8
Lower Seagry Wilts 33 J8
Lower Sheering Essex 51 L8
Lower Shelton C Beds 49 Q6
Lower Shiplake Oxon 35 L9
Lower Shuckburgh Warwks 48 E2
Lower Slaughter Gloucs 47 N10
Lower Soothill Kirk 90 H6
Lower Soudley Gloucs 32 C3
Lower Standen Kent 27 M3
Lower Stanton St Quintin Wilts 32 H8
Lower Stoke Medway 38 D6
Lower Stondon C Beds 50 E3
Lower Stone Gloucs 32 C6
Lower Stonnall Staffs 58 G4
Lower Stow Bedon Norfk 64 D3
Lower Street Dorset 12 D5
Lower Street E Susx 26 B9
Lower Street Norfk 77 K4
Lower Street Suffk 63 N10
Lower Street Suffk 64 G11
Lower Stretton Warrtn 82 D8
Lower Stroud Dorset 11 K5
Lower Sundon C Beds 50 C5
Lower Swanwick Hants 14 E5
Lower Swell Gloucs 47 N9
Lower Tadmarton Oxon 48 D7
Lower Tale Devon 9 Q4
Lower Tasburgh Norfk 64 H2
Lower Tean Staffs 71 J7
Lower Thurlton Norfk 65 N2
Lower Town Cnwll 2 H8
Lower Town Devon 7 J4
Lower Town Herefs 46 B6
Lower Town IoS 2 b2
Lower Town Pembks 41 J3
Lower Trebullett Cnwll 5 N6
Lower Treluswell Cnwll 3 K6
Lower Tysoe Warwks 48 B5
Lower Ufford Suffk 65 K11
Lower Upcott Devon 9 L8
Lower Upham Hants 22 F11
Lower Upnor Medway 38 C7
Lower Vexford Somset 18 F7
Lower Walton Warrtn 82 D7
Lower Waterston Dorset 12 B5
Lower Weare Somset 19 M4
Lower Weedon Nhants 60 D9
Lower Welson Herefs 45 K4
Lower Westmancote Worcs 46 H7
Lower Whatcombe Dorset 12 D4
Lower Whatley Somset 20 D5
Lower Whitley Ches W 82 D8
Lower Wick Gloucs 32 D5
Lower Wick Worcs 46 F4
Lower Wield Hants 22 H6
Lower Willingdon E Susx 25 N10
Lower Withington Ches E 82 H11
Lower Woodend Bucks 35 M7
Lower Woodford Wilts 21 M7
Lower Wraxhall Dorset 11 M4
Lower Wyche Worcs 46 E6
Lower Wyke C Brad 90 F5
Lowesby Leics 73 J9
Lowestoft Suffk 65 Q3
Loweswater Cumb 100 F6
Low Fell Gatesd 113 L9
Lowfield Heath W Susx 24 G3
Low Gartachorrans Stirlg 132 F10
Low Gate Nthumb 112 D8
Low Gettbridge Cumb 111 K9
Lowgill Cumb 102 B11
Lowgill Lancs 95 P8
Low Grantley N York 97 K6
Low Green N York 97 K9
Low Habberley Worcs 57 Q9
Low Ham Somset 19 M9
Low Harrogate N York 97 L9
Low Hawsker N York 105 P9
Low Hesket Cumb 111 J11
Low Hutton N York 98 F7
Lowick Cumb 94 F3
Lowick Nhants 61 L4
Lowick Nthumb 119 K3
Lowick Bridge Cumb 94 F3
Lowick Green Cumb 94 F3
Low Knipe Cumb 101 P7
Low Laithe N York 97 J8
Lowlands Dur 103 M5
Lowlands Torfn 31 J5
Low Langton Lincs 86 G5
Low Leighton Derbys 83 M7
Low Lorton Cumb 100 G5
Low Marishes N York 98 G5
Low Marnham Notts 85 P7
Low Middleton Nthumb 119 M3
Low Mill N York 105 J11
Low Moor C Brad 90 F5
Low Moorsley Sundld 113 M11
Low Moresby Cumb 100 C5
Low Newton Cumb 95 J4
Low Newton-by-the-Sea Nthumb 119 P6
Low Pittington Dur 104 B2
Low Row Cumb 100 G2
Low Row Cumb 101 L3
Low Row Cumb 111 L8
Low Row N York 103 J11
Low Salchrie D & G 106 D4
Low Santon N Linc 92 F8

Lowsonford Warwks 59 J11
Low Street Norfk 77 L7
Low Street Thurr 22 Q5
Low Tharston Norfk 64 H2
Lowther Cumb 101 P6
Lowthorpe E R Yk 99 M8
Lowton Devon 8 G4
Lowton Somset 18 G11
Lowton Wigan 82 D5
Lowton Common Wigan 82 D5
Lowton St Mary's Wigan 82 D5
Low Torry Fife 134 C10
Low Toynton Lincs 87 J6
Low Valley Barns 91 L10
Low Wood Cumb 94 G4
Low Worsall N York 104 C9
Low Wray Cumb 101 L10
Loxbeare Devon 18 B11
Loxhill Surrey 24 B3
Loxhore Devon 17 L4
Loxhore Cott Devon 17 L4
Loxley Warwks 47 Q4
Loxley Green Staffs 71 K8
Loxter Herefs 46 D6
Loxton N Som 19 L3
Loxwood W Susx 24 B4
Lubenham Leics 60 F3
Lucasgate Lincs 87 M11
Lucas Green Surrey 23 P2
Luccombe Somset 18 B6
Luccombe Village IoW 14 G11
Lucker Nthumb 119 N4
Luckett Cnwll 5 P7
Lucking Street Essex 52 D5
Luckington Wilts 32 F8
Lucklawhill Fife 135 L3
Lucknam Wilts 32 F10
Luckwell Bridge Somset 18 B7
Lucton Herefs 45 N2
Lucy Cross N York 103 P8
Ludag W Isls 168 c16
Ludborough Lincs 93 N11
Ludbrook Devon 6 H8
Ludchurch Pembks 41 M8
Luddenden Calder 90 C5
Luddenden Foot Calder 90 C5
Luddenham Court Kent 38 G9
Luddesdown Kent 37 Q7
Luddington N Linc 92 D7
Luddington Warwks 47 N4
Luddington in the Brook Nhants 61 P4
Ludford Lincs 86 G3
Ludford Shrops 57 J10
Ludgershall Bucks 49 J11
Ludgershall Wilts 21 Q4
Ludgvan Cnwll 2 E7
Ludham Norfk 77 M8
Ludlow Shrops 57 J9
Ludney Somset 10 H2
Ludwell Wilts 20 H10
Ludworth Dur 104 C2
Luffenhall Herts 50 D5
Luffincott Devon 5 N3
Luffness E Loth 128 D4
Lugar E Ayrs 115 L3
Luggate Burn E Loth 128 F5
Lugg Green Herefs 45 N2
Luggiebank N Lans 126 D3
Lugton E Ayrs 125 L7
Lugwardine Herefs 45 R6
Luib Highld 145 J2
Luing Ag & B 130 E5
Lulham Herefs 45 N6
Lullington Derbys 59 K2
Lullington E Susx 25 M10
Lullington Somset 20 E4
Lulsgate Bottom N Som 31 P11
Lulsley Worcs 46 D3
Lulworth Camp Dorset 12 D8
Lumb Calder 90 C6
Lumb Lancs 89 N6
Lumbutts Calder 90 B6
Lumby N York 91 M4
Lumphanan Abers 150 F7
Lumphinnans Fife 134 F9
Lumsden Abers 150 D3
Lunan Angus 143 M7
Lunanhead Angus 142 H7
Luncarty P & K 134 D2
Lund E R Yk 99 K11
Lund N York 91 R4
Lundie Angus 142 D10
Lundin Links Fife 135 L7
Lundin Mill Fife 135 L7
Lundy Devon 16 A2
Lundy Green Norfk 65 J3
Lunga Ag & B 130 E6
Lunna Shet 169 r7
Lunsford Kent 37 Q9
Lunsford's Cross E Susx 26 B9
Lunt Sefton 81 L4
Luntley Herefs 45 M3
Luppitt Devon 10 D3
Lupridge Devon 7 J8
Lupset Wakefd 91 J7
Lupton Cumb 95 M4
Lurgashall W Susx 23 P9
Lurley Devon 18 B11
Lusby Lincs 87 K7
Luscombe Devon 7 K7
Luskentyre W Isls 168 f8
Luson Devon 6 G8
Luss Ag & B 132 D9
Lussagiven Ag & B 130 C10
Lusta Highld 152 D6
Lustleigh Devon 9 J8
Luston Herefs 45 P2
Luthermuir Abers 143 N4
Luthrie Fife 135 J4
Lutley Dudley 58 D8
Luton Devon 9 M9
Luton Devon 10 B4
Luton Luton 50 C6
Luton Medway 38 C8
Luton Airport Luton 50 D6
Lutterworth Leics 60 B4
Lutton Devon 6 F7
Lutton Devon 6 H6
Lutton Lincs 74 H5
Lutton Nhants 61 P3
Luxborough Somset 18 C7
Luxulyan Cnwll 4 H10
Luxulyan Valley Cnwll 4 H10
Luzley Tamesd 83 L4
Lybster Highld 167 M9

Lydbury North Shrops 56 E7
Lydcott Devon 17 M4
Lydd Kent 26 H7
Lydd Airport Kent 27 J7
Lydden Kent 27 N2
Lydden Kent 39 Q8
Lyddington Rutlnd 73 M11
Lydd-on-Sea Kent 27 J8
Lydeard St Lawrence Somset 18 F8
Lyde Green Hants 23 K3
Lydford Devon 8 D7
Lydford on Fosse Somset 19 Q8
Lydgate Calder 89 Q5
Lydgate Rochdl 90 B7
Lydham Shrops 56 E6
Lydiard Green Wilts 33 L7
Lydiard Millicent Wilts 33 L7
Lydiard Tregoze Swindn 33 M8
Lydiate Sefton 81 M4
Lydiate Ash Worcs 58 E9
Lydlinch Dorset 12 B2
Lydney Gloucs 32 B4
Lydstep Pembks 41 L11
Lye Dudley 58 D8
Lye Cross N Som 19 N2
Lye Green Bucks 35 Q4
Lye Green E Susx 25 M4
Lye Green Warwks 59 J11
Lye Head Worcs 57 P10
Lye's Green Wilts 20 F5
Lyford Oxon 34 C6
Lymbridge Green Kent 27 K3
Lyme Regis Dorset 10 G6
Lyminge Kent 27 L3
Lymington Hants 13 P5
Lyminster W Susx 24 B10
Lymm Warrtn 82 E7
Lymm Services Warrtn 82 E8
Lympne Kent 27 K4
Lympsham Somset 19 K4
Lympstone Devon 9 N8
Lynbridge Devon 17 N2
Lynchat Highld 148 D7
Lynch Green Norfk 76 H10
Lyndhurst Hants 13 P3
Lyndon Rutlnd 73 N10
Lyndon Green Birm 58 H7
Lyne Border 117 J2
Lyne Surrey 36 B7
Lyneal Shrops 69 M8
Lyne Down Herefs 46 B8
Lyneham Devon 9 L9
Lyneham Oxon 47 Q10
Lyneham Wilts 33 K9
Lyneholmford Cumb 111 K6
Lynemouth Nthumb 113 L2
Lyne of Skene Abers 151 K5
Lynesack Dur 103 L5
Lyness Ork 169 c7
Lyng Norfk 76 F8
Lyng Somset 19 K9
Lynmouth Devon 17 N2
Lynn Staffs 58 G4
Lynn Wrekin 70 D11
Lynsted Kent 38 F9
Lynstone Cnwll 16 C10
Lynton Devon 17 N2
Lynton Cross Devon 17 J3
Lyon's Gate Dorset 11 P3
Lyonshall Herefs 45 L3
Lytchett Matravers Dorset 12 F5
Lytchett Minster Dorset 12 G6
Lyth Highld 167 N4
Lytham Lancs 88 D5
Lytham St Annes Lancs 88 C5
Lythbank Shrops 56 H3
Lythe N York 105 M8
Lythmore Highld 167 J3

M

Maaruig W Isls 168 h7
Mabe Burnthouse Cnwll 3 K7
Mablethorpe Lincs 87 P4
Macclesfield Ches E 83 K10
Macduff Abers 158 H5
Macharioch Ag & B 120 D10
Machen Caerph 30 H7
Machrie Ag & B 120 G5
Machrie Ag & B 136 b3
Machrihanish Ag & B 120 B7
Machrins Ag & B 136 b3
Machroes Gwynd 66 E9
Machynlleth Powys 54 G4
Machynys Carmth 28 F5
Mackworth Derbys 71 Q7
Macmerry E Loth 128 C5
Maddaford Devon 8 D6
Madderty P & K 134 B3
Maddington Wilts 21 L6
Maddiston Falk 126 G2
Madehurst W Susx 15 Q4
Madeley Staffs 70 D6
Madeley Wrekin 57 M4
Madeley Heath Staffs 70 D5
Madeley Park Wood Staffs 70 D6
Madford Devon 10 C2
Madingley Cambs 62 E8
Madley Herefs 45 N7
Madresfield Worcs 46 F5
Madron Cnwll 2 D7
Maenaddwyn IoA 78 H8
Maenan Conwy 79 P11
Maenclochog Pembks 41 L5
Maendy V Glam 30 D9
Maenporth Cnwll 3 K8
Maentwrog Gwynd 67 M6
Maen-y-groes Cerdgn 42 G3
Maer Cnwll 16 C10
Maer Staffs 70 D7
Maerdy Carmth 43 N9
Maerdy Conwy 68 D6
Maerdy Rhondd 30 C5
Maesbrook Shrops 69 K10
Maesbury Shrops 69 K9
Maesbury Marsh Shrops 69 K9
Maes-glas Newpt 31 J7
Maesgwynne Carmth 41 P4
Maeshafn Denbgs 68 H2
Maesllyn Cerdgn 42 G6
Maesmynis Powys 44 E5
Maesmynis Powys 44 E5
Maesteg Brdgnd 29 N6
Maesybont Carmth 43 L11

Maesycwmmer Caerph 30 G6
Magdalen Laver Essex 51 M9
Maggieknockater Moray 157 Q8
Maggots End Essex 51 L5
Magham Down E Susx 25 P8
Maghull Sefton 81 M4
Magna Park Leics 60 B4
Magor Mons 31 N7
Magor Services Mons 31 M7
Maidenbower W Susx 24 G3
Maiden Bradley Wilts 20 F7
Maidencombe Torbay 7 N5
Maidenhayne Devon 10 F5
Maiden Head N Som 31 Q11
Maidenhead W & M 35 N8
Maiden Law Dur 113 J11
Maiden Newton Dorset 11 M5
Maidens S Ayrs 114 D6
Maiden's Green Br For 35 P10
Maidenwell Lincs 87 K5
Maiden Wells Pembks 41 J11
Maidford Nhants 48 H4
Maids Moreton Bucks 49 K7
Maidstone Kent 38 C10
Maidstone Services Kent 38 D10
Maidwell Nhants 60 F5
Mail Shet 169 r9
Maindee Newpt 31 K7
Mainland Ork 169 d6
Mainland Shet 169 r8
Mainsforth Dur 104 B4
Mains of Balhall Angus 143 J5
Mains of Balnakettle Abers 143 L3
Mains of Dalvey Highld 157 L11
Mains of Haulkerton Abers 143 N3
Mains of Lesmoir Abers 150 D2
Mains of Melgunds Angus 143 J6
Mainsriddle D & G 109 K9
Mainstone Shrops 56 D7
Maisemore Gloucs 46 F10
Major's Green Worcs 58 H9
Makeney Derbys 72 B2
Malborough Devon 7 J11
Malcoff Derbys 83 N8
Malden Rushett Gt Lon 36 E8
Maldon Essex 52 E10
Malham N York 96 D8
Maligar Highld 152 H5
Mallaig Highld 145 L8
Mallaigvaig Highld 145 L8
Malleny Mills C Edin 127 M4
Mallows Green Essex 51 L5
Malltraeth IoA 78 G11
Mallwyd Gwynd 55 K2
Malmesbury Wilts 32 H7
Malmsmead Devon 17 P2
Malpas Ches W 69 N5
Malpas Cnwll 3 L5
Malpas Newpt 31 K6
Malshanger Hants 22 G4
Malswick Gloucs 46 D10
Maltby Lincs 87 K4
Maltby Rothm 84 H2
Maltby S on T 104 C8
Maltby le Marsh Lincs 87 N4
Malting Green Essex 52 G7
Maltman's Hill Kent 26 F3
Malton N York 98 F6
Malvern Worcs 46 E5
Malvern Hills 46 E5
Malvern Link Worcs 46 E5
Malvern Wells Worcs 46 E6
Mamble Worcs 57 M10
Mamhilad Mons 31 K4
Manaccan Cnwll 3 K9
Manafon Powys 55 Q4
Mànais W Isls 168 g9
Manaton Devon 9 J8
Manby Lincs 87 L3
Mancetter Warwks 59 M5
Manchester Manch 82 H5
Manchester Airport Manch 82 H8
Mancot Flints 81 L11
Mandally Highld 146 H7
Manea Cambs 62 G3
Maney Birm 58 H5
Manfield N York 103 P8
Mangersta W Isls 168 f4
Mangerton Dorset 11 K5
Mangotsfield S Glos 32 C9
Mangrove Green Herts 50 D6
Mangurstadh W Isls 168 f4
Manhay Cnwll 2 H7
Manish W Isls 168 g9
Mankinholes Calder 90 B6
Manley Ches W 81 Q10
Manmoel Caerph 30 G4
Mannal Ag & B 136 B7
Manningford Bohune Wilts 21 M3
Manningford Bruce Wilts 21 M3
Manningham C Brad 90 E3
Mannings Heath W Susx 24 F5
Mannington Dorset 13 J3
Manningtree Essex 53 K5
Mannofield C Aber 151 N7
Manorbier Pembks 41 L11
Manorbier Newton Pembks 41 K10
Manordeilo Carmth 43 N9
Manorhill Border 118 C4
Manorowen Pembks 40 H3
Manor Park Gt Lon 37 K3
Mansell Gamage Herefs 45 M6
Mansell Lacy Herefs 45 N5
Mansergh Cumb 95 N4
Mansfield E Ayrs 115 M5
Mansfield Notts 84 H8
Mansfield Woodhouse Notts 84 H8
Mansriggs Cumb 94 F4
Manston Dorset 20 F11
Manston Kent 39 P8
Manston Leeds 91 K4
Manswood Dorset 12 G3
Manthorpe Lincs 73 N3
Manthorpe Lincs 73 R7
Manton N Linc 92 F10
Manton Notts 85 K5
Manton Rutlnd 73 M10
Manton Wilts 33 N11
Manuden Essex 51 L5
Maperton Somset 20 C9
Maplebeck Notts 85 M8
Maple Cross Herts 36 B2
Mapledurham Oxon 35 J9
Mapledurwell Hants 23 J4
Maplehurst W Susx 24 E6

Maplescombe Kent 37 N8
Mapleton Derbys 71 M5
Mapleton Kent 37 L11
Mapperley Derbys 72 C2
Mapperley Park C Nott 72 F2
Mapperton Dorset 11 L5
Mappleborough Green Warwks 58 G11
Mappleton E R Yk 93 M2
Mapplewell Barns 91 J8
Mappowder Dorset 12 B3
Màraig W Isls 168 h7
Marazanvose Cnwll 3 K3
Marazion Cnwll 2 E7
Marbhig W Isls 168 j6
Marbury Ches W 69 Q5
March S Lans 116 D8
March Cambs 74 H11
Marcham Oxon 34 E5
Marchamley Shrops 69 Q9
Marchamley Wood Shrops 69 Q8
Marchington Staffs 71 L8
Marchington Woodlands Staffs 71 L9
Marchwiel Wrexhm 69 L5
Marchwood Hants 14 C4
Marcross V Glam 29 P11
Marden Herefs 45 Q5
Marden Kent 26 B3
Marden Wilts 21 L3
Marden Ash Essex 51 N10
Marden Beech Kent 26 B3
Marden's Hill E Susx 25 M4
Marden Thorn Kent 26 C3
Mardlebury Herts 50 G7
Mardy Mons 45 L11
Marefield Leics 73 J9
Mareham le Fen Lincs 87 J8
Mareham on the Hill Lincs 87 J7
Marehay Derbys 84 E11
Marehill W Susx 24 C7
Maresfield E Susx 25 L6
Marfleet C KuH 93 K5
Marford Wrexhm 69 L3
Margam Neath 29 L7
Margaret Marsh Dorset 20 F11
Margaret Roding Essex 51 N8
Margaretting Essex 51 Q10
Margaretting Tye Essex 51 Q10
Margate Kent 39 Q7
Margnaheglish N Ayrs 121 K5
Margrie D & G 108 C10
Margrove Park R & Cl 105 J7
Marham Norfk 75 P9
Marhamchurch Cnwll 16 C11
Marholm C Pete 74 B10
Marian-glas IoA 79 J8
Mariansleigh Devon 17 N7
Marine Town Kent 38 F7
Marionburgh Abers 151 J6
Marishader Highld 152 H5
Maristow Devon 6 D6
Marjoriebanks D & G 109 N4
Mark Somset 19 L5
Markbeech Kent 25 L2
Markby Lincs 87 N5
Mark Causeway Somset 19 L5
Mark Cross E Susx 25 N4
Markeaton C Derb 72 A3
Market Bosworth Leics 72 C10
Market Deeping Lincs 74 B8
Market Drayton Shrops 70 B8
Market Harborough Leics 60 F3
Market Lavington Wilts 21 K4
Market Overton Rutlnd 73 M7
Market Rasen Lincs 86 F3
Market Stainton Lincs 86 H5
Market Warsop Notts 85 J7
Market Weighton E R Yk 92 E2
Market Weston Suffk 64 D6
Markfield Leics 72 D9
Markham Caerph 30 G4
Markham Moor Notts 85 M6
Markinch Fife 134 H7
Markington N York 97 L7
Marksbury BaNES 20 C2
Mark's Corner IoW 14 E8
Marks Tey Essex 52 F7
Markwell Cnwll 5 P10
Markyate Herts 50 C7
Marlborough Wilts 33 N11
Marlbrook Herefs 45 Q4
Marlbrook Worcs 58 E10
Marlcliff Warwks 47 L4
Marldon Devon 7 M6
Marle Green E Susx 25 N7
Marlesford Suffk 65 L10
Marley Kent 39 L11
Marley Kent 39 P11
Marley Green Ches E 69 Q5
Marley Hill Gatesd 113 K9
Marlingford Norfk 76 G10
Marloes Pembks 40 E9
Marlow Bucks 35 M7
Marlow Herefs 56 G9
Marlow Bottom Bucks 35 M7
Marlpit Hill Kent 37 K11
Marlpits E Susx 25 L5
Marlpits E Susx 26 B9
Marlpool Derbys 84 F11
Marnhull Dorset 20 E11
Marple Stockp 83 L7
Marple Bridge Stockp 83 L7
Marr Donc 91 N9
Marrick N York 103 L11
Marros Carmth 41 P9
Marsden Kirk 90 C8
Marsden S Tyne 113 N8
Marsden Height Lancs 89 P3
Marsett N York 96 D3
Marsh Bucks 35 M3
Marsh C Brad 90 C3
Marsh Devon 10 F2
Marshall's Heath Herts 50 E8
Marshalswick Herts 50 E9
Marsham Norfk 76 H7
Marsh Baldon Oxon 34 G5
Marsh Benham W Berk 34 D11
Marshborough Kent 39 P10
Marshbrook Shrops 56 G7
Marshchapel Lincs 93 Q11
Marsh Farm Luton 50 C5
Marshfield Newpt 31 J8
Marshfield S Glos 32 E10
Marshgate Cnwll 5 K3

Marsh Gibbon Bucks 48 H10
Marsh Green Devon 9 P6
Marsh Green Kent 25 K2
Marsh Green Wrekin 57 L2
Marsh Lane Derbys 84 F5
Marsh Lane Gloucs 31 Q3
Marshside Sefton 88 D7
Marsh Street Somset 18 C6
Marshwood Dorset 10 H5
Marske N York 103 M10
Marske-by-the-Sea R & Cl 104 H6
Marsland Green Wigan 82 E9
Marston Ches W 82 E9
Marston Herefs 45 M3
Marston Lincs 73 M2
Marston Oxon 34 F3
Marston Staffs 58 B2
Marston Staffs 70 G9
Marston Warwks 59 K6
Marston Wilts 21 J3
Marston Green Solhll 59 J7
Marston Jabbet Warwks 59 N7
Marston Magna Somset 19 Q10
Marston Meysey Wilts 33 M5
Marston Montgomery Derbys 71 L7
Marston Moretaine C Beds 49 Q6
Marston on Dove Derbys 71 N9
Marston St Lawrence Nhants 48 F6
Marston Stannett Herefs 45 R3
Marston Trussell Nhants 60 E3
Marstow Herefs 45 R11
Marsworth Bucks 35 P2
Marten Wilts 21 Q2
Marthall Ches E 82 G9
Martham Norfk 77 P8
Martin Hants 21 L11
Martin Kent 27 P2
Martin Lincs 86 F9
Martin Lincs 86 H7
Martindale Cumb 101 M7
Martin Dales Lincs 86 G8
Martin Drove End Hants 21 L10
Martinhoe Devon 17 M2
Martin Hussingtree Worcs 46 G2
Martinscroft Warrtn 82 E7
Martinstown Dorset 11 N7
Martlesham Suffk 53 M2
Martlesham Heath Suffk 53 M2
Martletwy Pembks 41 K8
Martley Worcs 46 E2
Martock Somset 19 N11
Marton Ches E 83 J11
Marton Ches W 82 D11
Marton Cumb 94 E5
Marton E R Yk 93 L3
Marton E R Yk 99 Q7
Marton Lincs 85 P4
Marton Middsb 104 F7
Marton N York 97 P8
Marton N York 98 E4
Marton Shrops 56 D4
Marton Warwks 59 P11
Marton-le-Moor N York 97 N6
Martyr's Green Surrey 36 C9
Martyr Worthy Hants 22 F8
Marvig W Isls 168 j6
Marwell Wildlife Hants 22 F10
Marwick Ork 169 b4
Marwood Devon 17 J4
Marybank Highld 155 N7
Maryburgh Highld 155 P6
Marygold Border 129 L8
Maryhill C Glas 125 P4
Marykirk Abers 143 M4
Maryland Mons 31 P3
Marylebone Gt Lon 36 G4
Marylebone Wigan 88 H9
Marypark Moray 157 M10
Maryport Cumb 100 D3
Maryport D & G 106 F11
Marystow Devon 8 B8
Mary Tavy Devon 8 D9
Maryton Angus 143 M6
Marywell Abers 150 F8
Marywell Abers 151 N8
Marywell Angus 143 M9
Masham N York 97 K4
Mashbury Essex 51 Q8
Mason N u Ty 113 K6
Masongill N York 95 P5
Mastin Moor Derbys 84 G5
Matching Essex 51 M8
Matching Green Essex 51 M8
Matching Tye Essex 51 M8
Matfen Nthumb 112 G6
Matfield Kent 25 Q2
Mathern Mons 31 P6
Mathon Herefs 46 D5
Mathry Pembks 40 G4
Matlask Norfk 76 H5
Matlock Derbys 84 D9
Matlock Bank Derbys 84 D8
Matlock Bath Derbys 84 C9
Matlock Dale Derbys 84 C9
Matson Gloucs 46 G11
Matterdale End Cumb 101 L6
Mattersey Notts 85 L3
Mattersey Thorpe Notts 85 L3
Mattingley Hants 23 K3
Mattishall Norfk 76 F9
Mattishall Burgh Norfk 76 F9
Mauchline E Ayrs 115 J2
Maud Abers 159 M8
Maufant Jersey 11 c1
Maugersbury Gloucs 47 P9
Maughold IoM 80 g3
Mauld Highld 155 M10
Maulden C Beds 50 C3
Maulds Meaburn Cumb 102 B7
Maunby N York 97 N3
Maund Bryan Herefs 45 R4
Maundown Somset 18 E9
Mautby Norfk 77 P9
Mavesyn Ridware Staffs 71 K11
Mavis Enderby Lincs 87 L7
Mawbray Cumb 109 N11
Mawdesley Lancs 88 F8
Mawdlam Brdgnd 29 M8
Mawgan Cnwll 3 J8
Mawgan Porth Cnwll 4 D8
Maw Green Ches E 70 C3
Mawla Cnwll 3 J4
Mawnan Cnwll 3 K8

Mawnan Smith Cnwll 3 K8
Mawsley Nhants 60 H5
Mawthorpe Lincs 87 N6
Maxey C Pete 74 B9
Maxstoke Warwks 59 K7
Maxted Street Kent 27 K3
Maxton Border 118 B4
Maxton Kent 27 P3
Maxwelltown D & G 109 L5
Maxworthy Cnwll 5 M3
Mayals Swans 28 H7
May Bank Staffs 70 F5
Maybole S Ayrs 114 E6
Maybury Surrey 36 B9
Mayes Green Surrey 24 D3
Mayfield E Susx 25 N5
Mayfield Mdloth 128 B7
Mayfield Staffs 71 M5
Mayford Surrey 23 Q3
May Hill Gloucs 46 D10
Mayland Essex 52 F11
Maylandsea Essex 52 F11
Maynard's Green E Susx 25 N7
Maypole Birm 58 G9
Maypole Kent 39 M9
Maypole Mons 45 P11
Maypole Green Norfk 65 N2
Maypole Green Suffk 64 C10
Maypole Green Suffk 65 K8
May's Green Oxon 35 K8
May's Green Surrey 36 C9
Mead Devon 16 C8
Meadgate BaNES 20 C3
Meadle Bucks 35 M3
Meadowfield Dur 103 P3
Meadowtown Shrops 56 E4
Meadwell Devon 5 Q5
Meaford Staffs 70 F7
Mealabost W Isls 168 j4
Meal Bank Cumb 101 P11
Mealrigg Cumb 109 P11
Mealsgate Cumb 100 H2
Meanwood Leeds 90 H3
Mearbeck N York 96 B8
Meare Somset 19 N6
Meare Green Somset 19 J10
Meare Green Somset 19 K9
Mearns E Rens 125 N6
Mears Ashby Nhants 60 H7
Measham Leics 72 A8
Meath Green Surrey 24 G2
Meathop Cumb 95 J4
Meaux E R Yk 93 J3
Meavaig W Isls 168 f4
Meavy Devon 6 E5
Medbourne Leics 60 H2
Medburn Nthumb 112 H6
Meddon Devon 16 D8
Meden Vale Notts 85 J7
Medlam Lincs 87 K9
Medlar Lancs 88 E3
Medmenham Bucks 35 M8
Medomsley Dur 112 H10
Medstead Hants 23 J7
Medway Services Medway 38 D9
Meerbrook Staffs 70 H2
Meer Common Herefs 45 M4
Meesden Herts 51 K4
Meeson Wrekin 70 A10
Meeth Devon 17 J10
Meeting Green Suffk 63 M9
Meeting House Hill Norfk 77 L6
Meidrim Carmth 41 Q4
Meifod Powys 56 B2
Meigle P & K 142 D9
Meikle Carco D & G 115 Q5
Meikle Earnock S Lans 126 C7
Meikle Ferry Highld 162 G9
Meikle Kilmory Ag & B 124 D5
Meikle Obney P & K 141 P10
Meikleour P & K 142 B10
Meikle Wartle Abers 158 H11
Meinciau Carmth 28 E2
Meir C Stke 70 G6
Meir Heath Staffs 70 G6
Melbost W Isls 168 j4
Melbourn Cambs 51 J2
Melbourne Derbys 72 B5
Melbourne E R Yk 92 C2
Melbur Cnwll 3 N3
Melbury Devon 16 F8
Melbury Abbas Dorset 20 G10
Melbury Bubb Dorset 11 M3
Melbury Osmond Dorset 11 M3
Melbury Sampford Dorset 11 M3
Melchbourne Bed 61 M7
Melcombe Bingham Dorset 12 C4
Meldon Devon 8 E6
Meldon Nthumb 112 H4
Meldon Park Nthumb 112 H3
Meldreth Cambs 62 E11
Meldrum Stirlg 133 L8
Melfort Ag & B 130 G5
Meliden Denbgs 80 F8
Melinau Pembks 41 N8
Melin-byrhedyn Powys 55 J5
Melincourt Neath 29 M4
Melin-y-coed Conwy 67 Q2
Melin-y-ddol Powys 55 M9
Melin-y-wig Denbgs 68 D5
Melkinthorpe Cumb 101 Q5
Melkridge Nthumb 111 P8
Melksham Wilts 20 H2
Mellangoose Cnwll 2 H8
Mell Green W Berk 34 E9
Mellguards Cumb 110 H11
Melling Lancs 95 M6
Melling Sefton 81 M4
Melling Mount Sefton 81 N4
Mellis Suffk 64 F7
Mellon Charles Highld 160 C8
Mellon Udrigle Highld 160 D7
Mellor Lancs 89 K4
Mellor Stockp 83 L7
Mellor Brook Lancs 89 J4
Mells Somset 20 D5
Mells Suffk 65 N6
Melmerby Cumb 102 B3
Melmerby N York 96 G3
Melmerby N York 97 M5
Melness Highld 165 N4
Melon Green Suffk 64 A10
Melplash Dorset 11 K5
Melrose Border 117 Q4
Melsetter Ork 169 b8
Melsonby N York 103 N9

Meltham Kirk 90 E8
Meltham Mills Kirk 90 E8
Melton E R Yk 92 G5
Melton Suffk 65 K11
Meltonby E R Yk 98 F10
Melton Constable Norfk 76 E5
Melton Mowbray Leics 73 K7
Melton Ross N Linc 93 J8
Melvaig Highld 160 A9
Melverley Shrops 69 K11
Melverley Green Shrops 69 K11
Melvich Highld 166 E4
Membury Devon 10 F4
Membury Services W Berk 34 B9
Memsie Abers 159 N5
Memus Angus 142 G6
Menabilly Cnwll 4 H11
Menagissey Cnwll 3 J4
Menai Bridge IoA 79 K10
Mendham Suffk 65 K5
Mendip Hills 19 P4
Mendlesham Suffk 64 G8
Mendlesham Green Suffk 64 G9
Menheniot Cnwll 5 M9
Menithwood Worcs 57 N11
Menna Cnwll 3 N3
Mennock D & G 115 R6
Menston C Brad 90 F2
Menstrie Clacks 133 P8
Menthorpe N York 92 B4
Mentmore Bucks 49 P11
Meoble Highld 145 N10
Meole Brace Shrops 56 H2
Meonstoke Hants 22 H11
Meon Vale Warwks 47 N5
Meopham Kent 37 P7
Meopham Green Kent 37 P7
Meopham Station Kent 37 P7
Mepal Cambs 62 F4
Meppershall C Beds 50 D3
Merbach Herefs 45 L5
Mere Ches E 82 F8
Mere Wilts 20 F8
Mere Brow Lancs 88 E7
Mereclough Lancs 89 P4
Mere Green Birm 58 H5
Mere Green Worcs 47 J2
Mere Heath Ches W 82 E10
Meresborough Medway 38 D9
Mereworth Kent 37 Q10
Meriden Solhll 59 K8
Merkadale Highld 152 F11
Merley BCP 12 H5
Merlin's Bridge Pembks 40 H8
Merrington Shrops 69 N10
Merrion Pembks 40 H11
Merriott Somset 11 J2
Merrivale Devon 8 D9
Merrow Surrey 36 B10
Merry Field Hill Dorset 12 H4
Merry Hill Herts 36 D2
Merryhill Wolves 58 C5
Merry Lees Leics 72 D9
Merrymeet Cnwll 5 M8
Mersea Island Essex 52 H8
Mersey Crossing Halton 81 Q8
Mersham Kent 27 J3
Merstham Surrey 36 G10
Merston W Susx 15 N6
Merstone IoW 14 F9
Merther Cnwll 3 M5
Merthyr Carmth 42 G10
Merthyr Cynog Powys 44 D7
Merthyr Dyfan V Glam 30 F11
Merthyr Mawr Brdgnd 29 N8
Merthyr Tydfil Myr Td 30 D3
Merthyr Vale Myr Td 30 E5
Merton Devon 17 J9
Merton Gt Lon 36 G6
Merton Norfk 64 C2
Merton Oxon 48 G11
Meshaw Devon 17 P8
Messing Essex 52 E8
Messingham N Linc 92 E10
Metal Bridge Dur 103 Q4
Metfield Suffk 65 K5
Metherell Cnwll 5 Q8
Metheringham Lincs 86 E8
Methil Fife 135 K8
Methilhill Fife 135 K7
Methley Leeds 91 K5
Methley Junction Leeds 91 K5
Methlick Abers 159 L10
Methven P & K 134 C2
Methwold Norfk 63 M2
Methwold Hythe Norfk 63 M2
Mettingham Suffk 65 M4
Metton Norfk 76 H4
Mevagissey Cnwll 3 Q5
Mexborough Donc 91 M10
Mey Highld 167 N2
Meysey Hampton Gloucs 33 M4
Miabhaig W Isls 168 f4
Michaelchurch Herefs 45 Q9
Michaelchurch Escley
    Herefs 45 L8
Michaelchurch-on-Arrow
    Powys 45 J4
Michaelstone-y-Fedw
    Newpt 30 H8
Michaelston-le-Pit V Glam 30 G10
Michaelstow Cnwll 4 H6
Michaelwood Services
    Gloucs 32 D5
Michelcombe Devon 6 H5
Micheldever Hants 22 F6
Micheldever Station Hants 22 F6
Michelmersh Hants 22 B9
Mickfield Suffk 64 G9
Micklebring Donc 84 H2
Mickleby N York 105 M8
Micklefield Leeds 91 L4
Micklefield Green Herts 50 B11
Mickleham Surrey 36 E10
Mickleover C Derb 71 Q8
Micklethwaite C Brad 90 E2
Micklethwaite Cumb 110 E10
Mickleton Dur 103 J6
Mickleton Gloucs 47 N6
Mickletown Leeds 91 L5
Mickle Trafford Ches W 81 N11
Mickley Derbys 84 D5
Mickley N York 97 L5
Mickley Green Suffk 64 A10
Mickley Square Nthumb 112 G8
Mid Ardlaw Abers 159 M5

Midbea Ork 169 d2
Mid Beltie Abers 150 G7
Mid Bockhampton BCP 13 L5
Mid Calder W Loth 127 K4
Mid Clyth Highld 167 N9
Mid Culbeuchly Abers 158 G5
Middle Assendon Oxon 35 K7
Middle Aston Oxon 48 E9
Middle Barton Oxon 48 D9
Middlebie D & G 110 D5
Middlebridge P & K 141 L4
Middle Chinnock Somset 11 K2
Middle Claydon Bucks 49 K9
Middlecliffe Barns 91 L9
Middlecott Devon 8 H7
Middlecroft Derbys 84 F6
Middle Duntisbourne
    Gloucs 33 J3
Middleham N York 96 H3
Middle Handley Derbys 84 F5
Middle Harling Norfk 64 D4
Middlehill Cnwll 5 M8
Middlehill Wilts 32 F11
Middlehope Shrops 56 H7
Middle Kames Ag & B 131 J10
Middle Littleton Worcs 47 L5
Middle Madeley Staffs 70 D5
Middlemarsh Dorset 11 P3
Middle Mayfield Staffs 71 L6
Middle Mill Pembks 40 F5
Middlemoor Devon 6 D4
Middle Quarter Kent 26 E4
Middle Rasen Lincs 86 E3
Middle Rocombe Devon 7 N5
Middle Salter Lancs 95 N8
Middlesbrough Middsb 104 E7
Middlesceugh Cumb 101 M2
Middleshaw Cumb 95 M3
Middlesmoor N York 96 G6
Middle Stoford Somset 18 G10
Middle Stoke Medway 38 D6
Middlestone Dur 103 Q4
Middlestone Moor Dur 103 P4
Middle Stoughton Somset 19 M5
Middle Street Gloucs 32 E4
Middle Taphouse Cnwll 5 K9
Middlethird Border 118 C2
Middleton Ag & B 136 A7
Middleton Cumb 95 N3
Middleton Derbys 71 M2
Middleton Derbys 84 C9
Middleton Essex 52 E4
Middleton Hants 22 D6
Middleton Herefs 57 J11
Middleton Lancs 95 J9
Middleton Leeds 91 J5
Middleton N York 96 H11
Middleton N York 98 F3
Middleton Nhants 60 H3
Middleton Norfk 75 N7
Middleton Nthumb 112 G6
Middleton Nthumb 119 M3
Middleton P & K 134 E6
Middleton Rochdl 89 P9
Middleton Shrops 57 J9
Middleton Shrops 69 K9
Middleton Suffk 65 N8
Middleton Swans 28 D7
Middleton Warwks 59 J5
Middleton Cheney Nhants 48 E6
Middleton Green Staffs 70 H7
Middleton Hall Nthumb 119 J5
Middleton-in-Teesdale Dur 102 H5
Middleton Moor Suffk 65 N8
Middleton One Row Darltn 104 C8
Middleton-on-Leven N York 104 E9
Middleton-on-Sea W Susx 15 Q6
Middleton on the Hill
    Herefs 45 Q2
Middleton on the Wolds
    E R Yk 99 J11
Middleton Park C Aber 151 N5
Middleton Priors Shrops 57 L6
Middleton Quernhow N York 97 M5
Middleton Scriven Shrops 57 M7
Middleton St George Darltn 104 B8
Middleton Stoney Oxon 48 F10
Middleton Tyas N York 103 P9
Middletown Cumb 100 C9
Middle Town IoS 2 b3
Middletown N Som 31 N10
Middletown Powys 56 E2
Middle Tysoe Warwks 48 B6
Middle Wallop Hants 21 Q7
Middlewich Ches E 82 F11
Middle Winterslow Wilts 21 P8
Middlewood Cnwll 5 M6
Middlewood Herefs 45 K6
Middle Woodford Wilts 21 M7
Middlewood Green Suffk 64 F9
Middle Yard Gloucs 32 F4
Middlezoy Somset 19 L8
Middridge Dur 103 P5
Midford BaNES 20 E2
Midge Hall Lancs 88 G5
Midgeholme Cumb 111 M9
Midgham W Berk 34 G11
Midgley Calder 90 C5
Midgley Wakefd 90 H8
Mid Holmwood Surrey 36 E11
Midhopestones Sheff 90 G11
Midhurst W Susx 23 N10
Mid Lavant W Susx 15 N5
Midlem Border 117 Q5
Mid Mains Highld 155 M10
Midney Somset 19 N9
Midpark Ag & B 124 C6
Midsomer Norton BaNES 20 C4
Midtown Highld 165 N4
Midville Lincs 87 L8
Mid Yell Shet 169 s4
Migdale Highld 162 G8
Migvie Abers 150 C6
Milborne Port Somset 20 C11
Milborne St Andrew Dorset 12 D5
Milborne Wick Somset 20 C10
Milbourne Nthumb 112 H5
Milbourne Wilts 33 J7
Milburn Cumb 102 C5
Milbury Heath S Glos 32 C6
Milby N York 97 P7
Milcombe Oxon 48 D8
Milden Suffk 52 G2

Mildenhall Suffk 63 M6
Mildenhall Wilts 33 P11
Milebrook Powys 56 E10
Milebush Kent 26 C2
Mile Elm Wilts 33 J11
Mile End Essex 52 G6
Mile End Gloucs 31 Q2
Mile End Suffk 65 L4
Mile Oak Br & H 24 F9
Mile Oak Kent 25 Q2
Mile Oak Staffs 59 J4
Miles Hope Herefs 45 R2
Milesmark Fife 134 D10
Miles Platting Manch 83 J5
Mile Town Kent 38 F7
Milfield Nthumb 118 H4
Milford Derbys 84 E11
Milford Devon 16 C7
Milford Powys 55 P6
Milford Staffs 70 H10
Milford Surrey 23 P6
Milford Haven Pembks 40 H9
Milford on Sea Hants 13 N6
Milkwall Gloucs 31 Q3
Millais Jersey 11 a1
Milland W Susx 23 M9
Milland Marsh W Susx 23 M9
Mill Bank Calder 90 C6
Millbeck Cumb 101 J5
Millbreck Abers 159 P9
Millbridge Surrey 23 M6
Millbrook C Beds 50 B3
Millbrook C Sotn 14 C4
Millbrook Cnwll 6 C8
Millbrook Jersey 11 b2
Millbrook Tamesd 83 L5
Mill Brow Stockp 83 L7
Millbuie Abers 151 K6
Millbuie Highld 155 Q7
Millcombe Devon 7 L9
Mill Common Norfk 77 L11
Mill Common Suffk 65 N5
Millcorner E Susx 26 D7
Millcraig Highld 156 B3
Mill Cross Devon 7 J6
Milldale Staffs 71 L4
Mill End Bucks 35 L7
Millend Gloucs 32 D5
Mill End Herts 50 H4
Millerhill Mdloth 127 Q4
Miller's Dale Derbys 83 P10
Millers Green Derbys 71 P4
Miller's Green Essex 51 N9
Millgate Lancs 89 P7
Mill Green Cambs 63 K11
Mill Green Essex 51 P10
Mill Green Herts 50 F8
Mill Green Lincs 74 D6
Mill Green Norfk 64 G5
Mill Green Shrops 70 B9
Mill Green Staffs 58 G4
Mill Green Staffs 71 K10
Mill Green Suffk 52 G3
Mill Green Suffk 64 D10
Mill Green Suffk 64 G9
Mill Green Suffk 65 L9
Millhalf Herefs 45 K5
Millhayes Devon 10 E4
Millhead Lancs 95 K6
Millheugh S Lans 126 C7
Mill Hill E Susx 25 P9
Mill Hill Gt Lon 36 F2
Millhouse Ag & B 124 B3
Millhouse Cumb 101 L3
Millhousebridge D & G 109 P3
Millhouse Green Barns 90 G10
Millhouses Barns 91 L10
Millhouses Sheff 84 D4
Milliken Park Rens 125 L5
Millin Cross Pembks 41 J8
Millington E R Yk 98 G10
Mill Lane Hants 23 L4
Millmeece Staffs 70 E8
Millness Cumb 95 L4
Mill of Drummond P & K 133 N4
Mill of Haldane W Duns 132 D11
Millom Cumb 94 D4
Millook Cnwll 5 K2
Millpool Cnwll 2 F7
Millpool Cnwll 5 J7
Millport N Ayrs 124 F7
Mill Side Cumb 95 J4
Mill Street Kent 37 Q9
Mill Street Norfk 76 F8
Mill Street Suffk 64 F7
Millthorpe Derbys 84 D5
Millthrop Cumb 95 P2
Milltimber C Aber 151 M7
Milltown Abers 149 P6
Milltown Abers 150 D4
Milltown Cnwll 5 J10
Milltown D & G 110 F5
Milltown Derbys 84 E8
Milltown Devon 17 K4
Milltown Highld 153 N9
Milltown of Auchindoun
    Moray 157 R9
Milltown of Campfield
    Abers 150 H7
Milltown of Edinvillie
    Moray 157 P9
Milltown of Rothiemay
    Moray 158 D8
Milnathort P & K 134 E7
Milngavie E Duns 125 P3
Milnrow Rochdl 89 Q8
Milnthorpe Cumb 95 K4
Milnthorpe Wakefd 91 J7
Milovaig Highld 152 B8
Milson Shrops 57 L10
Milstead Kent 38 F10
Milston Wilts 21 N5
Milthorpe Lincs 74 B4
Milthorpe Nhants 48 G5
Milton C Stke 70 G4
Milton Cambs 62 G8
Milton Cumb 111 L8
Milton Cumb 106 H7
Milton D & G 108 H6
Milton Derbys 72 A7
Milton D & G 106 C3
Milton Highld 155 N11
Milton Highld 155 Q8
Milton Highld 156 D3
Milton Highld 167 P6

Milton Inver 125 K4
Milton Kent 37 Q6
Milton Moray 149 M4
Milton Moray 158 D5
Milton N Som 19 K2
Milton Newpt 31 L7
Milton Notts 85 M6
Milton Oxon 34 E6
Milton Oxon 48 E7
Milton P & K 141 Q5
Milton Pembks 41 K10
Milton Somset 19 N10
Milton Stirlg 132 G2
Milton W Duns 125 L3
Milton Abbas Dorset 12 D4
Milton Abbot Devon 5 Q6
Milton Bridge Mdloth 127 P5
Milton Bryan C Beds 49 Q8
Milton Clevedon Somset 20 C7
Milton Combe Devon 6 D5
Milton Common Oxon 35 J4
Milton Damerel Devon 16 F9
Milton End Gloucs 32 D2
Milton End Gloucs 33 M4
Milton Ernest Bed 61 M9
Milton Green Ches W 69 N3
Milton Hill Oxon 34 E6
Milton Keynes M Keyn 49 N7
Milton Lilbourne Wilts 21 N2
Milton Malsor Nhants 60 F9
Milton Morenish P & K 140 F10
Milton of Auchinhove Abers 150 F7
Milton of Balgonie Fife 135 J7
Milton of Buchanan Stirlg 132 E9
Milton of Campsie E Duns 126 B2
Milton of Finavon Angus 142 H6
Milton of Leys Highld 156 B9
Milton of Murtle C Aber 151 M7
Milton on Stour Dorset 20 E9
Milton Regis Kent 38 F9
Milton Street E Susx 25 M10
Milton-under-Wychwood
    Oxon 47 Q11
Milverton Somset 18 F9
Milverton Warwks 59 M11
Milwich Staffs 70 H8
Milwr Flints 80 H10
Minard Ag & B 131 K8
Minchington Dorset 12 G2
Minchinhampton Gloucs 32 G4
Mindrum Nthumb 118 F4
Minehead Somset 18 C5
Minera Wrexhm 69 J4
Minety Wilts 33 K6
Minffordd Gwynd 67 K7
Mingarrypark Highld 138 B4
Miningsby Lincs 87 K8
Minions Cnwll 5 M7
Minishant S Ayrs 114 F5
Minllyn Gwynd 55 K2
Minnigaff D & G 107 M4
Minnonie Abers 159 J5
Minshull Vernon Ches E 70 B2
Minskip N York 97 N8
Minstead Hants 13 N2
Minsted W Susx 23 N10
Minster Kent 39 P9
Minsterley Shrops 56 F3
Minster Lovell Oxon 34 B2
Minster-on-Sea Kent 38 G7
Minsterworth Gloucs 46 E11
Minterne Magna Dorset 11 P4
Minterne Parva Dorset 11 P4
Minting Lincs 86 G6
Mintlaw Abers 159 N8
Minto Border 117 R6
Minton Shrops 56 G6
Minwear Pembks 41 K8
Minworth Birm 59 J6
Mirehouse Cumb 100 C7
Mireland Highld 167 P4
Mirfield Kirk 90 G7
Miserden Gloucs 32 H3
Miskin Rhondd 30 D5
Miskin Rhondd 30 D8
Misson Notts 85 L2
Misterton Leics 60 C4
Misterton Notts 85 N2
Misterton Somset 11 K3
Mistley Essex 53 K5
Mistley Heath Essex 53 K5
Mitcham Gt Lon 36 G7
Mitcheldean Gloucs 46 C11
Mitchell Cnwll 3 M3
Mitchellslacks D & G 116 D11
Mitchel Troy Mons 31 N2
Mitford Nthumb 113 J3
Mithian Cnwll 3 J3
Mitton Staffs 70 F11
Mixbury Oxon 48 H8
Mixenden Calder 90 D5
Moats Tye Suffk 64 E10
Mobberley Ches E 82 G9
Mobberley Staffs 71 J6
Moccas Herefs 45 M6
Mochdre Conwy 79 Q9
Mochdre Powys 55 P5
Mochrum D & G 107 K8
Mockbeggar Hants 13 L3
Mockbeggar Kent 26 B2
Mockerkin Cumb 100 E6
Modbury Devon 6 H8
Moddershall Staffs 70 G7
Moelfre IoA 79 J7
Moelfre Powys 68 G9
Moel Tryfan Gwynd 67 J3
Moffat D & G 116 F9
Mogador Surrey 36 F10
Moggerhanger C Beds 61 P11
Moira Leics 71 Q11
Molash Kent 38 H11
Mol-chlach Highld 144 G5
Mold Flints 68 H2
Moldgreen Kirk 90 F7
Molehill Green Essex 51 N6
Molehill Green Essex 52 B7
Molescroft E R Yk 92 H2
Molesden Nthumb 112 H4
Molesworth Cambs 61 N5
Moll Highld 153 K11
Molland Devon 17 Q6
Mollington Ches W 81 M10
Mollington Oxon 48 D5
Mollinsburn N Lans 126 C3
Monachty Cerdgn 43 K2
Mondynes Abers 143 P2

284 Monewden – Nettleton

Monewden Suffk 65 J10
Moneydie P & K 134 D2
Moneyrow Green W & M 35 N9
Moniaive D & G 115 Q9
Monifieth Angus 142 H11
Monikie Angus 142 H10
Monimail Fife 134 H5
Monington Pembks 41 M2
Monk Bretton Barns 91 K9
Monken Hadley Gt Lon 50 F11
Monk Fryston N York 91 N5
Monkhide Herefs 46 B6
Monkhill Cumb 110 F9
Monkhopton Shrops 57 L6
Monkland Herefs 45 P3
Monkleigh Devon 16 H7
Monknash V Glam 29 P10
Monkokehampton Devon 8 E3
Monkseaton N Tyne 113 M6
Monks Eleigh Suffk 52 G2
Monk's Gate W Susx 24 F5
Monks Heath Ches E 82 H10
Monk Sherborne Hants 22 H3
Monks Horton Kent 27 K3
Monksilver Somset 18 E7
Monks Kirby Warwks 59 Q8
Monk Soham Suffk 65 J8
Monkspath Solhll 58 H9
Monks Risborough Bucks 35 M4
Monksthorpe Lincs 87 M7
Monk Street Essex 51 P5
Monkswood Mons 31 K4
Monkton Devon 10 D4
Monkton Kent 39 N9
Monkton S Ayrs 114 G2
Monkton S Tyne 113 M8
Monkton V Glam 29 P10
Monkton Combe BaNES 20 E2
Monkton Deverill Wilts 20 G7
Monkton Farleigh Wilts 32 F11
Monkton Heathfield Somset 19 J9
Monkton Up Wimborne Dorset 12 H2
Monkton Wyld Dorset 10 G5
Monkwearmouth Sundld 113 N9
Monkwood Hants 23 J8
Monmore Green Wolves 58 D5
Monmouth Mons 31 P2
Monnington on Wye Herefs 45 M6
Monreith D & G 107 L9
Montacute Somset 19 N11
Montcliffe Bolton 89 K8
Montford Shrops 56 G2
Montford Bridge Shrops 69 M11
Montgarrie Abers 150 F4
Montgomery Powys 56 C5
Monton Salfd 82 G5
Montrose Angus 143 N6
Mont Saint Guern 10 b2
Monxton Hants 22 B6
Monyash Derbys 83 Q11
Monymusk Abers 150 H4
Monzie P & K 133 P2
Moodiesburn N Lans 126 B3
Moonzie Fife 135 J4
Moor Allerton Leeds 91 J3
Moorbath Dorset 11 J5
Moorby Lincs 87 J8
Moorcot Herefs 45 M3
Moor Crichel Dorset 12 G3
Moordown BCP 13 J6
Moore Halton 82 C8
Moor End C Beds 49 Q10
Moor End Calder 90 D5
Moor End Devon 17 M10
Moorend Gloucs 32 D4
Moor End Lancs 88 D2
Moor End N York 91 Q3
Moorends Donc 92 A7
Moorgreen Hants 22 E11
Moor Green Herts 50 H5
Moorgreen Notts 84 G11
Moorhall Derbys 84 D6
Moorhampton Herefs 45 M5
Moorhead C Brad 90 E3
Moor Head Leeds 90 G5
Moorhouse Cumb 110 E10
Moorhouse Cumb 110 F9
Moorhouse Donc 91 M8
Moorhouse Notts 85 N7
Moorhouse Bank Surrey 37 K10
Moorland Somset 19 K8
Moorlinch Somset 19 L7
Moor Monkton N York 97 R9
Moor Row Cumb 100 D8
Moor Row Cumb 110 D11
Moorsholm R & Cl 105 J8
Moorside Dorset 20 E11
Moorside Dur 112 G11
Moor Side Lancs 88 E4
Moor Side Lancs 88 F3
Moorside Leeds 90 G3
Moor Side Lincs 87 J9
Moorside Oldham 89 Q9
Moorstock Kent 27 K4
Moor Street Medway 38 D8
Moorswater Cnwll 5 L9
Moorthorpe Wakefd 91 M8
Moortown Devon 6 E4
Moortown Hants 13 L4
Moortown IoW 14 D10
Moortown Leeds 90 H3
Moortown Lincs 93 J11
Moortown Wrekin 69 R11
Morangie Highld 162 H10
Morar Highld 145 L9
Morborne Cambs 61 P2
Morchard Bishop Devon 9 J3
Morchard Road Devon 9 J3
Morcombelake Dorset 11 J6
Morcott Rutlnd 73 N10
Morda Shrops 69 J9
Morden Dorset 12 F5
Morden Gt Lon 36 G7
Mordiford Herefs 45 R7
Mordon Dur 104 B5
More Shrops 56 E6
Morebath Devon 18 C9
Morebattle Border 118 E6
Morecambe Lancs 95 J8
Moredon Swindn 33 M7
Morefield Highld 161 J7
Morehall Kent 27 M4
Moreleigh Devon 7 K8
Morenish P & K 140 F10
Moresby Parks Cumb 100 C7
Morestead Hants 22 F9
Moreton Dorset 12 D7
Moreton Essex 51 M9
Moreton Herefs 45 Q2
Moreton Oxon 35 J4
Moreton Staffs 70 D11
Moreton Staffs 71 L9
Moreton Wirral 81 K7
Moreton Corbet Shrops 69 Q10
Moretonhampstead Devon 9 J7
Moreton-in-Marsh Gloucs 47 P8
Moreton Jeffries Herefs 46 B5
Moretonmill Shrops 69 Q10
Moreton Morrell Warwks 48 B3
Moreton on Lugg Herefs 45 Q5
Moreton Paddox Warwks 48 B4
Moreton Pinkney Nhants 48 G5
Moreton Say Shrops 70 A8
Moreton Valence Gloucs 32 E3
Morfa Cerdgn 42 F4
Morfa Bychan Gwynd 67 J7
Morfa Dinlle Gwynd 66 G3
Morfa Glas Neath 29 N3
Morfa Nefyn Gwynd 66 D6
Morganstown Cardif 30 F8
Morgan's Vale Wilts 21 N10
Morham E Loth 128 F5
Moriah Cerdgn 54 E9
Morland Cumb 102 B6
Morley Ches E 82 H8
Morley Derbys 72 B2
Morley Dur 103 M5
Morley Leeds 90 H5
Morley Green Ches E 82 H8
Morley St Botolph Norfk 64 F2
Mornick Cnwll 5 N7
Morningside C Edin 127 N3
Morningside N Lans 126 E6
Morningthorpe Norfk 65 J3
Morpeth Nthumb 113 J3
Morphie Abers 143 N5
Morrey Staffs 71 L11
Morridge Side Staffs 71 J4
Morriston Swans 29 J5
Morston Norfk 76 E3
Mortehoe Devon 16 H2
Morthen Rothm 84 G3
Mortimer W Berk 23 J2
Mortimer Common W Berk 35 J11
Mortimer's Cross Herefs 45 N2
Mortimer West End Hants 22 H2
Mortlake Gt Lon 36 F5
Morton Cumb 101 N3
Morton Cumb 110 G10
Morton Derbys 84 F8
Morton IoW 14 H9
Morton Lincs 74 A6
Morton Lincs 85 P2
Morton Lincs 85 Q8
Morton Notts 85 M10
Morton Shrops 69 J10
Morton-on-Swale N York 97 M2
Morton on the Hill Norfk 76 G8
Morton Tinmouth Dur 103 N6
Morvah Cnwll 2 C6
Morval Cnwll 5 M10
Morvich Highld 146 B3
Morville Shrops 57 M6
Morville Heath Shrops 57 M6
Morwenstow Cnwll 16 C8
Mosborough Sheff 84 F4
Moscow E Ayrs 125 M9
Mose Shrops 57 P6
Mosedale Cumb 101 L4
Moseley Birm 58 G8
Moseley Wolves 58 D5
Moseley Worcs 46 F3
Moses Gate Bolton 89 L9
Moss Ag & B 136 B7
Moss Donc 91 P8
Moss Wrexhm 69 K4
Mossat Abers 150 D4
Mossbank Shet 169 r6
Moss Bank St Hel 81 Q5
Mossbay Cumb 100 C5
Mossblown S Ayrs 114 H3
Mossbrow Traffd 82 F7
Mossburnford Border 118 C7
Mossdale D & G 108 E6
Mossdale E Ayrs 115 J7
Moss Edge Lancs 88 E2
Moss End Ches E 82 E9
Mossend N Lans 126 C5
Mosser Mains Cumb 100 F5
Mossley Ches E 70 F2
Mossley Tamesd 83 L4
Mosspaul Hotel Border 117 M11
Moss Side Cumb 110 C10
Moss-side Highld 156 F6
Moss Side Lancs 88 D4
Moss Side Sefton 81 M4
Mosstodloch Moray 157 Q6
Mossyard D & G 107 P7
Mossy Lea Lancs 88 G8
Mosterton Dorset 11 K3
Moston Manch 83 J4
Moston Shrops 69 Q9
Moston Green Ches E 70 C2
Mostyn Flints 80 H8
Motcombe Dorset 20 G9
Mothecombe Devon 6 G9
Motherby Cumb 101 M5
Motherwell N Lans 126 C6
Motspur Park Gt Lon 36 F7
Mottingham Gt Lon 37 K6
Mottisfont Hants 22 B9
Mottisfont Hants 22 B9
Mottistone IoW 14 D10
Mottram in Longdendale Tamesd 83 L5
Mottram St Andrew Ches E 83 J9
Mouilpied Guern 10 b2
Mouldsworth Ches W 81 Q10
Moulin P & K 141 M6
Moulsecoomb Br & H 24 H9
Moulsford Oxon 34 G8
Moulsoe M Keyn 49 P6
Moultavie Highld 156 A3
Moulton Ches W 82 E11
Moulton Lincs 74 F6
Moulton N York 103 P10
Moulton Nhants 60 G7
Moulton Suffk 63 L8
Moulton V Glam 30 E11
Moulton Chapel Lincs 74 E7
Moulton St Mary Norfk 77 M10
Moulton Seas End Lincs 74 F5
Mount Cnwll 4 B10
Mount Cnwll 5 J8
Mount Kirk 90 D7
Mountain C Brad 90 D4
Mountain Ash Rhondd 30 D5
Mountain Cross Border 127 M8
Mountain Street Kent 39 J11
Mount Ambrose Cnwll 3 J5
Mount Bures Essex 52 F5
Mountfield E Susx 26 B7
Mountgerald Highld 155 Q5
Mount Hawke Cnwll 3 J4
Mount Hermon Cnwll 2 H10
Mountjoy Cnwll 4 D9
Mount Lothian Mdloth 127 P6
Mountnessing Essex 51 P11
Mounton Mons 31 P6
Mount Pleasant Ches E 70 E3
Mount Pleasant Derbys 71 P11
Mount Pleasant Derbys 84 D11
Mount Pleasant Dur 103 Q4
Mount Pleasant E R Yk 93 N3
Mount Pleasant E Susx 25 K7
Mount Pleasant Norfk 64 D3
Mount Pleasant Suffk 63 M11
Mount Pleasant Worcs 47 K2
Mountsorrel Leics 72 F8
Mount Sorrel Wilts 21 K10
Mount Tabor Calder 90 D5
Mousehole Cnwll 2 D8
Mouswald D & G 109 N6
Mow Cop Ches E 70 F3
Mowhaugh Border 118 F6
Mowmacre Hill C Leic 72 F9
Mowsley Leics 60 D3
Moy Highld 147 L11
Moy Highld 156 D11
Moyle Highld 145 Q4
Moylegrove Pembks 41 M2
Muasdale Ag & B 120 C3
Muchalls Abers 151 N9
Much Birch Herefs 45 Q8
Much Cowarne Herefs 46 B5
Much Dewchurch Herefs 45 P8
Muchelney Somset 19 M10
Muchelney Ham Somset 19 M10
Much Hadham Herts 51 K7
Much Hoole Lancs 88 F6
Much Hoole Town Lancs 88 F6
Muchlarnick Cnwll 5 L10
Much Marcle Herefs 46 C8
Much Wenlock Shrops 57 L5
Muck Highld 144 F12
Mucking Thurr 37 Q4
Muckleburgh Collection Norfk 76 G3
Muckleford Dorset 11 N6
Mucklestone Staffs 70 C7
Muckley Shrops 57 L5
Muckton Lincs 87 L4
Muddiford Devon 17 K4
Muddles Green E Susx 25 M8
Mudeford BCP 13 L6
Mudford Somset 19 Q11
Mudford Sock Somset 19 Q11
Mudgley Somset 19 N5
Mud Row Kent 38 H7
Mugdock Stirlg 125 P2
Mugeary Highld 152 G10
Mugginton Derbys 71 P6
Muggintonlane End Derbys 71 P6
Muggleswick Dur 112 F11
Muirden Abers 158 H7
Muirdrum Angus 143 K10
Muiresk Abers 158 G8
Muirhead Angus 142 E11
Muirhead Fife 134 H6
Muirhead N Lans 126 B4
Muirhouses Falk 134 C11
Muirkirk E Ayrs 115 N2
Muirmill Stirlg 133 L11
Muir of Fowlis Abers 150 F5
Muir of Miltonduff Moray 157 M6
Muir of Ord Highld 155 P7
Muirshearlich Highld 146 E11
Muirtack Abers 159 N10
Muirton P & K 133 Q5
Muirton Mains Highld 155 N7
Muirton of Ardblair P & K 142 B9
Muker N York 102 H11
Mulbarton Norfk 76 H11
Mulben Moray 157 R7
Mulfra Cnwll 2 D7
Mull Ag & B 137 Q9
Mullacott Cross Devon 17 J3
Mullardoch Highld 154 H11
Mullion Cnwll 2 H10
Mullion Cove Cnwll 2 H10
Mumby Lincs 87 P6
Munderfield Row Herefs 46 B4
Munderfield Stocks Herefs 46 C4
Mundesley Norfk 77 L4
Mundford Norfk 63 P2
Mundham Norfk 65 L2
Mundon Hill Essex 52 E11
Mundy Bois Kent 26 F2
Mungrisdale Cumb 101 L4
Munlochy Highld 156 A7
Munnoch N Ayrs 124 H8
Munsley Herefs 46 C6
Munslow Shrops 57 J7
Murchington Devon 8 G7
Murcot Worcs 47 L6
Murcott Oxon 48 G11
Murcott Wilts 33 J6
Murkle Highld 167 L3
Murlaggan Highld 146 C9
Murrell Green Hants 23 K3
Murroes Angus 142 H10
Murrow Cambs 74 G9
Mursley Bucks 49 M9
Murston Kent 38 F9
Murthill Angus 142 H6
Murthly P & K 141 R10
Murton C York 98 C10
Murton Cumb 102 D6
Murton Dur 113 N11
Murton N Tyne 113 M6
Murton Nthumb 129 P10
Murton Swans 28 G7
Musbury Devon 10 F6
Muscoates N York 98 D5
Musselburgh E Loth 127 Q3
Muston Leics 73 L3
Muston N York 99 M5
Mustow Green Worcs 58 C10
Muswell Hill Gt Lon 36 G3
Mutehill D & G 108 E11
Mutford Suffk 65 P4
Muthill P & K 133 P4
Mutterton Devon 9 P3
Muxton Wrekin 57 N2
Mybster Highld 167 L6
Myddfai Carmth 43 Q8
Myddle Shrops 69 N10
Mydroilyn Cerdgn 43 J3
Myerscough Lancs 88 F3
Mylor Cnwll 3 L6
Mylor Bridge Cnwll 3 L6
Mynachlog ddu Pembks 41 M4
Myndd-llan Flints 80 H10
Myndtown Shrops 56 F7
Mynydd Bach Cerdgn 54 G9
Mynydd-bach Mons 31 N6
Mynydd-Bach Swans 29 J5
Mynyddgarreg Carmth 28 D3
Mynydd Isa Flints 69 J2
Mynydd Llandygai Gwynd 79 L11
Mynydd Mechell IoA 78 F6
Mynytho Gwynd 66 E8
Myrebird Abers 151 J8
Myredykes Border 118 A11
Mytchett Surrey 23 N3
Mytholm Calder 90 B5
Mytholmroyd Calder 90 C5
Mythop Lancs 88 D4
Myton-on-Swale N York 97 P7

N

Naast Highld 160 C10
Nab's Head Lancs 89 J5
Na Buirgh W Isls 168 f8
Naburn C York 98 B11
Naccolt Kent 27 J3
Nackington Kent 39 L11
Nacton Suffk 53 M3
Nafferton E R Yk 99 M9
Nag's Head Gloucs 32 G5
Nailbridge Gloucs 46 B11
Nailsbourne Somset 18 H9
Nailsea N Som 31 N10
Nailstone Leics 72 C9
Nailsworth Gloucs 32 F5
Nairn Highld 156 F6
Nalderswood Surrey 36 F11
Nancegollan Cnwll 2 G7
Nancledra Cnwll 2 D6
Nanhoron Gwynd 66 D8
Nannerch Flints 80 H11
Nanpantan Leics 72 E7
Nanpean Cnwll 4 F10
Nanquidno Cnwll 2 B8
Nanstallon Cnwll 4 G8
Nant-ddu Powys 30 D2
Nanternis Cerdgn 42 G3
Nantgaredig Carmth 43 J10
Nantgarw Rhondd 30 F7
Nant-glas Powys 55 M11
Nantglyn Denbgs 68 D2
Nantgwyn Powys 55 M9
Nant Gwynant Gwynd 67 L4
Nantlle Gwynd 67 J4
Nantmawr Shrops 69 J10
Nantmel Powys 55 N11
Nantmor Gwynd 67 L5
Nant Peris Gwynd 67 L3
Nantwich Ches E 70 B4
Nant-y-Bwch Blae G 30 F2
Nantycaws Carmth 43 J11
Nant-y-derry Mons 31 K3
Nant-y-ffin Carmth 43 L8
Nantyffyllon Brdgnd 29 N6
Nantyglo Blae G 30 G2
Nant-y-gollen Shrops 68 H9
Nant-y-moel Brdgnd 29 P6
Nant-y-pandy Conwy 79 M10
Naphill Bucks 35 M5
Napleton Worcs 46 G5
Nappa N York 96 C10
Napton on the Hill Warwks 48 E2
Narberth Pembks 41 M8
Narborough Leics 72 E11
Narborough Norfk 75 P8
Narkurs Cnwll 5 N10
Nasareth Gwynd 66 H5
Naseby Nhants 60 E5
Nash Bucks 49 L8
Nash Gt Lon 37 K8
Nash Herefs 45 L2
Nash Newpt 31 K8
Nash Shrops 57 L10
Nash End Worcs 57 P8
Nashes Green Hants 23 J5
Nash Lee Bucks 35 M3
Nash Street Kent 37 P7
Nassington Nhants 73 R11
Nastend Gloucs 32 E3
Nasty Herts 51 J6
Nateby Cumb 102 E9
Nateby Lancs 88 F2
National Memorial Arboretum Staffs 59 J2
National Motor Museum (Beaulieu) Hants 14 C6
National Space Centre C Leic 72 F9
Natland Cumb 95 L3
Naughton Suffk 52 H2
Naunton Gloucs 47 M10
Naunton Worcs 46 G7
Naunton Beauchamp Worcs 47 J4
Navenby Lincs 86 C9
Navestock Essex 51 M11
Navestock Side Essex 51 N11
Navidale Highld 163 N3
Navity Highld 156 D5
Nawton N York 98 D4
Nayland Suffk 52 G5
Nazeing Essex 51 K9
Nazeing Gate Essex 51 K9
Neacroft Hants 13 L5
Neal's Green Warwks 59 M8
Neap Shet 169 s8
Near Cotton Staffs 71 K5
Near Sawrey Cumb 101 L11
Neasden Gt Lon 36 F3
Neasham Darltn 104 B8
Neath Neath 29 L5
Neatham Hants 23 K6
Neatishead Norfk 77 L7
Nebo Cerdgn 54 C11
Nebo Conwy 67 Q3
Nebo Gwynd 66 H4
Nebo IoA 78 H6
Necton Norfk 76 B10
Nedd Highld 164 D10
Nedderton Nthumb 113 K4
Nedging Suffk 52 G2
Nedging Tye Suffk 52 H2
Needham Norfk 65 J5
Needham Market Suffk 64 F10
Needham Street Suffk 63 M7
Needingworth Cambs 62 D6
Neen Savage Shrops 57 M9
Neen Sollars Shrops 57 M10
Neenton Shrops 57 L7
Nefyn Gwynd 66 E6
Neilston E Rens 125 M6
Nelson Caerph 30 F5
Nelson Lancs 89 P3
Nemphlar S Lans 116 B2
Nempnett Thrubwell BaNES 19 P2
Nenthall Cumb 111 Q11
Nenthead Cumb 102 E2
Nenthorn Border 118 C3
Neopardy Devon 9 J5
Nep Town W Susx 24 F7
Nerabus Ag & B 122 B8
Nercwys Flints 68 H2
Nerston S Lans 125 Q6
Nesbit Nthumb 119 J4
Nesfield N York 96 G11
Ness Ches W 81 L9
Nesscliffe Shrops 69 L11
Neston Ches W 81 K9
Neston Wilts 32 G11
Netchwood Shrops 57 L6
Nether Abington S Lans 116 C6
Nether Alderley Ches E 82 H9
Netheravon Wilts 21 M5
Nether Blainslie Border 117 Q2
Netherbrae Abers 159 J6
Nether Broughton Leics 72 H5
Netherburn S Lans 126 D8
Netherbury Dorset 11 K5
Netherby Cumb 110 G6
Netherby N York 97 M11
Nether Cerne Dorset 11 P5
Nethercleuch D & G 109 P3
Nether Compton Dorset 19 Q11
Nethercote Warwks 60 B8
Nethercott Devon 5 P2
Nethercott Devon 16 H4
Nether Crimond Abers 151 L3
Nether Dallachy Moray 157 R5
Netherend Gloucs 31 Q4
Nether Exe Devon 9 M4
Netherfield E Susx 26 B8
Netherfield Leics 72 F7
Netherfield Notts 72 G2
Nether Fingland S Lans 116 C8
Nethergate N Linc 92 C11
Nethergate Norfk 76 F6
Netherhampton Wilts 21 M9
Nether Handley Derbys 84 F5
Nether Handwick Angus 142 F9
Nether Haugh Rothm 91 L11
Netherhay Dorset 11 J3
Nether Headon Notts 85 M5
Nether Heage Derbys 84 E10
Nether Heyford Nhants 60 E9
Nether Kellet Lancs 95 L7
Nether Kinmundy Abers 159 Q9
Netherland Green Staffs 71 L8
Nether Langwith Notts 84 H6
Netherley Abers 151 M9
Nethermill D & G 109 M3
Nethermuir Abers 159 M9
Netherne-on-the-Hill Surrey 36 G9
Netheroyd Hill Kirk 90 E7
Nether Padley Derbys 84 B5
Nether Poppleton C York 98 B10
Nether Row Cumb 101 K3
Netherseal Derbys 59 L2
Nether Silton N York 97 Q2
Nether Skyborry Shrops 56 D10
Nether Stowey Somset 18 G7
Nether Street Essex 51 N8
Netherstreet Wilts 21 J2
Netherthong Kirk 90 E9
Netherthorpe Derbys 84 F6
Netherton Angus 143 J6
Netherton Devon 7 M4
Netherton Dudley 58 D7
Netherton Hants 22 C3
Netherton Herefs 45 Q9
Netherton Kirk 90 E8
Netherton N Lans 126 D7
Netherton Nthumb 119 J9
Netherton Oxon 34 D5
Netherton P & K 142 A7
Netherton Sefton 81 M5
Netherton Shrops 57 N8
Netherton Stirlg 125 P2
Netherton Wakefd 90 H7
Netherton Worcs 47 J6
Nethertown Cumb 100 C9
Nethertown Highld 167 Q1
Nethertown Lancs 89 L3
Nethertown Staffs 71 L11
Netherurd Border 116 G2
Nether Wallop Hants 22 B7
Nether Wasdale Cumb 100 F10
Nether Welton Cumb 110 G11
Nether Westcote Gloucs 47 P10
Nether Whitacre Warwks 59 K6
Nether Whitecleuch S Lans 116 A7
Nether Winchendon Bucks 35 K2
Netherwitton Nthumb 112 G2
Nethy Bridge Highld 149 J3
Netley Hants 14 E5
Netley Marsh Hants 13 P2
Nettlebed Oxon 35 J7
Nettlebridge Somset 20 B5
Nettlecombe Dorset 11 L5
Nettlecombe IoW 14 F11
Nettleden Herts 50 B8
Nettleham Lincs 86 D5
Nettlestead Kent 37 Q10
Nettlestead Green Kent 37 Q10
Nettlestone IoW 14 H8
Nettlesworth Dur 113 L11
Nettleton Lincs 93 K10

Nettleton – North End 285

Nettleton Wilts 32 F9
Nettleton Shrub Wilts 32 F9
Netton Devon 6 F9
Netton Wilts 21 M7
Neuadd Carmth 43 P10
Neuadd-ddu Powys 55 L9
Nevendon Essex 38 C3
Nevern Pembks 41 L2
Nevill Holt Leics 60 H2
New Abbey D & G 109 L7
New Aberdour Abers 159 L5
New Addington Gt Lon 37 J8
Newall Leeds 97 J11
New Alresford Hants 22 G8
New Alyth P & K 142 C8
Newark C Pete 74 D10
Newark Ork 169 g2
Newark-on-Trent Notts 85 N10
New Arley Warwks 59 L7
New Arram E R Yk 92 H2
Newarthill N Lans 126 D6
New Ash Green Kent 37 P7
New Balderton Notts 85 P10
Newbarn Kent 27 L3
New Barn Kent 37 P7
New Barnet Gt Lon 50 G11
New Barnetby N Linc 93 J8
New Barton Nhants 61 J8
Newbattle Mdloth 127 Q4
New Bewick Nthumb 119 L6
Newbie D & G 110 C7
Newbiggin Cumb 94 B2
Newbiggin Cumb 94 F7
Newbiggin Cumb 101 N5
Newbiggin Cumb 102 B5
Newbiggin Cumb 111 L11
Newbiggin Dur 102 H5
Newbiggin Dur 112 H11
Newbiggin N York 96 E2
Newbiggin N York 96 F3
Newbiggin-by-the-Sea Nthumb 113 M3
Newbigging Angus 142 D9
Newbigging Angus 142 G10
Newbigging Angus 142 H10
Newbigging S Lans 127 J8
Newbiggin-on-Lune Cumb 102 D10
New Bilton Warwks 59 Q9
Newbold Derbys 84 E6
Newbold Leics 72 C7
Newbold on Avon Warwks 59 Q9
Newbold on Stour Warwks 47 P5
Newbold Pacey Warwks 47 Q3
Newbold Revel Warwks 59 Q8
Newbold Verdon Leics 72 C10
New Bolingbroke Lincs 87 K9
Newborough C Pete 74 D9
Newborough IoA 78 G11
Newborough Staffs 71 L9
Newbottle Nhants 48 F7
Newbottle Sundld 113 M10
New Boultham Lincs 86 C6
Newbourne Suffk 53 N3
New Bradwell M Keyn 49 M6
New Brampton Derbys 84 E6
New Brancepeth Dur 103 P2
Newbridge C Edin 127 L3
Newbridge Caerph 30 H5
Newbridge Cerdgn 43 K3
Newbridge Cnwll 2 C7
Newbridge Cnwll 3 K5
Newbridge D & G 109 K5
Newbridge Hants 21 Q11
Newbridge IoW 14 D9
New Bridge N York 98 G3
Newbridge Oxon 34 D4
Newbridge Wrexhm 69 J6
Newbridge Green Worcs 46 F7
Newbridge-on-Usk Mons 31 L6
Newbridge-on-Wye Powys 44 E3
New Brighton Flints 81 K11
New Brighton Wirral 81 L6
New Brinsley Notts 84 G10
New Brotton R & Cl 105 J6
Newbrough Nthumb 112 C7
New Broughton Wrexhm 69 K4
New Buckenham Norfk 64 F3
Newbuildings Devon 9 J4
Newburgh Abers 151 P2
Newburgh Abers 159 N6
Newburgh Fife 134 G4
Newburgh Lancs 88 F8
Newburn N u Ty 113 J7
New Bury Bolton 82 F4
Newbury Somset 20 C5
Newbury W Berk 34 E11
Newbury Wilts 20 F6
Newbury Park Gt Lon 37 K3
Newby Cumb 101 Q6
Newby Lancs 96 B11
Newby N York 95 Q7
Newby N York 99 L2
Newby N York 104 F8
Newby Bridge Cumb 94 H3
Newby Cross Cumb 110 G10
Newby East Cumb 111 J9
Newby Head Cumb 101 Q6
New Byth Abers 159 K7
Newby West Cumb 110 G10
Newby Wiske N York 97 N3
Newcastle Mons 45 N11
Newcastle Shrops 56 D8
Newcastle Airport Nthumb 113 J6
Newcastle Emlyn Carmth 42 F6
Newcastleton Border 111 J3
Newcastle-under-Lyme Staffs 70 E5
Newcastle upon Tyne N u Ty 113 K8
Newchapel Pembks 41 P3
Newchapel Staffs 70 F4
Newchapel Surrey 25 J2
Newchurch Blae G 30 G2
Newchurch Herefs 45 M4
Newchurch IoW 14 G9
Newchurch Kent 27 J5
Newchurch Mons 31 N5
Newchurch Powys 45 J4
Newchurch Staffs 71 L10
Newchurch in Pendle Lancs 89 N3
New Costessey Norfk 76 H9
New Cowper Cumb 109 P11
Newcraighall C Edin 127 Q3
New Crofton Wakefd 91 K7
New Cross Cerdgn 54 E9
New Cross Gt Lon 37 J5
New Cross Somset 19 M11
New Cumnock E Ayrs 115 M5
New Cut E Susx 26 D8
New Deer Abers 159 L8
New Delaval Nthumb 113 L5
New Delph Oldham 90 B9
New Denham Bucks 36 B4
Newdigate Surrey 24 E2
New Duston Nhants 60 F8
New Earswick C York 98 C9
New Eastwood Notts 84 G11
New Edlington Donc 91 N11
New Elgin Moray 157 N5
New Ellerby E R Yk 93 L3
Newell Green Br For 35 N10
New Eltham Gt Lon 37 K6
New End Worcs 47 L2
Newenden Kent 26 D6
New England C Pete 74 C10
New England Essex 52 B3
Newent Gloucs 46 D9
New Farnley Leeds 90 H4
New Ferry Wirral 81 L7
Newfield Dur 103 P4
Newfield Dur 113 K10
Newfield Highld 156 D2
New Fletton C Pete 74 C11
New Forest National Park 13 N3
Newfound Hants 22 G4
New Fryston Wakefd 91 M5
Newgale Pembks 40 G6
New Galloway D & G 108 D5
Newgate Norfk 76 E3
Newgate Street Herts 50 H9
New Gilston Fife 135 L6
New Grimsby IoS 2 b1
Newhall Ches E 69 R5
Newhall Derbys 71 P10
Newham Nthumb 119 N5
New Hartley Nthumb 113 M5
Newhaven C Edin 127 P2
Newhaven Derbys 71 M2
Newhaven E Susx 25 K10
New Haw Surrey 36 C8
New Hedges Pembks 41 M10
New Herrington Sundld 113 M10
Newhey Rochdl 89 Q8
New Holkham Norfk 76 B4
New Holland N Linc 93 J6
Newholm N York 105 N8
New Houghton Derbys 84 G7
New Houghton Norfk 75 Q5
Newhouse N Lans 126 D5
New Houses N York 96 B6
New Houses Wigan 82 C4
New Hutton Cumb 95 M2
New Hythe Kent 38 B10
Newick E Susx 25 K6
Newingreen Kent 27 K4
Newington Kent 27 L4
Newington Kent 38 E9
Newington Oxon 34 H5
Newington Shrops 56 G8
Newington Bagpath Gloucs 32 F6
New Inn Carmth 43 J7
New Inn Pembks 41 L4
New Inn Torfn 31 K5
New Invention Shrops 56 D9
New Lakenham Norfk 77 J10
New Lanark S Lans 116 B2
New Lanark Village S Lans 116 B2
Newland C KuH 93 J4
Newland Cumb 94 G5
Newland E R Yk 92 D5
Newland Gloucs 31 Q3
Newland N York 92 A6
Newland Oxon 34 C3
Newland Somset 17 Q4
Newland Worcs 46 E5
Newlandrig Mdloth 128 B7
Newlands Border 111 K2
Newlands Cumb 101 K3
Newlands Nthumb 112 G9
Newlands of Dundurcas Moray 157 P7
New Lane Lancs 88 E8
New Lane End Warrtn 82 D6
New Langholm D & G 110 G4
New Leake Lincs 87 M9
New Leeds Abers 159 N7
New Lodge Barns 91 K9
New Longton Lancs 88 G5
New Luce D & G 106 G5
Newlyn Cnwll 2 D8
Newmachar Abers 151 M4
Newmains N Lans 126 E6
New Malden Gt Lon 36 F7
Newman's End Essex 51 M8
Newman's Green Suffk 52 E3
Newmarket Suffk 63 K8
Newmarket W Isls 168 j4
New Marske R & Cl 104 H6
New Marston Oxon 34 F3
New Marton Shrops 69 K8
New Mill Abers 151 K11
Newmill Border 117 P8
New Mill Cnwll 2 D7
New Mill Herts 35 P2
New Mill Kirk 90 F9
Newmill Moray 158 B7
Newmillerdam Wakefd 91 J7
Newmill of Inshewan Angus 142 G5
Newmills C Edin 127 M4
New Mills Cnwll 3 M3
New Mills Derbys 83 M7
Newmills Fife 134 C10
Newmills Mons 31 P3
New Mills Powys 55 P4
Newmiln P & K 142 A11
Newmilns E Ayrs 125 N10
New Milton Hants 13 M5
New Mistley Essex 53 K5
New Moat Pembks 41 L5
Newnes Shrops 69 L8
Newney Green Essex 51 Q9
Newnham Hants 23 K4
Newnham Herts 50 F3
Newnham Kent 38 G10
Newnham Nhants 60 C9
Newnham Bridge Worcs 57 L11
Newnham on Severn Gloucs 32 C2
New Ollerton Notts 85 L7
New Oscott Birm 58 G6
New Pitsligo Abers 159 L6
New Polzeath Cnwll 4 E6
Newport Cnwll 5 N4
Newport Dorset 12 E5
Newport E R Yk 92 E4
Newport Essex 51 M4
Newport Gloucs 32 D5
Newport Highld 163 Q2
Newport IoW 14 F9
Newport Newpt 31 K7
Newport Norfk 77 Q8
Newport Pembks 41 L3
Newport Wrekin 70 C11
Newport-on-Tay Fife 135 L2
Newport Pagnell M Keyn 49 N6
Newport Pagnell Services M Keyn 49 N6
Newpound Common W Susx 24 C5
New Prestwick S Ayrs 114 F3
New Quay Cerdgn 42 G3
Newquay Cnwll 4 C9
New Quay Essex 52 H7
Newquay Zoo Cnwll 4 C9
New Rackheath Norfk 77 K9
New Radnor Powys 45 J2
New Rent Cumb 101 N3
New Ridley Nthumb 112 G9
New Road Side N York 90 B2
New Romney Kent 27 J7
New Rossington Donc 91 Q11
New Row Cerdgn 54 G10
New Row Lancs 89 J3
New Sauchie Clacks 133 P9
Newsbank Ches E 82 H11
Newseat Abers 158 H11
Newsham Lancs 88 G3
Newsham N York 97 N4
Newsham N York 103 M8
Newsham Nthumb 113 M5
New Sharlston Wakefd 91 K7
Newsholme E R Yk 92 B5
Newsholme Lancs 96 B10
New Shoreston Nthumb 119 N4
New Silksworth Sundld 113 N10
New Skelton R & Cl 105 J7
Newsome Kirk 90 F8
New Somerby Lincs 73 N3
New Springs Wigan 88 H9
Newstead Border 117 R4
Newstead Notts 84 H10
Newstead Nthumb 119 N5
New Stevenston N Lans 126 D6
New Street Herefs 45 L3
New Swanage Dorset 12 H8
New Swannington Leics 72 C7
Newthorpe N York 91 M4
Newthorpe Notts 84 G11
New Thundersley Essex 38 C4
Newtimber W Susx 24 G8
Newtoft Lincs 86 D3
Newton Ag & B 131 L8
Newton Border 118 B6
Newton Brdgnd 29 M9
Newton C Beds 50 F2
Newton Cambs 62 F11
Newton Cambs 74 H8
Newton Cardif 30 H9
Newton Ches W 69 P3
Newton Ches W 81 N11
Newton Ches W 82 B9
Newton Cumb 94 E6
Newton Derbys 84 F9
Newton Herefs 45 L8
Newton Herefs 45 Q4
Newton Herefs 56 F11
Newton Highld 155 Q7
Newton Highld 156 C8
Newton Highld 156 D4
Newton Highld 167 P7
Newton Lancs 88 C3
Newton Lancs 95 M6
Newton Lincs 73 Q3
Newton Mdloth 127 Q4
Newton Moray 157 M5
Newton Moray 157 Q5
Newton N York 98 H6
Newton Nhants 61 J4
Newton Norfk 76 A8
Newton Notts 72 H2
Newton Nthumb 112 F8
Newton Nthumb 118 H9
Newton S Lans 116 C4
Newton S Lans 126 B5
Newton Sandw 58 F6
Newton Shrops 69 M8
Newton Somset 18 F7
Newton Staffs 71 J9
Newton Suffk 52 F3
Newton W Loth 127 K2
Newton Warwks 60 B5
Newton Wilts 21 P10
Newton Abbot Devon 7 M4
Newton Arlosh Cumb 110 D9
Newton Aycliffe Dur 103 Q6
Newton Bewley Hartpl 104 E5
Newton Blossomville M Keyn 49 P4
Newton Bromswold Nhants 61 L7
Newton Burgoland Leics 72 B9
Newton by Toft Lincs 86 D3
Newton Ferrers Devon 6 F9
Newton Ferry W Isls 168 d10
Newton Flotman Norfk 65 J2
Newtongrange Mdloth 127 Q5
Newton Green Mons 31 P6
Newton Harcourt Leics 72 G11
Newton Heath Manch 83 J4
Newtonhill Abers 151 N9
Newton Hill Wakefd 91 J6
Newton-in-Bowland Lancs 95 P10
Newton Kyme N York 91 M2
Newton-le-Willows N York 97 K3
Newton-le-Willows St Hel 82 C5
Newtonloan Mdloth 127 Q5
Newton Longville Bucks 49 M8
Newton Mearns E Rens 125 N6
Newtonmill Angus 143 L5
Newtonmore Highld 148 C8
Newton Morrell N York 103 P9
Newton Mountain Pembks 41 J9
Newton Mulgrave N York 105 L7
Newton of Balcanquhal P & K 134 F5
Newton of Belltrees Rens 125 K6
Newton-on-Ouse N York 97 R9
Newton-on-Rawcliffe N York 98 G2
Newton on the Hill Shrops 69 N10
Newton-on-the-Moor Nthumb 119 N9
Newton on Trent Lincs 85 P6
Newton Poppleford Devon 10 B7
Newton Purcell Oxon 48 H8
Newton Regis Warwks 59 L3
Newton Reigny Cumb 101 N4
Newton St Cyres Devon 9 L5
Newton St Faith Norfk 77 J8
Newton St Loe BaNES 20 D2
Newton St Petrock Devon 16 G9
Newton Solney Derbys 71 P9
Newton Stacey Hants 22 D6
Newton Stewart D & G 107 M4
Newton Tony Wilts 21 P6
Newton Tracey Devon 17 J6
Newton under Roseberry R & Cl 104 G8
Newton Underwood Nthumb 112 H3
Newton upon Derwent E R Yk 98 E11
Newton Valence Hants 23 K8
Newton Wamphray D & G 109 P2
Newton with Scales Lancs 88 F4
Newtown BCP 12 H6
Newtown Blae G 30 G3
Newtown Ches W 82 B9
Newtown Cnwll 2 F8
Newtown Cnwll 5 M6
Newtown Cumb 101 P6
Newtown Cumb 109 P11
Newtown Cumb 110 G8
Newtown Cumb 111 K8
Newtown D & G 115 Q5
Newtown Derbys 83 L8
Newtown Devon 9 Q5
Newtown Devon 17 P6
Newtown Dorset 11 K4
New Town Dorset 12 G3
New Town Dorset 21 J11
New Town Dorset 21 J11
New Town E Susx 25 L6
Newtown Gloucs 32 C4
Newtown Hants 13 N2
Newtown Hants 14 H4
Newtown Hants 22 E2
Newtown Herefs 45 P3
Newtown Herefs 45 Q8
Newtown Herefs 46 B5
Newtown Highld 147 K7
Newtown IoW 14 D8
Newtown Nthumb 119 J4
Newtown Nthumb 119 K10
Newtown Nthumb 119 K5
Newtown Powys 55 Q6
Newtown Rhondd 30 E5
Newtown Shrops 69 M10
Newtown Shrops 69 N8
Newtown Somset 10 F2
Newtown Staffs 58 E4
Newtown Staffs 70 G2
Newtown Wigan 82 C4
Newtown Wilts 20 H9
Newtown Wilts 21 Q2
Newtown Worcs 46 G3
Newtown Worcs 58 D9
Newtown-in-St Martin Cnwll 3 J9
Newtown Linford Leics 72 E9
Newtown St Boswells Border 117 R4
Newtown Unthank Leics 72 D10
New Tredegar Caerph 30 F4
New Trows S Lans 126 E10
New Tupton Derbys 84 E7
Newtyle Angus 142 D9
New Walsoken Cambs 75 J9
New Waltham NE Lin 93 N10
New Whittington Derbys 84 E5
New Winton E Loth 128 C5
New Yatt Oxon 34 C2
Newyears Green Gt Lon 36 C3
Newyork Ag & B 131 K5
New York Lincs 86 H9
New York N Tyne 113 M6
New York N York 97 J8
New Zealand Wilts 33 K9
Nextend Herefs 45 L3
Neyland Pembks 41 J9
Niarbyl IoM 80 b6
Nibley Gloucs 32 C3
Nibley S Glos 32 C8
Nibley Green Gloucs 32 D5
Nicholashayne Devon 18 F11
Nicholaston Swans 28 F7
Nickies Hill Cumb 111 K7
Nidd N York 97 M8
Nigg C Aber 151 N7
Nigg Highld 156 E3
Nigg Ferry Highld 156 D4
Nimlet BaNES 32 D10
Ninebanks Nthumb 111 Q10
Nine Elms Swindn 33 M7
Nine Wells Pembks 40 E6
Ninfield E Susx 26 B9
Ningwood IoW 14 C9
Nisbet Border 118 C5
Nisbet Hill Border 129 K9
Niton IoW 14 F11
Nitshill C Glas 125 N5
Noah's Ark Kent 37 N9
Noak Bridge Essex 37 Q2
Noak Hill Gt Lon 37 M2
Noblethorpe Barns 90 H9
Nobold Shrops 56 H2
Nobottle Nhants 60 E8
Nocton Lincs 86 E8
Nogdam End Norfk 77 M11
Noke Oxon 34 F2
Nolton Pembks 40 G7
Nolton Haven Pembks 40 G7
No Man's Heath Ches W 69 P5
No Man's Heath Warwks 59 L3
No Man's Land Cnwll 5 M10
Nomansland Devon 9 K2
Nomansland Wilts 21 Q11
Noneley Shrops 69 N9
Nonington Kent 39 N11
Nook Cumb 95 L4
Nook Cumb 111 J5
Norbiton Gt Lon 36 E7
Norbreck Bpool 88 C2
Norbridge Herefs 46 D6
Norbury Ches E 69 Q5
Norbury Derbys 71 L6
Norbury Gt Lon 36 H7
Norbury Shrops 56 F6
Norbury Staffs 70 D10
Norbury Common Ches E 69 Q5
Norbury Junction Staffs 70 D10
Norchard Worcs 58 B11
Norcott Brook Ches W 82 D8
Norcross Lancs 88 C2
Nordelph Norfk 75 L10
Norden Rochdl 89 P8
Nordley Shrops 57 M5
Norfolk Broads Norfk 77 P10
Norham Nthumb 129 N10
Norland Town Calder 90 D6
Norley Ches W 82 C10
Norleywood Hants 14 C7
Norlington E Susx 25 K8
Normanby Lincs 86 C3
Normanby N Linc 92 E7
Normanby N York 98 E4
Normanby R & Cl 104 F7
Normanby le Wold Lincs 93 K11
Norman Cross Cambs 61 Q2
Normandy Surrey 23 P4
Normans Bay E Susx 25 Q9
Norman's Green Devon 9 Q4
Normanton C Derb 72 A4
Normanton Leics 73 L2
Normanton Notts 85 M10
Normanton Rutlnd 73 N9
Normanton Wakefd 91 K6
Normanton Wilts 21 M6
Normanton le Heath Leics 72 B8
Normanton on Cliffe Lincs 86 B11
Normanton on Soar Notts 72 E6
Normanton on the Wolds Notts 72 G4
Normanton on Trent Notts 85 N7
Normoss Lancs 88 C3
Norney Surrey 23 P6
Norrington Common Wilts 20 G2
Norris Green Cnwll 5 Q8
Norris Green Lpool 81 M6
Norris Hill Leics 72 A7
Norristhorpe Kirk 90 G6
Northacre Norfk 64 D2
Northall Bucks 49 Q10
Northallerton N York 97 N2
Northall Green Norfk 76 D9
Northam C Sotn 14 D4
Northam Devon 16 H6
Northampton Nhants 60 G8
Northampton Worcs 58 B11
Northampton Services Nhants 60 F9
North Anston Rothm 84 H4
North Ascot Br For 35 P11
North Aston Oxon 48 E9
Northaw Herts 50 G10
Northay Somset 10 F2
North Baddesley Hants 22 C10
North Ballachulish Highld 139 K5
North Barrow Somset 20 B9
North Barsham Norfk 76 C4
Northbay W Isls 168 c17
North Benfleet Essex 38 C4
North Berwick E Loth 128 E3
North Bitchburn Dur 103 N4
North Blyth Nthumb 113 M4
North Boarhunt Hants 14 H4
North Bockhampton BCP 13 L5
Northborough C Pete 74 C9
Northbourne Kent 39 P11
North Bovey Devon 8 H8
North Bradley Wilts 20 G3
North Brentor Devon 8 C8
North Brewham Somset 20 D7
North Bridge Surrey 23 Q7
Northbridge Street E Susx 26 B7
Northbrook Hants 22 F7
Northbrook Oxon 48 E10
North Brook End Cambs 50 G2
North Buckland Devon 16 H3
North Burlingham Norfk 77 M10
North Cadbury Somset 20 B9
North Carlton Lincs 86 B5
North Carlton Notts 85 J4
North Cave E R Yk 92 E4
North Cerney Gloucs 33 K3
North Chailey E Susx 25 J6
Northchapel W Susx 23 Q9
North Charford Hants 21 N11
North Charlton Nthumb 119 N6
North Cheam Gt Lon 36 F7
North Cheriton Somset 20 C9
North Chideock Dorset 11 J6
Northchurch Herts 35 Q3
North Cliffe E R Yk 92 E3
North Clifton Notts 85 P6
North Close Dur 103 Q4
North Cockerington Lincs 87 L2
North Connel Ag & B 138 G11
North Cornelly Brdgnd 29 M8
North Corner Cnwll 3 K10
North Cotes Lincs 93 P10
Northcott Devon 5 N3
Northcott Devon 10 B2
Northcott Devon 10 C3
North Country Cnwll 2 H5
Northcourt Oxon 34 E5
North Cove Suffk 65 P4
North Cowton N York 103 Q10
North Crawley M Keyn 49 P6
North Cray Gt Lon 37 L6
North Creake Norfk 76 B4
North Curry Somset 19 K9
North Dalton E R Yk 99 J10
North Deighton N York 97 N10
Northdown Kent 39 Q7
North Downs 38 F10
North Duffield N York 92 A3
Northedge Derbys 84 E7
North Elham Kent 27 L3
North Elkington Lincs 87 J2
North Elmham Norfk 76 D7
North Elmsall Wakefd 91 M8
Northend Bucks 35 K6
North End C Port 15 J6
North End Cumb 110 F9
North End Dorset 20 F9
North End E R Yk 93 L2
North End E R Yk 93 N4
North End Essex 51 Q7
North End Hants 21 M11
North End Hants 22 G9
North End Leics 72 F7
North End Lincs 74 D2

286 North End – Osterley

North End Lincs 87 M3
North End Lincs 92 H11
North End Lincs 93 P10
North End N Linc 93 K6
North End N Som 31 M11
North End Nhants 61 L7
North End Norfk 64 D3
North End Nthumb 119 M10
North End Sefton 81 L4
North End W Susx 15 Q6
North End W Susx 24 D9
Northend Warwks 48 C4
Northenden Manch 82 H7
Northend Woods Bucks 35 P7
North Erradale Highld 160 A10
North Evington C Leic 72 G10
North Fambridge Essex 38 E2
North Featherstone Wakefd 91 L6
North Ferriby E R Yk 92 G5
Northfield Birm 58 F9
Northfield C Aber 151 N6
Northfield E R Yk 92 H5
Northfields Lincs 73 Q9
Northfleet Kent 37 P6
North Frodingham E R Yk 99 N10
Northgate Lincs 74 C5
North Gorley Hants 13 L2
North Green Norfk 65 J4
North Green Suffk 65 L9
North Green Suffk 65 M8
North Greetwell Lincs 86 D6
North Grimston N York 98 G7
North Halling Medway 38 B8
North Hayling Hants 15 K6
North Hazelrigg Nthumb 119 L4
North Heasley Devon 17 N5
North Heath W Susx 24 C6
North Hele Devon 18 D10
North Hill Cnwll 5 M6
North Hillingdon Gt Lon 36 C4
North Hinksey Village Oxon 34 E3
North Holmwood Surrey 36 E11
North Huish Devon 7 J7
North Hykeham Lincs 86 B7
Northiam E Susx 26 D7
Northill C Beds 61 P11
Northington Gloucs 32 D3
Northington Hants 22 G7
North Kelsey Lincs 92 H10
North Kessock Highld 156 B8
North Killingholme N Linc 93 K7
North Kilvington N York 97 P3
North Kilworth Leics 60 D4
North Kingston Hants 13 L4
North Kyme Lincs 86 G10
North Lancing W Susx 24 E9
North Landing E R Yk 99 Q6
Northlands Lincs 87 K10
Northleach Gloucs 33 M2
North Lee Bucks 35 M3
North Lees N York 97 L6
Northleigh Devon 10 D5
Northleigh Devon 17 L5
North Leigh Kent 27 K2
North Leigh Oxon 34 C2
North Leverton with
Habblesthorpe Notts 85 N4
Northlew Devon 8 D5
North Littleton Worcs 47 L5
Northload Bridge Somset 19 N7
North Lopham Norfk 64 E5
North Luffenham Rutlnd 73 N10
North Marden W Susx 23 M11
North Marston Bucks 49 L10
North Middleton Mdloth 128 B8
North Middleton Nthumb 119 J6
North Millbrex Abers 159 K9
North Milmain D & G 106 E7
North Molton Devon 17 N6
Northmoor Oxon 34 D4
North Moreton Oxon 34 G7
Northmuir Angus 142 F6
North Mundham W Susx 15 N6
North Muskham Notts 85 N9
North Newbald E R Yk 92 F3
North Newington Oxon 48 D6
North Newnton Wilts 21 M3
North Newton Somset 19 K8
Northney Hants 15 K6
North Nibley Gloucs 32 D5
North Oakley Hants 22 F4
North Ockendon Gt Lon 37 N3
Northolt Gt Lon 36 D4
Northolt Airport Gt Lon 36 C3
Northop Flints 81 J11
Northop Hall Flints 81 K11
North Ormesby Middsb 104 F7
North Ormsby Lincs 87 J2
Northorpe Kirk 90 G6
Northorpe Lincs 74 A7
Northorpe Lincs 74 D3
Northorpe Lincs 92 E11
North Otterington N York 97 N3
Northover Somset 19 N7
Northover Somset 19 P10
North Owersby Lincs 86 E2
Northowram Calder 90 E5
North Perrott Somset 11 K3
North Petherton Somset 19 J8
North Petherwin Cnwll 5 M4
North Pickenham Norfk 76 B10
North Piddle Worcs 47 J4
North Poorton Dorset 11 L5
Northport Dorset 12 F7
North Poulner Hants 13 L3
North Queensferry Fife 134 E11
North Radworthy Devon 17 P5
North Rauceby Lincs 86 D11
Northrepps Norfk 77 J4
North Reston Lincs 87 L4
North Rigton N York 97 L11
North Ripley Hants 13 L5
North Rode Ches E 83 J11
North Roe Shet 169 q5
North Ronaldsay Ork 169 f1
North Ronaldsay Airport
Ork 169 g1
North Row Cumb 100 H4
North Runcton Norfk 75 M7
North Scale Cumb 94 D7
North Scarle Lincs 85 P7
North Seaton Nthumb 113 L3
North Seaton Colliery
Nthumb 113 L3
North Shian Ag & B 138 G9
North Shields N Tyne 113 N7
North Shoebury Sthend 38 F4
North Shore Bpool 88 C3
North Side C Pete 74 E11
North Side Cumb 100 C5
North Skelton R & Cl 105 J7
North Somercotes Lincs 93 R11
North Stainley N York 97 L5
North Stainmore Cumb 102 F7
North Stifford Thurr 37 P4
North Stoke BaNES 32 D11
North Stoke Oxon 34 H7
North Stoke W Susx 24 B8
Northstowe Cambs 62 F7
North Street Cambs 63 J7
North Street Hants 21 N11
North Street Hants 22 H8
North Street Kent 38 H10
North Street Medway 38 D7
North Street W Berk 34 H10
North Sunderland Nthumb 119 P4
North Tamerton Cnwll 5 N2
North Tawton Devon 8 G4
North Third Stirlg 133 M10
North Thoresby Lincs 93 N11
North Togston Nthumb 119 P10
North Tolsta W Isls 168 k3
Northton W Isls 168 e9
North Town Devon 17 J10
North Town Somset 19 Q6
North Town W & M 35 N8
North Tuddenham Norfk 76 E9
North Uist W Isls 168 c10
Northumberland National
Park Nthumb 111 Q4
North Walbottle N u Ty 113 J7
North Walsham Norfk 77 K5
North Waltham Hants 22 G5
North Warnborough Hants 23 K4
Northway Somset 18 F9
North Weald Bassett Essex 51 L10
North Wheatley Notts 85 N3
North Whilborough Devon 7 M5
Northwich Ches W 82 E10
North Wick BaNES 31 Q11
Northwick S Glos 31 Q7
Northwick Somset 19 L5
Northwick Worcs 46 F3
North Widcombe BaNES 19 Q3
North Willingham Lincs 86 G3
North Wingfield Derbys 84 F7
North Witham Lincs 73 N6
Northwold Norfk 75 Q11
Northwood C Stke 70 F5
Northwood Derbys 84 C8
Northwood Gt Lon 36 C2
Northwood IoW 14 E8
Northwood Shrops 69 N8
Northwood Worcs 57 P9
Northwood Green Gloucs 46 D11
North Wootton Dorset 11 P2
North Wootton Norfk 75 M6
North Wootton Somset 19 Q6
North Wraxall Wilts 32 F9
North Wroughton Swindn 33 M8
North York Moors National
Park 105 K10
Norton Donc 91 N7
Norton E Susx 25 L10
Norton Gloucs 46 G10
Norton Halton 82 C8
Norton Hants 22 E6
Norton Herts 50 F4
Norton IoW 13 P7
Norton Mons 45 N10
Norton N Som 19 K2
Norton Nhants 60 C8
Norton Notts 85 J6
Norton Powys 56 E11
Norton S on T 104 D6
Norton Sheff 84 E4
Norton Shrops 56 H8
Norton Shrops 57 K3
Norton Shrops 57 L8
Norton Shrops 57 N4
Norton Suffk 64 D8
Norton Swans 28 H7
Norton W Susx 15 P5
Norton Wilts 32 G8
Norton Worcs 46 G4
Norton Worcs 47 K5
Norton Bavant Wilts 20 H6
Norton Bridge Staffs 70 F8
Norton Canes Staffs 58 F3
Norton Canes Services
Staffs 58 F3
Norton Canon Herefs 45 M5
Norton Corner Norfk 76 F6
Norton Disney Lincs 85 Q9
Norton Ferris Wilts 20 E7
Norton Fitzwarren Somset 18 G9
Norton Green IoW 13 P7
Norton Hawkfield BaNES 19 Q2
Norton Heath Essex 51 P10
Norton in Hales Shrops 70 C7
Norton-Juxta-Twycross
Leics 59 M3
Norton-le-Clay N York 97 P6
Norton-le-Moors C Stke 70 F4
Norton Lindsey Warwks 47 P2
Norton Little Green Suffk 64 D8
Norton Malreward BaNES 20 B2
Norton Mandeville Essex 51 N10
Norton-on-Derwent N York 98 F6
Norton St Philip Somset 20 E3
Norton Subcourse Norfk 65 N2
Norton sub Hamdon Somset 19 N11
Norton Wood Herefs 45 M5
Norwell Notts 85 N8
Norwell Woodhouse Notts 85 M8
Norwich Norfk 77 J10
Norwich Airport Norfk 77 J9
Norwick Shet 169 t2
Norwood Clacks 133 P9
Norwood Derbys 84 G4
Norwood Kent 27 J5
Norwood End Essex 51 N9
Norwood Green Calder 90 E5
Norwood Green Gt Lon 36 D5
Norwood Hill Surrey 24 F2
Norwoodside Cambs 74 H11
Noseley Leics 73 J11
Noss Mayo Devon 6 F9
Nosterfield N York 97 L4
Nosterfield End Cambs 51 P2
Nostie Highld 145 Q2
Notgrove Gloucs 47 M10
Nottage Brdgnd 29 M9
Notter Cnwll 5 P9
Nottingham C Nott 72 F3
Nottington Dorset 11 P8
Notton Wakefd 91 J8
Notton Wilts 32 H11
Nounsley Essex 52 C9
Noutard's Green Worcs 57 Q11
Nowton Suffk 64 B9
Nox Shrops 56 G2
Nuffield Oxon 35 J7
Nunburnholme E R Yk 98 G11
Nuncargate Notts 84 H10
Nunclose Cumb 111 J11
Nuneaton Warwks 59 N6
Nuneham Courtenay Oxon 34 G5
Nunhead Gt Lon 36 H5
Nunkeeling E R Yk 99 N11
Nun Monkton N York 97 R9
Nunney Somset 20 D5
Nunney Catch Somset 20 D6
Nunnington Herefs 45 R6
Nunnington N York 98 D5
Nunsthorpe NE Lin 93 N9
Nunthorpe C York 98 C10
Nunthorpe Middsb 104 F8
Nunthorpe Village Middsb 104 F8
Nunton Wilts 21 N9
Nunwick N York 97 M6
Nunwick Nthumb 112 C6
Nupdown S Glos 32 B5
Nup End Bucks 49 N11
Nupend Gloucs 32 E3
Nuptown Br For 35 N10
Nursling Hants 22 C11
Nursted Hants 23 L10
Nursteed Wilts 21 K2
Nurton Staffs 58 B5
Nutbourne W Susx 15 L5
Nutbourne W Susx 24 C7
Nutfield Surrey 36 H10
Nuthall Notts 72 E2
Nuthampstead Herts 51 K4
Nuthurst W Susx 24 E5
Nutley E Susx 25 K5
Nutley Hants 22 H6
Nuttall Bury 89 M7
Nutwell Donc 91 Q10
Nybster Highld 167 Q4
Nyetimber W Susx 15 N7
Nyewood W Susx 23 M10
Nymans W Susx 24 G5
Nymet Rowland Devon 17 N10
Nymet Tracey Devon 8 H4
Nympsfield Gloucs 32 F4
Nynehead Somset 18 F10
Nythe Somset 19 M8
Nyton W Susx 15 P5

O

Oadby Leics 72 G10
Oad Street Kent 38 E9
Oakall Green Worcs 46 F2
Oakamoor Staffs 71 J6
Oakbank W Loth 127 K4
Oak Cross Devon 8 D5
Oakdale Caerph 30 G5
Oake Somset 18 G9
Oaken Staffs 58 C4
Oakenclough Lancs 95 L11
Oakengates Wrekin 57 N2
Oakenholt Flints 81 K10
Oakenshaw Dur 103 N3
Oakenshaw Kirk 90 F5
Oakerthorpe Derbys 84 E10
Oakford Cerdgn 43 J3
Oakford Devon 18 B10
Oakfordbridge Devon 18 B10
Oakgrove Ches E 83 K11
Oakham Rutlnd 73 M9
Oakhanger Ches E 70 D4
Oakhanger Hants 23 L7
Oakhill Somset 20 B5
Oakhurst Kent 37 N10
Oakington Cambs 62 F8
Oaklands Herts 50 F7
Oaklands Powys 44 E4
Oakle Street Gloucs 46 E11
Oakley BCP 12 H5
Oakley Bed 61 M10
Oakley Bucks 34 H2
Oakley Fife 134 C10
Oakley Hants 22 G4
Oakley Oxon 35 L4
Oakley Suffk 64 H6
Oakley Green W & M 35 P9
Oakley Park Powys 55 M7
Oakridge Lynch Gloucs 32 H4
Oaks Lancs 89 K4
Oaks Shrops 56 G4
Oaksey Wilts 33 J6
Oaks Green Derbys 71 M8
Oakshaw Ford Cumb 111 K5
Oakshott Hants 23 K9
Oakthorpe Leics 59 M2
Oak Tree Darltn 104 C8
Oakwood C Derb 72 B3
Oakwood Nthumb 112 D7
Oakworth C Brad 90 C3
Oare Kent 38 H9
Oare Somset 17 P2
Oare Wilts 21 N2
Oasby Lincs 73 Q3
Oath Somset 19 L9
Oathlaw Angus 142 H6
Oatlands Park Surrey 36 C7
Oban Ag & B 130 H2
Oban Airport Ag & B 138 G10
Obley Shrops 56 E9
Obney P & K 141 P10
Oborne Dorset 20 C11
Obthorpe Lincs 74 A8
Occold Suffk 64 H7
Occumster Highld 167 N9
Ochiltree E Ayrs 115 K3
Ockbrook Derbys 72 C3
Ocker Hill Sandw 58 E6
Ockeridge Worcs 46 E2
Ockham Surrey 36 C9
Ockle Highld 137 P1
Ockley Surrey 24 D2
Ocle Pychard Herefs 46 A5
Octon E R Yk 99 L7
Odcombe Somset 19 P11
Odd Down BaNES 20 D2
Oddendale Cumb 101 Q8
Oddingley Worcs 46 H3
Oddington Oxon 48 G11
Odell Bed 61 L9
Odham Devon 8 C4
Odiham Hants 23 K4
Odsal C Brad 90 F5
Odsey Cambs 50 G3
Odstock Wilts 21 M9
Odstone Leics 72 B9
Offchurch Warwks 59 N11
Offenham Worcs 47 L5
Offerton Stockp 83 K7
Offerton Sundld 113 M9
Offham E Susx 25 K8
Offham Kent 37 Q9
Offham W Susx 24 B9
Offleymarsh Staffs 70 D9
Offord Cluny Cambs 62 B7
Offord D'Arcy Cambs 62 B7
Offton Suffk 53 J2
Offwell Devon 10 D5
Ogbourne Maizey Wilts 33 N10
Ogbourne St Andrew Wilts 33 N10
Ogbourne St George Wilts 33 P10
Ogden Calder 90 D4
Ogle Nthumb 112 H5
Oglet Lpool 81 N8
Ogmore V Glam 29 N9
Ogmore-by-Sea V Glam 29 N9
Ogmore Vale Brdgnd 29 P6
Ogwen Bank Gwynd 79 L11
Okeford Fitzpaine Dorset 12 D2
Okehampton Devon 8 E5
Oker Side Derbys 84 C8
Okewood Hill Surrey 24 D3
Olchard Devon 9 L9
Old Nhants 60 G6
Old Aberdeen C Aber 151 N6
Old Alresford Hants 22 G8
Oldany Highld 164 C10
Old Arley Warwks 59 L6
Old Auchenbrack D & G 115 Q8
Old Basford C Nott 72 F2
Old Basing Hants 23 J4
Old Beetley Norfk 76 D8
Oldberrow Warwks 58 H11
Old Bewick Nthumb 119 L6
Old Bolingbroke Lincs 87 L7
Old Bramhope Leeds 90 G2
Old Brampton Derbys 84 D6
Old Bridge of Urr D & G 108 G7
Old Buckenham Norfk 64 F3
Old Burghclere Hants 22 E3
Oldbury Kent 37 N9
Oldbury Sandw 58 E7
Oldbury Shrops 57 N6
Oldbury Warwks 59 M6
Oldbury Naite S Glos 32 B6
Oldbury-on-Severn S Glos 32 B6
Oldbury on the Hill Gloucs 32 F7
Old Byland N York 98 B3
Old Cantley Donc 91 Q10
Old Cassop Dur 104 B3
Oldcastle Mons 45 L10
Oldcastle Heath Ches W 69 N5
Old Catton Norfk 77 J9
Old Churchstoke Powys 56 D6
Old Clee NE Lin 93 N9
Old Cleeve Somset 18 D6
Old Colwyn Conwy 80 B9
Oldcotes Notts 85 J3
Old Coulsdon Gt Lon 36 H9
Old Dailly S Ayrs 114 D8
Old Dalby Leics 72 H6
Old Dam Derbys 83 P9
Old Deer Abers 159 N8
Old Ditch Somset 19 P5
Old Edlington Donc 91 N11
Old Eldon Dur 103 P5
Old Ellerby E R Yk 93 L3
Old Felixstowe Suffk 53 P4
Oldfield C Brad 90 C3
Oldfield Worcs 46 F2
Old Fletton C Pete 74 C11
Oldford Somset 20 E4
Old Forge Herefs 45 R11
Old Furnace Herefs 45 P10
Old Glossop Derbys 83 M6
Old Goole E R Yk 92 B6
Old Grimsby IoS 2 b1
Old Hall Green Herts 51 J6
Oldhall Green Suffk 64 B10
Old Hall Street Norfk 77 L5
Oldham Oldham 83 K4
Oldhamstocks E Loth 129 J5
Old Harlow Essex 51 L8
Old Heath Essex 52 H7
Old Hunstanton Norfk 75 N2
Old Hurst Cambs 62 D5
Old Hutton Cumb 95 M3
Old Inns Services N Lans 126 D2
Old Kea Cnwll 3 L5
Old Kilpatrick W Duns 125 M3
Old Knebworth Herts 50 F6
Old Lakenham Norfk 77 J10
Oldland S Glos 32 C10
Old Langho Lancs 89 L3
Old Laxey IoM 80 f5
Old Leake Lincs 87 M10
Old Malton N York 98 F6
Oldmeldrum Abers 151 L2
Oldmill Cnwll 5 P7
Old Milverton Warwks 59 L11
Oldmixon N Som 19 K3
Old Newton Suffk 64 F9
Old Oxted Surrey 37 J10
Old Portlethen Abers 151 N8
Old Quarrington Dur 104 B3
Old Radford C Nott 72 F2
Old Radnor Powys 45 K3
Old Rayne Abers 150 H2
Old Romney Kent 26 H7
Old Shoreham W Susx 24 F9
Oldshoremore Highld 164 F5
Old Soar Kent 37 P10
Old Sodbury S Glos 32 E8
Old Somerby Lincs 73 P4
Oldstead N York 98 A5
Old Stratford Nhants 49 L6
Old Struan P & K 141 K4
Old Swarland Nthumb 119 N10
Old Swinford Dudley 58 D8
Old Tebay Cumb 102 B9
Old Thirsk N York 97 P4
Old Town Calder 90 C5
Old Town Cumb 95 M4
Old Town Cumb 101 N2
Old Town E Susx 25 N11
Old Town IoS 2 c2
Old Trafford Traffd 82 H5
Old Tupton Derbys 84 E7
Oldwall Cumb 111 J8
Oldwalls Swans 28 E6
Old Warden C Beds 50 D2
Oldways End Somset 17 R7
Old Weston Cambs 61 N5
Old Wick Highld 167 Q7
Old Windsor W & M 35 Q10
Old Wives Lees Kent 39 J11
Old Woking Surrey 36 B9
Old Wolverton M Keyn 49 M6
Old Woodhall Lincs 86 H7
Old Woods Shrops 69 N10
Olgrinmore Highld 167 J6
Olive Green Staffs 71 L11
Oliver's Battery Hants 22 E9
Ollaberry Shet 169 q5
Ollach Highld 153 J10
Ollerton Ches E 82 G9
Ollerton Notts 85 L7
Ollerton Shrops 70 A9
Olmarch Cerdgn 43 M3
Olmstead Green Cambs 51 P2
Olney M Keyn 49 N4
Olrig House Highld 167 L3
Olton Solhll 58 H8
Olveston S Glos 32 B7
Ombersley Worcs 46 F2
Ompton Notts 85 L7
Once Brewed Nthumb 111 P7
Onchan IoM 80 e6
Onecote Staffs 71 J3
Onehouse Suffk 64 E10
Onen Mons 31 M2
Ongar Street Herefs 56 F11
Onibury Shrops 56 H9
Onich Highld 139 J5
Onllwyn Neath 29 M2
Onneley Staffs 70 D6
Onslow Green Essex 51 Q7
Onslow Village Surrey 23 Q5
Onston Ches W 82 C10
Openwoodgate Derbys 84 E11
Opinan Highld 153 N3
Orbliston Moray 157 Q6
Orbost Highld 152 D9
Orby Lincs 87 N7
Orchard Portman Somset 18 H10
Orcheston Wilts 21 L5
Orcop Herefs 45 P9
Orcop Hill Herefs 45 P9
Ord Abers 158 F6
Ordhead Abers 150 H5
Ordie Abers 150 D7
Ordiequish Moray 157 Q6
Ordley Nthumb 112 D9
Ordsall Notts 85 M5
Ore E Susx 26 D9
Oreleton Common Herefs 56 H11
Oreton Shrops 57 M8
Orford Suffk 65 N11
Orford Warrtn 82 D6
Organford Dorset 12 F6
Orgreave Staffs 71 L11
Orkney Islands Ork 169 d6
Orkney Neolithic Ork 169 c5
Orlestone Kent 26 H5
Orleton Herefs 56 H11
Orleton Worcs 57 N11
Orlingbury Nhants 61 J6
Ormathwaite Cumb 101 J5
Ormesby R & Cl 104 F7
Ormesby St Margaret Norfk 77 P9
Ormesby St Michael Norfk 77 P9
Ormiscaig Highld 160 D8
Ormiston E Loth 128 C6
Ormsaigmore Highld 137 M3
Ormsary Ag & B 123 M5
Ormskirk Lancs 88 E9
Ornsby Hill Dur 113 J11
Oronsay Ag & B 136 b4
Orphir Ork 169 c6
Orpington Gt Lon 37 L7
Orrell Sefton 81 L5
Orrell Wigan 82 B4
Orrell Post Wigan 88 G9
Orrisdale IoM 80 d3
Orroland D & G 108 G11
Orsett Thurr 37 P4
Orsett Heath Thurr 37 P4
Orslow Staffs 70 E11
Orston Notts 73 K2
Orthwaite Cumb 101 J4
Ortner Lancs 95 L10
Orton Cumb 102 B9
Orton Nhants 60 H5
Orton Staffs 58 C5
Orton Longueville C Pete 74 C11
Orton-on-the-Hill Leics 59 M4
Orton Rigg Cumb 110 F10
Orton Waterville C Pete 74 C11
Orwell Cambs 62 E10
Osbaldeston Lancs 89 J4
Osbaldeston Green Lancs 89 J4
Osbaldwick C York 98 C10
Osbaston Leics 72 C10
Osbaston Shrops 69 K10
Osborne IoW 14 F8
Osborne House IoW 14 F8
Osbournby Lincs 73 R3
Oscroft Ches W 81 Q11
Ose Highld 152 E9
Osgathorpe Leics 72 C7
Osgodby Lincs 86 E2
Osgodby N York 91 Q4
Osgodby N York 99 M4
Oskaig Highld 153 J10
Oskamull Ag & B 137 M7
Osmaston Derbys 71 M6
Osmington Dorset 11 Q8
Osmington Mills Dorset 12 B8
Osmondthorpe Leeds 91 J4
Osmotherley N York 104 E11
Osney Oxon 34 E3
Ospringe Kent 38 H9
Ossett Wakefd 90 H6
Ossington Notts 85 N8
Ostend Essex 38 F2
Osterley Gt Lon 36 E5

Oswaldkirk – Pentre Bach 287

Oswaldkirk N York 98 C5
Oswaldtwistle Lancs 89 L5
Oswestry Shrops 69 J9
Otairnis W Isls 168 e10
Otford Kent 37 M9
Otham Kent 38 C11
Otham Hole Kent 38 D11
Othery Somset 19 L8
Otley Leeds 97 K11
Otley Suffk 65 J10
Otley Green Suffk 65 J10
Otterbourne Hants 22 E10
Otterburn N York 96 C9
Otterburn Nthumb 112 C2
Otter Ferry Ag & B 131 J11
Otterham Cnwll 5 K3
Otterhampton Somset 18 H6
Otterham Quay Kent 38 D8
Otterham Station Cnwll 5 K4
Otternish W Isls 168 e10
Ottershaw Surrey 36 B8
Otterswick Shet 169 s5
Otterton Devon 10 B7
Otterwood Hants 14 D6
Ottery St Mary Devon 10 C5
Ottinge Kent 27 L3
Ottringham E R Yk 93 N6
Oughterby Cumb 110 E9
Oughtershaw N York 96 C4
Oughterside Cumb 100 F2
Oughtibridge Sheff 84 D2
Oughtrington Warrtn 82 E7
Oulston N York 98 A6
Oulton Cumb 110 D10
Oulton Leeds 91 K5
Oulton Norfk 76 G6
Oulton Staffs 70 D10
Oulton Staffs 70 G7
Oulton Suffk 65 Q3
Oulton Broad Suffk 65 Q3
Oulton Street Norfk 76 H6
Oundle Nhants 61 M3
Ounsdale Staffs 58 C6
Our Dynamic Earth C Edin 127 P3
Ousby Cumb 102 B4
Ousden Suffk 63 M9
Ousefleet E R Yk 92 D6
Ouston Dur 113 L10
Outchester Nthumb 119 M4
Out Elmstead Kent 39 M11
Outgate Cumb 101 L11
Outhgill Cumb 102 E10
Outhill Warwks 58 H11
Outlands Staffs 70 D8
Outlane Kirk 90 D7
Out Newton E R Yk 93 Q6
Out Rawcliffe Lancs 88 E2
Out Skerries Shet 169 t6
Outwell Norfk 75 K10
Outwick Hants 21 M11
Outwood Surrey 36 H11
Outwood Wakefd 91 J6
Outwood Gate Bury 89 M9
Outwoods Leics 72 C7
Outwoods Staffs 70 D11
Ouzlewell Green Leeds 91 J5
Ovenden Calder 90 D5
Over Cambs 62 E6
Over Ches W 82 D11
Over Gloucs 46 F11
Over S Glos 31 Q8
Over Burrows Derbys 71 P7
Overbury Worcs 47 J7
Overcombe Dorset 11 P8
Over Compton Dorset 19 Q11
Over End Cambs 61 N2
Overgreen Derbys 84 D6
Over Green Warwks 59 J6
Over Haddon Derbys 84 B7
Over Hulton Bolton 82 E4
Over Kellet Lancs 95 L7
Over Kiddington Oxon 48 D10
Overleigh Somset 19 N7
Overley Staffs 71 M11
Over Monnow Mons 31 P2
Over Norton Oxon 48 B9
Over Peover Ches E 82 G10
Overpool Ches W 81 M9
Overscaig Highld 161 Q2
Overseal Derbys 71 P11
Over Silton N York 97 P2
Oversland Kent 39 J10
Oversley Green Warwks 47 L3
Overstone Nhants 60 G7
Over Stowey Somset 18 G7
Overstrand Norfk 77 J3
Over Stratton Somset 19 M11
Overstreet Wilts 21 L7
Over Tabley Ches E 82 F9
Overthorpe Nhants 48 E6
Overton C Aber 151 M5
Overton Ches W 81 Q9
Overton Hants 22 F5
Overton Lancs 95 J9
Overton N York 98 B9
Overton Shrops 57 J10
Overton Swans 28 E7
Overton Wakefd 90 H7
Overton Wrexhm 69 L6
Overton Bridge Wrexhm 69 L6
Overton Green Ches E 70 E2
Overtown Lancs 89 P5
Overtown Lancs 95 N5
Overtown N Lans 126 E7
Overtown Swindn 33 N9
Overtown Wakefd 91 K7
Over Wallop Hants 21 Q7
Over Whitacre Warwks 59 L6
Over Woodhouse Derbys 84 G6
Over Worton Oxon 48 D9
Overy Oxon 34 G6
Oving Bucks 49 L10
Oving W Susx 15 P6
Ovingdean Br & H 25 J10
Ovingham Nthumb 112 G8
Ovington Dur 103 M8
Ovington Essex 52 C3
Ovington Hants 22 G8
Ovington Norfk 76 C11
Ovington Nthumb 112 G8
Ower Hants 14 E6
Ower Hants 22 B11
Owermoigne Dorset 12 C7
Owlbury Shrops 56 E6
Owlerton Sheff 84 D3
Owlpen Gloucs 32 E5
Owl's Green Suffk 65 K8
Owlsmoor Br For 23 M2
Owlswick Bucks 35 L3
Owmby Lincs 86 D3
Owmby Lincs 93 J10
Owslebury Hants 22 F10
Owston Donc 91 P8
Owston Leics 73 K9
Owston Ferry N Linc 92 D10
Owstwick E R Yk 93 N4
Owthorne E R Yk 93 P5
Owthorpe Notts 72 H4
Owton Manor Hartpl 104 E5
Oxborough Norfk 75 P10
Oxbridge Dorset 11 K5
Oxcombe Lincs 87 K5
Oxcroft Derbys 84 G6
Oxen End Essex 51 Q5
Oxenholme Cumb 95 L3
Oxenhope C Brad 90 C4
Oxen Park Cumb 94 G3
Oxenpill Somset 19 M6
Oxenton Gloucs 47 J8
Oxenwood Wilts 22 B3
Oxford Oxon 34 F3
Oxford Airport Oxon 48 E11
Oxford Services Oxon 34 H4
Oxgangs C Edin 127 N4
Oxhey Herts 50 D11
Oxhill Dur 113 J10
Oxhill Warwks 48 B5
Oxley Wolves 58 D4
Oxley Green Essex 52 F9
Oxley's Green E Susx 25 Q6
Oxlode Cambs 62 G3
Oxnam Border 118 C7
Oxnead Norfk 77 J7
Oxshott Surrey 36 D8
Oxshott Heath Surrey 36 D8
Oxspring Barns 90 H10
Oxted Surrey 37 J10
Oxton Border 128 D9
Oxton N York 91 N2
Oxton Notts 85 K10
Oxton Wirral 81 L7
Oxwich Swans 28 E7
Oxwich Green Swans 28 E7
Oxwick Norfk 76 C6
Oykel Bridge Highld 161 P6
Oyne Abers 150 H2
Oystermouth Swans 28 H7
Ozleworth Gloucs 32 E6

P

Pabail W Isls 168 k4
Packers Hill Dorset 11 Q2
Packington Leics 72 B8
Packmoor C Stke 70 F4
Packmores Warwks 59 L11
Padanaram Angus 142 G7
Padbury Bucks 49 K8
Paddington Gt Lon 36 G4
Paddington Warrtn 82 D7
Paddlesworth Kent 27 L4
Paddlesworth Kent 37 Q8
Paddock Wood Kent 25 Q2
Paddolgreen Shrops 69 P8
Padfield Derbys 83 M5
Padgate Warrtn 82 D7
Padhams Green Essex 51 P11
Padiham Lancs 89 M4
Padside N York 97 J9
Padstow Cnwll 4 E6
Padworth W Berk 34 H11
Page Bank Dur 103 P3
Pagham W Susx 15 N7
Paglesham Essex 38 F3
Paignton Torbay 7 M6
Pailton Warwks 59 Q8
Paine's Cross E Susx 25 P6
Painleyhill Staffs 71 J8
Painscastle Powys 44 H5
Painshawfield Nthumb 112 G8
Painsthorpe E R Yk 98 G9
Painswick Gloucs 32 G3
Painter's Forstal Kent 38 G10
Paisley Rens 125 M5
Pakefield Suffk 65 Q3
Pakenham Suffk 64 C8
Pale Gwynd 68 C7
Pale Green Essex 51 Q2
Palestine Hants 21 Q6
Paley Street W & M 35 N9
Palfrey Wsall 58 F5
Palgrave Suffk 64 G6
Pallington Dorset 12 C6
Palmarsh Kent 27 K5
Palmersbridge Cnwll 5 K6
Palmers Green Gt Lon 36 H2
Palmerston E Ayrs 115 K4
Palmerstown V Glam 30 F11
Palnackie D & G 108 H9
Palnure D & G 107 N5
Palterton Derbys 84 G7
Pamber End Hants 22 H3
Pamber Green Hants 22 H3
Pamber Heath Hants 22 H2
Pamington Gloucs 46 H8
Pamphill Dorset 12 G4
Pampisford Cambs 62 G11
Panborough Somset 19 N5
Panbride Angus 143 K10
Pancrasweek Devon 16 D10
Pancross V Glam 30 D11
Pandy Caerph 30 G7
Pandy Gwynd 54 E4
Pandy Gwynd 68 A9
Pandy Mons 45 L10
Pandy Powys 55 L4
Pandy Wrexhm 68 G7
Pandy'r Capel Denbgs 68 E4
Pandy Tudur Conwy 67 R2
Panfield Essex 52 B6
Pangbourne W Berk 34 H9
Pangdean W Susx 24 G8
Panks Bridge Herefs 46 B5
Pannal N York 97 M10
Pannal Ash N York 97 L10
Pant Shrops 69 J10
Pantasaph Flints 80 H9
Panteg Pembks 40 H4
Pantersbridge Cnwll 5 K8
Pant-ffrwyth Brdgnd 29 P8
Pant Glas Gwynd 66 H5
Pantglas Powys 54 H5
Pant-Gwyn Carmth 43 L9
Pant-lasau Swans 29 J4
Pant Mawr Powys 55 J8
Panton Lincs 86 G5
Pant-pastynog Denbgs 68 D2
Pantperthog Gwynd 54 G4
Pantside Caerph 30 H5
Pant-y-caws Carmth 41 M5
Pant-y-dwr Powys 55 M10
Pant-y-ffridd Powys 56 B4
Pantyffynnon Carmth 28 H2
Pantygaseg Torfn 31 J5
Pantygelli Mons 45 L11
Pant-y-gog Brdgnd 29 P6
Pantymwyn Flints 68 G2
Panxworth Norfk 77 M9
Papa Stour Shet 169 n7
Papa Stour Airport Shet 169 n8
Papa Westray Ork 169 d1
Papa Westray Airport Ork 169 d1
Papcastle Cumb 100 F4
Papigoe Highld 167 Q6
Papple E Loth 128 F5
Papplewick Notts 84 H10
Papworth Everard Cambs 62 C8
Papworth St Agnes Cambs 62 C8
Par Cnwll 3 R3
Paramour Street Kent 39 N9
Parbold Lancs 88 F8
Parbrook Somset 19 Q7
Parbrook W Susx 24 C5
Parc Gwynd 68 A8
Parcllyn Cerdgn 42 D4
Parc Seymour Newpt 31 M6
Pardown Hants 22 G5
Pardshaw Cumb 100 E6
Parham Suffk 65 L9
Park D & G 109 K2
Park Nthumb 111 N8
Park Bottom Cnwll 2 H5
Park Bridge Tamesd 83 K4
Park Corner E Susx 25 M3
Park Corner Oxon 35 J7
Park Corner W & M 35 N8
Park End Bed 49 Q4
Parkend Gloucs 32 B3
Park End Nthumb 112 C5
Parker's Green Kent 37 P11
Parkeston Essex 53 M5
Parkeston Quay Essex 53 M5
Park Farm Kent 26 H4
Parkgate Ches W 81 K9
Parkgate Cumb 110 D11
Parkgate D & G 109 M3
Parkgate E Susx 26 B9
Parkgate Essex 51 Q5
Park Gate Hants 14 F5
Parkgate Kent 26 E5
Parkgate Kent 37 M8
Park Gate Leeds 90 F2
Parkgate Surrey 24 F2
Park Gate Worcs 58 D10
Park Green Essex 51 L5
Park Green Suffk 64 G9
Parkhall W Duns 125 M3
Parkham Devon 16 F7
Parkham Ash Devon 16 F7
Park Head Derbys 84 E10
Parkhill Dur 104 B3
Park Hill Gloucs 31 Q5
Parkhouse Mons 31 P4
Parkmill Swans 28 F7
Park Royal Gt Lon 36 E4
Parkside Dur 113 P11
Parkside N Lans 126 E6
Parkside Wrexhm 69 L3
Parkstone BCP 12 H6
Park Street Herts 50 D10
Park Street W Susx 24 D4
Parkway Herefs 46 D7
Parley Green BCP 13 K5
Parmoor Bucks 35 L7
Parracombe Devon 17 M2
Parrog Pembks 41 L3
Parsonby Cumb 100 F3
Parson Cross Sheff 84 D2
Parson Drove Cambs 74 G9
Parson's Heath Essex 52 H6
Parson's Hill Derbys 71 P9
Partick C Glas 125 N4
Partington Traffd 82 F6
Partney Lincs 87 M7
Parton Cumb 100 C6
Partridge Green W Susx 24 E7
Partrishow Powys 45 K10
Parwich Derbys 71 M4
Paslow Wood Common Essex 51 N10
Passenham Nhants 49 L7
Passfield Hants 23 M8
Passingford Bridge Essex 51 M11
Paston C Pete 74 C10
Paston Norfk 77 L5
Pasturefields Staffs 70 H10
Patchacott Devon 8 C5
Patcham Br & H 24 H9
Patchetts Green Herts 50 D11
Patching W Susx 24 C9
Patchole Devon 17 L3
Patchway S Glos 32 B8
Pateley Bridge N York 97 J7
Paternoster Heath Essex 52 F8
Pathe Somset 19 L8
Pathhead Fife 134 H9
Pathhead Mdloth 128 B7
Pathlow Warwks 47 N3
Path of Condie P & K 134 D5
Patmore Heath Herts 51 K5
Patna E Ayrs 114 H5
Patney Wilts 21 L3
Patrick IoM 80 b5
Patrick Brompton N York 97 K2
Patricroft Salfd 82 G5
Patrington E R Yk 93 P6
Patrington Haven E R Yk 93 P6
Patrixbourne Kent 39 L10
Patterdale Cumb 101 L7
Pattingham Staffs 57 Q5
Pattishall Nhants 49 J4
Pattiswick Green Essex 52 D7
Patton Shrops 57 K5
Patton Bridge Cumb 101 Q11
Paul Cnwll 2 D8
Paulerspury Nhants 49 K5
Paull E R Yk 93 L5
Paulton BaNES 20 C3
Paultons Park Hants 22 B11
Paunton Herefs 46 C4
Pauperhaugh Nthumb 119 M11
Pave Lane Wrekin 70 D11
Pavenham Bed 61 L9
Pawlett Somset 19 J6
Pawston Nthumb 118 G4
Paxford Gloucs 47 N7
Paxton Border 129 N9
Payden Street Kent 38 F11
Payhembury Devon 10 B4
Paynter's Lane End Cnwll 2 H5
Paythorne Lancs 96 B10
Paytoe Herefs 56 G10
Peacehaven E Susx 25 K10
Peak Dale Derbys 83 N9
Peak District National Park 83 Q6
Peak Forest Derbys 83 P9
Peak Hill Lincs 74 E7
Peakirk C Pete 74 C9
Pearson's Green Kent 25 Q2
Peartree Green Herefs 46 A8
Peasedown St John BaNES 20 D3
Peasehill Derbys 84 F11
Peaseland Green Norfk 76 F8
Peasemore W Berk 34 E9
Peasenhall Suffk 65 M8
Pease Pottage W Susx 24 G4
Pease Pottage Services W Susx 24 G4
Peaslake Surrey 24 C2
Peasley Cross St Hel 81 Q6
Peasmarsh E Susx 26 E7
Peasmarsh Somset 10 G2
Peasmarsh Surrey 23 Q5
Peathill Abers 159 M4
Peat Inn Fife 135 M6
Peatling Magna Leics 60 C2
Peatling Parva Leics 60 C3
Peaton Shrops 57 J7
Pebmarsh Essex 52 E5
Pebsham E Susx 26 C10
Pebworth Worcs 47 M5
Pecket Well Calder 90 B5
Peckforton Ches E 69 P3
Peckham Gt Lon 36 H5
Peckleton Leics 72 D10
Pedairffordd Powys 68 F10
Pedlinge Kent 27 K4
Pedmore Dudley 58 D8
Pedwell Somset 19 M7
Peebles Border 117 K2
Peel IoM 80 b5
Peel Lancs 88 D4
Peel Common Hants 14 G6
Peene Kent 27 L4
Peening Quarter Kent 26 E6
Peggs Green Leics 72 C7
Pegsdon C Beds 50 D4
Pegswood Nthumb 113 K3
Pegwell Kent 39 Q9
Peinchorran Highld 153 J11
Peinlich Highld 152 G6
Pelcomb Pembks 40 H7
Pelcomb Bridge Pembks 40 H7
Pelcomb Cross Pembks 40 H7
Peldon Essex 52 G8
Pell Green E Susx 25 P4
Pelsall Wsall 58 F4
Pelsall Wood Wsall 58 F4
Pelton Dur 113 L10
Pelton Fell Dur 113 L10
Pelutho Cumb 109 P11
Pelynt Cnwll 5 L10
Pemberton Carmth 28 F4
Pemberton Wigan 82 C4
Pembles Cross Kent 26 E2
Pembrey Carmth 28 D4
Pembridge Herefs 45 M3
Pembroke Pembks 41 J10
Pembroke Dock Pembks 41 J10
Pembrokeshire Coast National Park Pembks 40 F6
Pembury Kent 25 P2
Pen-allt Herefs 45 R9
Penallt Mons 31 P2
Penally Pembks 41 M11
Penare Cnwll 3 P5
Penarth V Glam 30 G10
Penblewin Pembks 41 M7
Pen-bont Rhydybeddau Cerdgn 54 F8
Penbryn Cerdgn 42 E4
Pencader Carmth 42 H7
Pencaenewydd Gwynd 66 G6
Pencaitland E Loth 128 C6
Pencarnisiog IoA 78 F10
Pencarreg Carmth 43 K5
Pencarrow Cnwll 5 J5
Pencelli Powys 44 F9
Penclawdd Swans 28 F5
Pencoed Brdgnd 30 C8
Pencombe Herefs 46 A4
Pencoyd Herefs 45 Q9
Pencraig Herefs 45 R10
Pencraig Powys 68 D9
Pendeen Cnwll 2 B7
Penderyn Rhondd 29 P3
Pendine Carmth 41 P9
Pendlebury Salfd 82 G4
Pendleton Lancs 89 M3
Pendock Worcs 46 E8
Pendoggett Cnwll 4 G6
Pendomer Somset 11 L2
Pendoylan V Glam 30 E9
Penegoes Powys 54 H4
Penelewey Cnwll 3 L5
Pen-ffordd Pembks 41 L6
Pengam Caerph 30 G5
Pengam Cardif 30 H9
Penge Gt Lon 37 J6
Pengelly Cnwll 4 H5
Pengenffordd Powys 44 H9
Pengorffwysfa IoA 78 H6
Pengover Green Cnwll 5 M8
Pen-groes-oped Mons 31 K3
Pengwern Denbgs 80 E9
Penhale Cnwll 2 H10
Penhale Cnwll 4 E10
Penhale Cnwll 4 H9
Penhale Cnwll 5 Q11
Penhallow Cnwll 3 K3
Penhalurick Cnwll 3 J6
Penhalvean Cnwll 3 J6
Penhill Swindn 33 N7
Penhow Newpt 31 M6
Penhurst E Susx 25 Q7
Peniarth Gwynd 54 E3
Penicuik Mdloth 127 N6
Peniel Carmth 42 H10
Peniel Denbgs 68 D2
Penifiler Highld 152 H9
Peninver Ag & B 120 E7
Penisarwaun Gwynd 67 K2
Penistone Barns 90 G10
Penjerrick Cnwll 3 K7
Penketh Warrtn 82 C7
Penkill S Ayrs 114 D8
Penkridge Staffs 58 D2
Penlean Cnwll 5 L2
Penleigh Wilts 20 G4
Penley Wrexhm 69 M6
Penllergaer Swans 28 H5
Pen-llyn IoA 78 F8
Penllyn V Glam 30 C9
Pen-lôn IoA 78 G11
Penmachno Conwy 67 P4
Penmaen Caerph 30 G5
Penmaen Swans 28 F7
Penmaenan Conwy 79 N9
Penmaenmawr Conwy 79 N9
Penmaenpool Gwynd 67 M11
Penmark V Glam 30 E11
Penmon IoA 79 L8
Penmorfa Gwynd 67 J6
Penmynydd IoA 79 J10
Penn Bucks 35 P6
Penn Wolves 58 C5
Pennal Gwynd 54 F4
Pennan Abers 159 K4
Pennant Cerdgn 43 K2
Pennant Denbgs 68 D8
Pennant Powys 55 K5
Pennant-Melangell Powys 68 D9
Pennar Pembks 41 J10
Pennard Swans 28 G7
Pennerley Shrops 56 F5
Pennicott Devon 9 L4
Pennines 90 B3
Pennington Cumb 94 F5
Pennington Hants 13 P5
Pennington Green Wigan 89 J9
Pennorth Powys 44 G9
Penn Street Bucks 35 P5
Pennsylvania S Glos 32 D10
Penny Bridge Cumb 94 G4
Pennycross Ag & B 137 N10
Pennygate Norfk 77 L7
Pennyghael Ag & B 137 N10
Pennyglen S Ayrs 114 E5
Penny Green Derbys 84 H5
Penny Hill Lincs 74 G5
Pennymoor Devon 9 L2
Pennywell Sundld 113 N9
Penparc Cerdgn 42 D5
Penparcau Cerdgn 54 D8
Penpedairheol Caerph 30 F5
Penpedairheol Mons 31 K4
Penpergwm Mons 31 K2
Penperlleni Mons 31 K4
Penpethy Cnwll 4 H4
Penpillick Cnwll 4 H10
Penpol Cnwll 3 L6
Penpoll Cnwll 5 J11
Penponds Cnwll 2 G6
Penpont Cnwll 4 H7
Penpont D & G 108 H2
Penpont Powys 44 D9
Penquit Devon 6 G8
Penrest Cnwll 5 N6
Penrherber Carmth 41 Q3
Pen-rhiw Pembks 41 P2
Penrhiwceiber Rhondd 30 E5
Pen Rhiwfawr Neath 29 K2
Penrhiwgoch Carmth 43 L11
Penrhiwllan Cerdgn 42 G6
Penrhiwpal Cerdgn 42 F5
Penrhos Gwynd 66 E8
Penrhos IoA 78 D8
Penrhos Mons 31 M2
Penrhos Powys 29 M2
Penrhos garnedd Gwynd 79 K10
Penrhyn Bay Conwy 79 Q8
Penrhyn-coch Cerdgn 54 E8
Penrhyndeudraeth Gwynd 67 L7
Penrhyn-side Conwy 79 Q8
Penrhys Rhondd 30 D6
Penrice Swans 28 E7
Penrioch N Ayrs 120 G3
Penrith Cumb 101 P4
Penrose Cnwll 4 D7
Penruddock Cumb 101 M5
Penryn Cnwll 3 K7
Pensarn Conwy 80 D9
Pensax Worcs 57 N11
Pensby Wirral 81 K8
Penselwood Somset 20 E8
Pensford BaNES 20 B2
Pensham Worcs 46 H6
Penshaw Sundld 113 M10
Penshurst Kent 25 M2
Penshurst Station Kent 37 M11
Pensilva Cnwll 5 M7
Pensnett Dudley 58 D7
Penstone Devon 9 J4
Penstrowed Powys 55 P6
Pentewan Cnwll 3 Q4
Pentir Gwynd 79 K11
Pentire Cnwll 4 B9
Pentlepoir Pembks 41 M9
Pentlow Essex 52 D3
Pentlow Street Essex 63 P11
Pentney Norfk 75 P8
Pentonbridge Cumb 110 H5
Penton Grafton Hants 22 B5
Penton Mewsey Hants 22 B5
Pentraeth IoA 79 J9
Pentre Denbgs 68 E2
Pentre Flints 81 L11
Pentre Mons 31 K3
Pentre Mons 31 M4
Pentre Powys 55 P7
Pentre Powys 56 B7
Pentre Powys 56 D6
Pentre Rhondd 30 C5
Pentre Shrops 69 L11
Pentre Wrexhm 69 J6
Pentre-bâch Cerdgn 43 L5
Pentre Bach Flints 81 J9

Place	Area	Page	Grid
Pentrebach	Myr Td	30	E4
Pentre-bach	Powys	44	C8
Pentrebeirdd	Powys	56	B2
Pentre Berw	IoA	78	H10
Pentre-bont	Conwy	67	N4
Pentre-cagel	Carmth	42	F6
Pentre-celyn	Denbgs	68	F4
Pentre-celyn	Powys	55	K3
Pentre-chwyth	Swans	29	J6
Pentre-clawdd	Shrops	69	J8
Pentre-cwrt	Carmth	42	G7
Pentredwr	Denbgs	68	G5
Pentrefelin	Carmth	43	J7
Pentrefelin	IoA	78	G6
Pentre Ffwrndan	Flints	81	K10
Pentrefoelas	Conwy	67	R4
Pentregalar	Pembks	41	N4
Pentregat	Cerdgn	42	G4
Pentre-Gwenlais	Carmth	43	M11
Pentre Gwynfryn	Gwynd	67	K9
Pentre Halkyn	Flints	81	J10
Pentre Hodrey	Shrops	56	E9
Pentre Isaf	Conwy	80	D10
Pentre Llanrhaeadr	Denbgs	68	E2
Pentre Llifior	Powys	56	B5
Pentre-llwyn-llwyd	Powys	44	D4
Pentre-llyn	Cerdgn	54	E9
Pentre-llyn-cymmer	Conwy	68	C4
Pentre-Maw	Powys	55	K4
Pentre Meyrick	V Glam	30	C9
Pentre-piod	Torfn	31	J4
Pentre-poeth	Newpt	31	J7
Pentre'rbryn	Cerdgn	42	G4
Pentre'r-felin	Cerdgn	43	M5
Pentre'r Felin	Conwy	79	Q11
Pentre'r-felin	Powys	44	C8
Pentre Saron	Denbgs	68	D2
Pentre-tafarn-y-fedw Conwy		67	Q2
Pentre ty gwyn	Carmth	43	R7
Pentrich	Derbys	84	E10
Pentridge	Dorset	21	K11
Pen-twyn	Caerph	30	H4
Pentwyn	Cardif	30	H8
Pen-twyn	Mons	31	P3
Pen-twyn	Torfn	31	J4
Pentwynmaur	Caerph	30	G5
Pentyrch	Cardif	30	F8
Penwithick	Cnwll	4	G10
Penwood	Hants	22	D2
Penwyllt	Powys	44	B11
Penybanc	Carmth	43	M10
Penybont	Powys	44	G2
Pen-y-bont	Powys	68	H10
Penybontfawr	Powys	68	E10
Pen-y-bryn	Pembks	41	N2
Pen-y-cae	Powys	44	M2
Penycae	Wrexm	69	J5
Pen-y-cae-mawr	Mons	31	M5
Pen-y-cefn	Flints	80	G9
Pen-y-clawdd	Mons	31	N3
Pen-y-coedcae	Rhondd	30	E7
Penycwm	Pembks	40	G6
Pen-y-fai	Brdgnd	29	N8
Pen-y-felin	Flints	80	H11
Penyffordd	Flints	69	K2
Pen-y-ffordd	Flints	80	G8
Penyffridd	Gwynd	67	J3
Pen-y-garn	Cerdgn	54	E7
Pen-y-Garnedd	Powys	68	F10
Pen-y-graig	Gwynd	66	C8
Penygraig	Rhondd	30	D6
Penygroes	Carmth	28	G2
Penygroes	Gwynd	66	H4
Pen-y-Gwryd	Gwynd	67	M3
Pen-y-lan	V Glam	30	C9
Pen-y-Mynydd	Carmth	28	E4
Penymynydd	Flints	69	K2
Pen-y-pass	Gwynd	67	L3
Pen-yr-Heol	Mons	31	M2
Penysarn	IoA	78	H6
Pen-y-stryt	Denbgs	68	H4
Penywaun	Rhondd	30	C4
Penzance	Cnwll	2	D7
Peopleton	Worcs	46	H4
Peover Heath	Ches E	82	G10
Peper Harow	Surrey	23	P6
Peplow	Shrops	70	A10
Pepper's Green	Essex	51	P8
Pepperstock	C Beds	50	C7
Perceton	N Ayrs	125	K9
Percyhorner	Abers	159	N4
Perelle	Guern	10	b2
Perham Down	Wilts	21	Q5
Periton	Somset	18	C5
Perivale	Gt Lon	36	E4
Perkins Village	Devon	9	P6
Perkinsville	Dur	113	L10
Perlethorpe	Notts	85	K6
Perranarworthal	Cnwll	3	K5
Perranporth	Cnwll	3	K3
Perranuthnoe	Cnwll	2	E8
Perranwell	Cnwll	3	K3
Perranwell	Cnwll	3	K6
Perran Wharf	Cnwll	3	K6
Perranzabuloe	Cnwll	3	K3
Perrott's Brook	Gloucs	33	K3
Perry	Birm	58	G6
Perry	Cambs	61	P7
Perry Barr	Birm	58	G6
Perry Green	Essex	52	D7
Perry Green	Herts	51	K7
Perry Green	Wilts	33	J7
Perrystone Hill	Herefs	46	B9
Perry Street	Somset	10	G3
Pershall	Staffs	70	E9
Pershore	Worcs	46	H5
Pertenhall	Bed	61	N7
Perth	P & K	134	E3
Perthy	Shrops	69	L8
Perton	Herefs	46	A6
Perton	Staffs	58	C5
Pertwood	Wilts	20	G7
Peterborough	C Pete	74	C11
Peterborough Services Cambs		61	P2
Peterchurch	Herefs	45	L7
Peterculter	C Aber	151	L7
Peterhead	Abers	159	R8
Peterlee	Dur	104	D2
Petersfield	Hants	23	K10
Peter's Green	Herts	50	D7
Petersham	Gt Lon	36	E6
Peters Marland	Devon	16	H9
Peterstone Wentlooge Newpt		31	J9
Peterston-super-Ely	V Glam	30	E9
Peterstow	Herefs	45	R11
Peters Village	Kent	38	B9
Peter Tavy	Devon	8	D9
Petham	Kent	39	K11
Petherwin Gate	Cnwll	5	M4
Petrockstow	Devon	17	J10
Petsoe End	M Keyn	49	N5
Pett	E Susx	26	E9
Pettaugh	Suffk	64	H10
Pett Bottom	Kent	39	L11
Petterden	Angus	142	G10
Pettinain	S Lans	116	D2
Pettistree	Suffk	65	L10
Petton	Devon	18	D10
Petton	Shrops	69	M9
Petts Wood	Gt Lon	37	L7
Pettycur	Fife	134	H10
Petty France	S Glos	32	E7
Pettymuk	Abers	151	N3
Petworth	W Susx	23	Q10
Pevensey	E Susx	25	P9
Pevensey Bay	E Susx	25	Q10
Pewsey	Wilts	21	N2
Pewsham	Wilts	32	H10
Pheasant's Hill	Bucks	35	L7
Phepson	Worcs	46	H3
Philadelphia	Sundld	113	M10
Philham	Devon	16	D7
Philiphaugh	Border	117	N5
Phillack	Cnwll	2	F6
Philleigh	Cnwll	3	M6
Phillpot End	Essex	51	P7
Philpstoun	W Loth	127	K2
Phocle Green	Herefs	46	B9
Phoenix Green	Hants	23	L3
Pibsbury	Somset	19	M9
Pica	Cumb	100	D6
Piccadilly	Warwks	59	K5
Piccotts End	Herts	50	B9
Pickburn	Donc	91	N9
Pickering	N York	98	F4
Picket Piece	Hants	22	C5
Picket Post	Hants	13	L3
Picket Twenty	Hants	22	C5
Pickford	Covtry	59	L8
Pickford Green	Covtry	59	L8
Pickhill	N York	97	M4
Picklescott	Shrops	56	G5
Pickmere	Ches E	82	E9
Pickney	Somset	18	G9
Pickstock	Wrekin	70	C10
Pickup Bank	Bl w D	89	L6
Pickwell	Devon	16	H3
Pickwell	Leics	73	K8
Pickwick	Wilts	32	G10
Pickworth	Lincs	73	Q4
Pickworth	RutInd	73	P8
Picton	Ches W	81	N10
Picton	Flints	80	G8
Picton	N York	104	D9
Piddinghoe	E Susx	25	K10
Piddington	Bucks	35	M6
Piddington	Nhants	49	M4
Piddington	Oxon	48	H11
Piddlehinton	Dorset	11	Q5
Piddletrenthide	Dorset	11	Q5
Pidley	Cambs	62	D5
Piercebridge	Darltn	103	P7
Pierowall	Ork	169	d2
Piff's Elm	Gloucs	46	H9
Pigdon	Nthumb	113	J3
Pigeon Green	Warwks	47	P2
Pig Oak	Dorset	12	H4
Pig Street	Herefs	45	M5
Pikehall	Derbys	71	M3
Pilford	Dorset	12	H4
Pilgrims Hatch	Essex	51	N11
Pilham	Lincs	85	Q2
Pill	N Som	31	N9
Pillaton	Cnwll	5	P9
Pillatonmill	Cnwll	5	P9
Pillerton Hersey	Warwks	47	Q5
Pillerton Priors	Warwks	47	Q5
Pilleth	Powys	56	D11
Pilley	Barns	91	J10
Pilley	Hants	13	P5
Pilley Bailey	Hants	13	P5
Pillgwenlly	Newpt	31	K7
Pillhead	Devon	16	H6
Pilling	Lancs	95	J11
Pilling Lane	Lancs	94	H11
Pilning	S Glos	31	Q7
Pilot Inn	Kent	27	J8
Pilsbury	Derbys	71	L2
Pilsdon	Dorset	11	J5
Pilsgate	C Pete	73	R9
Pilsley	Derbys	84	B6
Pilsley	Derbys	84	F8
Pilson Green	Norfk	77	M9
Piltdown	E Susx	25	K6
Pilton	Devon	17	K5
Pilton	Nhants	61	M4
Pilton	RutInd	73	N10
Pilton	Somset	19	Q6
Pilton Green	Swans	28	D7
Pimbo	Lancs	81	P4
Pimlico	Herts	50	C9
Pimlico	Lancs	89	L2
Pimlico	Lancs	48	H6
Pimperne	Dorset	12	F3
Pinchbeck	Lincs	74	D5
Pinchbeck Bars	Lincs	74	C5
Pincheon Green	Donc	91	R7
Pinchinthorpe	R & Cl	104	G8
Pincock	Lancs	88	G7
Pinfold	Lancs	88	D8
Pinford End	Suffk	64	A10
Pinged	Carmth	28	D4
Pingewood	W Berk	35	J11
Pin Green	Herts	50	G5
Pinhoe	Devon	9	N6
Pinkett's Booth	Covtry	59	L8
Pinkney	Wilts	32	G7
Pinkneys Green	W & M	35	N8
Pinley	Covtry	59	N9
Pinley Green	Warwks	59	N11
Pin Mill	Suffk	53	M4
Pinminnoch	S Ayrs	114	C9
Pinmore	S Ayrs	114	D9
Pinn	Devon	10	C7
Pinner	Gt Lon	36	D3
Pinner Green	Gt Lon	36	D2
Pinsley Green	Ches E	69	Q5
Pinvin	Worcs	47	J5
Pinwherry	S Ayrs	114	D10
Pinxton	Derbys	84	G10
Pipe and Lyde	Herefs	45	Q5
Pipe Aston	Herefs	56	H10
Pipe Gate	Shrops	70	C5
Pipehill	Staffs	58	G3
Piperdam	Angus	142	D11
Piperhill	Highld	156	F7
Pipers Pool	Cnwll	5	M5
Pipewell	Nhants	60	H3
Pippacott	Devon	17	J4
Pippin Street	Lancs	88	H6
Pipton	Powys	44	H7
Pirbright	Surrey	23	P3
Pirbright Camp	Surrey	23	P3
Pirnie	Border	118	C5
Pirnmill	N Ayrs	120	G3
Pirton	Herts	50	D4
Pirton	Worcs	46	G5
Pisgah	Cerdgn	54	F9
Pishill	Oxon	35	K7
Pistyll	Gwynd	66	E6
Pitblae	Abers	159	N5
Pitcairngreen	P & K	134	D2
Pitcalnie	Highld	156	E3
Pitcaple	Abers	151	J2
Pitchcombe	Gloucs	32	G3
Pitchcott	Bucks	49	L10
Pitcher Row	Lincs	74	E4
Pitchford	Shrops	57	J4
Pitch Green	Bucks	35	L4
Pitch Place	Surrey	23	N7
Pitch Place	Surrey	23	Q4
Pitchroy	Moray	157	M10
Pitcombe	Somset	20	C8
Pitcot	V Glam	29	N10
Pitcox	E Loth	128	G5
Pitfichie	Abers	150	H4
Pitglassie	Abers	158	G9
Pitgrudy	Highld	162	H11
Pitlessie	Fife	135	J6
Pitlochry	P & K	141	M6
Pitmachie	Abers	150	H4
Pitmain	Highld	148	C7
Pitmedden	Abers	151	M2
Pitmedden Garden	Abers	151	M2
Pitminster	Somset	18	H11
Pitmuies	Angus	143	K8
Pitmunie	Abers	150	H5
Pitney	Somset	19	N9
Pitroddie	P & K	134	G2
Pitscottie	Fife	135	L5
Pitsea	Essex	38	B4
Pitses	Oldham	83	K4
Pitsford	Nhants	60	G7
Pitstone	Bucks	49	P11
Pitt	Devon	18	D11
Pitt	Hants	22	E9
Pittarrow	Abers	143	N3
Pitt Court	Gloucs	32	D5
Pittenweem	Fife	135	P7
Pitteuchar	Fife	134	H8
Pittodrie House Hotel Abers		150	H1
Pitton	Wilts	21	P8
Pitt's Wood	Kent	37	P11
Pittulie	Abers	159	N4
Pityme	Cnwll	4	F7
Pity Me	Dur	113	L11
Pivington	Kent	26	F2
Pixey Green	Suffk	65	J6
Pixham	Surrey	36	E10
Plains	N Lans	126	D4
Plain Street	Cnwll	4	F6
Plaish	Shrops	57	J5
Plaistow	Gt Lon	37	K4
Plaistow	W Susx	24	B4
Plaitford	Hants	21	Q11
Plank Lane	Wigan	82	D5
Plas Cymyran	IoA	78	D9
Plastow Green	Hants	22	F2
Platt Bridge	Wigan	82	D4
Platt Lane	Shrops	69	P7
Platts Heath	Kent	38	E11
Plawsworth	Dur	113	L11
Plaxtol	Kent	37	P10
Playden	E Susx	26	F7
Playford	Suffk	53	M2
Play Hatch	Oxon	35	K9
Playing Place	Cnwll	3	L5
Playley Green	Gloucs	46	E8
Plealey	Shrops	56	G3
Plean	Stirlg	133	N10
Pleasance	Fife	134	G5
Pleasington	Bl w D	89	J5
Pleasley	Derbys	84	H8
Pleasleyhill	Notts	84	H8
Pleasurewood Hills	Suffk	65	Q2
Pleck	Dorset	11	Q2
Pledgdon Green	Essex	51	N5
Pledwick	Wakefd	91	J7
Pleinheaume	Guern	10	b1
Plemont	Jersey	11	a1
Plemstall	Ches W	81	N10
Plenmeller	Nthumb	111	P8
Pleshey	Essex	51	Q8
Plockton	Highld	153	Q11
Plowden	Shrops	56	F7
Plox Green	Shrops	56	F3
Pluckley	Kent	26	F2
Pluckley Station	Kent	26	F3
Pluckley Thorne	Kent	26	F3
Plucks Gutter	Kent	39	N9
Plumbland	Cumb	100	G3
Plumgarths	Cumb	95	K2
Plumley	Ches E	82	F10
Plump Hill	Gloucs	46	C11
Plumpton	Cumb	94	Q5
Plumpton	Cumb	101	N3
Plumpton	E Susx	25	J8
Plumpton	Nhants	48	G5
Plumpton End	Nhants	49	M6
Plumpton Green	E Susx	25	J7
Plumpton Head	Cumb	101	P3
Plumstead	Gt Lon	37	K5
Plumstead	Norfk	76	G5
Plumstead Green	Norfk	76	G5
Plumtree	Notts	72	G4
Plumtree Green	Kent	26	D2
Plungar	Leics	73	K4
Plurenden	Kent	26	F4
Plush	Dorset	11	Q4
Plusha	Cnwll	5	M5
Plushabridge	Cnwll	5	N7
Plwmp	Cerdgn	42	G4
Plymouth	C Plym	6	D8
Plympton	C Plym	6	E7
Plymstock	C Plym	6	E8
Plymtree	Devon	9	Q4
Pockley	N York	98	C3
Pocklington	E R Yk	98	G11
Pode Hole	Lincs	74	D6
Podimore	Somset	19	P10
Podington	Bed	61	K8
Podmore	Staffs	70	D7
Point Clear	Essex	53	K9
Pointon	Lincs	74	B4
Pokesdown	BCP	13	K6
Polbain	Highld	160	F4
Polbathic	Cnwll	5	N10
Polbeth	W Loth	127	J5
Polbrock	Cnwll	4	G8
Poldark Mine	Cnwll	2	H7
Polebrook	Nhants	61	N3
Pole Elm	Worcs	46	F4
Polegate	E Susx	25	N10
Pole Moor	Kirk	90	D7
Polesden Lacey	Surrey	36	D10
Polesworth	Warwks	59	L4
Polgigga	Cnwll	2	B9
Polglass	Highld	160	G5
Polgooth	Cnwll	3	P3
Polgown	D & G	115	P7
Poling	W Susx	24	B10
Poling Corner	W Susx	24	B9
Polkerris	Cnwll	4	H11
Pollard Street	Norfk	77	L5
Pollington	E R Yk	91	Q7
Polloch	Highld	138	D4
Pollokshaws	C Glas	125	P5
Pollokshields	C Glas	125	P5
Polmassick	Cnwll	3	P4
Polmear	Cnwll	4	H11
Polmont	Falk	126	G2
Polnish	Highld	145	N11
Polperro	Cnwll	5	L11
Polruan	Cnwll	5	J11
Polsham	Somset	19	P6
Polstead	Suffk	52	G4
Polstead Heath	Suffk	52	G3
Poltalloch	Ag & B	130	G8
Poltescoe	Cnwll	3	J10
Poltimore	Devon	9	N5
Polton	Mdloth	127	P5
Polwarth	Border	129	J9
Polyphant	Cnwll	5	M5
Polzeath	Cnwll	4	E6
Pomathorn	Mdloth	127	N6
Pomeroy	Derbys	83	P11
Ponde	Powys	44	G7
Pondersbridge	Cambs	62	C2
Ponders End	Gt Lon	51	J11
Ponsanooth	Cnwll	3	K6
Ponsonby	Cumb	100	E9
Ponsongath	Cnwll	3	K10
Ponsworthy	Devon	7	J4
Pont Abraham Services Carmth		28	G3
Pontac	Jersey	11	c2
Pontamman	Carmth	28	H2
Pontantwn	Carmth	28	D2
Pontardawe	Neath	29	K4
Pontarddulais	Swans	28	G4
Pont-ar-gothi	Carmth	43	K10
Pont-ar-Hydfer	Powys	44	B9
Pont-ar-llechau	Carmth	43	P10
Pontarsais	Carmth	42	H9
Pontblyddyn	Flints	69	J2
Pont Cyfyng	Conwy	67	N3
Pontcysyllte Aqueduct Wrexhm		69	J6
Pont Dolgarrog	Conwy	79	P11
Pontdolgoch	Powys	55	N6
Pont-Ebbw	Newpt	31	J7
Pontefract	Wakefd	91	M6
Ponteland	Nthumb	113	J6
Ponterwyd	Cerdgn	54	G8
Pontesbury	Shrops	56	F3
Pontesbury Hill	Shrops	56	F3
Pontesford	Shrops	56	G3
Pontfadog	Wrexhm	68	H7
Pontfaen	Pembks	41	K4
Pont-faen	Powys	44	D8
Pontgarreg	Cerdgn	42	F4
Pontgarreg	Pembks	41	M2
Ponthenri	Carmth	28	E3
Ponthir	Torfn	31	K6
Ponthirwaun	Cerdgn	42	E5
Pontllanfraith	Caerph	30	G5
Pontlliw	Swans	28	H4
Pontllyfni	Gwynd	66	G4
Pontlottyn	Caerph	30	F4
Pont Morlais	Carmth	28	F3
Pontnewydd	Torfn	31	J5
Pontnewynydd	Torfn	31	J4
Pont Pen-y-benglog	Gwynd	67	M2
Pontrhydfendigaid	Cerdgn	54	G11
Pont Rhyd-sarn	Gwynd	67	R9
Pont Rhyd-y-cyff	Brdgnd	29	N7
Pontrhydyfen	Neath	29	L6
Pont-rhyd-y-groes	Cerdgn	54	G10
Pontrhydyrun	Torfn	31	J5
Pontrilas	Herefs	45	M9
Pont Robert	Powys	55	Q2
Pont-rug	Gwynd	67	J2
Ponts Green	E Susx	25	Q7
Pontshaen	Cerdgn	42	H5
Pontshill	Herefs	46	B10
Pontsticill	Myr Td	30	E2
Pont Walby	Neath	29	N3
Pontwelly	Carmth	42	H6
Pontyates	Carmth	28	D3
Pontyberem	Carmth	28	E3
Pont-y-blew	Wrexhm	69	K7
Pontybodkin	Flints	69	J3
Pontyclun	Rhondd	30	D8
Pontycymer	Brdgnd	29	P6
Pontyglasier	Pembks	41	M3
Pontygwaith	Rhondd	30	D6
Pontymister	Caerph	30	H6
Pont-y-pant	Conwy	67	P4
Pontypool	Torfn	31	J4
Pontypridd	Rhondd	30	E7
Pont-yr-hafod	Pembks	40	H5
Pont-yr-Rhyl	Brdgnd	29	P7
Pontywaun	Caerph	30	H6
Pool	Cnwll	2	H5
Pool	IoS	2	b2
Poole	BCP	12	H6
Poole Keynes	Gloucs	33	J5
Poolewe	Highld	160	D10
Pooley Bridge	Cumb	101	N6
Pooley Street	Norfk	64	F5
Poolfold	Staffs	70	F3
Pool Head	Herefs	45	R4
Poolhill	Gloucs	46	D9
Pool in Wharfedale	Leeds	97	K11
Pool of Muckhart	Clacks	134	C7
Pool Quay	Powys	56	D2
Pool Street	Essex	52	C4
Pootings	Kent	37	L11
Popes Hill	Gloucs	32	C2
Popham	Hants	22	G6
Poplar	Gt Lon	37	J4
Poplar Street	Suffk	65	N8
Porchfield	IoW	14	D8
Poringland	Norfk	77	K11
Porkellis	Cnwll	2	H7
Porlock	Somset	18	A5
Porlock Weir	Somset	17	R2
Portachoillan	Ag & B	123	N8
Port-an-Eorna	Highld	153	P11
Port Appin	Ag & B	138	G8
Port Askaig	Ag & B	122	F6
Portavadie	Ag & B	124	A4
Port Bannatyne	Ag & B	124	D4
Portbury	N Som	31	P9
Port Carlisle	Cumb	110	D8
Port Charlotte	Ag & B	122	C8
Portchester	Hants	14	H5
Port Clarence	S on T	104	E6
Port Driseach	Ag & B	124	B3
Port Ellen	Ag & B	122	E10
Port Elphinstone	Abers	151	K3
Portencalzie	D & G	106	D3
Portencross	N Ayrs	124	F8
Port Erin	IoM	80	a8
Portesham	Dorset	11	N7
Portessie	Moray	158	B4
Port e Vullen	IoM	80	g3
Port Eynon	Swans	28	E7
Portfield Gate	Pembks	40	H7
Portgate	Devon	5	Q4
Port Gaverne	Cnwll	4	G5
Port Glasgow	Inver	125	J3
Portgordon	Moray	158	A5
Portgower	Highld	163	N4
Porth	Cnwll	4	C9
Porth	Rhondd	30	D6
Porthallow	Cnwll	3	K9
Porthallow	Cnwll	5	L11
Porthcawl	Brdgnd	29	M9
Porthcothan	Cnwll	4	D7
Porthcurno	Cnwll	2	B9
Porthdinllaen	Gwynd	66	D6
Port Henderson	Highld	153	P3
Porthgain	Pembks	40	F4
Porthgwarra	Cnwll	2	B9
Porthill	Staffs	70	E5
Porthkea	Cnwll	3	L5
Porthkerry	V Glam	30	E11
Porthleven	Cnwll	2	G8
Porthmadog	Gwynd	67	K7
Porthmeor	Cnwll	2	C6
Porth Navas	Cnwll	3	K8
Portholland	Cnwll	3	P5
Porthoustock	Cnwll	3	L9
Porthpean	Cnwll	3	Q3
Porthtowan	Cnwll	3	H4
Porthwgan	Wrexhm	69	L5
Porthyrhyd	Carmth	43	K11
Porth-y-Waen	Shrops	69	J10
Portincaple	Ag & B	131	Q9
Portinfer	Jersey	11	a1
Portington	E R Yk	92	C4
Portinnisherrich	Ag & B	131	K5
Portinscale	Cumb	101	J6
Port Isaac	Cnwll	4	F5
Portishead	N Som	31	N9
Portknockie	Moray	158	C4
Portland	Dorset	11	P10
Portlethen	Abers	151	N8
Portling	D & G	109	J10
Portloe	Cnwll	3	N6
Port Logan	D & G	106	E9
Portlooe	Cnwll	5	L11
Portmahomack	Highld	163	L10
Port Mary	D & G	108	F11
Portmeirion	Gwynd	67	K7
Portmellon	Cnwll	3	Q5
Port Mòr	Highld	144	F12
Portmore	Hants	13	P5
Port Mulgrave	N York	105	L7
Portnacroish	Ag & B	138	G8
Portnaguran	W Isls	168	k4
Portnahaven	Ag & B	122	A9
Portnalong	Highld	152	E11
Portnancon	Highld	165	K4
Port nan Giùran	W Isls	168	k4
Port nan Long	W Isls	168	d10
Port Nis	W Isls	168	k1
Portobello	Edin	127	Q3
Portobello	Gatesd	113	L9
Portobello	Wolves	58	E5
Port of Menteith	Stirlg	132	H7
Port of Ness	W Isls	168	k1
Porton	Wilts	21	N7
Portontown	Devon	5	Q6
Portpatrick	D & G	106	C7
Port Quin	Cnwll	4	F5
Port Ramsay	Ag & B	138	F8
Portreath	Cnwll	2	H4
Portreath Harbour	Cnwll	2	H4
Portree	Highld	152	H9
Port Righ	Ag & B	120	F4
Port St Mary	IoM	80	b8
Portscatho	Cnwll	3	M6
Portsea	C Port	14	H6
Portskerra	Highld	166	E3
Portskewett	Mons	31	N7
Portslade	Br & H	24	G9
Portslade-by-Sea	Br & H	24	G9
Portslogan	D & G	106	C6
Portsmouth	C Port	14	H7
Portsmouth	Calder	89	Q5
Portsmouth Arms	Devon	17	L8
Portsmouth Dockyard C Port		14	H6
Port Soderick	IoM	80	d7
Port Solent	C Port	14	H5
Portsonachan Hotel	Ag & B	131	L3
Portsoy	Abers	158	E4
Port Sunlight	Wirral	81	L8

Portswood C Sotn....14 D4
Port Talbot Neath....29 L7
Port Tennant Swans....29 J6
Portuairk Highld....137 L2
Portway Herefs....45 P6
Portway Herefs....45 P7
Portway Sandw....58 E7
Portway Worcs....58 G10
Port Wemyss Ag & B....122 A9
Port William D & G....107 K9
Portwrinkle Cnwll....5 P11
Portyerrock D & G....107 N10
Posbury Devon....9 K5
Posenhall Shrops....57 M4
Poslingford Suffk....63 N11
Posso Border....117 J4
Postbridge Devon....8 G9
Postcombe Oxon....35 K4
Post Green Dorset....12 G6
Postling Kent....27 K4
Postwick Norfk....77 K10
Potarch Abers....150 G8
Potsgrove C Beds....49 Q8
Potten End Herts....50 B9
Potten Street Kent....39 N8
Potter Brompton N York....99 K5
Pottergate Street Norfk....64 H3
Potterhanworth Lincs....86 E7
Potterhanworth Booths Lincs....86 E7
Potter Heigham Norfk....77 N8
Potterne Wilts....21 J3
Potterne Wick Wilts....21 J3
Potter Row Bucks....35 P4
Potters Bar Herts....50 F10
Potters Brook Lancs....95 K10
Potters Corner Kent....26 G3
Potter's Cross Staffs....58 B8
Potters Crouch Herts....50 D9
Potter's Forstal Kent....26 E2
Potters Green Covtry....59 N8
Potter's Green E Susx....25 M6
Potter's Green Herts....51 J6
Pottersheath Herts....50 F7
Potters Marston Leics....72 D11
Potter Somersal Derbys....71 L7
Potterspury Nhants....49 L6
Potter Street Essex....51 L9
Potterton Abers....151 N4
Potterton Leeds....91 L3
Potthorpe Norfk....76 C7
Pottle Street Wilts....20 F6
Potto N York....104 E10
Potton C Beds....62 B11
Pott Row Norfk....75 P6
Pott's Green Essex....52 F7
Pott Shrigley Ches E....83 K9
Poughill Cnwll....16 C10
Poughill Devon....9 L3
Poulner Hants....13 L3
Poulshot Wilts....21 J3
Poulton Gloucs....33 L4
Poulton Wirral....81 L6
Poulton-le-Fylde Lancs....88 C3
Poulton Priory Gloucs....33 L5
Pound Bank Worcs....57 N10
Poundbury Dorset....11 P6
Poundffald Swans....28 G6
Poundgate E Susx....25 L5
Pound Green E Susx....25 M6
Pound Green Suffk....63 M10
Pound Green Worcs....57 P9
Pound Hill W Susx....24 G3
Poundon Bucks....48 H9
Poundsbridge Kent....25 M2
Poundsgate Devon....7 J4
Poundstock Cnwll....5 L2
Pound Street Hants....22 E2
Pounsley E Susx....25 M6
Pouton D & G....107 N8
Pouy Street Suffk....65 M7
Povey Cross Surrey....24 G2
Powburn Nthumb....119 L7
Powderham Devon....9 N8
Powerstock Dorset....11 L5
Powfoot D & G....109 P7
Pow Green Herefs....46 D6
Powhill Cumb....110 D9
Powick Worcs....46 F4
Powmill P & K....134 C8
Poxwell Dorset....12 B8
Poyle Slough....36 B5
Poynings W Susx....24 G8
Poyntington Dorset....20 C10
Poynton Ches E....83 K8
Poynton Wrekin....69 Q11
Poynton Green Wrekin....69 Q11
Poyston Cross Pembks....41 J7
Poystreet Green Suffk....64 D10
Praa Sands Cnwll....2 F8
Pratt's Bottom Gt Lon....37 L8
Praze-an-Beeble Cnwll....2 G6
Predannack Wollas Cnwll....2 H10
Prees Shrops....69 Q8
Preesall Lancs....94 H11
Prees Green Shrops....69 Q8
Preesgweene Shrops....69 J7
Prees Heath Shrops....69 Q7
Prees Higher Heath Shrops....69 Q7
Prees Lower Heath Shrops....69 Q8
Prendwick Nthumb....119 K8
Pren-gwyn Cerdgn....42 H6
Prenteg Gwynd....67 K6
Prenton Wirral....81 L7
Prescot Knows....81 P6
Prescott Devon....10 B2
Prescott Shrops....57 M8
Prescott Shrops....69 M10
Presnerb Angus....142 B4
Pressen Nthumb....118 F3
Prestatyn Denbgs....80 F8
Prestbury Ches E....83 J9
Prestbury Gloucs....47 J2
Presteigne Powys....45 L2
Prestleigh Somset....20 B7
Prestolee Bolton....89 M9
Preston Border....129 K8
Preston Br & H....24 H9
Preston Devon....7 M4
Preston Dorset....11 Q8
Preston E R Yk....93 L4
Preston Gloucs....33 K4
Preston Herts....50 E6
Preston Kent....38 H9
Preston Kent....39 M9
Preston Lancs....88 G5

Preston Nthumb....119 N5
Preston Rutlnd....73 M10
Preston Shrops....57 J2
Preston Somset....18 F5
Preston Torbay....7 M6
Preston Wilts....33 N9
Preston Wilts....33 Q10
Preston Bagot Warwks....59 J11
Preston Bissett Bucks....49 J9
Preston Bowyer Somset....18 F9
Preston Brockhurst Shrops....69 P10
Preston Brook Halton....82 C8
Preston Candover Hants....22 H6
Preston Capes Nhants....48 G4
Preston Crowmarsh Oxon....34 H6
Preston Deanery Nhants....60 G9
Preston Green Warwks....59 J11
Preston Gubbals Shrops....69 N11
Preston Montford Shrops....56 G2
Preston on Stour Warwks....47 P5
Preston on Tees S on T....104 D7
Preston on the Hill Halton....82 C8
Preston on Wye Herefs....45 M6
Prestonpans E Loth....128 B5
Preston Patrick Cumb....95 L4
Preston Plucknett Somset....19 P11
Preston St Mary Suffk....64 C11
Preston Street Kent....39 N9
Preston-under-Scar N York....96 G2
Preston upon the Weald Moors Wrekin....70 B11
Preston Wynne Herefs....45 R5
Prestwich Bury....82 H4
Prestwick Nthumb....113 J6
Prestwick S Ayrs....114 G2
Prestwick Airport S Ayrs....114 G2
Prestwood Bucks....35 N4
Prestwood Staffs....58 C7
Price Town Brdgnd....29 P6
Prickwillow Cambs....63 J4
Priddy Somset....19 P4
Priestacott Devon....8 B3
Priestcliffe Derbys....83 P10
Priestcliffe Ditch Derbys....83 P10
Priest Hutton Lancs....95 L6
Priestland E Ayrs....125 P10
Priestley Green Calder....90 E5
Priest Weston Shrops....56 D5
Priestwood Green Kent....37 Q8
Primethorpe Leics....60 B2
Primrose Green Norfk....76 F8
Primrosehill Border....129 K8
Primrose Hill Cambs....62 E3
Primrose Hill Derbys....84 F9
Primrose Hill Dudley....58 D7
Primrose Hill Lancs....88 D9
Primsidemill Border....118 F5
Prince of Wales Bridge Mons....31 P7
Princes Gate Pembks....41 M8
Princes Risborough Bucks....35 M4
Princethorpe Warwks....59 P10
Princetown Devon....6 F4
Prinsted W Susx....15 L5
Prion Denbgs....68 E2
Prior Rigg Cumb....111 J7
Priors Halton Shrops....56 H9
Priors Hardwick Warwks....48 E3
Priorslee Wrekin....57 N2
Priors Marston Warwks....48 E3
Priors Norton Gloucs....46 G10
Priors Park Gloucs....46 G8
Priory Wood Herefs....45 K5
Prisk V Glam....30 D9
Priston BaNES....20 C2
Pristow Green Norfk....64 G4
Prittlewell Sthend....38 E4
Privett Hants....23 J9
Prixford Devon....17 K4
Probus Cnwll....3 M4
Prora E Loth....128 E4
Prospect Cumb....100 F2
Prospidnick Cnwll....2 G7
Protstonhill Abers....159 K5
Prudhoe Nthumb....112 G8
Prussia Cove Cnwll....2 F8
Pubil P & K....140 C9
Publow BaNES....20 B2
Puckeridge Herts....51 J6
Puckington Somset....19 L11
Pucklechurch S Glos....32 C9
Puckrup Gloucs....46 G7
Puddinglake Ches W....82 F11
Puddington Ches W....81 L10
Puddington Devon....9 K2
Puddledock Norfk....64 F3
Puddletown Dorset....12 C6
Pudleston Herefs....45 R3
Pudsey Leeds....90 G4
Pulborough W Susx....24 B7
Puleston Wrekin....70 C10
Pulford Ches W....69 L3
Pulham Dorset....11 Q3
Pulham Market Norfk....64 H4
Pulham St Mary Norfk....65 J4
Pullens Green S Glos....32 B6
Pulloxhill C Beds....50 C4
Pulverbatch Shrops....56 G4
Pumpherston W Loth....127 K4
Pumsaint Carmth....43 N6
Puncheston Pembks....41 K5
Puncknowle Dorset....11 M6
Punnett's Town E Susx....25 P6
Purbrook Hants....15 J5
Purfleet-on-Thames Thurr....37 N5
Puriton Somset....19 K6
Purleigh Essex....52 D11
Purley Gt Lon....36 H8
Purley on Thames W Berk....35 J9
Purlogue Shrops....56 D9
Purls Bridge Cambs....62 G3
Purse Caundle Dorset....20 C11
Purshull Green Worcs....58 C10
Purslow Shrops....56 F8
Purston Jaglin Wakefd....91 L7
Purtington Somset....10 H3
Purton Gloucs....32 C3
Purton Gloucs....32 C4
Purton Wilts....33 L7
Purton Stoke Wilts....33 L6
Pury End Nhants....49 K5
Pusey Oxon....34 C5
Putley Herefs....46 B7
Putley Green Herefs....46 B7
Putloe Gloucs....32 E3

Putney Gt Lon....36 F6
Putsborough Devon....16 G3
Puttenham Herts....35 N2
Puttenham Surrey....23 P5
Puttock End Essex....52 D3
Putton Dorset....11 N8
Putts Corner Devon....10 C5
Puxley Nhants....49 L6
Puxton N Som....19 M2
Pwll Carmth....28 E4
Pwllcrochan Pembks....40 H10
Pwll-du Mons....30 H2
Pwll-glâs Denbgs....68 F4
Pwllgloyw Powys....44 E8
Pwllheli Gwynd....66 F7
Pwllmeyric Mons....31 P6
Pwll-trap Carmth....41 Q7
Pwll-y-glaw Neath....29 L6
Pydew Conwy....79 Q9
Pye Bridge Derbys....84 F10
Pyecombe W Susx....24 G8
Pye Corner Newpt....31 K7
Pye Green Staffs....58 E2
Pyle Brdgnd....29 M8
Pyleigh Somset....18 F8
Pylle Somset....20 B7
Pymoor Cambs....62 G3
Pymore Dorset....11 K6
Pyrford Surrey....36 B9
Pyrton Oxon....35 J5
Pytchley Nhants....61 J6
Pyworthy Devon....16 E11

Q

Quabbs Shrops....56 C8
Quadring Lincs....74 D4
Quadring Eaudike Lincs....74 D4
Quainton Bucks....49 K10
Quaker's Yard Myr Td....30 E5
Quaking Houses Dur....113 J10
Quantock Hills Somset....18 G7
Quarff Shet....169 r10
Quarley Hants....21 Q6
Quarndon Derbys....72 A2
Quarr Hill IoW....14 G8
Quarrier's Village Inver....125 K4
Quarrington Lincs....73 R2
Quarrington Hill Dur....104 B3
Quarry Bank Dudley....58 D7
Quarrywood Moray....157 M5
Quarter N Ayrs....124 F5
Quarter S Lans....126 C7
Quatford Shrops....57 N6
Quatt Shrops....57 P7
Quebec Dur....103 N2
Quedgeley Gloucs....32 F2
Queen Adelaide Cambs....63 J4
Queenborough Kent....38 F7
Queen Camel Somset....19 Q10
Queen Charlton BaNES....32 B11
Queen Dart Devon....17 Q8
Queen Elizabeth Forest Park Stirlg....132 G7
Queen Elizabeth II Bridge Thurr....37 N5
Queenhill Worcs....46 G7
Queen Oak Dorset....20 E8
Queen's Bower IoW....14 G10
Queensbury C Brad....90 E4
Queensferry Flints....81 L11
Queensferry Crossing Fife....134 E11
Queen's Head Shrops....69 K9
Queen's Hills Norfk....76 H9
Queenslie C Glas....126 B4
Queen's Park Bed....61 M11
Queen's Park Essex....51 Q11
Queen's Park Nhants....60 G8
Queen Street Kent....37 Q11
Queen Street Wilts....33 K7
Queenzieburn N Lans....126 B2
Quendon Essex....51 M4
Queniborough Leics....72 G8
Quenington Gloucs....33 M4
Quernmore Lancs....95 L9
Queslett Birm....58 G6
Quethiock Cnwll....5 N9
Quick's Green W Berk....34 G9
Quidenham Norfk....64 E4
Quidhampton Hants....22 F4
Quidhampton Wilts....21 M8
Quina Brook Shrops....69 P8
Quinbury End Nhants....48 H4
Quinton Dudley....58 E8
Quinton Nhants....60 G9
Quinton Green Nhants....49 L4
Quintrell Downs Cnwll....4 C9
Quixhall Staffs....71 L6
Quixwood Border....129 K7
Quoditch Devon....5 Q2
Quoig P & K....133 N3
Quoisley Ches E....69 P5
Quorn Leics....72 F7
Quothquan S Lans....116 D3
Quoyburray Ork....169 e6
Quoyloo Ork....169 b4

R

Raasay Highld....153 K9
Rabbit's Cross Kent....26 C2
Rableyheath Herts....50 F7
Raby Cumb....110 C10
Raby Wirral....81 L9
Rachan Mill Border....116 G4
Rachub Gwynd....79 L11
Rackenford Devon....17 R8
Rackham W Susx....24 B8
Rackheath Norfk....77 K9
Racks D & G....109 M6
Rackwick Ork....169 b7
Radbourne Derbys....71 P7
Radcliffe Bury....89 M9
Radcliffe Nthumb....119 Q10
Radcliffe on Trent Notts....72 G3
Radclive Bucks....49 J8
Radcot Oxon....33 Q5
Raddery Highld....156 C6
Raddington Somset....18 D9
Radernie Fife....135 M6
Radford Covtry....59 M8
Radford Semele Warwks....48 B2

Radlet Somset....18 H7
Radlett Herts....50 E10
Radley Devon....17 N7
Radley Oxon....34 F5
Radley W Berk....34 C11
Radley Green Essex....51 P9
Radmore Green Ches E....69 Q3
Radnage Bucks....35 L5
Radstock BaNES....20 C4
Radstone Nhants....48 G6
Radway Warwks....48 C5
Radwell Bed....61 M9
Radwell Herts....51 F3
Radwinter Essex....51 P3
Radwinter End Essex....51 P3
Radyr Cardif....30 F8
RAF College (Cranwell) Lincs....86 D11
Rafford Moray....157 K6
RAF Museum Cosford Shrops....57 P3
RAF Museum Hendon Gt Lon....36 F2
Ragdale Leics....72 H7
Ragdon Shrops....56 H6
Raginnis Cnwll....2 D8
Raglan Mons....31 M3
Ragnall Notts....85 P6
Raigbeg Highld....148 G3
Rainbow Hill Worcs....46 G3
Rainford St Hel....81 P4
Rainford Junction St Hel....81 P4
Rainham Gt Lon....37 M4
Rainham Medway....38 D8
Rainhill St Hel....81 P6
Rainhill Stoops St Hel....81 Q6
Rainow Ches E....83 K9
Rainsough Bury....82 H4
Rainton N York....97 N5
Rainworth Notts....85 J9
Raisbeck Cumb....102 B9
Raise Cumb....111 P11
Raisthorpe N York....98 H8
Rait P & K....134 G2
Raithby Lincs....87 K4
Raithby Lincs....87 L7
Raithwaite N York....105 N8
Rake Hants....23 M9
Rakewood Rochdl....89 Q8
Ralia Highld....148 C8
Ram Carmth....43 L5
Ramasaig Highld....152 B9
Rame Cnwll....3 J7
Rame Cnwll....6 C9
Ram Hill S Glos....32 C9
Ram Lane Kent....26 G2
Rampisham Dorset....11 M4
Rampside Cumb....94 E7
Rampton Cambs....62 F7
Rampton Notts....85 P5
Ramsbottom Bury....89 M7
Ramsbury Wilts....33 Q10
Ramscraigs Highld....167 K11
Ramsdean Hants....23 K10
Ramsdell Hants....22 G3
Ramsden Oxon....48 C11
Ramsden Worcs....46 H5
Ramsden Bellhouse Essex....38 B3
Ramsden Heath Essex....38 B2
Ramsey Cambs....62 C3
Ramsey Essex....53 M5
Ramsey IoM....80 g3
Ramsey Forty Foot Cambs....62 D3
Ramsey Heights Cambs....62 B4
Ramsey Island Essex....52 F10
Ramsey Island Pembks....40 D6
Ramsey Mereside Cambs....62 C3
Ramsey St Mary's Cambs....62 C3
Ramsgate Kent....39 Q8
Ramsgill N York....96 H6
Ramshaw Dur....103 M5
Ramshaw Dur....112 E11
Ramsholt Suffk....53 P3
Ramshope Nthumb....118 D10
Ramshorn Staffs....71 K5
Ramsley Devon....8 G5
Ramsnest Common Surrey....23 P8
Ranby Lincs....86 H5
Ranby Notts....85 L4
Rand Lincs....86 F5
Randwick Gloucs....32 F3
Ranfurly Rens....125 K4
Rangemore Staffs....71 M10
Rangeworthy S Glos....32 C7
Rankinston E Ayrs....115 J5
Ranksborough RutInd....73 L8
Rank's Green Essex....52 B8
Rannoch Station P & K....140 B6
Ranscombe Somset....18 B6
Ranskill Notts....85 L3
Ranton Staffs....70 F10
Ranton Green Staffs....70 F10
Ranworth Norfk....77 M9
Raploch Stirlg....133 M9
Rapness Ork....169 e2
Rapps Somset....19 K11
Rascarrel D & G....108 G11
Rashfield Ag & B....131 N11
Rashwood Worcs....58 D11
Raskelf N York....97 Q6
Rassau Blae G....30 G2
Rastrick Calder....90 E6
Ratagan Highld....145 R4
Ratby Leics....72 E9
Ratcliffe Culey Leics....72 A11
Ratcliffe on Soar Notts....72 D5
Ratcliffe on the Wreake Leics....72 G8
Rathen Abers....159 N5
Rathillet Fife....135 K3
Rathmell N York....96 B9
Ratho C Edin....127 L3
Ratho Station C Edin....127 L3
Rathven Moray....158 B4
Ratlake Hants....22 D10
Ratley Warwks....48 C5
Ratling Kent....39 M11
Ratlinghope Shrops....56 G5
Rattar Highld....167 N2
Ratten Row Cumb....101 K2
Ratten Row Cumb....110 G11
Ratten Row Lancs....88 E2
Rattery Devon....7 J6
Rattlesden Suffk....64 D10
Ratton Village E Susx....25 N10
Rattray P & K....142 B8

Raughton Cumb....110 G11
Raughton Head Cumb....110 G11
Raunds Nhants....61 L6
Ravenfield Rothm....91 M11
Ravenglass Cumb....100 C11
Ravenhills Green Worcs....46 E3
Raveningham Norfk....65 M2
Ravenscar N York....105 Q10
Ravenscraig N Lans....126 D6
Ravensdale IoM....80 e3
Ravensden Bed....61 N10
Ravenseat N York....102 G10
Ravenshead Notts....85 J10
Ravensmoor Ches E....69 R4
Ravensthorpe Kirk....90 G6
Ravensthorpe Nhants....60 E6
Ravenstone Leics....72 C8
Ravenstone M Keyn....49 M4
Ravenstonedale Cumb....102 D10
Ravenstruther S Lans....126 G8
Ravensworth N York....103 M9
Raw N York....105 P9
Rawcliffe C York....98 B10
Rawcliffe E R Yk....92 A6
Rawcliffe Bridge E R Yk....92 A6
Rawdon Leeds....90 G3
Rawling Street Kent....38 F10
Rawmarsh Rothm....91 L11
Rawnsley Staffs....58 F2
Rawreth Essex....38 C3
Rawridge Devon....10 E3
Rawtenstall Lancs....89 N6
Raydon Suffk....52 H4
Raylees Nthumb....112 D2
Rayleigh Essex....38 D3
Raymond's Hill Devon....10 G5
Rayne Essex....52 B7
Raynes Park Gt Lon....36 F7
Reach Cambs....63 J7
Read Lancs....89 M4
Reading Readg....35 K10
Reading Services W Berk....35 J11
Reading Street Kent....26 F5
Reading Street Kent....39 Q8
Reagill Cumb....102 B7
Rearquhar Highld....162 G8
Rearsby Leics....72 H8
Rease Heath Ches E....70 A4
Reawla Cnwll....2 G6
Reay Highld....166 G3
Reculver Kent....39 M8
Red Ball Devon....18 E11
Redberth Pembks....41 L10
Redbourn Herts....50 D8
Redbourne N Linc....92 G11
Redbrook Gloucs....31 P3
Redbrook Wrexhm....69 P6
Redbrook Street Kent....26 F4
Redburn Highld....156 G8
Redburn Nthumb....111 Q8
Redcar R & C....104 H6
Redcastle D & G....108 H7
Redcastle Highld....155 Q8
Red Dial Cumb....110 E11
Redding Falk....126 G2
Reddingmuirhead Falk....126 G2
Reddish Stockp....83 J6
Redditch Worcs....58 F11
Rede Suffk....63 P9
Redenhall Norfk....65 K5
Redenham Hants....22 B5
Redesmouth Nthumb....112 C4
Redford Abers....143 P3
Redford Angus....143 K9
Redford W Susx....23 N9
Redfordgreen Border....117 M7
Redgate Rhondd....30 D7
Redgorton P & K....134 D2
Redgrave Suffk....64 E6
Redhill Abers....151 K7
Red Hill BCP....13 J5
Redhill Herts....50 H4
Redhill N Som....19 N2
Redhill Surrey....36 G10
Red Hill Warwks....47 M3
Redisham Suffk....65 N5
Redland Bristl....31 Q9
Redland Ork....169 c4
Redlingfield Suffk....64 H7
Redlingfield Green Suffk....64 H7
Red Lodge Suffk....63 L6
Red Lumb Rochdl....89 N7
Redlynch Somset....20 D8
Redlynch Wilts....21 P10
Redmain Cumb....100 F4
Redmarley Worcs....57 P11
Redmarley D'Abitot Gloucs....46 E8
Redmarshall S on T....104 C6
Redmile Leics....73 K3
Redmire N York....96 F2
Redmyre Abers....143 P2
Rednal Birm....58 F9
Rednal Shrops....69 L9
Redpath Border....118 A3
Red Point Highld....153 N4
Red Post Cnwll....16 D10
Red Rice Hants....22 B6
Red Rock Wigan....88 H9
Red Roses Carmth....41 P8
Red Row Nthumb....119 Q11
Redruth Cnwll....2 H5
Redstocks Wilts....20 H2
Redstone P & K....142 B11
Redstone Cross Pembks....41 M7
Red Street Staffs....70 E4
Redvales Bury....89 N9
Red Wharf Bay IoA....79 J8
Redwick Newpt....31 M8
Redwick S Glos....31 P7
Redworth Darltn....103 P6
Reed Herts....51 J3
Reedham Norfk....77 N11
Reedness E R Yk....92 D6
Reeds Beck Lincs....86 H7
Reeds Holme Lancs....89 N6
Reepham Lincs....86 D6
Reepham Norfk....76 G7
Reeth N York....103 K11
Reeves Green Solhll....59 L9
Regaby IoM....80 f2
Regil N Som....19 P2
Reiff Highld....160 F4
Reigate Surrey....36 G10
Reighton N York....99 N5
Reinigeadal W Isls....168 h7
Reisque Abers....151 M4

Reiss Highld 167 P6
Rejerrah Cnwll 4 B10
Releath Cnwll 2 H7
Relubbus Cnwll 2 F7
Relugas Moray 156 H8
Remenham Wokam 35 L8
Remenham Hill Wokam 35 L8
Rempstone Notts 72 F6
Rendcomb Gloucs 33 K3
Rendham Suffk 65 L9
Rendlesham Suffk 65 L11
Renfrew Rens 125 N4
Renhold Bed 61 N10
Renishaw Derbys 84 G5
Rennington Nthumb 119 P7
Renton W Duns 125 K2
Renwick Cumb 101 Q2
Repps Norfk 77 N8
Repton Derbys 71 Q9
Reraig Highld 145 P2
Resaurie Highld 156 C8
Rescassa Cnwll 3 P5
Rescorla Cnwll 3 P4
Resipole Burn Highld 138 C5
Reskadinnick Cnwll 2 G5
Resolis Highld 156 B4
Resolven Neath 29 M4
Rest and be thankful Ag & B 131 Q6
Reston Border 129 M7
Restronguet Cnwll 3 L6
Reswallie Angus 143 J3
Reterth Cnwll 4 E9
Retford Notts 85 M4
Retire Cnwll 4 G9
Rettendon Essex 38 C2
Retyn Cnwll 4 D10
Revesby Lincs 87 J8
Rew Devon 7 J11
Rew Devon 7 K4
Rewe Devon 9 M5
Rew Street IoW 14 E8
Rexon Devon 5 Q4
Reydon Suffk 65 P6
Reymerston Norfk 76 E10
Reynalton Pembks 41 L9
Reynoldston Swans 28 E7
Rezare Cnwll 5 P6
Rhadyr Mons 31 L4
Rhandirmwyn Carmth 43 Q6
Rhayader Powys 55 M11
Rheindown Highld 155 P8
Rhenigidale W Isls 168 h7
Rhes-y-cae Flints 80 H10
Rhewl Denbgs 68 F2
Rhewl Denbgs 68 G6
Rhewl Mostyn Flints 80 H8
Rhicarn Highld 164 C11
Rhiconich Highld 164 G6
Rhicullen Highld 156 B3
Rhigos Rhondd 29 P3
Rhives Highld 163 J6
Rhiwbina Cardif 30 G8
Rhiwbryfdir Gwynd 67 M5
Rhiwderyn Newpt 31 J7
Rhiwen Gwynd 67 K2
Rhiwinder Rhondd 30 D7
Rhiwlas Gwynd 68 B7
Rhiwlas Gwynd 79 K11
Rhiwlas Powys 68 G8
Rhiwsaeson Rhondd 30 E8
Rhode Somset 19 J8
Rhoden Green Kent 37 Q11
Rhodesia Notts 85 J5
Rhodes Minnis Kent 27 L3
Rhodiad-y-brenin Pembks 40 E5
Rhonehouse D & G 108 F9
Rhoose V Glam 30 E11
Rhos Carmth 42 G7
Rhos Denbgs 68 F2
Rhos Neath 29 K4
Rhosaman Carmth 29 K2
Rhosbeirio IoA 78 F6
Rhoscefnhir IoA 78 J9
Rhoscolyn IoA 78 D9
Rhoscrowther Pembks 40 H10
Rhosesmor Flints 81 J11
Rhos-fawr Gwynd 66 F7
Rhosgadfan Gwynd 67 J3
Rhosgoch IoA 78 G7
Rhosgoch Powys 44 H5
Rhos Haminiog Cerdgn 43 K2
Rhoshill Pembks 41 N2
Rhoshirwaun Gwynd 66 C9
Rhoslan Gwynd 66 H6
Rhoslefain Gwynd 54 D3
Rhosllanerchrugog Wrexhm 69 J5
Rhôs Lligwy IoA 78 H7
Rhosmaen Carmth 43 M10
Rhosmeirch IoA 78 H9
Rhosneigr IoA 78 E10
Rhosnesni Wrexhm 69 L4
Rhôs-on-Sea Conwy 79 Q8
Rhosrobin Wrexhm 69 K4
Rhossili Swans 28 D7
Rhostrehwfa IoA 78 G10
Rhostryfan Gwynd 66 H3
Rhostyllen Wrexhm 69 K5
Rhosybol IoA 78 G7
Rhos-y-brithdir Powys 68 F10
Rhosygadfa Shrops 69 K8
Rhos-y-garth Cerdgn 54 E10
Rhos-y-gwaliau Gwynd 68 B8
Rhos-y-llan Gwynd 66 C7
Rhosymedre Wrexhm 69 J6
Rhos-y-meirch Powys 56 D11
Rhu Ag & B 132 B11
Rhuallt Denbgs 80 F9
Rhubodach Ag & B 124 C3
Rhuddall Heath Ches W 69 Q2
Rhuddlan Cerdgn 43 J6
Rhuddlan Denbgs 80 E9
Rhue Highld 161 J7
Rhulen Powys 44 G5
Rhunahaorine Ag & B 123 M10
Rhyd Gwynd 67 L6
Rhydargaeau Carmth 42 H9
Rhydcymerau Carmth 43 L7
Rhydd Worcs 46 F5
Rhyd-Ddu Gwynd 67 K4
Rhydding Neath 29 K3
Rhydgaled Conwy 68 C2
Rhydlanfair Conwy 67 Q4
Rhydlewis Cerdgn 42 F5
Rhydlios Gwynd 66 B9
Rhydlydan Conwy 68 A4
Rhydowen Cerdgn 42 H5

Rhydroser Cerdgn 54 D11
Rhydspence Herefs 45 J5
Rhydtalog Flints 68 H4
Rhyd-uchaf Gwynd 68 A7
Rhyd-y-clafdy Gwynd 66 E8
Rhydycroesau Shrops 68 H8
Rhydyfelin Cerdgn 54 D9
Rhydyfelin Rhondd 30 E7
Rhyd-y-foel Conwy 80 C9
Rhydyfro Neath 29 K3
Rhyd-y-groes Gwynd 79 K11
Rhydmain Gwynd 67 Q10
Rhyd-y-meirch Mons 31 K3
Rhydymwyn Flints 81 J11
Rhyd-y-pennau Cerdgn 54 E7
Rhyd-yr-onnen Gwynd 54 E4
Rhyd-y-sarn Gwynd 67 M6
Rhyl Denbgs 80 E8
Rhymney Caerph 30 F3
Rhynd P & K 134 F3
Rhynie Abers 150 D2
Rhynie Highld 163 J11
Ribbesford Worcs 57 P10
Ribbleton Lancs 88 H4
Ribby Lancs 88 L4
Ribchester Lancs 89 K3
Riber Derbys 84 D9
Riby Lincs 93 L9
Riccall N York 91 Q3
Riccarton Border 111 K2
Riccarton E Ayrs 125 L10
Richards Castle Herefs 56 H11
Richings Park Bucks 36 B5
Richmond Gt Lon 36 E6
Richmond N York 103 N10
Richmond Sheff 84 F3
Rich's Holford Somset 18 F8
Rickerscote Staffs 70 G10
Rickford N Som 19 N3
Rickham Devon 7 K11
Rickinghall Suffk 64 E6
Rickling Essex 51 L4
Rickling Green Essex 51 M5
Rickmansworth Herts 36 C2
Riddell Border 117 Q6
Riddings Derbys 84 F10
Riddlecombe Devon 17 L9
Riddlesden C Brad 90 D2
Ridge BaNES 19 Q3
Ridge Dorset 12 F7
Ridge Herts 50 F10
Ridge Wilts 21 J8
Ridgebourne Powys 44 F2
Ridge Green Surrey 36 H11
Ridge Lane Warwks 59 L6
Ridge Row Kent 27 M3
Ridgeway Derbys 84 F4
Ridgeway Worcs 47 K3
Ridgeway Cross Herefs 46 D5
Ridgewell Essex 52 B3
Ridgewood E Susx 25 L7
Ridgmont C Beds 49 Q7
Riding Mill Nthumb 112 F8
Ridley Kent 37 P8
Ridley Nthumb 111 Q8
Ridley Green Ches E 69 Q4
Ridlington Norfk 77 L5
Ridlington Rutlnd 73 L10
Ridlington Street Norfk 77 L5
Ridsdale Nthumb 112 D4
Rievaulx N York 98 C11
Rigg D & G 110 E7
Riggend N Lans 126 D3
Righoul Highld 156 F7
Rigmadon Park Cumb 95 M4
Rigsby Lincs 87 M5
Rigside S Lans 116 B3
Riley Green Lancs 89 J5
Rileyhill Staffs 58 H2
Rilla Mill Cnwll 5 M7
Rillaton Cnwll 5 M7
Rillington N York 98 H6
Rimington Lancs 96 B11
Rimpton Somset 20 B10
Rimswell E R Yk 93 P5
Rinaston Pembks 41 J5
Rindleford Shrops 57 N5
Ringford D & G 108 E9
Ringinglow Sheff 84 C4
Ringland Norfk 76 G9
Ringles Cross E Susx 25 L6
Ringlestone Kent 38 E10
Ringmer E Susx 25 K8
Ringmore Devon 6 H9
Ringmore Devon 7 N4
Ringorm Moray 157 P9
Ring's End Cambs 74 Q10
Ringsfield Suffk 65 N4
Ringsfield Corner Suffk 65 N4
Ringshall Herts 35 Q2
Ringshall Suffk 64 E11
Ringshall Stocks Suffk 64 F11
Ringstead Nhants 61 L5
Ringstead Norfk 75 P2
Ringwood Hants 13 L3
Ringwould Kent 27 Q2
Rinmore Abers 150 C4
Rinsey Cnwll 2 F8
Rinsey Croft Cnwll 2 G8
Ripe E Susx 25 M8
Ripley Derbys 84 E10
Ripley Hants 13 L3
Ripley N York 97 L8
Ripley Surrey 36 C9
Riplingham E R Yk 92 G4
Riplington Hants 23 J10
Ripon N York 97 M6
Rippingale Lincs 74 A5
Ripple Kent 39 Q11
Ripple Worcs 46 G2
Ripponden Calder 90 C7
Risabus Ag & B 122 D11
Risbury Herefs 45 Q4
Risby N Linc 92 F8
Risby Suffk 63 P7
Risca Caerph 30 H6
Rise E R Yk 93 L2
Riseden E Susx 25 P4
Riseden Kent 26 B4
Risegate Lincs 74 D5
Risehow Cumb 100 D4
Riseley Bed 61 N8
Riseley Wokham 23 K2
Rishangles Suffk 64 H8

Rishton Lancs 89 L4
Rishworth Calder 90 C7
Rising Bridge Lancs 89 M5
Risley Derbys 72 D3
Risley Warrtn 82 E6
Risplith N York 97 K7
Rivar Wilts 22 B2
Rivenhall End Essex 52 D3
River Kent 27 N3
River W Susx 23 P10
River Bank Cambs 62 H7
Riverford Highld 155 P7
Riverhead Kent 37 M9
Rivers Corner Dorset 12 C2
Rivington Lancs 89 J8
Rivington Services Lancs 89 J8
Roachill Devon 17 N7
Roade Nhants 49 L4
Road Green Norfk 65 K3
Roadhead Cumb 111 K6
Roadmeetings S Lans 126 F3
Roadside E Ayrs 115 L4
Roadside Highld 167 L4
Roadwater Somset 18 D7
Roag Highld 152 D9
Roa Island Cumb 94 E7
Roan of Craigoch S Ayrs 114 E4
Roast Green Essex 51 L4
Roath Cardif 30 G9
Roberton Border 117 N8
Roberton S Lans 116 C5
Robertsbridge E Susx 26 B7
Roberttown Kirk 90 F6
Robeston Wathen Pembks 41 L7
Robgill Tower D & G 110 D6
Robin Hill Staffs 70 G3
Robin Hood Lancs 88 G8
Robin Hood Leeds 91 J5
Robinhood End Essex 52 B4
Robin Hood's Bay N York 105 P9
Roborough Devon 6 E6
Roborough Devon 17 K8
Robroyston C Glas 125 Q4
Roby Knows 81 N6
Roby Mill Lancs 88 G9
Rocester Staffs 71 L7
Roch Pembks 40 G6
Rochdale Rochdl 89 P8
Roche Cnwll 4 F9
Rochester Medway 38 B8
Rochester Nthumb 118 F11
Rochford Essex 38 E3
Rochford Worcs 57 L11
Roch Gate Pembks 40 G6
Rock Cnwll 4 E6
Rock Neath 29 L6
Rock Nthumb 119 P6
Rock W Susx 24 D8
Rock Worcs 57 N10
Rockbeare Devon 9 P6
Rockbourne Hants 21 M11
Rockcliffe Cumb 110 G8
Rockcliffe D & G 108 F10
Rockcliffe Cross Cumb 110 F8
Rock End Staffs 70 F3
Rockend Torbay 7 N6
Rock Ferry Wirral 81 L7
Rockfield Highld 163 L10
Rockfield Mons 31 N2
Rockford Devon 17 P2
Rockford Hants 13 L3
Rockgreen Shrops 57 J9
Rockhampton S Glos 32 C6
Rockhead Cnwll 4 H5
Rockhill Shrops 56 H9
Rock Hill Worcs 58 E11
Rockingham Nhants 61 J2
Rockland All Saints Norfk 64 D2
Rockland St Mary Norfk 77 L11
Rockland St Peter Norfk 64 D2
Rockley Notts 85 M6
Rockley Wilts 33 N10
Rockliffe Lancs 89 P6
Rockville Ag & B 131 Q9
Rockwell End Bucks 35 L7
Rockwell Green Somset 18 F10
Rodborough Gloucs 32 F4
Rodbourne Swindn 33 M7
Rodbourne Wilts 32 H8
Rodd Herefs 45 L2
Roddam Nthumb 119 K6
Rodden Dorset 11 M8
Roddymoor Dur 103 N3
Rode Somset 20 F4
Rode Heath Ches E 70 E3
Rode Heath Ches E 83 J11
Rodel W Isls 168 f9
Roden Wrekin 69 Q11
Rodhuish Somset 18 D7
Rodington Wrekin 57 K2
Rodington Heath Wrekin 57 K2
Rodley Gloucs 32 D2
Rodley Leeds 90 G3
Rodmarton Gloucs 32 H5
Rodmell E Susx 25 K9
Rodmersham Kent 38 F9
Rodmersham Green Kent 38 F9
Rodney Stoke Somset 19 N5
Rodsley Derbys 71 N6
Rodway Somset 19 J6
Roecliffe N York 97 N7
Roe Cross Tamesd 83 L5
Roe Green Herts 50 F9
Roe Green Herts 50 H4
Roe Green Salfd 82 F4
Roehampton Gt Lon 36 F6
Roffey W Susx 24 E4
Rogart Highld 162 G6
Rogate W Susx 23 M10
Roger Ground Cumb 101 L11
Rogerstone Newpt 31 J7
Roghadal W Isls 168 f9
Rogiet Mons 31 M7
Roke Oxon 34 H6
Roker Sundld 113 P9
Rollesby Norfk 77 N8
Rolleston Leics 73 J10
Rolleston Notts 85 M10
Rollestone Wilts 21 L5
Rolleston on Dove Staffs 71 N9
Rolston E R Yk 93 M2
Rolstone N Som 19 L2
Rolvenden Kent 26 D5
Rolvenden Layne Kent 26 D5
Romaldkirk Dur 103 J6
Rishangles Suffk 64 H8
Romanby N York 97 N2

Romanno Bridge Border 127 M8
Romansleigh Devon 17 N7
Romden Castle Kent 26 E3
Romesdal Highld 152 G7
Romford Dorset 13 J3
Romford Gt Lon 37 M3
Romiley Stockp 83 K6
Romney Street Kent 37 N9
Romsey Cambs 62 G9
Romsey Hants 22 C10
Romsley Shrops 57 P8
Romsley Worcs 58 E8
Rona Highld 153 L6
Rood Ashton Wilts 20 G3
Rookhope Dur 102 H2
Rookley IoW 14 F10
Rookley Green IoW 14 F10
Rooks Bridge Somset 19 L4
Rooks Nest Somset 18 E8
Rookwith N York 97 K3
Roos E R Yk 93 N4
Roose Cumb 94 E7
Roosebeck Cumb 94 F7
Roothams Green Bed 61 N9
Ropley Hants 22 H8
Ropley Dean Hants 22 H8
Ropley Soke Hants 23 J8
Ropsley Lincs 73 P4
Rora Abers 159 Q7
Rorrington Shrops 56 E4
Rosarie Moray 158 A7
Rose Cnwll 3 K3
Roseacre Lancs 88 E3
Rose Ash Devon 17 P7
Rosebank S Lans 126 E8
Rosebush Pembks 41 L5
Rosecare Cnwll 5 K2
Rosecliston Cnwll 4 C10
Rosedale Abbey N York 105 K11
Rose Green Essex 52 F6
Rose Green Suffk 52 F4
Rose Green Suffk 52 G3
Rose Green W Susx 15 P7
Rosehall Highld 162 B6
Rosehearty Abers 159 M4
Rose Hill E Susx 25 L7
Rose Hill Lancs 89 N4
Rosehill Shrops 69 N11
Roseisle Moray 157 L4
Roselands E Susx 25 P10
Rosemarket Pembks 41 J9
Rosemarkie Highld 156 C6
Rosemary Lane Devon 10 D2
Rosemount P & K 142 B9
Rosenannon Cnwll 4 F8
Rosenithon Cnwll 3 L9
Roser's Cross E Susx 25 M6
Rosevean Cnwll 4 G10
Rosevine Cnwll 3 M6
Rosewarne Cnwll 2 G6
Rosewell Mdloth 127 P5
Roseworth S on T 104 D6
Roseworthy Cnwll 2 G6
Rosgill Cumb 101 P7
Roskestal Cnwll 2 B9
Roskhill Highld 152 D9
Roskorwell Cnwll 3 K9
Rosley Cumb 110 F11
Roslin Mdloth 127 P5
Rosliston Derbys 71 N11
Rosneath Ag & B 132 B11
Ross D & G 108 D12
Ross Nthumb 119 M3
Rossett Wrexhm 69 L3
Rossett Green N York 97 L10
Rossington Donc 91 Q11
Ross-on-Wye Herefs 46 A10
Roster Highld 167 N9
Rostherne Ches E 82 F8
Rosthwaite Cumb 101 J8
Roston Derbys 71 L6
Rosudgeon Cnwll 2 G8
Rosyth Fife 134 E11
Rothbury Nthumb 119 L10
Rotherby Leics 72 H7
Rotherfield E Susx 25 N5
Rotherfield Greys Oxon 35 K8
Rotherfield Peppard Oxon 35 K8
Rotherham Rothm 84 F2
Rothersthorpe Nhants 60 F9
Rotherwick Hants 23 K3
Rothes Moray 157 P8
Rothesay Ag & B 124 D5
Rothiebrisbane Abers 158 H10
Rothiemurchus Lodge Highld 148 H6
Rothienorman Abers 158 H10
Rothley Leics 72 F8
Rothley Nthumb 112 F3
Rothmaise Abers 158 G11
Rothwell Leeds 91 J5
Rothwell Lincs 93 K11
Rothwell Nhants 60 H4
Rotsea E R Yk 99 M10
Rottal Lodge Angus 142 F4
Rottingdean Br & H 25 J10
Rottington Cumb 100 C8
Roucan D & G 109 M5
Roud IoW 14 F10
Rougham Norfk 76 A7
Rougham Suffk 64 C9
Rough Close Staffs 70 G7
Rough Common Kent 39 K10
Roughlee Lancs 89 N2
Roughpark Abers 149 Q5
Roughton Lincs 86 H8
Roughton Norfk 77 J4
Roughton Shrops 57 P6
Roughway Kent 37 P10
Round Bush Herts 50 D11
Roundbush Green Essex 51 N8
Round Green Luton 50 D6
Roundham Somset 11 J3
Roundhay Leeds 91 J3
Rounds Green Sandw 58 E7
Round Street Kent 37 Q7
Roundstreet Common W Susx 24 C4
Roundswell Devon 17 J5
Roundway Wilts 21 K2
Roundyhill Angus 142 F7
Rousay Ork 169 c3
Rousdon Devon 10 F6
Rousham Oxon 48 E10

Rous Lench Worcs 47 K4
Routenburn N Ayrs 124 F5
Routh E R Yk 93 J2
Rout's Green Bucks 35 L5
Row Cnwll 4 H6
Row Cumb 95 K3
Row Cumb 102 B4
Rowanburn D & G 110 H5
Rowardennan Stirlg 132 D8
Rowarth Derbys 83 M7
Row Ash Hants 14 F4
Rowberrow Somset 19 N3
Rowborough IoW 14 E10
Rowde Wilts 21 J2
Rowden Devon 8 F5
Rowen Conwy 79 P10
Rowfield Derbys 71 M5
Rowfoot Nthumb 111 N8
Rowford Somset 18 H9
Row Green Essex 52 B7
Rowhedge Essex 52 H7
Rowhook W Susx 24 D4
Rowington Warwks 59 K11
Rowland Derbys 84 B6
Rowland's Castle Hants 15 K4
Rowlands Gill Gatesd 113 J9
Rowledge Surrey 23 M6
Rowley Dur 112 G11
Rowley E R Yk 92 G4
Rowley Shrops 56 E3
Rowley Hill Kirk 90 F8
Rowley Regis Sandw 58 E7
Rowlstone Herefs 45 M9
Rowly Surrey 24 B2
Rowner Hants 14 G6
Rowney Green Worcs 58 F10
Rownhams Hants 22 C11
Rownhams Services Hants 22 C11
Rowrah Cumb 100 E7
Rowsham Bucks 49 M11
Rowsley Derbys 84 C7
Rowstock Oxon 34 E7
Rowston Lincs 86 E9
Rowthorne Derbys 84 G8
Rowton Ches W 69 M2
Rowton Shrops 56 F2
Rowton Shrops 56 G8
Rowton Wrekin 69 R11
Row Town Surrey 36 B8
Roxburgh Border 118 C4
Roxby N Linc 92 F7
Roxby N York 105 L7
Roxton Bed 61 Q10
Roxwell Essex 51 P9
Royal Leamington Spa Warwks 59 M11
Royal Oak Darltn 103 P6
Royal Oak Lancs 81 N4
Royal's Green Ches E 69 R6
Royal Sutton Coldfield Birm 58 H5
Royal Tunbridge Wells Kent 25 N3
Royal Wootton Bassett Wilts 33 L8
Royal Yacht Britannia C Edin 127 P2
Roy Bridge Highld 146 H11
Roydhouse Kirk 90 G8
Roydon Essex 51 K8
Roydon Norfk 64 G5
Roydon Norfk 75 P6
Roydon Hamlet Essex 51 K9
Royston Barns 91 K8
Royston Herts 51 J2
Royton Oldham 89 Q9
Rozel Jersey 11 c1
Ruabon Wrexhm 69 K6
Ruaig Ag & B 136 D6
Ruan High Lanes Cnwll 3 N6
Ruan Lanihorne Cnwll 3 M5
Ruan Major Cnwll 3 J10
Ruan Minor Cnwll 3 J10
Ruardean Gloucs 46 B11
Ruardean Hill Gloucs 46 B11
Ruardean Woodside Gloucs 46 B11
Rubery Birm 58 E9
Rubha Ban W Isls 168 c16
Ruckcroft Cumb 101 P2
Ruckhall Herefs 45 P7
Ruckinge Kent 26 H5
Ruckland Lincs 87 K5
Ruckley Shrops 57 J4
Rudbaxton Pembks 41 J6
Rudby N York 104 E9
Rudchester Nthumb 112 H7
Ruddington Notts 72 F4
Ruddle Gloucs 32 C2
Ruddlemoor Cnwll 3 Q3
Rudford Gloucs 46 E10
Rudge Somset 20 F4
Rudgeway S Glos 32 B7
Rudgwick W Susx 24 C4
Rudhall Herefs 46 B9
Rudheath Ches W 82 E10
Rudheath Woods Ches E 82 F10
Rudley Green Essex 52 D11
Rudloe Wilts 32 F10
Rudry Caerph 30 H7
Rudston E R Yk 99 M7
Rudyard Staffs 70 H3
Ruecastle Border 118 B6
Rufford Lancs 88 F7
Rufford Abbey Notts 85 K8
Rufforth C York 98 A10
Rug Denbgs 68 E6
Rugby Warwks 59 P9
Rugby Services Warwks 60 B5
Rugeley Staffs 71 J11
Ruigh'riabhach Highld 160 G7
Ruisgarry W Isls 168 e9
Ruishton Somset 19 J9
Ruisigearraidh W Isls 168 e9
Ruislip Gt Lon 36 C3
Rùm Highld 144 E8
Rumbach Moray 158 A7
Rumbling Bridge P & K 134 C2
Rumburgh Suffk 65 L5
Rumby Hill Dur 103 N4
Rumford Cnwll 4 D7
Rumford Falk 126 G2
Rumney Cardif 30 H9
Rumwell Somset 18 G10
Runcorn Halton 81 Q8
Runcton W Susx 15 N6
Runcton Holme Norfk 75 M9
Runfold Surrey 23 N5
Runhall Norfk 76 F10
Runham Norfk 77 P9
Runham Norfk 77 Q10

Runnington – Scholes 291

Runnington Somset 18 F10
Runsell Green Essex 52 C10
Runshaw Moor Lancs 88 G7
Runswick N York 105 M7
Runtaleave Angus 142 D4
Runwell Essex 38 C3
Ruscombe Wokham 35 L9
Rushall Herefs 46 B7
Rushall Norfk 64 H5
Rushall Wilts 21 M3
Rushall Wsall 58 F4
Rushbrooke Suffk 64 B9
Rushbury Shrops 57 J6
Rushden Herts 50 H4
Rushden Nhants 61 L7
Rushenden Kent 38 F7
Rusher's Cross E Susx 25 P5
Rushford Devon 8 C9
Rushford Norfk 64 C5
Rush Green Essex 53 L8
Rush Green Gt Lon 37 M3
Rush Green Herts 50 F6
Rush Green Warrtn 82 E7
Rushlake Green E Susx 25 P7
Rushmere Suffk 65 P4
Rushmere St Andrew Suffk 53 L2
Rushmoor Surrey 23 N6
Rushock Herefs 45 L3
Rushock Worcs 58 C10
Rusholme Manch 83 J6
Rushton Ches W 69 Q2
Rushton Nhants 60 H4
Rushton Shrops 57 L3
Rushton Spencer Staffs 70 G2
Rushwick Worcs 46 F4
Rushyford Dur 103 Q5
Ruskie Stirlg 133 J7
Ruskington Lincs 86 E10
Rusland Cross Cumb 94 G3
Rusper W Susx 24 F3
Ruspidge Gloucs 32 C2
Russell Green Essex 52 B9
Russell's Water Oxon 35 K7
Russel's Green Suffk 65 K7
Russ Hill Surrey 24 F2
Rusthall Kent 25 N3
Rustington W Susx 24 B10
Ruston N York 99 K4
Ruston Parva E R Yk 99 M8
Ruswarp N York 105 N9
Ruthall Shrops 57 K6
Rutherford Border 118 B4
Rutherglen S Lans 125 Q5
Ruthernbridge Cnwll 4 G8
Ruthin Denbgs 68 F3
Ruthrieston C Aber 151 N7
Ruthven Abers 158 D8
Ruthven Angus 142 D8
Ruthven Highld 148 D8
Ruthven Highld 156 E11
Ruthvoes Cnwll 4 E9
Ruthwaite Cumb 100 H3
Ruthwell D & G 109 N7
Ruxley Gt Lon 37 L6
Ruxton Green Herefs 45 Q11
Ruyton-XI-Towns Shrops 69 L10
Ryal Nthumb 112 F6
Ryall Dorset 11 J5
Ryall Worcs 46 G6
Ryarsh Kent 37 Q8
Rycote Oxon 35 J3
Rydal Cumb 101 L9
Ryde IoW 14 G8
Rye E Susx 26 F7
Ryebank Shrops 69 P8
Ryeford Herefs 46 B10
Rye Foreign E Susx 26 E7
Rye Harbour E Susx 26 F8
Ryehill E R Yk 93 M5
Ryeish Green Wokham 35 K11
Rye Street Worcs 46 E7
Ryhall Rutlnd 73 Q8
Ryhill Wakefd 91 K8
Ryhope Sundld 113 P10
Rylah Derbys 84 G7
Ryland Lincs 86 D5
Rylands Notts 72 E3
Rylstone N York 96 E9
Ryme Intrinseca Dorset 11 M2
Ryther N York 91 P3
Ryton Gatesd 113 J8
Ryton N York 98 F5
Ryton Shrops 57 P4
Ryton Warwks 59 P7
Ryton-on-Dunsmore Warwks 59 N10
Ryton Woodside Gatesd 112 H8
RZSS Edinburgh Zoo C Edin 127 N3

S

Sabden Lancs 89 M3
Sabine's Green Essex 51 M11
Sacombe Herts 50 H7
Sacombe Green Herts 50 H7
Sacriston Dur 113 K11
Sadberge Darltn 104 B7
Saddell Ag & B 120 E5
Saddington Leics 60 E2
Saddlebow Norfk 75 M7
Saddlescombe W Susx 24 G8
Sadgill Cumb 101 N9
Saffron Walden Essex 51 M3
Sageston Pembks 41 L10
Saham Hills Norfk 76 C11
Saham Toney Norfk 76 B11
Saighton Ches W 69 M2
St Abbs Border 129 N6
St Agnes Border 128 H7
St Agnes Cnwll 3 J3
St Agnes IoS 2 b3
St Agnes Mining District Cnwll 3 J4
St Albans Herts 50 D9
St Allen Cnwll 3 L3
St Andrew Guern 10 b2
St Andrews Fife 135 N4
St Andrews Botanic Garden Fife 135 N4
St Andrews Major V Glam 30 F10
St Andrews Well Dorset 11 K6
St Anne's Lancs 88 C5
St Ann's D & G 109 N2
St Ann's Chapel Cnwll 5 Q7
St Ann's Chapel Devon 6 H9
St Anthony-in-Meneage Cnwll 3 K8
St Anthony's Hill E Susx 25 P10
St Arvans Mons 31 P5
St Asaph Denbgs 80 E10
St Athan V Glam 30 D11
St Aubin Jersey 11 b2
St Austell Cnwll 3 Q3
St Bees Cumb 100 C8
St Blazey Cnwll 3 R3
St Blazey Gate Cnwll 3 R3
St Boswells Border 118 A4
St Brelade Jersey 11 a2
St Brelade's Bay Jersey 11 a2
St Breock Cnwll 4 F7
St Breward Cnwll 4 H6
St Briavels Gloucs 31 Q4
St Brides Pembks 40 F8
St Brides Major V Glam 29 N10
St Brides Netherwent Mons 31 M7
St Brides-super-Ely V Glam 30 E9
St Brides Wentlooge Newpt 31 J8
St Budeaux C Plym 6 D7
Saintbury Gloucs 47 M7
St Buryan Cnwll 2 C8
St Catherine BaNES 32 E11
St Catherines Ag & B 131 N6
St Chloe Gloucs 32 F4
St Clears Carmth 41 Q7
St Cleer Cnwll 5 L8
St Clement Cnwll 3 M5
St Clement Jersey 11 c2
St Clether Cnwll 5 L5
St Colmac Ag & B 124 C4
St Columb Major Cnwll 4 E9
St Columb Minor Cnwll 4 C9
St Columb Road Cnwll 4 E10
St Combs Abers 159 Q5
St Cross South Elmham Suffk 65 K5
St Cyrus Abers 143 N5
St David's P & K 133 Q3
St Davids Pembks 40 E5
St Davids Cathedral Pembks 40 E5
St Day Cnwll 3 J5
St Decumans Somset 18 E6
St Dennis Cnwll 4 F10
St Devereux Herefs 45 N8
St Dogmaels Pembks 42 C5
St Dogwells Pembks 41 J5
St Dominick Cnwll 5 Q8
St Donats V Glam 29 P11
St Edith's Marsh Wilts 21 J2
St Endellion Cnwll 4 F6
St Enoder Cnwll 4 D10
St Erme Cnwll 3 L4
St Erney Cnwll 5 P10
St Erth Cnwll 2 F6
St Erth Praze Cnwll 2 F6
St Ervan Cnwll 4 D7
St Eval Cnwll 4 D8
St Ewe Cnwll 3 P4
St Fagans Cardif 30 F9
St Fagans: National History Museum Cardif 30 F9
St Fergus Abers 159 Q7
St Fillans P & K 133 K3
St Florence Pembks 41 L10
St Gennys Cnwll 5 J2
St George Conwy 80 D9
St Georges N Som 19 L2
St George's V Glam 30 F9
St George's Hill Surrey 36 C8
St Germans Cnwll 5 P10
St Giles in the Wood Devon 17 J8
St Giles-on-the-Heath Devon 5 P3
St Gluvia's Cnwll 3 K7
St Harmon Powys 55 M10
St Helen Auckland Dur 103 N5
St Helens Cumb 100 D4
St Helen's E Susx 26 D9
St Helens IoW 14 H9
St Helens St Hel 81 Q5
St Helier Gt Lon 36 G7
St Helier Jersey 11 b2
St Hilary Cnwll 2 E7
St Hilary V Glam 30 D10
Saint Hill Devon 10 B3
Saint Hill W Susx 25 J3
St Illtyd Blae G 30 H4
St Ippolyts Herts 50 E5
St Ishmael's Pembks 40 F9
St Issey Cnwll 4 E7
St Ive Cnwll 5 N8
St Ive Cross Cnwll 5 N8
St Ives Cambs 62 D6
St Ives Cnwll 2 E5
St Ives Dorset 13 K4
St James Norfk 77 K7
St James's End Nhants 60 F8
St James South Elmham Suffk 65 L5
St Jidgey Cnwll 4 E8
St John Cnwll 5 Q11
St John Jersey 11 b1
St Johns Dur 103 L4
St John's E Susx 25 M4
St John's IoM 80 c5
St John's Kent 37 M9
St Johns Surrey 23 Q3
St Johns Worcs 46 F4
St John's Chapel Devon 17 J6
St John's Chapel Dur 102 G3
St John's Fen End Norfk 75 K8
St John's Highway Norfk 75 K8
St John's Kirk S Lans 116 D3
St John's Town of Dalry D & G 108 D4
St John's Wood Gt Lon 36 G4
St Judes IoM 80 e2
St Just Cnwll 2 B7
St Just-in-Roseland Cnwll 3 L6
St Just Mining District Cnwll 2 B7
St Katherines Abers 159 J11
St Keverne Cnwll 3 K9
St Kew Cnwll 4 G6
St Kew Highway Cnwll 4 G6
St Keyne Cnwll 5 L9
St Lawrence Cnwll 4 G8
St Lawrence Essex 52 G11
St Lawrence IoW 14 F11
St Lawrence Jersey 11 b1
St Lawrence Kent 39 Q8
St Leonards Bucks 35 P3
St Leonards Dorset 13 K4
St Leonards E Susx 26 D10
St Leonard's Street Kent 37 Q9
St Levan Cnwll 2 B9
St Lythans V Glam 30 F10
St Mabyn Cnwll 4 G7
St Madoes P & K 134 F3
St Margarets Herefs 45 M8
St Margarets Herts 51 J8
St Margaret's at Cliffe Kent 27 Q3
St Margaret's Hope Ork 169 d7
St Margaret South Elmham Suffk 65 L5
St Marks IoM 80 c7
St Martin Cnwll 3 J9
St Martin Cnwll 5 M10
St Martin Guern 10 b2
St Martin Jersey 11 c1
St Martin's IoS 2 c1
St Martin's P & K 142 B11
St Martin's Shrops 69 K7
St Martin's Moor Shrops 69 K7
St Mary Jersey 11 a1
St Mary Bourne Hants 22 D4
St Marychurch Torbay 7 N5
St Mary Church V Glam 30 D10
St Mary Cray Gt Lon 37 L7
St Mary Hill V Glam 30 C9
St Mary in the Marsh Kent 27 J6
St Mary's IoS 2 c2
St Mary's Ork 169 d6
St Mary's Bay Kent 27 J6
St Mary's Hoo Medway 38 D6
St Mary's Platt Kent 37 P9
St Maughans Mons 45 P11
St Maughans Green Mons 45 P11
St Mawes Cnwll 3 L7
St Mawgan Cnwll 4 D8
St Mellion Cnwll 5 P8
St Mellons Cardif 30 H8
St Merryn Cnwll 4 D7
St Mewan Cnwll 3 P3
St Michael Caerhays Cnwll 3 P5
St Michael Church Somset 19 K8
St Michael Penkevil Cnwll 3 M5
St Michaels Kent 26 E4
St Michaels Worcs 57 K11
St Michael's Mount Cnwll 2 E8
St Michael's on Wyre Lancs 88 F2
St Michael South Elmham Suffk 65 L5
St Minver Cnwll 4 F6
St Monans Fife 135 N7
St Neot Cnwll 5 K8
St Neots Cambs 61 Q8
St Newlyn East Cnwll 4 C10
St Nicholas Pembks 40 H3
St Nicholas V Glam 30 E10
St Nicholas-at-Wade Kent 39 N8
St Ninians Stirlg 133 M9
St Olaves Norfk 65 P2
St Osyth Essex 53 K8
St Ouen Jersey 11 a1
St Owen's Cross Herefs 45 Q10
St Paul's Cray Gt Lon 37 L7
St Paul's Walden Herts 50 E6
St Peter Jersey 11 a1
St Peter Port Guern 10 c2
St Peter's Guern 10 b2
St Peter's Kent 39 Q8
St Peter's Hill Cambs 62 B6
St Petrox Pembks 41 J11
St Pinnock Cnwll 5 L9
St Quivox S Ayrs 114 G3
St Ruan Cnwll 3 J10
St Sampson Guern 10 c1
St Saviour Guern 10 b2
St Saviour Jersey 11 b2
St Stephen Cnwll 3 N3
St Stephens Cnwll 5 N4
St Stephens Cnwll 5 Q10
St Teath Cnwll 4 H5
St Thomas Devon 9 M6
St Margaret's Bay Kent 27 Q3
St Tudy Cnwll 4 H6
St Twynnells Pembks 41 J11
St Veep Cnwll 5 J10
St Vigeans Angus 143 L9
St Wenn Cnwll 4 F9
St Weonards Herefs 45 P10
St Winnow Cnwll 5 J10
St y-Nyll V Glam 30 E9
Salcombe Devon 7 J11
Salcombe Regis Devon 10 D7
Salcott-cum-Virley Essex 52 F9
Sale Traffd 82 G6
Saleby Lincs 87 N5
Sale Green Worcs 46 H3
Salehurst E Susx 26 C7
Salem Carmth 43 M9
Salem Cerdgn 54 F8
Salen Ag & B 137 P7
Salen Highld 138 B5
Salesbury Lancs 89 K4
Salford C Beds 49 P7
Salford Oxon 47 Q9
Salford Salfd 82 H5
Salford Priors Warwks 47 L4
Salfords Surrey 36 G11
Salhouse Norfk 77 L9
Saline Fife 134 C9
Salisbury Wilts 21 M8
Salisbury Plain Wilts 21 L6
Salkeld Dykes Cumb 101 P3
Sallachy Highld 162 C5
Salle Norfk 76 G7
Salmonby Lincs 87 K6
Salperton Gloucs 47 L10
Salph End Bed 61 N10
Salsburgh N Lans 126 E5
Salt Staffs 70 H9
Salta Cumb 109 N11
Saltaire C Brad 90 E3
Saltaire C Brad 90 E3
Saltash Cnwll 6 C7
Saltburn Highld 156 C3
Saltburn-by-the-Sea R & Cl 105 J6
Saltby Leics 73 M5
Salt Coates Cumb 110 C10
Saltcoats Cumb 100 E11
Saltcoats N Ayrs 124 G9
Saltcotes Lancs 88 D5
Saltdean Br & H 25 J10
Salterbeck Cumb 100 C5
Salterforth Lancs 96 C11
Salterswall Ches W 82 D11
Salterton Wilts 21 M7
Saltfleet Lincs 87 N2
Saltfleetby All Saints Lincs 87 N2
Saltfleetby St Clement Lincs 87 N2
Saltfleetby St Peter Lincs 87 M3
Saltford BaNES 32 C11
Salthouse Norfk 76 F3
Saltley Birm 58 H7
Saltmarsh Newpt 31 K8
Saltmarshe E R Yk 92 C6
Saltney Flints 69 L2
Salton N York 98 E5
Saltrens Devon 16 H7
Saltwick Nthumb 113 J4
Saltwood Kent 27 L4
Salvington W Susx 24 D9
Salwarpe Worcs 46 G2
Salway Ash Dorset 11 K5
Sambourne Warwks 47 L2
Sambrook Wrekin 70 C10
Samlesbury Lancs 88 H4
Samlesbury Bottoms Lancs 89 J5
Sampford Arundel Somset 18 F11
Sampford Brett Somset 18 E6
Sampford Courtenay Devon 8 F4
Sampford Moor Somset 18 F11
Sampford Peverell Devon 9 P2
Sampford Spiney Devon 6 E4
Samsonlane Ork 169 f4
Samson's Corner Essex 53 J8
Samuelston E Loth 128 D5
Sanaigmore Ag & B 122 B5
Sancreed Cnwll 2 C8
Sancton E R Yk 92 E3
Sand Somset 19 M5
Sandaig Highld 145 M7
Sandale Cumb 100 H2
Sandal Magna Wakefd 91 J7
Sanday Ork 169 f2
Sanday Airport Ork 169 f2
Sandbach Ches E 70 D2
Sandbach Services Ches E 70 D2
Sandbank Ag & B 131 P11
Sandbanks BCP 12 H7
Sandend Abers 158 E4
Sanderstead Gt Lon 36 H8
Sandford Cumb 102 D7
Sandford Devon 9 K4
Sandford Dorset 12 F7
Sandford Hants 13 L4
Sandford IoW 14 F10
Sandford N Som 19 M3
Sandford S Lans 126 C9
Sandford Shrops 69 K10
Sandford Shrops 69 Q8
Sandford-on-Thames Oxon 34 F4
Sandford Orcas Dorset 20 B10
Sandford St Martin Oxon 48 D9
Sandgate Kent 27 M4
Sandhaven Abers 159 N4
Sandhead D & G 106 E8
Sandhill Rothm 91 L11
Sandhills Dorset 11 M4
Sandhills Dorset 11 P2
Sand Hills Leeds 91 K3
Sandhills Oxon 34 G3
Sandhills Surrey 23 P7
Sandhoe Nthumb 112 E7
Sandhole Ag & B 131 L8
Sand Hole E R Yk 92 D3
Sandholme E R Yk 92 D4
Sandholme Lincs 74 F3
Sandhurst Br For 23 M2
Sandhurst Gloucs 46 F10
Sandhurst Kent 26 D6
Sandhurst Cross Kent 26 C6
Sandhutton N York 97 N4
Sand Hutton N York 98 D9
Sandiacre Derbys 72 D3
Sandilands Lincs 87 P4
Sandiway Ches W 82 D10
Sandleheath Hants 21 M11
Sandleigh Oxon 34 E4
Sandley Dorset 20 E10
Sandling Kent 38 C10
Sandlow Green Ches E 82 G11
Sandness Shet 169 n8
Sandon Essex 52 B11
Sandon Herts 50 H4
Sandon Staffs 70 G9
Sandon Bank Staffs 70 G9
Sandown IoW 14 G10
Sandplace Cnwll 5 M10
Sandridge Herts 50 E8
Sandridge Wilts 32 H11
Sandringham Norfk 75 N5
Sands Bucks 35 M6
Sandsend N York 105 N8
Sand Side Cumb 94 E4
Sandside Cumb 95 K4
Sandtoft N Linc 92 B9
Sandway Kent 38 E11
Sandwich Kent 39 P10
Sandwich Bay Kent 39 Q10
Sandwick Cumb 101 M7
Sandwick Shet 169 r11
Sandwick W Isls 168 j4
Sandwith Cumb 100 C8
Sandwith Newtown Cumb 100 C8
Sandy C Beds 61 Q11
Sandy Bank Lincs 87 J9
Sandycroft Flints 81 L11
Sandy Cross E Susx 25 N6
Sandy Cross Herefs 46 C3
Sandyford D & G 110 D2
Sandygate Devon 7 M4
Sandygate IoM 80 e2
Sandy Haven Pembks 40 G9
Sandyhills D & G 109 J9
Sandylands Lancs 95 J8
Sandy Lane C Brad 90 E3
Sandylane Staffs 70 C7
Sandylane Swans 28 G7
Sandy Lane Wilts 33 J11
Sandy Lane Wrexhm 69 M6
Sandy Park Devon 8 H7
Sandysike Cumb 110 G7
Sandyway Herefs 45 P9
Sangobeg Highld 165 K3
Sangomore Highld 165 K3
Sankey Bridges Warrtn 82 C7
Sankyn's Green Worcs 57 P11
Sanna Highld 137 L2
Sanndabhaig W Isls 168 j4
Sannox N Ayrs 124 C8
Sanquhar D & G 115 Q6
Santon Cumb 100 F10
Santon IoM 80 d7
Santon Bridge Cumb 100 F10
Santon Downham Suffk 63 P3
Sapcote Leics 59 Q6
Sapey Common Herefs 46 D2
Sapiston Suffk 64 C6
Sapley Cambs 62 B6
Sapperton Derbys 71 M8
Sapperton Gloucs 32 H4
Sapperton Lincs 73 Q4
Saracen's Head Lincs 74 F5
Sarclet Highld 167 P8
Sarisbury Hants 14 F5
Sarn Brdgnd 29 P8
Sarn Powys 56 C6
Sarnau Carmth 42 F11
Sarnau Cerdgn 42 F4
Sarnau Gwynd 68 C7
Sarnau Powys 44 E8
Sarnau Powys 68 H11
Sarn Bach Gwynd 66 E9
Sarnesfield Herefs 45 M4
Sarn Mellteyrn Gwynd 66 C8
Sarn Park Services Brdgnd 29 P8
Sarn-wen Powys 69 J11
Saron Carmth 28 H2
Saron Carmth 42 G7
Saron Gwynd 66 H3
Saron Gwynd 79 J11
Sarratt Herts 50 B11
Sarre Kent 39 N8
Sarsden Oxon 47 Q10
Sarson Hants 22 B6
Satley Dur 103 M2
Satmar Kent 27 N4
Satron N York 102 H11
Satterleigh Devon 17 M7
Satterthwaite Cumb 94 G2
Satwell Oxon 35 K8
Sauchen Abers 151 J5
Saucher P & K 142 B11
Sauchieburn Abers 143 M4
Saul Gloucs 32 D3
Saundby Notts 85 N3
Saundersfoot Pembks 41 M10
Saunderton Bucks 35 L4
Saunderton Station Bucks 35 M5
Saunton Devon 16 H4
Sausthorpe Lincs 87 L7
Saverley Green Staffs 70 H7
Savile Town Kirk 90 G6
Sawbridge Warwks 60 B7
Sawbridgeworth Herts 51 L8
Sawdon N York 99 J4
Sawley Derbys 72 D4
Sawley Lancs 96 A11
Sawley N York 97 K7
Sawston Cambs 62 G11
Sawtry Cambs 61 Q4
Saxby Leics 73 L7
Saxby Lincs 86 D3
Saxby All Saints N Linc 92 G7
Saxelbye Leics 72 H6
Saxham Street Suffk 64 F9
Saxilby Lincs 85 Q5
Saxlingham Norfk 76 E4
Saxlingham Green Norfk 65 J2
Saxlingham Nethergate Norfk 65 J2
Saxlingham Thorpe Norfk 65 J2
Saxmundham Suffk 65 M9
Saxondale Notts 72 H3
Saxon Street Cambs 63 L9
Saxtead Suffk 65 K8
Saxtead Green Suffk 65 K9
Saxtead Little Green Suffk 65 J8
Saxthorpe Norfk 76 G5
Saxton N York 91 M3
Sayers Common W Susx 24 G7
Scackleton N York 98 C6
Scadabay W Isls 168 g8
Scadabhagh W Isls 168 g8
Scafell Pike Cumb 100 H9
Scaftworth Notts 85 L2
Scagglethorpe N York 98 G6
Scalasaig Ag & B 136 b3
Scalby E R Yk 92 D5
Scalby N York 99 L2
Scald End Bed 61 M9
Scaldwell Nhants 60 G6
Scaleby Cumb 110 H8
Scalebyhill Cumb 110 H8
Scale Houses Cumb 111 L11
Scales Cumb 94 F6
Scales Cumb 101 K5
Scalesceugh Cumb 110 H11
Scalford Leics 73 K6
Scaling N York 105 K8
Scaling Dam R & Cl 105 K8
Scalloway Shet 169 r10
Scalpay Highld 153 L11
Scalpay W Isls 168 h8
Scamblesby Lincs 87 J5
Scammonden Kirk 90 D7
Scamodale Highld 138 E3
Scampston N York 98 H5
Scampton Lincs 86 C5
Scaniport Highld 156 A10
Scapegoat Hill Kirk 90 D7
Scarba Ag & B 130 D7
Scarborough N York 99 L3
Scarcewater Cnwll 3 N3
Scarcliffe Derbys 84 G7
Scarcroft Leeds 91 K2
Scarfskerry Highld 167 N2
Scargill Dur 103 L8
Scarinish Ag & B 136 C7
Scarisbrick Lancs 88 D8
Scarness Cumb 100 H4
Scarning Norfk 76 D9
Scarrington Notts 73 J2
Scarth Hill Lancs 88 E9
Scarthingwell N York 91 M3
Scartho NE Lin 93 N9
Scatsta Airport Shet 169 q6
Scaur D & G 108 H10
Scawby N Linc 92 G9
Scawsby Donc 91 N10
Scawthorpe Donc 91 P9
Scawton N York 98 A4
Scayne's Hill W Susx 25 J6
Scethrog Powys 44 G9
Scholar Green Ches E 70 E3
Scholes Kirk 90 F5

Place	Page	Grid
Scholes Kirk	90	F9
Scholes Leeds	91	K3
Scholes Rothm	91	K11
Scholes Wigan	88	H9
School Aycliffe Dur	103	Q6
School Green C Brad	90	E4
School Green Ches W	70	A2
Schoolgreen Wokham	35	K11
School House Dorset	10	H4
Scissett Kirk	90	G8
Scleddau Pembks	40	H4
Scofton Notts	85	K4
Scole Norfk	64	H6
Scone P & K	134	E2
Sconser Highld	153	J11
Scoonie Fife	135	K7
Scopwick Lincs	86	E9
Scoraig Highld	160	G7
Scorborough E R Yk	99	L11
Scorrier Cnwll	3	J5
Scorriton Devon	7	J5
Scorton Lancs	95	L11
Scorton N York	103	Q10
Sco Ruston Norfk	77	K7
Scotby Cumb	110	H9
Scotch Corner N York	103	P9
Scotch Corner Rest Area N York	103	P9
Scotforth Lancs	95	K9
Scot Hay Staffs	70	D5
Scothern Lincs	86	D5
Scotland Lincs	73	Q4
Scotland Gate Nthumb	113	L4
Scotlandwell P & K	134	F7
Scot Lane End Bolton	89	J9
Scotscalder Station Highld	167	J5
Scotsdike Cumb	110	G6
Scot's Gap Nthumb	112	F3
Scotsmill Abers	150	F4
Scotstoun C Glas	125	N4
Scotswood N u Ty	113	K8
Scotter Lincs	92	E10
Scotterthorpe Lincs	92	E10
Scottlethorpe Lincs	73	R6
Scotton Lincs	92	E11
Scotton N York	97	M9
Scotton N York	103	N11
Scottow Norfk	77	K7
Scott Willoughby Lincs	73	R3
Scoulton Norfk	76	D11
Scounslow Green Staffs	71	K9
Scourie Highld	164	E8
Scourie More Highld	164	D8
Scousburgh Shet	169	q12
Scouthead Oldham	90	B9
Scrabster Highld	167	K2
Scraesburgh Border	118	C7
Scrafield Lincs	87	K7
Scrainwood Nthumb	119	J9
Scrane End Lincs	74	G2
Scraptoft Leics	72	G9
Scratby Norfk	77	Q8
Scrayingham N York	98	E9
Scrays E Susx	26	C8
Scredington Lincs	74	A2
Scremby Lincs	87	M7
Scremerston Nthumb	129	Q10
Screveton Notts	73	J2
Scrivelsby Lincs	87	J7
Scriven N York	97	M9
Scrooby Notts	85	L2
Scropton Derbys	71	M8
Scrub Hill Lincs	86	H9
Scruton N York	97	L2
Scuggate Cumb	110	H6
Scullomie Highld	165	P4
Sculthorpe Norfk	76	B5
Scunthorpe N Linc	92	E8
Scurlage Swans	28	E7
Sea Somset	10	G2
Seaborough Dorset	11	J3
Seabridge Staffs	70	E6
Seabrook Kent	27	L4
Seaburn Sundld	113	P9
Seacombe Wirral	81	L6
Seacroft Leeds	91	K3
Seacroft Lincs	87	Q8
Seadyke Lincs	74	F3
Seafield W Loth	127	J4
Seaford E Susx	25	L11
Seaforth Sefton	81	L5
Seagrave Leics	72	G7
Seagry Heath Wilts	33	J8
Seaham Dur	113	P11
Seahouses Nthumb	119	P4
Seal Kent	37	N9
Sealand Flints	81	M11
Seale Surrey	23	N5
Seamer N York	99	L4
Seamer N York	104	E8
Seamill N Ayrs	124	G8
Sea Palling Norfk	77	N6
Searby Lincs	93	J9
Seasalter Kent	39	J9
Seascale Cumb	100	D10
Seathwaite Cumb	100	H11
Seathwaite Cumb	100	H8
Seatle Cumb	94	H4
Seatoller Cumb	100	H8
Seaton Cnwll	5	N11
Seaton Cumb	100	D4
Seaton Devon	10	E6
Seaton Dur	113	N11
Seaton E R Yk	99	P11
Seaton Kent	39	M10
Seaton Nthumb	113	M5
Seaton Rutlnd	73	N11
Seaton Burn N Tyne	113	K6
Seaton Carew Hartpl	104	F5
Seaton Delaval Nthumb	113	M5
Seaton Ross E R Yk	92	C2
Seaton Sluice Nthumb	113	M5
Seatown Dorset	11	J6
Seatown Moray	157	N3
Seave Green N York	104	G10
Seaview IoW	14	H8
Seaville Cumb	110	C10
Seavington St Mary Somset	11	J2
Seavington St Michael Somset	19	M11
Sebastopol Torfn	31	J5
Sebergham Cumb	101	L2
Seckington Warwks	59	L3

Place	Page	Grid
Second Severn Crossing Mons	31	P7
Sedbergh Cumb	95	P2
Sedbury Gloucs	31	P6
Sedbusk N York	96	C2
Sedgeberrow Worcs	47	K7
Sedgebrook Lincs	73	M3
Sedge Fen Suffk	63	L4
Sedgefield Dur	104	C5
Sedgeford Norfk	75	P3
Sedgehill Wilts	20	G9
Sedgemoor Services Somset	19	L4
Sedgley Dudley	58	D6
Sedgley Park Bury	82	H4
Sedgwick Cumb	95	L3
Sedlescombe E Susx	26	C8
Sedrup Bucks	35	M2
Seed Kent	38	F10
Seend Wilts	20	H2
Seend Cleeve Wilts	20	H2
Seer Green Bucks	35	Q6
Seething Norfk	65	L2
Sefton Sefton	81	M4
Seghill Nthumb	113	L6
Seighford Staffs	70	F9
Seion Gwynd	79	J11
Seisdon Staffs	58	B5
Selattyn Shrops	69	J8
Selborne Hants	23	N8
Selby N York	91	Q4
Selham W Susx	23	P10
Selhurst Gt Lon	36	H7
Selkirk Border	117	P5
Sellack Herefs	45	R9
Sellafield Station Cumb	100	D10
Sellafirth Shet	169	s4
Sellan Cnwll	2	C7
Sellick's Green Somset	18	H11
Sellindge Kent	27	J4
Selling Kent	38	H10
Sells Green Wilts	20	H2
Selly Oak Birm	58	F8
Selmeston E Susx	25	M9
Selsdon Gt Lon	37	J8
Selsey W Susx	15	N8
Selsfield Common W Susx	24	H4
Selside Cumb	101	P11
Selside N York	96	A5
Selsley Gloucs	32	F4
Selsted Kent	27	M3
Selston Notts	84	G10
Selworthy Somset	18	B5
Semer Suffk	52	G2
Semington Wilts	20	G2
Semley Wilts	20	G9
Sempringham Lincs	74	B4
Send Surrey	36	B9
Send Marsh Surrey	36	B9
Senghenydd Caerph	30	F6
Sennen Cnwll	2	B8
Sennen Cove Cnwll	2	B8
Sennybridge Powys	44	C9
Serlby Notts	85	K3
Sessay N York	97	Q5
Setchey Norfk	75	M8
Setley Hants	13	P4
Seton Mains E Loth	128	C4
Settle N York	96	B8
Settrington N York	98	G6
Seven Ash Somset	18	G8
Sevenhampton Gloucs	47	K10
Sevenhampton Swindn	33	P3
Seven Kings Gt Lon	37	L3
Sevenoaks Kent	37	M9
Sevenoaks Weald Kent	37	M10
Seven Sisters Neath	29	M3
Seven Springs Gloucs	47	J11
Seven Star Green Essex	52	F6
Severn Beach S Glos	31	P8
Severn Bridge S Glos	31	Q6
Severn Stoke Worcs	46	G6
Severn View Services S Glos	31	Q7
Sevick End Bed	61	N10
Sevington Kent	26	H3
Sewards End Essex	51	N3
Sewardstonebury Essex	51	J11
Sewell C Beds	49	Q10
Sewerby E R Yk	99	P7
Seworgan Cnwll	3	J7
Sewstern Leics	73	M6
Sexhow N York	104	E9
Sgalpaigh W Isls	168	h8
Sgiogarstaigh W Isls	168	k1
Shabbington Bucks	35	J3
Shackerley Shrops	57	Q3
Shackerstone Leics	72	B9
Shacklecross Derbys	72	C4
Shackleford Surrey	23	P5
Shade Calder	89	Q6
Shader W Isls	168	i2
Shadforth Dur	104	B2
Shadingfield Suffk	65	N5
Shadoxhurst Kent	26	G4
Shadwell Leeds	91	J3
Shadwell Norfk	64	C5
Shaftenhoe End Herts	51	K3
Shaftesbury Dorset	20	G10
Shaftholme Donc	91	P9
Shafton Barns	91	K8
Shafton Two Gates Barns	91	K8
Shakerley Wigan	82	E4
Shalbourne Wilts	22	B2
Shalcombe IoW	14	C9
Shalden Hants	23	J4
Shalden Green Hants	23	K6
Shaldon Devon	7	N4
Shalfleet IoW	14	D9
Shalford Essex	52	B6
Shalford Surrey	36	B11
Shalford Green Essex	52	B6
Shallowford Staffs	70	F9
Shalmsford Street Kent	39	J11
Shalstone Bucks	48	H7
Shamley Green Surrey	24	B2
Shandford Angus	142	H5
Shandon Ag & B	132	B10
Shandwick Highld	156	F2
Shangton Leics	73	J11
Shankhouse Nthumb	113	L5
Shanklin IoW	14	G10
Shantron Ag & B	132	C10
Shap Cumb	101	Q7
Shapinsay Ork	169	e4
Shapwick Dorset	12	F4
Shapwick Somset	19	M7

Place	Page	Grid
Shard End Birm	59	J7
Shardlow Derbys	72	C4
Shareshill Staffs	58	D3
Sharlston Wakefd	91	K7
Sharlston Common Wakefd	91	K7
Sharmans Cross Solhll	58	H9
Sharnal Street Medway	38	C7
Sharneyford Lancs	89	P6
Sharnbrook Bed	61	L9
Sharnford Leics	59	Q6
Sharnhill Green Dorset	11	Q3
Sharoe Green Lancs	88	G4
Sharow N York	97	M6
Sharpenhoe C Beds	50	C4
Sharperton Nthumb	119	J10
Sharp Green Norfk	77	M7
Sharpness Gloucs	32	C4
Sharpthorne W Susx	25	J4
Sharptor Cnwll	5	M7
Sharpway Gate Worcs	58	E11
Sharrington Norfk	76	E4
Shatterford Worcs	57	P8
Shattering Kent	39	N10
Shatton Derbys	84	B4
Shaugh Prior Devon	6	E5
Shave Cross Dorset	11	J5
Shavington Ches E	70	B4
Shaw C Brad	90	C3
Shaw Oldham	89	Q9
Shaw Swindn	33	M7
Shaw W Berk	34	E11
Shaw Wilts	32	G11
Shawbirch Wrekin	57	L2
Shawbost W Isls	168	h3
Shawbury Shrops	69	Q10
Shawclough Rochdl	89	P8
Shaw Common Gloucs	46	C9
Shawdon Hill Nthumb	119	L8
Shawell Leics	60	B4
Shawford Hants	22	E9
Shawforth Lancs	89	P6
Shaw Green Herts	50	H4
Shaw Green Lancs	88	G7
Shaw Green N York	97	L10
Shawhead D & G	109	J5
Shaw Mills N York	97	L8
Shawsburn S Lans	126	D7
Shear Cross Wilts	20	G9
Shearington D & G	109	M7
Shearsby Leics	60	D2
Shearston Somset	19	J8
Shebbear Devon	16	G10
Shebdon Staffs	70	D9
Shebster Highld	166	H4
Shedfield Hants	14	G4
Sheen Staffs	71	L2
Sheepbridge Derbys	84	E6
Sheep Hill Dur	113	J9
Sheepridge Kirk	90	F7
Sheepscar Leeds	91	J4
Sheepscombe Gloucs	32	G2
Sheepstor Devon	6	F5
Sheepwash Devon	8	D2
Sheepwash Nthumb	113	L3
Sheepway N Som	31	N9
Sheepy Magna Leics	72	A10
Sheepy Parva Leics	72	A10
Sheering Essex	51	M8
Sheerness Kent	38	F7
Sheerwater Surrey	36	B8
Sheet Hants	23	L10
Sheffield Cnwll	2	D8
Sheffield Sheff	84	E3
Sheffield Bottom W Berk	34	H11
Sheffield Green E Susx	25	K5
Sheffield Park E Susx	25	K6
Shefford C Beds	50	D3
Shefford Woodlands W Berk	34	C10
Sheigra Highld	164	E4
Sheinton Shrops	57	L4
Shelderton Shrops	56	G9
Sheldon Birm	58	J8
Sheldon Derbys	83	Q11
Sheldon Devon	10	C3
Sheldwich Kent	38	H10
Sheldwich Lees Kent	38	H10
Shelf Calder	90	E5
Shelfanger Norfk	64	G5
Shelfield Warwks	47	M2
Shelfield Wsall	58	F4
Shelfield Green Warwks	47	M2
Shelford Notts	72	H2
Shelford Warwks	59	P7
Shellacres Nthumb	118	G2
Shelley Essex	51	N9
Shelley Kirk	90	G8
Shelley Suffk	52	H4
Shelley Far Bank Kirk	90	G8
Shellingford Oxon	34	B6
Shellow Bowells Essex	51	P9
Shelsley Beauchamp Worcs	46	D2
Shelsley Walsh Worcs	46	D2
Shelton Bed	61	M7
Shelton Norfk	65	J3
Shelton Notts	73	K2
Shelton Shrops	56	H2
Shelton Green Norfk	65	J3
Shelton Lock C Derb	72	B4
Shelton Under Harley Staffs	70	E7
Shelve Shrops	56	E5
Shelwick Herefs	45	Q6
Shenfield Essex	51	P11
Shenington Oxon	48	C6
Shenley Herts	50	E10
Shenley Brook End M Keyn	49	N7
Shenleybury Herts	50	E10
Shenley Church End M Keyn	49	N7
Shenmore Herefs	45	M7
Shennanton D & G	107	K5
Shenstone Staffs	58	H4
Shenstone Worcs	58	C10
Shenstone Woodend Staffs	58	H4
Shenton Leics	72	B11
Shenval Moray	149	N2
Shepeau Stow Lincs	74	F8
Shephall Herts	50	F6
Shepherd's Bush Gt Lon	36	F4
Shepherd's Green Oxon	35	K8
Shepherds Patch Gloucs	32	D4
Shepherdswell Kent	27	N2
Shepley Kirk	90	F9
Shepperdine S Glos	32	B5
Shepperton Surrey	36	C7
Shepperton Green Surrey	36	C7
Shepreth Cambs	62	E11
Shepshed Leics	72	D7

Place	Page	Grid
Shepton Beauchamp Somset	19	M11
Shepton Mallet Somset	20	B6
Shepton Montague Somset	20	C8
Shepway Kent	38	C11
Sheraton Dur	104	D3
Sherborne Dorset	20	B11
Sherborne Gloucs	33	N2
Sherborne Somset	19	Q3
Sherborne St John Hants	22	H3
Sherbourne Warwks	47	Q2
Sherburn Dur	104	B2
Sherburn N York	99	K5
Sherburn Hill Dur	104	B2
Sherburn in Elmet N York	91	M4
Shere Surrey	36	C11
Shereford Norfk	76	B6
Sherfield English Hants	21	Q10
Sherfield on Loddon Hants	23	J3
Sherfin Lancs	89	M5
Sherford Devon	6	F5
Sherford Devon	7	K10
Sherford Dorset	12	F6
Sheriffhales Shrops	57	P2
Sheriff Hutton N York	98	D7
Sheringham Norfk	76	H3
Sherington M Keyn	49	N5
Shermanbury W Susx	24	F7
Shernborne Norfk	75	P4
Sherrington Wilts	21	J7
Sherston Wilts	32	G7
Sherwood C Nott	72	F2
Sherwood Forest Notts	85	K8
Shetland Islands Shet	169	r8
Shettleston C Glas	125	Q5
Shevington Wigan	88	G9
Shevington Moor Wigan	88	G9
Shevington Vale Wigan	88	G9
Sheviock Cnwll	5	P10
Shibden Head C Brad	90	D5
Shide IoW	14	F9
Shidlaw Nthumb	118	F3
Shiel Bridge Highld	146	A4
Shieldaig Highld	153	Q7
Shieldhill D & G	109	M3
Shieldhill Falk	126	F2
Shieldhill House Hotel S Lans	116	E2
Shields N Lans	126	D6
Shielfoot Highld	138	B3
Shielhill Angus	142	G6
Shielhill Inver	124	G3
Shifford Oxon	34	C4
Shifnal Shrops	57	N3
Shilbottle Nthumb	119	N9
Shildon Dur	103	P5
Shillford E Rens	125	M6
Shillingford Devon	18	C10
Shillingford Oxon	34	G6
Shillingford Abbot Devon	9	M7
Shillingford St George Devon	9	M7
Shillingstone Dorset	12	D2
Shillington C Beds	50	D4
Shillmoor Nthumb	118	G9
Shilton Oxon	33	Q3
Shilton Warwks	59	P8
Shimpling Norfk	64	H5
Shimpling Suffk	64	B11
Shimpling Street Suffk	64	B11
Shincliffe Dur	103	Q2
Shiney Row Sundld	113	M10
Shinfield Wokham	35	K11
Shingay Cambs	62	D11
Shingle Street Suffk	53	Q3
Shinnersbridge Devon	7	K6
Shinness Highld	162	C4
Shipbourne Kent	37	N10
Shipdham Norfk	76	D10
Shipham Somset	19	M3
Shiphay Torbay	7	M5
Shiplake Oxon	35	L9
Shiplake Row Oxon	35	K9
Shiplate N Som	19	L3
Shipley C Brad	90	F3
Shipley Derbys	72	C2
Shipley Shrops	57	Q5
Shipley W Susx	24	D6
Shipley Bridge Surrey	24	H2
Shipley Hatch Kent	26	H4
Shipmeadow Suffk	65	M3
Shippea Hill Station Cambs	63	K4
Shippon Oxon	34	D5
Shipston-on-Stour Warwks	47	Q6
Shipton Bucks	49	L9
Shipton Gloucs	47	K11
Shipton N York	98	B9
Shipton Shrops	57	K6
Shipton Bellinger Hants	21	P5
Shipton Gorge Dorset	11	K6
Shipton Green W Susx	15	M7
Shipton Moyne Gloucs	32	G7
Shipton-on-Cherwell Oxon	48	E11
Shiptonthorpe E R Yk	92	E2
Shipton-under-Wychwood Oxon	47	Q11
Shirburn Oxon	35	J5
Shirdley Hill Lancs	88	D8
Shire Cumb	102	B3
Shirebrook Derbys	84	H7
Shiregreen Sheff	84	E2
Shirehampton Bristl	31	P9
Shiremoor N Tyne	113	M6
Shirenewton Mons	31	N6
Shire Oak Wsall	58	G4
Shireoaks Notts	85	J4
Shirkoak Kent	26	F4
Shirland Derbys	84	E9
Shirlett Shrops	57	L5
Shirley C Sotn	14	D4
Shirley Derbys	71	N6
Shirley Gt Lon	37	J7
Shirley Solhll	58	H9
Shirrell Heath Hants	14	G4
Shirwell Devon	17	L4
Shiskine N Ayrs	120	H6
Shittlehope Dur	103	K3
Shobdon Herefs	45	N2
Shobley Hants	13	L4
Shobrooke Devon	9	L4
Shoby Leics	72	H6
Shocklach Ches W	69	M5
Shocklach Green Ches W	69	M5
Shoeburyness Sthend	38	F3
Sholden Kent	39	Q11

Place	Page	Grid
Sholing C Sotn	14	E4
Shoot Hill Shrops	56	G2
Shop Cnwll	4	D7
Shop Cnwll	16	C9
Shopwyke W Susx	15	N5
Shore Rochdl	89	Q7
Shoreditch C Lon	36	H4
Shoreditch Somset	18	H10
Shoreham Kent	37	M8
Shoreham-by-Sea W Susx	24	F9
Shoreswood Nthumb	129	N10
Shorley Hants	22	G9
Shorncote Gloucs	33	K5
Shorne Kent	37	Q6
Shortacross Cnwll	5	M10
Shortbridge E Susx	25	L6
Shortfield Common Surrey	23	M6
Shortgate E Susx	25	L7
Short Heath Birm	58	G6
Shortheath Hants	23	L7
Short Heath Wsall	58	E4
Shortlanesend Cnwll	3	L4
Shortlees E Ayrs	125	L10
Shortstown Bed	61	N11
Shorwell IoW	14	E10
Shoscombe BaNES	20	D3
Shotesham Norfk	65	J2
Shotgate Essex	38	C3
Shotley Suffk	53	M4
Shotley Bridge Dur	112	G10
Shotleyfield Nthumb	112	G10
Shotley Gate Suffk	53	M5
Shottenden Kent	38	H11
Shottermill Surrey	23	N8
Shottery Warwks	47	N4
Shotteswell Warwks	48	D5
Shottisham Suffk	53	P3
Shottle Derbys	71	Q5
Shottlegate Derbys	71	Q5
Shotton Dur	104	C5
Shotton Dur	104	D3
Shotton Flints	81	L11
Shotton Nthumb	113	K5
Shotton Nthumb	118	F4
Shotton Colliery Dur	104	C2
Shotts N Lans	126	F6
Shotwick Ches W	81	L10
Shougle Moray	157	N6
Shouldham Norfk	75	N9
Shouldham Thorpe Norfk	75	N9
Shoulton Worcs	46	F3
Shover's Green E Susx	25	Q4
Shraleybrook Staffs	70	D5
Shrawardine Shrops	69	L11
Shrawley Worcs	46	Q11
Shreding Green Bucks	36	B4
Shrewley Warwks	59	K11
Shrewsbury Shrops	56	H2
Shrewton Wilts	21	L6
Shripney W Susx	15	P6
Shrivenham Oxon	33	P7
Shropham Norfk	64	D3
Shroton Dorset	12	E2
Shrub End Essex	52	G7
Shucknall Herefs	46	A6
Shudy Camps Cambs	51	P2
Shuna Ag & B	130	F6
Shurdington Gloucs	46	H11
Shurlock Row W & M	35	M10
Shurnock Worcs	47	K2
Shurrery Highld	166	H5
Shurrery Lodge Highld	166	H5
Shurton Somset	18	H6
Shustoke Warwks	59	K6
Shute Devon	9	L4
Shute Devon	10	F5
Shutford Oxon	48	C6
Shut Heath Staffs	70	F10
Shuthonger Gloucs	46	G7
Shutlanger Nhants	49	K5
Shutterton Devon	9	N9
Shutt Green Staffs	58	C3
Shuttington Warwks	59	L3
Shuttlewood Derbys	84	G6
Shuttleworth Bury	89	N7
Siabost W Isls	168	h3
Siadar W Isls	168	i2
Sibbertoft Nhants	60	E4
Sibdon Carwood Shrops	56	G8
Sibford Ferris Oxon	48	C7
Sibford Gower Oxon	48	C7
Sible Hedingham Essex	52	C5
Sibley's Green Essex	51	P5
Siblyback Cnwll	5	L7
Sibsey Lincs	87	L10
Sibsey Fenside Lincs	87	K10
Sibson Cambs	74	A11
Sibson Leics	72	B10
Sibster Highld	167	P6
Sibthorpe Notts	85	M6
Sibthorpe Notts	85	N11
Sibton Suffk	65	M8
Sicklesmere Suffk	64	B9
Sicklinghall N York	97	N11
Sidbrook Somset	19	J9
Sidbury Devon	10	C6
Sidbury Shrops	57	M7
Sid Cop Barns	91	K9
Sidcot N Som	19	M3
Sidcup Gt Lon	37	L6
Siddick Cumb	100	D4
Siddington Ches E	82	H10
Siddington Gloucs	33	K5
Sidemoor Worcs	58	E10
Sidestrand Norfk	77	K4
Sidford Devon	10	C6
Sidlesham W Susx	15	N7
Sidlesham Common W Susx	15	N7
Sidley E Susx	26	B10
Sidmouth Devon	10	C7
Siefton Shrops	56	H8
Sigford Devon	7	K4
Sigglesthorne E R Yk	99	P11
Sigingstone V Glam	30	C10
Signet Oxon	33	P2
Silchester Hants	22	H2
Sileby Leics	72	G7
Silecroft Cumb	94	C4
Silfield Norfk	64	G2
Silian Cerdgn	43	L4
Silkstead Hants	22	D10
Silkstone Barns	90	H9
Silkstone Common Barns	90	H10
Silk Willoughby Lincs	73	R2
Silloth Cumb	109	P10
Silpho N York	99	K2

Silsden – Spean Bridge 293

Silsden C Brad 96 F11
Silsoe C Beds 50 C3
Silton Dorset 20 E9
Silverburn Mdloth 127 N5
Silverdale Lancs 95 K6
Silverdale Staffs 70 E5
Silver End Essex 52 D8
Silverford Abers 159 J5
Silvergate Norfk 76 H6
Silverlace Green Suffk 65 L9
Silverley's Green Suffk 65 K6
Silverstone Nhants 49 J6
Silver Street Kent 38 E9
Silver Street Somset 19 P8
Silverton Devon 9 N4
Silverwell Cnwll 3 J4
Silvington Shrops 57 L9
Simister Bury 89 N9
Simmondley Derbys 83 M6
Simonburn Nthumb 112 C6
Simonsbath Somset 17 P4
Simonsburrow Devon 18 F11
Simonstone Lancs 89 M4
Simonstone N York 96 C2
Simprim Border 129 L11
Simpson M Keyn 49 N7
Simpson Cross Pembks 40 G7
Sinclair's Hill Border 129 L9
Sinclairston E Ayrs 115 J4
Sinderby N York 97 M4
Sinderhope Nthumb 112 B10
Sinderland Green Traffd 82 F7
Sindlesham Wokham 35 L11
Sinfin C Derb 72 A4
Singleborough Bucks 49 L8
Single Street Gt Lon 37 K9
Singleton Kent 26 H3
Singleton Lancs 88 D3
Singleton W Susx 15 N4
Singlewell Kent 37 Q6
Sinkhurst Green Kent 26 D3
Sinnahard Abers 150 D5
Sinnington N York 98 E3
Sinope Leics 72 C7
Sinton Worcs 46 F2
Sinton Worcs 46 F2
Sinton Green Worcs 46 F2
Sipson Gt Lon 36 C5
Sirhowy Blae G 30 F2
Sissinghurst Kent 26 C4
Siston S Glos 32 C9
Sitcott Devon 5 P3
Sithney Cnwll 2 G8
Sithney Common Cnwll 2 G8
Sithney Green Cnwll 2 G8
Sittingbourne Kent 38 F9
Six Ashes Shrops 57 P7
Six Bells Blae G 30 H4
Six Hills Leics 72 G6
Sixhills Lincs 86 G3
Six Mile Bottom Cambs 63 J9
Sixmile Cottages Kent 27 K3
Sixpenny Handley Dorset 21 J11
Six Rues Jersey 11 b1
Sizewell Suffk 65 P9
Skaill Ork 169 e6
Skara Brae Ork 169 b5
Skares E Ayrs 115 K4
Skateraw Abers 151 N9
Skateraw E Loth 129 J5
Skeabost Highld 152 G8
Skeeby N York 103 N10
Skeffington Leics 73 J10
Skeffling E R Yk 93 Q7
Skegby Notts 84 G8
Skegby Notts 85 N7
Skegness Lincs 87 Q8
Skelbo Highld 162 H7
Skelbo Street Highld 162 H8
Skelbrooke Donc 91 N8
Skeldyke Lincs 74 F3
Skellingthorpe Lincs 86 B6
Skellorn Green Ches E 83 K8
Skellow Donc 91 N8
Skelmanthorpe Kirk 90 G8
Skelmersdale Lancs 88 F9
Skelmorlie N Ayrs 124 F4
Skelpick Highld 166 B5
Skelston D & G 108 H3
Skelton C York 98 B9
Skelton Cumb 101 M3
Skelton E R Yk 92 C5
Skelton N York 103 L10
Skelton R & Cl 105 J7
Skelton on Ure N York 97 N7
Skelwith Bridge Cumb 101 K10
Skendleby Lincs 87 M7
Skene House Abers 151 K5
Skenfrith Mons 45 P10
Skerne E R Yk 99 L9
Skerray Highld 165 Q4
Skerricha Highld 164 F6
Skerton Lancs 95 K8
Sketchley Leics 59 P6
Sketty Swans 28 H6
Skewen Neath 29 K5
Skewsby N York 98 C6
Skeyton Norfk 77 J6
Skeyton Corner Norfk 77 K6
Skiall Highld 166 H3
Skidbrooke Lincs 87 M2
Skidbrooke North End Lincs 93 R11
Skidby E R Yk 92 H4
Skigersta W Isls 168 k1
Skilgate Somset 18 C9
Skillington Lincs 73 M5
Skinburness Cumb 109 P9
Skinflats Falk 133 Q11
Skinidin Highld 152 C8
Skinners Green W Berk 34 D11
Skinningrove R & Cl 105 K7
Skipness Ag & B 123 R8
Skipper's Bridge D & G 110 G4
Skiprigg Cumb 110 G11
Skipsea E R Yk 99 P10
Skipsea Brough E R Yk 99 P10
Skipton N York 96 E10
Skipton-on-Swale N York 97 N5
Skipwith N York 91 R3
Skirlaugh E R Yk 93 K3
Skirling Border 116 F3
Skirmett Bucks 35 L6
Skirpenbeck E R Yk 98 E9
Skirwith Cumb 102 B4
Skirwith N York 95 Q6
Skirza Highld 167 Q3
Skitby Cumb 110 H7
Skittle Green Bucks 35 L4
Skokholm Island Pembks 40 D10
Skomer Island Pembks 40 D9
Skulamus Highld 145 L3
Skyborry Green Shrops 56 D10
Skye Green Essex 52 E7
Skye of Curr Highld 148 H3
Skyreholme N York 96 G8
Slack Calder 90 B5
Slackbuie Highld 156 B9
Slackcote Oldham 90 B9
Slack Head Cumb 95 K5
Slackholme End Lincs 87 P6
Slacks of Cairnbanno Abers 159 K8
Slad Gloucs 32 G3
Slade Devon 10 C3
Slade Devon 17 J2
Slade Devon 17 Q6
Slade End Oxon 34 G6
Slade Green Gt Lon 37 M5
Slade Heath Staffs 58 D3
Slade Hooton Rothm 84 H3
Sladesbridge Cnwll 4 G7
Slades Green Worcs 46 F8
Slaggyford Nthumb 111 N10
Slaidburn Lancs 95 Q10
Slaithwaite Kirk 90 D8
Slaley Derbys 84 C9
Slaley Nthumb 112 E9
Slamannan Falk 126 F3
Slapton Bucks 49 P10
Slapton Devon 7 L9
Slapton Nhants 48 H5
Slattocks Rochdl 89 P9
Slaugham W Susx 24 G5
Slaughterford Wilts 32 F10
Slawston Leics 60 G2
Sleaford Hants 23 M7
Sleaford Lincs 86 E11
Sleagill Cumb 101 Q7
Sleap Shrops 69 N9
Sleapford Wrekin 70 A11
Sleapshyde Herts 50 E9
Sleasdairidh Highld 162 E7
Slebech Pembks 41 K7
Sledge Green Worcs 46 F8
Sledmere E R Yk 99 J8
Sleetbeck Cumb 111 K5
Sleight Dorset 12 G5
Sleightholme Dur 103 J8
Sleights N York 105 N9
Slepe Dorset 12 F6
Slickly Highld 167 N3
Sliddery N Ayrs 120 H7
Sligachan Highld 144 G2
Sligrachan Ag & B 131 P9
Slimbridge Gloucs 32 D4
Slindon Staffs 70 E8
Slindon W Susx 15 Q5
Slinfold W Susx 24 D4
Sling Gloucs 31 Q3
Sling Gwynd 79 L11
Slingsby N York 98 D6
Slip End C Beds 50 C7
Slip End Herts 50 G3
Slipton Nhants 61 L5
Slitting Mill Staffs 71 J11
Slockavullin Ag & B 130 G8
Sloley Norfk 77 K7
Sloncombe Devon 8 H7
Sloothby Lincs 87 N6
Slough Slough 35 Q9
Slough Green Somset 19 J11
Slough Green W Susx 24 G5
Slumbay Highld 154 A10
Slyfield Surrey 23 Q4
Slyne Lancs 95 K7
Smailholm Border 118 B3
Smallbridge Rochdl 89 Q7
Smallbrook Devon 9 L5
Smallbrook Gloucs 31 Q4
Smallburgh Norfk 77 L7
Smallburn E Ayrs 115 N2
Smalldale Derbys 83 N9
Smalldale Derbys 83 Q8
Small Dole W Susx 24 F8
Smalley Derbys 72 C2
Smalley Common Derbys 72 C2
Smalley Green Derbys 72 C2
Smallfield Surrey 24 H2
Smallford Herts 50 E9
Small Heath Birm 58 H7
Small Hythe Kent 26 E5
Smallridge Devon 10 G4
Smallthorne C Stke 70 F4
Smallways N York 103 M8
Smallwood Ches E 70 E2
Small Wood Hey Lancs 94 H11
Smallworth Norfk 64 E5
Smannell Hants 22 C5
Smardale Cumb 102 D9
Smarden Kent 26 E3
Smarden Bell Kent 26 E3
Smart's Hill Kent 25 M2
Smeafield Nthumb 119 L3
Smeatharpe Devon 10 D2
Smeeth Kent 27 J4
Smeeton Westerby Leics 60 E2
Smelthouses N York 97 J8
Smerral Highld 167 L10
Smestow Staffs 58 C6
Smethwick Sandw 58 F7
Smethwick Green Ches E 70 E2
Smirisary Highld 138 A2
Smisby Derbys 72 A7
Smith End Green Worcs 46 E4
Smithfield Cumb 110 H7
Smith Green Lancs 95 K9
Smithies Barns 91 J9
Smithincott Devon 9 Q2
Smith's End Herts 51 K3
Smith's Green Essex 51 N6
Smith's Green Essex 51 Q2
Smithstown Highld 160 B11
Smithton Highld 156 C8
Smithy Bridge Rochdl 89 Q7
Smithy Green Ches E 82 F10
Smithy Green Stockp 83 J7
Smithy Houses Derbys 84 E11
Smockington Leics 59 Q7
Smoo Highld 165 K3
Smythe's Green Essex 52 F8
Snade D & G 108 H3
Snailbeach Shrops 56 F4
Snailwell Cambs 63 K7
Snainton N York 99 J4
Snaith E R Yk 91 Q6
Snake Pass Inn Derbys 83 P6
Snape N York 97 L4
Snape Suffk 65 M10
Snape Green Lancs 88 D8
Snape Street Suffk 65 M10
Snaresbrook Gt Lon 37 K3
Snarestone Leics 72 A9
Snarford Lincs 86 D4
Snargate Kent 26 G6
Snave Kent 26 H6
Sneachill Worcs 46 H4
Snead Powys 56 E6
Sneath Common Norfk 64 H4
Sneaton N York 105 N9
Sneatonthorpe N York 105 P9
Snelland Lincs 86 E4
Snelson Ches E 82 H10
Snelston Derbys 71 M6
Snetterton Norfk 64 D3
Snettisham Norfk 75 N4
Snibston Leics 72 C8
Snig's End Gloucs 46 E9
Snitter Nthumb 119 K10
Snitterby Lincs 86 C2
Snitterfield Warwks 47 P3
Snitterton Derbys 84 C8
Snitton Shrops 57 K9
Snoadhill Kent 26 F3
Snodhill Herefs 45 L6
Snodland Kent 38 B9
Snoll Hatch Kent 37 Q11
Snowden Hill Barns 90 H10
Snowdon Gwynd 67 L4
Snowdon Kent 39 M11
Snowdonia National Park 67 Q9
Snow End Herts 51 K4
Snowshill Gloucs 47 L8
Snow Street Norfk 64 F5
Soake Hants 15 J4
Soar Cardif 30 E8
Soar Devon 7 J11
Soar Powys 44 D8
Soay Highld 144 F5
Soberton Hants 22 H11
Soberton Heath Hants 14 H4
Sockbridge Cumb 101 N5
Sockburn Darltn 104 B9
Sodom Denbgs 80 F10
Sodylt Bank Shrops 69 K7
Soham Cambs 63 J6
Soham Cotes Cambs 63 J5
Solas W Isls 168 d10
Solbury Pembks 40 G8
Soldon Devon 16 E9
Soldon Cross Devon 16 E9
Soldridge Hants 23 J7
Sole Street Kent 27 J2
Sole Street Kent 37 Q7
Solihull Solhll 59 J9
Sollas W Isls 168 d10
Sollers Dilwyn Herefs 45 N3
Sollers Hope Herefs 46 B8
Sollom Lancs 88 F7
Solva Pembks 40 F6
Solwaybank D & G 110 F5
Somerby Leics 73 K8
Somerby Lincs 93 J9
Somercotes Derbys 84 F10
Somerford BCP 13 L6
Somerford Keynes Gloucs 33 K5
Somerley W Susx 15 M7
Somerleyton Suffk 65 P2
Somersal Herbert Derbys 71 L7
Somersby Lincs 87 K6
Somersham Cambs 62 E5
Somersham Suffk 53 J2
Somerton Oxon 48 E9
Somerton Somset 19 N9
Somerton Suffk 63 P10
Somerwood Shrops 57 K2
Sompting W Susx 24 E9
Sompting Abbotts W Susx 24 E9
Sonning Wokham 35 L9
Sonning Common Oxon 35 K8
Sonning Eye Oxon 35 K9
Sontley Wrexhm 69 K5
Sopley Hants 13 L5
Sopwell Herts 50 E9
Sopworth Wilts 32 F7
Sorbie D & G 107 M8
Sordale Highld 167 K4
Sorisdale Ag & B 136 H3
Sorn E Ayrs 115 L2
Sornhill E Ayrs 125 N11
Sortat Highld 167 N4
Sotby Lincs 86 H5
Sots Hole Lincs 86 F8
Sotterley Suffk 65 N5
Soughton Flints 81 J11
Soulbury Bucks 49 N9
Soulby Cumb 101 N5
Soulby Cumb 102 D8
Souldern Oxon 48 F8
Souldrop Bed 61 L8
Sound Ches E 70 A5
Sound Muir Moray 157 R7
Soundwell S Glos 32 C9
Sourton Devon 8 D6
Soutergate Cumb 94 E4
South Acre Norfk 75 R8
South Alkham Kent 27 M3
Southall Gt Lon 36 D5
South Allington Devon 7 K11
South Alloa Falk 133 P9
Southam Gloucs 47 J9
Southam Warwks 48 D2
South Ambersham W Susx 23 P10
Southampton C Sotn 14 D4
Southampton Airport Hants 22 E11
South Anston Rothm 84 H4
South Ascot W & M 35 P11
South Ashford Kent 26 H3
South Baddesley Hants 14 C7
South Bank C York 98 B10
South Bank R & Cl 104 F6
South Barrow Somset 20 B9
South Beddington Gt Lon 36 G8
South Beer Cnwll 5 N3
South Benfleet Essex 38 C4
South Bockhampton BCP 13 L5
Southborough Gt Lon 37 K7
Southborough Kent 25 N2
Southbourne BCP 13 K6
Southbourne W Susx 15 L5
South Bowood Dorset 11 J5
South Bramwith Donc 91 Q8
South Brent Devon 6 H6
South Brewham Somset 20 D7
South Broomhill Nthumb 119 P11
Southburgh Norfk 76 E10
South Burlingham Norfk 77 M10
Southburn E R Yk 99 K10
South Cadbury Somset 20 B9
South Carlton Lincs 86 B5
South Carlton Notts 85 J4
South Cave E R Yk 92 F4
South Cerney Gloucs 33 K5
South Chailey E Susx 25 J7
South Chard Somset 10 G3
South Charlton Nthumb 119 N6
South Cheriton Somset 20 C10
South Church Dur 103 P5
Southchurch Sthend 38 F4
South Cleatlam Dur 103 M7
South Cliffe E R Yk 92 E3
South Clifton Notts 85 P6
South Cockerington Lincs 87 L3
South Cornelly Brdgnd 29 M8
Southcott Cnwll 5 K2
Southcott Devon 8 D5
Southcott Devon 9 J8
Southcott Devon 16 G8
Southcott Wilts 21 N3
Southcourt Bucks 35 M2
South Cove Suffk 65 P5
South Creake Norfk 76 B4
South Crosland Kirk 90 E8
South Croxton Leics 72 H8
South Dalton E R Yk 99 K11
South Darenth Kent 37 N7
South Dell W Isls 168 j1
South Downs National Park 25 J9
South Duffield N York 92 A4
South Earlswood Surrey 36 G11
Southease E Susx 25 K9
South Elkington Lincs 87 J3
South Elmsall Wakefd 91 M8
Southend Ag & B 120 C10
South End E R Yk 93 Q7
South End Hants 21 M11
South End Herefs 46 D6
South End N Linc 93 K6
South End Norfk 64 D3
Southend Wilts 33 N10
Southend Airport Essex 38 E4
Southend-on-Sea Sthend 38 E4
Southernby Cumb 101 L3
Southernden Kent 26 E2
Southerndown V Glam 29 N10
Southerness D & G 109 L10
South Erradale Highld 153 N3
Southerton Devon 10 B6
Southery Norfk 63 K2
South Fambridge Essex 38 E3
South Fawley W Berk 34 C8
South Ferriby N Linc 92 G6
South Field E R Yk 92 H5
Southfield Falk 126 E3
Southfleet Kent 37 P6
Southford IoW 14 F11
Southgate Gt Lon 36 G2
Southgate Norfk 75 N4
Southgate Norfk 76 B4
Southgate Norfk 76 G7
Southgate Swans 28 G7
South Godstone Surrey 37 J11
South Gorley Hants 13 L2
South Gosforth N u Ty 113 K7
South Green Essex 37 Q2
South Green Essex 52 H8
South Green Kent 38 E9
South Green Norfk 76 F9
South Green Suffk 64 H6
South Gyle C Edin 127 M3
South Hanningfield Essex 38 B2
South Harting W Susx 23 L11
South Hayling Hants 15 K7
South Hazelrigg Nthumb 119 L4
South Heath Bucks 35 P4
South Heighton E Susx 25 K10
South Hetton Dur 113 N11
South Hiendley Wakefd 91 K8
South Hill Cnwll 5 N7
South Hill Somset 19 N9
South Hinksey Oxon 34 F4
South Hole Devon 16 C7
South Holmwood Surrey 24 E2
South Hornchurch Gt Lon 37 M4
South Horrington Somset 19 Q5
South Huish Devon 6 H10
South Hykeham Lincs 86 B8
South Hylton Sundld 113 N9
Southill C Beds 50 E2
Southington Hants 22 F5
South Kelsey Lincs 92 H11
South Kessock Highld 156 B8
South Killingholme N Linc 93 K7
South Kilvington N York 97 P4
South Kilworth Leics 60 D4
South Kirkby Wakefd 91 L8
South Knighton Devon 7 L4
South Kyme Lincs 86 G11
Southleigh Devon 10 E6
South Leigh Oxon 34 C3
South Leverton Notts 85 N4
South Littleton Worcs 47 L5
South Lopham Norfk 64 E5
South Luffenham Rutlnd 73 N10
South Lynn Norfk 75 M7
South Malling E Susx 25 K8
South Marston Swindn 33 N7
South Merstham Surrey 36 G10
South Middleton Nthumb 119 J6
South Milford N York 91 M4
South Milton Devon 6 J10
South Mimms Herts 50 F10
South Mimms Services Herts 50 F10
Southminster Essex 38 G2
South Molton Devon 17 N6
South Moor Dur 113 J10
Southmoor Oxon 34 C5
South Moreton Oxon 34 G7
Southmuir Angus 142 F7
South Mundham W Susx 15 N6
South Muskham Notts 85 N9
South Newbald E R Yk 92 F3
South Newington Oxon 48 D8
South Newton Wilts 21 L8
South Nitshill C Glas 125 N6
South Normanton Derbys 84 F9
South Norwood Gt Lon 36 H7
South Nutfield Surrey 36 H11
South Ockendon Thurr 37 N4
Southoe Cambs 61 Q8
Southolt Suffk 64 H8
South Ormsby Lincs 87 L5
Southorpe C Pete 74 A10
South Ossett Wakefd 90 H7
South Otterington N York 97 N3
Southover Dorset 11 N6
Southover E Susx 25 Q5
South Owersby Lincs 86 E2
Southowram Calder 90 E6
South Park Surrey 36 F11
South Perrott Dorset 11 K3
South Petherton Somset 19 M11
South Petherwin Cnwll 5 N5
South Pickenham Norfk 76 B11
South Pill Cnwll 5 Q10
South Pool Devon 7 K10
South Poorton Dorset 11 L5
Southport Sefton 88 C7
South Queensferry C Edin 127 L2
South Radworthy Devon 17 N5
South Rauceby Lincs 86 D11
South Raynham Norfk 76 B7
South Reddish Stockp 83 J6
Southrepps Norfk 77 K4
South Reston Lincs 87 M4
Southrey Lincs 86 F7
South Ronaldsay Ork 169 d8
Southrop Gloucs 33 N4
Southrope Hants 23 J6
South Runcton Norfk 75 M9
South Scarle Notts 85 P8
Southsea C Port 15 J7
Southsea Wrexhm 69 K4
South Shian Ag & B 138 G9
South Shields S Tyne 113 N7
South Shore Bpool 88 C4
Southside Dur 103 M5
South Somercotes Lincs 87 M2
South Stainley N York 97 M8
South Stifford Thurr 37 N5
South Stoke BaNES 20 D2
South Stoke Oxon 34 G8
South Stoke W Susx 24 B9
South Stour Kent 26 H4
South Street Kent 37 P8
South Street Kent 39 J10
South Street Kent 39 K8
South Tarbrax S Lans 127 J7
South Tawton Devon 8 G6
South Tehidy Cnwll 2 H5
South Thoresby Lincs 87 M5
South Thorpe Dur 103 M8
South Town Hants 23 J7
Southtown Norfk 77 Q10
Southtown Somset 19 K11
South Uist W Isls 168 d14
Southwaite Cumb 110 H11
Southwaite Services Cumb 110 H11
South Walsham Norfk 77 M9
Southwark Gt Lon 36 H5
South Warnborough Hants 23 K5
Southwater W Susx 24 E5
Southwater Street W Susx 24 E5
Southway C Plym 6 D6
Southway Somset 19 P6
South Weald Essex 37 N2
Southwell Dorset 11 P10
Southwell Notts 85 L10
South Weston Oxon 35 K5
South Wheatley Cnwll 5 L3
South Wheatley Notts 85 N3
Southwick Hants 14 H5
Southwick Nhants 61 M2
Southwick Somset 19 L5
Southwick Sundld 113 N9
Southwick W Susx 24 F9
Southwick Wilts 20 F3
South Widcombe BaNES 19 Q3
South Wigston Leics 72 F11
South Willingham Lincs 86 G4
South Wingate Dur 104 D4
South Wingfield Derbys 84 E9
South Witham Lincs 73 N7
Southwold Suffk 65 Q6
South Wonston Hants 22 E7
Southwood Norfk 77 M10
Southwood Somset 19 Q8
South Woodham Ferrers Essex 38 D2
South Wootton Norfk 75 M6
South Wraxall Wilts 20 F2
South Zeal Devon 8 G6
Sovereign Harbour E Susx 25 P10
Sowerby Calder 90 C6
Sowerby N York 97 P4
Sowerby Bridge Calder 90 D6
Sowerby Row Cumb 101 L2
Sower Carr Lancs 88 D2
Sowerhill Somset 18 A10
Sowhill Torfn 31 J4
Sowley Green Suffk 63 M10
Sowood Calder 90 D7
Sowton Devon 6 E5
Sowton Devon 9 N6
Soyland Town Calder 90 C6
Spa Common Norfk 77 K5
Spain's End Essex 51 Q3
Spalding Lincs 74 D6
Spaldington E R Yk 92 C4
Spaldwick Cambs 61 P6
Spalford Notts 85 P7
Spanby Lincs 74 A3
Spanish Green Hants 23 J3
Sparham Norfk 76 F8
Sparhamill Norfk 76 F8
Spark Bridge Cumb 94 G4
Sparket Cumb 101 M5
Sparkford Somset 20 B9
Sparkhill Birm 58 H8
Sparkwell Devon 6 F7
Sparrow Green Norfk 76 C9
Sparrowpit Derbys 83 N8
Sparrows Green E Susx 25 P4
Sparsholt Hants 22 D8
Sparsholt Oxon 34 B7
Spartylea Nthumb 112 C11
Spath Staffs 71 K7
Spaunton N York 98 E3
Spaxton Somset 18 H7
Spean Bridge Highld 146 G11

Spear Hill W Susx 24 D7
Spearywell Hants 22 B9
Speen Bucks 35 M5
Speen W Berk 34 E11
Speeton N York 99 P6
Speke Lpool 81 N8
Speldhurst Kent 25 N2
Spellbrook Herts 51 L7
Spelmonden Kent 26 B4
Spelsbury Oxon 48 B10
Spen Kirk 90 F5
Spencers Wood Wokham 35 K11
Spen Green Ches E 70 E2
Spennithorne N York 96 H3
Spennymoor Dur 103 Q4
Spernall Warwks 47 L2
Spetchley Worcs 46 G4
Spetisbury Dorset 12 F4
Spexhall Suffk 65 M5
Spey Bay Moray 157 R4
Speybridge Highld 149 J2
Speyview Moray 157 P9
Spilsby Lincs 87 M7
Spindlestone Nthumb 119 N4
Spinkhill Derbys 84 G5
Spinningdale Highld 162 F9
Spion Kop Notts 85 J7
Spirthill Wilts 33 J9
Spital Wirral 81 L8
Spital Donc 85 K2
Spital in the Street Lincs 86 C2
Spithurst E Susx 25 K7
Spittal E Loth 128 D4
Spittal E R Yk 98 F10
Spittal Highld 167 L6
Spittal Nthumb 129 Q9
Spittal Pembks 41 J6
Spittalfield P & K 141 R9
Spittal of Glenmuick Abers 149 Q10
Spittal of Glenshee P & K 141 R4
Spittal-on-Rule Border 118 A7
Spixworth Norfk 77 J8
Splatt Cnwll 4 E6
Splatt Cnwll 5 L4
Splatt Devon 8 F3
Splayne's Green E Susx 25 K6
Splott Cardif 30 H9
Spofforth N York 97 N10
Spondon C Derb 72 C3
Spon Green Flints 69 J2
Spooner Row Norfk 64 F2
Sporle Norfk 76 A9
Spott E Loth 128 H4
Spottiswoode Border 128 G10
Spratton Nhants 60 F7
Spreakley Surrey 23 M6
Spreyton Devon 8 G5
Spriddlestone Devon 6 E8
Spridlington Lincs 86 D4
Springburn C Glas 125 Q4
Springfield D & G 110 F7
Springfield Essex 52 B10
Springfield Fife 135 J5
Springhill Staffs 58 E4
Springhill Staffs 58 G3
Springholm D & G 108 H6
Springside N Ayrs 125 K10
Springthorpe Lincs 85 Q3
Spring Vale Barns 90 H10
Springwell Sundld 113 L9
Sproatley E R Yk 93 L4
Sproston Green Ches W 82 F11
Sprotbrough Donc 91 N10
Sproughton Suffk 53 K3
Sprouston Border 118 E3
Sprowston Norfk 77 K9
Sproxton Leics 73 M6
Sproxton N York 98 C4
Spunhill Shrops 69 M8
Spurstow Ches E 69 Q3
Spyway Dorset 11 L6
Square and Compass
 Pembks 40 F4
Stableford Shrops 57 P5
Stableford Staffs 70 E7
Stacey Bank Sheff 84 C2
Stackhouse N York 96 B7
Stackpole Pembks 41 J11
Stackpole Elidor Pembks 41 J11
Stacksford Norfk 64 F3
Stacksteads Lancs 89 P6
Staddiscombe C Plym 6 E8
Staddlethorpe E R Yk 92 D5
Staden Derbys 83 N10
Stadhampton Oxon 34 H5
Stadhlaigearraidh W Isls 168 c14
Staffield Cumb 101 P2
Staffin Highld 152 H4
Stafford Staffs 70 G10
Stafford Services
 (northbound) Staffs 70 F8
Stafford Services
 (southbound) Staffs 70 F8
Stagsden Bed 49 Q5
Stainborough Barns 91 J10
Stainburn Cumb 100 D5
Stainburn N York 97 L11
Stainby Lincs 73 N6
Staincross Barns 91 J8
Staindrop Dur 103 M6
Staines-upon-Thames
 Surrey 36 B6
Stainfield Lincs 74 A6
Stainfield Lincs 86 F6
Stainforth Donc 91 Q8
Stainforth N York 96 B7
Staining Lancs 88 C3
Stainland Calder 90 D7
Stainsacre N York 105 P9
Stainsby Derbys 84 G7
Stainton Cumb 95 L3
Stainton Cumb 101 N5
Stainton Cumb 110 G9
Stainton Donc 85 J2
Stainton Dur 103 L7
Stainton Middsb 104 E8
Stainton N York 103 M11
Stainton by Langworth
 Lincs 86 E5
Staintondale N York 105 Q11
Stainton le Vale Lincs 86 G2
Stainton with Adgarley
 Cumb 94 E6
Stair Cumb 100 H6
Stair E Ayrs 114 H3
Stairfoot Barns 91 K9

Stairhaven D & G 106 H7
Staithes N York 105 L7
Stakeford Nthumb 113 L3
Stake Pool Lancs 95 J11
Stakes Hants 15 J5
Stalbridge Dorset 20 D11
Stalbridge Weston Dorset 20 D11
Stalham Norfk 77 M6
Stalham Green Norfk 77 M7
Stalisfield Green Kent 38 G11
Stallen Common Norfk 64 E2
Stallen Dorset 20 B11
Stallingborough NE Lin 93 L8
Stalling Busk N York 96 D3
Stallington Staffs 70 G7
Stalmine Lancs 94 H11
Stalmine Moss Side Lancs 94 H11
Stalybridge Tamesd 83 L5
Stambourne Essex 52 B4
Stambourne Green Essex 51 Q3
Stamford Lincs 73 Q9
Stamford Nthumb 119 P7
Stamford Bridge Ches W 81 P11
Stamford Bridge E R Yk 98 E9
Stamfordham Nthumb 112 G6
Stamford Hill Gt Lon 36 H3
Stanah Lancs 88 D2
Stanborough Herts 50 F8
Stanbridge C Beds 49 Q10
Stanbridge Dorset 12 H4
Stanbury C Brad 90 C3
Stand Bury 89 M9
Stand N Lans 126 D4
Standburn Falk 126 G3
Standeford Staffs 58 D3
Standen Kent 26 C3
Standen Street Kent 26 D5
Standerwick Somset 20 F4
Standford Hants 23 M8
Standingstone Cumb 100 E3
Standish Gloucs 32 E3
Standish Wigan 88 H8
Standish Lower Ground
 Wigan 88 H9
Standlake Oxon 34 C4
Standon Hants 22 D9
Standon Herts 51 J6
Standon Staffs 70 E7
Standon Green End Herts 51 J7
Standwell Green Suffk 64 G8
Stane N Lans 126 F6
Stanfield Norfk 76 C7
Stanford C Beds 50 E2
Stanford Kent 27 K4
Stanford Shrops 56 E2
Stanford Bishop Herefs 46 C4
Stanford Bridge Worcs 57 N11
Stanford Bridge Wrekin 70 C10
Stanford Dingley W Berk 34 G10
Stanford in the Vale Oxon 34 B6
Stanford le Hope Thurr 37 Q4
Stanford on Avon Nhants 60 C5
Stanford on Soar Notts 72 E6
Stanford on Teme Worcs 57 N11
Stanford Rivers Essex 51 M10
Stanfree Derbys 84 G6
Stanghow R & Cl 105 J7
Stanground C Pete 74 D11
Stanhill Lancs 89 L5
Stanhoe Norfk 75 R3
Stanhope Border 116 G5
Stanhope Dur 103 J3
Stanhope Kent 26 H3
Stanhope Bretby Derbys 71 P10
Stanion Nhants 61 K3
Stanklin Worcs 58 C10
Stanley Derbys 72 C2
Stanley Dur 113 J10
Stanley Notts 84 G8
Stanley P & K 141 R11
Stanley Shrops 57 N8
Stanley Staffs 70 G4
Stanley Wakefd 91 J6
Stanley Common Derbys 72 C2
Stanley Crook Dur 103 N3
Stanley Ferry Wakefd 91 K6
Stanley Gate Lancs 88 E9
Stanley Moor Staffs 70 G4
Stanley Pontlarge Gloucs 47 K8
Stanmer Br & H 24 H9
Stanmore Gt Lon 36 E2
Stanmore Hants 22 E9
Stanmore W Berk 34 E9
Stannersburn Nthumb 111 P3
Stanningfield Suffk 64 B10
Stanningley Leeds 90 G4
Stannington Nthumb 113 K5
Stannington Sheff 84 D3
Stannington Station
 Nthumb 113 K4
Stansbatch Herefs 45 L2
Stansfield Suffk 63 N10
Stanshope Staffs 71 L4
Stanstead Suffk 52 D2
Stanstead Abbotts Herts 51 J8
Stansted Kent 37 P8
Stansted Airport Essex 51 N6
Stansted Mountfitchet
 Essex 51 M5
Stanton Derbys 71 P11
Stanton Gloucs 47 L8
Stanton Mons 45 L10
Stanton Nthumb 112 H4
Stanton Staffs 71 L5
Stanton Suffk 64 D7
Stanton by Bridge Derbys 72 B5
Stanton by Dale Derbys 72 D3
Stanton Drew BaNES 19 Q2
Stanton Fitzwarren Swindn 33 N6
Stanton Harcourt Oxon 34 D3
Stanton Hill Notts 84 G8
Stanton in Peak Derbys 84 B8
Stanton Lacy Shrops 56 H9
Stanton Lees Derbys 84 C8
Stanton Long Shrops 57 K6
Stanton-on-the-Wolds
 Notts 72 G4
Stanton Prior BaNES 20 C2
Stanton St Bernard Wilts 21 L2
Stanton St John Oxon 34 G3
Stanton St Quintin Wilts 32 H9
Stanton Street Suffk 64 D8
Stanton under Bardon Leics 72 D8
Stanton upon Hine Heath
 Shrops 69 Q10
Stanton Wick BaNES 20 B2

Stantway Gloucs 32 D2
Stanwardine in the Field
 Shrops 69 M10
Stanwardine in the Wood
 Shrops 69 M9
Stanway Essex 52 F7
Stanway Gloucs 47 L8
Stanway Green Essex 52 G7
Stanway Green Suffk 65 J7
Stanwell Surrey 36 C6
Stanwell Moor Surrey 36 B6
Stanwick Nhants 61 L6
Stanwick St John N York 103 N8
Stanwix Cumb 110 H9
Staoinebrig W Isls 168 c14
Stape N York 98 F2
Stapehill Dorset 13 J4
Stapeley Ches E 70 B5
Stapenhill Staffs 71 P10
Staple Kent 39 N10
Staple Cross Devon 18 D10
Staplecross E Susx 26 C7
Staplefield W Susx 24 G5
Stapleford Cambs 62 G10
Stapleford Herts 50 H7
Stapleford Leics 73 L7
Stapleford Lincs 85 Q9
Stapleford Notts 72 D3
Stapleford Wilts 21 L7
Stapleford Abbotts Essex 37 M2
Stapleford Tawney Essex 51 M11
Staplegrove Somset 18 H9
Staplehay Somset 18 H10
Staple Hill Worcs 58 E10
Staplehurst Kent 26 C3
Staplers IoW 14 F9
Staplestreet Kent 39 J9
Stapleton Cumb 111 K6
Stapleton Herefs 56 E11
Stapleton Leics 72 C11
Stapleton N York 103 N8
Stapleton Shrops 56 H4
Stapleton Somset 19 N10
Stapley Somset 10 D2
Staploe Bed 61 Q8
Staplow Herefs 46 C6
Star Fife 135 J7
Star IoA 79 J10
Star Pembks 41 P4
Star Somset 19 M3
Starbeck N York 97 M9
Starbotton N York 96 E6
Starcross Devon 9 N8
Stareton Warwks 59 N10
Starkholmes Derbys 84 D9
Starlings Green Essex 51 L4
Starr's Green E Susx 26 C8
Starston Norfk 65 J5
Start Devon 7 L10
Startforth Dur 103 M7
Startley Wilts 32 H8
Statenborough Kent 39 P10
Statham Warrtn 82 E7
Stathe Somset 19 L9
Stathern Leics 73 K4
Station Town Dur 104 D3
Staughton Green Cambs 61 P7
Staughton Highway Cambs 61 P8
Staunton Gloucs 31 Q2
Staunton Gloucs 46 B9
Staunton in the Vale Notts 73 L2
Staunton on Arrow Herefs 45 M2
Staunton on Wye Herefs 45 M6
Staveley Cumb 101 N11
Staveley Derbys 84 F7
Staveley N York 97 N8
Staveley-in-Cartmel Cumb 94 H3
Staverton Devon 7 K6
Staverton Gloucs 46 G10
Staverton Nhants 60 B8
Staverton Wilts 20 G2
Staverton Bridge Gloucs 46 G10
Stawell Somset 19 L7
Stawley Somset 18 E10
Staxigoe Highld 167 Q6
Staxton N York 99 L5
Staylittle Cerdgn 54 E7
Staylittle Powys 55 K6
Staynall Lancs 88 D2
Staythorpe Notts 85 N10
Stead C Brad 96 H11
Stean N York 96 G6
Stearsby N York 98 C6
Steart Somset 19 J5
Stebbing Essex 51 Q6
Stebbing Green Essex 51 Q6
Stechford Birm 58 H7
Stede Quarter Kent 26 E4
Stedham W Susx 23 N10
Steel Nthumb 112 D9
Steel Cross E Susx 25 M4
Steelend Fife 134 C9
Steele Road Border 111 K2
Steel Green Cumb 94 D5
Steel Heath Shrops 69 P7
Steen's Bridge Herefs 45 Q3
Steep Hants 23 K9
Steephill IoW 14 F11
Steep Lane Calder 90 C6
Steeple Dorset 12 F8
Steeple Essex 52 F11
Steeple Ashton Wilts 20 H3
Steeple Aston Oxon 48 E9
Steeple Barton Oxon 48 D10
Steeple Bumpstead Essex 51 Q2
Steeple Claydon Bucks 49 K9
Steeple Gidding Cambs 61 P4
Steeple Langford Wilts 21 K7
Steeple Morden Cambs 50 G2
Steep Marsh Hants 23 L9
Steeton C Brad 90 C2
Stein Highld 152 D6
Stella Gatesd 113 J8
Stelling Minnis Kent 27 K2
Stembridge Somset 19 M10
Stenalees Cnwll 4 G10
Stenhouse D & G 115 R9
Stenhousemuir Falk 133 P11
Stenigot Lincs 86 H4
Stenscholl Highld 152 H4
Stenson Fields Derbys 72 A4
Stenton E Loth 128 G5
Steornabhagh W Isls 168 j4
Stepaside Pembks 41 M9
Stepford D & G 109 J4

Stepney Gt Lon 37 J4
Stepping Hill Stockp 83 K7
Steppingley C Beds 50 B3
Stepps N Lans 126 B4
Sternfield Suffk 65 M9
Stert Wilts 21 K3
Stetchworth Cambs 63 K9
Stevenage Herts 50 F5
Steven's Crouch E Susx 26 B8
Stevenston N Ayrs 124 H9
Steventon Hants 22 F5
Steventon Oxon 34 E6
Steventon End Essex 51 N2
Stevington Bed 49 Q4
Stewartby Bed 50 B2
Stewartfield S Lans 125 Q6
Stewarton Ag & B 120 C8
Stewarton E Ayrs 125 L8
Stewkley Bucks 49 N9
Stewley Somset 19 K11
Stewton Lincs 87 L3
Steyne Cross IoW 14 H9
Steyning W Susx 24 E8
Steynton Pembks 40 H9
Stibb Cnwll 16 C9
Stibbard Norfk 76 D6
Stibb Cross Devon 16 G9
Stibb Green Wilts 21 P2
Stibbington Cambs 74 A11
Stichill Border 118 D3
Sticker Cnwll 3 P3
Stickford Lincs 87 L8
Sticklepath Devon 8 F6
Sticklepath Somset 18 D7
Stickling Green Essex 51 L4
Stickney Lincs 87 K9
Stiffkey Norfk 76 D3
Stifford Clays Thurr 37 P4
Stifford's Bridge Herefs 46 D5
Stiff Street Kent 38 E9
Stile Bridge Kent 26 C2
Stileway Somset 19 N6
Stillingfleet N York 91 P2
Stillington N York 98 B7
Stillington S on T 104 C6
Stilton Cambs 61 Q3
Stinchcombe Gloucs 32 D5
Stinsford Dorset 11 Q6
Stiperstones Shrops 56 F4
Stirchley Birm 58 G8
Stirchley Wrekin 57 M3
Stirling Abers 159 R9
Stirling Stirlg 133 M9
Stirling Castle Stirlg 133 M9
Stirling Services Stirlg 133 N10
Stirtloe Cambs 61 Q7
Stirton N York 96 E10
Stisted Essex 52 D7
Stitchcombe Wilts 33 P11
Stithians Cnwll 3 J6
Stivichall Covtry 59 M9
Stixwould Lincs 86 G7
St Michaels Fife 135 L3
Stoak Ches W 81 N10
Stobo Border 116 H3
Stoborough Dorset 12 F7
Stoborough Green Dorset 12 F7
Stobs Castle Border 117 Q9
Stobswood Nthumb 119 P11
Stock Essex 51 Q11
Stock N Som 19 N2
Stockbridge Hants 22 C7
Stockbridge W Susx 15 N6
Stockbriggs S Lans 126 D10
Stockbury Kent 38 D9
Stockcross W Berk 34 D11
Stockdalewath Cumb 110 G11
Stocker's Head Kent 38 G11
Stockerston Leics 73 L11
Stock Green Worcs 47 J3
Stocking Herefs 46 B8
Stockingford Warwks 59 M6
Stocking Pelham Herts 51 L5
Stockland Devon 10 E4
Stockland Bristol Somset 18 H6
Stockland Green Kent 25 N2
Stockleigh English Devon 9 L3
Stockleigh Pomeroy Devon 9 L4
Stockley Wilts 33 J11
Stockley Hill Herefs 45 M7
Stocklinch Somset 19 L11
Stockmoor Herefs 45 M4
Stockport Stockp 83 J6
Stocksbridge Sheff 90 H11
Stocksfield Nthumb 112 G8
Stockton Herefs 45 Q2
Stockton Norfk 65 M3
Stockton Shrops 56 D4
Stockton Shrops 57 N5
Stockton Warwks 48 D2
Stockton Wilts 21 J7
Stockton Wrekin 70 D11
Stockton Brook Staffs 70 G4
Stockton Heath Warrtn 82 D7
Stockton-on-Tees S on T 104 D7
Stockton on Teme Worcs 57 N11
Stockton on the Forest
 C York 98 D9
Stockwell Gloucs 32 H2
Stockwell End Wolves 58 C4
Stockwell Heath Staffs 71 K10
Stockwood Bristl 32 B11
Stockwood Dorset 11 M3
Stock Wood Worcs 47 K3
Stodday Lancs 95 K9
Stodmarsh Kent 39 M9
Stody Norfk 76 F4
Stoer Highld 164 B11
Stoford Somset 11 M2
Stoford Wilts 21 L7
Stogumber Somset 18 E7
Stogursey Somset 18 H6
Stoke Covtry 59 N9
Stoke Devon 16 C9
Stoke Hants 15 K6
Stoke Hants 22 D4
Stoke Medway 38 D7
Stoke Abbott Dorset 11 K4
Stoke Albany Nhants 60 H3
Stoke Ash Suffk 64 G7
Stoke Bardolph Notts 72 G2
Stoke Bliss Worcs 46 C2
Stoke Bruerne Nhants 49 K5
Stoke-by-Clare Suffk 52 B3
Stoke-by-Nayland Suffk 52 G4

Stoke Canon Devon 9 M5
Stoke Charity Hants 22 E7
Stoke Climsland Cnwll 5 P7
Stoke Cross Herefs 46 B4
Stoke D'Abernon Surrey 36 D9
Stoke Doyle Nhants 61 M3
Stoke Dry Rutlnd 73 M11
Stoke Edith Herefs 46 B6
Stoke End Warwks 59 J5
Stoke Farthing Wilts 21 L9
Stoke Ferry Norfk 75 P10
Stoke Fleming Devon 7 M9
Stokeford Dorset 12 E7
Stoke Gabriel Devon 7 M7
Stoke Gifford S Glos 32 B9
Stoke Golding Leics 72 B11
Stoke Goldington M Keyn 49 M5
Stoke Green Bucks 35 Q8
Stokeham Notts 85 N5
Stoke Hammond Bucks 49 N9
Stoke Heath Shrops 70 B9
Stoke Heath Worcs 58 D11
Stoke Holy Cross Norfk 77 J11
Stokeinteignhead Devon 7 N4
Stoke Lacy Herefs 46 B5
Stoke Lyne Oxon 48 G9
Stoke Mandeville Bucks 35 M2
Stokenchurch Bucks 35 L5
Stoke Newington Gt Lon 36 H3
Stokenham Devon 7 L10
Stoke-on-Trent C Stke 70 F5
Stoke Orchard Gloucs 46 H9
Stoke Poges Bucks 35 Q8
Stoke Pound Worcs 58 E11
Stoke Prior Herefs 45 Q3
Stoke Prior Worcs 58 D11
Stoke Rivers Devon 17 L4
Stoke Rochford Lincs 73 N5
Stoke Row Oxon 35 J8
Stoke St Gregory Somset 19 K9
Stoke St Mary Somset 19 J10
Stoke St Michael Somset 20 C5
Stoke St Milborough Shrops 57 K8
Stokesay Shrops 56 G8
Stokesby Norfk 77 N9
Stokesley N York 104 F9
Stoke sub Hamdon Somset 19 N11
Stoke Talmage Oxon 35 J5
Stoke Trister Somset 20 D9
Stoke upon Tern Shrops 70 A9
Stoke-upon-Trent C Stke 70 F5
Stoke Wake Dorset 12 C3
Stoke Wharf Worcs 58 E11
Stolford Somset 18 H5
Stondon Massey Essex 51 N10
Stone Bucks 35 L2
Stone Gloucs 32 C5
Stone Kent 37 N6
Stone Rothm 85 J3
Stone Somset 19 Q8
Stone Staffs 70 G8
Stone Worcs 58 C9
Stonea Cambs 62 G2
Stone Allerton Somset 19 L4
Ston Easton Somset 20 B4
Stonebridge N Som 19 L3
Stonebridge Norfk 64 C3
Stonebridge Warwks 59 K8
Stone Bridge Corner C Pete 74 E10
Stonebroom Derbys 84 F9
Stone Chair Calder 90 E5
Stone Cross E Susx 25 M5
Stone Cross E Susx 25 P10
Stone Cross E Susx 25 P4
Stone Cross Kent 25 M3
Stone Cross Kent 26 H4
Stone Cross Kent 39 P10
Stonecross Green Suffk 63 P9
Stonecrouch Kent 26 B5
Stone-edge-Batch N Som 31 N10
Stoneferry C KuH 93 K4
Stonefield Castle Hotel
 Ag & B 123 Q5
Stonegate E Susx 25 Q5
Stonegate N York 105 L9
Stonegrave N York 98 D5
Stonehall Worcs 46 G5
Stonehaugh Nthumb 111 Q5
Stonehaven Abers 151 M10
Stonehenge Wilts 21 M6
Stone Hill Donc 92 A9
Stonehouse C Plym 6 D8
Stone House Cumb 95 R3
Stonehouse Gloucs 32 F3
Stonehouse Nthumb 111 N9
Stonehouse S Lans 126 D8
Stone in Oxney Kent 26 F6
Stoneleigh Warwks 59 M10
Stoneley Green Ches E 69 R4
Stonely Cambs 61 P7
Stoner Hill Hants 23 K9
Stonesby Leics 73 L6
Stonesfield Oxon 48 C11
Stones Green Essex 53 L6
Stone Street Kent 37 N10
Stone Street Suffk 52 G4
Stone Street Suffk 65 H3
Stone Street Suffk 65 M5
Stonestreet Green Kent 27 J4
Stonethwaite Cumb 101 J8
Stonewells Moray 157 P4
Stonewood Kent 37 N6
Stoneybridge W Isls 168 c14
Stoneybridge Worcs 58 D9
Stoneyburn W Loth 126 H5
Stoney Cross Hants 13 N2
Stoneygate C Leic 72 G10
Stoneyhills Essex 38 G2
Stoneykirk D & G 106 E7
Stoney Middleton Derbys 84 B5
Stoney Stanton Leics 59 Q6
Stoney Stoke Somset 20 D7
Stoney Stratton Somset 20 C7
Stoney Stretton Shrops 56 F3
Stoneywood C Aber 151 M5
Stonham Aspal Suffk 64 G10
Stonnall Staffs 58 G4
Stonor Oxon 35 K7
Stonton Wyville Leics 73 J11
Stonybreck Shet 169 t14
Stony Cross Herefs 45 D5
Stony Cross Herefs 57 J11
Stonyford Hants 22 B11
Stony Houghton Derbys 84 G7
Stony Stratford M Keyn 49 L6

Stonywell Staffs 58 G2
Stoodleigh Devon 17 M5
Stoodleigh Devon 18 B11
Stop 24 Services Kent 27 K4
Stopham W Susx 24 B7
Stopsley Luton 50 D6
Stoptide Cnwll 4
Storeton Wirral 81 L8
Storeyard Green Herefs 46 D6
Storey Arms Powys 44 D10
Stornoway W Isls 168 j4
Stornoway Airport W Isls 168 j4
Storridge Herefs 46 E5
Storrington W Susx 24 C8
Storth Cumb 95 K5
Storwood E R Yk 92 B2
Stotfield Moray 157 N3
Stotfold C Beds 50 F3
Stottesdon Shrops 57 M8
Stoughton Leics 72 G10
Stoughton Surrey 23 Q4
Stoughton W Susx 15 M4
Stoulton Worcs 46 H5
Stourbridge Dudley 58 C8
Stourhead Wilts 20 E8
Stourpaine Dorset 12 E3
Stourport-on-Severn Worcs 57 Q10
Stour Provost Dorset 20 E10
Stour Row Dorset 20 F10
Stourton Leeds 91 J4
Stourton Staffs 58 C8
Stourton Warwks 47 Q7
Stourton Wilts 20 E8
Stourton Caundle Dorset 20 D11
Stout Somset 19 M8
Stove Shet 169 r11
Stoven Suffk 65 N5
Stow Border 117 P2
Stow Lincs 85 Q4
Stow Bardolph Norfk 75 N10
Stow Bedon Norfk 64 D2
Stowbridge Norfk 75 M9
Stow-cum-Quy Cambs 62 H8
Stowe Gloucs 31 Q3
Stowe Shrops 56 E10
Stowe-by-Chartley Staffs 71 J9
Stowehill Nhants 60 D9
Stowell Somset 20 C10
Stowey BaNES 19 Q3
Stowford Devon 8 B5
Stowford Devon 8 B7
Stowford Devon 10 C7
Stowford Devon 17 M3
Stowlangtoft Suffk 64 D8
Stow Longa Cambs 61 P6
Stow Maries Essex 38 D2
Stowmarket Suffk 64 E10
Stow-on-the-Wold Gloucs 47 N9
Stowting Kent 27 K3
Stowting Common Kent 27 K3
Stowupland Suffk 64 F9
Straad Ag & B 124 C5
Straanruie Highld 148 H4
Strachan Abers 150 H9
Strachur Ag & B 131 M7
Stradbroke Suffk 65 J7
Stradbrook Wilts 20 H4
Stradishall Suffk 63 N10
Stradsett Norfk 75 N9
Stragglethorpe Lincs 86 B10
Stragglethorpe Notts 72 H3
Straight Soley Wilts 34 B10
Straiton Mdloth 127 P4
Straiton S Ayrs 114 G7
Straloch Abers 151 M3
Straloch P & K 141 P5
Stramshall Staffs 71 K7
Strang IoM 80 e6
Strangeways Salfd 82 H5
Strangford Herefs 46 A9
Stranraer D & G 106 E5
Strata Florida Cerdgn 54 G11
Stratfield Mortimer W Berk 23 J2
Stratfield Saye Hants 23 J2
Stratfield Turgis Hants 23 J3
Stratford C Beds 61 Q11
Stratford Gt Lon 37 J4
Stratford St Andrew Suffk 65 M9
Stratford St Mary Suffk 52 H5
Stratford sub Castle Wilts 21 M8
Stratford Tony Wilts 21 L9
Stratford-upon-Avon Warwks 47 P3
Strath Highld 160 B11
Strathan Highld 160 H2
Strathan Highld 165 N4
Strathaven S Lans 126 C9
Strathblane Stirlg 125 P2
Strathcanaird Highld 161 K6
Strathcarron Highld 154 B9
Strathcoil Ag & B 138 B11
Strathdon Abers 150 B5
Strathkinness Fife 135 M4
Strathloanhead W Loth 126 G3
Strathmashie House Highld 147 P9
Strathmiglo Fife 134 G6
Strathpeffer Highld 155 N6
Strathtay P & K 141 M7
Strathwhillan N Ayrs 121 K4
Strathy Highld 166 D3
Strathy Inn Highld 166 D3
Strathyre Stirlg 132 H4
Stratton Cnwll 16 C10
Stratton Dorset 11 P6
Stratton Gloucs 33 K4
Stratton Audley Oxon 48 H9
Stratton-on-the-Fosse Somset 20 C4
Stratton St Margaret Swindn 33 N7
Stratton St Michael Norfk 65 J3
Stratton Strawless Norfk 77 J7
Stream Somset 18 E7
Streat E Susx 25 J7
Streatham Gt Lon 36 H6
Streatley C Beds 50 C5
Streatley W Berk 34 G8
Street Devon 10 D7
Street Lancs 95 L10
Street N York 105 K10
Street Somset 19 N7
Street Ashton Warwks 59 Q8
Street Dinas Shrops 69 K7
Street End E Susx 25 P6
Street End Kent 39 K11
Street End W Susx 15 N7
Street Gate Gatesd 113 K9

Streethay Staffs 58 H2
Street Houses N York 98 A11
Streetlam N York 104 B11
Street Lane Derbys 84 E11
Streetly Wsall 58 G5
Streetly End Cambs 63 K11
Street on the Fosse Somset 20 B7
Strefford Shrops 56 G7
Strelitz P & K 142 B10
Strelley Notts 72 E2
Strensall C York 98 C8
Strensham Worcs 46 H6
Strensham Services (northbound) Worcs 46 G6
Strensham Services (southbound) Worcs 46 H6
Stretcholt Somset 19 J6
Strete Devon 7 L9
Stretford Herefs 45 N3
Stretford Herefs 45 Q3
Stretford Traffd 82 G6
Strethall Essex 51 L3
Stretham Cambs 62 H6
Strettington W Susx 15 N5
Stretton Ches W 69 M4
Stretton Derbys 84 E8
Stretton Rutlnd 73 N7
Stretton Staffs 58 C2
Stretton Staffs 71 P9
Stretton Wartn 82 D8
Stretton en le Field Leics 59 M2
Stretton Grandison Herefs 46 B6
Stretton-on-Dunsmore Warwks 59 P10
Stretton on Fosse Warwks 47 P7
Stretton Sugwas Herefs 45 P6
Stretton under Fosse Warwks 59 Q8
Stretton Westwood Shrops 57 K5
Strichen Abers 159 M6
Strines Stockp 83 L7
Stringston Somset 18 G6
Strixton Nhants 61 K8
Stroat Gloucs 31 Q5
Strollamus Highld 145 J2
Stroma Highld 167 Q1
Stromeferry Highld 153 R11
Stromness Ork 169 b6
Stronaba Highld 146 G11
Stronachlachar Stirlg 132 E5
Stronafian Ag & B 131 L11
Stronchrubie Highld 161 L3
Strone Ag & B 131 P11
Strone Highld 146 E11
Stronmilchan Ag & B 131 P2
Stronsay Ork 169 f4
Stronsay Airport Ork 169 f4
Strontian Highld 138 E5
Strood Kent 26 E5
Strood Medway 38 B8
Strood Green Surrey 36 F11
Strood Green W Susx 24 B6
Stroud Gloucs 32 G3
Stroud Hants 23 K10
Stroude Surrey 36 B7
Stroud Green Essex 38 E3
Stroud Green Gloucs 32 F3
Stroxton Lincs 73 N4
Struan Highld 152 E10
Struan P & K 141 K4
Strubby Lincs 87 N4
Strumpshaw Norfk 77 L10
Strutherhill S Lans 126 D8
Struthers Fife 135 K6
Struy Highld 155 M9
Stryd-y-Facsen IoA 78 E8
Stryt-issa Wrexhm 69 J5
Stuartfield Abers 159 N8
Stubbers Green Wsall 58 F4
Stubbington Hants 14 G6
Stubbins Lancs 89 M7
Stubbs Cross Kent 26 G4
Stubbs Green Norfk 65 K2
Stubhampton Dorset 12 F2
Stubley Derbys 84 D5
Stubshaw Cross Wigan 82 C5
Stuckton Hants 13 L2
Studfold N York 96 B7
Stud Green W & M 35 N9
Studham C Beds 50 B7
Studholme Cumb 110 E9
Studland Dorset 12 H8
Studley Warwks 47 L2
Studley Wilts 33 J10
Studley Common Warwks 47 L2
Studley Roger N York 97 L7
Studley Royal N York 97 L6
Studley Royal Park & Fountains Abbey N York 97 L7
Stuntney Cambs 63 J5
Stunts Green E Susx 25 P8
Sturbridge Staffs 70 E8
Sturgate Lincs 85 Q3
Sturmer Essex 51 Q2
Sturminster Common Dorset 12 C2
Sturminster Marshall Dorset 12 G4
Sturminster Newton Dorset 12 C2
Sturry Kent 39 L9
Sturton N Linc 92 G10
Sturton by Stow Lincs 85 Q4
Sturton le Steeple Notts 85 N4
Stuston Suffk 64 G6
Stutton N York 91 M2
Stutton Suffk 53 L5
Styal Ches E 82 H8
Stydd Lancs 89 K3
Stynie Moray 157 Q5
Styrrup Notts 85 K2
Succoth Ag & B 132 B6
Suckley Worcs 46 D4
Suckley Green Worcs 46 D4
Sudborough Nhants 61 L4
Sudbourne Suffk 65 N11
Sudbrook Lincs 73 P2
Sudbrook Mons 31 P7
Sudbrooke Lincs 86 D5
Sudbury Derbys 71 M8
Sudbury Gt Lon 36 E3
Sudbury Suffk 52 E3
Sudden Rochdl 89 P8
Sudgrove Gloucs 32 H3
Suffield N York 99 K2

Suffield Norfk 77 J5
Sugdon Wrekin 69 R11
Sugnall Staffs 70 D8
Sugwas Pool Herefs 45 P6
Suisnish Highld 145 J4
Sulby IoM 80 e3
Sulgrave Nhants 48 G6
Sulham W Berk 34 H10
Sulhamstead W Berk 34 H11
Sulhamstead Abbots W Berk 34 H11
Sulhamstead Bannister W Berk 34 H11
Sullington W Susx 24 C8
Sullom Shet 169 q6
Sullom Voe Shet 169 r6
Sully V Glam 30 G11
Sumburgh Airport Shet 169 q12
Summerbridge N York 97 K8
Summercourt Cnwll 4 D10
Summerfield Norfk 75 Q3
Summerfield Worcs 58 B10
Summer Heath Bucks 35 K6
Summerhill Pembks 41 N9
Summerhill Staffs 58 G3
Summer Hill Wrexhm 69 K4
Summerhouse Darltn 103 P7
Summerlands Cumb 95 L3
Summerley Derbys 84 E5
Summersdale W Susx 15 N5
Summerseat Bury 89 M8
Summertown Oxon 34 F3
Summit Oldham 89 Q9
Summit Rochdl 89 Q7
Sunbiggin Cumb 102 C9
Sunbury-on-Thames Surrey 36 D7
Sundaywell D & G 108 H4
Sunderland Ag & B 122 B7
Sunderland Cumb 100 G3
Sunderland Lancs 95 J9
Sunderland Sundld 113 N9
Sunderland Bridge Dur 103 Q3
Sundhope Border 117 L5
Sundon Park Luton 50 C5
Sundridge Kent 37 L9
Sunk Island E R Yk 93 N7
Sunningdale W & M 35 Q11
Sunninghill W & M 35 P11
Sunningwell Oxon 34 E4
Sunniside Dur 103 M3
Sunniside Gatesd 113 K9
Sunny Brow Dur 103 N4
Sunnyhill C Derb 72 A4
Sunnyhurst Bl w D 89 K6
Sunnylaw Stirlg 133 M8
Sunnymead Oxon 34 F3
Sunton Wilts 21 P4
Surbiton Gt Lon 36 E7
Surfleet Lincs 74 E5
Surfleet Seas End Lincs 74 E5
Surlingham Norfk 77 L10
Surrex Essex 52 E7
Sustead Norfk 76 H4
Susworth Lincs 92 D10
Sutcombe Devon 16 E9
Sutcombemill Devon 16 E9
Suton Norfk 64 F2
Sutterby Lincs 87 L6
Sutterton Lincs 74 E3
Sutton C Beds 62 B11
Sutton C Pete 74 A11
Sutton Cambs 62 F5
Sutton Devon 7 J10
Sutton Devon 8 H4
Sutton Donc 91 P8
Sutton E Susx 25 L11
Sutton Gt Lon 36 G8
Sutton Kent 27 P2
Sutton N York 91 M5
Sutton Norfk 77 M7
Sutton Notts 73 K3
Sutton Oxon 34 D3
Sutton Pembks 40 H7
Sutton Shrops 57 J2
Sutton Shrops 57 N7
Sutton Shrops 69 L9
Sutton Shrops 70 B8
Sutton St Hel 82 B6
Sutton Staffs 70 D10
Sutton Suffk 53 P2
Sutton W Susx 23 Q11
Sutton Abinger Surrey 36 D11
Sutton-at-Hone Kent 37 N7
Sutton Bassett Nhants 60 G2
Sutton Benger Wilts 32 H9
Sutton Bingham Somset 11 L2
Sutton Bonington Notts 72 E6
Sutton Bridge Lincs 75 J6
Sutton Cheney Leics 72 C10
Sutton Coldfield Birm 58 H5
Sutton Courtenay Oxon 34 F6
Sutton Crosses Lincs 74 H6
Sutton cum Lound Notts 85 L4
Sutton Fields Notts 72 D5
Sutton Green Surrey 36 B10
Sutton Green Wrexhm 69 M5
Sutton Heath Suffk 53 P2
Sutton Howgrave N York 97 M6
Sutton-in-Ashfield Notts 84 G9
Sutton-in-Craven N York 90 C2
Sutton in the Elms Leics 60 B2
Sutton Lane Ends Ches E 83 K10
Sutton Maddock Shrops 57 N4
Sutton Mallet Somset 19 L7
Sutton Mandeville Wilts 21 J9
Sutton Manor St Hel 81 Q6
Sutton Marsh Herefs 45 R6
Sutton Montis Somset 20 B10
Sutton-on-Hull C KuH 93 K4
Sutton on Sea Lincs 87 P4
Sutton-on-the-Forest N York 98 B8
Sutton on the Hill Derbys 71 N8
Sutton on Trent Notts 85 N7
Sutton Poyntz Dorset 11 P8
Sutton St Edmund Lincs 74 G8
Sutton St James Lincs 74 G7
Sutton St Nicholas Herefs 45 Q5
Sutton Scotney Hants 22 E7
Sutton Street Kent 38 D10
Sutton-under-Whitestonecliffe N York 97 Q4
Sutton upon Derwent E R Yk 98 E11
Sutton Valence Kent 26 D2
Sutton Veny Wilts 20 H6

Sutton Waldron Dorset 20 G11
Sutton Weaver Ches W 82 B9
Sutton Wick BaNES 19 Q3
Sutton Wick Oxon 34 E6
Swaby Lincs 87 L5
Swadlincote Derbys 71 P11
Swaffham Norfk 75 R9
Swaffham Bulbeck Cambs 63 J8
Swaffham Prior Cambs 63 J8
Swafield Norfk 77 K5
Swainby N York 104 E10
Swainshill Herefs 45 P6
Swainsthorpe Norfk 77 J11
Swainswick BaNES 32 E11
Swalcliffe Oxon 48 C7
Swalecliffe Kent 39 K8
Swallow Lincs 93 L10
Swallow Beck Lincs 86 B7
Swallowcliffe Wilts 21 J9
Swallowfield Wokham 23 K2
Swallownest Rothm 84 G3
Swallows Cross Essex 51 P11
Swampton Hants 22 D4
Swanage Dorset 12 H9
Swanbourne Bucks 49 M9
Swanbridge V Glam 30 G11
Swancote Shrops 57 N6
Swan Green Ches W 82 F10
Swanland E R Yk 92 G5
Swanley Kent 37 M7
Swanley Village Kent 37 M7
Swanmore Hants 22 G11
Swannington Leics 72 C7
Swannington Norfk 76 G8
Swanpool Lincs 86 C7
Swanscombe Kent 37 P6
Swansea Swans 29 J6
Swansea Airport Swans 28 G6
Swansea West Services Swans 28 H5
Swan Street Essex 52 E6
Swanton Abbot Norfk 77 K6
Swanton Morley Norfk 76 E8
Swanton Novers Norfk 76 E5
Swanton Street Kent 38 E10
Swan Valley Nhants 60 F9
Swan Village Sandw 58 E6
Swanwick Derbys 84 F10
Swanwick Hants 14 F5
Swarby Lincs 73 Q2
Swardeston Norfk 77 J11
Swarkestone Derbys 72 B5
Swarland Nthumb 119 N10
Swarraton Hants 22 G7
Swartha C Brad 96 G11
Swarthmoor Cumb 94 F5
Swaton Lincs 74 B3
Swavesey Cambs 62 E7
Sway Hants 13 N5
Swayfield Lincs 73 P6
Swaythling C Sotn 22 D11
Sweet Green Worcs 46 B2
Sweetham Devon 9 L5
Sweethaws E Susx 25 M5
Sweetlands Corner Kent 26 C2
Sweets Cnwll 5 K2
Sweetshouse Cnwll 4 H9
Swefling Suffk 65 L9
Swepstone Leics 72 B8
Swerford Oxon 48 C8
Swettenham Ches E 82 H11
Swffryd Blae G 30 H5
Swift's Green Kent 26 E3
Swilland Suffk 64 H11
Swillbrook Lancs 88 F4
Swillington Leeds 91 K4
Swimbridge Devon 17 L5
Swimbridge Newland Devon 17 L5
Swinbrook Oxon 33 Q2
Swincliffe Kirk 90 G5
Swincliffe N York 97 K9
Swincombe Devon 17 M3
Swinden Cumb 101 P8
Swinden N York 96 C10
Swinderby Lincs 85 Q8
Swindon Gloucs 46 H9
Swindon Nthumb 119 J11
Swindon Staffs 58 C6
Swindon Swindn 33 M8
Swine E R Yk 93 K3
Swinefleet E R Yk 92 C6
Swineford S Glos 32 C11
Swineshead Bed 61 N7
Swineshead Lincs 74 D2
Swineshead Bridge Lincs 74 D2
Swiney Highld 167 M9
Swinford Leics 60 C5
Swinford Oxon 34 D3
Swingate Notts 72 E2
Swingfield Minnis Kent 27 M3
Swingfield Street Kent 27 M3
Swingleton Green Suffk 52 G2
Swinhoe Nthumb 119 P5
Swinhope Lincs 93 M11
Swinithwaite N York 96 F3
Swinmore Common Herefs 46 C6
Swinscoe Staffs 71 L5
Swinside Cumb 100 H6
Swinstead Lincs 73 Q6
Swinthorpe Lincs 86 E4
Swinton Border 129 L10
Swinton N York 97 K5
Swinton N York 98 F6
Swinton Rothm 91 M11
Swinton Salfd 82 G4
Swiss Valley Carmth 28 F4
Swithland Leics 72 E8
Swordale Highld 155 Q4
Swordland Highld 145 N9
Swordly Highld 166 B4
Sworton Heath Ches E 82 E8
Swyddffynnon Cerdgn 54 F11
Swyncombe Oxon 35 J6
Swynnerton Staffs 70 F7
Swyre Dorset 11 L7
Sychant Powys 68 M9
Sychtyn Powys 55 M3
Sydallt Wrexhm 69 K3
Syde Gloucs 33 J2
Sydenham Gt Lon 37 J6
Sydenham Oxon 35 K4
Sydenham Damerel Devon 5 Q6
Sydenhurst Surrey 23 N9
Syderstone Norfk 76 A5
Sydling St Nicholas Dorset 11 N5

Sydmonton Hants 22 E3
Sydnal Lane Shrops 57 Q3
Syerston Notts 85 M11
Syke Rochdl 89 P7
Sykehouse Donc 91 Q7
Syleham Suffk 65 J6
Sylen Carmth 28 F3
Symbister Shet 169 s7
Symington S Ayrs 125 K11
Symington S Lans 116 D3
Symondsbury Dorset 11 J6
Symonds Yat (East) Herefs 45 R11
Symonds Yat (West) Herefs 45 R11
Sympson Green C Brad 90 F3
Synderford Dorset 10 H4
Synod Inn Cerdgn 42 H4
Syre Highld 165 Q8
Syreford Gloucs 47 K10
Syresham Nhants 48 H6
Syston Leics 72 G8
Syston Lincs 73 N2
Sytchampton Worcs 58 B11
Sywell Nhants 60 H7

T

Tabley Hill Ches E 82 F9
Tackley Oxon 48 E11
Tacolneston Norfk 64 G2
Tadcaster N York 91 M2
Taddington Derbys 83 P10
Taddington Gloucs 47 L8
Taddiport Devon 16 H8
Tadley Hants 22 H2
Tadlow Cambs 62 C11
Tadmarton Oxon 48 C7
Tadpole Swindn 33 M6
Tadwick BaNES 32 D10
Tadworth Surrey 36 F9
Tafarnaubach Blae G 30 F2
Tafarn-y-bwlch Pembks 41 L4
Tafarn-y-Gelyn Denbgs 68 G2
Taff's Well Rhondd 30 F8
Tafolwern Powys 55 K4
Taibach Neath 29 L7
Tain Highld 162 H10
Tain Highld 167 M3
Tai'n Lôn Gwynd 66 G4
Tai'r Bull Powys 44 D9
Tairgwaith Neath 29 K2
Takeley Essex 51 N6
Takeley Street Essex 51 M6
Talachddu Powys 44 F8
Talacre Flints 80 G8
Talaton Devon 9 Q5
Talbenny Pembks 40 F8
Talbot Green Rhondd 30 D8
Talbot Village BCP 13 J6
Taleford Devon 10 B5
Talerddig Powys 55 L4
Talgarreg Cerdgn 42 H4
Talgarth Powys 44 H8
Talisker Highld 152 E11
Talke Staffs 70 E4
Talke Pits Staffs 70 E4
Talkin Cumb 111 L9
Talladale Highld 154 B3
Talla Linnfoots Border 116 G6
Tallaminnock S Ayrs 114 H8
Tallarn Green Wrexhm 69 M6
Tallentire Cumb 100 F3
Talley Carmth 43 M8
Tallington Lincs 74 A9
Tallwrn Wrexhm 69 J5
Talmine Highld 165 N4
Talog Carmth 42 F9
Talsarn Cerdgn 43 K3
Talsarnau Gwynd 67 L3
Talskiddy Cnwll 4 E8
Talwrn IoA 78 H9
Talwrn Wrexhm 69 L5
Tal-y-bont Cerdgn 54 F7
Tal-y-Bont Conwy 79 P11
Talybont Powys 67 K10
Tal-y-bont Gwynd 67 K10
Tal-y-bont Gwynd 79 L10
Talybont-on-Usk Powys 44 G10
Tal-y-Cafn Conwy 79 P10
Tal-y-coed Mons 45 N11
Tal-y-garn Rhondd 30 D8
Tal-y-llyn Gwynd 54 G3
Tal-y-Waun Torfn 31 J4
Talywern Powys 55 J4
Tamar Valley Mining District Devon 6 C5
Tamer Lane End Wigan 82 D4
Tamerton Foliot C Plym 6 D6
Tamworth Staffs 59 K4
Tamworth Green Lincs 74 E2
Tamworth Services Warwks 59 K4
Tancred N York 97 Q9
Tancredston Pembks 40 G5
Tandridge Surrey 37 J10
Tanfield Dur 113 J9
Tanfield Lea Dur 113 J10
Tangasdale W Isls 168 b17
Tangiers Pembks 41 J7
Tangley Hants 22 B4
Tangmere W Susx 15 P5
Tan Hill N York 102 G9
Tankerness Ork 169 e6
Tankersley Barns 91 J11
Tankerton Kent 39 K8
Tannach Highld 167 P7
Tannachie Abers 151 K11
Tannadice Angus 142 H6
Tanner's Green Worcs 58 G10
Tannington Suffk 65 J8
Tannochside N Lans 126 C5
Tansley Derbys 84 D9
Tansor Nhants 61 N2
Tantobie Dur 113 J10
Tanton N York 104 F8
Tanwood Worcs 58 D10
Tanworth in Arden Warwks 58 H10
Tan-y-Bwlch Gwynd 67 M4
Tan-y-fron Conwy 68 C2
Tan-y-fron Wrexhm 69 J4
Tan-y-grisiau Gwynd 67 M5
Tan-y-groes Cerdgn 42 E5
Taobh Tuath W Isls 168 e9
Taplow Bucks 35 P8
Tarbert Ag & B 123 L9
Tarbert Ag & B 123 Q6

Tarbert W Isls...168 g7	Terrington St Clement Norfk...75 L6	Thingwall Wirral...81 K8	Thorpe N York...96 F8	Thurning Norfk...76 F6
Tarbet Ag & B...132 C7	Terrington St John Norfk...75 K8	Thirkleby N York...97 Q5	Thorpe Norfk...65 N2	Thurnscoe Barns...91 M9
Tarbet Highld...145 N9	Terry's Green Warwks...58 H10	Thirlby N York...97 Q4	Thorpe Notts...85 N11	Thurrock Services Thurr...37 N5
Tarbet Highld...164 E7	Teston Kent...38 B11	Thirlestane Border...128 F10	Thorpe Surrey...36 B7	Thursby Cumb...110 F10
Tarbock Green Knows...81 P7	Testwood Hants...14 C4	Thirn N York...97 K3	Thorpe Abbotts Norfk...64 H6	Thursden Lancs...89 Q4
Tarbolton S Ayrs...114 H2	Tetbury Gloucs...32 G6	Thirsk N York...97 P4	Thorpe Acre Leics...72 E7	Thursford Norfk...76 D5
Tarbrax S Lans...127 J6	Tetbury Upton Gloucs...32 G5	Thirtleby E R Yk...93 L4	Thorpe Arnold Leics...73 K6	Thursley Surrey...23 P7
Tardebigge Worcs...58 E11	Tetchill Shrops...69 L8	Thistleton Lancs...88 E3	Thorpe Audlin Wakefd...91 M7	Thurso Highld...167 K3
Tarfside Angus...142 H2	Tetcott Devon...5 N2	Thistleton Rutlnd...73 N7	Thorpe Bassett N York...98 H6	Thurstaston Wirral...81 J8
Tarland Abers...150 D7	Tetford Lincs...87 K6	Thistley Green Suffk...63 L5	Thorpe Bay Sthend...38 F4	Thurston Suffk...64 C8
Tarleton Lancs...88 F6	Tetney Lincs...93 P10	Thixendale N York...98 G8	Thorpe by Water Rutlnd...73 M11	Thurston Clough Oldham...90 B9
Tarlscough Lancs...88 E8	Tetney Lock Lincs...93 P10	Thockrington Nthumb...112 E5	Thorpe Common Rothm...91 K11	Thurstonfield Cumb...110 F9
Tarlton Gloucs...33 J5	Tetsworth Oxon...35 J4	Tholomas Drove Cambs...74 H9	Thorpe Constantine Staffs...59 L3	Thurstonland Kirk...90 F8
Tarnock Somset...19 L4	Tettenhall Wolves...58 C4	Tholthorpe N York...97 Q7	Thorpe End Norfk...77 K9	Thurston Planche Suffk...64 C9
Tarns Cumb...109 P11	Tettenhall Wood Wolves...58 C5	Thomas Chapel Pembks...41 M9	Thorpe Green Essex...53 L7	Thurton Norfk...77 L11
Tarnside Cumb...95 J2	Teversal Notts...84 G8	Thomas Close Cumb...101 M2	Thorpe Green Lancs...88 H6	Thurvaston Derbys...71 N7
Tarporley Ches W...69 Q2	Teversham Cambs...62 G9	Thomastown Abers...158 G10	Thorpe Green Suffk...64 C11	Thuxton Norfk...76 E10
Tarr Somset...17 R5	Teviothead Border...117 N9	Thompson Norfk...64 C2	Thorpe Hesley Rothm...91 K11	Thwaite N York...102 G11
Tarrant Crawford Dorset...12 F4	Tewin Herts...50 G8	Thomshill Moray...157 N6	Thorpe in Balne Donc...91 P8	Thwaite Suffk...64 G8
Tarrant Gunville Dorset...12 F2	Tewin Wood Herts...50 G7	Thong Kent...37 Q6	Thorpe Langton Leics...60 F2	Thwaite Head Cumb...94 G2
Tarrant Hinton Dorset...12 F2	Tewkesbury Gloucs...46 G8	Thongsbridge Kirk...90 F9	Thorpe Larches Dur...104 C5	Thwaites C Brad...90 D2
Tarrant Keyneston Dorset...12 F4	Teynham Kent...38 G9	Thoralby N York...96 F3	Thorpe Lea Surrey...36 B6	Thwaite St Mary Norfk...65 L2
Tarrant Launceston Dorset...12 F3	Thackley C Brad...90 F3	Thoresby Notts...85 K6	Thorpe le Fallows Lincs...86 B4	Thwaites Brow C Brad...90 D2
Tarrant Monkton Dorset...12 F3	Thackthwaite Cumb...100 F6	Thoresthorpe Lincs...87 N5	Thorpe-le-Soken Essex...53 L7	Thwing E R Yk...99 L6
Tarrant Rawston Dorset...12 F3	Thackthwaite Cumb...101 M5	Thoresway Lincs...93 L11	Thorpe le Street E R Yk...92 D2	Tibbermore P & K...134 C3
Tarrant Rushton Dorset...12 F3	Thainstone Abers...151 K4	Thorganby Lincs...93 M11	Thorpe Malsor Nhants...60 H5	Tibbers D & G...116 B11
Tarring Neville E Susx...25 K10	Thakeham W Susx...24 D7	Thorganby N York...92 A2	Thorpe Mandeville Nhants...48 F6	Tibberton Gloucs...46 E10
Tarrington Herefs...46 B6	Thame Oxon...35 K3	Thorgill N York...105 K11	Thorpe Market Norfk...77 J4	Tibberton Worcs...46 H3
Tarskavaig Highld...145 J5	Thames Ditton Surrey...36 E7	Thorington Suffk...65 N7	Thorpe Marriot Norfk...76 H8	Tibberton Wrekin...70 B10
Tarves Abers...159 L11	Thamesmead Gt Lon...37 L4	Thorington Street Suffk...52 H4	Thorpe Morieux Suffk...64 C11	Tibenham Norfk...64 G4
Tarvin Ches W...81 P11	Thamesport Medway...38 E7	Thorlby N York...96 E10	Thorpeness Suffk...65 P10	Tibshelf Derbys...84 F8
Tarvin Sands Ches W...81 P11	Thanington Kent...39 K10	Thorley Herts...51 L7	Thorpe on the Hill Leeds...91 J5	Tibshelf Services Derbys...84 F8
Tasburgh Norfk...65 J2	Thankerton S Lans...116 D3	Thorley IoW...14 C9	Thorpe on the Hill Lincs...86 B7	Tibthorpe E R Yk...99 K9
Tasley Shrops...57 M6	Tharston Norfk...64 H3	Thorley Houses Herts...51 L7	Thorpe Park Surrey...36 B7	Ticehurst E Susx...25 Q4
Taston Oxon...48 C10	Thatcham W Berk...34 F11	Thorley Street IoW...14 C9	Thorpe St Andrew Norfk...77 K10	Tichborne Hants...22 G8
Tatenhill Staffs...71 N10	Thatto Heath St Hel...81 Q6	Thormanby N York...97 Q6	Thorpe St Peter Lincs...87 N8	Tickencote Rutlnd...73 P9
Tathall End M Keyn...49 M5	Thaxted Essex...51 P4	Thornaby-on-Tees S on T...104 E7	Thorpe Salvin Rothm...84 H4	Tickenham N Som...31 N10
Tatham Lancs...95 N7	Theakston N York...97 M3	Thornage Norfk...76 F4	Thorpe Satchville Leics...73 J8	Tickford End M Keyn...49 N6
Tathwell Lincs...87 K4	Thealby N Linc...92 E7	Thornborough Bucks...49 K8	Thorpe Thewles S on T...104 C6	Tickhill Donc...85 J2
Tatsfield Surrey...37 K9	Theale Somset...19 N5	Thornborough N York...97 L5	Thorpe Tilney Lincs...86 F9	Ticklerton Shrops...56 H6
Tattenhall Ches W...69 N3	Theale W Berk...34 H10	Thornbury C Brad...90 F4	Thorpe Underwood N York...97 Q9	Ticknall Derbys...72 B6
Tatterford Norfk...76 B6	Thearne E R Yk...93 J3	Thornbury Devon...16 G10	Thorpe Underwood Nhants...60 G4	Tickton E R Yk...93 J2
Tattersett Norfk...76 A6	The Bank Ches E...70 E3	Thornbury Herefs...46 B3	Thorpe Waterville Nhants...61 M4	Tidbury Green Solhll...58 H9
Tattershall Lincs...86 H9	The Beeches Gloucs...33 K4	Thornbury S Glos...32 B6	Thorpe Willoughby N York...91 P4	Tidcombe Wilts...21 Q3
Tattershall Bridge Lincs...86 G9	The Bog Shrops...56 F5	Thornby Cumb...110 E10	Thorpland Norfk...75 M9	Tiddington Oxon...34 H4
Tattershall Thorpe Lincs...86 H9	The Bourne Worcs...47 J3	Thornby Nhants...60 E5	Thorrington Essex...53 J8	Tiddington Warwks...47 P3
Tattingstone Suffk...53 K4	The Braes Highld...153 J11	Thorncliff Staffs...71 J3	Thorverton Devon...9 M4	Tiddleywink Wilts...32 G9
Tattingstone White Horse Suffk...53 K4	The Bratch Staffs...58 C6	Thorncombe Dorset...10 H4	Thrales End C Beds...50 D7	Tidebrook E Susx...25 P5
Tatton Park Ches E...82 F8	The Bridge Kent...37 M5	Thorncombe Street Surrey...23 Q6	Thrandeston Suffk...64 G6	Tideford Cnwll...5 P10
Tatworth Somset...10 G3	The Broad Herefs...45 P2	Thorncott Green C Beds...61 Q11	Thrapston Nhants...61 L5	Tideford Cross Cnwll...5 N9
Tauchers Moray...157 R8	The Broads...77 P10	Thorncross IoW...14 D10	Threapland Cumb...100 G3	Tidenham Gloucs...31 Q5
Taunton Somset...18 H10	The Brunt E Loth...128 H5	Thorndon Suffk...64 G8	Threapland N York...96 E8	Tideswell Derbys...83 Q9
Taunton Deane Services Somset...18 G10	The Bryn Mons...31 K3	Thorndon Cross Devon...8 D2	Threapwood Ches W...69 M6	Tidmarsh W Berk...34 H10
Taverham Norfk...76 H9	The Bungalow IoM...80 e4	Thorne Donc...92 A8	Threapwood Staffs...71 J6	Tidmington Warwks...47 Q7
Taverners Green Essex...51 N7	The Burf Worcs...57 Q11	Thorne Coffin Somset...19 P11	Threapwood Head Staffs...71 J6	Tidpit Hants...21 L11
Tavernspite Pembks...41 N8	The Camp Gloucs...32 H3	Thornecroft Devon...7 K5	Threave S Ayrs...114 F6	Tidworth Wilts...21 P5
Tavistock Devon...6 D4	The Chequer Wrexhm...69 N6	Thornehillhead Devon...16 G8	Three Ashes Herefs...45 Q10	Tiers Cross Pembks...40 H8
Tavistock Devon...6 D4	The City Bed...61 P9	Thorner Leeds...91 K2	Three Bridges W Susx...24 G3	Tiffield Nhants...49 K4
Taw Green Devon...8 G5	The City Bucks...35 L5	Thornes Staffs...58 G4	Three Burrows Cnwll...3 K4	Tigerton Angus...143 J5
Tawstock Devon...17 K6	The Common Oxon...47 Q9	Thornes Wakefd...91 J7	Three Chimneys Kent...26 D9	Tigh a' Ghearraidh W Isls...168 c10
Taxal Derbys...83 M9	The Common Wilts...21 P8	Thorne St Margaret Somset...18 F10	Three Cocks Powys...44 H7	Tigharry W Isls...168 c10
Tay Bridge C Dund...135 L2	The Common Wilts...33 K7	Thorney Bucks...36 B5	Three Crosses Swans...28 G6	Tighnabruaich Ag & B...124 B3
Taychreggan Hotel Ag & B...131 L3	The Corner Kent...26 B3	Thorney C Pete...74 E10	Three Cups Corner E Susx...25 P6	Tilbrook Cambs...61 N7
Tay Forest Park P & K...141 J5	The Cronk IoM...80 d2	Thorney Notts...85 Q6	Three Gates Worcs...46 C2	Tilbury Thurr...37 P5
Tayinloan Ag & B...123 L10	Theddingworth Leics...60 E3	Thorney Somset...19 M10	Threehammer Common Norfk...77 L8	Tilbury Dock Thurr...37 P5
Taynton Gloucs...46 D10	Theddlethorpe All Saints Lincs...87 N3	Thorney Hill Hants...13 M5	Three Hammers Cnwll...5 L4	Tilbury Green Essex...52 B3
Taynton Oxon...33 P2	Theddlethorpe St Helen Lincs...87 N3	Thorney Island W Susx...15 L6	Three Holes Norfk...75 K10	Tilbury Juxta Clare Essex...52 C3
Taynuilt Ag & B...139 J11	The Deep C KuH...93 J5	Thorney Toll Cambs...74 F10	Threekingham Lincs...74 A3	Tile Cross Birm...59 J7
Tayport Fife...135 M2	The Den N Ayrs...125 J7	Thornfalcon Somset...19 J10	Three Leg Cross E Susx...25 Q4	Tile Hill Covtry...59 L9
Tayvallich Ag & B...130 E10	The Forge Herefs...45 L3	Thornford Dorset...11 N2	Three Legged Cross Dorset...13 J3	Tilehouse Green Solhll...59 J9
Tealby Lincs...86 G2	The Forstal Kent...26 H4	Thorngrafton Nthumb...111 Q7	Three Mile Cross Wokham...35 K11	Tilehurst Readg...35 J10
Tealing Angus...142 G10	The Fouralls Shrops...70 B8	Thorngrove Somset...19 L8	Threemilestone Cnwll...3 K4	Tilford Surrey...23 N6
Team Valley Gatesd...113 K9	The Green Cumb...94 D4	Thorngumbald E R Yk...93 M5	Threemiletown W Loth...127 K2	Tilgate W Susx...24 G4
Teangue Highld...145 L6	The Green Essex...52 C8	Thornham Norfk...75 P2	Three Oaks E Susx...26 D9	Tilgate Forest Row W Susx...24 G4
Teanord Highld...155 Q5	The Green N York...105 L9	Thornham Magna Suffk...64 G7	Threlkeld Cumb...101 K5	Tilham Street Somset...19 Q7
Tebay Cumb...102 B10	The Green Wilts...20 G8	Thornham Parva Suffk...64 G7	Threshers Bush Essex...51 L9	Tillers Green Gloucs...46 C8
Tebay Services Cumb...102 B9	The Grove Dur...112 G10	Thornhaugh C Pete...73 R10	Threshfield N York...96 E8	Tillicoultry Clacks...133 Q8
Tebworth C Beds...49 Q9	The Grove Worcs...46 G6	Thornhill C Sotn...14 E4	Thrigby Norfk...77 P9	Tillietudlem S Lans...126 E8
Tedburn St Mary Devon...9 K6	The Haven W Susx...24 C4	Thornhill Caerph...30 G8	Thringarth Dur...102 H6	Tillingham Essex...52 G11
Teddington Gloucs...47 J8	The Haw Gloucs...46 F9	Thornhill Cumb...100 D9	Thringstone Leics...72 C7	Tillington Herefs...45 P6
Teddington Gt Lon...36 E6	The Headland Hartpl...104 F4	Thornhill D & G...116 B11	Thrintoft N York...97 M2	Tillington W Susx...23 Q10
Tedstone Delamere Herefs...46 C3	The Hendre Mons...31 N2	Thornhill Derbys...83 Q8	Thriplow Cambs...62 F11	Tillington Common Herefs...45 P5
Tedstone Wafer Herefs...46 C3	The Hill Cumb...94 D4	Thornhill Kirk...90 H7	Throapham Rothm...84 H3	Tillybirloch Abers...150 H6
Teesport R & Cl...104 F6	The Holt Wokham...35 M9	Thornhill Stirlg...133 K7	Throckenhalt Lincs...74 G9	Tillyfourie Abers...150 G5
Teesside Park S on T...104 E7	The Hundred Herefs...45 Q2	Thornhill Lees Kirk...90 G7	Throcking Herts...50 H4	Tillygreig Abers...151 M3
Teeton Nhants...60 E6	Thelbridge Cross Devon...9 J2	Thornhills Calder...90 F6	Throckley N u Ty...113 J7	Tillyrie P & K...134 E6
Teffont Evias Wilts...21 J8	The Leacon Kent...26 G5	Thornholme E R Yk...99 N8	Throckmorton Worcs...47 J5	Tilmanstone Kent...39 P11
Teffont Magna Wilts...21 J8	The Lee Bucks...35 P4	Thornicombe Dorset...12 E4	Throop BCP...13 K5	Tilney All Saints Norfk...75 L7
Tegryn Pembks...41 P4	The Lhen IoM...80 e1	Thornington Nthumb...118 G4	Throop Dorset...12 D6	Tilney High End Norfk...75 L7
Teigh Rutlnd...73 M7	Thelnetham Suffk...64 E6	Thornley Dur...103 M3	Throphill Nthumb...112 H3	Tilney St Lawrence Norfk...75 K8
Teigncombe Devon...8 G7	The Lochs Moray...157 Q5	Thornley Dur...104 C3	Thropton Nthumb...119 K10	Tilshead Wilts...21 K5
Teigngrace Devon...7 M4	Thelveton Norfk...64 H5	Thornley Gate Nthumb...112 E9	Throsk Stirlg...133 P9	Tilstock Shrops...69 P7
Teignmouth Devon...7 N4	Thelwall Warrtn...82 E7	Thornliebank E Rens...125 P6	Througham Gloucs...32 H3	Tilston Ches W...69 N4
Teindside Border...117 N9	The Marsh Powys...56 E5	Thorns Suffk...63 M9	Throughgate D & G...109 J4	Tilstone Bank Ches W...69 Q3
Telford Wrekin...57 M3	Themelthorpe Norfk...76 F7	Thornsett Derbys...83 M7	Throwleigh Devon...8 G6	Tilstone Fearnall Ches W...69 Q2
Telford Services Shrops...57 N3	The Middles Dur...113 K10	Thorns Green Ches E...82 G8	Throwley Kent...38 G10	Tilsworth C Beds...49 Q10
Telham E Susx...26 C9	The Moor Kent...26 C6	Thornthwaite Cumb...100 H5	Throwley Forstal Kent...38 G11	Tilton on the Hill Leics...73 J9
Tellisford Somset...20 F3	The Mumbles Swans...28 H7	Thornthwaite N York...97 J9	Thrumpton Notts...72 E4	Tiltups End Gloucs...32 F5
Telscombe E Susx...25 K10	The Murray S Lans...125 Q7	Thornton Angus...142 F8	Thrumpton Notts...85 M4	Tilty Essex...51 N5
Telscombe Cliffs E Susx...25 K10	The Mythe Gloucs...46 G8	Thornton Bucks...49 K7	Thrunscoe NE Lin...93 P9	Timberland Lincs...86 F9
Tempar P & K...140 G6	The Narth Mons...31 P3	Thornton C Brad...90 D4	Thrunton Nthumb...119 L8	Timbersbrook Ches E...70 F2
Templand D & G...109 N3	The Neuk Abers...151 J8	Thornton E R Yk...98 F11	Thrup Oxon...33 Q5	Timberscombe Somset...18 C6
Temple Cnwll...5 J7	Thenford Nhants...48 F6	Thornton Fife...134 H8	Thrupp Gloucs...32 G4	Timble N York...97 J10
Temple Mdloth...127 Q6	Theobald's Green Wilts...33 K11	Thornton Lancs...88 C2	Thrupp Oxon...48 E11	Timewell Devon...18 C9
Temple Balsall Solhll...59 K9	The Quarry Gloucs...32 D5	Thornton Leics...72 D9	Thrushelton Devon...8 B7	Timpanheck D & G...110 F6
Temple Bar Cerdgn...43 K4	The Quarter Kent...26 E3	Thornton Lincs...86 H7	Thrussington Leics...72 H7	Timperley Traffd...82 G7
Temple Cloud BaNES...20 B3	The Reddings Gloucs...46 H10	Thornton Middsb...104 E8	Thruxton Hants...21 Q5	Timsbury BaNES...20 C3
Templecombe Somset...20 D10	Therfield Herts...50 H4	Thornton Nthumb...129 P10	Thruxton Herefs...45 N8	Timsbury Hants...22 B10
Temple End Suffk...63 L10	The Rhôs Powys...44 H8	Thornton Pembks...40 H9	Thrybergh Rothm...91 M11	Timsgarry W Isls...168 f4
Temple Ewell Kent...27 N3	The Ross P & K...133 M3	Thornton Sefton...81 L4	Thulston Derbys...72 C4	Timsgearraidh W Isls...168 f4
Temple Grafton Warwks...47 M3	The Sands Surrey...23 N5	Thornton Curtis N Linc...93 J7	Thundersley Essex...38 C4	Timworth Suffk...64 B8
Temple Guiting Gloucs...47 L9	The Shoe Wilts...32 F10	Thorntonhall S Lans...125 P6	Thurcaston Leics...72 F8	Timworth Green Suffk...64 B8
Temple Herdewyke Warwks...48 C4	The Smithies Shrops...57 M5	Thornton Heath Gt Lon...36 H7	Thurcroft Rothm...84 G3	Tincleton Dorset...12 C6
Temple Hirst N York...91 Q6	The Spring Warwks...59 L10	Thornton Hough Wirral...81 L8	Thurdon Cnwll...16 D9	Tindale Cumb...111 M9
Temple Normanton Derbys...84 F7	The Square Torfn...31 J5	Thornton-in-Craven N York...96 D11	Thurgarton Norfk...76 H5	Tingewick Bucks...49 J8
Temple of Fiddes Abers...151 L11	The Stair Kent...37 P11	Thornton in Lonsdale N York...95 P6	Thurgarton Notts...85 L11	Tingley Leeds...90 H5
Temple Sowerby Cumb...102 B5	The Stocks Kent...26 F6	Thornton-le-Beans N York...97 N2	Thurgoland Barns...90 H10	Tingrith C Beds...50 B4
Templeton Devon...9 L2	The Straits Hants...23 L7	Thornton-le-Clay N York...98 D7	Thurlaston Leics...72 E11	Tingwall Airport Shet...169 r9
Templeton Pembks...41 M8	The Strand Wilts...20 H3	Thornton-le-Dale N York...98 G4	Thurlaston Warwks...59 Q10	Tingwell Ork...169 d4
Templetown Dur...112 H10	Thetford Norfk...64 B5	Thornton le Moor Lincs...92 H11	Thurlbear Somset...19 J10	Tinhay Devon...5 P4
Tempsford C Beds...61 Q10	Thetford Forest Park...63 P3	Thornton-le-Moor N York...97 N3	Thurlby Lincs...74 A7	Tinker's Hill Hants...22 D5
Tenbury Wells Worcs...57 K11	Thethwaite Cumb...101 L2	Thornton-le-Moors Ches W...81 N10	Thurlby Lincs...86 B8	Tinkersley Derbys...84 C8
Tenby Pembks...41 M10	The Towans Cnwll...2 F5	Thornton-le-Street N York...97 P3	Thurlby Lincs...87 N5	Tinsley Sheff...84 F2
Tendring Essex...53 K7	The Vauld Herefs...45 Q5	Thorntonloch E Loth...129 K5	Thurleigh Bed...61 N9	Tinsley Green W Susx...24 G3
Tendring Green Essex...53 K6	The Wyke Shrops...57 N3	Thornton Rust N York...96 E3	Thurlestone Devon...6 H10	Tintagel Cnwll...4 H4
Tendring Heath Essex...53 K6	Theydon Bois Essex...51 K11	Thornton Steward N York...97 J3	Thurloxton Somset...19 J8	Tintern Mons...31 P4
Ten Mile Bank Norfk...75 L11	Theydon Mount Essex...51 L11	Thornton Watlass N York...97 K3	Thurlstone Barns...90 G10	Tintinhull Somset...19 N11
Tenpenny Heath Essex...53 J7	Thicket Priory N York...92 A2	Thornwood Common Essex...51 L10	Thurlton Norfk...65 N2	Tintwistle Derbys...83 M5
Tenterden Kent...26 E5	Thickwood Wilts...32 F10	Thornydykes Border...128 G10	Thurlwood Ches E...70 E3	Tinwald D & G...109 M4
Terling Essex...52 C8	Thimbleby Lincs...86 H6	Thornythwaite Cumb...101 L6	Thurmaston Leics...72 G9	Tinwell Rutlnd...73 Q9
Tern Wrekin...69 R11	Thimbleby N York...104 D11	Thoroton Notts...73 K2	Thurnby Leics...72 G10	Tippacott Devon...17 P2
Ternhill Shrops...70 A8		Thorp Arch Leeds...97 P11	Thurne Norfk...77 N8	Tiptoe Hants...13 M5
Terregles D & G...109 K5		Thorpe Derbys...71 M4	Thurnham Kent...38 D10	Tipton Sandw...58 E6
Terrington N York...98 D6		Thorpe E R Yk...99 K11	Thurning Nhants...61 N4	Tipton Green Sandw...58 E6
		Thorpe Lincs...87 N4		

Tipton St John – Tullynessle 297

Tipton St John Devon 10 B6
Tiptree Essex 52 E8
Tiptree Heath Essex 52 E8
Tirabad Powys 44 B6
Tircoed Swans 28 H4
Tiree Ag & B 136 C7
Tiree Airport Ag & B 136 C7
Tiretigan Ag & B 123 M7
Tirley Gloucs 46 F9
Tiroran Ag & B 137 M10
Tirphil Caerph 30 F4
Tirril Cumb 101 P5
Tir-y-fron Flints 69 J3
Tisbury Wilts 20 H9
Tisman's Common W Susx 24 C4
Tissington Derbys 71 M4
Titchberry Devon 16 C6
Titchfield Hants 14 F5
Titchfield Common Hants 14 F5
Titchmarsh Nhants 61 M5
Titchwell Norfk 75 Q2
Tithby Notts 72 H3
Titley Herefs 45 L2
Titmore Green Herts 50 F5
Titsey Surrey 37 K10
Titson Cnwll 16 C11
Tittensor Staffs 70 F7
Tittleshall Norfk 76 B7
Titton Worcs 58 B11
Tiverton Ches W 69 Q2
Tiverton Devon 9 N2
Tivetshall St Margaret Norfk 64 H4
Tivetshall St Mary Norfk 64 H4
Tivington Somset 18 B5
Tivy Dale Barns 90 H9
Tixall Staffs 70 H10
Tixover Rutlnd 73 P10
Toab Shet 169 q12
Toadhole Derbys 84 E9
Toadmoor Derbys 84 D10
Tobermory Ag & B 137 N4
Toberonochy Ag & B 130 E6
Tobha Mòr W Isls 168 c14
Tocher Abers 158 G11
Tochieneal Moray 158 D4
Tockenham Wilts 33 K9
Tockenham Wick Wilts 33 K8
Tocketts R & Cl 104 H7
Tockholes Bl w D 89 K6
Tockington S Glos 32 B7
Tockwith N York 97 Q10
Todber Dorset 20 E11
Todburn Nthumb 119 M11
Toddington C Beds 50 B5
Toddington Gloucs 47 K8
Toddington Services C Beds 50 B5
Todds Green Herts 50 F5
Todenham Gloucs 47 P7
Todhills Angus 142 G10
Todhills Cumb 110 G8
Todhills Dur 103 P4
Todhills Rest Area Cumb 110 G8
Todmorden Calder 89 Q6
Todwick Rothm 84 G4
Toft Cambs 62 E9
Toft Ches E 82 G9
Toft Lincs 73 R7
Toft Shet 169 r6
Toft Warwks 59 Q10
Toft Hill Dur 103 N5
Toft Hill Lincs 86 H8
Toft Monks Norfk 65 N3
Toft next Newton Lincs 86 D3
Toftrees Norfk 76 B6
Toftwood Norfk 76 D9
Togston Nthumb 119 P10
Tokavaig Highld 145 K5
Tokers Green Oxon 35 K9
Tolastadh bho Thuath W Isls 168 k3
Toldish Cnwll 4 E10
Tolland Somset 18 F8
Tollard Farnham Dorset 21 J11
Tollard Royal Wilts 20 H11
Toll Bar Donc 91 P9
Tollbar End Covtry 59 N9
Toller Fratrum Dorset 11 M5
Toller Porcorum Dorset 11 M5
Tollerton N York 97 R8
Tollerton Notts 72 G4
Toller Whelme Dorset 11 L4
Tollesbury Essex 52 G9
Tolleshunt D'Arcy Essex 52 F9
Tolleshunt Knights Essex 52 F9
Tolleshunt Major Essex 52 F9
Tollingham E R Yk 92 D3
Toll of Birness Abers 159 P11
Tolpuddle Dorset 12 C6
Tolworth Gt Lon 36 E7
Tomatin Highld 148 E2
Tomchrasky Highld 146 H5
Tomdoun Highld 146 F7
Tomich Highld 147 J2
Tomich Highld 155 P8
Tomich Highld 156 B3
Tomich Highld 162 E5
Tomintoul Moray 149 M4
Tomlow Warwks 48 E2
Tomnacross Highld 155 P9
Tomnavoulin Moray 149 N2
Tompkin Staffs 70 G4
Ton Mons 31 K4
Ton Mons 31 L5
Tonbridge Kent 37 N11
Tondu Brdgnd 29 N8
Tonedale Somset 18 F10
Tonfanau Gwynd 54 D4
Tong C Brad 90 G4
Tong Kent 38 G10
Tong Shrops 57 P3
Tong W Isls 168 j4
Tonge Leics 72 C6
Tong Green Kent 38 G11
Tongham Surrey 23 N5
Tongland D & G 108 E10
Tong Norton Shrops 57 P3
Tongue Highld 165 N5
Tongue End Lincs 74 C7
Tongwynlais Cardif 30 F8
Tonmawr Neath 29 M5
Tonna Neath 29 L5
Ton-teg Rhondd 30 E7
Tonwell Herts 50 H7
Tonypandy Rhondd 30 C6
Tonyrefail Rhondd 30 D7
Toot Baldon Oxon 34 G4
Toot Hill Essex 51 M10
Toothill Hants 22 C11
Toothill Swindn 33 M8
Tooting Gt Lon 36 G6
Tooting Bec Gt Lon 36 G6
Topcliffe N York 97 N5
Topcroft Norfk 65 K3
Topcroft Street Norfk 65 K3
Top End Bed 61 M8
Topham Donc 91 Q7
Top of Hebers Rochdl 89 P9
Toppesfield Essex 52 B4
Toprow Norfk 64 H2
Topsham Devon 9 N7
Top-y-rhos Flints 69 J3
Torbeg N Ayrs 120 G6
Torboll Highld 162 H7
Torbreck Highld 156 A9
Torbryan Devon 7 L5
Torcastle Highld 139 L2
Torcross Devon 7 L10
Tore Highld 155 R7
Torfrey Cnwll 5 J11
Torinturk Ag & B 123 P7
Torksey Lincs 85 P5
Torlundy Highld 139 L2
Tormarton S Glos 32 E9
Tormore N Ayrs 120 G5
Tornagrain Highld 156 D7
Tornaveen Abers 150 G6
Torness Highld 147 P2
Toronto Dur 103 N4
Torpenhow Cumb 100 H3
Torphichen W Loth 126 H3
Torphins Abers 150 G7
Torpoint Cnwll 6 C7
Torquay Torbay 7 N6
Torquhan Border 128 C10
Torr Devon 6 F8
Torran Highld 153 K8
Torrance E Duns 125 Q3
Torranyard N Ayrs 125 K9
Torre Somset 18 D7
Torridon Highld 154 B6
Torridon House Highld 153 R6
Torrin Highld 145 J3
Torrisdale Ag & B 120 E4
Torrisdale Highld 165 Q4
Torrish Highld 163 M3
Torrisholme Lancs 95 K8
Torrobull Highld 162 D6
Torry C Aber 151 N6
Torryburn Fife 134 C10
Torteval Guern 10 a2
Torthorwald D & G 109 M5
Tortington W Susx 24 B9
Torton Worcs 58 B10
Tortworth S Glos 32 D6
Torvaig Highld 152 H9
Torver Cumb 94 F2
Torwood Falk 133 N11
Torwoodlee Border 117 P3
Torworth Notts 85 L3
Tosberry Devon 16 D7
Toscaig Highld 153 N10
Toseland Cambs 62 B8
Tosside Lancs 95 R9
Tostock Suffk 64 D9
Totaig Highld 152 C7
Tote Highld 152 G8
Tote Highld 153 J5
Tote Hill W Susx 23 N10
Totford Hants 22 G7
Tothill Lincs 87 M4
Totland IoW 13 P7
Totley Sheff 84 D5
Totley Brook Sheff 84 D4
Totnes Devon 7 L6
Toton Notts 72 E4
Totronald Ag & B 136 F4
Totscore Highld 152 F4
Tottenham Gt Lon 36 H2
Tottenhill Norfk 75 M8
Totteridge Gt Lon 36 F2
Totternhoe C Beds 49 Q10
Tottington Bury 89 M8
Tottleworth Lancs 89 L4
Totton Hants 14 C4
Touchen End W & M 35 N9
Toulston N York 91 M2
Toulton Somset 18 G8
Toulvaddie Highld 163 K10
Tovil Kent 38 C11
Towan Cnwll 3 Q4
Towan Cnwll 4 D7
Toward Ag & B 124 E4
Toward Quay Ag & B 124 E4
Towcester Nhants 49 J5
Towednack Cnwll 2 D6
Tower of London Gt Lon 36 H4
Towersey Oxon 35 K3
Towie Abers 150 C5
Tow Law Dur 103 M3
Town End Cambs 74 H11
Town End Cumb 95 J4
Town End Cumb 101 K9
Town End Cumb 102 B5
Townend W Duns 125 K2
Towngate Cumb 111 K11
Towngate Lincs 74 B8
Town Green Lancs 88 E9
Town Green Norfk 77 M9
Townhead Barns 83 Q4
Townhead Cumb 100 E3
Town Head Cumb 101 M10
Townhead Cumb 102 B4
Townhead D & G 109 M3
Town Head N York 96 B9
Townhead of Greenlaw D & G 108 F8
Townhill Fife 134 E10
Town Kelloe Dur 104 C3
Townlake Devon 5 Q7
Town Lane Wigan 82 E5
Town Littleworth E Susx 25 K7
Town of Lowton Wigan 82 D5
Town Row E Susx 25 N4
Towns End Hants 22 G3
Townsend Somset 10 H2
Townshend Cnwll 2 F7
Town Street Suffk 63 N3
Townwell S Glos 32 D6
Town Yetholm Border 118 F5
Towthorpe C York 98 C9
Towthorpe E R Yk 98 H8
Towton N York 91 M3
Towyn Conwy 80 D9
Toxteth Lpool 81 M7
Toynton All Saints Lincs 87 L8
Toynton Fen Side Lincs 87 L8
Toynton St Peter Lincs 87 M8
Toy's Hill Kent 37 L10
Trabboch E Ayrs 114 H3
Trabbochburn E Ayrs 115 J3
Traboe Cnwll 3 J9
Tracebridge Somset 18 E10
Tradespark Highld 156 F6
Trafford Park Traffd 82 G5
Trallong Powys 44 D9
Tranent E Loth 128 C5
Tranmere Wirral 81 L7
Trantelbeg Highld 166 E6
Trantlemore Highld 166 E6
Tranwell Nthumb 113 J4
Trap Carmth 43 N11
Traprain E Loth 128 F4
Trap's Green Warwks 58 H11
Trapshill W Berk 22 C2
Traquair Border 117 L4
Trash Green W Berk 35 J11
Trawden Lancs 89 Q3
Trawscoed Cerdgn 54 F10
Trawsfynydd Gwynd 67 N7
Trealaw Rhondd 30 D6
Treales Lancs 88 E4
Trearddur Bay IoA 78 D9
Treator Cnwll 4 E6
Tre Aubrey V Glam 30 D10
Trebanog Rhondd 30 D6
Trebanos Neath 29 K4
Trebartha Cnwll 5 M6
Trebarwith Cnwll 4 H4
Trebeath Cnwll 5 M4
Trebetherick Cnwll 4 E6
Treborough Somset 18 D7
Trebudannon Cnwll 4 D9
Trebullett Cnwll 5 N6
Treburgett Cnwll 4 H6
Treburley Cnwll 5 P6
Treburrick Cnwll 4 D7
Trebyan Cnwll 4 H9
Trecastle Powys 44 B9
Trecogo Cnwll 5 N5
Trecott Devon 8 F4
Trecwn Pembks 41 J4
Trecynon Rhondd 30 C4
Tredaule Cnwll 5 L5
Tredavoe Cnwll 2 D8
Tredegar Blae G 30 F3
Tredethy Cnwll 4 H7
Tredington Gloucs 46 H9
Tredington Warwks 47 Q6
Tredinnick Cnwll 4 E7
Tredinnick Cnwll 4 G10
Tredinnick Cnwll 5 K8
Tredinnick Cnwll 5 L10
Tredinnick Cnwll 5 M10
Tredomen Powys 44 G8
Tredrizzick Cnwll 4 F6
Tredunnock Mons 31 L6
Tredustan Powys 44 G8
Treen Cnwll 2 B9
Treen Cnwll 2 C6
Treesmill Cnwll 4 H10
Treeton Rothm 84 F3
Trefasser Pembks 40 G3
Trefdraeth IoA 78 G10
Trefecca Powys 44 G8
Trefechan Myr Td 30 D3
Trefeglwys Powys 55 M6
Trefenter Cerdgn 54 E11
Treffgarne Pembks 41 J6
Treffgarne Owen Pembks 40 G5
Treffynnon Pembks 40 G5
Trefil Blae G 30 F2
Trefilan Cerdgn 43 K3
Trefin Pembks 40 F4
Treflach Shrops 69 J9
Trefnannau Powys 68 H11
Trefnant Denbgs 80 F10
Trefonen Shrops 69 J9
Trefor Gwynd 66 F5
Trefor IoA 78 F8
Treforest Rhondd 30 E7
Trefrew Cnwll 5 J5
Trefriw Conwy 67 P2
Tregadillett Cnwll 5 M5
Tre-gagle Mons 31 P3
Tregaian IoA 78 H8
Tregare Mons 31 M2
Tregarne Cnwll 3 K9
Tregaron Cerdgn 43 N3
Tregarth Gwynd 79 L11
Tregaswith Cnwll 4 D9
Tregatta Cnwll 4 H4
Tregawne Cnwll 4 G8
Tregeare Cnwll 5 L4
Tregeiriog Wrexhm 68 G8
Tregele IoA 78 F6
Tregellist Cnwll 4 G6
Tregenna Cnwll 3 M5
Tregeseal Cnwll 2 B7
Tregew Cnwll 3 L7
Tre-Gibbon Rhondd 30 C3
Tregidden Cnwll 3 K9
Tregiskey Cnwll 3 Q4
Treglemais Pembks 40 F5
Tregole Cnwll 5 K2
Tregolls Cnwll 3 J6
Tregonce Cnwll 4 E7
Tregonetha Cnwll 4 F9
Tregonning & Gwinear Mining District Cnwll 2 F7
Tregony Cnwll 3 N5
Tregoodwell Cnwll 5 J5
Tregorrick Cnwll 3 Q3
Tregoss Cnwll 4 F9
Tregoyd Powys 44 H7
Tregrehan Mills Cnwll 3 Q3
Tre-groes Cerdgn 42 H6
Tregullon Cnwll 4 H9
Tregunna Cnwll 4 F7
Tregunnon Cnwll 5 L5
Tregurrian Cnwll 4 D8
Tregynon Powys 55 P5
Tre-gynwr Carmth 42 H11
Trehafod Rhondd 30 D6
Trehan Cnwll 5 Q10
Treharris Myr Td 30 E5
Treharrock Cnwll 4 G6
Trehemborne Cnwll 4 D7
Treherbert Carmth 43 L5
Treherbert Rhondd 29 P5
Trehunist Cnwll 5 N9
Trekenner Cnwll 5 N6
Treknow Cnwll 4 H4
Trelan Cnwll 3 J10
Trelash Cnwll 5 K3
Trelassick Cnwll 3 M3
Trelawne Cnwll 5 L11
Trelawnyd Flints 80 F9
Treleague Cnwll 3 K9
Treleaver Cnwll 3 K10
Trelech Carmth 41 Q4
Trelech a'r Betws Carmth 42 F9
Treleddyd-fawr Pembks 40 E5
Trelew Cnwll 3 L6
Trelewis Myr Td 30 F5
Treligga Cnwll 4 G5
Trelights Cnwll 4 F6
Trelill Cnwll 4 G6
Trelinnoe Cnwll 5 N5
Trelion Cnwll 3 N3
Trelissick Cnwll 3 L6
Trellech Mons 31 P3
Trelleck Grange Mons 31 N4
Trelogan Flints 80 G8
Trelow Cnwll 4 E8
Trelowarren Cnwll 3 J9
Trelowia Cnwll 5 M10
Treluggan Cnwll 3 M6
Trelystan Powys 56 D4
Tremadog Gwynd 67 K7
Tremail Cnwll 5 K4
Tremain Cerdgn 42 D5
Tremaine Cnwll 5 L4
Tremar Cnwll 5 M8
Trematon Cnwll 5 P10
Trembraze Cnwll 5 M8
Tremeirchion Denbgs 80 F10
Tremethick Cross Cnwll 2 C7
Tremore Cnwll 4 G9
Tre-Mostyn Flints 80 G9
Trenance Cnwll 3 L9
Trenance Cnwll 4 D8
Trenance Cnwll 4 E7
Trenarren Cnwll 3 Q4
Trench Wrekin 57 M2
Trench Green Oxon 35 J9
Trendeal Cnwll 3 M3
Trendrine Cnwll 2 D6
Treneague Cnwll 4 F7
Trenear Cnwll 2 H7
Treneglos Cnwll 5 L4
Trenerth Cnwll 2 G6
Trenewan Cnwll 5 K11
Trenewth Cnwll 4 H6
Trengune Cnwll 5 K3
Treninnick Cnwll 4 C9
Trenowah Cnwll 4 B10
Trenoweth Cnwll 3 K7
Trent Dorset 19 Q11
Trentham C Stke 70 F6
Trentishoe Devon 17 L2
Trentlock Derbys 72 D4
Trent Port Lincs 85 P4
Trent Vale C Stke 70 F6
Trenwheal Cnwll 2 G7
Treoes V Glam 29 P9
Treorchy Rhondd 30 C5
Trequite Cnwll 4 G6
Tre'r-ddol Cerdgn 54 F6
Trerhyngyll V Glam 30 D9
Trerulefoot Cnwll 5 N10
Tresaith Cerdgn 42 E4
Tresawle Cnwll 3 M4
Tresco IoS 2 b2
Trescott Staffs 58 C5
Trescowe Cnwll 2 F7
Tresean Cnwll 4 B10
Tresham Gloucs 32 E6
Treshnish Isles Ag & B 136 G7
Tresillian Cnwll 3 M4
Tresinney Cnwll 5 J5
Treskinnick Cross Cnwll 5 L2
Tresmeer Cnwll 5 L4
Tresparrett Cnwll 5 J3
Tressait P & K 141 K5
Tresta Shet 169 q8
Tresta Shet 169 t4
Treswell Notts 85 N5
Treswithian Cnwll 2 G5
Tre Taliesin Cerdgn 54 F6
Trethevey Cnwll 4 H4
Trethewey Cnwll 2 B9
Trethomas Caerph 30 G7
Trethosa Cnwll 3 N3
Trethurgy Cnwll 4 G10
Tretio Pembks 40 E5
Tretire Herefs 45 Q10
Tretower Powys 44 H10
Treuddyn Flints 69 J3
Trevadlock Cnwll 5 M6
Trevalga Cnwll 4 H3
Trevalyn Wrexhm 69 L3
Trevanger Cnwll 4 F6
Trevanson Cnwll 4 F7
Trevarrack Cnwll 2 D7
Trevarren Cnwll 4 E9
Trevarrian Cnwll 4 D8
Trevarrick Cnwll 3 P5
Trevarth Cnwll 3 J5
Trevaughan Carmth 41 P7
Tre-vaughan Carmth 42 G10
Treveal Cnwll 2 D5
Treveal Cnwll 4 B10
Treveighan Cnwll 4 H6
Trevellas Downs Cnwll 3 J3
Trevelmond Cnwll 5 L9
Trevemper Cnwll 4 C10
Treveor Cnwll 3 P5
Treverbyn Cnwll 3 M4
Treverbyn Cnwll 4 G10
Treverva Cnwll 3 K7
Trevescan Cnwll 2 B9
Trevethin Torfn 31 J4
Trevia Cnwll 4 H5
Trevigro Cnwll 5 N8
Trevilla Cnwll 3 L6
Trevilson Cnwll 4 C10
Treviscoe Cnwll 4 E10
Treviskey Cnwll 3 N5
Trevithick Cnwll 3 P4
Trevithick Cnwll 4 D9
Trevoll Cnwll 4 C10
Trevone Cnwll 4 D6
Trevor Wrexhm 69 J6
Trevorgans Cnwll 2 C8
Trevorrick Cnwll 4 E7
Trevose Cnwll 4 D6
Trew Cnwll 2 G8
Trewalder Cnwll 4 H5
Trewalkin Powys 44 H8
Trewarmett Cnwll 4 H4
Trewassa Cnwll 5 J4
Trewavas Cnwll 2 F8
Trewavas Mining District Cnwll 2 F8
Treween Cnwll 5 L5
Trewellard Cnwll 2 B7
Trewen Cnwll 5 M5
Trewennack Cnwll 2 H8
Trewent Pembks 41 K11
Trewern Powys 56 D2
Trewetha Cnwll 4 G5
Trewethern Cnwll 4 G6
Trewidland Cnwll 5 M10
Trewillis Cnwll 3 K10
Trewint Cnwll 5 L5
Trewint Cnwll 5 M9
Trewithian Cnwll 3 M6
Trewoodloe Cnwll 5 N7
Trewoon Cnwll 2 H10
Trewoon Cnwll 3 P3
Treworga Cnwll 3 M5
Treworgan Cnwll 3 L4
Treworlas Cnwll 3 M6
Treworld Cnwll 5 J3
Treworthal Cnwll 3 M6
Tre-wyn Mons 45 L10
Treyarnon Cnwll 4 D7
Treyford W Susx 23 M11
Trickett's Cross Dorset 13 J4
Triermain Cumb 111 L7
Triffleton Pembks 41 J6
Trillacott Cnwll 5 M4
Trimdon Dur 104 C4
Trimdon Colliery Dur 104 C3
Trimdon Grange Dur 104 C3
Trimingham Norfk 77 K4
Trimley Lower Street Suffk 53 N4
Trimley St Martin Suffk 53 N4
Trimley St Mary Suffk 53 N4
Trimpley Worcs 57 P9
Trimsaran Carmth 28 E4
Trims Green Herts 51 L7
Trimstone Devon 17 J3
Trinafour P & K 140 H5
Trinant Caerph 30 H5
Tring Herts 35 P2
Tringford Herts 35 P2
Tring Wharf Herts 35 P2
Trinity Angus 143 L5
Trinity Jersey 11 b1
Trinity Gask P & K 134 B4
Triscombe Somset 18 G7
Trislaig Highld 139 K3
Trispen Cnwll 3 L3
Tritlington Nthumb 113 K2
Troan Cnwll 4 D10
Trochry P & K 141 N9
Troedrhiwfuwch Caerph 30 F4
Troedyraur Cerdgn 42 F5
Troedyrhiw Myr Td 30 E4
Trofarth Conwy 80 B10
Trois Bois Jersey 11 b1
Troon Cnwll 2 H6
Troon S Ayrs 125 J11
Tropical World Roundhay Park Leeds 91 J3
Trossachs Stirlg 132 G6
Trossachs Pier Stirlg 132 F6
Troston Suffk 64 B7
Troswell Cnwll 5 M3
Trotshill Worcs 46 G3
Trottiscliffe Kent 37 P8
Trotton W Susx 23 M10
Troughend Nthumb 112 C2
Trough Gate Lancs 89 P6
Troutbeck Cumb 101 L5
Troutbeck Cumb 101 M10
Troutbeck Bridge Cumb 101 M10
Troway Derbys 84 E5
Trowbridge Wilts 20 G3
Trowell Notts 72 D3
Trowell Services Notts 72 D2
Trowle Common Wilts 20 F3
Trowley Bottom Herts 50 C8
Trowse Newton Norfk 77 J10
Troy Leeds 90 G3
Trudoxhill Somset 20 D6
Trull Somset 18 H10
Trumfleet Donc 91 Q8
Trumpan Highld 152 C5
Trumpet Herefs 46 C7
Trumpington Cambs 62 F10
Trumpsgreen Surrey 35 Q11
Trunch Norfk 77 K5
Trunnah Lancs 88 C2
Truro Cnwll 3 L5
Truscott Cnwll 5 M4
Trusham Devon 9 L8
Trusley Derbys 71 P7
Trusthorpe Lincs 87 P4
Trysull Staffs 58 C6
Tubney Oxon 34 D5
Tuckenhay Devon 7 L7
Tuckhill Shrops 57 P7
Tuckingmill Cnwll 2 H5
Tuckingmill Wilts 20 H9
Tuckton BCP 13 K6
Tucoyse Cnwll 3 P4
Tuddenham Suffk 53 L2
Tuddenham Suffk 63 M6
Tudeley Kent 37 P11
Tudhoe Dur 103 Q3
Tudorville Herefs 46 A10
Tudweiliog Gwynd 66 C7
Tuesley Surrey 23 Q6
Tuffley Gloucs 32 F2
Tufton Hants 22 E5
Tufton Pembks 41 K5
Tugby Leics 73 K10
Tugford Shrops 57 K7
Tughall Nthumb 119 P5
Tullibody Clacks 133 P8
Tullich Abers 150 B8
Tullich Highld 147 Q2
Tullich Highld 156 F2
Tulliemet P & K 141 P7
Tulloch Abers 159 K11
Tullochgorm Ag & B 131 K8
Tulloch Station Highld 147 K11
Tullymurdoch P & K 142 B7
Tullynessle Abers 150 F4

Tulse Hill Gt Lon....36 H6
Tumble Carmth....28 F2
Tumbler's Green Essex....52 D6
Tumby Lincs....86 H9
Tumby Woodside Lincs....87 J9
Tummel Bridge P & K....141 J6
Tunbridge Wells Kent....25 N3
Tundergarth D & G....110 C4
Tunga W Isls....168 j4
Tungate Norfk....77 K6
Tunley BaNES....20 C3
Tunstall C Stke....70 F4
Tunstall E R Yk....93 P4
Tunstall Kent....38 E9
Tunstall Lancs....95 N6
Tunstall N York....103 P11
Tunstall Norfk....77 N10
Tunstall Staffs....70 D9
Tunstall Suffk....65 M10
Tunstall Sundld....113 N10
Tunstead Derbys....83 P10
Tunstead Norfk....77 K7
Tunstead Milton Derbys....83 M8
Tunworth Hants....23 J5
Tupsley Herefs....45 Q6
Turgis Green Hants....23 J3
Turkdean Gloucs....47 M11
Turleigh Wilts....20 F2
Turleygreen Shrops....57 P7
Turn Lancs....89 N7
Turnastone Herefs....45 M7
Turnberry S Ayrs....114 D6
Turnchapel C Plym....6 D8
Turnditch Derbys....71 P5
Turner Green Lancs....89 J4
Turner's Green E Susx....25 P7
Turner's Green Warwks....59 J11
Turners Hill W Susx....24 H3
Turners Puddle Dorset....12 D6
Turnford Herts....51 J10
Turnhouse C Edin....127 M3
Turnworth Dorset....12 D3
Turriff Abers....158 H7
Turton Bottoms Bl w D....89 L7
Turves Cambs....74 F11
Turvey Bed....49 P4
Turville Bucks....35 L6
Turville Heath Bucks....35 K6
Turweston Bucks....48 H7
Tushielaw Inn Border....117 L7
Tutbury Staffs....71 N9
Tutnall Worcs....58 E10
Tutshill Gloucs....31 P6
Tuttington Norfk....77 J6
Tutts Clump W Berk....34 G10
Tutwell Cnwll....5 P6
Tuxford Notts....85 M6
Twatt Ork....169 b4
Twatt Shet....169 q8
Twechar E Duns....126 B2
Tweedbank Border....117 Q4
Tweedmouth Nthumb....129 P9
Tweedsmuir Border....116 G6
Twelveheads Cnwll....3 K5
Twelve Oaks E Susx....25 Q6
Twemlow Green Ches E....82 G11
Twenty Lincs....74 C6
Twerton BaNES....20 D2
Twickenham Gt Lon....36 E6
Twigworth Gloucs....46 F10
Twineham W Susx....24 G7
Twineham Green W Susx....24 G6
Twinhoe BaNES....20 E3
Twinstead Essex....52 E4
Twitchen Devon....17 P5
Twitchen Shrops....56 F9
Twitham Kent....39 N10
Two Bridges Devon....6 G4
Two Dales Derbys....84 C8
Two Gates Staffs....59 K4
Two Mile Ash W Susx....24 D5
Two Mile Oak Cross Devon....7 J3
Two Pots Devon....17 J3
Two Waters Herts....50 C9
Twycross Leics....72 A10
Twycross Zoo Leics....59 M3
Twyford Bucks....49 J9
Twyford Hants....22 E10
Twyford Leics....73 J8
Twyford Lincs....73 N6
Twyford Norfk....76 E7
Twyford Wokham....35 L9
Twyford Common Herefs....45 Q7
Twyn-carno Caerph....30 F3
Twynholm D & G....108 E10
Twyning Green Gloucs....46 H7
Twynllanan Carmth....43 Q10
Twyn-yr-Odyn V Glam....30 F10
Twyn-y-Sheriff Mons....31 M3
Twywell Nhants....61 L5
Tyberton Herefs....45 M7
Tyburn Birm....58 H6
Tycroes Carmth....28 H2
Ty Croes IoA....78 E10
Tycrwyn Powys....68 F11
Tydd Gote Lincs....75 J7
Tydd St Giles Cambs....74 H7
Tydd St Mary Lincs....74 H7
Tye Hants....15 K6
Tye Green Essex....51 M6
Tye Green Essex....51 N3
Tye Green Essex....52 C7
Tyersal C Brad....90 F4
Tyldesley Wigan....82 E4
Tyler Hill Kent....39 K9
Tylers Green Bucks....35 P6
Tyler's Green Essex....51 M9
Tylers Green Surrey....37 J10
Tylorstown Rhondd....30 D5
Tylwch Powys....55 M8
Ty-nant Conwy....68 C6
Ty-nant Gwynd....68 B9
Tyncelyn Cerdgn....43 M2
Tyndrum Stirlg....139 Q11
Ty'n-dwr Denbgs....68 H6
Tyneham Dorset....12 E8
Tynemouth N Tyne....113 N7
Tyne Tunnel S Tyne....113 M7
Tynewydd Rhondd....29 P5
Tyninghame E Loth....128 G4
Tynron D & G....115 R9
Ty'n-y-bryn Rhondd....30 D7
Ty'n-y-coedcae Caerph....30 G7
Tynygongl IoA....79 J8
Tynygraig Cerdgn....54 F11

Ty'n-y-Groes Conwy....79 P10
Tyn-y-nant Rhondd....30 E7
Tyrie Abers....159 M5
Tyringham M Keyn....49 N5
Tyseley Birm....58 H8
Tythegston Brdgnd....29 N9
Tytherington Ches E....83 K9
Tytherington S Glos....32 C7
Tytherington Somset....20 E6
Tytherington Wilts....20 H6
Tytherleigh Devon....10 G4
Tytherton Lucas Wilts....32 H10
Tyttenhanger Herts....50 E9
Tywardreath Cnwll....4 H11
Tywardreath Highway Cnwll....4 H10
Tywyn Conwy....79 P9
Tywyn Gwynd....54 D4

U

Ubbeston Green Suffk....65 L7
Ubley BaNES....19 P3
Uckerby N York....103 P10
Uckfield E Susx....25 L6
Uckinghall Worcs....46 G7
Uckington Gloucs....46 H10
Uckington Shrops....57 K2
Uddingston S Lans....126 B5
Uddington S Lans....116 B4
Udimore E Susx....26 E8
Udny Green Abers....151 M2
Udny Station Abers....151 N3
Uffcott Wilts....33 M9
Uffculme Devon....9 Q2
Uffington Lincs....73 R9
Uffington Oxon....34 B7
Uffington Shrops....57 J2
Ufford C Pete....74 A10
Ufford Suffk....65 K11
Ufton Warwks....48 C2
Ufton Nervet W Berk....34 H11
Ugadale Ag & B....120 E6
Ugborough Devon....6 H7
Uggeshall Suffk....65 N5
Ugglebarnby N York....105 N9
Ughill Sheff....84 C2
Ugley Essex....51 M5
Ugley Green Essex....51 M5
Ugthorpe N York....105 L8
Uibhist A Deas W Isls....168 d14
Uibhist A Tuath W Isls....168 c10
Uig Ag & B....136 F5
Uig Highld....152 B7
Uig Highld....152 F5
Uig W Isls....168 f4
Uigshader Highld....152 G8
Uisken Ag & B....137 K12
Ulbster Highld....167 P8
Ulcat Row Cumb....101 M6
Ulceby Lincs....87 M6
Ulceby N Linc....93 K8
Ulceby Skitter N Linc....93 K7
Ulcombe Kent....26 D2
Uldale Cumb....100 H3
Uley Gloucs....32 E5
Ulgham Nthumb....113 K2
Ullapool Highld....161 J8
Ullenhall Warwks....58 H11
Ullenwood Gloucs....46 H11
Ulleskelf N York....91 N3
Ullesthorpe Leics....60 B3
Ulley Rothm....84 G3
Ullingswick Herefs....46 A5
Ullinish Lodge Hotel Highld....152 E10
Ullock Cumb....100 E6
Ullswater Cumb....101 M6
Ullswater Steamers Cumb....101 L7
Ulnes Walton Lancs....88 G7
Ulpha Cumb....94 D2
Ulpha Cumb....95 K4
Ulrome E R Yk....99 P9
Ulsta Shet....169 r5
Ulting Wick Essex....52 D10
Ulva Ag & B....137 K7
Ulverley Green Solhll....58 H8
Ulverston Cumb....94 F5
Ulwell Dorset....12 H8
Ulzieside D & G....115 Q6
Umberleigh Devon....17 L7
Unapool Highld....164 F10
Underbarrow Cumb....95 K2
Under Burnmouth Border....111 J4
Undercliffe C Brad....90 F4
Underdale Shrops....57 J2
Underling Green Kent....26 C2
Underriver Kent....37 N10
Underwood Newpt....31 L7
Underwood Notts....84 G10
Undley Suffk....63 L4
Undy Mons....31 M7
Union Mills IoM....80 e6
Union Street E Susx....26 B5
Unst Shet....169 s3
Unstone Derbys....84 E5
Unstone Green Derbys....84 E5
Unthank Cumb....101 N3
Unthank Cumb....102 B2
Unthank Cumb....110 G11
Unthank Derbys....84 D5
Unthank Nthumb....129 P10
Upavon Wilts....21 M4
Up Cerne Dorset....11 P4
Upchurch Kent....38 D8
Upcott Devon....17 P6
Upcott Herefs....45 L4
Upend Cambs....63 M9
Up Exe Devon....9 M4
Upgate Norfk....76 G8
Upgate Street Norfk....64 F3
Upgate Street Norfk....65 K3
Uphall Dorset....11 M4
Uphall W Loth....127 K3
Upham Devon....9 L3
Upham Hants....22 F10
Uphampton Herefs....45 M2
Uphampton Worcs....46 F2
Uphill N Som....19 K3
Up Holland Lancs....88 G9
Uplawmoor E Rens....125 L6
Upleadon Gloucs....46 E9
Upleatham R & Cl....104 H7
Uplees Kent....38 H9
Uploders Dorset....11 L6
Uplowman Devon....18 D11

Uplyme Devon....10 G6
Up Marden W Susx....15 L4
Upminster Gt Lon....37 N3
Up Mudford Somset....19 Q11
Up Nately Hants....23 J4
Upottery Devon....10 E3
Upper Affcot Shrops....56 G7
Upper Arley Worcs....57 P8
Upper Arncott Oxon....48 H11
Upper Astrop Nhants....48 F7
Upper Badcall Highld....164 B8
Upper Basildon W Berk....34 G9
Upper Batley Kirk....90 G5
Upper Beeding W Susx....24 E8
Upper Benefield Nhants....61 L3
Upper Bentley Worcs....58 E11
Upper Bighouse Highld....166 E5
Upper Birchwood Derbys....84 F9
Upper Boat Rhondd....30 F7
Upper Boddington Nhants....48 E4
Upper Borth Cerdgn....54 E7
Upper Brailes Warwks....48 B7
Upper Breinton Herefs....45 P6
Upper Broadheath Worcs....46 F3
Upper Broughton Notts....72 H5
Upper Bucklebury W Berk....34 F11
Upper Burgate Hants....21 N11
Upper Bush Medway....37 Q7
Upperby Cumb....110 H10
Upper Caldecote C Beds....61 Q11
Upper Canada N Som....19 L3
Upper Canterton Hants....13 N2
Upper Catesby Nhants....60 B9
Upper Catshill Worcs....58 E10
Upper Chapel Powys....44 E6
Upper Cheddon Somset....18 H9
Upper Chicksgrove Wilts....21 J8
Upper Chute Wilts....21 Q4
Upper Clapton Gt Lon....36 H3
Upper Clatford Hants....22 C6
Upper Coberley Gloucs....47 J11
Upper Cotton Staffs....71 K5
Upper Cound Shrops....57 K3
Upper Cudworth Barns....91 K9
Upper Cumberworth Kirk....90 G9
Upper Dallachy Moray....157 R5
Upper Deal Kent....39 Q11
Upper Dean Bed....61 M7
Upper Denby Kirk....90 G9
Upper Denton Cumb....111 M7
Upper Dicker E Susx....25 N9
Upper Dinchope Shrops....56 H8
Upper Dounreay Highld....166 H3
Upper Dovercourt Essex....53 M5
Upper Drumbane Stirlg....133 L4
Upper Dunsforth N York....97 P8
Upper Eashing Surrey....23 Q6
Upper Eathie Highld....156 D5
Upper Egleton Herefs....46 B6
Upper Elkstone Staffs....71 K3
Upper Ellastone Staffs....71 L6
Upper End Derbys....83 N9
Upper Enham Hants....22 C4
Upper Farmcote Shrops....57 P6
Upper Farringdon Hants....23 K7
Upper Framilode Gloucs....32 E2
Upper Froyle Hants....23 L6
Upperglen Highld....152 E7
Upper Godney Somset....19 N6
Upper Gravenhurst C Beds....50 D3
Upper Green Mons....45 M11
Upper Green Suffk....63 M8
Upper Green W Berk....22 C2
Upper Grove Common Herefs....45 P9
Upper Hackney Derbys....84 C8
Upper Hale Surrey....23 M5
Upper Halliford Surrey....36 C7
Upper Halling Medway....37 Q8
Upper Hambleton Rutlnd....73 N9
Upper Hardres Court Kent....39 L11
Upper Hardwick Herefs....45 N3
Upper Hartfield E Susx....25 L4
Upper Hartshay Derbys....84 E10
Upper Hatherley Gloucs....46 H10
Upper Hatton Staffs....70 E7
Upper Haugh Rothm....91 L11
Upper Hayton Shrops....57 J8
Upper Heaton Kirk....90 F7
Upper Helmsley N York....98 D9
Upper Hergest Herefs....45 K4
Upper Heyford Nhants....60 E9
Upper Heyford Oxon....48 E9
Upper Hill Herefs....45 P4
Upper Hockenden Kent....37 M7
Upper Hopton Kirk....90 F7
Upper Howsell Worcs....46 E5
Upper Hulme Staffs....71 J2
Upper Ifold Surrey....24 B4
Upper Inglesham Swindn....33 P5
Upper Kilcott Gloucs....32 E7
Upper Killay Swans....28 G6
Upper Kinchrackine Ag & B....131 P2
Upper Knockando Moray....157 M9
Upper Lambourn W Berk....34 B8
Upper Landywood Staffs....58 E3
Upper Langford N Som....19 N3
Upper Langwith Derbys....84 G7
Upper Largo Fife....135 L7
Upper Leigh Staffs....71 J7
Upper Littleton N Som....19 Q2
Upper Lochton Abers....150 H8
Upper Longdon Staffs....58 G2
Upper Ludstone Shrops....57 Q5
Upper Lybster Highld....167 N9
Upper Lydbrook Gloucs....46 B11
Upper Lyde Herefs....45 P6
Upper Lye Herefs....56 F11
Upper Maes-coed Herefs....45 L8
Upper Marham Norfk....75 P9
Upper Midhope Sheff....90 G11
Uppermill Oldham....90 B9
Upper Milton Worcs....57 Q10
Upper Minety Wilts....33 K6
Upper Moor Worcs....47 J5
Upper Moor Side Leeds....90 G4
Upper Mulben Moray....157 R7
Upper Netchwood Shrops....57 L6
Upper Nobut Staffs....71 J7
Upper Norwood W Susx....23 P11
Upper Oddington Gloucs....47 P9
Upper Padley Derbys....84 B5
Upper Pennington Hants....13 P5
Upper Pollicott Bucks....35 K2
Upper Poppleton C York....98 B10

Upper Quinton Warwks....47 N5
Upper Ratley Hants....22 B10
Upper Rissington Gloucs....47 P11
Upper Rochford Worcs....57 L11
Upper Ruscoe D & G....108 C8
Upper Sapey Herefs....46 C2
Upper Saxondale Notts....72 H3
Upper Seagry Wilts....32 H8
Upper Shelton C Beds....49 Q6
Upper Sheringham Norfk....76 G3
Upper Skelmorlie N Ayrs....124 D3
Upper Slaughter Gloucs....47 N10
Upper Soudley Gloucs....32 C2
Upper Spond Herefs....45 L4
Upper Standen Kent....27 M3
Upper Staploe Bed....61 P9
Upper Stoke Norfk....77 K11
Upper Stondon C Beds....50 D3
Upper Stowe Nhants....60 D9
Upper Street Hants....21 N11
Upper Street Norfk....64 H6
Upper Street Norfk....77 M8
Upper Street Suffk....53 K5
Upper Street Suffk....63 N10
Upper Street Suffk....64 G11
Upper Strensham Worcs....46 G7
Upper Sundon C Beds....50 B5
Upper Swell Gloucs....47 N9
Upper Tankersley Barns....91 J11
Upper Tean Staffs....71 J7
Upperthong Kirk....90 E9
Upperthorpe Derbys....84 G4
Upperthorpe N Linc....92 C10
Upper Threapwood Ches W....69 M5
Upperton W Susx....23 Q10
Upper Town Derbys....71 N4
Uppertown Derbys....84 D8
Upper Town Dur....103 L3
Upper Town Herefs....46 A5
Upper Town Highld....167 Q1
Upper Town N Som....31 P11
Upper Town Suffk....64 C8
Upper Tumble Carmth....28 F2
Upper Tysoe Warwks....48 B6
Upper Ufford Suffk....65 K11
Upperup Gloucs....33 K5
Upper Upham Wilts....33 P9
Upper Upnor Medway....38 C7
Upper Victoria Angus....143 J10
Upper Vobster Somset....20 D5
Upper Wardington Oxon....48 E5
Upper Weald M Keyn....49 M7
Upper Weedon Nhants....60 D9
Upper Welland Worcs....46 E6
Upper Wellingham E Susx....25 K8
Upper Weston BaNES....32 D11
Upper Weybread Suffk....65 J6
Upper Wick Worcs....46 F4
Upper Wield Hants....22 H7
Upper Winchendon Bucks....35 K2
Upperwood Derbys....84 C9
Upper Woodford Wilts....21 M7
Upper Woolhampton W Berk....34 G11
Upper Wootton Hants....22 G4
Upper Wraxall Wilts....32 F10
Upper Wyche Worcs....46 E6
Uppincott Devon....9 M3
Uppingham Rutlnd....73 M11
Uppington Dorset....12 H3
Uppington Shrops....57 K3
Upsall N York....97 Q3
Upsettlington Border....129 M10
Upshire Essex....51 K10
Up Somborne Hants....22 C8
Upstreet Kent....39 M9
Up Sydling Dorset....11 N4
Upthorpe Suffk....64 D7
Upton Bucks....35 L2
Upton C Pete....74 B10
Upton Cambs....61 Q5
Upton Ches W....81 N11
Upton Cnwll....5 M7
Upton Cnwll....16 C11
Upton Cumb....101 K3
Upton Devon....7 J10
Upton Devon....10 B4
Upton Dorset....12 B8
Upton Dorset....12 G6
Upton E R Yk....99 N10
Upton Halton....81 P7
Upton Hants....22 C11
Upton Hants....22 C11
Upton Leics....72 B11
Upton Lincs....85 Q3
Upton Nhants....60 F9
Upton Norfk....77 M9
Upton Notts....85 M10
Upton Notts....85 M5
Upton Oxon....33 P2
Upton Oxon....34 F7
Upton Pembks....41 K10
Upton R & Cl....105 K7
Upton Slough....35 Q9
Upton Somset....18 C9
Upton Somset....19 N9
Upton Wakefd....91 M8
Upton Warwks....47 M3
Upton Wilts....20 G8
Upton Wirral....81 K7
Upton Bishop Herefs....46 C9
Upton Cheyney S Glos....32 C10
Upton Cressett Shrops....57 M6
Upton Crews Herefs....46 B9
Upton Cross Cnwll....5 M7
Upton End C Beds....50 D4
Upton Grey Hants....23 J5
Upton Heath Ches W....81 N11
Upton Hellions Devon....9 K4
Upton Lovell Wilts....20 H6
Upton Magna Shrops....57 K2
Upton Noble Somset....20 D7
Upton Pyne Devon....9 M5
Upton St Leonards Gloucs....46 G11
Upton Scudamore Wilts....20 G5
Upton Snodsbury Worcs....46 H4
Upton Towans Cnwll....2 F5
Upton-upon-Severn Worcs....46 G6
Upton Warren Worcs....58 D11
Upwaltham W Susx....15 P4
Upware Cambs....62 H6
Upwell Norfk....75 J10
Upwey Dorset....11 P7
Upwick Green Herts....51 L5
Upwood Cambs....62 C4

Urchfont Wilts....21 K3
Urdimarsh Herefs....45 Q5
Ure Bank N York....97 M6
Urlay Nook S on T....104 D8
Urmston Traffd....82 G6
Urpeth Dur....113 L10
Urquhart Moray....157 P5
Urquhart Castle Highld....147 N2
Urra N York....104 G10
Urray Highld....155 P7
Uryside Abers....151 K3
Usan Angus....143 N7
Ushaw Moor Dur....103 P2
Usk Mons....31 L4
Usselby Lincs....86 E2
Usworth Sundld....113 M9
Utkinton Ches W....82 B11
Utley C Brad....90 D2
Uton Devon....9 K5
Utterby Lincs....87 K2
Uttoxeter Staffs....71 K8
Uwchmynydd Gwynd....66 B9
Uxbridge Gt Lon....36 C4
Uyeasound Shet....169 s3
Uzmaston Pembks....41 J8

V

Vale Guern....10 c1
Valley IoA....78 D9
Valley End Surrey....23 Q2
Valley Truckle Cnwll....4 H5
Valtos Highld....153 J5
Valtos W Isls....168 f4
Vange Essex....38 B4
Varteg Torfn....31 J3
Vatsetter Shet....169 s5
Vatten Highld....152 D9
Vaynor Myr Td....30 D2
Vazon Bay Guern....10 b2
Veensgarth Shet....169 r9
Velindre Powys....44 H7
Vellow Somset....18 E7
Velly Devon....16 D7
Venngreen Devon....16 F9
Vennington Shrops....56 E3
Venn Ottery Devon....10 B6
Venny Tedburn Devon....9 K5
Venterdon Cnwll....5 P7
Ventnor IoW....14 G11
Venton Devon....6 F7
Vernham Dean Hants....22 B3
Vernham Street Hants....22 B3
Vernolds Common Shrops....56 H8
Verwood Dorset....13 J3
Veryan Cnwll....3 N6
Veryan Green Cnwll....3 N5
Vicarage Devon....10 E7
Vickerstown Cumb....94 D7
Victoria Barns....90 F9
Victoria Blae G....30 G3
Victoria Cnwll....4 F9
Vidlin Shet....169 r7
Viewfield Moray....157 P5
Viewpark N Lans....126 C5
Vigo Kent....37 P8
Village de Putron Guern....10 c2
Ville la Bas Jersey....11 a1
Villiaze Guern....10 b2
Vinehall Street E Susx....26 C7
Vines Cross E Susx....25 N7
Virginia Water Surrey....36 B7
Virginstow Devon....5 P3
Vobster Somset....20 D5
Voe Shet....169 r7
Vowchurch Herefs....45 M7
Vulcan Village St Hel....82 C6

W

Waberthwaite Cumb....94 C2
Wackerfield Dur....103 N6
Wacton Norfk....64 H3
Wadborough Worcs....46 H5
Waddesdon Bucks....49 K11
Waddeton Manor Bucks....49 K11
Waddeton Devon....7 M7
Waddicar Sefton....81 M5
Waddingham Lincs....92 G11
Waddington Lancs....89 L2
Waddington Lincs....86 C8
Waddon Devon....9 L9
Waddon Dorset....11 N7
Waddon Gt Lon....36 H8
Wadebridge Cnwll....4 F7
Wadeford Somset....10 G2
Wadenhoe Nhants....61 M4
Wadesmill Herts....51 J7
Wadhurst E Susx....25 P4
Wadshelf Derbys....84 D6
Wadswick Wilts....32 F11
Wadworth Donc....91 P11
Waen Denbgs....68 C2
Waen Denbgs....80 G11
Waen Powys....68 H11
Waen Fach Powys....68 H11
Waen-pentir Gwynd....79 K11
Waen-wen Gwynd....79 K11
Wagbeach Shrops....56 F4
Wainfelin Torfn....31 J4
Wainfleet All Saints Lincs....87 N9
Wainfleet Bank Lincs....87 N9
Wainfleet St Mary Lincs....87 N9
Wainford Norfk....65 L3
Wainhouse Corner Cnwll....5 K2
Wainscott Medway....38 B7
Wain's Hill N Som....31 L10
Wainstalls Calder....90 C5
Waitby Cumb....102 E9
Waithe Lincs....93 N10
Wakefield Wakefd....91 J6
Wake Green Birm....58 G8
Wakehurst Place W Susx....24 H4
Wakerley Nhants....73 P11
Wakes Colne Essex....52 E6
Walberswick Suffk....65 P7
Walberton W Susx....15 Q5
Walbottle N u Ty....113 J7
Walbutt D & G....108 F7
Walby Cumb....110 H8
Walcombe Somset....19 Q5
Walcot Lincs....73 R3

Walcot – West Derby 299

Walcot N Linc 92 E6
Walcot Shrops 56 E7
Walcot Shrops 57 K2
Walcot Swindn 33 N8
Walcote Leics 60 C4
Walcote Warwks 47 M3
Walcot Green Norfk 64 G5
Walcott Lincs 86 F9
Walcott Norfk 77 M5
Walden N York 96 F4
Walden Head N York 96 E4
Walden Stubbs N York 91 P7
Walderslade Medway 38 C9
Walderton W Susx 15 L4
Walditch Dorset 11 K6
Waldley Derbys 71 L7
Waldridge Dur 113 L11
Waldringfield Suffk 53 N2
Waldron E Susx 25 M7
Wales Rothm 84 G4
Wales Somset 19 Q10
Walesby Lincs 86 F2
Walesby Notts 85 L6
Walford Herefs 46 A10
Walford Herefs 56 F10
Walford Shrops 69 M10
Walford Staffs 70 E8
Walford Heath Shrops 69 M11
Walgherton Ches E 70 B5
Walgrave Nhants 60 H6
Walhampton Hants 13 P5
Walkden Salfd 82 F4
Walker N u Ty 113 L8
Walkerburn Border 117 M3
Walker Fold Lancs 89 K2
Walkeringham Notts 85 N2
Walkerith Lincs 85 N2
Walkern Herts 50 G5
Walker's Green Herefs 45 Q5
Walker's Heath Birm 58 G9
Walkerton Fife 134 G7
Walkford BCP 13 M6
Walkhampton Devon 6 E5
Walkington E R Yk 92 G3
Walkley Sheff 84 D3
Walk Mill Lancs 89 P5
Walkwood Worcs 47 K2
Wall Nthumb 112 D7
Wall Staffs 58 H3
Wallacetown S Ayrs 114 E7
Wallacetown S Ayrs 114 F3
Wallands Park E Susx 25 K8
Wallasey Wirral 81 K6
Wallasey (Kingsway) Tunnel Wirral 81 L6
Wall End Cumb 94 E4
Wall End Herefs 45 N3
Wallend Medway 38 E6
Waller's Green Herefs 46 C7
Wallhead Cumb 111 J8
Wall Heath Dudley 58 C7
Wall Houses Nthumb 112 F7
Wallingford Oxon 34 H7
Wallington Gt Lon 36 G8
Wallington Hants 14 G5
Wallington Herts 50 G4
Wallington Heath Wsall 58 E4
Wallis Pembks 41 K5
Wallisdown BCP 13 J6
Walliswood Surrey 24 D3
Walls Shet 169 p9
Wallsend N Tyne 113 L7
Wallthwaite Cumb 101 L5
Wall under Haywood Shrops 57 J6
Wallyford E Loth 128 B5
Walmer Kent 39 Q11
Walmer Bridge Lancs 88 F6
Walmersley Bury 89 N8
Walmestone Kent 39 N10
Walmley Birm 58 H6
Walmley Ash Birm 58 H6
Walmsgate Lincs 87 L5
Walney Cumb 94 D7
Walpole Somset 19 K6
Walpole Suffk 65 M7
Walpole Cross Keys Norfk 75 K7
Walpole Highway Norfk 75 K8
Walpole St Andrew Norfk 75 K7
Walpole St Peter Norfk 75 K7
Walrow Somset 19 K5
Walsall Wsall 58 F5
Walsall Wood Wsall 58 F4
Walsden Calder 89 Q6
Walsgrave on Sowe Covtry 59 N8
Walsham le Willows Suffk 64 E7
Walshaw Bury 89 M8
Walshford N York 97 P10
Walsoken Norfk 75 J8
Walston S Lans 127 K8
Walsworth Herts 50 E4
Walter's Ash Bucks 35 M5
Walters Green Kent 25 M2
Walterston V Glam 30 E10
Walterstone Herefs 45 L9
Waltham Kent 27 K2
Waltham NE Lin 93 N10
Waltham Abbey Essex 51 J10
Waltham Chase Hants 14 G4
Waltham Cross Herts 51 J10
Waltham on the Wolds Leics 73 L6
Waltham St Lawrence W & M 35 M9
Waltham's Cross Essex 51 Q4
Walthamstow Gt Lon 37 J3
Walton C Pete 74 C10
Walton Cumb 111 K8
Walton Derbys 84 E7
Walton Leeds 97 P11
Walton Leics 60 C3
Walton M Keyn 49 N7
Walton Powys 45 K3
Walton Shrops 56 H9
Walton Somset 19 N7
Walton Staffs 70 F8
Walton Staffs 70 F9
Walton Suffk 53 N4
Walton W Susx 15 M6
Walton Wakefd 91 K7
Walton Warwks 47 Q4
Walton Wrekin 69 Q11
Walton Cardiff Gloucs 46 H8
Walton East Pembks 41 K6
Walton Elm Dorset 20 E11
Walton Grounds Nhants 48 F8
Walton Highway Norfk 75 J8
Walton-in-Gordano N Som 31 M10
Walton-le-Dale Lancs 88 H5
Walton-on-Thames Surrey 36 D7
Walton-on-the-Hill Staffs 70 H10
Walton-on-the-Hill Surrey 36 F9
Walton-on-the-Naze Essex 53 N7
Walton on the Wolds Leics 72 F7
Walton-on-Trent Derbys 71 N11
Walton Park N Som 31 M10
Walton West Pembks 40 G8
Walwen Flints 80 G9
Walwen Flints 80 H10
Walwen Flints 81 J9
Walwick Nthumb 112 D6
Walworth Darltn 103 P7
Walworth Gt Lon 36 H5
Walworth Gate Darltn 103 P6
Walwyn's Castle Pembks 40 G8
Wambrook Somset 10 F3
Wampool Cumb 110 D10
Wanborough Surrey 23 P5
Wanborough Swindn 33 P8
Wandon End Herts 50 D6
Wandsworth Gt Lon 36 G6
Wangford Suffk 65 P6
Wanlip Leics 72 F8
Wanlockhead D & G 116 B8
Wannock E Susx 25 N10
Wansford C Pete 73 R11
Wansford E R Yk 99 M9
Wanshurst Green Kent 26 C2
Wanstead Gt Lon 37 K3
Wanstrow Somset 20 D6
Wanswell Gloucs 32 C4
Wantage Oxon 34 C7
Wants Green Worcs 46 E3
Wapley S Glos 32 D9
Wappenbury Warwks 59 N11
Wappenham Nhants 48 H5
Warbleton E Susx 25 P7
Warborough Oxon 34 G6
Warboys Cambs 62 D4
Warbreck Bpool 88 C3
Warbstow Cnwll 5 L3
Warburton Traffd 82 F7
Warcop Cumb 102 D7
Warden Kent 38 H7
Warden Nthumb 112 D7
Ward End Birm 58 H7
Warden Street C Beds 50 D2
Ward Green Suffk 64 E9
Ward Green Cross Lancs 89 J3
Wardhedges C Beds 50 C3
Wardington Oxon 48 E5
Wardle Ches E 69 R3
Wardle Rochdl 89 Q7
Wardley Gatesd 113 M8
Wardley Rutlnd 73 L10
Wardley Salfd 82 G4
Wardlow Derbys 83 Q10
Wardsend Ches E 83 K8
Wardy Hill Cambs 62 G4
Ware Herts 51 J8
Wareham Dorset 12 F7
Warehorne Kent 26 G5
Warenford Nthumb 119 M5
Waren Mill Nthumb 119 M4
Warenton Nthumb 119 M4
Wareside Herts 51 J7
Waresley Cambs 62 C10
Waresley Worcs 58 B10
Ware Street Kent 38 C10
Warfield Br For 35 N10
Warfleet Devon 7 M8
Wargate Lincs 74 D4
Wargrave Wokham 35 L9
Warham Herefs 45 P7
Warham Norfk 76 D3
Wark Nthumb 112 C5
Wark Nthumb 118 F3
Warkleigh Devon 17 L7
Warkton Nhants 61 J5
Warkworth Nhants 48 E6
Warkworth Nthumb 119 P9
Warlaby N York 97 M2
Warland Calder 89 Q6
Warleggan Cnwll 5 K8
Warleigh BaNES 20 E2
Warley Town Calder 90 D6
Warlingham Surrey 37 J9
Warmbrook Derbys 71 P4
Warmfield Wakefd 91 K6
Warmingham Ches E 70 C2
Warmington Nhants 61 N2
Warmington Warwks 48 D5
Warminster Wilts 20 G5
Warmley S Glos 32 C10
Warmsworth Donc 91 N10
Warmwell Dorset 12 C7
Warndon Worcs 46 G3
Warner Bros. Studio Tour Herts 50 C10
Warnford Hants 22 H10
Warnham W Susx 24 E4
Warnham Court W Susx 24 E4
Warningcamp W Susx 24 B9
Warninglid W Susx 24 F5
Warren Ches E 83 J10
Warren Pembks 40 H11
Warrenby R & Cl 104 G5
Warrenhill S Lans 116 C3
Warren Row W & M 35 M8
Warren's Green Herts 50 G5
Warren Street Kent 38 F11
Warrington M Keyn 49 N4
Warrington Warrtn 82 D7
Warriston C Edin 127 P2
Warsash Hants 14 E5
Warslow Staffs 71 K3
Warsop Vale Notts 84 H7
Warter E R Yk 98 H10
Warthermaske N York 97 K5
Warthill N York 98 D9
Wartling E Susx 25 Q9
Wartnaby Leics 73 J6
Warton Lancs 88 E5
Warton Lancs 95 K6
Warton Nthumb 119 K10
Warton Warwks 59 L4
Warwick Warwks 59 L11
Warwick Bridge Cumb 111 J9
Warwick Castle Warwks 47 Q2
Warwick-on-Eden Cumb 111 J9
Warwick Services Warwks 48 B3
Warwicksland Cumb 111 J5
Wasbister Ork 169 c3
Wasdale Head Cumb 100 G9
Wash Derbys 83 N8
Washall Green Herts 51 K4
Washaway Cnwll 4 G8
Washbourne Devon 7 K8
Washbrook Somset 19 M4
Washbrook Suffk 53 K3
Washfield Devon 18 B11
Washfold N York 103 L10
Washford Somset 18 E6
Washford Pyne Devon 9 K2
Washingborough Lincs 86 D6
Washington Sundld 113 M9
Washington W Susx 24 D8
Washington Services Gatesd 113 L9
Washwood Heath Birm 58 H7
Wasing W Berk 22 G2
Waskerley Dur 112 F11
Wasperton Warwks 47 Q3
Wasps Nest Lincs 86 E8
Wass N York 98 B5
Wast Water Cumb 100 G9
Watchet Somset 18 E6
Watchfield Oxon 33 P6
Watchfield Somset 19 K5
Watchgate Cumb 101 P11
Watchill Cumb 100 G2
Watcombe Torbay 7 N5
Watendlath Cumb 101 J7
Water Devon 9 J8
Water Lancs 89 N5
Waterbeach Cambs 62 G7
Waterbeach W Susx 15 N5
Waterbeck D & G 110 D5
Waterden Norfk 76 B4
Water Eaton Oxon 34 F2
Water Eaton Staffs 58 D2
Water End Bed 61 P10
Water End Bed 61 P11
Water End C Beds 50 C3
Waterend Cumb 100 F6
Water End E R Yk 92 C3
Water End Essex 51 N2
Water End Herts 50 B8
Water End Herts 50 F10
Waterfall Staffs 71 K4
Waterfoot Ag & B 120 F4
Waterfoot E Rens 125 P6
Waterfoot Lancs 89 N6
Waterford Herts 50 H8
Water Fryston Wakefd 91 M5
Watergate Cnwll 5 J5
Waterhead Cumb 101 L10
Waterheads Border 127 N7
Waterhouses Dur 103 N2
Waterhouses Staffs 71 K4
Wateringbury Kent 37 Q10
Waterlane Gloucs 32 H4
Waterloo Cnwll 5 J7
Waterloo Derbys 84 F8
Waterloo Herefs 45 L5
Waterloo Highld 145 L3
Waterloo N Lans 126 E7
Waterloo Norfk 77 J8
Waterloo P & K 141 Q10
Waterloo Pembks 41 J10
Waterloo Sefton 81 L5
Waterloo Cross Devon 9 Q2
Waterloo Port Gwynd 66 H2
Waterlooville Hants 15 J5
Watermead Bucks 49 M11
Watermillock Cumb 101 M6
Water Newton Cambs 74 B11
Water Orton Warwks 59 J6
Waterperry Oxon 34 H3
Waterrow Somset 18 E9
Watersfield W Susx 24 B7
Waterside Bl w D 89 L6
Waterside Bucks 35 Q4
Waterside Cumb 110 D11
Waterside Donc 91 R8
Waterside E Ayrs 114 H6
Waterside E Ayrs 125 M9
Waterside E Duns 126 B3
Water's Nook Bolton 89 K9
Waterstein Highld 152 A8
Waterstock Oxon 34 H3
Waterston Pembks 40 H9
Water Stratford Bucks 49 J8
Water Street Neath 29 M8
Waters Upton Wrekin 70 A11
Water Yeat Cumb 94 F3
Watford Herts 50 D11
Watford Nhants 60 D7
Watford Gap Services Nhants 60 D7
Wath N York 96 H7
Wath N York 97 M5
Wath upon Dearne Rothm 91 L10
Watlington Norfk 75 M8
Watlington Oxon 35 J6
Watnall Notts 84 H11
Watten Highld 167 M6
Wattisfield Suffk 64 E7
Wattisham Suffk 64 E11
Watton Dorset 11 K6
Watton E R Yk 99 L10
Watton Norfk 76 C11
Watton-at-Stone Herts 50 H7
Watton Green Norfk 76 C11
Wattons Green Essex 51 M11
Wattston N Lans 126 D3
Wattstown Rhondd 30 D6
Wattsville Caerph 30 H6
Wauldby E R Yk 92 G5
Waulkmill Abers 150 G9
Waunarlwydd Swans 28 H5
Waun Fach Powys 44 H9
Waunfawr Cerdgn 54 E8
Waunfawr Gwynd 67 J3
Waungron Swans 28 G4
Waunlwyd Blae G 30 G3
Wavendon M Keyn 49 P7
Waverbridge Cumb 110 D11
Waverton Ches W 69 N2
Waverton Cumb 110 D11
Wawne E R Yk 93 J3
Waxham Norfk 77 N6
Waxholme E R Yk 93 P5
Way Kent 39 P8
Waye Devon 7 K4
Wayford Somset 11 J3
Waytown Dorset 11 K5
Way Village Devon 9 L2
Way Wick N Som 19 L2
Weacombe Somset 18 F6
Weald Oxon 34 B4
Wealdstone Gt Lon 36 E3
Weardley Leeds 90 H2
Weare Somset 19 M4
Weare Giffard Devon 16 H7
Wearhead Dur 102 G3
Wearne Somset 19 M9
Weasdale Cumb 102 C10
Weasenham All Saints Norfk 76 A7
Weasenham St Peter Norfk 76 B7
Weaste Salfd 82 H5
Weatheroak Hill Worcs 58 G10
Weaverham Ches W 82 D10
Weaverslake Staffs 71 L11
Weaverthorpe N York 99 K6
Webbington Somset 19 L3
Webb's Heath S Glos 32 C10
Webheath Worcs 58 F11
Webton Herefs 45 N7
Wedderlairs Abers 159 L11
Wedding Hall Fold N York 96 D11
Weddington Kent 39 N10
Weddington Warwks 59 N6
Wedhampton Wilts 21 L3
Wedmore Somset 19 M5
Wednesbury Sandw 58 E5
Wednesfield Wolves 58 D4
Weecar Notts 85 P7
Weedon Bucks 49 M11
Weedon Bec Nhants 60 D9
Weedon Lois Nhants 48 H5
Weeford Staffs 58 H4
Week Devon 7 K6
Week Devon 17 K6
Week Devon 17 N8
Weeke Devon 9 J3
Weeke Hants 22 E8
Weekley Nhants 61 J4
Week St Mary Cnwll 5 L2
Weel E R Yk 93 J3
Weeley Essex 53 K7
Weeley Heath Essex 53 L7
Weem P & K 141 K8
Weeping Cross Staffs 70 G10
Weethley Warwks 47 L3
Weeting Norfk 63 N3
Weeton E R Yk 93 Q6
Weeton Lancs 88 D4
Weeton N York 97 L11
Weetwood Leeds 90 H3
Weir Lancs 89 P5
Weirbrook Shrops 69 K10
Weir Quay Devon 6 C5
Weisdale Shet 169 q8
Welborne Norfk 76 F9
Welbourn Lincs 86 C10
Welburn N York 98 E7
Welbury N York 104 C10
Welby Lincs 73 P3
Welches Dam Cambs 62 G3
Welcombe Devon 16 C8
Weldon Nhants 61 K3
Weldon Bridge Nthumb 119 M11
Welford Nhants 60 D4
Welford W Berk 34 D10
Welford-on-Avon Warwks 47 M4
Welham Leics 60 G2
Welham Notts 85 M4
Welham Bridge E R Yk 92 C4
Welham Green Herts 50 F9
Well Hants 23 L5
Well Lincs 87 M6
Well N York 97 L4
Welland Worcs 46 E6
Wellbank Angus 142 H10
Well End Bucks 35 N7
Well End Herts 50 F11
Wellesbourne Warwks 47 Q3
Wellesbourne Mountford Warwks 47 Q3
Well Head Herts 50 E5
Well Hill Kent 37 L8
Wellhouse W Berk 34 F10
Welling Gt Lon 37 L5
Wellingborough Nhants 61 J7
Wellingham Norfk 76 B7
Wellingore Lincs 86 C9
Wellington Cumb 100 E10
Wellington Herefs 45 P5
Wellington Somset 18 F10
Wellington Wrekin 57 M2
Wellington Heath Herefs 46 D6
Wellington Marsh Herefs 45 P5
Wellow BaNES 20 D3
Wellow IoW 14 C9
Wellow Notts 85 L7
Wellpond Green Herts 51 K6
Wells Somset 19 P5
Wellsborough Leics 72 B10
Wells Green Ches E 70 B4
Wells Head C Brad 90 D4
Wells-next-the-Sea Norfk 76 C3
Wellstye Green Essex 51 P7
Well Town Devon 9 M3
Welltree P & K 134 B3
Wellwood Fife 134 D10
Welney Norfk 62 H2
Welshampton Shrops 69 M7
Welsh Bicknor Herefs 46 A11
Welsh End Shrops 69 P7
Welsh Frankton Shrops 69 L8
Welsh Hook Pembks 40 H5
Welsh Newton Herefs 45 Q11
Welshpool Powys 56 C3
Welsh St Donats V Glam 30 D9
Welton Cumb 101 L2
Welton E R Yk 92 G5
Welton Lincs 86 D5
Welton Nhants 60 C7
Welton le Marsh Lincs 87 N7
Welton le Wold Lincs 87 J3
Welwick E R Yk 93 P6
Welwyn Herts 50 F7
Welwyn Garden City Herts 50 F8
Wem Shrops 69 P9
Wembdon Somset 19 J7
Wembley Gt Lon 36 E3
Wembury Devon 6 E9
Wembworthy Devon 17 M10
Wemyss Bay Inver 124 F4
Wenallt Cerdgn 54 F10
Wendens Ambo Essex 51 M3
Wendlebury Oxon 48 G11
Wendling Norfk 76 C9
Wendover Bucks 35 N3
Wendron Cnwll 2 H7
Wendron Mining District Cnwll 2 H7
Wendy Cambs 62 D11
Wenfordbridge Cnwll 4 H6
Wenhaston Suffk 65 N6
Wennington Cambs 62 B5
Wennington Gt Lon 37 M4
Wennington Lancs 95 N7
Wensley Derbys 84 C8
Wensley N York 96 G3
Wentbridge Wakefd 91 M7
Wentnor Shrops 56 F6
Wentworth Cambs 62 G5
Wentworth Rothm 91 K11
Wentworth Castle Barns 91 J10
Wenvoe V Glam 30 F10
Weobley Herefs 45 N4
Weobley Marsh Herefs 45 N4
Wepham W Susx 24 B9
Wereham Norfk 75 N10
Wergs Wolves 58 C4
Wern Gwynd 67 J7
Wern Powys 44 G11
Wern Powys 56 D2
Wern Shrops 69 J8
Werneth Low Tamesd 83 L6
Wernffrwd Swans 28 F6
Wern-Gifford Mons 45 L10
Wern-y-gaer Flints 81 J11
Werrington C Pete 74 C10
Werrington Cnwll 5 N4
Werrington Staffs 70 G5
Wervin Ches W 81 N10
Wesham Lancs 88 E4
Wessington Derbys 84 E9
West Aberthaw V Glam 30 D11
West Acre Norfk 75 Q7
West Allerdean Nthumb 129 P10
West Alvington Devon 7 J10
West Amesbury Wilts 21 M6
West Anstey Devon 17 R6
West Appleton N York 97 K2
West Ashby Lincs 87 J6
West Ashling W Susx 15 M5
West Ashton Wilts 20 G3
West Auckland Dur 103 N5
West Ayton N York 99 K4
West Bagborough Somset 18 G8
West Bank Blae G 30 H3
West Bank Halton 81 Q8
West Barkwith Lincs 86 G4
West Barnby N York 105 M8
West Barns E Loth 128 H4
West Barsham Norfk 76 C5
West Bay Dorset 11 K6
West Beckham Norfk 76 G4
West Bedfont Surrey 36 C6
Westbere Kent 39 L9
West Bergholt Essex 52 G6
West Bexington Dorset 11 L7
West Bilney Norfk 75 P7
West Blatchington Br & H 24 G9
West Boldon S Tyne 113 N8
Westborough Lincs 73 M2
Westbourne BCP 13 J6
Westbourne W Susx 15 L5
West Bourton Dorset 20 E9
West Bowling C Brad 90 F4
West Brabourne Kent 27 J3
West Bradenham Norfk 76 C10
West Bradford Lancs 89 L2
West Bradley Somset 19 Q7
West Bretton Wakefd 90 H8
West Bridgford Notts 72 F3
West Briscoe Dur 103 J7
West Bromwich Sandw 58 F6
Westbrook Kent 39 P7
Westbrook W Berk 34 D10
Westbrook Wilts 33 J11
West Buckland Devon 17 M5
West Buckland Somset 18 G10
West Burrafirth Shet 169 p8
West Burton N York 96 F3
West Burton W Susx 15 Q4
Westbury Bucks 48 H7
Westbury Shrops 56 F3
Westbury Wilts 20 G4
Westbury Leigh Wilts 20 G5
Westbury-on-Severn Gloucs 32 D2
Westbury-on-Trym Bristl 31 Q9
Westbury-sub-Mendip Somset 19 P5
West Butsfield Dur 103 M2
West Butterwick N Linc 92 D9
Westby Lancs 88 D4
West Byfleet Surrey 36 B8
West Cairngaan D & G 106 F11
West Caister Norfk 77 Q9
West Calder W Loth 127 J5
West Camel Somset 19 Q10
West Chaldon Dorset 12 C8
West Challow Oxon 34 C7
West Charleton Devon 7 K10
West Chelborough Dorset 11 L3
West Chevington Nthumb 119 P11
West Chiltington W Susx 24 C7
West Chinnock Somset 11 K2
West Chisenbury Wilts 21 M4
West Clandon Surrey 36 B10
West Cliffe Kent 27 P3
Westcliff-on-Sea Sthend 38 E4
West Clyst Devon 9 N5
West Coker Somset 11 L2
West Combe Devon 7 K6
Westcombe Somset 20 C7
West Compton Somset 19 Q6
West Compton Abbas Dorset 11 M6
Westcote Gloucs 47 P10
Westcote Barton Oxon 48 D9
Westcott Bucks 49 K11
Westcott Devon 9 P4
Westcott Surrey 36 D11
West Cottingwith N York 92 A2
Westcourt Wilts 21 P2
West Cowick E R Yk 91 Q6
West Cross Swans 28 H7
West Curry Cnwll 5 M3
West Curthwaite Cumb 110 F11
Westdean E Susx 25 M11
West Dean W Susx 15 N4
West Dean Wilts 21 Q9
West Deeping Lincs 74 B9
West Derby Lpool 81 M6

West Dereham Norfk....75 N10
West Ditchburn Nthumb....119 M10
West Down Devon....17 J3
Westdown Camp Wilts....21 K5
Westdowns Cnwll....4 H5
West Drayton Gt Lon....36 C5
West Drayton Notts....85 M6
West Dunnet Highld....167 M4
Wested Kent....37 M7
West Ella E R Yk....92 H5
West End Bed....49 Q4
West End Br For....35 N10
West End Caerph....30 H5
West End Cumb....110 H9
West End E R Yk....92 F4
West End E R Yk....93 L4
West End E R Yk....93 N5
Westend Gloucs....32 E3
West End Hants....14 E4
West End Hants....22 H7
West End Herts....50 G9
West End Herts....50 H9
West End Lancs....89 L5
West End Leeds....90 G3
West End Lincs....93 Q11
West End N Som....31 N11
West End N York....91 N2
West End Norfk....76 C10
West End Norfk....77 Q9
West End Oxon....34 G7
West End S Glos....20 D7
West End Somset....20 C8
West End Surrey....23 P2
West End Surrey....36 D8
West End W & M....35 M9
West End W Susx....24 F7
West End Wilts....20 H10
West End Wilts....21 J10
West End Wilts....33 J9
West End Green Hants....23 J2
Westend Town Nthumb....111 Q7
Westenhanger Kent....27 K4
Wester Aberchalder Highld....147 P3
Westerdale Highld....167 K6
Westerdale N York....105 J9
Westerfield Suffk....53 L2
Westergate W Susx....15 P5
Westerham Kent....37 K10
Westerhope N u Ty....113 J7
Westerland Devon....7 M6
Westerleigh S Glos....32 C9
Western Isles W Isls....168 f8
Wester Ochiltree W Loth....127 J3
Wester Pitkierie Fife....135 P6
Wester Ross Highld....160 F11
Westerton W Susx....15 N5
Westerton of Rossie Angus....143 M7
Westerwick Shet....169 p9
West Ewell Surrey....36 F8
West Farleigh Kent....38 B11
West Farndon Nhants....48 F4
West Felton Shrops....69 K9
Westfield BaNES....20 C4
Westfield Cumb....100 C5
Westfield E Susx....26 D8
Westfield Highld....167 J4
Westfield N Lans....126 C3
Westfield Norfk....76 D10
Westfield Surrey....36 B9
Westfield W Loth....126 G3
Westfields Dorset....12 B3
Westfields Herefs....45 P6
Westfields of Rattray P & K....142 B8
Westfield Sole Kent....38 C9
West Flotmanby N York....99 M5
Westford Somset....18 F10
Westgate Dur....102 H3
Westgate N Linc....92 C9
Westgate Norfk....76 D3
Westgate Hill C Brad....90 G5
Westgate-on-Sea Kent....39 P7
Westgate Street Norfk....76 H7
West Ginge Oxon....34 D7
West Grafton Wilts....21 P2
West Green Hants....23 K3
West Grimstead Wilts....21 P9
West Grinstead W Susx....24 E6
West Haddlesey N York....91 P5
West Haddon Nhants....60 D6
West Hagbourne Oxon....34 F7
West Hagley Worcs....58 D8
Westhall Suffk....65 N5
West Hallam Derbys....72 C2
West Hallam Common Derbys....72 C2
West Halton N Linc....92 F6
Westham Dorset....11 P9
Westham E Susx....25 P10
West Ham Gt Lon....37 J4
Westham Somset....19 M5
Westhampnett W Susx....15 N5
West Handley Derbys....84 E5
West Hanney Oxon....34 D6
West Hanningfield Essex....38 B2
West Harnham Wilts....21 M9
West Harptree BaNES....19 Q3
West Harting W Susx....23 L10
West Hatch Somset....19 J10
West Hatch Wilts....20 H9
West Haven Angus....143 K10
Westhay Somset....19 M6
Westhead Lancs....88 E9
West Head Norfk....75 L9
West Heath Birm....58 F9
West Heath Hants....22 G3
West Helmsdale Highld....163 N3
West Hendred Oxon....34 D7
West Heslerton N York....99 J5
West Hewish N Som....19 L2
Westhide Herefs....46 A6
Westhill Abers....151 L6
West Hill Devon....9 Q6
Westhill Highld....156 C9
West Hoathly W Susx....25 J4
West Holme Dorset....12 E7
Westholme Somset....19 Q6
Westhope Herefs....45 P4
Westhope Shrops....56 H7
West Horndon Essex....37 P3
Westhorp Nhants....48 F4
Westhorpe Lincs....74 D4
Westhorpe Suffk....64 E8
West Horrington Somset....19 Q5
West Horsley Surrey....36 C10
West Horton Nthumb....119 K4
West Hougham Kent....27 N3

Westhoughton Bolton....89 K9
Westhouse N York....95 M6
Westhouses Derbys....84 F9
West Howe BCP....13 J5
West Howetown Somset....18 B8
Westhumble Surrey....36 G10
West Huntingtower P & K....134 D3
West Huntspill Somset....19 K6
West Hyde C Beds....50 D7
West Hyde Herts....36 B3
West Hythe Kent....27 K5
West Ilkerton Devon....17 N2
West Ilsley W Berk....34 E8
West Itchenor W Susx....15 L6
West Keal Lincs....87 L8
West Kennett Wilts....33 M11
West Kilbride N Ayrs....124 G8
West Kingsdown Kent....37 N8
West Kington Wilts....32 F9
West Kirby Wirral....81 J7
West Knapton N York....98 H5
West Knighton Dorset....12 B7
West Knoyle Wilts....20 G8
West Kyloe Nthumb....119 L2
Westlake Devon....6 G8
West Lambrook Somset....19 M11
Westland Green Herts....51 L6
West Langdon Kent....27 P2
West Lavington W Susx....23 N10
West Lavington Wilts....21 K4
West Layton N York....103 M8
West Leake Notts....72 E5
West Learmouth Nthumb....118 F3
West Lees N York....104 E10
West Leigh Devon....8 G3
Westleigh Devon....16 H6
Westleigh Devon....18 E11
West Leigh Somset....18 F8
Westleton Suffk....65 N8
West Lexham Norfk....76 A8
Westley Shrops....56 F3
Westley Suffk....63 P8
Westley Waterless Cambs....63 K9
West Lilling N York....98 C8
Westlington Bucks....35 L2
West Linton Border....127 M7
Westlinton Cumb....110 G8
West Littleton S Glos....32 E9
West Lockinge Oxon....34 D7
West Lulworth Dorset....12 D8
West Lutton N York....99 J7
West Lydford Somset....19 Q8
West Lyn Devon....17 N2
West Lyng Somset....19 K9
West Lynn Norfk....75 M6
West Malling Kent....37 Q9
West Malvern Worcs....46 E5
West Marden W Susx....15 L4
West Markham Notts....85 M6
Westmarsh Kent....39 N9
West Marsh NE Lin....93 N9
West Marton N York....96 C10
West Melbury Dorset....20 G10
West Melton Rothm....91 L10
West Meon Hants....22 H10
West Meon Hut Hants....23 J9
West Meon Woodlands Hants....22 H9
West Mersea Essex....52 H9
Westmeston E Susx....24 H8
West Mickley Nthumb....112 G8
West Midland Safari Park Worcs....57 Q9
Westmill Herts....50 H7
Westmill Herts....51 J5
West Milton Dorset....11 L5
Westminster Gt Lon....36 G5
Westminster Abbey & Palace Gt Lon....36 G5
West Molesey Surrey....36 D7
West Monkton Somset....19 J9
West Moors Dorset....13 J4
West Morden Dorset....12 F5
West Morriston Border....118 B2
West Morton C Brad....90 D2
West Mudford Somset....19 Q10
Westmuir Angus....142 F7
West Ness N York....98 D5
West Newbiggin Darltn....104 C7
Westnewton Cumb....100 F2
West Newton E R Yk....93 M3
West Newton Norfk....75 N5
West Newton Somset....19 J9
West Norwood Gt Lon....36 H6
Westoe S Tyne....113 N7
West Ogwell Devon....7 L4
Weston BaNES....32 D11
Weston Ches E....70 C4
Weston Devon....10 C4
Weston Devon....10 D7
Weston Dorset....11 P10
Weston Halton....81 Q8
Weston Hants....23 K10
Weston Herefs....45 M3
Weston Herts....50 G4
Weston Lincs....74 E6
Weston N York....97 J11
Weston Nhants....48 G5
Weston Notts....85 N7
Weston Shrops....56 E10
Weston Shrops....57 L6
Weston Shrops....69 J9
Weston Staffs....70 H9
Weston Suffk....65 N4
Weston W Berk....34 C10
Weston Beggard Herefs....46 A6
Westonbirt Gloucs....32 G7
Weston by Welland Nhants....60 G2
Weston Colley Hants....22 F7
Weston Colville Cambs....63 K10
Weston Corbett Hants....23 J5
Weston Coyney C Stke....70 G6
Weston Favell Nhants....60 G8
Weston Green Cambs....63 K10
Weston Heath Shrops....57 P2
Weston Hills Lincs....74 E6
Weston in Arden Warwks....59 N7
Westoning C Beds....50 B4
Weston-in-Gordano N Som....31 N10
Westoning Woodend C Beds....50 B4
Weston Jones Staffs....70 D10
Weston Longville Norfk....76 G8
Weston Lullingfields Shrops....69 M10
Weston-on-Avon Warwks....47 N4
Weston-on-the-Green Oxon....48 F11

Weston Park Staffs....57 Q2
Weston Patrick Hants....23 J5
Weston Rhyn Shrops....69 J7
Weston-sub-Edge Gloucs....47 M6
Weston-super-Mare N Som....19 K2
Weston Turville Bucks....35 M3
Weston-under-Lizard Staffs....57 Q2
Weston under Penyard Herefs....46 B10
Weston-under-Redcastle Shrops....69 Q9
Weston under Wetherley Warwks....59 N11
Weston Underwood Derbys....71 P6
Weston Underwood M Keyn....49 N4
Weston-upon-Trent Derbys....72 C5
Westonzoyland Somset....19 L8
West Orchard Dorset....20 F11
West Overton Wilts....33 M11
Westow N York....98 F7
West Panson Devon....5 N3
West Park Abers....151 K8
West Parley Dorset....13 J5
West Peckham Kent....37 P10
West Peeke Devon....5 N3
West Pelton Dur....113 K10
West Pennard Somset....19 P7
West Pentire Cnwll....4 B9
West Pinchbeck Lincs....74 D6
West Porlock Somset....17 R2
Westport Somset....19 L10
West Pulham Dorset....11 Q3
West Putford Devon....16 F9
West Quantoxhead Somset....18 F6
Westquarter Falk....126 E2
West Raddon Devon....9 L4
West Rainton Dur....113 M11
West Rasen Lincs....86 E3
West Ravendale NE Lin....93 M11
Westray Ork....169 d2
Westray Airport Ork....169 d1
West Raynham Norfk....76 B6
West Retford Notts....85 L4
Westridge Green W Berk....34 G9
Westrigg W Loth....126 G4
Westrop Swindn....33 P6
West Rounton N York....104 D10
West Row Suffk....63 L5
West Rudham Norfk....75 R5
West Runton Norfk....76 H3
Westruther Border....128 G10
Westry Cambs....74 H11
West Saltoun E Loth....128 D6
West Sandford Devon....9 K4
West Sandwick Shet....169 r5
West Scrafton N York....96 G4
West Sleekburn Nthumb....113 L4
West Somerton Norfk....77 P7
West Stafford Dorset....11 Q7
West Stockwith Notts....92 C11
West Stoke W Susx....15 M5
West Stonesdale N York....102 G10
West Stoughton Somset....19 M5
West Stour Dorset....20 E10
West Stourmouth Kent....39 N9
Stow Suffk....63 P6
West Stowell Wilts....21 M2
West Stratton Hants....22 F6
West Street Kent....38 F11
West Street Kent....39 P11
West Street Medway....38 B6
West Street Suffk....64 D7
West Tanfield N York....97 L5
West Taphouse Cnwll....5 J9
West Tarbert Ag & B....123 Q6
West Tarring W Susx....24 D10
West Thirston Nthumb....119 N11
West Thorney W Susx....15 L6
Westthorpe Derbys....84 G5
West Thorpe Notts....72 G5
West Thurrock Thurr....37 N5
West Tilbury Thurr....37 Q5
West Tisted Hants....23 J9
West Torrington Lincs....86 F4
West Town BaNES....19 P2
West Town Hants....15 K7
West Town Herefs....45 N2
West Town N Som....31 N11
West Town Somset....19 P7
West Town Somset....20 D6
West Tytherley Hants....21 Q9
West Walton Norfk....75 J8
Westward Cumb....101 J2
Westward Ho! Devon....16 G6
Westwell Kent....26 A2
Westwell Oxon....33 P3
Westwell Leacon Kent....26 A2
West Wellow Hants....21 Q11
West Wembury Devon....6 E9
West Wemyss Fife....135 J9
Westwick Cambs....62 F7
Westwick Dur....103 L7
West Wick N Som....19 L2
West Wickham Cambs....63 K11
West Wickham Gt Lon....37 J7
West Williamston Pembks....41 K9
West Winch Norfk....75 M7
West Winterslow Wilts....21 P8
West Wittering W Susx....15 L7
West Witton N York....96 G3
Westwood Devon....9 P5
Westwood Kent....37 P6
Westwood Kent....39 Q8
Westwood Notts....84 G10
Westwood Nthumb....111 Q7
Westwood Wilts....20 F3
West Woodburn Nthumb....112 C3
Westwood Heath Covtry....59 L9
West Woodlands Somset....20 E6
Westwoodside N Linc....92 B10
West Worldham Hants....23 K7
West Worthing W Susx....24 D10
West Wratting Cambs....63 K10
West Wycombe Bucks....35 M6
West Wylam Nthumb....112 H8
West Yatton Wilts....32 G9
West Yoke Kent....37 P7
West Youlstone Cnwll....16 D8
Wetham Green Kent....38 D8
Wetheral Cumb....111 J10
Wetherby Leeds....97 P11
Wetherby Services N York....97 P10
Wetherden Suffk....64 E9

Wetheringsett Suffk....64 G8
Wethersfield Essex....52 B5
Wetherup Street Suffk....64 G9
Wetley Rocks Staffs....70 H5
Wettenhall Ches E....69 R2
Wetton Staffs....71 L3
Wetwang E R Yk....99 J9
Wetwood Staffs....70 D8
Wexcombe Wilts....21 Q3
Wexham Slough....35 Q8
Wexham Street Bucks....35 Q8
Weybourne Norfk....76 G3
Weybourne Surrey....23 N5
Weybread Suffk....65 J5
Weybread Street Suffk....65 J6
Weybridge Surrey....36 C8
Weycroft Devon....10 G5
Weydale Highld....167 L4
Weyhill Hants....22 B5
Weymouth Dorset....11 P9
Whaddon Bucks....49 N8
Whaddon Cambs....62 E11
Whaddon Gloucs....32 F2
Whaddon Wilts....20 G2
Whaddon Wilts....21 N9
Whale Cumb....101 P6
Whaley Derbys....84 H6
Whaley Bridge Derbys....83 M8
Whaley Thorns Derbys....84 H6
Whaligoe Highld....167 P8
Whalley Lancs....89 L3
Whalley Banks Lancs....89 L3
Whalsay Shet....169 s7
Whalton Nthumb....112 H4
Whaplode Lincs....74 F6
Whaplode Drove Lincs....74 F8
Wharf Warwks....48 D4
Wharfe N York....96 A7
Wharles Lancs....88 E3
Wharley End C Beds....49 P6
Wharncliffe Side Sheff....84 C2
Wharram-le-Street N York....98 H7
Wharton Ches W....82 E11
Wharton Herefs....45 Q3
Whashton N York....103 N9
Whasset Cumb....95 L4
Whatcote Warwks....47 Q6
Whateley Warwks....59 K5
Whatfield Suffk....52 H2
Whatley Somset....10 H3
Whatley Somset....20 D5
Whatley's End S Glos....32 C8
Whatlington E Susx....26 C8
Whatsole Street Kent....27 K3
Whatstandwell Derbys....84 D10
Whatton-in-the-Vale Notts....73 J3
Whauphill D & G....107 M8
Whaw N York....103 J10
Wheal Peevor Cnwll....3 J5
Wheal Rose Cnwll....3 J5
Wheatacre Norfk....65 P3
Wheatfield Oxon....35 J5
Wheathampstead Herts....50 E8
Wheathill Shrops....57 L8
Wheathill Somset....19 Q8
Wheatley Hants....23 L6
Wheatley Oxon....34 G3
Wheatley Hill Dur....104 C3
Wheatley Hills Donc....91 P10
Wheatley Lane Lancs....89 N3
Wheaton Aston Staffs....58 C2
Wheddon Cross Somset....18 B7
Wheelbarrow Town Kent....27 K2
Wheeler End Bucks....35 M6
Wheeler's Green Wokham....35 L10
Wheelerstreet Surrey....23 P6
Wheelock Ches E....70 D3
Wheelock Heath Ches E....70 D3
Wheelton Lancs....89 J6
Wheldale Wakefd....91 M5
Wheldrake C York....92 A2
Whelford Gloucs....33 N5
Whelpley Hill Bucks....35 Q4
Whelpo Cumb....101 K3
Whelston Flints....81 J9
Whempstead Herts....50 H6
Whenby N York....98 C7
Whepstead Suffk....64 A10
Wherstead Suffk....53 L3
Wherwell Hants....22 C6
Wheston Derbys....83 P9
Whetsted Kent....37 Q11
Whetstone Gt Lon....36 G2
Whetstone Leics....72 F11
Wheyrigg Cumb....110 C11
Whicham Cumb....94 C4
Whichford Warwks....48 B8
Whickham Gatesd....113 K8
Whiddon Devon....8 C5
Whiddon Down Devon....8 G6
Whigstreet Angus....142 H9
Whilton Nhants....60 D8
Whimble Devon....16 F11
Whimple Devon....9 P5
Whimpwell Green Norfk....77 M6
Whin Lane End Lancs....88 D2
Whinnieliggate D & G....108 F10
Whinnow Cumb....110 F10
Whinnyfold Abers....159 Q11
Whinny Hill S on T....104 C7
Whippingham IoW....14 F8
Whipsnade C Beds....50 B7
Whipsnade Zoo ZSL C Beds....50 B7
Whipton Devon....9 M6
Whirlow Sheff....84 D4
Whisby Lincs....86 B7
Whissendine Rutlnd....73 L8
Whissonsett Norfk....76 C7
Whistlefield Ag & B....131 Q9
Whistlefield Inn Ag & B....131 N9
Whistley Green Wokham....35 L10
Whiston Knows....81 P6
Whiston Nhants....60 H8
Whiston Rothm....84 F3
Whiston Staffs....58 C2
Whiston Staffs....71 J5
Whiston Cross Shrops....57 P4
Whiston Eaves Staffs....71 J5
Whitacre Fields Warwks....59 K6
Whitbeck Cumb....94 C4
Whitbourne Herefs....46 D3
Whitburn S Tyne....113 P8
Whitburn W Loth....126 G3
Whitby Ches W....81 M9
Whitby N York....105 N8

Whitbyheath Ches W....81 M10
Whitchester Border....129 J8
Whitchurch BaNES....32 B11
Whitchurch Bucks....49 M10
Whitchurch Cardif....30 G9
Whitchurch Devon....6 D4
Whitchurch Hants....22 E5
Whitchurch Herefs....45 R11
Whitchurch Oxon....34 H9
Whitchurch Pembks....40 D5
Whitchurch Shrops....69 P6
Whitchurch Canonicorum Dorset....10 H5
Whitchurch Hill Oxon....34 H9
Whitcombe Dorset....11 Q7
Whitcot Shrops....56 F6
Whitcott Keysett Shrops....56 D8
Whiteacre Kent....27 K2
Whiteacre Heath Warwks....59 K6
Whiteash Green Essex....52 C5
White Ball Somset....18 F11
Whitebridge Highld....147 M4
Whitebrook Mons....31 P3
Whitebushes Surrey....36 G11
Whitecairns Abers....151 N4
Whitechapel Gt Lon....36 H4
White Chapel Lancs....88 H2
Whitechurch Pembks....41 N3
Whitecliff Gloucs....31 Q3
White Colne Essex....52 E6
White Coppice Lancs....89 J7
Whitecraig E Loth....127 Q3
Whitecroft Gloucs....32 B3
Whitecrook D & G....106 G6
Whitecross Cnwll....2 E7
White Cross Cnwll....2 H9
Whitecross Cnwll....4 F7
Whitecross Falk....126 H2
White End Worcs....46 E8
Whiteface Highld....162 G9
Whitefarland N Ayrs....120 G3
Whitefaulds S Ayrs....114 G6
Whitefield Bury....89 N9
Whitefield Devon....17 N4
Whitefield Somset....18 E9
Whitefield Lane End Knows....81 P7
Whiteford Abers....151 J2
Whitegate Ches W....82 D11
Whitehall Hants....23 K4
Whitehall Ork....169 f4
Whitehall W Susx....24 D6
Whitehaven Cumb....100 C7
Whitehill Hants....23 L8
Whitehill Kent....38 H10
Whitehill Leics....72 C8
Whitehills Abers....158 G4
Whitehouse Abers....150 G5
Whitehouse Ag & B....123 P7
Whitehouse Common Birm....58 H5
Whitekirk E Loth....128 F3
White Kirkley Dur....103 K3
White Lackington Dorset....11 Q5
Whitelackington Somset....L11
White Ladies Aston Worcs....46 H4
Whiteleaf Bucks....35 M4
White-le-Head Dur....113 J10
Whiteley Hants....14 F5
Whiteley Bank IoW....14 G10
Whiteley Green Ches E....83 K9
Whiteley Village Surrey....36 C8
Whitemans Green W Susx....24 H5
White Mill Carmth....43 J10
Whitemire Moray....156 H7
Whitemoor C Nott....72 E2
Whitemoor Cnwll....3 N4
Whitemoor Derbys....84 E11
Whitemoor Staffs....70 F2
Whiteness Shet....169 q9
White Notley Essex....52 C8
Whiteoak Green Oxon....34 B2
White Ox Mead BaNES....20 D3
Whiteparish Wilts....21 P10
White Pit Lincs....87 L5
Whiterashes Abers....151 M3
White Roding Essex....51 N8
Whiterow Highld....167 Q7
Whiterow Moray....157 J6
Whiteshill Gloucs....32 F3
Whitesmith E Susx....25 M8
White Stake Lancs....88 G5
Whitestaunton Somset....10 F2
Whitestone Devon....9 L6
Whitestone Herefs....45 R6
Whitestone Warwks....59 N7
Whitestone Cross Devon....9 L6
Whitestreet Green Suffk....52 G4
Whitewall Corner N York....98 F7
White Waltham W & M....35 M9
Whiteway BaNES....20 D2
Whiteway Gloucs....32 H2
Whitewell Lancs....95 P11
Whiteworks Devon....6 G4
Whitfield C Dund....142 G11
Whitfield Kent....27 P2
Whitfield Nhants....48 H7
Whitfield Nthumb....111 Q9
Whitfield S Glos....32 C6
Whitfield Hall Nthumb....111 Q9
Whitford Devon....10 F5
Whitford Flints....80 G9
Whitgift E R Yk....92 D6
Whitgreave Staffs....70 G9
Whithorn D & G....107 M9
Whiting Bay N Ayrs....121 K6
Whitkirk Leeds....91 K4
Whitland Carmth....41 N7
Whitlaw Border....117 Q8
Whitletts S Ayrs....114 G3
Whitley N York....91 P6
Whitley Readg....35 K10
Whitley Sheff....84 D2
Whitley Wilts....32 G11
Whitley Bay N Tyne....113 N6
Whitley Chapel Nthumb....112 D9
Whitley Heath Staffs....70 E9
Whitley Lower Kirk....90 G7
Whitley Row Kent....37 L10
Whitlock's End Solhll....58 H9
Whitminster Gloucs....32 E3
Whitmore Dorset....13 J3
Whitmore Staffs....70 E6
Whitnage Devon....18 D11
Whitnash Warwks....48 B2
Whitney-on-Wye Herefs....45 K5
Whitrigg Cumb....100 H3
Whitrigg Cumb....110 D9

Whitrigglees Cumb......110 D9
Whitsbury Hants......21 M11
Whitsome Border......129 M9
Whitson Newpt......31 L8
Whitstable Kent......39 K8
Whitstone Cnwll......5 M2
Whittingham Nthumb......119 L8
Whittingslow Shrops......56 G7
Whittington Derbys......84 E5
Whittington Gloucs......47 K10
Whittington Lancs......95 N5
Whittington Norfk......75 P11
Whittington Shrops......69 K8
Whittington Staffs......58 C8
Whittington Staffs......59 J3
Whittington Warwks......59 L5
Whittington Worcs......46 G4
Whittington Moor Derbys......84 E6
Whittlebury Nhants......49 J8
Whittle-le-Woods Lancs......88 H6
Whittlesey Cambs......74 E11
Whittlesford Cambs......62 G11
Whittlestone Head Bl w D......89 L7
Whitton N Linc......92 F6
Whitton Nthumb......119 L10
Whitton Powys......56 D11
Whitton S on T......104 C6
Whitton Shrops......57 K10
Whitton Suffk......53 K2
Whittonditch Wilts......33 Q10
Whittonstall Nthumb......112 H9
Whitway Hants......22 E3
Whitwell Derbys......84 H5
Whitwell Herts......50 E6
Whitwell IoW......14 F11
Whitwell N York......103 Q11
Whitwell Rutlnd......73 N9
Whitwell-on-the-Hill N York......98 E7
Whitwell Street Norfk......76 G7
Whitwick Leics......72 C7
Whitwood Wakefd......91 L6
Whitworth Lancs......89 P7
Whixall Shrops......69 P8
Whixley N York......97 P9
Whorlton Dur......103 M8
Whorlton N York......104 E10
Whyle Herefs......45 R2
Whyteleafe Surrey......36 H9
Wibdon Gloucs......31 Q5
Wibsey C Brad......90 E4
Wibtoft Warwks......59 Q7
Wichelstowe Swindn......33 M8
Wichenford Worcs......46 E2
Wichling Kent......38 F10
Wick BCP......13 L6
Wick Devon......10 D4
Wick Highld......167 Q6
Wick S Glos......32 D10
Wick Somset......18 H6
Wick Somset......19 M9
Wick V Glam......29 P10
Wick W Susx......24 B10
Wick Wilts......21 N10
Wick Worcs......47 J5
Wicken Cambs......63 J6
Wicken Nhants......49 K7
Wicken Bonhunt Essex......51 L4
Wickenby Lincs......86 G4
Wick End Bed......49 Q4
Wicken Green Village Norfk......76 A5
Wickersley Rothm......84 G2
Wicker Street Green Suffk......52 G3
Wickford Essex......38 B3
Wickham Hants......14 G4
Wickham W Berk......34 C10
Wickham Bishops Essex......52 D9
Wickhambreaux Kent......39 M10
Wickhambrook Suffk......63 N10
Wickhamford Worcs......47 L6
Wickham Green Suffk......64 F8
Wickham Green W Berk......34 D10
Wickham Heath W Berk......34 D11
Wickham Market Suffk......65 L10
Wickhampton Norfk......77 N10
Wickham St Paul Essex......52 D4
Wickham Skeith Suffk......64 F8
Wickham Street Suffk......63 N10
Wickham Street Suffk......64 F8
Wickhurst Green W Susx......24 D4
Wick John o' Groats Airport Highld......167 Q6
Wicklewood Norfk......76 F11
Wickmere Norfk......76 H5
Wick St Lawrence N Som......31 L11
Wicksteed Park Nhants......61 J5
Wickstreet E Susx......25 M9
Wickwar S Glos......32 D7
Widdington Essex......51 M4
Widdop Calder......89 Q4
Widdrington Nthumb......119 Q11
Widdrington Station Nthumb......113 K2
Widecombe in the Moor Devon......8 H9
Widegates Cnwll......5 M10
Widemouth Bay Cnwll......16 C11
Wide Open N Tyne......113 K6
Widford Essex......51 Q10
Widford Herts......51 K7
Widham Wilts......33 L7
Widley Hants......15 J5
Widmer End Bucks......35 N5
Widmerpool Notts......72 G5
Widmore Gt Lon......37 K7
Widnes Halton......81 Q7
Widworthy Devon......10 E5
Wigan Wigan......88 H9
Wigborough Somset......19 M11
Wiggaton Devon......10 C6
Wiggenhall St Germans Norfk......75 L8
Wiggenhall St Mary Magdalen Norfk......75 L8
Wiggenhall St Mary the Virgin Norfk......75 L8
Wiggenhall St Peter Norfk......75 M8
Wiggens Green Essex......51 Q2
Wiggenstall Staffs......71 K2
Wiggington Shrops......69 K7
Wigginton C York......98 C9
Wigginton Herts......35 P2
Wigginton Oxon......48 C8
Wigginton Staffs......59 K3
Wigginton Bottom Herts......35 P3
Wigglesworth N York......96 B9

Wiggonby Cumb......110 E10
Wiggonholt W Susx......24 C7
Wighill N York......97 Q11
Wighton Norfk......76 C4
Wigley Derbys......84 D6
Wigley Hants......22 B11
Wigmore Herefs......56 G11
Wigmore Medway......38 C9
Wigsley Notts......85 Q6
Wigsthorpe Nhants......61 M4
Wigston Leics......72 G11
Wigston Fields Leics......72 G10
Wigston Parva Leics......59 Q7
Wigthorpe Notts......85 J4
Wigtoft Lincs......74 E3
Wigton Cumb......110 E11
Wigtown D & G......107 M6
Wigtwizzle Sheff......90 G11
Wike Leeds......91 J2
Wilbarston Nhants......60 H3
Wilberfoss E R Yk......98 E10
Wilburton Cambs......62 G5
Wilby Nhants......61 J7
Wilby Norfk......64 E4
Wilby Suffk......65 J7
Wilcot Wilts......21 M2
Wilcott Shrops......69 L11
Wilcove Cnwll......6 C7
Wilday Green Derbys......84 D6
Wildboarclough Ches E......83 L11
Wilden Bed......61 N9
Wilden Worcs......58 B10
Wilde Street Suffk......63 M5
Wildhern Hants......22 C4
Wildhill Herts......50 G9
Wildmanbridge S Lans......126 E7
Wildmill Brdgnd......29 P8
Wildmoor Hants......23 J3
Wildmoor Worcs......58 E9
Wildsworth Lincs......92 D11
Wilford C Nott......72 F3
Wilkesley Ches E......70 A6
Wilkhaven Highld......163 L9
Wilkieston W Loth......127 L4
Wilkin's Green Herts......50 F9
Wilksby Lincs......87 J8
Willand Devon......9 P2
Willards Hill E Susx......26 B7
Willaston Ches E......70 B4
Willaston Ches W......81 L9
Willen M Keyn......49 N6
Willenhall Covtry......59 N9
Willenhall Wsall......58 E5
Willerby E R Yk......92 H4
Willerby N York......99 L5
Willersey Gloucs......47 M7
Willersley Herefs......45 L5
Willesborough Kent......26 H3
Willesborough Lees Kent......26 H3
Willesden Gt Lon......36 F4
Willesleigh Devon......17 L5
Willesley Wilts......32 G7
Willett Somset......18 F8
Willey Shrops......57 M5
Willey Warwks......59 Q8
Willey Green Surrey......23 P4
Williamscot Oxon......48 E5
Williamstown Rhondd......30 D6
Willian Herts......50 F4
Willicote Warwks......47 N5
Willingale Essex......51 N9
Willingdon E Susx......25 N10
Willingham Cambs......62 F6
Willingham by Stow Lincs......85 Q4
Willingham Green Cambs......63 K10
Willingham St Mary Suffk......65 N5
Willington Bed......61 P10
Willington Derbys......71 P9
Willington Dur......103 N3
Willington Kent......38 C11
Willington N Tyne......113 M7
Willington Warwks......47 Q7
Willington Corner Ches W......82 B11
Willitoft E R Yk......92 B4
Williton Somset......18 E6
Willoughby Lincs......87 N6
Willoughby Warwks......60 B7
Willoughby Hills Lincs......87 L11
Willoughby-on-the-Wolds Notts......72 G5
Willoughby Waterleys Leics......60 C2
Willoughton Lincs......86 B2
Willow Green Ches W......82 D9
Willows Green Essex......52 B8
Willsbridge S Glos......32 C10
Willsworthy Devon......8 D8
Willtown Somset......19 L10
Wilmcote Warwks......47 N3
Wilmington BaNES......20 C2
Wilmington Devon......10 E5
Wilmington E Susx......25 M10
Wilmington Kent......37 M6
Wilmslow Ches E......82 H8
Wilnecote Staffs......59 K4
Wilpshire Lancs......89 K4
Wilsden C Brad......90 D3
Wilsford Lincs......73 Q2
Wilsford Wilts......21 M3
Wilsford Wilts......21 M7
Wilsham Devon......17 P2
Wilshaw Kirk......90 E9
Wilsill N York......97 J8
Wilsley Green Kent......26 C4
Wilsley Pound Kent......26 C4
Wilson Herefs......45 R10
Wilson Leics......72 C6
Wilsontown S Lans......126 G6
Wilstead Bed......50 C2
Wilsthorpe Lincs......74 A8
Wilstone Herts......35 P2
Wilstone Green Herts......35 P2
Wilton Cumb......100 D8
Wilton Herefs......46 A10
Wilton N York......98 H4
Wilton R & Cl......104 G7
Wilton Wilts......21 L8
Wilton Wilts......21 Q2
Wilton Dean Border......117 P8
Wimbish Essex......51 N3
Wimbish Green Essex......51 P3
Wimbledon Gt Lon......36 F6
Wimblington Cambs......62 F2
Wimboldsley Ches W......70 B2
Wimborne Minster Dorset......12 H5

Wimborne St Giles Dorset......12 H2
Wimbotsham Norfk......75 M9
Wimpole Cambs......62 E11
Wimpstone Warwks......47 P5
Wincanton Somset......20 D9
Winceby Lincs......87 K7
Wincham Ches W......82 E9
Winchburgh W Loth......127 K3
Winchcombe Gloucs......47 K9
Winchelsea E Susx......26 F8
Winchelsea Beach E Susx......26 F8
Winchester Hants......22 E9
Winchester Services Hants......22 F7
Winchet Hill Kent......26 B3
Winchfield Hants......23 L4
Winchmore Hill Bucks......35 P5
Winchmore Hill Gt Lon......36 H2
Wincle Ches E......83 L11
Wincobank Sheff......84 E2
Winder Cumb......100 D7
Windermere Cumb......101 M11
Windermere Jetty Cumb......101 M11
Winderton Warwks......48 B6
Windhill Highld......155 P8
Windlehurst Stockp......83 L7
Windlesham Surrey......23 P2
Windmill Cnwll......4 D7
Windmill Derbys......83 Q9
Windmill Hill E Susx......25 P8
Windmill Hill Somset......19 K11
Windrush Gloucs......33 N2
Windsole Abers......158 E5
Windsor W & M......35 Q9
Windsor Castle W & M......35 Q9
Windsoredge Gloucs......32 F4
Windsor Green Suffk......64 B11
Windygates Fife......135 J7
Windyharbour Ches E......82 H10
Windy Hill Wrexhm......69 K4
Wineham W Susx......24 F6
Winestead E R Yk......93 N6
Winewall Lancs......89 Q2
Winfarthing Norfk......64 G4
Winford IoW......14 G10
Winford N Som......19 P2
Winforton Herefs......45 K5
Winfrith Newburgh Dorset......12 D8
Wing Bucks......49 N10
Wing Rutlnd......73 M10
Wingate Dur......104 D3
Wingates Bolton......89 K9
Wingates Nthumb......119 L11
Wingerworth Derbys......84 E7
Wingfield C Beds......50 B5
Wingfield Suffk......65 J6
Wingfield Wilts......20 F3
Wingfield Green Suffk......65 J6
Wingham Kent......39 M10
Wingland Lincs......75 J6
Wingmore Kent......27 L2
Wingrave Bucks......49 N11
Winkburn Notts......85 M9
Winkfield Br For......35 P10
Winkfield Row Br For......35 N10
Winkhill Staffs......71 K4
Winkhurst Green Kent......37 L11
Winkleigh Devon......17 L10
Winksley N York......97 L6
Winkton BCP......13 L5
Winlaton Gatesd......113 J8
Winlaton Mill Gatesd......113 J8
Winless Highld......167 P6
Winmarleigh Lancs......95 K11
Winnall Hants......22 E9
Winnersh Wokham......35 L10
Winnington Ches W......82 D10
Winscales Cumb......100 D5
Winscombe N Som......19 M3
Winsford Ches W......82 E11
Winsford Somset......18 B8
Winsham Devon......17 J4
Winsham Somset......10 H3
Winshill Staffs......71 P10
Winshwen Swans......29 J5
Winskill Cumb......101 Q4
Winslade Hants......23 J5
Winsley Wilts......20 E2
Winslow Bucks......49 L9
Winson Gloucs......33 L3
Winsor Hants......13 P2
Winster Cumb......95 J2
Winster Derbys......84 B8
Winston Dur......103 M7
Winston Suffk......64 H9
Winstone Gloucs......33 J3
Winston Green Suffk......64 H9
Winswell Devon......16 H9
Winterborne Came Dorset......11 Q7
Winterborne Clenston Dorset......12 D4
Winterborne Herringston Dorset......11 P7
Winterborne Houghton Dorset......12 D4
Winterborne Kingston Dorset......12 E5
Winterborne Monkton Dorset......11 P7
Winterborne Stickland Dorset......12 D4
Winterborne Tomson Dorset......12 E5
Winterborne Whitechurch Dorset......12 D4
Winterborne Zelston Dorset......12 E5
Winterbourne S Glos......32 B8
Winterbourne W Berk......34 E10
Winterbourne Abbas Dorset......11 N6
Winterbourne Bassett Wilts......33 L10
Winterbourne Dauntsey Wilts......21 N8
Winterbourne Earls Wilts......21 N8
Winterbourne Gunner Wilts......21 N7
Winterbourne Monkton Wilts......33 L10
Winterbourne Steepleton Dorset......11 N7
Winterbourne Stoke Wilts......21 L6
Winterbrook Oxon......34 H7
Winterburn N York......96 D9
Winteringham N Linc......92 F6
Winterley Ches E......70 C3
Wintersett Wakefd......91 K7
Winterslow Wilts......21 P8
Winterton N Linc......92 F7
Winterton-on-Sea Norfk......77 P8

Winthorpe Lincs......87 Q7
Winthorpe Notts......85 P9
Winton BCP......13 J6
Winton Cumb......102 E8
Winton E Susx......25 M10
Winton N York......104 D11
Wintringham Cambs......62 B9
Wintringham N York......98 H6
Winwick Cambs......61 P4
Winwick Nhants......60 D6
Winwick Warrtn......82 D6
Wirksworth Derbys......71 P4
Wirral......81 K7
Wirswall Ches E......69 P6
Wisbech Cambs......75 J9
Wisbech St Mary Cambs......74 H9
Wisborough Green W Susx......24 C5
Wiseman's Bridge Pembks......41 M9
Wiseton Notts......85 M3
Wishanger Gloucs......32 H3
Wishaw N Lans......126 D6
Wishaw Warwks......59 J6
Wisley Surrey......36 C9
Wisley Garden RHS Surrey......36 C9
Wispington Lincs......86 H6
Wissenden Kent......26 F3
Wissett Suffk......65 M6
Wissington Norfk......75 N11
Wissington Suffk......52 G5
Wistanstow Shrops......56 G7
Wistanswick Shrops......70 B9
Wistaston Ches E......70 B4
Wistaston Green Ches E......70 B4
Wisterfield Ches E......82 H10
Wiston Pembks......41 K7
Wiston S Lans......116 D4
Wiston W Susx......24 D8
Wistow Cambs......62 C4
Wistow Leics......72 G11
Wistow N York......91 P3
Wiswell Lancs......89 L3
Witcham Cambs......62 G4
Witchampton Dorset......12 G3
Witchford Cambs......62 H5
Witcombe Somset......19 N10
Witham Essex......52 D9
Witham Friary Somset......20 D6
Witham on the Hill Lincs......73 Q7
Witham St Hughs Lincs......85 Q8
Withcall Lincs......87 J4
Withdean Br & H......24 H9
Witherenden Hill E Susx......25 P5
Witheridge Devon......9 K2
Witherley Leics......72 A11
Withern Lincs......87 M4
Withernsea E R Yk......93 P5
Withernwick E R Yk......93 L2
Withersdale Street Suffk......65 K5
Withersfield Suffk......63 L11
Witherslack Cumb......95 J4
Withiel Cnwll......4 F8
Withiel Florey Somset......18 C8
Withielgoose Cnwll......4 G8
Withington Gloucs......47 K11
Withington Herefs......45 R6
Withington Manch......82 H6
Withington Shrops......57 K2
Withington Staffs......71 J7
Withington Green Ches E......82 H10
Withington Marsh Herefs......45 R6
Withleigh Devon......9 M2
Withnell Lancs......89 J6
Withnell Fold Lancs......89 J6
Withybed Green Worcs......58 F10
Withybrook Warwks......59 P8
Withycombe Somset......18 D6
Withyham E Susx......25 L3
Withy Mills BaNES......20 C3
Withypool Somset......17 Q4
Withywood Bristl......31 Q11
Witley Surrey......23 P7
Witnesham Suffk......64 H11
Witney Oxon......34 C2
Wittering C Pete......73 R10
Wittersham Kent......26 F6
Witton Birm......58 G6
Witton Norfk......77 L10
Witton Norfk......77 L5
Witton Gilbert Dur......113 K11
Witton Green Norfk......77 N11
Witton le Wear Dur......103 M4
Witton Park Dur......103 N4
Wiveliscombe Somset......18 E9
Wivelrod Hants......23 J7
Wivelsfield E Susx......24 H6
Wivelsfield Green E Susx......25 J7
Wivelsfield Station W Susx......24 H7
Wivenhoe Essex......52 H7
Wivenhoe Cross Essex......52 H7
Wiveton Norfk......76 E3
Wix Essex......53 L6
Wixams Bed......50 C2
Wixford Warwks......47 L4
Wix Green Essex......53 L6
Wixhill Shrops......69 Q9
Wixoe Suffk......52 B3
Woburn C Beds......49 P8
Woburn Safari Park C Beds......49 Q8
Woburn Sands M Keyn......49 P7
Wokefield Park W Berk......35 J11
Woking Surrey......36 B9
Wokingham Wokham......35 M11
Wolborough Devon......7 M4
Woldingham Surrey......37 J9
Wold Newton E R Yk......99 L6
Wold Newton NE Lin......93 M11
Wolfclyde S Lans......116 E3
Wolferlow Herefs......46 C2
Wolferton Norfk......75 N5
Wolfhampcote Warwks......60 B7
Wolfhill P & K......142 B11
Wolf Hills Nthumb......111 P9
Wolf's Castle Pembks......41 J5
Wolfsdale Pembks......40 H6
Wollaston Dudley......58 C8
Wollaston Nhants......61 K8
Wollaston Shrops......56 E2
Wollaton C Nott......72 E3
Wollaton Hall & Park C Nott......72 E3
Wolleigh Devon......9 K8
Wollerton Shrops......69 R8
Wollescote Dudley......58 D8
Wolseley Bridge Staffs......71 J10
Wolsingham Dur......103 L3
Wolstanton Staffs......70 F5
Wolston Warwks......59 P9

Wolston Warwks......59 P9
Wolsty Cumb......109 P10
Wolvercote Oxon......34 E2
Wolverhampton Wolves......58 D5
Wolverhampton Halfpenny Green Airport Staffs......58 B6
Wolverley Shrops......69 N8
Wolverley Worcs......58 B9
Wolverton Hants......22 G3
Wolverton Kent......27 N3
Wolverton M Keyn......49 M6
Wolverton Warwks......47 P2
Wolverton Wilts......20 E8
Wolverton Common Hants......22 G3
Wolvesnewton Mons......31 N5
Wolvey Warwks......59 P7
Wolvey Heath Warwks......59 P7
Wolviston S on T......104 E5
Wombleton N York......98 D4
Wombourne Staffs......58 C6
Wombwell Barns......91 L10
Womenswold Kent......39 M11
Womersley N York......91 N7
Wonastow Mons......31 N2
Wonersh Surrey......36 B11
Wonford Devon......9 M6
Wonson Devon......8 G7
Wonston Dorset......12 B3
Wonston Hants......22 E7
Wooburn Bucks......35 P7
Wooburn Green Bucks......35 P7
Wooburn Moor Bucks......35 P7
Woodacott Devon......16 F10
Woodale N York......96 F5
Woodall Rothm......84 G4
Woodall Services Rothm......84 G4
Woodbank Ches W......81 M10
Woodbastwick Norfk......77 L8
Woodbeck Notts......85 N5
Wood Bevington Warwks......47 L4
Woodborough Notts......85 K11
Woodborough Wilts......21 M3
Woodbridge Devon......10 D5
Woodbridge Dorset......20 G11
Woodbridge Suffk......53 N2
Wood Burcote Nhants......49 J5
Woodbury Devon......9 P7
Woodbury Salterton Devon......9 P7
Woodchester Gloucs......32 F4
Woodchurch Kent......26 F5
Woodchurch Wirral......81 K7
Woodcombe Somset......18 C5
Woodcote Gt Lon......36 G8
Woodcote Wrekin......70 D11
Woodcote Green Worcs......58 D10
Woodcott Hants......22 D4
Woodcroft Gloucs......31 P5
Woodcutts Dorset......21 J11
Wood Dalling Norfk......76 F6
Woodditton Cambs......63 L9
Woodeaton Oxon......34 F2
Wood Eaton Staffs......70 E11
Wooden Pembks......41 M9
Wood End Bed......61 M11
Wood End Bed......61 N7
Wood End C Beds......49 Q6
Wood End Cambs......62 E5
Wood End Gt Lon......36 D4
Wood End Herts......50 H5
Woodend Highld......138 D5
Woodend Nhants......48 H5
Woodend Staffs......71 M9
Woodend W Loth......126 G4
Woodend W Susx......15 M5
Wood End Warwks......58 H10
Wood End Warwks......59 K5
Wood End Warwks......59 L7
Wood End Wolves......58 D4
Wood Enderby Lincs......87 J8
Woodend Green Essex......51 N5
Woodfalls Wilts......21 N10
Woodford Cnwll......16 C9
Woodford Devon......7 K8
Woodford Gloucs......32 C5
Woodford Gt Lon......37 K2
Woodford Nhants......61 L5
Woodford Stockp......83 J8
Woodford Bridge Gt Lon......37 K2
Woodford Green Gt Lon......37 K2
Woodford Halse Nhants......48 H4
Woodford Wells Gt Lon......37 K2
Woodgate Birm......58 E8
Woodgate Devon......18 F11
Woodgate Norfk......76 B8
Woodgate Norfk......76 E8
Woodgate W Susx......15 P6
Woodgate Worcs......58 E11
Wood Green Gt Lon......36 H2
Woodgreen Hants......21 N11
Woodgreen Oxon......34 C2
Woodhall N York......96 E3
Woodhall Hill Leeds......90 G3
Woodhall Spa Lincs......86 G8
Woodham Bucks......49 K11
Woodham Dur......103 Q5
Woodham Surrey......36 B8
Woodham Ferrers Essex......38 C2
Woodham Mortimer Essex......52 D11
Woodham Walter Essex......52 D10
Wood Hayes Wolves......58 E4
Woodhead Abers......159 J10
Woodhill Shrops......57 N8
Woodhill Somset......19 L9
Woodhorn Nthumb......113 L3
Woodhorn Demesne Nthumb......113 M3
Woodhouse Leeds......90 H4
Woodhouse Leics......72 E8
Woodhouse Sheff......84 F4
Woodhouse Wakefd......91 K6
Woodhouse Eaves Leics......72 E8
Woodhouse Green Staffs......70 G2
Woodhouselee Mdloth......127 N5
Woodhouselees D & G......110 G6
Woodhouse Mill Sheff......84 F3
Woodhouses Oldham......83 K4
Woodhouses Staffs......58 G3
Woodhouses Staffs......71 M11
Woodhuish Devon......7 N6
Woodhurst Cambs......62 D5
Woodingdean Br & H......25 J9
Woodkirk Leeds......90 H5
Woodland Abers......151 M3
Woodland Devon......6 G7

Woodland Devon 7 K5
Woodland Dur 103 L5
Woodland Kent 27 K3
Woodland S Ayrs 114 C8
Woodland Head Devon 9 J5
Woodlands Donc 91 N9
Woodlands Dorset 13 J3
Woodlands Hants 13 P2
Woodlands Kent 37 N8
Woodlands N York 97 M10
Woodlands Somset 18 G6
Woodlands of Durris Abers 151 K8
Woodlands Park W & M 35 N9
Woodlands St Mary W Berk 34 B9
Woodland Street Somset 19 P7
Woodland View Sheff 84 D3
Wood Lane Shrops 69 M8
Wood Lane Staffs 70 E5
Woodleigh Devon 7 J9
Woodlesford Leeds 91 K5
Woodley Stockp 83 K6
Woodley Wokham 35 L10
Woodmancote Gloucs 32 E5
Woodmancote Gloucs 33 K3
Woodmancote Gloucs 47 J9
Woodmancote W Susx 15 L5
Woodmancote W Susx 24 F8
Woodmancote Worcs 46 H6
Woodmancott Hants 22 G6
Woodmansey E R Yk 93 J3
Woodmansgreen W Susx 23 N9
Woodmansterne Surrey 36 G9
Woodmanton Devon 9 P7
Woodmarsh Wilts 20 G3
Woodmill Staffs 71 L10
Woodminton Wilts 21 K10
Woodnesborough Kent 39 P10
Woodnewton Nhants 61 M2
Woodnook Notts 84 G10
Wood Norton Norfk 76 E6
Woodplumpton Lancs 88 F4
Woodrising Norfk 76 D11
Wood Row Leeds 91 K5
Woodrow Worcs 58 C9
Wood's Corner E Susx 25 Q7
Woods Eaves Herefs 45 K5
Woodseaves Shrops 70 B8
Woodseaves Staffs 70 D9
Woodsend Wilts 33 P9
Woodsetts Rothm 84 H4
Woodsford Dorset 12 C6
Wood's Green E Susx 25 P4
Woodside Br For 35 P10
Woodside Cumb 100 D4
Woodside Essex 51 L10
Woodside Fife 135 L6
Woodside Gt Lon 36 H7
Woodside Hants 13 P6
Woodside Herts 50 F9
Woodside P & K 142 C10
Woodside Green Kent 38 F11
Woodstock Oxon 48 D11
Woodstock Pembks 41 K5
Woodston C Pete 74 C11
Wood Street Norfk 77 M7
Wood Street Village Surrey 23 Q4
Woodthorpe Derbys 84 G6
Woodthorpe Leics 72 E7
Woodthorpe Lincs 87 M4
Woodton Norfk 65 K3
Woodtown Devon 16 G7
Woodvale Sefton 88 C8
Woodville Derbys 71 Q11
Woodwall Green Staffs 70 D8
Wood Walton Cambs 62 B4
Woodyates Dorset 21 K11
Woody Bay Devon 17 M2
Woofferton Shrops 57 J11
Wookey Somset 19 P5
Wookey Hole Somset 19 P5
Wool Dorset 12 D7
Woolacombe Devon 16 H3
Woolage Green Kent 27 M2
Woolage Village Kent 39 M11
Woolaston Gloucs 31 Q5
Woolaston Common Gloucs 31 Q4
Woolavington Somset 19 K6
Woolbeding W Susx 23 N10
Woolbrook Devon 10 C7
Woolcotts Somset 18 C8
Wooldale Kirk 90 F9
Wooler Nthumb 119 J5
Woolfardisworthy Devon 9 K3
Woolfardisworthy Devon 16 E7
Woolfold Bury 89 M8
Woolfords S Lans 127 J4
Woolhampton W Berk 34 G11
Woolhope Herefs 46 B7
Woolland Dorset 12 C3
Woollard BaNES 20 B2
Woollensbrook Herts 51 J9
Woolley BaNES 32 D11
Woolley Cambs 61 Q6
Woolley Cnwll 16 D8
Woolley Derbys 84 E8
Woolley Wakefd 91 J8
Woolley Bridge Derbys 83 M6
Woolley Edge Services Wakefd 91 J8
Woolley Green W & M 35 M8
Woolmere Green Worcs 47 J2
Woolmer Green Herts 50 G7
Woolmerston Somset 19 J8
Woolminstone Somset 11 J3
Woolpack Kent 26 E4
Woolpit Suffk 64 D9
Woolpit Green Suffk 64 D9
Woolscott Warwks 60 B7
Woolsgrove Devon 9 J4
Woolsington N u Ty 113 J6
Woolstaston Shrops 56 H5
Woolsthorpe by Belvoir Lincs 73 L4
Woolsthorpe-by-Colsterworth Lincs 73 N6
Woolston C Sotn 14 D4
Woolston Devon 7 J10
Woolston Devon 7 J8
Woolston Shrops 56 E7
Woolston Shrops 69 K10
Woolston Somset 18 E7
Woolston Somset 20 C9
Woolston Warrtn 82 D7
Woolstone Gloucs 47 J8
Woolstone M Keyn 49 N7
Woolstone Oxon 33 Q7

Woolston Green Devon 7 K5
Woolton Lpool 81 N7
Woolton Hill Hants 22 D2
Woolverstone Suffk 53 L4
Woolverton Somset 20 E4
Woolwich Gt Lon 37 K5
Woonton Herefs 45 M4
Woonton Herefs 45 R2
Wooperton Nthumb 119 K6
Woore Shrops 70 C6
Wootten Green Suffk 65 J7
Wootton Bed 50 B2
Wootton Hants 13 M5
Wootton Herefs 45 L4
Wootton IoW 14 F8
Wootton Kent 27 M2
Wootton N Linc 93 J7
Wootton Nhants 60 G9
Wootton Oxon 34 E4
Wootton Oxon 48 D11
Wootton Shrops 69 K9
Wootton Staffs 70 E9
Wootton Staffs 71 L6
Wootton Bassett Wilts 33 L8
Wootton Bridge IoW 14 F8
Wootton Broadmead Bed 50 B2
Wootton Common IoW 14 F8
Wootton Courtenay Somset 18 B6
Wootton Fitzpaine Dorset 10 H5
Wootton Rivers Wilts 21 N2
Wootton St Lawrence Hants 22 G4
Wootton Wawen Warwks 47 N2
Worcester Worcs 46 G4
Worcester Park Gt Lon 36 F7
Wordsley Dudley 58 C7
Worfield Shrops 57 P5
Worgret Dorset 12 F7
Workhouse End Bed 61 P10
Workhouse Green Suffk 52 F4
Workington Cumb 100 D5
Worksop Notts 85 J5
Worlaby Lincs 87 K5
Worlaby N Linc 92 H8
Worlds End Bucks 35 N3
Worlds End Hants 14 H4
World's End W Berk 34 E9
Worlds End W Susx 24 H6
Worle N Som 19 L2
Worleston Ches E 70 B3
Worlingham Suffk 65 N4
Worlington Devon 9 J2
Worlington Suffk 63 L6
Worlingworth Suffk 65 J8
Wormald Green N York 97 M7
Wormbridge Herefs 45 N8
Wormegay Norfk 75 N8
Wormelow Tump Herefs 45 P8
Wormhill Derbys 83 P10
Wormhill Herefs 45 N7
Wormingford Essex 52 F5
Worminghall Bucks 34 H3
Wormington Gloucs 47 K7
Worminster Somset 19 Q6
Wormit Fife 135 L2
Wormleighton Warwks 48 E4
Wormley Herts 51 J9
Wormley Surrey 23 P7
Wormleybury Herts 51 J9
Wormley Hill Donc 91 R7
Wormshill Kent 38 E10
Wormsley Herefs 45 N5
Worplesdon Surrey 23 Q4
Worrall Sheff 84 D2
Worrall Hill Gloucs 32 B2
Worsbrough Barns 91 K10
Worsbrough Bridge Barns 91 K10
Worsbrough Dale Barns 91 K10
Worsley Salfd 82 G4
Worstead Norfk 77 L6
Worsthorne Lancs 89 P4
Worston Devon 6 F8
Worston Lancs 89 M2
Worth Kent 39 P10
Worth Somset 19 P5
Worth W Susx 24 H3
Wortham Suffk 64 F6
Worthen Shrops 56 E4
Worthenbury Wrexhm 69 M5
Worthing Norfk 76 D8
Worthing W Susx 24 D10
Worthington Leics 72 C6
Worth Matravers Dorset 12 G9
Worthybrook Mons 31 N2
Worting Hants 22 G4
Wortley Barns 91 J11
Wortley Gloucs 32 E6
Wortley Leeds 90 H4
Worton N York 96 E3
Worton Wilts 21 J3
Wortwell Norfk 65 K5
Wotherton Shrops 56 D4
Wothorpe C Pete 73 Q9
Wotter Devon 6 F6
Wotton Surrey 36 D11
Wotton-under-Edge Gloucs 32 E6
Wotton Underwood Bucks 49 J11
Woughton on the Green M Keyn 49 N7
Wouldham Kent 38 B9
Woundale Shrops 57 P6
Wrabness Essex 53 L5
Wrafton Devon 16 H4
Wragby Lincs 86 F5
Wragby Wakefd 91 L7
Wramplingham Norfk 76 G10
Wrangaton Devon 6 H7
Wrangbrook Wakefd 91 M8
Wrangle Lincs 87 M10
Wrangle Common Lincs 87 M10
Wrangle Lowgate Lincs 87 M10
Wrangway Somset 18 F11
Wrantage Somset 19 K10
Wrawby N Linc 92 H9
Wraxall N Som 31 N10
Wraxall Somset 20 B7
Wray Lancs 95 N7
Wray Castle Cumb 101 L10
Wraysbury W & M 36 B6
Wrayton Lancs 95 N6
Wrea Green Lancs 88 D4
Wreaks End Cumb 94 E3
Wreay Cumb 101 M6
Wreay Cumb 110 H11
Wrecclesham Surrey 23 M6
Wrekenton Gatesd 113 L9
Wrelton N York 98 F3

Wrenbury Ches E 69 Q5
Wrench Green N York 99 K3
Wreningham Norfk 64 H2
Wrentham Suffk 65 P5
Wrenthorpe Wakefd 91 J6
Wrentnall Shrops 56 G4
Wressle E R Yk 92 B4
Wressle N Linc 92 G9
Wrestlingworth C Beds 62 C11
Wretton Norfk 75 N10
Wrexham Wrexhm 69 K4
Wrexham Industrial Estate Wrexhm 69 L4
Wribbenhall Worcs 57 P9
Wrickton Shrops 57 L7
Wrightington Bar Lancs 88 G8
Wright's Green Essex 51 M7
Wrinehill Staffs 70 D5
Wrington N Som 19 N2
Writhlington BaNES 20 C4
Writtle Essex 51 Q9
Wrockwardine Wrekin 57 L2
Wroot N Linc 92 B10
Wrose C Brad 90 F3
Wrotham Kent 37 P9
Wrotham Heath Kent 37 P9
Wroughton Swindn 33 M8
Wroxall IoW 14 G11
Wroxall Warwks 59 K10
Wroxeter Shrops 57 K3
Wroxham Norfk 77 L8
Wroxton Oxon 48 D6
Wyaston Derbys 71 M6
Wyatt's Green Essex 51 N11
Wyberton Lincs 74 F2
Wyboston Bed 61 Q9
Wybunbury Ches E 70 B5
Wychbold Worcs 58 D11
Wych Cross E Susx 25 K4
Wychnor Staffs 71 M11
Wychwood Ches E 70 C4
Wyck Hants 23 L7
Wyck Rissington Gloucs 47 N10
Wycliffe Dur 103 M8
Wycoller Lancs 89 Q3
Wycomb Leics 73 K6
Wycombe Marsh Bucks 35 N6
Wyddial Herts 51 J4
Wye Kent 27 J2
Wyesham Mons 31 P2
Wyfordby Leics 73 K7
Wyke C Brad 90 F5
Wyke Devon 9 L5
Wyke Devon 10 F5
Wyke Dorset 20 E9
Wyke Shrops 57 L4
Wyke Surrey 23 P4
Wyke Champflower Somset 20 C8
Wykeham N York 99 K4
Wyken Covtry 59 N8
Wyken Shrops 57 P5
Wyke Regis Dorset 11 P9
Wykey Shrops 69 L10
Wykin Leics 72 C11
Wylam Nthumb 112 H8
Wylde Green Birm 58 H6
Wylye Wilts 21 K7
Wymeswold Leics 72 G6
Wymington Bed 61 L8
Wymondham Leics 73 L7
Wymondham Norfk 76 G11
Wyndham Brdgnd 29 P6
Wynford Eagle Dorset 11 M5
Wynyard Park S on T 104 D5
Wynyard Village S on T 104 D5
Wyre Piddle Worcs 47 J5
Wysall Notts 72 G5
Wyson Herefs 57 J11
Wythall Worcs 58 G9
Wytham Oxon 34 E3
Wythburn Cumb 101 K8
Wythenshawe Manch 82 H7
Wythop Mill Cumb 100 G5
Wyton Cambs 62 C6
Wyton E R Yk 93 L4
Wyton on the Hill Cambs 62 C6
Wyverstone Suffk 64 E8
Wyverstone Street Suffk 64 E8
Wyville Lincs 73 M5

Y

Yaddlethorpe N Linc 92 E9
Yafford IoW 14 D10
Yafforth N York 97 M2
Yalberton Torbay 7 M7
Yalding Kent 37 Q10
Yanwath Cumb 101 P5
Yanworth Gloucs 33 L2
Yapham E R Yk 98 F10
Yapton W Susx 15 Q6
Yarborough N Som 19 L3
Yarbridge IoW 14 H9
Yarburgh Lincs 87 L2
Yarcombe Devon 10 E3
Yard Devon 17 P7
Yardley Birm 58 H7
Yardley Gobion Nhants 49 L6
Yardley Hastings Nhants 61 J9
Yardley Wood Birm 58 H9
Yardro Powys 45 J3
Yarford Somset 18 H9
Yarkhill Herefs 46 B6
Yarley Somset 19 P6
Yarlington Somset 20 C9
Yarm S on T 104 D8
Yarmouth IoW 14 C9
Yarnacott Devon 17 L5
Yarnbrook Wilts 20 G4
Yarner Devon 9 J9
Yarnfield Staffs 70 F8
Yarnscombe Devon 17 K7
Yarnton Oxon 34 E2
Yarpole Herefs 45 P2
Yarrow Border 117 M5
Yarrow Somset 19 L5
Yarrow Feus Border 117 L5
Yarrowford Border 117 N4
Yarsop Herefs 45 N5
Yarwell Nhants 73 R11
Yate S Glos 32 D8
Yateley Hants 23 M2

Yatesbury Wilts 33 L10
Yattendon W Berk 34 G10
Yatton Herefs 56 G11
Yatton N Som 31 M11
Yatton Keynell Wilts 32 G9
Yaverland IoW 14 H9
Yawl Devon 10 G6
Yawthorpe Lincs 85 Q2
Yaxham Norfk 76 E9
Yaxley Cambs 61 Q2
Yaxley Suffk 64 G7
Yazor Herefs 45 N5
Yeading Gt Lon 36 D4
Yeadon Leeds 90 G2
Yealand Conyers Lancs 95 L6
Yealand Redmayne Lancs 95 L5
Yealand Storrs Lancs 95 K5
Yealmbridge Devon 6 F8
Yealmpton Devon 6 F8
Yearby R & Cl 104 G6
Yearngill Cumb 100 F2
Yearsley N York 98 B6
Yeaton Shrops 69 M11
Yeaveley Derbys 71 M6
Yeavering Nthumb 118 H4
Yedingham N York 98 H5
Yelford Oxon 34 C4
Yell Shet 169 r5
Yelland Devon 16 H5
Yelling Cambs 62 C8
Yelvertoft Nhants 60 C5
Yelverton Devon 6 E5
Yelverton Norfk 77 K11
Yenston Somset 20 D10
Yeoford Devon 9 J5
Yeolmbridge Cnwll 5 N4
Yeo Mill Devon 17 Q6
Yeo Vale Devon 16 G7
Yeovil Somset 19 Q11
Yeovil Marsh Somset 19 P11
Yeovilton Somset 19 P10
Yerbeston Pembks 41 L9
Yesnaby Ork 169 b5
Yetminster Dorset 11 M2
Yetson Devon 7 L7
Yettington Devon 9 Q7
Yetts o'Muckhart Clacks 134 C7
Yews Green C Brad 90 D4
Yew Tree Sandw 58 F5
Y Felinheli Gwynd 79 J11
Y Ferwig Cerdgn 42 C5
Y Ffôr Gwynd 66 F7
Yielden Bed 61 M7
Yieldingtree Worcs 58 C9
Yieldshields S Lans 126 F7
Yiewsley Gt Lon 36 C4
Y Nant Wrexhm 69 J4
Ynys Gwynd 67 K8
Ynysboeth Rhondd 30 E5
Ynysddu Caerph 30 G6
Ynysforgan Swans 29 J5
Ynyshir Rhondd 30 D6
Ynyslas Cerdgn 54 E6
Ynysmaerdy Rhondd 30 D8
Ynysmeudwy Neath 29 K3
Ynystawe Swans 29 J4
Ynyswen Powys 29 M2
Ynyswen Rhondd 30 C5
Ynysybwl Rhondd 30 E6
Ynysymaengwyn Gwynd 54 D4
Yockenthwaite N York 96 D5
Yockleton Shrops 56 F2
Yokefleet E R Yk 92 D6
Yoker C Glas 125 N4
York C York 98 C10
York Lancs 89 L4
Yorkletts Kent 39 J9
Yorkley Gloucs 32 B3
Yorkshire Dales National Park 96 C5
York Town Surrey 23 N2
Yorton Heath Shrops 69 P10
Youlgreave Derbys 84 B8
Youlthorpe E R Yk 98 F9
Youlton N York 97 Q8
Youngsbury Herts 51 J7
Young's End Essex 52 B8
Yoxall Staffs 71 L11
Yoxford Suffk 65 M8
Y Rhiw Gwynd 66 C9
Ysbyty Cynfyn Cerdgn 54 H9
Ysbyty Ifan Conwy 67 Q5
Ysbyty Ystwyth Cerdgn 54 G10
Ysceifiog Flints 80 H10
Ysgubor-y-Coed Cerdgn 54 F5
Ystalyfera Neath 29 L3
Ystrad Rhondd 30 C5
Ystrad Aeron Cerdgn 43 K3
Ystradfellte Powys 29 P2
Ystrad Ffin Carmth 43 Q5
Ystradgynlais Powys 29 L2
Ystrad Meurig Cerdgn 54 G11
Ystrad Mynach Caerph 30 F6
Ystradowen V Glam 30 D9
Ystumtuen Cerdgn 54 G9
Ythanbank Abers 159 M11
Ythanwells Abers 158 F10
Ythsie Abers 159 L11

Z

Zeal Monachorum Devon 8 H4
Zeals Wilts 20 E8
Zelah Cnwll 3 L3
Zennor Cnwll 2 D6
Zoar Cnwll 3 K10
Zouch Notts 72 E6
ZSL London Zoo Gt Lon 36 G4
ZSL Whipsnade Zoo C Beds 50 B7